THE LIFE OF AUGUST WILHELM SCHLEGEL

The Life of
August Wilhelm Schlegel

Cosmopolitan of Art and Poetry

Roger Paulin

http://www.openbookpublishers.com

© 2016 Roger Paulin

This work is licensed under a Creative Commons Attribution 4.0 International license (CC BY 4.0). This license allows you to share, copy, distribute and transmit the text; to adapt the text and to make commercial use of the text providing attribution is made to the author (but not in any way that suggests that he endorses you or your use of the work). Attribution should include the following information:

Paulin, Roger, *The Life of August Wilhelm Schlegel, Cosmopolitan of Art and Poetry*. Cambridge, UK: Open Book Publishers, 2016. http://dx.doi.org/10.11647/OBP.0069

Further details about CC BY licenses are available at http://creativecommons.org/licenses/by/4.0/

Please see the list of illustrations for attribution relating to individual images. Every effort has been made to identify and contact copyright holders and any omission or error will be corrected if notification is made to the publisher. For information about the rights of the Wikimedia Commons images, please refer to the Wikimedia website (the relevant links are listed in the list of illustrations).

In order to access detailed and updated information on the license, please visit http://www.openbookpublishers.com/isbn/9781909254954#copyright

All external links were active on 12/01/2016 and archived via the Internet Archive Wayback Machine: https://archive.org/web/

Digital material and resources associated with this volume are available at http://www.openbookpublishers.com/isbn/9781909254954 resources

ISBN Paperback: 978-1-909254-95-4
ISBN Hardback: 978-1-909254-96-1
ISBN Digital (PDF): 978-1-909254-97-8
ISBN Digital ebook (epub): 978-1-909254-98-5
ISBN Digital ebook (mobi): 978-1-909254-99-2
DOI: 10.11647/OBP.0069

The Department of German and Dutch, University of Cambridge, and Trinity College, Cambridge, have generously contributed towards the publication of this volume.

Cover image: background: Map of Central and Southern Europe (1855) from Wikimedia, http://commons.wikimedia.org/wiki/File:Central_and_Southern_Europe_Map_1855.jpg. Portrait of Schlegel in the 1840s from Flickr Commons, in the Internet Archive Book Images collection, https://www.flickr.com/photos/internetarchivebookimages/14777435381

All paper used by Open Book Publishers is SFI (Sustainable Forestry Initiative), PEFC (Programme for the Endorsement of Forest Certification Schemes) and Forest Stewardship Council(r)(FSC(r)) certified.

Printed in the United Kingdom, United States, and Australia
by Lightning Source for Open Book Publishers (Cambridge, UK).

Contents

Acknowledgements — xi
List of Abbreviations — xiii
Introduction — 1

1. Family, Childhood and Youth (1767-1794) — 11
    Antecedents — 11
    'From One House Four Such Marvellous Minds' — 13
    Johann Adolf Schlegel — 17
    Growing Up in Hanover — 20
    Siblings — 23
    Childhood and Schooling — 27
    Göttingen — 30
    Gottfried August Bürger: 'Young Eagle' — 37
    The First Translations — 46
    Johann Dominik Fiorillo — 48
    Caroline Michaelis-Böhmer — 50
    Summer 1791-Summer 1795: Amsterdam, Mainz, Leipzig — 52
    Caroline's Tribulations — 54
    Schlegel in Amsterdam — 59
    'Du, Caroline und ich': Friedrich Schlegel — 62

2. Jena and Berlin (1795-1804) — 65
    2.1 Jena — 70
        Die Horen — 74
        Goethe and Schiller on the Attack: The *Xenien* — 79
        Schlegel's Reviews: Language, Metrics — 83
        Dante — 88
        The Shakespeare Translation — 91
        The *Wilhelm Meister* Essay — 99
        The Jena Group — 109
        The Genesis of the *Athenaeum* — 115

	The Group Meets in Dresden	121
	Professor in Jena	125
	The Fichte Affair	129
	The Scandal of *Lucinde*	132
	Foregathering in Jena	135
	The First Strains	139
	The Death of Auguste Böhmer	143
	Elegies for the Dead and the Living	146
	Schlegel's Contributions to the *Athenaeum*	154
	The Essays on Art	159
	Schlegel's Lectures in Jena	166
2.2	Berlin (1801-1804)	169
	The End of Jena: Controversies and Polemics	169
	The Essay on Bürger	172
	Sophie Tieck-Bernhardi	182
	The *Ion* Fiasco	186
	Polemics, Caricatures and Lampoons	189
	Friedrich Schlegel's *Europa*	192
	Calderón	198
2.3	The Berlin Lectures	202
3. The Years with Madame de Staël (1804-1817)		221
	Holding Things Together	221
	Germaine de Staël-Holstein	225
	Madame de Staël and Germany	230
	The Meeting of Staël and Schlegel	234
	Schlegel in Coppet	240
	In Italy with Madame de Staël 1804-1805	249
3.1	With Madame de Staël in Coppet and Acosta 1805-1807	260
	The Writer in Diaspora	260
	Considérations sur la civilisation en général	267
	On some Tragic Roles of Madame de Staël	269
	Corinne, ou l'Italie	273
	Swiss Journeyings with Albert de Staël	279
	Comparaison entre la Phèdre de Racine et celle d'Euripide (1807)	281
3.2	Vienna	290
	Travelling to Vienna with Madame de Staël	293
	Friedrich Schlegel: Rome and India	296
	The Vienna Lectures	299

	Lectures on Dramatic Art and Literature	302
	Further Travels	314
	Back to Coppet	318
	De l'Allemagne	325
	Holed up in Berne	330
	The Dash to Vienna	334
	De l'Allemagne: The Book Itself	337
	The Last Days in Coppet	341
3.3	The Flight: Caught Up in History	345
	Through Germany, Austria and Russia, to Sweden	349
	In the Service of Bernadotte: The Political Pamphleteer	356
	Political and Military Developments 1813-1814	364
	England and France 1814	376
	The Return to Scholarship	380
	Italy, Coppet, Paris: The Death of Madame de Staël	383
3.4	Scholarly Matters	393
	Learned Reviews	397
	Medieval Studies	407
	The *Nibelungenlied*	409
4.	**Bonn and India (1818-1845)**	**415**
4.1	Bonn	415
	'Chevalier de plusieurs ordres'	415
	Auguste and Albertine	417
	The European Celebrity	421
	Friedrich Schlegel in Frankfurt	430
	Marriage	435
	The University of Bonn	442
	The Bonn Professor	448
	The Carlsbad Decrees	453
	The Professor's Day	458
	Teacher and Taught	463
	The Content of the Lectures	471
4.2	India	478
	The *Indische Bibliothek*	490
	Paris and London 1820-1823	497
	Educating the Young	504
	Paris and London Again	509
	The Sanskrit Editions	515

5. The Past Returns	521
Friedrich Schlegel	522
Ludwig Tieck	526
Goethe	529
The 1827 Art Lectures in Berlin	536
Heinrich Heine	540
5.1 The Last Years 1834-1845	546
The Works of Frederick the Great	557
Illness and Death	560
Epilogue	563
Short Biographies	567
Select Bibliography	603
List of Illustrations	617
Index	625

The true translator, one could state boldly, who is able to render not just the content of a masterpiece, but also to preserve its noble form, its peculiar idiom, is a herald of genius who, over and beyond the narrow confines set by the separation of language, spreads abroad its fame and broadcasts its high gifts. He is a messenger from nation to nation, who mediates mutual respect and admiration, where otherwise all is indifference or even enmity.

August Wilhelm von Schlegel

The Schlegel Coat of Arms ('Schlegel von Gottleben').
© SLUB Dresden, all rights reserved

Acknowledgements

Work on this project has been greatly assisted by my easy access to the large Schlegel holdings in Cambridge University Library and in the Wren Library, Trinity College, Cambridge. David Lowe and Christian Staufenbiel of Cambridge University Library and Sandy Paul and the staff of the Wren Library have been of invaluable help in my researches.

I am grateful to the following institutions for allowing me to consult and/or refer to unpublished material in their possession: Edinburgh, National Library of Scotland (Murray Archives); Bonn, Universitätsbibliothek, Handschriftenabteilung; Bonn, Universitätsarchiv; Coburg, Landesarchiv; Dresden, Sächsische Staats- Landes- und Universitätsbibliothek; Kupferstich-Kabinett, Staatliche Kunstsammlungen Dresden; Hanover, Landeskirchliches Archiv; Hanover, Ev. Lutherische Stadtkirchenkanzlei; Heidelberg, Universitätsbibliothek; Jena, Universitätsarchiv; Wolfenbüttel, Herzog August Bibliothek. Hans-Joachim Dopfer (Sigmaringen) kindly permitted me to use the portrait drawing of Schlegel.

I am indebted to fellow scholars working in the same field: Claudia Becker, who generously placed Ernst Behler's *Nachlass* at my disposal; Anil Bhatti; Cornelia Bögel, who in addition gave me great assistance with my manuscript; Ralf Georg Czapla; Christoph Jamme; Stefan Knödler; Margaret Rose; Jochen Strobel; Rosane and Ludo Rocher kindly gave me much useful advice on Sanskrit and answered my questions; Roger Dawe gave me guidance in matters relating to Classics, Pat Boyde with regard to Italian. Stephen Fennell encouraged me to start writing; Julia Allen, David Blamires, Barry Nisbet, Helmut Pfotenhauer, and my wife, Traute, read all or part of the manuscript and made helpful suggestions towards its improvement. Responsibility for what is written lies with me alone.

Anne and Thomas Bürger extended kind hospitality to me during my various visits to Dresden; Rolf Herrfahrdt similarly in Hanover.

The Fellows' Research Fund of Trinity College kindly met the costs of my archival visits to Bonn, Dresden, Heidelberg and Hanover.

I wish to record my grateful thanks to Trinity College and to the Deparment of German, University of Cambridge (Schröder Fund) who made generous grants towards the production of this book.

A final word of cordial thanks to all at Open Book Publishers, who have seen this book through its various stages to its conclusion.

October 2015, Trinity College Cambridge

List of Abbreviations

Athenaeum: *Athenaeum. Eine Zeitschrift von August Wilhelm Schlegel und Friedrich Schlegel*, 3 vols (Berlin: Vieweg, 1798; Frölich, 1799-1800).

Bonstettiana: *Bonstettiana. Historisch-kritische Ausgabe der Briefkorrespondenzen Karl Viktor von Bonstettens und seines Kreises, 1753-1832*, ed. Doris and Peter Walser-Wilhelm, 14 vols in 27 (Berne: Peter Lang, 1996-2011).

Briefe: *Briefe von und an August Wilhelm Schlegel*, ed. Josef Körner, 2 vols (Zurich, Leipzig, Vienna: Amalthea, 1930).

Carnets de voyage: Simone Balayé (ed.), *Les carnets de voyage de Madame de Staël. Contribution à la genèse de ses oeuvres* (Geneva: Droz, 1971).

Caroline: *Caroline. Briefe aus der Frühromantik*. Nach Georg Waitz vermehrt hg. von Erich Schmidt, 2 vols (Leipzig: Insel, 1913).

Correspondance générale: Madame de Staël, *Correspondance générale*, ed. Béatrice W. Jasinski and Othenin d'Haussonville, 7 vols (Paris: Pauvert; Hachette; Klincksieck, 1962-; Geneva: Champion-Slatkine, 1962-2008).

Die Horen: Die Horen eine Monatsschrift herausgegeben von Schiller (Tübingen: Cotta, 1795-97*)*.

Jenisch: *August Wilhelm Schlegels Briefwechsel mit seinen Heidelberger Verlegern*, ed. Erich Jenisch (Heidelberg: Winter, 1922).

Journaux intimes: Benjamin Constant, *Journaux intimes*, ed. Alfred Roulin and Charles Roth (Paris: Gallimard, 1952).

Justi: Carl Justi, *Winckelmann und seine Zeitgenossen*, 3rd edn, 3 vols (Leipzig: Vogel, 1923).

KA: *Kritische Friedrich-Schlegel-Ausgabe*, ed. Ernst Behler *et al*., 30 vols (Paderborn, Munich, Vienna: Schöningh; Zurich: Thomas, 1958- in progress).

KAV: August Wilhelm Schlegel, *Kritische Ausgabe der Vorlesungen* (Paderborn, etc.: Schöningh, 1989- in progress): I: *Vorlesungen über Ästhetik I* (1798-1803), ed. Ernst Behler (1989); II, i: *Vorlesungen über Ästhetik* (1803-27), ed. Ernst Behler, then Georg Braungart (2007); III: *Vorlesungen über Encyklopädie* (1803), ed. Frank Jolles and Edith Höltenschmidt (2006).

Krisenjahre: *Krisenjahre der Frühromantik. Briefe aus dem Schlegelkreis*, ed. Josef Körner, 3 vols (Brno, Vienna, Leipzig: Rohrer, 1936-37; Berne: Francke, 1958).

Leitzmann: *Briefwechsel zwischen Wilhelm von Humboldt und August Wilhelm Schlegel*, ed. Albert Leitzman (Halle: Niemeyer, 1908).

Lohner: *Ludwig Tieck und die Brüder Schlegel. Briefe.* Auf der Grundlage der von Henry Lüdeke besorgten Edition neu herausgegeben und kommentiert von Edgar Lohner (Munich: Winkler, 1972).

Mix-Strobel: York-Gothart Mix and Jochen Strobel (eds.), *Der Europäer August Wilhelm Schlegel. Romantischer Kulturtransfer—romantische Wissenswelten*, Quellen und Forschungen 62 (296) (Berlin, New York: de Gruyter, 2010).

Oeuvres: *Oeuvres de M. Auguste-Guillaume de Schlegel écrites en français*, ed. Édouard Böcking, 3 vols (Leipzig: Weidmann, 1846).

Opuscula: *Opuscula quae Augustus Guilelmus Schlegelius Latine scripta reliquit*, ed. Eduardus Böcking (Lipsiae: Weidmann, 1848).

Pange: Comtesse Jean de Pange, née Broglie, *Auguste-Guillaume Schlegel et Madame de Staël. D'après des documents inédits*, doctoral thesis University of Paris (Paris: Albert, 1938).

Sulger-Gebing: Emil Sulger-Gebing, *Die Brüder A. W. und F. Schlegel in ihrem Verhältnisse zur bildenden Kunst*, Forschungen zur neueren Litteraturgeschichte, 3 (Munich: Haushalter, 1897).

SW: August Wilhelm Schlegel, *Sämmtliche Werke*, ed. Eduard Böcking, 12 vols (Leipzig: Weidmann, 1846-47).

Walzel: *Friedrich Schlegels Briefe an seinen Bruder August Wilhelm*, ed. Oskar F. Walzel (Berlin: Speyer & Peters, 1890).

Wieneke: *August Wilhelm und Friedrich Schlegel im Briefwechsel mit Schiller und Goethe*, ed. Josef Körner and Ernst Wieneke (Leipzig: Insel, 1926).

Introduction

The idea for this biography arose out of a specific situation, the first conference ever devoted to August Wilhelm Schlegel, in Dresden in 2008.[1] The relatively late date might suggest decades of neglect of Schlegel's life and works, an indifference or nescience in the academy and in general cultural consciousness. Despite a corpus of studies extending back well over a century, it is indeed true to say that August Wilhelm Schlegel, unlike his brother Friedrich, has not been in the forefront of German critical awareness and is in great need of a general reappraisal. My own task at the conference was to set out some thoughts on how one approaches writing Schlegel's life.[2] I ended with the question: Who is to do it? My colleagues agreed that I should. This biography is the result.

There has never been a full-scale biography of Schlegel in any language. (The language factor is not irrelevant, for Schlegel wrote in French as well as German and lived for thirteen years in a French-speaking environment.) The first attempt in German so far, Bernhard von Brentano's short biography (originally 1943) was a popular account that restricted itself to printed sources,[3] many of them available since the nineteenth century. There is also an enormous amount of information tucked away in the many editions

---

1   The proceedings of the conference were published by York-Gothart Mix and Jochen Strobel (eds), *Der Europäer August Wilhelm Schlegel. Romantischer Kulturtransfer— romantische Wissenswelten*, Quellen und Forschungen 62 (296) (Berlin, New York: de Gruyter, 2010), esp. 1-10.
2   Roger Paulin, 'August Wilhelm Schlegel: Die Struktur seines Lebens', *ibid.*, 309-318.
3   Bernhard von Brentano, *August Wilhelm Schlegel. Geschichte eines romantischen Geistes* (Stuttgart: Cotta, 1943) and subsequently reprinted. See Konrad Feilchenfeldt, 'Bernhard von Brentanos August Wilhelm Schlegel-Biographie', Mix/Strobel, 295-307. An American master's thesis covers essentially the same material as Brentano (i.e. no unpublished sources). Effi Irmingard Kosin, 'Vorstudie zu einer Biographie von August Wilhelm Schlegel', M.A. thesis Stanford University 1965.

of his correspondence and lectures, as well as in major monographs on individual aspects of his life and works—Körner on the Vienna Lectures,[4] Pange on Madame de Staël,[5] Nagavajara on his reputation in France,[6] Höltenschmidt on his medieval studies[7] are but a few—that open up a wealth of intellectual and historical detail relevant to his life. Yet there is no account that joins up these spheres of activity as one narrative whole.

Perhaps the length of Schlegel's life (1767-1845) and the breadth of his interests, far from being a stimulus, have deterred potential biographers. It may seem on the face of it hard to define what makes him biography-worthy: there are simply so many sides to his intellectual interests and too many loose ends to his life. 'I have to admit to myself that I have undertaken a great deal and completed very little',[8] says the man whose works in German take up twelve volumes in the standard edition. But proudly listing his achievements, he nevertheless is justified in calling himself a 'cosmopolitan of art and poetry'.[9] For he is at once poet, dramatist, critic, translator, editor, philosopher, historian, philologist, an 'érudit' in the eighteenth century's sense of the word; and is it symptomatic that a French name seems best suited to sum up his character and achievement. Being a cosmopolitan meant publishing in German, French and Latin;[10] his ideal biographer—and I certainly do not claim to fulfil that role—as well as being versed in the classical and Romance languages, should also know Sanskrit.

Might a man with such an extraordinary mind and range not spend his hours closeted with books and papers and have no real life to speak of? There are times when Schlegel seems to fit this description. Not, however, when he is visiting the capitals of Europe or rattling in a chaise across

---

4   Josef Körner, *Die Botschaft der deutschen Romantik an Europa*, Schriften zur deutschen Literatur für die Görresgesellschaft, 9 (Augsburg: Filser, 1929).
5   Comtesse Jean de Pange, née Broglie, *Auguste-Guillaume Schlegel et Madame de Staël. D'après des documents inédits*, doctoral thesis University of Paris (Paris: Albert, 1938).
6   Chetana Nagavajara, *August Wilhelm Schlegel in Frankreich. Sein Anteil an der französischen Literaturkritik 1807-1835*, intr. Kurt Wais, Forschungsprobleme der vergleichenden Literaturgeschichte, 3 (Tübingen: Niemeyer, 1966).
7   Edith Höltenschmidt, *Die Mittelalter-Rezeption der Brüder Schlegel* (Paderborn, etc.: Schöningh, 2000).
8   'Je dois m'avouer à moi-même que j'ai beaucoup entrepris, et achevé peu de chose'. *Oeuvres de M. Auguste-Guillaume de Schlegel écrites en français*, ed. Édouard Böcking, 3 vols (Leipzig: Weidmann, 1846), I, 10.
9   'Kosmopolit der Kunst und Poesie/Verkündigt' ich in allen Formen sie'. August Wilhelm Schlegel, *Sämmtliche Werke* [SW], ed. Eduard Böcking, 12 vols (Leipzig: Weidmann, 1846-47), III, 3.
10 *Opuscula quae Augustus Guilelmus Schlegelius Latine scripta reliquit*, ed. Eduardus Böcking (Lipsiae: Weidmann, 1848).

the steppes with Madame de Staël (and her lover), having saved a copy of *De l'Allemagne* from Napoleon's censors, or when he joins Marshal Bernadotte's suite as a political pamphleteer. These are of course high moments, but the circumstances that brought about the works for which he is chiefly remembered today—his translation of Shakespeare, and the Vienna Lectures on Dramatic Art and Literature that were read from 'Cadiz to Edinburgh, Stockholm and St Petersburg'[11]—are also the stuff of biography.

The main problem has nevertheless been his reputation in his own country. Despite a renewal of interest in him during the twentieth century and impressive editions of his lectures and correspondence—the initiatives of Josef Körner or Ernst Behler, to mention but two—Schlegel has generally not been well served by his fellow-countrymen. In the German lands, his reputation has never quite recovered from Heinrich Heine's devastating attack in *Die Romantische Schule* of 1835; memoirs in the later nineteenth century did him hardly better service. He failed to be enshrined in the national canon, being perceived as having sold his soul to France, the 'traditional enemy'. In the strident years after 1871, he became a symbol of effeteness, lacking 'vital forces'; even Brentano's biography, when speaking of his Shakespeare translation, can only find a 'feminine capacity for empathy', not life-giving originality.[12]

Writing a biography to counter prejudice and neglect is doubtless laudable, but it is not enough. Schlegel himself knew this. In the sole biographical essay from his own pen, a defence of his former mentor Gottfried August Bürger, he wrote that 'it is a forlorn hope to impute to a human work a higher reputation than it deserves, through keeping silent about its faults'.[13] It is a warning against the temptation to compensate for perceived injustices. Schlegel nevertheless believed in preserving a self-image and was ever ready to justify himself. He wrote a total of four autobiographical pieces (two in German, one in French and one in Latin), setting out his credentials, respectively, as a poet,[14] as a man of action and political conscience (not merely a sedentary man of letters),[15] and a man

---

11 *SW*, VII, 285.
12 Sources set out in Paulin, 'Struktur', 312f.
13 August Wilhelm Schlegel, 'Bürger. 1800', *SW*, VIII, 64-139, ref. 73.
14 [Sketch of a Biography]. (undated). Cornelia Bögel, 'Fragment einer unbekannten autobiographischen Skizze aus dem Nachlass August Wilhelm Schlegels', *Athenäum*, 22 (2012), 165-180.
15 'Oratio cum magistratum academicum die XVIII. Octobris anni MDCCCXXIV. deponeret habita', *Opuscula*, 385-392; 'Berichtigung einiger Mißdeutungen', *SW*, VIII, 239-258.

of mature reflection.¹⁶ The modern biographer will not wish to follow implicitly these directives from his biographical subject, but by the same token he will not wish to brush them aside as irrelevant.

The biographer also has the task of seeing his subject in his times. Politically, Schlegel was born in a part of that conglomeration of German states still owing allegiance to a Holy Roman Emperor (he still had the last Emperor's name on his doctoral diploma from the University of Jena). Growing up in the Hanover of George III, he experienced the last years of this political system, before the French Revolution, the Revolutionary Wars, and the rise of Napoleon destroyed the old order and imposed a new one on Europe. The circumstances of his thirteen-year association with Madame de Staël saw him in the opposite camp to Napoleon, forced with her into exile and a wandering existence. His travels with her took him to France, Switzerland, Italy, Austria, Russia, Sweden and England, all during times of political or military turmoil. The reaction in the German lands after the Restoration of 1815 left him culturally and intellectually oriented to France, despite his being a professor in Prussian service.

A life that extended from the reigns of Frederick the Great, George III and Louis XV in the 1760s to those of Frederick William IV, Victoria and Louis-Philippe in the 1840s involved not just political change and upheaval, but irreversible social and technological revolutions. Much of this was to occupy his two best-known pupils at the University of Bonn, Karl Marx and Heinrich Heine. (Not to be outdone, Schlegel himself wrote an ode in Latin marking the arrival of the first steamboat on the Rhine; in the year before he died, the railway reached Bonn.) He did not see all of this necessarily as progress. Towards the end of his life listing (in no particular order) the 'achievements' of the last half-century, he was wryly ambiguous as to their benefits: beet sugar, the free press, gas lighting, centralization, steam engines, lithography, daguerrotypes, metres and hectares, stearin candles, the rights of man, Chartism, socialism, and much else besides.¹⁷ He could have added: the July Revolution, the British Empire, the Carlsbad Decrees, the subject of trenchant comment elsewhere. The role of the intellectual, the scholar, the writer was, as he saw it, to preserve some integrity and self-esteem when everything else about him was restless and shifting.

Yet these factors alone do not necessarily warrant a biography. I believe Schlegel to have been an interesting man in his own right and a

---

16   'Fragments extraits du porte-feuille d'un solitaire contemplatif', *Oeuvres*, I, 189-194.
17   'Formule d'abjuration', *Oeuvres*, I, 83.

leading intellectual in his day—not always likeable, but few of his great contemporaries, Goethe or Schiller, Madame de Staël or Heine, would necessarily qualify in those terms. I seek to strip away the accumulation of prejudices that have accompanied his reputation and present him, not as he was (that no biographer can do) but as he might reasonably be seen, with all of his faults and also his virtues. To this end, I make extensive use of a mass of archival material, much of which presents a Schlegel different from the image in printed sources.

This biography identifies the high points of Schlegel's life, the major influences on it, the places and persons affected by his presence and personality. These are, as I see it, the years in Jena, his Shakespeare translation, the Berlin and Vienna Lectures, and the years as a professor in Bonn. I have devoted over a quarter of my account to his association with Madame de Staël (1804-17), not least because that extraordinary woman said that she could not live without him, but also because Staël studies tend to sideline him in favour of other members of the 'Groupe de Coppet'. Thus I have drawn on the material afforded by recent Staël scholarship in order to place Schlegel more centrally in the account of her life and works. I regard his Lectures on Dramatic Art and Literature as commensurate with Staël's De l'Allemagne, part of the recognition of Schlegel's pivotal role as a representative figure of both German and European Romanticism, sometimes even as the man who held everything together when politics forced so much apart.

An equally long section is devoted to his years as a professor in Bonn, for here Schlegel achieved prominence—fame even—as a Sanskrit scholar, and it is a claim to eminence that in its time could compete with his renown as a translator and as the voice of Romanticism.

I see Schlegel as a professional writer for a large part of his career. His publications did not exist in a vacuum. His dealings with publishers, the sums that they paid, the position of the author in the book trade, the vicissitudes of publishing in Napoleonic Germany and also later: all these are concerns of special interest to the biographer.

Heinrich Heine grievously wronged Schlegel, and the victim has had very little opportunity for redress. I come to his defence against his calumniator-in-chief, endeavouring also to find some sympathy for the man, who without children of his own, showed genuine affection for the young and devoted much time and care to them. He was not only the travelling companion to Madame de Staël but also the tutor to her three children, all of whom have their part in this narrative.

His poetry—today little appreciated—I make use of, not so much for any intrinsic qualities that it may have, but as a accompaniment to the biography, and where I think it has merit, I also quote it.

Finally, a biography of August Wilhelm Schlegel must be in part also the life narrative of his brother Friedrich. The different trajectories of their respective reputations, the greater availability of printed sources for Friedrich, his subsequent advancement to spokesman and representative of German Romanticism, even to being hailed as a father of modern critical theory, mean that August Wilhelm sometimes is apportioned a secondary role. I have tried to give as balanced a narrative as I can of their relationship, its interactions, and its tensions.

A Note on Sources

The textual situation with Schlegel is far from satisfactory. There has been no standard edition of his works since that produced by Eduard Böcking in 1846-48, and it is far from complete. It is, however, the main source from which I cite his poetry, his translations, and his criticism. His lectures, those given in Jena, Berlin, Vienna, and Bonn, are not yet edited in their entirety, and at least three of them I quote from the original manuscripts. Even the great Vienna Lectures on Dramatic Art and Literature have not yet been the subject of a modern critical edition. Schlegel scholars are nevertheless grateful for the three volumes of Berlin Lectures edited in the 1880s by Jakob Minor,[18] the Lectures on German Language edited by Josef Körner in 1913,[19] the Lectures on Academic Study edited by Frank Jolles in 1971,[20] and the three volumes of the *Kritische Ausgabe der Vorlesungen* (*KAV*), originally under the aegis of Ernst Behler and subsequently of Georg Braungart, that have appeared so far (1989-2007)[21] and of which further volumes are promised shortly.

---

18 August Wilhelm Schlegel, *Vorlesungen über schöne Litteratur und Kunst*, ed. Jakob Minor, Deutsche Litteraturdenkmale des 18. und 19. Jahrhunderts, 17-19 (Heilbronn: Henninger, 1884).

19 August Wilhelm Schlegel, *Geschichte der Deutschen Sprache und Poesie. Vorlesungen, gehalten an der Universität Bonn seit dem Wintersemester 1818/19*, ed. Josef Körner, Deutsche Literaturdenkmale des 18. und 19. Jahrhunderts, 147 (Berlin: Behr, 1913).

20 August Wilhelm Schlegel, *Vorlesungen über das akademische Studium*, ed. Frank Jolles, Bonner Vorlesungen, 1 (Heidelberg: Stiehm, 1971).

21 August Wilhelm Schlegel, *Vorlesungen über Ästhetik I (1798-1803)*, ed. Ernst Behler, Kritische Ausgabe der Vorlesungen [*KAV*], I (Paderborn, etc.: Schöningh, 1989); *Vorlesungen über Encyklopädie* [1803], ed. Frank Jolles and Edith Höltenschmidt, *KAV*, III (ibid., 2006); *Vorlesungen über Ästhetik* II, i, ed. Ernst Behler, then Georg Braungart, *KAV*, II, i (ibid., 2007).

The Schlegel scholar faces a similar situation in respect of his correspondence. The great scholar-editor Josef Körner produced a two-volume collection of Schlegel's letters in 1930[22] which is still a standard tool, followed by the three-volume *Krisenjahre der Frühromantik* (1936-37, 1958).[23] The *Kritische Ausgabe* of Friedrich Schlegel (1958-, in progress) brings together in a modern edition sources otherwise scattered and not of easy access.[24] One is grateful for continuing editorial work on the correspondence, for instance the recent specialized editions of letters produced by Ralf Georg Czapla and Franca Victoria Schankweiler,[25] Rosane and Ludo Rocher,[26] and Cornelia Bögel,[27] which cast light on important aspects of Schlegel's life and works. Above all, the Digital Edition of Schlegel's letters, under the aegis of the Deutsche Forschungsgemeinschaft and carried out at the Sächsische Landesbibliothek—Staats- und Universitätsbibliothek in Dresden (SLUB) in collaboration with the Universities of Marburg and Trier, will, when completed, give a complete conspectus and image of Schlegel's correspondence, as far as it is known.[28] Much nevertheless remains unedited, but important tracts of correspondence, Madame de Staël's letters to Schlegel, for example, and most of his letters to his brother Friedrich, must unfortunately be considered lost.

Schlegel himself threw nothing away. His papers (*Nachlass*) in the SLUB in Dresden (Mscr. Dresd. e. 90), amounting to 78 sections, contain everything from personal items (such as tailors' bills) to large unpublished drafts of significant research projects (*Nibelungenlied*, Provençal) as well as the bulk of his correspondence. Further archival material, from Coppet and relating to the years 1804-12, was purchased by the SLUB in 1998 (Mscr. Dresd. App. 2712). Two specialized (on-line) catalogues itemize these

---

22 *Briefe von und an August Wilhelm Schlegel*, ed. Josef Körner [*Briefe*], 2 vols (Zurich, Leipzig, Vienna: Amalthea, 1930).
23 *Krisenjahre der Frühromantik. Briefe aus dem Schlegelkreis*, ed. Josef Körner [*Krisenjahre*], 3 vols (Brno, Vienna, Leipzig: Rohrer, 1936-37; Berne: Francke, 1958).
24 *Kritische Friedrich-Schlegel-Ausgabe*, ed. Ernst Behler *et al.*, 30 vols [*KA*] (Paderborn, Munich, Vienna: Schöningh; Zurich: Thomas, 1958- in progress).
25 'Meine liebe Marie' — 'Werthester Herr Professor'. *Der Briefwechsel zwischen August Wilhelm von Schlegel und seiner Bonner Haushälterin Maria Löbel*. Historisch-kritische Ausgabe, ed. Ralf Georg Czapla and Franca Victoria Schankweiler (Bonn: Bernstein, 2012).
26 *Founders of Western Indology. August Wilhelm von Schlegel and Henry Thomas Colebrooke in Correspondence 1820-1837*, ed. Rosane Rocher and Ludo Rocher, Abhandlungen für die Kunde des Morgenlandes, 84 (Wiesbaden: Harrassowitz, 2013).
27 Cornelia Bögel, '*Geliebter Freund und Bruder*'. *Der Briefwechsel zwischen Christian Friedrich Tieck und August Wilhelm Schlegel in den Jahren 1804 bis 1811*, Tieck Studien 1 (Dresden, Thelem, 2015).
28 Jochen Strobel, 'Eine digitale Edition der Korrespondenzen August Wihelm Schlegels', *Athenäum*, 22 (2012), 145-151.

8   *The Life of August Wilhelm Schlegel*

holdings.[29] There is also a significant amount of archival material in Bonn University Library. I have made the fullest possible use of this corpus, in both Dresden and Bonn, and elsewhere.

A Note on Money[30]

Money plays in important part in Schlegel's life, not least for his being a professional writer and translator for a part of his life. The standard currency in the German lands was the taler, a silver coin, also the coinage in which he was mainly paid. There were 24 groschen to one taler. Publishers also used the gold Friedrichsd'or, worth 5 talers, or the Louisd'or, also worth 5 talers. Other coins in use were the ducat (Dukaten), worth $3^{1/2}$ talers, or the Carolin, worth 6 talers. In the southern territories and in Austria, the standard currency was the florin or Gulden, worth one half of a taler; there were 60 Kreutzer to one Gulden. During his years with Madame de Staël, Schlegel was paid in Louisd'or or francs. There were 20 francs to the Louis, 20 francs 80 centimes to one Friedrichsd'or and 3 francs to the taler. During his visits to England (1814, 1823, 1832), he was using pounds sterling or guineas (£1.1.0).

Schlegel's publishers paid him in most of these currencies, never in paper money. Some examples: in the 1790s Cotta (through Schiller) paid 4 Louisd'or per sheet for his contributions to the periodical *Die Horen*;[31] from Unger he received 120 talers per volume for his Shakespeare translation (1797-1810);[32] in 1808, Mohr und Zimmer in Heidelberg could offer him $2^{1/2}$ Carolins per sheet for his famous Lectures on Dramatic Art and Literature

---

29 *Rekonstruierter Spezialkatalog (Inhaltskonspekte der 78 Gruppen) des Nachlasses von August Wilhelm v. Schlegel*, ed. Helmut Deckert (Sächsische Landesbibliothek, 1981); August Wilhelm Schlegel, *Spezialkatalog zum schriftlichen Nachlass*, ed. Perk Loesch (SLUB Dresden, 2000); see Perk Loesch, 'Der Nachlass August Wilhelm Schlegels in der Handschriftensammlung der Sächsischen Landesbibliothek- Staats- und Universitätsbibliothek Dresden', in: Ludger Syré (ed.), *Dichternachlässe. Literarische Sammlungen und Archive in den Regionalbibliotheken von Deutschland, Österreich und der Schweiz* (Frankfurt am Main: Klostermann, 2009), 183-193.

30 Useful guides to currency and prices may be found in W. H. Bruford, *Germany in the Eighteenth Century: The Social Background of the Literary Revival* (Cambridge: Cambridge UP, 1935), 329-332 (Bruford converts the sums of the late 18th century into the sterling equivalents of 1935); Bernd Sprenger, *Das Geld der Deutschen. Geldgeschichte Deutschlands von den Anfängen bis zur Gegenwart* (Paderborn, etc.: Schöningh, 1991).

31 *Caroline. Briefe aus der Frühromantik. Nach Georg Waitz vermehrt hg. von Erich Schmidt*, 2 vols (Leipzig: Insel, 1913), I, 419.

32 *Krisenjahre*, I, 89.

(at 24 sheets per volume).³³ Reimer paid 40 Friedrichsd'or or 200 talers for the collection called *Blumensträuße* in 1804.³⁴ In 1828, he agreed with Reimer for 2 Friedrichsd'or per sheet (a total of 1,200 talers) for his *Kritische Schriften*.³⁵

These sums make no sense in themselves unless related to the cost of living. His brother Friedrich, never provident with money, suggested in 1793 that a single man in Dresden, with meals and a servant, would need 80 talers annually, a married couple 250 talers, to live as a professional writer and in the appropriate style.³⁶ Schiller at the same time is said to have needed 1,400 talers, and that was in provincial Jena. In 1803, it was claimed that a family, with servants, clothing and entertaining, needed at least 2,000 talers per annum to live in Berlin.³⁷ That was the sum that Schlegel received as a professor in Bonn, from 1817 onwards, augmented of course by the pension from the Staël estate. During Madame de Staël's lifetime, from 1804 to 1817, he had received 10 Carolins or 240 francs monthly.³⁸

By contrast, in 1764, a manual labourer in Dresden earned 4 groschen per day; in 1829-31, it was 6 groschen.³⁹ A bricklayer at the same time earned 6-7 groschen and later 8. The basic annual income for a working-class family in Berlin around 1800 was 200 talers. Preachers and teachers could expect 500 talers. A common soldier's pay was 24 talers (over and above lodgings and keep). Professors at the newly-founded University of Berlin in 1810 could expect a maximum of 2,500 talers (augmented of course by student fees for lectures). Goethe, as 'Exzellenz' and minister of state in Saxe-Weimar had an annual income of 3,000 talers in 1816.⁴⁰

In Dresden in 1764 a kilo of butter cost 6 groschen (11 groschen in 1829-31), 60 eggs 9 groschen (later, 25 groschen), a bushel of wheat cost 3 talers 4 groschen (later, 4 talers 12 groschen).⁴¹These do not differ greatly from prices in Weimar around 1790.⁴² In Berlin in 1802, one paid 3 talers for the

---

33 *August Wilhelm Schlegels Briefwechsel mit seinen Heidelberger Verlegern*, ed. Erich Jenisch (Heidelberg: Winter, 1922), 23, 38.
34 Doris Reimer, *Passion & Kalkül. Der Verleger Georg Andreas Reimer (1776-1842)* (Berlin: de Gruyter, 1999), 278.
35 *Ibid.*, 294.
36 KA, XXIII, 198.
37 Reimer, 31.
38 *Krisenjahre*, I, 88, 183; III, 68.
39 Sprenger, 150, 161.
40 These figures in Reimer, 29f.
41 Sprenger, 150, 161.
42 Bruford, 329-332.

two volumes of Novalis's works, edited by Friedrich Schlegel and Tieck and published by Reimer (4 talers 12 groschen on better paper). For just a little more money one could also purchase 45 kilos of white bread and 58 of rye bread, or 28 kilos of beef. A luxury item like an umbrella cost $10^{1/2}$ talers.[43] In 1820, a traveller in Ulm paid 1 Gulden 30 Kreuzer for a meal in his rooms, 1 Gulden 12 Kreuzer for a bottle of Neckar wine, 30 Kreuzer for coffee and bread, and 1 Gulden 15 Kreuzer for lodgings.[44]

For France or French-speaking Switzerland we have records of luxury items purchased by Schlegel. A beaver hat cost him 33 francs,[45] four pairs of silk stockings (white) 48 francs, and two in black 30 francs.[46] In London in 1832, he paid £1.3.0 for a hat, and £5.17.6 for lodgings from 11-17 March.[47] For comparison, a carpenter's wages were 25/- (£1.5.0) per week, those of bookseller's apprentices 4/- and knitters' 5/-. An upper-middle class family would reckon to live on £5 per week (£300 per annum). The two volumes of Schlegel's Lectures, translated by John Black, cost 21/- (£1.1.0) unbound and 27/- (£1.7.0) bound.[48] The subscription price for his *Râmâyana* edition was £4 for one volume in two parts.[49]

How well did Schlegel live? Unlike his brother Friedrich, he knew how to combine a comfortable life-style with some necessary economies. He supported his mother (until 1811), Sophie Tieck-Bernhardi (especially around 1804-05) and his brother Friedrich (up to 1818), later various nieces and nephews. As a professor in Bonn, he had his salary and his pension from Madame de Staël, but he had also purchased his own house (for 7,000 talers). In addition, he paid for the production and publication of his three Sanskrit editions, estimating in 1829 that he had spent 5,000 talers, while by 1844 he was talking of 30,000 francs, roughly the equivalent of 10,000 talers.[50]

---

43   Reimer, 30f.
44   Bill pasted into a copy of [Heinrich August Ottokar Reichard], *Guide des voyageurs en Allemagne, en Hongrie at à Constantinople* (Weimar: Bureau d'Industrie, 1817), Trinity College U. 8. 90.
45   SLUB Dresden, Mscr. Dresd. App. 2712, B31, 36.
46   *Ibid.*, B31, 61.
47   Mscr. Dresd. e. 90. II, 51.
48   This information in William St Clair, *The Reading Nation in the Romantic Period* (Cambridge: Cambridge UP, 2004), 194-196.
49   Advertisement to *Râmâyana, id est carmen epicum* […], issued by Treuttel & Würtz in London and dated 'London, November, 1823', 7.
50   *Briefe*, I, 612f.

1. Family, Childhood and Youth (1767-1794)

Antecedents

August Wilhelm Schlegel was inordinately proud of his ancestry.[1] Writing in 1828 to defend himself against allegations of crypto-Catholicism, he could lay claim to a two-hundred-year line of Protestant pastors.[2] His niece, Auguste von Buttlar, incurring her uncle's displeasure for having converted to Catholicism, was similarly reminded in 1827 of those generations of Protestant ministers of word and sacrament, sober in Lutheran black.[3]

As we shall see, Schlegel invoked his Protestantism only when it suited him, and his ancestor-worship was similarly selective. Since 1813, he had been calling himself 'von Schlegel' (full title 'Schlegel von Gottleben'). He had had an ornate copy made of the letters patent of nobility issued in 1651 to his great-grandfather, 'Christophorus Schlegel a Gottleben', adding portraits of three clergymen, 'Martinus Schlegel', the said Christoph, and his own father, 'Johannes Adolphus Schlegel'. It suggested a pedigree of religious orthodoxy and ennoblement in office.[4]

Not all of this was strictly true. In one way, his family was even more interesting than Schlegel imagined. For his grandfather Johann Friedrich

---

[1] On the Schlegel family see K. F. von Frank, 'Schlegel von Gottleben', *Seftenegger Monatsblatt für Genealogie und Heraldik* 5 (1960-65), col. 314.

[2] [SW, VIII, 221, 263. On AWS's ancestry see Konrad Seeliger, 'Johann Elias Schlegel', *Mitteilungen des Vereins f. Geschichte der Stadt Meißen* 2, Heft 2 (1888), 145-188.

[3] *Briefe von und an August Wilhelm Schlegel*, ed. Josef Körner, 2 vols (Zurich, Leipzig, Vienna: Amalthea, 1930), I, 460f.

[4] Bound in the Schlegel family psalter (Nuremberg, 1525), Bonn, Universitätsbibliothek, S 1640.

© Roger Paulin, CC BY   http://dx.doi.org/10.11647/OBP.0069.01

had married a descendant of the great German (and Protestant) painter, Lukas Cranach. His descendant August Wilhelm Schlegel would later, in 1797, pass unmoved though the Cranach collection in the Dresden gallery: it was not a good year for the appreciation of that kind of Renaissance painting by the Romantic generation.

Christoph Schlegel had most certainly been a Lutheran clergyman, and he had been ennobled by Emperor Ferdinand III, also king of Hungary. He had been court preacher, Gymnasium professor, doctor of theology, and pastor in Leutschau (today's Levoča in Slovakia), at that time in the kingdom of Hungary (whence came the ennoblement). The letters patent— in Latin—were signed by the bishop of Nyitra and the archbishop of Esztergom, as well as by several Hungarian grandees, among them a Pálffy and a Batthyány. In 1808, descendants of these grand families were in the audience in Vienna when August Wilhelm Schlegel delivered his Lectures on Dramatic Art and Literature. The crest of the family arms showed a male figure holding a miner's hammer: the German word for this tool is 'Schlegel'.

The next two generations saw the Schlegels in Saxony, but as jurists. Christoph's son Johann Elias—the double names start here—was a lawyer in Saxon service. His son held high legal titles ('Hof- und Justizrat'), becoming 'Stiftssyndikus' (senior jurist in the foundation) in Meissen cathedral in the electoral territory of Saxony, and it was with him that the family abandoned its noble title. Titles of nobility were useful in the seventeenth century, where a new *noblesse de robe* needed to be created. They mattered rather less in the eighteenth, when the middle classes dominated corporate and intellectual life, and towns like Leipzig or Hamburg—not royal residences—supplied so much of the intellectual energy, and the books that went with it. For August Wilhelm's generation, however, with greater upward mobility, with careers opening up that were hitherto unheard of, an ennoblement had its uses—or the revival of a lapsed title. August Wilhelm and Friedrich von Schlegel were the only members of the family to benefit, and with their deaths, the title also became extinct.

It was Johann Friedrich who married Rebekka Wilke, the descendant of Cranach. She died at the birth of their thirteenth child. August Wilhelm's grandfather was not cut out for a legal career, preferring instead the pleasures of his vineyard in Sörnewitz, near Meissen: the pretty little village produces a good crisp white wine still to this day. He spent the time with studies and country pursuits, among beehives. His superiors had less time for such Virgilian idylls and sacked him in 1741. Funds were to be short for his sons, August Wilhelm's father and his uncles, Johann Elias, Johann Heinrich and Johann August

Their lives showed no such disorder. There have been those who have seen in Johann Friedrich's grandson, Karl Wilhelm Friedrich Schlegel, shortened to Friedrich, and his unregulated lifestyle and frenetic bursts of intellectual energy, something of his grandfather's inheritance.[5] True, Friedrich's life was a kind of fever chart; but outward circumstances also played their part in it. He stands out all the more when compared with the ordered lives of his older brothers.

Of Johann Friedrich's and Rebekka's thirteen children,[6] we are concerned with three only, at a pinch four, all Saxons born in Meissen, three of them part of German literary history, one (Johann Heinrich) a mere footnote, while the other two (Johann Elias and Johann Adolf) are rather more substantially represented. Their nephews, August Wilhelm and Friedrich, found it convenient to cite them when it suited their purposes. August Wilhelm was from an early age conscious of the family legacy: as a Göttingen student he wrote to Johann Joachim Eschenburg, the earlier Shakespeare translator, with the pious wish that he might live up to the name;[7] he kept a piece of paper on which he jotted down the names of the dramatists by the name of Schlegel,[8] himself and his brother of course—the authors of those dismal failures, *Ion* and *Alarcos*—but also his two uncles Johann Elias and Johann Heinrich. Friedrich Schlegel, in 1796 sidling up to another member of his father's generation, Christoph Martin Wieland, expressed his pride in a family that had made its contribution to the 'dawn of German art' and the 'first formation of taste in Germany'.[9] No matter that it was pure hypocrisy: the young Romantics all abhorred Wieland.

'From One House Four Such Marvellous Minds'

'From one house four such marvellous minds' and 'paragons of taste and virtue' was how Christian Fürchtegott Gellert poet, writer of fables and sermons, later a professor in Leipzig, characterised the Schlegel brothers

---

5 Such as Ernst Behler, *Friedrich Schlegel in Selbstzeugnissen und Dokumenten*, rowohlts monographien (Reinbek: Rowohlt, 1966), 8.
6 Listed in Seeliger, 149f.
7 *Briefe*, I, 5f.
8 SLUB Dresden, Mscr. Dresd. e. 90, II, 6 (VIa, VIII).
9 *Kritische Friedrich-Schlegel-Ausgabe* [KA], ed. Ernst Behler *et al.*, 30 vols (Paderborn, Munich, Vienna: Schöningh; Zurich: Thomas, 1958– in progress), XXIII, 288.

whom he had met at the élite school of St Afra in Meissen or at the University of Leipzig in the 1730s and 1740s.[10] In fact, only one (Johann Heinrich) was sent to St Afra, where Gellert—and more famously Lessing—had been pupils. Two (Johann Elias and Johann Adolf) attended the no less renowned Pforta school in Naumburg, alma mater to Klopstock (and to Nietzsche). Much later, when delivering a Latin oration in Bonn, August Wilhelm Schlegel could not resist informing his audience that his own father had been a pupil and then a teacher at the Pforta.[11] These schools produced scholars and young gentlemen (in that order) trained in the classics and rhetoric, Euclid and world history and much more besides. One is tempted to paraphrase Carl Justi's words in his great biography of Winckelmann, that attending these schools had 'nothing youthful about it except the ability to cope with work, and lots of it'.[12]

Johann Elias[13] was by far the most interesting and the most talented of the three. It was his great misfortune to die young. He had not been well served by embarking as a poet and critic under the tutelage of Johann Christoph Gottsched, the Leipzig pundit of French models of taste, or by being overshadowed by the young Gotthold Ephraim Lessing, his main rival as a writer of tragedies and comedies—and also Gottsched's nemesis. The German stage had not been receptive to him, forcing him to find employment in Copenhagen until his early death. His critical writings on the limits of imitation and on the formation of a national style have earned him the title of a 'pioneer in German aesthetics',[14] and that is in good part true. He came closer to his nephew August Wilhelm as a translator (from the French and Danish) and as an adaptor of Greek drama; and closest as the first real German voice to attempt an appreciation of Shakespeare. In his review of Johann Friedrich von Borck's translation of *Julius Caesar* (1741), he rose above the conventional debates on merits and faults with a definition of genius as a 'spirit that grows within itself' ('selbstwachsender

---

10   Christian Fürchtegott Gellert, *Werke*, Sammlung der besten deutschen prosaischen Schriftsteller und Dichter, 10 parts (Carlsruhe: Schmieder, 1774), X, 43.
11   *Opuscula quae Augustus Guilelmus Schlegelius Latine scripta reliquit*, ed. Eduardus Böcking (Lipsiae: Weidmann, 1848), 416f.
12   Carl Justi, *Winckelmann und seine Zeitgenossen*, 3rd edn, 3 vols (Leipzig: Vogel, 1923), I, 49.
13   JES was born in 1718, not 1719, as is often assumed. For dating I rely on Seeliger, who consulted the relevant parish registers (153).
14   See Elizabeth M. Wilkinson, *Johann Elias Schlegel: a German Pioneer in Aesthetics* (Oxford: Blackwell, 1945).

Geist'), and pointed forward to Edward Young's notion of an '*Original*' that '*grows*; it is not *made*',[15] and through him, to Herder's organicist thinking.

Johann Heinrich, a close friend of Lessing's at St Afra, was also a translator from the English;[16] he, too, went to Copenhagen, becoming a professor of history and geography at the university and royal librarian and historian.[17] To him we owe the edition of Johann Elias's works (1764-73)[18] that also contains material about the family. There is also his footnote in literary history, a minuscule one perhaps, for the preface to his translation of James Thomson's *Sophonisba* (1758)[19] was the first attempt to explain to the Germans the rudiments of English blank verse. Thomson's orderly neo-classical tragedy is a long way from Shakespeare, but the iambic pentameter of German classical drama has an Augustan ring, and August Wilhelm's translation of Shakespeare is not altogether free of it. Uncle and nephew never met, although their antiquarian interests were similar.[20] The two cousins, August Wilhelm Schlegel and Johan Frederik Wilhelm Schlegel must have, as both were studying in Göttingen at the same time before the one became a law professor in Copenhagen, indeed the kind of professor that Schlegel might have become had Madame de Staël not entered his life. Later they found themselves on opposing sides as Denmark sided with Napoleon against Sweden (in 1800 he produced a memorandum on the boarding of neutral vessels, while August Wilhelm was to polemicize against the Continental System and specifically against Danish politics).[21] The fourth brother, Johann August, from whom August

---

15 [Edward Young], *Conjectures on Original Composition* (London: Dodsley, 1759), 12.
16 He translated James Thomson's tragedies *Agamemnon*, *Sophonisba* and *Coriolanus*, and Edward Young's *The Brothers*.
17 On Johann Heinrich see *Dansk Biografisk Leksikon*, ed. C. F. Bricka, cont. Poul Engelstoft and Svend Dahl, 27 vols (Copenhagen: Schultz, 1887-1944), XXI, 190-194; Leopold Magon, *Ein Jahrhundert geistiger und literarischer Beziehungen zwischen Deutschland und Skandinavien 1750-1850* (Dortmund: Ruhfus, 1926), I, 268-274; J.W. Eaton, *The German Influence in Danish Literature in the Eighteenth Century: The German Circle in Copenhagen 1750-1770* (Cambridge: Cambridge UP, 1929), 148-151.
18 Johann Elias Schlegel, *Werke*, ed. Johann Heinrich Schlegel, 5 vols (Copenhagen and Leipzig: Mumm; Prost u. Rothens Erben, 1764-73).
19 *Jakob Thomson's Sophonisba ein Trauerspiel aus dem Englischen übersetzt und mit Anmerkungen erläutert* [...] *von Johann Heinrich Schlegeln* (Leipzig: Hahn, 1758), [xxif.].
20 Cf. *Ioannis Henrici Schlegelii observationes criticae et historicae in Cornelium Nepotem* [...] (Havniae: Philibert, 1778).
21 J. F. W. Schlegel, *Sur la visite de vaisseaux neutres sous convoi* [...] (Copenhagen: Cohen, 1800), subsequently in English. He also published the codex of Old Icelandic Law. On Johan Frederik Wilhelm see *Neuer Nekrolog der Deutschen*, 14. Jg., 2 Th. (1836) (Weimar: Voigt, 1838), 936-943; *Dansk Biografisk Leksikon*, ed Cedergreen Beck, 16 vols (Copenhagen: Gyldendahl, 1979-84), XIII, 122-123.

Wilhelm perhaps took his second name, was the kindly uncle who for a time took in his wayward nephew Friedrich in his country pastorate at Rehburg near Hanover.[22]

We need not dwell too long on the poetic merits of the ten-page elegy that Johann Adolf Schlegel wrote on his brother Johann Elias's death.[23] Its biographical content is of interest, tracing as it does patterns of destitution: emotional (and economic) through the death of his father, then the departure of his university friends, and now the death of his brother. The 'friends' catch the eye.[24] In the style of eighteenth-century poetry, they are named: Christian Fürchtegott Gellert, Johann Arnold Ebert, Gottlieb Wilhelm Rabener, Nikolaus Dietrich Giseke, Johann Andreas Cramer. They are members of the so-called 'Bremer Beiträger' [Bremen Contributors], the group of young writers in Leipzig who were the first to challenge Gottsched's authority. One name is missing: Friedrich Gottlieb Klopstock, whose meteoric rise as Germany's greatest lyric and epic poet of his generation overshadowed all their efforts. They remained *poetae minores*, versatile in a variety of styles, grave and gay as the occasion demanded: his was the grand style alone and the inspired tone. Their names occur in an altogether different context, Klopstock's great Alcaic ode, 'Auf meine Freunde' [To My Friends] (1749). Here Klopstock is in grand Dionysian flight—at least as the eighteenth century understood it—and turns impeccably respectable friends into a herd of goat-footed, thyrsus-brandishing fauns. Johann Adolf Schlegel comes off more lightly; still we do not know whether he was comfortable with being apostrophised as a priest at the wine-god's altar.[25] But friendship, 'Seul mouvement de l'âme où l'excès soit permis' [the sole emotion where excess is allowed],[26] in Voltaire's formulation, surely permitted it.

Klopstock hoped—against all hope—to keep his friends assembled round him, as in his other great ode, on the Lake of Zurich (1750), 'Were you here, we would build tabernacles of friendship, we would live here forever'.[27] The reality was different, although Klopstock asked Johann Adolf in 1754 whether he would consider exchanging his position in Zerbst

---

22 'Joh. Adolf Schlegel', Friedrich Schlichtegroll, *Nekrolog auf das Jahr 1793. Enthaltend Nachrichten von dem Leben merkwürdiger in diesem Jahre verstorbener Personen* (Gotha: Perthes, 1794), 71-121, ref. 91; Carl Enders, *Friedrich Schlegel. Die Quellen seines Wesens und Werdens* (Leipzig: Haessel, 1913), 169.
23 Johann Elias Schlegel, *Werke*, V, liii-lxiv; also in Johann Adolf Schlegel, *Vermischte Gedichte*, 2 vols (Carlsruhe: Schmieder, 1788-90), I, 222-243.
24 Johann Elias Schlegel, *Werke*, V, lviii.
25 Friedrich Gottlieb Klopstock, *Werke und Briefe. Historisch-kritische Ausgabe*, ed. Horst Gronemeyer *et al.*, 21 vols in 25 (Berlin, New York: de Gruyter, 1974- in progress), I, i, 28.
26 Voltaire, *Discours en vers sur l'homme* (1734-37).
27 Klopstock, I, i, 97.

for the pastorate of St Catherine in Hamburg: it would bring him nearer to Copenhagen, where Klopstock was (and Johann Heinrich).[28] Johann Adolf remained loyal to his friends and they to him: there are several poems by him addressing them. They stayed together in word and spirit if not in body; they provided important networks. Towards the end of his life Johann Adolf was still in touch with Johann Arnold Ebert, one of 'the Poet's Friends' and now a professor in Brunswick and well-disposed to his son August Wilhelm, just out of university.[29] And through Ebert, he knew his influential colleague, the Shakespeare translator Eschenburg. Even later, Klopstock himself, doubtless displeased at having his verse quantities criticised by a young upstart, may have been in some measure mollified in learning that the author was Johann Adolf's clever son, August Wilhelm.

Otherwise, these friends saw little of each other. Their letters tried to relive a lost presence and were passed on from hand to hand as sacred relics. The next generation, Goethe's, but especially the circle around August Wilhelm's later mentor, Gottfried August Bürger in Göttingen, outdid each other in an exuberance from which Klopstock's generation would have recoiled. For the Romantics, too, friendship was an uninhibiting factor, as their letters testify. Not August Wilhelm's, of course, but it is worth advancing the view that for him friendship was the closest he ever came to real intimacy, real exchange of minds, that the relationships that mattered and lasted were with friends, the Tieck brothers, Ludwig and Friedrich, later, Madame de Staël and her children; his dealings with his brother Friedrich ('my oldest and most exacting friend'),[30] have elements of this. Even his wife Caroline's form of address to him, 'mein guter Freund' ['my good friend'][31] may tell us something of the nature of their relationship.

Johann Adolf Schlegel

The Schlegel family reverted to type with Johann Adolf, the clergyman and theologian.[32] He held on to the accepted tenets of the Christian faith and its Lutheran doctrinal basis—even accepting eternal damnation[33]—indeed

---

28   *Ibid.*, III, Briefe 1753-58, 24f.
29   SLUB Dresden, Mscr. Dresd. e. 90, XIX (21), 5.
30   *KA*, XXIII, 298.
31   As in *Caroline. Briefe aus der Frühromantik*. Nach Georg Waitz vermehrt hg. v. Erich Schmidt, 2 vols (Leipzig: Insel, 1913), I, 432.
32   On JAS see Schlichtegroll, *Nekrolog*, and esp. the exhaustive study by Joyce S. Rutledge, *Johann Adolph Schlegel*, German Studies in America, 18 (Berne, Frankfurt am Main: Herbert Lang, 1974).
33   As instanced by his poem, 'Von der Hölle', *Vermischte Gedichte*, I, 130-133.

he would not have found high office without general orthodoxy in such matters. A typical eighteenth-century career unfolded, where church and state, poetry and criticism, the pulpit and the study, held a not always easy balance. But with this generation, as almost everywhere in Europe, an independent career as a writer was almost impossible without private means or patronage—or a prodigious industry that could compromise literary standards. The three greatest representatives of Johann Adolf's generation are instructive: Klopstock lived off a royal pension; Wieland had to write and write and write, and not all of it was good; as for Lessing, he was burnt up by projects and the fits and starts of a literary career. A generation on, Schiller could not exist without patronage, a university post, and a position at court, and he had to write for all he was worth. If the brothers Schlegel, Friedrich and August Wilhelm, like so many of their Romantic contemporaries, had to turn in later life to the state for their support, it is a measure of how much and how little had changed. In their father's generation, the state, universities (especially a small group in Protestant territories), the school and the church were distributors of security. Elsewhere, Edward Young and Thomas Gray in England knew this to be true, as did the host of abbés in France.

Johann Adolf knew hard grind and self-discipline, the drudgery of a house tutor, until he was appointed a teacher at his old school, the Pforta in Naumburg. There, he married Johanna Christiane Erdmuthe Hübsch, the daughter of the mathematics master Johann Georg Gotthelf Hübsch. Before becoming 'Mutter Schlegel' and the matriarch who bore ten children, she was briefly 'Muthchen' in letters from the Klopstock circle.[34] In 1754 Johann Adolf accepted a post at the petty ducal residence of Zerbst in Anhalt (a Zerbst princess was to become Catherine the Great), with a church ministry and a professorship of theology and aesthetics at the Gymnasium. Gerlach Adolf von Münchhausen, first 'Kurator' of Göttingen university, then George III's minister of finance in Hanover, heard of Johann Adolf's powers as a preacher and in 1759 offered him either a pastorate at Göttingen or the Marktkirche in Hanover. He chose Hanover, bringing with him his brother Johann August to nearby Pattensen, then Rehburg. In 1775, he became 'Superintendent' and pastor of the Hof- und Stadtkirche, the court and city church in the Hanover New Town, later still adding the title of 'Generalsuperintendent' of Hoya (1782) and Calenberg (1787).[35]

---

34 Klopstock, III, Briefe 1753-58, 25.
35 See Rudolf Steinmetz, 'Die Generalsuperintendenten von Calenberg', *Zeitschrift der Gesellschaft für niedersächsische Kirchengeschichte* 13 (1908), 25-267, on JAS 192-201.

Yet these bare facts need qualifying and extending. Johann Adolf was called to these high ecclesiastical appointments on the strength of his skills as a preacher and as a writer of sermons. One of Hanover's sons, the great actor-dramatist August Wilhelm Iffland, much later to cross paths with our Schlegel, remembered Johann Adolf's oratorical powers—he preached from a memorised text, which he later published[36]—the warmth of his exposition, but also his Saxon dialect and his spare physical frame.[37] His sermons follow orthodox teaching and homiletics, but they are not mere rhetorical exercises; the text of the day is central and its direct application to the faithful. August Wilhelm and Friedrich Schlegel certainly picked up some tips for their own kind of secular predication, August Wilhelm's Shakespeare essay, Friedrich's 'sermon' on mythology, and the many courses of lectures that both brothers gave.

Two portraits of Johann Adolf represent the different sides of his personality: one, by Johann Gerhard Wilhelm Thielo, also the basis for the image in the family psalter, has him as a Lutheran pastor with preaching bands; the other, by Caroline Rehberg, shows high forehead and ascetic features, suggesting self-discipline, while the large eyes betoken a ready intelligence. A sober and scholarly figure, one who kept aloof where he could from the 'Connexionen' in the residence city,[38] he retreated where possible to his 'Official-Garten' and was able to work impervious to children milling around him.[39] But contemporaries also remembered his sense of duty, his application, his love of order, qualities that seem to recur in his second-youngest son, August Wilhelm. He, in 1828 reaffirming his Protestant roots (if not their doctrinal stance) described his father as 'learned, pious, and a man of worth'.[40] Learning and piety certainly characterised his collections of sermons and hymns, to which he devoted himself in later life, as an adjunct to his many pastoral duties. There was also a textbook for confirmands. At least two generations of Hanoverian worshippers would have sung the standard repertoire of German Protestant hymnody, like 'Ein' feste Burg' or 'Wie schön leuchtet der Morgenstern', in hymnals edited by Johann Adolf, shorn of much of their original theological content and poetic language and

---

36 As: *Neue Sammlung einiger Predigten über wichtige Glaubens- und Sittenlehren*, 2 vols (Leipzig: Crusius, 1778).
37 August Wilhelm Iffland, *Ueber meine theatralische Laufbahn*, ed. Hugo Holstein, Deutsche Litteraturdenkmale des 18. und 19. Jahrhunderts, 24 (Heilbronn: Henninger, 1886), 14.
38 Steinmetz, 196.
39 Schlichtegroll, 100.
40 *SW*, VIII, 221.

reduced to virtue and morality.⁴¹ His sons, the one in his Catholicising phase, the other in his outright conversion to Catholicism, would—like most of their generation—react against this Enlightenment theology.

Above all, he was known as a poet. The principle of versatility, poetic *silvae*, that characterised so much eighteenth-century poetry, applied in full measure to him: occasional poems (an ode to his temporal overlord, King George III, for instance, declaimed in 1770 'by one of my sons'),⁴² religious (on Christian devotion), didactic, fables, verse *contes*, and pastoral, fugitive, light-footed verse in the manner of Anacreon or Horace. It was restrained rococo, Phyllis never lifting her skirts indecorously. He was still issuing these poems as the young Goethe began to write in this vein. Then there was his translation of Charles Batteux's normative *Les beaux-arts réduits à un même principe* [The Fine Arts Reduced to One and the Same Principle] (1746), that came out in three editions, one as late as 1770, and which, despite his attempts to modify the Frenchman's rigidity, incurred Herder's thunderous ire.⁴³ Such texts could no longer hold their own in the years of the 'Sturm und Drang'. Or his part-translation of Antoine Banier's *La Mythologie et les fables expliquées par l'histoire* [Mythology and Fables Explained by History] (1754-64), that found Lessing's immediate approval and later Herder's. One might be permitted the fantasy of imagining the young August Wilhelm absorbing his later knowledge of comparative mythology from these volumes in his father's study. All this reflects both the contentments of ecclesiastical office and also the wider explorations of the intellect. Herder, later superintendent in Weimar, was to know their tensions; Johann Adolf was able to keep them in check.

Growing Up in Hanover

'I am a Hanoverian, born a subject of the king of Great Britain, who always showed great respect for my father'.⁴⁴ Writing thus in 1813 from Stockholm to Count Sickingen, a high Austrian official, Schlegel was making two

---

41 On JAS's hymnody see John Julian, *A Dictionary of Hymnology* [...] (London: Murray, 1892), 1009-1010; Inge Mager, 'Die Rezeption der Lieder Paul Gerhardts in niedersächsischen Gesangbüchern', *Zeitschrift der Gesellschaft für niedersächsische Kirchengeschichte* 80 (1982), 121-146, ref. 137-140.
42 'Auf die Geburtstagsfeyer Georg des Dritten [...]', *Vermischte Gedichte*, II, 345-358.
43 Rutledge, 197-221.
44 Ludwig Schmidt, 'Ein Brief August Wilhelm v. Schlegels an Metternich' [*recte* Sickingen], *Mitteilungen des Instituts f. Österreichische Geschichtsforschung* 23 (1902), 490-495, ref. 495.

points. Despite being a 'cosmopolitan' in the close company of Madame de Staël, he maintained a sense of loyalty to Hanover, his birthplace, and to the kingdom of Hanover, that had been occupied by foreign forces during the Napoleonic troubles and whose fate as an integral German territory was his present concern. He had of course meanwhile moved on, to the great capitals of Europe, but his family name still remained linked to the administration and polity of the Hanoverian state,[45] where his father had had high ecclesiastical office, his brother Moritz similarly, and his brother Karl was a jurist in the church consistory. His late brother Carl, too, had joined a Hanoverian regiment. It reminds us as well that Schlegel's life is part of a family chronicle: there were significant moments when family concerns overrode all else, when the dutiful and obedient son or the solicitous brother dropped everything and interrupted an otherwise orderly life; or when August Wilhelm and Friedrich almost assumed a common identity of aim and purpose.

Schlegel's childhood was spent within the confines of the residence town of Hanover, where on 5 September, 1767 he was born. Whereas Zerbst was a smallish ducal seat with a huge Schloss, Hanover was different. True: it was no longer the seat of the duke-electors of Brunswick-Lüneburg, for they were now kings of Great Britain and Ireland; but there was still a palace, the Leineschloss, where the viceroy resided, where he received royal visitors progressing through their German territories, such as the sons of King George III, who underwent their military training in Hanover or attended the university at Göttingen. Thus Hanover enjoyed a special status in the eighteenth and early nineteenth centuries: in personal union with one of the great extraterritorial powers, but locally administered according to German conventions. The population was 18,000 (Weimar's: 8,000); there was a musical culture; there were frequent enough visits from theatre troupes to catch the young Iffland's imagination. Johann Adolf Schlegel, as a church dignitary ('Generalsuperintendent'), was in the hierarchy of the Hanoverian administration the ecclesiastical servant of King George III, and it was the same monarch who in 1775 signed the letters patent

---

45 Reinhard Oberschelp, *Niedersachsen 1760-1820. Wirtschaft, Gesellschaft, Kultur im Land Hannover und Nachbargebieten*, Veröffentlichungen der historischen Kommission für Niedersachsen und Bremen, XXXV (Quellen und Untersuchungen zur allgemeinen Geschichte Niedersachsens in der Neuzeit, 4, i), 2 vols (Hildesheim: Lax, 1982), II, 261-264.

appointing him to the Court Church[46] or who in 1786 'assures him of our affection' when granting him a pension of 200-300 talers.[47]

Not that this Hanoverian connection ever made his son August Wilhelm into an anglophile. Perhaps only his later visits to the country and his acquaintance with the solidity of its institutions enabled him in some measure to overcome his prejudices: against, as he saw them, English coldness and superficiality, their inadequate system of education, their commercial mentality, the 'impurity' of their language. The list may be extended. But then there was Shakespeare: the 'mixed' language would be worth learning for his sake. Also, Madame de Staël was a staunch anglophile; it was she who introduced him to the *haute volée* in London. When London became the greatest repository of Sanskrit manuscripts outside of India, Schlegel willingly went there and enjoyed being feted. He was the proud recipient of the Royal Hanoverian Guelphic Order[48] (the white horse of Hanover is visible among his many other decorations on Hohneck's portrait). And when in 1832 he was received by the Duke of Sussex, George III's only studious son,[49] they had in common that both had studied at the illustrious University of Göttingen, founded by His Royal Highness's great-grandfather, King George II.

Rapid urbanisation and the Second World War mean that there is now but little to recognise of Schlegel's birthplace, today's city. The town itself then was dominated by its four main city churches and the elaborate gables of the old town hall. Johann Adolf's first appointment was to the big city church in Hanover, the Marktkirche, and it was in the pastorate that his younger children were born. This huge brick Gothic church of St George and St James was the tallest of the four spires that the beholder saw when approaching Hanover from outside. It still maintained its medieval character, dominating the market place and its old high-fronted houses.

The Old Town, with its fine medieval and Renaissance half-timbered fronts, lived in somewhat uneasy union with the ducal residence that Hanover had become when the house of Brunswick-Lüneburg made its seat there in 1636. This event had made it necessary to create a ducal palace, the Leineschloss, and indeed to extend the whole town across to the west of the river Leine. In the eighteenth century this was enclosed

---

46 Hanover, Landeskirchliches Archiv, A 07 Nr. 0892.
47 SLUB Dresden, Mscr. Dresd. e. 90, VI (5).
48 *Ibid.*, II (5).
49 *Ibid.*, XI, V (B).

within a system of defence walls, beyond which was open country. In this New Town, the Neustadt, was built in 1666-70 the Neustädter Hof- und Stadtkirche, to which Johann Adolf Schlegel was appointed as pastor and superintendent in 1775. It was the parish church for the court officials and employees, their tradesmen and servants. A baroque building designed by an Italian architect, it was a hall church with galleries, good for carrying the voice. Memorials to court officials, preachers and 'Generalsuperindenten' covered the floor; but none could compete with the grave of its most famous parishioner, Gottfried Wilhelm Leibniz. The young Iffland, whose father worked in the Hanoverian war chancellery,[50] thus had not far to go to hear Johann Adolf Schegel, whose sermons so warmed his heart.[51] There were close links with the families of other leading Hanoverian citizenry: Johann Adolf knew Karl August von Hardenberg, the future Prussian chancellor; later August Wilhelm was to use this connection as an entrée.[52] Heinrich Christian Boie, one of the Göttingen circle around Bürger, was for a time the secretary to a general in Hanover[53] and founded the influential periodical *Deutsches Museum*. This may well have forged the link with Bürger when August Wilhelm went to Göttingen to study.

Siblings

Thus far, men have been to the fore. Johanna Christiane Erdmuthe Schlegel, 'Mutter Schlegel', as she signed herself in letters, was the matriarch of this remarkable family, as 'Frau Generalsuperintendentin' part of the ruling administration of the city and aware of the 'Connexionen' this afforded.[54] Johann Adolf was absorbed by his pastoral duties, latterly, by his religious poetry. The practical concerns he left to his wife. It was she who held things together. The touches of Saxon dialect in her letters bring her speech alive. August Wilhelm, in his turn, did everything to support his widowed mother, whom he saw but rarely in the later years of her life. But in 1808, on his return from the triumph of the Vienna Lectures, despite rumours of war and armies on the move, he made a quick dash across from Weimar to Hanover just to see her.

---

50   Iffland, vi.
51   *Ibid.*, 6.
52   *Briefe*, I, 65, II, 25f.
53   Enders, 83.
54   As she writes. SLUB Dresden, Mscr. Dresd. e. 90, XIX (21), 16.

According to Schlichtegroll's *Nekrolog*,[55] there were ten children, of whom four predeceased their parents: if this is true, there are records only of nine.[56] The pattern (for the sons at least) of lawyers, theologians, and writer-academics that applied to Johann Adolf's generation, seemed to be perpetuated in Moritz the pastor, Karl the jurist, August Wilhelm the academic, but then there was Carl August the soldier—and Friedrich, not trained for anything. The two eldest, born in Zerbst, were Karl August Moritz, known as Moritz, and Johann Karl Fürchtegott, known as Karl (Fürchtegott a tribute to Gellert). Moritz was first a pastor in Bothfeld near Hanover, then superintendent in Göttingen, finally superintendent-general in Harburg. Friedrich Schlegel, the 'problem child', found a kind of second father in Moritz. Moritz surprised everyone by producing a volume of sermons to mark the political events leading up to 1814.[57] It was his mentally disturbed son Johann August Adolph for whom his uncle August Wilhelm later accepted responsibility in Bonn. His wife Charlotte survived all of the Schlegels of this generation. Karl was a 'Konsistorialrat', a jurist in the church administration in Hanover: their family circumstances, especially the letters written by his wife Julie during the Napoleonic occupation of Hanover tell us much of its cost to the civilian population. His history of the church in Hanover, not least of the Reformation, will not have pleased his younger brother Friedrich (August Wilhelm subscribed to a set on finer paper),[58] while his compendium of church law in Hanover[59] set out the respective spheres of competence of the spiritual and secular authorities (Karl knew from close observation of his father what the responsibilities of a pastor were). Karl's works are still cited.

But what of Carl August Schlegel, the brother who embodied—tragically—the link between Hanover and England? This mathematically

---

55 Schlichtegroll, 119.
56 I have only been able to trace records of two sons who predeceased their parents, in Hanover: Georg Adolph Bonaventura, died 20 April 1782, and Friedrich Anton Heinrich, died 31 July 1784. Hanover, Ev. Luth. Stadtkirchenkanzlei. A third is Carl Christian August (1762-89), who died at Madras.
57 Karl August Moriz [sic] Schlegel, *Auswahl einiger Predigten in Beziehung auf die bisherigen Zeitereignisse, und nach wichtigen Zeitbedürfnissen* (Göttingen: Vandenhoek und Ruprecht, 1814).
58 Johann Karl Fürchtegott Schlegel, *Kirchen- und Reformationsgeschichte von Norddeutschland und den Hannoverschen Staaten*, 3 vols (Hanover: Helwing, 1828-32). AWS's order I, xviii. A short characteristic of JAS III, 471, 486.
59 Johann Karl Fürchtegott Schlegel, *Churhannöversches Kirchenrecht*, 5 vols (Hanover: Hahn, 1801-06).

and technically endowed brother (the grandson of a mathematician on his mother's side, the nephew of an officer of engineers on his father's)[60] became a lieutenant in a Hanoverian regiment in 1782, while his young brothers were still at school. With it, he travelled to India in the service of the East India Company.[61] Behind these bare facts stands a personal link with wider historical and political developments that was to colour August Wilhelm Schlegel's view of European involvement in India.

To augment the forces available for their wars against the French and against insurgent Indian rulers, the British in 1781 raised two infantry regiments in Hanover. They consisted of volunteers, who in their turn had to sign up for eight years, seven of these to be spent in India. They went in ships inadequately protected first against cold and then heat, the men packed in like sardines, illness and shipwreck a constant threat during the six months' journey. Once arrived, they were prey to the extreme climate, pests and wild animals. The pay was good, if one survived, and only one in three did. General Stuart, commanding at Fort St George, immediately used his Hanoverians against the French, against the great Tipu Sultan and against mutinying Indian troops.

Carl Schlegel's commanding general, realising his talents, sent him on a surveying expedition from Madras into the Carnatic, as far as the mountain region (his cartographic survey is today in Göttingen university library). All was not well with the young Hanoverian lieutenant: a charge of misconduct (later quashed) caused him distress and depression. Like so many Europeans, he was fired by the adventure of India; like so many, he never returned. He fell victim to a tropical disease and died at Madras, aged only twenty-eight. The letter of condolence from his superior officer calls him 'extremely esteemed, and equally regretted by his brother Officers and friends', and 'Lines written on the death of Lieutenant Schlegel' appeared in the *Madras Courier* for 21 October 1789.[62]

---

60   A brother of his father's, Johann Karl Schlegel (born 1727), is said to have been an officer of engineers. Seeliger, 150.

61   Carl Schlegel served in the 14th Regiment, commanded first by Colonel Reinbold, then by Colonel von Wangenheim. Information about Hanoverians in the service of the East India Company in E. von dem Knesebeck, *Geschichte der churhannoverschen Truppen in Gibraltar, Minorca und Ostindien* (Hanover: Helwing, 1845), 123-183, ref. 182f.; also Oberschelp, *Niedersachsen*, I, 350-352.

62   *SW*, II, 13; *Briefe*, I, 6-9; see Rosane Rocher and Ludo Rocher, *Founders of Western Indology. August Wilhelm von Schlegel and Henry Thomas Colebrooke in Correspondence 1820-1837*, Abhandlungen für die Kunde des Morgenlandes, 84 (Wiesbaden: Harrassowitz, 2013), 1f.

Carl had found time to write affectionately to his younger brother Wilhelm, encouraging him in his poetry, rather as Johann Adolf might have, promising him funds out of the bounty that he was never to receive, and, from Fort St George, describing a Brahmin funeral.[63] Eleven years later, when the death of his step-daughter Auguste Böhmer plunged him into grief, August Wilhelm extended the mourning process to include his brother, in the elegy 'Neoptolemus an Diocles'. It would be reductive and simplistic to attribute the two younger brothers' fascination with India solely to this family link, yet Carl Schlegel found mention in the preface to Friedrich's *Ueber die Sprache und Weisheit der Indier* [On the language and Wisdom of the Indians] of 1808,[64] while August Wilhelm referred to his brother in his first letter to the great Indologist Henry Thomas Colebrooke.[65] Schlegel, not surprisingly, hardly ever had a good word to say about the East India Company. Coleridge and Schlegel, otherwise associated through a common way of seeing creative processes in art (those 'borrowings' with which Coleridge is taxed) were further linked, in that both lost an older brother, lieutenants in the Company service.[66]

Schlegel's two sisters, Henriette and Charlotte, married two brothers Ernst. Charlotte's husband Ludwig Emanuel, a secretary in the Dresden court bursary and later second court chamberlain there, moved with the Saxon royal household between its residences in Dresden and Pillnitz. Their daughter was the talented painter Auguste von Buttlar, the niece for whom her uncle Wilhelm did so much in the 1820s. The Ernst household in Dresden was a place of refuge and repose for brothers ever on the move, Friedrich especially. Charlotte was intelligent, and a shrewd judge of character; she knew what drove her brothers, even if they did not. She was level-headed and sensible; she needed to be when one brother (August Wilhelm) married a 'lady with a past' (Caroline) or when another (Friedrich) was living in open liaison with a divorcee who happened also to be Jewish (Dorothea).

---

63 Oskar Walzel, 'Neue Quellen zur Geschichte der älteren romantischen Schule', *Zeitschrift für die Österreichischen Gymnasien* 43 (1892), 289-296.
64 Friedrich Schlegel, *Ueber die Sprache und Weisheit der Indier* (Heidelberg: Mohr u. Zimmer, 1808), xiif.
65 Rocher and Rocher, 30.
66 Richard Holmes, *Coleridge: Early Visions* (London, etc.: Hodder & Stoughton, 1989), 10.

Childhood and Schooling

August Wilhelm's birth was recorded in the parish register of the Marktkirche on 5 September, 1767.[67] Godparents were his uncle Johann August's wife, and a daughter of the mayor of Zerbst. In September, 1813, in the uniform of a Swedish 'Regeringsråd', Schlegel found his aged godmother still alive in Zerbst, now blind and arthritic. She reminded him of his nurse's prophecy that he would travel abroad: the tide of war had swept him back to the place where his father had ministered.[68]

How does one write the childhood of a man about whom the only anecdotes or other sources are scholastic, who seemed almost by parthenogenesis to have become a scholar, to emerge from a chrysalis as a fully-formed savant? Must one not move on swiftly to the Man? Already his position in the family, as the studious and industrious and talented second-youngest son, contrasted with the youngest sibling, Friedrich, the problem child of already elderly parents, handed over for a while, first to his uncle, then to his much older brother Moritz in his country parish.[69] August Wilhelm, or Wilhelm, as he was more commonly called, secured a special place in his mother's affections. He was reliable, orderly, punctual, particularly when after Johann Adolf's death in 1793 the sons needed to support their mother financially (and Friedrich was constantly in debt).

We have to begin with education. The latter part of the eighteenth century was dominated by debates about the 'bud-time of childhood', as Jean Paul's treatise *Levana* (1807) called it. The educational theorists of the day, Johann Bernhard Basedow and Johann Heinrich Pestalozzi especially, proceeded directly or indirectly from engagement with Rousseau's *Émile*; all reacted in some way against the incarceration of children in former monastic buildings, their early years spent in drudgery, rote learning, hardly seeing the light of day, the miserable childhood suffered by two of

---

67 'Pastoris Joh. Adolph Schlegel Söhnlein August Wilhelm. Paten Frau Wilhelmine Sophie Pastor: Schlegel in Rehburg Eheliebste. Demoiselle Auguste Sophie Weissen Oberbürgermeister in Zerbst dritte Tochter'. Hanover, Ev. Lutherische Stadtkirchenkanzlei.
68 Comtesse Jean de Pange née Broglie, *Auguste-Guillaume Schlegel et Madame de Staël. D'Après des documents inédits*, doctoral thesis University of Paris (Paris: Albert, 1938), 458.
69 Enders, 169.

Schlegel's scholarly mentors, one, Johann Joachim Winckelmann by proxy, the other, the great Göttingen classicist Christian Gottlob Heyne, directly.

Schlegel's was a privileged childhood, and he would not disappoint that line of pastors and lawmen whose spiritual presence others might find daunting. In that sense he conformed to type: he did not shift radically from the family's traditions; he was not like his Romantic contemporaries for whom the reformed Gymnasium in Berlin meant social change or social mobility, like Ludwig Tieck or Achim von Arnim; or like those remarkable brothers Humboldt, whose private tutoring extended to its limits the range of their intellectual and physical pursuits. But neither was he presumably a '*Monstrum eruditionis*': the great eighteenth-century macrobiotic physician Christoph Wilhelm Hufeland warned his readers in 1797 that their children would become this if closeted with books too early.[70]

A 'monstrum' he was certainly was not, but doubtless a kind of prodigy. His father Johann Adolf taught his own sons (there is no mention of his daughters) until they were ready for the Lyceum. There seems also to have been a tutor.[71] From his own translations of Batteux and also of the French children's writer Marie Leprince de Beaumont, we can extrapolate a kind of direct method that appealed to the senses as well as to the intellect, that taught social forms of behaviour as well as facts, that tried to bring grammar and language paradigms alive. Not all of his sons may have needed this. When briefly a professor in Jena, then in Berlin and Bonn, August Wilhelm was to express thoughts on language, its origin and acquisition. The effortless assimilation of language by children[72]—like wet clay ready to receive all impressions, as he was to write much later[73]—even by imitation, was a sign of unconscious and innate powers at work; in each child were repeated the earliest processes of human language invention. In another context, he criticised Rousseau's educational theories for their emphasis on sensory connotations and their neglect of moral and religious inculcation under parental guidance. But he did concede Rousseau's concern for children's physical welfare.[74] He doubtless came closer to personal experience when

---

70 Christoph Wilhelm Hufeland, *Die Kunst das menschliche Leben zu verlängern*, 2 parts (Vienna, Prague: Haas, 1797), II, 108.
71 'August Wilhelm und Friedrich Schlegel', *Zeitgenossen. Biographieen und Charakteristiken*, vol. 1 (Leipzig and Altenburg: Brockhaus, 1816), 80.
72 Walter Jesinghaus, 'August Wilhelm von Schlegels Meinungen über die Ursprache', doctoral thesis University of Leipzig (Düsseldorf: C. Jesinghaus, 1913), 41.
73 *Indische Bibliothek*, 3 vols (Bonn: Weber, 1820-30), II (1827), 17.
74 *Vorlesungen über das akademische Studium*, ed. Frank Jolles, Bonner Vorlesungen, 1 (Heidelberg: Stiehm, 1971), 49-52.

he recommended the early acquisition of languages, and stressed the need to train the memory from childhood, to profit from the child's natural aptitude for learning, by teaching him the classical languages:[75] there was no royal road to Latin à la Comenius or Basedow, and Latin was the basis of the Gymnasium, the foundation of grammar and rhetoric—and of good style in the vernacular. Schlegel's crisp, elegant, well-modulated sentences owed much to this, and Latin remained for him the vehicle for much of his scholarly discourse.

All this was doubtless reflected in the curriculum of the old Lyceum in Hanover, founded in 1583, the Gymnasium that Schlegel attended, like before him Iffland, like Karl Philipp Moritz, the novelist and aesthetician.[76] To reach it, he would have to cross the river Leine and walk into the Old Town, where a somewhat dilapidated half-timbered building stood next to the Marktkirche. It is not clear at what age his father released his sons for further schooling (Friedrich was never sent at all), but they would have experienced the Lyceum essentially as the Latin school that its name suggests. The old curriculum—it is worth listing it in its entirety—had been theology, catechism, Latin, Greek, universal history, Bible history, geography, arithmetic, logic, oratory, classical antiquities, Hebrew, writing and reading. French was added in 1761, English in 1773. In 1774, there were 170 pupils (including Karl Philipp Moritz and Iffland). The new rector, Johann Daniel Schumann, preferred over Herder's head, complained of too much learning by rote. (It was the same Schumann who had an exchange with Lessing over the tenets of Christianity against perceived threats to the authenticity of revelation.) A directive of 1775 called for more lessons in the mother tongue and more 'Realien'. These latter were supplied by the abbé Pluche's *Spectacle de la nature*, in Johann Georg Sulzer's version. Schumann taught English privately, and there was a French instructor. His successor, Julius Bernhard Ballenstedt, won the post in 1780 in contention with the schoolman, poet and translator Johann Heinrich Voss, and Karl Philipp Moritz. Competition indeed! The last rector in Schlegel's time, Christian

---

75 *Ibid.*, 55; see also his 'Abriß vom Studium der classischen Philologie', published by Josef Körner, 'Ein philologischer Studienplan August Wilhelm Schlegels', *Die Erziehung* 7 (1932), 373-379.

76 For what follows see Franz Bertram, *Geschichte des Ratsgymnasiums (vormals Lyceum) zu Hannover*, Veröffentlichungen zur niedersächsischen Geschichte, 10 (Hanover: Gersbach, 1915), 256-284; also Hugo Eybisch, *Anton Reiser. Untersuchungen zur Lebensgeschichte von K. Ph. Moritz und zur Kritik seiner Autobiographie*, Probefahrten, 14 (Leipzig: Voigtländer, 1909), 18-53; Oberschelp, *Niedersachsen*, II, 183-191.

Friedrich Rühlmann, continued the move from excessive teaching of the classics to more geography and history. In his semi-autobiographical novel *Anton Reiser* (1785), Karl Philipp Moritz left his undisguised memories of his time under Schumann and his predecessor (1771-76), the sheer joy of being taught well and being encouraged, but also the miseries inflicted by insensitive pedagogues.

As good Hanoverians, the school, its staff and pupils, celebrated the king's birthday with poems, music and orations. On one of these occasions, the young Schlegel recited his own history of German literature in hexameters.[77] There were also theatrical performances, no doubt fired by the great actors Friedrich Ludwig Schröder and Johann Franz Brockmann visiting Hanover and playing Hamlet in guest roles. Moritz's *Anton Reiser* told of the draw of the theatre on the young and excitable mind; Iffland needed no encouragement.[78] We learn that schoolboys performed Fresny's *Die Widersprecherin* [The Lady Contradicts] in Luise Gottsched's translation.[79] No-one was bothered that the nine-year-old Schlegel's father had once been an adversary of Gottsched's: the boy was given a female role in the performance.

The boy's powers of concentration were such that his tutor had trouble rousing him to take exercise.[80] Thus one can only hope that there was ample use of the 'Official-Garten', or excursions outside the city ramparts and into the open country, perhaps with the children of other officials, or even an expedition to Bothfeld, where his brother Moritz was the pastor. We have no evidence at this stage: only later, when he did walking tours in the Alps with the Staël boys, or took seriously to horse-riding, do we see another, less bookish side to Schlegel.

Göttingen

For Schlegel, Göttingen would always mean two things: an idea of scholarship, an institution of minds, a notion of method, a school of thought; but also the plain and unadorned university town of the kingdom

---

77 *Zeitgenossen*, 180; Enders, 181f.
78 Cf. Doris Olsen, Linda Bock, Ralf Lubnow, 'Theaterleidenschaft', in: 'Eine Jugend in Niedersachsen im 18. Jahrhundert', in: Silvio Vietta (ed.), *Romantik in Niedersachsen. Der Beitrag des protestantischen Nordens zur Entstehung der literarischen Romantik in Deutschland* (Hildesheim, Zurich, New York: Olms, 1986), 100-111.
79 Iffland, ix.
80 *Zeitgenossen*, 180.

of Hanover, and its professors. It was set, as German universities then were, at a suitable distance from the royal or ducal residence, to keep student rowdiness at bay: Schlegel's matriculation diploma of 3 May 1786 adjured him in the king's name to 'piety, sobriety, modesty', to abstain from duelling and debts; should he commit any of these things ('which heaven forfend')[81] he was to be relegated in perpetuity. For him, it was to be a place associated with scholarly mentors, one or two of whom welcomed him into their closer circles; but also the place where he first caught sight of a bright and intelligent professor's daughter, Caroline Michaelis. He was later to marry her.

He would have known from his older brothers' example that Göttingen, like German universities in general, was a place where one received one's training in law or theology for a later career in administration or in the church. He may specifically have known that Münchhausen, the 'Kurator' of the university, had offered his father, Johann Adolf, the choice of either a pastorate at Göttingen or one in Hanover; and he would have shared in the family honour when the university awarded his father an honorary doctorate in 1787.[82] It was August Wilhelm's good fortune that Göttingen was Germany's premier university: for a Hanoverian subject there was little or no choice. As it was, he was inscribed as a student of theology,[83] moving gradually and decisively over into philology and philosophy.[84] Later, his ever practical mother wished that he had studied something useful like law, but by then it was too late.

And yet this Göttingen had a double aspect. It was a small town (8,600), its numbers swollen by 850 students. If its professors were guaranteed greater freedom of opinion in teaching than elsewhere, there was also a care for public morals.[85] The 'Kurator' of the kingdom of Hanover was also the 'Prorektor' of the university. It was not good when professors (like Gottfried August Bürger) involved themselves in marital scandal;

---

81   'quod DEVS avertat', SLUB Dresden, Mscr. Dresd. e. 90, VI (7).
82   Schlichtegroll, 104; Rutledge, 30.
83   'August Wilhelm Schlegel, Hannoveranus, theol.' Götz von Selle, *Die Matrikel der Georg-August-Universität zu Göttingen 1734-1837*, 2 vols, Veröffentlichungen der historischen Kommission für Hannover, Oldenburg, Braunschweig, Schaumburg-Lippe und Bremen, 9 (Hildesheim, Leipzig: Lax, 1937), I, 294.
84   'in Göttingen dem Studium der Theologie durch den Reitz des Sprachstudiums entzogen'. Cornelia Bögel, 'Fragment einer unbekannten autobiographischen Skizze aus dem Nachlass August Wilhelm Schlegels', *Athenäum*, 22 (2012), 165-180, ref. 168.
85   Luigi Marino, *Praeceptores Germaniae. Göttingen 1770-1820*, Göttinger Universitätsschriften, A, 10 (Göttingen: Vandenhoek u. Ruprecht, 1995), 61.

or when professors' daughters were wittingly or unwittingly caught up in revolution (like Therese Forster, née Heyne, or Caroline Böhmer, née Michaelis). But that was only one side. Göttingen had Germany's largest university library, with the great classicist Christian Gottlob Heyne as its director. It had some international flair, with its contingents of English, Russian or French students, British royal princes among them: in 1813, Prince Adolphus, duke of Cambridge told Madame de Staël that he had known Schlegel in Göttingen and had formed a high opinion of him.[86] It was home to Germany's premier scholarly review, the *Göttinger Gelehrte Anzeigen*, to which the young Schlegel was to contribute. And there was the 'Göttingen school', a branch of the international community of savants, the republic of letters; institutionalised, it is true, but linked by correspondence and contact with its peers throughout Europe. There had of course been German scholars who were independent of the university, Winckelmann or Lessing or Herder among them, but they formed part of this wider confraternity nevertheless.

Put at its simplest, the 'Göttingen school' stood for history.[87] That did not merely mean those lectures on 'Historische Enzyklopädie' that the Kurator Münchhausen had made compulsory back in 1756 and that the historian Johann Christoph Gatterer would have been delivering in August Wilhelm's time.[88] It had to do rather with a general insight that all academic disciplines, whether law or politics or geography or classical philology, grew out of an awareness of human origins and development; that none was an end in itself but conformed to general patterns of knowledge about mankind. Thus all forms of historical knowledge were intrinsically of worth, whether Gatterer's or August Ludwig von Schlözer's great systemisations of the historical method (or the details, the historical documents and relics, the archaeological remains, works of art, in short, any testimony of human activity). Two of Göttingen's greatest humanities scholars, Gatterer and Heyne, shared this largeness of view, as did Johann David Michaelis (Schlegel's future father-in-law) or Johann Gottfried Eichhorn, both

---

86 *Lettres inédites de Mme. de Staël*, ed. Paul Usteri and Eugène Ritter (Paris: Hachette, 1903), 261.
87 Antony Grafton, *What Was History? The Art of History in Early Modern Europe* (Cambridge: Cambridge UP, 2007), 190-193; Gerhard Oexle, 'Aufklärung und Historismus: Zur Geschichtswissenschaft in Göttingen um 1800', in: Antje Middeldorf Kosegarten (ed.), *Johann Domenicus Fiorillo und die romantische Bewegung um 1800* (Göttingen: Wallstein, 1997), 28-56.
88 Marino, 261; Horst Walter Blanke, *Historiographiegeschichte als Historie*, Fundamenta Historica, 3 (Stuttgart-Bad Canstatt: Frommann-Holzboog, 1991), 136.

propounders of historical biblical criticism, even the 'German Buffon', the great comparative anatomist Johann Friedrich Blumenbach, with his 'vital energy', whose work on fossils and crania Schlegel was later to cite (and whose *laudatio* he was to write in Latin for the university in Bonn).[89]

Thus the Seminarium Philologicum that Schlegel joined, Johann Matthias Gesner's creation and now Heyne's inheritance,[90] was not merely a place of textual study (it was certainly that); it was also a workshop of historical method, historical fact, historical commentary; the creative use of the old antiquarian sources—which of course one had to know[91]—but expanding them in all directions, giving them system, understanding their relationships and rapports. Winckelmann, free of the academy's restraints, had had no other aim when he subjected classical archaeology to factors like climate and *moeurs* and historical contingency. Mythology, too, would be of interest to the classical scholar, not only for learned commentary, but for its opening up of 'primitive', 'ancient' cultures.

It was Göttingen that made Schlegel a scholar and a historian (Gatterer himself signed the pass that admitted him to the Historical Institute of Göttingen and permitted him use of maps, inscriptions etc.).[92] It also made him a critic. This involved sheer expertise, be it linguistic, textual, archaeological, as those later formidable reviews of Winckelmann, Grimm and Niebuhr testify (and which some waspish comments in the earliest reviews from his student years already demonstrated), but also the requisites of good style. The smooth, elegant prose, with just the right touch of emotion, that carried along his *Nibelungenlied* lecture in Berlin is written by the same man who laboriously collated antiquarian notes and sources on the identical epic.

He was, as his 'Zeitrechnung' (a rough chronological guide up to 1812) records,[93] eighteen and a half when he became a student at the place that seemed so promising for his talents. With little evidence of anything but a studious boyhood and youth, it comes as a relief to read in letters (a little later) of a walking tour in the Harz (including the ascent of the Brocken), or of riding part of the way home when accompanying a student friend.[94] His

---

89 *Opuscula*, 397-399.
90 Grafton, 190f.
91 Marino, 269-273.
92 SLUB Dresden, Mscr. Dresd. e. 90, VI (8).
93 Bögel (2012), 179.
94 *Briefe*, I, 10.

first letter from Göttingen, to his brother Karl,[95] was a mixture of nature observation, conventional with 'fresh' and 'green' and 'prospect' (perhaps it would be read to his father); a castle ruin evoked echoes of Goethe's *Götz von Berlichingen*, and he had been reading Homer and Ossian (in that order), regretting the passing of the heroic age. Just the sort of thing that this Romantic generation, force-fed on books, was prone to writing. But he had taken his lodgings in the town, where he had a good view of the gardens and the hills beyond; he had even heard a nightingale. Nature was however never enough: he looked forward to the discipline of new rules of conduct, which his brother the jurist will have noted with satisfaction. He had presented the letter of recommendation that his father had written to the great Heyne, but even the son of Johann Adolf Schlegel must earn his place in the Seminarium Philologicum and serve a trial period of six months.

He certainly proved himself worthy. From 1788 until his departure in the summer of 1790, he actually lived in Heyne's house,[96] something not uncommon in the eighteenth century, and became a kind of personal assistant. The Heyne and Michaelis houses in the Mühlenpforte (today's Prinzenstrasse) stood in close proximity: the daughters of both families, Therese Heyne and Caroline Michaelis, were extremely well read and knew all the eligible (and ineligible) young men who passed through their fathers' houses. In Heyne's seminar Schlegel met Wilhelm von Humboldt, born in the same year, later a Sanskritist and much else besides, but also a strict linguistician in the way Schlegel never was to be. His circumstances were different from Schlegel's: he was wealthy, noble, not dependent on patronage or office (although he would accept high positions within the Prussian monarchy). Privately educated, he was for the first time free of the tutor who shadowed him.[97] He moved in and out of the Heyne household as a matter of right; he consorted with British royal princes and nobles; he knew

---

95   *Ibid.*, 3f.
96   Achim Hölter,'August Wilhelm Schlegels Göttinger Mentoren', in: York-Gothart Mix and Jochen Strobel (eds), *Der Europäer August Wilhelm Schlegel. Romantischer Kulturtransfer—romantische Wissenswelten*, Quellen und Forschungen 62 (296) (Berlin, New York: de Gruyter, 2010), 13-29, ref. 16f. Another source has AWS living first in the Alleestrasse 15, then in Heyne's house, Papendiek 17, then as tutor, in the Buchstrasse (today's Prinzenstrasse) 6. Ida Hakemeyer, *Das Michaelis-Haus zu Göttingen* (Göttingen: Kaestner, 1947), 20.
97   Paul Robinson Sweet, *Wilhelm von Humboldt: A Biography*, 2 vols (Columbus: Ohio State UP, 1979-80), I, 35; Wilhelm von Humboldt, *Gesammelte Schriften*, ed. Albert Leitzmann *et al.* for Königlich Preußische Akademie der Wissenschaften, 17 vols in 18 (Berlin: Behr, 1903-36), XIV (=Tagebücher, I), 66-75.

women and was sexually experienced. From Göttingen, he would embark on a Grand Tour that took in Paris and Switzerland. He and Heyne's other daughter Marianne found Schlegel rather dull. There is no record of Schlegel having met Alexander von Humboldt, the other near-contemporary, whom he was to single out for praise and admiration and whose explorations were a model for his later studies on the origins of humanity.

By contrast, Schlegel found himself with several others helping Heyne to index his great Virgil edition of 1788-89: Heyne praised him to the skies in his preface,[98] for what was essentially learned hackwork (Johann Adolf had also known such drudgery with an index to Bayle's *Dictionnaire*),[99] but he could learn how editions are made and how they in their turn depend on other editions. He had had to sort out the incomplete work of two predecessors, and there had been inconsistencies to surmount. As late as 1827, defending such indices for Sanskrit texts, he pleaded indulgence for the young 'accessory of learning' ['Handlanger der Gelehrsamkeit'].[100]

Towards the end of his studies, from Easter 1790, Schlegel became tutor to a fifteen-year-old Englishman named George Thomas Smith.[101] It had been arranged through 'Connexionen', this time with another prominent Hanoverian, Johann Georg Zimmermann, personal physician to King George III and author of the much-read *On Solitude*. All had not gone well. In a letter to a Mr Hutton (whether the famous geologist James Hutton is not clear),[102] Zimmermann explained why. Young Smith had come to Göttingen to study Persian. Heyne had recommended Schlegel as a tutor, but Smith had given 'M. Schlegel' nothing but trouble.[103] An undated and unsigned letter, in halting English, 'You will excuse, I hope, my troubling you', was Schlegel's account to Mrs Smith of these burdensome matters.[104] Zimmermann knew Schlegel to be 'as virtuous as he is reasonable and well-bred' and hinted that he would be happy to add to his already considerable knowledge by coming to England. Mr Hutton did not take the hint. Schlegel

---

98 'Debetur autem ille studio *Aug. Guil. Schlegel*, Hannoverani, ad praeclarum laudem exquisitioris doctrinae eximiis ingenii et animi viribus annitentis'. *P. Virgilii Maronis Opera, varietate lectionis et perpetua adnotatione illustrata a Christ. Gottl. Heyne* […], 4 vols (Londini: Rickaby, 1793), IV, [vi].
99 Schlichtegroll, 83; Enders, 6.
100 *Indische Bibliothek*, II, 5f.
101 Selle, I, 321.
102 J. H. Scholte assumes that it is he. 'August Wilhelm Schlegel in Amsterdam', *Jaarboek van het Genootschap Amstelodamum* 41 (Amsterdam: de Bussy, 1949), 102-146, ref. 123.
103 *Briefe*, II, 3f.
104 *Ibid.*, I, 625-627.

was tutor to two further young gentlemen, the one English, the other French, and seems to have tutored them in their own languages, Josiah Dornford, lawyer and translator,[105] and Count Ferdinand de Broglie, the son of a distinguished French general and diplomat, from a junior branch of the family Schlegel would know through Madame de Staël, and a soldier under Louis XVI.[106] Dornford knew German sufficiently well to translate into English the huge work on the constitution of the Holy Roman Empire by the Göttingen jurist Johann Stephan Pütter.[107]

Clearly, however, Schlegel was profiting from Heyne's classical seminar and the methods being practised there. In June 1787, he was runner-up to the prize-winner in the competition set by the Philosophical Society in Göttingen, with the dissertation *De geographia Homerica commentatio*.

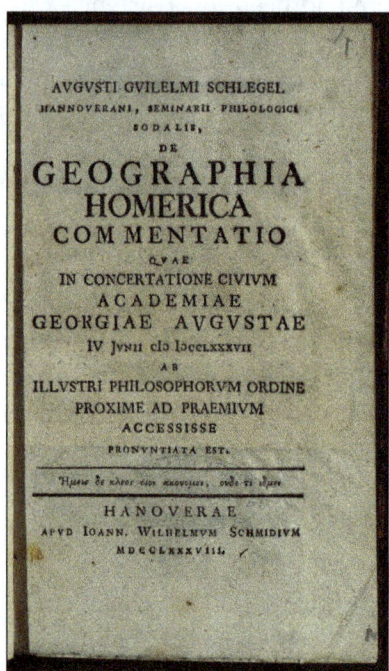

Fig. 1 August Wilhelm Schlegel, *De geographia Homerica* (Hanover, 1788). Title page.
© and by kind permission of the Master and Fellows of Trinity College, Cambridge,
CC BY-NC 4.0

---

105 'jur., ex ac. Oxford.' 1786. Selle, I, 295.
106 Broglie came in 1788 from Paris to Göttingen. Selle, I, 309.
107 As: *An Historical Development of the Present Constitution of the Germanic Empire*, 3 vols (London: Payne etc.; Oxford: Fletcher, 1790). Letters of Dornford to AWS SLUB Dresden, Mscr. Dresd. e. 90, XIX (6), 19-20; see also Oskar Walzel, 'Neue Quellen zur Geschichte der älteren romantischen Schule', *Zeitschrift für die Österreichischen Gymnasien* 42 (1891), 486-493, ref. 490.

This duly came out in a small duodecimo volume of 198 pages with the publisher Schmid in Hanover in 1788, his first substantial independent publication.[108] One should not approach this treatise with too high expectations: it is essentially a listing of the ships in *Iliad* Book Two, their putative origins, and of the peoples and places mentioned in the *Odyssey*. There is heavy reliance on Strabo as an external source. But one notes in the preface the name of 'vir illustris Gatterer',[109] acknowledging his work on Herodotus and Thucydides and the new standards of historical enquiry set in it. The names of the Homeric scholars Robert Wood and Thomas Blackwell show that the young scholar was using the resources of Europe's finest classical seminar; both were noted for their historical and geographical approach to Homer. What strikes us is his early interest in the origins and movements of peoples, their overlaps and admixtures. Who were the Pelasgians or the Scythians? What was the status in the Mediterranean of the Phoenicians and Egyptians and Libyans? What cultures converged on Sicily; which peoples sailed beyond the Pillars of Hercules out into 'Oceanus'? Later, in a much wider context of the origins of mankind's civilisation, languages and religion, Schlegel came back to the basic questions which his early dissertation had posed: those Pelasgians are there almost at the end of his Bonn lectures on general world history (1821), and the same issues were raised in his unpublished review of Alexander von Humboldt's *Vues des cordillères*. (1817). When in 1797 he was supplicating for a doctorate *honoris causa* from Jena university and for the right to lecture there, he cited *De geographia Homerica* in support of his application. As well he might.

Gottfried August Bürger: 'Young Eagle'

With Gottfried August Bürger, whose acquaintance he seems to have made soon after his arrival in Göttingen, Schlegel entered a world where the spheres of the academy and poetry merged in personal union. Bürger was *the* poet of the German Sturm und Drang, or more accurately the German Sturm und Drang without Goethe. Bürger, and the poets of the Göttingen *Musenalmanach* of the 1770s—Ludwig Heinrich Hölty, Johann Heinrich

---

108 Full title: Augusti Guilelmi Schlegel, Hannoverani, seminarii philologici sodalis, *De geographia Homerica commentatio quae in concertatione civium academiae Georgiae Augustae IV Junii clc lccclxxxvii ab illustri philosophorum ordine proxime ad praemium accessisse pronuntiata est* (Hanoverae: Schmid, 1788). *Opuscula*, 1-144. The winner of the competition wrote on the geography of the Argonauts.
109 *Opuscula*, 3.

Voss, Friedrich Leopold von Stolberg, and others—had been less inventive than Goethe and represented a kind of 'middle tone' in German poetry. Bürger had followed Thomas Percy—and Herder—in bringing both the form and tone of folk poetry into the stream of the German lyric; Hölty and Voss had seized on Klopstock's formal experiments with Greek and Latin ode stanzas and had made them into a vehicle for the poetry of sentiment and friendship. Goethe had advanced, they rather less, although Voss was to be a highly innovative translator of Homer to whom Goethe in the 1790s was much indebted. Bürger the folk balladeer had not changed greatly, but he had experimented widely: with the Petrarchan sonnet, with a translation of the *Iliad* (in iambic verse), with a prose version of *Macbeth*. A classical scholar and popular philosopher in his own right, he had secured the right to teach in Göttingen. There was much here that was congenial to the young Schlegel. It was the other side of Göttingen, the place where poetry was forged and published, in a town where otherwise learning dominated. The attractions of poetry and learning had kept Bürger in Göttingen, where Voss, Stolberg and the others had moved on, as indeed Schlegel in his turn was to do.

This was but one side of Bürger. The other side was unfortunate—or unedifying—depending on how one looked at it. His life seemed to be one set of contradictions. Though a trained jurist, Bürger was saddled with debt; a Petrarchan lover in his own poetry, he lived—in small-town Göttingen— in a ménage à trois (with sisters, both of whom died in childbirth) and then contracted a marriage, which ended in disaster. Everyone knew about these irregularities; gossipy letters between friends made sure of that. Heyne did what he could on the university front, and it was not much. Help from outside was not forthcoming. Goethe showed the stiff, glacial ministerial aspect that he adopted when it suited him: there were to be no more lame-duck Sturm und Drang poets in Weimar. What then came was even worse. In 1791 Schiller, unprompted by Goethe, for the period of their close association had not yet begun, took upon himself to review the revised edition of Bürger's poems brought out by Dieterich in Göttingen in 1789. It so happens that the young August Wilhelm Schlegel had done a brief unsigned notice of the same edition in the *Göttinger Gelehrte Anzeigen* in the year of its publication.[110]

---

110 *Göttinger Anzeigen von gelehrten Sachen* 109 (1789), 1089-1092 (not in *SW*).

1. Family, Childhood and Youth

Much has been written about Schiller's devastating review of Bürger. It may be that Bürger's poetry reminded him uncomfortably of a period in his own development, but that is surely only one factor. Comparing it with another famous review of another *poète maudit*, Samuel Johnson's Life of Richard Savage, one might say that human compassion was in short supply in Schiller's Jena (or in nearby Weimar). While Johnson was not making a case for Savage's poetry, he was pleading for a sympathetic understanding of the man. The later reactions by the English Romantics to the 'marvellous boy' Chatterton would not differ in this respect. Schiller duly reviewed the poetry, but he also introduced the fatal juxtaposition of 'sittlich' and 'aesthetisch', the 'moral' and the 'aesthetic'. Not that he suggested for one moment that Bürger's poetry was, by virtue of being its author's own expression, morally compromised; but readers—and that is *all* readers— would have known the truth about Bürger's private catastrophes. The word, once spoken, the association once hinted at, was enough.

As a masterly demolition, Schiller's review shows that the fine art of trashing literary reputations, so expertly exemplified by Lessing's stiletto-work on Gottsched in 1759, was not dead. It takes its place among the line that would lead eventually to Heine's assassination of Platen (and of Schlegel himself). For Schiller's readers of 1791, there was the common, if tacit, understanding that a tribune of the people's sentiments ['Wortführer der Volksgefühle'] should also prove worthy of that office. Schlegel noted this life-and-works definition. It made him wary of Schiller, but also of the hagiography practised in his own day: Lessing panegyrized as a latter-day Elijah, Winckelmann deified by Goethe, or Novalis sanctified by Ludwig Tieck. His own answer to Schiller would have to wait until he had won his first spurs as a critic, but even then he refused to eulogise Bürger. As yet, it was but an early encounter in the uneasy relationship with Schiller that was to extend beyond the great dramatist's death.[111]

In his review, Schiller mentioned Schlegel as one of Bürger's friends and a 'fellow devotee of the Pythian oracle'. It was a reference to the sonnet 'An August Wilhelm Schlegel', proclaiming to the world that Schlegel was Bürger's 'disciple'. Such vocabulary was typical of the Göttingen fraternity of the 1770s; its use in 1789 was a sign that some brothers had not quite grown up. 'My beloved son in whom I am well pleased' was another

---

111 A succinct account of their relationship in: *Friedrich Schiller-August Wilhelm Schlegel. Der Briefwechsel*, ed. Norbert Oellers (Cologne: DuMont, 2005), 5-15.

appellation with which Bürger invested Schlegel;[112] changing mythologies, Schlegel became 'junger Aar' (young eagle).[113] This was hardly Schlegel's style, then or later. Leaving aside Bürger's extravagant imagery, he did learn all that could be learned about the craft of the Petrarchan sonnet. All this indicated that Schlegel, in a relatively short space of time since his arrival in Göttingen, had found his way into the literary world with some ease and alacrity. Nor would this surprise one in Johann Adolf's son and the pupil of a leading Latin school, a young man who, it seemed, had already read everything.

In addition to indexing Virgil and investigating Homeric geography, this young man, hardly more than twenty years old, had added poetry and criticism to his list of attainments. He had Bürger's active encouragement for all this. There is no documentary evidence, but we may safely assume that it was Bürger's influence that induced him to pick up Italian along the way, not just from any source, but from Dante himself. Then Bürger, whose English was excellent, saw in this student a likely collaborator in a translation of Shakespeare. Entering Bürger's world involved indulging in the occasionally forced jokiness and infantilism of their discourse ('Ew. Poetisirlichkeit' [Your Poetedness]) and the like.[114] More importantly, it meant accepting the older poet's willingly proffered hand, first of all on his terms, then—if the 'young eagle' image is not too far-fetched—taking to his own wings.

Bürger, whatever his marital and monetary disarray, was still the editor of the influential Göttingen *Musenalmanach*, and had been since 1777.[115] He had had trouble with his publisher Dieterich over the monetary side, but he alone had the running of the publication and secured its contributors. We need to note the term *Musenalmanach*. Under its various guises—and these can be *Taschenbuch, Taschenkalender, Blumenlese*—it was essentially an anthology of what was best and most entertaining (or edifying) by way of poetic production in a given year. It took short poems—the Muses preferred these—and in the variety that the later eighteenth century and the early nineteenth found so agreeable. Everybody had a go at it. It

---

112 *Briefe von und an Gottfried August Bürger. Ein Beitrag zur Literaturgeschichte seiner Zeit.* Aus dem Nachlasse Bürger's und anderen, meist handschriftlichen Quellen hg. von Adolf Strodtmann, 4 vols (Berlin: Paetel, 1874), III, 211.
113 *Ibid.*, 268.
114 *Ibid.*, IV, 102.
115 York-Gothart Mix, *Die deutschen Musenalmanache des 18. Jahrhunderts* (Munich: Beck, 1987), 52.

brought Schlegel into the company of such shaky talents as Caroline von Dacheröden, later married to Wilhelm von Humboldt, Friedrich Wilhelm August Schmidt von Werneuchen, whom Schlegel was to parody, or Friedrich Ludwig Wilhelm Meyer, to whom Caroline Michaelis poured out her soul and wit in letters. It was the title that Schlegel and Ludwig Tieck chose for their miscellany of 1802, which was also a Romantic memorial to the early dead. As late as the 1830s, Schlegel was joined by a younger generation of poets when he published satirical verse in periodicals still calling themselves *Musenalmanach*.

Much of Bürger's poetic output—ballads, Lieder, romances, epigrams— had first been published in the *Musenalmanach* with which he is usually associated. Why not encourage a young man, a 'junger Aar' indeed, with poetic talent, a good ear for rhyme, a sense of metre, and a head full of classical and mythological *loci*? None of these qualities alone, not even their totality, necessarily makes a good poet. No-one was ever going to call Schlegel that; a competent one perhaps, a correct one, a learned one— these are the qualities that spring to mind. They are also useful ones for the translator, who needs to rise above the limited store of his own poetic inspiration. Although he did not yet know it, this was to be his forte.

The poetry by Schlegel that got published in Bürger's *Musenalmanach* or allied almanacs[116]—mainly narrative poems with the light eroticism that the late rococo still enjoyed—showed him mastering the models available, nothing more.[117] He did not emulate Bürger at his most innovative, the ballad in the mode of Percy's *Reliques*, or the Lied, perhaps rightly sensing that it was better to restrict oneself to 'safe' subjects, bosky shades, Bacchus and Ariadne, sibyls, ruminations on the poetic office. The sonnet was a very different proposition altogether.

Bürger may take much of the credit for the reintroduction of the sonnet into the mainstream of German literature. It had once enjoyed a vogue in the seventeenth century, but critical opinion early in the eighteenth century inimical to the baroque style had ensured its virtual disappearance from the assortment of available lyrical forms (there were hardly any by Johann Adolf Schlegel and his contemporaries). Thus it was not by chance that Bürger's preface to his *Gedichte* of 1789 (the edition reviewed by Schiller)

---

116 *SW*, I, 7-27, 180-203, 328; II, 345-357, 360-364.
117 Hans Grantzow, *Geschichte des Göttinger und des Vossischen Musenalmanachs*, Berliner Beiträge zur germanischen und romanischen Philologie, 22 (Berlin: Ebering, 1909), 149-166.

paid tribute to young Schlegel, his 'beloved disciple' (that tiresome vocabulary again), who with 'poetic talent, taste and criticism' had given him the necessary encouragement. He quoted in full a sonnet by Schlegel, 'Das Lieblichste' [The Most Pleasing] and one admires its neatness. 'A very satisfactory form for presenting material in brief compass' and 'very agreeable withal'; suitable for the lyric or the didactic veins, for 'occasional poems for friends of both sexes'. This was Bürger's version of 'Scorn not the Sonnet', and it is a very reasonable working definition, too. Both master and pupil only ever used the Petrarchan model: Schlegel was never really interested in Shakespeare's sonnets. It was in the form of a sonnet, from 1810, 'An Bürgers Schatten' [To Bürger's Shade], that he acknowledged his debt to the older man, his inner awareness of Bürger's lasting legacy but also his own poetic apostasy.

There was much in these early poems that pointed towards the future. The sonnet on Guido Reni's Cleopatra, for instance, or the poem 'Adonis',[118] on a mythological and painterly subject, suggested that he was absorbing some of the lessons given by the university's drawing instructor, Johann Dominik Fiorillo. The three metrical translations of Spanish romances showed that things Hispanic were being cultivated in Göttingen:[119] it was here that this generation, that included Ludwig Tieck and the Humboldt brothers, gained their facility in the language. The poem, 'Die Bestattung des Braminen' [The Brahmin's Funeral],[120] in regular eight-line stanzas, addressed to his brother in India (Carl Schlegel had supplied the material for his young brother to commit to verse),[121] is, together with his reference to *Śakuntalâ*, the first indication of Schlegel's interest in things Indian and his respect for Brahmanic wisdom.

This was not a young man merely willing to try out any literary genre that entered his head, unlike his younger contemporaries, or his younger brother Friedrich, who was about to begin omnivorously ingesting all the latest philosophy. There is no evidence of his having attended Bürger's much-frequented lectures on Kant, the first offered in the university and a

---

118 *SW*, I, 328; II, 352-354. Cf. Emil Sulger-Gebing, *Die Brüder A. W. und F. Schlegel in ihrem Verhältnisse zur bildenden Kunst*, Forschungen zur neueren Litteraturgeschichte, 3 (Munich: Haushalter, 1897), 16f.

119 *SW*, IV, 169-171; see Wilhelm Schwartz, *August Wilhelm Schlegels Verhältnis zur spanischen und portugiesischen Literatur*, Romanistische Arbeiten, 3 (Halle: Niemeyer, 1914), 6f.

120 *SW*, I, 82-86.

121 Writing from Fort St George in Madras 1 February 1784. Oskar Walzel, 'Neue Quellen zur Geschichte der älteren romantischen Schule', *Zeitschrift für die Österreichischen Gymnasien* 43 (1892), 289-296, ref. 291-293.

source of envy among his academic colleagues. That would change when he himself became a professor, but in the Kant-charged atmosphere of the university in Jena.

For the time being, he stuck to what came naturally, poetry of course, but also increasingly criticism and translation. As a critic, he was prepared to take on anything, however obscure—or however well-known. It also meant making use of one connections: Heyne's good offices secured him access to the *Göttinger Gelehrte Anzeigen*. In 1789, he reviewed that new edition of Bürger's poems,[122] favourably of course ('one of our best-loved poets'), taking note of the older man's use of metre.[123] His review of Bürger's long love poem 'Das Hohe Lied' [Song of Songs] in Heinrich Christian Boie's *Neues Deutsches Museum*,[124] was, however, set up by Bürger himself, showing off his young prodigy to as wide a circle of his literary friends as possible. Boie was told of Schlegel's 'youth, power, imagination, language and versification';[125] in his turn, he paid well (17 Reichstaler and 17 Groschen) which was money from a more congenial employ than looking after Master Smith. The review itself satisfied both Bürger's and Schlegel's priorities, doing justice to this love elegy and also analysing how this 'monument to passion' is also an enshrinement of poetic form.

The review appeared in two sections. Between these, Boie the editor inserted an account of the French Revolution. It seemed very remote from Göttingen, where Bürger's latest misadventure was of greater interest to its academic citizenry. Schlegel would have an opportunity to observe the ever-widening circles of the Revolution after his departure for Holland the following Easter. Meanwhile, his Göttingen mentors, Heyne and Bürger, were enabling him to cast a critical eye over the literary production in Germany as a whole, even of Europe. For the twenty-five reviews that he provided for *Göttinger Gelehrte Anzeigen* between 1789 and 1791[126] dealt with books in four different languages (German, French, Italian, English), with some names then resonant in German literature but now less so (Langbein, Thümmel), but also with Wieland, Goethe and Schiller.

---

122 'Gedichte von Gottfried August Bürger', *Göttinger Anzeigen von gelehrten Sachen*, 109 (1789), 1089.
123 *Ibid.*, 1091.
124 'Ueber Bürgers hohes Lied', *Neues Deutsches Museum* 11 (Leipzig: Göschen, 1790), 205-214, 306-348 (not *SW*).
125 Strodtmann, IV, 42.
126 *SW*, X, 3-56.

A 'young eagle' could scarcely mount higher—even as a reviewer. In view of the Schlegel brothers' later plans for an 'annihilation' of Wieland, the older man came off quite lightly in 1790. How Wieland felt when told that his revised translation of Horace's *Epistles* had gained in 'poise, correctness and exactness',[127] is not recorded. In the manner of the young, Schlegel spotted an error. He reviewed Wieland's Lucian translation almost as one expert to another. What of Goethe, whose works, his *Schriften* of 1787-91, announced that he had returned from Italy and was back in the literary scene? Of Volume Eight Schlegel noted that Goethe had carried out welcome revisions to his poetry, not least in matters metrical. Goethe's 'individuality', that which rendered his poetry immortal, could be seen both in poems that were fully worked through or only just 'hingeschüttet' ('thrown off'), a compliment capable of two different readings.[128] In his review of *Torquato Tasso* he was on sure ground, knowing the biographical sources and notes.[129] It conferred on him, in his eyes, the right to be fairly dismissive of the play itself. This was the first of his several reviews of Goethe, that recorded his continuing deference and then his gradual disenchantment.

Schiller was a different proposition, especially when Schlegel, already in Amsterdam, was pushing Bürger to reply to the infamous review.[130] His *Musenalmanach* poem 'An einen Kunstrichter' [To a Critic] can be read as a stiff address to Schiller to stick to his métier and not involve himself in moral issues.[131] By then, however, there were indications enough that he needed to go beyond Bürger's intellectual and poetic ambit and step out of the narrow confines of Göttingen. By the time Bürger died, in 1794, Schlegel had moved on, closer to Schiller. Given that Schiller was only eight years older than Schlegel and that he enjoyed a very cordial relationship with Schlegel's exact contemporary Wilhelm von Humboldt, there is no reason on the face of it why Schiller and this older Romantic generation should not have made common cause, or at least in part. Their collaboration in Schiller's periodical *Die Horen* was such an indication. Schlegel had much to share with the concerns of the older generation in general—Voss, Bürger, and others—in their search for new rhythms in poetic language, their

---

127 Ibid., 29.
128 Ibid., 4.
129 Ibid., 4-8.
130 Strodtmann, IV, 124.
131 SW, I, 8f.; Carl Alt, *Schiller und die Brüder Schlegel* (Weimar: Böhlau, 1904), 39f.; Josef Körner, *Romantiker und Klassiker. Die Brüder Schlegel in ihren Beziehungen zu Schiller und Goethe* (Berlin: Askanischer Verlag, 1924), 12f.

classical learning (far superior to Schiller's), and in some cases their interest in aesthetic theory. But that family business of the 1790s, the Brothers Schlegel, set out to forge quite different alliances, and they would be with those of their own generation, not with Schiller.

The two reviews of Schiller that Schlegel produced (one appeared after he had left Göttingen) belonged essentially to the last years at the university. The notice in the *Göttinger Gelehrte Anzeigen* of both parts of Schiller's short-lived periodical *Thalia* (1785-91), where of course not everything was by Schiller himself, served basically to inform the reader of the contents, with only the barest of comment ('Profound thoughts presented with surprising novelty and warmth').[132] He was hardly interested in Schiller's *Dom Karlos* (the first version of that play), or the stories that made *Thalia* so special. Schiller may not have been best pleased to be pulled up over his 'impure rhymes', less still over his 'provincialisms'[133] (Hanoverians to this day pride themselves on their 'pure' German). He did note especially Georg Forster's translation of scenes from *Śakuntalā* (based on Sir William Jones) and rightly commented how they alien they were to the European ear,[134] a modest step towards his later Sanskrit studies.

The altogether much more substantial review of Schiller's great philosophical poem 'Die Künstler' [The Artists] did come to Schiller's notice, and he would have had no cause to be dissatisfied with it. There was, however, no question of a young reviewer seeking to ingratiate himself with the author of *Don Carlos*. He noted what for him were obscurities and impurities in the diction: having been told that 'Fechter' ['fighter'] had associations with ignoble gladiatorial contests, Schiller actually changed it to 'Ringer' ['wrestler'], presumably at the reviewer's prompting.[135] Schlegel could not suppress the view, one that would occur in Schiller's periodical of the 1790s, *Die Horen*, that spoken rhythms and poetic language were humanity's oldest expression, not the urge to draw or build, as Schiller would have it. What he most admired was how Schiller had taken material that was otherwise the stuff of didactic poetry or even art appreciation (Winckelmann or Mengs) and had made it into a rhapsody whose poetic expression and energy and the flow of whose language had enabled philosophical and aesthetic seriousness to be transmitted with such conviction.

---

132 *SW*, X, 30-36, ref. 31.
133 Ibid., 32.
134 Ibid., 34.
135 Ibid., VII, 3-23, ref. 19.

The First Translations

To review Goethe and Schiller meant ascending heady enough heights for a twenty-two-year-old 'young eagle', but aspiring to Petrarch, Dante and Shakespeare suggested Icarus instead. For anyone as careful as Schlegel, such an analogy is of course far-fetched, yet some surprise is justified nevertheless. Göttingen stood for two things: the historical accuracy of texts as they have come down to us, their integrity, the painstaking work of editors (Heyne)—and the perceived need to make the texts of world literature available in translation (Bürger). Nobody at that time was of course speaking publicly of 'world literature', but Wieland had used the word 'Weltliteratur' privately,[136] and Georg Forster was saying essentially the same thing: it was not Goethe's later invention. Mere translation was not enough; versions that did justice to the original in form and tone were needed. There was nothing extraordinary about this: debates had been going on throughout the century on the proprieties and practicalities. Where there were no debates, there were versions themselves, and plenty of them. Schlegel's reviews in the *Göttinger Gelehrte Anzeigen* drew attention to the latest efforts from at least three languages, one of which was Sanskrit.

Bürger himself was an inveterate translator. Before Schlegel appeared on the scene to brighten up his last years, he had done versions of the *Pervigilium Veneris*, the *Iliad*, and *Macbeth*, an impressive list. But an *Iliad* in iambic verse was already a compromise, an anachronism even, when Klopstock and Voss were demonstrating how much in common Greek and German had (this would be Schlegel's own later position). A prose *Macbeth* took its place among several such, notably Wieland's and Eschenburg's, and was unremarkable enough in that company (unless one cared for Bürger's rumbustious witches). From writing sonnets in the Petrarchan style it was for Schlegel but a step to versions of the original, Petrarch himself.[137] The handful of sonnets by Petrarch that he translated, mainly in Bürger's *Musenalmanach*, together with one of the *canzone*, are not exciting reading, if proof enough that he could handle the stanzaic forms with early mastery. As yet there was no attempt at Dante's verse, but an introductory essay *Ueber die göttliche Komödie* [On the Divine Comedy] that came out just after his departure from Göttingen,[138] enunciated some important

---

136 Hans-J. Weitz, '"Weltliteratur" zuerst bei Wieland', *Arcadia* 22 (1987), 206-208.
137 *SW*, IV, 9, 22, 41, 47, 51, 53, 57, 59, 63, 68, 74, 76.
138 *SW*, III, 199-230.

principles for the translator. The *Divine Comedy* was, says Schlegel, a work so much bound up with the personality and experience of its poet, so inextricably one with him, that the translator must render all of its characteristics and form and idiosyncrasies.[139] They are the *aerugo nobilis*, the patina that declares an ancient coin to be genuine.[140] Thus only a poetic translation, one that respects the character of the original, blemishes and all, is acceptable. It was his first formulation of the translation principles that he set out in Schiller's *Die Horen* in 1796. Yet already Schlegel was in danger of overreaching himself, for these efforts were fragments of a general study of Italian poetry that got lost in other and more pressing enterprises.[141]

Did he and Bürger, on their moonlit walks or as they took tea, make plans for a Shakespeare translation?[142] It is unlikely to have been anything so ambitious, but the choice of *A Midsummer Night's Dream* for a joint translation effort was in itself noteworthy. An interest in Dryden and Addison's 'fairy way of writing' among critical connoisseurs had kept interest in this play and *The Tempest* alive. These included Wieland, who had produced a verse translation in 1762, improved by Eschenburg in 1775. These two plays were also by tradition those that one found when opening the first volume of a Shakespeare edition. Even so, it was a measure of Wieland's self-confidence that he submitted his versifying skills to this ultimate test. Bürger and Schlegel had a similarly high opinion of their capacities when they attempted the same task, but with Wieland and Eschenburg as guides. It was an important exercise, for it immediately showed up Bürger's inadequacies, and yet in the same process convinced Schlegel that this might well be his own poetic métier.[143] How far his thoughts went at this stage is unclear, but he took their joint translation with him and it found its way eventually to Jena when things Shakespearean resurfaced. It spoke for Bürger that he did not force his versions or his style on the younger man: he simply recognised superior talent when he saw it. Where in the opening scenes they were still competing, Schlegel by the close had the field to himself, with this, for example:

---

139 *Ibid.*, 226f.
140 *Ibid.*, 229.
141 Michael Bernays, *Zur Entstehungsgeschichte des Schlegelschen Shakespeare* (Leipzig: Hirzel, 1872), 89.
142 Frank Jolles, *A.W. Schlegels Sommernachtstraum in der ersten Fassung vom Jahre 1789 nach den Handschriften herausgegeben*, Palaestra, 244 (Göttingen: Vandenhoek & Ruprecht, 1967), 22-31.
143 *Ibid.*, 28f.

The poet's eye, in a fine frenzy rolling,	Des Dichters Aug' in schönem Wahnsinn rollend,
Doth glance from heaven; to earth, from earth to heaven,	Blitzt auf zum Himmel, blitzt zur Erd' herab,
And, as imagination bodies forth The forms of things unknown, the poet's pen	Und wie die schwangre Fantasie Gebilde Von unbekannten Dingen ausgebiert,
Turns them to shapes, and gives to airy nothing A local habitation, and a name.	Gestaltet sie des Dichters Kiel, und giebt Dem luft'gen Unding Wohnsitz, Ort und Nahmen.
Such tricks hath strong imagination; That, if it would but apprehend some joy, It comprehends some bringer of that joy; Or, in the night, imagining some fear, How easy is a bush suppos'd a bear?[145]	So gaukelt die allmächtige Einbildung: Daß sie, sobald sie eine Freude fühlt Auch einen Freudenbringer sich gedenkt; Und in der Nacht, wenn uns ein Graun befällt, Wie leicht, daß man den Busch für einen Bären hält![146]

What matter if Schlegel made borrowings here and there from Wieland. What better source? And with this prentice work, under Bürger's benevolent eye, he was in the process of consigning Wieland to history.

Johann Dominik Fiorillo

Yet it would be misleading to attribute all the mentorship and guidance given to the young Schlegel entirely to Heyne and Bürger. How much he learned from Friedrich Bouterwek, a near-contemporary with whom he overlapped in Göttingen, is hard to assess.[146] Also a member of Bürger's circle, a minor poet (very minor), he shared Schlegel's interest in the Romance languages (Italian, Spanish) and was, as Schlegel was preparing to leave Göttingen, beginning to give the first of the many systematic lectures on literature and philosophy that he was later to publish as compendia. For Bouterwek is the great compiler of facts, the systematizer, of his generation. Schlegel, too, needed facts when it suited him, but his narrative was organic, followed the natural development of human endeavours in the arts, the processes of change; it was never merely linear. Yet when Schlegel later needed to set out the history of the Spanish drama, it was to Bouterwek and his like that he turned (not always acknowledged)—but always in the interests of

---

144 *The Dramatick Writings of Will. Shakspere* […], 20 vols (London: Bell, 1788), V, 73.
145 Jolles, 120.
146 On Bouterwek and Schlegel see Achim Hölter, 'August Wilhelm Schlegels Göttinger Mentoren', esp. 20-22.

making known the poetry and the historical and social developments that produced it. With this difference in method went a mutual animosity. But were parts of Schlegel's lectures in Bonn on German literature—the later sections in particular—all that better than Bouterwek's undifferentiated accounts?

Johann Dominik Fiorillo (spellings of his second name vary) was a different proposition.[147] It was he who kindled Schlegel's life-long interest in the fine arts and helped to make him, with his brother Friedrich, into formidable art connoisseurs and critics. Fiorillo, an artist in his own right (he had been in Pompeo Batoni's studio) first came to Göttingen in 1781, becoming in 1782 drawing master and then in 1784 the inspector of the collection of engravings, much later, well after Schlegel's time, a professor. From 1786 he gave private lectures on the history and theory of painting, although there is no evidence that Schlegel actually attended these. Fiorillo was a protégé of Heyne's, doing the engravings for the Virgil edition for which Schlegel had performed more mundane services; he knew Bürger;[148] he knew Bürger's publisher Dieterich. We do not know with any certainty what Fiorillo specifically passed on to Schlegel: a couple of sonnets based on Titian or Guido Reni may not seem to amount to much, except that they do show knowledge of Italian painting, and the Italian schools were to be ever in the forefront of Schlegel's art connoisseurship, not the Netherlandish, the Flemish, the French. Assuming, as we safely can, that Fiorillo showed Schlegel the prints and drawings of which he was the custodian, he would have seen sheets after the major Italian masters (including Raphael, Michelangelo, Bandinelli, Giulio Romano, Polidoro, Parmigianino, Correggio, the Carracci).[149] What Schlegel did not receive were the systematic private lectures on art that his younger contemporaries Ludwig Tieck and Wilhelm Heinrich Wackenroder were to have from Fiorillo when they studied in Göttingen in 1792-93. They had already been to galleries: Schlegel had not. Whereas Tieck's and Wackenroder's early

---

147 On Fiorillo see esp. Claudia Schrapel, *Johann Domenicus Fiorillo. Grundlagen zur wissenschaftsgeschichtlichen Beurteilung der 'Geschichte der zeichnenden Künste in Deutschland und den vereinigten Niederlanden'*, Studien zur Kunstgeschichte, 155 (Hildesheim, Zurich, New York: Olms, 2004); on his relation to AWS see Hölter, 'Mentoren', 25-29.

148 Strodtmann, IV, 138, 216.

149 See Jochen Wagner, 'Katalog der Druckgraphik und Handzeichnungen', in: Manfred Boetzkes, Gerd Unverfehrt, Silvio Vietta (eds), *Renaissance in der Romantik. Johann Domenicus Fiorillo, italienische Kunst und die Georgia Augusta. Druckgraphik und Handzeichnungen aus der Kunstsammlung der Universität Göttingen* (Hildesheim: Roemer-Museum, 1993), 33-241.

output as writers (especially the latter's) was heavily slanted towards art appreciation, Schlegel's was as yet unfocused. He only started to show art connoisseurship in his reviews and his Dante essays from the 1790s. Meanwhile, he had to acquire the knowledge of originals, which no print collection could supplant. We do not know what he saw in Amsterdam; we can assume that he looked at the collections in Düsseldorf on his return journey to the Netherlands in 1794, the ones so recently praised by Wilhelm Heinse and Friedrich Leopold von Stolberg (although Schlegel never liked Rubens, the pride of Düsseldorf); with Caroline, he saw the collection of the dukes of Brunswick at Salzdahlum in 1795. It was however not until the crucial visit to the Dresden gallery in 1797 that his art appreciation began to take on a distinct profile.

Fiorillo must nevertheless have formed a favourable impression of Schlegel the Göttingen student, for in 1797 he entrusted him with the manuscript of the first volume of his monumental history of graphic art (Fiorillo was never quite secure in German) and thanked him publicly for his assistance with the language.[150] Schlegel in his turn thought of Fiorillo when in 1803 he was charged with finding suitable copy for the new Jena *Allgemeine Literatur-Zeitung* and wondered if his old master could review art publications.[151]

Caroline Michaelis-Böhmer

Two names are largely missing in this account of Schlegel's Göttingen years: his brother Friedrich, and Caroline Böhmer, née Michaelis, later to be his wife. Friedrich was in many ways still a child when his older brother left for university, difficult, intractable, the afterthought of elderly parents, and what was worse in the Schlegel family, unstudious. Hardly grown up, at the age of fifteen, this 'problem child' had been sent to Leipzig to learn the banking trade. But Friedrich, whom his mother was soon to call 'kein Wirth' ('cannot cope with money'), was constitutionally unsuited to this profession, or, one is tempted to say, any kind of fixed employment. It may have been the example of his older brother, or the awakening of his intellectual powers with puberty (his friend Novalis was to experience something similar): whatever, it sparked off the wish to go to the same

---

150 Johann Dominik Fiorillo, *Geschichte der zeichnenden Künste von ihrer Wiederauflebung bis auf die neuesten Zeiten* […], 5 vols (Göttingen: Rosenbusch, 1798-1808), I, xx.

151 Letter of Fiorillo to AWS 7 October 1803, Schrapel, 489-490.

university as August Wilhelm. His father had despaired of teaching him, and he had not been sent to the Lyceum. In a spate, an orgy, of reading, Friedrich in a few months seemingly devoured what his older brother had acquired in more systematic fashion. That may be an exaggeration, but he did read the whole of Plato in Greek. Armed with this, he was able to matriculate in 1790, attending lectures in mathematics and medicine, reading Herder, Kant, Winckelmann, Hemsterhuis as well. Friedrich does not feature in Bürger's letters, so we may assume that he was not admitted to this poetic circle, but August Wilhelm did succeed in securing him an entrée to Heyne's Seminarium Philologicum. Their ways parted at Easter 1791, and from that time the brothers' letters keep us informed of the crisscrossing of their paths.

Caroline Michaelis was by now 'Mad. Böhmer'. In Göttingen, she had seen, some of them even in her father's house, the explorers Georg Forster and Carsten Niebuhr, the publisher and author Friedrich Nicolai, the Princess Gallitzin (she had missed Goethe); she had kept up with all the developments in literature and the theatre, was competent in English, French and Italian, English especially. It was spoken in the house (her father had translated from the English); the royal princes were frequent guests.[152] Yet in 1784 she married—was married off to—Johann Franz Wilhelm Böhmer, the son of another Göttingen professor. Böhmer was a doctor in Clausthal, the mining town in the Harz, sixty kilometres from Göttingen and a narrow provincial nest. She hated it.[153] Their daughter Auguste was born in 1785. In that year, Therese Heyne, the daughter of her father's colleague and a close but unreliable friend, married Georg Forster. These events were to have consequences for all of them. Another daughter was born. Then Böhmer died of an illness in 1788.

She would have seen Schlegel on her periodic visits home to Göttingen, indeed the young student living in the Heyne household came in useful when she needed a poem of congratulation for her father's seventy-second birthday.[154] In his way, he paid court to this widow, young still, but older and more experienced than he, her letters showing a psychological sophistication that his never did. His journey on foot through the Harz included a visit to Clausthal,[155] but one cannot imagine this bookish student,

---

152 Hakemeyer, 19f.
153 *Caroline*, I, 77.
154 *Ibid.*, I, 182, 688.
155 *Briefe*, I, 10.

doubtless with good manners, making any kind of impression, certainly not a favourable one. He, twenty years later, noted in his 'Zeitrechnung' that she left Göttingen in the summer of 1789—she is the only person apart from himself that he mentions[156]—for Marburg, to stay with her brother, a medical professor. Her second child died there, under distressing circumstances. She returned to Göttingen: Schlegel records that he saw her before his departure for Holland at Easter 1791. It would have been devotion at a distance, a Petrarchan or Dantean worship from afar. For in Göttingen, Caroline, the young widow, had a romantic attachment to Georg Tatter,[157] the tutor to the three British royal princes studying there; Friedrich Ludwig Wilhelm Meyer, 'Kustos' of the university library and a professor extraordinarius in philosophy and history, a man of considerable charm but of uncertain character, was her confidant in a stream of letters. She knew all the town scandal, not least the unedifying story of Bürger's disastrous third marriage. She was still in Göttingen when August Wilhelm Schlegel left at Easter 1791. Their paths were not to cross again until 1793.

Summer 1791-Summer 1795: Amsterdam, Mainz, Leipzig

These were not unproductive years—with Schlegel there was no danger of that—yet they were the space between the first unfolding of his poetic and critical talents, and the achievement of their first maturity of expression. They saw him cutting the cord that bound him to Gottfried August Bürger and accepting the hand of the same Schiller whose review, in Caroline's words, had taken 'all the human honour out of him' ['Bürgern um alle menschliche Ehre recennsirt'].[158] As for Caroline, he was not taking 'no' for an answer; as a consequence, much of his time and energy would be devoted to extricating her from the toils spun by the French Revolution. It was a time of close meeting of souls with his brother Friedrich, but also of paying off his improvident brothers' debts.

Most of this was conducted at a distance. We know of most of his doings through others' letters. He was in a self-imposed exile from Germany, in Amsterdam. Not eating the bread of affliction: quite the contrary, for those useful 'Connexionen' (this time, Eschenburg in Brunswick) had secured him the post of tutor to the only son of the 'Counsellor and Magistrate', Henric Muilman.[159] Muilman's business interests extended to England,

---

156 Bögel (2012), 179.
157 *Caroline*, I, 686f.
158 *Ibid.*, 225.
159 Cf. Eschenburg's letter to AWS of 30 April 1791, SLUB Dresden, Mscr. Dresd. e. 90,

the East and West Indies, and he could afford to pay well. Schlegel was no longer dependent on sums like the '9 Rthl.' that he got from *Göttinger Gelehrte Anzeigen* for 1791[160] or even the one or two Louisd'ors per sheet that Schiller could offer.[161] Schlegel travelled from Göttingen via Osnabrück to Amsterdam in the spring of 1791 and remained there until the summer of 1795. His letters to his Göttingen mentors, Heyne and Bürger, tell of his first impressions. The house at Herengracht 476 was remarkable for two reasons: its opulence, compared at least with anything that Schlegel would have been accustomed to, and its extended family, a daughter each from Muilman's and Madame Muilman's first marriages, and two children from their second. It was Willem Ferdinand Mogge Muilman, a wide-awake boy of 13, to whom Schlegel was tutor and with whom, if later letters are anything to go by, he seems to have had a good relationship.[162] The idea was that Willem should emerge with the necessary skills in French and English that a young gentlemen and man of affairs must have—and much more besides. This Schlegel delivered. Thus when Schlegel later stated views on education, he knew what he was talking about. The household was comfortable; he was warmly clad (his mother saw to this) and well fed.

It was, however, no more than a temporary arrangement until something permanent turned up. His father had been trying to pull strings to secure him a teaching position;[163] and in letters from his mother we are kept posted about the health of professors at the Collegium Carolinum in Brunswick, where some of his father's elderly contemporaries were ending their careers as professors.[164] Their mental horizon did not extend beyond the usual eighteenth-century notions of 'Amt', the security afforded by fixed tenure. There were even hints—from his mother—that his family were glad to know that he was free of Bürger's direct influence. Otherwise, there were parental admonitions to prudence, frugality and economy, qualities already abundant in Holland and ones that their son already possessed in large measure. Not so 'Fritz', now a student in Leipzig, 'kein Wirth' and a burden on their exchequer,[165] in fact already in debt to the tune of 300

XIX, 7 (84), which makes it clear that Eschenburg was behind AWS's appointment and makes Scholte's (1949) remarks on this subject redundant (105f). Scholte otherwise the main source of information on AWS in Amsterdam.
160 Walzel (1891), 490.
161 *KA*, XXIII, 19.
162 Letters (in extract) of Muilman Sr. and Willem Muilman to AWS in Scholte (1949), 134-146.
163 Walzel (1891), 487f.
164 SLUB Dresden, Mscr. Dresd. e. 90, XIX, 12 (21).
165 *Ibid*. (15).

talers. But Friedrich discovered his now absent brother as a source of true friendship; a correspondence ensued, which is one of the most important and revealing documents of these years. We owe this to the tidiness of August Wilhelm: he kept Friedrich's letters, while his own were lost.

Caroline's Tribulations

Lost, too, are his letters to Caroline Böhmer, née Michaelis, that young widow so much older in human experience and general sophistication than he. Had they survived, we would know for certain how earnestly and assiduously August Wilhelm had asked for Caroline's hand. We would know whether those poems in Bürger's *Musenalmanach* were mere exercises in style and versification or addresses of devotion to Caroline. We would know whether she ever wrote to him letters of such verve, of such stylistic accomplishment and vividness, as her friend Meyer or her sister Lotte Michaelis were to receive. In the spring of 1789, tired of Göttingen, she moved with her children to Marburg, where her brother was a medical professor. She met there the *grande dame* of German letters, Sophie von La Roche. For the moment, life seemed one late rococo *fête champêtre*. But in this atmosphere, away from the Hanoverian realms, she could only exclaim: 'Schlegel and me? Not a chance!'[166]

Caroline needed all of her considerable powers of description to relate what happened next, the harrowing death of her two-year-old daughter Therese in December 1789.[167] Eighteenth-century therapeutics could only try the standard cures, and they were fruitless; her brother the professor could not save the child. Then, for almost two years, she moved between Marburg and Göttingen, trying to pick up the pieces of her life. It was at Easter 1791, as Schlegel recorded in his 'Zeitrechnung',[168] that he last saw her before his departure for Holland. In March 1791, she spent a month in Mainz with her old childhood friend, Therese Forster, née Heyne, and her family. In December of that year, she made the momentous—or fatal—decision to join Therese and all the Forsters, Georg, Therese and the children. It was to bring her, and the Schlegel brothers, face to face with the Revolutionary Wars and the consequences of the French Revolution. This deserves mention, as Friedrich's later attitude to the Revolution, his articles on Condorcet and Forster, his elevation of the Revolution to one of

---

166 *Caroline*, I, 191.
167 *Ibid.*, 195-199.
168 Bögel (2012), 179.

the 'tendencies of the age', had as their author someone whose sister-in-law had escaped the siege of Mainz and had seen the inside of a prison. It was all very different from their friend Ludwig Tieck, a Göttingen student in 1793 and singing 'Ça ira' at a safe distance.

But why Mainz? With a population of 25,000, it was the capital of the archdiocese and electoral territory of Mainz ('Kurmainz') that took in not just the substantial ancient city but other territories, such as Erfurt in Thuringia. With its position on the Rhine, it had commercial significance, but as events would soon show, also strategic value. For the city lay on that bank of the Rhine that was soon to change hands. The court and its appurtenances attracted men of culture. Wilhelm Heinse (Hölderlin's 'Heinze'), novelist and art critic, found a niche there before the troubles saw him removing to yet another court. The Elector of Mainz, Baron Friedrich Karl Joseph von Erthal, saw no contradiction between the opulence of his palace, and the spirit of enlightenment in his university. Even Germany's Catholic universities, such as the one founded in nearby Bonn, were not immune to *lumières*: among those whom the Elector brought to Mainz, the anatomist Samuel Thomas Sömmering and the university librarian, Georg Forster, stand out.

Forster might have become one of those universal figures like Goethe or Alexander von Humboldt, had he made the necessary accommodations to courts and state institutions that they—with varying degrees of reluctance—submitted to. With his life ending in ruins in the Paris of the Terror, he seemed in the 1790s to be a warning example of where revolutionary ardour or a belief in unending human progress led to. Goethe's and Schiller's heartless *Xenion* of 1796[169] has to be seen in this context, but also Friedrich Schlegel's essay of 1797, that sprang to his defence. Yet the Goethe of the 1820s, by now the author of the upliftingly anti-revolutionary *Hermann und Dorothea* but also of the cynical political allegory *Reineke Fuchs*, when writing the selective and embellished account of his own involvement in the Revolutionary Wars, avoided disparaging reference to Forster in *Campagne in Frankreich* [The Campaign in France]; he made no secret of the fact that in August 1792, on his way to the disastrous encounter with revolutionary forces, he spent convivial evenings with him and friends in Mainz (a draft even added 'Mad. Böhmer').

---

169 *Phlegyasque miserrimus omnes admonet.*
O ich Tor! Ich rasender Tor! Und rasend ein jeder,
Der, auf des Weibes Rat horchend, den Freiheitsbaum pflanzt!
Johann Wolfgang Goethe, *Gedenkausgabe der Werke, Briefe und Gespräche*, ed. Ernst Beutler, 3rd edn, 27 vols (Zurich: Artemis, 1986 [1949]), II, 489.

One could not overlook Forster. When in March to May 1773 Goethe was just back from his unhappy sojourn in Wetzlar and Herder was chafing in Bückeburg, Forster was with James Cook in Dusky Bay in New Zealand, collecting plants, birds and native artefacts, all of which would go into his epoch-making *Journey Round the World* of 1777 (his *Reise um die Welt* of 1778-80.) He was Alexander von Humboldt's mentor, and his *Ansichten vom Niederrhein* [Views of the Lower Rhine], as significant as anything at all by Goethe or Schiller at the time, showed Humboldt how one could amalgamate topography, politics and culture in one narrative. Forster won August Wilhelm Schlegel's later approval when he sided with Forster's (and Blumenbach's) views against Kant's on racial types.[170] He was the German translator of Sir William Jones's *Śakuntalâ*, which for Schlegel merited mention among the pioneering history of German Indology.

But in 1791, Caroline, and by extension the brothers Schlegel, knew this wide-ranging genius only for his human frailty. Caroline had chosen Mainz as opposed to the minor residences of Gotha or Weimar, where everyone would have known who she was. That was in itself an error. The Forster marriage, never happy—only later would Therese confess to its full wretchedness—had collapsed.[171] Therese was conducting an open affair with the Saxon legation secretary Ludwig Ferdinand Huber, later her husband. It was Huber, with Sömmering, who were to spread some of the gossip that led to Caroline being declared *persona non grata* in so many territories. Caroline was aware of the delicacy of her position.[172] These were not normal times: the city was full of French émigrés, and the league of German princes that included Duke Carl August of Saxe-Weimar-Eisenach was about to move its armies down towards Verdun and Valmy to counter the revolutionary armies. She was reading Mirabeau, sensing the momentousness of the times she lived in. In words not unreminiscent of Goethe's in *Campagne in Frankreich*—'Here begins a new epoch in world history, and you can say that you were present at it'—she imagines telling her grandchildren of the 'highly interesting moment in politics' unfolding around her.[173] But a few days before Goethe's visit to Mainz, she was writing of the hatred felt in Mainz towards the émigrés and the imperial troops. On October 6, the French enemy was at the gates; on 21 October, the princes' armies dispersed, and General Adam Philippe de Custine's forces occupied

---

170 'Einleitung in die allgemeine Weltgeschichte', SLUB Dresden, Mscr. Dresd. e. 90, XXVIII, esp. [64-68].
171 *Caroline*, I, 324f.
172 *Ibid.*, 242.
173 *Ibid.*, 250. Goethe's words in *Gedenkausgabe*, XII, 289.

Mainz. 'What a change in events in 8 days',[174] she wrote on 27 October, with Custine in the Elector's palace and a garrison of 10,000 men of the French Revolutionary Army in the city. A Jacobin Club was set up: Forster joined. A proponent of political union with France, he was sent in March 1793 to Paris as a delegate of the German National Convention. He was now alone, Therese and the children having left for Strasbourg, she to marry Huber, and then make a career as an independent writer. Caroline was one of Forster's few remaining friends: later rumours, all of them malicious, would differ as to the degree of 'comfort' she is alleged to have afforded him. What is certain, is that she met a young French officer, Jean-Baptiste Dubois de Crancé, the nephew of Custine's successor, General François-Ignace Ervoil d'Oyré, and that she surrendered to his advances, 'an event that was very significant for her honour', as Therese Huber later wrote.[175]

With Forster gone, or about to go, Caroline secured a pass to leave Mainz with her six-year-old daughter Auguste and two other women. The intention was to reach Gotha, and her friend Luise Gotter, and eventually Göttingen. What then happened is unclear: Sömmering, no friend of Jacobins—he reinstalled himself immediately after the siege was lifted—claimed that Caroline had tried to be witty with some Prussian officers—never a wise thing—and was promptly arrested.[176] The latter part is certainly true. She thus escaped the bombardment and reduction of the city in July, that assault by the German princes on the ragtag defenders that formed the basis of Goethe's wry account in *Belagerung von Mainz*. And she was spared Georg Forster's death in Paris in January 1794, in isolation and sickness, dying for the principles of 'communal spirit' that the Revolution was in the process of betraying.

What was certain was that a small company of women found themselves arrested and incarcerated in the fortress of Königstein, in the Taunus hills above Frankfurt. 'This is a most unfortunate state of affairs';[177] 'Dear Caroline has not acted as she would have had she had all her wits about her'[178] are words in an exchange of letters between her sister Luise Michaelis and August Wilhelm Schlegel. Caroline, now ill, had to spend nine weeks sharing a room with seven others. She was not denied pen and paper, and sent out pleas for help.[179] She needed to, as she was proscribed and in danger

---

174 *Ibid.*, 274.
175 *Ibid.*, I, 302, 695; KA, XXIII, 431.
176 *Caroline*, I, 694f.
177 *Ibid.*, 656.
178 *Ibid.*, 650.
179 *Ibid.*, 292, 657.

of being treated as a hostage. *Le Moniteur* in Paris already referred to her as 'la veuve Böh. amie du Citoyen Forster' [the widow Böhmer, friend of Citizen Forster],[180] and Friedrich Schlegel picked up a rumour that she was Custine's mistress.[181] We do not have the letters that she wrote, only the responses to them. She wrote to her family, to the Gotters in Gotha—and to August Wilhelm in Amsterdam. Friedrich Schlegel, apprised by a network of informants in Leipzig, wrote to his brother that 'something must be done'. Proscribed or not, she was still a Göttingen professor's daughter and a Hanoverian subject. The historian Schlözer, her father's colleague, took up her cause;[182] the dramatist Friedrich Wilhelm Gotter in Gotha was to approach Karl Theodor von Dalberg in Erfurt, 'Coadjutor', prince of the church, and the representative there of the Elector of Mainz;[183] Schlegel wrote to Wilhelm von Humboldt, Dalberg's protégé, only to learn that the Elector himself made the decisions.[184] Finally, it was her brother Philipp, himself a doctor, who secured her release; he petitioned the commander in chief of the military alliance, King Frederick William II of Prussia, and learned that it was not 'My will' that the innocent should suffer. An adjutant was to issue passes for her safe conduct home.[185]

But it was less simple than that. The 'illness' proved to the first stages of pregnancy: she was carrying Crancé's child. Her letter to Schlegel had, it seems, contained the request for poison, 'to escape the shame through death'.[186] 'I have nothing more to live for in Germany'.[187] Where was she to go? Prussia would not have her; Saxe-Gotha similarly; her 'shame' prevented her from returning to Göttingen. Her friends the Gotters used their influence with the publisher Georg Joachim Göschen in Leipzig.[188] There she could stay for a brief time, provided that the Saxon authorities did not get wind. But how was this distressed person, five months pregnant and with a small daughter, to accomplish this? Their saviour proved to be none other than August Wilhelm Schlegel. 'Of his own accord, not thinking of himself, and making no claims', is how Caroline wrote in August of that year.[189] Forgetting rebuffs and discouragements, he had come in July from

---

180 *Ibid.*, 290.
181 *KA*, XXIII, 89, 416.
182 *Caroline*, I, 656.
183 *Ibid.*, 288.
184 Sweet, I, 98.
185 *Caroline*, I, 702.
186 *Ibid.*, 696.
187 *Ibid.*, 298.
188 *KA*, XXIII, 424,
189 *Caroline*, I, 309.

Amsterdam (Muilman had granted him leave)[190] and had accompanied Caroline from Frankfurt to Leipzig. There, his brother Friedrich had his meditations on Hamlet and other subjects rudely interrupted by the arrival of the small party; indeed August Wilhelm more or less handed Caroline over to him and returned to his duties with the Muilmans in Amsterdam. Not, however, before having installed Caroline in the small town of Lucka. 'Kleinstaaterei', Germany's many pocket-handkerchief states, proved this time to have advantages: although close to Leipzig, Lucka was in the territory of Saxe-Altenburg and thus a safe haven. She was quartered in a doctor's house, awaiting her confinement. August Wilhelm sent her the portrait of himself he had had done in Amsterdam, to remind her of his continuing devotion; Friedrich came in person. The 'petit citoyen' Wilhelm Julius Kranz was born on 3 November 1793 and baptised 'the same day'.[191] Fictitious parental names for 'Crancé' were signed in the parish register, but as one of the godparents we find the non-fictitious 'Friedrich Schlegel, *stud. jur.* in Leipzig'.[192] The child was fostered, its upkeep paid for by the ever-provident August Wilhelm Schlegel.[193]

Schlegel in Amsterdam

This was the only dramatic event in the four years that August Wilhelm Schlegel spent in Amsterdam. Yet late in 1792 and early in 1793, it seemed for a time that even the peace of that solid city was about to be disturbed by General Dumouriez's incursions into the Low Countries (during which a young lieutenant colonel named Arthur Wesley, later Wellesley, then Wellington, first saw action). In the event, Schlegel seems to have settled down to a routine, not with any enthusiasm, for his letters to Heyne and Bürger evinced little inclination for the Dutch, their language, their culture, their political factions, in short, he seemed bored. Indeed as early as December 1791[194] he wrote to his brother that he was prepared to abandon everything and move to Mainz to be near Caroline. The libraries, he claimed, were not adequate for the kind of intensive study of Italian literature that he wished to undertake (later, Friedrich sent him the necessary books). And yet the essential groundwork was laid for the big essays, on Dante and on

---

190 Cf. Muilman's letter of 19 July, 1793, Scholte (1949), 134f.
191 *Caroline*, I, 703; Erich Schmidt, the editor of Caroline's letters, Prussian professor and civil servant, observed in 1913 that such irregularities 'would not happen today'.
192 *Ibid.*, 704.
193 *KA*, XXIII, 192, 455.
194 Strodtmann, IV, 125, 139.

language and metrics, that started coming out in Schiller's periodical *Die Horen* in 1795. As early as the summer of 1791, we learn through Friedrich that Schiller wanted contributions to *Die Neue Thalia*, which *Die Horen* was to succeed.[195] But Schlegel bided his time. References in Friedrich's letters to his brother's sample versions from *Hamlet* and *Romeo and Juliet*, to a whole translation of Shakespeare, indicated that the break with Bürger had not spelled an end to such ambitions.

And yet he could not avoid getting involved in the affairs that exercised the Muilman household, such as a schism in the Lutheran church (things like that did not happen in Hanover).[196] It also produced Schlegel's most unlikely publication. A brother-in-law of Muilman's, Joachim Rendorp, had become embroiled in the issue of the regency during Stadholder William V's minority and in particular against the regent himself, duke Ludwig Ernst of Brunswick. This elicted a defence from the Göttingen historian Schlözer, a protégé of the Brunswicker. Mr Rendorp wrote a spirited reply; Schlegel was asked to translate it into German for the publisher Heinsius in Leipzig—anonymously, so as not to offend Schlözer personally. These *Nachrichten* were essentially hack work and were discontinued after the first part (they are today a rarity).[197] The 60 talers due for the work went straight into the insatiable maw of his debt-ridden brother Friedrich.

Fig. 2 Portrait drawing of August Wilhelm Schlegel as a young man, by unknown artist, undated [early 1790s]. © and by kind permission of Hans-Joachim Dopfer, all rights reserved.

---

195 *KA*, XXIII, 19.
196 *Briefe*, I, 14.
197 Full title: (Anon.), *Joachim Rendorps geheime Nachrichten zur Aufklärung der Vorfälle während des letzten Krieges zwischen England und Holland, aus dem Holländ. mit erläuternden Anmerkungen* (Leipzig: Heinsius, 1793); *KA*, XXIII, 412.

Despite his protestations of love and devotion to Caroline, there was talk of a 'Sophie', a singer in Amsterdam; indeed his brother counselled him not to mention her name in letters that Caroline might also see.[198] But we must assume that it was for Caroline that August Wilhelm had his portrait painted by Johann Friedrich August Tischbein, in 1793, during one of that painter's sojourns in Amsterdam. It is that slightly sensuous, effete and stylised portrait, with the modish high stock, that hitherto was our only image of the young Schlegel.[199]

Fig. 3 Portrait in oils of August Wilhelm Schlegel, by Johann Friedrich August Tischbein [1793]. Image in the public domain.

How good a likeness it is can only be gauged from Friedrich's reactions, with which Caroline also agreed: forehead, nose and general area successful, but not the mouth; he had not captured the natural fire of the eyes and had substituted some significance perceptible only to himself. The sitter seems to have been satisfied, otherwise he would not have sent it. Perhaps it is

---

198 *KA*, XXIII, 75.
199 Now in the Freies Deutsches Hochstift, Frankfurt am Main. Cf. *Freies Deutsches Hochstift Frankfurter Goethe-Museum. Katalog der Gemälde*, ed. Sabine Michaelis (Tübingen: Niemeyer, 1982), 162f. The new edition of the catalogue retracts the attribution to Tischbein on the grounds of the paint quality and dates it at around 1800, the artist unidentified. This being outside of my sphere of competence, I leave the matter open. *Freies Deutsches Hochstift—Frankfurter Goethe-Museum. Die Gemälde. 'Denn was wäre die Welt ohne Kunst?'. Bestandskatalog*, ed. Petra Maisak and Gerhard Kölsch (Frankfurt am Main: Freies Deutsches Hochstift—Frankfurter Goethe-Museum, 2011), 365-367.

the first sign of the vanity with which he later was taxed and which some detected as early as 1791.[200]

'Du, Caroline und ich': Friedrich Schlegel[201]

What of Friedrich, plunged into a broil of human affairs for which he was emotionally, perhaps even constitutionally, not prepared? The four years of correspondence with his brother August Wilhelm reveal the many sides of his character, by no means all of them flattering; but we do well to remember that this was a young man, a late developer, given to mood swings and dark reflections that only just recoiled from suicide. When these young (and not so young) men in the 1790s turned their attention to the figure of Hamlet, they revealed much of themselves: Goethe had his Wilhelm Meister believe in the Prince's innate nobility; Christian Garve the popular philosopher found a balance between reason and unreason; Ludwig Tieck was fascinated by the phenomenon of madness; August Wilhelm saw a 'surfeit of the rational'. Only Friedrich Schlegel saw 'endless destruction, breakdown, of the very highest powers' ('unendliche Zerrüttung an den allerhöchsten Kräften'), a 'fearful void', and there was a sense of identification that the others lacked.[202] When he learned in 1792 that Schiller had called him a 'kalter Witzling' ('smart alec'),[203] we perceive something of that inner insecurity that sought compensation in superficial brilliance or the parading of knowledge. It was a hasty judgement, a weakness to which Schiller inclined. It did not for the moment diminish Friedrich's admiration for Schiller, but both brothers would learn to be wary of the older man's prickliness.

This inner insecurity may be a reason why Friedrich elevated friendship as he did, not just as his father's generation had done, but following Burke and Kant, to the sublime itself.[204] He said this in 1791 and repeated it substantially in 1794. Yet these heady notions of friendship also had their feet on the ground of reality. It was not by chance that concrete sums of

---

200 KA, XXIII, 14.
201 For an account of Friedrich Schlegel's early development see Enders, 200-277; Franz Futterknecht, 'Zur Herkunft romantischen Geistes im Werk Friedrich Schlegels— Blumenbachs "Bildungstrieb" und das Elternhaus in Kurhannover', in: *Romantik in Niedersachsen*, 175-232; Harro Zimmermann, *Friedrich Schlegel oder die Sehnsucht nach Deutschland* (Paderborn, etc.: Schöningh, 2009), 30-37.
202 KA, XXIII, 104f.
203 Ibid., 51.
204 Ibid., 33, 176.

money occurred frequently in these fraternal letters. By the end of 1793, he was hopelessly in debt: his creditors were gathering round to prevent his departure from Leipzig for Dresden, and he desperately needed 500 talers. His brother in Amsterdam managed to raise this huge sum, using wealthy 'Connexionen' but also drawing on his own savings. It was to be the first of several quite hefty sums that Friedrich was to receive from this source, even when relations between the brothers later were strained. We wonder therefore how accurate Friedrich's estimate of May 1794 was, computing the annual cost of living in Dresden: for a single man, his meals and a servant, 80 talers, for a married couple perhaps 250 talers.²⁰⁵ Later in the year, he saw no reason why August Wilhelm, once he had returned to Germany, should not be able to earn 1,000 talers from his writings (at roughly the same time, Schiller claimed to need 1,400 talers to live in an appropriate style).²⁰⁶ It is clear that Friedrich envisaged a future unburdened by 'Amt' and tenure, where the talers and Louisd'ors would be earned by the pen alone. The model was certainly Schiller, but even he was never a completely 'independent writer', never without a helping hand from some prince or other. It was a perilous path to follow, and not even his provident brother was able to pursue it consistently. The Romantic generation needed professional qualifications, or academic posts, or private estates, or patrons, or combinations of all of these. Not a single one of them was ever financially independent. The irony is that Friedrich Schlegel, who believed longer than most that he could be a writer and nothing else, was also the one whose finances were always in the greatest disarray.

One does not wish to reduce the many heady literary plans, feverishly communicated to his brother in Amsterdam, to the level of mere income sources. They came bubbling up out of his fertile intelligence: 'My hidden powers are alive, everything in me is active, and I only seek that which will ease, urge and channel the plenitude within me'.²⁰⁷ We do note their ambitiousness and their desire to supplant what was already published and articulated by others: the Roman republic (abandoned), the history of Greek poetry (reduced in scope), the Greeks and Romans compared with the Moderns (adapted). They involved absolute definitions of the nature of poetry: the inner unity of the disparate, the harmony of inner fullness, and attempt to express the many-sided as a system. Eventually, he came down

---

205 *Ibid.*, 198.
206 *Ibid.*, 211.
207 *Ibid.*, 51.

to the amalgamation of the essentially modern ('das Wesentlich-Moderne') with the essentially ancient ('das Wesentlich-Antike').[208] Big names cropped up: the Greeks, of course, for he was still in the grip of a kind of Graecomania, but also Dante, Shakespeare, Goethe, as a post-classical canon. The formulations came in rapid succession; one touched off the next. Thus Hamlet, so close to Friedrich's own mood, was the archetypical figure of the modern, the merely 'interesting' and sensational, the nihilistic and destructive. These notions pushed him closer to an examination of his own times and sparked off the essays on Condorcet, Lessing and Forster.

But his letters were not without their propaedeutic side and their tendency towards absolute pronouncements. His older brother, never as philosophically inclined as he, was treated to several philosophy lessons. He was frequently enjoined to complete his Dante project, which of course he duly did. The translator of Petrarch must learn that the 'ideal' could only be found in tragedy; he must be told that Bürger, the sponsor of those translations, was merely a poet of 'life', not, by implication, of anything higher. But Friedrich did call on August Wilhelm's superior knowledge of Homer or of Greek grammarians. He passed on comments from Caroline: August Wilhelm's samples of Shakespeare contained, for her taste, too many archaisms, a negative effect of translating Dante.[209] But both welcomed his new prose style, she noting that it had a polemically sharp edge, he finding elements of Herder and Johannes von Müller, high praise indeed.[210] They seemed to form an ideal combination: 'Du, Caroline und ich'.[211] If only they could all be together in one place, Rome for instance, where they could complete Winckelmann's work by supplying the poetic dimension to his history of Greek art![212]

By then, however, August Wilhelm was being published in Schiller's *Die Horen*. Caroline was urging Friedrich to read Condorcet. August Wilhelm was willing to work for the *Allgemeine Literatur-Zeitung* in Jena. And at the end of 1795, he returned to Germany from Amsterdam. Muilman had treated him well, in a business-like fashion. Willem's later letters to his former tutor are chatty: on his grand tour, which included England and Germany, he visited Schlegel, now a professor in Jena. In England, Willem had his portrait painted by Sir Thomas Lawrence.[213]

---

208 *Ibid.*, 185.
209 *Ibid.*, 138.
210 *Ibid.*, 218.
211 *Ibid.*, 160.
212 *Ibid.*, 227.
213 Scholte, 141-146.

2. Jena and Berlin (1795-1804)

'Devoting Myself Exclusively to the Profession of a Writer'

In the preface to his *Kritische Schriften* of 1828, taking stock of his career as a critic, Schlegel identified the years 1795 to 1804 as those in which he had 'devoted himself solely to writing as a profession' ('wo ich mich ausschließend dem Schriftstellerberuf widmete').[1] 1828 was by coincidence also the year in which Goethe began issuing his correspondence with Schiller, documents that suggested a wide disparity of interest between them and Schlegel's generation. The reality was of course different: these years brought Schlegel into close contact with the great Dioscuri of Weimar and Jena, Goethe and Schiller. The decision to live by his pen involved to some extent hitching his wagon to their star, exploiting the openings that they afforded, pursuing aims that coincided with theirs, and using them, Goethe especially, as tutelary geniuses. This Classical and Romantic decade is rightly seen as the great time of intellectual and poetic ferment that produced the *Letters on Aesthetic Education, Wallenstein, Wilhelm Meister* and *Hermann und Dorothea, Die Horen* and *Athenaeum*, to cite but a few. It is proper to mention the titles of Goethe's and Schiller's works in one breath with the Schlegel brothers': they all share in the creativity, the desire to achieve new standards and perceive new norms, the 'aesthetic revolution' (Friedrich Schlegel's phrase), the zest for all things new. This is what the modern historian Reinhold Koselleck meant when he saw this period as a 'Sattelzeit', rising up to an 'eminence', or as the threshold to a new age ('Epochenschwelle').

There was a human side to all this, and a human cost. Movements involve real people, competing and jostling, urging themselves to bursts

---

1 *SW*, VII, xxxi.

of creativity, sparing neither their nerves nor their physical energies, nor those closest to them. 'Do not distract yourself with reading literary trifles. Force yourself. […] Schiller has to pump the thoughts up out of himself with the greatest effort. And Goethe's lightness of touch is often the fruit of immense diligence and great strain',[2] was the advice Friedrich Schlegel gave to his brother on 17 August 1795, at the outset of that decade of professional writing. Georg Forster's death, in the clash of critical and political forces, had been a warning example; but even Schiller, who insisted on keeping politics out of critical discourse, found his creativity constantly interrupted by chronic bouts of illness; Goethe's otherwise robust frame almost succumbed. The new Romantic movement was soon to have its own necrology: two promising young men of the new generation died, respectively, in 1798 and 1801, Wackenroder and Novalis; Caroline was often ill, surely a contributory factor to the breakdown of her marriage with Schlegel; Ludwig Tieck ruined his health in damp and insanitary Jena. When in the summer of 1799, the young Friedrich Carl von Savigny, the later distinguished jurist, attended August Wilhelm's lectures in Jena, he saw before him a man marked by a 'destructive force',[3] the result of over-exertion and economic pressure, in modern parlance, 'burned out'.

Being a professional writer meant for Schlegel producing in the space of a few years four major and several minor contributions to Schiller's periodical *Die Horen*[4] (which included a large section of translation from the *Divine Comedy*), some of this running parallel with the versions of sixteen Shakespearean plays up to 1802—he told Schiller that he might spend hours just on one line—and nearly three hundred reviews for the *Allgemeine Literatur-Zeitung* in Jena. Then there were lectures at Jena university, followed by the cycle in Berlin (this does not take contributions to *Musenalmanache* into account). Small wonder that his 1828 preface spoke

---

2   *Kritische Friedrich-Schlegel-Ausgabe* [KA], ed. Ernst Behler *et al.*, 30 vols (Paderborn, Munich, Vienna: Schöningh; Zurich: Thomas, 1958- in progress), XXIII, 247.

3   Adolf Stoll, *Der junge Savigny. Kinderjahre, Marburger und Landshuter Zeit Friedrich Karl von Savignys. Zugleich ein Beitrag zur Geschichte der Romantik* (Berlin: Heymann, 1927), 118.

4   *Die Horen eine Monatsschrift herausgegeben von Schiller* (Tübingen: Cotta, 1795-97). AWS's contributions are: 'Dante's Hölle', 1. Bd., Jg. 1795, 3. Stück, 22-69, 2. Bd. Jg. 1795, 4. Stück, 1-13, Bd. 3, Jg. 1795, 7. Stück, 31-49, Jg. 1795, 8. Stück, 35-74; 'Briefe über Poesie, Silbenmaaß und Sprache', Jg. 1795, 11. Stück, 77-103, Bd. 5, Jg. 1796, 1. Stück, 54-74, Jg. 1796, 2. Stück, 56-73; 'Scenen aus Romeo und Julie von Shakespeare', Jg. 1796, 3. Stück, 92-104; 'Etwas über William Shakespeare bey Gelegenheit Wilhelm Meisters', Jg. 1796, 4. Stück, 57-112; 'Szenen aus Shakespeare. Der Sturm', Jg. 1796, 6. Stück, 61-82; 'Aus Shakespeares Julius Cäsar', Jg. 1797, 4. Stück, 17-42; 'Ueber Shakespeare's Romeo und Julia', Jg. 1797, 6. Stück, 18-48.

of 'difficulties and restrictions', the 'demands of the moment' that inhibited 'objects of wide compass'.[5] Listed like this, his achievement in these years appears anything but fragmentary. But, transpose it on to a day-to-day basis, as has been done for Goethe, and it is a story of overlapping demands, pressures and conflicts, commitments and deadlines. Not for nothing did his brother Friedrich—hardly suppressing a touch of fraternal disrespect— call him the 'great schoolmaster of the universe',[6] knowing him capable of prodigies of sheer hard work that drew on the reservoirs of knowledge accumulated in his years in Hanover, in Göttingen and in Holland.

Yet Friedrich Schlegel, writing in November 1795, could claim with some justification that he already had three and a half years as a writer to his credit: August Wilhelm was in these terms a relative novice.[7] Friedrich had lived from his writing (conveniently forgetting those loans, but no matter). His letters seemed to be flares shooting in all directions, firecrackers and showers of sparks, but there were also some concrete results as well: his work on the schools of Greek poetry, for instance, his essay on republicanism, the monograph-length essay on the study of the Greeks and Romans, soon to be joined by his essays on Condorcet, on Lessing, on Forster. He was still overflowing with ideas, a refutation of Kant, a study of Greek music, an essay on Caesar and Alexander, a history of mankind even; he was entering into his phase of close study of Fichte, and had revived his friendship with the young inspector of salt mines, Friedrich von Hardenberg, known as Novalis. Much would remain fragmentary, work in progress, the products of a young man in a hurry, always picking up the next project and so often publishing several drafts too soon. Schiller spotted this particular weakness and lampooned him for it. He could also be a menace. He was an unruly presence when he moved from Dresden to Jena in the summer of 1796 and effectively destroyed August Wilhelm's good working relationship with Schiller. Transferring to Berlin a summer later, he was immediately at home in the salons and societies that provincial Jena did not offer and was quite the man about town.

In the spring of 1795, August Wilhelm's time in Holland was drawing to a close. Caroline was still sequestered in Lucka. During her absence on a visit to Gotha, her small son Wilhelm Julius died, aged a year and a half. He was buried without ceremony;[8] the cause of death was given

---

5   SW, VII, xxxi.
6   KA, XXIII, 252.
7   Ibid., 260.
8   Caroline. Briefe aus der Frühromantik. Nach Georg Waitz hg. von Erich Schmidt, 2 vols (Leipzig: Insel, 1913), I, 704, 708; KA, XXIII, 469.

as purpura. A child, not of love (or perhaps just), but of the Revolution, Friedrich Schlegel's godchild, poor little Julius passes out of our account. But what would have become of him; might he not have been a hindrance, a reminder of an episode best forgotten? Yet his death meant, as Caroline wrote, the end of her inner peace and happiness, leaving only a kind of stoical acceptance. There was no material or political security, either. Leaving Lucka, she headed for Göttingen, and her family, only to find that the writ against her staying in the kingdom of Hanover was still in force. Brunswick, the dukedom next door, dynastically allied with Hanover, proved to be more welcoming (and more cultivated): Lessing had found refuge there twenty years earlier. Schlegel returned from Holland in June, and in August, Caroline, her mother, and her daughter Auguste moved to Brunswick. In the same letter (to Göschen) she wrote of the consolation of having Schlegel there until he found his destination. His mother, meanwhile, needed careful handling before the nature of their relationship became open news.

The residence town of Brunswick, with its French theatre and Italian opera, its polished court—the culture-loving Duchess Anna Amalia of Saxe-Weimar had been a Brunswick princess—certainly had its attractions. In addition, survivors of Johann Adolf Schlegel's generation lived there, 'Mamselle Jerusalem' (her brother had been the model for Goethe's Werther), or 'Mad. Ebert', the widow of Johann Arnold Ebert, Johann Adolf's friend and professor at the Collegium Carolinum academy. Another professor, Johann Joachim Eschenburg, the translator of Shakespeare and professor, was a further useful link: Schlegel was nevertheless about to supplant his translation. With Ebert dead there was talk of Schlegel succeeding him. Opinions differed as to what he should do. A family friend from Hanover advised him not to commit himself and to wait until a favourable moment made it opportune.[9] His brother Moritz for his part warned against the perils of journalism ('journaliere Schriftstellerey') and the 'superficial philosophy' that Schiller was purveying in *Die Horen*.[10] It was too late for such admonitions. Even before he left Holland, Schlegel had already signed up as a contributor to Schiller's periodical *Die Horen*, and Schiller had introduced him to Christian Gottfried Schütz, university professor and editor of the *Allgemeine Literatur-Zeitung* in Jena for which Schlegel

---

9   *August Wilhelm und Friedrich Schlegel im Briefwechsel mit Schiller und Goethe*, ed. Josef Körner and Ernst Wieneke [Wieneke] (Leipzig: Insel, 1926), 192.

10 *Briefe von und an August Wilhelm Schlegel*, ed. Josef Körner [*Briefe*], 2 vols (Zurich, Leipzig, Vienna: Amalthea, 1930), I, 24-26, ref. 25.

was to write those nearly three hundred reviews;¹¹ he was still in contact with his old publisher, Wilhelm Gottlieb Becker, who had published some of his poems and the first part of his Dante.¹² He was clearly on the way to becoming a free-lance writer, even if the prospect of 1,000 talers a year that his brother Friedrich had once dangled before him was to be seldom fulfilled. Should they all make a fresh start and go to America? A plan emerged and was dropped almost as soon as it was mentioned.¹³ America was, in Goethe's phrase, 'here or nowhere' [hier oder nirgend].¹⁴

At first, Caroline seems to have accepted Schlegel's presence. To her confidant Luise Gotter in Gotha she stated that the basis of her attachment to Schlegel was friendship, and the need for protection.¹⁵ She had her ten-year-old daughter Auguste to consider, and her education. This precocious and talented child (the grand-daughter of two Göttingen professors) was showing musical gifts; later, her step-father and step-uncle, the Schlegel brothers, would be giving her Greek lessons. There is a slightly stiff letter to her signed, 'Your friend Wilhelm', suggesting that Schlegel was at least making the effort to be amicable.¹⁶

That autumn he and Caroline made the short journey to Salzdahlum, the slightly ramshackle lodge that at the time housed the ducal Brunswick art collection (now in the Herzog Anton Ulrich Museum). We do not know what they saw, but it doubtless extended what he knew from Holland or Düsseldorf. Over a year earlier, two Göttingen students, Ludwig Tieck and Wilhelm Heinrich Wackenroder, had made the same journey; but they had already seen the Dürers in Nuremberg and the dubious 'Raphael' in Pommersfelden. In his preface of 1828, Schlegel stated that his real aim had been to write a history of the fine arts, but that 'demands of the moment' kept him from it.¹⁷ It is therefore all the more frustrating that there is a blank in our knowledge of the visit to Salzdahlum, especially noted for its Netherlandish collection, and what caught their eye.

One of the more pressing 'demands of the moment' was of course Schlegel's collaboration on Schiller's *Die Horen*, that lasted from 1795 to 1797. Schiller went even further. On December 10, 1795, he wrote to

---

11 *Ibid.*, 28f.
12 *Ibid.*, 27f.
13 *Caroline*, I, 374; *KA*, XXIII, 469.
14 *Wilhelm Meisters Lehrjahre*. Johann Wolfgang Goethe, *Gedenkausgabe der Werke, Briefe und Gespräche*, ed. Ernst Beutler, 3rd edn, 27 vols (Zurich: Artemis, 1986 [1949]), VII, 464.
15 *Caroline*, I, 376.
16 *Ibid.*, 378.
17 *SW*, VII, xxxi.

Schlegel in Brunswick suggesting that they come and live in Jena. Surely, he said, letters were no substitute for conversation.[18] Over a year earlier, Friedrich Schlegel had urged him to consider these twin towns of Jena and Weimar as a base. But first, August Wilhelm was married to Caroline. Their wedding took place on 1 July, 1796 in the St Catherine church in Brunswick.[19] His devotion to Caroline, her sense of gratitude to him, and the awareness that their destinies coincided, had led them to this step. She went into the union with her eyes open; it was not primarily a love relationship, but one of mutual respect, a good working arrangement, nothing more, free of any romantic illusions. She brought with her a sharp critical mind, but abandoned such literary ambitions as she may have had (there is the fragment of a novel).[20] Schlegel's multifarious projects took precedence. Her wit and perspicacity were undiminished: surveying Schiller's *Musenalmanach* for 1796, she immediately spotted the wicked *Xenien*. Her description of these epigrams by Goethe and Schiller, forming their own section in the almanac, as 'piglets enclosed in their own sty',[21] does not feature in the critical literature. No-one in Jena or Weimar could overlook 'Mad. Schlegel'.

2.1 Jena

The ancient university town of Jena, set romantically between hills in the valley of the river Saale, was on the face of it not a natural choice for an up-and-coming man of letters. Once Germany's premier university, it had lost ground to Göttingen. By the end of the 1780s Jena was facing bankruptcy, and with a population of only 4,500, it was being deserted by its students, the sustainers of its livelihood, whose numbers dropped to as low as 850. Those that remained gave Jena the unenviable reputation of being Germany's rowdiest university. Student corporations, bizarrely uniformed and armed to the teeth, flouted civil authority when it suited them.[22] The troops sent by Duke Carl August of Saxe-Weimar in the summer of 1792 to quell a student riot, knew this to their cost when they were forced to withdraw; another stand-off occurred in 1795. Unpopular professors—and others—were liable to have their windows broken (it happened to

---

18 Wieneke, 19; *KA*, XXIII, 211.
19 *Caroline*, I, 712.
20 Ibid., 662-664.
21 Ibid., 382.
22 Ernst Borkowsky, *Das alte Jena und seine Universität. Eine Jubiläumsgabe zur Universitätsfeier* (Jena: Diederichs, 1908), 129-131; W. H. Bruford, *Culture and Society in Classical Weimar 1775-1806* (Cambridge: Cambridge UP, 1962), 377f.

Fichte, to Goethe's secret pleasure). Caroline wrote with some relief in September 1796 that they were living above a courtyard and thus unlikely to have their glassware smashed.[23] The town itself was unprepossessing; it could be noted that prominent citizens, Schiller being the most famous, moved outside the town to summerhouses as soon as the weather allowed, indeed the macrobiotic physician, Christoph Wilhelm Hufeland, himself based in Jena, recommended such 'Rusticationen' as an antidote to the insalubriousness of towns.[24]

If Jena proved attractive to the Schlegel brothers, it was very largely Goethe's good work. As Saxe-Weimar's minister of state responsible for educational matters, assisted by the excellent government official, Christian Gottlob Voigt, he set to work in the 1790s to improve the university's image.[25] That meant first of all winning round Duke Carl August, who was inclined to see Jena as a hotbed of sedition—a professor was actually lecturing on the French Revolution—and then securing new blood among the professoriate. Of course Schiller himself had been a *professor extrordinarius* in Jena since 1789, and his lectures on world history had been filled with enthusiastic hearers, but he was unable to sustain these numbers, and his health forced him to abandon lecturing altogether. Yet Schiiller's intellectual presence was a draw-card in itself: Wilhelm von Humboldt stayed in Jena at various times between 1794 and 1797. Then in 1794 came Goethe's coup in securing Johann Gottlieb Fichte's appointment to the main chair of philosophy.[26] This unkempt and farouche figure lectured to huge audiences, some even sitting on the window-sills of the auditorium, holding them in the palm of his hand through the force of his oratory. It was he who had given those seditious lectures on the Revolution and on freedom of thought; his calls for independence of mind among his young hearers, on 'Man's Vocation' ('Die Bestimmung des Menschen') appealed to students coming to terms with their own moral selves. He also challenged what he saw as the reactionary spirit of the student corporations: they promptly smashed his windows. Very few may have understood his new philosophical terminology: Friedrich Schlegel and Novalis were enthusiastic Fichteans,

---

23 *Caroline*, I, 397.
24 Christoph Wilhelm Hufeland, *Die Kunst das menschliche Leben zu verlängern*, 2 parts (Vienna and Prague: Haas, 1797), I, 153, 155.
25 Friedrich Sengle, *Das Genie und sein Fürst. Die Geschichte der Lebensgemeinschaft Goethes mit dem Herzog Carl August von Sachsen-Weimar-Eisenach. Ein Beitrag zum Spätfeudalismus und zu einem vernachlässigten Thema der Goetheforschung* (Stuttgart, Weimar: Metzler, 1993), 142-152.
26 Theodore Ziolkowski, *Das Wunderjahr in Jena. Geist und Gesellschaft* (Stuttgart: Klett-Cotta, 1998), 40-61.

while August Wilhelm never was, and their relationship was never close; in that he would be seconded by Schiller.

Besides Fichte, the Jena professors included Schütz, professor of rhetoric, who with the jurist Gottlieb Hufeland edited the *Allgemeine Literatur-Zeitung*. This review periodical was part of the realm of the Weimar entrepreneur Friedrich Justin Bertuch and helped to put Jena on the map.[27] But Heinrich Eberhard Gottlob Paulus, the theologian and orientalist, deserves mention, and his young wife, with whom August Wilhelm allegedly flirted,[28] not least because their daughter Sophie would have been five in 1796. In 1818, she was to be the partner of his second, ill-starred marriage. It was largely the result of Goethe's ministrations that this whole galaxy had been brought together, and it was fortunate for the Schlegels that Goethe in 1795-96 spent a disproportionate amount of time in Jena itself, or was occupied with university affairs. Goethe knew, as August Wilhelm was to find out in 1798, that university matters required tact and diplomacy. Weimar the residence town of a petty dukedom was open to all kinds of social and intellectual currents, but some aspects of Jena university's administration suggested deepest provinciality and small-town mentality. Goethe had general oversight, but four Thuringian dukes, all members of the Ernestine branch of the Saxon house, also had their say in university appointments. These *Serenissimi Nutritores*, 'Sovereign Providers', were Saxe-Coburg, Saxe-Meiningen, Saxe-Gotha, and of course Saxe-Weimar itself.

It said much for Goethe's conciliatory and persuasive skills that the university had the professors that it did. Just before his marriage and their move to Jena, Schlegel had supplicated to an even smaller Thuringian court, Schwarzburg-Rudolstadt, for the style of 'Rat' [counsellor], duly conferred on 28 May 1796.[29] Titles were to prove important in Jena.

First, Schlegel had to associate with Jena's notabilities and luminaries and join in the literary and intellectual scene. Some of these people he had only known by correspondence: he had been in touch with Schiller by letter since the summer of 1795, and with Schütz since the end of that year. For the time being, they were his main providers: *Die Horen* paid four Louisd'ors a sheet,[30] and the *Allgemeine Literatur-Zeitung* brought in a steady income.

Schiller had of course known about Schlegel since 1791; his name was among the array of potential contributors to *Die Horen*, linking generations

---

27 Bruford, *Culture and Society*, 297-308.
28 KA, XXIII, 376.
29 SLUB Dresden, Mscr. Dresd. e. 90, II (9) (the actual document is now lost); Briefe, II, 14.
30 *Caroline*, I, 419.

and philosophical schools, listed when the journal was announced in 1794. Not all of these names were of course actually to feature in the pages of *Die Horen* (Fichte was a prominent absentee). Schlegel could be relied upon right through from the earliest issues in 1795, until the enterprise began to falter, then to collapse in 1797. Meanwhile, Schlegel was a regarded as an 'Acquisition'; both Humboldt and Schütz used the word.[31] From his experience in Göttingen and Amsterdam, Schlegel knew a little about how journals and reviews functioned; they set out with great intentions and then got stuck in details; editors changed tack and went in for 'deals': Schiller, for instance, as editor of *Die Horen*, had 'set up' reviews of his own journal and had them paid for by his own publisher, Cotta in Tübingen.[32] There were often divided loyalties: Schlegel found himself writing for the one (*Die Horen*) and then reviewing what he had written in the other (*Allgemeine Literatur-Zeitung*).[33] Schütz had even asked him to review the 'poetic' material of the first few issues of *Die Horen*, which meant Goethe's *Roman Elegies* and *Conversations of German Exiles*.

All of Schlegel's writings at this stage—whether for *Die Horen* or for the *Allgemeine Literatur-Zeitung*—pursued a strategy of their own or exploited others' strategies for their own purposes. He dressed up in more accessible form some notes made originally for his brother Friedrich in order to help him formulate ideas on two of his preoccupations: the origin of language and the development of rhythm and metre. *Die Horen* was not the place for too technical a discussion, but reviews in the *Allgemeine Literatur-Zeitung*, of Voss's Homer translation and later of Goethe's *Hermann und Dorothea*,[34] provided the appropriate forum. These, in their turn, dovetailed into his later contributions to the *Athenaeum* (1798-1800), co-edited with his brother. Similarly, reviews in the *Allgemeine Literatur-Zeitung* enabled him to note other translations of Shakespeare (Tieck's of *The Tempest* in 1796, for instance),[35] or to spot talent, Tieck's *Volksmährchen* [Folktales][36] or Tieck's

---

31   *Briefe*, I, 28; *Briefwechsel zwischen Schiller und Wilhelm v. Humboldt. Mit einer Vorerinnerung über Schiller und den Gang seiner Geistesentwicklung von W. von Humboldt* (Stuttgart and Tübingen: Cotta, 1830), 312, 347.
32   Raymond Heitz, 'Publizistik, Politik und die Weimarer Klassik. *Die Horen* im Kreuzfeuer von Schillers Zeitgenossen', in: Raymond Heitz and Roland Krebs (eds), *Schiller publiciste/Schiller als Publizist*, Convergences, 42 (Berne, etc.: Peter Lang, 2007), 357-384, ref. 362f.
33   *SW*, X, 59-90.
34   *Ibid.*, XI, 185-221.
35   *Ibid.*, 16-22.
36   *Ibid.*, 136-146.

and Wackenroder's *Herzensergiessungen* [Heart's Outpourings][37] or even odes and elegies by the young Hölderlin. It was part of the programmatic Romantic movement in making. His Dante and Shakespeare projects followed similar patterns. Bürger's and Becker's journals had given him the outlet for his first ideas on Dante and how to translate him; now *Die Horen* enabled him to publish long extracts in metrical form. As for Shakespeare, Schiller's journal gave him the chance to to set out his translation principles (the *Wilhelm Meister* essay), to provide a piece of model criticism (the *Romeo and Juliet* essay) and to demonstrate in chosen extracts how Shakespeare might actually look in German. There was no need for Schlegel to tell Schiller directly that he was using *Die Horen* in order to provide publicity for the Shakespeare translation that started coming out in 1797.

Die Horen

Fig. 4 *Die Horen eine Monatsschrift herausgegeben von Schiller* (Tübingen, 1795-98). Title page of vol. 1. Image in the public domain.

---

37   Ibid., X, 363-371.

Schiller's *Die Horen* [The Hours] with Goethe as right-hand man and star contributor, began by appealing to a 'Societät' of 'all men of good will',[38] but was from its inception elitist to a fault in concept and practice. Schiller almost immediately departed from the general accord that his 'Announcement' of 1794 had promised. There was talk of a cultural, intellectual and aesthetic consensus, but only on its own strict terms. Although Cotta originally wanted a journal of general European interest,[39] Schiller insisted on excluding any kind of political debate—and got his way. From its very inaugural number (1795) it set its sights too high, placing strains on its readers' capacities for abstract thought (Schiller's *Letters on the Aesthetic Education of Man*) or on their moral sensibilities (Goethe's *Roman Elegies*). It was clear that *Die Horen* would be hard going for those unwilling to follow Schiller's lead, to the heights of ideal abstraction, or Goethe's, into the hidden places of passion. In publishing terms, *Die Horen* was a total failure. It is remembered today precisely because of those bold forays and affronts to the 'Zeitgeist', not for the many pieces that merely provided copy (which include Goethe's translation of Benvenuto Cellini). In this context, August Wilhelm Schlegel's contributions are very much worth looking at.

They came very close to the ideal that Schiller enunciated in his 'Announcement', of 'breaking down the barrier between the aesthetic world and the learned', 'imparting sound knowledge into social intercourse and taste into scholarship',[40] thus effectively removing the differences between the arts and the sciences. Schlegel, when in October 1795 he sent Schiller a contribution, the *Briefe über Silbenmaß* [Letters on Metrics], very much hoped that he had found the right tone of 'thoroughness combined with an entertaining style', avoiding the 'dry and technical'.[41] And so the undoubted quality of Schlegel's pieces for *Die Horen* singles him out as a major contributor, but also what he was trying to do through them. His articles represent 'genuine criticism' ('ächtere Kritik')[42] that combines the poetic and the intellectual, accessible in style yet not written for a generality of readers either; text-based, not abstract; making alien poetry available through an 'answerable style' of translation, and postulating a kind of 'musée imaginaire' of great poetry. All these points the later *Athenaeum*

---

38 *Die Horen*, 1. Bd., 1. Stück (1795), ix.
39 Helmut Koopmann, 'Schillers *Horen* und das Ende der Kunstperiode', in: *Schiller publiciste*, 219-230, ref. 223.
40 *Die Horen*, v.
41 Wieneke, 12.
42 *SW*, VII, 25.

would develop more confidently, so that despite enormous personal and ideological differences, it is legitimate to link these two periodicals.

Once settled in the Döderlein house in the Leutragasse in the centre of Jena,[43] Caroline, Auguste and August Wilhelm quickly adjusted to life in a university town. It was, after years of interruption, what Caroline was used to, with the sole difference that Jena was not Göttingen. The house was small but 'pleasant', her husband showing a love of domestic order and even 'elegance'.[44] In the first confusion of moving in, they had to borrow some tea from the Schillers, and soon they were visiting the Schiller family, the poet, his wife Charlotte, and their two small sons. Then it would be the Hufelands' turn, and other tea-parties. Soon, Schiller and Schlegel were exchanging notes similar to those that passed between Schiller and Goethe. Schiller was paying well (a Shakespeare extract brought in seven-and-a-half Louisd'ors).[45] All seemed set for the future. But Schiller had other correspondents, and to them he wrote of different things. Wilhelm von Humboldt was told on 23 July, 1796 that one could have a good conversation with Caroline, but she could also be sharp and prickly.[46] Humboldt, in his turn warned Schiller that she was 'cold, vain, and a bad influence on Schlegel' (these were letters that Humboldt suppressed, when in 1830 he published his correspondence with Schiller, to spare Schlegel's feelings and maintain his working friendship). Through his friend Christian Gottfried Körner in Leipzig and his circle, Schiller was in any case predisposed against Caroline: the sobriquet 'Madame Lucifer' would not be long in coming. Clever, witty and articulate women, it seemed, represented a kind of threat to male-dominated Jena. Schiller meanwhile was prepared to tolerate Caroline so long as her husband gave sustenance to the already ailing *Horen*.

Things were not made better by the arrival—incursion—of Friedrich Schlegel in Jena from the summer of 1796 until the summer of 1797. Friedrich had been publishing in the Jena-based *Philosophisches Journal*, part-edited by Fichte, and in Johann Friedrich Reichardt's magazine *Deutschland*.[47] The composer Reichardt played an important intermediary role in the lives of the young Romantics. His incidental music to Shakespeare and his settings of Goethe were significant musically and culturally. As Kapellmeister in

---

43 As established by Peer Kösling, 'Die Wohnungen der Gebrüder Schlegel in Jena', *Athenäum*, 8 (1998), 97-110.
44 *Caroline*, I, 389.
45 Wieneke, 37.
46 *Caroline*, I, 712.
47 KA, XXIII, 320f.

Berlin, he had introduced the young Ludwig Tieck into soirees and circles otherwise closed to him (he even became his brother-in-law). But he had also spoken unwisely of the French Revolution—at a time of political reaction in Berlin—and had lost his post. Now he was settled romantically at Giebichenstein, near Halle, on a promontory above the river Saale. Giebichenstein became a synonym for sociability, conviviality, meetings of minds: Friedrich Schlegel, drawn to agreeable company, found his way there.

Reichardt's short-lived periodical *Deutschland* (1796) was conceived very much as a counter to Weimar and Jena. Perhaps injudiciously, he engaged the Schlegel brothers: Friedrich wrote an essay on republicanism, August Wilhelm produced an extract from his translation of *Romeo and Juliet*, so short as hardly to be noticed. Then Reichardt published his own review of *Die Horen*.[48] It seized on the feature that for many was its chief weakness: its rejection of any debate whatsoever on political events, in an age when the map of Europe was being redrawn and old verities were no longer secure. Reichardt, not surprisingly, singled out Goethe's 'aristocratic' *Conversations of German Emigrés* for criticism. Schiller, who stood on his dignity, was incensed: Reichardt and his periodical, he wrote to Goethe, was a 'biting insect' that must be stamped upon.[49] This was already in June, 1796, before Friedrich Schlegel's own massive indiscretion, his review of *Die Horen* in *Deutschland*.

Schiller never had a high opinion of Friedrich Schlegel and denied him any talent as a writer.[50] When his friend Körner mentioned Friedrich as a possible contributor to *Die Horen* and sent Schiller the draft of Friedrich's *Studium* essay, Schiller never even bothered to read it through.[51] With both Schlegel brothers in Jena during the later months of 1796, Schiller, despite having an aristocratic wife, may have felt a sense of social unease in the presence of these two highly self-aware and self-possessed superintendent's sons, too clever by half, formidably erudite and informed, moving without effort in all social circles while Caroline, too, was a Göttingen professor's daughter and frequented them as of right. As yet, however, August Wilhelm was all deference.

To Goethe, however, these matters were as nothing. The minister of state, the courtier, the representative in one person of an aristocracy of

---

48   *Deutschland*, 4 parts (Berlin: Unger, 1796), I, i, 55-90.
49   18 June, 1796. Gräf-Leitzmann, I, 164.
50   *Caroline*, I, 710.
51   *KA*, XXIII, 482.

the mind and of station, the director of the court theatre—there seemed no end to his attainments—could afford to be all things to all men (and women). The intensity of his correspondence with Schiller, the almost daily notes that crossed between Jena and Weimar, could give the impression of an exclusivity, of a preoccupation with the aesthetic and the intellectual. But in Goethe's case they shut out much of his persona, his domestic and administrative duties, the tiresome details of everyday life in Weimar;[52] they made no mention of Weimar's open secret, his mistress, Christiane Vulpius. Goethe tried to keep on good terms with Weimar's other luminaries, Wieland and Herder; he encouraged young genius like Alexander von Humboldt, or later, Schelling. And he was welcoming to the Schlegel brothers.

To Caroline, he was distinctly affable.[53] They had not met for three years, since the days in Mainz, and neither had any wish to remind the other of their respective involvements. Goethe was however no longer the lithe young man of his early Weimar years and with the gravitas of office he had put on weight. His 'Corpulenz' was not such as to prevent him from riding over to Jena to discuss with Schiller his latest draft of *Wilhelm Meister*. In the winter of 1796, August Wilhelm and Caroline were in Weimar.[54] First they were in the theatre. There was dinner at Goethe's (but no sign of Christiane). They visited Herder, whom they knew to be touchy and querulous, but found him charming and his Baltic accent delightful. Wieland, visiting Weimar from his self-imposed exile in nearby Ossmannstedt, was in a witty frame of mind. Not all of this was innocent. Polemics were in the air; reputations were to be 'adjusted'. Both Friedrich and Caroline were conspiring in an 'Annihilation' of Wieland.[55] As one classical scholar to another,[56] August Wilhelm conducted a friendly correspondence with Karl August Böttiger, 'Konsistorialrat' in Weimar. Not everyone found Böttiger so amenable: Ludwig Tieck lampooned him; he was Weimar's 'Magister Ubique', an ever-present and indefatigable purveyor of gossip (for which Goethe consigned him to the Walpurgis Night's Dream in *Faust*). But for Schlegel, he was a useful link with Weimar, especially with Herder and Wieland, who saw themselves overshadowed by Goethe and Schiller and generally unappreciated.

---

52 Sengle, *Das Genie und sein Fürst*, 147-164.
53 *Caroline*, I, 391.
54 Ibid., 408-413.
55 As Friedrich Schlegel later puts it. *Caroline*, I, 465; KA, XXIV, 185.
56 AWS's correspondence with Böttiger in *Briefe*, I, 35-37, 48-52, 55f., 58-60, 63-67.

Goethe and Schiller on the Attack: The *Xenien*

For all the good relations and the general tone of bonhomie, controversy was in the air. Already towards the end of 1795, Schiller was writing to Goethe of 'times of feud' and a 'church militant'.[57] They felt embattled. Neither *Die Horen* nor the first parts of *Wilhelm Meister* had been well enough received for Goethe's satisfaction nor was this state of affairs to improve substantially. Excellence was not being given its due; German literary discourse was dominated by the ill-disposed, by mediocrities, by superannuated talents, by mere specialists. Schiller named them: Nicolai, Manso, Eschenburg, Ramdohr and *tutti quanti*. Philosophy was wreathed in Fichtean obnubilations. There were direct opponents, the hated Reichardt for instance, who had dared to remark 'deficiencies' in *Die Horen*, and there were those all-too-clever young men, the brothers Schlegel.

Such indignation could not be contained in letters. Already in 1795, it spilled over into the 'unpolitical' pages of *Die Horen*. Goethe, in his short polemic *Literarischer Sansculottismus*[58] threw down the gauntlet to the detractors of *Die Horen*, the snipers, the deniers; those who would not allow that Germany might some day, like France and England, be secure in a culture supported by a mature society. Small wonder, where the literary scene was dominated by such an untalented bunch; with them setting the tone, there could be no 'classical' literature, no centre, no nation with an attendant high degree of culture. None of this was new. Friedrich Nicolai had said substantially the same thing back in 1755: now, he was to be a prominent target in the frontal attack that was marshalled by Goethe and Schiller in 1796, the 414 epigrammatic distichs known as *Xenien* (Offerings), published, not in *Die Horen*, but in Schiller's *Musenalmanach* for 1797.

It was more scatter-shot than directed fire: almost anyone who mattered (notable exceptions were Fichte and Voss) received a burst of Goethe's and Schiller's disdainful—but often delightfully wicked—epigrammatic wit. The *Xenien* made clear to August Wilhelm Schlegel which side Goethe and Schiller were on: his mentor Heyne (nos. 366-70), his publisher Becker (no. 132), his patron Eschenburg (no. 159) came under fire, the Bürger review was revisited (no. 345) and his wife's alleged association with Forster was rehearsed (no. 347) (there was even a light-hearted *Xenion* on Johann Elias

---

57   Schiller to Goethe 1 November, 1795. *Der Briefwechsel zwischen Schiller und Goethe*, ed. Hans Gerhard Gräf and Albert Leitzmann, 3 vols (Leipzig: Insel, 1955), 112.
58   *Die Horen*, Jg. 1795, 5. Stück, 50-56.

Schlegel and his nephews [no. 341]). But the twenty-one in total devoted to Friedrich showed the extent of Schiller's exasperation with Schlegel's 'Gräkomanie', his rejection of modern poetry, his unacknowledged borrowings, his all-too fertile pen, his hasty, impetuous writing:

> *Die höchste Harmonie*
> [The height of harmony]
>
> Ödipus reißt die Augen sich aus, Jocasta erhenkt sich,
> Beide schuldlos; das Stück hat sich harmonisch gelöst.[59]
>
> [Oedipus tears out his eyes, and Jocasta's body dies hanging,
> Both without guilt; the play ends harmoniously.]

This was a travesty, of course, of Friedrich Schlegel's contrast between Greek harmony and the frenzied, dissonant, 'atroce' world of modern art and letters, his critique of Shakespeare and Hamlet.

This attention lavished on Friedrich Schlegel may surprise: even the detested Reichardt received fewer *Xenien*. For the time being, both brothers (and Caroline) nevertheless enjoyed good personal relations with Schiller, observing the proprieties of polite sociability.[60] Privately, Friedrich did his best to shrug off the *Xenien*, consoling himself with the thought that he must expect some grapeshot from an opponent like Schiller.[61] It was no more than an uneasy truce. Now, Friedrich, taking over from where Reichardt had left off, began to review the 1796 issues of *Die Horen* in the much-disliked *Deutschland*.[62] These reviews were, to say the least, partial. He praised his own brother at Schiller's expense, made impudent remarks about Schiller's poetry, found good words for Goethe's wonderful elegy *Alexis und Dora*, but made impertinent comments on Goethe's translation of Benvenuto Cellini. There were two-edged comments on the *Xenien* and their effect on the more sensitive reader, for privately Friedrich was up in arms at their treatment of Reichardt. He was in good company: by no means everyone had enjoyed reading these 'Offerings', and the Weimar and Gotha courts had been scandalised.[63] His account of the eighth number

---

59 Goethe, *Gedenkausgabe*, II, 486.
60 *Caroline*, I, 401-404.
61 KA, XXIII, 344.
62 *Deutschland*, III, 74-97.
63 *Goethe in vertraulichen Briefen seiner Zeitgenossen*, ed. Wilhelm Bode, 3 vols (Berlin, Weimar: Aufbau, 1979), II, 81; Sengle, *Das Genie und sein Fürst*, 144f.

of the 1796 *Horen* was little better: there was talk of mediocrity and even plagiarism. The Hours [*Horen*], he said, had diverged from their orbit and had entered their 'translation phase' — translation was beginning to dominate (nearly half) — and suggested that the supply of more imaginative copy was beginning to run dry.

Schiller's reaction was instantaneous and Olympian. Not being able to harm Friedrich, who was excluded from *Die Horen*, he hurled his bolts at August Wilhelm instead. On 31 May, 1797, August Wilhelm received this astringent message:

> It was my pleasure to afford you a chance to make an income, not given to many, in my Horen, by publishing your translations of Dante and Shakespeare, but now that I hear that Herr Friedrich Schlegel, even as I am rendering you this favour, is abusing them publicly and finds too many translations in the Horen, you must accept my excuses for the future. And to release you once and for all from a relationship that must inhibit the frank and sensitive exchange of thought and opinion, permit me to break off an arrangement that under such circumstances is no longer natural and which already has too often compromised my trust.[64]

This glacially imperious letter thus removed with immediate effect an important source of income from Schlegel. Shaken, he wrote straight away to Schiller, protesting his innocence, claiming not to have seen the review, disavowing any personal influence over his brother:

> If ever you have felt any bond of friendship for me, then please do not refuse my request to speak to you as soon as possible and plead my innocence in this most unfortunate mishap [...][65]

Caroline added a postscript, similarly penitent,[66] but Schiller remained inexorable:

> In the circle of my close acquaintances I must have implicit and absolute trust, and after what has happened, that cannot be the case between you and me.

Schlegel was not entirely blameless.[67] In his *Horen* review in the *Allgemeine Literatur-Zeitung*, he had praised Goethe to the exclusion of Schiller. He

---

64 Wieneke, 38.
65 *Ibid.*, 38-40, ref. 39.
66 *Ibid.*, 40; *Caroline*, I, 420.
67 Josef Körner, *Romantiker und Klassiker. Die Brüder Schlegel in ihren Beziehungen zu Schiller und Goethe* (Berlin: Askanischer Verlag, 1924), 40f.

may well have been behind the disrespectful mention of Schiller's less than good poem *Würde der Frauen* [Women's Worth] and indeed his parody of it,[68] which produced gales of laughter in the *Athenaeum* circle, may date from this time. He had not restrained Friedrich when he went over to the anti-Schiller faction, but then again there was Schiller's behaviour in the *Xenien*. There was fault on both sides.

Clearly, there was no trifling with Schiller's sensitivities. Despite the apparent finality of this exchange of letters, Schiller in fact did not bar Schlegel from further collaboration on *Die Horen*, or on his *Musenalmanach*, both of which were at any rate moribund and about to expire. But the damage was done: the relationship never recovered. This was immediately visible when Schiller demanded changes to August Wilhelm's contributions to the *Musenalmanach*.[69] There was his distinctly un-Promethean poem *Prometheus*, that Goethe, his artistic advisor Heinrich Meyer, Wilhelm von Humboldt, and now Schiller, had all found unreadable; and here Schiller was surely the expert in matters relating to philosophical or allegorical poetry. Schlegel did not take kindly to criticism. It brought out a less attractive side: he marshalled all of his formidable philological knowledge (all of his pedantry), knowing that Schiller was at a disadvantage in these matters.

From now on, Schlegel was not capable of objective or reasonable comment on Schiller (Schiller returning the compliment in his letters to Goethe). He was to be represented almost always to his disfavour or he was written out of the account altogether: the *Athenaeum*, which wreathed Goethe in clouds of incense, was to mention Schiller but once, and then only incidentally.

Friedrich Schlegel, meanwhile, was throwing Goethe's and Schiller's own parlance back in their faces by reviewing Georg Forster in another of Reichardt's periodicals.[70] What is more: Forster, far from being the failed revolutionary, was for Schlegel a 'classic', a 'citizen of the world', a 'true patriot'. There was, of course, some self-projection involved in this, the intellectual with universal sweep, radical, progressive. It did not mean that either Schlegel brother was about to abandon the security of his own studies and engage in active politics (Friedrich much later saw fit to suppress his Forster review). In fact, their interests were still fairly and squarely in

---

68 *SW*, II, 172.
69 Wieneke, 44-48.
70 Friedrich Schlegel, 'Georg Forster. Fragment einer Karakteristik der deutschen Klassiker', *Lyceum der schönen Künste* (Berlin: Unger, 1797), I, i, 32-78.

literature or poetry in their widest sense, but nothing illustrates better their as yet divergent approaches, that were to complement each other in the *Athenaeum*, than their respective reviews of Herder: Friedrich's of parts of the *Humanitätsbriefe* [Letters on Humanity] in 1796,[71] and August Wilhelm's of *Terpsichore* in 1797.[72] Where Friedrich recognised a fellow-spirit 'writing fragments of an uncompleted whole', wrestling with the large issues of the Ancient and Modern in poetry and as yet finding no solution, casting his gaze over the widest range of poetic traditions, August Wilhelm seized on questions of poetic language and prosody.

Schlegel's Reviews: Language, Metrics

'Force yourself' had been Friedrich Schlegel's advice to his brother as he embarked on a career as a professional writer.[73] Writing under pressure involved drawing on existing sources of knowledge and insight, the things that Bürger and Heyne had taught him in Göttingen, the notions garnered from his wide reading in Holland: the theory and practice of translation, the origins of language, prosody and metrics, the relationship of the arts to each other, anthropology and human character, criticism, its proprieties and limits, the history of poetry. There could at this juncture be no question of a system, but a network of ideas was nevertheless emerging, fragmentary adumbrations of comparative literature, even of 'Weltliteratur'.

Was there not something calculated and careerist about Schlegel's abandoning the ailing Bürger and embracing his adversary Schiller? But both he and Bürger knew that there was nothing to retain him in Göttingen: the 'young eagle' had to take flight. He might seem now to be accommodating to Schiller, especially the Schiller of the 'naïve' and the 'sentimental', those critical categories that he set out in his great *Horen* essay of 1795-96.[74] For Schlegel was praising three great 'naïve' poets, Homer, Dante, and Shakespeare, and dispraising Klopstock, a prime representative of the modern and the 'sentimental'. On the other hand all of these figures had in their time also been dear to Bürger's heart and were central to his writings. Schlegel was of course venturing into terrain never traversed by Bürger; yet while his major articles for *Die Horen* showed Schlegel moving far beyond his old mentor, the many reviews for Schütz contained

---

71 *Deutschland*, III, ix, 326-336 ref. 326.
72 *SW*, X, 376-413.
73 *KA*, XXIII, 247.
74 *Die Horen*, Jg. 1795, 11. Stück, 43-76; 12. Stück, 1-55; Jg. 1796, 1. Stück, 75-122.

occasional references to the whole question of a poet's life and works,[75] that pointed forward to that great biographical and critical essay of 1801, with its speaking title, *Bürger*.

It was not Bürger, but Friedrich Schlegel, who prompted Schlegel's first article for *Die Horen*, *Briefe über Poesie, Sylbenmaß und Sprache* [*Letters on Poetry, Prosody and Language*] (1795-96).[76] It used Schiller's 'house style', a series of fictitious letters, although Schlegel's model is most likely to have been Frans Hemsterhuis, the Dutch philosopher (who wrote in French) whose Platonic dialogues and letters were to influence his aesthetic and historical writings. He admired Hemsterhuis's ability to express philosophical truths in an accessible fashion,[77] the stated aim also of *Die Horen*. He did not subscribe to Hemsterhuis's notion of a Golden Age with the enthusiasm that his brother's friend Novalis was to do, but it did inform his thinking about historical origins nevertheless.

'Amalie', the imaginary recipient of these letters, cannot have been a philosophical novice. She was taken, in eclectic fashion, through the various theories of language, the Platonic notion of an ideal language, Rousseau's on the passions as the source of linguistic articulation, de Brosses's on infant intuition, Fulda's etymologies, Hemsterhuis's views on the psychological roots of language, and Herder's 'inner language' that becomes poetic expression.[78]

Amalie would, however, learn that Schlegel's real point of departure was primitive humankind, driven still by its senses, where joy and pain provided the first and basic articulations common to all, and where the human ability to express feelings through sounds and bodily movements led over to rhythm and dance. It could be observed in the most primitive of peoples (Amalie would have read Georg Forster). It followed that rhythmic utterance, and eventually metre, were not later refinements, but belonged to the basic needs of human articulation. Thus all poetry, in terms of these origins, was essentially lyrical, with dance and song as the expressive form of what later became dignified with the name of myth.

---

75 As for instance *SW*, X, 232f., 284, 354.
76 *SW*, VII, 98-154.
77 Cf. Klaus Hammacher, 'Hemsterhuis und seine Rezeption in der deutschen Philosophie und Literatur des ausgehenden achtzehnten Jahrhunderts', in: Marcel F. Fresco *et al.* (ed.), *Frans Hemsterhuis (1721-1790). Quellen, Philosophie und Rezeption* […], Niederlande-Studien, 9 (Münster, Hamburg: LIT, 1995), 405-432, ref. 412; Heinz Moenckemeyer, *François Hemsterhuis*, Twayne's World Author Series, 277 (Boston: Twayne, 1975), 28.
78 Cf. Walter Jesinghaus, 'August Wilhelm von Schlegels Meinungen über die Ursprache', doctoral dissertation University of Leipzig (Düsseldorf: C. Jesinghaus, 1913), 5-24.

In December 1795 Friedrich could write to his brother that he had achieved 'complete clarity' in matters of language and metre,[79] which suggests that he had received from August Wilhelm a long letter, only much later published in the standard edition of 1846 as *Betrachtungen über Metrik* [*Considerations on Metre*] but datable to this period.[80] It says much for the relationship between the brothers that August Wilhelm took the effort to commit to paper almost thirty pages of thoughts that both reacted to Friedrich's notions but also went far beyond them. It is as if Friedrich, exuberantly postulating a history of Greek poetry, had need of some elementary instruction in metrical matters. These his brother duly supplied. Addressing Friedrich in these private *Considerations*, he needed to become more technical.

While he was at it, he treated Friedrich to one of the eighteenth century's more extraordinary theories, the relationship between vowel sound and colour,[81] the *clavecin oculaire* [ocular harpsichord] pioneered by the abbé Louis Bertrand Castel and continued in Schlegel's day by the physicist Ernst Florens Friedrich Chladni with his *Farbklavier* [colour pianoforte]. It is however interesting to note that none of these theories on synaesthesia and language colouration went into writings published in his own lifetime or into his lectures on prosody. It is not to Schlegel that we look for the link between these experiments and Charles Baudelaire's later 'correspondences'.

It is therefore instructive to see Schlegel applying some of his more general insights on language and metre to a specific case, his 70-page review of Johann Heinrich Voss's translation of Homer that appeared in the *Allgemeine Literatur-Zeitung* in 1796.[82] It was too technical for *Die Horen*, still hoping to capture a general readership. The length of the review may surprise, but Homer had now come into his own; he was everywhere, an almost measureless subject. He was Klopstock's model; he was for Schiller the 'naïve' poet *tout court*; poets, among them Bürger, had been rendering him into German. The year 1795 had seen the publication of Friedrich August Wolf's *Prolegomena ad Homerum*, which challenged for ever the notion of one single blind singer as the author of Homer's songs. Goethe was beginning his 'Homeric' phase that saw his verse epics *Hermann und Dorothea* and

---

79 KA, XXIII, 263-267, ref. 265.
80 SW, VII, 155-196.
81 *Ibid.*, 175f.
82 SW, X, 115-195.

Achilleis. What is more: Voss was one of the few contemporary poets not to be treated with disfavour in the *Xenien*, indeed his epic poem *Luise*, that Homerized domestic life, had found high praise there. The Weimar Friday club had spent the winter months discussing Voss's translation.[83] Into this chorus of praise Schlegel was to introduce a note of discord.

Schlegel, too, had of course made his critical début with Homer, that Latin *De geographia Homerica* in Göttingen. Now, Voss's translation gave him the opportunity to expand and expound. It was a review of which he was inordinately proud. He republished it twice in his lifetime—once in 1801 in *Charakteristiken und Kritiken*, once in 1828, in his *Kritische Schriften*— and once in Voss's. Looking back in 1828, after Voss's death, he was able to assess its status: it had been his first major piece of criticism and he had devoted months to it. It had also been generally well received. He could now state what he would not have dared to say in 1796: that Goethe's and Schiller's admiration of Voss had gone hand in hand with their own laxity in metrical matters, however readable the results.[84] In 1801, he had inserted a kind of apology. He had not always done Voss justice and—a valid point— he had in 1796 done little translating himself, at least of this kind.[85] That was, of course, to change very soon. The fact nevertheless remained that he had challenged the authority of a significant poet of Goethe's generation and a former friend of Bürger's. Seen historically, it was the critique offered by the author of the standard German translation of Shakespeare (which Schlegel's undoubtedly is) to the creator of the standard German Homer (Voss still remains supreme).

Voss, difficult and querulous by nature, an inveterate bearer of grudges, never forgave Schlegel and sought every opportunity to cause him annoyance and embarrassment. It confirmed him as a great Romantic-hater.[86] There can be no doubt that his later decision (with his sons) to translate Shakespeare, was informed by the desire to 'get even' with Schlegel. Schlegel, in his turn, never mentioned in print a factor of which he was subsequently aware and which could have mitigated some of his

---

83 Bruford, *Culture and Society*, 386; Ernst Friedrich Sondermann, *Karl August Böttiger. Literarischer Journalist der Goethezeit in Weimar*, Mitteilungen zur Theatergeschichte der Goethezeit, 7 (Bonn: Bouvier, 1983), 188f.
84 SW, X, 185.
85 Ibid., 182.
86 There is a nice irony in the fact that Schlegel's later father-in-law, the appalling Heinrich Eberhard Gottlob Paulus, spoke the funeral address for Voss in 1826. *Lebens- und Todeskunden über Johann Heinrich Voß. Am Begräbnisstage gesammelt für Freunde von Dr. H. E. G. Paulus* (Heidelberg: Winter, 1826), 34-65.

strictures: Voss in 1796 had been ill and the review had served to compound his physical and mental discomfort.[87]

If some readers of the review found it too harsh (Friedrich August Wolf was one),[88] they could not deny that Schlegel spoke with considerable technical authority. This for the moment set him apart from his brother Friedrich, yet it could be said that both brothers as reviewers complemented each other, the one in the universality of his claims, the other in the precision of his arguments. There was much in Schlegel's review that was generally acceptable: the assertion, for instance, that German had a special affinity with Greek and a structure that facilitated its rendition into the modern medium. And who better than Voss ('learned', 'noble', 'manly') to accomplish this with Homer? There was also a need for 'consistent and accurate correctness',[89] and there followed a detailed critique, often line-by-line, some of it relating to passages that still defy modern scholars, much of it merely captious. It might be fair to single out Voss's occasional use of the lexis of modern sensitivity, where Homer's original is robust and simple, but that same charge could be levelled at Schlegel's own Shakespeare, and Voss was later to do it; indeed it has often been a complaint of critics since then that Schlegel's Shakespeare approximates more to the dramatic language of his own day and does not bring across the sheer challenge of the Elizabethan original.

There was nothing in principle wrong with comparing Voss with his predecessors among Homer translators, but when one of these was Bürger this was special pleading and *pro domo*. For Schlegel knew, and indeed went on to say, that Voss's versification was exemplary. In view of what Schlegel was to write in 1796 in Schiller's *Horen* about translating Shakespeare ('everything that the German language is capable of'), it is interesting to find him here pronouncing on the limitations of translation: a translation can never be more than an 'imperfect approximation', with 'established borders' that may not be transgressed;[90] above all, it must not read like some 'translationese', some invented language that is neither the original nor its modern rendition. This was directed against Voss's idiosyncratic use of German word order, compounds and archaisms to convey what was for him the Homeric essence: hence the untypical negativeness of Schlegel's pronouncements.

---

87 *Briefe*, I, 57.
88 *SW*, X, 186.
89 *Ibid.*, 117, 122.
90 *Ibid.*, 149f.

For all that, Voss's translation and his *Luise* have stayed in print, as has *Hermann und Dorothea*. Friedrich August Wolf was always to remain for Schlegel an authority in matters of editorial philology:[91] his name recurs later in the edition of the *Râmâyana*. No-one could hold back the tide of Homerizing. Schlegel in effect never returned to Homer criticism. A pattern was establishing itself already in the 1790s: the overlapping of projects, brief spasms of attention, then abrupt abandonments. The Dante project is one of these, competing with Homer, then pushed aside as the next idea caught his imagination. It did not mean that he was a fragmentist by nature, like his brother Friedrich: it was not the way August Wilhelm worked. He simply took on too many commitments: a too crowded writing and reviewing programme saw flagging interests, as personal crises also supervened. A history of Italian poetry, with Dante at its centre, and a translation of Shakespeare, simply could not coexist. Furthermore, both Dante and Shakespeare involved verse translations, requiring concentration and attention to the minutest detail; they could not be hurried. Eschenburg, living in different times, had managed to produce a complete Shakespeare in the space of a few years, but he was not driven by Schlegel's ambition and—crucially—was translating into prose.

The subject of Dante had the high praise of both Herder and Schiller:[92] for Herder, he was a mighty voice in the historical cycle of poetry; one can imagine Schiller, already seized by the extreme situations in Shakespeare, equally fascinated by the disturbing scenes in Dante (Goethe was at this stage largely indifferent).[93]

Dante[94]

There were important differences between Dante and Shakespeare. In Germany, people had been writing about Shakespeare for most of the eighteenth century and there had been two major attempts at translation (Wieland and Eschenburg). Dante, by contrast, was hardly known. True,

---

91 *Ibid.*, 186.
92 Wieneke, 5.
93 Emil Sulger-Gebing, *Goethe und Dante. Studien zur vergleichenden Literaturgeschichte*, Forschungen zur neueren Literaturgeschichte, 32 (Berlin: Muncker, 1907), 50.
94 On the general background to AWS's Dante studies see Eva Hölter, *'Der Dichter der Hölle und des Exils'. Historische und systematische Profile der deutschsprachigen Dante-Rezeption*, Epistemata, 382 (Würzburg: Königshausen & Neumann, 2002), 27-59.

there had been prose versions in the 1760s—by Johann Nicolaus Meinhard and Leberecht Bachenschwanz[95]—but Schlegel was the first actually to put Dante into German verse. This deserves to be given its due, in the face of assertions that his translation is archaizing, uniformly elevated and stiff, where in fact it actually reads quite well.[96] It is also correct; it matches line for line, even if it makes concessions, such as adopting for the rhyme scheme of his *terza rima* one different from Dante's. He could show his contemporaries, Goethe among them, that this technically demanding verse was possible in German and worthy of creative imitation.

The Dante project was nevertheless terminated even as it was published. Its very publication seemed haphazard.[97] The historical introduction had been written in Göttingen and had appeared in Bürger's *Akademie der schönen Redekünste* in 1791 and Becker's almanac in 1794; the main section, the *Inferno* translation, came out in *Die Horen* in 1795 and was welcome copy for Schiller; while sections from *Purgatorio* and *Paradiso*, of dwindling length, were again entrusted to the ever-enterprising Becker in 1795-97, first in a journal called *Leipziger Monatsschrift für Damen*, then in *Erholungen*, and finally in *Taschenbuch zum geselligen Vergnügen*, all titles that suggested pastimes remote from the sombre world of Dante. With that, the Dante project was forced out by his fellow-genius Shakespeare. We know that Caroline, the co-translator of Shakespeare, also helped to keep the guttering flame of Dante alight before its final extinction.[98]

Schlegel was not merely content to translate. Dante provided too good an opportunity for excursions. Thus readers of *Die Horen* could learn that *Inferno* was different from *Paradise Lost* or *Der Messias*, its characters human, its world restricted to Earth (in the centre of which was Hell), not domiciled in some extraterrestrial sphere. In Dante, our senses, reason and principles are not offended by the spectacle of 'pure,

---

95 Johann Nicolaus Meinhard in the 1760s published some specimen passages, including the Ugolino section, commending Dante as one with Homer, the Greek tragedians, and Shakespeare. Leberecht Bachenschwanz, following the practice of the times, had even translated the whole *Divine Comedy* into prose (1769). See *Weltliteratur. Die Lust am Übersetzen im Jahrhundert Goethes*, ed. Reinhard Tgahrt *et al.*, Marbacher Kataloge, 17 (Munich: Kösel, 1982), 563f.

96 Dispraised for instance by Jürgen von Stackelberg, *Weltliteratur in deutscher Übersetzung. Vergleichende Analysen* (Munich: Fink, 1978), 10-19, 20-29.

97 Set out in detail by Emil Sulger-Gebing, 'August Wilhelm Schlegel und Dante', in: Andreas Heusler *et al.*, *Germanistische Abhandlungen Hermann Paul zum 17. März 1902 dargebracht* (Strasbourg: Trübner, 1902), 99-134 and esp. 107f. Complete text in SW, III, 169-381.

98 SW, III, 369.

absolute evil' that Milton and Klopstock unfold.[99] Here Schlegel was not merely denying legitimacy to these modern epics; he was finding fault with Protestant poetry as represented by his father's generation. As yet, he did not postulate a Catholic alternative, but that would come soon enough in the pages of the *Athenaeum*.

The terrible story of Ugolino, incarcerated with his sons and grandsons and left to starve to death, brought Schlegel hard up against the limits of his translation powers. So great was the 'appalling truth' of this story that the translator would rather be silent.[100] Because Dante's 'unstinting humanity' shone through all the horror,[101] because there was heroism and virtue without which the atrocious would be merely gratuitous, he was able to complete the task. Schlegel, moving on to more congenial territory, cited Philoctetes and Laocoön as analogies, thereby stepping into the debate on the depiction of physical suffering in art that had been exercising critical minds since Winckelmann and Lessing in the 1760s. Dante had also inspired Michelangelo: Schlegel mentions a terracotta basrelief of Ugolino and his sons by the Renaissance master.[102] This was an over-eager attribution, for the sculpture now hardly rates a mention by scholars: the art appreciation of this young Romantic generation was too often informed by enthusiasms (like Tieck and Wackenroder seeing a 'Raphael' in 1793). It was not, however, allowed to invalidate Schlegel's general point that Laocoön or Ugolino in artistic representation impress us, take hold of us, not because of who they are (the legend or story) but for what they represent, the stoic acceptance of the inevitable.

We glimpse here nevertheless some of the inhibitions that later caused Schlegel to leave *King Lear* or *Macbeth* or *Othello* untranslated. For him horror in Greek tragedy was embedded in mythology and ancient beliefs; Dante's *Inferno* displayed 'an indestructible force' for justice and virtue;[103] but Shakespeare, rooted as he was in the irrationalities of human behaviour, never provided such a convenient conceptual basis. Schiller, more robust, wanted to see *Macbeth* and *Othello* performed on the Weimar stage, but Schlegel could not or would not supply them. Horror and cruelty did not feature in his later lectures on Classical and Romantic literature, either; already his account of Dante in the *Athenaeum* in 1799 was much blander, smoother, Hemsterhuisian, while his discomfort with the aesthetically

---

99   Ibid., 290f.
100 Ibid., 327.
101 Ibid., 328.
102 Ibid., 336.
103 Ibid., 330f.

compromising in Shakespeare was still evident in his Vienna Lectures in 1808. The selections from *Purgatorio* and *Paradiso* meanwhile brought Schlegel on to more familiar and acceptable ground: the Platonism employed by his mentor Hemsterhuis to demonstrate the existence of God in us.

The Shakespeare Translation

If Dante was edged aside by Shakespeare, if Shakespeare even had to compete with Homer, there was to be no doubt that these 'great names' were to exemplify a notion of poetry that the Romantics were to espouse, pristine, organic, originating in nature, rooted in the people or nation, in the widest sense mythological. Of course no-one had yet applied the term 'Romantic' to this great historical strand of poetry; the attribution would however not be long in coming. Much of what Schiller had called 'naïve' or Goethe 'classical' could be subsumed under it, but it would first have to enter the national consciousness through translation. Schlegel's Shakespeare was to do no more nor less than that: by 1801, when nearly all of this translation was available,[104] it could claim to align Shakespeare with the greatest in the national tradition, Goethe and Schiller. It provided the centrepiece of a German mythology that declared the Englishman 'ours', enshrined him, in the familiar phrase from Goethe's *Faust* as 'the third in the alliance' ['der Dritte im Bund'].

As is usual with such visions, the unreal mingled with the real; Schlegel's name was lost in an ideological haze, and the true circumstances of his achievement became obscured. Meanwhile, for a German Shakespeare to come anywhere near the original, it needed an adequate language, an 'answerable style'. Nearly fifty years of critical discussion of Shakespeare in Germany had been inhibited by the perceived failure of German as an adequate medium to convey 'natural genius'. No-one had known this better than Schlegel's own uncle Johann Elias when in 1741 he had found fault with a *Julius Caesar* in alexandrines that succeeded in confining any Shakespearean 'extravagance'; or his other uncle, Johann Heinrich, in 1758 presenting his blank-verse translation of James Thomson's *Sophonisba* and commending to the Germans this as yet untried verse form. True, Thomson's

---

104 *Shakespeare's dramatische Werke, übersetzt von August Wilhelm Schlegel*, 9 vols (Berlin: Unger, 1797-1810). The plays translated by Schlegel, in order of volumes, are: I: *Romeo and Juliet, A Midsummer Night's Dream* (1797); II: *Julius Caesar, Twelfth Night* (1797); III: *The Tempest, Hamlet* (1798); IV: *The Merchant of Venice, As You Like It* (1799); V: *King John, King Richard II* (1799); VI: *King Henry IV*, 1 and 2 (1800); VII: *King Henry V, King Henry VI*, 1 (1801), VIII: *King Henry VI*, 2 and 3; IX: *King Richard III* (1810).

verse was many removes from Shakespeare, but it did offer some freedom from the imprisonment of rhyme. A generation of translators, like Wieland or Eschenburg, would need to arise, or dramatists like Lessing, Goethe and Schiller, before blank verse could become established in German letters, and then often more Augustan than Shakespearean. In all this Schlegel acknowledged Schiller as a model or mentor, if only grudgingly, especially after their estrangement.[105] Yet, even when one allows for the expanded lexis and the enhanced range of expression inherent in Shakespeare, Schlegel's translation has a Schillerian ring to it, an echo of the 1790s that saw its origins.

The Shakespeare project brought out most but not all sides of Schlegel: the translator, of course, the critic, the analyst, the historian rather less. In the writings devoted exclusively to Shakespeare, we have none of the historical background that informs his Dante, such as the circumstantial recounting of the true story of Ugolino; there is, for instance, only the briefest of information about the sources of *Romeo and Juliet*, and then not the crucial point that it is an early play. Schlegel was not a Shakespearean scholar of the stamp of Eschenburg or—even allowing for his sometimes freakish attributions—Ludwig Tieck. Unlike Tieck, who at the age of 20 owned the Fourth Folio, he had no significant collection (Eschenburg was a prodigious collector.) The editions that Schlegel is known to have used, Rivington's printing of Malone, and Bell's Johnson-Steevens, while containing the essential texts and commentary (Malone's especially), were made-up sets and of no particular textual distinction;[106] indeed in one of his few public defences of his translation, he reserved the right to set aside even Malone as a final authority.[107] Unlike Eschenburg and later Tieck, he was not interested in a scholarly apparatus and was concerned, as he said, only 'to present the poet in his true guise'.

Late in life, surveying the Shakespeare project in a long letter to his publisher Reimer,[108] not without its element of self-justification, Schlegel employed only the first person, conveniently overlooking the roles of two

---

105 *SW*, VII, 66f.
106 *The Plays of William Shakespeare. Accurately printed from the text of Mr Malone's edition* […] (London: J. Rivington, vol. 1 [1790], vols 2-7 [1786]) and *The Dramatick Writings of Will. Shakspere, With the notes of all the various Commentators* […] ed. Sam. Johnson and Geo. Steevens, 20 vols (London: J. Bell, 1788) (two odd vols dated 1785 [17] and 1786 [15]). Michael Bernays, *Zur Entstehungsgeschichte des Schlegelschen Shakespeare* (Leipzig: Hirzel, 1872), 217f.
107 *Athenaeum. Eine Zeitschrift von August Wilhelm Schlegel und Friedrich Schlegel*, 3 vols (Berlin: Vieweg, 1798; Frölich, 1799-1800), III, 335.
108 *SW*, VII, 281-291.

persons now dead, Friedrich and Caroline, whose part in the Shakespeare project had been considerable. There were, of course, personal reasons for their omission. Looking at the nine volumes of the Schlegel translation and assessing their significance, we may easily overlook the actual circumstances and the element of the haphazard and the adventitious that accompanied them and their occasionally cooperative origins. As we have seen, being a professional writer meant grasping every opportunity. Yet Shakespeare seems to have been the 'main task', the work that would establish Schlegel's reputation once and for all, not, say, the 'occasional' work for *Die Horen*, the Dante essay, the letters on language. We know that he took with him to Holland his and Bürger's version of *A Midsummer Night's Dream*; in 1793 Friedrich had shown Caroline a draft translation of *Hamlet* and *Romeo and Juliet* that she found too archaic.[109] That would suggest intensive work in Holland, competing with other projects there, including Dante.

By 1796, however, well into his working association with Schiller, he missed no chances, supplying sample passages of *Romeo and Juliet* and *The Tempest* for *Die Horen*, but also a passage from *Romeo and Juliet* to its hated rival, Reichardt's *Deutschland*;[110] in 1797 there were scenes from *Julius Caesar* for Schiller. In 1796 also, perhaps opportunistically, he published his major statement on translating Shakespeare, also in *Die Horen*, invoking Goethe's *Wilhelm Meister* (just completed). He followed this in 1797 with his fine critical essay on *Romeo and Juliet*. Letters from this period suggest Friedrich's close involvement with this play and Caroline's hand in drafting the actual essay.[111] But translation and criticism were to be kept apart, as two separate but complementary processes; the one was not to detract from the other. The choice of *Romeo and Juliet* and *Julius Caesar* as 'tasters' was no doubt influenced by a general sense around 1790 that these two plays were Shakespeare's most accessible and had a long history of critical reception and adaptation to prove it. The sample from *The Tempest* in *Die Horen*, with 'Full fathom five', could show how much better Schlegel was than Wieland or Eschenburg (if in their debt) and superior to a recent anonymous version called *Der Sturm*, which Tieck had just published in Berlin. It would appeal to those for whom the 'fairy way of writing', not passion or statecraft, was their way of access into Shakespeare.

---

109 KA, XXIII, 138.
110 'Probe einer neuen Uebersetzung von Shakespeare's Werken', *Deutschland*, II, v, 248-259.
111 KA, XXIV, 364; *Caroline*, I, 426-432.

The first Shakespeare extract in *Die Horen* (*Romeo and Juliet* II, ii, i-iii) called itself a 'sample of a new metrical translation of this poet',[112] which suggested a translation already in being. In June of the same year, writing from Jena to the publisher Göschen in Leipzig, he could report that he had read the whole version to Goethe and had met with his approval.[113] The question of a publisher had, however, not yet been clarified. He had negotiated with his brother Friedrich's publisher, Salomon Heinrich Michaelis in Neustrelitz, setting his price at 150 talers per play, and even sent *Romeo and Juliet* and *A Midsummer Night's Dream* to him.[114] This was too high a price for Michaelis, who was in fact in the process of going bankrupt. Schlegel's newly-won colleague in Weimar, Böttiger, was willing to use his good offices with Wieland, whose son-in-law Gessner was a partner in the Zurich firm of Orell, Füssli.[115] It was with this publisher that both Wieland and Eschenburg had brought out their respective translations. Wieland's was long since out of print, but Eschenburg was thinking of revising his for a new edition.[116] In the event, nothing came of this approach; in 1797, however, out of courtesy sending the first volume of his Shakespeare to Eschenburg, Schlegel wrote a long and not entirely sincere letter explaining the circumstances of his own enterprise.[117] Eschenburg's twenty-year-old version had been the best available hitherto, and here Schlegel was in the process of undermining it: he knew perfectly well what he was doing.

Eschenburg's response was gracious, but he did not neglect to mention the forthcoming revision of his own translation, which duly appeared between 1798 and 1806. Not only that: his friend Friedrich Nicolai in Berlin, the particular abhorrence of Goethe and Schiller and soon of the young Romantics, had been supplying him with material for the updated apparatus to this edition, including information about Schlegel's own extracts in *Die Horen*.[118] The indefatigable Eschenburg even went on to write a whole book on the Ireland Shakespeare forgery; its preface is the proud statement of a Shakespeare scholar 'whose annotations have never been bettered', and who accepts the challenge of 'another and more able hand'.[119]

---

112 *Die Horen*, Jg. 1796, 3. Stück, 92.
113 *Briefe*, I, 33.
114 *Ibid.*, II, 17f.
115 *Ibid.*, I, 43.
116 As indeed is made clear in AWS's letter to Eschenburg, Bernays, 255-259.
117 Eschenburg responding with his new edition, Bernays, 259f.
118 Nicolai to Eschenburg 24 June, 1796. Herzog August Bibliothek Wolfenbüttel, Cod. Guelf. 622 Novi.
119 Johann Joachim Eschenburg, *Ueber den vorgeblichen Fund Shakspearischer Handschriften* (Leipzig: Sommer, 1797), 3.

It needs to be said that readers who wanted a complete Shakespeare were still dependent on Eschenburg's prose version and made-up editions like that of the entrepreneur Carl Joseph Meyer, until the syndicate of Voss father and sons finished their verse translation in 1829.[120] By then Schlegel had given up any idea of a whole version.

Even if Schlegel's emerges from all this ruck as better than those of his rivals, it is because time has dealt less kindly with them, who were once very present and active and vociferous. Pushing Eschenburg aside was one thing, and here Schiller was only too willing to abet Schlegel by publishing his extracts in *Die Horen*. Anything that suggested a new beginning, a Weimar-sponsored break with the past, was to be encouraged, while Eschenburg, in Schiller's eyes, stood for 'mediocrity', mere 'scholarship' that failed to differentiate genius, that espoused parity and relativeness of esteem, comprehensiveness, not the high points of excellence. It was to know no mercy; only the creative forces of the century were to have recognition. The Schlegel brothers, the one exalting Lessing and Kant, the other extolling Shakespeare, both elevating Goethe, gladly joined in this chorus until they found a voice of their own. At no stage, however, did they admit how useful they had found the corpus of knowledge patiently collated by painstaking scholars like Eschenburg, whom Goethe and Schiller were in the process of excoriating. Herder was to write ruefully and resignedly to Eschenburg in 1799 that they both now belonged to a past era in literature and taste, and for the moment, that was true.[121]

As it was, Schlegel turned to Johann Friedrich Unger in Berlin to publish *Shakespeare's dramatische Werke*. Unger already had some interesting authors: Goethe had entrusted *Wilhelm Meister* to him, while two young men in Berlin, Tieck and Wackenroder, lightly disguised as a self-effacing and art-loving friar, had brought out their *Herzensergiessungen* with him, a work that was to change the nature of art appreciation. Unger was also in the process of enshrining himself in the history of book production and printing, having developed a new clean and elegant face for the German black-letter type, known as 'Unger-Fraktur'.[122] These things mattered.

---

120 On this see Christine Roger, *La Réception de Shakespeare en Allemagne de 1815 à 1850. Propagation et assimilation de la référence étrangère*, Theatrica, 24 (Berne, etc.: Peter Lang, 2008), esp. 363-369.

121 Johann Gottfried Herder, *Briefe. Gesamtausgabe*, ed. Karl-Heinz Hahn *et al.* for Nationale Forschungs- und Gedenkstätten der Klassischen Deutschen Literatur in Weimar (Goethe- und Schiller-Archiv), 16 vols (Weimar: Böhlau, 1977- in progress), VIII, 51.

122 Georg Kurt Schauer, 'Schrift und Typologie', in: Ernst L. Hauswedell and Christian Voigt (eds), *Buchkunst und Litteratur, 1750 bis 1850*, 2 vols (Hamburg: Maximilian-Gesellschaft, 1977), I, 7-57, esp. 29.

When Eschenburg saw the first volume of Schlegel's Shakespeare, he initially asked Orell, Füssli to use Roman type instead for his revised edition. Despite hesitations, it came out in 'Fraktur',[123] and so it was two Shakespeare editions in black-letter type, Schlegel's and Eschenburg's, that were to vie for the reading public's favour.

The transition process from writing-desk to readable typeface was, however, seemingly chaotic and haphazard. The manuscripts of the twelve plays that have survived, tell their own tale.[124] Schlegel folded down a margin on his manuscript sheet to allow for corrections, but the frenetic hatchings, scorings, overwritings (doodlings) speak of late vigils, candles burning low, the desperate hours spent in search of the right word (as he wrote to Schiller),[125] the dissatisfactions and self-doubts as the Shakespeare text seemed to prove intractable. The creative process can be seen in the successive drafts. Attached to the manuscript of *The Tempest* is the version of 1796 printed in *Die Horen*.[126] There, Schlegel does not even attempt a literal 'Full fathom five', and is content with the rather lame 'Tief in Meeres Grund gefallen', but for the 'final' version, the one published in 1798, he is more precise. Is 'fathom' German 'Klafter' (which can also mean 'a cord of wood')? 'Faden' is the nautical term (and the cognate of Shakespeare's word). Yet the manuscript still shows the translator's indecision: both words are left standing there, but it is 'Faden' that goes into the printed version. In *King John*, there are new sections pasted over. The two *Midsummer Night's Dream* manuscripts reflect the heavy reworkings of the old Göttingen text now to emerge as Schlegel's own in 1797.[127] *Romeo and Juliet*, by contrast, is less heavily annotated or crossed out. Did the 'ideal' Shakespeare, that this play seemed to represent for Schlegel, also pose fewer linguistic problems? (In fact he left out some intractable punnings and some ruderies.) Caroline made a clean copy for the printer. We also recognize her hand on the manuscripts of *As You Like It*, *Hamlet*, *The Merchant of Venice* and *Julius Caesar*. Ludwig Tieck

---

123 Thomas Bürger, *Aufklärung in Zürich. Die Verlagsbuchhandlung Orell, Gessner, Füssli & Comp. in der zweiten Hälfte des 18. Jahrhunderts, Mit einer Bibliographie der Verlagswerke 1761-1798* (Frankfurt am Main: Buchhändler-Vereinigung GmbH, 1997), 74.
124 SLUB Dresden, Mscr. Dresd. e. 90, XXII, 1-14.
125 Wieneke, 29.
126 *Die Horen*, Jg. 1796, 6. Stück, 77f.
127 The older text published by Frank Jolles, *A. W. Schlegels Sommernachtstraum in der ersten Fassung vom Jahre 1798 nach den Handschriften herausgegeben*, Palaestra, 244 (Göttingen: Vandenhoek & Ruprecht, 1967), 55-135.

much later at least had the grace to admit that a 'friend' had helped him with his revision of Shakespeare (his daughter Dorothea): Schlegel never made even that concession. And so 'Übersetzt [Translated] von August Wilhelm Schlegel' on the title page should rightly read 'Translated with Caroline Schlegel's assistance'.

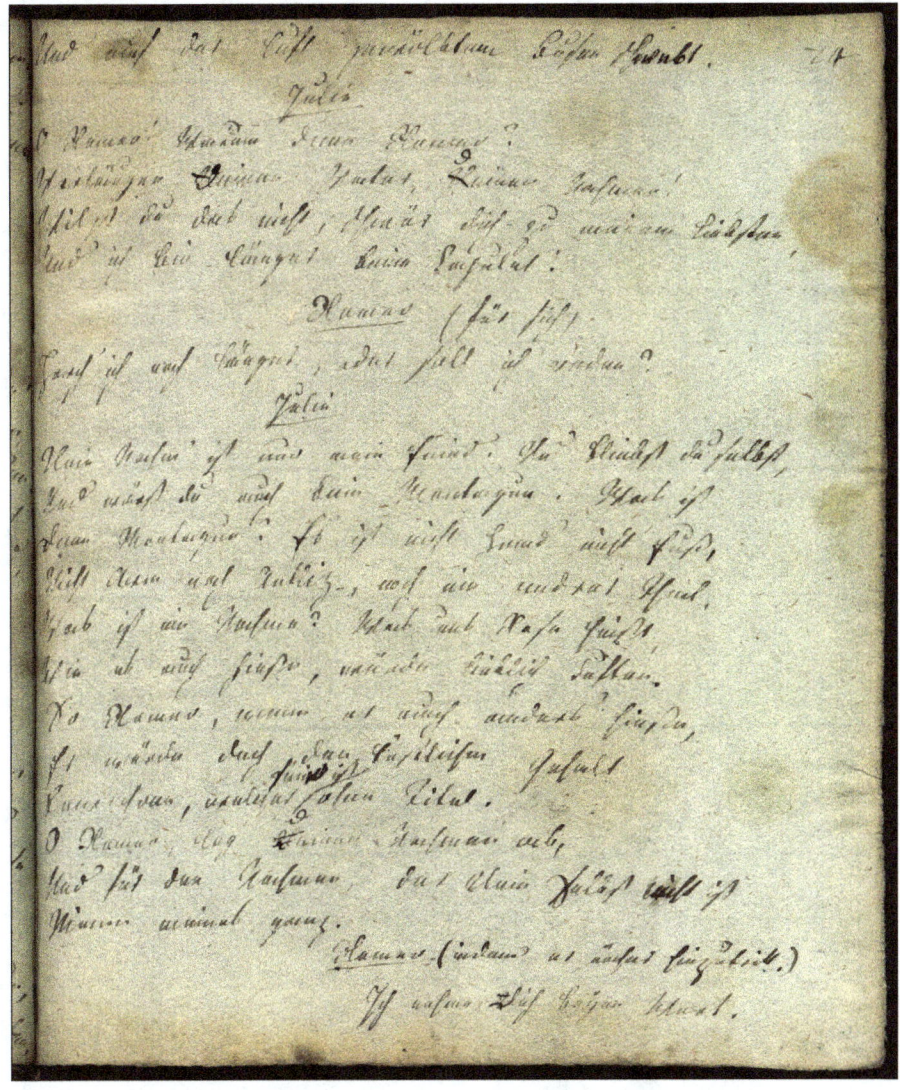

Fig. 5 Manuscript page of Schlegel's and Caroline's translation of Shakespeare's *Romeo and Juliet* (1797), in Caroline's hand, open at Act 2, Scene 1 ('O Romeo, Romeo, wherefore art thou Romeo?'). © SLUB Dresden, all rights reserved.

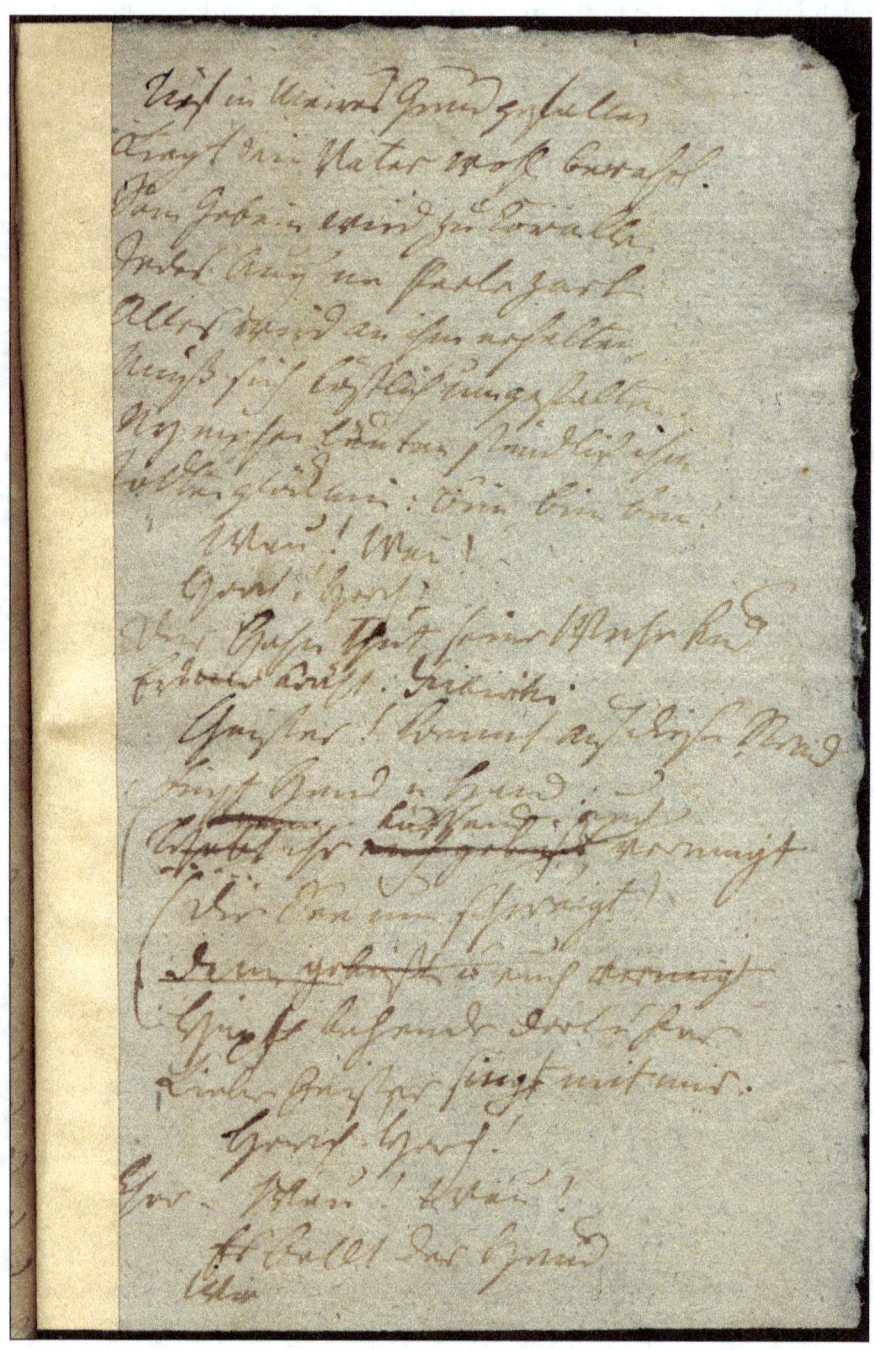

Fig. 6 Manuscript page of Schlegel's translation of Shakespeare's *The Tempest* (1798), open at Act 1, Scene 2 ('Full fathom five'). © SLUB Dresden, all rights reserved.

Friedrich, too, had his part in this family enterprise. In Berlin from July 1797 until September 1799, he was sent the manuscript packages and passed them on to Unger. He seems even to have done the proof-reading.[128] Or maybe there was none, for this historic translation is marred by printer's errors.[129] It is from Friedrich that we learn of the first enthusiastic reactions from leading figures in the Berlin cultural scene, Schleiermacher the preacher, Alois Hirt the classicist, Johann Gottfried Schadow the sculptor, Friedrich Fleck the actor. August Wilhelm, as well, had been assiduous in self-promotion. Putting first things first, he sent a copy of Volume One (*Romeo and Juliet, A Midsummer Night's Dream*) to Duke Carl August in Weimar, but also to his fellow-Hanoverian, Karl August von Hardenberg, now Prussian minister in charge of Ansbach-Bayreuth and much later Prussian chancellor. Wieland, Herder and Böttiger in Weimar, Eschenburg in Brunswick, Heyne in Göttingen, were other 'strategic' recipients.[130] In due course, another son of Hanover, the actor-producer Iffland, expressed his admiration.[131] It was to begin Schlegel's never trouble-free association with the theatre.

The *Wilhelm Meister* Essay

Schlegel nevertheless felt the need to establish his credentials beyond the scope of mere translation. He wished to set out his translation principles, not in any systematic way, but in the free flow of critical writing. If the Voss review had been closely argued, rigorous, stiff (pedantic, too), he would treat Shakespeare in more associative and accessible fashion. Schiller's *Die Horen*, now less demanding after its taxing debut in 1795, provided the adequate forum. What better way to cause pleasure in both Jena and Weimar than by invoking Goethe himself? Thus came about Schlegel's essay *Etwas über William Shakespeare bei Gelegenheit Wilhelm Meisters* [Some Remarks on William Shakespeare Occasioned by Wilhelm Meister], 'classic' for its stylistic elegance, its freedom from factual ballast, and its claims for both writer and translator.[132] In the 1796 volume of *Die Horen*, it is nicely balanced between the continuation and conclusion of Schiller's *On Naïve and Sentimental Poetry* and Schlegel's own *Letters on Poetry*, both of them

---

128 *KA*, XXIV, 4f.
129 Bernays, 173-216.
130 *Briefe*, I, 61f., 65; Bernays, 254.
131 *Briefe*, I, 74.
132 *Die Horen*, Jg. 1796, 4. Stück, 57-112; *SW*, VII, 24-70.

theoretical, occasionally abstract, and Schlegel's own first sample of *Romeo and Juliet*, and his second example, from *The Tempest*. There is no evidence that Schiller, ever desirous of copy, had planned it this way, but it worked fortuitously to Schlegel's advantage. Observers might also remark that the essay was interspersed between sections of Goethe's version of Benvenuto Cellini's life, that had elicited Friedrich's insolent remarks about the journal's 'translation phase'. Unlike Shakespeare, who could not be turned out to order, this was hackwork, if hackwork with Goethe's own touch.

Like so many programmatic statements, especially those from the 1790s, the *Wilhelm Meister* essay dealt in absolutes and was short on nuances. There was Schlegel's opening gambit: *Wilhelm Meister* had caused Shakespeare to 'rise from the dead and walk among the living'.[133] It was manifestly untrue, or at most half true, a formulation whose ultimate analogies may not have resonated well with Wieland or Eschenburg, neither of whom saw themselves in such salvific terms (and who in the essay were dealt with fairly perfunctorily). The assertion that Shakespeare was not a 'mere episode' in the novel was, to say the least, open to challenge,[134] indeed it soon became clear that Schlegel was not primarily concerned with Wilhelm Meister or even with his obsession, Hamlet. The view that *Hamlet* was a 'Gedankenschauspiel' ['thought play],[135] brought no incisively new insights to Shakespeare criticism. Rather, Schlegel was concerned with the nature of creative genius itself: he invoked that quasi-mystical language of 'divine spark', 'deep waters', 'sounding depths' that goes some way towards explaining the essence and mystery of genius.[136] These processes Schlegel was concerned to align with the métier of criticism: it was not judgmental or atomising, not Johnsonian (and for Johnson read also Eschenburg):

> What it best does is to seize and give meaning to the real sense that creative genius places in its works and which is there as they take body in their essential shape, in complete, untainted form, in sharp profile, and thus to raise beholders who are less acute, but are receptive, to a higher state of perception. But only rarely has it achieved this. And why? Because perceiving the essential make-up of others in close and direct contemplation, as if it were a very part of one's own consciousness, is bound up as one with the capacity for creation itself.[137]

---

133 *SW*, VII, 24f.
134 *Ibid.*, 24.
135 *Ibid.*, 31.
136 *Ibid.*, 30f.
137 *Ibid.*, 26.

There is here some of that distinction between mere 'philological' and 'interpretative' criticism, that informs the later Vienna Lectures, itself based on the opposites of 'mechanical' and 'organic'. But in 1796 this proud formulation both defined limits, those of a finite mind like Wilhelm Meister's, and opened up the limitless spaces of genius, the 'forces' (Herder's favourite word, 'Kräfte') and secrets of nature.[138] These could not be compromised. Thus, in an essay ostensibly devoted to Wilhelm Meister the man of the theatre, we learn that genius imparts itself through the integrated whole work of art, not through its 'contaminated' form on the stage.[139]

Two thirds of the essay were devoted to the means of transferring to an alien medium the expressive powers of consummate genius. The Germans need have no fear, for Shakespeare was 'completely ours' ('ganz unser');[140] no other nation had such a sense of identification with him, had studied and admired him in such depth. Intrinsic to the German language must therefore be the capacity to express this affinity through a translation that observed and respected the structures and nuances of the original, in verse where verse was required, not in a prose approximation; stretching to its limits the native tongue and its range and inner resources, but always within due limits ('alles im Deutschen Thunliche') [everything feasible in German].[141] The translator would have to compromise and compensate, but he (or she: Caroline) would be motivated by what he could do, not discouraged by what ultimately eluded him.

All this needed to be restated, for there were restraining and sceptical voices, such as Wilhelm von Humboldt's, writing to Schlegel on 23 July 1796 from Berlin, having just read the two extracts in *Die Horen*, and counselling caution.[142] Translation was an elusive and ultimately impossible undertaking, and Schlegel should concentrate instead on an original work, not the mere transmission of the alien. In this matter, the two were never to see eye to eye, Humboldt never diverging from his conviction that translation (if one were to do it at all) must always contain a 'tinge of the foreign' ('Farbe der Fremdheit'), Schlegel forever stressing the resources of the native language. Indeed Schlegel's later view, stated with some nobility, that the translator

---

138 *Ibid.*, 30.
139 *Ibid.*, 36.
140 *Ibid.*, 38.
141 *Ibid.*, 62.
142 Anton Klette, *Verzeichniss der von A. W. v. Schlegel nachgelassenen Briefsammlung* (Bonn: [n.p.], 1868), vf.

is the ultimate ambassador and mediator between cultures, was written in response to Humboldt's sceptical utterances in the *Indische Bibliothek* in 1827,[143] when Shakespeare and his like were far from his mind.

Only the manuscripts of Schlegel's translation reveal the struggles and agonizings over the alien text, with Caroline offering her voice, both discerning and reasonable. We must imagine them at a table strewn with the untidy harvest of a day's or week's work, scratching out and overwriting until the result sounded like the 'nearest best' that it would always be. The printed text was final, if the result of those compromises and accommodations, compensations and approximations. Only in critical reviews was Schlegel willing to pass on insights into the actual translation process. Reviewing Tieck's version of *The Tempest*, he remarked that Tieck had translated 'lord of weak remembrance' with 'Angedenken', where it should be 'Gedächtnis' (both can mean 'memory'). He knew this from translating *Hamlet* (but did not say so).[144] There, the original's word-play on 'remember' and 'remembrance' foundered on the preciser distinctions of its German equivalents, but for readers of German this was of course an added enrichment. In 1797, in a review of a periodical devoted to language,[145] he rejected the linguistic purism that would not sanction in German the phrase 'mein tiefstes Herz' ['my deepest heart'] and asked what the author would have made of Hamlet's

In my heart's core, ay, in my heart of heart

Schlegel had already translated this line as

Im Herzensgrund, ja in des Herzens Herzen[146]

a more regular line that Shakespeare's (as is often the case), but notable for that 'Herzensgrund' whose religious and mystical echoes opened up associations that the original did not. When on the other hand 'Not a mouse stirring' at the opening of *Hamlet* became 'Alles mausestill',[147] with a commendable neatness and naturalness in the German, the omission

---

143 *Indische Bibliothek. Eine Zeitschrift von August Wilhelm von Schlegel*, 3 vols (Bonn: Weber, 1820-30), II, 254f.
144 SW, XI, 19. In fact he translates it as 'Erinnrung'. *Shakespeare's dramatische Werke*, III, 57.
145 SW, XI, 169f.
146 *Shakespeare's dramatische Werke*, III, 243.
147 *Ibid.*, 140.

of 'stirring' blurred the sense that another 'Thing' was on the move. But let Shakespeare scholars concern themselves with these nuances. The translation can still stand up to any kind of analysis, the most favourable and even the most stringent or unfriendly. Wherever translated poetry is recognized as poetry in its own right, Schlegel's name must always be in the first rank, and with this translation he enters into the main stream of the German poetic tradition.

Schlegel was, however, not content merely to postulate criticism as part of the creative process. He must deliver an example: it was *Ueber Shakespeares Romeo und Julia* [On Shakespeare's Romeo and Juliet], the last contribution that he was to send to *Die Horen*.[148] Everyone seemed to be reacting to *Romeo and Juliet*. Caroline had copied it out for the printer; it opened the first volume of the Shakespeare translation in 1797. August Wilhelm, temporarily in Dresden, asked his brother Friedrich to present Schiller with a copy.[149] It was despatched in mid-May 1797, only a matter of days before Schiller's terrible letter of the 30th of the same month. Schiller did not react, and his correspondence with Goethe did not mention it; it was also not one of the Shakespeare plays with which he felt a close bond. Goethe, who had known it from his formative years, noted it for a possible stage adaptation in 1797, but the death of the designated actress caused him to defer the idea, eventually until 1812.[150]

In May, Friedrich had sent his precious presentation copy of *Romeo and Juliet* to his friend Novalis in Tennstedt in Thuringia. It went accompanied by his intense feelings about the play, 'like a lowering thunderstorm amid the splendours of the spring day', full of antitheses: the 'rose of life' but also the thorn that goes to the quick.[151] Re-reading it (he had Eschenburg among his books) Novalis confessed to Shakespeare's 'powers of divination'.[152] Of greater interest were two letters from Caroline to August Wilhelm, that have survived only in a fragmentary state.[153] Why she should be writing is unclear, and the dating is uncertain, but these letters were essentially a draft of his *Horen* essay, disposed differently and with other emphases,

---

148 *Die Horen*, Jg. 1797, 6. Stück, 18-48; *SW*, VII, 71-97 (where the title has 'Shakspeares').
149 *KA*, XXIII, 366.
150 Heinrich Huesmann, *Shakespeare-Inszenierungen unter Goethe in Weimar*, Österreichische Akademie der Wissenschaften, Phil.-hist. Klasse, Sitzungsberichte, 258, Bd. 2, 2. Abh. (Vienna: Böhlau, 1968), 148-154.
151 *KA*, XXIII, 364.
152 Novalis, *Schriften. Die Werke Friedrich von Hardenbergs*, ed. Paul Kluckhohn and Richard Samuel, 6 vols in 7 [*HKA*] (Stuttgart: Kohlhammer, 1960-2006), IV, 227f.
153 *Caroline*, I, 426-432.

meaning that Caroline was not acting merely as an amanuensis, but as a co-author.

For her it was a play that broke with all modern notions of dramatic economy and overflowed in all directions, yet with study, one could uncover its inner harmony (what he calls its 'inner unity'). It contained discords and dark melancholy[154] (Schlegel saw instead 'gentle enthusiasm'). His concern in the essay was a 'creative criticism' that 'fathomed' (German 'ergründen')[155] the process of composition and laid down notions of the organic, unified whole that is the work of art, bringing out Shakespeare's artistry, the conscious inventions that held everything in place. Where we see clashes and disharmonies, Shakespeare employs the contrasting 'devices' of romantic passion (Romeo) and innocent simplicity (Juliet), balancing one against the other. True, the tragic outcome was inevitable, but so was the resolution and reconciliation of the action beyond the grave.

The 'antitheses' that had seized his brother Friedrich could not of course be wished away. August Wilhelm was, however, concerned to resolve them. One way was to place the lovers in some kind of capsule, emotionally, spiritually, linguistically set apart from the world and its conventions, even from the machinations of fate. Their language, which may strike others as mannered and self-indulgent, makes sense only to them; it is part of their fulfilled 'white-hot passion'. For Schlegel, it was not the dark, wild, doom-ridden strand of the play that was in the foreground, rather 'Love was the poetry of life'.[156] He used Friedrich's image of the thunderstorm, but left out the 'thorn' that went with it.[157] Among their contemporaries, Ludwig Tieck had already acknowledged the play's sombre aspect in notes made in Göttingen in 1792, while Coleridge was later to diverge radically from Schlegel's interpretation.

How much of this reading was informed by the desire to enter into the creative processes of composition through his newly-formulated 'better criticism', finding resolutions and hidden harmonies where others stressed 'There never was a story of more woe'; and how much was motivated by the wish to believe in young, unadulterated and ideal love that lived in its own world and was oblivious to real circumstances? Seen in terms of their life together, his and Caroline's, did it mean that despite the strand of practical realism in his relationship with her, he believed nevertheless in a romantic love that rose above actualities? Not just the use made of

---

154 Ibid., 429.
155 SW, VII, 76.
156 Ibid., 94.
157 Ibid., 77.

Caroline's draft is interesting (or that Caroline took the initiative in writing it); it was also her sense that Romeo's and Juliet's love, which she defended, was subjected to 'dissonances' ('Mislaute' [sic]), even 'asperities' ('Härten') and yet emerged triumphant. She concluded: 'You two [sc. presumably August Wilhelm and Friedrich] will have to decide whether or not Romeo and Juliet is a tragedy'.[158] There could be no answer to all these questions. The fascination with *Romeo and Juliet* did not end with *Die Horen*.

Schlegel, concurrently with his criticism and translation, had also been writing poetry. It was part of the professional writer's métier, especially one who had gone through Bürger's school. As already remarked, little of Schlegel's poetry warms the heart, uplifts the senses, raises the hopes. Perhaps it is wrong in the first place to apply Wordsworthian (or Goethean) criteria to it. It was not just a question of the formal devices that he used: when Goethe used regular metrical verse like the classical elegy—a favoured form in the 1790s—he never abandoned the personal note, while Schlegel, in this and other metres, was correct, learned—and soulless.[159] Where Schiller brought his own moral and philosophical energy to bear in didactic poetry, Schlegel lacked the other man's essential dynamism. The correspondence with Schiller over the poem *Prometheus*—in the *terza rima* so recently displayed in the Dante translation—is not agreeable reading and shows Schlegel trying to worst Schiller with pedantry and pedagoguery.[160] Schiller, who was also editing a *Musenalmanach* and needed copy, did eventually accept it, the same Schiller whose versification Schlegel had openly criticised. Schlegel the poet did not shine with general subjects, those so current in aesthetic and poetological debate, like the role of the artist as creator and shaper of higher truth. Occasional poems, those dedicated to a person or object, did however bring out the best of his poetic powers, as indeed translation also did. His poetic powers looked different to aspiring poets: the young Friedrich Hölderlin, after so much disparagement from Schiller, was greatly heartened by a few encouraging words by Schlegel in a review,[161] and it may have been one spur among many for him to write some of the finest elegies in the language.

---

158 *Caroline*, I, 431, 429, 432.
159 On AWS's poetry see Klaus Manger, 'Statt "Kotzebuesieen" nur Poesie? Zu den lyrischen Dichtungen August Wilhelm Schlegels', in: York-Gothart Mix and Jochen Strobel (eds), *Der Europäer August Wilhelm Schlegel. Romantischer Kulturtransfer— romantische Wissenswelten*, Quellen und Forschungen, 62 (296) (Berlin, New York: de Gruyter, 2010), 77-92.
160 Wieneke, 42-48.
161 *SW*, XI, 363-365; Friedrich Hölderlin, *Stuttgarter Ausgabe*, ed. Friedrich Beissner *et al.*, 8 vols in 15 (Stuttgart: Kohlhammer, 1946-85), XI, 11-13.

It was verse directed at an object that found Schiller's approval for his *Musenalmanach* for 1798 (issued in late 1797): *Zueignung des Trauerspiels Romeo und Julia* [Dedication of the Tragedy Romeo and Juliet], written in correct *ottava rima*—and actually a good poem:[162]

Zueignung des Trauerspiels Romeo und Julia

Nimm dieß Gedicht, gewebt aus Lieb' und Leiden,
Und drück' es sanft an deine zarte Brust.
Was *dich* erschüttert, regt sich in uns beiden,
Was *du* nicht sagst, es ist mir schon bewußt.
Unglücklich Paar! und dennoch zu beneiden;
Sie kannten ja des Daseins höchste Lust.
Laß süß und bitter denn uns Thränen mischen,
Und mit dem Thau der Treuen Grab erfrischen.

Den Sterblichen ward nur ein flüchtig Leben:
Dieß flücht'ge Leben, welch ein matter Traum!
Sie tappen, auch bei ihrem kühnsten Streben,
Im Dunkel hin, und kennen selbst sich kaum.
Das Schicksal mag sie drücken oder heben:
Wo findet ein unendlich Sehnen Raum?
Nur Liebe kann den Erdenstaub beflügeln,
Nur sie allein der Himmel Thor entsiegeln.

Und ach! sie selbst, die Königin der Seelen,
Wie oft erfährt sie des Geschickes Neid!
Manch liebend Paar zu trennen und zu quälen
Ist Haß und Stolz verschworen und bereit.
Sie müßen schlau die Augenblicke stehlen,
Und wachsam lauschen in der Trunkenheit,
Und, wie auf wilder Well' in Ungewittern,
Vor Todesangst und Götterwonne zittern.

Doch der Gefahr kann Zagheit nur erliegen,
Der Liebe Muth erschwillt, je mehr sie droht.
Sich innig fest an den Geliebten schmiegen,
Sonst kennt sie keine Zuflucht in der Noth.
Entschloßen sterben, oder glücklich siegen
Ist ihr das erste, heiligste Gebot.
Sie fühlt, vereint, noch frei sich in den Ketten,
Und schaudert nicht bei Todten sich zu betten.

---

162 *SW*, I, 35-37.

2. Jena and Berlin (1795-1804)

Ach! schlimmer droh'n ihr lächelnde Gefahren,
Wenn sie des Zufalls Tücken überwand.
Vergänglichkeit muß jede Blüth' erfahren:
Hat aller Blüthen Blüthe mehr Bestand?
Die wie durch Zauber fest geschlungen waren,
Löst Glück und Ruh und Zeit mit leiser Hand,
Und, jedem fremden Widerstand entronnen,
Ertränkt sich Lieb' im Becher eigner Wonnen.

Viel seliger, wenn seine schönste Habe
Das Herz mit sich in's Land der Schatten reißt,
Wenn dem Befreier Tod zur Opfergabe
Der süße Kelch, noch kaum gekostet, fleußt.
Ein Tempel wird aus der Geliebten Grabe,
Der schimmernd ihren heil'gen Bund umschleußt.
Sie sterben, doch im letzten Athemzuge
Entschwingt die Liebe sich zu höherm Fluge.

Dieß mildert dir die gern erregte Trauer,
Die Dichtung führt uns in uns selbst zurück.
Wir fühlen beid' in freudig stillem Schauer,
Wir sagen es mit schnell begriffnem Blick:
Wie unsers Werths ist unsers Bundes Dauer,
Ein schön Geheimniß sichert unser Glück.
Was auch die ferne Zukunft mag verschleiern,
Wir werden stets der Liebe Jugend feiern.

[Dedication of the Tragedy Romeo and Juliet

Receive this poem, woven of love and travail,
And press it gently to your tender breast.
What moves your soul is feeling that we share,
What you withhold, I know it all the same.
Unhappy pair! And yet one to be envied;
They knew the heights of joy that life can give.
Then let us mingle sweet and bitter tears,
And with this dew refresh these true ones' grave.

These mortals' portion was a fleeting life:
Their lives, they vanished like a soulless dream!
They feel their way, even in their boldest strivings,
In darkness, and themselves they hardly know.
Fate may oppress them or it may inspire them:
Can longing without end be once contained?
Love can alone give wing to earthly dust,
And she alone unseal the door to heaven.

Alas, for her, the monarch of the souls,
How often is she prone to envious fate!
To part and to torment so many pairs
Hate and pride conspire time and again.
They must use stealth to seize a moment's bliss,
When drunk with love be watchful and alert,
And, like on storm-tossed waves mid peals of thunder,
Tremble in deathly fear and heavenly joy.

Danger, though, the weak will overcomes,
While love is bold and full, when dangers press.
To nestle close in the beloved's arms
Is the sole refuge when all else oppresses.
To will to die, or rise victorious,
Is love's command, its first and its most sacred,
It feels, when joint, still free in fetters' bonds,
And knows no terrors bedded in the grave.

But smiling dangers threaten her with worse,
When she has conquered all the wiles of chance,
And every flower learns of transience:
Is there a hope then for the flower of flowers?
They, as by magic caught in soft embrace,
By fortune, peace and time are drawn apart,
And, slipping free when others bear them down,
Love drowns in bliss inside its very chalice.

But greater joys, when what one treasures most
The heart tears with it to the realm of shades,
And like a sacrifice to all-releasing death,
The cup of joy, scarce touched, is poured away.
The lovers' grave becomes their only temple
And is the shining tomb to sacred vows.
They die, but in their very dying breath
Love takes them up into the higher spheres.

All this may help you to assuage your sorrow,
The poem brings us back into ourselves.
We feel it both, the thrill and joy of love,
We speak it, knowing what the other kens:
Together, bonded, is our lasting worth,
A secret known to us secures our bliss.
May distant future hide behind its veil,
We celebrate forever love's fair youth.]

Is it because of the distinctly Goethean echoes, associations with a poem written in that same stanzaic form but not yet published, *Warum gabst du uns die tiefen Blicke* [Why did you gaze on us so deeply], Goethe's confession of love to Frau von Stein from the 1770s, or with one not yet written, *Urworte. Orphisch* [Deep Orphic Words]? If so, it shows both poets operating within similar conventions, while at the same time transcending them. We recognize Schlegel's own emphases. He could not resist the chance of transfiguring the Shakespearean lovers' untimely deaths, but there is also an underlying antithesis between the erotic language of longing and ecstasy ('Ertränkt sich Lieb' im Becher eigner Wonnen' ['Love drowned in the chalice of its own bliss'], and the lexis of fate, chance, and transience. Schlegel was in reality dedicating this poem to Caroline: the final stanza told of *their* love, *their* union, *their* mystery, *their* youthful passion that would never die. The threefold anaphoric 'We' in the final stanza brings them, as it says, from the realm of poetry into the reality of their present lives. Professor Schlegel in love? It seems so. But Caroline? Of that we can be less certain.

The Jena Group

Conventional sociological wisdom informs us that groups are both cohesive and fissiparous entities, held together by a consensus and a common identity, but they are also fluid and fragile, subject to inner tensions and threats to unity.[163] Often cliquish, they rarely speak in unison. A joint bond of sympathy and purpose unites them, but strong personalities can unfold and dominate the common endeavour. Does this describe the association in Jena from 1798 to 1800? Can one even legitimately speak of a 'Jena group'? Older scholarship had no hesitation in positing (a French example) 'Frédéric Schlegel et son groupe', even 'la doctrine de l'Athenaeum'.[164] Today, we might wish rather to content ourselves with words like 'circle' or 'association' and might be less eager to identify a unifying 'doctrine', for even words such as this have their own problems. Yet what was it that enabled people of the most disparate backgrounds to coalesce; what was the cement

---

163 Cf. Friedhelm Neidhardt, 'Das innere System sozialer Gruppen', *Kölner Zeitschrift für Soziologie und Sozialpsychologie* 31 (1979), 639-660, esp. 642, 644, 649.

164 Alfred Schlagdenhauffen, *Frédéric Schlegel et son groupe. La doctrine de l'Athenaeum, 1798-1800*, Publications de la Faculté des Lettres de l'Université de Strasbourg, 64 (Paris: Les Belles Lettres, 1934).

that bonded them socially and intellectually: one a ribbon-weaver's son (Fichte), another the son of a poor Silesian preacher (Schleiermacher), yet another an impoverished Thuringian aristocrat (Novalis), two of them sons of a Hanoverian superintendent and poet (the Schlegel brothers), another the product of a Swabian vicarage (Schelling), yet another the scion of a Berlin rope-maker, now *embourgeoisé* (Tieck), not to speak of a Göttingen professor's daughter (Caroline Schlegel) or the daughter of the celebrated Berlin Jewish philosopher, Moses Mendelssohn (Dorothea Veit)? What was there that transcended this disparity of background, religion—Dorothea in 1799 still had to pay a 'toll for Jews' if she crossed from Prussia to Saxony— education, dialect even (think of Dorothea's written Berlinisms or the thick Swabian that Schelling must have spoken)?

On the intellectual level, there seemed to be a common meeting of minds. Friedrich Schlegel and Novalis favoured words prefixed by 'sym-', 'Symphilosophieren', 'Symbiblismen', 'Sympoesie', 'Symphysik', 'Sympraxis', even 'symfaulenzen' ('sym'-lazing),[165] that connoted not only some kind of togetherness but also a universal range of mind and spirit, bespeaking 'community' in its widest sense. As Novalis's *Athenaeum* fragment put it, an intellectual association of persons of spirit.[166] Indeed Friedrich's famous 116th *Athenaeum* Fragment that sought to define 'romantic poetry' did this inclusively, in terms of the most audacious combinations, mixes, syntheses, extensions and linkings.[167]

The biographical facts, with which we are alone concerned here, suggest a much looser and more extemporised association. It is not even possible to bring all these characters together in one place (unless we use the convenient—if endearing—chronological liberties and rearrangements that Penelope Fitzgerald employs for Novalis in her novel *The Blue Flower*). Fichte had already been dismissed from his university post in Jena before the association had even begun to form and had moved to Berlin; Schleiermacher never left his post as preacher at the Charité hospital there. Novalis was based at the mining academy in Freiberg in Saxony, then the salt inspectorate in Weissenfels, and was only an occasional visitor in Jena. Moreover he knew practical science where Friedrich Schlegel wrote gaseously of 'Chemie' and 'Physik'.[168] Friedrich Schlegel and Dorothea Veit

---

165 *Caroline*, I, 453f., 481, 518.
166 KA, II, 182f.
167 *Athenaeum*, I, i, 86.
168 Theodore Ziolkowsi, *German Romanticism and Its Institutions* (Princeton UP, 1990), 27-63.

were resident in Berlin until the autumn of 1799, Ludwig Tieck similarly. Only August Wilhelm and Caroline Schlegel and Schelling were actually domiciled in Jena for the whole period of 1798 to 1800.

These dates, 1798 to 1800, are decisive, for they saw the production and publication of the enterprise that served as a focus and a common purpose for this circle: the periodical *Athenaeum. Eine Zeitschrift von August Wilhelm und Friedrich Schlegel*.[169] Some words of caution are needed. Fichte, Tieck and Schelling actually wrote nothing for it, Schleiermacher and Dorothea Veit relatively little, Caroline contributed only anonymously, leaving Novalis and above all the brothers Schlegel as authors, with a few associated friends joining in towards the end. The original contexts and contiguities were soon lost sight of. In the course of publication history the three original octavo volumes of the *Athenaeum* were recontextualised and their contents scattered. Enshrined in editions of Novalis, Friedrich and August Wilhelm Schlegel, as we have them now, it is often hard to envisage the mixture of plan and improvisation that is the essence of a literary periodical. For all that, the *Athenaeum* concentrated the energies of the brothers and their closest associates and gave them a method and a tone and a way of seeing that, almost by accident, became known as 'Romantic'. That word, meaning—depending on its context—'Romance' in the linguistic sense, therefore modern, post-medieval, 'romantick', fantastic, pertaining to the 'romance' of the Middle Ages and Renaissance, then to the novel ('Roman'), became in the usage of the group a universal term for everything progressive, modern, inclusive, universal, poetic.[170] The *Athenaeum* was not a mere general hold-all for Romantic writing; it

---

169 AWS's contributions to the *Athenaeum* were as follows (original titles): 'Die Sprachen. Ein Gespräch über Klopstocks grammatische Gespräche' (I, i, 3-69), 'Elegien aus dem Griechischen' (with Friedrich Schegel) (I, i, 107-140), 'Beyträge zur Kritik der neuesten Sprachen' (I, i, 141-177), 'Fragmente' (with Friedrich Schlegel and Friedrich Schleiermacher) (I, ii, 179-322), 'Die Gemählde. Gespräch' (with Caroline Schlegel) (II, i, 39-151), 'Die Kunst der Griechen. An Goethe. Elegie' (II, ii, 181-192), 'Ueber Zeichnungen zu Gedichten und John Flaxman's Umrisse' (II, ii, 193-246), 'Der rasende Roland. Eilfter Gesang' (II, ii, 247-284), 'Notizen' (with Friedrich Schlegel, Friedrich Schleiermacher, Dorothea Veit, Karl Gustav von Brinkman) (II, ii, 285-327), 'Literarischer Reichsanzeiger oder Archiv der Zeit und ihres Geschmacks' (II, ii, 328-340), [Matthisson, Voss und Schmidt] (III, i, 139-164), 'Vollständiges Verzeichniß meiner zur Allg. Lit. Zeit. beygetragenen Rezensionen' (III, i, [165-168]), 'Idyllen aus dem Griechischen' (with Friedrich Schlegel) (III, ii, 216-232), 'Sonette, Von A. W. Schlegel' (III, ii, 233-237), 'Notizen' (with Dorothea Veit, Friedrich Schleiermacher, August Ferdinand Bernhardi) [AWS did 'Parny's Guerre des Dieux'], 252-268, ['Soltau's Don Quixote'], 297-329, ['Notiz'], 329- 336).

170 *KA*, II, lii-lxiv.

defined itself primarily as a focal point for critical and creative forces. Readers searching for instance for a corpus of original poetry (as opposed to translation), narrative fiction or systematic philosophy, would have to look elsewhere, for there were only occasional glimpses of these, a notable example being Novalis's poetic *Hymnen an die Nacht* [Hymns to the Night].

Friedrich Schlegel, apart from the calamitous interlude in Jena in the summer of 1796 to July 1797 that forfeited Schiller's goodwill, was with short interruptions based on Berlin until the autumn of 1799. It was in Berlin that he had the oversight of the Shakespeare translation and where he negotiated with Unger, its publisher. In fact, he had more dealings with Unger's wife, Friederike Helene, who featured in his letters under various disrespectful appellations.[171] His initial task in Berlin was to assist Johann Friedrich Reichardt with his periodical *Lyceum*, and it was in that short-lived journal (1797) that his essays on Lessing and on Georg Forster appeared, as well as his first collection of 'fragments', the aphorisms that were to characterise him and his circle. Reichardt himself was persona non grata in Berlin, but his house at Giebichenstein near Halle, romantically overlooking the river Saale, was, as already mentioned, a meeting-place at various times for most of the Romantics. He doubtless gave Schlegel recommendations to various societies in Berlin, and Schlegel, gregarious and sociable by nature, would have taken them up. These contacts in themselves showed that Berlin was quite a different place from Jena or even Weimar: with its 170,000 inhabitants it was a royal capital, an administrative and cultural centre, and as such it put provincial Thuringian ducal residences in the shade.

Where Jena had tea-parties and Weimar even small literary and philosophical societies, these were inevitably limited to, respectively, the university professors and their wives, and the senior court officials or prominent residents.[172] Berlin, as yet without a university, still offered a wider range of intellectual and cultural circles. Some, like those restricted to the aristocracy, admitted only their own kind. The 'Mittwochsgesellschaft' [Wednesday Club] only received high state administrators or leading intellectuals. Yet to this last-named Schlegel secured an entrée. It was no doubt there that he met the redoubtable and influential Friedrich Nicolai, publisher and sturdy defender of the Enlightenment, ever on the lookout for young talent. When in October 1797 Friedrich reported that

---

171 Cf. *KA*, XXIV, 355.
172 Bruford, *Culture and Society*, 380-388.

the 'Mitwochsgesellschaft' was reading his brother's Shakespeare, we notice the name of Friedrich Schleiermacher. Schleiermacher had come from being an impoverished military chaplain's son, then associated with the Moravian Brethren, to the position of preacher at the Charité hospital in Berlin. Schleiermacher and Schlegel found an immediate bond of companionship—indeed for a while they lived together in Schleiermacher's quarters at the Charité near the Oranienburg Gate—and shared with each other questions of ethics, friendship and love, in their widest philosophical and moral connotations. Whereas Friedrich saw in Schleiermacher all 'Sinn und Tiefe' [depth of mind],[173] this closeness of association was not shared by August Wilhelm, either in Jena or later in Berlin. The most one can say is that he was loyal to his brother's friends.

Berlin had at that time around 3,600 Jews, still subject to social restrictions and discriminations, but already dominant in the mercantile and banking life of the city. 'Pluralist' Berlin might be as a city, but it was not until two salons, or societies, were created by Jewish hostesses, that aristocrats, intellectuals, artists, writers and cognoscenti were able to meet on a basis of equality.[174] These were the salons of Henriette Herz and Rahel Levin (later Varnhagen). At their soirees, respectively in the Neue Friedrichsstrasse and the Jägerstrasse, one could rub shoulders with Prince Louis Ferdinand of Prussia or the Humboldt brothers or the Swedish envoy Karl Gustav von Brinkman and the intellectual *haute volée* of the city. It was here that Friedrich Schlegel first met the three Tiecks, Ludwig, Sophie and Friedrich, who were to play a prominent part in the affairs of the extended Schlegel family. Ludwig, who was to survive them all, was also the closest associate of both Schlegel brothers, but Sophie the writer and Friedrich the sculptor would intervene disproportionately in the artistic and emotional life of August Wilhelm.

The Berlin salons were places of liberality and social ease, where barriers of class counted as little, and wit and soul and an ability to converse were all that mattered. Yet the tone in Friedrich's letters to his brother in Jena is that of the clique or the conventicle, the 'ecclesia pressa' (his own phrase),[175] turned inwards, satisfied, sometimes insufferably so, with its own resources

---

173 KA, XXIV, 22.
174 Peter Seibert, *Der literarische Salon. Literatur und Gesellschaft zwischen Aufklärung und Vormärz* (Stuttgart, Weimar: Metzler, 1993), 151-161; Petra Wilhelmy, *Der Berliner Salon im 19. Jahrhundert (1780-1914)*, Veröffentlichungen der Historischen Kommission zu Berlin, 73 (Berlin: de Gruyter, 1989), 868-873.
175 KA, XXIV, 42.

and its own cleverness. Nowhere is this more noticeable than in his attitude to Ludwig Tieck, outwardly friendly, but in private letters condescending to an extreme ('only half a gentleman', 'does not know Henriette Herz' etc.).[176] This may surprise, given that Tieck had been early initiated into social decorum by Reichardt when Kapellmeister in Berlin, and after study in Halle and Göttingen was now a young man very much talked about in Berlin literary circles. Of course only initiates would know that he was the author of the 800-page *roman noir William Lovell*, the ironically titled *Volksmährchen* [Folk Tales] that included the witty and satirical comedy *Der gestiefelte Kater* [Puss in Boots], was the co-author of those extraordinary effusions on art, the *Herzensergiessungen*, and had translated *The Tempest*. For all of these works appeared anonymously. It may be that Friedrich was too preoccupied with his intellectual exchange with Schleiermacher, or Tieck with his close friend and co-writer of those outpourings, Wilhelm Heinrich Wackenroder, soon to die tragically young and to be the first in that Romantic necrology.

August Wilhelm meanwhile had reviewed the *Herzensergiessungen*, Tieck's Bluebeard adaptation (*Ritter Blaubart*), the *Kater*, and *The Tempest*, all for the *Allgemeine Literatur-Zeitung*, their first serious publicity.[177] The *Herzensergiessungen* he had greeted with an enthusiasm tempered with some misgivings about its religious tone. On Tieck's version of *The Tempest* he was more severe, for this was a prose version in the style of Eschenburg and a competitor with his own, one moreover that took liberties with the text. But the author of the comedies—he did not know that it was Tieck— was a 'poet among poets' ('ein dichtender Dichter')[178] equipped with wit and verve and a nice disrespect. Writing in 1828, Schlegel would claim that he was the first to draw attention to Tieck and give him his due, and this was largely true. A lively correspondence ensued between Tieck and August Wilhelm Schlegel, from December 1797. Tieck, who knew his Shakespeare at least as well as the older man, asked deferential questions about points of text or matters of authorship; while Schlegel, punctiliously 'inaugurating' their exchange on 11 December 1797,[179] encouraged Tieck in his planned translation of *Don Quixote*. Tieck would have agreed with his

---

176 Ibid., 41.
177 SW, X, 363-371; XI, 16-22, 136-146.
178 Ibid., 136.
179 *Ludwig Tieck und die Brüder Schlegel. Briefe.* Auf der Grundlage der von Henry Lüdeke besorgten Edition neu herausgegeben und kommentiert von Edgar Lohner (Munich: Winkler, 1972), 22.

correspondent that the English had no real idea of Shakespeare, but he may have been less prepared when Schlegel dropped his guard and asked: 'How ever did he chance among the frigid and stupid souls on that brutal island?'[180]

Friedrich's view of Tieck *de haut en bas* (no 'character', 'no intelligence or inner worth')[181] may also have been conditioned by his elevation of another person in the scale of his esteem and affections. This was Dorothea Veit, née Mendelssohn. He had met her in the summer of 1797 in the salon of Henriette Herz. Chafing under a loveless marriage—she had been married off to the banker Simon Veit and had two sons (both in their turn to become leading Romantic painters)—she had been attracted to this witty and brilliant younger man, while he, crushed since his teens under the weight of books, suddenly felt the forces of a belated youth bursting forth. Writing in February 1798, not to his brother, but to his sympathetic sister-in-law Caroline, he set out Dorothea's qualities: simplicity, a heart and mind open to love, music, wit and philosophy (he was later to add: religion).[182] That was as yet seeing her very much in his own terms. While nobody would call Dorothea a beauty, her bright dark eyes compensated for conventional good looks, and her conversation and letters betrayed a sharp mind, and a skill with words. One would expect no less from Moses Mendelssohn's daughter. As yet there was no question of separation or even divorce. Friedrich and Dorothea lived in open liaison (not yet under one roof: even Berlin's tolerance had its limits). If there were not enough scandal adhering to a relationship with a married woman seven years older than himself, her being Jewish added an extra element of piquancy.

The Genesis of the *Athenaeum*

It was clear that Friedrich would not long be content with writing for Reichardt or correcting his brother's Shakespeare proofs. He needed an outlet for his own writings, now that *Die Horen*—to which he had no access as it was—had finally collapsed. In a long letter of 31 October, 1797 to August Wilhelm, he set out his views on a remedy to the situation. It was, he averred, a 'sin and shame' that people like them were reduced to writing for the *Allgemeine Literatur-Zeitung*.[183] What was needed was a periodical

---

180 *Ibid.* 23.
181 *KA*, XXIV, 85f.
182 *Ibid.,* 86.
183 *Ibid.,* 29-35.

produced by themselves. It should run to six parts annually, each of twelve sheets (and at three Louisd'ors a sheet). He had a publisher in mind, Friedrich Vieweg in Berlin. That was the practical part. As for the content, the tone was to be one of 'sublime insolence', 'open war', establishing them as 'critical dictators' and working the destruction of the *Literatur-Zeitung*. Who were to be the contributors? Themselves of course, perhaps Fichte or Novalis or Schleiermacher; they were to ask Tieck and hoped for Goethe.[184] What was it to be called? 'Herkules' perhaps (clubbing its adversaries or cleansing the Augean stable), or 'Freya' (with her chariot), 'Dioskuren' (the twins, now stars in the firmament) or 'Parzen' (the Fates dealing out life and death). 'Schlegeleum' was briefly considered,[185] then finally rejected in favour of the eventual title 'Athenaeum', the ever-prudent August Wilhelm's suggestion.

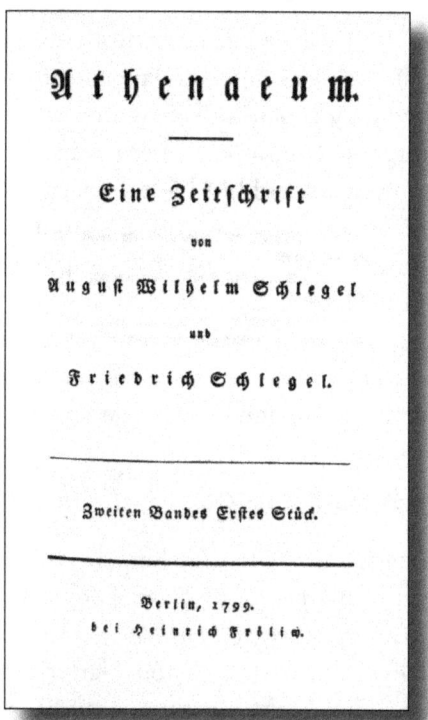

Fig. 7 *Athenaeum. Eine Zeitschrift von August Wilhelm und Friedrich Schlegel* (Berlin, 1798-1800). Title page of vol. 2. Image in the public domain.

---

184 *Ibid.*, 55.
185 General strategy, *ibid.*, 48-54, 72-76; 'Herkules', 'Freya', 37; 'Dioskuren', 'Parzen', 43; 'Schlegeleum', 'Athenaeum', 53.

By December of 1797, Friedrich was giving thought to the journal's organisation. It was to represent the closest association, the union of two minds. There was to be an absolute consensus between them on matters of content (perhaps with Caroline mediating in cases of disagreement). No form or subject was in principle to be excluded, but the pieces accepted should be units in themselves, not extracts from some larger or more extensive 'work in progress'. That would explain why even the groups of fragments that are a distinguishing feature of the *Athenaeum*, form entities in themselves, in the same way that the disparate items of criticism are marshalled into a coherent corpus. Above all—and this is crucial for our understanding of this extraordinary journal—it meant that August Wilhelm, whose style and approach tended rather towards the systematic and the critical, effectively placed his seal of approval on the more open, radical, experimental, 'revolutionary' contributions of his brother and his associates,[186] and was prepared, even where it was not his personal preference, to sanction any combination of ideas, any synthesis, any extension of the intellect. It did not mean that the brothers put their all into this enterprise. There was clearly enough copy available for the 1798 number without the need for them to extend themselves.[187] Soon it had to jostle in competition with Friedrich's novel *Lucinde* (1799) or with August Wilhelm's continued reviewing for the *Allgemeine Literatur-Zeitung* (until late 1799), his Shakespeare translation, and his courses of lectures at the university in Jena. Whatever its claims, and the 'Vorerinnerung' [Preliminary Note] to the reader suggested that these were of the widest degree,[188] it could only represent one side of a movement, many of whose representatives—Fichte, Schelling, Wackenroder, Tieck—never found their way into its pages and whose important works ran parallel with it. This might suggest a publication that took notice only of its own kind. There would however be plenty of references to contemporary literature, those 'Notizen', most of them disrespectful, it is true: Schiller was punished with total silence, Wieland was threatened with a 'massacre' (which in the event never happened), Voss was ridiculed, while Goethe was to be elevated at every possible opportunity.

The proofs of the first part of the 1798 number were ready by the end of March of that year, containing August Wilhelm's *Die Sprachen* [Languages],

---

186 *Ibid.*, 102-106.
187 *Ibid.*, 110.
188 *Athenaeum*, I, [i and ii].

a critique of Klopstock's theories on language, Novalis's collection of aphorisms entitled *Blütenstaub* [Pollen], Friedrich and August Wilhelm's translations of Greek elegies, and August Wilhelm's conspectus of the latest literature, with its significant review of Tieck. There, August Wilhelm had stressed how different their own enterprise was from the run-of the-mill 'critical institutes' (Nicolai's *Allgemeine Deutsche Bibliothek* or, by implication, the *Allgemeine Literatur-Zeitung*), with their levelling 'tone'.[189] The 'Vorerinnerung' would in any case have made this clear.

If one were to apply to the *Athenaeum* the distinction later made by Thomas De Quincey between the 'literature of knowledge' (mere information) and 'the literature of power' (universal and timeless insights),[190] one would find both, comments on an ephemeral contemporary literary scene, and—more prominently and memorably—wide-ranging statements about poetry, about art, about their relationship to philosophy. There would be much however that reminded one of *Die Horen*, of so recent expiry, the confident statements of intent, the bold opening forays—and the gradual loss of élan. In style, it used programmatically the same letters and conversations that characterised Schiller's publication. It did not share his stated aim of breaking down the barriers between learned and literary discourse. Instead, readers must be 'à la hauteur' (one of Friedrich's expressions) and expect 'rhapsodic reflexions and aphoristic fragments', the general and the particular, theory and history, national German aspirations and those of other nations, the present and the past, not least classical antiquity. The focus was to be on art and philosophy, not, by implication, on political affairs, history, or religion, although these might feature under different guises. There was no interdict on contemporary events such as Schiller had imposed, although the journal was in no direct sense political, either. Thus the famous aphorism 216 in the first part for 1798, 'The French Revolution, Fichte's Doctrine of Knowledge, and Goethe's Wilhelm Meister are the major tendencies of our age',[191] that upset Friedrich Nicolai and so many others, challenged the reader to consider the meaning of the word 'tendency' itself, rather than merely summon up the recent cataclysm. The mention of the Revolution, here and in other fragments, even once or twice the naming of Robespierre or Bonaparte, was part of the desire to affront,

---

189 *Ibid.*, I, i, 144-145.
190 Thomas De Quincey, *The Collected Writings*, ed. David Masson, 14 vols (London: A. & C. Black, 1889-90), XI, 59.
191 *KA*, II, 198; *Athenaeum*, I, ii, 232.

to cock a snook, *épater le bourgeois*. There is much in the *Athenaeum* that is impudent, much that contemporaries did not like and said so, but nothing that is directly seditious.

Above all, August Wilhelm's prefatory statement made it clear that this was a journal BY August Wilhelm and Friedrich Schlegel, not merely edited by them. Thus it differed from Schiller's *Horen*. It was also different from another periodical with the same dates and duration as *Athenaeum*, *Propyläen*, that came out in 1798-1800 under Goethe's editorship. Unlike Goethe's and Schiller's journals, and notably unlike the *Allgemeine Literatur-Zeitung*, there was to be no anonymity; one was to know the identity of the contributors immediately from the contents page. The author no longer spoke for a collective, such as Schiller's 'Societät' or Goethe's 'friends united', but in his own name.[192]

At first there was general satisfaction with the *Athenaeum* on the brothers' part. A copy of the first issue went of course to Goethe, then to Fichte, Schütz, Hufeland. The whole Jena establishment, Schiller even, received theirs.[193] Whereas Schiller claimed to feel almost physically ill at the 'over-clever, discriminatory, cutting and one-sided manner of the fragments',[194] Goethe had every reason to be pleased with it, as with subsequent parts.[195] It was not merely that the *Athenaeum*, in its three yearly issues, plied him with gross flattery, Friedrich Schlegel reviewing *Wilhelm Meister*, August Wilhelm elevating him in verse to the successor of the ancient elegists (*Die Kunst der Griechen* [The Art of the Greeks]) and Friedrich offering a conspectus of Goethe's poetic development; there was more to it than plurality of mention. By placing emphasis on the autonomy of art, on an ironic, worldly-wise 'hovering' above events, on the renewal in modern guise of ancient form, on Goethe's protean recreations of his own self, the brothers, separately and jointly, were presenting Goethe as a universal manifestation. This was set out in 1798 in Friedrich's Fragment 247:

> Dante's prophetic poem is the sole system of transcendental poetry, still the highest of its kind. Shakespeare's universality is the focal point of romantic art. Goethe's purely poetic poetry is the utterest poetry of poetry. This is

---

192 Stefan Matuschek, 'Epochenschwelle und prozessuale Verknüpfung. Zur Position der *Allgemeinen Literatur-Zeitung* zwischen Aufklärung und Frühromantik', in: Stefan Matuschek (ed.), *Organisation der Kritik. Die* Allgemeine Literatur-Zeitung *in Jena 1785-1803* (Heidelberg: Winter, 2004), 7-21.
193 *KA*, XXIV, 141f.
194 Schiller to Goethe 23 July, 1798; Gräf-Leitzmann, II, 120.
195 *Caroline*, I, 455-462.

the great triad of modern poetry, the inmost and most sacred circle of the classics of modern poesy.[196]

Here, Goethe was being elevated to one of those 'archpoets' (Tieck's word)[197] of the Romantic canon. He was not entirely averse to this odorous incense offering, displeased as he was at the otherwise unenthusiastic reception of *Wilhelm Meister* (which the *Allgemeine Literatur-Zeitung* had taken no notice of). While the Schlegels furthered their ambitions of being Germany's 'kritische Dictatoren', he believed that his *Propyläen* would dominate discourse in the arts.[198]

None of them took to heart the recent warning example of *Die Horen* and its demise. For Friedrich was fast learning that running an avant-garde periodical involved not only the high ground of an elite and its intellectual risk-taking. One had to contend with more mundane matters, the tergiversations of a publisher, a diminishing stock of copy, and the hostility of the general public. The new king of Prussia, Frederick William III, nonplussed at the political manifesto, *Glaube und Liebe* [Faith and Love], that Novalis had dedicated to him, claimed that one of the Schlegels must have been the author, for 'what a Schlegel writes is incomprehensible'.[199] Friedrich complained of a 'Berlin clique' and the threat of stricter censorship there.[200] The publisher Vieweg was causing trouble, having printed too many copies, not having enough of the right paper, and being under suspicion of sharp practice.[201] By November, Friedrich was putting to August Wilhelm the possibility of changing publishers. The choice fell on Heinrich Frölich, also in Berlin.

Yet, with the appearance of Volume One of the *Athenaeum*, the brothers had every reason to be satisfied with the first products of their 'Fraternität'.[202] It could nevertheless be said of it that it was heavily—unrelievedly—literary, critical, philosophical, and its prefatory statement had promised nothing different. Volume Two, once the practical matters

---

196 *KA*, II, 206; *Athenaeum*, I, ii, 244.
197 Lohner, 25.
198 Sengle, *Das Genie und sein Fürst*, 147; Kurt Krolop, 'Geteiltes Publikum, geteilte Publizität: "Wilhelm Meisters" Aufnahme im Vorfeld des "Athenaeums" (1795-1797)', in: Hans-Dieter Dahnke and Bernd Leistner (eds), *Debatten und Kontroversen. Literarische Auseinandersetzungen in Deutschland am Ende des 18. Jahrhunderts*, 2 vols (Berlin, Weimar: Aufbau, 1989), I, 270-384.
199 *KA*, XXIV, 154; *HKA*, IV, 497.
200 *KA*, XXIII, 159.
201 *Ibid.*, 186f., 193.
202 *Ibid.*, 133.

were sorted out, was to be more varied, with more poetry and a large section of art criticism. This criticism, the larger portion of which, *Die Gemälde* [The Paintings], was written by August Wilhelm and Caroline (if published under his name only), was ready by November 1798 but had to wait until quite late in 1799 to make its appearance.[203] This had certain unexpected advantages: inside the Romantic camp, there was now Tieck's novel *Franz Sternbalds Wanderungen* [Franz Sternbald's Journeyings] that Unger in Berlin had brought out in the autumn of 1798. Written by the co-author of the *Herzensergiessungen* and of its sequel *Phantasien über die Kunst*, it concentrated on the development of a young painter living in the age of Raphael and Dürer, and stressed atmosphere, inner visions, the right religious frame of mind, rather than technicalities or historical frameworks. There was also Goethe's periodical, *Propyläen*, appearing concurrently with the *Athenaeum*. Its message, set out stringently in the introduction (and in larger print, for emphasis) was mastery of the aesthetic and artistic basics, entering the temple forecourt (propylea), before proceeding to the inner sanctum of art, which could only be achieved by a proper study of ancients and moderns alike.[204] The art criticism of the *Athenaeum* would stand somewhere between these two positions, the one consciously religious and Catholicizing, the other neo-classical and pagan. This would, as said, not become evident until late in 1799.

The Group Meets in Dresden

There was meanwhile a general wish to look at works of painting and sculpture in situ. This led to the first Romantic gathering, not in Jena, but in Dresden, and it was to involve Caroline, August Wilhelm and Friedrich Schlegel, Johann Diederich Gries, Novalis, and Schelling. That the choice fell on Dresden comes as no surprise, for this 'Florence on the Elbe' held one of the finest art collections north of the Alps. It was also where the Schlegels' sister lived, the hospitable and long-suffering Charlotte Ernst, with her husband, the court official, and their small daughter Auguste. Moving as

---

203 *HKA*, IV, 514.
204 *Propyläen. Eine periodische Schrift herausgegeben von Goethe*, 3 vols (Tübingen: Cotta, 1798-1800), I, iii-xxxviii; Richard Benz, *Goethe und die romantische Kunst* (Munich: Piper, 1940), 69. A full documentation of the respective views on art of Goethe and the Romantics in: Christoph Perels (ed.), *'Ein Dichter hatte uns alle geweckt'. Goethe und die literarische Romantik*, exhibition catalogue (Frankfurt am Main: Freies Deutsches Hochstift Frankfurter Goethe-Museum, 1999), esp. 72-103.

they did between the main residence in Dresden and the summer palace at Pillnitz, a few miles upstream, the Ernsts somehow provided a base for their extended family.[205] They knew the Dresden painters and academy professors;[206] the inspector of the antique collection was the same Wilhelm Gottlieb Becker who in a different guise had published so much of August Wilhelm's works. They knew the same aristocratic circle of friends that Novalis frequented. It was in such company that Caroline met Germany's most popular novelist, Jean Paul Richter, and made polite conversation over dinner (his popularity did not extend to the *Athenaeum*). The group around Schiller's friends, the Körners, kept their distance.[207]

First, however, August Wilhelm left in May for Berlin to spend five weeks in the Prussian capital. Passing through Leipzig, he met the young Friedrich Wilhelm Joseph Schelling who was successfully negotiating for a post as professor extrordinarius of philosophy at Jena.[208] Schelling would discover that Schlegel, too, had been appointed to a similar position in literature and aesthetics and that from the winter semester of 1798-99 they would be colleagues—and, as it turned out, much else besides.

Schlegel was introduced to Dorothea Veit, meeting his brother's friends Schleiermacher and especially Ludwig Tieck, now the author of *Sternbald*, with whom he had been corresponding for six months. As an experienced critic, he encouraged him to send a copy of the novel to Goethe.[209] Cutting a figure in the salons,[210] August Wilhelm allowed himself to be feted as the translator of Shakespeare and the co-editor of the *Athenaeum*. Sensing the historic moment of Frederick William III's and Queen Louise's accession to the throne, he produced the first of his several poems in homage to the Prussian royal house.[211] It was also a necessary corrective to the reputation the Schlegels enjoyed. His main business in Berlin was, however, to negotiate with his fellow-Hanoverian and now famous actor-producer August Wilhelm Iffland. He had renewed his acquaintance with Iffland

---

205 Günter Jäckel (ed.), *Dresden zur Goethezeit 1760-1815* (Hanau: Dausien, 1988), 234; *KA*, XXIV, 312; *Krisenjahre der Frühromantik. Briefe aus dem Schlegelkreis*, ed. Josef Körner, 3 vols (Brno, Vienna, Leipzig: Röhrer, 1936-37; Berne: Francke, 1958), III, 12.
206 *Ibid.*
207 *Caroline*, I, 723.
208 F. W. J. Schelling, *Briefe und Dokumente*, ed. Horst Fuhrmans, 3 vols (Bonn: Bouvier, 1962-75), I, 154.
209 Lohner, 227.
210 *Krisenjahre*, I, 6; III, 12, 211.
211 *SW*, I, 160-162.

at a guest performance earlier that year in Weimar.²¹² Now, he sought to interest him in a stage performance of *Hamlet*, reading him his translation.²¹³ It was another year, October 1799, before this came about and then without any success.²¹⁴ Meanwhile, he had to make do with the present reality of the Berlin theatre, Gotter's adaptation of *The Tempest*, with music by Reichardt.²¹⁵ He paid court to and flirted with Friederike Unzelmann, the premier actress in Berlin: Caroline accepted these tendernesses for the 'Diabolino' (her soubriquet for Unzelmann)²¹⁶ as part of the realistic view of their partnership.

It was not until July that August Wilhelm arrived in Dresden for the gallery visit, bringing with him his brother Friedrich, without Dorothea. The moment for introductions was not yet opportune, and there was the 'Jews' tax' to consider. At the beginning of August, Schelling announced his intention of coming,²¹⁷ whereupon Friedrich wrote to Novalis, a day's journey away at the mining academy in Freiberg.²¹⁸ Caroline and Auguste had been accompanied to Dresden by Johann Diederich Gries, then a student at Jena but soon to be the standard translator of Ariosto, Tasso and Calderón. On 25 and 26 August, for just two days, the circle was united in Dresden. We only have Gries's account of the hoped-for 'philosophisches Convent',²¹⁹ but Novalis jotted down aphorisms on art that went beyond personal details.²²⁰ Friedrich and Novalis did not become converts overnight to Schelling's notion of the 'Weltseele';²²¹ while August Wilhelm and Caroline were more interested in art, indeed that was the primary reason for their coming.²²²

Their visits to the Dresden gallery and their social life in general in the city differed somewhat from the later stylised art conversations in

---

212 *Krisenjahre*, III, 12.
213 *Caroline*, I, 450, 452.
214 15 October, 1799. See Ella Horn, 'Zur Geschichte der ersten Aufführung von Schlegel's Hamlet-Übersetzung auf dem Kgl. Nationaltheater zu Berlin. Mit unveröffentlichten Briefen Ifflands und seiner Frau an A. W. Schlegel', *Jahrbuch der Deutschen Shakespeare-Gesellschaft*, 51 (1915), 34-52. AWS also issued *Hamlet* separately, with Iffland's needs in mind. *Shakspeare's Hamlet. Übersetzt von A. W. Schlegel* (Berlin: Unger, 1800).
215 *KA*, XXIV, 143-144.
216 *Caroline*, I, 452.
217 Fuhrmans, I, 155, 157.
218 *HKA*, IV, 496.
219 *KA*, XXIV, 161.
220 *HKA*, II, 648-651.
221 Fuhrmans, I, 155.
222 *KA*, XXIV, 145.

Die Gemälde. There, as in so many reactions to the Dresden collections, the beholders saw only what seemed essential, what struck the senses, what seized and overpowered the beholder with awe and reverence and the frisson of religious devotion. Others' reactions were no different, not least Goethe's. Thirty years earlier, the Dresden gallery had been for him a 'temple, a 'house of God'. Such paintings as he had had 'eyes to see' had not been Italian,[223] and although a young devotee of Winckelmann, he had not walked the mile or so to see the antique sculptures (until 1785 outhoused).[224] Writing of this in 1813 in his autobiography, he was passing on the insight that young temple worshippers see only what they wish to see, and these remarks would be directed at the devotees of Romantic art appreciation. Still, it was clear that Goethe, in 1798 so wryly dismissive of youthful ardour and recommending those 'forecourts' (*Propyläen*), had himself not always been subject to the dictates of balanced maturity. Thus in 1793 Wackenroder and Tieck had in Dresden seen the Sistine Madonna: little else mattered. Again Goethe in 1794 made a long list of the Dresden paintings and included almost none that the Schlegel group was impressed by.[225] Wilhelm von Humboldt in 1797 was struck by the contrast that the gallery afforded between ancient and modern, 'ideal and individual'.[226] Schiller, slightly later, felt more at home in the world of ancient sculpture than among the paintings.

The aesthetic arguments of the century—sculpture versus painting, repose versus movement, plasticity versus colour—were rehearsed, as it were, in front of the Dresden collections. The lighting could contribute. Inspecting the statuary by torchlight, as the Romantics and also Schiller did, softened contours and accentuated forms.[227] One could overlook the physical surroundings, the so-called 'stablings' ('Stallgebäude', today's Johanneum), where the paintings were hung according to a rough approximation of historical schools and where the jewel, the Sistine Madonna herself, was grouped among works from different Italian periods.[228] If one was, like Schlegel, a pupil of Fiorillo in Göttingen, and had studied Caylus and

---

223 *Dichtung und Wahrheit*, Part 2, book 8. Goethe, *Gedenkausgabe*, X, 352f., 355.
224 Carl Justi, *Winckelmann und seine Zeitgenossen*, 3rd edn, 3 vols (Leipzig: Vogel, 1923), I, 296.
225 Goethe, *Gedenkausgabe*, XIII, 91-108.
226 Jäckel, 191.
227 *Ibid.*, 192f.; Lothar Müller in AWS, *Die Gemählde. Gespräch*, ed. Lothar Müller, Fundus-Bücher, 143 (Dresden: Verlag der Kunst, 1996), 176.
228 Angelo Walter, 'Die Hängung der Dresdner Gemäldegalerie zwischen 1765 und 1832', *Dresdner Kunstblätter* 29 (1981), 76-87, ref. 78; Justi, III, 89-103.

Winckelmann (while not always acknowledging their authority), one knew what belonged where.

Did it really matter? The collection assembled by the Electors of Saxony, mainly up to 1763, was an eighteenth-century creation and as such suitably eclectic. It had benefited from the connoisseurship of Francesco Algarotti, known to so many courts in Europe; it was strong on colour, with not just Raphael's masterpiece, but also Correggio, Veronese, Guido Reni, Palma, Maratta. There was much that the late eighteenth century had as yet no eye for—the Cranachs, the Dürers—or the Mannerists, or Velásquez or the French pastellists. There was little sense that the gallery formed part of a baroque residence, as captured by Bellotto's famous panorama of 1748, where the court was Catholic, the citizenry Protestant, or that its most famous Catholic convert, Winckelmann, had written his epoch-making Gedanken, his thoughts on the works of the ancients, in this very city.[229] Winckelmann had of course not converted out of spiritual considerations: his dogma was aesthetic, his longing for Rome pagan.[230] Nevertheless, the visit of the Schlegel brothers did coincide with their renewed interest in religion. *Die Gemälde* is the most Catholicisizing (as opposed to religious) text in the *Athenaeum*. It coincided with August Wilhelm's remarkable poem on the *Union of the Church with the Arts*, that came out in 1800. Yet it would be Friedrich, motivated by urges quite different from Winckelmann's, who found his way to Rome, not August Wilhelm. The other convert from the Schlegel family was to be the daughter of the staunchly Protestant Ernsts in Dresden, Auguste von Buttlar. It was in Dresden that Friedrich died in 1829, in the arms of his niece, and it is here that he is buried.

Professor in Jena

The efficient team of August Wilhelm and Caroline had *Die Gemälde* ready by November of 1798.[231] The Dresden circle had dispersed, Friedrich back to Berlin, Novalis to Freiberg, Gries to Göttingen. In Jena, there were August Wilhelm and Caroline—and Schelling. In a letter to Novalis, of some considerable frankness, Caroline dropped her guard and took stock of the situation. The *Athenaeum* had in her view come to a standstill. It had in any case been a mistake for the brothers to have got involved with a journal,

---
229 *Ibid.*, I, 359.
230 *Ibid.*, 323f.
231 *Caroline*, I, 473f.; *HKA*, IV, 505.

and August Wilhelm should not have become a professor. Lecturing consumed his energies, so that there was little time for the journal, indeed, she would have been content to offer *Die Gemälde* to Goethe's *Propyläen* (Goethe was, as always, at the centre of her admiration). There was also the 'cussed' [trotzig] Schelling. This young academic, whom Caroline a month earlier had characterised as an 'Urnatur' [a piece of primal nature], a 'chip of granite', was now their midday guest and needed, as she put it, 'taking in hand'.[232]

Caroline had never been keen on what Friedrich called his brother's 'professorale Energie und Expansivität',[233] and it is hard not to share her point of view. The *Athenaeum* became more and more Friedrich's concern, until he too found other and more pressing outlets for his restless energy, notably the novel *Lucinde*. Ultimately, all this was to cost August Wilhelm his health and his marriage. For even a free and tolerant association like theirs could not survive such multitudinousness, where one partner was translating Shakespeare, writing lectures, reviewing, editing his poems, never able to resist additional tasks on the side (such as helping Fiorillo with his proofs,[234] or, most unnecessary of all, translating a selection of Horace Walpole's writings).[235] Where Caroline was increasingly being taken for granted as an amanuesis or even a ghost-writer (she wrote most of *Die Gemälde*), was it surprising that she sought ways of bringing about a chemical change in that 'chip of granite'?

The *Athenaeum*, despite its declared universal scope, could never possibly provide more than 'échappées de vue', in one of Friedrich's more famous formulations.[236] It could never satisfy the urge to systematise knowledge, to expand encyclopaedically, to bring scholarly and scientific discourse alive, to broaden the limits of the academy. In August Wilhelm's case, he could not easily shake off his Göttingen experience. There was something of Heyne, of Fiorillo, above all of Bürger, in his nature. It was Bürger, after all, who had provided the model of a professional writer with one foot

---

232 *Caroline*, I, 459; Fuhrmans, I, 154f.
233 *KA*, XXIV, 199.
234 See above.
235 *Historische literarische und unterhaltende Schriften von Horatio Walpole, übersetzt von A. W. Schlegel* (Leipzig: Hartknoch, 1800). The preface is in *SW*, VIII, 58-63. See *Briefe*, II, 33. The Hartknoch edition is a one-volume selection based on the five-volume folio edition, *The Works of Horatio Walpole, Earl of Orford*, 5 vols (London: C. G. & J. Robertson, & J. Edwards, 1798). AWS's main interest in Walpole seems to have been in his remarks on garden design.
236 *Athenaeum*, I, ii, 234.

in the university, Schiller likewise. Readers of the letters on language in *Die Horen* or of the Dante sections there, readers of Schlegel's reviews, too, could sense that there was a corpus of knowledge kept in check only by the dictates of the journal medium, while much of *Die Gemälde* would need only to be systematised to take on the lineaments of a lecture. This expansiveness of communication, that reached its height in Berlin in 1801-04 or in Vienna in 1808 and that went far beyond a student audience, sat perhaps uneasily with the polished and elegantly crafted essay—the *Horen* articles or the Bürger review of 1801—and it might be said that Schlegel only reconciled these two approaches later in his great reviews for the *Heidelberger Jahrbücher*. For all that, university lecturing was not merely a matter of holding forth. It involved a rapport with one's hearers, something that Fichte and Schelling in Jena excelled at, using transcriptions of their lecture notes as a means of disseminating their ideas.[237] They were of course not poets, or if so, only rarely. One did not go to their lectures, as one might to Schlegel's, to hear a professional translator or the co-editor of an avant-garde journal discoursing on the history of German poetry or on aesthetics.

It seems that Schlegel's negotiations with the university began already in 1797, ultimately through the minister Voigt and always in consultation with Goethe.[238] One learns here something of the creaking mechanisms of the eighteenth-century university. During the spring and summer of 1798 a series of florid communications went to and fro between the rector's and dean's offices and those *Serenissimi nutritores* in the Thuringian courts.[239] Schlegel was well enough known in Saxe-Weimar, but perhaps not in Saxe-Meiningen, where he had to present his scholarly credentials. A warm testimonial on his behalf by Schütz stressed his mastery of German style as a poet and translator, his solidity as a classical scholar (*De geographia Homerica*), his 'Genialität' [touch of genius] and 'Fleiß' [studiousness].[240] Although the subjects he hoped to profess in Jena were not new to the institution (German poetry, and aesthetics), he would stand in nicely for 'Hofrat Schiller' whose health no longer permitted him to lecture.[241] There

---

237 Ziolkowski, *German Romanticism*, 254.
238 *Goethes Briefwechsel mit Christian Gottlob Voigt*, 4 vols, Schriften der Goethe-Gesellschaft, 53-56 (Weimar: Böhlau, 1949-62). I, 353.
239 *Ibid*, II, 80. Jena, Universitätsarchiv, A 621; Coburg, Staatsarchiv, Min K Nr. 35 and LA E Nr. 2059.
240 Jena, Universitätsarchiv, A 621, M 208, 5-7, 18; also SLUB Dresden, Mscr. Dresd. e. 90, VI (11).
241 Jena, Universitätsarchiv A 621, M 208, 18; hand-written list of proposed lectures *ibid.*, M 210, 75.

is an irony in that Schlegel was to quarrel spectacularly with Schütz in 1799, and that the imperial diploma ('Auctoritate Sacrae Caesareae Maiestatis') granting him the style of doctor of philosophy and professor extraordinarius was in the name of the pro-rector Eberhard Gottlob Paulus,[242] later his father-in-law in his calamitous second marriage.

As was quite common at the time, Schlegel held his lectures in a colleague's house, that of the jurist Gottlieb Hufeland (with whom he also fell out) in the 'Döderlein house in the Leutragasse', the same building in fact in which he and Caroline lived.[243] Between the winter semester of 1798-99 and the summer of 1801 he gave courses of lectures on the history of German poetry, German style, the history of Greek and Roman literature, Horace's Epistles and satires, and on aesthetics, overlapping with other professors such as Schütz and Eichstädt and standing in as it were for the absent Schiller. When lecturing on aesthetics, he appeared on the lecture lists under philosophy with Fichte and Schelling.[244] Yet Schlegel, unlike them, never seems to have had more than twelve listeners,[245] and the effort he put into his lectures—they were said to be in publishable form—was out of all proportion to their intellectual or even financial benefits.[246] Friedrich Hölderlin's friend Friedrich Muhrbeck, writing in September, 1799, found Schlegel's content 'half intellect, half spirit, without emphasis and without feeling and life'.[247] But two, possibly three, of his auditors later went on to greater things, the distinguished jurist Carl Friedrich von Savigny,[248] Friedrich Ast, the Platonist and aesthetician,[249] and most likely also August Klingemann, now agreed to be the anonymous author of the black and nihilistic *Nachtwachen des Bonaventura* [Bonaventura's Night Watches]. Ast

---

242 *Ibid.*, M 209, 23; SLUB Dresden, Mscr. Dresd. e. 90, VI (12).
243 *Briefe*, II, 31; I, 78-81: Jena, Universitätsarchiv M 210, 75; Ute Fritsch, 'Wohnorte der Dichter und Gelehrten in Jena um 1800', in: Friedrich Strack (ed.), *Evolution des Geistes: Jena um 1800. Natur und Kunst, Philosophie und Wissenschaft im Spannungsfeld der Geschichte*, Deutscher Idealismus, 17 (Stuttgart: Klett-Cotta, 1994), 689-717.
244 Horst Neuper et al. (ed.), *Das Vorlesungsangebot an der Universität Jena von 1749 bis 1854* (Weimar: Verlag und Datenbank für Geisteswissenschaften, 2003), I, 312-328.
245 Ernst Behler, 'August Wilhelm Schlegels Vorlesungen über philosophische Kunstlehre Jena 1798, 1799', in: Strack, 412-433.
246 *Ibid.*, 219.
247 Hölderlin, *GStA*, VII, i, 142.
248 Stoll, I, 118f.
249 Rudolf Haym, *Die romantische Schule. Ein Beitrag zur Geschichte des deutschen Geistes* (Berlin: Gaertner, 1870), 764-768; *Briefe*, II, 35; *KA*, XXV, 484; Hugo Burath, *August Klingemann und die deutsche Romantik* (Braunschweig: Vieweg, 1948), 55-61; *Allgemeine Deutsche Biographie*, ed. Historische Kommission der Königl. Akademie der Wissenschaften, 56 vols (Leipzig: Duncker & Humblot, 1875-1912), XVI, 187.

handed his notes over to Karl Christian Friedrich Krause, later a philosopher influential in the Hispanic world, and these are the only full transcripts to survive.[250] Yet another, Heinrich Schmidt, left a disrespectful account of Schlegel proudly listing his poetic ancestors.[251] Ast's transcription of Schlegel's lectures may not be verbatim, for comparing it with a short sample from Savigny we find agreement in subject-matter if not in formulation. Given Schlegel's unwillingness to discard the merest scrap of paper, it is possible that he used the material of his Jena lectures on German poetry and Greek and Roman literature for similar lectures in Bonn after 1819, but of that we cannot be certain. The other lectures we must assume to be lost.

It was Savigny, too, who noted Schlegel's physical appearance. The 'handsome young man' was no more: one saw instead marked on his face 'over-exertion' and its 'destructive force'. Thus it comes as no surprise that once *Die Gemälde* and the closely related essay on Flaxman had been delivered to Friedrich, August Wilhelm's contributions to the *Athenaeum* became more sparse and that the original resolve of fraternal collaboration had to undergo some accommodation. It is even fair to say that these two pieces of art criticism are what put his personal stamp on the periodical. It was small wonder, too, that Caroline complained to Novalis that she had hardly been out of her husband's study since the beginning of the year, translating 'the second play of Shakespeare' (there were four, *The Merchant of Venice, As You Like It, King John* and *King Richard II*, that came out in 1799, not counting the reviews for the *Allgemeine Literatur-Zeitung*).

The Fichte Affair

A further distraction from the 'main task' came with the Fichte affair in 1799,[252] the so-called 'atheism controversy' that demonstrated how much the University of Jena, despite the distinction of its professors— Schiller, Paulus, Hufeland, Schelling, above all Fichte himself—was an

---

250 These were published as: *Aug. Wilhelm Schlegels Vorlesungen über Philosophische Kunstlehre* [...], ed. Aug. Wünsche (Leipzig: Dieterich, 1911), then AWS, *Kritische Ausgabe der Vorlesungen [KAV]*, ed. Ernst Behler *et al.*, 3 vols (Paderborn, Munich, Vienna, Zurich: Schöningh, 1989- in progress), I (Vorlesungen über Ästhetik, I), 3-177.
251 Heinrich Schmidt, *Erinnerungen eines Weimarer Veteranen aus dem geselligen, literarischen und Theater-Leben* [...] (Leipzig: Brockhaus, 1856), 53f.
252 Set out by Waldtraut Beyer, 'Der Atheismusstreit um Fichte', in: Dahnke and Leistner, II, 154-245; Sengle (1993), 168-175.

eighteenth-century institution and subject to the political will of its ruler, Duke Carl August of Saxe-Weimar. Of course this was not essentially to change under the so-called 'reformed' university of the nineteenth century, as Schlegel's own agitated correspondence with the Prussian minister Altenstein over the Carlsbad Decrees attests, and as the 'Göttingen Seven' were to learn from hard experience. Officially, Carl August was subject to the authority of the Holy Roman Emperor (the last of his kind), whose name appeared at the top of the university's decrees and diplomas,[253] The 'affair' was, however, more about the issue of censorship and the right to publish, ultimately the question of academic freedom. Whereas academic freedom was something that the nineteenth-century universities had to fight hard to achieve, Fichte in the eighteenth believed it was already his by right. None of these was an issue to which the Schlegel brothers, one already a professor and the other aspiring to be one, could be indifferent.

It needs also to be said that Fichte had not always displayed prudence as a professor in Jena. The Weimar publisher Bertuch remarked in 1799 that those professing wisdom ('Weltweise', philosophers) were seldom worldly-wise.[254] It was all very well for Fichte to play the public intellectual and appeal to an audience of reasonable, enlightened and tolerant men and women beyond the university confines. Carl August had never been happy with his appointment, and Fichte's debut in Jena, lecturing on a Sunday—and on the subject of the French Revolution—had required all of Goethe's diplomatic skills to placate his blunt and forthright sovereign and master. This was only the beginning.

The background, briefly, is this. Fichte had seized the opportunity of becoming co-editor of the *Philosophisches Journal* in 1797. In 1798 his former colleague Friedrich Karl Forberg sent him a contribution that seemed to postulate a moral and religious existence without the necessity of a belief in God. Alarmed at what seemed to be the reduction of faith to a mere incidental, but reluctant to stifle philosophical debate, Fichte decided to append an essay of his own, setting out the notion of a world order dependent on the idea of God.

The ideas set out here and their dependence (or not) on Kant are not the issue. No sooner had the journal appeared, than the Lutheran consistory in Dresden apprised the Elector of Saxony of the 'irreligious' nature of

---

[253] As on another diploma granting AWS his honorary doctorate of philosophy, 'Auctoritate Sacrae Caesareae Maiestatis Francisci II. Imperatoris Romano-Germanici'. Jena, Universitätsarchiv, M 213, 7.

[254] *KA*, XXIV, 271.

Forberg's article and recommended not only the confiscation of the journal but the censure of those at the university in Jena responsible for teaching philosophy. Otherwise, Saxon students would be forbidden attendance at Jena. This was the main Saxon ducal house dictating to its Ernestine laterals in Thuringia. Like Tsar Paul's similar decree recalling Russian students home from Germany's 'nest of sedition',[255] this was a provocative and even extortionate step, directed against a fellow ruler but also the material existence of the Jena academy. On hearing the words 'Fichtean atheism' being used, Fichte set out to justify and defend himself. In considerable haste, he penned a brochure, extending to 114 pages of print, his *Appellation an das Publikum* that came out in January 1799, in 2,500 copies and with a double impress, Jena and Leipzig. It appeared also in Tübingen, Fichte having brought the mighty South German publisher Cotta on to his side and thereby securing the widest possible dissemination in the German-speaking lands.[256] To make his point, Fichte ensured that copies were sent to Germany's rulers and to leading intellectuals, Goethe and Schiller among them. August Wilhelm and Caroline each received one, accompanied by a printed but hand-signed letter appealing to the 'thinking public' and alluding to the gravity of the issue.[257]

There is no record of any immediate action by Schlegel, but those more wary of the ways of courts, like Schiller,[258] may have sensed that Fichte's rhetoric had got somewhat out of hand. As it was, only Hanover followed the example of the Saxon and Thuringian courts. The ban on Hanoverian students studying in Jena, and the possible silencing of its star professor, would still have serious consequences for the university, the town, and the state at large. Above all, Fichte chose badly his time to appeal over the heads of rulers to some notional 'Volk', some popular mandate. In 1808, with his famous *Speeches to the German Nation*, events would be on his side, but not now.

It was his political naivete that was to cost him his post in Jena. He wrote to the minister Voigt stating that he would rather seek dismissal than accept censure. Carl August, a dislike of intellectual demagoguery deep in his heart, found this a convenient means of being rid of a turbulent professor. And so,

---

255 *Briefe*, I, 79.
256 J. G. *Fichte-Gesamtausgabe der Bayerischen Akademie der Wissenschaften*, ed. Reinhard Lauth *et al.*, 42 vols in 4 sections (Stuttgart-Bad Canstatt: Frommann, 1962-2012), III, iii, 174f.
257 *Ibid.*, 183f.
258 Cf. Schiller to Goethe 14 June, 1799; Gräf-Leitzmann, II, 223.

on 1 April 1799, having had 400 students in the previous semester, Fichte found himself dismissed, shunned and humiliated.[259] Caroline divined correctly the duke's hand in the affair and Voigt's duplicity (he need not have treated Fichte's letter as an official document), while Friedrich rightly noted Fichte's general lack of political astuteness. He wondered, too, about Goethe's role. As well he might, for Goethe, while not doing nothing, had done little and had effectively bowed to his ducal master's will. It was, as Caroline averred, 'bad for all friends of frank and courageous bearing'.[260] Friedrich contemplated a counter-brochure, even wrote a few draft pages, but it was essentially too late.[261] Friedrich and Dorothea could offer practical help. The authorities in late-Enlightenment Berlin saw no threat to church and state in Fichte's writings and welcomed him in the Prussian capital. For a while, until he found suitable quarters for his family, Fichte actually shared lodgings with Dorothea in the Ziegelstrasse, an act of kindness but also of some forbearance, for Fichte held strongly anti-Semitic opinions.[262]

Nobody emerged very well from the 'atheism controversy'. Life returned to normal in Jena (and Weimar). Nobody resigned in protest, although Fichte's dismissal was the first step towards the grand exodus from Jena that by 1803 saw most of the university's luminaries—Paulus, Hufeland the medical professor, and Schelling among them—depart elsewhere. The *Athenaeum* circle's adulation of Goethe was undiminished. They could conveniently separate out the 'archpoet' from the courtier and minister of state. Other pressing plans, of which part two of the *Athenaeum* was but one, crowded in. Schlegel took note of one thing. When in his later Berlin lectures on 'encyclopedia' he cited Fichte as one of the models for his own approach to knowledge and its systematisation, he was referring not only to the other man's metaphysical and epistemological system but also to his appeal beyond a purely academic audience to an imagined 'nation' of auditors.

The Scandal of *Lucinde*

There was no direct connection between the 'atheism affair' and the continuing fortunes of the *Athenaeum* except in the sense that the unity of purpose that had given the original enterprise its nerve and energy and

---

259 *KA*, XXIV, 278.
260 *Caroline*, I, 535-538.
261 *KA*, XVIII, 522-525.
262 *Caroline*, I, 738.

drive, was now sheering off in all directions. In August Wilhelm's case, it had always been in competition with the multiform commitments of the professional writer, whereas Friedrich, charged with the energy of his intellectual friendships with Schleiermacher and Novalis, regenerated by his love for Dorothea, had put his heart and soul into the journal. Under different circumstances, this had also been the pattern of *Die Horen*. The problem was sustaining the élan, keeping the pace going. In the brothers' letters from 1799, Friedrich's especially, we see their minds already running ahead to projects that would mature in 1800 or even 1802, their collected essays, to be published as *Charakteristiken und Kritiken*, August Wilhelm's edition of his own poems, and the *Musen-Almanach*, the tone and purport of which were to be transformed by the tragic events of the summer of 1800. Above all, for six months, the *Athenaeum* had to compete with Friedrich's novel *Lucinde*.

On a pragmatic level, Friedrich took advantage of the switch from Vieweg to Frölich to interest his new publisher in something quite different, what was to become the 300 pages of *Lucinde. Ein Roman von Friedrich Schlegel*. Intellectually, philosophically, the novel belongs in the world that Schleiermacher, Novalis and Friedrich Schlegel himself inhabited, where history, science and nature (Novalis), religion and morals (Schleiermacher) and love (Schlegel) were elevated to universals and absolutes. In one sense it is right to associate *Lucinde* with Schleiermacher's *Reden über die Religion* [Discourses on Religion] that came out in the same year, in that Schleiermacher was seeking to free religion from rationalism and morals, from institutions, to present it as the 'sense of the universal', here and now, in the embrace of the eternal in an all-feeling sense of love and dependence. Such ideas were to the fore when Schleiermacher produced his defence of his friend's novel in 1800, the *Vertraute Briefe über Friedrich Schlegels Lucinde* [Private Letters] and employed quasi-mystical language to express love growing into endlessness [wachsende Unendlichkeit].[263] Similarly, if one reduced the novel to its philosophical import, it would propound a unity of spiritual and sensual love, a synthesis of these two main forces of existence, above human sanctions and conventional morals, the elevation of love to a religious as well as a physical experience; culturally, the breaking down of gender barriers, equal respect for the sexes.[264]

---

263 [Friedrich Schleiermacher], *Vertraute Briefe über Friedrich Schlegels Lucinde* (Lübeck and Leipzig: Bohn, 1800), 141.
264 Paul Kluckhohn, *Die Auffassung der Liebe in der Literatur des 18. Jahrhunderts und in der deutschen Romantik*, 3rd edn (Halle: Niemeyer 1966), 362-365.

Clearly this novel was not *Wilhelm Meister* or, closer to hand, even Tieck's *William Lovell*, with its cold and cynical seductions, or *Sternbald*, ever aware of the perils to the artist of fleshly allurements. These novels had plots (of a sort), whereas *Lucinde* was episodic and unsequent. The reader might be drawn inexorably to scenes where the newly emancipated flesh and sportive sexual encounters caught the attention, not the philosophical and Intellectual arguments. Would it not, feared Novalis, remind readers of *Ardinghello*, Wilhelm Heinse's novel of 1785, noted for its amorous high jinks (for the prudish Coleridge an 'abomination')?[265] Did it not show up as hypocritical the Romantics' moral indignation at the hetaerist world of Wieland—whom the *Athenaeum* circle vowed to 'annihilate'[266]—or the lascivious Frenchmen Crébillon and Parny?

Above all, there was the autobiographical factor. It did not require much ingenuity to recognize Friedrich Schlegel and Dorothea Veit as the main protagonists, but the discerning would also spot Caroline, even little Auguste Ernst, Friedrich's niece. Dorothea had given up everything for the man whom she adored and worshipped,[267] her civil status, her reputation and her material security. Caught between her religion and his, she did not wish to affront further her family by baptism, the necessary step to marriage. Moreover her estranged husband demanded custody of both of their sons should she take this step.[268] It was all very well for Friedrich to write to Novalis of her 'religious nature'—she would choose Indian-style self-immolation if ever she lost him[269]—and then put this straight into the text of the novel. Both Caroline and Dorothea wished that the novel had never been published, setting out as it did what was intimate and private and beyond articulation.[270] The eventual scandal that the novel produced—Schiller spoke for many in seeing 'modern lack of form and contrary to nature'[271]—affected them personally and was easily transferred to the *Athenaeum*, involving the whole Romantic circle in polemics, libel and slander.[272]

---

265 *Collected Letters of Samuel Taylor Coleridge*, ed. Earl Leslie Griggs, 6 vols (Oxford: Clarendon, 1956-71), IV, 793.
266 *Caroline*, I, 465; Friedrich Sengle, *Wieland* (Tübingen: Metzler, 1949), 510-513.
267 *KA*, XXIV, 249.
268 *Ibid.*, 202.
269 *Ibid.*, 215.
270 *Ibid.*, 266; *Caroline*, I, 732; *Lucinde ein Roman von Friedrich Schlegel* (Berlin: Frölich, 1799), 23, 26.
271 Schiller to Goethe, 19 July, 1799; Gräf-Leitzmann, II, 242.
272 Kluckhohn, *Auffassung der Liebe*, 414-424.

A common sense of purpose, the awareness of a 'good cause', a sharing in the fate of a journal to which no-one could be indifferent, putting on a bold front to charges of incomprehension or even immorality: all of these factors convinced the *Athenaeum* circle—the Romantics—that they should not merely form a coalition of the mind and spirit but should constitute a living community in one place, under one roof. This was the germ of the Jena circle. It was the Berlin fraction that was initially so much in favour of this togetherness, for they were already accepted in the circles that mattered to them and—not insignificantly—they were dealing with publishers there. Fichte even called for 'one big family' in Berlin,[273] but of course he had by then shaken the dust of Jena off his feet; while Schleiermacher had his chaplain's duties—and, a subject of some malicious comment—was involved in a platonic attachment with the Jewish *salonnière* Henriette Herz. Caroline, no doubt speaking for all in Jena, had no intention of removing to a city that she did not know, with her husband a professor in Jena, as was Schelling. They had their own circle of friends and acquaintances, the publisher Frommann and his open hospitality, or the Paulus family. In Jena, one could meet Goethe, usually over from Weimar on visits of two weeks at a time.[274] Novalis, moving around in the course of his professional duties, was now in Weissenfels, but a short journey away.

Foregathering in Jena

Thus it was agreed that they should foregather in Jena. Friedrich entrusted the *Athenaeum* to Schleiermacher, and it is in letters to him that we learn the most of events in Jena. Nearly all of the 1799 number was ready by July of that year, and the rest, for the remainder of its short existence, was effectively edited from a distance. Friedrich arrived in Jena on 2 September, Dorothea and her small son Philipp on 6 October, the Tieck family on 17 October, while Novalis was in Jena only from 11-14 November. Friedrich and Dorothea shared part of the house in the Leutragasse, while the Tiecks had quarters in the Fischergasse, and Schelling in the Fürstengraben, all short distances in a small university town like Jena.[275] There was open house in the Leutragasse and meals were taken there. The young Norwegian nature philosopher Henrik Steffens moved in and out of this

---

273 *Caroline*, I, 740.
274 Thomas Pester, 'Goethe und Jena. Eine Chronik seines Schaffens in der Universitätsstadt', in: Strack (1994), 663-688, esp. 672f.
275 Peer Kösling, 'Die Wohnungen der Gebrüder Schlegel in Jena', *Athenäum*, 8 (1998), 97-110; *KA*, XXIV, 300f.

Romantic circle, sensing the 'ferment of a new age', although for him it was the galvanic experiments by the young physical chemist Johann Wilhelm Ritter, to whom Friedrich and Novalis were also drawn, that was the main attraction.[276] For an impressionable young man at the outset of his scientific and literary career, it was still 'bliss to be alive'.

Doubtless that was true: one could hear Tieck reading from his own works or from Holberg (taking all the roles) or listen to one of the discourses on religion or poetry or galvanism (or all three) that dominated proceedings. Religion was to be the keynote of Jena. Already in May of that year Friedrich had told his brother August Wilhelm that the time had come to found a new religion.[277] The years of travail that had brought forth the French Revolution would accomplish it. This, somewhat toned down, merged into his call for a new poetic mythology that the *Gespräch über die Poesie* [Conversation on Poetry] in the last part of the *Athenaeum* would adumbrate. Novalis's much more radical rewriting of history, finished early in 1800 but held back from publication on Goethe's advice, his *Die Christenheit oder Europa* [Christendom or Europe] demanded the emphatic reinstatement of the Christian Middle Ages into the historical narrative, with vast visions of a Golden Age to come.[278] Like this religious homily by Novalis, two other overtly Catholicizing works by members of the circle did not appear in the journal: August Wilhelm's *Der Bund der Kirche mit den Künsten* [The Church's Alliance with the Arts], the long ottava rima poem that later caused him some embarrassment,[279] and Tieck's archly medievalising martyr tragedy on the life and death of St Genevieve, *Leben und Tod der heiligen Genoveva*, with its sophisticated religiosity. Two works that the journal did publish, the poems appended to *Die Gemälde*, harked back to times when religion and the arts had been under one hierarchical aegis, and the section of the *Gespräch* called *Epochen der Dichtkunst* [Periods of Poetry] placed Dante in a similar cultural context.

Dorothea Veit, her attention often drawn to more mundane matters, commented wryly to Schleiermacher: 'Christianity is à l'ordre du jour; the gentlemen are slightly crazed'.[280] With so many strong and productive personalities—a 'Despoten Republik'[281]—it was not surprising that the

---

276 Henrich Steffens, *Was ich erlebte*, 10 vols (Breslau: Max, 1840-44), IV, 83.
277 *KA*, XXIV, 273, 284.
278 *KA*, XXV, 23.
279 AWS, 'Berichtigung einiger Mißdeutungen', *SW*, VIII, 225.
280 *KA*, XXV, 23.
281 *Ibid.*, 71.

Jena circle began to fray from its inception. The two 'grandes dames'—the professor's daughter and the philosopher's daughter—at first sized each other up warily and were initially on their best behaviour.[282] Both agreed that Tieck's wife Amalia, the hapless 'Mad. Tieck', a pastor's daughter, was not in their class.[283] There were soon tensions between Friedrich and Caroline. Despite the loose bonds of Caroline's and August Wilhelm's marriage arrangements, it was evident that she was making advances to Schelling— 'strong, rough, noble, intractable, like a French general', in Dorothea's words[284]—and that her husband either did not notice or chose not to notice. There were children milling around in the extended households, some to go on to greater things, like Philipp Veit, the Nazarene painter (and cousin of Felix Mendelssohn Bartholdy) or Dorothea Tieck, the Shakespeare translator, some whose lives were tragic, like Sophie Paulus or short, like Caroline's daughter Auguste Böhmer. There were compensations: Goethe, the god of their idolatry—'die alte göttliche Excellenz'[285]—was gracious and gave sound advice to the editors of the *Athenaeum*. Ludwig Tieck in December of 1799 read his drama *Genoveva* to a spellbound Goethe who was still working on his *Faust*, in its way also a 'romantic tragedy'. Schiller they did not visit, and they affected indifference to the first performance of his *Wallenstein* in Weimar, while the whole group fell out of their chairs with laughter at his *Lied von der Glocke* [Song of the Bell].[286] Later, the group would add Schiller's *Macbeth* translation to its objects of ridicule, for how could someone with so little English presume to such heights? Yet Schiller's *Macbeth* has its moments, and it is at least better than the *Macbeth* that Schlegel never got round to doing.

It was all very well to poke fun at Schiller's old-fashioned and homespun views on the family and its traditional hierarchies (August Wilhelm had already parodied the even more crass *Würde der Frauen* [Women's Worth]), considering that the same Schlegel was prepared to exalt the identical domestic virtues when they were formulated by Goethe, in his reverential review of *Hermann und Dorothea*. Were Fichte's views on the role of women more progressive? Hardly. Was not Friedrich Schlegel luxuriating in Dorothea's devoted submission (while not averse to a *petite*

---

282 *Caroline*, I, 564.
283 *Ibid.*, 569; KA, XXV, 18.
284 *Ibid.*, 17.
285 *Ibid.*, 23, 26.
286 *Caroline*, I, 570.

amie on the side), setting her to work as a translator (for that is what literate women did),[287] even publishing her novel *Florentin* in his own name when it came out in 1801 (in many ways a better read than *Lucinde*)? What of Novalis's, for his time, unexceptionable child bride, Sophie von Kühn,[288] now mystically transformed with death fantasies and visions in *Hymnen an die Nacht*, the last major work in the *Athenaeum*? At her death she was hardly older than Caroline's Auguste (fourteen), who the malicious believed was to be 'procured' for Schelling?[289] At least Caroline knew what she wanted, a lustier man and one who would free her from the treadmill of being her husband's secretary. Everyone seems to have known except August Wilhelm himself. He maintained excellent outward relations with Schelling, the man who was in reality cuckolding him.[290]

There would be those, like Goethe when later less well-disposed to the Romantics, who drew conclusions from the *Athenaeum* or from *Lucinde* about their views on love and marriage. What was one to expect when Friedrich Schlegel in a fragment declared nearly all marriages to be but concubinage?[291] Yet that same journal found (qualified) praise for Mary Wollstonecraft, even (from Schleiermacher) a celebration of love in marriage.[292] Clearly an experimental journal was not intended to establish guidelines for marital behaviour, any more than Schleiermacher's important essay of 1799 on social decorum and the balance of discourse (*Versuch einer Theorie des geselligen Betragens* [An Essay on the Theory of Social Behaviour]) was a prescription for real gregarious behaviour. It said nothing about the realities of communal living, the debts that Friedrich and Dorothea had run up (selling their 'meubles' to Fichte), the real quarrels, the bitterly cold Jena winter that caused Ludwig Tieck to go down with a rheumatic complaint from which he never recovered, effectively ruining his health. In an alarmingly frank letter to his sister Sophie in Berlin he reduced the whole Jena circle to a 'pigsty'.[293] For his part, August Wilhelm wrote a poem lampooning Tieck's 'free-loading' tendencies,[294] for everyone was expected to contribute to a common exchequer and not all did.

---

287 *KA*, XXV, 63.
288 Kluckhohn, *Auffassung*, 465.
289 *Caroline*, I, 755f.
290 *KA*, XXV, 65.
291 *Athenaeum*, I, ii, 187f.
292 *Ibid.*, II, ii, 312f.
293 Gotthold Klee, 'Ein Brief Ludwig Tiecks aus Jena vom 6. Dezember 1799', *Euphorion*, 3. Ergänzungsheft (1897), 211-215, ref. 212.
294 Josef Körner, 'Romantiker unter sich. Ein Spottgedicht A. W. Schlegels auf L. Tieck', *Die Literatur* 26 (1923), 271-273, ref. 272.

The First Strains

What now held the *Athenaeum* circle together intellectually and emotionally was less the celebration of a 'good cause' than an embattled gathering of ranks against an increasingly hostile reading public, both in Jena and outside. We need however to see all this in perspective. The literary feuds of the years 1795 to about 1803—and we are not concerned here with rehearsing all of their tiresome and repetitive details—were just that: literary. They were a Battle of the Books brought up to date. They bore only the most tenuous of links with those seditious political *libelles* that both scandalized and delighted pre-Revolutionary France or with the hurly-burly of Grub Street in London. Goethe and Schiller in their *Horen* had wanted to be above the political fray. The most political contribution to their journal, Goethe's *Literarischer Sansculottismus*, used a word charged with political associations to make a point about literature and its national, classical status. The *Xenien* waged war inside the Republic of Letters, while the *Athenaeum* steered clear of politics altogether, at most wrapping its historical and social discourse in poetry and myth. This was all to change once the Romantics had dispersed, the Schlegel brothers to France, and especially after 1806, when poetry and art would be invoked to counter the humiliations visited by Napoleon on the German nation. But one is tempted to adapt Heinrich Heine's later *mot* that the *Xenien*—and by extension the Romantics' literary polemics—were but the 'Kartoffelkrieg' (the 'potato war', the popular name for the War of the Bavarian Succession, when the armies never fired a shot) before the great political events supervened.[295]

As it was, the case of Fichte showed what could happen when one was perceived to be a threat to church, state and public morals, and August Wilhelm, among all his literary attainments also a professor, had no wish to be thus tainted. His poem of homage to the royal house of Prussia was opportunistic enough, but writing a sonnet to Bonaparte in 1800 (and in Italian) for his friend Friedrich Tieck to hand to the First Consul in Paris, was keeping one's political options very wide open indeed.[296] It was in fact

---

[295] Heinrich Heine, *Säkularausgabe*, hg. von den Nationalen Forschungs- und Gedenkstätten der klassischen deutschen Literatur in Weimar und dem Centre National de la Recherche Scientifique in Paris, 27 vols (Berlin: Akademie-Verlag; Paris: Éditions du CNRS, 1970-), XX, 385.

[296] Josef Körner, 'Neues von August Wilhelm und Caroline Schlegel', *Zeitschrift für Bücherfreunde* NF 17 (1925), 143-145, ref. 144; Barbara Besslich, *Der deutsche Napoleon-Mythos. Literatur und Erinnerung 1800-1945* (Darmstadt: Wissenschaftliche Buchgesellschaft, 2007), 52f.

the threat of disapproval from on high that first nerved him into polemical action. The hack-writer Garlieb Merkel had spread a rumour that Duke Carl August had reprimanded the editors of the *Athenaeum*.[297] August Wilhelm had sixty copies of a sonnet rushed off the press in which the originator of the canard found his name rhymed with 'Ferkel' [swine].[298] Friedrich Nicolai's *roman à clef Vertraute Briefe von Adelheid B** an ihre Freundinn Julie S*** [Private Letters of Adelheid B** to her Friend Julie S**] of 1799 was also one of the first anti-Romantic voices, but then again Nicolai had been writing satirical novels for decades about things that he did not like. Already in 1799 the Romantics in Jena and Berlin had a foretaste of more scurrilous lampoons when Daniel Jenisch in his *Diogenes Laterne*, with singular nastiness, caricatured Friedrich and Schleiermacher for their association with Jewish women (Dorothea and Henriette Herz, respectively).

It was different when their opponent was August von Kotzebue, Germany's—Europe's—most-performed dramatist (the *Athenaeum* carried a report on a performance in Paris).[299] He was also its most disliked. Unscrupulous, treacherous, servile to princes—the attributes which eventually earned him the assassin's knife—Kotzebue captured Europe's stages through a mixture of sentiment and dubious morality. It says much that the German Romantics' aversion was also shared by Coleridge.[300] August Wilhelm did not care much for Kotzebue's nearest rival Iffland either, with the actor-producer's well-attested penchant for young men; but Iffland was a Shakespearean actor and must be cultivated. Kotzebue had a history of calumniations, and to these he now added Friedrich Schlegel. It was Kotzebue in satirical and largely non-offensive mode, for his play, *Der hyperboräische Esel* [The Hyperboreal Ass] (1799) featured a young man who, to everyone's consternation, quoted passages verbatim from the *Athenaeum* and from *Lucinde*. Friedrich Schlegel should of course never be quoted out of context, and this Kotzebue knew. It was not good for the Romantics' self-esteem to know that this lampoon was being performed with some success in Leipzig; even worse to learn that Schütz, the editor of the *Allgemeine Literatur-Zeitung*, had had it performed in his own house in

---

297 KA, XXV, 11, 377, 381.
298 SW, II, 201; Friedrich Daniel Ernst Schleiermacher, *Kritische Gesamtausgabe*, ed. Hans-Joachim Birkner and Gerhard Ebeling, 22 vols in 5 sections (Berlin, New York: de Gruyter, 1980- in progress), V, iii, 227.
299 *Athenaeum*, II, ii, 321.
300 Samuel Taylor Coleridge, *Lectures 1808-1819 On Literature*, ed. Reginald Foakes, 2 vols (*The Collected Works of STC*, Bollingen Series, LXXV, 5) (Princeton: Princeton UP; London: Routledge & Kegan Paul, 1987), I, 514.

Jena, but a few streets away.[301] It led August Wilhelm abruptly to end his association with the *Literatur-Zeitung*, a relationship that had been strained to breaking-point more than once already. His swansong for it had been a review of Tieck's translation of *Don Quixote*, an act of friendship but also part of the Romantics' elevation of Cervantes to classical status.[302] His response to Kotzebue, his piece of 'devilment' as he called it, would have to wait until the end of 1800.

Schlegel owed much to the *Allgemeine Literatur-Zeitung*, and he had given much to it in his turn. At its best, it had a wide distribution (2,000 subscribers) and had maintained high standards of writing, as opposed to specialised scholarly discourse; and it had been a major force in the dissemination of Kant. For all Schlegel's later strained relationship with the *Allgemeine Literatur-Zeiltung*, and his acrimonious correspondence with Schütz, its co-editor, it had been Schiller's anonymous review of Bürger in the journal that had first brought Schlegel's name before a discerning reading public. He in his turn had taken over most of the journal's belles-lettres reviewing, including the pieces on Voss and *Hermann und Dorothea*, and to make his point, he listed all of these reviews in the *Athenaeum*.[303] It was time to free himself from the tutelage of editors and 'house style': the *Athenaeum* placed no such constraints upon its reviewers.[304] Things were not helped when Ludwig Ferdinand Huber, Caroline's erstwhile friend from Mainz days,[305] did an unflattering anonymous review, first of the *Athenaeum*, then of *Lucinde*, in the *Allgemeine Literatur-Zeitung*. Schlegel initially considered seeking redress from Schütz through the courts, only to be told by Goethe that such 'public recriminations' were forbidden by decree.[306]

As it was, Schlegel was no longer interested in piecemeal reviewing. Both he and Fichte came up with ideas, with slightly different emphases,

---

301 Rainer Schmitz (ed.), *Die ästhetische Prügeley. Streitschriften der antiromantischen Bewegung* (Göttingen: Wallstein, 1992), 318; Heinz Härtl, '"Athenaeum"-Polemiken', in: *Dahnke and Leistner*, I, esp. 292-357; Steffens, *Was ich erlebte*, IV, 264; *Caroline*, I, 577-580, 749f.
302 *SW*, XI, 427-430; *Briefe*, I, 99f.
303 *Athenaeum*, III, i, [165-168].
304 Stefan Matuschek, 'Epochenschwelle und prozessuale Verknüpfung. Zur Position der *Allgemeinen Literatur-Zeitung* zwischen Aufklärung und Frühromantik', in: Stefan Matuschek (ed.), *Organisation der Kritik*. Die Allgemeine Literatur-Zeitung *in Jena 1785-1803* (Heidelberg: Winter, 2004) 9-11.
305 *Caroline*, I, 577-580.
306 *Goethes Briefwechsel mit Christian Gottlob Voigt*, II, 452; *KA*, XXV, 459.

for a so-called *Kritisches Institut*, a review journal that would reflect a more systematic ordering of knowledge and would accommodate the various encyclopaedic ambitions that the Jena circle entertained.[307] These *Jahrbücher der Wissenschaft und Kunst für Deutschland* [Yearbooks of Science and the Arts] were without doubt the most ambitious plan to emanate from Jena. Its editorial board was to consist of both Schlegel brothers, Schleiermacher, Schelling, Tieck, and August Ferdinand Bernhardi, the Berlin schoolman and husband of Sophie Tieck, who was proving himself useful as an editor and reviewer. The break-up of the Jena circle put paid to the project. It would in any case have been difficult to tie some of its editorial board down, notably Tieck, who had promised contributions for the *Athenaeum* and had never delivered. Schlegel, for his part, was to find himself setting out the order and subdivisions of knowledge, not in a review journal, but in his lectures in Jena and Berlin.

Dorothea Veit rightly sensed that the *Allgemeine Literatur-Zeitung* affair simply consumed misspent energy.[308] Even as the Jena circle began to dissolve, it was augmented by the young Clemens Brentano, a 'witty scatterbrain',[309] caught between the study of medicine and his real avocation of poetry. The last part of the *Athenaeum* appeared in March of 1800. It was, as it turned out, a symbolic closure, if memorable for the *Gespräch über die Poesie* and the *Hymnen an die Nacht*. Caroline then fell seriously ill. Dorothea, a shrewd, although hardly objective observer of humanity and its frailties, tried to be even-handed towards her sister-in-law. Despite the differences in their personalities and backgrounds, Caroline had been the first to recognize Dorothea publicly and to ensure her acceptance in Jena circles. She conceded to Caroline wit and spirit, but no understanding of art (she had clearly not read *Die Gemälde*). August Wilhelm, she continued, had not been an easy partner to live with, but he loved Caroline after his own fashion and in a way that she never did in return. She had never been open about her relationship with Schelling, who had kept up a front of politeness to August Wilhelm while disliking him in private.[310] Was August Wilhelm 'surfeitet, preoccupied or blind? 'All three'.[311] What is more, he had been affectionate to his step-daughter Auguste in his own avuncular style while not noticing how little this was in reality reciprocated.

---

307 *KA*, XXV, 33-38, 58f., 419; *SW*, VIII, 50-57.
308 *KA*, XXV, 18.
309 *Ibid.*, 76.
310 *Ibid.*, 109.
311 *Ibid.*, 116.

The Death of Auguste Böhmer

The events of the spring and summer of 1800 throw light on human relationships and emotional entanglements, but also on the sheer precariousness of life itself at the turn of the eighteenth to the nineteenth century. Caroline's illness,[312] described as 'Nervenfieber', the catch-all name for dysenteric infections, refused to improve. Christoph Wilhelm Hufeland, the great Jena doctor and father of macrobiotics, treated her according to his tried and conventional methods, but Schelling, who in addition to the nature philosophy that he professed also had some knowledge of medicine, insisted that Hufeland try the fashionable therapeutics of the Brownian method. Brownism or Brunonism, named after the Scottish doctor John Brown,[313] saw health as the median state of excitability, based on the fundamental doctrine of life as a state of excitation produced by external agents upon the body, and perceived disease as consisting in excess or deficiency of such stimulants. Novalis was also a Brownian. His recommendation to Tieck that he try 'electricity, guaiacum, tafia, acids and mercurial substances' for his rheumatism[314] was essentially Brownist but also typical of the insouciance with which contemporaries passed on their patent cures, or doctors sent prescriptions without first having seen the patient.

Caroline did not respond to counter-stimulants. It was agreed that she should take the waters in Bad Bocklet in Franconia, known for their curative qualities for women's complaints; while Schelling, to acquaint himself further with Brownian medicine, should go to nearby Bamberg to study. An elaborate charade was set up, with Schelling leaving first for Saalfeld, a convenient half-way house. On May 5, Caroline and Auguste left, accompanied as far as Saalfeld by Schlegel, after which they were to proceed independently to Bamberg. Schlegel returned to Jena, taking a detour via Leipzig, while Schelling, of course, was waiting in Saalfeld and saw Caroline and Auguste to quarters in Bamberg. Early in July, all three of them were in Bocklet, the Paulus family from Jena also. There was no

---

312 Documentation in: Wulf Segebrecht *et al.*, *Romantische Liebe und romantischer Tod. Über den Bamberger Aufenthalt von Caroline Schlegel, Auguste Böhmer, August Wilhelm Schlegel und Friedrich Wilhelm Schelling im Jahre 1800*, Fussnoten zur Literatur, 48 (Bamberg: Universität Bamberg, 2001).
313 Cf. John Neubauer, 'Dr. John Brown (1735-88) and Early German Romanticism', *Journal of the History of Ideas* 28 (1967), 367-382, esp. 372f.
314 *HKA*, IV, 521f.

secrecy, for on 6 July Schelling wrote to Schlegel that Auguste had taken ill. The words 'Ruhr' and 'Nervenfieber' were used, indicating diarrhoea. Schelling apparently used Brownian methods, including the standard stimulant of opium, to try to bring her back to health. It was to no avail. On 12 July, 1800 she died, aged 15. She was buried in the churchyard at Bocklet. One will not find there either of the two monuments commissioned from sculptors of European rank in her memory and executed by both of them (Friedrich Tieck's is in Copenhagen, Schadow's is lost): she is only memorialised in poetry.

Caroline had buried her sole surviving child. She returned to Bamberg with Schelling, Schlegel hurrying there as soon as he heard the news.[315] He made a 'pilgrimage' to Auguste's grave, today a remote and romantic spot, for him then merely a country churchyard, 'narrow and mean'. It was in the territory of the prince-bishop of Würzburg and subject to Catholic jurisdiction. Very much later, at the distance of thirty-eight years, writing to Albertine de Broglie, Madame de Staël's daughter, he recalled seeking solace 'in an episcopal seat'[316] (Bamberg) and finding some consolation in the high mass performed there. The accident of this Franconian journey, calamitous for all who took part in it, had brought him to the same South German cultural landscape that Wackenroder and Tieck had already experienced in 1793, both of them Berlin Protestants brought face to face with the aesthetic splendours of the rite. For Schlegel, if one excludes Mainz in 1793, when visits to cathedrals were far from his mind, this was effectively the first visit to a Catholic environment (Dresden was decidedly Protestant apart from the Catholic court) where he could see 'religion majestically clad in its best finery, instead of the monotonous mourning that it wears in Protestant churches'.[317] We have no reason to doubt the genuineness of these sentiments as here expressed, and it may be that the sound and pomp was a distraction for his thoughts, rather than the meditative silence that churches may also offer. It was however a far cry from this brief soul-enrichment to the flirtations with Catholicism that his poems, issued in April 1800, evidenced and which were later, to his indignation, to nourish his alleged reputation as 'half-Catholic'.[318]

---

315 *Caroline*, I, 606f.
316 *Oeuvres de M. Auguste-Guillaume de Schlegel écrites en français*, ed. Édouard Böcking, 3 vols (Leipzig: Weidmann, 1846), I, 191.
317 *Ibid.*
318 *SW*, VIII, 220.

He had known all three of Caroline's children to various degrees. Therese Böhmer, who had died eleven years previously, he knew only at a distance. Poor little Julius Crancé had been briefly in his charge. Auguste he had loved as his own daughter and it was to him that the extended Jena circle expressed their condolences. Now was the time for his friends to recollect his genuine paternal affection, not to consider whether this had been on his side only. The brief notes to Auguste from her step-father and her step-uncle 'Fritz' that we have are documents of their time and as such are not safe indicators of feeling. Yet this stiff, formal, professorial man loved children and wished to have children of his own. It was the hope of founding a family after his *années de pèlerinage* with Madame de Staël that motivated his unhappy decision to marry in 1818. As it was, his affections had to be lavished on others' children, Willem Muilman, the Staëls, the Colebrooke and Johnston boys in Bonn, his niece Auguste von Buttlar, even his unfortunate nephew Johann August Adolph, and there is no doubt that Auguste de Staël and Albertine de Broglie, née Staël, later saw him as a kind of second father.

To Ludwig Tieck, who had now advanced to a closeness and intimacy that not even his unreliability and dilatoriness could shatter, Schlegel wrote of 'having saved up all his tears'.[319] To a grieving step-father one could not express doubts or reservations, but they did arise nevertheless, in the privacy of the correspondence between Friedrich and Dorothea. Novalis, writing to Friedrich, wondered whether there was not some causal link between Caroline's 'affair' and Auguste's passing, her turning back, Eurydice-like, at the threshold of life.[320] Dorothea, now making no secret of her detestation of Caroline, spelled this out, less poetically than Novalis, attributing the weakening of Auguste's system to the onset of the menarche.[321] Above all, she claimed, Schelling's quack doctoring had been a contributory cause, and Dorothea was certainly the source of this persistent and malicious allegation.[322]

Schelling returned alone to Jena. Caroline and Schlegel travelled to Gotha, where her close friend Luise Gotter took her in. From now on they journeyed together, even slept under the same roof. Their letters remained friendly and tolerant, as they had been all along; but the marriage was over.

---

319 Lohner, 45.
320 *HKA*, IV, 333.
321 *KA*, XXV, 162.
322 *Ibid.*, 146, 162.

From Gotha, they went to Brunswick, to allow Caroline to see her mother and sister. The Jena circle was effectively at an end. The Tiecks had left in June; Schelling continued as a professor, not in any close association with the Schlegel brothers, but not estranged from them either. The 'Kritisches Institut' foundered on differences between Fichte and Schelling. Friedrich Schlegel was beginning his brief and ill-starred career as 'Privatdozent' in philosophy in Jena, while his brother August Wilhelm continued to lecture there until the summer of 1801. But Jena, as a metonymic association of minds as they had known it, was over. Its last symbolic act was perhaps the publication of August Wilhelm's replique to Kotzebue, *Ehrenpforte und Triumphbogen für den Theater-Präsidenten von Kotzebue* [Gate of Honour and Triumphal Arch for the Theatre-Director von K.], printed, as the title page stated, 'at the beginning of the new century'. Yet it was only as Schlegel shook off these idle polemics, the irksome attendants of the Jena association, that he could turn, symbolically as well as in reality, to face the challenges of that new nineteenth century.

Elegies for the Dead and the Living

Even as the tears were drying on the letter that Schlegel wrote to Tieck from Bamberg on 14 September 1800, he was full of literary plans.[323] Ever aware that the emotional and the practical are two sides of the one person, he was in the same letter drafting a *Musen-Almanach* (with Cotta in Stuttgart, twelve sheets, at five Louisd'ors the sheet) that would eventually be the memorialisation of Auguste, so recently dead. He announced, also in the same letter, the *Ehrenpforte*, of which he was to be so inordinately proud and which would go on to take pride of place in his *Poetische Werke* in 1811. In a sense that had its justification, for it showed what he could do, and all in a comic vein: sonnets, ballads, romances, epigrams, plus the parody of a sentimental comedy, and what not. One senses his urge to display versatility and if need be virtuosity. It was part of a self-image that his autobiographical sketch of around 1811 sought to perpetuate. There, he characterized his poetic products by many-sided attainments, grace, lightness of touch, fire and emotion even, with virtuosic use of 'Harmonien'.[324] While still in the phase of co-writing the *Athenaeum* he had been already looking ahead to

---

323 Lohner, 45-49.
324 Cornelia Bögel, 'Fragment einer unbekannten autobiographischen Skizze aus dem Nachlass August Wilhelm Schlegels', *Athenäum*, 22 (2012), 165-180, ref. 173.

further critical endeavour, but in fact the *Charakteristiken und Kritiken*, as they were to become, were a restatement of what had been, brilliant some of it, it is true, rather than a fresh new venture. The only major new essay for that collection, the one on Bürger, was in so many ways a coming to terms with Schlegel's own personal development, his own poetic and critical persona from 1786 to 1800, a critical self-examination through the guise of biography.

Given this penchant towards self-projection (self-monumentalisation) at the turn of the new century, it may be instructive to see what at this stage he considered could stand and what should be discarded. The *Athenaeum*, which, as we saw, was for August Wilhelm a joint enterprise and only one of several undertakings, contained some short and more ephemeral pieces of comment and criticism by him that had little sense outside of their original context, and these he never re-edited. The large and substantial contributions, like *Die Gemälde*, went on to have a separate existence inside his oeuvre. The lectures that he gave in Jena seemed to have served if anything as drafts for later series in Berlin; but most of this material was never edited in his lifetime. The edition of his poems was, however, different, those *Gedichte von August Wilhelm Schlegel*, that came out in April of 1800. For this edition, Schlegel had turned, not to Vieweg or Frölich—good enough for the *Athenaeum*—but to the mighty Cotta in Tübingen, Goethe's and also Schiller's publisher.[325] This immediately gave him a certain cachet that his brother Friedrich's disparate works did not possess, or Tieck's, that is, if one took publisher's impress as any guide to status. Publication by Cotta was however not synonymous with success, as the recent examples of *Die Horen* and *Propyläen* and their early termination would show. Although the *Athenaeum* did contain certain of his more important poems, there was evidence that he was also writing poetry for a different audience, one more generally receptive and perhaps less aesthetically discriminating than the readership of an avant-garde periodical. It may be significant that when his *Gedichte* first appeared in 1800, copies were immediately sent to Duke Carl August, Goethe, and Schiller. First things first.[326]

The reader of this quarto volume in roman type (Cotta's house style) would remark that these poems were an unrepentant self-statement. Schlegel had not drawn a line under his youthful poems for the Göttingen

---

325 First approaches August 1799. *Briefe an Cotta. Das Zeitalter Goethes und Napoleons 1794-1815*, ed. Maria Fehling (Stuttgart, Berlin: Cotta, 1925), 256.
326 Wieneke, 101f.

Musen-Almanach, for they were here again in collected, edited form, the sonnet *An Bürger*, or the poem that had impertinently told Schiller to keep personalities out of his criticism; also more recent works, those long and ever so slightly dreary philosophical poems like *Pygmalion* or *Prometheus*, or that dedicatory poem to *Romeo and Juliet*, whose addressee, Caroline, had now left him, or a sonnet *An Schelling* (not an especially good one) that expressed Romantic solidarity rather than the non-poetic reality. Readers with some knowledge of the *Athenaeum* would have noted that the romance on St Luke, the patron saint of painting, that concluded *Die Gemälde*, was there, as well as the nine sonnets inspired by religious paintings in Dresden, but now augmented. The subject of one of these new poems, on St Sebastian, would hardly have qualified as a suitable subject for painting according to the criteria laid down in *Propyläen* by Goethe's arch-classicist acolyte in art matters, Heinrich Meyer.[327] Meyer would have been more affronted by that extraordinary hymn to the co-existence of the church and the arts, *Der Bund der Kirche mit den Künsten*, that here first saw the light of day. It would confirm the Catholicizing nature of those *Gemälde* conversations. The few hearers of Schlegel's university lectures would recognise a similar emphasis there on the civilising force of religion, together with the feudal system, as a factor in bringing about the efflorescence of poetry in the European Middle Ages. The inclusion of a cycle of six sonnets on the great Italian poets and of a further six on Cervantes, was also in keeping with the thrust of the *Athenaeum*, with Schlegel's own essay there on Flaxman's Dante, the long passage of Ariosto in translation, his slating of Soltau's version of *Don Quixote*, so different from his laudatory review of Tieck's translation in the *Allgemeine Literatur-Zeitung*.

That was only one side. This was a Romantic canon set out in poetry, that Friedrich's *Gespräch über die Poesie* was also adumbrating, here more formally and perhaps more accessibly. These poets, too, were the names that his Jena lectures were beginning to enshrine and that his Berlin lectures were to canonise. The sonnets were also, most of them, about fellow-sonneteers, and with them Schlegel was affirming but also extending widely his early discipleship of Bürger. There was even a sonnet called *Das Sonett* that was both a poetic and also a prosodic demonstration of the Petrarchan form.[328] Not all sonneteers were treated even-handedly. Paul Fleming, the seventeenth-century sonnet writer, was celebrated as an 'old

---
327 Cf. *Propyläen*, I, ii, 66f.
328 *SW*, I, 304.

German' poet, as part of the nation's heritage that the eighteenth century had wanted to deny and that was now beginning to be appreciated in terms of an organic continuity of poetry. Shakespeare's sonnets—themselves the subject of a Petrarchan, not a Shakespearean, sonnet—Schlegel found deficient, early 'mannered' poetry compared with the dramatist who could both cause suffering and also resolve it. Here spoke the same Schlegel who so eloquently praised the 'Petrarchan' *Romeo and Juliet* but who also shared the eighteenth century's indifference to Shakespeare's poetry.

But what were readers to make of the two long elegies that seemed to take up a disproportionate amount of space in the collection, *Neoptolemus an Diocles* and *Die Kunst der Griechen* [The Art of the Greeks]? The second of these poems they might know if they were also readers of the *Athenaeum*,[329] but the other one was new. Who was Neoptolemus? The classically educated would recognise that the 'young warrior' was another name for Pyrrhus, the son of Achilles. The reference to a long footnote made it clear that the Greek name stood for Schlegel's own brother Carl,[330] the Hanoverian lieutenant who had died in the service of the East India Company—the hated British— in 1789. Carl addresses his surviving younger brother, classical-style, from the land of the dead. One may guess at its motivation: the desire to commemorate the brother whom he had last seen as a schoolboy of fifteen. Also perhaps the wish to show the world that the Schlegels were not all bookmen, but men of action as well. For the generally elegiac tone of the poem does not exclude a certain expansiveness of detail, the raising of the Hanoverian regiment, the touching farewell scene, with his only mention of both of his parents:[331]

> Aber ich stürmte hinein, den letzten Moment zu verkürzen,
>   Heiß geschäftig, wo schon alle sie meiner geharrt.
> Brünstig segnete mich der fromm ehrwürdige Vater,
>   Schwestern hiengen an mir, Brüder umarmten mich fest.
> Aber vor allem die Mutter, die liebende Mutter! an ihrem
>   Herzen zerfloß ich, und wand, kaum noch besonnen, mich los.
> Wie ich mich innerlich schalt, mir sagte die ahnende Seele:
>   Nie mehr soll ich mit euch tauschen den innigen Gruß.
> Doch die Mutter ergriff ein unwiderstehliches Drängen,
>   Einmal ihn nur, den Sohn, noch den geliebten zu sehn.

---

329 *Athenaeum*, II, ii, 181-192.
330 Manger in Mix/Strobel, 89-91.
331 The poem is in *SW*, II, 13-20, ref. 15f.

Und sie machte sich auf, von bangenden Töchtern begleitet,
  Schaute vom Fenster am Platz, wo sich die Schaaren gereiht.
Bei den Gefährten stand ich, und, ob ich gleich sie bemerkte,
  Hob ich den Blick nicht auf, mich zu erweichen besorgt.
Viel durchlief ich die Reih'n beschleunigend, brachte Befehle
  Hin vom Führer und her, auf das Geschäft nur bedacht.
Schwang dann schnell mich zu Pferd, voreilend dem Zug, der begonnen,
  Und erst außen am Tor wandt' ich die Blicke noch heim.
Alles Trauren erstickte das muntere Spiel der Hoboen,
  Und der Morgengesang männlicher Kehlen darein.

[But I rushed inside, to shorten the time of leave-taking,
Found things to do, with everyone waiting for me.
My good pious father gave me his heartfelt blessing,
Sisters crowded around, brothers embracing me.
But our so loving mother, I broke down in tears on her bosom,
Only just tearing myself from her arms in confusion.
How I reproached myself later, for a sixth sense foretold me
Never again would I answer your dearest greetings.
But our mother could not hold back the urge that possessed her
Just to see her beloved son this once more.
She made her way, her daughters came with her,
Looked down on the square from the window, the ranks all assembled,
I stood with my brothers in arms, and though I could see her,
I never raised an eye, to preserve my composure.
I went through the lines and hurried them on, took orders,
Passed them on, immersing myself in military business,
Mounted my horse, taking the lead of the marching column,
And only looked homeward when we were outside the gate.
The fifes and drums drowned out any sad thoughts that I might have
And the song of the men who were greeting the morning.]

Then came the long ocean haul via Trinidad to pick up the trade winds for India, regimental service, explorations (facing down tigers), the study of Indian customs and religion, then Carl Schlegel's dishonouring, rehabilitation and death. All this in 198 verses of elegiac couplets. It is a good poem, almost the only one by him that breathes genuine feeling.

He may perhaps have sensed the need to compete with his ultimate rival. Goethe's elegy *Euphrosyne* of 1798 (and one of those that Goethe asked Schlegel to 'correct' metrically), more varied in structure than this poem, had also used the device of an address to the speaker by the commemorated dead. Above all it had combined the poetic with the real and autobiographical. Schlegel could not resist inserting a further link with the times, the 'Zeitgeist'. Carl Schlegel had died in the symbolic year 1789, and Neoptolemus in the elegy recalled how the political turmoil and chaos of the revolutionary years had brought ever more dead to join him in the realm of the shades. This, at least, would be a sentiment that could appeal to the Goethe of *Hermann und Dorothea*. It is not safe to see this poem as pointing to Schlegel the later Sanskrit scholar except in the sense that both Friedrich and August Wilhelm later were to cite their brother's name as part of their credentials, so to speak, their only real link with a country that never directly revealed its mysteries to them. In 1811, in its reissue in his re-named *Poetische Werke*, Schlegel separated his documentation (Carl's posthumous papers are lost) from his elegy and let it stand on its own poetic merits, leaving to the reader,[332] as Goethe did in *Euphrosyne*, to distinguish poetic truth from a more mundane reality. Schlegel of course would never have begun an elegy seemingly in mid-sentence, as *Euphrosyne* does. That was the privilege of genius.

Die Kunst der Griechen was but one of several testimonies from the *Athenaeum* years of 1798 to 1800 to the sedulous Romantic cult of Goethe. Even he knew that they were laying it on thickly, disingenuously assuring Schiller that it was 'only a literary relationship and not one of friendship'.[333] To other contemporaries in or visiting Weimar, like Herder or Wieland or Jean Paul, it seemed that the Romantics had subsumed modern German literature under the one sole name of Goethe (and themselves, of course).[334] The *Athenaeum* would have done little to disabuse them of that impression. Goethe was pleased with Schlegel's review of *Hermann und Dorothea* in the *Allgemeine Literatur-Zeitung* in 1798, a journal that had not seen fit to review *Wilhelm Meister*. It enshrined Goethe's work as the legitimate successor to the Homeric epic and applied the same categories and epithets to it: pure, perfect, simple, harmonious, natural. Like Homer's it was based on reality, it reflected the needs and concerns of its day (the background of revolutionary war and turmoil), and was thus truly national, close to the needs and aspirations of the people. Following the *Odyssey* (the *Iliad* rather less), it was also private and domestic, with characters who displayed a heart-warming sincerity and directness. As a renewal of Homer, it had

---

332 AWS, *Poetische Werke*, 2 parts (Heidelberg: Mohr und Zimmer, 1811), II, 293-295.
333 Schiller to Countess Schimmelmann 23 November 1800, Friedrich Schilller, *Werke. Nationalausgabe*, ed. Julius Petersen *et al.*, 42 vols (Weimar: Böhlau, 1943- in progress), XXX, 214.
334 Schmitz, *Die ästhetische Prügeley*, 274f.

an unforced epic tone, and its rhythm was unconstrained by any too punctilious adaptation of the ancient hexameter. *Hermann und Dorothea* was 'vaterländisch', and with that word Schlegel said more for Goethe's standing than the more abstract formulations of his brother.

This was the background to August Wilhelm's poem *Die Kunst der Griechen* that appeared in the second volume of the *Athenaeum*. It is as much a didactic poem in distichs as an elegy proper, for it rehearses at some considerable length the now lost world of Greece—mythology, art, poetry— with Goethe, 'the devotee of the Hellenic muse', as the consecrated high priest of its renewal. As such, it could apply equally to Goethe the reviver of Greek poetry and to the editor of the *Propyläen*. It is the same lost ancient world that Hölderlin's elegies of 1799-1800 summoned up, but without Schlegel's parade of knowledge or his systematic insistence on learning— and with infinitely more poetic power. At most one can say that Hölderlin's sense of loss leads to the hymnic visions of his late poetry, Schlegel's to the historical pessimism that informs his elegy *Rom* of 1805.

When reviewing *Die Horen* in 1796 August Wilhelm had already praised Goethe as the renewer of the Roman elegy.[335] Friedrich Schlegel, in his preface to *Elegien aus dem Griechischen* [Elegies from the Greek], their joint effort in the opening volume of the *Athenaeum*,[336] had reiterated this in fulsome terms that echoed his brother's vision of Shakespeare: 'dwelling amongst us'. Goethe's elegies had helped to redefine the genre: his renewal of Propertius did not involve the 'klagende Empfindsamkeit' [soulful complaint][337] that Schiller had recently claimed for the elegy in general (in keeping with *Athenaeum* practice, Schiller's name was not mentioned). Goethe's *Roman Elegies*, by contrast, had celebrated fulfilment in the here and now, as had his classical models, the old Latin 'triumvirs' (Propertius, Tibullus and Ovid). They did not however represent the sum of the elegiac tradition, and so Friedrich Schlegel reminded him of the thematic variety of the much less-known and imperfectly edited Greek elegy (all in extracts translated by August Wilhelm). A fragment of Phanokles, for instance, could show the 'naturalness' of Greek boy-love,[338] or Hermesianax the universal and not always auspicious power of Eros, or Callimachus a florid celebration of Pallas Athene bathing. These poems were learned

---

335 *SW*, X, 62.
336 *Athenaeum*, I, i, 107-112.
337 *Ibid.*, 108-110, ref. 110.
338 *Ibid.* 111f.

and replete with allusions: both Schlegels were very much at home in this world, classical philologists in effect,[339] ever so slightly parading their knowledge.[340] Goethe was distinctly less *au fait*. It was that philological, learned side of the Schlegel brothers, that has travelled rather less well. Nevertheless it formed part of their sense of poetic continuities, their ultimately Herderian awareness of the historical rhythms and patterns of rise and fall, efflorescence and decay, that record the Alexandrian desiccations (as here) as well as the new risings of sap. Such an exercise also appealed to August Wilhelm's prosodic punctiliousness as a translator from ancient languages.

It was one thing to exalt Goethe, but quite another to presume to correct his verse. It has always mildly scandalised Goethe scholarship that in 1799-1800 he allowed Schlegel to approach his epic and elegiac verse with a critical eye and permitted him to treat this poetry, not as a monument already cast, but (to adapt one of Schlegel's most famous images) as clay in the mass still being formed. It is also fair to say that Schlegel's reputation was at its lowest point when the extent of his 'interventions' became known in 1887 with the publication of the first volume of the Weimar edition. Goethe had an explanation. Reflecting over twenty years later, in *Campagne in Frankreich* (1822), he recalled the general laxity in the writing of hexameters when, as a distraction from the Revolutionary Wars of 1793, he first sat down to retell the story of Reynard the Fox in classical verse, as *Reineke Fuchs*. Schlegel, when in 1796 praising the first number of *Die Horen* and Goethe's *Roman Elegies* especially, had not hesitated to express some doubts about the verse and had even appended 'remarks of a prosodic nature' to his section on Schiller.[341] When Goethe's thoughts first turned seriously to revising his classical verse and making it metrically more correct, Schlegel immediately sprang to mind. Schlegel's review of the Propertius translation by Knebel (a close friend of Goethe) in the *Allgemeine Literatur-Zeitung* was a further reminder.[342] Schlegel had the added advantage of being on the spot; moreover the new professor in Jena

---

339 'virtuelle Altphilologen'. Joachim Wohlleben, 'Beobachtungen über eine Nicht-Begegnung Welcker und Goethe', in: William M. Calder III *et al.*, *Friedrich Gottlieb Welcker. Werk und Wirkung* [...], Hermes Einzelschriften, 49 (Stuttgart: Franz Steiner, 1986), 3-34, ref. 16.
340 Cf. Friedrich Beissner, *Geschichte der deutschen Elegie*, 3rd edn, Grundriss der germanischen Philologie, 14 (Berlin: de Gruyter, 1965), 162.
341 *SW*, X, 59-90, ref. 62.
342 *Ibid.*, 337-346.

included 'prosody' in his lectures on language and poetics.[343] During his visits to Jena in February, March to April, and September 1799, Goethe discussed with Schlegel his 'metrical doubts'; they took hour-long walks, a good stimulus for measuring rhythmical feet.

We are not concerned here with recording the full extent of Schlegel's suggestions, nor their details.[344] Goethe submitted for the other man's scrutiny his substantive poetic oeuvre from the 1790's, his three verse epics, *Reineke Fuchs*, *Hermann und Dorothea* and *Achilleis*, and all of the long elegies, including *Alexis und Dora* and *Euphrosyne*. The point has been made that, whether or not Goethe acted upon Schlegel's suggestions—on incorrect caesuras, spondees versus trochees, impure dactyls and the like—his revisions, where made, were done in the spirit of Schlegel's advice, if perhaps not always to the letter. It is also certain that they disagreed on the extent to which metre may have priority over sense. Goethe where possible allowed himself to be guided by the natural rhythm of the language rather than its purely metrical patterns.[345] All this needs to be said, as the later cooling of relations between the two men—their two schools of thought—did not make for objective comment. Goethe's later disrespectful remark about 'strict-observance metricists' came after the fiasco in Weimar with Schlegel's overly neoclassical verse play *Ion* and after Schlegel himself had seen his own protégé Wilhelm von Schütz descend into extreme areas of Graecizing verse. It is symptomatic of the low temperature between Goethe and Schlegel that Schlegel, when reissuing his review of Voss in 1828, could say openly in print that both Goethe and Schiller had been 'lax and negligent' in matters of metre and quantity.[346] Goethe's response was to publish the whole of his correspondence with Schiller—with all their remarks about Schlegel.

Schlegel's Contributions to the *Athenaeum*

All this might suggest a Schlegel grappling with a many-headed hydra of poetry, criticism, academic discourse and much else besides, grasping here metrics, there Renaissance painting, in another place a history of poetics, in yet another the contemporary literary scene. He himself saw none of

---

343 *KAV*, I, 33-46.
344 For these see John William Scholl, 'August Wilhelm Schlegel and Goethe's Epic and Elegiac Verse', *Journal of English and Germanic Philology* 7, iii (1907-08), 61-98, iv, 54-86.
345 Scholl, iv, 80.
346 *SW*, X, 184.

these activities in isolation. He never put himself into compartments. All areas of endeavour had their place but were also interdependent: philology and antiquarian scholarship, the creative use of language in translation, art appreciation, the writing of poetry (yes, even this). It was a style that he had developed earlier in the decade: his lecture-like letters to Friedrich, for instance, replete with prosodic detail, were intended in the last analysis to raise his brother's awareness of the subtleties of the Greek language and its poetry.

There were underlying principles that linked and combined and gave mutual enlightenment to the different strands of endeavour. They could be expressed as a philosophical principle, referring all art forms to an original ideal or model, from which all else emanated, a neo-platonic (or Hemsterhuisian) notion of beauty, the outward manifestation seen as but a mirror image of the inner. These notions informed the staid verses of those didactic or poetological poems, *Prometheus* or *Pygmalion*, of which Schlegel was so proud.[347] Or, drawing on Fichte's more recent philosophy, he could advance the hypothesis that notions of beauty and art do not exist outside of the human mind ('Geist').[348] It is there, in humankind, that the absolute is posited, and it follows that if art is an absolute purpose of mankind, it is in the mind of man or woman that we should seek it. This, too, would guarantee its autonomy and also the validity and truthfulness of human feelings.

Thus one could underwrite central tenets of the *Athenaeum*: the unity of the art forms in time and space, never seen in isolation, the interdependence of their functions, whether simultaneous (like the plastic arts) or successive (like poetry or music); or their 'progressive' quality, seen in terms of the development of human speech and gesture into rhythm, then musical expression, and finally into myth;[349] or in the more modern sense of a freedom from notions of achieved perfection ('classical') and a shift to notions of process, a striving towards new forms of expression with a new mythology undergirding them ('modern').[350] All this need not be expressed abstractly: that 'ideological' poem about the unity of the arts under the aegis of the church, for instance, was historically anchored in the Middle Ages but it also had an inner dynamic that linked past, present and future.

Schlegel had formulated these ideas in the lectures that he gave at Jena. They were not however generally available outside of that narrow academic

---

347 Manger in Mix/Strobel, 85-90.
348 *KAV*, I, i, 128f.
349 Jesinghaus, 24-36.
350 *KAV*, I, i, 109f.

circle. His hearers may in any case not have been aware of the extent of his borrowings from existing material. An example was his use of his *Horen* essay as the source for his notions on language, not substantially altered. His ideas on euphony and musicality in language drew on his opening contribution to the *Athenaeum*, *Die Sprachen* [The Languages]. Sections on Greek poetry had been copied straight from his brother Friedrich. The passage on Shakespeare was little advance on Eschenburg. He did refer by name to his brother's essay on *Wilhelm Meister*, but he had *Don Quixote* in mind when he identified 'situation' (Friedrich's key term) as the structural principle behind that novel.[351]

It means, as said, that we cannot easily subdivide the output of the *Athenaeum* years into poetry, journalistic discourse and criticism, and systematic statements of knowledge. All contain elements of the others. Take poetry. A didactic poem like *Die Kunst der Griechen* [The Art of the Greeks] was both a threnody for a lost past and also a statement positing the centrality of Greek culture for a post-classical age. It could also point beyond all this to the living, present and 'progressive' example of Goethe. The sonnets in *Die Gemälde* were miniature analyses of paintings in their own right and extended the canon of what the viewer endowed with modern sensitivities must see. Or criticism. Schlegel's review of Parny's mock-heroic epic *La Guerre des dieux* [The War of the Gods] in the *Athenaeum* in 1799[352] indulged the by now ritual denigration of things French and was as such a step towards its 'classic' formulation in *Comparaison entre la Phèdre de Racine et celle d'Euripide* of 1807. It also prefigured Schlegel's remarks on Aristophanes, his 'brawling chaos' or 'absolute subjective freedom', that he set out in his lectures in Jena, Berlin and Vienna.

He never further developed the seemingly 'throw-away' remark that the clash of mythologies would provide an excellent subject for a Romantic tragedy, but two dramatists who deferred to him, Friedrich de la Motte Fouqué and Zacharias Werner, were later to seize on it. His translation of the eleventh canto of Ariosto's *Orlando Furioso* in the 1799 issue of the *Athenaeum*, so agreeable to read and in such impeccable *ottava rima*, was a reminder of his linguistic versatility but also of the sheer hard grind of translating (one canto was enough). At the same time he was linking the art of good translation—his own, Tieck's of *Don Quixote* and eventually Gries's of Ariosto—to the notion of a Romance, 'Romantic' canon of poetry,

---

351 *Ibid.*, 113f.
352 *Athenaeum*, III, ii, 252-268; *SW*, XII, 92-106.

equal, in some respects superior, to the ancients, from a golden age when chivalry and legend, folk tradition and piety blended into a national literature. Friedrich Schlegel, too, while editing the 1799 and 1800 numbers of the *Athenaeum*, had privately been catching up on his reading of the sixteenth and seventeenth-century Italian and Spanish classics. His brother meanwhile in his university lectures in Jena was setting out the notion of a modern, 'Romantic' literature that was not fixed in the past like its classical forebears, but was 'progressive', active, self-renewing.

If one were nevertheless to select Schlegel's major achievements from the *Athenaeum* years that were also contributions to the periodical itself, the choice must fall on the piece that inaugurated the whole enterprise in 1798, *Die Sprachen*, and the two pieces of art criticism that provided the substantial copy for 1799, *Die Gemälde* [The Paintings] and *Über Zeichnungen zu Gedichten und John Flaxmans Umrisse* [On Drawings for Poems and John Flaxman's Outlines]. Both *Die Sprachen* and *Die Gemälde* were cast in the form of conversations, the 'causerie', the social exchange that set positions one against each other, while a lightness of touch avoided all too learned and technical details or too dogmatic conclusions. That at least was the theory: not all eighteenth-century 'entretiens' achieved it. One knew it from Lessing, from Hemsterhuis, from *Die Horen*—and now from Klopstock. For the full title of *Die Sprachen* was *Ein Gespräch über Klopstocks grammatische Gespräche* [A Conversation About Klopstock's Conversations on Grammar] (later altered, more aggressively, to *Der Wettstreit der Sprachen* [The Contest of the Languages]).[353]

Klopstock, whose *Der Messias* [The Messiah] in twenty cantos had once ranked just below the Bible in general esteem, had seen a slump in his reputation in the 1790s. In the old days, as Schlegel's old mentor Heyne wrote to him in 1798, one would have been in serious trouble if had one written about Klopstock in the disrespectful tone now adopted a younger generation.[354] It needs to be said that these young people were generally allergic to Klopstock, the 'sacred singer'. There was an element of rivalry in all this, a break with paternal authority, challenging their father Johann Adolf's old friend but also those avid Klopstockians Bürger and Voss. For August Wilhelm, Dante had seemed preferable, despite his eccentric theology. At least the characters in the *Inferno* had flesh and blood. True, much offended the sensitivities (Ugolino, for instance), but it was

---

353 *Athenaeum*, I, i, 3-69; *SW*, VII, 197-268.
354 *Briefe*, I, 75.

preferable to the exsangious creations of *Der Messias* (and by extension, his model, Milton).

Klopstock had once had a revolutionary effect on the German poetic language—that could not be denied—but now he was using his authority as a divine bard to pronounce on the qualities of the German language in general. For in 1794 Klopstock had surprised everyone by issuing his various ideas on language, as *Grammatische Gespräche*. Its two major reviewers were, not surprisingly, Schlegel and Voss. Some would have feared the worst, for Klopstock was emerging from a 'Bardic' phase, de-Graecising some of his best poems while re-germanising them (including the hymn in which Johann Adolf Schlegel had made his brief appearance, now translating him to the 'grove of Thuiskon') and celebrating the exploits of Hermann/Arminius.[355] The tone of the *Grammatische Gespräche* was stridently anti-French (that is, against Frederick the Great's French-language hegemony), and Klopstock was contorting the German language to create Germanic grammatical terms, as opposed to Latin ones. There was therefore much that Schlegel did not like: Klopstock's 'permissive' use in the hexameter of trochees instead of spondees; his *idée fixe* with brevity ('Kürze') as the chief virtue of the poetic language, not least of German.[356] German for him in many ways 'outdid' Greek. Much of the *Grammatische Gespräche* was devoted to sample translations from the Greek and Latin to prove this very point.[357]

Schlegel, of course, could also do that sort of thing when pressed, but unlike Klopstock he never set up hypotheses—on language of all things— without the necessary philological and historical foundation. For there were absurdities in Klopstock, not least his imagined link between Greek and German (fanciful ideas involving the Thracian Getae). This Schlegel could easily rectify. If one wanted brevity, better examples could be found in Aeschylus rather than in Homer, on whom Klopstock seemed to be fixated. Above all he challenged Klopstock's one-sided patriotism, setting against it the general point that all languages have the potential for melody and poetic utterance. True, English and French had their limits as poetic languages, but Italian certainly did not.

Reissuing this conversation in 1828, over a generation later, Schlegel was inclined to conciliation. Himself now aware of the status of his own

---

355 Friedrich Gottlieb Klopstock, *Werke und Briefe. Historisch-kritische Ausgabe*, ed. Horst Gronemeyer *et al.*, 21 vols in 25 (Berlin: de Gruyter, 1974- in progress), I, i, 29.
356 *SW*, VII, 244.
357 Schlegel nevertheless later (1827) compares versions of *Aeneid* VI, 847-853 ('Excudent alii spirantia mollius aera […]') by Klopstock, Voss, and himself. It hardly needs saying that all three manage these seven verses in seven German hexameters.

critical writings as monuments of good style, he praised Klopstock as one of the great German prose writers, nowhere better than in the *Grammatische Gespräche*. He could now see much in perspective: Klopstock's xenophobia had been but a passing phase, quite different from his genuine patriotism. Klopstock had also lived in an age unfazed by manifest improbabilities, happily linking druids and bards, German and Celt, Greek and Goth as one linguistic community. We (1828) knew better, especially since the appearance of Jacob Grimm's comparative grammar. This in its turn was an olive branch to the same Grimm whom Schlegel had exquisitely torn to pieces in his massive review of 1815.[358] Klopstock's main fault had been to set aside the rules of Greek and Latin prosody and their quantitative system and to base classical verse in German on the accent, not on the quantity. He would now learn that the great mother language, Sanskrit, followed Greek, Gothic perhaps as well (had its poetry survived). In 1820, but addressing the specialist audience of his fellow-Sanskritists and linguisticians in his *Indische Bibliothek*,[359] Schlegel had been yet more even-handed towards Klopstock, to Goethe and Schiller also, knowing that neither Klopstock nor Schiller were alive to appreciate this irenic gesture. Seen in these terms, *Die Sprachen* of 1798 came at the beginning of a long process of learning and assimilation of knowledge that was to eventually occupy much of his time in Madame de Staël's household and form the basis of his later career as a university professor in Bonn.

The Essays on Art

Caroline had seen no reason why *Die Gemälde*,[360] that conversation on painting, should not go to Goethe's *Propyläen*. It was both a shrewd and a naïve remark. The objections to youthful enthusiasms raised in that periodical's prologue had not been directed against the Schlegel brothers, who as yet had no art criticism to show for themselves, but at Wackenroder and Tieck, who did. It was at their door—and much later at Friedrich

---

358 *SW*, XII, 383-426.
359 *Indische Bibliothek*, I (1820), 40-46, esp. 42f.
360 *Athenaeum*, II, i, 39-151; *SW*, IX, 3-101 (minus the poems). For remarks of relevance on *Die Gemälde* see Margaret Stoljar, *Athenaeum: A Critical Commentary*, Australian and New Zealand Studies in German Language and Literature, 4 (Berne and Frankfurt am Main: Herbert Lang, 1973), 53-76; Claudia Becker, 'Bilder einer Ausstellung. Literarische Bildkunstkritik in A. W. Schlegels *Gemälde*-Gespräch', in: Paul Gerhard Klussmann *et al.* (eds), *Das Wagnis der Moderne. Festschrift für Marianne Kesting* (Frankfurt am Main etc.: Peter Lang, 1993), 143-155; Lothar Müller in *Die Gemählde* (1996), 165-196.

Schlegel's—that Goethe was to lay the blame for the 'Catholicizing, neo-germanising' art that so displeased him in the first decade and a half of the nineteenth century. His outburst in 1817 (or rather, Heinrich Meyer's) only made brief mention of August Wilhelm and then only of those slightly compromising poems on Christian art. *Die Gemälde* was different: it was not like Wackenroder and Tieck, writing uncritically and even hagiographically about artists. It still had its gaze firmly fixed on the works of art themselves and the things to be observed as one stood in front of them. Only after this necessary analysis did the discourse merge into poetic utterance. Whether *Die Gemälde* could be accommodated in *Propyläen*, a periodical whose aim was to bring some system, some order, some terminological clarity, into matters of artistic taste and practice, was to say the least questionable.

There were of course agreements here and there. They had similar views on the Laocoön group, and both accorded faint praise to Diderot's discursive *Salon*. They all accepted Winckelmann's position on Greek statuary: that one must penetrate beyond the outer surface to its 'heart' and essential inner 'repose'. But there were also immediate differences between the Romantics and Goethe. *Die Gemälde* placed painting, not sculpture, in the centre and thus reversed Winckelmann's order of priorities. There were disparaging remarks on neo-classical landscape, Claude and Poussin, especially on Philipp Hackert, Goethe's much-revered colleague from Italian days. Moreover it is worth noting that *Die Gemälde* had much to say about schools of Italian painting (Venetian, Bolognese, Tuscan) about which Goethe when a traveller in Italy had not been universally enthusiastic (or so he was later to aver).

Above all, *Die Gemälde* was cast around a gallery walk by informed— highly informed—cognoscenti[361] who knew their Vasari and their Fiorillo, who were nevertheless not art historians (insofar as this term existed), whose eyes were caught by what they related to, and that was the power in a painting to produce emotion and to give that emotion poetic expression. Their remarks reflected existing hierarchies within art discourse or engaged with these. Historical painting ranked as superior to landscape or seascape, genre or still life. Venetian, Bolognese, and French schools stood in that order of esteem. Generally these connoisseurs followed their own dictates and looked or overlooked as they chose. If that meant more Venetians and almost no Dutch, well and good. They were dependent on

---

361 Sulger-Gebing, *Die Brüder Schlegel*, 59; Wilhelm Waetzoldt, 'August Wilhelm und Friedrich Schlegel', in: WW, *Deutsche Kunsthistoriker*, 2 vols (Berlin: Spiess, 1986 [1921, 1924]), I, 233-241.

eighteenth-century attributions, so that praise was lavished on a Holbein that was but a copy or on a 'Leonardo', even then considered dubious, that is now certainly a Holbein.³⁶²

Who actually wrote *Die Gemälde*? The question of authorship arose in 1828 when Schlegel finally admitted that a large part had been written by 'a clever woman'. The dialogue and the poems he had written, the descriptions of paintings were by the said lady.³⁶³ That had been the division of labour over the *Romeo and Juliet* essay of 1797. One can draw inferences from the respective contributions of the three interlocutors in the conversation: Louise, generally accepted as being Caroline herself, Waller, who is August Wilhelm, and Reinhold, a kind of collective figure for the remaining friends. Certainly Louise's participations bulk large in the general scheme of the work. Of course Friedrich, Schelling and Novalis had their own views, Novalis noting that 'The art gallery is a storehouse of all kinds of indirect stimuli for the poet'.³⁶⁴ They all shared the conversations' general emphasis on the interrelation and interdependence of the art forms, the ability of language adequately to express the 'spirit' of the work of art (not mere description), the power of a piece of sculpture or a painting to collapse the borders between poetry and music, to produce 'Übergänge' (transitions, transgressions).

First, there was a brief look at sculpture. Waller summed up the general consensus—quoting Herder or Hemsterhuis in all but name—that statuary was not a mere question of shape or contour or mass or repose. It was also 'in movement', 'organic', a 'beseelte Einheit' [a unity with life and soul], and that was almost to a word what August Wilhelm would be telling his student audience in Jena in 1799-1800.³⁶⁵ It was also related to Goethe's remarks in *Propyläen* about the 'dynamism' of the Laocoön group. The whole conversation was, however, called *The Paintings*, and so the visitors walked on towards the painting galleries, their real goal.

Their movements did not reflect the traditional subject rankings in art discourse, for instead of heading directly for the religious or mythological subjects, the 'historical paintings', the group halted at a section of landscapes. These were in reality scattered, but the essay conveniently assembled them, one Italian (Salvator Rosa), one French (Claude), one Dutch (Ruysdael). Total coverage was not their aim. Where Goethe later

---

362 Stoljar, 67.
363 AWS, *Kritische Schriften*, 2 vols (Berlin: Reimer, 1828), I, xviii.
364 *HKA*, II, 648.
365 *KAV*, I, 122-124.

discussed Dresden's three Ruysdaels, they were content with one. Nor were they interested in rehearsing the century's notions on landscape (questions of 'factual' or 'ideal' or 'horror and immensity'). They were content to dispraise a Claudesque painting by Hackert as being essentially lifeless if it suited them. Instead they attempted a close, sometimes quite technical, analysis of the three paintings. In their view, the painter's art and sense of proportion reduce the huge scale of nature to humanly accessible form. He puts his 'soul' into it as his personal impress. Faced with the measurelessness of nature, he can only select and group, but in the process he restores a sense of nature's original unity. If—they concluded—painting is the art of appearance ('Schein') the painter gives substance and body to appearance and confers on it its own legitimate existence. The Romantics' enhancement of landscape had two aspects. It used specific examples, as here, to validate aesthetic categories, whereas in Tieck's novel *Sternbald* of 1798 it postulated a symbolic, 'hieroglyphic' landscape, not based so much on seeing as on imagining. It was to be Tieck's approach that would lead directly to the painters Philipp Otto Runge or Caspar David Friedrich or the poet Joseph von Eichendorff envisioning their respective landscapes in paint or word.

Once within the Dresden gallery's collection of 'historical' and portrait paintings—Holbein, Andrea del Sarto, Correggio, Paolo Veronese, Annibale Carracci and the crowning glory of Raphael's Sistine Madonna— the tone and the language of the conversation changed. They sought inner qualities such as 'stillness', 'nobility', 'grace' or 'inner beauty', the common-currency Winckelmannian language of the late eighteenth century, but always in combination with an analysis of technique or colour or positioning of figures. It was never supercharged, as in Wackenroder, so as to crowd out these technical features as mere 'incidentals'. This could be seen increasingly in the accounts of Correggio, who was beginning here his advance in Romantic esteem to become the equal of Raphael. There were outright condemnations, too, that amounted to blanket rejections of schools or centuries: the Flemish (Rubens), French neo-classicism (Poussin), the eighteenth century in general (Batoni, Mengs).

It is therefore interesting to find them invoking briefly the ideal Renaissance categories of beauty, as applied to the male features,[366] in their discussion of Annibale Carracci's head of Christ. Waller listed them: technically, the right balance of facial details formed a harmonious whole (he never mentions the crown of thorns); aesthetically, it produced repose,

---

366 Stoljar, 71; Becker (1998), 153.

dignity, greatness, and serenity. Above all it led the discussion to the question of the highest in (Christian) art, the ultimate icon of Raphael's Sistine Madonna. Was one (like Wackenroder) simply to 'take the shoes from off one's feet' and declare critical language, any kind of language, redundant? Or was one to make the attempt nevertheless to describe 'the divine in child-like guise', the commingling of the two natures, godlike and human, the Madonna standing (or rather floating on a cloud) before us, the handmaid of the divine and above all earthly functions? Louise confessed to tears. Was she in danger of becoming Catholic? But art never lost its autonomy. It was not so suffused with feeling as to become something vague and indefinable. It did not inhibit further analysis (of the supporting figures), but it raised two important issues. The first was the close relationship of the fine arts to poetry. The other was the inner attitude that must accompany the account of sacred art, the need to reinstall the 'mythological order' ('mythologischer Kreis') that is the basis of all religious veneration, the reinstatement of that old devotion, of all of those venerable Christian legends that the Reformation had banished. These were also to be the sentiments that Friedrich's 'mythology speech' in the last number of the *Athenaeum* in 1800 was to express even more eloquently.

By way of demonstrating these points, the conversation ceased to be a discussion and became instead poetry: eight sonnets that traced the life of the Virgin. Formally always contained and ordered (they were by Schlegel, after all), their subject matter went beyond what was available in Dresden and invoked a 'musée imaginaire' that involved memories (presumably from 1793) of the Düsseldorf collection.[367] The concluding 'legend', a romance reliving St Luke's vision of the Virgin and his consecration as the patron saint of painters, brought together the Madonna, St Luke and Raphael. For the later Nazarene painters in Rome, the 'brotherhood of St Luke' (that included Schlegel's step-nephew Philipp Veit) this was 'all ye need to know'. August Wilhelm saw the matter less extravagantly. In a much later letter to Albertine de Broglie he sought to explain it in terms of 'artist's predilection':[368] 'Catholic' subjects and an awareness of the patronage of the arts by the church were second nature to the artist and did not require any

---

367 Such as the poem 'Johannes in der Wüste', based on the painting, once attributed to Raphael, now in the Alte Pinakothek in Munich but still in Düsseldorf when AWS presumably saw it. Most recently described in 1791 by Friedrich von Stolberg, *Reise in Deutschland, der Schweiz, Italien und Sizilien in den Jahren 1791-92, Gesammelte Werke der Brüder Christian und Friedrich Leopold Grafen zu Stolberg*, 20 vols (Hamburg: Perthes u. Besser, 1820-25), VI, 11f.
368 *Oeuvres*, I, 191; Sulger-Gebing, 56.

accompanying affirmation of faith, let alone conversion. This was also the uncle of Auguste von Buttlar speaking, displeased at her embrace of Rome.

Schlegel's contribution to the art appreciation of the *Athenaeum* did not however end there. There was his Flaxman essay as well.[369] It linked up with *Die Gemälde* by reiterating the notion of a mutual interrelation of the arts. The artist 'gives us a new perceptory sense for appreciating the poet' and the poet creates a new language of 'ciphers' or 'hieroglyphs' that acts on the imagination and stimulates it to further creative insights ('plastisches Dichtergefühl'). This was not achieved by conventional engravings, Hogarth (Schlegel's special *bête noire*) or Boydell's Shakespeare Gallery (Tieck had already reviewed its singular horrors) or Chodowiecki's illustrations of modern German literature. One needed a radical approach, and this was furnished by John Flaxman's outline engravings to Dante, Homer and Aeschylus.

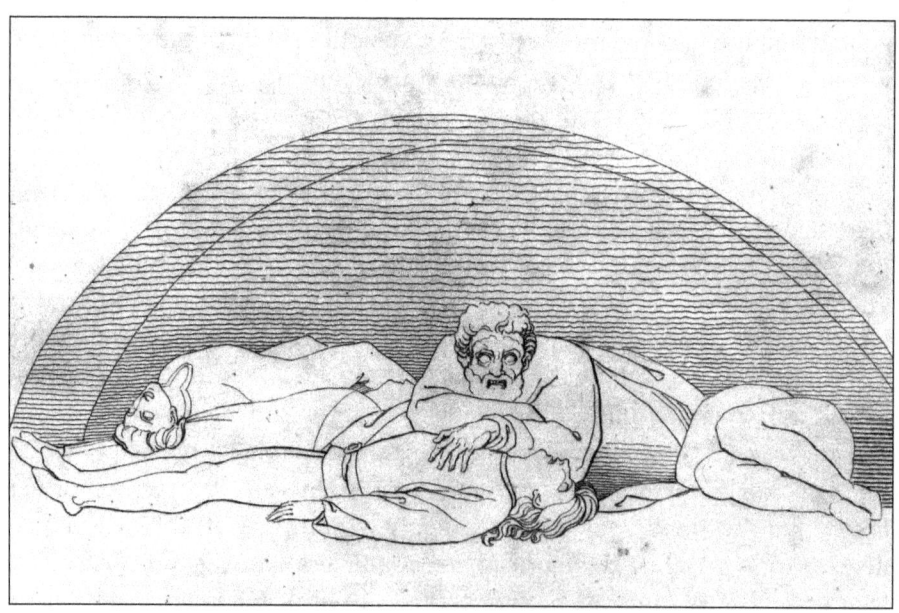

Fig. 8 John Flaxman: illustration of Dante, *Inferno*, Canto 33 (Rome[?], 1802), showing Ugolino and his sons. © and by kind permission of the Master and Fellows of Trinity College, Cambridge, CC BY-NC 4.0.

Flaxman had not yet begun his triumphant progress through the academies or his conquest of European art taste. The engravings, first produced by Tommaso Piroli in Rome in 1793, were expensive and copies were initially

---

369 *Athenaeum*, II, ii, 193-246; *SW*, IX, 102-157.

hard to come by.[370] Schlegel borrowed his from the librarian in Dresden, Johann August Heine, who seems to have been planning a German edition under Böttiger's guidance and who had not completely given up the hope of Schlegel producing a work on Dante.[371] Goethe's first (unpublished) note on Flaxman also dated from 1799.[372] Indeed, it was not until reissues were made available and artists were beginning to copy and adapt the 'outline style' that Flaxman's advance began in earnest. It was not long in coming: Runge's Hamburg teacher Gerdt Hardorff, for instance, was already encouraging his pupil, now in Copenhagen, in this direction.[373] Goethe's 'friends of art in Weimar', at least as far as Homeric subjects were concerned, were for the time being advocating the full-bodied sculptural approach to drawing, as evidenced by the competitions for young artists on motifs from the *Iliad*, that were one of the less auspicious things to be announced in the *Propyläen*.[374] Goethe, despite misgivings, could not be indifferent to Flaxman. How far Schlegel's essay had a part in all of these processes is hard to say;[375] there is no evidence that Runge read it (with the original Flaxman, or copies from it, he hardly needed to), but Friedrich Tieck in Weimar, soon to depart for Louis David's studio in Paris, certainly did.[376]

Goethe, who up to this time had shown no great interest in Dante, expressed himself in cautiously neo-classical terms about Flaxman's Dante engravings ('simplicity', 'serenity'). He noted, too, their proximity to the 'innocence, naivety and naturalness' of the old Italian pre-Raphaelite schools. All this one could read in Schlegel as well, but charged with a veneration for Dante, the 'great prophet of Catholicism', the 'Raphael and Michelangelo of poetry'. Gone were the reservations that he had expressed but a few years ago. This may have had to do with Flaxman's handling of situation, figure and costume, as for instance in the second Ugolino engraving, where the grouping and positioning mitigated some of the horror of the original. Schlegel could be more open about Dante's mysticism. In those sections where Dante went beyond the powers of human expression, Flaxman used

---

370 Sulger-Gebing, 62-67.
371 *Ibid.*, 63f.
372 Goethe, *Gedenkausgabe*, XIII, 183-188.
373 Werner Hofmann (ed.), *Runge in seiner Zeit*, exhibition catalogue Hamburg Kunsthalle, Kunst um 1800 (Munich: Prestel, 1977), 21, 99.
374 William Vaughan, *German Romantic Painting* (New Haven and London: Yale UP, 1980), 46f.
375 Cf. Klaus-Peter Schuster, '"Flaxman der Abgott aller Dilettanten". Zu einem Dilemma des klassischen Goethe und den Folgen', in: Werner Hofmann (ed.), *John Flaxman. Mythologie und Industrie*, exhibition catalogue Hamburg Kunsthalle, Kunst um 1800 (Munich: Prestel, 1979) 32-35, esp. 33f.
376 *Caroline*, II, 213.

geometrical figures (circle, triangle), themselves mystical symbols of the godhead, and passed beyond mere representation. There was Flaxman's title page to *Purgatorio*, with its representation of the triumph of the church and its saints. Schlegel praised it in neo-classical vocabulary, but also in language where 'simplicity' became 'simple-heartedness', 'naivety' was coupled with 'humility', and all of these virtues with 'piety'. Friedrich Schlegel was to take up this strain in 1804-05 when his periodical *Europa* made the same connections with the Italian and Flemish primitives. In that sense, this *Athenaeum* essay was entering regions where Goethe already had reservations and later was to see merely superstition.

Schlegel's further remarks, on Homer, stressing as they did the special suitability of Flaxman's reductive outline technique for the expression of what was quintessentially ancient and Greek, its symmetry, its repose, would have elicited Goethe's qualifications, his doubts perhaps, but not his disapproval. For Schlegel's essay ended with an appeal to German artists to make this style their own. Both Goethe and Schlegel were in their own ways to be astonished by Runge's Flaxmanian *Times of Day*.[377] When reissuing this essay in 1828, Schlegel drew attention to two other highly accomplished sets of outline engravings, by Peter Cornelius,[378] the one, of *Faust* (1810), which could claim Goethe as its ultimate inspiration, the other, of the *Nibelungenlied* (1822), had as its originating influence Schlegel himself. It is worth recording that when Schlegel visited London in 1823, he made no attempt to visit Lawrence or Haydon or any other members of the English art establishment, but sought out 'Mr Flaxman Buckingham St Portland Place'.[379] It was an act of loyalty to Flaxman and also to himself, although by then Flaxman's reputation was firmly established as a sculptor, rather less as an engraver.

Schlegel's Lectures in Jena

There remain the lectures that Schlegel delivered in Jena from the autumn of 1798[380] and which, as we have seen, overlapped in many respects with his other writings and with the *Athenaeum* in particular. Their effect was

---

377 Hofmann, *Flaxman*, 24.
378 *SW*, IX, 156f.
379 SLUB Dresden, Mscr. Dresd. e. 90, IX (IV)b. AWS's own account of this visit in *Kritische Schriften*, II, 306.
380 Friedrich Ast's transcripts were passed on to Karl Christian Friedrich Krause and published by Aug. Wünsche in 1911, then *KAV*, I, 3-177. See Behler, 'A. W. Schlegels Vorlesungen über philosophische Kunstlehre' (1994); Claudia Becker, 'Naturgeschichte der Kunst'. August Wilhelm Schlegels ästhetischer Ansatz im Schnittpunkt zwischen Aufklärung und Frühromantik (Munich: Fink, 1998), 93-107.

of necessity limited, for students did not flock to Schlegel as they did to Schelling and as they had done to Fichte, and it is only through the initiatives of two promising and intelligent young men, Ast and Savigny, that we have any record at all. Even then they have only handed down to us those lectures now called *Philosophische Kunstlehre* [Philosophical Art Theory]. These contain sections dealing with German literature, but they are presumably different from the lectures on the history of German poetry (now lost) that he also announced. From the examples of German literature cited there we may infer that Klopstock and Goethe commanded the greatest esteem, Klopstock the author of the *Grammatische Gespräche,* but also (with Goethe) the renewer of modern German poetic expression. Such coverage of the older stages of German/Germanic literature as there was, in the account of poetic genres and in the remarkable section on 'romantische Poesie', suggested that Otfrîd (whom both Schlegels read as their token Old High German text), the *Nibelungenlied,* the *Heldenbuch* and *Minnesang* featured. Of Schlegel's lectures on Horace we know nothing.

We saw that Schlegel's lectures ranged in the university calendar between 'Philologie' and 'Philosophie', with his course on aesthetics falling into the second category. If this brought him into a proximity with Schiller, who had ceased lecturing but who nevertheless still featured in the university's programme, or with Fichte, who had now left, or with Schelling, very definitely present, it should not be forgotten that he was also a colleague of lesser figures like Schütz (of the *Allgemeine Literatur-Zeitung*), or Eichstädt. In keeping with other German universities,[381] Jena had been offering lectures on aesthetics (not necessarily under this exact title) for decades. Schlegel could therefore be seen as a versatile and reliable colleague in both classical and modern literatures and was also the man best suited to inject the central tenets of transcendental idealism into the academic teaching of aesthetics.

As such, the lectures did two things. They posited absolute statements and manifest, 'incontrovertible', truths while also explaining the processes by which these ideas achieved their incontrovertibility. Aesthetics, as the philosophical study of human awareness of art and beauty, dealt with such absolutes, themselves the absolute aims of humanity. A sense of beauty is innate to humankind, does not exist outside of the human mind, and is mankind's absolute aim.[382] As part of original human nature and the destination of mankind, the aesthetic sense is postulated as a given, it is

---

381 H. S. Reiss, 'The Naturalisation of the Term "Ästhetik" in Eighteenth-Century German: Alexander Gottlieb Baumgarten and his Impact', *Modern Language Review* 89 (1994), 645-658.
382 Jesinghaus, 25.

'to be'. As man becomes aware of his ultimate purpose, so he grows in his awareness of art and beauty. Art is by this definition no mere accessory, has no ancillary function, is no frill or furbelow. These are ideas firmly rooted in Schiller or Fichte.

Schlegel was also concerned to show how man came to this awareness and what manifestations it took as a historical process. On one level, this meant setting out the history of aesthetics from Plato and Aristotle to Baumgarten, Winckelmann and Kant. On a more general plane, it involved a history of humanity—Schlegel used roughly Herder's scheme but differed as to where the march of history was leading—which was co-terminous with the natural history of art. Unlike his *Horen* essay of 1795-96, his lectures were less concerned with rehearsing theories of language than with linking the speech act to the first beginnings of poetry, with 'Naturpoesie'. We study Homer, he said, because he was closest to this primeval poetry before it became the preserve of a chosen few and was changed into art. Although climate and physical or phonetic differences lead to disparity, all language is by nature rhythmical, musical or image-laden. Image is the essential of myth, and myth is the product of the powers of human expression. Here Schlegel first developed the basically anthropological ideas (human figure, oracle, fate, belief in life after death, the golden age) that were to form part of his Romantic mythology but also informed his later Bonn lectures on ancient history.

From there, it was a logical step to an historical account of the various forms of poetic expression, the literary genres (epic, lyric, dramatic). Again, there were many prefigurations here of his later Berlin and Vienna lectures. Surely the part that could make the greatest claim to being a new approach was the section on 'modern poetic forms', where he developed first his view of the Middle Ages as a fusion of religion, chivalry and feudalism, both morally upright (courtly love) but also prone to fantasy and play with the imagination (Arthurian romance, fairy tale). The 'Romantic' genres were therefore the romance and ballad, the novella, the novel and the 'romantic drama' and as such they overthrew old neoclassical hierarchies and scales of esteem. Here for the first time Schlegel set out a general view of Shakespeare in a wider context (as indeed before him Wieland, Herder and Eschenburg had done); but with the reference to *Śakuntalā* and Goethe it now contained the germ of a suggestion that a dramatic form that mixed and commingled the poetic styles, that was both comic and tragic, loved complexities but was 'open' in form, might not have ceased with Shakespeare but could be creatively revived in Germany in their own day.

2.2 Berlin (1801-1804)

The End of Jena: Controversies and Polemics

The death of Auguste Böhmer in the summer of 1800 marked in real and in symbolic terms the end of the Romantics' association in Jena. A personal tragedy for her mother Caroline, but also for her step-father August Wilhelm, Auguste's loss had the effect of awakening old enmities and shaking existing relationships. It was to be followed by another gap in the Romantic ranks when early in 1801 Novalis succumbed to the tuberculosis that had been undermining his frail constitution. These were not 'romantic' deaths, certainly not for the sufferers: Auguste dosed with opium against the diarrhoea that was killing her (her mother was to die in identical circumstances nine years later); Novalis, a Keatsian phthisic, not in Rome but in wintry Weissenfels. Yet here was a Romantic necrology—in Jena, Wackenroder's early death in 1798 went largely unnoticed—that would also furnish an instant Romantic mythology, the creation of a semblance of unity in mourning and memorialisation where the real edifice showed cracks and fissures. In the case of Novalis it provided a convenient hagiography that could later compete with Goethe's elevation of Winckelmann and Schiller.

As already recounted, poor Auguste never had the grave monument designed for her, that might have become a tiny neo-classical enclave in a corner of Catholic Franconia. Tieck and August Wilhelm quarrelled over Novalis's 'sacred relics' (their term), over the abhorrent thought of 'continuing' his unfinished novel *Heinrich von Offterdingen*. August Wilhelm, never especially close to Novalis, allowed Tieck and Friedrich Schlegel to issue Novalis's works. Significantly, they did not include his radical *Die Christenheit oder Europa* [Christendom or Europe], a vision of history too controversial for readers in the new nineteenth century. Despite differences, personal between Caroline and Dorothea, ideological between Friedrich Schlegel and Schelling, the former Romantic circle was nevertheless able to show a united front when it suited, as in the two volumes called *Charakteristiken und Kritiken* in 1801. These assembled the Schlegel brothers' best works of criticism. Or the *Musen-Almanach für das Jahr 1802* (issued late in 1801) edited by Tieck and August Wilhelm, that commemorated the recent and early Romantic dead.

The circle's letters now reflect much more of current events than before. During the *Athenaeum* years one would hardly have known that the map of Europe was being redrawn or that tumultuous events were happening, in the far-off Mediterranean or Egypt, so absorbed had these men and women of letters been with matters of the mind or wars with literary rivals. These were now the times of Marengo and Hohenlinden, of the occupation of Hanover, of the peace treaties of Lunéville and Amiens, then of the division of the German lands themselves. We hear much more now of the threats, real or imagined, of armies on the move, of real captures and quarterings imposed on the civil population. In 1801, Caroline experienced the political repercussions of the times at first hand in Harburg, with the cession of the Hanoverian lands to Prussia.[383] Caroline's and August Wilhelm's mothers were directly affected. Yet the postal service still functioned. During the peace interludes Friedrich and Dorothea travelled unhindered to Paris and set themselves up there, relying on the *diligence* to get letters, proofs and packets of books from one land to another. Indeed it had been Bonaparte's pillages in the Near East and in Italy (later in Germany) that had made Paris so attractive as a place in which to study the arts.

Caroline needed to regain her health and recuperate, first in Bocklet and then with Schelling and August Wilhelm in Bamberg. Artists were commissioned to do a drawing of Auguste (with halo), then a portrait in oils (only Johann Friedrich August Tischbein's portrait of 1798 survives). The sculptors, Gottfried Schadow, then Friedrich Tieck, the latter due back imminently from Louis David's studio in Paris, were to produce a memorial, of which only Tieck's drawing[384] and a plaster bust by him are extant.[385] Thus Auguste, at the edge of a circle that was discovering Renaissance and Catholic portraiture, is commemorated in a bust of neo-classical lineaments, her eyes left blank, her plaited hair tied up with a ribbon, her shoulders covered with the barest outline of a Greek cloak, a young Iphigenia perhaps, or even a Persephone.

Once restored, Caroline set out to visit her mother and sister in Göttingen. It was in more ways than one a repetition of the journey in the same direction she had once made from Mainz. She was, as then, accompanied by August Wilhelm, now as ever linked by bonds of friendship and respect, devotion even. Once more, she found herself subject to the same decree as then banning her from the Hanoverian university town (the 'immoral' Friedrich

---

383 *Caroline*, II, 90-93.
384 SLUB Dresden, Mscr. Dresd. App. 2712, B17, 25 and 26.
385 Bernhard Maaz, *Christian Friedrich Tieck 1776-1851. Leben und Werk unter besonderer Berücksichtigung seines Bildnisschaffens, mit einem Werkverzeichnis*, Bildhauer des 19. Jahrhunderts (Berlin: Gebr. Mann, 1995), 270f; Cornelia Bögel, *'Geliebter Freund und Bruder'. Der Briefwechsel zwischen Christian Friedrich Tieck und August Wilhelm Schlegel in den Jahren 1804 bis 1811*, Tieck Studien 1 (Dresden: Thelem, 2015), 143-152.

Schlegel was subject to the same interdict).[386] Yet again, they had to opt for Brunswick, the more tolerant ducal residence that also had a French theatre. August Wilhelm, not affected, had visited his mother in Hanover, no doubt to reassure her that her sons' marital affairs were not leading them to perdition.

Their marriage was over. There remained still a strong residue of the affection, solicitude and camaraderie that had once been the mainstay of their relationship. They used the intimate 'Du' form until their formal separation and divorce. Schelling in Jena could read in a letter from Caroline 'Mein Herz, mein Leben' [My heart, my life],[387] Schlegel in Berlin might note 'O wie sehr fehltest Du mir' [How much I need you],[388] when things were really earnest and she needed his succour and support. He was still helping her financially. She, as before, could still be relied upon to pass on her critical and practical insights and her encouragement, as Schlegel sought to forge for himself a career as a dramatist and as a public lecturer in Berlin. It was she who advised him not to break with his publisher Unger over a breach of contract with the Shakespeare edition, shrewdly noting that no-one else would take on this enterprise with a litigious translator.[389] He should keep out of business affairs and concentrate on the task in hand, consider whether he wanted to make a name as a dramatist or earn a useful income from Shakespeare. On the last-named subject, she asked the pertinent question why he was still dashing off the Histories when he could have done *Macbeth, Othello* and *Lear*, where Schiller had produced a *Macbeth* well below Schlegel's standards.[390] As in 1801 the two quarto volumes of *Charakteristiken und Kritiken* appeared, with the Schlegel brothers' best critical offerings, she may have reflected that August Wilhelm's essay on Bürger contained much of herself (she had known Bürger longer than he had). When the final volumes of Shakespeare appeared in 1801-02, she knew that the whole undertaking was a part-monument to her own skills.

For a publisher for *Charakteristiken und Kritiken* they had gone to one of Friedrich's contacts, Friedrich Nicolovius in Königsberg, a sign that the Romantics still had to 'shop around' to sell even their best wares. It also represented a leave-taking from Jena and its associations. Friedrich had become 'habilitiert' in the university in 1800; 'Dr. Schlegel' could be heard in the winter semester of 1800-01 lecturing on 'Transcendentalphilosophie' (in

---

386 *Caroline*, II, 3f.
387 *Ibid.*, 4.
388 *Ibid.*, 75.
389 *Ibid.*, 138-147.
390 *Ibid.*, 152.

competition with Schelling) and on 'Principles of Philosophy' in the summer of 1801.[391] August Wilhelm, although still officially on the lecture list offering aesthetics and Horace,[392] never in fact returned as a professor to Jena after Caroline's departure, now setting his sights on greater things in Berlin. Friedrich's academic career was brief and inauspicious, part of the general break-up that hastened his and Dorothea's departure for Paris in 1802.

The Essay on Bürger

The brothers talked desultorily of continuing the *Athenaeum*.[393] It was not to be: the original élan was no longer there. *Charakteristiken und Kritiken* reprinted only one piece from that earlier periodical, Friedrich's essay on *Wilhelm Meister*.

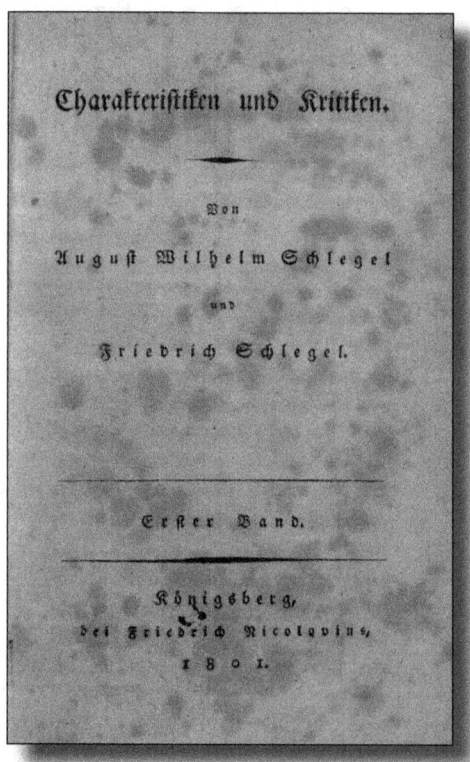

Fig. 9 August Wilhelm and Friedrich Schlegel, *Charakteristiken und Kritiken* (Königsberg, 1801), Title page of vol. 1. © and by kind permission of the Master and Fellows of Trinity College, Cambridge, CC BY-NC 4.0.

---

391 Leuper, *Vorlesungsangebot*, I, 326, 328.
392 *Ibid.*, 328.
393 *KA*, XXV, 250f.

August Wilhelm republished his essay on *Romeo and Juliet*—his set piece of critical analysis—and his *Horen* dialogue on language, his stated position on the inner link between language, rhythm, poetry and mythology, to be reiterated in Berlin. Of his reviews he reprinted those of Voss (somewhat toned down), of Goethe's *Roman Elegies* and *Hermann und Dorothea*, of Wackenroder and Tieck's *Herzensergiessungen*, and of Tieck's *Don Quixote*. Here one could read a continuing solidarity with the Romantic movement's main living poet, Ludwig Tieck, and with the *spiritus rector*, patron and idol of their endeavours, Goethe.

There were two new contributions, Friedrich's essay on Boccaccio, and August Wilhelm's on Bürger. The Schlegel brothers wrote no novellas, but they knew that Goethe had consciously revived this Renaissance narrative form in 1795, and they were to see its explosive expansion during their own lifetime. August Wilhelm's remarks on the genre in his Berlin lectures remained unpublished, but in Friedrich's essay readers could learn of the link between the novella's 'subjective' story matter and the 'objective' brevity of its form, how a mere anecdote could achieve mastery in the hands of a Boccaccio or a Cervantes. The essay is part of the Romantic discovery and rehabilitation of Italian and Spanish literature as sources of original, vital poetry, that saw Cervantes placed on the same scale of esteem as Dante and Shakespeare.

Unlike Friedrich's on the novella, August Wilhelm's Bürger essay[394] was not forward-looking. It harked back to Gottfried August Bürger, the man who had first opened up these realms of gold, the long shadow over his work and career whose influence he now needed to exorcise. It was a leave-taking from his poetic childhood, the infantilisms of Bürger's circle, as the seriousness of maturity became his tone. While going through the requisite rites of mourning he emancipated himself once and for all from mentoring and tutoring. It is surely no coincidence that Schlegel performed this deed of stringent filial piety just as he was about to step out in to the wide stage in Berlin and become a public persona untrammelled by the narrow provincialities of Göttingen or Jena. As a now established critic and poet, he could also savour the opportunity of delivering a delayed riposte to Schiller's attack of 1791.

Had the circumstances and the subjects not been widely different, the essay was the nearest that the long eighteenth century in Germany came

---

394 'Ueber Bürgers Werke'. *Charakteristiken und Kritiken. Von August Wilhelm Schlegel und Friedrich Schlegel*, 2 vols (Königsberg: Nicolovius, 1801), II, 3-96; as 'Bürger', in AWS, *Kritische Schriften*, II, 1-81 and *SW*, VIII, 64-139.

to Samuel Johnson's famous Life of Richard Savage (1744). Johnson was of course defending the memory of a *poète maudit* whose unfortunate and dissolute circumstances had prevented his unfolding as an artist. In Johnson's eyes, he nevertheless deserved sympathy and understanding from posterity. This Johnson did with some nobility. The Germans, it seems, had been less generous to their downtrodden artists. Schiller knew that Bürger's private circumstances were unedifying when in 1791 he had kicked him down for not conforming to his own notion of the poetic office. There had been voices during the eighteenth century raised in defence of Johann Christian Günther, the nearest German equivalent to Savage, but Goethe's autobiography of 1811-14 concentrated on Günther's perceived inadequacies, not his brief achievements, and Goethe was to compound this with an ungracious account of his slightly younger contemporary Johann Reinhold Michael Lenz, a poor fish in real life but an innovator and *frondeur* nevertheless.

By the same token, there were in the same elongated century also hagiographies, with improbable attributions and equations, Schink's of Lessing, Friedrich Schlegel's of Georg Forster, Goethe's of Winckelmann, raising their subjects to the heights of mythological enshrinement and quasi-religious apotheosis. Friedrich Schlegel, as seen, put into his Forster essay many of his own aspirations and strivings, and some of that is true also for August Wilhelm's account of Bürger. Schlegel clearly did not wish to kick a fallen man, but neither did he wish to write a hagiography. He did not strive to overpraise his subject, as if to compensate for Schiller's inclemency and ungenerousness. 'It is a forlorn hope', he says', to accord more fame to a man's work than it deserves, by withholding its faults'.[395] This was his stringent judgment on Bürger and the extent of his compensating generosity. His aim was to be fair, even if fairness involved the occasional severity. Schlegel's later calumniator Heinrich Heine was to accuse him of committing parricide, but Heine, himself adept at the black arts of character assassination, must have known that this was not true. Yet Schlegel did not wish to be too closely associated with Bürger's reputation, either. His few scattered defences of his mentor during the 1790s had not amounted to a rehabilitation of his memory, although one or two reviews (notably those of Salomon Gessner and the *Éloges*) had shown him pondering the essential structures of a poet's life, the approach that is needed to do justice

---

395 'Zudem ist es eine vergebliche Hoffnung, einem menschlichen Werke durch Verschweigung der Mängel einen höheren Ruhm fristen zu wollen, als der ihm zukommt'. *SW*, VIII, 73.

to the private and public sides of artistic existence. Lest he might be seen as merely following leads or initiatives proceeding from Bürger, he was quick to press his own independence. The short preface to the first volume of the Shakespeare translation in 1797 stressed that it contained 'not a word' of Bürger.[396] His own sonnets consciously followed the high models of the Renaissance, not Bürger's. The unfinished romance *Tristan*, on which he was working at the time, aligned itself with medieval subject-matter, not with the pseudo-folksy subjects in which Bürger indulged in his less vigilant moments.

Schlegel made it clear that he had no wish to concentrate on a life that was in many ways unfulfilled and hemmed about with adversities. Thus his essay should not be read as a direct reply to the points raised by Schiller. Instead he singled out Bürger's absolute dedication to poetry and his essential fulfilment in that avocation, although his was a satisfaction won only amid life-threatening tensions and the constant struggle against pressing circumstances. The times had not been favourable to him, says Schlegel, in that the period of his greatest influence was the immediate aftermath of the Sturm und Drang, in the 1780s, not the high-pitched turbulence of the 1770s. Here Schlegel was overlooking Bürger's decisive role in the brotherhood of the Göttingen 'Hain' [Grove]; and he was situating Bürger, for strategic reasons, in the years of his own early poetic development and of his association with the older man. In characterising the 1780s as 'lethargic' and not conducive to the higher aspirations of poetry, he was thinking too much of Goethe's silences during that period, but was by implication also describing the formative years of Schiller, Bürger's later nemesis. Schlegel was at pains never to compare Bürger directly with Goethe. Similarly, although he spoke of the 'cruelty' of Schiller's review, he maintained a diplomatic silence about the 'reviewer'. He was after all still close to Weimar. In 1828, when reissuing the essay,[397] he marred its generally even-handed tone with querulous and carping comments on Schiller, who was no longer able to answer.

Thus it happened, says Schlegel, that Bürger, most of whose best poems were written in the 1770s, returned in the 1780s to revise many of them, forfeiting in the process much of their original freshness and at most imbibing the spirit of the later, less 'poetic' decade. This suggested by implication that the 1790s, after Bürger's death, were the real years of

---

396 *Shakespeare's dramatische Werke*, I, [iiif.].
397 *Kritische Schriften*, II, 1-80.

fulfilment, a view since vindicated by history. Bürger was not (like, say, Goethe, although Schlegel mentions no names) 'one favoured by nature'. He sought for two things that in many ways cancelled each other out: popularity and correctness. Popularity was fine, but it could have the effect of depressing the level of quality, of being poetically all things to all men. The great names of Romantic poetry (this is the Schlegel of the *Athenaeum* and the later Berlin lectures speaking), from the Troubadours to Shakespeare, had never been in any sense 'popular'. Bürger strove to be both a folk poet and a correct one at that. This paradox also contained a fatal contradiction. On the one hand, it was Bürger who rediscovered the old ballads and romances, many of English, Scottish and Scandinavian provenance, and made them accessible in creative recastings. This service to poetry, says Schlegel the historian of the romance form, cannot be praised too highly. Yet these modernisations had often gone against the spirit of the seemingly naïve and unsophisticated originals, had been often too explicit, too crude, too mannered ('Manier' was not a term of praise in Schlegel's— or Goethe's—terminology). There had been great poetry nevertheless, such as that ballad *Lenore*, that Schlegel could not praise enough, that had taken the English by storm. Bürger's attempts at *Minnesang* were laudable, and contained fine musical poetry. Still, Bürger could not let well alone: he would 'correct' his own poetry and forfeit some of its freshness and originality. All the same, Schlegel found some kind words for Bürger's love poetry and for his sonnets, even for his fragmentary versification of Homer (Voss was not to have all the credit). He totally rejected Bürger's prose *Macbeth*. Even if he never himself attempted a translation of this play, he was not willing to compromise the standards of Shakespearean rendition that he himself had established in theory and even more so in practice.

Schlegel's *envoi* made some amends for the severity of his judgments. He accorded Bürger 'freshness', 'power', 'clarity', 'elegance', even a 'rare greatness'. He had reviewed Bürger's works on their merits, not confusing the work with the man, and had avoided all moral strictures except those relating to poetry itself. He had not attempted to raise Bürger to any kind of canonical status. He was clearly no 'archpoet' in the spirit of the *Athenaeum*. One could not apply to him the high standards that the Berlin lectures were to require of great and lasting poetry, but he was accorded a place, more modest but not without its own honour, in the national literature. Yet one senses that Schlegel with this essay had not quite got Bürger out of his system. How else can one explain the sonnet of 1810 called *An Bürgers Schatten* [To Bürger's Shade] that went into his *Poetische Werke* of 1811:

2. Jena and Berlin (1795-1804)

An Bürgers Schatten

Mein erster Meister in der Kunst der Lieder,
    Der über mich, als meiner Jugend Morgen
    Noch meinen Namen schüchtern hielt verborgen,
Der Weihung Wort sprach, väterlich und bieder!

Den deutschen Volksgesang erschufst du wieder,
    Und durftest nicht gelehrte Weisen borgen;
    Doch Müh, verworrne Leidenschaften, Sorgen,
Sie drückten früh dein krankend Leben nieder.

Zürnst du, daß ich zu männlich strenger Sichtung
    Des reinen Golds von minder edlen Erzen
    An deines Geists Gepräge mich entschloßen?

In dumpfen Tagen schien der Quell der Dichtung
    Dir schon versiegt; er hat sich neu ergossen,
    Doch tragen wir dein wackres Thun im Herzen.[398]

[My early master in the art of song,
Who in the first morning of my youth,
When shyness did not let me name my name,
Blessed me as father, spoke kind words to me.

You brought the German folksong back to life
And did not need to borrow learned tones;
But travail, cares and passion's ravages
Oppressed you and made your heart sick.

Do you resent that my stern critic's eye
Is sifting the pure gold from baser ores
And doing this on your own spirit's coin?

On dark dull days you felt the wells of song
Dried up in you; but now they flow again,
And in our hearts we bear your deeds and worth.]

In February of 1801, Schlegel went to Berlin. It was to be his base until 1804. A short exception was the brief return visit to Jena in the late summer of 1801. It was troubled by recriminations between Caroline and Dorothea over 'meubles', also over Dorothea's alleged rumour-mongering about Auguste. Friedrich and Dorothea were in debt, borrowing from

---

398 AWS, *Poetische Werke*, 2 parts (Heidelberg: Mohr und Zimmer, 1811), I, 334 (as here); *SW*, I, 375.

any forthcoming lenders, Friedrich already showing the 'embonpoint' produced by his compulsive eating.³⁹⁹ The subject of Auguste was always sensitive. August Wilhelm had rejected a poem of Friedrich's, *Der welke Kranz* [The Wilted Wreath] for inclusion in the *Musen-Almanach*, allegedly at Caroline's prompting.⁴⁰⁰ Friedrich in his turn had also been reading the proofs of Schleiermacher's translation of Plato, and he had written the tragedy *Alarcos*, the failure of which in Weimar was to hasten their departure for Paris in 1802. He had managed to reach an agreement with Ludwig Tieck—no easy task—over the edition of Novalis's works. After a final journey to Berlin and Dresden (where his sister Charlotte Ernst unwisely lent them money), Friedrich and Dorothea left in stages for Paris. There was, he said, no chance of earning a living in Germany, with them constantly on the move—a wanderlust occasioned by his creditors, one might add. He would be able to use his writings in Paris and work from that base. The much-admired Georg Forster had existed in this fashion,⁴⁰¹ an analogy that even Friedrich must have known to be unfortunate in all of its associations. Yet the Schlegel brothers, while never agreeing on the subject of their respective partners or spouses, could in many ways not live without each other. When Friedrich's periodical *Europa*, the only substantial product of his Paris years, began to appear in 1803, it contained a major input from August Wilhelm.

Thus Jena now ceased to be the base of their literary association. Does that validate the thesis, advanced in the 1920s,⁴⁰² that Jena stood for 'literary Romanticism' while the newly reformed and reconstituted (1802) University of Heidelberg represented its 'religious' (thus ideological) side? A kind of exodus from Jena to Heidelberg did take place. Overtures were made to Tieck; Paulus eventually went there; Schelling at one stage showed interest (the Schlegel brothers never). It might instead be fair to say that the content of the *Athenaeum* had been determined, dictated even, by the arguments of the 1790s, by associations, like those with Fichte, Schleiermacher or Novalis, that no longer held in the new century. Or that Goethe, and the desire to please him, had absorbed a disproportionate amount of its attention. If anything, we could say

---

399   *KA*, XXV, 308.
400   *Ibid.*, 296f.
401   *Ibid.*, 331.
402   Cf. Julius Petersen, *Wesensbestimmung der deutschen Romantik. Eine Einführung in die moderne Literaturwissenschaft* (Leipzig: Quelle & Meyer, 1926), 134f.

that the dissolution of the Jena circle did paradoxically produce in the Schlegel brothers the desire to systematize the achievement of Jena, to give it a historical foundation, a firm basis in fact, and this one could see, not in Heidelberg, but in August Wilhelm's Berlin lectures and the private course which Friedrich gave in Paris. If one were searching for a manifesto of things new, as opposed to the old order, one would not look to the artificial divide between Jena and Heidelberg, but to the works of the circle itself. The last poem of the *Musen-Almanach für das Jahr 1802*—a year late—contained August Wilhelm's Shrovetide parody on the old and new centuries.[403] It was an unrepentant credo to the new spirit of the new age, young, disrespectful of mediocrity, intolerant of mere enlightenment, open to the glories of the past, great deeds martial and spiritual. The 'new century' stood in effect for the *Athenaeum*, whether one felt its influence in Jena, Heidelberg or Berlin. This was where the future lay.

Leaving Jena for Berlin did not mean August Wilhelm cutting off his ties with Weimar. His début as a writer for the stage was made there, not in Berlin, and Goethe's patronage and benevolence was something that he could not easily forfeit. Yet as other Romantics, his brother Friedrich, Schleiermacher, Ludwig Tieck among them, were removing themselves from Berlin, it seemed as if August Wilhelm was trying to reconstitute the Prusssian capital as a focal point for the movement. In this he also found himself being drawn into the turbulent affairs of the Tieck family, the three siblings, Ludwig, Sophie, and Friedrich. It could be said that all three possessed to a degree the charm, the ease of movement and conversation, the affability and savoir-vivre that came from early contact with Berlin culture and its salons (August Wilhelm spoke of Friedrich Tieck's '*tournure*').[404] But all three were subject variously to mood swings, dilatoriness, frenetic bursts of creative energy followed by torpor and lassitude, which may be symptomatic of a manic-depressive condition. In fairness, Ludwig's health had been ruined in that Jena winter of 1799-1800, while Sophie had to contend with three difficult pregnancies and the loss of her second child Ludwig. Friedrich, in his turn, not always through his own fault, was at times reduced to a hand-to-mouth existence.

---

403 'Ein schön kurzweilig Fastnachtspiel vom alten und neuen Jahrhundert', *Musen-Almanach für das Jahr 1802. Herausgegeben von A. W. Schlegel und L. Tieck* (Tübingen: Cotta, 1802), 274-295; *SW*, II, 149-162.
404 *Briefe*, I, 137.

Take Ludwig first. He was no longer in Berlin, having spent himself in polemics and controversies directed at the anti-Romantic clique there. Now he was in Dresden, but in 1802 he was to move even further east to a friend's estates beyond the Oder. He and August Wilhelm had agreed soon after Auguste Böhmer's death that there should be a kind of poetic memorial, a 'Todten-Opfer'.[405] Sacred memory did not rule out very business-like calculations. It would fill the gap in the market that Schiller's *Musenalmanach* usually took up (Schiller had now given up this kind of literary work), would become the 'Musenalmanach par excellence', amounting to thirteen to fourteen duodecimo sheets of Romantic poetry. August Wilhelm, now an author with Johann Friedrich Cotta, also publisher to Goethe and Schiller, had negotiated terms: an almanac of 1,500 copies at a basic royalty of 60 Louisd'ors, authors to be paid for their contributions.[406] From Dresden and Berlin, Tieck and Schlegel were to use their influence in their respective circles to produce a volume of verse in keeping with its appointed task. With the death of Novalis in March 1801, a double memorialisation seemed called for. Novalis's *Geistliche Lieder* [Devotional Hymns] were to provide its centre, together with Schlegel's sonnet cycle on Auguste. Tieck and both Schlegel brothers were to be the main contributors, but anyone capable of acceptable verse and of the right disposition might also be invited. Thus we find in the almanac an array of major and minor names, Schelling (as 'Bonaventura'), Sophie Tieck, Karl von Hardenberg (Novalis's brother), Wilhelm von Schütz, briefly August Wilhelm's protégé, and others. An engraving of Goethe by the neo-classical painter Friedrich Bury, one of Schlegel's new Berlin friends, was to form the frontispiece, in the forlorn hope that the great man might also contribute (the almanac appeared plate-less). Despite dealing with sacred remains, the editors quarrelled over Tieck's tardiness. As usual, it was Schlegel who saw the little volume through the press.[407]

---

405 See generally Roger Paulin, '*Der Musen-Almanach für das Jahr 1802*. Herausgegeben von A. W. Schlegel und L. Tieck', in: York-Gothart Mix (ed.), *Kalender? Ey, wie viel Kalender! Literarische Almanache zwischen Rokoko und Klassizismus*, exhibition catalogue (Wolfenbüttel: Herzog August Bibliothek, 1986), 179-183.

406 Lohner, 49f., 65; York-Gothart Mix, 'Kunstreligion und Geld. Ludwig Tieck, die Brüder Schlegel und die Konkurrenz auf dem literarischen Markt um 1800', in: Heidrun Markert *et al.* (eds), *'lasst uns, da es uns vergönnt ist, vernüftig seyn!'—Ludwig Tieck (1773-1853)*, Publikationen zur Zeitschrift für Germanistik NF, 9 (Berne etc.: Peter Lang, 2004), 241-258, ref. 244f.

407 Lohner, 49-95.

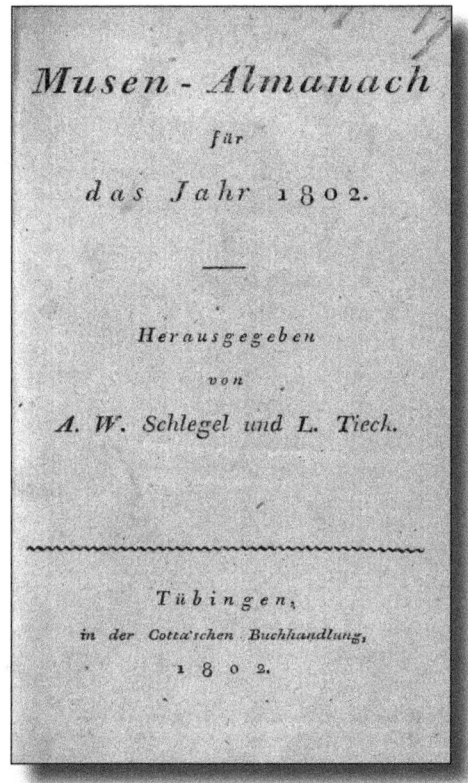

Fig. 10 A. W. Schlegel and L. Tieck, *Musenalmanach auf das Jahr 1802* (Tübingen, 1802). Title page. © and by kind permission of the Master and Fellows of Trinity College, Cambridge, CC BY-NC 4.0.

If the *Athenaeum*'s verse offerings had not been typical of the movement's capabilities, the *Musen-Almanach* was to make good this deficiency. It was 'Romantic' to a fault, in that Romance verse forms (sonnet, canzone, terza rima, ottava rima) were to the fore. Ballads or religious verse stanzas from different traditions, Catholic and Protestant, were also prominent. Religious the almanac certainly was, with those extraordinary poems by Novalis as its centrepiece, a kind of ecumenical religiosity that took in elements of whatever provenance and reflected the sense, formulated by Schleiermacher, that all facets of intellectual and cultural life were subject to a spiritual dimension. Thus even Schelling's ballad (rather good) and Tieck's romance (less good) had religious themes.[408] One could find the

---

408 Schelling (pseud. Bonaventura), 'Die letzten Worte des Pfarrers zu Drottning auf Seeland', *Musen-Almanach*, 218-228; Tieck, 'Die Zeichen im Walde', *ibid.*, 2-24.

theosophical imagery of the old mystagogue Jacob Böhme in both Tieck's and Novalis's verse. The Schlegels translated the swooning cadences of the medieval hymn and the devotional verse of the Spanish Baroque. Yet few readers would have been receptive to the daring eucharistic eroticism of Novalis's communion hymn that draws on the mystical imagery of the Moravian Brethren among whom he was nurtured:

> Einst ist alles Leib,
> Ein Leib,
> In himmlischem Blute
> Schwimmt das selige Paar.—
> O! daß das Weltmeer
> Schon erröthete,
> Und in duftiges Fleisch
> Aufquölle der Fels!
> Nie endet das süße Mahl
> Nie sättigt die Liebe sich.[409]

> [Once all is body,
> One body,
> In heavenly blood
> Swim the two blissful ones.—
> O that the ocean
> Were already red
> And as sweet-scented flesh
> The rock were to spring up!
> The blessed feast never ends,
> Love is never sated.]

August Wilhelm's nine sonnets of 'Todten-Opfer', his offering to the dead, was altogether more decorous and eclectic in its mythology. A classicizing element was rarely absent from any of Schlegel's enterprises. In one sonnet, Auguste is likened to Eurydice, in another she is safe in the Virgin's arms.

Sophie Tieck-Bernhardi

Ludwig Tieck and Schlegel made up their quarrel and returned to exchanging letters about more congenial things, about Shakespeare, about the Middle Ages. Tieck's modernising anthology of Minnesang, *Minnelieder aus dem Schwäbischen Zeitalter* [Love Songs from the Swabian Era] of 1803 was an influential authority for Schlegel's Berlin lectures. Still, it is

---

409 *Musen-Almanach*, 203; *HKA*, I, 167 (with different stanza pattern).

noticeable, when at the end of 1803 Tieck showed all the signs of crisis and nervous collapse, that it was Friedrich Schlegel to whom he wrote a great confessional letter, not August Wilhelm.[410] Sophie Tieck[411] had contributed both to the *Athenaeum* and to the *Musen-Almanach*, a short essay for the one and two poems for the other. In fact, she had been included anonymously in publications by her brother and her husband August Ferdinand Bernhardi since at least 1795, mostly as 'Sophie B.'. Whereas the Schlegels did not go in for sibling rivalry, with the Tiecks it assumed textbook dimensions. At first together in Berlin, then separated by study or marriage, they repulsed each other and yet became inextricably implicated in each others' fates and misfortunes. Those who defend Sophie (mostly women) point to her invidious position as the middle sibling between two brothers, hemmed in by domesticity, marriage and childbearing, disparaged and exploited by writers in her immediate entourage. A woman writer unappreciated, even compared with her contemporaries Caroline von Wolzogen, Therese Huber, Sophie Mereau or Karoline von Günderode, with whom she bears equal rank, her publications were mainly anonymous: her full name appeared but once on a title page (Dorothea Schlegel's never did). Those who do not defend her (largely men) find her neurotic, exploitative, rapacious, vampiric even, and these are the terms that one tends to hear in the Schlegel narrative (not of course from August Wilhelm himself). In that context, she did not possess Caroline's strength of character, Dorothea's devotion, or Madame de Staël's sheer hugeness of personality. Yet in 1801-02, she and Schlegel were lovers.

He had met her on his previous visit to Berlin, as Ludwig Tieck's sister and as Bernhardi's wife. Bernhardi, a classicist and schoolmaster at the Friedrichswerder Gymnasium in Berlin, was a friend of her brother Ludwig, and his marriage to Sophie in 1799 seemed a natural consequence. Their first child, Wilhelm, was born in 1800, but the marriage failed. Bernhardi had few friends. He may have had an unpleasant and unattractive personality, but he surely does not deserve the demonisation visited on him by the Tieck-Schlegel circle. It was easy to overlook that he had contributed to the *Athenaeum* (Tieck had not) and that he had been drawn into the various plans for a 'Kritisches Institut'. Schlegel was to do a long review of his important handbook on language for *Europa*. Yet a messy divorce and court cases over custody of his children seem to be Bernhardi's personal legacy.

---

410 Lohner, 137-147.
411 Cf. Ewa Eschler, *Sophie Tieck-Bernhardi-Knorring (1775-1833). Das Wanderleben und das vergessene Werk* (Berlin: trafo, 2005), 111-123.

Bernhardi could also be generous, gregarious (he went drinking with Fichte) and hospitable. When Schlegel arrived in Berlin, the Bernhardis took him in for the duration of his lectures, in their quarters in the Oberwasserstrasse (or Jungfernbrücke),[412] on the Kupfergraben canal and not far from the Tieck family home. The Bernhardis, with their wide circle of friends, did all they could to assist Schlegel's adjustment to the capital city. He needed no introductions to the world of the theatre: Madame Unzelmann was very glad of his company, more than glad, some alleged. He commemorated her acting in prose and verse.[413] Relations with Iffland, the director of the Royal Theatre, were cooler. He did not care for Schlegel's particular brand of neo-classical drama, his verse play *Ion*, and did nothing for its success in Berlin. Through the Bernhardis, Schlegel found a lawyer willing to take the publisher Unger to court (unsuccessfully, as it turned out). Thus the Shakespeare project, one of the few great things still associated with Schlegel's name, so proudly inaugurated in 1797, ended in litigation and recrimination, and in a truncated state, with most of the great tragedies and the 'problem plays' untranslated. Only in 1810 did he give in to Madame Unger's importunings[414] and finish *King Richard III*.

Above all, the Bernhardis were assiduous in finding a venue and drumming up an audience for the lectures that Schlegel was to give in Berlin from the end of 1801 until the winter of 1804. Almost at the same time as Schlegel was 'brouillirt' with her brother Ludwig over literary matters, he fell in love with Sophie. No doubt it began with friendship, doubtless also with Schlegel's chivalrous concern for her condition—her second child, Ludwig, was born in August, 1801. Perhaps also solicitude when this little mite died the following February. The letters that they exchanged from the period of his absence in Jena, from August until October 1801, are, however, full of passion.

In 1811, sorting through his papers before his imminent and hasty departure from Coppet, Schlegel placed a double seal on the packet of letters to and from Sophie, with the instruction 'à bruler [sic] après ma mort sans ouvrir le paquet' [to be burned unopened after my death].[415] Her letters, in a spidery hand and in uncertain spelling, speak of passion

---

412 Location described in Friedrich Nicolai, *Wegweiser für Fremde und Einheimische durch die Königl. Residenzstädte Berlin und Potsdam* [...] (1793), *Gesammelte Werke*, ed Bernhard Fabian *et al.*, vol. 6 (Hildesheim, etc.: Olms, 1987), 32; *Caroline*, II, 177.
413 As in *SW*, I, 235-243, II, 37-38, IX, 227-230.
414 These letters SLUB Dresden, Mscr. Dresd. App. 2712, IVe, 1-33.
415 SLUB Dresden, Mscr. Dresd. App. 2712, B15, 1 and 2. He adds in German 'S. T. nach meinem Tod uneröffnet zu verbrennen'.

and longing, his of devotion. Using lovers' ruses, hers alternate between 'Du' and 'Sie', intimate when Bernhardi was absent, formal and factual when Bernhardi was at home and could surprise her at her writing-desk.[416] The frequent allusions to pain and melancholy, the mention of opium-taking, that punctuate her letters, now and later, may be real. They may also be manipulative, self-stylisation, as when she compares herself with Aurelie, Goethe's neurotic heroine in *Wilhelm Meister*.[417] One can but guess. Bernhardi was of course to be kept in the dark. So was Caroline: Schlegel still had too much affection for her. In the autumn of 1802 Schlegel waxed lyrical in a poem to Sophie with perhaps a veiled reference to a child that she was carrying,[418] and when in November 1802 Felix Theodor Bernhardi was born, Schlegel had reason to believe that he was the father. That conflicted with Bernhardi's justified belief in his own paternity, but also with a second rival, Karl Gregor von Knorring. Knorring, a Baltic nobleman, had been taking private Greek lessons with Bernhardi, perhaps a little more than that. Schlegel, together with the two Tieck brothers, was one of Felix Theodor's godparents. Yet it was in Knorring's company that Sophie, in the summer of 1803, fled to Dresden from her loveless marriage, then a year later finally abandoned her husband and began a wandering existence that took her first to Weimar and then eventually to Rome, to separation and divorce. Schlegel, it hardly needs to be said, made regular contributions to her exchequer.

Schlegel had at this stage not met the third Tieck sibling, Friedrich the sculptor. Friedrich had been absent from Berlin since 1797. His travelling scholarship to Rome fell victim to Bonaparte's campaign in Italy and was taken up instead in the studio of Louis David in Paris.[419] Wilhelm von Humboldt had kept a benevolent eye on him there and had reported favourably to Goethe on his progress.[420] The Weimar ducal palace had been destroyed by fire in 1774, and its replacement, a neo-classical building of impressive dimensions, had been coming along gradually since 1789. Tieck's return in the summer of 1801 coincided very nicely with the latest phase, and through Goethe's good offices he was entrusted with the basreliefs on the main staircase. Tieck also did busts of Goethe (commemorated in

---

416 *Krisenjahre*, I, 17, 19.
417 *Ibid.*, 17.
418 *Ibid.*, III, 29f.
419 Maaz, 23-26.
420 *Briefe*, II, 55.

a distich by Schlegel)[421] and of members of the ducal house and court.[422] Commissions also came in from Berlin, indeed there was talk of him doing the queen's portrait,[423] ahead of Johann Gottfried Schadow, his nearest rival. Had Tieck possessed the determination of Schadow or Christian Daniel Rauch, his work would be more widely known. He did not, suffering as he did from the Tiecks' more than occasional fecklessness and lack of staying-power. Yet it was not entirely his fault that the monument to Auguste Böhmer never came to fruition: the plans kept changing.[424] In Weimar, he did a portrait drawing of Schelling[425] and did the costume designs for Schlegel's play *Ion*. These showed the five main characters in different forms of Greek dress, the royal figures, the priestess, the old man, each in a symbolic colour relating to rank and status.[426]

The *Ion* Fiasco

Ion. Schauspiel in fünf Aufzügen [Play in Five Acts] is not one of Schlegel's more memorable or even readable works. But for him it was his only serious dramatic product, the testimony that he need not be ashamed in the company of Goethe's *Iphigenie auf Tauris* or Schiller's *Die Braut von Messina*, the high points of German neo-classicism on the stage. Of course it is but one further example of those classicizing adaptations for which in the eighteenth century the English, the Italians, the French—and now the Germans—had such a weakness and in which those Schlegel uncles, Johann Elias and Johann Heinrich, had had a minor part, a footnote in the family chronicle. There were no incompatibilities between neo-classicism and Romanticism, as Schlegel's admiration for Flaxman had shown, indeed as Friedrich Tieck's career was to demonstrate. As for neo-classical dramas, the Romantic generation felt no inhibitions: Tieck was writing a *Niobe* (unfinished), while Schlegel's acolyte Wilhelm von Schütz actually finished one of the same name in 1807, and the genre proved resilient enough to withstand Kleist's *Penthesilea* of 1810, his ferocious reworking of the *Bacchae*.

Of course one could not confuse this kind of dramatic writing with the French *drame classique*, for which Schlegel had only contempt (except when

---

421 *SW*, II, 37.
422 Maaz, 26-30.
423 Lohner, 109.
424 Bögel (2015), 143-152.
425 *Caroline*, II, 212.
426 Georg Reichard, *August Wilhelm Schlegels 'Ion'. Das Schauspiel und die Aufführungen unter der Leitung von Goethe und Iffland*, Mitteilungen zur Theatergeschichte der Goethezeit, 9 (Bonn: Bouvier, 1987), 176, and for subsequent remarks on *Ion*.

declaimed by Madame de Staël). He could hardly conceal his dismay that Goethe had translated Voltaire and was having him staged in Weimar, in order to train his actors in proper declamation and harmonious unity of movement, the kind of thing that Schlegel himself so admired in Friederike Unzelmann in Berlin. Nor was there any question of his own *Ion* being merely another adaptation of Euripides, whom he had called a 'chattering rhetorician'[427] and whose achievements his lectures in Berlin sought to disparage as against those of Aeschylus or Sophocles. Schlegel did not wish to come over as a mere professor passing on insights, a kind of Euripides at the lectern, if one will. When his audience in Berlin heard about Greek drama, they were to know that Schlegel himself had attempted a completely new creation in the Greek style, a 'neues Original-Schauspiel' [new original play], not some Euripidean pastiche.[428] The man who was lecturing was therefore a poet in his own right, a translator too, a critic, but not least a poet. The two forums of public performance, the stage and the rostrum, therefore complemented each other.

No-one could be unaware that Schlegel was following Goethe's lead when he had 'sanitized' Euripides' *Iphigenia in Tauris* of those elements of Greek culture that remained problematic to eighteenth-century taste: deceit, blood sacrifice, the malevolence of the gods, and suchlike.[429] Thus, too, Schlegel tones down Euripides' *Ion*. Apollo's rape of Kreusa becomes a mere passing incontinence; he removes the lie by which Xuthus believes Ion to be his own son; he humanizes, and creates bonds of sympathy where Euripides has none, awakening pity for the wronged Kreusa and for her female fragility. There is recognition and reconciliation; Ion's divine parentage is no obstacle to family harmony (he allows Xuthus to adopt him); Apollo's appearance at the end removes all doubt about the validity of oracles. As in Goethe's play, the main formal vehicle is blank verse, but Schlegel cannot resist the occasional opportunity to display his skills with trimeters and other classical metres. Like Goethe, Schlegel has no chorus, but Ion sings a song (the music by Johann Friedrich Reichardt) to be accompanied by that most un-Greek of instruments, the pianoforte. The style was uniformly elevated, reinforced by the use of masks. If there were concessions to sentiment, they were not couched in the vaguely Christian sensibility that marks Goethe's first neo-classical drama.

---

427 *SW*, II, 35.
428 As he points out in his own review in *Zeitung für die elegante Welt*, 6 January 1802, 322-325. *Caroline*, II, 590-592.
429 Reichard (1987), 34-55.

Goethe—perhaps against his better judgment—was not merely prepared to countenance Schlegel's play. He was willing to have it performed in Weimar as part of the new regimen of 'anti-naturalistic' acting style that he was seeking to enforce.[430] Schlegel kept Goethe posted on its progress, from February 1801 until its completion in October, and he read it to Goethe in Weimar before his return to Berlin. He was therefore not present when it was duly performed on 2 January 1802. Caroline and Schelling were, and they even enjoyed the privilege of sharing Goethe's own box.[431] They had a good view of the audience. It was a full house, the stalls packed with students, the boxes taken by Weimar notabilities, Herder and his wife Caroline, Bertuch the publisher, Schütz and Hufeland from Jena, Meyer the art connoisseur, Böttiger. Even Schiller attended, despite his perennial illness.

Schiller's instincts, warning Goethe against this production, proved to be accurate. True, the great Weimar actress Karoline Jagemann was praised in the title role. There were however elements in the audience inimical to both Goethe and Schlegel. These centred on Kotzebue, and they planned mischief. There were titters and whisperings, then jeers. Goethe had to rise in his box, Jupiter-like, and command 'Man lache nicht!' [No laughing].[432] For the Herders it had been no laughing matter: they were shocked at the explicit terms used by Kreusa to recall her encounter with the god Apollo. A second performance on 4 January was a failure, although the play had some success later in the year at the summer theatre at Bad Lauchstädt near Leipzig.

There was a conspiracy of silence over the identity of the author. So strong was the anti-Goethe and anti-Romantic faction in both Weimar and Berlin that Schlegel wished to preserve his anonymity, at least until the play was performed in Berlin. Friedrich Schlegel unwisely told Dorothea, and then the secret was out. Kotzebue knew, Böttiger knew.[433] Böttiger, who had not forgiven the editors of the *Athenaeum* for their unflattering remarks about him, planned a disrespectful review in Bertuch's periodical *Journal des Luxus und der Moden*. Hearing of this, Goethe confronted Bertuch, threatening to go to the duke with his resignation as director of the court theatre if he proceeded. Bertuch backed down. It was remarkable what one could achieve if one was the major name in a minor ducal residence.

---

430 W. H. Bruford, *Theatre, Drama and Audience in Goethe's Germany* (London: Routledge & Kegan Paul, 1950), 288-319.
431 Their account in *Caroline*, II, 248-262.
432 The source for this anecdote Eduard Genast, *Aus Weimars klassischer und nachklassischer Zeit*, Memoirenbibliothek, 5 (Stuttgart: Lutz, 1905), 76-78.
433 Sondermann, *Karl August Böttiger* (1983), 200.

Caroline wrote a very positive anonymous review for the *Zeitung für die elegante Welt* in Berlin.[434] Schlegel did not find it sufficiently accurate and by August of 1802 had written a total of three 'correctives' to the newspaper's editor,[435] a record even for someone as concerned with his self-image as he was. Iffland had shown far less enthusiasm for the play than Goethe. He did nevertheless have it performed twice in May, taking himself the role of Xuthus, with the celebrated Friederike Unzelmann in the title role. The neo-classical architect Hans Christian Genelli, a member of Schlegel's Berlin circle, had designed the décor. Iffland's acting style was less formal than Weimar's, but even it could not capture the hearts of the Berlin audience. Nor could the book edition of 1803 rescue its reputation; printing the play in his poetic works in 1811 did not help either. *Ion* remained a dismal flop.

Polemics, Caricatures and Lampoons

In 1800, Schlegel's wise sister Charlotte Ernst had written: why waste your time on pointless controversies when you could be writing poetry.[436] Over three years later, Madame de Staël could inform a visitor to Coppet that she had achieved the sacrifice of his polemics'.[437] What of the time in between? It is fair to say that in this intervening period those Romantics still actively involved were subjected to a barrage of polemics—lampoons, parodies, caricatures—that threatened to consume their energies. Both sides spoke of 'warfare'. Ludwig Tieck had actually withdrawn from Berlin to Dresden and then to remotest Ziebingen partially to escape from this tiresome business. Friedrich Schlegel had not helped matters by persuading Goethe to have his tragedy *Alarcos* performed in Weimar in April, 1802. There were scenes similar to the *Ion* fiasco, Goethe as then prompted to Olympian pronouncements. There are those who defend *Alarcos* in preference to *Ion*, but the choice is essentially one between two evils.[438] Like his brother with *Ion*, if surely with even less justification, Friedrich was inordinately proud of his dramatic and poetic achievements, sending copies to all who

---

[434] Published in *Caroline*, II, 585-590.
[435] One published in *Caroline*, II, 590-592, one in *SW*, IX, 193-209. Also in *Zeitung für die elegante Welt*, 21 and 24 August, 1802. Reichard, 263-269.
[436] *Briefe*, I, 123.
[437] Ludwig Geiger, *Dichter und Frauen. Abhandlungen und Mittheilungen. Neue Sammlung* (Berlin: Paetel, 1899), 124.
[438] The whole dismal story available in the documentation to Friedrich Schlegel, *Alarcos. Ein Trauerspiel*. Historisch-kritische Edition mit Dokumenten, ed. Mark-Georg Dehrmann *et al.* (Hanover: Wehrhahn, 2013), 103-185.

mattered.⁴³⁹ It is also fair to say that his and Dorothea's departure for Paris was in some measure hastened by the dismal *Alarcos* affair. The Weimar audience took itself less seriously than its authors. Already in February 1801 there had been a masque performed in honour of the duchess's birthday, with Harlequin travestying Lucinde and all of the 'new aesthetics'. The duke had had a good laugh.⁴⁴⁰

Until his removal to Switzerland in 1804, Schlegel had to contend with a background noise of controversy involving the same tedious array of minor names that had begun to harry the Jena circle in 1799-1800: Nicolai, Böttiger, Merkel, Kotzebue, Falk, and others. Were one even to list the titles of all the anti-Romantic ephemera and squibs (many of them damp) from 1798 to 1804 one would fill several pages.⁴⁴¹ It could be said that Schlegel provoked some of this with his 'Gate of Honour' and 'Triumphal Arch' for Kotzebue, when silence would have been the preferable option. He had not refrained from adding his name to Fichte's polemic against Friedrich Nicolai (1801).⁴⁴² At least no-one broke up his Berlin lectures: entry was by ticket only. There were, as said, burlesques and parodies, but also deliberate and malicious disinformation, at which the Schlegels' old adversary Karl August Böttiger was a past master. His links with the English literary scene enabled him to achieve an even wider circle of dissemination. The *Monthly Review* in London purveyed Böttiger's version of the German literary scene and was talking freely of the 'lubricities' of *Ion* and the 'ridiculo-horrid monster' that was *Alarcos*.⁴⁴³ Goethe was brought in by association, for by no means everyone found to their taste his protection of the Jena 'clique' and their contingent gross flattery of him. One did not however spoil with Goethe; besides he was quite capable of delivering his own brand of polemics, witness his treatment of Nicolai and Böttiger in the first part of *Faust*.

Perhaps it is the pictorial polemics, the caricatures, that have emerged best from all of this frenzied activity. The artists involved were no Gillrays or Rowlandsons, nor would German censorship have permitted such excesses. It was entertaining when an artist of Gottfried Schadow's standing did a rough private sketch⁴⁴⁴ depicting Goethe on his Olympian throne, the Schlegels standing on a pile of books (where else?), Novalis on stilts, and Schelling

---

439 *KA*, XXV, 338-339.
440 *Der Briefwechsel zwischen Friedrich Nicolai und Carl August Böttiger*, ed. Bernd Maurach (Berne, etc.: Peter Lang, 1996), 28-31, 39.
441 Listed by Wolfgang Pfeiffer-Belli, 'Antiromantische Streitschriften und Pasquille (1798-1804)', *Euphorion*, 26 (1925), 602-630.
442 For which he supplied the preface. *SW*, VIII, 140f.
443 Sondermann (1985), 238f.
444 Schmitz, *Die ästhetische Prügeley*, 428.

as a barking dog. Novalis also appears on the published broadsheet *Versuch auf den Parnass zu gelangen* [Attempt to Reach Parnassus], again on stilts, and as the author of those eucharistic hymns, hanging with chalices, while Schlegel, armed to the teeth, brandishes a crucifix, Tieck, astride Puss in Boots, similarly, Wilhelm von Schütz (whose name means 'archer') is taking aim with bow and arrow[445] (and poor hunchbacked little Schleiermacher has his nose in a book). On Parnassus itself Kotzebue, modishly dressed in the new *pantalon*, is wielding a flail in defence. But *Die neuere Aesthetik* [The New Aesthetics] is altogether more entertaining, not least for having affinities with a French carnival print.[446] On a triumphal chariot are to be seen a corpulent Friedrich Schlegel, with papal tiara, while leaning against a close stool is a harridan Caroline, between them a partially-veiled female figure, revealing bosom and buttocks, who is of course Lucinde. The artist knew his stuff, for the car, drawn by asses, is crushing under its wheels the works of Wieland, Klopstock, Milton, Euripides, Voltaire, but also Kotzebue and Böttiger, while in a corner, August Wilhelm and Tieck are crowning each other with laurels and Jacob Böhme is emerging from the mystical depths. These engravings have maintained their wit, which cannot be said for the other polemical ephemera of the period. The Romantics could not respond in kind.

Fig. 11 'Schlegel and Tieck Crowning Each Other With Laurels'. Extract from the caricature 'Die neuere Ästhetik' (1803). Courtesy of Wallstein Verlag, image in the public domain.

---

445 Helmut Sembdner, *Schütz-Lacrimas. Das Leben des Romantikerfreundes, Poeten und Literaturkritikers Wilhelm von Schütz (1776-1847)* (Berlin: Erich Schmidt, 1974), 26f.

446 See Robert Darnton, *The Great Cat Massacre and Other Episodes in French Cultural History* (Harmondsworth: Penguin, 2001 [1984]), ill. 84. Revolutionary prints are another possible source.

Friedrich Schlegel's *Europa*

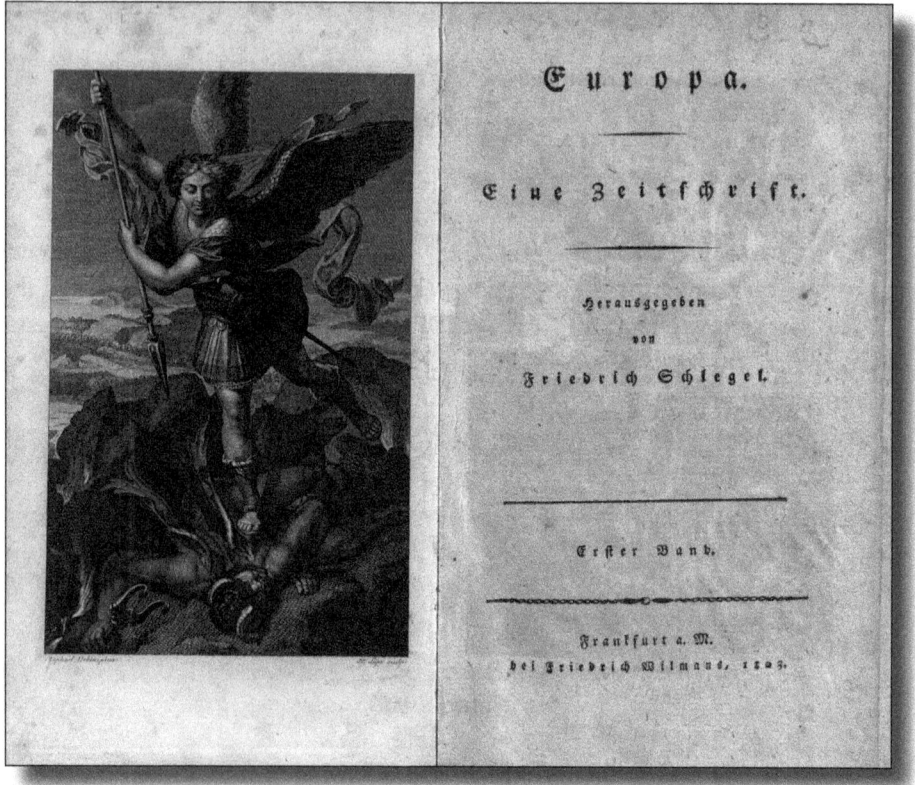

Fig. 12 *Europa. Eine Zeitschrift. Herausgegeben von Friedrich Schlegel* (Frankfurt am Main, 1803, 1805). Frontispiece and title page. © and by kind permission of the Master and Fellows of Trinity College, Cambridge, CC BY-NC 4.0.

All this may have prompted the Schlegel brothers to detach themselves spiritually but also physically from their German homeland. As said, by late 1802, Friedrich and Dorothea were in Paris. It was in some measure a parting of the ways for the two brothers. Of course there were enough protestations of solidarity: August Wilhelm's poem *An Friedrich Schlegel. Im Herbst* 1802 [To Friedrich Schlegel. In the Autumn of 1802], but not published until 1808 when the brothers were together for a brief time in Vienna,[447] seemed to suggest a common purpose, a conjoint effort, but with a division of labour. Friedrich was to pursue Oriental studies in Paris, August Wilhelm Spanish translations in Berlin. The poetic images

---

447 *SW*, I, 244-250.

speak of one brother (Friedrich) putting down roots, steering the course, delving in the innermost parts of the earth, the other (August Wilhelm) as rising sap, trimming the sails, tending the products of the soil. Both, in the terms of the poem, would return to their homeland to enjoy the fruits of their labours. It was not to be. Does this poem not confirm what so many have since maintained: that the younger brother had the ideas (mined the ores) while the elder merely gave them formulation (reaped the harvest), the one a thinker, the other a mere translator (in all senses of that word)? These are ultimately sterile debates, and above all they do not reflect what the brothers thought. Let each one pursue his sphere of the intellect and of poetry, was Friedrich's response in 1808. In an image reminiscent of Goethe, he saw himself as the unruly element, the wild stream, his brother the broad reflecting surface of the lake into which it flows.[448]

Putting first things first, Friedrich had by April of 1803 set up a periodical, *Europa*, published by Friedrich Wilmans in Frankfurt, the first of the three that he was eventually to edit. Needing money and seeing publishers somewhat grandly as mere commodity suppliers, he harried Wilmans for cash on the nail.[449] It was not until a year later that Dorothea was baptised in the Protestant rite and the two were married—in the chapel of the Swedish envoy, the same sanctuary where in 1786 Germaine Necker had entered into her union with Baron de Staël-Holstein.[450] There had simply been too much else to do for an 'idealist or poet in partibus infidelium',[451] as Friedrich described himself. There was a Provençal project that would investigate the roots of Romance poetry. He was learning Persian with the orientalist Antoine-Léonard de Chézy. Alexander Hamilton,[452] a Scotsman formerly in the employ of the East India Company and caught by the accident of war in Paris, was teaching him Sanskrit. 'Encyclopädie' was in the air.[453] There were plans to use Paris as a stepping-stone to the south of

---

448 The poem, 'An A. W. Schlegel', *ibid.*, 250-253.
449 *Krisenjahre*, I, 42-45; Doris Reimer, *Passion & Kalkül. Der Verleger Georg Andreas Reimer (1776-1842)* (Berlin, New York: de Gruyter, 1999), 259.
450 *Krisenjahre*, I, 70f., III, 58.
451 *Friedrich Schlegels Briefe an seinen Bruder August Wilhelm*, ed. Oskar F. Walzel [Walzel] (Berlin: Speyer & Peters, 1890), 498-510, ref. 501.
452 On Hamilton see Rosane Rocher, 'Alexander Hamilton (1762-1824). A Chapter in the Early History of Sanskrit Philology', *American Oriental Series*, 51 (New Haven: American Oriental Society, 1968), 44-52; Chen Tzoref-Ashkenazi, *Der romantische Mythos vom Ursprung der Deutschen. Friedrich Schlegels Suche nach der indogermanischen Verbindung*, trans. Markus Lemke, Schriftenreihe des Minerva Instituts für deutsche Geschichte der Universität Tel Aviv, 29 (Göttingen: Wallstein, 2009), 117-120.
453 Walzel, 518.

France, to Spain, to Italy. Would August Wilhelm not join them? Of course money was the problem. Were someone to give him a thousand francs per annum for two or three years, all would be well. Not that they were living in straitened circumstances—they never did—but at the edge of town, in the rue Clichy, in an elegant *hôtel* with garden.[454] To ease the exchequer, they took in a number of paying guests, the said Alexander Hamilton, presiding over the beginnings of German Sanskrit studies, in addition the young Hanoverian Gottfried Hagemann, another student of Sanskrit,[455] but also three young sons of Cologne patricians, Sulpiz and Melchior Boisserée, later under Friedrich's guidance to be the revivers of German medieval art and architecture, and their friend Johann Baptist Bertram. These three young gentlemen were receiving private lectures from Schlegel on the history of literature and art (and paying well), balancing in some respect the public lecture course that August Wilhelm was delivering in Berlin.

All this would seem to indicate that Paris, the cosmopolitan metropolis of the Consulate, was about to become the centre of German Romanticism. There was of course nothing new in Germans coming to terms with themselves and their culture in a great foreign city, be it Rome or London or Paris. Already a cohort loosely associated with the Romantic circle had been to Paris: Wilhelm von Humboldt, the Tiecks' schoolfriend Wilhelm von Burgsdorff, who had reported back on the Paris theatre scene, and Friedrich Tieck himself, in the centre of French neo-classicism. The painter Gottlieb Schick, whose work in Rome Schlegel was to praise, had also studied with David. And the year 1804 would see the most famous German of his time—Alexander von Humboldt—fresh from his epoch-making journeys to the 'equinoctial regions' of America, choosing Paris as his place of abode for the next nearly twenty years. The loot and plunder from French military successes in Italy was rolling in—already in 1798 the bronze horses of St Mark's in Venice had bowed to Bonaparte's yoke—and by 1803, when *Europa* was appearing, the greatest assemblage of Western art ever seen was being put together by courtesy of the First Consul.[456]

---

454 *Ibid.*, 510-518.
455 Rocher (1968), 54.
456 Ingrid Oesterle, 'Paris—das moderne Rom?', in: Conrad Wiedemann (ed.), *Rom-Paris-London. Erfahrung und Selbsterfahrung deutscher Schriftsteller und Künstler in den fremden Metropolen. Ein Symposion*, Germanistische Symposien. Berichtsbände, 8 (Stuttgart: Metzler, 1988), 375-419, ref. 388; Thomas W. Gaehtgens, 'Das Musée Napoléon und sein Einfluß auf die Kunstgeschichte', in: Antje Middeldorf Kosegarten (ed.), *Johann Dominicus Fiorillo und die romantische Bewegung um 1800* (Göttingen: Wallstein, 1997), 339-369.

2. Jena and Berlin (1795-1804)

Thus it is that the art criticism of *Europa* could draw on, among others, the Lucien Bonaparte collection[457] and a far greater array of excellence than the *Athenaeum* had been able to cite. While not caring for French neo-classical painting itself, Friedrich Schlegel had to admit that the lack of a 'Central-Stadt'[458] in Germany was an inhibiting factor for German artists' development. Berlin, where his brother was lecturing, was, despite being a major city, only *A* capital, not *THE* capital.

And so *Europa* was to do two things. It was to report on the sheer richness, vibrancy, plenitude of Paris in all areas of the mind and the arts, the advances in archaeology since the Egyptian campaign, those in the physical sciences, or in philology, the *république des lettres* gathered in Paris,[459] while a name like Cuvier[460] indicated a focal point in the sciences. Producing grand syntheses and unities was however something given to the Germans, not the French, 'Ganzes', 'Einheit', not a mere conglomerate of various branches of knowledge.[461] If this was consciously overlooking the *Encyclopédie* or Buffon, it was also part of a general disparagement of French literary culture, past and present.

With this, Friedrich Schlegel struck the other dominant note in *Europa*, the one that echoed with his brother in Berlin. First, there was the theme of loss that formed the immediate historical background to *Europa*. France, with Paris as its centre, was a nation forged by the French Revolution. Germany by contrast, lay in ruin: the Principal Resolution of the Imperial Deputation (*Reichsdeputationshauptschluss*) of 1803, spelled formally the end of the old Holy Roman Empire, the final push that Bonaparte had given to the tottering edifice. The emphasis was therefore on Europe, but on the Europe that once was. In the important introductory section, Friedrich recorded his real and symbolic journey from Berlin to Paris.[462] He had seen past greatness only in medieval vestiges and remains in Germany, like the Wartburg, like the Rhine and its castles, evidence of a time that had once enjoyed political and spiritual unity, a Europe that had once embraced North and South, German and Romance. Thus on the one hand the discourse was one of decay, *déchéance* and disunity. What had held

---

457 *Europa. Eine Zeitschrift. Herausgegeben von Friedrich Schlegel* (Frankfurt: Wilmans, 1803, 1805) I, i, 112.
458 *Ibid.*, 105.
459 *Ibid.*, I, ii, 107-16.
460 *Ibid.*, 124.
461 *Ibid.*, 132f.
462 *Ibid.*, I, i, 5-40.

Europe together at the time of its greatness (the Middle Ages) had been the union of the church and the arts (quoting August Wilhelm's poem on this subject with approval) within the culture of chivalry. The subsequent interruptions and losses of continuity, whether caused by the downfall of the old Holy Roman Empire or by the Reformation, or the much-hated Enlightenment and its child, the French Revolution, had left the Germans with a past and its poetry and painting, an uncertain present, and an even more dubious future.

But that was only one side. The tone was also aggressive, adversarial and triumphant. The frontispiece, an engraving by Lips based on Raphael's archangel Michael vanquishing Satan, made that clear. There could be no discourse with those who were 'not for us', let alone those against us. The one-sided deference to Goethe was now a thing of the past, and there was much in *Europa* that Goethe would find unappealing (Schiller, predictably, was mentioned just once). *Europa* was nevertheless also a prophetic text: in the present state of separation the seeds of a unity—yet to be regained— might be discerned. The spur to higher endeavours, to a real revelation, were the literatures and cultures of the North and South that in the past had provided us with inspiration, and their cultural representatives— Boccaccio, Cervantes, Calderón, Shakespeare, Raphael, Correggio, Dürer, the civilisation of India. Cultural and artistic manifestations—in France or Germany—that did not measure up to these standards were to be exposed and identified.

If Friedrich Schlegel furnished most of the ideological—and prophetic— statements for *Europa*, his brother August Wilhelm was also an active contributor to the journal, in fact over a hundred pages of the second number were by him. It was to him that Friedrich wrote, urging the widest possible distribution of *Europa*: to Copenhagen, to Stockholm, to St Petersburg.[463] It was a forum, too, for younger talents who were later to disseminate Romanticism through their own poetry, not through theoretical pronouncements, the young Achim von Arnim,[464] fresh from his grand tour, or August Wilhelm's protégé Friedrich de la Motte Fouqué.[465] Friedrich's articles reflected in unsystematic fashion the more ordered discourse that his pupils the Boisserées and Bertram were receiving in Paris, to be

---

463 Walzel, 509.
464 The author of *Erzählungen von Schauspielen* in *Europa*, I, ii, 140-192.
465 The author of *Der gehörnte Siegfried an der Schmiede* in *Europa*, II, i, 82-91 and *Der alte Held an der Schmiede, ibid.*, 91-94.

continued in Cologne, but the private nature of these lectures prevented their publication in his lifetime.[466] August Wilhelm by contrast sent to his brother what are in effect discrete sections from his much-publicised Berlin lectures. His review of Bernhardi's treatise on language, *Sprachlehre* (1801, 1803),[467] covered very largely the same points as his remarks on language in his first lecture cycle. There, his discussion of the theories of the origin of language was intended to merge into an account of the human urge for rhythm and poetry and the different manifestations, historical and cultural, that these may take. Reviewing Bernhardi, he examined the latter's views on an inner language structure that was, as it were, part of the human intellect, that referred back to the origins of mankind but also looked forward to communication among a community. It is in the discussion of poetry's origins that Berlin and *Europa* have most in common:[468] poetry evolved through separating itself from quotidian matters, by evolving a mathematically determined accent and a rhythmical unity. In the ancient world prosody, metre, and verse were kept severely distinct: in the modern they are subject to 'mixtures'. The Vienna Lectures in 1808 were to elevate this to a principle determining and distinguishing the 'Classical' and the 'Romantic'.

The other extract from Berlin struck a more sombre note, contrasting with the generally positive and forward-looking tone of *Europa*. *Ueber Litteratur, Kunst und Geist des Zeitalters* [On Literature, Art and the Spirit of the Age] repeated very largely what his second course of 1802-3 had said[469] and anticipated some of the tone of the final set, the *Enzyclopädie* of 1803. Whereas the first part of the periodical had contained a generally upbeat account by Friedrich, simply called *Literatur*,[470] essentially setting out the achievements in poetry, philosophy and science of the Romantic school (not forgetting Goethe or even Schiller), August Wilhelm offered a *tabula rasa* of the century that had so recently ended. Apart from a few notable exceptions—and they, Winckelmann, Lessing, Hemsterhuis and Goethe, were very few indeed—Schlegel found no modern literature to speak of and—not surprisingly—no satisfactory national traditions of poetry or criticism. As against the mere indifferentism, tolerance, utilitarianism and

---

466 These comprise *KA*, XI.
467 *Europa*, I, ii, 193-204; *SW*, XII, 141-153.
468 *KAV*, I, 394-429; Jesinghaus, 36-42.
469 *Europa*, I, ii, 3-95; *KAV*, II, i, 195-253.
470 *Europa*, I, i, 41-63.

general 'enlightenment' of his own day, he harked back instead to a past unity of religion, philosophy and morals, held together by mythology, now lost in this age; the religious nature of culture, the 'wonder' of scientific discovery, the sense of magic, of the chaotic and ever-changing nature of originary being. But like Friedrich, August Wilhelm also perceived signs of regenerating processes, mostly among the like-minded Romantic poets to whom he belonged. The context was important: the remarks made by August Wilhelm in Berlin prefaced a general account of the poetry of the Greeks and Romans; his general catalogue of German non-achievement and 'Nullität' for Paris came after Friedrich's generally positive account of German achievements.

August Wilhelm's other major contribution to *Europa*, *Ueber das spanische Theater*,[471] actually supplied what his third Berlin cycle did not say. For the account of Spanish drama there was scrappy, to say the least, whereas here was an informative survey of plays by Cervantes, Lope de Vega and Calderón, patterns of development, the general structures that he was to fill out in detail in Vienna. Spain had what many other literatures (French and German among them) no longer had: the magical and imaginary, the fiercely patriotic, the deeply religious. Schlegel picked up the common eighteenth-century cliché that saw the drama of the Spanish and the English as a valid alternative to the neo-classicism and French *bienséances* that had dominated other literary cultures, a point that would become the structuring principle of his Vienna lectures.

Calderón

Schlegel had also been in the process of translating Calderón.[472] The perfunctoriness of his remarks on Calderón in the Berlin lectures, but also on Shakespeare, may be another way of saying: read my translations, they contain all you need to know. If today Schlegel's *Spanisches Theater* is less well-known than his Shakespeare, this may have to do with the diverging paths the two dramatists were to take in their subsequent reception in

---

471 *Europa*, I, ii, 72-87.
472 Part 1 published as: *Spanisches Theater. Herausgegeben von August Wilhelm Schlegel* (Berlin: Reimer, 1803), part 2 (with a reprint of part 1) as: *Schauspiele von Don Pedro Calderon de la Barca. Übersetzt von August Wilhelm Schlegel* (Berlin: Hitzig, 1809). See in general Henry W. Sullivan, *Calderón in the German Lands and the Low Countries: His Reception and Influence, 1654-1980* (Cambridge, etc.: Cambridge UP, 1983), esp. 169-183; Christoph Strosetzki, 'August Wilhelm Schlegels Rezeption spanischer Literatur', in: Mix/Strobel (2010), 144-157.

Germany. Unlike Shakespeare, Calderón was never 'ganz unser'. But it is also true to say that no other single work by Schlegel went through so many later editions (but with different publishers), including three different Viennese pirates.[473] Yet stage adaptations of Calderón in the eighteenth century had made him better known than Shakespeare; similar 'big names' (Voltaire, Lessing) had had significant things to say about him. Göttingen in Schlegel's student days had been a centre of German Hispanism, and he, like the Humboldt brothers and Ludwig Tieck, knew both the basics of Spanish and also its refinements before he left university, indeed there had been those three metrical renderings of Spanish romances by him in the Göttingen *Musenalmanach* for 1792, another part of Bürger's legacy.[474] As yet there was no reference to sources: these he would supply in Vienna, even acknowledging his debt to the dry-as-dust Göttingen professor Friedrich Bouterwek, whose compendious account of Spanish literature also appeared in 1804.

For the translation enterprise itself, Schlegel showed again some of that hard-headedness that the Romantics often displayed in publishing matters. He transferred his loyalties from Cotta to Georg Andreas Reimer in Berlin, who used the impress 'Realschulbuchhandlung'. Still based on the premises at the corner of Kochstrasse and Friedrichstrasse ('Checkpoint Charlie' in less happy times) and before he moved to a grand *palais* in the Wilhelmstrasse,[475] Reimer counted most of the prominent Romantics (Fichte, Schleiermacher, Tieck, later Arnim) among his authors, and now added Schlegel. Not for long, as the story of their slightly stormy relationship was to show. Reimer attended Schlegel's lectures and may have spotted the need for a Calderón translation. It did not sell well (although Schlegel received over 300 talers for it), and the whole enterprise ended in acrimony.[476] Schlegel's Calderón had also to compete with other

---

473 There were pirate editions of *El principe constante* (*Der standhafte Prinz*) in Vienna 1813, 1826, and 1828, and in Leipzig 1845. Information in Sullivan (1983), 438.

474 *SW*, IV, 169-171. Wilhelm Schwartz, *August Wilhelm Schlegels Verhältnis zur spanischen und portugiesischen Literatur*, Romanistische Arbeiten, 3 (Halle: Niemeyer 1914), 6f.

475 Reimer, 62, 119.

476 Schlegel translated *La devoción de la Cruz* (as *Die Andacht zum Kreuze*), *El mayor encanto Amor* (as *Über allen Zauber Liebe*), *La Vanda y la flor* (as *Die Schärpe und die Blume*) for the *Spanisches Theater* (Berlin 1803). A further two plays appeared in the second volume of the reuissue, *Schauspiele des Don Pedro Calderon de la Barca* (Berlin 1809): *El principe constante* (as *Der standhafte Prinz*), *La puente de Mantible* (as *Die Brücke von Mantible*). On the relationship with Reimer and the publication history see Reimer (1999), 62, 74, 81, 278-292. A poem by Gries on the tribulations of translating Spanish for the book market in Reinhard Tgarht (1983), 532-534.

versions and adaptations, beginning in 1815 with that by Johann Diederich Gries, his Jena pupil.

In the process, however, Schlegel had introduced Goethe to Calderón,[477] sending him his version of *La devoción de la cruz* [The Devotion of the Cross] in manuscript in September of 1802. This was almost the last area in which their interests fully coincided before irreconcilable differences obtruded. Goethe was delighted, amazed; Schiller, despite his dislike of Schlegel, similarly. Of *El princípe constante* [The Constant Prince] Goethe wrote in 1804 that 'if poetry were to be temporarily lost, one could restore it from this play'. High praise indeed. Goethe, the Weimar theatre director, immediately saw possibilities here: the formality, 'artificiality', splendour of Calderón's verse, the religious ceremonial, the conflict of cultures (Christianity versus paganism) stood in marked contrast to Shakespeare's unruliness and lack of religion (Goethe had had to rewrite almost a third of *Romeo and Juliet* to make it acceptable for the Weimar audience, indeed he was inclining more and more to the view that Shakespeare was not a dramatist for the theatre at all). Calderón appealed to his interest in the Orient: he cited him in the same breath as Hafiz. There were even fragments of a religious drama in the Calderonian style. At the first Weimar performance of *El princípe constante*, in 1811, Goethe was moved to tears, as never with Shakespeare. Of course later—much later—he would say that both Calderón and Shakespeare were 'will o' the wisps', leading the unwary into uncharted perils, but who could deny the influence of both of them on the second part of *Faust*?

Of course no-one was more enthusiastic about Calderón than the Romantics themselves. Tieck's huge, sprawling, kaleidoscopic dramas *Genoveva* and *Kaiser Octavianus* fairly luxuriated in the poetic forms to be found in the Spanish dramatist, *redondillas, silvas, octavas reales*, the *glosas*. Zacharias Werner, whose bizarre paths were to cross with Schlegel's in Coppet, found Calderonian inspiration for the religious and mythological pageants of his plays and their lush and varied versification. Even the unhappy *Alarcos* was also a misbegotten child of Calderón's, and Wilhelm von Schütz, a friend of Tieck's and then of Schlegel's, issued—with Schlegel's misguided encouragement (his name appears as 'editor' on the title page)—his tragedy *Lacrimas* in 1803,[478] all orientally odorous but

---

477 For the following see the useful article by Hans-Jürgen Lüsebrink, 'Pedro Calderón de la Barca', in: Bernd Witte *et al.*, *Goethe-Handbuch*, 4 vols in 5 (Stuttgart, Weimar: Metzler, 1996-98), IV, i, 149-150.

478 [Wilhelm von Schütz], *Lacrimas, ein Schauspiel. Herausgegeben von August Wilhelm Schlegel* (Berlin: Realschulbuchhandlung, 1803); Sembdner, *Schütz-Lacrimas*, 21-31.

without Calderón's religious substance. There were to be later recantations (notably by Tieck himself). The genie was however well and truly out of the bottle, and the mode for Calderonian drama in the nineteenth century stems from this generation. For Schlegel, the chance of showing his mastery of rhyming verse was too good to be missed: his verse technique in the Calderón translations has been described as virtuosic,[479] and it was he who introduced into German dramatic versification the trochaic tetrameter that has not always been his best legacy.

If Schegel's Shakespeare translation was originally planned to take in all thirty-six plays (or forty and more, according to some adventuresome Romantic attributions) there was no question of him rendering over two hundred by Calderón. Some have said that the sheer quality of Schlegel's Shakespeare deterred nineteenth-century dramatists and inhibited the unfolding of the genre. That certainly could not be claimed for his Calderón. On the contrary, his preference for *La devoción de la cruz* may well have led unwittingly to a rash of so-called 'fate dramas'[480] whose loss would not be a great impoverishment for German letters. It was all too easy for dramatists, Tieck, Friedrich Schlegel and Wilhelm von Schütz among them, to apply a formal sheen and create a vaguely Catholicizing or chivalric atmosphere, allegedly Calderonian, without an understanding of the courtly and aristocratic culture out of which Calderón had emerged and in which he operated. For all that, the plays that Schlegel actually chose for translation[481] encompassed the drama of fate and redemption (*La devoción de la cruz*), an allegorical *Festspiel* displaying the 'types' of virtue (Ulysses) in conflict with its opposite (Circe) (*El mayor encanto amor*), a *comedia de capa y espada* [cloak and dagger] on the theme of love and honour (with homage to the ruler) (*La banda y la flor*) and the great baroque drama of constancy and magnanimity, its action both 'historical' and exemplary (*El príncipe constante*).

If Schlegel can be said to have inaugurated a 'Spanish decade' [482]with his advocacy of Calderón, it is equally clear why—apart from purely pragmatic factors—the Shakespeare translation could not flourish in his scheme of things. With Schlegel in 1811 still writing of himself to Goethe—not in

---

479 Sullivan (1983), 174f.
480 Swana L. Hardy, *Goethe, Calderon und die romantische Theorie des Dramas*, Heidelberger Forschungen, 10 (Heidelberg: Winter, 1965), 53f.
481 *Ibid.*, 61-76.
482 *Ibid.*, 21.

all seriousness—as a 'missionary' for Calderón[483] and the Vienna lectures having stressed the southern Catholicism of the great Spanish dramatist, it was evident that not even Madame de Staël's Swiss Protestantism could effect a cure overnight. 'He inclines towards Catholicism and talks nonsense on the subject of religion' was her assessment in 1804.[484] It was, as we shall see, only one side, but it was his public aspect. It also meant that Schlegel, as a drama critic in Berlin in the years 1802-3, was even more impatient than before with the fare on the stage,[485] with the things that Shakespeare or Calderón would have done so much better, further signs of that 'Nullität' of which *Europa* had so eloquently spoken. Madame Unzelmann's acting would be excepted from these strictures, but that was another matter.

2.3 The Berlin Lectures

Which brings us to the principal reason for Schlegel being in Berlin in the first place, his so-called Berlin Lectures (1801-04).[486] He had had no salary

---

483 Wieneke, 157.
484 Geiger, *Dichter und Frauen*, 125.
485 This drama criticism, written for the *Zeitung für die elegante Welt*, is in *SW*, IX, 181-230.
486 The publication history of the Berlin lectures is complex and is set out as follows. The first cycle (1801-02) remained unpublished during Schlegel's lifetime and was published as: *A. W. Schlegels Vorlesungen über schöne Litteratur und Kunst. Erster Teil (1801-1802). Die Kunstlehre* [ed. Jakob Minor], Deutsche Litteraturdenkmale des 18. und 19 Jahrhunderts, 17 [DLD] (Heilbronn: Henninger, 1884) [Minor I]; (*KAV*, I, 179-472), except that sections on art had been incorporated into the later *Vorlesungen über Theorie und Geschichte der bildenden Künste*, given in Berlin in 1827 (*KAV*, II, i, 289-348), variants and extensions to the original lectures set out in Minor, I, xxxi-lxxi. A small section, called *Ueber das Verhältniß der schönen Künste zur Natur; über Täuschung und Wahrscheinlichkeit; über Stil und Manier. Aus Vorlesungen, gehalten in Berlin im Jahre 1802*, was published in 1808 in Seckendorf's and Stoll's periodical *Prometheus* (5.-6. Heft, 1-28; *SW*, IX, 295-319) (variants set out in Minor, I, xxvii-xxxi).
The second cycle (1802-03) was published as: *A. W. Schlegels Vorlesungen über schöne Litteratur und Kunst. Zweiter Teil (1802-03), Geschichte der klassischen Literatur*, DLD, 18 (Heilbronn: Henninger, 1884) [Minor, II]; (*KAV*, I, 472-781), except that the section *Allgemeine Übersicht des gegenwärtigen Zustandes der deutschen Literatur* had been published separately in *Europa* II, i (1803), 3-95 as *Ueber Litteratur, Kunst und Geist des Zeitalters. Einige Vorlesungen in Berlin, zu Ende des J. 1802, gehalten von A. W. Schlegel* (*KAV*, II, i, 197-253), the variants set out in Minor, II, xvi-xx.
The third cycle (1803-04) was published as: *A. W. Schlegels Vorlesungen über schöne Literatur und Kunst. Dritter Teil (1803-04) Geschichte der romantischen Litteratur*, DLD, 19 (Heilbronn: Henninger, 1884) [(Minor, III]; (*KAV*, II, i, 1-194), except that the section *Ueber das Mittelalter, Eine Vorlesung, gehalten 1803, von A. W. Schlegel*, had been published in Friedrich Schlegel's *Deutsches Museum* in 1812 (II, 11, 432-462), variants in Minor III, xii-xvi, the whole text in *KAV*, II, i, 256-288.
A fourth lecture, held privately and not part of the other series, *Vorlesungen über Encyclopädie* (1803), remained unpublished until 2006 (*KAV, III*).

in Jena. Public lectures were a source of emolument, and an independent writer and scholar had to be both astute and versatile. They saw him, although billed as 'Herr Professor A.W. Schlegel aus Jena',[487] breaking out of that enclosed academic world into the public sphere, where the audience was now drawn from the widest circles of educated and literate society, the *monde* of a capital city, with its court, its salons, its diplomatic corps, its institutions of higher learning. With Berlin still without a university, and with few German universities situated in large towns, there was a need for this form of public discourse. The academy lectures on classical antiquity by Karl Philipp Moritz that Tieck and Wackenroder had attended in Berlin from 1789 to 1792 before they went off to university, are an example, indeed Friedrich Nicolai's vademecum, his *Wegweiser* of 1793, lists nearly thirty lecture series.[488] Fichte's later *Addresses to the German Nation* in 1808 with their message not just for Berlin but for all who called themselves German, are another instance. It has even been suggested that Schlegel's lectures attracted some competition in Berlin itself during the period 1802-5, not least from Fichte himself and from Gall the phrenologist.[489] Dresden, also a royal capital but not a university city, was the venue for several important lecture series in this decade, and Karl August Böttiger, now taking sides against the Romantics, was to inaugurate them in 1806. There was an international aspect to this desire for public lectures. Cuvier was to give cycles in Paris, Coleridge and Humphry Davy in London, Alexander von Humboldt in Berlin—and of course August Wilhelm Schlegel himself in Vienna.

There was much that overlapped with the other great projects on which he was as ever working concurrently. They coincided with his last burst of poetic writing, up to 1805, when he was still seeking to demonstrate an undiminished belief in his own poetic powers (or his powers of versification), whether in original form or in translation. Hence his remarks on Euripides, in the second cycle of lectures in 1802-3, coincided with his

---

487 Minor, I, viif.
488 Nicolai, *Wegweiser*, 132-133.
489 Minor, I, xiii. The later educator Heinrich Friedrich Theodor Kohlrausch states that Fichte lectured to an audience not dissimilar to Schlegel's (but without women), on 'Wisssenschaftslehre', in the winter of 1802-03, on 'Anweisung zum seligen Leben' the following winter, and 'Grundzüge des gegenwärtigen Zeitalters' the winter after that. Gall was lecturing on craniology. Fr. Kohlrausch, *Erinnerungen aus meinem Leben* (Hanover: Hahn, 1863), 65-69, 74. Kohlrausch was joined by Wolf von Baudissin and others. Bernd Goldmann, *Wolf Heinrich von Baudissin. Leben und Werk eines großen Übersetzers* (Hildesheim: Gerstenberg, 1981), 28.

own *Ion*. His comments on Romantic poetry in the third cycle interlocked with his own versions of Dante's *Vita nuova*, Petrarch and others in his volume *Blumensträuße italienischer, spanischer und portugiesischer Poesie* [Nosegays of Flowers from Italian, Spanish and Portuguese Poetry] of 1804 (another ill-starred enterprise with Reimer),[490] and these are most likely the poems that he read out to his audience. When they heard the section on sculpture in the first series, the audience might know that the lecturer had also reviewed the latest art exhibition in Berlin and had discussed the respective merits of Schadow and Friedrich Tieck.[491] In some cases, the Berlin Lectures took their place in a discourse that extended from the 1790s into the second decade of the nineteenth century (his medieval studies are a good instance); in other cases, they contained the only definitive remarks ever made by him on certain themes, on the *novella*, for example. All this is by way of saying that the Berlin Lectures should ideally be read as a continuum with *Die Horen*, the *Athenaeum* and, to some extent, the Jena lectures, for these are often the spoken or unspoken authorities to which he refers. They stand for attitudes that he presupposed even as the audience changed from students in Jena, who were supposed to be learning something, to a Berlin *monde*, generally receptive to literature and culture, but who wanted their instruction admixed with a little pleasure.

It is important to grasp that these lectures, despite the enormous effort of study and formulation and the frequent incisiveness of utterance, were not always final and definitive statements. From the Berlin cycle he selected only relatively small extracts for publication, proof that they were in his eyes not yet ready for wider distribution. Their inner relationship with the later series in Vienna is complex and will occupy us in due course. In some cases—the fine arts are one—he went on to frame things more systematically in a different context. In others—Dante for instance—different and more pressing needs crowded in and caused a project to be left effectively in an abandoned state. The historical model that he used to reinstate the Middle Ages (third cycle) as a force for political, social and cultural cohesion, was to recur in variations, first formulated in the lectures on *Encylopädie*, then in Vienna. Yet we also see him moving away from this eurocentric view and seeking increasingly to accommodate Sanskrit into his general scheme of things.

---

490 Untypically, Reimer miscalculated the print runs and had 1,600 copies done, leaving 358 remaining. Schlegel received 40 Friedrichsd'or. Reimer (1999), 74, 279.
491 *SW*, IX, 158-179.

Even as we have them, these lectures, with a sophistication of formulation over long sections, must have tested his Berlin audience, much as his earlier ones had extended his students in Jena. Where Fichte's lectures were rhetorically sustained, Schlegel's style was uneven and he did not always hold his hearers.[492] Some even nodded off.[493] His notes can also tail off into keywords and jottings, suggesting a more off-the-cuff, extemporised approach. The aides-mémoire referring to passages to be read aloud suggest that he frequently interrupted his technical or historical explication to give the audience an opportunity to savour his own renditions of texts from Homer, Aeschylus, Sophocles, or the *Nibelungenlied*. These readings—we unfortunately no longer have all of his versions[494]— were a concession to a more popular, non-academic style. One hearer even remarked that Schlegel's own lecturing style flagged when he was dealing with material that he found of lesser interest.[495] Despite bold and challenging forays into aesthetics and the philosophy of history and even a scheme for a systematic organisation of knowledge on art and poetry, the private series called *Encyclopädie*, the overall impression is also increasingly one of fragmentation, of leads and approaches that are severed, almost in mid-sentence.

As said, most of this corpus of material was not published in Schlegel's own lifetime: it was left to others to pass on its insights. Only very selected extracts in Seckendorf's periodical *Prometheus* and his brother's *Deutsches Museum* reached an immediate readership, limited of course to subscribers. Unlike the Vienna cycle of 1808, which were followed almost immediately by publication (and translation into French and English), the Berlin Lectures had their greatest effect on those who were actually there. This could apply even to seminal sections, like his remarks on the Middle Ages: the rightly famous section *Über das Mittelalter*, delivered in 1803, was not published until 1812, and then in one of his brother's short-lived periodicals. Much had happened by then to bring the Middle Ages to a wider national consciousness, not least the humiliations wrought by Napoleon and the perceived need for a revival of the nation's cultural heritage. Schlegel's was by then only one voice (if one with authority), along with Tieck's more

---

492 Kohlrausch, 72f.
493 *Caspar Voght und sein Hamburger Freundeskreis. Briefe aus einem tätigen Leben*, ed. Kurt Detlev Möller and Anneliese Tecke, 3 vols, Veröffentlichung des Vereins für Hamburgische Geschichte, 15, i-iii (Hamburg: Christians, 1959-67), II, 123.
494 Caspar Voght, for one, did not enjoy the Pindar renditions. *Ibid.*, 107.
495 Kohlrausch, 72f.

accessible selection *Minnelieder aus dem Schwäbischen Zeitalter* [Love-Songs from the Swabian Period] of 1803 (to which Schlegel frequently refers) or Arnim and Brentano's popularising anthology *Des Knaben Wunderhorn* [Youth's Magic Horn] of 1806. Antiquarian endeavours by others, too, played their part in evoking and rediscovering this past poetic age, its magic and charm and its occasional barbarities. It is doubtful whether his unflattering conspectus of the contemporary literary scene in Germany, *Allgemeine Übersicht des gegenwärtigen Zustandes der deutschen Literatur* [General Overview of the Contemporary State of German Literature], which was the opening blast of his 1802-03 series and which was inserted in *Europa* under a different title and with some reformulation, actually reached the wider audience in Copenhagen or St Petersburg that his brother Friedrich hoped for (although Friedrich Gentz read it in Vienna).[496]

As said, the lectures often hark back to earlier criticism and translations and also refer forward to plans yet to be realised. One example: his remarks on the history and theory of language in two of the Berlin cycles (and in *Europa*) draw heavily on material from *Die Horen* and the Jena lectures and have a certain finality. Then there are nearly two decades of silence on the subject until he starts corresponding with Wilhelm von Humboldt in the 1820s. Sometimes the emphasis in Berlin is different from what went before. His successive remarks on Dante in the 1790s had been a semi-biographical account, then translations in extract (mainly from *Inferno*), with his remarks in the *Athenaeum* tending more towards the religious content. Now, in Berlin, Dante was to be enshrined as the pivotal figure of a 'Romantic' Middle Ages and a central witness in Catholic mysticism (mainly drawing on *Purgatorio* and *Paradiso*). For all that, there was never to be a linked-up account of the great Italian poet, nor did he ever reissue any of his earlier writing on Dante (or Calderón).

Certain major figures of Romantic poetry he chose not to treat in lecture form at all, leaving his own translations, or those by others whom he trusted (Gries, Tieck) to make the essential statement. Thus these lectures contain very little about Shakespeare, whom he was (just) still translating, or Calderón, whose translation appeared more or less to coincide with his remarks, or Cervantes, Tieck's version of *Don Quixote* having already been the subject of Schlegel's very favourable review. Shakespeare and Calderón would have to wait until Vienna in 1808 for a fuller treatment,

---

496 *Briefe von und an Friedrich von Gentz*, ed. Friedrich Carl Wittichen, 3 vols in 4 (Munich and Berlin: Oldenbourg, 1909-13), II, 121.

for the times in Vienna required emphases different from those in Berlin, when these poets' respective religious and national messages would have more direct relevance than in 1802-03. Aristophanes, deftly characterised in the Parny review in the *Athenaeum*, but perfunctorily dealt with in Berlin, would similarly have to wait until Vienna for a fuller treatment. Euripides, dispraised both in Berlin and in Vienna, would be used for different ideological purposes in the *Comparaison entre la Phèdre de Racine et celle d'Euripide* of 1807.

Where were the lectures held, and who came? With his accustomed meticulousness, Schlegel planned his four lecture cycles, three in public and one in private, well in advance. The public lectures were billed for Sundays and Wednesdays in the winters of 1801-02, 1802-03, and 1803-04, the private one for May, 1803, roughly to coincide with the long academic winter semester (November-Easter), but also with the ball season and the opera and theatre, when people would be 'in town'. These were not idle considerations, for Schlegel went to considerable pains to make his offerings rather better than those of some professor or other from a *Gymnasium* or academy.[497] What he called the 'junta' of his Berlin friends (Schleiermacher, both Bernhardis, Schütz) received exact instructions about the invitation cards to be printed, the paper, the form of words.[498] The lectures seem to have taken place at various venues: the printed invitations for the first cycle request the audience's presence in the Luisenstrasse, then newly formed and newly named, of easy access to those living in the elegant private *palais* in the Wilhelmstrasse. But we also hear of a lecture hall in the Französische Strasse,[499] more central, and then the Hôtel de Paris in the Brüderstrasse, near the royal palace.[500] It may have been where the Berlin jurist Karl Wilhelm Grattenauer lived: he is mentioned as making himself generally useful. The Brüderstrasse was also right under the nose of its other prominent denizen, Friedrich Nicolai. Thus these Berlin lecture cycles were 'set up' carefully, like the later ones in Vienna, even those in Bonn that elicited Heine's malicious comments. Entrance cost two Friedrichsd'or: Caroline said in jest that the queen herself might have come had the price

---

497 Minor, I, v.
498 An entrance ticket for the Lectures is reproduced at *Krisenjahre*, III, 19.
499 *Briefe*, II, 60; Karl Ende, 'Beitrag zu den Briefen an Schiller aus dem Kestner Museum', *Euphorion*, 12 (1905), 364-402, ref. 397.
500 Wilhelm Schoof, 'Briefwechsel der Brüder Grimm mit Ernst v. d. Malsburg', *Zeitschrift für deutsche Philologie* 36 (1904), 173-232, ref. 214; *Krisenjahre*, III, 25 opts (inconsistently) for the venue in the Französische Strasse.

(expensive enough) been double!⁵⁰¹ As it was, Schlegel had to defer the start from November to December 1801 until he had the necessary audience of forty to fifty to make the whole effort viable. The takings from the first three lectures, at, say, 100 Friedrichsd'or per lecture, would have been in the vicinity of 1,500 talers, even then somewhat short of the 2,000 talers that one needed annually to live comfortably in Berlin.⁵⁰²

To achieve those numbers, the doors were open to women. If the queen did not attend, at least ladies from the court did,⁵⁰³ certainly also those Jewish salonnières Henriette Herz and Rahel Levin (later Varnhagen).⁵⁰⁴ Not only did Rahel attend the first series: she came in grand company, with one of her salon habitués, Prince Louis Ferdinand of Prussia, Frederick the Great's nephew, composer, and general. With him and Friedrich Gentz, Rahel whiled away the time with the written equivalent of noughts and crosses, but when alone she jotted down key words and phrases from Schlegel's first cycle (she seems not to have attended the rest).⁵⁰⁵ There would have been some fine carriages at the door: the young Prince August of Prussia came, Louis Ferdinand's brother and later a general,⁵⁰⁶ members of the diplomatic corps also, not least Karl Friedrich von Brinkman, Swedish envoy, friend of the Romantics and of Madame de Staël and sometime contributor to the *Athenaeum*. We hear of two Polish counts.⁵⁰⁷ The young Danish-German Count Wolf Heinrich von Baudissin, still accompanied by his tutor, attended the later cycle.⁵⁰⁸ Baron Caspar von Voght, the cultivated Hamburg merchant, philanthropist and traveller, managed to find time from his duties and diversions in high society to attend these lectures from January to March of 1803 and hear the section on Greek poetry.⁵⁰⁹ Wilhelm

---

501 *Caroline*, II, 225.
502 Reimer, 31.
503 *Krisenjahre*, I, 28.
504 *Rahel-Bibliothek. Rahel Varnhagen. Gesammelte Werke*, ed. Konrad Feilchenfeldt, Uwe Schweikert and Rahel E. Steiner, 10 vols (Munich: Matthes & Seitz, 1983), I, 257.
505 Renata Buzzo Màrgari, 'Schriftliche Konversation im Hörsaal. "Rahels und Anderer Bemerkungen in A. W. Schlegels Vorlesungen zu Berlin 1802"', in: Barbara Hahn and Ursula Isselstein (eds), *Rahel Levin Varnhagen. Die Wiederentdeckung einer Schriftstellerin*, *Zeitschrift für Literaturwissenschaft und Linguistik*, Beiheft, 14 (Göttingen: Vandenhoek & Ruprecht, 1987), 104-127.
506 Otto Brandt, *August Wilhelm Schlegel. Der Romantiker und die Politik* (Stuttgart, Berlin: Deutsche Verlags-Anstalt, 1919), 37.
507 *Krisenjahre*, I, 20.
508 Lohner, 149; Goldmann (1981), 27f.
509 Voght, II, 95-138. He reports on the lectures on epic (95f.), lyric (100), Anacreon (103), Pindar (107), elegy (117), Aeschylus (123), Sophocles (130), Euripides (132), the three versions of Elektra (133) and Aristophanes (138).

Körte, a young literary historian with time on his hands, even transcribed Schlegel's text for possible publication.[510] Two young men who were to make a fast career in the Austrian state service, converted and ennobled, dropped in occasionally: Friedrich Gentz,[511] already the translator of Edmund Burke's *Reflections on the Revolution in France*, and Adam Müller.[512] Wilhelm von Humboldt may have come in the brief interval between his time in Paris and his appointment as Prussian envoy in Rome. The publisher Reimer attended.[513]

Some members of a group of young cadets in the Prussian civil service, fresh from university—who, is not always clear—could be seen: Karl August Varnhagen von Ense, diplomat, writer, gossip, Karl Wilhelm Ferdinand Solger, later to review Schlegel's Vienna lectures,[514] Friedrich von Raumer, Friedrich Heinrich von der Hagen, Johann Gustav Büsching. All of these were later to play larger or smaller roles in Schlegel's life. Of course one could rely on most of Schlegel's Berlin circle: Schütz, Genelli, Bernhardi, Buri; the assiduous Friedrich de la Motte Fouqué came over from his estate at Nennhausen in the Mark of Brandenburg; Wilhelm von Burgsdorff from distant Ziebingen when 'in town'. Fichte and Schleiermacher were notable absentees, the former no longer close to Schlegel and working on his own series of lectures (which, it is claimed, both Schlegel and Kotzebue attended),[515] the latter, now a pastor in Stolpe in Pomerania, morally disapproving of Schlegel's liaison with Sophie Bernhardi. Schlegel sent a transcript of his first lecture cycle to Schelling in Jena, who used it for his own lectures on the philosophy of art in 1802.

For all that his audience included names later prominent in political and intellectual life in Germany, Schlegel was also lecturing to a general public, not to specialists. No-one would have expected absolute originality from his remarks (his section on music is largely taken from Rousseau, for

---

510 SLUB Dresden, Mscr. Dresd. e. 90. XXXIII. 1-2. Minor, I, xvii-xviii.
511 Gentz, *Briefe*, II, 85, 89.
512 Adam Müller, *Lebenszeugnisse*, ed. Jakob Baxa, 2 vols (Munich etc.: Schöningh, 1966), I, 63.
513 Reimer (1999), 83.
514 He most likely attended the second and third cycles, if his remarks on the *Nibelungenlied* and Dante may be cited as evidence. *Solger's nachgelassene Schriften und Briefwechsel*, ed. Ludwig Tieck and Friedrich von Raumer, 2 vols (Leipzig, 1826), I, 97, 124.
515 *Johann Gottlieb Fichte's Leben und litterarischer Briefwechsel*, ed. I. H. Fichte, 2 parts (Sulzbach: Seidel, 1830-31), I, 448. Kohlrausch vouches for Kotzebue. *Erinnerungen aus meinem Leben*, 66.

instance).⁵¹⁶ Why should he, so eminent a critic and translator, not indulge in self-references and self-quotations? Still, it is not too fanciful to imagine some of those present having implanted in them the first germ of their later avocations and professions of political faith: those three young men who later became professors at the University of Berlin, Solger the aesthetician and translator of Sophocles, Raumer the historian of the Middle Ages, von der Hagen the medieval antiquarian and editor of the *Nibelungenlied*; Gentz and Müller confirmed in their restorative conservatism by Schlegel's remarks on the Middle Ages; even a royal prince hearing of the Gothic style that would flourish in Berlin under his cousin, King Frederick William III. Two young men may even have been confirmed in their later literary careers: Wolf von Baudissin as the translator who put into German verse most of the Shakespeare plays that Schlegel had not tackled; and Friedrich de la Motte Fouqué, already featuring in *Europa* and, under Schlegel's guidance, an important disseminator of Germanic mythology through his plays and prose works.

Yet, despite their appeal to some future university figures, these were not academic lectures in the strict sense. Non-academic listeners might have to strain at times, but the elegance of Schlegel's prose, his frequent citation of poetic examples, helped to make them more generally accessible. The more academically inclined were also catered for. The first cycle, of 1801-02, announced the 'theory, history, and criticism of the fine arts',⁵¹⁷ and a systematic ordering of knowledge ['geordnetes Ganzes, System']. The initiated were reminded of those systematisations of 'science' (in the widest sense), those 'trees of knowledge' of the French Enlightenment,⁵¹⁸ Herder's macrohistorical accounts (or even Friedrich August Wolf's lectures on 'Enzyklopädie der Altertumswissenschaft' [classical scholarship] that some of them had so recently heard in Halle). Readers of the writings of the Romantics would be aware that Fichte, Friedrich Schlegel, Novalis, Schelling were aiming at an encyclopaedic encompassment of knowledge. There were of course differences. Where the Enlightenment narratives were predicated on progress, from the 'long intervalle d'ignorance' that for

---

516 Clémence Couturier-Heinrich, 'Die Schriften Rousseaus als musikgeschichtliche Quelle für A. W. Schlegels Jenaer und Berliner Ästhetik-Vorlesungen', in: Mix/Strobel (2010), 185-197.
517 *KAV*, I, 181.
518 Darnton, *Cat Massacre*, 191-218.

d'Alembert was the Middle Ages,[519] Schlegel reversed this forward time-flow and placed the Middle Ages in the centre of his historical account.

Without a sense of history there could be no survey of the various art forms and their development or of the national cultures that nurtured them. Schlegel is concerned that theory (what should be) is always linked with history (what was). It is history that imposes a system on the chaos of individual manifestations. This is central to his approach, breaking down the traditional classifications in aesthetics and finding mixtures, syntheses, overlaps between the art forms, 'medial' combinations involving the different senses: sculpture, for instance, 'caught' between the fluid and the solid, architecture that combines organic geometrical form with art, painting that needs our sense of proportion and distance, dance which combines poetry and music. Above all, poetry—the real subject of these lectures—cannot exist unless language and imagination come together in mythology,[520] that state where reality is suspended and human intuition recreates a new unity of nature and mind, a sense of the essential and ultimate truths of human existence. Without mythology—and each lecture cycle states this categorically—there can be no poetry. The Greeks had it, the Middle Ages knew it, we must recapture it through the creative imagination in poetry. For poetry in its true sense brings together in a synthesis philosophy, moral awareness and religion.

All this was not to be seen in the abstract or couched in generalities. There were clear examples to be cited and distinctions to be made. When he spoke of the pure and ultimate forms of art, unattainable in imitation, he invoked the ancient world of the Greeks, their language showing the highest development, their mythology predicated on the noblest ideals of humanity. Their art forms had each a distinct purpose, without admixture or contamination. The Moderns, by contrast, those whom Schlegel defined as 'Romantic' (essentially the Middle Ages and what we now call the Renaissance) started from a position of loss and inferiority—the threnody of this Classical and Romantic generation—the attenuation of language, the suppression of the senses. The Moderns' portion is striving for 'mystery', especially in the Catholic Middle Ages, the mixing of all poetic elements as an expression of a longing for the infinite, the hope of some fulfilment in distant and imperceptible time. It is the statement that comes near the

---

519 Jean le Rond d'Alembert, *Discours préliminaire de l'Encyclopédie*, ed. Michel Malherbe (Paris: Vrin, 2000), 117.
520 *KAV*, I, i, 441.

end of the first cycle, before it abruptly ends, and it is one that Schlegel develops into a principle in his Vienna Lectures.

True, Schlegel briefly resumed those points as he took up the next cycle in November, 1802: 'homogeneous' (ancient) versus 'heterogeneous' (modern). All was not lost: translations, properly conceived, especially those into German, might retrieve some of the texture of past cultures. Here Schlegel breaks off and launches into that philippic on modern German literature, a version of which was to feature so prominently in *Europa*. One can only guess at the motives behind the scission of his lecture course into two disjunct sections. The past winter had seen the *Ion* fiasco in Weimar and Berlin; 1802-03 was also the climax of the 'literary war' with the opponents of all things Romantic. It was time to tell some home truths, to set out positions, to distinguish the excellent from the mediocre. But Schlegel also reminded his hearers that there were, and always had been, higher universal principles of renewal,[521] the phoenix arising from the ashes, ebb and flow, expansion and contraction, and that is why he could end this section with the names of Winckelmann, Lessing, Hemsterhuis, and Goethe.

Compared with the extended corpus of criticism by Schlegel up to 1800, not least his writings on Homer, the second section of this lecture, on 'Greek Poetry' (which also includes Latin), may disappoint those looking for a definitive statement. It should not be forgotten that he was also reading out extracts in translation to his audience,[522] not all of whom would be conversant with Greek. Thus his relatively short section on Aeschylus presupposes his quoting aloud of a passage from the *Eumenides*. When explicating Greek metres, he could read his own examples. He had of course already stated unequivocally in the previous cycle that the Greeks were unsurpassable, so that when he went through their achievement, genre by genre, and compared it with what had come since, no further elucidation was necessary. By excluding oratory, rhetoric and historiography, he may have been unfair to the Romans. Only Horace and Propertius emerge really unscathed. By contrast, he had praise for their didactic poetry, but of course he was himself a practitioner of the genre. Homer, emerging from a dark 'Urzeit' of priestly song and referring back to it, remained the pinnacle of epic poetry for all time. There was little hope for Virgil, not to speak of later aberrations like Milton or *Der Messias*.

---

521 *Ibid.*, 537-540.
522 These in *SW*, III, 101-102, 129-153.

For the author of *Ion*, however, Greek tragedy had to be of primary interest. Even it was not a 'pure' genre, rising as it did out of the congruence of myth (as in the epic) and human subjectivity (as in the lyric). Tragedy is based on the conflict of these principles, but—here again the recreator of *Ion* speaks—it need not end in unhappiness. Simlarly, the theatre of the Greeks is an 'organic whole' made up of the interconnecting elements of music, dance and architecture.

From here on, the text becomes more shorthand than fully formulated expository prose. The essentials were, however, there. Greek mythology expressed the force of higher necessity; it involved human sacrifice; its beginnings were darkly orgiastic. It was this mythology that informed Greek tragedy, in conflict with human striving. The section on Sophocles makes it clear where his preferences in tragedy lie. The renewer of *Ion* does not see only starkness and bleakness. When discussing the Oedipus cycle, he opts for *Oedipus in Colonos*, with its 'mildness of humanity',[523] where the Furies lead the hero away from the horror into a blissful Grecian grove. With the tragic effect of Sophocles thus diminished—as indeed Schelling was to do in his lectures on the philosophy of art—there was little to stress in Euripides except his decadence, gratuitous terror, and sophistry, which of course also applied to the *Ion* which Schlegel had sought to 'improve'. There are some brief remarks on comedy, on Aristophanes, who breaks down all the barriers raised by the mind and presents us in our animal or 'democratic' aspect,[524] a point that his review of Parny in 1800 had made at greater length. The brief survey of modern comedy that follows mentions the Spaniards briefly, without a word on Shakespeare: it reflects Schlegel's preoccupations at the time.

The third cycle, from 1803 to 1804, was also in some respect an account of the priorities of his Berlin years. As a statement of 'modern' European poetry, it had its deficiencies. We have already noted the effective absence of Calderón and Shakespeare and the one-sided etherealities of the Dante section. The things that he was doing as a sideline to the lectures now found their way into his general definition of Romanticism in the preamble of 1803. Romantic poetry arose out of the fusion of the Romance and the Germanic, the interaction of the North and South (pagan and Christian, if one will). It reflected his interest in both the Nordic and Germanic and the southern Romance. His correspondence with Tieck in these Berlin years speaks of

---

523 *KAV*, I, i, 744.
524 *Ibid.*, 770.

studies of the *Nibelungenlied*—Tieck was preparing an edition—and the need to procure copies of Icelandic sagas for comparison and collation, or of the Latin *Waltharius* epic. Schlegel himself was working on a 'romance', simply called *Tristan* (to remain unpublished until 1811), his own retelling of Gottfried von Strassburg, and evidence of his lively interest in the Grail and Lancelot cycles. As yet, Schlegel could not learn enough about the 'Matter of Britain': his scepticism towards anything Celtic would come later. The autumn of 1803 saw the publication of the work that was in a sense conceived as the poetic accompaniment to his remarks on Romance poetry, those *Blumensträuße* [Nosegays][525] from Italian, Spanish and Portuguese, that showed—yet again—his virtuosic command of the various verse and stanza forms. This time his emphasis was as much on the cadences of lyrical and pastoral poetry (Dante's *Rime*, Tasso's *Amyntas*, Guarini's *Pastor Fido*) as on the narrative (selections from Ariosto's *Orlando Furioso* or Camões' *Lusiadas*). Readers of this duodecimo volume could enjoy Friedrich Tieck's Flaxman-like vignettes and note the easy conexistence of neo-classicism and Romance poetry.

Whereas the two earlier cycles could draw confidently on centuries of classical scholarship and decades of codifications of aesthetics, the lectures on Romantic literature represented in part 'work in progress' or accounts of texts in the process of discovery. Schlegel was much more dependent on other authorities, eighteenth-century pioneers like Thomas Warton or Jean-Baptiste de La Curne de Sainte-Palaye. He mentions in a letter to Tieck having met the Swiss historian Johannes von Müller, one of the originators of the comparison of the *Nibelungenlied* with Homer.[526] Above all, one recognises the influence of Herder, those chains of historical events, those 'Kräfte' [forces] bringing about ferment and change, indeed he is indebted to Herder's insights on the meeting of Orient and Occident in the poetry of the Spanish romance. His remarks on the *Nibelungenlied*, kept accessible to the needs of the audience, were to be backed up privately by a battery of notes and collations towards the establishment of a definitive text. It was yet another project that was destined eventually to fall by the wayside.

And so this cycle is not a grand, systematic, encompassing, definitive statement of Romantic literature. Rather it is disjunct and often repetitive,

---

525 See AWS, *Blumensträuße italiänischer, spanischer und portugiesischer Poesie*. Nach dem Erstdruck [1803] neu hg. von Jochen Strobel (Dresden: Thelem, 2007), with introduction and commentary.
526 Lohner, 151.

overlapping with earlier sections. Romantic poetry did not emerge as some gathered, phalanx-like entity, some mass with but a few national divergences. Its terms of reference were still very wide. It encompassed the Middle Ages. That was itself a period of time that extended from the migrations and Late Latin until (in Germany at least) the late sixteenth century. It was subject to all manner of incursions and influences and coincidences. Dante's position in thirteenth-century Europe provided a prime example; the continuation of medieval themes in the Italian Renaissance or in Shakespeare would be another. There were different strands—Nordic, Celtic, Provençal— whose influence irradiated in the different language areas. Genres, like the romance and the chap book, extended beyond any linguistic barriers. The Middle Ages, as Schlegel conceived them, were the synthesis of many disparate forces. They were Christian, chivalrous, monastic. The Crusades brought in the Orient. The feudal system fostered a code of honour, of courtly love, of pious devotion to the Virgin. It was as if those Herderian 'Kräfte' enabled assimilations to a general religious mentality, extracting poetry wherever their influence held sway.

Schlegel must nevertheless account for certain developments in later national literary cultures. It brings him to the first formulations of a project that would recur at various later stages in his life (and engender masses of unpublished papers), one that pursued him into the 1830s: Provençal. The Provençal lyric represents for Schlegel the highest development of any Romance language and is the mother of all modern poetry and versification. It is crucial for the later development of Italian and Spanish (and to some extent Middle High German). It must not be confused with French, an 'aberrant' Romance culture. Thus the lecture on Provençal serves as a kind of general preamble to his remarks on the great Italians, Dante and Boccaccio, and indeed what he might have gone on to say about the Italian and Spanish Renaissance.

Where did that leave Germanic and the Germans? In contrast with the querulous tone of his previous cycle, Schlegel is prepared, in this his last one, to be more conciliatory and more even-handed. In his short conspectus of older German literature, he already retracts the assertion, made in 1802, that German literature as such is hardly more than seventy years old. For he now gives an account of older figures who in 1803 would not be household names (if indeed they ever were). Those who did know of Hans Sachs and Dürer would learn that they represented the last extensions of the Middle Ages, the end of the age of chivalry. There then ensued a period of 'learned poetry', for which Schlegel, not surprisingly, has some sympathy. Like his brother Friedrich in another context, he is mapping out lines of continuity in German poetry, not registering its breaks (such as the Reformation). Thus his audience could hear praise for the old *poeta doctus* Martin Opitz, the founder of modern German poetics, and would note less familiar names like Weckherlin, Fleming, Hofmannswaldau, Lohenstein, even the Jesuit poet Spee, for the Romantics are among the first to point out that German religious poetry is not all Protestant. What follows in the next century can be subsumed under 'bürgerlich' [civic, middle-class], with praise for Klopstock and dispraise for Wieland. If only, Schlegel perorates, we could renew all of these forces and bring them together—learned, chivalric, 'bürgerlich'—we would achieve that universality of the mind and intellect that is the aim of a poetic culture.

Where did the German Middle Ages stand in relation to other linguistic cultures? The answer to this is to be found in the important lecture on the *Nibelungenlied*.[527] This national epic fulfils all the criteria set up in the lectures on Classical and Romantic poetry. It is mythical, Christianising older myths and legends and weaving several historical strands into one. It is ancient, drawn from a putative Latin original, linguistically archaic (possibly translated from older sources); like Homer, it is co-authored. It combines the moral sense of justice done and the Christian notion of divine retribution. Schlegel is content to add his voice to the current view, already advancing to cliché status, that this was an epic commensurate with Homer, indeed his Germanic counterpart. This was heady ideology indeed, significant when but a few years ahead cultural rallying-points were needed amid national downfall and national renewal. Schlegel is still, perhaps *faute de mieux*, prepared to praise the *Heldenbuch*, for these attenuated heroic lays did not yet have to face the competition of Wolfram von Eschenbach, Hartmann von Aue or Gottfried von Strassburg, whose Grail cycles were far less known at the turn of the century.

Schlegel was clearly running out of time when he came at last to Italian 'Romantic' literature. Dante was supremely the Christian, Catholic poet, ethereal, mystical, arcanely symbolic. The *Inferno*, like Greek tragedy at its starkest, no longer formed part of the narrative. The name of Petrarch

---

527 Edith Höltenschmidt, *Die Mittelalter-Rezeption der Brüder Schlegel* (Paderborn, etc.: Schöningh, 2000), 46-53, 172-186; *ibid.*, 'Homer, Shakespeare und die Nibelungen. Aspekte romantischer Synthese in A. W. Schlegels Interpretation des Nibelungenliedes in den Berliner Vorlesungen', in: Mix/Strobel (2010), 215-235.

gave him the opportunity for a highly technical discussion of the sonnet and its 'architectural' form, and while he was at it, the canzone, the ode, even the entwined complexities of the sestina. In the rather perfunctory account of Boccaccio's *Decameron* we find his excellent working definition of the novella. It is fair to say that, had this text been available during the nineteenth century (the twentieth took almost no notice of it), we might have been spared much idle theorizing and symbol-hunting. For Schlegel restates what the Italian, Spanish and French Renaissance knew, what Goethe and Wieland knew, what Tieck knew. The novella recounts a real happening, factual, everyday, but also out of the ordinary, tragic even. It is also companionable, chatty, but it needs a central episode ('something has to happen') and a turn of events that makes it extraordinary. No more is necessary.

Much of this lecture material was confusing and unsystematic, but who expected Romantic doctrine to adhere to a system? How many of his audience sat it out to the very end, attended every lecture, we do not know (Bernhardi springs to mind). And yet this being the Schlegel that he was, he could not leave these matters hanging in the air, unjoined and unconnected. For those willing to hear lectures that were altogether much harder going— and we have little idea who that audience was—he gave another series, on 'Enzyclopädie', this time in private, at a venue not specified, in May of 1803. It has taken over two hundred years for them to be edited: establishing their relationship to the 'Romantic' series was not a priority for Schlegel's nineteenth-century editors. They point, not to Vienna, as the main Berlin cycle does, but much further forward in time, to Bonn, to the professor who seemed to have put so much of Romanticism behind him. They are not for the uninitiated or the faint-hearted, which is not to say that everything that they contained was original—far from it—but there were no concessions made for those not prepared for a heavy dose of philosophy, history, and philology.

His audience needed first of all to be disabused of the common associations of 'encyclopedia' or 'encyclopedic'. It was not the polymath laboriousness of eighteenth-century German scholarship that had once oppressed the young Winckelmann;[528] it was not an 'aggregate', a mere accumulation of facts such as in his own Göttingen days Heeren and Tychsen's *Bibliothek der alten Literatur und Kunst* had offered. Instead,

---

528 Cf. 'schwerfällige Polymathie', Justi, I, 5.

Schlegel moves from compendiousness to a system, one that takes in all the disciplines. He comes closest to Bacon's 'tree of knowledge'[529] (with an unacknowledged side glance at d'Alembert) in positing a triad of history, poetry and philosophy, 'observation' and 'classification', where 'language' and 'grammar' mediate between philosophy and history. Philosophy is the basis of the truth that reveals itself in art and poetry; history needs cognition ('Wahrnehmung') through observation and classification. Extending the tree to its side branches, Schlegel places mythology as the mediating factor between philosophy and poetry, that which produces 'nationaler Geist'. 'Nation' is in its turn to be understood as an original geographical and political unity, the 'motherland' of a linguistic culture. (When later writing in French, Schlegel used 'nationalité' in this sense, indeed he is credited with having introduced the word into that language.)[530]

The history of Europe was in these terms one of growing disparity, as it moved away from Asia, its natural 'heartland', the area of primeval unity. This notion—a scattered Europe versus a monolithic Asia—may not be Schlegel's first borrowing from Herder's *Ideen*, following as they do the commonplaces of eighteenth-century orientalism.[531] In the light of his later development, it is a significant one, as India in these lectures achieves the status of the mother culture, the originator of myth, the cradle of mankind, the space of a language even more venerable than Greek.

Turning to history proper, Schlegel rejects the traditional 'universal historiography', that had tried vainly to encompass the history of mankind. A much more useful mode of explanation for the processes in history can be found in nature, in antagonism and cohesion, pull and thrust, forces that produce an inner unity. More concretely: only nations that combine mythology and poetry with their oral traditions deserve that name in its full sense. The history of Germany, for instance, shows the gradual loss of those unifying factors (enshrined in the narrative of the Middle Ages and the feudal system) down to our present 'Nullität' and lack of a sense of national community. Few other nations have achieved it either, not Austria,

---

529 Darnton, 212.
530 Comtesse Jean de Pange, née Broglie, *Auguste-Guillaume Schlegel et Madame de Staël. D'après des documents inédits*, doctoral dissertation University of Paris (Paris: Albert, 1938), 234.
531 See R. Rocher, 'The Knowledge of Sanskrit in Europe Until 1800', in: Sylvain Auroux et al., *The History of the Language Sciences* [...], 3 vols, Handbücher zur Sprach- und Kommunikationswissenschaft, 18, 1-3 (Berlin, New York: de Gruyter, 2000), II, 1156-1163; Tzoref-Ashkenazi (2009), 66-71.

not France, not England or Italy (perhaps only Spain under the Inquisition), not the Slavic nations (an anti-Slavonic *parti pris* that will become a regular theme),[532] at most Prussia, with its concern for a 'national confederation' (he did not say that it was swallowing his native Hanover). A name does however occur which will later enshrine his ideal of national history: Johannes von Müller, the historiographer of the Swiss. When it comes to the creation of historical narrative, Schlegel invokes the principles that will later dominate his thinking, the history of the earth (geology, physics) and the 'sense of the divine', the two forces that rise above the mere recounting of empirical fact.

On language (the section on philology), Schlegel stresses the centrality of 'families', not least that confederation of 'Indo-European' languages that Charles de Brosses and above all Sir William Jones had demonstrated and that his brother Friedrich would soon be expounding. Greek, of course, enjoys a superiority above all others in this family. Yet German, once similarly pristine and pure, stands out from all other modern European languages for its syncretism, its adaptability, the 'universality' by which it is capable of taking the good features of the other nations, to 'enter into their thought processes and feelings and thus create a cosmopolitan focus for the human spirit'.[533] Georg Forster had said something similar in 1791, in the preface to his German translation of Sir William Jones's version of the *Śakuntalâ*.[534] Friedrich Schlegel's *Europa* was articulating analogous sentiments. Before such notions could become reality, there must be criticism, grammatical study, hermeneutic endeavours, the processes that Winckelmann once had used for the study of art, and in our day Friedrich Schlegel was applying to poetry.

It is not by chance that the trajectory of many of these ideas points them a decade, sometimes nearly two decades, forward in time, to the life of a celibate professor in Bonn.[535] In what was clearly the *envoi* to these lectures, Schlegel postulated the ideal life in which such studies might

---

532 Dorota Masiakowska-Osses, 'August Wilhelm Schlegel und Polen: Gegenseitige Rezeption', in: Mix/Strobel (2010), 199-213.
533 *KAV*, III, 336.
534 Georg Forster, *Werke. Sämtliche Schriften, Tagebücher, Briefe*, ed. Deutsche Akademie der Wissenschaften zu Berlin, 16 vols in 20 (Berlin: Akademie, 1958-85), VII, 285.
535 On the links between AWS's lecture series see Frank Jolles, 'August Wilhelm Schlegel und Berlin: Sein Weg von den Berliner Vorlesungen von 1801-04 zu denen vom Jahre 1827', in: Otto Pöggeler *et al.* (eds), *Kunsterfahrung und Kulturpolitik im Berlin Hegels*, Hegel-Studien, Beiheft 22 (Bonn: Bouvier, 1983), 153-173 plus [2].

flourish.[536] He invoked the philosophical asceticism of the ancient Stoics (or their neo-stoic descendants in the seventeenth century), their minds lifted above material concerns, passions or pleasures, their bodies subjected to moderation, cleanliness and order. It was not unlike the culture of the Brahmins that he was later so to admire. Berlin had not been conducive to such self-abnegation, such anchorite retreat from the real world, nor could it be said that the next decade and a half were any more amenable to this ideal life of scholarly contemplation.

---

536 *KAV*, III, 371.

3. The Years with Madame de Staël (1804-1817)

Holding Things Together

August Wilhelm Schlegel and Caroline were formally divorced in the summer of 1803.[1] Herder, before he died in 1803, had had to give his approval as superintendent-general of the Lutheran church and the ducal consistory in Saxe-Weimar, and Goethe used his good offices with Voigt the minister to see the matter to its conclusion. In their petition to the duke, the divorcing couple cited as grounds 'diverging aims in life, forced on the undersigned [him] by the pursuit of his literary avocation and [her] by the state of her health, [that] make it impossible for them to live in one and the same place'. If there was more to it than that, and the duke would have been in the know, nobody let on. From now on, Caroline and Schlegel used the formal 'Sie' in their letters, but the tone remained friendly. She was now free to marry Schelling, who in 1803 joined the great exodus from Jena, that saw him, Paulus, both Hufelands and others move to universities elsewhere. His career took him first to Würzburg, now the premier Bavarian university, then to Munich as secretary of the Academy of Sciences. Schlegel was to see Caroline again only twice, once in Würzburg in 1804 and once in Munich early in 1808, and on both occasions he was in the company of Madame de Staël.

If Schlegel sought solace with other women, he kept quiet about it. His name would be linked by some with the actress Madame Unzelmann or

---

1   The documents are in SLUB Dresden, Mscr. Dresd. e. 90, XIX (22), 43-58. Herder's signature on 45. *Caroline. Briefe aus der Frühromantik*. Nach Georg Waitz vermehrt hg. von Erich Schmidt, 2 vols (Leipzig: Insel, 1913), II, 342-345. *Goethes Briefwechsel mit Christian Gottlieb Voigt*, Schriften der Goethe-Gesellschaft, 53-56, 4 vols (Weimar: Böhlau, 1949-62), II, 314, 326, 329.

with Elisabeth Wilhelmine (Minna) van Nuys, but we need not attach too much to such rumours. As for Sophie Tieck-Bernhardi, she was now seeking comfort with Karl Gregor von Knorring, ever willing however to receive monetary assistance from Schlegel. At the end of 1804, she began her flight from Berlin and Bernhardi, into scandal and divorce. She would meet up with Schlegel again in 1805, in Rome, finding her way there through monies flowing into the voracious Tieck exchequer. Again, he was there by courtesy of Madame de Staël.

These are not years in which the Tieck family appeared in the best of lights. Ludwig, ensconced in farthest Ziebingen beyond the Oder, wrote almost no letters to his friend Schlegel, tried the patience of several publishers (to whom he never delivered), and took a countess as a mistress. Friedrich, once the work on the Weimar palace was completed, did write letters to Schlegel, but they were full of self-pity and informed by those alternations of frenzied activity and depressive torpor that was the Tiecks' trademark. Both did what they could for their sister, and both were agreed that their brother-in-law Bernhardi was a brute, a beast and a monster[2] and that Sophie was right in fleeing him with her children—to Weimar, to Munich, and finally to Rome. To be fair: Sophie undoubtedly suffered from bad health and had good reasons for moving to a warmer climate. She was also trying to revive her career as a writer, which with the demands of two small children and ill-health was not easy. One can understand the persistence with which she pressed Schlegel and others to find a publisher for her drama *Egidio und Isabella*.[3] Yet her frequent letters to him from 1804 to 1808 are by the same token begging and manipulative (still hinting darkly that he might be Felix Theodor's father) and inveterately mercenary (pleading poverty). Schlegel, otherwise ever tidy with his finances, was for most of these years in debt. There were debts going back to 1802, funds raised for Caroline,[4] and he had run up more in Berlin (there is in the tiresome and unedifying correspondence with Sophie a recurrent 'tailor's

---

2   Expressions which they use at various times.
3   *Egidio und Isabella, Ein Trauerspiel in drei Aufzügen von Sophie B.* was finally published in *Dichter-Garten. Erster Gang. Violen*. Herausgegeben von Rostorf [Novalis's brother Karl von Hardenberg] (Würzburg: Stahel, 1807), 183-334. The periodical was the subject of one of AWS's reviews in the Jena *Allgemeine Literatur-Zeitung*. AWS, *Sämmtliche Werke*, ed. Eduard Böcking [*SW*], 12 vols (Leipzig: Weidmann, 1846-47), XII, 208-216.
4   Cf. the letter of Paulsen in Brunswick to AWS of 14 January, 1802, about repayment of 100 talers. SLUB Dresden, Mscr. Dresd. e. 90, XIX (17), 30. He had borrowed 600 Reichstalers from Schelling and took nearly ten years to pay it off. *Briefe von und an August Wilhelm Schlegel*, ed. Josef Körner, 2 vols (Zurich, Leipzig, Vienna: Amalthea, 1930), II, 79. *Dreihundert Briefe aus zwei Jahrhunderten*, ed. Karl von Holtei, 2 vols in 4 parts (Hanover: Rümpler, 1872), III, 71, on debts.

bill' from Berlin that Bernhardi had paid on his behalf). Thus the chance to join Madame de Staël was an opportunity to put his finances on a firm footing, but Sophie's importunings meant that even the Staël money was not sufficient. It may explain in part why he, who was usually so punctilious, withheld for longer than was proper the repayment of an advance from the publisher Reimer for which he never delivered the manuscript; and it doubtless accounts partly for his journalistic work and occasional poetry, with those 'Friedrichsd'or per sheet' that came in so handy.

His brother Friedrich also needed money. Now in Cologne, giving private lectures on literature to the brothers Sulpiz and Melchior Boisserée and their friend Johann Baptist Bertram, he was suffering from his perennial insouciance in financial matters, but it was also true that there was little money to be careless with. His periodical *Europa* survived into 1805 and then ceased publication, its sections on Renaissance Christian art in Paris and on medieval painting in Cologne not coming at a moment opportune for a larger readership (which included Madame de Staël). Aghast when he heard that his brother August Wilhelm had accepted a 'tutor's post' with Madame de Staël (he used the word 'Hofmeister' which had associations of penurious theological students tutoring the children of the aristocracy), he found himself, when the Boisserée money ceased, teaching classics, then philosophy, in a Lyceum in Cologne, hoping that the French might found a university there or in nearby Düsseldorf. He needed to be in Paris to consult the Persian and Sanskrit manuscripts on which he was working, but he could not afford to live there for any length of time. He too found himself the occasional recipient of Madame de Staël's largesse, and two longer stays, at Coppet and Auxerre, were a welcome respite. She entrusted to him (in fact to Dorothea) the German translation of her novel *Corinne*. He even pinned his hopes on some kind of pension from her, in desperation not even despising the chance of a post of 'Hofmeister' with a noble family in Rome (it came to nothing). It was not until Madame de Staël went to Vienna in 1808 that she was able to use her considerable influence with high-placed persons to secure Friedrich a post in the Austrian administration.

Then there was his aged mother in Hanover. The last years of her life were overshadowed by war and its attendant dangers for the civilian populace: the occupation of Hanover by Prussians, French, Russians, requisitions, the quartering of troops, the devaluation of currency (her 'Pancion'), shortage of food and the threat of real penury. Her letters, which are a challenge to decipher, deal mainly with her family and their careers and prospects, and with money, of necessity her priorities. Yet amid the mass of Schlegel's correspondence, with its all-consuming and unrelenting literary professionalism, it is heart-warming to find a simple letter from his mother: 'My dear, best son. I can find no words to tell you how great my joy was when I received your letter'.[5] Thus his former lover, his brother, and his mother all received monies, the source of much of which was Madame de Staël.

Yet before we embark on the account of the thirteen years of his association with her, the major climacteric of his life,[6] we need to see the years 1804-07 and indeed those up to 1812 in their proper perspective. They were years of crisis, unrest, journeyings, abrupt changes of domicile, the years of Austerlitz, Jena, Wagram, then the Russian campaign. Hanover, as said, was full of troops, but so was Berlin; Weimar was sacked; Caroline and Schelling lived through a French occupation of Würzburg; the country houses of Schlegel's friends and correspondents Countess Voss and Friedrich de la Motte Fouqué in the Mark of Brandenburg were plundered. Spies and secret police were everywhere. Caroline spoke for everyone when she wrote in 1808 of the Tiecks: 'These people are always on the move, and the other good friends live a nomadic existence'.[7] Those who could found bolt holes: the ancient university town of Heidelberg, protected from Napoleon's armies by Baden's astute politics, was one. Coppet was another, but even it proved not to be safe in the long run. On a personal level, the groups associated with Jena and Berlin split into two camps, depending on how they stood in the matter of the Bernhardi divorce: Fichte, Schleiermacher, Fouqué, Schütz against the Tiecks and Schlegels.

Yet somehow one person held all this together: Schlegel. Leaving aside material and personal matters, it was he who acted as a focal point for so many, not of course in matters of philosophy, where Schelling and Fichte (and to some extent Friedrich Schlegel) went their own ways, but in formulating and stating the purpose and message of poetry. Goethe

---

5   The letters from his mother (only one of his has survived), mostly unpublished, are in SLUB Dresden and are divided between Mscr. Dresd. e. 90, XIX, 4-66 and Mscr. Dresd. App. 2712, B18, 20-43. Letter quoted of 29 March, 1810.
6   For much of my account of Madame de Staël I have found Christopher Herold's entertaining, informative, and slightly outrageous study very useful. His disrespect is refreshing but has its limits. Above all, a considerable amount of material has come to light since its publication, the *Correspondance générale* and the *Cahiers de voyage*, for instance. J. Christopher Herold, *Mistress to an Age. A Life of Madame de Staël* (London: Hamish Hamilton 1958). A more recent popular biography in French is Michel Winock, *Madame de Staël* (Paris: Fayard, 2010), a more recent study in English Angelica Gooden, *Madame de Staël. The Dangerous Exile* (Oxford: Oxford UP, 2008).
7   *Caroline*, II, 536.

had always done this, but after Schiller's death in 1805 he was to find the Romantic generation ever less to his taste, especially its older representatives and most particularly those who affected a Catholicizing attitude to art. The *Elective Affinities*, the *Italian Journey*, his autobiographical writings, were to record his growing disenchantment, and his correspondence with Schlegel all but ceased. Thus people turned to Schlegel, younger writers, editors, publishers, despite his being in distant Coppet. Some of the Romantic message of Jena and Berlin was getting through, even if in fragmentary form (such as the excerpts from Schlegel's Berlin lectures in periodicals); his Shakespeare and Calderón translations were still present in people's minds (and in print), and his publishers pressed him for more. When Friedrich de la Motte Fouqué wrote to him in 1806 about his plans for dramas on Germanic themes, he received the makings of a lecture on patriotic poetry and on the continuing solidarity of the Romantic school.[8] Goethe in 1805 was to learn that the artists working in Rome were no longer beholden to the doctrines of Weimar. German readers of the works that emerged in the Coppet circle, the elegy *Rom* dedicated to Madame de Staël, or the controversial *Comparaison entre la Phèdre de Racine et celle d'Euripide*, would see a distinctly German approach to issues that resonated differently in France, while his Vienna Lectures of 1808 would be a proclamation of the German view of drama and the creative processes associated with it.

Germaine de Staël-Holstein

There was nothing inevitable about his joining the circle of a celebrity like Madame de Staël. Although but one year older than Schlegel, her name already had so many resonances as a political and cultural cipher in both ancien-régime and post-Revolutionary France, her presence and personality were so dominating and powerful, her career, even up to 1804 when they first met, had been so turbulent and not without its brushes with the authorities and even with death. The Baroness Germaine de Staël-Holstein was a person so utterly different from Schlegel that the events surrounding his career might seem petty and insignificant by contrast. Were not the doings in Jena or Weimar or Berlin, the literary polemics, the frenzied exchanges of insults, the Fichte affair, the *Ion* fiasco, but storms in a teacup when compared with her close run with the Terror, clandestine

---

8 'August Wilhelm Schlegel an Fouqué. Genf, 12. März 1806', *SW*, VIII, 142-153.

escape, exile in England, playing for high stakes in the Directory and then being in the bad books of the First Consul? There was her very background: Edward Gibbon had (unsuccessfully) wooed her mother; as a child she had accompanied her father, the Genevan banker Jacques Necker, to England. He in his turn was to become Louis XVI's minister of finances, leaving patrician Geneva for the uncertainties of 1780s Paris and the still greater incertitudes of the early 1790s. Their name might not be aristocratic, but it denoted one of the first families of a Swiss city-state, and a style of living that was in every respect noble. Marrying the Swedish envoy to France, Baron Erik Magnus Staël von Holstein in 1786 made Germaine a baroness, but it was not long before she was a *grande dame* in her own right and running a political salon without the baron's assistance. There was around her, too, the aura, the whiff of scandal.

She had as well the knack of being there when great things were happening, seeing the procession of the Estates General in 1789, the march on Versailles and the return of the royal family to Paris, the sight of the distraught queen in July 1792; there was her own escape from the mob in the same year, her first exile in England, coming back under the Directory. She had had a tête-à-tête with Bonaparte before the great events of 1799 and had returned from Coppet to Paris to coincide with the 18th Brumaire. She had not heeded Bonaparte's pronouncement to another lady, 'Madame, je n'aime pas que les femmes se mêlent de politique' ['Madam, I do not like women meddling in politics'],[9] and had found herself banished from Paris and eventually in a second exile.

But how was it that this highly politicised personality, with her finger on the cultural pulse of the Directory and of Consular France yet writing against the grain of its official culture, became involved with a figure so different as Schlegel? Or that he, hitherto sedulously unpolitical (if one overlooked those unfortunate poems of homage), became totally, abjectly devoted to her up to her death in 1817, dependent on her movements, propelled to the most unlikely places because of promulgations against her, sharing her exiles, reliant on her largesse, so that even the work most associated with his name, the Vienna Lectures on Dramatic Art and Literature of 1808, might not have come about without her intervention?

It has been rightly remarked that intercultural transfers—for that is the grand name for Madame de Staël's whole involvement with Germany—do not come about in the abstract: they require key persons to experience the

---

9   Madame de Staël, *Considérations sur la Révolution française*, ed. Jacques Godechot (Paris: Tallandier, 1983), 340.

alien culture at first hand.[10] But in her case—for her motives were never simple—the circumstances were complex: they involved the genuine desire to make herself acquainted with Germany and things German, her relations with the political powers that be (Bonaparte), the search for a suitable tutor for her sons, companionship—the list does not end there. It is not easy to separate strands which in real life are closely interwoven.

She had already shared a forum with Schlegel when Goethe translated her *Essai sur les fictions* (as *Versuch über die Dichtungen*) for inclusion in *Die Horen* in 1796 (in the same year as Schlegel's *Wilhelm Meister* essay), Schiller having overcome Goethe's misgivings about 'French lack of clarity'.[11] It was a relatively conventional tract when compared with the experiments Goethe himself was conducting with the novel, not to speak of the young Romantics. But whereas for Goethe and Schiller these were times for throwing down the gauntlet in literary feuds,[12] she—and her lover Benjamin Constant—were deep in real politics in Paris.

She knew such recent literature on Germany as there was in France (Marmontel, La Harpe, Grimm),[13] and her Swiss friend Henri Meister was a useful intermediary between the two cultures. Having had the *Essai sur les fictions* published by Goethe and being flattered by his attention, she arranged through Meister to have a copy of her *De l'influence des passions* sent to him in October of 1796; Schiller showed some interest, but never included it in *Die Horen*. Goethe in his turn sent her *Wilhelm Meister*, which she could not read. In Wilhelm von Humboldt, who spent the years 1797 to 1801 in Paris, she found someone to help her with the rudiments of the German language, or most likely the second envoy in the Swedish embassy, Karl Gustav von Brinkman,[14] whom she would also later meet in Berlin and Stockholm. Humboldt would do his best to introduce her to Kant, Fichte and Schiller and wean her away from her indebtedness to French

---

10 Werner Greiling, 'Die "Deutsch-Franzosen". Agenten des französisch-deutschen Kulturtransfers um 1800', in: Gerhard R. Kaiser and Olaf Müller (eds), *Germaine de Staël und ihr erstes deutsches Publikum. Literaturpolitik und Kulturtransfer um 1800* (Heidelberg: Winter, 2008), 45-59, ref. 51.

11 'französische Unbestimmtheit'. Goethe to Schiller 6 October, 1795. *Der Briefwechsel zwischen Schiller und Goethe*, ed. Hans Gerhard Gräf and Albert Leitzmann, 3 vols (Leipzig: Insel, 1955), I, 104.

12 'Zeiten der Fehde', Schiller to Goethe 1 November, 1795. Gräf-Leitzmann, I, 112.

13 Comtesse Jean de Pange, *Mme de Staël et la découverte de l'Allemagne* (Paris: Malfère, 1929), 11-15.

14 She met Humboldt in Paris in 1798 through the good offices of the Swedish legation secretary Karl Gustav von Brinkman. Paul Robinson Sweet, *Wilhelm von Humboldt: A Biography*, 2 vols (Columbus: Ohio State UP, 1978-80), I, 218.

sensualism,¹⁵ even producing for her a French version of his *Ueber Göthes Hermann und Dorothea* where she could read that 'German poetry is still unknown in the greater part of Europe. Only a few chosen authors are known by name, themselves only in largely inadequate translations [...] Rich in profound thoughts and in noble and delicate sentiments, it is rising daily to the greatest simplicity and elegance of ancient forms'.¹⁶

But Humboldt was equally caught up in observing the heady politics of the Directory and Consulate, noting astutely the rising career of General Bonaparte.¹⁷ Charles de Villers, a French émigré in Germany and an enthusiast for things German, especially Kant, on whom he wrote the first book in French, had a circle of contacts that included Friedrich Heinrich Jacobi, Goethe's old friend. The links strengthened when Jacobi came to Paris in 1801. It was through Jacobi that Villers was apprised of two very different, but related, matters: Staël's wish to be acquainted with the doctrines of Kant and her search for a suitably qualified young German to act as a tutor to her sons.¹⁸

All this would not of itself have produced a German journey in the form that it did. The fact was that Madame de Staël did precisely what Napoleon Bonaparte said women should not do: she meddled in politics. And she wrote books that could be construed as a critique of the society in which she was living. Her lover Benjamin Constant was directly involved in politics not of Bonaparte's liking. Her salon in Paris was frequented by persons from all political spectrums, even the Bonaparte brothers, Joseph and Lucien, but it had the reputation of being disrespectful of authority and generally indiscreet. She was close to the generals who were plotting against Napoleon: one of them, Jean Baptiste Bernadotte, was later to play a central role in her life and in Schlegel's. She did not heed warnings. Bonaparte did not want her in Paris and encouraged her to join her father and her children in Coppet on Lake Geneva (she was by now estranged from her husband). She came back nevertheless. Napoleon had her placed under the surveillance of his minister of police, Joseph Fouché. Back she went to Coppet. Matters came to a head when, in the late summer of 1803,

---

15 Axel Blaeschke, 'Über Individual- und Nationalcharakter, Zeitgeist und Poesie. *De l'influence des passions* und *De la littérature* im Urteil Wilhelm von Humboldts und seiner Zeitgenossen', in: Kaiser/Müller (2008), 145-161, ref. 152.
16 Passage quoted in Kurt Müller-Vollmer, *Poesie und Einbildungskraft. Zur Dichtungstheorie von Humboldt. Mit der zweisprachigen Ausgabe eines Aufsatzes Humboldts für Frau von Staël* (Stuttgart: Metzler, 1967), 204f.
17 Sweet, I, 225-227.
18 *Madame de Staël, Charles de Villers, Benjamin Constant. Correspondance*, ed. Kurt Kloocke et al. (Frankfurt am Main etc.: Peter Lang, 1993), 19-22.

she settled at a distance of ten leagues from Paris, the precinct to which she was relegated, then gradually but unwisely moving closer to Paris itself. Fouché informed her that she would be conveyed under military escort back to Coppet. A direct appeal to Napoleon himself was rebuffed; an officer in civilian dress appeared, to carry out the order. She appealed to the respective 'bonté' of the First Consul and his brother Joseph,[19] but the only concession that she received was the granting of a passport to visit the German lands.

Napoleon had not enjoyed the two major works of the period 1800-03, her treatise *De la littérature considérée dans ses rapports avec les institutions sociales* [On Literature Considered in Relation to Social Institutions] (1800) and her novel *Delphine* (1803). There was, as we shall see, much in *De la littérature* that would appear inadequate or dated to a reader acquainted with the new German literary criticism. Napoleon would however have noted its cosmopolitan outreach, its admiration for England and its civilisation (and for a Germany as yet but imperfectly understood), along with its occasionally qualified affirmation of French classicism. Her belief in progress contained a critique of autocratic institutions. Her praise of the Middle Ages as a force for civilisation in its time broke with the view of monkish retardation put about by the French Enlightenment. Her enthusiasm for the North (including Napoleon's favourite, Ossian) might be construed as allowing dark forces into the classical light of the South, the Midi. Despite her defence of the novel as a force for the depiction and the uplifting of *moeurs*, *Delphine* seemed to present a society in turmoil, and one that exacted its punishment on female nonconformity.

Thus, having not read the signs and unwilling to compromise with what she saw as tyranny, Madame de Staël landed in exile. There was nothing unfamiliar in this. Necker had been exiled in 1787, at forty leagues from Paris[20] (as she would again in 1807), and she had spent part of 1792-93 in England, an exile from the Terror. Now began those 'ten years of exile' that her later book, *Dix années d'exil*, would document with fervid and righteous indignation. She would not live in Paris again for any length of time until 1814: at most she would savour the life of the French provinces. When not actually travelling—in Germany, in Italy, in the Austrian lands—she was in the family château of Coppet. She affected to dislike this residence, but there,

---

19 Letter to First Consul 13-24 September, 1803. Madame de Staël, *Correspondance générale*, ed. Béatrice W. Jasinski and Othenin d'Haussonville, 7 vols (Paris: Pauvert; Hachette; Klincksieck, 1962-; Geneva: Champion-Slatkine, 1962-2008), V, i, 18-19; to Joseph Bonaparte 4 or 5 October, 1803, *ibid.*, 39-41.
20 *Considérations*, 111.

as in nearby Geneva, which also she claimed to hate, would foregather the most extraordinary cosmopolitan group of European Romanticism. It was all very well making dramatic postures—'I have a sorrow gnawing at the bottom of my heart for that France, for that Paris, which I love more than ever'[21]—with attendant self-stylisations and identifications with the great exiles (Ovid, Dante) or great tragic heroines.[22] Another side of her saw the chance that exile afforded: already in November of 1803 she could write of 'mon voyage littéraire',[23] a preformulation of the later *De l'Allemagne*.

There were practical considerations for her attention. She would go where she knew people. She need not have given it a thought: the news that this famous authoress and adversary of Napoleon had arrived would open doors anywhere and at the highest levels.[24] She wanted to discuss Kant with Villers in Metz; Frankfurt would be the next stage, then Gotha, where Baron Melchior Grimm, an old survivor of the *siècle des lumières* and a former friend of her father's, was now living; Weimar was a 'must', and Berlin, where Brinkman now was, would surely receive her in style. And so it was. The journey into exile had much of a royal progress into the highest echelons of German society. Already in her *De la littérature* she had spoken of Germany's 'feudal regime',[25] and the nature of her contacts was not likely to alter that impression. If she saw the common people—landlords, ostlers, chambermaids, scullions—they did not merit mention.

Madame de Staël and Germany

Madame de Staël, Benjamin Constant, two children and a bevy of servants left the vicinity of Paris on 23 October 1803 on their way to Germany. She took with her her eldest, Auguste, the slightly staid and unimaginative but essentially reliable boy of thirteen, later to be her standby, and the youngest, Albertine, still a small girl, not yet the vivacious teenager who would grow up to become the duchess de Broglie. The middle son, Albert, the problem child, unpredictable and scatterbrained, stayed in Coppet

---

21   To Necker, 27 October, 1803, *Correspondance générale*, V, i, 85.
22   Simone Balayé, *Madame de Staël. Écrire, lutter, vivre*. Pref. Roland Mortier, afterword Frank Paul Bowman, Historie des idées et critique littéraire (Geneva: Droz, 1994), 52.
23   To J.-B.-A. Suard, 4 November, 1803, *Correspondance générale*, V, i, 92.
24   The day-to-day itinerary can be traced in Simone Balayé (ed.), *Les carnets de voyage de Madame de Staël. Contribution à la genèse de ses oeuvres* (Geneva: Droz, 1971), 435f. and *Correspondance générale*, V, i, Calendrier staëlien, vii-viii.
25   Madame de Staël, *De la littérature considérée dans ses rapports avec les institutions sociales*, ed. Axel Blaeschke (Paris: Garnier, 1998), 237.

with his grandfather Necker. The welfare and education of these boys was to be the immediate reason for Schlegel's joining Madame de Staël.

Although no ordinary traveller, she was to know the travails of journeying with small children, inns, squalor, and deep winter snow. Constant's presence as far as Weimar was reassuring,[26] and his spoken German was better than hers. Ten days were spent at Metz, where Charles de Villers gave her a crash course on Kant, not leaving her much the wiser. The sojourn in Frankfurt was extended to three weeks: Albertine went down with scarlet fever (or so it was believed). She was fortunate to be in Frankfurt and to be Madame de Staël's daughter, for one of Germanys' greatest physicians, Samuel Thomas Sömmering, lived there and attended her. The banker Bethmann, once less welcoming to an impecunious Friedrich Schlegel, received her. Bettina Brentano—if she was not embellishing as usual—remembered *Delphine* being read aloud in Bethmann's house.

Friedrich Schlegel's progress to Paris had been a symbolic journey. Hers to Germany may be compared with his in the other direction, except that his was voluntary, hers enforced. Both were driven by curiosity, he filled with the sense that the wealth of knowledge amassed in Paris should be made available to the Germans (and on their terms), she with the awareness that the French needed to be made acquainted with the philosophy and literature of what was for so many an unknown country. The product of his journey was the essentially German-centred periodical *Europa*, while *De l'Allemagne*, yet to emerge, was to be an account of Germany skewed by her own experience. For it needs to be said that the recital there of German institutions—literary, educational, political—had a marked slant towards those persons and those places that she actually visited; and as with England there was to be next to no reference to the lower orders.[27] For how else could one account for the mention of minor figures like Tiedge, Böttiger or Knebel, all of whom she met. The hope of meeting Jacobi[28] never came about.

As they progressed through the snow to the residence of Gotha, she could write to her father that 'There is something Gothic in their way of living, although something of the eighteenth century in their knowledge and insights',[29] a very fair summing up of an ancien régime just still in existence. But Weimar (14 December 1803 to 1 March 1804) was different.

---

26 To Necker, *Correspondance générale*, V, i, 135.
27 *Carnets de voyage*, 381.
28 1 January, 1804. *Correspondance générale*, V, i, 174-176.
29 *Ibid.*, 135.

Separating briefly from Constant, who joined them discreetly in Weimar, installed in the 'Werthernhaus', she waited for doors to open, which they duly did. We may pass lightly over her unconventional attire and headdress, her volubility, her receiving visitors in bed—for a celebrity need not be conventional. There was no love for the First Consul in Weimar, and everyone seemed to have read *Delphine*. Karl August and his duchess, Louise (she would correspond with the duchess over a longer period), also the dowager duchess Anna Amalia[30] received her graciously. There were visits to the theatre: Schiller's *Maria Stuart* and *Die Jungfrau von Orleans* [Joan of Arc] and Goethe's *Die natürliche Tochter* [The Natural Daughter] were promised, but they saw instead *Andromaque* and some comedies, even a piece by Kotzebue.[31] Goethe, once he could be persuaded to come over from Jena, she found 'had put on weight',[32] and conversation was strained (Constant, reading Herder's *Ideen*, confiding in his journal, found Goethe tainted by Spinozism and Schellingian mysticism and indifferent to politics).[33] Schiller in court dress she mistook for a general and found that he spoke indifferent French. To show her good will, she translated ballads by both into French.[34]

Yet there was no doubting their pre-eminence and significance. As if to reinforce this, the ubiquitous Böttiger, 'without taste and ponderous in his manners' (Constant)[35] persuaded the translator Karl Ludwig von Knebel, whose Propertius Schlegel had once reviewed,[36] to produce a short account of German literary culture.[37] It established a hierarchy of Klopstock, Lessing, Wieland (who had charmed Madame de Staël), Herder and Goethe (not Schiller) and had issued the usual lament on German insularity and Germany's lack of a capital, history and a culture comparable with the French and English. Then there was Kant. Henry Crabb Robinson, diarist,

---

30 Benjamin Constant, *Journaux intimes*, ed. Alfred Roulin and Charles Roth (Paris: Gallimard, 1952), 54.
31 *Ibid.*, 53, 59.
32 *Correspondance générale*, V, i, 179.
33 *Journaux intimes*, 54.
34 Goethe's 'Der Gott und die Bajadere' and 'Die Braut von Korinth', 'Der Fischer', and Schiller's 'Siegesfest'. Alfred Götze, *Ein fremder Gast. Frau von Staël in Deutschland 1803/04. Nach Briefen und Dokumenten* (Jena: Frommann, 1928), 70f., 88.
35 *Journaux intimes*, 53.
36 *SW*, XI, 337-346.
37 Originally published by Karl Emil Franzos, 'Eine Denkschrift Knebels über die deutsche Literatur', *Goethe-Jahrbuch*, 10 (1889), 117-138; more recently in *Goethe Almanach auf das Jahr 1968* (Berlin and Weimar, 1967), 208-221. French translation by Andrée Denis, 'Un tableau de la littérature allemande de Klopstock à Goethe, en 1804', *Cahiers staëliens*, 35 (1984), 77-94.

gossip, and connoisseur of things German, 'cultural transfer' in person, once a student of Schelling's in Jena, undertook to explain the Kantian system.³⁸ If she comprehended anything, it was that the beautiful 'must have no object outside of itself', which Constant reformulated as 'l'art pour l'art'.³⁹ He also gave her a short run-down of the main features and works of the Schlegel brothers, 'the most *piquans* in the whole compass of German Criticism', whose 'criticisms are written with more *esprit* than almost any german Works'.⁴⁰ Historiography also made an appearance in Weimar in the person of Johannes von Müller, the author of the history of the Helvetic republic, now quitting Austrian service to become court historian in Berlin and later a visitor in Coppet. The same Böttiger also assiduously wrote down what he saw and heard of Madame de Staël.⁴¹ Lacking good looks, she was reliant on her conversation to charm others and on her frankness to conquer convention. That it seems is how she managed to raise the subject of 'feudalism' with the duke, missing as she did the free exchange of public opinion that she knew and loved in England and the gallantry towards ladies that made French salon culture so agreeable.

Weimar also produced an account of the Romantic school that had once been assembled in nearby Jena. Robinson certainly explained Schelling's system to her. She also mentioned her search for a tutor for her sons. Goethe believed that Schlegel would be the right man, and Crabb Robinson went even further: 'It was I who first named [Schlegel] to Madame de Staël and who gave Madame de Staël her first ideas of German literature'.⁴² The second statement is certainly true. One wonders what criteria were behind these sponsorships. Goethe, having seen Schlegel in Jena with Auguste Böhmer, would have known that he was fond of children. Schlegel doubtless kept quiet about his time as a 'Hofmeister' in Göttingen and Amsterdam, securely in the past. Now, he was a professor.

---

38 See James Vigus, 'Zwischen Kantianismus und Schellingianismus: Henry Crabb Robinsons Privatvorlesungen für Madame de Staël 1804 in Weimar', in: Kaiser/Müller (2008), 355-391.
39 *Journaux intimes*, 58.
40 Henry Crabb Robinson, *Essays on Kant, Schelling, and German Aesthetics*, ed. James Vigus, Modern Humanities Research Association Critical Texts, 18 (London: MHRA, 2010), 137f., ref. 137.
41 Ernst Behler, 'Madame de Staël à Weimar: 1803-1804. Un témoignage inconnu de K. A. Böttiger et deux billets de Madame de Staël', *Studi Francesci* 37 (Jan.-Apr. 1969), 59-71.
42 Goethe to Schlegel 1 March, 1804. *August Wilhelm Schlegel und Friedrich Schlegel im Briefwechsel mit Schiller und Goethe*, ed. Josef Körner and Ernst Wieneke (Leipzig: Insel, 1926) [Wieneke], 156; Robinson quoted in Vigus, 356.

Constant accompanied them from Weimar to Leipzig and returned via Weimar to Coppet. The diminished party left for Berlin on 1 March 1804. She did not come unannounced. The Berlin gazette gave news of her impending arrival, and she came armed with letters of introduction—as if she needed them—from Duke Karl August, while Brinkman, Johannes von Müller and the Prince of Orange (an old Paris acquaintance) were there to receive her.[43] Were one to take the account in *Dix Années d'exil* as a guide, one might assume that she spent most of her time at court or with the high nobility, such as Princess Radziwill, the duchess of Courland or duke Ferdinand of Brunswick, the entrées secured by Brinkman.[44] It might account for her later view, expressed in *De l'Allemagne*, that Berlin seemed to be preoccupied with enjoying itself. That source would not tell us that Prince Louis Ferdinand of Prussia—to die a hero's death at the battle of Saalfeld in 1805—was habitually drunk,[45] or that Albertine at a court party slapped the face of a small boy who was later to be king of Prussia. She does mention the Moreau-Pichegru conspiracy against Napoleon, word of which reached her in Berlin, and it was Prince Louis Ferdinand who brought her in person the news of the execution on 20 March, 1804 of the duke d'Enghien—further examples of Napoleon's tyranny.

She also attended the salons of the duchess of Courland and of Rahel Varnhagen (she and Rahel were later to diverge in their political and ethical views). She met Nicolai, Goethe's friend Zelter, and Fichte, whose attempt to explain his system in 'a matter of a quarter of an hour' failed dismally,[46] even Kotzebue. And she met August Wilhelm Schlegel.

The Meeting of Staël and Schlegel

The first mention of Schlegel's name was in a note to Brinkman of 14 March, inviting him to her apartment, where Schlegel already was. First impressions were more than favourable and she could write to her father on 23 March in these terms:

> I have met here a man who displays more knowledge and wit in literary matters than anyone I know; it is Schlegel. Benjamin will tell you that he has some standing in Germany, but what Benj. does not know is that he speaks French and English like a Frenchman and an Englishman, and that he has

---

43 Götze, 101.
44 *Correspondance générale*, V, i, 259f., 262.
45 *Carnets de voyage*, 445.
46 The source of this much-quoted anecdote seems to be George Ticknor, *Life, Letters and Journals*, 2 vols (London: Sampson Low, Marston, 1876) I, 410.

read everything under the sun, although he is only 36. I am doing what I can to urge him to come with me. He will not be my children's tutor; he is too distinguished for that, but he will give lessons: Albert during the months he spends at Coppet, and I will gain a great deal for the work that I am planning. Benjamin will enjoy his conversation on the subjects close to his heart, and most importantly, I am sure that he will not displease you, as his manners are simple and discreet, and it will give you pleasure to see each one of us in his study hard at work.[47]

The points that Madame de Staël makes in this letter are, in order, Schlegel's reputation in Germany (another 'prize' for her group), his fluency in French and English (effectively giving her the linguistic advantage nevertheless), not a mere teacher (but one with pedagogical experience: she had attended the very end of his Berlin Lectures),[48] a right-hand man for the projected *De l'Allemagne*, and a conversationalist. A few days later she could add that she was receiving lessons in German literature from Schlegel and was 'charmed by his wit'.[49] On 31 March,[50] there were certain qualifications: she still needed a 'a musician secretary and someone to take the boys for walks' (Schlegel would function as the latter), but all would be perfect, Schlegel was just the right man, no beauty and hardly seductive, but inexhaustible in conversation, more than a match for the assembled wiseacres in Geneva, and someone to ward off the solitude of Coppet. Thus Schlegel appeared as the ideal person for the scholarly retreat which she and the circle must now inhabit, not so much for the 'monde' that also formed an essential part of it. It was an arrangement that suited the situation of exile, where in his own way Schlegel would become indispensable. On the practical side, her son Auguste had been placed in one of Berlin's top Gymnasien: six months of Latin and Greek would set him up to take the entrance examination for the École polytechnique for which he was destined.[51]

As yet, all seemed so smooth and unproblematic. But there were lessons to be learned and manners to be acquired. Schlegel, in accepting employment and companionship with Madame de Staël, would have to keep back some of the prejudices that his reviews and his lectures in Berlin had so forthrightly expressed, against French classicism (not

---

47 *Correspondance générale*, V, i, 284.
48 *Briefe*, II, 79.
49 *Correspondance générale*, V, i, 300, 304.
50 *Ibid.*, 300.
51 Auguste was at school at the Graues Kloster with Alexander von der Marwitz and the eldest son of the then colonel Scharnhorst. Theodor Fontane, *Wanderungen durch die Mark Brandenburg: Das Oderland. Werke, Schriften und Briefe*, ed. Walter Keitel and Helmuth Nürnberger, 4 sections, 21 vols in 22 (Munich: Hanser, 1962-97), Abt. 2, i, 787.

against neo-classicism as such), against the eighteenth century, against a facile belief in progress, against English literature and culture after Shakespeare. Whereas his statements effectively placed a caesura between all pre-Romantic German literature (before Goethe) and what followed, he would have to find a means of coexistence with a patroness who respected Wieland and Schiller, who was on good terms with Böttiger, who had visited Nicolai; for whom French classical drama was still part of a living continuity and which she herself performed; who revered all things English; who when in Italy was as much interested in the Italian late Enlightenment, Alfieri, Cesarotti, above all Vincenzo Monti, as she was in Dante, Petrarch or Ariosto. He would soon establish that she and her circle evinced a good deal of scepticism (and worse) for the cherished notions of poetry and art that he had been expounding in Jena and Berlin and were much more open in their judgments on things German and far less censorious. The Coppet circle was not to be a continuation of Jena, nor was it a salon.[52] It was, as he soon found out, a place for discussions, not for holding forth. Dogmatism, over-eager insistence, intolerance, gratuitous acerbity and polemics were not part of this style, as they had been in Jena and still were in Berlin.

Doubtless he was at first dazzled by her presence and her conversation, she by his erudition. There would be time to think over the details of their working relationship. Assuming that she attended the very last part of his Berlin Lectures, and assuming that she was able to follow them, she would have heard his section on Italian poetry of which she was a ready recipient and on which she had already pronounced. Had they thought about their differences? For if one were to take the respective works by Schlegel and Madame de Staël that might be at all comparable, these would be *De la littérature considérée dans ses rapports avec les institutions sociales* (1800) and the Berlin lectures. Except, of course, that both authors had moved on since then, or were in the process of so doing. She may not yet have read the *Athenaeum* and *Charakteristiken und Kritiken*, but she knew their main thrust; all that she could have known of the Berlin Lectures that was in print was his philippic against modern German literature and his expanded piece on Calderón, both in *Europa*. His shrill anti-Enlightenment tone in the one and his warm affirmation in the other would inform her that this was no admirer of the *siècle des lumières* but by the same token one unworried

---

52 Cf. Madeleine Bertrand, 'Conclusions', in: Roger Marchal (ed.), *Vie des salons et activités littéraires, de Marguerite de Valois à Mme de Staël* [...], Collection Publications du Centre d'Étude des Milieux Littéraires, 2 (Nancy: Presses Universitaires de Nancy, 2001), 320.

by the Spanish Inquisition. Clearly, their notions of human progress diverged irreconcilably. She in her turn had meanwhile been attacked by Chateaubriand and was allergic to the aesthetic Christianity that he was propounding. This may explain some of the challenges issued initially by the Coppet circle to Schlegel's Catholicizing and medievalizing views.

But it is also more than likely that these things did not worry her and were not an obstacle to his being part of her entourage. They had probably not had time to discuss politics, but he doubtless never mentioned that embarrassing Italian sonnet to Bonaparte, or another in German to a thinly-veiled 'hero'.[53] It is hardly conceivable that Schlegel—knowing of him what we do—had not read *De la littérature* and had not registered the affronts to his beliefs that much of it represented. They could not even begin to agree on most of the crucial points for which she stood. She had sought to extract from the French Revolution as much as might be beneficial for France and for humankind in general, even when this involved perilous engagement in politics. He knew from the bans and edicts issued against Caroline and from the Fichte affair that German professors had to steer clear of political entanglements. For Schlegel at this stage was not interested in questions of liberty, the cosmopolitan connotations of literature, or the social values of the novel, in old issues that still echoed in France under new guise, such as the *Querelle des anciens et des modernes* or the divide between North and South, especially a notion of the North that had Bards, Skalds, Danes, Scots and Ossian in unhistorical hugger-mugger. There would be time for their views to converge on some points: for instance, knowing that she was concerned with the relation of Racine to Euripides may have been one factor among many in his decision to compare the two Phaedra stories.[54] In Schlegel's eyes—and others'—she clearly would have a lot to learn about German literature, although she did already sense that German ideas were 'less practical' and the German lands subject to a 'feudal regime'.[55] Take human progress: for her, something continuous, uninterrupted, towards perfection; for him an undulating process, subject to rise and fall (Herder), or elliptical, as one moved towards the sun or away from it (Hemsterhuis). On French culture in general, there was his ostinato voice of hostility; and there was more to come in that *Comparaison* of 1807 and in the Vienna

---

53 'An einen Helden', *SW*, I, 356. See Barbara Besslich, *Der deutsche Napoleon-Mythos. Literatur und Erinnerung 1800-1945* (Darmstadt: Wissenschaftliche Buchgesellschaft, 2007), 53.
54 Madame de Staël, *De la littérature*, 66.
55 Ibid., 239, 237.

Lectures. He might agree with her on the creative encounter of North and South, one of her main theses, but he was not troubled, at least at this stage, by the 'servitude of the South' that so exercised her. Then there were the real red rags like her bracketing of Homer and Ossian! There would be time for both of them to become somewhat more accommodating. The great work that was to become *De l'Allemagne* was already taking shape in her mind and would advance views on religion, art, and education that in 1800 had not yet been developed. Like her heroine Corinne in Italy she would become more conciliatory towards Catholicism.

There was no question of his ever becoming her *cicisbeo*, her *cavaliere servente*, her Hausfreund, although tongues wagged in Berlin when their association became known. At most perhaps Benjamin Constant, who spent the rest of the years after 1804 agonizing over whether he should or should not marry her, saw Schlegel as a potential rival. But anyone trying to press for her attentions would soon discover that she was capricious in her emotional attachments and allowed herself to be captivated by men who, on the face of it, were unsuited to her (after 1804, Monti, Souza, O'Donnell, then Rocca). Their relationship has been seen as slavish devotion (his to her), but also an increasing dependence (she on him). It has led to all kinds of speculation about his sexuality (or its lack), his willing domination, his submission to women, pathological traits which he may or not have had, his failure to enter into any kind of lasting bond. It has permeated an old-fashioned vitalist literary criticism that sees Schlegel the translator or commentator as merely receptive, not creative.[56] It lays too much store by malicious gossip. It takes us into areas which the modern biographer treads at his or her peril. Above all, it overlooks the sheer extraordinariness of Germaine de Staël. For Schlegel was not the only man who was to be driven to near-distraction by her. She overturns biographical certitudes; she is a phenomenon of nature.

Both sides—the mutual dependence—need to be emphasised, for he was always there (the 2,000 francs salary was an incentive), unlike the inconstant Benjamin Constant, or Prosper de Barante or Mathieu de Montmorency, ex-lovers and friends who moved in and out of the Coppet circle as their inclinations and activities—in Constant's case the hope of emotional

---

56 It is already there in Haym, Minor and Ricarda Huch, informs much of Josef Körner, 'August Wilhelm von Schlegel und die Frauen. Ein Gedenkblatt zum 150. Geburtstag des Romantikers', *Donauland* 1 (1918), 1219-1227, and is alive and well in Georges Solovieff, 'Mme de Staël et August Wilhelm Schlegel. Natures complémentaires et/ou antinomiques?', *Cahiers staëliens*, 37 (1985-86), 97-106.

favours—took them. Thus in one sense Schlegel was bound, yet in another he was free, free of the pressing need for ready income. He was no longer beholden to publishers and review editors, all and sundry, and could pick and choose, except of course when the subject was her Racinian roles or her novel *Corinne*. It gave him security in uncertain times. His movements in the years 1804-08 were determined by her itineraries and her exiles. There were none of the frantic peregrinations of his brother Friedrich or the Tieck family. He escaped the worst of the political turmoil in Germany after 1806 (and indeed until 1812). If there were frequent journeyings with Madame de Staël, at least they did not involve his own exchequer and they always had a firm domestic base that involved both adults and children. Thus it was that Schlegel could provide a solid ground, a focal point, moral and financial support even, for an extended Romantic circle, a Jena in diaspora.

The real conditions of his service were set out before he left Berlin with her and her two children. If he were to stay for only six months, he would receive 60 louis, if permanently 120 louis annually (about 240 francs monthly).[57] Other teachers would take the burden off him and leave his mornings undisturbed. Once the children's education was completed, he would be free to remain with her on the same footing, with a pension of 120 louis or, should he leave, either with an annuity of 60 louis or a lump sum of 10,000 livres de France. She hoped for the former, for 'as long as I live, he will have contributed effectively to my happiness, which will perhaps prolong my life'.[58] These were perhaps very Neckerian calculations, predicated on his not marrying and his living a life of service and devotion. That devotion was soon to be put to the test.

Already in Berlin, she had learned that her father was gravely ill. This led to a hasty departure for Weimar on 19 April. Her father meanwhile had died in Geneva on 9 April. Constant, hardly arrived back in Coppet, left at breakneck speed for Weimar, reaching there at midnight on 20 April. The Staël party was there on 22 April, and it was he who had to break the news the next day and witness the scene of grief.[59] It was now that he met Schlegel, whose attempts to console Madame de Staël he found as admirable as they were futile. Schlegel meanwhile had been presented to

---

57 The fabulous sum of 12,000 francs annually, in the literature since Pange, has been corrected by Körner upon scrutiny of the Coppet account books. *Krisenjahre der Frühromantik. Briefe aus dem Schlegelkreis*, ed. Josef Körner, 3 vols (Brno, Vienna, Leipzig: Rohrer, 1936-37; Berne: Francke, 1958), III, 68. The Louisd'or was worth 20 francs or 11 talers.
58 Letter to Brinkman of 12 or 13 April, 1804, *Correspondance générale*, V, i, 324.
59 *Journaux intimes*, 80f. and 80-89 for the remainder.

the duke and had met Goethe and Böttiger in society, a small foretaste of the social accommodations he would have to learn to make. They left for Gotha on 1 May and again were received at court. Constant had begun to converse with Schlegel and discovered that he was a follower of the 'abstruse and absurd' philosophy of Schelling (whom he had attempted to read without success). With his interest in comparative religion, Constant found Schlegel's admiration for the Middle Ages extraordinary for someone who seemed not to have any personal religious belief (a very percipient observation). He found Schlegel hypersensitive if one of his favourite theories or poets was challenged, taking it as a personal affront. Clearly the German professor and the Franco-Swiss private scholar had yet to find the measure of each other. Schlegel for his part had commented on Constant's esprit and wit.[60]

In Würzburg, where they remained one day, Schlegel saw Caroline in society, but not Schelling. Constant did, and found his person as unappealing as his philosophy. But their main task was to distract Madame de Staël, which Schlegel did by reading Goethe to her and translating him into French. In Ulm, they visited Caroline's old friends, the Hubers, Therese Huber remarking that Schlegel looked washed out and the worse for taking opium. From Schaffhausen, they proceeded to Zurich, where Madame de Staël's cousin by marriage, Albertine Necker de Saussure, met them, the daughter of the scientist and alpinist Horace-Bénédicte de Saussure, later the translator of Schlegel's Vienna Lectures and still later the author of the first short official biography of Madame de Staël herself. She had brought Albert de Staël with her, a 'pretty blond wild boy of twelve'. Schlegel travelled with the boys in a separate chaise via Lucerne and Küssnacht to Coppet and another harrowing emotional scene when they arrived, yet another when her father was interred in the mausoleum that he had had built specially for his wife and himself in the grounds of the château.

Schlegel in Coppet

It was time for Schlegel to take in his surroundings, the feudal mansion that Jacques Necker had bought for his family in 1784.[61] Not surprisingly, he was overwhelmed by the view over Lake Geneva to the mountains, which, while screening Mont Blanc itself, were still spectacular. But landscape for

---

60 *Krisenjahre*, I, 78; 78-82 for the rest.
61 Cf. generally Pierre Kohler, *Madame de Staël au château de Coppet* (Lausanne: Éditions SPES, 1929).

Schlegel was not just a question of 'nature experience': as a contemporary of Saussure, of Hutton, of Cuvier, of Sedgwick, of Alexander von Humboldt (the last three of whom he knew personally), he saw in it like them also the textbook of physical science, the 'map of natural knowledge',[62] the 'record of the rocks', the cradle of human settlement and habitation. Nevertheless he could not be aesthetically indifferent to his physical environment, the park, the bosky landscape extending to the lake, mountains such as he had never seen before. It was his late equivalent of the Berliners Tieck and Wackenroder being overwhelmed by the Franconian countryside in 1793, but this was on an altogether grander scale. He even discovered (or rediscovered) physical exercise, on horseback perhaps for the first time since his Göttingen days (and the subject of Constant's malice),[63] even doing a walking tour in the Jura with the Staël boys and a Necker cousin in June of 1804, seeing the otherwise elusive Mont Blanc,[64] and, without the boys, another more extensive journey to the Savoyan Alps in August.[65] Like most things that he undertook, this and subsequent expeditions were to find expression in published form when in 1808 he did a series of sketches of the Swiss landscape, its most prominent features, its language and customs, later (1812) printed in the periodical *Alpenrosen*.[66] Think, too, of the extraordinary passage very much later in the *Indische Bibliothek*, describing a mountain torrent in Switzerland, but trying withal to evoke the even more spectacular landscape of the Himalayas, which he was never to see.[67] Already in May of 1804 he was reporting to Sophie Bernhardi on how much better he was feeling, no longer taking opium (for medicinal purposes only) and wishing he could already bathe in the lake.[68]

In the same letter, he would say to Sophie that Coppet was 'not like Nennhausen'. What did he mean? Nennhausen was Fouqué's country house in the flatness of the Mark of Brandenburg, with a grand façade and an English park, full of associations with Frederick the Great's generals and run on suitably hierarchical lines. But Coppet, even with its massive

---

62 See generally Martin J. S. Rudwick, *Bursting the Limits of Time. The Reconstruction of Geohistory in the Age of Revolution* [...] (Chicago and London: Chicago UP, 2005), esp. 48-52.
63 'prétentions à la virilité, à l'équitation et au courage'. *Journaux intimes*, 127.
64 *Krisenjahre*, I, 113-116.
65 Ibid., 148.
66 'Umriße, entworfen auf einer Reise durch die Schweiz'. SW, VIII, 154-176.
67 'Neueste Mittheilungen der Asiatischen Gesellschaft zu Calcutta', *Indische Bibliothek*, I (1820), 388.
68 *Krisenjahre*, I, 90f.

corner towers and its donjon, betraying its origins as a 'château-fort', had been purchased by Jacques Necker as a retreat from France and its political affairs: 'a fine refuge for my father, solitude in a free country, after having served a king!', as his daughter had written.[69] He did not make use of the barony that went with it and he did undertake some alterations in the interests of style and comfort and planted an avenue of trees to screen the view. But Coppet, a short journey from Geneva, meant retirement, not Rousseau's communion with nature, not Voltaire's grandseigneurial set-up at Ferney, but choosing one's own company, reading from one's own library. The 'free country', that 'pays libre' of course not longer existed in 1804, the Directory in 1798 having annexed Geneva to France and having appointed a prefect. Madame de Staël, inclined to melancholy when left alone, detested solitude (and nature), especially the solitude of exile, and was determined to fill the house with interesting people. In the first few months that Schlegel spent in Coppet, he was to experience how often the mistress of the house moved between Coppet and Geneva, sometimes Lausanne, on business, as the administrator of an estate and of her father's legacy and investments, or simply to be in a different society. He might write in August 1804 of the 'dry economical republicanism of the Genevans' and their general dreadfulness,[70] but it was the nearest place with a scholarly library. In fact he was to rely on two Genevan scholars, his fellow comparative linguist Marc-Auguste Pictet [71] and the immensely learned Guillaume Favre[72] to supply him with recondite antiquarian details.

Sophie was to be his main correspondent before he left for Italy later in the year, and it was to her that he gave an account of his day-to-day routine. He had been allocated the bedroom formerly belonging to Madame Necker. He took his breakfast in his room at seven, not being required to appear with the rest of the company. At three-thirty was the midday meal, at ten supper. He had the mornings free until one, taught till three, with another hour later in the afternoon.[73] He does not give details of the boys' lessons,

---

69 Quoted in Pierre Kohler, *Madame de Staël et la Suisse. Étude biographique et littéraire avec de nombreux documents inédits* (Lausanne and Paris: Payot, 1916), 78, and subsequently 78-80.
70 *Krisenjahre*, I, 136, also 91.
71 Cf. *Oeuvres de M. Auguste-Guillaume de Schlegel écrites en français*, ed. Édouard Böcking, 3 vols (Leipzig: Weidmann, 1846), III, 83.
72 For AWS's correspondence with Favre cf. *Mélanges d'histoire littéraire par Guillaume Favre avec des lettres inédites d'Auguste-Guillaume Schlegel et d'Angelo Mai receuilllis par sa famille et publiés par J. Adert*, 2 vols (Geneva: Ramboz & Schuchardt, 1856).
73 *Krisenjahre*, I, 90f., 105.

but one may assume that they took in Greek and Latin and much else besides (mathematics was taught by a tutor). These ancient languages were for him the basis of all learning, especially for the young, and he had little time for Rousseau's methods. Thus Schlegel, his paternal feelings cruelly dashed when Auguste Böhmer died, found them revived and reciprocated through his contact with the Staël children. As said, we do not know exactly what was the nature of his tutoring, and with his views on education he may have needed to rein in his learning. Auguste and Albertine de Staël never ceased to show affection for him to the end of their lives. True, Albertine later confessed that she failed to see the Homeric qualities in the *Nibelungenlied*,[74] which suggests a Berlin lecture scaled down for children. It is the human side of Schlegel, which tends to be lost sight of, the aspect that those many later testimonies to his vanity and self-importance either did not know about or chose to ignore.

The frequency of letters from Sophie meant that he could not be completely absorbed by his new surroundings, nor was this to change as family, friends, publishers sought him out in his Genevan fastness. Sophie, not surprisingly, wanted money. He had received his first quarterly payment from Madame de Staël and reminded Sophie that there were others who had a prior claim on his generosity (Friedrich, his mother).[75] He unwisely told her that he expected to be able to put 100 talers per annum aside, precisely the sum that she was to ask for in July.[76] He apprised her of Madame de Staël's plans for Italy and hoped that she, too, might be able to go there for her health and escape Bernhardi's claims for the custody of his children. Schlegel in his turn saw an opportunity for Friedrich Tieck: Madame de Staël wanted a sculptor to do a bas-relief in the Necker mausoleum, in the antique style that was already his specialty. It would not be done until 1806-07.[77] His publisher Reimer in Berlin was sending consignments of books that would stock the Coppet library with German literature, asking also for the rest of the Calderón translation. Unger was

---

74 *Lettres de la duchesse de Broglie 1814-1838 publiées par son fils le duc de Broglie* (Paris: Calmann-Lévy, 1896), 283.
75 *Krisenjahre*, I, 89.
76 Ibid., 130.
77 Bernhard Maaz, *Christian Friedrich Tieck 1776-1851. Leben und Werk unter besonderer Berücksichtigung seines Bildnisschaffens, mit einem Werkverzeichnis*, Bildhauer des 19. Jahrhunderts (Berlin: Mann, 1995), 72f., 283; letter of Friedrich Tieck to AWS, 6 August, 1804, Cornelia Bögel, *'Geliebter Freund und Bruder'. Der Briefwechsel zwischen Christian Friedrich Tieck und August Wilhelm Schlegel in den Jahren 1804 bis 1811*, Tieck Studien, 1 (Dresden: Thelem, 2015), 71-75.

hoping for volume nine of Shakespeare,[78] that was to contain *King Richard III*, a request Schlegel would be five years in fulfilling. Friedrich Schlegel wrote that letter that expressed his dismay at August Wilhelm's demeaning himself as 'Hofmeister', secretly envious perhaps that his brother had a fixed income and security where he was stuck in Cologne, without friends, without his brother's stimulating presence, but brimming over with ideas for Persian, for a chrestomathy of Indian texts, for the *Nibelungenlied*.[79] It led to Friedrich spending five weeks in Coppet, from early October to early November of 1804.[80] Heinrich Karl Albrecht Eichstädt, the editor of the new Jena *Allgemeine Literatur-Zeitung*, asked for contributions.[81] Schlegel had already sent him a review of Friedrich Leopold von Stolberg's metrical version of Aeschylus, more conciliatory in its views on translation than his account of Voss, but equally severe on 'Laxitäten'.[82] The Italian journey would provide more copy for Eichstädt.

This was to be the pattern for Schlegel's years with Madame de Staël: the engagement with her circle and his continuing concern with the 'Vaterland'. It is difficult to place them in order of priority, for so often her schemes and plans opened up opportunities for him to make statements on his own native national literature. First he had to surmount some adjustments to the life-style of Coppet. How much Schlegel knew of the company that he would be sharing, is open to question. He may not have been prepared for what seemed like a constant stream of visitors.[83] Benjamin Constant was to be in Coppet or nearby for most of the remainder of 1804. Johannes von Müller spent two weeks in June in the area. Three figures who were or were to become major members of the Coppet group put in an appearance during the same summer. They would make Schlegel acutely aware of how different his background was from theirs and, despite his professorial erudition, how narrowly provincial in some respects. Karl Viktor von Bonstetten had studied at Leyden, Cambridge and Paris and had lived in Copenhagen and Italy before settling in Geneva. He was about to publish

---

78   *Krisenjahre*, I, 119f.
79   *Ibid.*, 125-128.
80   Béatrice W. Jasinski, 'Liste des principaux visiteurs qui ont séjourné à Coppet de 1799 à 1816', in: Simone Balayé and Jean-Daniel Candaux (eds), *Le Groupe de Coppet. Actes et documents du deuxième colloque de Coppet 1974* [...], Bibliothèque de la littérature comparée, 118 (Geneva and Paris: Slatkine, 1977), 461-492, ref. 469.
81   *Krisenjahre*, I, 124.
82   *SW*, XII, 157-169.
83   Visitors for 1804 listed in Jasinski (1977), 468f.

an account of his Italian journey.⁸⁴ He would later expand the Staëlian contrast of the 'Midi' and the 'Nord' into a psychological system. Benjamin Constant had studied at Oxford, Erlangen and Edinburgh and had had a rapid career as a political publicist until Bonaparte put paid to it. Jean-Charles-Léonard Simonde de Sismondi had studied in Italy and was to become the premier historian of the Italian republics and of the literatures of the Romance lands (he did draw on Schlegel's knowledge).⁸⁵ All three were Swiss Calvinists associated with Geneva and not given to Catholicizing freakishness. Hardly any of the remarks about Schlegel in their journals or correspondence is respectful. A fourth, Mathieu de Montmorency, from one of the great French aristocratic houses, had served in the American War of Independence and had been deeply involved in the French Revolution. Rescued from the Terror by Madame de Staël herself, he had shared her English exile and was ever devoted to her. It was to him that Schlegel later addressed the extraordinary letter of August 1811 in which he contemplated a return to the bosom of the church.⁸⁶ In quite a different category was the visit of the duchess of Courland and her entourage, Madame de Staël reciprocating the hospitality extended in Berlin.

Coppet may have been a free association of minds, famously in Stendhal's words, 'the estates general of European opinion';⁸⁷ sociologically however it was a gathering-place of the titled, the privileged, never descending lower than 'grande bourgeoisie'.⁸⁸ Schlegel, belonging to the German *Mittelstand*, as most of his peers did, some of them indeed elevated to this status through intellectual merit (Schleiermacher or Fichte), came from the pastorate and the professoriate for whom certain standards of ease and comfort of living were an entitlement. But he could not compete with, say, Goethe in his ministerial *palais* in Weimar, and he could not be

---

84 Reviewed by AWS. *SW*, XII, 169-177.
85 G. C. L. Sismondi, *Epistolario*, ed. Carlo Pellegrini, 4 vols (Florence: La Nuova Italia, 1933-1954), I, xxix.
86 [Charles Lenormant], *Coppet et Weimar. Madame de Staël et la grande-duchesse Louise* (Paris: Lévy, 1862), 194-202.
87 Stendhal, *Rome, Naples et Florence en 1817*, in: *Voyages en Italie*, ed. V. del Litto, Bibliothèque de la Pléiade (Paris: Gallimard, 1973) 155.
88 Simone Balayé, 'Le Groupe de Coppet: conscience d'une mission commune', in: *Le Groupe de Coppet. Colloque 1974*, ed. Simone Balayé and Jean-Daniel Candaux (Geneva: Slatkine; Paris: Champion, 1977), 29-45, ref. 32. Further discussion in: Roland Mortier, 'Les Etats généraux et l'opinion européenne', in: *Le Groupe de Coppet et l'Europe 1789-1830. Colloque de Coppet 1993*, ed. Kurt Kloocke and Simone Balayé, Annales Benjamin Constant, 15-16 (Lausanne: Institut Benjamin Constant; Paris: Touzot, 1994), 17-24, ref. 19.

received as of right at court, his grandfather having considered the family's ennoblement to be superfluous. His manners were good, and he took a certain pride in his appearance[89] (vanity, some said), but he lacked the nobleman's ease and poise—and he was in employment at Coppet, not free to move as were Constant, Bonstetten or Sismondi. Free social and intellectual concourse Coppet and its circle certainly afforded, yet it had occasionally also the atmosphere of a court presided over in regal style by One who yielded only to Napoleon—and that unwillingly. Thus it is still an open question whether Schlegel belongs to the 'Cercle de Coppet' as more rigidly defined, its 'noyau central'.[90] His thirteen-year association with Madame de Staël, and his presence in Coppet for much of that time, would seem to guarantee him membership of this exclusive club and to separate him from the great and famous who merely put in an appearance, whether Byron or Chateaubriand or Clausewitz, Humphry Davy, Guizot or Barbara von Krüdener. But his dogged loyalty did not necessarily admit him as of right to the very inner circle in which Constant, Sismondi or Bonstetten found favour. That would only happen once Madame de Staël came to depend on him.

It is clear that Constant, Bonstetten and Sismondi, French intellectuals, wished to test the mettle of the German professor. Having just lectured to a receptive audience in Berlin, he was not best pleased when they advanced disrespectful views on subjects sacred to the German Romantics or when Madame de Staël herself drew attention to his social inadequacies. Constant noted with some malice that Schlegel could afford to advance untenable theories because he had never lived in the real world (i. e. the French Revolution).[91] While it is true that Schlegel never really believed in a restoration of the Middle Ages and was aware that one must live in actualities, he did not always have an answer for Constant's searching questions which were prompted by a more general interest in the

---

89 If his tailor's bills in Coppet are any indication. SLUB Dresden, Mscr. Dresd. App. 2712, 5-16.
90 The doyenne of Staëlien studies and the author of the indispensable monograph on Schlegel and Staël, Comtesse Jean de Pange (1938) saw Schlegel as part of the circle but understandably restricted herself to those aspects of Schlegel's life and works that impinged on Coppet. Simone Balayé, on whom Pange's mantle has fallen, has doubts, on account of Schlegel's social subservience. It may be significant that there is, as far as I can see, only one article in the whole of *Cahiers staëliens* devoted to Staël and Schlegel alone (Solovieff), and not a single one in the various *Colloques* dealing exclusively with him.
91 *Journaux intimes*, 91.

3. *The Years with Madame de Staël (1804-1817)* 247

phenomenon of religion. (Later, Bonstetten would blame Schlegel for the outbreak of religious mysticism to which Coppet succumbed in 1809.) Predictably, they disagreed about French classical tragedy.⁹² A discussion on Moses, Homer and Ossian between Johannes von Müller, Paul-Henri Mallet, the author of the famous *Northern Antiquities*, Bonstetten and Schlegel collapsed in disorder because Schlegel, who had read Michaelis, Herder and Friedrich August Wolf, did not believe in the historical reality of any of these figures.⁹³ It was no better when Friedrich Schlegel arrived. Constant left a highly unflattering description of his exterior, 'inordinately fat', and of the 'absurdity' of his views and his arrogation of a new religion.⁹⁴ He wondered that Schlegel was already hankering after Catholic Vienna, where not a line of Romantic doctrine would be tolerated by the censor. They did find common ground on India, not on the view that everything had its origin there, but on the awareness that Indian religion had advanced from polytheism to theism.⁹⁵ On that point Schlegel was treating Constant to a preview of the theories to be set out in his *Ueber die Sprache und Weisheit der Indier* of 1808. Through Pictet's good offices, he was able to borrow a set of the *Asiatick Researches*,⁹⁶ and one can imagine not just Friedrich, but both Schlegel brothers consulting them.

All this may account for the more than occasional gruffness, huffiness and touchiness that Schlegel seems to have displayed, especially at the beginning of his association with the Coppet circle.⁹⁷ We have this account from a visitor to Coppet in 1804:

> Finally about Schlegel. St[aël] asked me what they would think about it in Germany. And I answered straight: people have thought, and I have hardly thought, that it would be lasting; but it was very natural to both and must indeed be so. She, despite her wide knowledge (which I knew of and could vouch for with a good conscience) would gain much from S[chlegel]'s wide reading. He, on the other hand, would be drawn out of his quarrels and learn more taste, etc. She seems to have a great respect for his learning and says, now she knows *qu'elle ne sait que lire* [that she must do nothing but read]. She also likes him, and he must feel very much at home there. He

---

92 Ibid., 143.
93 *Bonstettiana. Historisch-kritische Ausgabe der Briefkorrespondenzen Karl Viktor von Bonstettens und seines Kreises, 1753-1832*, ed. Doris and Peter Walser-Wilhelm, 14 vols in 27 (Berne: Peter Lang, 1996-2011), IX, ii, 711.
94 *Journaux intimes*, 145.
95 Ibid., 151-160.
96 *Briefe*, I, 190.
97 Cf. *Coppet et Weimar*, 63 as one account among many.

does not talk much, but when he does it is forthright and well-judged. But *impar congressus* [mismatch] the moment he strays from his scholarship. He is not adroit enough—perhaps language is part of the problem despite his generally speaking it well. Then she soon shuts him up—*ces jeunes allemands, cette nouvelle école—ça vous a des idées etc.—mais, mon cher Schlegel, vous dites des bêtises ah ça finissez vous ête[s] ridicule—mais je m'abandonne—oh! vous ne paraissez pas à votre avantage, quand vous vous abandonnez.* [These young Germans, this new school, such ideas etc.—but, my dear Schlegel, you talk nonsense, do stop, you are ridiculous—but I'm losing hold on myself, oh you do not appear at your best when you lose control]. All half in jest, half with a certain tenderness. She said, *la [première] chose que j'ai exigé (amicalement) de lui, c'est le sacrifice de ses polémiques, et sous ce rapport je crois avoir rendu service à l'Allemagne*—[the first thing that I required (amicably) of him was for him to give up his polemics and in that connection I believe I have done Germany a favour] true enough.

Asked whether Schlegel was an atheist and thus unsuitable as a tutor to her children, she replied:

> *Au contraire, il penche vers le Catholicisme, il dit des bêtises quand il parle de r[e] ligion etc. mais pour athée—oh non, etc.—et plus je parlais des absurdités de S. et plus cette brave femme me répondait: oh, mon Dieu, que j'en suis bien aise.*[98]
> [On the contrary, he leans towards Catholicism. He talks nonsense when he speaks of religion, but an atheist—oh no—and the more I spoke of S's absurdities this fine lady replied, o goodness, they don't worry me at all]

This was after a dinner at which Constant, Sismondi and Schlegel had maintained an uneasy conversation. Faced with challenges to his most cherished ideas, and surrounded by her circle and its own historical and cultural emphases, Schlegel had various options at his disposal. It was not difficult to assume the role of the encyclopaedic German professor whose caricature pops up at given moments in much of the literature on Madame de Staël. But that was clearly not a satisfactory mode of existence, and even the material comfort that his tutorship or companionship afforded would be no compensation if he was always being belittled or disadvantaged by the company—all aristocrats as well as intellectuals. He could take comfort in the fact that—as our extract showed—Madame de Staël, despite everything, already had some genuine affection for him.

---

98   Ludwig Geiger, *Dichter und Frauen. Abhandlungen und Mittheilungen. Neue Sammlung* (Berlin: Paetel, 1899), 124. But cf. Bonstetten: 'Ist S[chlegel] nicht artig, so kriegt er entsetzlich die Ruthe, und das artigste ist, wenn die Staël ihn straft: dann verdreifacht sich ihr Witz, S[chlegel] antwortet bald die witzigsten, bald die galantesten Sachen, und beide werden bei diesem Kampf entzückt'. *Bonstettiana*, IX, ii, 693.

In Italy with Madame de Staël 1804-1805

No doubt Madame de Staël would some day have fulfilled her heartfelt wish to visit Italy even without the agency of Napoleon Bonaparte. Bonstetten and Sismondi moved between Switzerland and Italy as a matter of course, and Wilhelm von Humboldt was actually in Rome.[99] Like her third sojourn in England (1814) and all of the time she spent in the German lands, her first Italian journey was forced on her by Napoleon's attentions She and her son Auguste, in the text he edited as *Dix Années d'exil*, would always write 'Bonaparte', but when in the winter of 1804 she set out for Italy, he was already Napoleon, Emperor of the French, and soon to be King of Italy. He and his agents had her completely in their power, banning her from Paris, exiling her to Coppet, and capable of any arbitrary measure that they chose to implement. Although much of Italy owed allegiance to Napoleon, he chose not to pursue her beyond the Alps, indeed Auguste later claimed that Joseph Bonaparte (not yet king of Naples) had provided letters of recommendation to make her stay in Rome more agreeable.[100]

Thus we may speak of her Italian Journey, as we speak of Goethe's, like his a progress through a politically fragmented land, but with Piedmont now part of France, a northern republic of Italy based on Milan, a protectorate of Genoa, a kingdom of Etruria, Venetia incorporated into Austria, leaving the Papal States, and the kingdom of the Two Sicilies.[101] All of these territories she was to traverse—accompanied by Auguste, Albert, Albertine, Schlegel, (and from Turin) Sismondi, and a train of servants. Political and territorial differences apart, this Italian Journey conformed to certain patterns. Like Friedrich Leopold von Stolberg's in 1791-92, it went over Mont Cenis into Northern Italy, unlike Goethe's, who descended into Venetia and went to Sicily as well.

It would in time inevitably give rise to comparisons with other French journeys, Bonstetten's, Chateaubriand's or Stendhal's, for Madame de Staël (through her novel *Corinne*), while sitting among ruins or climbing Vesuvius as did all travellers, was also a trend-setter in the understanding of national temperaments. Again, her Italian Journey was different from

---

99 *Carnets de voyage*, 93.
100 Madame de Staël, *Dix années d'exil*, ed. Simone Balayé (Paris: Bibliothèque 1018, 1966), 96.
101 Geneviève Gennari, *Le premier voyage de Madame de Staël en Italie et la genèse de* Corinne (Paris: Boivin, 1947), 46. Cf. the opening of *War and Peace*: 'Eh bien, mon prince, Gênes et Luques ne sont plus que des apanages [...] de la famille Buonaparte'.

theirs, in its scale and the range of experience. Above all, it was to provide material for a notional and never-written *De l'Italie*, a *De l'Allemagne* of the 'Midi' if one will, which was to assume a quite different guise as the novel of 1807, *Corinne, ou l'Italie*.

On the German side, there had been at various times Friedrich Schlegel's vague and heady talk of their circle's decamping to Italy, the ultimate Romantic destination. With his finances always limping behind his dreams, Friedrich was not to see Italy until 1819, and then tagging along as secretary to the Austrian emperor and his chancellor, Metternich. By then, his brother August Wilhelm had seen Italy twice, all paid for out of the plenteous bounty of Madame de Staël. How different, too, from the Tieck family, in Rome at roughly the same time (1805), but dependant on money largely not theirs and disliked for their importuning.[102] For some of the sums disbursed by August Wilhelm to Sophie Tieck-Bernhardi in Rome in 1805 came ultimately from Madame de Staël.

Madame de Staël's interest in Italy, as defined by her *De la littérature* of 1800, was as political as it was literary. There had been great writers, but the disaggregation of Italy into small states had produced no national sense of a cohesive culture. Here she was seeing Italy very much in contrast with France and England. But it was also part of that 'Midi', 'romantic' if not yet 'Romantic': she could still find an appreciative word for eighteenth-century figures like Metastasio or Alfieri. Her taste in art was not yet highly developed. All this was to change as it found its expression in that extraordinary novel *Corinne*.

Schlegel's, by contrast, was more deeply informed, but in accordance with the doctrines of Jena ultimately infused with the awareness that Italy had contributed to the Romantic canon some 'archpoets' like Dante or Ariosto and that the union of language and poetry sufficed to define a nation. But so much of his appreciation of antiquity, his aesthetic of painting, even his theory of language, was predicated on things Italian. He would inform Goethe that Rome, not Weimar, was where the emergent schools of German painting and sculpture were situated. Being in Italy would add observed detail to his archaeological knowledge and his art criticism. In that sense he was following in Goethe's footsteps, but he lacked Goethe's instinctive sense of a classical landscape. Rather he might be seen as treading in Winckelmann's path, to whom he was much more beholden, indeed he met

---

102 See Roger Paulin, *Ludwig Tieck. A Literary Biography* (Oxford: Clarendon, 1985), 166-173.

Carlo Feà, his Italian translator,[103] making notes that would come in useful for the review of Winckelmann's works that he was eventually to write in 1812, a moment of classical repose among the political turmoil of that year. But if we seek for some account of Schlegel's Italian Journey, we are left with just a few letters and a few odd asides (such as meeting Alexander von Humboldt in Rome), a number of scattered reviews of an art critical or archaeological nature, but little sense of the criss-crossing of the peninsula that happened in real terms. His elegy, *Rom*, dedicated to Madame de Staël, would be no different.

One may regret this, as Schlegel has the makings of a good travel writer, varying the precise with the general or the sublime, so unlike their friend Hülsen who had provided copy for the *Athenaeum* with a description of Switzerland where one cliché is piled on another.[104] Schlegel's account in a letter to Sophie of his trip to the Savoyan Alps[105] has a nice balance between precise observation (granite outcrops) and poetic embellishment (men like ants before the massif of Mont Blanc) that reminds one of Alexander von Humboldt at his best. 'You will not expect a travel account from me', he wrote to his brother Karl from Rome on 27 March 1805, but he could not conceal his excitement at being in Italy nevertheless.[106] And Sophie was treated to this short characterisation of the land and its attractions: 'The mild and short winter, fruit in all seasons, a more carefree style of life, wonderful music, beautiful paintings, stern ruins, prodigal nature, being away from so many memories that oppressed you in Germany, occupying oneself with poetry in these surroundings'.[107] To his brother he could admit that his main interests in Italy were the fine arts, the study of classical antiquities and learning to speak the language fluently—and the opportunity of meeting the most important persons from all classes. To fill in the details of all this, one has to look at the works that are a direct reflection or result of his Italian Journey, his letter to Goethe about artists living in Rome, his review of *Corinne*, and his critique of Winckelmann, all of course carefully edited. The more extensive and informed remarks about architecture, painting and sculpture in his later Bonn and Berlin lectures

---

103 *SW*, XII, 334.
104 'Natur-Betrachtungen auf einer Reise durch die Schweiz', *Athenaeum. Eine Zeitschrift von August Wilhelm Schlegel und Friedrich Schlegel*, 3 vols (Berlin: Vieweg, 1798; Frölich, 1799-1800), III, i, 34-57.
105 *Krisenjahre*, I, 148f.
106 *Briefe*, I, 191.
107 *Krisenjahre*, I, 183.

on the fine arts are another direct reflection of the Italian experience.[108] One would also learn in the letter to Goethe that he had visited Sophie Bernhardi in Rome, the author of the as yet unpublished epic *Flore und Blanscheflur*,[109] but his private papers would tell of a continuing emotional attachment deepened by seeing her.

For Madame de Staël of course it was different. On the one hand her journey was another royal progress.[110] From Turin to Milan, to Bologna, to Rome and Naples, and back via Rome to Florence, Bologna, Padua and Venice, Padua again to Milan and Turin, with smaller sojourns in between, she was received, as appropriate, by generals, prelates, royalty, dilettanti and cognoscenti, and poets. This account inevitably has several sides. On the purely physical, we hear of the floods that prevented them from coming directly to Rome; being in Rome itself in cooler February, but in Naples in a balmier March; the carnivals in both cities; climbing Vesuvius by mule and on foot, accompanied by Schlegel and Sismondi—the source of that hellish set-piece vision at the opening of Book 13 of *Corinne*—scrambling on to the acropolis at Cumae, her various excursions among the Roman ruins. There was the political and social: being received at court in Naples, meeting the Countess of Albany in Florence (the widow of the Young Pretender), being in Milan almost, but not quite, to coincide with Napoleon's crowning as king of Italy. There was the emotional: a platonic attachment to the much older Italian poet Vincenzo Monti, the translator of Homer, and a closer bond with the young Portuguese nobleman Dom Pedro de Souza e Holstein. It was at times hard to distinguish this from the literary, for Monti was but one Italian neo-classical poet who received her; in Rome she was admitted, as Goethe once had been, to the Accademia Arcadiana;[111] in Padua she met the aged Melchiorre Cesarotti who had once translated Ossian (the Countess of Albany had been the protectress of Alfieri). Schlegel needed to rein in his prejudices against Italian neo-classicism, and Monti took the opportunity of reminding him of the injustice of foreigners towards Italian men of letters.[112] There were the 'courses d'antiquité' [explorations

---

108 The works of architecture and art concerned are listed in: *A. W. Schlegels Vorlesungen über schöne Litteratur und Kunst*, ed. Jakob Minor, 1. Teil, Deutsche Litteraturdenkmale des 18. und 19. Jahrhunderts, 17 (Heilbronn: Henninger, 1884), xxxvii-xliii, liv-lvii.
109 *SW*, IX, 264f.
110 The exact stages are set out in Gennari, *Le Premier voyage*, 15-120; *Carnets de voyage*, 93-259 and *Correspondance générale*, V, ii, Calendrier staëlien, ix-xi.
111 *Carnets de voyage*, 179.
112 Letter to Luigi Bossi, quoted in translation by Gennari, 51.

of antiquities] with Wilhelm von Humboldt, now Prussian envoy to the Vatican,[113] with Giuseppe Antonio Guattani whose *Roma descritta ed illustrata* was just appearing, with the French envoy and connoisseur Alexis-François Artaud de Montor and the Danish archaeologist Johann Georg Zoëga; Easter 1805 saw her in the Sistine Chapel and at high mass at St Peter's. They delayed their departure from Rome to meet Alexander von Humboldt. There were personal touches at all levels: the Staël and Humboldt children played together, Albert and Albertine even met the Bernhardi boys.[114] Staël herself, making up for her previous indifference in some areas, was all the time making assiduous notes on classical antiquity, on Italian literature, painting, folklore, landscape and society that would find their way into *Corinne*.

Schlegel was not a passive observer in all this. We know that he passed on his considerable knowledge to the travelling party even without the 'courses' by those distinguished cicerone. A malicious letter from Sismondi to Bonstetten of 20 March, 1805 refers to Schlegel as the 'materialist in our society', a description conferred on him because of his enthusiasm and his attention to detail but also his ability to provoke dispute ('four paradoxes a day'), his eye for niceties such as the 'basalt' lions on the Capitol (not porphyry, as Sismondi laxly remarks).[115] For Schlegel was not content merely with archaeological facts and evidence; the connoisseur needed to draw on other disciplines to establish periods and styles. The party was to wait in Rome until Alexander von Humboldt arrived at the end of April 1805.[116] He, fresh from his South and Central American journeys, was travelling through Italy on a mainly geological trip.[117] Schlegel, becoming increasingly aware that historical record is a matter of tradition, language, archaeology, climate, materials, geography, could not have been more fortunate than to meet up with Humboldt, whose method he was largely to adopt in his Bonn lectures and for whom he had a great personal admiration.[118] With Humboldt's help he would establish that the lions were 'hornblende with veins of felspar',[119] not basalt, and that one could thus

---

113 Sweet, I, 271f.
114 Wilhelm Bernhardi to AWS, SLUB Dresden, Mscr. Dresd. App. 2712, B15, 57.
115 Sismondi, *Epistolario*, I, 57.
116 *Carnets de voyage*, 255.
117 Leopold von Buch, *Geognostische Beobachtungen auf Reisen durch Deutschland und Italien*, 2 vols (Berlin: Haude und Spener, 1803, 1809), II, 44.
118 See esp. his unpublished review of Humboldt's *Vues des cordillères* in around 1818. *SW*, XII, 513-528.
119 As set out in his review of Winckelmann in 1812. *SW*, XII, 359.

establish with greater accuracy their place of origin (Egypt). This would run counter to Winckelmann's (and Goethe's) anti-Egyptian bias in favour of 'pure' Greek forms. Such geological evidence would reveal a much more dynamic interaction between the cultures of the Mediterranean rim than previously entertained. (The lions are duly mentioned in *Corinne*, which suggests that Madame de Staël was more attentive than Sismondi.) This did not mean that Schlegel did not indulge in speculations himself. Meeting the scholarly antiquarian Luigi Bossi in Milan, he advanced views on the origins of the two lions in the Venice Arsenale, on the basis of inscriptions at their side. Some said the inscriptions were runic; Bossi said they must be Etruscan. Schlegel, at this stage not yet conversant enough with Etruscan, opted (wrongly) for runic, eliciting from Bossi a learned riposte.[120]

Thus we must assume that Schlegel took in and absorbed all that Madame de Staël also remarked. The days of religious-inspired art criticism in *Die Gemälde* were essentially over; with very few exceptions (such as his later article on Fra Angelico), he was to concentrate much more on the general history of form and style rather than on its individual manifestations and their effect on the receptive beholder. It is significant, for instance, that Schlegel later only makes passing mention of Domenichino, who forms the basis of the famous set-piece section on painting in Tivoli in *Corinne* (although he does praise George Augustus Wallis, the other artist in that passage, in his letter to Goethe). Madame de Staël, too, was seeing works of art very much in terms of their moral effect, showing her to be an attentive reader of Friedrich Schlegel's later sections in *Europa*[121] rather than of his brother. August Wilhelm's lectures in Bonn and Berlin would in their turn benefit from his having seen examples, say, of the Byzantine style (St Mark's in Venice), or of Italian Gothic. There is even a sonnet devoted to Milan cathedral,[122] claiming it unhistorically for 'deutsche Kunst': this also duly finds its way into *Corinne* (its source is ultimately Fiorillo). His remarks would benefit from his having seen Mantegna, for instance, while Correggio, to whom they made the obligatory pilgrimage in Parma,[123] would recede in significance. His observations on the development of painting in antiquity gained from him and his companions having actually been in Pompeii and Herculanaeum.

---

120 *Lettre de Mr. Louis Bossi, de Milan, [...] sur deux inscriptions prétendues runiques trouvées à Venise [...]* (Turin: Imprimerie départementale, 1805).
121 Which are acknowledged in a note in the novel.
122 *SW*, I, 373.
123 Mentioned briefly *SW*, IX, 262.

Were one however to take as a guide the article in the Jena *Allgemeine Literatur-Zeitung* that Schlegel wrote shortly after his return from Italy, one might assume that he had spent a good part of his time in the company of modern artists working in Rome. It is that *Schreiben an Goethe über einige Arbeiten in Rom lebender Künstler. Im Sommer 1805* [Letter to Goethe on Some Works by Artists Living in Rome. In the Summer of 1805].[124] It could be read as a replique to Goethe's essay on Winckelmann of the same year, *Winckelmann und sein Jahrhundert* [Winckelmann and his Century] that had elevated his Greekness and his paganism and had treated the circumstances of his life and death in hagiographic fashion. Schlegel did not mention the real reason why he could not subscribe to Goethe's Winckelmann cult, which had as much to do with Winckelmann's inadequate archaeological knowledge as with his doctrinaire neo-classicism. Nevertheless the sequence of his remarks indicates a strategy: praise for Canova, yet tempered with the remark that Italian sculpture from Donatello onwards had moved away from true classical norms; then approval of Thorwaldsen, who did conform to them. The next section, on French neo-classical artists in Rome, asks for more sentiment in expression and refers to Chateaubriand's *Le Génie du christianisme*, which cannot have been well received in Weimar. The critique is more pointed when the French academic style, still represented by Louis David's school, is accused of too closely following the dictates of Winckelmann and Mengs (Goethe had planned an article on David for his *Propyläen*).[125] It is now time for Schlegel to state his real position; there is a long section on Gottlieb Schick, a pupil of David's but now branching out into the 'true revelation that is the purpose of all art', represented by his painting of Noah's first sacrifice.[126] Schlegel approves of this move away from classical to religious subject matter, while being fully aware that Schick is in every other respect a neo-classical artist. In landscape painting he praises Johann Anton Koch for his heroic and monumental style: this might be seen as belittling Goethe's favoured painters Reinhart and Hackert. A section on writers in Rome appears relatively conciliatory until one notices the prominence given to the Middle Ages and its Christian culture, represented by the *Nibelungenlied*. For the Vatican Library held

---

124 *Ibid.*, 231-266.
125 Johann Wolfgang Goethe, *Gedenkausgabe der Werke, Briefe und Gespräche*, ed. Ernst Beutler, 3rd edn, 27 vols (Zurich: Artemis, 1986 [1949]), XIII, 157.
126 On Schick see the catalogue from the Staatsgalerie Stuttgart *Gottlieb Schick. Ein Maler des Klassizismus* (Stuttgart: Staatsgalerie, 1976).

manuscripts of the so-called *Heldenbuch,* and one of Schlegel's tasks was to consult them. Rome, whether Goethe liked it or not, was becoming the centre of things Romantic.

There is also a short section on Sophie Bernhardi-Tieck and her epic poem *Flore und Blancheflur*. She, her two children and her lover Knorring, had by now reached Rome, ostensibly for the sake of her health but also to escape from Bernhardi's court order.[127] She frequented the house of the Humboldts and anyone else of prominence to whom she had access, in order to forestall the Prussian authorities[128]—and to borrow money. When later in the year the Tieck cavalcade arrived, with Ludwig and Friedrich, the borrowing was on a large scale. By that time, Schlegel and Madame de Staël had left Rome and were on their way home from Italy. Friedrich was using the time in Rome to make a start on the Necker memorial.[129] Sophie was not above using her son Felix Theodor's paternity as a means to Schlegel's heart and purse strings, but the sonnet which he wrote on leaving Rome spoke only of the former:

> Mir schlug das Herz, es rasselte der Wagen:
>   Der Abschied tönt es mir vom hohen Rom;
>   Und an der Engelsburg und Petersdom
>   Ward ich in raschem Flug vorbeygetragen.
>
> Ist es die Kunst aus alt- und neuen Tagen,
>   Die sieben Hügel und der gelbe Strom,
>   Ist es der Weltbeherrscherin Fantom,
>   Dem ich so tief erschüttert mußt' entsagen?
>
> Ach nein, ach nein! und wär' es nichts als dieß:
>   Ich bin ein Mann, u[nd] sah schon manche Zeiten,
>   Und litt wie mich mein Schicksal unterwies.
>
> Es ist ein lallend Kind, das ich verließ.
>   Du wirst nicht mehr die Arme nach mir breiten:
>   Leb wohl, mein Cherub, und mein Paradies![130]

---

127 Ewa Eschler, *Sophie Tieck-Bernhardi-Knorring, 1775-1833. Das Wanderleben und das vergessene Werk* (Berlin: Trafo, 2005), 181-184.
128 Bernhardi was to accuse AWS of being an accessory to kidnapping. SLUB Dresden, Mscr. Dresd. App. 2712, B15, 2 (2).
129 Cf. his letters from Munich and Rome to AWS. Bögel (2015), 100, 103, 107f., 110.
130 *Krisenjahre,* I, 195f; quoted here as in original SLUB Dresden, Mscr. Dresd. App. 2712, B15 (97). I would take the addressee to be both mother and child.

> [My heart leapt up, the carriage rattled on;
> I take my leave from lofty mother Rome;
> And past St Angelo and Peter's dome
> I was borne on in swift flight.
>
> Is it the art from now and days of old,
> The seven hills and the yellow stream,
> The phantom of the conqueror of the world,
> That I must now give up with broken heart?
>
> O no alas, if only it were this!
> I am a man experienced in time
> And taking what my fate dealt out.
>
> It is a babbling child I left behind.
> You will not stretch your arms out to me more,
> Farewell my cherub and my paradise.]

Schlegel never published these verses, and it may be hard now to defend them on purely aesthetic grounds (especially the borrowing from Goethe in the first line), but there is no doubting that the sentiments were heartfelt. Yet Schlegel was not the only one whom leave-taking moved to poetic utterance. Madame de Staël had written the poem known as *Épitre sur Naples* [Epistle on Naples] with its evocation of the sensuous delights of the southern landscape but also the awareness of past tyranny and bloodshed. Then in a letter to de Souza came an equally long poem that starts 'Il faut donc quitter Rome, il faut donc vous quitter' [One must take leave of Rome, take leave of you].[131] This was the other side of the Roman experience, evoked especially at moments of parting and regret, for Schlegel no doubt the realisation that the love which he may well have believed was his had been transferred to another, for Madame de Staël the coming to terms with the hard fact that Pedro de Souza could not be hers, despite a bond of sympathy and fleeting happiness. 'Ah! I have felt it, that god, in the ruins of Rome that I have wandered through with you in the moonlight and almost at the moment of leave-taking. My whole soul is pierced with longing, tenderness and admiration. We were together in time amid the ruins of centuries, we were united by the worship of all that is beautiful', she wrote to Souza on 15 May 1805.[132]

---

131 *Correspondance générale*, V, ii, 349-351.
132 *Ibid.*, 557.

That was perhaps the romantic aspect of moonlit promenades in the Roman ruins. She slips, however, very easily into the other side of the cult of ruins that Byron's *Childe Harold's Pilgrimage* was to typify, with its 'Lone mother of dead empires!', 'The Niobe of nations!'[133], the dwelling on a dead past than enables the easy transition to a general *mal du siècle*, the 'dream-like and melancholy pleasure' of which she also writes.[134] But with her there was also a moral aspect to these contemplations: the contrast between then and now, the realisation nurtured by Constantin-François Volney and his *Les Ruines* (1791) that mismanagement, bad governance and tyranny were the causes of the downfall of empires, leaving us only ruins bereft of their possessors. For her the contrast would not just be between Roman grandeur and its *déchéance*, but with the present state of Italy, politically divided and a nation only in name. Much of this would go into her novel *Corinne*.

Some of this enters into the 296 verses of Schlegel's elegy *Rom*, written and published in 1805 with a dedication to Madame de Staël.[135] Schlegel was inordinately proud of this poem (the only one so dedicated), written in such correct elegiac couplets that it was translated into Latin during his lifetime.[136] In many ways *Rom* marks the high point and the effective end of the Schlegel brothers' efforts in the field of neo-classical poetry, as contained in the *Athenaeum* and in August Wilhelm's *Gedichte* of 1800. For the younger Romantic generation, Achim von Arnim and Clemens Brentano in Heidelberg, it represented the 'fettering' of a poetic language that they were expanding in all directions.[137] Yet for Schlegel the language was right and appropriate, in contrast with Wilhelm von Humboldt's elegy of the same name but in ottava rima, compared with whose frigid verses Schlegel's are light-footed. (Madame de Staël, who received both,

---

133 From Cantos 78 and 79.
134 *Correspondance générale*, V, ii, 543. See Roland Mortier, *La poétique des ruines en France. Ses origines, ses variations de la Renaissance à Victor Hugo*, Histoire des ideés et critique littéraire, 144 (Geneva: Droz, 1974), 193-200; Joseph Luzzi, *Romantic Europe and the Ghost of Italy* (New Haven and London: Yale UP, 2008), esp. 53-76.
135 *SW*, II, 21-31. Published originally as a 19-page brochure in Roman type: *Rom. Elegie von August Wilhelm Schlegel* (Berlin: Unger, 1805).
136 *Roma, elegia Augusti Guilelmi Schlegel, latinitate donata, notisque illustrata a J. D. Fuss* [...] (Coloniae Agrippinae: Rommerskirchen, 1817), and subsequent editions.
137 Clemens Brentano to Achim von Arnim, 20 December, 1805. Ludwig Achim von Arnim, *Werke und Briefwechsel*. Historisch-kritische Ausgabe ed. with Klassik Stiftung Weimar by Roswitha Burwick *et al.*, 8 vols in 11 (in progress) (Berlin, Boston: de Gruyter 2000-), XXXII, 110.

would form her own judgment.) Not only was the language 'correct' in more senses than one, but Schlegel could claim to Fouqué in 1806 that this was no mere 'metrical exercise': like the elegy in memory of his brother Carl and the garland for Auguste Böhmer, it expressed personal feeling, not directly like those other poems, but through a sense of awe generated by the remains of a past and once proud history.[138] With our knowledge of his unpublished sonnet to Sophie Bernhardi, we may perhaps feel tempted to attribute some of the elegy's melancholy and impotent languor to that emotional experience, now over, and to see the address to Germaine de Staël in its final section as an admission that she alone was to be his future companion, as the chaste 'expresser of great thoughts'.

Yet, try as we may, it is hard not to read much of this poem as the 'course de M. Schlegel', his conducted tour of Roman mythology, history and architecture (not forgetting those basalt lions and the granite sphinx). One baulks at learned if properly scanned words like 'Amphitryoniades' (meaning Hercules), even if the historical account, from mythical beginnings to the barbarian invasions, is factually impeccable. It is difficult to rescue much of the poem aesthetically even if we know that Schlegel would later declare those incursions into the Roman Empire to be the catalyst of modern European history.[139] But it joins the European poetry of ruins in its later sections, in its meditation among the tombs on what 'was' ('"Gewesen"/Ist Roms Wahlspruch' ['Rome's motto is/'What was']), its discourse on loss and decadence at the foot of the pyramid of Cestius in the dusk of the Roman day. Not even the Renaissance, Raphael or Michelangelo, is spared these depredations of time: perhaps this prompted him to hope that Vincenzo Monti might translate *Rom* into Italian.[140] Yet the poem, like so many such reveries, returns at the end to the present, the friendship, the great thoughts, the poetic magic and colour, all of which he associates with Madame de Staël. To show how heartfelt these sentiments are, he summons up the ultimate name in her personal configuration: her father Jacques Necker. For had he, Schlegel, not also played his modest part in Necker's memorialisation by securing the services of his friend Friedrich Tieck for the Coppet mausoleum?

---

138 *SW*, VIII, 146.
139 In his Bonn lectures on World History.
140 Comtesse Jean de Pange, née Broglie, *Auguste-Guillaume Schlegel et Madame de Staël d'après des documents inédits* [Pange], doctoral thesis University of Paris (Paris: Albert, 1938), 171.

3.1 With Madame de Staël in Coppet and Acosta 1805-1807

The Writer in Diaspora

Writing from Naples on 27 February, 1805 to Sophie Bernhardi, Schlegel had this to say about Rome: 'It is a wonderful place for a quiet and solitary life devoted to all that is beautiful and great'.[141] There are echoes here of Winckelmann and his dedication to beauty and grace and harmony, his placing of the aesthetic before the personal, that Goethe in his Winckelmann hagiography of 1805 was to elevate to superhuman dimensions. Unlike Winckelmann for whom the male form was everything, Schlegel was here writing to a woman who would not let him go, while he was in the entourage of another woman whose imperious claims had brought him to Italy in the first place. He was well advised to leave the former and cleave (chastely) to the latter. For Sophie, once installed in Rome in 1806, was all for having him come there for what would in effect be a ménage à trois.[142] It would be Caroline and Schelling all over again, only worse. And so Schlegel returned to Coppet with Madame de Staël and her children and resumed his duties and his social responsibilities.

He knew what these were, and he was aware that he would continue to be subject to the desires and whims of the capricious and mercurial mistress of the house. Already in the first full letter he had written from Coppet on his arrival in May 1804, he had recounted how he had had to drop his own work and be present when visitors arrived, first Bonstetten, then the prefect.[143] It applied of course to other members of the 'groupe de Coppet', those newly arrived like Prosper de Barante, later a respected historian but now still young enough to fall in love with the thirty-five-year-old Germaine de Staël; or to Elzéar de Sabran, a friend and indifferent writer who put in occasional appearances. Even Benjamin Constant, still making serious claims on her heart and hand, was similarly constrained.

Coppet seemed to afford the refuge and solitude that Madame de Staël and by implication also the members of her circle needed. For her, the first priorities were writing up the Italian experience as the novel *Corinne*, and the continuing work on the future *De l'Allemagne*. As we shall see, the large

---

141 *Krisenjahre*, I, 187.
142 Ibid., 371.
143 Ibid., 97.

bulk of the work on those projects was not actually carried out at Coppet at all and seemed to be fitted into a peripatetic lifestyle that took in several venues. While she was able to write in almost any place and at any time, it was not so easy for her circle, not least for Schlegel, indeed he was later to stress that his major work of the period 1805-07, the *Comparaison entre la Phèdre de Racine et celle d'Euripide*, was the product of unsettled times uncongenial to sustained work. Whatever the truth of that statement, and it is not without its element of *captatio benevolentiae*, Schlegel was to be subjected to several changes of scene in these years and, without yet knowing it, was on the threshold of even more 'années de pèlerinage'.

Unlike Winckelmann, who had effectively become a Greek (if an Italian one) and who had broken off the only journey back to Germany that he made, Schlegel always felt the draw of his native land and saw himself as part of a kind of diaspora. There would inevitably be tensions between his adherence to a 'group' and his consciousness of belonging to another culture and another language. While it is legitimate for later generations to see Schlegel as part of a nascent French Romanticism and to claim some of his major works, closely associated with Madame de Staël, as part of it,[144] it is by the same token also true that he had never abjured membership of the Jena circle. If that involved bringing to French-language readers what was now common knowledge in Germany, well and good.

There is no lack of evidence that he now saw himself primarily as a 'national poet', and it may be significant that he was dissociating himself more and more from translation. He kept Reimer waiting for the second volume of the Calderón and then never delivered; he was unworried that the Voss sons were now continuing his Shakespeare in the style and according to the principles that he himself had laid down. He approached Cotta about a reissue of his poems.[145] His letters contained protestations of 'national sympathies'[146] and reassured recipients that he was not in the process of becoming a French writer.[147]

The long letter that he wrote from Geneva to Friedrich de la Motte Fouqué in Prussian Nennhausen on 12 March 1806,[148] was essentially a call to abandon the languorous and sensuous sound-play of Calderonian (and

---

144 As stressed notably by Simone Balayé in several publications on the 'Groupe de Coppet'.
145 *Briefe*, I, 202f.
146 *Ibid.*, 200, 205, 213.
147 *Ibid.*, 200.
148 *SW*, VIII, 142-153, refs 145, 149.

Tieckian) imitation and to embrace instead a more 'direct, energetic and patriotic poetry'. Written just a few months before the downfall of Prussia at the battles of Jena and Auerstädt, it invoked the robust tones of Johannes von Müller's Helvetic history. Fouqué's task would be to seize the 'ancient documents of our poetry and history' and lift the national consciousness out of its torpor ('Versunkenheit'). It was the spur to Fouqué's Siegfried trilogy *Der Held des Nordens* [The Hero of the North] (1808-10) and much else in the nineteenth century.

A series of poems (none of especial aesthetic merit) showed him unrepentantly returning to the themes that had always preoccupied him, love, both ideal ('Minne') and real, chivalry, 'Vaterland',[149] as a further reminder that he was 'still there', that patriotic virtues were undiminished *in partibus infidelium*, even a longing for the sound of his native tongue in a Romance exile. Perhaps it gave him some satisfaction to have himself named, along with his brother Friedrich, in Adam Müller's Dresden lectures in 1807 on 'deutsche Wissenschaft und Literatur' [German Science and Literature] and see himself invoked there as one of those forces instrumental in national regeneration and renewal.[150]

For only months after their return from Italy in 1805, the precarious peace that had enabled their journey south was shattered by the resumption of the continental war. The Austrians were routed at Ulm in October, the Russians and Austrians at Austerlitz in December. The peace of Pressburg in the same month imposed Napoleon's terms on the Austrians—and gave Hanover to the Prussians. For the time being there was nothing Schlegel could do to help his family except send sums of money to his needy mother through the war zones. The catastrophe of Jena and Auerstädt in October of 1806, the total defeat of the Prussian army, had all the symbolic and real lineaments of a national disaster. Napoleon rode through Weimar and Jena, prompting Hegel's remark about seeing the 'Weltseele' in person.[151] It was also the end of Jena: Heinrich Luden, a history professor there, who had had his house pillaged and had lost his papers, spoke for many in summoning up a 'stream that surged through the lands of the world with

---

149 Such as 'In der Fremde', 'An die Jungfrau von Orleans', 'Glaube', 'Tells Kapelle, bei Küßnacht', *SW*, I, 258, 259-261, 264f., 280f.
150 Adam H. Müller, *Vorlesungen über die deutsche Wissenschaft und Literatur. Zweite vermehrte und verbesserte Auflage* (Dresden: Arnold, 1807), 44.
151 For this and other references cf. Roger Paulin, '1806/7—ein Krisenjahr der Frühromantik?', *Kleist-Jahrbuch*, 1993, 137-151, ref. 138.

a terrible roar and swept away thrones and swallowed up much that we cherished'.[152]

What could Schlegel effectively do? In practical terms, nothing. Much later, he would respond to Johann Heinrich Voss's rampageous anti-Romantic polemics by saying that at least he had been involved intellectually in the struggle against Napoleon, whereas Voss, in pro-Napoleonic Baden, had not seen a foreign foot set in his kitchen garden in Heidelberg.[153] But now at most he could share in the process of organic renewal and recovery that Goethe privately spoke of,[154] meet the 'cognitive challenge of war'[155] through intellectual and poetic means. It was a question of 'Gesinnungen', those 'convictions' that crop up in his letters. In October 1807 he sympathised with Countess Voss, who had actually suffered under the French occupation of Prussia, sensing that 'the ground is giving way under one's feet' and that one will never see familiar places as they once were. How different his recent journey through Switzerland, that 'citadel of freedom'. The letter had its symbolic side, for the bearer was Carl von Clausewitz, not yet the theoretician of war, but the aide-de-camp to Prince August of Prussia. Once a member of Schlegel's audience at the Berlin Lectures, now a lieutenant colonel, the prince had been captured at Prenzlau, with the capitulation of the remaining Prussian forces after Jena and Auerstädt and had come to France, and thence to Coppet, as a prisoner of war.[156] It was Clausewitz who would write to Schlegel early in 1808 about the 'unsteady' ground of the political and military situation and the need for a moral regeneration from which all else would proceed.[157]

In his letter of 1807, Schlegel mentions the *Dichter-Garten von Rostorf* [Poets' Garden], the mayfly almanac edited by Karl von Hardenberg, Novalis's brother and a noted convert to Catholicism. Reviewing it in the same year, Schlegel singled out the collection's tone of earnestness and patriotic piety, not least the (rather indifferent) poems by his brother Friedrich and the largest contribution by far, Sophie Bernhardi's *Egidio und Isabella*. Friedrich had not succeeded in extricating himself from Cologne. He was to complain that circumstances were forcing them apart, where they naturally belonged

---

152 *Ibid.*, 144.
153 'Berichtigung einiger Mißdeutungen', *SW*, VIII, 243.
154 Paulin, 144.
155 Using Peter Paret's phrase. *The Cognitive Challenge of War: Prussia 1806* (Princeton and Oxford: Princeton UP, 2009).
156 They were in Coppet from August until October 1807. Jasinski, 'Liste des principaux visiteurs', 473.
157 *Krisenjahre*, I, 496f.

together.[158] While August Wilhelm expressed a more general 'Gesinnung', Friedrich's views were more focused and more pronounced: against Protestantism, classicism, the Enlightenment, for Austria and above all for 'one constitution' and 'one Church', which could only mean 'Catholic'. Even in his comparative language studies he was inclined towards speculation where his brother was now and later much more cautious and 'philological'. He denied for instance the theory that the American peoples may once have crossed the Bering Strait from Asia and embraced instead wilder notions of Indian colonies in Peru and Germanic settlements in Mexico.[159] These ideas, given new currency by Alexander von Humboldt's journeys and indeed referred to (with due scepticism) in *Vues des cordillères*, were the less ordered side of the ideas on language families that Jean-Sylvain Bailly and Sir William Jones had given rise to in the late eighteenth century. Fortunately Friedrich was able to rein them in somewhat when writing his important *Ueber die Sprache und Weisheit der Indier* of 1808.

In Coppet meanwhile life was returning to some kind of routine, if that is ever a word that can properly be applied to Madame de Staël. In the first instance, Auguste de Staël was to be prepared for the entrance examinations to the École polytechnique, with Schlegel giving him extended Greek lessons. The boy then left for Paris in August, and Napoleon in the event intervened to put a stop to his admission. The letters with which she bombarded her unfortunate son, full of exhortations and expectations, not least the hope that this fifteen-year-old might put in a word for her in the highest circles (Fouché), suggest a fraught and frazzled state of mind. Things were not improved by Napoleon continuing his injunction banning her from Paris and restricting her to a precinct of forty leagues from the capital while graciously allowing her the provinces. 'But where can one live without the language, without my friends':[160] the tone is querulous and self-pitying. For the life-style of Coppet continued unabated: guests in 1805 included the prince of Mecklenburg-Schwerin, Prince Esterházy and Crown Prince Ludwig of Bavaria, names useful in the not too distant future. But other visitors involved emotional tangles: Prosper de Barante, immediately falling in love, Monti, to whom she was platonically attached, while Benjamin Constant saw himself as the lover *en titre*. When not thus engaged, she was writing *Corinne*. For Schlegel the shine was already wearing off Coppet.

---

158 *Ibid.*, 464.
159 *Ibid.*, 216.
160 *Correspondance générale*, V, ii, 673.

Whereas once he had been regarded as a favoured member of the household (or so he thought), he sensed that he was being relegated, misunderstood, made to feel what he effectively was, a foreigner, a German, a scholar-academic, a bourgeois. There were quarrels and exchanges of notes that might have been resolved in amicable fashion, coming to a head in a long letter in which he talked of breaking his chains, rehearsed her reproaches and begged her (quoting *Julius Caesar* for good measure) not to 'hurl them in my teeth'.[161] It seems to have had its effect, for the next note was couched in quite different tones. It is worth quoting it in the original:

> Je déclare que vous avez tous les droits sur moi et que je n'en ai aucun sur vous. Disposez de ma personne et de ma vie, ordonnez, défendez, je vous obéirai en tout. Je n'aspire à aucun bonheur que celui que vous voudrez me donner; je ne veux rien posséder, je veux tenir tout de votre générosité. Je consentirais volontiers à ne plus penser tout à ma célébrité, à vouer exclusivement à votre usage particulier ce que je peux avoir de connoissances et le talens. Je suis fier de vous appartenir en propriété'.[162] [I declare that you have all rights over me and that I have none over you. Dispose of my person, of my life, demand, forbid, I shall obey you in everything. I do not aspire to any happiness but what you care to bestow on me; I do not wish to possess anything, I wish to keep everything out of your generosity. I shall of my own free will consent to think no more wholly of my celebrity, to devote exclusively to your own use whatever I have by way of knowledge and talents. I am proud of belonging to you as your own possession.]

With this he moves from the harsh speech of *Julius Caesar* to the dulcet tones of courtly love, to *Minnesang*, to Petrarch, in a letter that is also a fine piece of rhetorical construction. On that level, it is one writer addressing another, each aware of the conventions and proprieties. It is also an admission of resignation and defeat, of the powerlessness of resistance, the realisation that his life, for the time being at least, was to be determined by her movements, her preferences, her dispensations. He had in effect nowhere else to turn: she offered security, but on her terms. Seen thus, it need not be read merely as the craven and obeisant act of submission that many have judged it to be. It does also suggest that an intervening letter or conversation had promised to make amends, to repair their relationship, and her solicitude for his welfare in the next years, and his willingness to undertake acts of sacrifice on her behalf, would bear this out. While Schlegel

---

161 Pange, 151f., ref. 152.
162 *Ibid.*, 153.

went through these rites of acquiescence and homage, accepting his role in a court where all was free but by the same token all was subtly controlled, at his desk, in those hours when there were no conversations and no social duties, he was able to perform some small acts of insubordination.

Meanwhile, it was a question of solidarity with Germaine, while reminding the reading public at home that, although physically absent from his native soil, he was still part of its national cultural patrimony and its discourse. By no means everyone, it seems, was edified by his association with Madame de Staël. A caricature of Schlegel in Rome—its circulation and date are uncertain—blindfolded, with ass's ears and a goose dictating a text which contained allusions of a sexually obscene nature, showed a less decorous attitude to his relationship.[163] The ubiquitous Kotzebue, also a visitor to Rome in 1805, wrote a disrespectful account of artistic life there and one that deliberately contradicted Romantic emphases.[164]

Fig. 13 'Artem penetrat'. Caricature drawing, undated [1805?]. Orphan work.

---

163 Not all of the iconography is clear, but the caption 'Artem penetrat' refers to the figure of Schlegel putting his foot through a canvas. What he is depicted as writing ('La carne mia e rimista da M. Schuwitz') is a reference to a notorious brothel madam in late 18th-century Berlin. Reproduced in J. G. van Gelder, 'Artem Penetrat', in: *Dancwerc. Opstellen aangeboden aan Prof. Dr. D. Th. Enklaar ter gelegenheid van zijn vijfenzestige verjaardag* (Groningen: Wolters, 1959), 308-317, ill. facing 312.

164 August von Kotzebue, *Erinnerungen von einer Reise aus Liefland nach Rom und Neapel*, 3 parts (Berlin: Frölich, 1805), II, 245-274, especially critical of Koch (266f.) and Schick (267f.).

Considérations sur la civilisation en général

Schlegel could show his good will by reviewing texts by authors close to her circle or her affections, by avoiding points of disagreement, or by agreeing to differ. They were often tucked away in German journals, mainly the *Allgemeine Literatur-Zeitung* in Jena.[165] He reviewed favourably Bonstetten's book tracing the footsteps of Virgil's Aeneas in Italy, but as one who also had been there and was just as good a Latinist (a pupil of Heyne's). His praise for Monti's treatise on a passage in Catullus was from one classical scholar to another, while he used Monti's defence elsewhere of Italian culture and *scienza nuova* as a stick to beat French snobbery towards both Italy and Germany. When he reviewed the posthumous papers of Jacques Necker,[166] he found the same hagiographical tone appropriate that Germaine always employed with reference to her father. He also started writing in French.

Considérations sur la civilisation en général et sur l'origine et la décadence des religions,[167] which Eduard Böcking his editor dated at 1805, is the first of the two major French texts from these earlier Staëlian years. It is a thirty-to-forty-page fragment that Schlegel never published in his lifetime, much of it derivative and not all of its arguments sustained. We do not know for whom or for what occasion it was written. It has echoes here and there of *Rom*, from the same year. Its title, *Considérations*, might suggest a companion piece, or even a critique, of Madame de Staël's own work of 1800 and indeed this may be the reason for his never issuing it. It has echoes of Herder's *Ideen*, of Johannes von Müller, of Schlegel's own lectures on *Enzyklopädie*; it cites Jean-Sylvain Bailly and Sir William Jones, all texts or authors that trace the development—material, linguistic, religious—of humankind from its notional origins.

It has two strands, neither of which is satisfactorily integrated into a consecutive argument: a critique of the eighteenth-century notion of progress, and an examination of the origins of civilization. Take first the cherished eighteenth-century view of progress, of human perfectibility,[168] especially its French variant, represented by Turgot and Condorcet

---

165 *SW*, XII, 169-188.
166 *Ibid.*, 177-182.
167 *Oeuvres*, I, 277-316.
168 On this see Ernst Behler, 'La doctrine de Coppet d'une perfectibilité infinie et la Révolution française', in: *Le Groupe de Coppet et la Révolution française. Colloque 1988*, ed. Étienne Hofmann and Anne-Lise Delacrétaz, Annales Benjamin Constant 8-9 (Lausanne: Institut Benjamin Constant; Paris: Touzot, 1988), 255-274.

(unnamed) and also Staël and Constant (also unidentified). Schlegel rebuts the claims of what he sees as sensualist, rationalist and egoistical philosophy by invoking the counter-claims of idealism (again, no names), which, far from denying the existence of the physical world, '[consists] solely in recognising the primacy of the intellect or of morals over the physical'.[169] Progress—which Schlegel does not deny—is not merely a matter of resisting earlier enthusiasms, but is contingent on the achievement of wisdom and of control over the passions. Thus we cannot speak of progress in our own age, when experience tells us that it is the first, primeval movements that count, not mere later 'raisonnements' and refinements of taste. We have lost original unities—those of philosophy with poetry or law-making with cosmogony—and our scientific discoveries serve only to make the material world available. 'Man becomes a machine',[170] words which echo the anti-rationalist, anti-mechanical theme running through the late eighteenth century in Germany; man loses the sense of poetry, loses the 'centre', the belief in some kind of providence.

None of this would be alien to Herder, to Schiller, to Friedrich Schlegel, if differently focused and formulated. He comes closer to Romantic doctrine in rejecting the Voltairean and Humean view of a primeval 'brutish state'.[171] Against it he sets early mankind's reliance on myth (Egyptian, Greek, American) as an explanation of natural phenomena and human achievement (poetry, agriculture, cultivation). The old idea of a Golden Age expressed this in terms of a primal energy, organic forces at work in natural rhythms, traces of which can be found in most ancient cultures. In deepest time, there must have existed a people of extreme wisdom and enlightenment who took uncivilized nature in hand and colonized it (the theme of migration from his Göttingen dissertation). We know this, he says, through the discoveries made by scholars like Bailly and Sir William Jones: India is the 'cradle of the human race', Sanskrit the mother of all languages, where the word, spoken or written, affords control over the terrestrial world, social institutions, astronomy and religion. This 'sacred language' is notable for its sophisticated structure and its range of expression, both concrete and abstract. It is the language of the Brahmins, in which still today there survives wisdom, calm, contemplation, paternalistic authority, as against 'our frantic perfectibility'.[172] They have seen the need to pass on

---

169 *Oeuvres*, I, 280.
170 *Ibid.*, 289.
171 *Ibid.*, 293.
172 *Ibid.*, 315.

to their descendants the traditions, monuments and precepts that our age, fixated as it is on the future, has forgotten.

This is Schlegel before he had learned a word of Sanskrit, combining Hermsterhuisian ideas with the eighteenth century's reverence for India and all things Indian, or rather, the clichés associated with it. It can be related to his polemical rejection of the 'shallow' optimism and utilitarianism of much of eighteenth-century German literary culture, from which judgment, it may be remembered, he had excluded those idealisers of past myth and past civilisations, Winckelmann and Hemsterhuis. That is one side. It is a first, tentative formulation of ideas that would find expression in his later lectures in Bonn on ancient history and Graeco-Roman culture, and it informs his later notions on language unities and linguistic structures. There is no evidence that he ever produced it in the Coppet circle,[173] even as a subject of discussion, for it would have elicited counter-arguments from Madame de Staël and from Constant. Its being drafted in French, and its clear engagement with the French 'idéologues' would have ensured this.

On some Tragic Roles of Madame de Staël

Madame de Staël was bored. Boredom was another form of melancholy and depression. Something had to be done to ward it off. Apart from writing frequent letters to Auguste in Paris, there was her other, slightly brainless, son Albert to consider. Knowing Schlegel's newly-discovered love of the outdoor life, she sent them on a journey on foot round parts of Lake Geneva, accompanied by Elzéar de Sabran. We know very little of this except what Schlegel tells us in a letter to his sister-in-law in Hanover, and a few lines to Sophie.[174] Taking their tutorial duties seriously, they showed Albert not only the sights in nature but those connected with Rousseau's *La Nouvelle Héloïse*, a reminder that the Neckers had once known Jean-Jacques and that Germaine's near-debut as a writer had been *Lettres sur les ouvrages et le caractère de J. J. Rousseau* in 1788.[175]

A distraction which never failed to revive Madame de Staël was the theatre, acting or declamation. It had been a very serious diversion since her childhood, when she had some lessons in the speaking of verse from the celebrated actress Mademoiselle Clairon.[176] Since then, in her first

---

173 Although he seems to have let Zacharias Werner see it. *Briefe*, II, 99.
174 *Briefe*, I, 194f., II, 84.
175 Pierre Kohler, *Madame de Staël et la Suisse*, 92-115.
176 Martine de Rougemont, 'Pour un répertoire des rôles et des représentations de Mme de Staël', *Cahiers staëliens*, 19 (1974), 79-92, ref. 80.

English exile, in Weimar, Berlin and Rome, she had given 'performances', either taking an acting part or reading, mainly Voltaire and Racine, and for preference the roles of Andromaque or Phèdre. In Germany, it had added to her reputation for eccentric celebrity, as it would later in Vienna and Stockholm.

In November of 1805, she, Constant and Schlegel moved to Geneva where they stayed until the end of March 1806. She hired the 'théâtre au Molard' in the centre of the city and immediately set about arranging productions in which her circle and her friends (notably Constant, Prosper de Barante and Sabran) were involved. This also meant Schlegel. We can imagine him as a lecturer in Jena or Berlin reading verse with good accentuation and even with feeling; and we know of his concern—also shared by Goethe— that the actors in *Ion* in Weimar should speak their lines well. Of his acting skills we know less. The ever-malicious Benjamin Constant claimed that he was comical in tragedy and not happy in comedy, but that we may largely discount.[177] In the letter to Julie Schlegel he spoke of the difficulty of acting in a foreign language, despite his 'almost impeccable' accent. Meanwhile, he was also to be a kind of wardrobe manager, so that presumably his brief even extended to the lavish 'Greek' and 'Spanish' attire of Madame de Staël to which he later made reference.[178] If Schlegel had little taste for the actual dramatic fare, at least he knew that the costumes were historically 'correct'.

The first play performed was Voltaire's *Mérope*. Schlegel knew, as probably no-one else present did, that Lessing had once subjected this play to one of his elegant demolitions in the *Hamburgische Dramaturgie*, and Schlegel had already made no secret of his disdain for French neo-classicism. But part of the new accommodation to circumstances meant pitching in with a will, in this case as the minor figure Euryclès. There was more Voltaire to follow in 1806, *Mahomet* and *Alzire* in January, *Zaïre* in March. In March, it was also the turn of Racine, first the comedy *Les Plaideurs*, with Schlegel in an unspecified role, and then the great performance of *Phèdre*. Earlier in the same month, Madame de Staël's own play, *Agar dans le désert*,

---

177 *Journaux intimes*, 282.
178 Cf. Friederike Brun: 'Die Kleidungen auf diesem Privattheater, die Beobbachtung [sic] des Costume, ließ die großen Theather [sic] hinter sich zurück—und dies war A.W. Schlegels Werk der ein feiner Kenner des Alterthums ist.' *Bonstettiana*, X, i, 77. One member of the audience did refer to the 'costumes très riches'. Jean-Daniel Candaux, 'Le théâtre de Mme de Staël au Molard (1805-6). Témoignages d'auditeurs genevois et calendrier des spectacles', *Cahiers staëliens*, 14 (1972), 19-32, ref. 24. See also Martine de Rougemont, 'L'activité théâtrale dans le Groupe de Coppet: la dramaturgie et le jeu', *Colloque 1974*, 263-283, ref. 270.

had been staged, with Germaine in the title role, Albertine as Ismaël, and Albert as the angel.

Whatever Schlegel may have said during this theatrical season, what he actually wrote about it made his views quite clear. This was in the article that he sent to the *Berliner Damen-Kalender* for 1807 (thus late in 1806), *Ueber einige tragische Rollen von Frau v. Staël dargestellt* [On Some Tragic Roles Represented by Madame de Staël].[179] The addressee was 'Madame Bethmann', who insiders knew was Friederike Unzelmann, the well-known Berlin actress, now remarried since 1803 and using a new name. She had of course been romantically associated with Schlegel in Berlin, and he had paid court to her in verse[180] — and, who knows, perhaps in other form. For all of these reasons it is interesting to have Schlegel's published account of Madame de Staël's acting. The context is crucial. On the one hand, he would not wish to diminish by association the artistry of the great *diva* who had excelled in Mozart operas, in Shakespearean roles, and who as Schiller's Maria Stuart had moved the audience to tears in the leave-taking scene in Act Five. By the same token, he was concerned not to disparage Madame de Staël's acting talent, which, while impressive, was 'natural', not 'professional'. Similarly, he would be careful not to display too many of the prejudices against French and to some extent Italian neo-classicism to which his Berlin lectures had most recently given expression. He was aware that Goethe had translated Voltaire's *Tancrède* and *Mahomet* and Schiller Racine's *Phèdre* for the needs of the Weimar stage and its actors' perceived deficiencies in speaking verse.

Thus it was a delicate balancing act, between rejection of false declamation and admiration for an acting performance that had taken provincial Geneva by storm (if not Paris or Vienna or Berlin). There was, too, the question of whether her acting was remarkable *per se* or whether it was the sight, the spectacle, of the writer 'whose works are already in everyone's hands' appearing in dramatic roles. Schlegel assured his German readers that she possessed the poise, the ease of movement and gesture, the mastery of spoken language, that the actor must have, but above all the ability to make the poetic character her own, to act from within the dictates

---

179 SW, IX, 267-281. Cf. the closely related review by Friederike Brun, also in 1806. *Bonstettiana*, X, i, 91-97.

180 Notably 'An Friederike Unzelmann bei Uebersendung meiner Gedichte' (*SW*, I, 240f.), 'Die Schauspielerin Friederike Unzelmann an das Publikum, als sie am Schluß des Schauspiels herausgerufen wurde' (*ibid.*, 242) and 'An Friederike Unzelmann als Nina' (*ibid.*, 243); there is also an unpublished sonnet in French, 'A Madame Unzelmann à son logis', full of Petrarchan extravagance. SLUB Dresden, Mscr. Dresd. e. 90, XX, Kapsel I, Bd. 2. Beilage 1a (10).

of her own heart, to empathise, to draw the audience into her own pain and suffering. There was none of the alleged forced declamation of some of the leading Paris actors.

So far, so good. How was Schlegel to reconcile his admiration for 'tragic roles' in plays by Voltaire and Racine for which he had to date mainly evinced contempt? He succeeded in praising *Mérope* by concentrating on Madame de Staël's mastery of the role, rather than discussing the play's intrinsic merits, and of course he himself had been Euryclès to her Mérope in December, 1805. This approach did not work for the 'irreligious' *Mahomet*, whereas *Alzire*, with its clash between the old and the new worlds (and Madame de Staël in Spanish costume) found his favour. Not so *Zaïre*: only the 'grace and tenderness' of her acting could redeem an otherwise 'unnatural' drama.

There then follows a section on *Phèdre*, which, when placed alongside the *Comparaison* of 1807, reads like a first draft of some of that essay's points: some only, as he reserves for that later work the reasons for Euripides' superiority over Racine. Here, he merely states that, by changing the role of Euripides' Hippolytus, Racine has placed Phèdre instead in the full centre of the action; a figure of almost morbid passion, pathological imagination and seductive power has pushed the borders of dramatic representation to their farthest extent without causing offence to our moral sensitivities. Not wishing to pursue this point further, Schlegel concentrates on Madame de Staël's use of gesture and voice modulation, above all her figure in 'Greek' costume that the author of *Ion* finds part of the 'grand style' of her performance.

Interestingly, however, he finds the real pathos, the tears of sympathy and empathy, not in Racine, but in Madame de Staël's own *Agar dans le désert*, performed by herself with Albertine and Albert. Apart from its ability to move (Schlegel found words in French verse),[181] the play has the merit of breaking with the conventions of the French stage, being in prose, allowing for mime, and with instrumental interludes between the speeches. It was a step, he says, towards the reformation of the French theatre, once attempted unsuccessfully by Diderot, but now restoring 'nature' to its proper place. No doubt the Staël family, even an angelic Albert, had the power to move, but his (German) readers may have wondered all the same at this elevation of Hagar to the level of Phèdre.

---

181 'A Madame de Staël après la représentation d'Agar. 1806'. *Oeuvres*, I, 84.

But the Staëlian theatre was also open for other talents. The poetess Friederike Brun brought her talented daughter Ida to Geneva that winter, where with Madame de Staël's encouragement the not quite fourteen-year-old girl performed pantomime dances to music, with representations of figures from classical mythology. Schlegel had referred briefly to this kind of performance in his Berlin lectures,[182] but here was 'attitude', rhythm, physical movement, ideal form, grace, expressiveness, plasticity, all in one action, abstract notions come alive, symbols made real, Pygmalion's ideal realised. Diana, Aurora, Atalanta, Althea—the gamut of mythological emotion, terror, dignity, fury, despair—came easily to Ida. Schlegel wrote a poem in her honour.[183] With the article on Madame de Staël's acting, it shows Schlegel postulating a kind of theatrical 'Gesamtkunstwerk' *avant la lettre*.

Corinne, ou l'Italie

These distractions could not last. By April of 1806, the Staël ménage was on the move again,[184] Albert and Albertine, Schlegel, to be joined again by Dom Pedro de Souza, with Auguste still in Paris. It is not easy to keep abreast with Madame de Staël's movements during this time, involving as they did various journeyings and sojourns in provincial France and over a year's absence from Coppet. First, they went to Lyon, then to Auxerre. From there it was Vincelles on the Yonne, where they settled in the small château. She had little eye for its scenic position above the river: it was 'a real Ovidian Scythia',[185] a not altogether unfitting analogy in that it was forty-one leagues from Paris. Paris itself remained out of reach: she sent Souza in the hope that he might negotiate some deal with Fouché, to get her to the capital and settle the two-million-franc loan that Necker had selflessly made to the French state (she would not get this back until the Restoration). She disclaimed any interest in politics, only a wish to live in the metropolis, but

---

182 AWS, *Kritische Ausgabe der Vorlesungen*, ed. Ernst Behler *et al.*, 3 vols [*KAV*] (Paderborn, etc.: Schöningh, 1989- in progress), I, 383. Cf. Claudia Albert, 'Bild, Symbol, Allegorie, Zeichen. Schlegels Ästhetik der Moderne', in: York-Gothart Mix and Jochen Strobel (eds), *Der Europäer August Wilhelm Schlegel. Romantischer Kulturtransfer—romantische Wissenswelten*, Quellen und Forschungen, 62 (296) (Berlin: de Gruyter, 2010), 107-123 (does not discuss the poem).
183 'An Ida Brun'. *Poetische Werke*, I, 227-230; *SW*, I, 254-257, with accompanying note. *Bonstettiana*, X, i, 82-97, with illustrations.
184 The account of her movements based on *Correspondance générale*, Calendrier staëlien, VI, xvii-xxii.
185 *Ibid.*, VI, 83.

Napoleon and his agents were inexorable. She was bored, taking opium, despite at various times Auguste, Mathieu de Montmorency, Elzéar de Sabran, and the amorous Prosper de Barante coming to keep her company.

She could at least send Schlegel and Albert to Paris for ten days, which happened in May. 'Be nice to him',[186] 'he is much more of a friend than the tutor to my children', is how she wrote on 8 May of Schlegel. The addressee was Juliette, the famous Madame Récamier. Prince August of Prussia was to fall seriously in love with her,[187] Auguste de Staël would be adolescently enamoured, and Schlegel was duly charmed. Writing to the permanent secretary of the Académie Française and the editor of *Le Publiciste*, Jean-Baptiste-Antoine Suard, she went further, qualifying Schlegel as 'the most extraordinary man as a philologist, clever and learned as a man of letters, that it is possible to meet'.[188] It is uncertain whom Schlegel met on this occasion, but this first encounter with the world of French academic scholarship was of symbolic importance for the future.

Germaine could not easily stay in one place and we find her making several short forays away from Vincelles, leaving the two younger children, Schlegel, Souza and Constant, who had been installed there since the summer of 1806. In August, however, Schlegel fell ill.[189] It was a tertian fever, most likely malarial, as the pattern of relapses (recorded by Constant and Madame de Staël) would indicate. While Constant saw Schlegel's prostration as mere 'pusillanimité',[190] there is no doubt that his condition was serious, so much so that Staël summoned a doctor from Paris. This was no ordinary physician, and he would play a role in Schlegel's later life disproportionate to his medical ministrations. David Ferdinand Koreff[191] had had a brilliant career in Berlin and had now launched himself in the 'grand monde' of Paris. There is something of the *Wunderdoktor* and charlatan about him, especially his magnetic cures; there is also no doubt that he was skilled at his profession. His approach to Schlegel was holistic, prescribing what was thought appropriate at the time (and rightly warning

---

186 *Ibid.*
187 Her picture by François Gérard is to be seen in the background of Franz Krüger's official portrait (c. 1817) of the prince (Berlin: Alte Nationalgalerie). He never married.
188 *Correspondance générale*, VI, 83.
189 First reference 8 August, Constant, *Journaux intimes*, 292; Sismondi, *Epistolario*, I, 85.
190 *Journaux intimes*, 292.
191 Cf. Simone Balayé, 'Madame de Staël et le docteur Koreff', *Cahiers staëliens*, 3 (1965), 15-32, and generally Friedrich v. Oppeln-Bronikowski, *David Ferdinand Koreff. Serapionsbruder, Magnetiseur, Geheimrat und Dichter. Der Lebensroman eines Vergessenen* (Berlin: Paetel, 1928).

him not to take too much quinine),[192] also probing into his state of mind. Could there not be some hidden cause for this persistent fever, some worry or anxiety or grief? Madame de Staël was in no doubt that Schlegel's jealousy of the amorous Barante was the cause.[193] If one were to adduce psychological causes for something so clearly physical, one might just as easily mention the barrage of letters from Sophie Bernhardi in Rome and their catalogue of woes as a contributory factor.

Schlegel only gradually got better; his brother Friedrich, alarmed at not hearing from him, actually came to be with him, extending the visit for a whole six months.[194] It relieved his strained exchequer, while he in his turn gave Madame de Staël a private lecture on metaphysics.[195] She had meanwhile removed to Rouen, from September to November, then to the (quite modest) Château d'Acosta in Aubergenville, where the valleys of the Mauldre and the Seine meet, forty-five kilometres from Paris and thus inside the forbidden zone. Fouché, for the meanwhile, left her in peace. She was to be there from the end of November 1806 until April 1807.

The Schlegel brothers were subject to no such constraints and were able to spend some time in Paris, taking the 'diligence-éclair' from Rouen. At least two notes that we can date from this time[196] suggest that they enjoyed the agreeable company of Madame Récamier. The rest of the time was more disciplined, with museums, libraries, theatre. It was August Wilhelm's first contact with the orientalists with whom Friedrich had already been working, Antoine-Léonard de Chézy and Louis-Mathieu Langlès.[197] They also met the Austrian ambassador, Count Metternich, whose name had not yet begun to resonate throughout Europe but who would prove useful towards the end of that same year. August Wilhelm saw the celebrated Mademoiselle Georges in Voltaire's *Tancrède*.[198] His remarks on the Paris theatre were not flattering and can have left his patroness in no doubt

---

192 *Krisenjahre*, I, 374f. Prescriptions in 'Briefe und medizinische Vorschriften von Koreff', *ibid.*, III, 196, 203f. and SLUB Dresden, Mscr. Dresd., App. 2712, B26, 1-19. These may well be placebos for a valetudinarian patient and should not be taken too literally.
193 *Krisenjahre*, I, 345f.
194 Pange, 178f.
195 Jan Urbich,'De profundis. Mme de Staël und Friedrich Schlegel', in: Kaiser/Müller (2008), 163-187, ref. 168f.
196 SLUB Dresden, Mscr. Dresd. App. 2712, B29, 1, 2. One is addressed to the 'hôtel de Suède' where they stayed (Pange, 179), the other is from the 'rue de la Loi', which changed its name back to rue de Richelieu in 1806. Part of a packet of 'Lettres et billets de Mad. R.'
197 Pange, 181.
198 *Ibid.*, 187.

about his views. He would have finished the piece on Madame de Staël's performances by then and was most likely already working on the more extensive *Comparaison*. She in her turn was taking Schlegel more and more into her confidence, using him as a signatory on documents for loans with an eye to purchasing property in France (Acosta was one possibility). Her main occupation in Acosta was finishing *Corinne ou l'Italie*, the novel that she had been planning since the Italian journey. She signed a contract with the publisher Nicolle, and arranged with Cotta for the German translation to be done by Friedrich Schlegel (in fact, by Dorothea).[199]

Personal and public matters intertwined. She was sending Auguste back to Geneva to prepare him for his confirmation, the religious education of her children being something that she took very seriously. Having had his entry to the École polytechnique blocked from on high, there was the question of Auguste's further education. Should it be in Germany (Friedrich Schlegel's suggestion), or America, or Edinburgh? His mother meanwhile was not making it easy for those around her. She was putting out feelers to Metternich (if only by sending him a copy of *Corinne*) and other Austrian grandees.[200] Time was up for her sojourn in Acosta, and officialdom was exerting pressure. In April, 1807 she made two clandestine forays into Paris, to meet up with Madame Récamier and Constant. They did not remain secret from Napoleon's spy network, and the Emperor, pausing between the battles of Eylau and Friedland, was displeased.

He had not enjoyed reading *Corinne*, either, a copy of which was sent to him on the Prussian-Russian front.[201] It had no flattering preface, which might have been enough to mitigate his displeasure and gain her return to Paris or its environs. It was a novel about Italy, and essentially about two English characters in Italy, not French, and the main French character was largely unflattering. The Italy of its sub-title was ante-bellum, an aristocratic capsule, not the kingdom of Napoleon's creation; it lamented the lost greatness of Italy, Dante's, but also Alfieri's (and Monti's). Its Anglophile sentiments, which admittedly did not extend to all the characters or all the moral situations, were another source of irritation. She would not back down, and the price was further exile. The extended family made its way back to Coppet in May-June, 1807.

---

199 *Correspondance générale*, VI, 200.
200 *Ibid*., VI, 212.
201 *Ibid*., 220. Simone Balayé, 'Corinne. Histoire du roman', in: SB (ed.), *L'Éclat et le silence. 'Corinne ou l'Italie' de Madame de Staël* (Paris: Champion, 1999), 7-38, ref. 28-31.

3. The Years with Madame de Staël (1804-1817)

Already as they were moving back into exile, Schlegel inserted a short notice on *Corinne* into Cotta's *Morgenblatt* on 26 May, 1807. He would follow it up with the longer and more sustained review of the novel which appeared later in the year in the Jena *Allgemeine Literatur-Zeitung*.[202] It was evident that he wished to do two things: to show up the obtuseness of the French critics whose voices were already being heard; and more importantly, to prepare the ground for a favourable reception in the German-speaking lands. The first point could be dealt with in a few masterful and disdainful sentences; the second would require more circumspection. For this was the fulfilment of her months in Italy and of her love declaration, already expressed in *De la littérature*, for all things Italian, the novel of which Monti, Humboldt, Chateaubriand, La Fayette, Jefferson, various German sovereigns, and Goethe had received a copy.[203] Schlegel also knew much about the real circumstances, political and emotional, the real *affaires du coeur* (the real 'courses') that had found their way into its texture, and the real travail that had accompanied its various drafts. While not being exactly the Oswald to her Corinne—far from it—he had been her companion through much that was here translated into fiction, and he had helped to ease the pangs of its creation.

Thus the important thing for Schlegel was to make this cosmopolitan novel, one with European dimensions, appeal to German taste and sensitivities. The Germans, who like no other literary nation had placed artists in the centre of their drama and fiction, might be expected to be sympathetic to a novel about an artist, Corinne the chosen vessel of providence. They could take in their stride a many-stranded text that took a love story, a travelogue, and long passages of art criticism, and interlaced them into a successful whole, a balanced ensemble (aspects that even well-intentioned readers today do not find easy to reconcile). As for those 'courses', the Germans, from Winckelmann to Goethe, had a special affinity with Italy and its culture and would bring a sympathy to bear that would make its past and present alive. Schlegel devoted sections to Corinne's improvisations, to the 'träumerische Lust', the dream-like desire, engendered by the southern landscape, the works of art that Corinne and Oswald behold and which the party with Madame de Staël had similarly

---

202 Briefe, II, 84, 91. Jan Röhnert, 'Weibliches Genie und männlicher Blick. Paradigmen und Paradoxien in der frühen deutschen *Corinne*-Rezeption', in: Kaiser/Müller (2008), 189-210, esp. 198-201.
203 Balayé (1999), 27.

seen. He was perhaps on less secure ground with the emotional content of the novel, but he made his position on Oswald clear (immature and unsteady), and hoped that his female readers would agree.

Of course he could not resist the opportunity of inferring some German input into the novel. The mention of the performance in Italian of *Romeo and Juliet*, that in many ways sums up Oswald's and Corinne's tragic love, gave Schlegel an opportunity to disprase Italian (and French) neo-classicism and to promote Shakespeare and Calderón (and perhaps by extension himself). The definition of a novel that he offered has little to do with *Corinne* but much more with his brother Friedrich's assertion in *Europa* that legend or the romance of chivalry should be the stuff of modern fiction, indeed one might also read into it the Romantic predilection for *Don Quixote*. The envoi of the review was puzzling. Was he piqued that, say, Monti was directly quoted in the text, while he and his brother Friedrich, whose Romantic art appreciation from *Europa* certainly informed passage after passage of the novel, were sidelined in a note each? It seemed that he was. The real Corinne would have forgiven him this little touch of personal vanity.

His was a positive voice nevertheless. Others would soon approach the novel with a definite parti pris.[204] Adam Müller, once a member of Schlegel's Berlin audience, but now delivering his own lectures in Dresden and promoting in them forces for the moral and political renewal of a Germany humiliated by the French, read the novel in terms of French 'frivolity' and German 'depth'. Jean Paul, a fellow-novelist, and, let it be said, one better than Madame de Staël ever was, had no reason to be favourable to a product of the extended Schlegel circle. He had been relegated by Jena's cultivation of Goethe and by its own self-promotion. Moreover, in his huge novel *Titan* of 1801-03 he relied on travel accounts by others to summon up a fabled Italy, where there were large passions, high politics—and fewer 'courses'. While admiring the character of Corinne herself, as is only right and proper, he was unrelentingly hard on Oswald, on the novel's indulgence of longing, suffering and pain, and its alleged unwillingness to seek or find fulfilment. Jean Paul's review is all the more telling in that its acerbity, its dismissal of the wimpish Oswald, is couched in feline irony.

---

204 Röhnert, 201-210.

Swiss Journeyings with Albert de Staël

In June 1807, Madame de Staël could write of being installed in 'the majestic solitude of Coppet'.[205] She had returned with her retinue, first of all via Lyon. They paused here long enough for Schlegel to meet the librarian and to be shown two Roman mosaics in the city. It gave him the opportunity for his first piece of sustained archaeological description:[206] a longer account of the scene of a chariot race on the one surface, and a shorter section on an allegorical scene of sensual and spiritual love. Schlegel shows here that he can be technical and learned, while also giving a spirited portrayal of the scenes depicted. It was to be his last contribution to the *Allgemeine Literatur-Zeitung* before his attentions were dispersed and he finally settled on the *Heidelberger Jahrbücher* for his reviewing needs.

Once at Coppet however there were love scenes of a different kind: Madame de Staël's show-down with Benjamin Constant, tempestuous and theatrical protestations, threats of suicide, of which Schlegel was a witness.[207] Madame Récamier and Elzéar de Sabran also arrived. The two ladies made an excursion to the glaciers at Chamonix: the reflected sunlight threatened to ruin their complexions. Schlegel and especially Albert de Staël did not have that problem. To use up the boy's surplus energy and to instruct him in 'the map of natural knowledge', the two were sent on a walking holiday through German-speaking Switzerland.[208]

It was indeed mostly on foot, as the conditions of those days demanded, at least from Berne, where the serious walking began. We have his account in letters to Albert's mother. There is something both amusing and touching in the spectacle of these two travellers, so different in temperament yet somehow making good companions; the one a chatterbox, the other studious, looking for 'beauty, horror and immensity' (and also the 'silence and solitude' that sublime nature afforded) yet being distracted from these by Albert's prattle. The savant-traveller was also—how could it be otherwise?—planning 'un petit livre' on their journey, rhapsodic reflections, descriptions of nature and of customs. He kept his ears open for gradations in dialect: knowing Middle High German, he would spot

---

205 *Correspondance générale*, VI, 262.
206 *Krisenjahre*, III, 81-86, not in SW. *Allgemeine Literatur-Zeitung*, Intelligenzblatt 50, 28 June, 1807, col. 433-437, 'Brief eines Reisenden aus Lyon. Im May 1807'.
207 Kohler, *Madame de Staël et la Suisse*, 337f.
208 The letters which trace this tour in Pange, 198-207.

the affinities of Swiss German and this older form. And so the two walked — Thun, Unterseen, Lauterbrunn, the Staubbach Fall ('in all its beauty'), to the 'icy and solitary horrors' of the Grimsel, into the valley of the Ticino ('romantic') (he was tempted to proceed to Lago Maggiore), on horseback over the St Gothard to Uri and Lucerne (the Rigi was overcast and invisible), Berne, Fribourg and Vevey.

It showed Schlegel, otherwise presented as bookish and retiring, to be the most physically fit of his Romantic generation; of those once outdoor-going friends, Wackenroder was prematurely dead, and Tieck was crippled; Novalis had died of consumption; Friedrich Schlegel was grossly corpulent; Fichte was to die after imprudently joining the militia in 1813. Schlegel did not have the poetic talent of his friend Tieck, who profited from his (vehicular) journey to Italy to produce his *Reisegedichte eines Kranken* [Travel Poems of an Invalid], but it seems that he did really plan a 'book in its own right'.[209] Those were the words that he used when writing in 1812 to Johann Rudolf Wyss, the editor of the important Swiss periodical *Alpenrosen* (and of his father's *Swiss Family Robinson*).

Schlegel entrusted a much shorter and far less comprehensive account of Switzerland to Wyss, having already published parts in Seckendorf's *Prometheus*, his major outlet for the year 1808. These *Umriße, entworfen auf einer Reise durch die Schweiz* [Outlines Sketched During a Journey Through Switzerland], lacking the spontaneity of his letters to Madame de Staël, had now become an ideologically slanted account of a land exhibiting qualities and virtues that Germany no longer possessed. The journey on foot was also a progression through pristine nature and uncorrupted morals. True, there were three set-piece descriptions that showed an eye for both nature and human customs; and there was disapproval of the tourism that had already sprung up. The dates of publication, 1812-13, brought with them reminders that this was the land of ancient freedom: it had once thrown off the oppressors' yoke, and still spoke a language that was not a mere regional dialect but a survival of Minnesang.

Albert and Schlegel returned first to Lausanne, then to Ouchy, the nearby port where Madame de Staël had rented a house for the summer, Molin de Montagny. Not only was there emotional turbulence between her and Constant, who was secretly finding comfort elsewhere, but Madame Récamier found herself the object of attention. Prince August of Prussia,

---

209 *SW*, XIII, 154.

who was forced to spend six weeks in Coppet while waiting for passports for himself and Clausewitz, fell passionately in love with her during the time he spent at Coppet (they later vowed eternal love, without marriage). Ouchy-Coppet proved itself to be a 'château dramatique'[210] in more ways than one, for a performance of Racine's *Andromaque* at Ouchy, put on as a distraction from fraying emotions, led to Staël (as Hermione) and Constant (as Pyrrhus) slanging each other in alexandrines. Before the year was out they would be performing Voltaire's *Sémiramis*, above all *Phèdre*, with Staël and Récamier, the second performance almost as the Staël ménage started on its next journey, to Vienna. There were also readings of Constant's new play, *Wallstein*.

Comparaison entre la Phèdre de Racine et celle d'Euripide (1807)

Schlegel wrote on both *Wallstein* and *Phèdre*, but it was Racine's play that had occupied him since earlier that year. During the spring of 1807, while Madame de Staël herself was barred from the capital or only clandestinely and furtively a visitor, Schlegel had used his weeks in Paris to negotiate publication of his famous—infamous—*Comparaison entre la Phèdre de Racine et celle d'Euripide*,[211] the 108-page brochure that came out later in 1807 with Turneisen (Tourneisen to his French readers).[212] Later (1842) he would claim that it was merely something 'that I found amusing to do on literary opinion',[213] and in the same context he saw it as a product of a time of social distractions and voyagings that allowed him little time for sustained work.[214] It is true that it does draw largely on existing insights and indeed is not free of signs of haste. Closer in time, he would state to his sister-in-law Dorothea Schlegel that he merely wanted to stir things up, get people annoyed,[215] and to Goethe he used a similar tone.[216] Except that when writing to Goethe, on 31 January 1808, he was already in Vienna,

---

210 *Correspondance générale*, VI, 315; Rougemont, 'Pour un répertoire', 86f.
211 *Comparaison entre la Phèdre de Racine et celle d'Euripide, par A. W. Schlegel* (Paris: Tourneisen fils, 1807). *Oeuvres*, II, 333-405.
212 He refers to the proofs in a letter of 10 August to Madame de Staël. Pange, 204.
213 A. W. de Schlegel, *Essais littéraires et historiques* (Bonn: Weber, 1842), Avant-propos, xiv; *Oeuvres*, I, 3.
214 *Ibid.*, 2.
215 *Dorothea von Schlegel geb. Mendelssohn und deren Söhne Johannes und Philipp Veit. Briefwechsel im Auftrag der Familie Veit*, hg. v. J. M. Raich, 2 vols (Mainz: Kirchheim, 1881), I, 211.
216 Wieneke, 157.

playing down French reactions to the work as mere 'spasms' and hoping for a more considered and balanced judgment from the Germans. That in its turn was somewhat disingenuous: Schlegel was at that moment waiting for the Austrian emperor to issue the *fiat* enabling him to deliver the course of lectures that would set out more comprehensively and systematically what the *Comparaison* was stating in less ordered aperçus. When these lectures were available, first in German, then in French, the full extent of his thinking on the notion of the classic, on classicism, on neo-classicism, would be shown in its widest context.

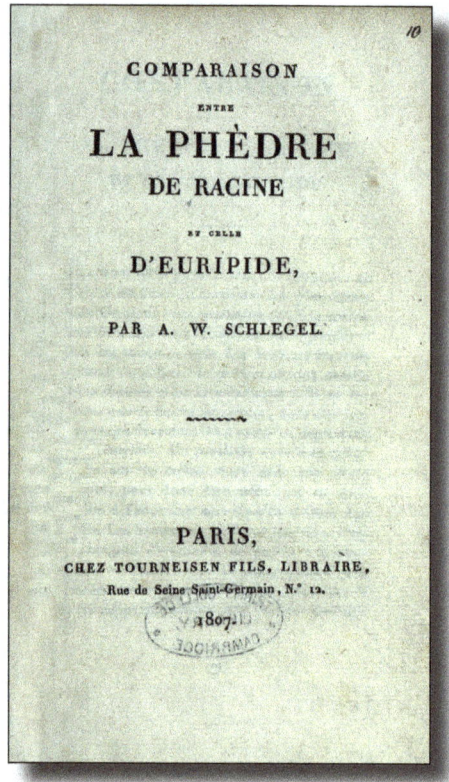

Fig. 14 August Wilhelm Schlegel, *Comparaison entre la Phèdre de Racine et celle d'Euripide* (Paris, 1807). Title page. © and by kind permission of the Master and Fellows of Trinity College, Cambridge, CC BY-NC 4.0.

In the same letter Schlegel mentioned in one breath his epistle to Goethe from Rome, the elegy *Rom*, and the *Comparaison*, which suggested that he saw some kind of inner link between these three products of his first years with Madame de Staël. They are all in their way an unrepentant affirmation of neo-classicism, either in style (the artists in Rome), in verse recreation (*Rom*) or in adaptation (the Euripidean-style *Ion*). It was a question of how one approached revival or recrudescence, not the principle itself. How else could one explain Schlegel's continuing admiration for Friedrich Tieck and his concern for his wellbeing, an artist who combined Greek strictness of form with modern elegance and subtlety? Goethe, predictably, did not care for Schlegel's kind of neo-classicism, and Schlegel in his turn was dismayed to find himself in 1808 sharing Seckendorf's periodical *Prometheus* with Goethe's most radical classicizing experiment, the dramatic fragment *Pandora*.

But Goethe would certainly have recognized, in the middle of the *Comparaison*, this reference: 'energetic souls, a great connoisseur of the classics has said, are like the sea, always calm at the bottom, though the surface be troubled by storms'.[217] It is the most famous passage from Winckelmann's *On the Imitation of the Greek Works*, long since available in French and Italian and thus quoted here without acknowledgement. If Goethe idolized Winckelmann, Schlegel certainly deeply respected him, and they differed only over the extent of Winckelmann's antiquarian knowledge. By placing this passage in the centre of his treatise, Schlegel was aligning himself with someone who had entered the Greek world with heart and mind and soul and spirit. He differed too in degree from those French abbés, Pierre Brumoy and Charles Batteux, whom Schlegel mentions at the opening of the *Comparaison*, for whom the world of the Greeks was not our world or our manners, its mythology too bizarre, its barbarities too patent; we must instead elevate its beauties, recreate its harmonies. Thus Schlegel was echoing debates that had coursed through the eighteenth century, on how to reconcile Greek harmony and repose with its concomitant pain and suffering and their expression, the question that had informed Lessing's *Laokoon* in 1766 and that was still not resolved in 1807.

For the moment it was a question of reasoned debate, but also of polemic. For it was no coincidence that Schlegel in 1842 invoked—by association, of course—the example of Lessing's *Hamburgische Dramaturgie* of 1767-69, where Voltaire's neo-classical efforts had been 'cudgelled' (Schlegel's word).[218] Naturally Schlegel would not have recourse to such tactics, but a combative edge would not be missing either: Schlegel, like Lessing, cut

---

217   *Oeuvres*, II, 366.
218   Avant-propos, xvi; *Oeuvres*, I, 4.

corners in argument, overlooked inconsistencies that did not suit him, and was often plainly unfair once he had his teeth in an opponent.

The choice of his comparison of Euripides and Racine made perfect sense to readers of his account of Madame de Staël's acting roles, where *Phèdre* was in pride of place. Some German readers would have been aware that Schiller had translated Racine's play for the Weimar stage, first performed in 1805, the year of his death. There had been disrespectful (but private) verses in 1799—that Schlegel was to publish in 1832[219]—relating to Schiller's translation of Euripides' *Iphigenia in Aulis*, for which he had relied largely on French sources. Schlegel, as was his policy, never mentioned Schiller in this connection, but readers of *Europa*, that recent work from the Schlegel circle, would be left in no doubt as to its position: the first number (1803) stated that the Paris theatre was performing—declaiming— an 'imperfect and debased' version of the *Iphigenia*, and in 1805 Achim von Arnim's article *Erzählungen von Schauspielen* [Conversations about Plays] stated that *Phèdre* was a 'mutilated' version of Euripides' *Hippolytus*.[220] Above all there had been Friedrich's translation of an extract from Racine's *Bajazet* in which both author and play were damned with faint praise.[221] (He may not have known that his uncle Johann Elias had also translated a fragment of *Bajazet* in 1749 and had found it rather better.)[222]

It has been argued that there were French voices during the eighteenth century, authorities like Fénelon or Marmontel, who had been critical of aspects of *Phèdre*'s characterization. Madame de Staël for her part postulated in *De la littérature* the general principle of 'progress' for all national literatures, which applied even to something as sacrosanct as the *drame classique*. She did not place Racine on a pinnacle for all time, as Voltaire had done. All the same, when directing the same notion of progress towards Greek drama, she placed the trio Aeschylus, Sophocles and Euripides in descending order of merit. There were further contradictions. While correctly seeing that Euripides and Racine are basically different, she was unable to suppress the insight that only a Frenchman, not a Greek, could have written

---

219 'Ohn' alles Griechisch hab ich ja/Verdeutscht die Iphigenia', *SW*, II, 212.
220 *Europa*, II, i, 155f.
221 Ibid., 117-139.
222 AWS's list of all plays written or translated by Schlegels (undated). SLUB Dresden, Mscr. Dresd., e. 90, II (VIa). Alexander Nebrig, *Rhetorizität des hohen Stils. Der deutsche Racine in französischer Tradition und romantischer Modernisierung*, Münchener Komparatistische Studien, 10 (Göttingen: Wallstein, 2007), 344.

>   'Ils ne se verront plus:—
>   Ils s'aimeront toujours!'[223]
>
> ['They will see each other no more/
> They will love each other forever] from Act IV of *Phèdre*.

It may not be fair to adduce *De la littérature* of 1800, knowing Madame de Staël's extensive and omnivorous programme of reading since then and the stimuli of Coppet, Weimar and Italy. Still, in keeping with the insights of that work, Staël felt herself in sympathy with the eighteenth century, the *siècle des lumières*, and felt strongly its progressive belief in humanity, the freedom and independence of the writer, the distinction made in the *Encyclopédie* between 'nation' and 'state', the one an entity with history, culture, memory and myth, the other a political construct. Thus Louis XIV's neo-classicism had also been an expression of political hegemony. Napoleon was now doing the same, reviving literary rules that were sterile for the modern writer,[224] producing the 'immobility' of which Benjamin Constant complained.[225] This placed her in opposition to Napoleon, and Schlegel remarked retrospectively in 1842 that 'Bonaparte [...] issued orders for us to admire again the century of Louis XIV, and the public, having obeyed in matters of quite different importance, was obsequious in its admiration'.[226]

And so if the *Comparaison* is an 'insubordination' in that it attacks cherished notions of seventeenth-century tragedy, it is also an act of solidarity with Schlegel's patroness. Hence it is written in French, primarily for French readers, while developing insights from his German-language writings, the reviews from the 1790s, recast in Jena and Berlin and taken up by Friedrich's *Europa*. Napoleon's hegemony was not just cultural but political, and it now extended to the German-speaking lands and the *pax romana* imposed on his terms. Yet the political message of the *Comparaison* was not overt, for everyone knew without being told that Schlegel was the companion of the proscribed Madame de Staël. He could be more outspoken before the audience of his Vienna Lectures a year later.

---

223 *Considérations*, 68.
224 See the important article by Simone Balayé, 'Les rapports de l'écrivain et du pouvoir: Madame de Staël et Napoléon', in: Balayé (1994), 137-154.
225 Benjamin Constant, *Mélanges de Littérature et de politique* (Paris: Pichon et Didier, 1829), 293.
226 Avant-propos, xivf.; *Oeuvres*, I, 3.

The *Comparaison* may also be seen as a much expanded version of his review for the *Damen-Kalender* on Madame de Staël's acting in *Phèdre*, but with the heat very much turned up. As said, it stands essentially between the Berlin Lectures and those in Vienna, rehearsing some insights of the one and anticipating views expressed later. The Berlin Lectures had established a hierarchy of Greek tragedians, the robust Aeschylus, the harmonious Sophocles, the ornate and over-sophisticated Euripides, the 'chattering rhetorician' of his epigram. Schlegel's recasting of the Euripidean *Ion* also belonged to this complex. In the *Comparaison* we have the same gradation of esteem but also for the sake of his argument an implicit equality. Inconsistencies creep in. On the one hand he calls Euripides a 'sophist' and enunciates a theory of decline.[227] But on the other Schlegel also needs to pit the Greeks against modern dramatic realisations based on ancient mythology. And so Euripides becomes 'THE Greek' against whom he measures Racine. He does not bring out essential but equally valid differences, as Herder had done forty years earlier when comparing Sophocles with Shakespeare. He is always at pains to show how Racine, in recasting Euripides' *Hippolytus* as *Phèdre*, is inferior not only to his specific Greek source but to 'the Greeks' themselves. Whereas Euripides in the Berlin Lectures stood for 'üppige Weichlichkeit' [decadent sensuality],[228] with the *Bacchae* as chief witness, now in Paris his *Hippolytus* is accorded the lineaments of a 'model' Greek tragedy, indeed Schlegel states that it is legitimate to compare the 'favourite' tragedian of the Greeks with the one most esteemed by the French.[229]

Clearly some legerdemain was required to achieve this—and some unfairness. Nowhere does Schlegel acknowledge why it was that Racine wanted to write a *Phèdre*, not an *Hippolyte*; or why he wished to shift the emphasis away from the vows tragically sworn to Greek divinities (Euripides) to an intense tragedy of passion, where Venus clutches her prey ('Vénus toute entière à sa proie attachée'). He notes rather how much Racine has borrowed from his Greek source and how much he has changed, not why a seventeenth-century dramatist would find many motifs from Greek tragedy unsuitable or why he would read them differently from antiquity (or from the early nineteenth century), bound as he was by the conventions of his own theatre that called for a love intrigue quite impossible in Athens but permissible in Paris. Of course it is legitimate to question whether a

---

227 *Oeuvres*, II, 338f.
228 *KAV*, I, 748.
229 *Oeuvres*, II, 336f.

modern adaptation of the Hippolytus-Phaedra-Theseus triangle actually works, whether or not it produces inconsistencies or moral velleities (such as those arising from Racine's characters Oenone and Aricie), as indeed one might still today ask whether Goethe's *Iphigenie auf Tauris* owes more to Christian sentiment than to the inexorabilities of its original Greek source.

Schlegel cannot deny that the play has great beauty of verse and diction,[230] but that is about all he is prepared to concede. Hippolyte is 'polite, well brought-up' but 'unnatural',[231] Thésée an amorous 'vagabond',[232] while Phèdre herself is seductive, ruled by 'a purely sensual passion'; the play's moral message is 'dubious', it 'glosses over vice'. Why this is so, he never discusses; there is no mention of the Jansenist doctrines of Port-Royal or of exemplary states of grace. He never concedes that sexual passion may burst forth inside the very bonds and formal limitations imposed by convention, even where Greek heroes are 'civilised' by speaking in French alexandrines. There is another factor as well: Schlegel's dislike of extreme tragedy. As we have seen, he preferred *Oedipus in Colonos* to *Oedipus Rex, Paradiso* to *Inferno, Romeo and Juliet* to *Lear* or *Macbeth*; he abhorred the orgiastic *Bacchae*, and thus he disliked Racine's heroine, caught as she is at the mercy of deep urges that she can no longer withstand.

With the Greeks, says Schlegel, there can be no love, only 'the dignity of human nature'.[233] The purpose of tragedy is for them not the 'effeminate emotion'[234] of European neo-classicism (including Staël's favourite Alfieri), not even the spectacle of suffering, but the 'awareness of human worth' when faced with the 'order of things supernatural' in divine ordinance. It is not 'accidental' but based on destiny, fatality, forcing the characters back on to their own human and moral resources. It is not Christian: a closest approximation would be the idea of a providence and the sublimities and inscrutablities it invokes (as in Calderón). The modern dramatist (Shakespeare) touches on issues that address the very aim of existence, human despair, 'fate' (Shakespeare's *Hamlet, Lear* and *Macbeth*—not, we note, the once so favoured 'love tragedy' *Romeo and Juliet*). Here Schlegel is rehearsing arguments that inform the second cycle of his Vienna Lectures.

To 'prove' all these points, Schlegel cites in French translation the whole final scene from Euripides between Hippolytus and the goddess Diana, its

---

230 *Ibid.*, 370.
231 *Ibid.*, 359.
232 *Ibid.*, 374.
233 *Ibid.*, 339.
234 *Ibid.*, 392.

'divine serenity'.[235] He compares and contrasts with *Phèdre*, where Hippolyte must die without his innocence being acknowledged. Where Euripides brings about a catastrophe wrought by divine agency, uninvolved with human passions, Racine is forced to reposition his material and make Phèdre's guilt and death the real tragic outcome.

Schlegel liked to think that he had stirred up a hornets' nest with this seeming attack on a hallowed institution,[236] the preface to his *Essais littéraires et historiques* of 1842 quoting the French critic Jean-Joseph-François Dussault in the official *Journal de l'Empire* ('M. Schlegel gives the impression of only having designs on Racine, but basically he is out to devalue all of French literature').[237] Indeed it was Dussault who ratcheted up the rhetoric by noting Schlegel's association with the dissident Madame de Staël.[238] It is also true that the *Comparaison* was adduced in 1812 as a reason for requiring Schlegel to leave French soil, and very much later he would attribute his blackballing by the Institut to the rancour engendered by the long memories of certain French colleagues. But by that time Stendhal's *Racine et Shakespeare* and the Schlegel reception of the young French Romantics made that argument hardly plausible, even Constant's more cautious *Wallstein*. The fact was that the French critics of the years 1807-08, while expressing indignation, as they must, were also prepared to acknowledge Schlegel's classical scholarship, and even the rightness of some of his arguments.[239]

The important thing was that Madame de Staël herself was not affronted. She in her turn was immersed in the task of writing *De l'Allemagne*, with all the reconsideration of existing positions that that involved. For Schlegel had not questioned the legitimacy of performing *Phèdre*, to which audiences from Vienna to Stockholm would later be treated. While placing Schlegel's Vienna Lectures in the forefront of *De l'Allemagne*, she did also devote a footnote to the *Comparaison*: 'it caused a great stir in Parisian literary circles, but nobody could deny that W. Schlegel, although a German, wrote

---

235 *Ibid.*, 402.
236 The reactions discussed in full by Chetana Nagavajara, *August Wilhelm Schlegel in Frankreich. Sein Anteil an der französischen Literaturkritik 1807-1835*, intr. Kurt Wais, Forschungsprobleme der vergleichenden Literaturgeschichte, 3 (Tübingen: Niemeyer, 1966), 21-44. See also Martine de Rougemont, 'Schlegel ou la provocation: une expérience sur l'opinion littéraire', *Romantisme* 51 (1986), 49-61.
237 Avant-propos, xv; *Oeuvres*, I, 4.
238 Navagajara, 28.
239 *Ibid.*, 36-43.

French sufficiently well for him to be permitted to speak of Racine'.[240] The context makes it clear that this was not intended as faint praise. It would be Schlegel's German detractors, such as Rahel Levin and her friend and later husband Karl August Varnhagen von Ense, who would try to disparage him by counting the alleged 'Solözismen' in his French.[241]

Not surprisingly, the 'groupe de Coppet' tried very hard not to be impressed. Constant noted nothing in his journal. Barante was displeased.[242] Sismondi, writing to the Countess of Albany, acknowledged its verve, but saw it essentially as an attack on 'what the nation regards as the glory of its literature',[243] to which he appended the unexceptionable remark that each nation must define its own theatrical taste. Schlegel had of course never alluded to 'nation' and certainly not to 'glory': Sismondi's use of these words merely shows that Schlegel had succeeded in ruffling sensitivities.

There was no mention in the *Comparaison* that translations from the French, not just from Racine, had been a staple of the German theatre, the 'national theatre', as it liked to call itself. Performances of French tragedies, such as Lessing had objected to in Hamburg forty years earlier, were still by no means uncommon in 1807:[244] there were seven Racine translations into German between 1800 and 1812 alone, including Schiller's *Phädra*[245] and two with Austrian and Russian impresses, from lands that Schlegel would be visiting with Madame de Staël in the not too distant future.[246] The Viennese dramatist Heinrich Joseph von Collin—best known today for the *Coriolan* for which Beethoven furnished the overture—in fact illustrated this nicely. He had once started and then abandoned a translation of *Phèdre* for the stage in Vienna. He then became first the reviewer and then the translator into German of Schlegel's *Comparaison*[247] and an enthusiastic follower of

---

240 Madame de Staël, *De l'Allemagne*, ed. Comtesse Jean de Pange and Simone Balayé, 5 vols (Paris: Hachette, 1958-60), III, 340.

241 Josef Körner, *Die Botschaft der deutschen Romantik an Europa*, Schriften zur deutschen Literatur für die Görresgesellschaft, 9 (Augsburg: Filser, 1929), 11. *Rahel-Bibliothek. Rahel Varnhagen. Gesammelte Werke*, ed. Konrad Feilchenfeldt, Uwe Schweikert and Rahel E. Steiner, 10 vols (Munich: Matthes & Seitz, 1983), I, 398.

242 Pange, 193f.

243 Sismondi, *Epistolario*, I, 235.

244 Nebrig, *Rhetorizität*, 368-371 lists them.

245 *Ibid.*, 394-399.

246 One by Ayrenhoff (Pressburg, 1804) and one by Nicolay (St Petersburg, 1812). *Ibid.*, 395, 397f.

247 *Ibid.*, 412. *Vergleichung der Phädra des Racine mit der des Euripides von A. W. Schlegel. Uebersetzt, und mit Anmerkungen und einem Anhange begleitet von H. J. v. Collin* (Vienna: Pichler, 1808). *Briefe*, II, 115; *Krisenjahre*, I, 535f., 543-545: Körner, *Botschaft*, 84.

the Vienna Lectures. Once Schlegel found himself in the imperial capital, these two enterprises became joined in one effort.

3.2 Vienna

If ever there was a time for Schlegel to break his connection with Madame de Staël, it was in these years that produced the two works on which their fame, his and hers, were to be based: his Vienna Lectures and her *De l'Allemagne*. The choice was put to him by his ever-wise sister, Charlotte Ernst in Dresden, as she heard of his impending departure for America with the Staël ménage. Either he must adopt the lifestyle of an abstracted scholar, with his personal and domestic needs attended to (she had no illusions about her brothers' marriages), or he must continue to live in the refined circles of 'this most interesting person'. She continues, knowing his response in advance: if his choice does fall on Staël, then he must give up all hopes of reciprocity and must live in devotion, drawing inner rewards and satisfaction from it.[248] There was no middle path. This he already knew, and in a sense the rumour—for it was no more than that—of his sailing to America provided the answer. He was willing to cross oceans in the service of this mercurial and hyperactive woman, in whose heart he could never claim pride of place (that was still reserved for Benjamin Constant)[249] but in whose mind Schlegel was 'a noble creature'[250] for whom she had 'a fraternal affection'; she could never imagine willingly separating from him; they would live and die together.[251] Yet the thought of America did for a brief moment awaken Humboldtian vistas in Schlegel, of Mexico, Brazil or even the Ganges.[252] The reality was to be different, and it would be European: Switzerland, occasionally France, Austria and Germany, before the great flight to Russia and Sweden in 1812.

True, there would be brief moments of disloyalty, the quarrels and sulks of which their relationship was never free, or amours, if they are worthy of such a description: the billets doux exchanged with the adventuress Minna van Nuys[253] in Vienna, his admiration (nothing more)

---

248 *Krisenjahre*, II, 97f.
249 'l'être le plus cher pour moi', *Correspondance générale*, VI, 386.
250 *Ibid.*, 496.
251 *Ibid.*, 367.
252 *Briefe*, I, 249.
253 On her cf. Josef Körner, 'Carolinens Rivalin', *Preußische Jahrbücher*, 198 (Oct.-Dec., 1924), 27-52.

for the irresistible Madame Récamier, the importunings and promptings of Sophie Tieck-Bernhardi, the exchange of letters (now lost) with Marianne Haller in Berne in 1811-12, a married woman and essentially beyond his reach. Sophie of course wanted money: divorce was an expensive business, especially a messy one involving custody of children.

His own brother Friedrich Schlegel had cause to be alarmed at the prospect of August Wilhelm leaving Europe: 'we need you everywhere'[254] is but one plea among many for financial and professional succour amid the tribulations that were to befall him and Dorothea in these years. On the one hand, it was his wonted dependence on a more reliable and more stable older sibling; yet there was also just a hint of the desire to prise August Wilhelm away from Madame de Staël and set up again those 'Schlegel Brothers' who had once astounded the world with their meteoric *Athenaeum* and their rather less siderial *Europa*. August Wilhelm had to hear promptings from his brother about his talent as a dramatist, about careers in new universities like Berlin, just being founded. Dorothea, extending her rapt admiration for Friedrich to her brother-in-law, averred that the two would be the pyramids that would outlast everything of their age.[255] Staying in the sphere of grandiose images, Friedrich claimed to Madame de Staël that he and his brother were 'one and indivisible'.[256]

And yet it is fair to say that Schlegel was in these years closer to his brother Friedrich than ever again. We cannot of course overlook the litany of querulous and self-pitying communications from Friedrich, but two symbolic confraternal gestures do stand out: they featured together in the Viennese periodical *Prometheus* in 1808, and the two poems that they had once addressed to each other, 'An Friedrich Schlegel' and 'An A.W. Schlegel' now stood conjoined in the first number.[257] It was as August Wilhelm was about to make Vienna the base for those Lectures that were to echo round the cultivated world as far as it extended; while Friedrich was stating that the visible institutions of culture, language, religion, mythology, law and literature were but earthly manifestations of the divine and invisible. August Wilhelm was to give his poem a prominent position in the reissue of his poetic works that he oversaw in 1811.[258] And when Friedrich's

---

254 *Krisenjahre*, I, 571.
255 *Ibid.*, II, 63.
256 *Ibid.*, I, 491.
257 *Prometheus. Eine Zeitschrift. Herausgegeben von Leo v. Seckendorf und Jos. Lud. Stoll* (Vienna: Geistinger, 1808), I, i, 57-65, 66-69.
258 *Poetische Werke* (Heidelberg: Mohr und Zimmer, 1811), 2 parts, I, 218-226.

Ueber die Sprache und Weisheit der Indier [On the Language and Wisdom of the Indians] came out, also in 1808, the first significant voice in German Sanskrit studies, it received a favourable notice in *Prometheus*. Was August Wilhelm the author?[259] Certainly in private he defended its basic theses.

Schlegel's Vienna Lectures and Madame de Staël's *De l'Allemagne* may stand out as the symbolic pinnacles of achievement of their oddly imbalanced relationship, tilted always towards her necessities and her whims, determined by her movements and—in these years—by the decrees of Napoleon and his willing agents. This is only one side. The record of Schlegel's correspondence in this period gives another account, of frenetic activity in all directions, not just occasioned by his brother or by Sophie Tieck or her brother Friedrich. *Prometheus* competed for his critical energy even as he was writing and delivering his Vienna Lectures; there are as well letters to and from review editors who wanted copy, notably the *Heidelberger Jahrbücher*, founded in 1808 by Johann Georg Zimmer, who was also to publish the Lectures. For this periodical Schlegel produced a corpus of learned reviews that must rank as a scholarly achievement almost commensurate with the more accessible Vienna Lectures. He could not resist a short contribution to Achim von Arnim's mayfly periodical *Zeitung für Einsiedler* [*Journal for Anchorites*] that Zimmer brought out also in 1808, a poem that praised William Tell's defiance of the tyrant (meaning the ultimate Tyrant, Napoleon).[260] There were pressures to complete the Calderón and to finish the Shakespeare. He was in addition collating the manuscripts of the *Nibelungenlied* and preparing a scholarly edition, but his medieval interests also extended to Provençal and the Troubadours. The list does not necessarily end there. It shows, as ever, that Schlegel was not merely a member of the 'Groupe de Coppet', sometimes seemingly no more than an adjunct, but a figure for whom German 'National-Geist'[261] was a paramount concern.

And so there is only a limited sense in bracketing the two famous works, the one by Schlegel, the other by Madame de Staël, as some apotheosis of that 'Groupe de Coppet'. Their renown extended much farther, as Schlegel's own words on the Vienna Lectures later attest, from 'Edinburgh and St

---

259 *Prometheus*, 5.-6. Heft, Anzeiger, 3-9. Attributed by the editor of *KA* to Wilhelm von Schütz. *Kritische Friedrich-Schlegel-Ausgabe*, ed. Ernst Behler et al., 30 vols (Paderborn, Munich, Vienna: Schöningh; Zurich: Thomas, 1958- in progress), VIII, ccxx. AWS cannot be ruled out.

260 'Tells Kapelle, bei Küssnacht', *Zeitung für Einsiedler* (Heidelberg: Mohr und Zimmer, 1808), No. 36, 281. *Poetische Werke*, I, 259-261; *SW*, I, 280f.

261 *Briefe*, I, 214, 269.

Petersburg to Stockholm and Cadiz'.²⁶² Yet it is also true that Schlegel could never have given his lectures without the ministrations of Madame de Staël, nor would the audience to which he delivered them have been such as it was without her contacts in highest Viennese society. By the same token, it is also without doubt that Schlegel certainly gave advice on German literature and thought to his benefactress (which she in fact acknowledged). He was also instrumental in saving a copy of *De l'Allemagne* after the first print-run was banned and destroyed. But each work was nevertheless its author's own and bore its inimitable and indelible stamp.

Travelling to Vienna with Madame de Staël

Far from being the 'Elisium' that his sister Charlotte claimed it would become,²⁶³ Coppet was for Schlegel in these years but one station among many, as Madame de Staël hurried from refuge to refuge or as the buffets of fate administered by Napoleon hastened her to unexpected destinations.

The plan of a comprehensive work on Germany—its people, culture, letters, *moeurs*, in brief whatever the French needed to learn about this fascinating nation in the north that was paradoxically not yet a nation— had never left her. Her journey of 1803-04, so fateful for Schlegel, had essentially been through west and central Germany, Berlin being as far north as she was to get, and the real north she was never to see. Now, there was the south, and there was Austria. While the section in *De l'Allemagne* on the south is effectively co-extensive with that on Jacobi, Vienna forms an important part of the work as completed.

But the south—Munich—was really only a stage towards the real destination of Vienna. For there lived Count Maurice O'Donnell. They had met in Venice in 1805, and she had not forgotten him. The disparity in their ages was no hindrance, as other admirers and lovers knew or were to know. The scion of an old Irish family, 'wild geese' in Austrian service, he was ideally situated, being charming, aristocratic, and extremely well-connected. Her plans for Vienna now had a treble thrust: to experience Austrian society; to place her son Albert in a military school where he might learn German and be less of a harum-scarum; and to enjoy the Count's agreeable society.²⁶⁴ The 'grand Viennese enterprise'²⁶⁵ got under way on 30

---

262 *SW*, VII, 285.
263 *Krisenjahre*, I, 573.
264 *Correspondance générale*, VI, 314.
265 *Ibid.*, 330.

November 1807, with a cavalcade of Madame de Staël, her children Albert and Albertine, her secretary and amanuensis Eugène Uginet, Schlegel, and the usual servants.²⁶⁶ Auguste, as we shall see, stayed behind, as did the most recent addition to her household, Albertine's English governess, Fanny Randall.²⁶⁷ They proceeded from Berne and Zurich to Augsburg, to their first longer staging-post, Munich.

Friedrich Heinrich Jacobi, her old friend, now President of the Bavarian Academy of Sciences, and Schelling, now its Secretary, received them cordially. Schelling and Schlegel were on their best behaviour and discoursed amicably, while agreeing to differ in private. Caroline, now Madame Schelling, had no rancour for Schlegel, if a little for Madame de Staël. It was also to be the last time that he saw her. Staël was feted, received by the wife of the chief minister Montgelas. But Munich also had its drawbacks: the Montgelas administration was pro-French; the Elector Max Joseph of Bavaria was now king by the grace of Napoleon.

It was time to move on to more congenial surroundings. Meanwhile, almost as they arrived in Vienna on 28 December, Auguste de Staël was having the most extraordinary meeting of his life and certainly the most unforgettable. Napoleon was reported to be returning from Italy via Spain; Auguste was to wait in Chambéry in Savoy to obtain an audience. This was granted, and the seventeen-year-old boy made his request: the repayment of the two million francs that his grandfather Jacques Necker had placed at the disposal of the French exchequer, and permission for his mother, Madame de Staël, to reside in France. The Emperor, as so often, was forthright, blunt and rude; he then relented and adopted a more kindly tone. He flatly refused both petitions, adding the much-quoted words, 'as long as I live, she will not return to Paris'.²⁶⁸ The boy had emerged well from his ordeal, steeled perhaps by Neckerian powers of utterance. Might not a little credit accrue to his tutor Schlegel? 'Do not tell people that the Emperor brushed you off; say instead that he received you with kindness', was his mother's advice.²⁶⁹

Vienna, where they arrived on 28 December 1807, received them with open arms: 'I have had a wonderful reception here', she wrote on 14 January 1808,²⁷⁰ not merely by Maurice O'Donnell, but by Count Stadion,

---

266 For the Munich sojourn see Pange, 212-216.
267 Her letters to Schlegel in SLUB Dresden, Mscr. Dresd. e. 90, XIX, 18 (1-8).
268 'Aussi, dites à votre mère que tant que je vivrai, elle ne rentrera pas à Paris'. Henri Welschinger, *La Censure sous le Premier Empire avec documents inédits* (Paris: Charavay, 1882), 173. The Emperor also chivalrously suggested that she take up knitting (175).
269 *Correspondance générale*, VI, 363.
270 Ibid., 359.

the foreign minister, and by her old admirer, the Prince de Ligne, sometime Austrian field marshal and once a favourite at the courts of Versailles, the Hermitage and Sanssouci.[271] Through O'Donnell's good offices, Albert was installed in a school from which he could take the examination for the military academy. Within a week, she had been received by the Emperor Francis and two royal archdukes. Her letters are studded with other grand names—Lobkowitz, Lichtenstein, Lubomirski, Potocki. She in her turn was giving a round of 'thés' and 'dîners'[272] and—it could not be otherwise— dramatic performances: mainly of her own plays[273] (with herself and her children, occasionally even Schlegel) for Countess Zamoiska, for Countess Zinzendorf, for Countess Potocka, at the Palais Lichtenstein, where in a performance of Molière's *Les Femmes savantes* the only roles played by those below the rank of prince or count were by herself and Sismondi. He, at her prompting, had joined them in March:[274] the 'Groupe de Coppet' had the habit of re-forming in foreign parts.

High life—the whole of Europe seemed to be dancing that winter[275]— was only one side. The serious business in Vienna was threefold: first, to complete the work that in a letter to the Prince de Ligne she called 'my testament',[276] *De l'Allemagne*, and this involved acquaintance with both political and literary circles; second, to enable Schlegel to give a series of public lectures, and third, to find some post in the Austrian service for Friedrich Schlegel. It needs to be said that her every step was followed by the assiduous Austrian police,[277] they having taken over from the equally zealous (but more efficient) Napoleonic surveillance system.[278] They probably bribed one of her servants; they certainly knew all about her and O'Donnell or about Schlegel and Minna van Nuys, and later about their dealings with Friedrich Gentz.[279]

---

271 Cf. Maria Ullrichová, *Lettres de Madame de Staël conservées en Bohème* (Prague: Czech Academy of Sciences, 1959), 15-81.
272 *Correspondance générale*, VI, 361.
273 Martine de Rougemont, 'Pour un répertoire des rôles et des représentations de Mme de Staël', 79-92, ref. 87f.
274 Sismondi, *Epistolario*, I, 232.
275 *Correspondance générale*, VI, 393.
276 *Ibid.*, 538-540.
277 Georges Solovieff, 'Madame de Staël et la police autrichienne', *Cahiers staëliens*, 41 (1989-1990), 13-54.
278 Simone Balayé and Norman King *et al.*, 'Madame de Staël et les polices françaises sous la Révolution et l'Empire', *Cahiers staëliens*, 44 (1992-93), 3-153, ref. 96.
279 For the police records relating to their movements between Vienna and Prague, Ullrichová, 106-123.

Friedrich Schlegel: Rome and India

Friedrich Schlegel, as always, provided the most difficult proposition of the three. This was partly his own doing, and partly because, as so often, he was ahead of his times. He and Dorothea were still stuck in Cologne in the French-ruled Rhineland, 'waiting for something to turn up', not living modestly, for that they never could do, encumbered as ever with debts and without any real professional prospects for him. With Madame de Staël in Vienna, who had helped him out of more than one crisis, also his ever-provident brother August Wilhelm, could there be some preferment in the imperial Austrian capital? There were however problems: both he and Dorothea were officially Protestants (she only since 1804); he had the dubious legacy of those 'early writings' that had propounded republicanism and licentiousness.[280] It was important now to show a different countenance. Ever since their removal to Paris and then Cologne, Friedrich had been doing just that. Of his Germanic and patriotic sentiments there could be no doubt; his letters, such as the one that he wrote to his brother in 1806, were beginning to express notions of spiritual authority and order—one church, one constitution, one faith—that suggested the hierarchy of Rome.[281] It was certainly not the same as August Wilhelm's aesthetic Catholicizing. Rediscovering his exiguous dramatic talents, he was drafting a historical play on Charles V. Could he consult the imperial archives in Vienna? August Wilhelm, using all of the Staëlien influence at his disposal and his own authority as a public lecturer, succeeded in gaining an audience with the Emperor on 6 May 1808.[282] From this time on, there is regular mention in their letters of the revival of the Schlegels' noble title, the imperial 'Schlegel von Gottleben' that their grandfather had allowed to lapse.

Friedrich and Dorothea were received into the Roman Catholic church in Cologne on 16 April 1808.[283] Friedrich left it to Dorothea to break the news, fearing it might cause heart-ache to the family. But it was by now fairly conditioned to Friedrich's deviations from the perceived norms of Protestant respectability. As it was, Dorothea's first, Jewish, marriage was declared to be null and void, and a dispensation was required to make the second valid according to canon law. She temporarily lost custody of her

---

280 Cf. *Briefe*, I, 224.
281 *Krisenjahre*, I, 321.
282 Ibid., 541.
283 Ibid., 564.

talented son Philipp Veit, the later Nazarene painter.[284] Friedrich now set out for Vienna, to be followed by Dorothea once he had established himself. The Staël cavalcade had by then moved on, but the brothers did meet briefly in Dresden, where the ever-sensible Charlotte Ernst put Friedrich (and later Dorothea) at their ease in the matter of the family's sensitivities. But for nearly a year Friedrich was dependent on others' hospitality and largesse.

The Charles V drama was never completed. By the time of his arrival in Vienna Friedrich had seen the publication of a work that towered in significance over almost anything that he had produced that decade: *Ueber die Sprache und Weisheit der Indier*.[285] With this work, Friedrich might otherwise have expected a university chair of oriental studies, but the times were not propitious and the Habsburgs were a safer proposition than the Hindus. This study was the product of his years in Paris with Hamilton and Chézy; it was to bring to a German readership ideas that had become current in English and French through Sir William Jones or Jean-Sylvain Bailly. While it did not involve the very first publication in German of a Sanskrit text, it was the first comprehensive survey of comparative mythology, migration theory, and the principles and origins of language, that was also a chrestomathy, a selection of Sanskrit religious and poetic texts in a German translation. August Wilhelm had at this stage not brought together in any kind of systematic statement his disparate ideas on the Indian origins of language and civilization (as formulated in his *Considérations*) or given shape to his interest in etymology, notably Gothic, his awareness of the centrality of historical geography as the key to the study of human beginnings.[286] Above all, he had not acquired a knowledge of Sanskrit. This Friedrich had, during the extraordinary six-month burst of creative energy—and sheer concentration—after their arrival in Paris.

---

284 Who rejoined them in Dresden, was baptized, and continued his art studies. Norbert Suhr, *Philipp Veit (1793-1877). Leben und Werk eines Nazareners. Monographie und Werkverzeichnis* (Weinheim: VCH, Acta humaniora, 1991), 7.

285 Full title: *Ueber die Sprache und Weisheit der Indier. Ein Beitrag zur Begründung der Alterthumskunde* (Heidelberg: Mohr und Zimmer, 1808). Schlegel appends extracts in metrical translation from the *Râmâyana, Manu, Bhagavad-Gîtâ* and *Sakuntalâ*. See KA, VIII, clxxxvii-ccxxx; 105-433; Schlegel's notes in KA, XV, i, 1-82. A full discussion of this work is far beyond the scope of this present study. I refer to Ursula Oppenberg, *Quellenstudien zu Friedrich Schlegels Übersetzungen aus dem Sanskrit*, Marburger Beiträge zur Germanistik, 7 (Marburg: Elwert, 1965); and Chen Tzoref-Ashkenazi, *Der romantische Mythos vom Ursprung der Deutschen. Friedrich Schlegels Suche nach der indogermanischen Verbindung*, Schriftenreihe des Minerva Instituts für deutsche Geschichte der Universität Tel Aviv (Göttingen: Wallstein, 2009).

286 Cf. his letter to Auguste de Staël, *Krisenjahre*, II, 250-252.

While still bringing out *Europa*, Friedrich in effect conceived this work on Indian language and lore. After approaches to Reimer and eventual successful negotiations with Zimmer, it was not to come out until 1808. Friedrich's Sanskrit did have its imperfections and its misapprehensions, and the texts on which he based his selections were not philologically reliable,[287] but at least here were texts in modern translation which were also embedded in an account of their linguistic and religious origins. August Wilhelm, in his later career as a Sanskritist, published full scholarly Sanskrit editions of the very same texts selected by his brother for translation—the *Bhagavad-Gîtâ*, the *Râmâyana*—stepping in as it were where Friedrich, with the enthusiasm of the innovator, had made a first major statement without refining the details and the philological base. Yet in many ways Friedrich had succeeded in bringing together in one volume aspects of India that would occupy August Wilhelm in what was ultimately a never-ending quest.

Friedrich drew the analogy between the rediscovery of Greek and Hebrew in the Renaissance and the emergence of Sanskrit studies in his own century.[288] This analogy went in reality even deeper, and its scope was wider. The work had two major thrusts. It was a study in comparative grammar, which enabled two language groups or families to emerge, equally venerable as organs of sacred truths (Hebrew and Sanskrit) but divergent in terms of structure. There was the 'Ursprache' of Sanskrit, related to the great family of languages that proceeded from these primeval origins, the one that now included Persian, Greek, Latin—and the Germanic dialects. This enabled him to isolate two different language groups, based on grammatical principles, the 'organic' (the Indo-European, as they would later be called), and the 'mechanical' (including the Semitic languages). Alexander von Humboldt's first explorations in the Orinoco regions had confirmed that these linguistic principles extended to the new world; they bore out earlier speculations about the migrations of peoples, away from a central 'Urheimat' westwards, towards Europe, and eastwards, towards the Americas. Human history could be traced to movements and removals, of place, language, belief and culture, away from the Centre, the simple and undivided Whole of primeval origins, as disorders and disruptions forced mankind in all directions.

But whereas Friedrich in his first Paris years was concerned to find some common ground between ancient Indian mythology and the Judaeo-Christian tradition, he now identified emanation, the transmigration of

---

287 Cf. *KA*, VIII, ccvi.
288 *Ibid.*, 309.

souls, and what he chose to call 'pantheism' as the fundamental doctrines of the Indian 'Urreligion'. These, although ultimately of divine origin, were nevertheless essentially 'aberrations' from the real Truth that in 1808 he now saw enshrined only in the traditions he had now so recently embraced. The work shows the comparative religionist, that Friedrich once was, in conflict with the believer on One faith and order.

His brother August Wilhelm was later to be more interested in the phenomenon of religion than in its particular manifestations or their respective verities. What linked the brothers at this stage, in 1808, as they both gave expression to the widest of generalities and postulated mythical or historical polarities, was their use of the organicist language of natural growth and development, the Herderian imagery of biological process, coupled with the analogy of cellular wholeness and integration ('unteilbares Ganzes').[289] Where Friedrich divides language families into 'organic' and 'mechanical', August Wilhelm makes this division a basic principle of art and poetry, the touchstone of all aesthetic awareness.

The Vienna Lectures

It is not clear when the idea of a series of lectures in Vienna occurred to Schlegel. There is no hint of any preparatory work, but coincidences and overlaps between Berlin and Vienna suggest that he had to hand notes from the earlier series and that he used these, suitably adapted, for his new audience. There is evidence that he wanted his lectures to reach a wider public: in 1808 he entrusted to Leo von Seckendorf's periodical *Prometheus* a whole section from the Berlin cycle, the part that deals with illusion and reality, style and manner that had featured in 1802's series.[290] Whereas this extract was theoretical and abstract and needed to be read, the Vienna Lectures, which Schlegel had most likely finished by now, were for hearers.

There is also no doubt that the quickly-forged links with the literary world of Vienna gave some immediacy to his lecturing plans. Leo von Seckendorf, who was to die of his wounds suffered at the battle of Aspern a year later, had won him over for *Prometheus*; Heinrich von Collin was already translating the *Comparaison*; the novelist and salonnière Caroline Pichler welcomed him. There was no attempt to present him as the voice

---

289 *Ibid.*
290 'Über das Verhältniß der schönen Kunst zur Natur; über Täuschung und Wahrscheinlichkeit; über Styl und Manier. (Aus Vorlesungen, gehalten in Berlin im Jahre 1802)'. *Prometheus*, 5.-6. Heft, 1-28. *KAV*, I, 252-266.

of a faction, a school, as he had been in Berlin. The preface to *Prometheus* made due reference to the gravity of the times and the needs of the 'geistiges Vaterland', and the periodical itself was widely embracing in its contributors and coverage. How else could Goethe have been persuaded to offer his 'Festspiel' *Pandora*, a work that made no concessions to readership or convention and represented an esoteric refinement of the German classical tradition,[291] or Johann Heinrich Voss extracts from his translation of Aeschylus? Or Böttiger, once the scourge of the Schlegels? But there was no overlooking the Schlegel presence in *Prometheus*, either: there was publicity for the *Comparaison* translation, and for the Lectures, plus a very positive review of Friedrich's *Ueber die Sprache und Weisheit der Indier*. The review of a performance in Vienna of *Macbeth* in Schiller's version adopted a line very similar to Schlegel's own critical position in his Lectures. His own contribution to *Prometheus*[292] was in itself not inconsiderable: not just the extract from his Berlin Lectures, and four poems, but also an account of the festivities connected with the (third) marriage of the Emperor Francis, the masked ball and gala operas, the celebratory verses. It was in a sense the Vienna that August Wilhelm was poised to conquer.

All this may have affected his resolve to concentrate on drama and theatre in his Lectures. It was a limitation when compared with the wide thematic sweep of Berlin, but otherwise his endeavours had always had a strong dramatic thrust, his pieces on Madame de Staël's acting, the *Comparaison* itself, or indeed the very choice of Shakespeare and Calderón for his translation projects. Furthermore, if one looked at the repertoire of the Burgtheater, just one of Vienna's theatres, for the crucial period January to March 1808, it might seem that the Viennese were in need of a little education in higher or more refined theatrical taste:[293] just two performances of Shakespeare, and one of

---

291 In fact Schlegel wrote a review of *Prometheus* for the Jena *Allgemeine Literatur-Zeitung*, commenting favourably on *Pandora*, having been distinctly cool in his Vienna Lectures on the subject of Goethe's other plays. The review of Schlegel's poems is by another hand. SW, XII, 216-221.
292 Apart from 'An Friedrich Schlegel', it included the essay 'Die deutschen Mundarten' (i, 73-78), the report 'Ueber die Vermählungsfeyer Sr. K. K. Majestät Franz I. mit I. Königl. Hoheit Maria Ludovica Beatrix von Oesterreich' (i, Anzeiger, 2-19), 'Montbard' (ii, 15-20, an extract from the Swiss journey), the poem 'Lied' ('Laue Lüfte, Blumendüfte') (*ibid.*, 70f.), 'Ueber das Verhältniß der schönen Kunst zur Natur [...]', and the poem 'Der Dom zu Mailand' (5.-6. Heft, 170).
293 Franz Hadamowsky, *Die Wiener Hoftheater (Staatstheater) 1776-1966. Verzeichnis der aufgeführten Stücke mit Bestandsnachweis und täglichem Spielplan. I: 1776-1810*, Museion NF I, 1. Reihe, Bd. 4, i (Vienna: Prachner, 1966). 'Täglicher Spielplan der Hoftheater (1776 bis Ende 1810)', 56-59.

those was Schiller's *Macbeth*, the other *Othello* in Wieland's translation and in Brockmann's adaptation, with the Kärntnertor theatre offering Schröder's happy-ended *Hamlet*. (At the end of the year there was *Phèdre* in Schiller's version.) Otherwise, it seemed like a triumph of Kotzebue and Iffland and their dubious sentimentality; or a riot of frivolous comedy after the French, and, this being Vienna, lots of opera.

But there were also distractions from the main task. Elisabeth Wilhelmine van Nuys, a beauty and of independent means (she had moved in high circles in north Germany and had been to England) had already attracted Schlegel's attention, for this 'adventuress' (Caroline's word) had turned up in Jena and Brunswick and rumours linked her with Schlegel. Now in 1808 she appeared in Vienna, moving in the Staël and Pichler circles. We have billets doux from Schlegel to her, mainly in English, 'to my sweet charming Minna', 'my dearest M.', arranging meetings at Count Stadion's or at Collin's, or assignations at the Prater (when not prevented by Lecture preparation).[294] Doubtless Madame de Staël tolerated these flirtations.

An altogether more disruptive presence was Sophie Tieck-Bernhardi, who had left Rome in the summer of 1807 and had proceeded via Munich and Prague now to Vienna. Her divorce from Bernhardi had been finally decreed, and the courts had awarded custody of her two sons to him. Essentially now a fugitive from Prussian justice, she moved with Wilhelm and Felix Theodor and her lover Karl Gregor von Knorring from Prague to Vienna, where their sojourn overlapped with Schlegel's Lectures. Using her contacts with Madame de Staël and Caroline Pichler, she was able to find protection in high places and ward off Bernhardi's attempts to remove the boys. After the Staëls and Schlegel left, a whole drama unfolded, with both Tieck brothers, Ludwig and Friedrich, converging on Munich. There Ludwig succumbed again to the rheumatic complaint that regularly laid him low in moments of stress; while Friedrich Tieck, his artistic career compromised and his finances exhausted, sent more and more desperate letters to the all-provident Schlegel. At the end of 1808, Bernhardi appeared in person and took his elder son Wilhelm back with him to Berlin, leaving Felix Theodor, who Schlegel had once believed was his, with his mother. Importunings and bad debts gave the Tieck-Bernhardi ménage a bad name from which it would scarcely recover. Sophie and Knorring finally married in 1810, but it was not until 1812 that she and Felix made the long journey

---

294 *Krisenjahre*, I, 530, 545f., 559-562; III, 308-311; also SLUB Dresden, Mscr. Dresd. e. 90, XX, 5 (46).

to the Knorring estates in farthest Estonia. Thus in that same year a bizarre near-coincidence saw both Sophie and the Staël cavalcade each heading separately across central Europe, Austria, Bohemia, Galicia, Poland, the one to Riga, the other to Moscow.

This whole divorce scandal, unedifying and squalid in itself, had the effect of polarizing the old associates of Jena and of alienating the younger generation of Romantic writers. It brought odium to the name of Tieck, singly and collectively. Friendships and collaborations stood or fell according to their stance towards the affair: Schelling and Fouqué were considered to be supportive, and so they received copies of the second volume of Calderón when it came out, but Schleiermacher and Fichte did not.[295] Especially not Bernhardi's friend Fichte. For later in 1808 Schlegel drafted a letter to him, which he had the good sense never to send, in which he alluded to Fichte's proletarian origins and his general unsuitability to be 'one of ours'.[296] All this may partly explain why Schlegel in these years leading up to 1812 was more than usually willing to support tried connections, his own brother Friedrich, but also that much-wronged Tieck sibling, the sculptor.

Lectures on Dramatic Art and Literature

Schlegel may, as said, have felt a particular need to remind the Viennese of the serious traditions of the theatre, to state some positions finally and authoritatively. The medium to be adopted was another matter. The public lecture was a means of achieving the widest publicity and dissemination, especially with Madame de Staël's energies behind it. The lecture was a social event, sometimes a political statement; it reached a female audience, unlike universities; like his father Johann Adolf's set-piece sermons in Hanover—an analogy only—it could be a rhetorical occasion aimed at winning hearts and minds. Schlegel was there at the outset of an era that saw, Europe-wide, the great wave of public lectures associated with Cuvier, Humboldt, Davy or Coleridge, and his must take their place in that lineage. But even as he was delivering his lectures in Vienna, others closer to hand were also using the public rostrum: Fichte, in Berlin, had been delivering his *Reden an die deutsche Nation* [*Speeches to the German Nation*] since the winter, and they represented in many ways the antithesis of what Schlegel stood for. Even more was happening in Dresden. As *Prometheus* announced

---

295 *Krisenjahre*, II, 30.
296 *Ibid.*, I, 654-657.

in its pages, Adam Müller in Dresden was just concluding his lectures on 'the sublime and the beautiful' there; Böttiger's on the archaeology of art were still continuing, as were Gotthilf Heinrich Schubert's, published under the title of *Ansichten von der Nachtseite der Naturwissenschaft* [*Views of the Night-Side of Science*] that were to fascinate Heinrich von Kleist and to provide stimulus for E. T. A. Hoffmann.

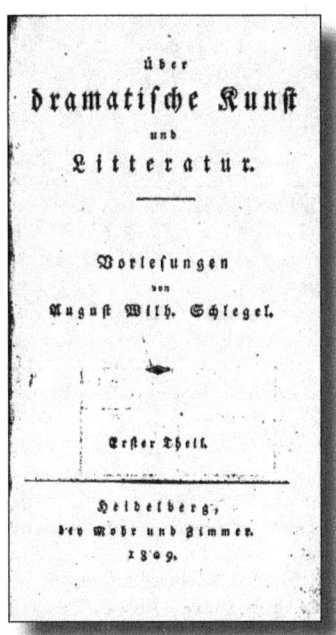

Fig. 15 August Wilhelm Schlegel, *Über dramatische Kunst und Litteratur* (Heidelberg, 1809, 1811). Title page of vol. 1. Image in the public domain.

And so Schlegel's Vienna Lectures are part of the *annus mirabilis* of 1808 which saw their delivery but also the publication of Friedrich's *Ueber die Sprache und Weisheit der Indier* and Fichte's *Reden an die deutsche Nation*. Towering above them all was, however, the first part of Goethe's *Faust*, with *Pandora* a lesser pinnacle. While *Faust* was for most common readers as yet a mystery and to translators still a stumbling-block, Schlegel's lectures had an almost immediate appeal,[297] first in their German published form in 1809-

---

297 The breakdown of the Lectures is as follows: 1: The Classical and the Romantic defined. 2. The nature of dramatic genres. 3. The Greek theatre. 4. Greek tragedy (Aeschylus, Sophocles). 5. Euripides. 6. Greek comedy (Aristophanes). 7. Comedy of the Greeks and Romans. 8. Roman and Italian theatre. 9. French theatre. 10. The *drame classique* in France (Corneille, Racine, Voltaire). 11. French comedy. 12. The Spanish and English stage. Shakespeare. 13. Other English dramatists. 14. Spanish theatre. Calderón. 15. The German theatre and its future.

11,[298] and soon in the other major European languages.[299] They were not an enigma like *Faust*; they did not require of the reader the same intellectual and linguistic effort that *Ueber die Sprache und Weisheit* demanded; they were not esoteric and speculative like Schubert's;[300] and while extolling the virtues of the nation, they never descended to the occasional anti-humanist and xenophobic rant of Fichte's inflammatory periods.

There was to be nothing common in Schlegel's lectures, and no demagoguery. If national values were to be addressed, they were always those that issued from the identity of nations and culture, not merely

---

298 The publication history of the Vienna Lectures is complex and is set out as follows. They were initially published as *Über dramatische Kunst und Litteratur. Vorlesungen von August Wilh. Schlegel* in Heidelberg by Mohr and Zimmer in 1809 (first part in two sections) and 1811 (second part), each with a separate title page. They were reissued, with minor emendations (such as an index), in 1817 as *Ueber dramatische Kunst und Litteratur. Vorlesungen von August Wilhelm von Schlegel*, also in Heidelberg, now with Mohr and Winter. The Swedish publisher Bruzelius issued an unauthorised edition of the Lectures in 1817: August Wilhelm Schlegel, *Werke*, 2 vols (Uppsala: Bruzelius, 1817), II, i-ii. A pirated version of the 1809-11 edition, by the publisher Christian Friedrich Schade, appeared in Vienna in 1825 in the *Classische Cabinets-Bibliothek oder Sammlung auserlesener Werke der deutschen und Fremd-Literatur*, vols 8-11. During the late 1830s Schlegel revisited the Lectures and made alterations and additions (adding notably a whole new section on the Greek theatre) and signed a contract with Winter, but was unable to oversee their publication. This was entrusted to his executor Eduard Böcking, who incorporated this edition into the *SW* (as V-VI), where the original 15 lectures were expanded to 37. The translations done into French, English and other languages are thus based on the 1809-11 or 1817 editions, so that there is justification for regarding them as the *editio princeps* for any critical edition. The Lectures were not reissued between 1846 (*SW*) and 1923, when Giovanni Vittorio Amoretti produced an annotated edition, based on the 1817 reprinting (2 vols, Bonn and Leipzig: Schroeder, 1923). As a critical edition (the first ever) it has its faults, not having taken into account Schlegel's later additions and emendations or the manuscript material in the Goethe-Schiller-Archiv in Weimar or the Sächsische Landesbibliothek in Dresden (now SLUB). For this he was much taken to task by Josef Körner, whose *Die Botschaft der deutschen Romantik an Europa* of 1929 is effectively a critique of Amoretti and its alleged defects, not without a touch of professional jealousy (Amoretti was a pupil of the great Italian comparatist Arturo Farinelli). For all its defaults (and its being long since out of print) Amoretti's edition contains much useful information and it will continue to serve its purpose until, we hope, the corresponding volume of the *KAV* appears. Edgar Lohner, meanwhile, reissued the 1846 edition in two paperback volumes (Stuttgart, etc.: Kohlhammer, 1966-67) as parts 5 and 6 of his six-volume selection, *Kritische Schriften und Briefe* (1962-1974). This edition, while not in the strict sense scholarly, has at least made a version of the famous Lectures available for a general readership.
299 Cf. Schlegel's proud statement in the edition of 1817 (second preface, p. [i]) that the Lectures had already been translated into French, English and Dutch (he had not registered the Italian translation of 1817). On the translation history, see Amoretti, I, xcii, and Körner, *Botschaft*, 56-74, 93-104.
300 Or like Adam Müller's *Vorlesungen über die deutsche Wissenschaft und Literatur*, his Dresden lectures recently reissued in 1807.

the 'Deutsche Nation'. Schlegel deliberately chose the word 'Nation' as distinct from Fichte's preferred term 'Staat', as covering all the aspects of a nation's cultural manifestations that contribute to its ultimate expression in drama and theatre. If Schlegel in his peroration commended the Romantic historical drama to the German nation—in its widest sense—it was in the awareness that this form of dramatic art had evolved in the crucible of other national cultures, the English and Spanish, and hence drew on both North and South for its inspiration, while appealing to the Germanic facility for assimilation and creative adaptation.

One might even say that some of Madame de Staël's sense of the 'spirit of a nation' had come to temper Schlegel's earlier strictures about German (and other) cultures and had imparted a tolerance not found in Jena or Berlin. For in introducing himself to his audience and readers, he could claim to be both a 'citizen of the world' and a German. Connoisseurs and insiders might spot a veiled homage to the values of Coppet, the *châteleine* of which was still working hard on the draft of *De l'Allemagne*. There, one nation would be seen through the eyes of another; but here was a German claiming insights into the drama and theatre of the whole of Europe.

Of course, as said, the Lectures would not have come about without Madame de Staël's contacts in high places, her manipulations and string-pullings (her romantic attachment to Maurice O'Donnell). There was the usual malicious talk of 'le professeur Staël', of his lectures being merely a *divertissement* for high society during the season of Lent.[301] But they were essentially his lectures, and not hers.[302]

The audience was another matter. Words in season eventually secured Schlegel permission to lecture in the capital city, and the university was the first chosen venue.[303] This fell through, and a grander place was found, 'in der Himmelpfortgasse Nr. 1023 bey Hoftraiteur Jahn', the ballroom owned by a restaurateur 'by appointment' to the court and otherwise used for high society occasions. A princely twenty-five florins was charged for fifteen lectures, three per week.[304] It is also fair to say that without Madame

---

301 Roger Bauer, 'Die "Neue Schule" der Romantik im Urteil der Wiener Kritik', in: Herbert Zeman (ed.), *Die österreichische Literatur. Ihr Profil im 19. Jahrhundert (1830-1880)* (Graz: Akademische Druck- und Verlagsanstalt, 1982), 221-229, ref. 222.
302 The relatively mild treatment of Voltaire and the coded remarks on a 'more profound' style of French acting, might for instance be attributed to her.
303 *Prometheus*, 3. Heft, Anzeiger, 24.
304 Three admission tickets have survived in SLUB, Mscr. Dresd. App. 2712, A8, 5 (1-3). Announcement in *Krisenjahre*, III, 301f.

de Staël's assiduous networking, the *haute volée* of Viennese society might not have turned out in the numbers that it did.

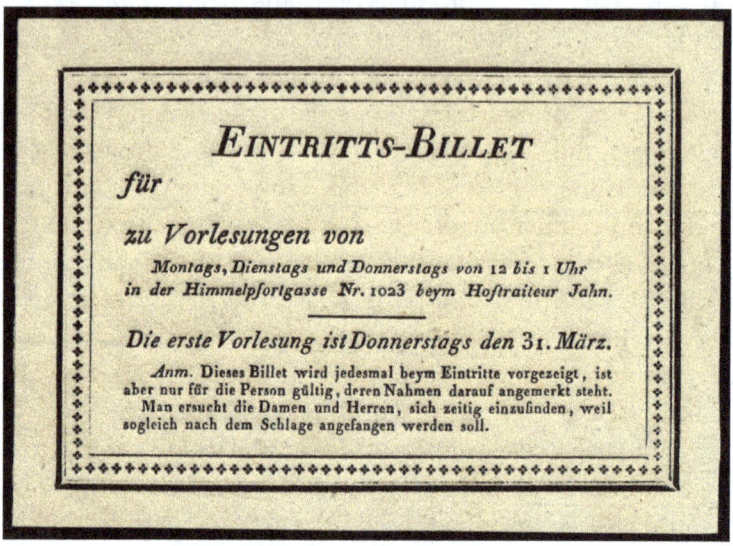

Fig. 16 'Eintritts-Billett'. Admission ticket for Schlegel's lectures on Dramatic Art and Literature, Vienna 1808. © SLUB Dresden, all rights reserved.

It reads like the Almanach de Gotha[305]—Schwarzenberg,[306] Lobkowitz, Kinsky, Schönborn, Liechtenstein—with some grand Polish names thrown in (Lubomirski, Jablonowski), soon to be of use to the fugitive Madame de Staël, and some Hungarian grandees (Pálffy, Batthyány) whose ancestors back in 1651 had signed Christoph von Schlegel's letters patent of nobility; the state chancellor Metternich was there, despite being no great friend of women in politics and of Madame de Staël in particular; Count Sickingen, Schlegel's later intermediary with Metternich, as well. (One notices also the state censor, perhaps making notes in the back row.) Nobles jostled to secure tickets, including Count Wrbna-Freudenthal[307] who later signed the letter granting Schlegel his imperial audience in April. These were the people with the time and the leisure, who would not miss 25 florins. Small wonder that Schlegel was gratified with his more than 250 hearers and all

---

305 The complete list *ibid.*, III, 302-306.
306 Cf. Schlegel's later obeisant letter to Prince Schwarzenberg, Ullrichová, 85. He was but one of several high-placed persons whose assistance was later to be useful to the Staël ménage.
307 SLUB Dresden, Mscr. Dresd. App. 2712, A8, 25.

that 'haute noblesse',[308] not forgetting names closer to home, like 'Madame Sophie Bernhardi', 'Freiherr Karl Gregor von Knorring', 'Frau Minna von Nuys', 'Hr. Simonde de Sismondi' and 'Carolina Pichler, geb. von Greiner', who has left us a description. Even among the nodding feather headdresses or the ribbons on coats, Schlegel's 'fashionable' appearance stood out—a silver-grey coat, straw-coloured breeches and an extravagantly high stock (she does not mention the stray cats which for a time competed for the audience's attention)[309]—Pichler went on to say:

> Schlegel's delivery is not pleasing, he does not speak freely, sometimes losing his way and searching for an expression; then he has another look at his written text and reads a few lines from it and speaks from memory until he is stuck again, etc. *What* he has to say, however, is very much to my liking, e.g. romantic poetry, the effects of the Christian religion on the changes in human thought, the character of the Spanish nation, of the Roman, on German literature, etc., especially our German identity which soon will be completely lost. I can say that I attended the lectures with great pleasure.[310]

Selective listening, no doubt, but interesting nevertheless as coming from someone so alert and intelligent. If Fichte's main device in capturing his Berlin audience was rhetoric and oratory, Schlegel's tone was more measured. It suited his hearers better and was more appropriate to his subject-matter. He had now found the right medium, not academic discourse as in Jena, or that demanding section in *Prometheus* taken from his Berlin cycle. He would have to make concessions and keep technicalities to a minimum: some of his exalted audience would be more conversant with French as a language of discourse. Romantic doctrine would have to be made accessible to princes and counts of the Empire, a balancing-act that required considerable skill and tact. In a sense, of course, he was not proclaiming Romanticism as something radically new or—the ultimate horror in Vienna—revolutionary. Much of his material was recycled from his own earlier lectures and publications. Very few, possibly none, of his audience would have been present in all three places, Jena, Berlin and now Vienna, and not many would have noticed how much had already been

---

308 *Briefe*, I, 220.
309 Caroline Pichler, *Denkwürdigkeiten aus meinem Leben*, ed. Emil Karl Blümml, 2 vols (Munich: Georg Müller, 1914), I, 312f.; *Krisenjahre*, I, 536.
310 *Charakteristiken. Die Romantiker in Selbstzeugnissen und Äußerungen ihrer Zeitgenossen*, ed. Paul Kluckhohn, Deutsche Literatur in Entwicklungsreihen, Reihe Romantik, 1 (Darmstadt: Wissenschaftliche Buchgesellschaft, 1964), 73.

enunciated in those earlier venues,[311] for instance most of the long sections on the Greeks. Much drew on existing published material, the Parny review in the *Athenaeum* (on Aristophanes), the article on the Spanish theatre in *Europa*, or the recent *Comparaison* of 1807 that Heinrich von Collin (also present) was in the process of translating.

The Jena and Berlin lectures remained largely unpublished and thus generally inaccessible: Schlegel had passed on but few of their insights in isolated publications, and Schelling, without acknowledgment, had done the same. In Vienna, Schlegel had to take a lot for granted, and he was sparing in his citation of sources. It was not the real point. In the terminology that he uses in Vienna, the study of sources—the study of the dry-as-dust Bouterwek on the Spanish drama or Malone on Shakespeare—would be mere 'philologische Kritik'. His own, by contrast, was 'vermittelnde Kritik', a criticism that crossed borders, made connections, established links, set up opposites, confronted, challenged. While philology could never be an irrelevance for Schlegel, the circumstances of the Lectures required large generalisations, relativisms, eye-catching juxtapositions and sweeping conclusions, the most famous of which is this section from the Twelfth Lecture:

> Ancient art and poetry strives for the strict severance of the disparate, the Romantic delights in indissoluble mixtures: all opposites, nature and art, poetry and prose, the grave and the gay, memory and intuition, the intellectual and the sensuous, the earthly and the divine, life and death, it stirs and dissolves into one solution. As the oldest law-givers proclaimed and set out their teachings and precepts in modulated harmonies, as Orpheus, the first tamer of the still wild human race, is praised in fable; in the same way the whole of ancient poetry and art is like a cadenced set of prescriptions, the harmonious proclamation of the eternal precepts of a world, finely ordered, that reflects the eternal archetypes of things. The Romantic, by contrast, is the expression of the mysteries of a chaos that is struggling to bring forth ever new and wondrous births, that is hidden under the order of nature, in its very womb: the life-giving spirit of primal love hovers anew over the waters. The one is simpler, clearer and more akin to nature in the self-sufficient perfection of its single works; the other, despite its fragmentary appearance, is closer to the secret of the universe.[312]

---

311 The overlaps conveniently listed in Körner, *Botschaft*, 109-112.
312 *Über dramatische Kunst und Litteratur. Vorlesungen von August Wilh. Schlegel*, 2. Theil, 2. Abt. (Heidelberg: Mohr und Zimmer, 1811), 13-15.

No-one had confronted Ancient and Modern, Classical and Romantic, in quite this way before, or on such a scale. True, Herder's seminal essay on Shakespeare of 1773 had showed Sophocles and Shakespeare—despite gulfs in form and content—to be equally valid in their respective cultures and historically justified in their dramatic expressions, but Schlegel is adumbrating even larger concepts. As with all generalisations, they blur details and occlude nuances; they force contrasting elements into contiguities that set off their essential differences: sculpture (Greek/Classical) versus painting (the Romantic/Modern); clay in the mass as opposed to clay hardened into form (the image that so seized Coleridge),[313] the mechanical as against organic, living form, the ideal versus the mystical. This technique can produce surprising insights of detail, as when Schlegel compares and contrasts Aeschylus and *Macbeth,* or brackets Shakespeare and Calderón as the quintessentially Romantic dramatists, which no-one to date had done in that fashion (and few since).

Thus we should not be looking for originality of basic ideas in these Lectures so much as originality of association. For instance, the images of biological organic growth as opposed to the mechanical and ordered, are common currency in the language of German idealism: Schlegel applies them to whole periods and styles. They harden (to use Schlegel's own image of clay) into fixed categories, but perhaps Schlegel had no option when dealing with the wide range of material at his disposal and faced with the need to make complex and nuanced processes comprehensible to a non-specialist audience. In matters of presentation and disposition, he had learned some lessons from Berlin; while in terms of his general attitudes, he had not greatly changed. The main addition, and one that was anticipated with some eagerness, were the sections on Shakespeare and Calderón, squeezed out of the account of Romantic literature in the earlier lectures.

Much would be familiar to those who had kept abreast with his publications. There was, for instance, the unrepentant preference of Aeschylus and Sophocles over the 'decadent' Euripides, a distinction now freed of the constraints of the *Comparaison* and its more than occasional equivocations. Aristophanes emerges as the supreme comic dramatist of all time (Shakespeare is too complex to be labelled merely 'comic or 'tragic'). Post-Athenian Greek drama receives little praise, as does Roman, but the

---

313 Which may owe its origin partly to Winckelmann. Justi, III, 72.

greatest stringencies are reserved for European neo-classicism, Italian, French or English, Schlegel now effectively writing off the French *drame classique*, but even its comic equivalent, Molière. In many ways, this section would command as much attention in continental Europe as his remarks on Shakespeare, for the subsequent debate on 'Racine et Shakespeare' (to use Stendhal's speaking title) affected not only dramatic practice and criticism in France but also in countries, like Italy or Russia, where the French model still had validity. Goethe would have no cause to be pleased with the relatively perfunctory section devoted to him and to German drama in general, and his displeasure extended to Schlegel's remarks on Schiller, which one can only describe as ungenerous. Old enmities ran deep.

Those expecting great new insights into Calderón would be disappointed: there was no history of Spanish drama as once (rashly) promised, and his relatively short section on Calderón limits itself to generalities about his religious and national virtues. Shakespeare, by contrast, the object of such a disproportionate amount of Schlegel's time and energy, required to be treated with a greater attention in detail. His Twelfth Lecture is a 'last word' in the sense that Schlegel never again returned to Shakespeare as a whole: he finished *King Richard III* in 1810, after years of distraction, but still leaving the translation enterprise incomplete; his *Kritische Schriften* of 1828 reprinted his early Shakespeare essays whose purpose had been quite different. Yet in 1808, to deal with Shakespeare as a general phenomenon, he nevertheless had recourse to a phrase from 1796, too good not to be repeated, 'risen from the dead', a reminder of how much the Germans, or Schlegel himself, had contributed to that resurrection. Thus to introduce the essential Shakespeare, Schlegel reformulated the insight, not new or original, which the Germans (Herder, Goethe, Eschenburg, Tieck, Schlegel himself) had made their own: that Shakespeare is the natural inerrant genius who essentially has nothing to learn, but who submits to the discipline of form and art to achieve true greatness.

So much had been written about Shakespeare that he could not brush aside the history of Shakespearean criticism and textual scholarship. Little of what he says in a couple of chosen pages goes beyond Augustan conventions—Shakespeare's learning, knowledge of humanity, variety of styles, etc.—but at least it is free of Johnsonian caveats. Unlike Calderón's enormous output, each play by Shakespeare (even the suppositious) merited discussion, the Comedies (a fluid term that ranges from *Measure to Measure* to *A Midsummer Night's Dream*), the Tragedies, the Roman Plays, and Schlegel's declared favourites, the Histories.

It has been remarked that Schlegel's comments on the individual plays lack Coleridge's originality,[314] but many in his audience would have been unfamiliar with the basic essentials of Shakespeare, and such plays as they knew would have been in those dubious stage adaptations in Viennese theatres. Whereas Coleridge's insights are based on close textual reading, Schlegel's are couched more generally and do not involve the interrogation of individual loci, are not 'practical criticism'. Schlegel will always disappoint those who want clarification of niceties, but the translator and the critic were 'one and indivisible'. When opting for a specific reading, his translation had already stated what Shakespeare's text 'meant'; translating was in itself a hermeneutic act; the translator's craft was not mere mechanical rendition, as those agonized manuscript scrabblings testified. Read my Shakespeare, is the unspoken message of his Shakespeare lecture to his German audience, an instruction of less relevance for later French, English or other readers. Certain Schlegelian preferences or prejudices nevertheless emerge: for *A Midsummer Night's Dream* and *The Tempest* among the Comedies, for *Romeo and Juliet* among the tragedies (still the 'sigh' of youthful love); in the question of Hamlet's 'qualities' he is now equivocal, and he finds the Prince much less attractive than in 1796; *Macbeth* or *Lear* produce 'terror', 'abhorrence' or sheer 'horror', and few mitigating features. The Histories, to which, as Caroline had remarked, he devoted more time and energy than to the great Tragedies, now emerge in their true glory, and what he says about them and about Shakespeare's place in the history of his nation, are also the remarks that bind together the various sections of the whole Lecture cycle.

Shakespeare, Schlegel says, had lived in stirring times (Calderón, too); like Calderón's, his theatre was truly national and popular. Shakespeare had links with both the intellectual (Bacon) and the political strivings of his age, but there was in his account of the English nation still some of that spirit of chivalry and feudalism, independence of mind and action, that had animated the Middle Ages. Furthermore: the Histories, taken as a cycle, could be read as heroic epic in dramatic form: it was not Spenser, not Milton (especially not he), but Shakespeare who through the unconsciousness of genius had supplied the English with their national epic. Not for the first time German ideas were being assimilated to the

---

314 Cf. Reginald Foakes, 'Samuel Taylor Coleridge', in: *Great Shakespeareans, III: Voltaire, Goethe, Schlegel, Coleridge*, ed. Roger Paulin (New York, London: Continuum, 2010), 128-172, ref. 162f.

processes of foreign literature: Schlegel was clearly finding analogies with the *Nibelungenlied*, one of his current preoccupations. There were echoes of Friedrich August Wolf's *Prolegomena ad Homerum*, that had postulated the multiple authorship of Homer's songs. It was analogous to Barthold Georg Niebuhr's later 'lay theory' for Roman history—that Schlegel was to excoriate—wishing 'Urtexte' into being where none existed.

Once having enunciated the idea of the 'nation', Schlegel could introduce into his lectures some ideas that linked poetry and politics.[315] Of course, with spy networks operating in Vienna and Paris, he could not say anything directly seditious, nor would it have been in his nature to do so. His audience contained ministers and ambassadors, who knew what Napoleon had done at Jena, at Tilsit, at Erfurt, in imposing his iron will on any 'Nation' that chose to resist him. The 'spirit of the age', the direct reference to drama as a nation-building influence, the praise of Greek drama as an expression of Athenian freedom and national pride and patriotic common endeavour and civil polity, would not be lost on those with ears to hear. Roman theatre was not like this: rather it reflected tyranny, the imposition of the will of the state on the populace (a veiled reference to Napoleon's Caesarism). Aeschylus and Sophocles had been Athenian citizens, Seneca the court philosopher of Nero.

French classical drama, for Schlegel, had not been national, either; it was prescriptive, courtly, not popular; even Molière had written to order 'from above'. Hence the amount of space, seemingly beyond all proportion (three lectures out of fifteen), that Schlegel devotes to the disqualification of the neo-classical, the need to deny it houseroom in the wide scheme of European drama that he unfolds, one that also obliquely takes in the Indians, who with the Greeks were the only ancient people with a native dramatic tradition. Spanish drama, too, spoke of 'Vaterland', a heroic nation (reinforced by the Germanic Goths), religious to the core, without the Enlightenment. It reflected national characteristics and virtues (love, honour). But above all Shakespeare's Histories were written in response to their own times; they were a mirror for princes, imparting political wisdom. In discussing them Schlegel could use words like 'usurpation', 'tyranny' or 'despotism', that suggested the ultimate Usurper himself.

Adam Müller in his Dresden lectures of 1806 had established in Shakespeare's historical dramas a pattern that saw the political upheavals

---

315 Herold's assertion, that the Vienna Lectures are unpolitical, is plain wrong. *Mistress to an Age*, 356.

in the reigns of King John and King Richard II, the struggles of York and Lancaster, leading over to their culmination in the establishment of a Henrician order. It was part of his conservative and restorative political vision after the catastrophes of 1805-06. Schlegel is less specific, but the model of Henry VIII's settlement might suggest an analogy with the Austrian emperor (as he now was) Francis I, who had emerged from the loss of the Holy Roman Empire to preside over the Germanic lands (and many others). While Schlegel's real hero is Henry V, his real villain is Richard III; he pits medieval chivalric ideals (Henry) against Machiavellian (Richard). Much of this would take on a peculiar relevance as the Lectures appeared in print, the sections up to and including European neo-classicism in 1809, followed in 1811 by the sections on Romantic drama. For readers by then would know that Spain, that nation called 'doughty and bold' in Schlegel's fourteenth Lecture, had later in 1808 risen up in revolt and was now a Napoleonic fief; they would remember the second heavy defeat that Napoleon had inflicted on the Austrians, at Wagram in 1809, or their own partial victory at Aspern, where Leo von Seckendorf had met his death.

Schlegel's envoi in the fifteenth Lecture, his call for a German historical drama, not along slavishly Shakespearean lines, but recording patterns of national history and its ascendance nevertheless, must be seen in this light. Angevins and Plantagenets would give way to Hermann the Cheruscan, the Hohenstaufen, or even the house of Habsburg, whose gracious permission had enabled the Lectures to come about in the first place (perhaps his brother's play on Charles V). National drama would also be nation-building: it is not by coincidence that the only play by Schiller to attract Schlegel's favour was *Wilhelm Tell*, with its 'old German' struggle for Helvetic national freedom (now a land under Napoleon's yoke). These political aspirations (as opposed to legal, military and educational reforms) were of course not to be fulfilled in the German lands, and Prince Metternich, no doubt sitting in the front row of the lecture hall, would be the author of the later reaction that saw their frustration. It may help to explain in part why Schlegel was later so willing to be involved in the political arena in 1813-14, but in the service of the Swedish Prince Royal, Bernadotte.

No-one surveying the German drama of the nineteenth century could say that Schlegel's advocacy of the Histories had been his best legacy. Here and there one finds a good historical drama, but rarely one as good as Schiller's, and the average seems to bear out those 'Hohenstaufen tapeworms'[316] which in Friedrich Hebbel's unpleasant phrase reflect the greater part of German practice.

Further Travels

Madame de Staël left Vienna on 22 May, 1808 in the company of Maurice O'Donnell, to be joined by the rest of her party, minus the reluctant cadet, Albert. Their journey took them into the Bohemian lands: Goethe was rumoured to be in Carlsbad. This meeting never eventuated, but in Prague, where they arrived on 26 May, they hoped to meet Friedrich Gentz. This translator of Edmund Burke and sometime member of Schlegel's Berlin audience, bon viveur and frequenter of literary and political salons, had lent his pen to the cause of both Prussian and Austrian anti-revolutionary and anti-Napoleonic politics. The British were paying him handsome retainers, which supported his extravagant and raffish life-style (later, as Metternich's right-hand man). Above all, he was in Napoleon's bad books, being suspected of having had a hand in the Prussian manifesto that had led to war in 1806. He chose therefore to lie low in Prague. He was also an admirer of Madame de Staël.[317] They finally met up in the watering-place of Teplitz (today's Teplice). At their meeting, they got on famously: 'a man of the first class' is her verdict;[318] 'one could spend an eternity with her' is his.[319] He was similarly taken with Schlegel, 'cultivated' 'socially at ease'.[320] The meeting, which so impressed the worldly-wise Gentz, was however ill-advised. Napoleon's agents knew all about it,[321] convincing the Emperor that banishment of this troublesome woman was the only solution.

They proceeded to Dresden. Adam Müller, another survivor of Berlin, was now tutor there to Prince Bernhard of Weimar and was attracting attention through his series of lectures. The January number of his

---

316 Friedrich Hebbel, preface to *Maria Magdalene*, *Werke*, ed. Gerhard Fricke *et al.*, 5 vols (Munich: Hanser, 1963-66), I, 325.
317 Cf. Maria Ullrichová, 'Mme de Staël et Frédéric Gentz', in: *Madame de Staël et l'Europe, Colloque de Coppet* (1966) (Paris: Klincksieck, 1970), 81-91; Norman King, 'De l'enthousiasme à la réticence: Germaine de Staël et Friedrich von Gentz (1808-1813)', *Cahiers staëliens*, 41 (1989-90), 55-72.
318 *Correspondance générale*, VI, 438.
319 Adam Müller, *Lebenszeugnisse*, ed. Jakob Baxa, 2 vols (Munich, etc.: Schöningh, 1966), I, 415.
320 *Ibid.* Welschinger, *La Censure*, 174, quotes the Emperor as saying 'Ces relations ne peuvent être que nuisibles'.
321 King (1989-90), 61.

periodical *Phöbus*, co-edited by Heinrich von Kleist and published in Dresden in 1808, had extracts from these, but also a highly flattering article on Madame de Staël (if later a less ingratiating review of *Corinne*) and, still later, one of her translations of Schiller's poems.[322] Articles on the Spanish theatre and on the drama of the Greeks were a reminder that Schlegel did not have a monopoly of these subjects in 1808.[323] Neither she nor Schlegel noticed the towering presence of Kleist, whose contributions make this periodical memorable. Müller, already an astute political rhetorician (but not yet Metternich's acolyte) found himself silenced and overwhelmed by Staël's sheer presence; she could out-talk and out-argue anyone who was theorizing, like him, about the 'elements of statecraft'.[324] She already knew what these were.

In Dresden Friedrich Schlegel was staying with his sister Charlotte Ernst, as he made his way towards Vienna in search of preferment. He had to borrow money from his brother to get this far, and more would be needed to see him to his ultimate destination. His first communication from Vienna, in July 1808,[325] would inaugurate a litany recounting his tribulations, his waiting in the antechambers of the influential, his harassments, real and imagined, by the secret police. He also caught up in Vienna with the extended Schlegel-Staël circle and its ramifications. His first quarters were with Karl Gregor von Knorring: there is a certain poetic justice in the Tieck-Bernhardi ménage giving support to a member of the Schlegel family, not the other way round. With Maurice O'Donnell, Friedrich was charged with keeping an eye on Albert de Staël, reporting to his mother about his Latin lessons and also his escapades. She even asked Friedrich to intervene when her short-lived romance with O'Donnell came to its inevitable end.[326] Dorothea did not join him until later in the year, making the journey from Cologne to Dresden amid troop movements.[327] By November she was finally installed in Vienna.

Leaving the Saxon capital, the Staëls moved on, amid rumours of war, to Weimar. The duke and duchess received them, as did Schiller's widow. Wieland was gracious, even to Schlegel. Schlegel left the party at Weimar

---

[322] *Phöbus. Ein Journal für die Kunst. Herausgegeben von Heinrich v. Kleist und Adam H. Müller* (Dresden: Gärtner, 1808), 1. Stück, 54-56, 2. Stück, 42-47, 6. Stück, 3-8.
[323] *Ibid.*, 7. Stück, 3-12, 8. Stück, 10-18.
[324] Baxa, 424.
[325] *Krisenjahre*, I, 550.
[326] *Correspondance générale*, VI, 542.
[327] *Krisenjahre*, I, 606.

and made a quick dash across to Hanover. Madame de Staël meanwhile was granted an insight into German religious life which was to inform one of the more extraordinary passages in *De l'Allemagne*. It was part of her discovery that the Germans were a profoundly religious people (Protestant Germans, that is, for Catholics formed a disproportionately shorter part of the narrative).[328] One may, if one will, discern Schlegel's hand in her chapter, 'Du Protestantisme', with its two-edged account of the Reformation and its trinity of theologians, Michaelis (Caroline's father), Herder, and Schleiermacher.[329] Her assertion that the North was more inclined to religious feeling than the Catholic South was the kind of insouciance that has given *De l'Allemagne* a bad name. (She may not even have appreciated the differences inside German Protestantism.) But the visit to the Moravian Brethren in Neudietendorf near Erfurt[330] struck a different note. She described the communal life and worship of the Brethren, their regularity and tranquility, the harmony of their inner feelings and their outward conduct. In comparing them with Quakers, whom she knew from England (or from Voltaire),[331] she was showing her indifference in matters both of doctrine and observance: for her the touchstone of religious experience, at its most basic, was 'emotion'.[332]

For Schlegel, too, at this time it was feeling, 'sentiments', that animated matters of belief. This would not be in the forefront as he revisited his Protestant homeland of Hanover and found himself back in the world of Lutheran polity, represented by his two brothers, the one in Göttingen, the other in Hanover, and by his mother, the superintendent-general's widow. Hanover had in 1807 experienced occupations and troop billetings (not least under Marshal Bernadotte):[333] Schlegel's regular money drafts to his mother had meant the difference between penury and survival. If Madame de Staël was the source of much of this (his publishers, too), it was also a reminder that his patroness could move as she chose from one bolt hole to the other, whereas the Schlegel family in Hanover could not. It was to be the last time that he saw his cherished and devoted mother.

---

328 John Isbell, *The Birth of European Romanticism. Truth and Propaganda in Staël's 'De l'Allemagne'*, Cambridge Studies in French, 49 (Cambridge: Cambridge UP, 1994), 175.
329 *De l'Allemagne*, V, 41-47.
330 The correct name of the village. Not in the former Erfurt territory, which was Catholic, but in Gotha. *De l'Allemagne*, V, 56-62.
331 Isbell, 180.
332 *De l'Allemagne*, V, 62.
333 Family letters from this period in SLUB Dresden, Mscr. Dresd. App. 2712, B18, 26-36. His own account in Pange, 225.

3. The Years with Madame de Staël (1804-1817)

His return journey, to rejoin Madame de Staël, took him to Kassel, since 1807 capital of the Kingdom of Westphalia and the seat of Napoleon's brother, King Jerome. (Hanover had been swallowed up by this Napoleonic creation.) There he met Johannes von Müller, now a privy counsellor at this court. He had made the political journey from Austrian service to Prussian, and now to Napoleon's. Johann Friedrich Reichardt, the Schlegel brothers' old associate from the 1790s, had traversed different political territory, and he too was also (briefly) in Kassel. For Schlegel, it was Müller's Helvetic history that mattered, its chronicle of fierce independence, not its author's political manoevrings and personal frailties.[334] In times like these it did not do to be too censorious. Madame de Staël thought similarly,[335] and it may well be at Schlegel's prompting that Müller emerges in *De l'Allemagne* as a historian commensurate with Herder.[336]

Schlegel found the Staël party again in Heidelberg. Heidelberg, through the grand duke of Baden's judicious dynastic policies (marrying his heir to Napoleon's adopted Beauharnais daughter),[337] had been spared troop movements and occupations. It was in this haven of peace, with its venerable setting and its newly reconstituted university, that the younger Romantics Achim von Arnim and Clemens Brentano had been able to produce works like the *Wunderhorn* or *Zeitung für Einsiedler*. He also met their publisher, Johann Georg Zimmer, of the firm Mohr and Zimmer: they were to bring out his Vienna Lectures.[338] But the Romantics' chief adversary, Johann Heinrich Voss, was now also a professor there. Only later, in response to Voss's calumniations, would Schlegel contrast his own banishment and exile with Voss's academic idyll in Heidelberg.[339] A meeting with the old curmudgeon went off surprisingly well, also with his son Heinrich.[340]

---

334 *Correspondance générale*, VI, 467f.
335 'dont la vie peut être diversement jugée'. *De l'Allemagne*, III, 301.
336 Cf. his later mention of Johannes von Müller in his Bonn lectures on World History, as a proponent of 'res gestae' as opposed to Herder's 'Ideen'. SLUB Dresden, Mscr. Dresd. e. 90, XXVIII, second lecture [p. 12].
337 Friedrich Strack, 'Historische und poetische Voraussetzungen der Heidelberger Romantik', in: idem (ed.), *200 Jahre Heidelberger Romantik, Heidelberger Jahrbücher*, 51 (2007), 23-40, ref. 33.
338 *August Wilhelm Schlegels Briefwechsel mit seinen Heidelberger Verlegern*, ed. Erich Jenisch (Heidelberg: Winter, 1922), 22f.
339 'Beleuchtung der Beschuldigungen in der Anti-Symbolik von J. H. Voss', second part of 'Berichtigung einiger Mißdeutungen' (1828), *SW*, VIII, 230-284, ref. 243 ('Die anrückenden Heere hatten seine Kohlpflanzen noch nicht zertreten [...] die Wehklagen der Völker drangen nicht bis zu seinem Ohr').
340 *Briefe*, II, 107-109 on his subsequent relations with Voss.

Schlegel was not unaware that the younger Voss had translated *Othello* and *King Lear* in 1806, in a style situated somewhere between Schiller's and his own; indeed Voss and his brother Abraham were soon to set themselves up in earnest competition with Schlegel's own Shakespeare enterprise, in sharp opposition even, once their father's astringent voice was added.[341] Schlegel was content to yield to Madame Unger's urgings and complete *King Richard III* in 1810. It marked for all intents and purposes the end of that great enterprise, begun in Jena and by an irony terminated a year after Caroline's death.

Back to Coppet

Coppet, where they returned in July, 1808, was with a few interruptions to be collectively and severally a safe place and centre of study, conviviality, and contemplation from the autumn through to the summer of 1809. Outside, Spain rose in revolt; later, Austria prepared for war. These were the last months of the 'Groupe de Coppet' as originally constituted, before circumstances brought about its disruption. With such a *châtelaine* things could never be exactly tranquil, still clinging to Maurice O'Donnell in Vienna but having the (secretly married) Benjamin Constant as her guest in Coppet. Prosper de Barante, Mathieu de Montmorency, Sismondi, Elzéar de Sabran and Bonstetten were joined by a new house guest, Baron Caspar von Voght, the attentive listener to Schlegel's Berlin lectures, who now became a major informant for *De l'Allemagne*. For these months were to be devoted to things German and a variety of German visitors, but also to *De l'Allemagne* itself. She would write this 'testament'—as she told the Prince de Ligne—and then she would leave for America.[342]

As usual Schlegel found himself torn between Coppet's preoccupations and his own perception of himself as a German man of letters, one of those 'wide-awake and German-minded writers'[343] of which the nation had such need in these days. But one act of fealty towards Coppet stands out: his review of Benjamin Constant's tragedy *Wallstein*. *Wallstein, tragédie en cinq actes et en vers, précédée de quelques réflexions sur le théâtre allemand, suivie de notes historiques*, to give it its full title,[344] was not merely Schiller's *Wallenstein*

---

341 Details in Roger Paulin, *The Critical Reception of Shakespeare in Germany 1682-1914. Native Literature and Foreign Genius*, Anglistische und amerikanistische Texte und Studien, 11 (Hildesheim, Zurich, New York: Olms, 2003), 335-244.
342 *Correspondance générale*, VI, 539.
343 *Briefe*, I, 225.
344 Modern critical edition ed. by Jean-René Derré, Bibliothèque de la Faculté des Lettres de Lyon, [10] (Paris: Les Belles Lettres, 1965).

recast in French alexandrines: it reduced the whole of that trilogy to five acts, it shrank its many places of action to one, it cut down the dramatis personae to the requirements of the French stage. Constant had avoided 'mixtures' of style or lapses of decorum (Schiller's occasional concessions to Shakespeare). Admitting that his play could not satisfy the strictest theoretical norms of the French 'drame classique', he thereby offered a critique of its stringencies, but he did not aim to overthrow its conventions either.[345] The fact that Madame de Staël in her section on *Wallenstein* in *De l'Allemagne* largely repeats Constant's own arguments, shows how problematic German drama was for a French readership and audience, not just Schiller's.[346] Hence Madame de Staël's preference there for the more regular *Maria Stuart*, which with its theme of regicide also suited her ideological purposes.

One might expect Schlegel, fresh from his recent severe judgment on neo-classicism, to find little merit in *Wallstein*,[347] but here loyalties to Coppet asserted themselves. He is more conciliatory in the matter of national dramatic styles, provided that none claims a monopoly of taste or excellence (the second part of his Vienna Lectures, published later in the same year, would adopt a different tone). Instead, he uses Constant to diminish Schiller. Schiller had not succeeded in containing his material in five acts; his trilogy was not, like those of the Greeks, the product of inner necessity, but of despair. Shakespeare, for instance, could have done the opening part, *Wallensteins Lager* [Wallenstein's Camp], in a few deft strokes. Had Schiller been a more experienced dramatist, had he spent less time on philosophical or historical studies, he might have achieved the same five-act solution as Constant. This was the delayed critical voice of Jena.

There were quite enough matters of his own to occupy Schlegel in these months, first of all publishing. With other things occupying his time and energy, he had not sent Reimer the promised second part of Calderón. An agitated correspondence ensued, Schlegel finally capitulating and returning Reimer's advance. Reimer in his turn handed Schlegel over to Julius Hitzig in Berlin, a new publisher looking for copy and very glad to

---

345 *Ibid.*, 66-67.
346 Voght discusses a reading of *Wallstein* by Constant, Staël and Sabran. He criticizes the French tendency to exposition in preference to action. *Caspar Voght und sein Hamburger Freundeskreis. Briefe aus dem tätigen Leben*, ed. Kurt Detlev Möller, then Annelise Tecke, Veröffentlichungen des Vereins für Hamburgische Geschichte, 15, i-iii, 3 vols (Hamburg: Christians, 1959-67), III, 225.
347 The actual review is in *Morgenblatt für gebildete Stände* 41, 17 February, 1809, 161-163. Not in *SW*. Text (German and French) in: Norman King, 'Deux critiques de Wallstein', *Annales Benjamin Constant* 4 (1984), 90-95.

add the famous translator to his list. Sophie Bernhardi had not forgotten her poetic ambitions amid her family affairs. Could Schlegel find a publisher for her verse epic *Flore und Blanscheflur*? He remembered Zimmer in Heidelberg. Zimmer was not interested, but he sensed a real prize when Schlegel offered him his Vienna Lectures. Schlegel had wanted them to appear in Vienna itself, but publishers there would only pay in paper money. Zimmer could offer proper currency, two and a half Carolins per sheet for a print-run of 1,250.[348] The first part was ready by October, 1809. Zimmer was also the publisher of the *Heidelberger Jahrbücher*, edited by the Heidelberg professors Karl Daub and Friedrich Creuzer, which began its long and distinguished life in 1808. This review periodical would deal with many of the important publications of this second wave of Romanticism, and for about five years it was to be the major outlet for Schlegel's own scholarly interests.

These of course included the *Nibelungenlied*. The visit to Munich at the end of 1807 had a fortunate consequence when in the summer of 1808 Schlegel was elected a corresponding member of the newly constituted Royal Bavarian Academy of Sciences (he would have loved the Academy's splendid uniform, but never got to wear it). Doubtless Schelling had a hand in this. There was an academy project on standard German grammatical usage. Could he be persuaded? In fact Schlegel was far more interested in borrowing the Munich manuscript of the *Nibelungenlied*. To Crown Prince Ludwig of Bavaria, the restless and untiring patron of the arts, he wrote, assuring his devotion, but his real hope was that with Madame de Staël they might find royal patronage for Friedrich Tieck.[349]

The opportunity for devotion presented itself for Madame de Staël in August 1808, at the folk festival at Interlaken. Schlegel had remained behind while she, Sabran and Montmorency set out for the event, which took place on 17 August. It forms of course one of the great set pieces of *De l'Allemagne*, part of its commodious attitude to the notion of 'Germany' or 'German-ness'. It was the only folk event that she in fact seems to have seen and it suited her purposes admirably. It was, as it were, Johannes von Müller brought to life, William Tell (the legend, or Schiller's version of it) re-enacted: here the people were freedom-loving, robust, given to song and dance—in short a nation that resisted despots. And so the Swiss (not, say, the Tyroleans, who were engaged in active revolt) stood in *De l'Allemagne* for the independent Germanic virtues that had once elicited the

---
348 Jenisch, 23-29.
349 *Briefe*, I, 226.

admiration of a Tacitus. A similar agenda informs her choice of Pestalozzi and his system for her long section on German education in *De l'Allemagne*.

There were other spectators of note at Interlaken. That great royal traveller Crown Prince Ludwig was there. It was the moment to intercede for Friedrich Tieck, still in Rome. Having done the busts of the Weimar notabilities and some in Munich, would Tieck not be the ideal sculptor for the Walhalla, the monument to German greatness that was to arise on the banks of the Danube near Regensburg? It little mattered that the Crown Prince's notions of 'German-ness' were as accommodating as Madame de Staël's, for even she was considered for inclusion.

The Crown Prince, himself a poetaster, was in his turn able to introduce her to a fellow-poet: Friedrich Ludwig Zacharias Werner. Thus ensued one of the more bizarre episodes in the history of Coppet. Werner, on his way through Switzerland to northern Italy, had met up with the Crown Prince's entourage. Ludwig or Madame de Staël had most likely heard of him, and one did not forget his actual physical presence, wild, farouche, outlandish, overwhelming; a man with a mission not just to fill Schiller's vacant dramatic throne, but through mystical unions and androgynous celestial resolutions to bring salvation to the world. He did not practise ethereality: no serving-wench was safe from his attentions. Goethe had been equally fascinated and repelled by him, but the periodical *Prometheus* expressed itself more drastically: sampling his works was like enjoying a banquet where one had unwittingly been eating human flesh.[350] His *Martin Luther* drama had been performed amid scandal in Berlin in 1806; and his *Attila* tragedy of 1807, as yet unperformed, would lead Madame de Staël to the most problematical of her indiscretions in *De l'Allemagne*. For Napoleon—or his censors—did not enjoy comparisons, however veiled, with the 'scourge of God'.[351]

Madame de Staël was fascinated by Werner, and Werner knelt in homage before her.[352] After his journey to Milan and Genoa, he was a welcome guest at Coppet from 14 October to 3 November, 1808, and the account in his diaries of life there is highly informative. He noted the presence of the Danish poet Adam Oehlenschläger, rude and malicious, who was to stay in Coppet or Geneva until the spring of 1809. Madame de Staël was

---

350 'Über die Tendenz der Wernerschen Schriften', *Prometheus*, 5.-6. Heft, 35-50, ref. 44.
351 Besslich, 79-82.
352 'Knie vor ihr nieder', *Die Tagebücher des Dichters Zacharias Werner (Texte)*, ed. Oswald Floeck, Bibliothek des Literarischen Vereins in Stuttgart, 289 (Leipzig: Hiersemann, 1939), 32-41, ref. 41. Werner's effusive correspondence with Madame de Staël, his 'Aspasia', published by Fernand Baldensperger, 'Lettres inédites de Zacharias Werner à Madame de Staël', *Revue de Littérature Comparée* 3 (1923), 112-133.

sufficiently taken with him to include him (and his fellow-countryman Jens Baggesen) in her widely-cast notion of German poetry in *De l'Alllemagne*. Werner also spent hours in conversation with Schlegel. He heard him read Calderón; Schlegel lent him—and nobody else—his *Considérations*; they talked about Catholicism and discoursed at length about the relationship of the plant and animal world to the divine. It was clear that they were both reading Louis Claude de Saint-Martin, the French mystical philosopher ('le philosophe inconnu').

What was happening in Coppet? Was Schlegel no longer talking nonsense when the subject was religion, as Madame de Staël had once averred? It is fair to say that an interest in mysticism and quietism—terms that she used indiscriminately—was never far from Madame de Staël's mind, but that it was not at all times equally active. Maybe she needed a catalyst such as Werner or Schlegel.[353] Certainly in a much-quoted letter from Bonstetten it is Schlegel who is deemed responsible: 'these people will all be turning Catholic, Böhmians, Martinists, mystics, all thanks to Schlegel; and on top of all that, everything is turning German'.[354] Clearly, distinctions between various kinds of spirituality were not Coppet's forte.

Saint-Martin had done the French translation of the works of Jacob Böhme, the mystagogue and heresiarch who had enjoyed such a vogue in Jena. Tieck, Novalis and Friedrich Schlegel had been attracted to the Silesian theosophist, whereas August Wilhelm had been less drawn. Now after his return from Vienna we find him ordering Böhme and Saint-Martin from booksellers.[355] Werner's religious notions were at this stage so heterodox that he could easily accommodate Saint-Martin—and much else—into his system. That was only to cease with his conversion to Catholicism in 1810. Schlegel was not to take such a step. Was the potential rift with Madame de Staël too grave to contemplate? For there is enough evidence from his correspondence up to the Russian journey of a searching for spiritual satisfaction, for an easing of soul, but not necessarily inside

---

353 *De l'Allemagne*, V, 96f.; Isbell, 184-191. 'Schlegel und Werner an der Spitze der speculation [sic] und Mystiker, mit dem Unterschied, das dieß bey Werner *Gefühl*, bey Schlegel *Einbildungskraft* ist'. Voght, III, 241. For Voght the Hamburg Protestant, Schlegel represents *'mystischen Papismus'* (*ibid.*, 217), 'Bekehrungs Eifer' (232). See Nicole Jacques-Chaquin and Stéphane Michaud, 'Saint-Martin dans le Groupe de Coppet et le cercle de Frédéric Schlegel', *Colloque 1974* (1977), 113-134.

354 Karl Viktor von Bonstetten to Friederike Brun, 12 October 1809. *Bonstettiana*, X, ii, 654.

355 SLUB Dresden, Mscr. Dresd. App. 2712, B 21 (68-72). By 1811, he had nine items by Saint-Martin plus S-M's translation of Böhme, in his library. 'Verzeichniß meiner Bücher im December 1811', Mscr. Dresd. e. 90, XV.

an ecclesiastical or hierarchical framework. At this stage he was willing to defend the speculations of his brother Friedrich in *Ueber die Sprache und Weisheit* against the likes of Schelling; indeed in an important letter to the latter of 19 August 1809[356] he saw philosophy as but one way towards truth, not an end in itself; it alone—not even Kant—could not open up the ultimate secrets. Whereas later it would be history, historical record, the examination of sources on the broadest of bases that would inform his method of study, he was now prepared to entertain hidden links between the spiritual and material world that would not sustain historical or philological analysis.

Another visitor to Coppet just before Werner had noticed religious stirrings in Schlegel. This was Barbara von Krüdener,[357] the itinerant visionary who was later to become the spiritual counsellor of Tsar Alexander I and the inspirer of the Holy Alliance. Madame de Staël, who was reading nothing more extreme than Fénelon, was on her list of potential converts; of Schlegel she observed that 'he believed Protestantism to be in decline and that he will find repose in the Catholic religion'.[358] Hankerings, longings, a search for inward peace, but no active steps taken towards the Church's formal embrace: this seemed to be the extent of Schlegel's Catholic leanings. He was still the tutor to Madame de Staël's sons, who had been confirmed into the Calvinist faith; he was very close to his mother and doubtless did not wish to add to the heart-ache of Friedrich's conversion; and there was the memory of his father, to whom he had owed so much and whom Friedrich, as the youngest sibling, had not known to this degree.

The third important guest at Coppet in this autumn and winter of 1808-09 was Friedrich Tieck.[359] He had left Rome in August and had made his way via Genoa and Turin to Munich, where he caught up with the Tieck family's untidy affairs, but was also commissioned to do Schelling's bust.[360] Tieck, who in his letters comes over as hang-dog, ever sorry for himself, was emerging as the major recorder in marble or plaster of the personal images of Berlin, of Jena, of Weimar, and now of Coppet. Or even of the German nation,

---

356 Krisenjahre, II, 66-71.
357 Jasinski, 'Liste des principaux visiteurs', 475.
358 Francis Ley, *Bernardin de Saint-Pierre, Madame de Staël, Chateaubriand, Benjamin Constant et Madame de Krüdener (d'après des documents inédits)* (Paris: Aubier, 1967), 142. Bonstetten predictably scathing on Frau von Krüdener: 'Sie ist ganz närrisch und sprach mit der Staël nur von Himmel und Hölle. Mich stinkt das Unwesen an'. *Bonstettiana*, X, ii, 655.
359 Jasinski, 475.
360 Maaz, 110f.; Bögel (2015), 169, 183.

for twenty-four of the busts in Crown Prince (and later King) Ludwig's Walhalla were to be by him,[361] those alternately glabrous or hirsute marble monuments to German greatness, whose provenance as routine commissions is all too evident. But where personal involvement or friendship entered into it he could be relied upon to produce a striking image that comes over to us as authentic. To him we owe the only portrait of Wackenroder that we have, the sole record of Ludwig and Sophie Tieck as young writers, the only convincing memorial to Auguste Böhmer. He filled niches in the Weimar palace, not only with Goethe and Schiller, but with Klopstock and Voss. His Schelling breathes energy and intelligence;[362] his Alexander von Humboldt has something of the freshness and determination of the young voyager.[363] Not everyone could perhaps enter into the spirit of the Necker mausoleum in Coppet (closed to all but the family), where a veiled and draped Suzanne Necker leads her husband Jacques, nude, but discreetly covered, to Elysium, with their daughter Germaine kneeling, her face hidden in her hands.[364]

Her features were revealed in the bust that Tieck did of her in 1808, with her ample figure, part décolletée, the head bare, not festooned with the toques or turbans that are a feature of her other portraits, the mouth slightly open, as if in the act of speech, about to articulate the latest aperçu or witticism.[365] Not so the bust of Schlegel.[366] He himself claimed that it was a 'speaking likeness',[367] recognizing in his image the seriousness, severity even, of the scholar and translator. The Grecian herm could not of course display the sitter's sartorial vanity, those silk breeches and embroidered waistcoats that his tailor's bills record.[368] Compared with his last formal representation, that slightly androgynous portrait by Tischbein, here was a display of maturity and achievement. The bust seen in profile shows a family resemblance to Caroline Rehberg's portrait of his father Johann Adolf. Of course the son's hair is swept forward, not tied back, eighteenth-century fashion, but each has a high forehead and prominent nose and large eyes. Johann Adolf's mouth expresses the kindliness that most witnesses attribute to him; August Wilhelm's is firm and determined and not a little defiant.

---

361 Full list in Bögel (2015), 197. They include Goethe, Schiller and Herder.
362 Maaz, 287.
363 *Ibid.*, 281f.
364 *Ibid.*, 282f.
365 Illustration *ibid.*, 109, description 285f.
366 *Ibid.*, 286f., with an account of the copies made.
367 *Briefe*, I, 226.
368 SLUB Dresden, Mscr. Dresd., App. 2712, B31 (5-16).

3. *The Years with Madame de Staël (1804-1817)*

Fig. 17 August Wilhelm Schlegel, marble bust by Friedrich Tieck 1816-30.
Image in the public domain.

De l'Allemagne

It was time at last for Madame de Staël to finish *De l'Allemagne*, time, too, for Schlegel to see his Vienna Lectures to press, indeed to oversee their translation into French. But even now there were distractions; everyone seemed to be busy at something, as Baron Voght wrote to Juliette Récamier: 'In every corner there is somebody composing a work. She herself is writing her *Letters on Germany*, Constant and Auguste a tragedy each, Sabran a comic opera, Sismondi his History, Schlegel his translation, Bonstetten his philosophy, and me my letter to Juliette'.[369] Apart from the usual stream of visitors, there was still play acting.

This would be as nothing compared with the return visit of Zacharias Werner in September to November of 1809,[370] when Coppet saw the first reading and then performance of his 'fate tragedy' *Der vierundzwanzigste Februar* [The Twenty-Fourth of February]. Werner himself played Kuntz, the old father, Schlegel Kurt the son, and a 'Fräulein von Zeuner' Trude the mother. Schlegel 'performed well', no doubt noting the superiority of his verse over Werner's semi-doggerel. Madame de Staël registered 'un

---

[369] Quoted in Georges Solovieff, 'Scènes de la vie de Coppet (récits d'hôtes européens)', *Cahiers staëliens*, 45 (1993-94), 46-66, ref. 50f.
[370] Jasinski, 478. *Briefe des Dichters Friedrich Ludwig Zacharias Werner*, ed. Oswald Floeck, 2 vols (Munich: Georg Müller, 1914), II, 212f.

effet terrible'.[371] The plot is simple: two family tragedies repeat themselves, at intervals, on the same fatal day; only in this way is the family curse lifted and grace triumphs. That was certainly the way that Werner, the later convert to Catholicism and ordained priest, wished to see it. But not all contemporaries shared this reading, especially after its performance in Weimar, perhaps abetted by the reading of Schlegel's translation of Calderón's *La devoción de la cruz*. The German stage meanwhile saw tokens of atavistic criminality invade its repertoire, as Adolf Müllner wrote *Die Schuld* [Guilt] and *Der neunundzwanzigste Februar* [29th of February] and Franz Grillparzer the sin of his youth, *Die Ahnfrau* [The Ancestress]. It had not been Werner's intention nor it was Schlegel's direct fault: minor or budding talents were simply unable to desist.

It was to be a year of removals and uncertainties. For Madame de Staël it involved the revelation of Benjamin Constant's marriage to Charlotte von Hardenberg; it saw the bewitching presence of Madame Récamier; it had Schlegel holding the fort at Coppet or wherever else his mistress required him to be. Albert returned from Vienna in April and was in Schlegel's care. The 'Groupe' only reconvened at Coppet during the summer months; otherwise it was fragmented, desultorily in Geneva or in Lyon. In 1809 her resolve to finish *De l'Allemagne* became more firm, but also her stated resolution to go to America after its completion. This would not be the hardship it might seem to be, for her father had presciently purchased property there. In *Dix Années d'exil* she even spoke of going to England via America.[372]

The work was however completed, not at Coppet but in France itself—Napoleon had only banned her from Paris—at the château of Chaumont on the Loire near Blois, the owner of which was absent in America.[373] To his sister-in-law Julie in Hanover Schlegel wrote describing the romantic setting and the historic associations; but his letter also contained echoes of French exile and the wistful hope of some day being in charge of his own fate.[374] For not only was Schlegel heavily committed to the proof-reading of *De l'Allemagne*: he was also superintending the French translation of his own Lectures. The fates of these two enterprises were soon to be intertwined.

We have to imagine not just one, but two, authors at Chaumont at work on the redaction of their important works. Madame de Staël and Schlegel

---

371 *Correspondance générale*, VI, 73.
372 *Dix Années*, 106.
373 Jasinski, 'Liste des principaux visiteurs à Chaumont et à Fossé', *Correspondance générale*, VII, 591-601.
374 *Briefe*, I, 253.

would both need the iron self-discipline of which they were both capable if need be. Around them was gathered the 'Groupe',[375] augmented by Madame Récamier, with whom just about everyone fell in love (Auguste de Staël especially). The young French émigré Adelbert de (later 'von') Chamisso was there, before writing *Peter Schlemihl*, circumnavigating the globe, and supplying Robert Schumann with the text of *Frauenliebe und –leben*, but now enjoying Madame de Staël's 'confidence'. There was time and leisure for the famous 'petite poste': the company would sit round a table and write letters to each other, or indeed from room to room. Perhaps the note from Madame Récamier to Schlegel is one such: 'Do you wish me to come and read English with you at 4 o'clock; if you are busy, we will choose another time—'.[376] Schlegel witnessed an altogether unusual event: the baptism of a twenty-two-year-old black man, 'born in Africa' ('un nègre né en Afrique' in the language of the time).[377] Who was he? Was he the property of the Franco-American owner of Chaumont and a reminder that slavery was still being practised in both countries? He had the honour of having Madame Récamier and Mathieu de Montmorency as godparents, and Schlegel wrote a sonnet in commemoration. The poem states that the slave was set free, and it affirms his belief (still) in the efficacy of the sacraments.[378] It confirmed Madame de Staël's opposition to the slave trade[379] and may well have been the germ of Auguste's and Albertine's later campaign against it, afforced when they met Wilberforce in England.

The translation of the Lectures was entrusted to Helmine de Chézy ('von' after her divorce from the orientalist) in Paris, once Schlegel had ascertained that she was linguistically competent; but the larger part was done by Chamisso (Helmine and Chamisso had an affair on the side); Prosper de Barante and even Madame de Staël herself are mentioned as helping.[380] This translation, which one can reconstruct from its later state, was making good progress, when it was hit by two related contingencies. A minor disruption occurred already in June, 1810, when the owner of Chaumont unexpectedly returned from America and they needed to shift camp to Fossé, near Blois. More serious altogether was the dismissal of Fouché as Napoleon's minister of police. Always a repulsive figure, he had

---

375 These in extenso *Correspondance générale*, VII, 209-243.
376 SLUB Dresden, Mscr. Dresd. App. 2712, B29 (5).
377 Pange, 265.
378 'Auf die Taufe eines Negers'. *Poetische Werke*, I, 333 (II, 292 has a note of the circumstances); *SW*, I, 374 (Böcking has added a wrong date).
379 [Charles Lenormant], *Coppet et Weimar*, 272.
380 Körner, *Botschaft*, 58f.; Pange, 273.

nevertheless not pursued Madame de Staël with the zeal that his superior expected. That would not apply to his replacement, René Savary, duke of Rovigo. Having presided at the execution of the duke d'Enghien, he was someone whom Napoleon could implicitly trust.

The manuscript of *De l'Allemagne* was for all intents and purposes finished early in 1810, having been copied out by Fanny Randall. For a publisher the author went to Gabriel-Henri Nicolle, who had also brought out *Corinne*.[381] Parts of the text went back as far as 1804, while other sections were of more recent provenance and reflected events and personages (such as Werner) at closer hand. Schlegel, whose knowledge and erudition were of great benefit to Madame de Staël, although occupied with his own translation and with the publication of the second part of his Lectures, played his part in the final proof-reading, as indeed anyone did who was in Chaumont or Fossé.

Censorship had been in operation in the Directory and then in imperial France certainly since 1800: Chateaubriand, Nodier, Marie-Joseph Chénier, even Kotzebue in translation had fallen foul of it, and it had been stepped up by the decree of 5 February in the very year 1810. Staël cannot have believed that her book would escape the attentions of the state authorities, especially since she and her family had been excluded from the amnesty extended on the occasion of Napoleon's marriage to Marie-Louise of Austria.[382] She had made it clear that she would sail for America once *De l'Allemagne* was out. Her every movement—Schlegel's too—was known to the secret police; Corbigny, the prefect of Loir-et-Cher, although well-disposed to Staël, was required nevertheless to report regularly to Savary. They knew of her unrepentant interest in politics, for instance her concern as the widow of a Swedish diplomat at the outcome of the succession to the Swedish throne. No sooner were the proofs of *De l'Allemagne* ready, than the book was placed under seal and passed on to the censors.[383]

They did their work thoroughly, but with a marked *parti pris*: they claimed to detect the hand of August Wilhelm Schlegel, 'the detractor of

---

[381] The contract in *De l'Allemagne*, I, xxv. The main sources of what follows are the Preface to *De l'Allemagne*, *Dix Années d'exil* (polemical and coloured by recent events), Henri Welschinger, *La Censure*, and the most recent and the most authoritative account, by Simone Balayé, 'Madame de Staël et le gouvernement impérial en 1810, le dossier de la suppression de *De l'Allemagne*', *Cahiers staëliens*, 19 (1974), 3-77. *Correspondance générale*, VII, xxiii-xxxiii (Chronologie staëlienne) gives details of Staël's movements.

[382] There is a letter of Staël to Prince Schwarzenberg written in the hope of his securing some intervention in her favour with the new Empress. Ullrichová, 86; *Correspondance générale*, VII, 137.

[383] Welschinger, *La Censure*, 176f.

French literature' (only partly true); they noted that the Emperor's role as patron of the arts and sciences had been played down (true); they read criticism of Austria into her remarks on that country (largely untrue); the section on Kant, they averred, lacked 'method and logic' (how true). Their recommendation was: publication, but with changes to the offending passages. Staël complied. The proofs then went to the highest authority himself: Napoleon. His main instruction was the removal of the section favourable to England. Sensing danger, Madame de Staël wrote directly to the Emperor and to Savary.[384] Savary replied with the austere and disdainful letter that now forms part of the Preface to *De l'Allemagne*. It is clear from that context that Auguste, not subject to the same ban as his mother, had taken the letter in person; Schlegel had sought to intervene with Corbigny.[385] Savary's letter cited in response her 'silence with regard to the Emperor' and treated her exile as a 'natural consequence' of the course that she had chosen.[386] He then invited her to select between Lorient, La Rochelle, Bordeaux and Rochefort as places of embarkation, all Atlantic ports from which she could sail to America.

On the same day that Savary saw Auguste and dispatched this letter, he also gave the order for the destruction of the proofs of *De l'Allemagne* and of all copies held by the printer. The proofs were then pulped. Napoleon's word was final: 'There is to be no further talk of this work or of that wretched woman'. Pleas for an audience fell on deaf ears.[387] Corbigny wrote to Savary, stating that Madame de Staël had passports and was about to embark for America with Schlegel. In fact she received a visa for Coppet and decided to return there instead. Nicolle the publisher was ruined and filed for bankruptcy (he had lost over 900,000 francs; Staël reimbursed the immediate expenses incurred).[388] It also spelled an end for the time being to any hopes Schlegel might have of seeing his Vienna Lectures published in France. Would they, with their marked anti-French bias, their praise of the Spanish and English nations (this section of course did not appear until 1811) not attract the same kind of unfavourable attention that *De l'Allemagne* was to receive in 1809-10? Was it not naïve to suppose that both works would not be heavily censored—or worse? And was it not clear that Schlegel, the author of the *Comparaison*, was regarded as her accomplice? Fortunately

---

384 Her letters to Napoleon *Correspondance générale*, VII, 258-260, 262-264, to Savary, 265-267.
385 Pange, 273; Welschinger, 184.
386 *De l'Allemagne*, I, 5-7.
387 Cf. to Napoleon *Correspondance générale*, VII, 273, 275f., to Queen Hortense 274f., 276f.
388 15,000 francs. *Ibid.*, 319.

the French translation had not reached the production stage, and Chamisso was able to retain his manuscript for future use. Schlegel himself wrote a fragment on the destruction of the first edition of *De l'Allemagne*, [389] which under the political circumstances had to remain anonymous.

The position late in 1810 was this. Barante Senior, the prefect of Léman, was instructed to prevent Madame de Staël from returning to France (she was to spend most of late 1810 and the spring of 1811 in Geneva). The French police bulletins of October and November 1810 were notable in drawing attention to the ideological dangers filtering in from Germany: Werner, with his offensive *Attila*; Fichte (of the *Reden an die deutsche Nation*), Gentz (in the pay of the English), and the Schlegel brothers. It was clear that Madame de Staël was associating with and even praising forces subversive of the French state. But *De l'Allemagne*, the seditious text, had not as Savary and Napoleon believed been totally suppressed. Nor with a print run of 5,000 and several sets of proofs in existence was this humanly possible. Both Nicolle and the printer seem to have colluded in this, and Madame de Staël—understandably—had not been absolutely open with the authorities. Three manuscript copies of *De l'Allemagne* and several sets of proofs have survived.[390] Publication would have to wait until 1813, and it would be in London, not in Paris.

Holed up in Berne

Writing to Schlegel from Paris on 5 December 1810, Henriette Mendelssohn, Dorothea Schlegel's sister, had this to say: 'How and where are you living? Some say, in Lausanne, Humboldt is supposed to have said it. Do you not have any bright new plans for next spring?'[391] Henriette was by no means the only correspondent left guessing as to Schlegel's whereabouts, and any plans that he had would have to coincide with Madame de Staël's own. She had meanwhile decided that it would be prudent for him to absent himself from Coppet or Geneva for a couple of months. It was in fact the first stage of planning for their eventual escape and for the preservation of a manuscript of *De l'Allemagne*. Thus began Schlegel's enforced sojourn in Berne,[392] which with intervals was to last until the summer of 1812. This

---

389 Untitled. SLUB Dresden, Mscr. Dresd. App. 2712, A11, 26. The publishing history of this fragment will be discussed by Stefan Knödler (forthcoming).
390 *De l'Allemagne*, I, i-iii; Balayé (1974), 72.
391 *Krisenjahre*, II, 185.
392 *Correspondance générale*, VII, 332.

exile ceased to be voluntary when early in January 1811, Barante was replaced as Léman prefect by the altogether more assiduous Guillaume Antoine Benoît Capelle, charming but ruthless.[393] He knew Schlegel to be the author of the *Comparaison* and thus no friend of the French nation. It all added to the precariousness of their situation.

From the relative security of Berne Schlegel could oversee the issue of passports for possible longer journeys. He could enjoy such local company as he found congenial; one such was Dr Koreff, from whom Madame de Staël had requested information about the 'new science' in Germany for her great work; another was Mathieu de Montmorency (also banned from Geneva),[394] with whom Schlegel had serious conversations about religion, as part of a general renewal of interest in things spiritual in the now fragmented Coppet circle. In the summer of 1811 and lasting into 1812, there was even an infatuation: with the admirable and gifted Marianne Haller,[395] the wife of the city architect and very much his junior. Schlegel could only enjoy her charms, her intelligence and her talk at a distance. It is certainly no coincidence that the two poems that he addressed to her[396] adopt the conventions of Minnesang, one of them even in an approximation to Middle High German stanzaic form, for this was the lady untouchable and inviolate whom one could approach only in verse.

It doubtless suited his general frame of mind, for Berne saw a last flurry of activity on the medieval front. It was to the robuster *Nibelungenlied* that Schlegel now devoted time and leisure, to collate the various manuscripts. Bernhard Joseph Docen, the Munich librarian and antiquarian and the subject of one of Schlegel's first reviews for the *Heidelberger Jahrbücher*, sent him material.[397] Friedrich Tieck, held up in Zurich by illness and lack of funds, inspected Bodmer's *Nachlass* on his behalf and sent copies of the *Heldenbuch* and other rare material.[398] The publisher Fuessli in Zurich had similar instructions, as did Mohr and Zimmer in Heidelberg.[399] Reimer

---

393 *Ibid.*, 338, 388.
394 As she wrote to Napoleon, *ibid.*, 461.
395 *Briefe*, II, 129; Pange, 349-351.
396 'Der Besuch und Abschied des Wanderers. 1812', which remained unpublished in his lifetime (*SW*, I, 286-288), and 'Thränen und Küße' and 'Der Abschied', published in Friedrich Schlegel's *Deutsches Museum* (1812), 179f. (*SW*, I, 291f.). Copies of the poems seem to have been in circulation. SLUB Dresden, Mscr. Dresd. e. 90, 21.
397 *Krisenjahre*, II, 203.
398 Bögel (2015), 242, 258, 262, 271. Schlegel also made a direct approach to the librarian in Zurich, Johann Jacob Horner. H. Blümner, 'Aus Briefen an J. J. Horner (1773-1831)', *Zürcher Taschenbuch auf das Jahr 1891* (Zurich: Höhr, 1891), 1-26, ref. 3-6.
399 Jenisch, 77.

even expressed an interest in publishing the *Nibelungenlied*.[400] Prosper de Barante and Sismondi were supplying him with information on the Troubadours.[401] But his present circumstances and those of the next years were neither congenial nor conducive to sustained study.

Reimer, who had acquired the rights of the Shakespeare translation from Madame Unger, was pleased with the sales of *Richard III* (a Machiavellian figure for the times, perhaps) and wondered if *Henry VIII* or *Macbeth* might be forthcoming. It was, however, to Mohr and Zimmer that Schlegel turned for the works that for him mattered in these last Swiss years: the completed Vienna Lectures and the *Poetische Werke*, both of which came out in 1811. These were not good times for publishers or for authors. North Germany, a market that a bookseller overlooked at his peril, was subject to the decree of 5 February 1810 that extended across the French imperial territories to all those under its jurisdiction; Zimmer, in neutral Baden, went ahead with the *Poetische Werke* nevertheless. Those who remembered the *Gedichte*, the first collection of his poetry, would note a few additions: the great Roman elegy for the—now proscribed— Madame de Staël, for instance, but also the threnody for Auguste Böhmer, now ten years dead but memorialized for as long as her step-father's poetry was read. They would see much with which they were familiar, the distichs for his brother Carl Schlegel, with whose name Friedrich Schlegel had ended the preface to *Ueber die Sprache und Weisheit der Indier*; the poetry from the *Athenaeum*, those sonnets of solidarity and friendship; the impudent attack on Kotzebue, who was still flourishing, luxuriating even, in the theatres of Europe; one would see a few patriotic poems, above all 'An Friedrich Schlegel' from *Prometheus* and an expression of fraternal loyalty. *Die Kunst der Griechen*, that elegy that had once adulated Goethe, was still there, more on account of its correct versification than its genuine sentiments. For Schlegel in 1812 joined with a number of his old Romantic associates in finding fault with Goethe's self-representation and self-stylisation in his autobiographical *Dichtung und Wahrheit* [Poetry and Truth]. He would have even more pleasure when in the same year Ludwig Tieck, a notoriously bad correspondent, surprised him by dedicating to him his collection *Phantasus* and reawakening the memory of Jena.

The collection also included the most intimate poem to the now dead Caroline, while the dedicatory poem, 'Zuschrift', spoke of the changes in life

---
400 *Briefe*, I, 274.
401 *Krisenjahre*, II, 220f. 226-228, 229-231.

and love, the ripening effects of time, too, the poet's gaining of maturity—in the wider interests of his fellow-countrymen.[402] Only a few compatriots now qualified for complimentary copies, though:[403] his family, of course, Heyne, his Göttingen teacher, Crown Prince Ludwig of Bavaria, Fouqué, Karl von Hardenberg, Ludwig Tieck, Goethe, Schelling—and Minna van Nuys. Here were some political tactics, some acts of deference, but also an acknowledgement of who belonged together, who had stood up for the other over the years—and there were not many of them left. The volumes sold well: Zimmer called for a reprinting in 1815;[404] the Swedish publisher Bruzelius issued it in 1812, as if anticipating Schlegel's arrival,[405] and in the same year a Viennese pirate edition, in handy duodecimo, indicated a similar need.[406] Perhaps Franz Schubert used it for the settings he made of poems by Schlegel.[407]

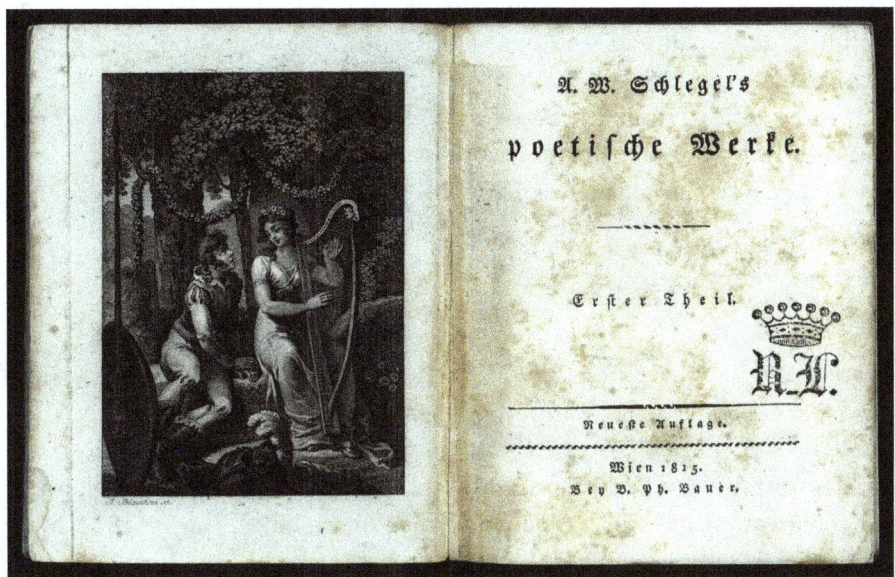

Fig. 18 August Wilhelm Schlegel, *Poetische Werke* (Vienna, 1815). Frontispiece and title page. Image in the public domain.

---

402 'Zuschrift', *Poetische Werke*, I, [iii]; *SW*, I, [3].
403 Jenisch (1922), 95.
404 *Ibid.*, 118 (not fulfilled).
405 August Wilhelm Schlegel, *Poetische Werke*, 2 vols (Uppsala: Bruzelius, 1812).
406 *A. W. Schlegel's poetische Werke. Neueste Auflage*, 2 parts (Vienna: B. Ph. Bauer, 1815).
407 These are: 'Abendlied für die Entfernte', 'Die gefangenen Sänger', 'Die verfehlte Stunde', 'Lob der Tränen', Sonett I, II, III (Petrarch), 'Sprache der Liebe', 'Wiedersehen'.

One poem, 'Tristan', newly added, but in no sense 'new', having been written in 1800, summed up what it had once meant to be Romantic.[408] It is essentially the account of Tristan's childhood and youth as recounted by Gottfried von Strassburg,[409] but now modernized, Gottfried in Ariostian stanzas. It was a reminder of how medieval chivalry and fable still informed the Renaissance (Ariosto, Tasso, Shakespeare, Cervantes), how the canonical poets all proceeded from the same sources and substance. Schlegel's own verse—a little arch and archaizing—shows the same competence that his sample from Ariosto in the *Athenaeum* had once displayed. It also brings out the Romantic dichotomy: on the one hand the call for the philological and scholarly establishment of old texts, the collating of variants that he was at that moment indulging in,[410] his etymological and grammatical study; and on the other the wish to communicate the spirit and essence of the Middle Ages through accessible modernisations—by Tieck, Görres, von der Hagen, Fouqué—that would reach the Germans, so much in need of cultural and political identity. It was—no-one said it aloud—also Wieland's legacy, the Ariostian hippogryph saddled up for the 'ride into the old romantic land'.[411] Schlegel's pirate publisher, Bauer in Vienna, saw the commercial potential of this when he issued his *Poetische Werke* with a frontispiece indebted—altogether more decorously, of course—to the engravings that had once added piquancy to Wieland's verse romances.

The Dash to Vienna

All of this was by way of a reminder to the Germans that he was 'still there' and not sequestered in remotest French Switzerland. It was Madame de Staël who in 1811 actually brought him back to the German lands, for the briefest duration and under hazardous circumstances, indeed a practice run for the great escape of the Staël entourage in the late spring of 1812. Most likely, Schlegel's stay in Berne had involved securing one of the manuscript copies of *De l'Allemagne* from possible police searches in Coppet. In June, 1811, while he was briefly back in Coppet, she decided on an altogether more adventuresome and risky operation: she asked Schlegel to travel

---

408 *Poetische Werke*, I, 98-134 (date given II, 284); *SW*, I, 100-126.
409 Up to verse 2325, Tristan's abduction by the merchants.
410 There is, for instance, a whole folder in the Nachlass devoted to Tristan. SLUB Dresden, Mscr. Dresd. e. 90. LXXIV, 2. Edith Höltenschmidt, *Die Mittelalter-Rezeption der Brüder Schlegel* (Paderborn etc.: Schöningh, 2000), 29-34.
411 As in the opening of Wieland's verse epic *Oberon*.

from Berne to Vienna with a copy, to be deposited in the safe hands of Friedrich Schlegel and to be recovered on their way eventually to Russian or Swedish asylum. The route to be taken was at this stage not clear, but Vienna would in all likelihood be the point of departure.

Schlegel set out at breakneck speed, taking little or no rest, often sleeping in the chaise conveying him—through Zurich, Munich, Braunau to Vienna (we do not have exact dates). In Vienna, he found his brother, doubtless told in advance of this imminent incursion, and not a little surprised.

Friedrich, after many frustrations and setbacks, had at last secured a post in Vienna.[412] It was not without the usual financial embarrassments or constant changes of domestic quarters; it did at least provide security. It bound him to a political ideology—that of the Habsburg state, its aspirations and its myths—yet who in these years could live free of such allegiances? Ludwig Tieck, living in his bolt hole in remotest Brandenburg, perhaps, or those two footloose if very different figures, Clemens Brentano and Zacharias Werner, until Rome claimed them, but most others could not afford that luxury.

Friedrich had hoped to give lectures in Vienna, and indeed the assiduous attendance that he danced on those in influence—Maurice O'Donnell included—was essentially to that end. The outbreak of war between Austria and Napoleon in the spring of 1809 put paid to such hopes; instead, he found himself a 'Hofsekretär' under Count Stadion, the minister for foreign affairs, with uniform (green coat with yellow buttons, red waistcoat with gold edging, braided tricorne, sword). One must picture—if one can—a corpulent Friedrich festooned in this finery, on horseback, in the rain, mud, heat and dust of armies on the march. It was his task to produce an army newspaper. Napoleon pushed back the Austrian troops, took Vienna, and forced the armies to retreat, first to Znaim in Moravia (today's Znojmo). Then followed the battles of Aspern and Wagram, an armistice, and the peace of Schönbrunn. The Austrian army had meanwhile withdrawn to Hungary. Friedrich suffered privations: with his usual intellectual curiosity he nevertheless explored in Buda the antiquities of the kingdom and met scholars and writers. He was not back in Vienna until the end of 1809. By now, the war gazette had become the *Österreichische Zeitung* and its purpose was to reach the general reading public and mould its political and cultural opinions. Under Metternich's guidance this merged into the

---

412 Most of what follows is based on the account in *KA*, VII, xlv-xciii.

Österreichischer Beobachter [Austrian Observer], for which Friedrich wrote a number of important articles and reviews. More significant for him were the lectures on history which he gave in Vienna from 19 February to 9 May, 1810. Not having a Madame de Staël to drum up princes and counts, his lectures were not quite the social spectacle that his brother August Wilhelm's had been; still, the audience included 'twenty duchesses and princesses' nevertheless.

They were 'Lectures on Modern History' [*Vorlesungen über die neuere Geschichte*], which meant simply European history since the barbarian invasions. And these lectures, delivered in the fine historiographical prose of which Friedrich was capable, had a distinctly Austrian accent. Out of the decline and fall of the old order would emerge figures who symbolized the movements of the times: Arminius, Attila (but a Hunnish leader quite different from Madame de Staël's), Charlemagne (the imperial political and ecclesiastical order and the rise of chivalry), Rudolf of Habsburg, Maximilian, Charles V, and so on. There were of course setbacks to the Habsburg narrative, such as the Reformation or the Thirty Years' War, there were 'might have beens', alliances which could have ensured a European *pax romana*, had French ambitions not frustrated them. And the fine rhetoric of delivery did not conceal a historical teleology and a message for the times, something that a political journalist and intellectual was expected to supply.

Friedrich was able to send a copy of these lectures to his brother on 29 April, 1811,[413] and in one of his notes to Madame de Staël on his way home August Wilhelm wrote from Zurich that he would have secured more copies had he known that people were scrambling to secure one.[414] Otherwise he found no time for distractions in Vienna, no theatre, no Prater, not even the leisure to read Friedrich's various political writings,[415] just enough for Friedrich's stepson Philipp Veit to do his portrait.[416] The brothers had time to talk about their respective present positions: of course Friedrich wanted August Wilhelm to stay in Austria, certainly not to enter into the service of one of those kings enthroned by the grace of Napoleon (August Wilhelm pointedly did not return via Munich, the seat of one such monarch). The

---
413 *Krisenjahre*, II, 199. Published as *Ueber die neuere Geschichte. Vorlesungen gehalten in Wien im Jahre 1810* (Vienna: Karl Schaumburg, 1811).
414 Pange, 302.
415 *Ibid.*, 302f.
416 Suhr, *Philipp Veit* (1991), 21. The portrait has not survived, *ibid.*, 339.

rest of August Wilhelm's letter strikes a much more sombre, even pathetic note:

> It is for us brothers of course a great privation to be separated from each other without any prospect of meeting again; he was quite hypochondriac and in lowest spirits before I arrived, but our conversations picked him up again. When I left, he went with me and then he turned back, alone, on foot across a bare and treeless plain, a truly sad image of our separation.[417]

When they did meet again, a year later, August Wilhelm was on his way to embark on a short political career that bore some similarity to his brother's. Unlike Friedrich, who was to deliver three more big lecture cycles in Vienna and Dresden, August Wilhelm was only once again to lecture to a general public, much later in Berlin. His lectures on history embraced the ancient world, not the modern, and they were for a university audience.

De l'Allemagne: The Book Itself

The text deposited with his brother Friedrich, *De l'Allemagne*, was a familiar one, for August Wilhelm's hand was evident in some of the sections, and we know of his presence during the process of composition, redaction and publication. By the same token there was much that was alien, for their work methods, Madame de Staël's and his, and their modes of expression, were their own. *De l'Allemagne* was idiosyncratically and unrepentantly hers: he would never have written anything containing sections so uncoordinated, garrulous, anecdotal or unsystematic. It was a reflection of her own experience, sometimes even shared with him, yet it was so much limited to what she had actually seen and taken in,[418] was so ideologically slanted to her needs, that questions of mere attributions or informants— who helped her with this part or that—became largely irrelevant. There were others of course who had filled in details, Baron Voght for instance, Dr Koreff in her account of the 'new science'; Schlegel (who else?) certainly gave her guidance on German versification and German art, indeed he received frequent honorific mention, even a short section on himself and his brother Friedrich, citing them as Germany's premier critics.[419] The main

---

417 Pange, 300.
418 As shown by Melitta Wallenborn, *Deutschland und die Deutschen in Mme de Staëls De l'Allemagne*, Europäische Hochschulschriften Reihe XIII, 232 (Frankfurt am Main etc.: Peter Lang, 1998).
419 *De l'Allemagne*, III, 329-348.

thrusts, emphases, the misapprehensions, wilful or unconscious, as said, were her own. There was little point in asking, as some contemporaries were to do, whether Schlegel had checked it through.[420] Yet it may not be by pure coincidence that the following words occur in the concluding remarks to her section on Schlegel, of a certain dignity and nobility and summing up this enterprise and those that had come before it, *De la littérature*, and *Corinne*, the book on Italy that was resolved as fiction:

> Nations should serve as guides one to one another, and they would all be wrong were they to deprive each other of the enlightenment that they can afford one another mutually. There is something very strange about the difference between one people and another: climate, landscape, language, government, above all the events of history, a force ranking above all others, contribute to these diversities, and no-one, however superior he may be, can guess at what is going on naturally in the mind of the one who lives on a different soil and breathes a different air: one will do well in every country to receive alien thoughts; for, in this way hospitality makes the fortune of the one who receives it.[421]

These were certainly words that Schlegel could affirm, and the reference to hospitality could have been designed to suit him. He had been with her in a significant number of the places that she had visited and which featured in *De l'Allemagne*, Berlin: Weimar, Dresden, Vienna. He had, however, not been at her side when she encountered the persons and places that provide some of the great set-pieces: the Moravian colony in Thuringia, the festival at Interlaken, Pestalozzi's educational institute. He knew also which places and which persons she chose to omit (no Munich, no Berlin salons, no Gentz, for instance) and which individuals she chose to elevate to a status largely ordained by her and her own personal acquaintance. Thus there is far more on Jacobi than on Schelling, for example, or almost as much on Johannes von Müller as on Herder; there is a section on Jean Paul, whom Schlegel disliked; there is certainly more on Zacharias Werner than perhaps he merited, but that is doubtless preferable to the almost total neglect from which he has subsequently suffered.

---

420 Bonstetten, expressing his concern in 1808 about possible Schlegel influence, need not have worried: 'nous craignons tous et toutes que dans votre ouvrage sur la litterature [sic] allemande vous ne vous soyez entrainée [sic] dans les idées des Schlegel et à la Schlegel'. *Bonstettiana*, X, i, 517.
421 *De l'Allemagne*, III, 352f.

Schlegel's own style was different, the Vienna Lectures with their crisp distinctions, their systematic structural and chronological approach, compared with the more impressionistic, associative and eclectic manner of *De l'Allemagne*. He might also have reflected that his material, his insights, his plot-summaries could be implicitly relied upon for their accuracy, while hers could not, being often second-hand, tailored to her needs, and sometimes wilfully wrong (as in her account of the plot of *Faust*).[422] He may have approved of the general principle enunciated in *De l'Allemagne* that the theatre is a school of political education, but it is doubtful whether he would have sanctioned the large and disproportionate amount of space devoted to the plays of Goethe and Schiller, whom he had treated rather peremptorily in Vienna. He did not share the admiration of England that is the largely unspoken sub-text of *De l'Allemagne*. He may have despaired at her account of Kant, until he recognized, as one must, that she was using him, as so many other figures and ideas, to further her own cultural and political aims,[423] or that she was calling for the study of serious philosophy as opposed to frivolous scepticism or materialism.[424]

Schlegel's Vienna Lectures were undergirded by the idea of the 'Nation' and had maintained that the drama, in order to reflect the spirit of a people, had to be truly national. There were allusions enough to the times in which they were delivered, arguments for the audience to understand why Germany in its present state could not emulate Athens or Golden Age Spain or Elizabethan England. In that sense his Lectures were a continuation of debates and agonizings since 1806 over what had gone wrong, why the old order had collapsed, why the German lands had fallen to Napoleon one after the other and had been divided and ruled as he saw fit. In postulating how the theatre might contribute to the building of the nation, Schlegel was doing his patriotic duty, less outspokenly of course than political voices like, say, Arndt, Gentz, or Stein, while performing it nevertheless.

The Staëlian view was different, not of course its opposition to Napoleon and its veiled, and sometimes even explicit, references to tyranny and

---

422 Isbell (1994), 70-90.
423 Julia von Rosen, 'Deutsche Ästhetik in *De l'Allemagne*: Eine Transferstudie am Beispiel der Kant-Interpretation Mme de Staëls', in Udo Schöning and Frank Seemann (eds), *Madame de Staël und die Internationalität der europäischen Romantik. Fallstudien zur interkulturellen Vernetzung*, Göttinger Beiträge zur Nationalität, Internationalität und Intermedialität von Literatur und Film, 2 (Göttingen: Wallstein, 2003), 173-202, ref. 198.
424 Balayé, 'À propos du "Préromantisme": continuité ou rupture chez Madame de Staël', in: Balayé (1994), 291-306, ref. 304.

despotism (as in her analysis of Goethe's *Egmont*, Schiller's *Wilhelm Tell*, or most notably of Werner's *Attila*).[425] But hers was essentially a pre-Jena-Auerstädt, pre-Wagram Germany, reflecting her own experience of 1803-04 and the precarious peace of those days. True, with its territorial divisions, it had then as now lacked a capital city, something that the Germans themselves had been deploring for several generations and that Friedrich Schlegel had noted with regret in *Europa*. While Berlin, Vienna and Weimar had been a kind of political, cultural and intellectual substitute for a metropolis, they were in 1810, and certainly in 1813 when *De l'Allemagne* appeared, very different places from those that she described in the ever so slightly roseate hues of 1803 or 1808. The idea that she enunciated of the individual liberty of the intellectual or writer—something, she averred, that the Germans enjoyed while the French did not—took little account of recent events, conveniently overlooked the stultifying censorship in Austria, or failed to acknowledge that Germany's very fragmentation into different centres of academic or intellectual concentration, or the flexibility of its book trade, had something to do with such freedom of expression as there was. For her part, she was not interested in institutions or society other than its highest echelons, or indeed too many tiresome factual details. The important thing was to point to what France did not have, but might have, if it let another nation be its guide and inspiration. It might see alternatives to centralism, control, despotism and acts of arbitrary tyranny. Readers in France might have cause to ponder issues that were not specific to Germany, but which might acquire a new urgency through an openness to another culture: reason, intelligence, faith, imagination, philosophy, mental energy.[426]

Schlegel of course had never been inhibited by the lack of a cultural or political centre, and one side of him remained a loyal Hanoverian, but his emphasis on German 'National-Geist' went hand in hand easily with a more cosmopolitan lifestyle (writing in French), looking beyond frontiers to a community of scholars, a *république des lettres*. It had been a way of transcending the provincial narrowness of Jena and it would also overcome the restrictions of Bonn, for his later scholarly career was oriented as much to Paris and London as to the Prussian university where he was to live and work.

---

425 Isbell, 94f.
426 Balayé (1994), 302.

The Last Days in Coppet

There were perhaps very good reasons for Schlegel to keep his distance from Coppet in the final twelve or so months in Switzerland. In fact he was only there from October to November, 1811, and from March to May in 1812.[427] He was not welcome to the French authorities, Capelle the prefect stating in a confidential note that Schlegel, while not a man of malice, was nevertheless imbued with the German spirit, thus anti-French and ready to carry out the every wish of 'la dame de Staël'.[428] These were excellent grounds for wishing him out of the Léman department.[429] Already in August Schlegel had warned Madame de Staël that Capelle was her 'gaoler', intent in keeping such an important person as herself under lock and key.[430] As 1811 merged into 1812, she was more and more on tenterhooks, in fear of prison,[431] planning a means of escape, but by which route? America was now ruled out, although as late as November 1811 she was contemplating it.[432] Italy seemed a possibility, but events supervened to prevent that outlet. They became more and more dependent on snippets of news regarding the political situation in Europe. Could Turkey be a route, once the Russo-Turkish border was secure? Or heartland Russia itself, when Napoleon's Russian campaign made a traverse from Galicia and Poland to Riga impossible?

She tried distractions, a last flurry of theatre,[433] but the great days of Coppet were essentially over.[434] She drafted something on Richard Coeur de Lion; she even completed articles for Michaud's *Biographie Universelle*, on Aspasia and on Camões, even on her Necker parents (under a pseudonym). The Schlegel brothers' erudition on Camões—Friedrich's article in *Europa*, and August Wilhelm's personal assistance—eased the way. Hearing of the death of Heinrich von Kleist in November, 1811, she began to draft those *Réflexions sur le suicide* that would come out in Stockholm in 1812,

---

427 Jasinski, 480.
428 Pange, 328.
429 But cf. Sismondi: 'l'on a forcé à éloigner d'elle M[onsieur] Schlegel, qui certainement ne devait pas s'attendre à exciter l'animadversion d'aucune autorité, et qui, perdu dans des travaux purement littéraires, étranger à toute politique même spéculative, n'a pu que par une erreur bien étrange devenir un moment suspect'. *Bonstettiana*, X, ii, 1124.
430 Pange, 315.
431 'menaces de prison', *Correpondance générale*, VII, 503.
432 *Ibid.*, 486, 508.
433 Rougemont, 90.
434 Cf. Bonstetten: 'Schlegel ist weg, der Hof von Coppet ist nun öde, verlassen'. *Bonstettiana*, X, ii, 1118, also 1140.

questioning the motives of those who take their own lives when there is a fatherland to die for. (It would be Tieck and Fouqué who would take the first steps to rehabilitate Kleist's memory.) When Capelle used chicanery to challenge the validity of the original purchase of Coppet by the Neckers, it was Schlegel who was able to use the good offices of his Heidelberg publisher to secure the deeds.[435]

The reason for the delay in leaving Coppet for the next stage of exile was however Albert-Jean-Michel de Rocca. Known as John, a young lieutenant invalided home from the guerilla wars in Spain (he needed the support of a crutch), dashing, handsome, and hardly twenty-three, Madame de Staël first saw him in the winter of 1810-11, and it was love at first sight. Discrepancy of age had never been a barrier to her emotional attachments (witness Maurice O'Donnell). Whereas O'Donnell was prudent enough to avoid a love entanglement with a woman twenty-two years his senior, Rocca had no such inhibitions, and she did not discourage him. There was no question of his being her intellectual equal, on the contrary, but Byron's later testimony to Rocca's good manners and poise (both had triumphed over disability) cannot be brushed aside.[436]

It made Schlegel's position in Coppet invidious, his enforced stay in Berne more attractive, and the presence of Madame Haller there all the more welcome. It also brought the nature of his relationship with Madame de Staël to a head. On his side, he could not aspire to claiming her affection, let alone her love; he was merely indispensable and fraternally so; on her side she permitted no rivals, but at the same time she was free to indulge her passions as she chose. Small wonder that he in a letter of April or May, 1811[437] reproached her with folly and heartlessness towards him. For was he not now the butt of everyone's malice, the aspirant lover, as it were cuckolded by a stripling of twenty-two? One can understand why he always referred to Rocca as 'Caliban' and why this name stuck.

Worse—for Schlegel at least—was to follow. Already in May, 1811 Germaine and Rocca entered into a solemn engagement to marry, and in the late summer she found herself pregnant—in her forty-sixth year. Of the official Coppet circle only Fanny Randall was party to the secret; Schlegel never found out while there. Germaine was to the outside world

---

435 Pange, 331; Jenisch, 101.
436 *Byron's Letters and Journals*, ed. Leslie A. Marchand, 12 vols plus 1 supplement (London: Murray, 1973-1994), III, 231; Pange, 288.
437 Pange, 287.

suffering from dropsy: even Zacharias Werner in Rome heard of it.[438] The authorities however did know and did nothing to prevent the circulation of ribald verses on the subject.[439] There was of course now no question of an Italian journey, for on April 7, 1812 she gave birth to a son. (Schlegel, on his last visit to Coppet, had not noticed anything unusual, nor had the Staël sons.)[440] Louis-Alphonse, the poor, frail, semi-retarded late love-child was taken to the village of Nyon, baptized under an assumed name and fostered with the pastor and his wife until such time as his parents were to return—in 1814. This was 'Alphonse', the half-sibling whose welfare later fell to Albertine's responsibility as duchess of Broglie, and who features frequently in her letters to Schlegel.

Schlegel meanwhile received visitors in Berne, Koreff, Prince Albrecht of Prussia, and Mathieu de Montmorency. He was gratified to hear that Madame Necker de Saussure, a Staël cousin, had agreed to take over from Chamisso the translation of his Vienna Lectures. It was in Berne, too, that he received through his sister-in-law Julie Schlegel in Hanover the news of the death of his mother, on 21 January, 1811.[441] She had reached the age of 76, but her last months had been full of suffering; she joined her husband Johann Adolf and two of her sons in the burial-ground of the Court and Town Church in the Hanover Neustadt. A letter from Mathieu de Montmorency of 3 March tried to offer him consolation for his loss: 'religion alone can sustain the soul in these great trials'.[442] It may have been in response to this letter of condolence that Schlegel wrote the (undated) long reply which is both a spiritual confession but in effect also a leave-taking from the religious urgings of the last decade.[443] He alludes to his reading of mystical and theosophical authors (Guyon, Fénelon, Saint-Martin) and to his once expressed aim of returning to the bosom of the Church (from his disparaging remarks about the Reformation, it is clear which 'church' is meant). Protestant worship no longer met the needs of his heart: it was in Catholic shrines that he found a first solace. What is more, he had come to see the role of religion as leading the seeker, through philosophy, to the

---

438 Baldensperger, 128f.
439 Pierre Kohler, *Madame de Staël et la Suisse*, 603.
440 *Ibid*.
441 Letter of 20 February, 1811, Mscr. Dresd. e. 90, XIX, 23 (53). Date in Hanover, Ev. Luth. Stadtkirchenkanzlei.
442 *Krisenjahre*, II, 191.
443 *Coppet et Weimar*, 194-202. A very different account of Schlegel's religious development is offered by Josef Körner, 'August Wilhelm Schlegel und der Katholizismus', *Historische Zeitschrift* 139 (1928-29), 62-83.

'gate of the sanctuary'; art and poetry, similarly, were but a reflection of the 'celestial beauty'. Nevertheless he had remained undecided, despite voices urging him, his brother's, Karl von Hardenberg's and others'. Nowhere is there a word about confession or doctrine: the outward signs and symbols manifested in the act of worship, he claimed, brought us an assurance of the divine presence. Much of this was familiar and would not have been out of place in *Die Gemälde*. A year later, he was looking for a church in which to meditate and express grief over his mother's death:[444] more than ten years earlier, he had sought similar solace over Auguste. With his mother now dead, a major barrier to his conversion was removed, but yet he never acted on what in the last analysis were feelings (French 'sentiments'). His remarks in 1812 on the reasons for Winckelmann's conversion—for him frivolous and unworthy[445]—suggested that 'sentiments' could not suffice, nor would they be enough to sustain him during the forthcoming tests on his physical, mental and intellectual energies.

During the last brief sojourn in Coppet he set his house in order, sorting through letters and documents, placing seals on correspondence that was to remain unopened until after his death, leaving behind a tidy settlement of his affairs. He must have assumed that he would never return, for this cache was to remain undiscovered for over 130 years. He left behind too his 1,083-volume library, carefully ordered according to incunables, quartos, and octavos. One could see here the books that had occupied him during this part of his career—the material on Dante, Shakespeare, Homer, Roman antiquities, the *Nibelungenlied*, the fine arts—and some, like the 1806 volumes of the *Asiatick Researches*, that pointed to future preoccupations.[446]

Madame de Staël, hardly recovered from her confinement and her health compromised for the remaining five years of her life, was now making serious plans for escape, to meet Schlegel at Berne and receive the passports that he had obtained. Rocca and Albert would join them later. No-one must suspect anything: there were to be no visible preparations for departure. On the afternoon of 23 May, 1812, Madame de Staël, Auguste, Albertine and Uginet went out for a carriage drive in Coppet. It was to end in St Petersburg.

---

444 Pange, 351.
445 *SW*, XII, 382.
446 'Verzeichniß meiner Bücher im December 1811'.

3.3 The Flight: Caught Up in History

The carriage drive to Moscow, St Petersburg and Stockholm did not mean that Schlegel and Madame de Staël took leave of their immediate pasts or embarked on a completely new phase of life. In a sense she had been traversing Europe since late 1803. Schlegel was in her company for a large part of that time. Why not an even grander tour? Yet this journey was in every other respect different. French sources speak of a 'fuite' or 'évasion', German of an 'Entrinnen', 'Entweichen' or 'Verschwinden', thus flight, release, escape, getaway.[447] She saw no option but to remove herself and those nearest to her to the safety of countries where Napoleon's writ did not run. Stockholm lent itself, because she was the widow of a Swedish envoy and baron. Her children were technically Swedish citizens, and she wished to see her sons employed in the service of their adopted country.[448] There too her old friend Marshal Bernadotte, through tricks of fortune characteristic of this Napoleonic age, was now the Prince Royal and the heir presumptive to the Swedish throne. He would later reign (1818-44) as King Charles XIV John. Her ultimate goal was however England, the land that in her eyes could do no wrong (or very little).[449] While she was there, Schlegel was for the first time since 1804 really his own master, staying in Germany as the Prince Royal's amanuensis and right-hand man.

Of course neither Staël nor Schlegel could separate themselves from their literary reputations, bound up as they were with their political confessions of allegiance, her defiantly anti-Napoleonic stance, his evocations of the German past. These were the years of Europe-wide engagement with Staël's and Schlegel's texts. He was already the much-celebrated author of the Vienna Lectures, which had been published in full in 1811, and were to appear in French in 1813 and in English in 1815. His highly patriotic contributions to his brother's periodical *Deutsches Museum* (1812) could be read even as their author was passing through the Austrian lands and into the Russian Empire. She was to bring out her *Réflexions sur le suicide* in 1813

---

447 Cf. *Bonstettiana*, XI, i, 119.
448 Cf. her letter to Bernadotte of 19 August, 1812. Torvald Höjer, 'Madame de Staëls brev till Kronprins Carl Johan 1812-1816', *Historisk Tidskrift* 80 (1960), 156-176, ref. 159.
449 John Quincy Adams, the American minister to St Petersburg, representing a nation technically at war with Great Britain, remarked wryly: 'She is one of the highest enthusiasts for the English cause that I have ever seen'. *The Russian Memoirs of John Quincy Adams. His Diary from 1809 to 1814* (New York: Arno, 1970), 401.

while they were still in Sweden (with a fulsome dedication to Bernadotte). However, the world had to wait until late 1813 for the appearance of *De l'Allemagne*. It would be issued in London by John Murray.

Somewhere along the road, perhaps already in Coppet, perhaps later, Schlegel had written an account of himself and his literary persona ('Selbstbeschreibung').[450] It was an unashamed self-affirmation of his past achievements, of his collaborations with his brother Friedrich, above all of his powers as a poet, a reminder to himself that this was perhaps his real métier.[451] Whatever history's judgment on Schlegel the poet may be, this document does make one wonder. For these were years that saw him producing not poetry but a great deal of prose, political rhetoric in fact. True, his Vienna Lectures[452] or his reviews for the *Heidelberger Jahrbücher* could be said to have a generally patriotic tenor, but Schlegel's writings in the years 1812-14—pamphlets and broadsheets—were overtly political, and it is conceivable that these ephemera in their various manifestations reached a wider readership than anything poetic or academic that he wrote. After this interlude of roughly two years, Schlegel was to turn again to pure scholarly activity, involving learning the basics of Sanskrit. This was to form the foundation of the academic career that opened up to him— perhaps *faute de mieux*—after Madame de Staël's death in 1817.

As for Staël, her hold on him remained a strong as ever, even during the time of their separation, while she was in England and he in Germany. Like her he was a fugitive from Napoleon. His association with her had seen him banned from Geneva. Now he was fleeing in her company, finding refuge in Russia, a country at war with Napoleon, and then in Sweden, where the Prince Royal and the Tsar had just concluded a treaty. Once Sweden and France were formally at war, Schlegel had no option but to stay close to Bernadotte. To what extent the political opinions that he expressed were the Prince Royal's, Madame de Staël's, or his own, will concern us later. For Napoleon and his agents they were seditious, insurrectionary even. Savary intercepted their—often indiscreet—letters and passed on all the essential information to his master: Staël's factotum Eugène Uginet was given an unnerving police interrogation when he

---

450 Cornelia Bögel, 'Fragment einer unbekannten autobiographische Skizze aus dem Nachlass August Wilhelm Schlegels', *Athenäum*, 22 (2012), 165-177.
451 There were plans to issue a third volume of his poetry in 1812. Jenisch, 109.
452 Stressed later in his 'Berichtigung einiger Mißdeutungen', *SW*, VIII, 251 ('vaterländische Gesinnung').

returned to France in 1813,⁴⁵³ showing that they knew everything. When later comparing his own career in these years with the academic idyll in Heidelberg enjoyed by his old adversary Johann Heinrich Voss, Schlegel was not exaggerating in saying that he could have been arrested for treason in French territory.⁴⁵⁴

Emotionally, he seemed as bound as ever. While even in the company of John Rocca, the father of her child, Madame de Staël put it to him that he was 'part of the family' and should 'return to the nest on the completion of your noble task. [...] I need so very much to believe that I am not separated from you'.⁴⁵⁵ Who could resist this and other such blandishments, even if Schlegel hated the 'Caliban' at her side, if she sought to undermine his hopes of marriage, if she belittled his philological studies? It was also tempered with a sobering knowledge: however much Madame de Staël might want his presence, when together they could never agree, they jarred on each other.⁴⁵⁶

Of course, during the years 1812-14, when he was effectively homeless and stateless,⁴⁵⁷ there was no other option open to him. Being a 'part of the family' also meant sharing its losses. Poor, feckless Albert de Staël, on whom Schlegel had lavished so much attention, was to be killed in a duel in 1813. In 1815, Albertine, now sixteen and a young beauty, was married to Victor, duke of Broglie. There were other reminders. He would learn that Schelling had remarried and had taken as his wife Pauline Gotter, who had once played with Auguste, Schlegel's beloved step-daughter.⁴⁵⁸ He seemed destined—the future would bear this out—to see those entrusted to his charge die premature deaths or elude his affections. All this may help in part to explain the tone in his letters, not without some self-pity, of stoical acceptance of an unfulfilled lot, the sense that one had to accommodate to what life had in store and not expect happiness.

---

453 Norman King, 'Un récit inédit du grand voyage de Madame de Staël (1812-1813)', *Cahiers staëliens*, 4 (1966), 4-23, esp. 22-23.
454 *SW*, VIII, 243.
455 Pange, 407. The French original reads: 'Songez que vous êtes de la famille; et revenez au nid quand vous aurez terminé votre noble entreprise. [...] J'ai tant besoin de ne pas me croire séparée de vous!'
456 *Ibid.*, 438.
457 Something that he stresses repeatedly. Cf. *Briefe*, I, 292; Norman King, 'A. W. Schlegel et la guerre de libération: le mémoire sur l'état de l'Allemagne', *Cahiers staëliens*, 16 (1973), 1-31, ref. 30.
458 Pange, 440.

But what of Schlegel the private secretary to the Prince Royal? A secret political agent, following armies on horseback;[459] wearing a splendid uniform,[460] in court dress;[461] rubbing shoulders with the high and mighty, corresponding with the Tsar, Metternich (Bernadotte as a matter of course); formulating state policy, like Stein or Gentz? There was nothing new in these associations: the visits to Italy, Germany and Austria, while under different circumstances, had been a first habituation. In a way the rest simply followed. In these years people changed in station and allegiance as chance and circumstances demanded. This applied not only to Bernadotte, but also to his fellow general from the Revolution, Moreau, later killed in battle at Tsar Alexander's side; the Corsican Pozzo di Borgo was a Russian envoy; the German-born generals Tettenborn and Bennigsen were commanding Russian armies. Why could not Schlegel the Hanoverian write pamphlets in Swedish service?

The Wars of Liberation saw men of letters or science pitched into political and military action regardless of their background. Fouqué the Prussian baron and the Jewish-born Philipp Veit were comrades-in-arms. The middle-aged Fichte ruined his health as an academic firebrand in Berlin. Younger men, some of whom had heard Schlegel in Jena or Berlin, rallied to the colours. Fouqué had a horse shot under him;[462] the 'Sekonde-Lieutenant und Professor'[463] Henrik Steffens became one of the more unlikely members of Scharnhorst's, Gneisenau's and Blücher's suite; Karl August Varnhagen von Ense, a survivor of Wagram, witnessed the battle for Hamburg in 1813; Wolf von Baudissin was imprisoned while a Danish diplomat; Ernst Moritz Arndt, later Schlegel's colleague in Bonn, went to Moscow and St Petersburg and from there eventually to Paris as the secretary to Baron Stein; Schlegel's step-nephew Philipp Veit served under Lützow. Only the unmartial Ludwig Tieck, dedicating his collection *Phantasus* to Schlegel in 1812 and evoking the great days of Jena, kept well out of the fray in his bolt hole in the Mark of Brandenburg. Unlike some of these, Schlegel did not see action and generally kept back with the headquarters staff. Not for him

---

459 Or, to his displeasure, with the baggage train. Pange, 454.
460 As reported by his step-nephew Philipp Veit. Raich, II, 226.
461 Which is what he was wearing in Ernst Moritz Arndt's malicious account. Ernst Moritz Arndt, *Meine Wanderungen und Wandelungen, Ausgewählte Werke*, ed. Heinrich Meisner and Robert Geerds, 16 vols (Leipzig: Hesse, [1908]), VIII, 45f.
462 Pange, 447.
463 Henrich Steffens, *Was ich erlebte. Aus der Erinnerung niedergeschrieben*, 12 vols (Breslau: Max, 1840-44), VIII, 152. He gives a brief account of his military service in a letter to Friedrich Schlegel. *KA*, XXIX, 35f.

the mud, the dust, the fleas, the corpses, the dead horses, the Cossacks, the detritus of the battlefield, the first-hand narratives of great encounters. In the rearguard, he would exchange the sword for the pen,[464] as a forceful writer in both German and French. Perhaps among all these men only Henrik Steffens could claim to have been present both at one of the great intellectual events of the age, the gathering of the Jena circle in 1798, and also 'the focus of one the greatest historical happenings of our times', the battle of Leipzig.[465]

Through Germany, Austria and Russia, to Sweden[466]

On 5 May, 1812 Madame de Staël, Albertine, Auguste, her factotum Uginet and his wife, plus two servants, set off through Switzerland in the direction of Berne. Here, they were joined by Rocca, Albert, and Schlegel, who had been entrusted with securing passports for the next leg of the journey. Auguste then left them, to return eventually to Paris and the irresistible charms of Madame Récamier. He would rejoin them in Stockholm. Here too Staël told Schlegel the truth about her recent confinement. He had no option but to swallow his chagrin and concentrate on the main task of their all somehow reaching Sweden. It would be different from their previous journeyings, for she was now in poor health and less able to withstand discomforts. Schlegel was in effect a proscribed person, Rocca was a French citizen. It seemed prudent to separate them from the Staël family party and for them all to meet up in Vienna. Thus Schlegel the 'ami de mon âme' shared a carriage with the lover *en titre*. From Berne they went via Zurich and Winterthur and then briefly through the Bavarian controlled Tyrol.

There they encountered the realities of Napoleonic redistributions of territory, for the old imperial city of Innsbruck, with its associations with Maximilian, was now Bavarian. Rather than reflect on the recent fate of Andreas Hofer and his Tyrolean uprising, it was expedient to pass quickly through to Salzburg and Munich and gain Austrian soil. The parties met up at Linz and proceeded to Vienna. She would soon realize that Austria had changed since 1808. Military defeats and the marriage of Napoleon with the emperor's daughter Marie-Louise were the chief political reasons for Austria's official pro-French policies. Austria's restraint in the struggle

---

464 An expression which he frequently uses. Cf. *Briefe*, I, 299f.
465 Steffens, *Was ich erlebte*, VII, 69.
466 The main sources for this section are *Dix Années d'exil*, *Carnets de voyage*, Ullrichová.

against Napoleon's 'world domination' was to be a subject of frustration for Staël and for Schlegel the budding political pamphleteer.

During their short visit to Vienna (6-22 June) they slipped without effort into the life of the *grand monde* which they had so enjoyed in 1808. They could renew contact with the Prince de Ligne, or with Friedrich Gentz; Wilhelm von Humboldt was now Prussian envoy. The Schlegel brothers saw each other for the last time until 1818. There was however the need to obtain passports for their forward journey: visits to the Russian and Swedish ambassadors became as much a necessity as a social duty. They were soon to learn the unpalatable fact that Austria could present a different aspect if one came as a fugitive, even one of fame and high rank. It was not the same nation as set out in the somewhat idealized pages of *De l'Allemagne*. It had a secret police, not as efficient as Savary's in France— it bumbled, it circumlocuted—but unpleasant nevertheless. They were subjected to constant surveillance, and it was even to emerge that one of their servants was in police pay. Gentz, Madame de Staël's old admirer, did what he could. His master Metternich, less enamoured than he, was absent and did nothing.

Which route would they take? Peace had been concluded between Russia and Turkey. It would now be technically possible to travel via Constantinople to England, but Madame de Staël hated the sea. It was one reason why she had preferred exile in Coppet to banishment in America. The only option was a journey across Prussian Silesia and Poland to St Petersburg. Napoleon however put paid to that particular scheme by declaring war on Russia. Earlier in the year Sophie Tieck-Bernhardi-Knorring had with her husband just managed to reach Estonia by that route. Ernst Moritz Arndt, only a few weeks before the Staëls, had had to opt for Galicia, the Ukraine and Moscow as he journeyed to meet up with Baron Stein, his master. The Staël-Schlegel cavalcade would have to follow suit. There were harassments and petty inconveniences along the way, with uncertainties about passports (Schlegel had been left in Vienna to sort these out) as they passed through Moravia (Brno, Olomouc) and Galicia. The monotony of the landscape depressed her. There were however compensations. They could descend on the palaces of the grand nobility (if accompanied by rude Austrian officials), like the Lubomirskis, both of whom had attended Schlegel's lectures in 1808. People lined the roads to see the progress of this 'queen of Sheba'. With great relief they arrived at Brody, the Austrian-Russian border station, on 13 July.

3. The Years with Madame de Staël (1804-1817) 351

Moscow was still a thousand kilometres away, but Staël's mood changed the moment she stepped on to Russian soil. In her account she dwells much on the 'Russian soul', on the splendours and miseries of this 'exotic people'. The governors of Kiev, Orel and Tula received them. Then, on 2 August, the golden cupolas of Moscow came into sight. There is no description from Schlegel's pen of this remarkable journey, apart from one reference to this same vista in a letter and a passage in his Latin valedictory address as rector of the University of Bonn.[467] But what is that? One may regret this, for the Staël party was one of the last to see the old Moscow, her 'Tartar Rome', before its destruction by fire later in the same year. Except in a political context, he rarely wrote anything complimentary about the Slavs. Whether the journey through the Slavonic lands was the cause, must remain a conjecture. Perhaps he lacked the sheer physical energy of Madame de Staël: she seemed able to fill notebooks after—or even during—a rattling carriage journey. For German readers Ernst Moritz Arndt's account of Russia is a kind of compensation, more picaresque than Staël's—squalid inns, vermin—and setting out a very different political agenda.

The visit to Moscow lasted a brief few days (2-7 August). They had time to take in the ancient city, to meet its most famous literary personage, Nikolai Karamzin, and its governor, Count Rostopchin, who was soon to give the order for its destruction. They then travelled across the endless plain, through Novgorod and thus to St Petersburg, where they arrived on 11 August. The month in the Russian capital was to be the first of her late triumphs, with Stockholm, London and Paris to follow.

Madame de Staël reconvened a kind of salon. This meant that Schlegel inevitably receded into the background, while she shone all the more refulgently. Arndt mentions him only by name,[468] Stein similarly,[469] John Quincy Adams, who had two animated conversations with her, not at all.[470] These were heady times: Kutuzov had just been appointed commander-in-chief of the Russian armies; the French were in retreat. St Petersburg was

---

467 Ludwig Schmidt, 'Ein Brief August Wilhelm v. Schlegels an Metternich', *Mitteilungen des Instituts für Österreichische Geschichtsforschung*, 23 (1902), 490-495, ref. 491. (The addressee is actually Count Sickingen), *Opuscula quae Augustus Guilelmus Schlegelius Latine scripta reliquit*, ed. Eduardus Böcking (Lipsiae: Weidmann, 1848), 389f. He also mentions having seen 'indecent' Indian figures in a Moscow museum. *Indische Bibliothek*, II, 434.
468 Arndt, VII, 146.
469 Freiherr vom Stein, *Briefe und amtliche Schriften*, ed. Erich Botzenhart and Walther Hubatsch, 10 vols (Stuttgart: Kohlhammer, 1957-74), III, 716.
470 Adams, *Russian Memoirs*, 399-401.

offering asylum to notable ruling spirits in the opposition against Napoleon. Chief among these was Baron Stein, the Freiherr vom Stein, the principal agent in the Prussian reforms after 1807, whose later dismissal and exile came about at the Emperor's insistence. Arndt had made his journey to Moscow and to St Petersburg to join Stein and become his private secretary. Stein was among the first to hear Madame de Staël read from *De l'Allemagne* in manuscript.[471] Yet there were already signs of later disagreement when he noted 'imprudences in her conduct and what she had to say'.[472] Her preoccupation at this stage was England: Adams noted how much time she spent in the company of the British envoy Lord Cathcart and of his staff assistant, Admiral Bentinck, and expressed 'in warm terms her admiration of the English nation as the preservers of social order and the saviors of Europe'.[473] The bombardment of Copenhagen did not seem to bear this out, nor would one expect Adams, as a representative of a nation technically at war with Britain, to share her enthusiasm.

Staël was received by the Tsarina and then by the Tsar himself, and with them she could discuss serious politics. Tsar Alexander was not present in St Petersburg during all of her stay, having left for Åbo (today's Turku) in Finland for a high-level meeting with the Swedish Prince Royal, Bernadotte. Lord Cathcart, the Russian general Count Suchtelen, and Kutuzov had also been present. A treaty had been signed there on 30 August, leaving Sweden free to pursue its policies against Denmark, suitably assisted by a Russian loan. The Tsar had charmed his Swedish partner, but had not committed himself to concrete undertakings. Did Madame de Staël influence the decisions taken at Åbo? Savary certainly thought so. More probably she put in a good word for Bernadotte during her audience with Alexander.[474] The stay in St Petersburg nevertheless ended for her on a sour note. The French theatre put on a performance of *Phèdre*. To her distress it was booed. Anti-French feelings might run high, but surely French culture was excepted. It clearly was not. Arndt, the great French-hater, noted with some glee that this incident merely proved that Madame de Staël was anti-Napoleon, but not, like himself, anti-French. In that assumption he was correct.[475]

Apart from reaching England, the real purpose of this long anabasis through the Russian Empire had been to see the Staël sons placed in

---

471 Stein, 719. Paul Gautier, *Madame de Staël et Napoléon* (Paris: Plon, 1921), 313.
472 Stein, 716.
473 Adams, 399.
474 Gabriel Girod de l'Ain, *Bernadotte, chef de guerre et chef d'état* (Paris: Perrin, 1968), 413f.; Gautier, 318f.
475 Arndt, VII, 146.

Swedish service. This meant leaving the splendours of St Petersburg for the more sober grandeur of Stockholm. Above all, it meant meeting Bernadotte, the Prince Royal of Sweden: Jean Baptiste Bernadotte, the son of a petty law official in Pau, Marshal of the Empire, Prince of Pontecorvo. The trajectory of his career saw him a divisional general of the Revolutionary armies by 1794, the first Republican French ambassador to Vienna, governor of Hanover, then of the Hanseatic towns, a 'Royal Highness' and 'cousin' of the Emperor (at whose coronation he had held the collar of state). If one wanted an illustration of how the French Revolution had shaken up the old political and social order of Europe, he would provide it. Bernadotte was above all the army commander at Austerlitz, at Jena, at Eylau, at Wagram, yet Napoleon was never satisfied with his performance at these battles, and what is more he did not trust him.[476] How far Bernadotte was involved in intrigues against Bonaparte during the Directory, or the so-called 'fronde des généraux' of 1802 and above all the plot of 1804 that saw the execution of the duke d'Enghien and the disgrace of Pichegru and Moreau, is a matter open to question. Whether he knew of the involvement of Madame Récamier or even Madame de Staël in some of this, remains conjecture.[477]

When in 1810 the Swedish royal house of Holstein-Gottorp was threatened with extinction, Bernadotte emerged as a suitable candidate to succeed the childless King Charles XIII. He had commended himself as a humane governor in Lübeck—and he was already a royal prince by the grace of Napoleon. The Emperor had no objection to his marshals becoming kings or princes (Joachim Murat was king of Naples, for instance), and he readily assented to Bernadotte's candidature. Nor did the thought of a parvenu on the Swedish throne worry him. In Metternich's Austria the new Prince Royal was regarded with less favour, something that would emerge again in 1814.

Arriving in Stockholm in October 1810, not knowing a word of the language (and never learning it) but using his many talents, his diplomatic skills, and his personal charm to good effect, Bernadotte was soon made aware of the peculiar problems of recent Swedish history and politics. Or indeed of older Swedish history: the remembrance of the Treaty of Kalmar of 1397, for instance, that had once united the three Scandinavian nations

---

476 Cf. Napoleon to Fouché: 'Il a toujours l'oreille ouverte aux intrigants qui inondent cette grande capitale'. Quoted in Girod de l'Ain, 288.
477 Cf. Torvald Torvaldson Höjer, *Carl XIV Johan*, 3 vols (Stockholm: Norstedt, 1939-60). I: *Den franska tiden* (1939), 259-261. Girod de l'Ain, 179, 185. Gautier, 324 makes claims for an involvement.

under one throne, or of Gustavus Adolphus, or even of Charles XII. He would have learned that Sweden was still smarting under the loss of its large eastern buffer province of Finland, which had been wrested from it by Russia in 1809 after a brief campaign. It was all the more necessary to ensure good relations with Russia in the east and to secure territorial guarantees in the west. The simple solution was to take Norway from Napoleon's ally Denmark and to compensate the Danes with Swedish Pomerania. This policy of annexation, together with the integrity of the German lands (of which both Denmark and Sweden had their small share), and the formation of an alliance against Napoleon, were to be the three issues that exercised Madame de Staël, and thus Schlegel, after their arrival in Stockholm.

Meanwhile, there were the pressing realities of Napoleonic hegemony. He had forced Sweden to declare war on Britain (no shots were actually ever fired), then he had invaded Swedish Pomerania preparatory to his Russian campaign in the summer of 1812. Secret negotiations, involving Count Suchtelen for Russia, Lord Cathcart for Britain and Count Karl Löwenhielm for Sweden (Count Neipperg for Austria observing), ensured cordial, if private, relations between the three powers. It was the background to the Treaty of Åbo that was concluded during Madame de Staël's sojourn in St Petersburg and whose implications were to be the subject of her frenetic rush of activity in Stockholm.

Already before their departure from St Petersburg, Madame de Staël had begun her politicking. On 19 August she could write to His Royal Highness in Stockholm in anticipation of 'seeing him again' in his exalted status and of her hope of rejoining her sons with their father's country[478] (she did not mention Rocca, who had served briefly under Bernadotte in the Low Countries).[479] Shortly after Staël's arrival, another letter to Bernadotte showed the extent of her networking: she knew all about a Swedish mission to Denmark, and she could claim that the news of Åbo had reached France through her[480] (she underestimated Savary).[481]

There was, however, the question of getting to Stockholm. For the first time since Vienna, Schlegel emerged from the shadows. The party left St

---

478 Höjer, 'Madame de Staëls brev' (1960), 159.
479 Girod de l'Ain, 413f.
480 Höjer (1960), 159.
481 Cf. Norman King, 'Un récit inédit' (1966), which makes it clear that their every move was watched and recorded.

3. *The Years with Madame de Staël (1804-1817)* 355

Petersburg on 7 September, proceeding through Finland to Åbo, where they embarked for Sweden. Her customary intrepidity deserted her when she left dry land, and her fears were compounded on seeing the frail vessel that was to transport them. It hardly helped when Schlegel, pointing to the fortress at Åbo, asked her if she preferred incarceration, her other phobia.[482] Yet few journeys with Madame de Staël were free of unlikely incidents or chance meetings. On board the same ship were also Madame Henriette Hendel-Schütz, the celebrated performer of attitudes and *tableaux vivants*,[483] and her husband. It was, as it were, Lady Hamilton translated to the Baltic. A storm rose, the ship was forced to take shelter near a rocky island. Later Schlegel was gallantly to give Albertine the credit for calming her mother's nerves as the party disembarked,[484] and servants (unmentioned) produced a fire and sustenance. Madame Hendel-Schütz then gave an improvised dramatic performance. Under such bizarre and slightly hilarious circumstances were Niobe or Iphigenia seen in the Gulf of Bothnia. Schlegel produced a poem for the occasion—it could not be otherwise—adding it to his earlier homage to the young dancer Friederike Brun.[485] It was a prelude to Madame Hendel-Schütz's triumphant reception in Stockholm. There too Madame de Staël, Albertine and Wolf von Baudissin were to regale high society with the theatricals of Coppet.[486]

Their arrival in Stockholm coincided with the news of the fall of Moscow. It set the scene for a flurry of political activity in the Staël circle. The Prussian envoy claimed that her house was the centre of anti-Napoleonic intrigue in the city.[487] That did not exclude social contact with those of a different political persuasion. Wolf von Baudissin, one of the youngest in Schlegel's audience at the Berlin Lectures in 1803, now advanced in the Danish diplomatic service, found himself representing Denmark in Stockholm. It was a post calling for some delicacy and tact: Denmark officially was an

---

482 *Dix Années*, 244.
483 On her and on the incident in the Gulf of Bothnia, see Kirsten Gram Holmström, *Monodrama, Attitudes, Tableaux Vivants. Studies on Some Trends of Theatrical Fashion 1770-1815*, Stockholm Studies in Theatrical History, 1 (Stockholm: Almquist & Wiksell, 1967), esp. 184f. An account by Madame Hendel-Schütz herself in *Bonstettiana*, XI, i, 266f.
484 Pange, 397.
485 'An Frau Händel-Schütz, früher Schauspielerin des königl. Theaters in Berlin. Auf der Ueberfahrt von Finnland nach Schweden, beim Zusammentreffen an einem Ankerplatz'. *SW*, I, 293f.
486 Rougemont, 'Pour un répertoire', 90f. She declaimed scenes from Racine's *Athalie* and *Iphigénie*, while they all played in comedy.
487 Gautier, 325.

ally of Napoleon, whereas Baudissin's preference was for an alliance with Sweden and Britain. Nor did he support the Danish initiatives to secure concessions from the British,[488] which later elicited sarcastic comments from Schlegel.[489] It did not prevent social contacts, acting in Madame de Staël's theatrical evenings, indeed for a while she wondered whether Baudissin would not make a suitable match for Albertine.

In the Service of Bernadotte: The Political Pamphleteer

There were, first of all, her sons to think of, then Schlegel. Auguste, still in Paris, was to enter the Swedish diplomatic service, while Albert was appointed an officer, a 'sous-lieutenant', or cornet, the most junior rank in the hussars of the royal guard.[490] Schlegel was made private secretary to the Prince Royal. No doubt Madame de Staël, who thought nothing of forcing her way into the royal presence,[491] was behind this appointment. Bernadotte, as a man of very considerable ability and judgment, could form his own opinions on Schlegel's capacities as 'Minister of Propaganda and Enlightenment for Germany' and did not need to take Madame de Staël's word on trust. That he later accorded to Schlegel the Swedish title of 'Regeringsråd' (state counsellor)[492] suggests that Bernadotte had every reason to be pleased with him.

To account for Schlegel's assumption of this role and his success at it, it is not enough to say that he had always been interested in history and politics, or that as a Hanoverian he had a special insight into the structures of the old Holy Roman Empire. Of course he had in various contexts expressed quite pronounced views on the development of the modern state, its tendency to centralism, bureaucracy, standing armies. For him the Reformation was the source of many of these evils, which (as he saw it) had brought the

---

488 Bernd Goldmann, *Wolf Heinrich Graf Baudissin. Leben und Werk eines großen Übersetzers* (Hildesheim: Gerstenberg, 1981), 46f. Bengt Hasselrot, *Nouveaux documents sur Benjamin Constant et Mme de Staël* (Copenhagen: Munksgaard, 1952), 53-64. The point is made (64) that Baudissin was an envoy of a country that was Staël's and Bernadotte's worst enemy.
489 [AWS], *Betrachtungen über die Politik der dänischen Regierung* (s.l., s.n.), 8.
490 King, 'Un récit inédit', 14.
491 Cf. the account in Sheilagh Margaret Riordan and Simone Balayé, 'Un manuscrit inédit sur le séjour de Madame de Staël à Stockholm', *Cahiers staëliens*, 48 (1996-97), 69-102, ref. 86f.
492 See the important article by Franklin D. Scott, 'Propaganda Activities of Bernadotte, 1813-1814', in: Donald C. McKay (ed.), *Essays in the History of Modern Europe* (Freeport, NY: Books For Libraries, 1968 [1936]), 16-30, ref. 24f.

Middle Ages proper to a symbolic end. His Vienna Lectures, by restricting themselves to the history of drama, did not praise the Middle Ages as such except as the forcing-ground of later national sentiment, but his articles in Friedrich's *Deutsches Museum* in 1812 were much more explicit celebrations of things medieval. They had less to do with the 'Union of the Church with the Arts' that had once preoccupied him in the days of the *Athenaeum*, than with the links between monarchy, chivalry, and the feudal system. They were not and never had been, a plea for restoration, a turning back of the clock, even less for a *faux* medievalism in the style of his former protégé Fouqué. Rather—in the year 1812—they were a call for reflection on the past as a guide to present uncertainties. Real politics were, as ever, best left to those who knew its practical limits and who did not go into reveries about what once was. His brother Friedrich meanwhile had been called upon to formulate general policies of state according to Austrian doctrine and had assumed the role of a political propagandist for the Habsburg cause.

Above all, most of these writings by August Wilhelm, inasmuch as they were published, were formulated for a specialized audience, some of it academic, all of it generally educated in literary matters. They were very largely in German, a language that Bernadotte did not read. The Vienna Lectures, the best proof of the man and his style, were not to appear in French until later in 1813. Bernadotte, who had a good 'style classique' himself, clearly saw in Schlegel a man with whom he could work, who wrote French well, who moved easily between the languages, and who could put into words—into good prose—ideas that expressed the wishes of his political master. The 'private' letters that Schlegel wrote to people in places of political influence (Gentz, Sickingen, Münster), while unsuperintended and thus not an officially sponsored part of state correspondence in the strict sense, articulated executive standpoints nevertheless. Thus General Suchtelen was more or less right when he saw in Schlegel a man whose talents and whose knowledge of Germany made him ideally suitable.[493]

It cannot be said that Schlegel was slow off the mark in joining the cause of political change in Germany. Already on 4 October 1812 he was able to 'lay at the feet' of the Prince Royal a confidential memorandum on the state of Germany. It had not been solicited by Bernadotte himself; rather, Madame de Staël, his sponsor, was behind it. Thus it lacked official status and

---

493 Suchtelen to Rumianstev November 1812. Torvald Torvaldson Höjer, *Carl Johan i den stora koalitionen mot Napoleon* […] (Uppsala: Almquist & Wiksell, 1935), 405. Cf. Höjer's description of AWS as Bernadotte's 'litterära väpnare' [literary armour-bearer], 103.

remained a draft. The reasons for this are not difficult to see. It represented the Staël-Schlegel view of the struggle against Napoleon, with Germany—suitably reconstituted along lines of their own imagining—in the centre. It begged questions and made sweeping assumptions. No-one doubted that a campaign against Napoleon would have to be initiated in the German lands: opinions differed on the details. Bernadotte himself was really only marginally interested in Germany. When he did go there, he used Swedish territory in Pomerania as his base. Baron Stein, and later Prince Metternich, also had very different notions of how Germany would look during and after a campaign against Napoleon, and they were not especially interested in a Swedish role in these processes except in a minor capacity. At the time of Schlegel's writing, Prussia and Austria were of course still technically Napoleon's allies. The question—an eminently fair one—was how these nations should behave in the light of Napoleon's recent reversals in Russia. That is the background to *Mémoire sur l'état de l'Allemagne et sur les moyens d'y former une insurrection nationale* [Memorandum on the state of Germany and on the means of creating a national uprising there].[494]

Schlegel was proposing nothing less than a general insurrection against Napoleon, a *levée en masse*. He knew that, rhetorically, the case had to be prepared with care. The mention of Walcheren, the British fiasco of 1809, suggested that small (and badly organised) expeditions were unlikely to succeed. It would by the same token remind the Prince Royal that he, as Marshal Bernadotte, had once been largely instrumental in that particular British defeat. There was no question of building on past or present political structures—and here the memorandum already went far beyond *De l'Allemagne*, the text being read in manuscript in St Petersburg and Stockholm. What was needed was the revival of the German empire itself. Of course it would be an empire that reflected the present state of Germany, its sophistication in political and philosophical thought, not some entity in the past. At most one might wish an existing royal house to assume leadership, such as Habsburg. Only here did the memorandum pick up some of the medievalisings of the *Deutsches Museum*. 'Empire' would of course be defined in the most generous territorial terms, to include Germanic territories ruled by powers strictly speaking outside of its ambit: the Hanoverian author naturally mentioned his own English-ruled native

---

[494] The text is published by King, 'A. W. Schlegel et la guerre de libération' (1973), text 14-28. See also Otto Brandt, *August Wilhelm Schlegel. Der Romantiker und die Politik* (Stuttgart, Berlin: Deutsche Verlags-Anstalt, 1919), 117-125. It is not the same as a 13-pp. draft in AWS's hand, in SLUB Dresden, Mscr. Dresd. e. 90, II (23), an exposé of the political situation in Europe and dated '17 Septembre 1812 St. Petersbourg' [sic].

land, and he thought too of Swedish Pomerania (not however Danish Schleswig-Holstein).

The present Confederation of the Rhine would be dissolved and the Germanic lands would form a league, with a diet and chancellor. This latter would be no other than Baron Stein (with whom, Schlegel reminded the Prince, he had had conversations in St Petersburg). Switzerland would form part of it, the Hanseatic towns as well (they would make it a sea power). Without realizing it, Schlegel was coming close to the pan-German visions to be formulated in mid-century and beyond. The envoi of the memorandum was addressed to Sweden and to the Prince Royal himself. It invoked the ultimate example of Gustavus Adolphus, whose worthy successor it suggested Bernadotte was. It pointed to Denmark, Napoleon's ally, as ready for the taking. A good command of (selected) facts, a well-presented argument (however shaky in parts), and some gross flattery: all of these factors combined to make this a skilfully written political pamphlet.

It was, as said, a draft, destined for the eyes of the Prince Royal only, but Schlegel clearly had the authority to make some of its general thrust known in other quarters. His letter to Count Franz von Sickingen, written on 14 January 1813,[495] was intended to acquaint the highest circles in Austria with Bernadotte's political vision. Sickingen, an imperial chamberlain and a good friend of the Emperor Francis I, had been in Schlegel's audience in Vienna in 1808. It was now opportune to make use of these contacts. Schlegel did little more than pass on the Prince Royal's views on Austria's position. Should Napoleon not be vanquished, it would be hemmed in by the constraints of a French alliance. How much more attractive an association with Russia, Britain and Sweden that would guarantee the balance of power but also enable a German league against Napoleon to be constituted. There follow the usual flatteries about the Emperor Francis, Sickingen himself, and the Prince Royal. There was still opposition in Vienna to Bernadotte, the perceived upstart.[496]

Concluding his letter, Schlegel claimed that, as a subject of His Majesty King George III, his natural place of refuge in these troubled times would be England. Perhaps at this stage he did not himself know, but as the year 1813 advanced it was clear that his paths and Madame de Staël's were about to diverge. She would be free to move as ever, to England, while

---

495 Ludwig Schmidt, 'Ein Brief August Wilhelm v. Schlegels an Metternich' [recte Sickingen] (1902), 490-495; published in a French version by King, 'A. W. Schlegel et la guerre de libération' (1973), 32-39.
496 On the low opinion of Bernadotte in Vienna see Höjer, *Carl Johan i den stora koalitionen*, 248.

he, now the committed amanuensis and propagandist of Bernadotte, must remain behind. Nothing made this clearer than the pamphlet *Sur le système continental et sur ses rapports avec la Suède* [On the Continental System and its Relations with Sweden], that appeared in 'Hambourg' in February, 1813.[497] It is fair to say that nothing written by Schlegel ever had such an immediate and widespread effect as this ephemeral broadsheet.

It was also seditious, not of course in Sweden, where it actually appeared,[498] nor in London, where it was soon translated,[499] but in the territories of Napoleon and his allies. It was to this pamphlet that Schlegel was later referring when he claimed that he could have been arrested in the Kingdom of Westphalia into which his native Hanover had been incorporated.[500] There was also no question of its being immediately translated into German until the Wars of Liberation made it safe to do so.[501] Why was this 92-page brochure so dangerous?

There was no dearth of other pamphlets on the subject, pointing out the harm being done by Napoleon's blockade, the loss of British markets, the rise of smuggling. It had been a sensitive subject over ten years earlier when Schlegel's Danish cousin Johan Frederik Schlegel had challenged the British right to board neutral vessels.[502] Henrik Steffens, a Norwegian by birth and mistrustful of Swedish-British rapprochements, had read Francis d'Ivernois's much-translated *Effets du blocus continental* [Effects of the Continental Blockade] on this subject.[503] In Germany, Ludwig Lüders had

---

497 The publication and translation history of this pamphlet would demand a bibliographical study of its own. Schlegel himself (*SW*, VIII, 255f.) noted that it had been translated into Swedish (Stockholm, 1813), Russian, German (Berlin, 1813) and English (London, 1813). It was issued in London in French in 1813. There is also a Dutch translation (1814). Not in *SW* (as are none of the political pamphlets); a shortened version in AWS, *Essais littéraires et historiques* (Bonn: Weber, 1842), 1-70. Some information in J. M. Heberle, *Katalog der von Aug. Wilh. von Schlegel nachgelaßenen Büchersammlung* (Bonn, 1845), XVIIf.; Brandt, 140-152; and esp. in Bengt Hasselrot, *Nouveaux documents*, 27-52. AWS kept all the relevant printed and draft material, and this cache of political writings, by AWS and others, in SLUB Dresden is invaluable, Mscr. Dresd. e. 90, VII (1-13), VIII (1-14) and IX. They remain unedited.

498 *SW*, VIII, 255.

499 As: *An Appeal to the Nations of Europe Against the Continental System: Published at Stockholm by Authority of Bernadotte, In March 1813. By Madame de Staël Holstein* (London: Richardson, 1813). Also: *The Continental System, and its Relations with Sweden. Translated From the French* (London: Stockdale, 1815).

500 *SW*, VIII, 256.

501 *Briefe*, I, 298f., 300; II, 126f.

502 J. F. W. Schlegel, *Sur la visite des vaisseaux neutres sous convoi* […] (Copenhagen: Cohen, 1800). English 1801.

503 Francis d'Ivernois, *Effets du blocus continental sur le commerce, les finances, le crédit et la prospérité des Isles Britanniques* (London: Vogel & Schulze, 1809), then English, German and Swedish in 1811. Steffens, *Was ich erlebte*, VII, 58.

set out the case against British 'intransigence'.⁵⁰⁴ Schlegel, however, turned the tables. The system was causing misery to French-occupied Europe itself (including still 'Hambourg') and Napoleon alone was the originator of this commercial ruination. Not only that, Schlegel used the pamphlet as an opportunity to dilate on Napoleon's predatory and usurpatory career, in terms that only Staël's *Dix Années d'exil* would surpass. Indeed it was assumed by many that she was the author (the English translation actually said so). There was even a public retraction.⁵⁰⁵ She then wrote privately to her publisher, with some little disingenuousness, that she 'did not get involved in politics in this fashion'.⁵⁰⁶

Schlegel may have had to suppress his own private sentiments when, dropping all subtleties, he embarked on a eulogistic account of British virtues (his only really anglophile text). His grand gesture of praise for Sweden and its 'Bayard' Prince Royal was doubtless more sincere. The preface to Madame de Staël's *Réflexions sur le suicide*, just published, had been similarly florid. His aim was to show that neutrality was ineffectual in the face of the dangers of Napoleonic domination. The case of the 'craven' Denmark proved his point. There was the need for an alliance that would strengthen the three main powers as yet unaffected by French occupation: Russia, Britain, and Sweden itself. To that effect, Sweden must extend its border to the west: it should take Norway from Denmark and incorporate it into an aggrandized Swedish kingdom.

The pamphlet may therefore be seen as a preparatory for the actual political decisions made soon after. A triple alliance was signed on 3 March 1813 at Örebro between Sweden, Russia and Britain, agreeing on a Russo-Swedish pact, the annexation of Norway and—no less important—a grant of one million pounds sterling. The notions of a German confederation that had informed Schlegel's first memorandum to Bernadotte were now less to the fore: this was primarily a document of Swedish policy. There were conflicts of interest. Both Sweden and Britain of course had a territorial stake in Germany, but Prussia had no intention of allowing its interests to be subordinated to theirs. Baron Stein, who had little respect for German territorial princes, had been conducting a robust correspondence with Hanover's minister in London, Count Münster, on Prussia's proposals to

---

504 [Ludwig Lüders], *Das Continental-System* [...] (Leipzig: Kunst- und Industrie-Comptoir, 1812).
505 Hasselrot, 51f.
506 Gautier, 353.

divide up the German lands among the main contenders.[507] Schlegel the Hanoverian also disagreed with Stein, but to no avail.[508]

Schlegel even gave the impression of being more Swedish than the Swedes. Writing in May 1813 to Gentz he stated bluntly that the Prince Royal 'wants Norway, he absolutely wants it, and nothing will deter him'.[509] To Madame de Staël's Danish friends however it seemed as if the rapacities attributed to Napoleon in Schlegel's pamphlet were about to be perpetrated in Denmark by Bernadotte.[510] (We may safely assume that Schlegel's Danish cousin, the 'Etatsråd' Johan Frederik Wilhelm, disagreed with the Swedish 'Regerungsråd', August Wilhelm.) Certainly nobody asked the Norwegians how they felt.[511] Madame de Staël's response—'there are overriding necessities in politics'[512]—is not one of her most endearing. In the circle around Rahel Varnhagen, at a time when French troops were beginning to leave Berlin and Russians to occupy it, Schlegel's pamphlet was dismissed as 'émigré language' (and bad French at that), lacking conviction, merely 'his master's voice'.[513] Compared with Varnhagen, about to join in the battle for Hamburg, the views expressed in Stockholm might seem like arm-chair patriotism. There was a further matter of contention. For Rahel the defender of Heinrich von Kleist, Madame de Staël's *Réflexions sur le suicide*, for all their talk of 'devotion' to a righteous cause, had failed to understand that Kleist's suicide in 1811 had also been a kind of despairingly patriotic act.

If Sweden were to be seen as politically and morally justified in annexing Norway, the case would have to be prepared through further propaganda. Comparisons between Sweden and Denmark would have to be made, contrasts between recent Swedish behaviour in the struggle against Napoleon, and Danish compliance in the Usurper's 'monarchie universelle'. To prise Norway away from Denmark, one would need to appeal to older links between Sweden and its western neighbour. Or overriding issues of maritime security would have to be cited. The issues of Schleswig and Holstein, of the Hanseatic towns, would have to be addressed. This Schlegel did in a draft called *Réflexions sur la situation politique du Danemarc* [Reflexions

---

507 Stein, *Briefe*, IV, 2-8, 162-164, 210-212.
508 Ludwig Schmidt, 'Drei Briefe Aug. Wilh. Schlegels an Gentz', *Mitteilungen des Instituts für Österreichische Geschichtsforschung* 24 (1903), 412-423, ref. 416f.
509 *Ibid.*, 413.
510 Reactions, some irate, in *Bonstettiana*, XI, i, 306, 310f., 316f., 336.
511 Something later noted bitterly by Steffens, *Was ich erlebte*, VIII, 133-135.
512 'enfin il est des nécessités impérieuses en politique'. *Bonstettiana, ibid.*, 336.
513 *Rahel-Bibliothek*, V, i, 60.

on the Political Situation in Denmark] and what are some rough, possibly stenographed notes of 'comments' and 'opinions'.[514]

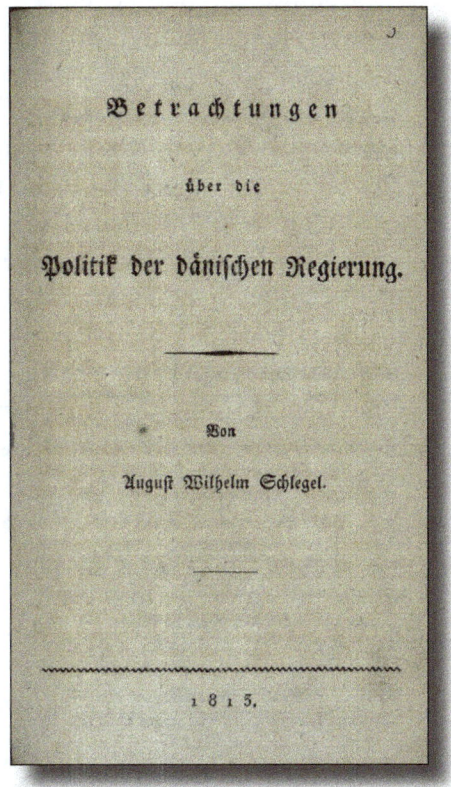

Fig. 19 August Wilhelm Schlegel, *Betrachtungen über die Politik der dänischen Regierung* ([Stockholm], 1813). Title page. © and by kind permission of the Master and Fellows of Trinity College, Cambridge, CC BY-NC 4.0.

There was all the more reason for this, as Denmark was anything but willing to surrender Norway, which had been hers since 1536. If so, there would have to be compensations, such as the Hanseatic cities.[515] This forms the background to, and also the immediate cause for, the 48-page pamphlet *Betrachtungen über die Politik der dänischen Regierung* [Considerations on the Politics of the Danish Government] that came out in German, with Schlegel's name on the title page, and in French anonymously.[516] Schlegel's

---

514 SLUB Dresden, Mscr. Dresd. e. 90, VII (8, 9). Brandt, 154.
515 *Ibid.*
516 The translation is *Considérations sur la politique du gouvernement danois. Par un Allemand* (s.l., s.n., 1813). Pange, 437.

task was to disqualify Denmark in terms of its political fabric and its recent history: an absolute monarchy (as opposed to a constitutional Swedish state), duplicitous in its dealings with other nations (there was the matter of the recent Danish re-occupation of Hamburg, after the French had left), oppressive of the Norwegians (who—surely an ill-chosen analogy—would under Swedish rule enjoy a status akin to Scotland or Ireland under the British). Schlegel then addressed the contentious issue of the duchies of Schleswig and Holstein, since 1806 united with the Danish crown, but historically part of the old Holy Roman Empire. Did they want to remain Danish, to live under despotism, or return to the embrace of the 'Germanic confederation' (an entity that he chose not to describe in detail)?

This was not all rhetoric, for his animus against the Danes ('whom heaven confound'), was repeated in his private correspondence,[517] even to the extent of quoting Cato's famous imprecation against Carthage.[518] It was not well received in Vienna: it was not to be until 12 August that Austria declared war on Napoleon. It led to ripostes and charges of venality, that the cosmopolitan savant was lending his pen to whoever paid best.[519] Schlegel was to return to harrying the Danes towards the end of 1813. Bernadotte meanwhile was preparing to bring Sweden directly into the campaign against Napoleon in the German lands.

Political and Military Developments 1813-1814

The general historical and political background needs a few words of explanation. Bernadotte had taken advantage of Napoleon's defeat in Russia to secure his own aims for his adopted Sweden. The treaties with Russia and Britain, nations at war with Napoleon, were a means of taking action against Denmark, France's ally, and of securing the prize of Norway. Compromises were however necessary. Sweden agreed in the Örebro declaration to place 30,000 troops at the Allies' disposal on the European mainland. The agreement between Russia and Prussia at Kalisch on 25 March, 1813 brought Sweden into a further net of alliances, with the guarantee that Prussia would offer Bernadotte an army, a joint

---

517 *Briefe*, I, 291.
518 'Praeterea censeo, Daniam esse delendam'. Pange, 424.
519 Cf. [Johann Daniel Timotheus Manthey], *Épître à Monsieur Auguste Guill. Schlegel, bel-esprit, actuellement aux gages de Son Altesse le Prince Royal de Suède. Par un Suédois* (Stockholm, 1813, German translation Copenhagen 1813). Brandt, 162-166.

force of Swedish, Russian and Prussian troops under his command and based in the first instance in Swedish Pomerania. It was at the same time that Bernadotte formally broke off diplomatic relations with France, in a written declaration to the Emperor.

Not all of this went as smoothly as Bernadotte might have wished. He was not best pleased when he heard of a Russian initiative to win Denmark for the Allied cause, with a diplomatic mission to Copenhagen. Without consulting Bernadotte, there was talk of a compromise over Norway. In the event, Denmark remained intransigently on Napoleon's side.

It was to emerge that Sweden was but a minor player in the great diplomatic and military operations of 1813-14. The Allies' placing an army under Bernadotte's command was more a tribute to a former Marshal of the Empire than a recognition of Sweden's status. In the event, he was not to prove to be the successor to Gustavus Adolphus, who had faced up to Tilly and Wallenstein. There was mistrust on all sides. Bernadotte feared that Prussia, Russia or Austria might broker a peace with Napoleon without consulting him. Prussia especially suspected that Bernadotte was holding back his Swedish contingent from the thick of the fighting. Henrik Steffens picked up conversations in the Prussian headquarters that were disparaging of the French general in their midst. He was even deputed to deliver a rousing speech in Norwegian to the Swedish troops, intended to remind them of past greatness.[520]

Schlegel was about to embark on a new phase of his career as private secretary to Bernadotte. It was to be a wandering existence,[521] one that often involved not knowing exactly where he was and what was actually happening.[522] Between his arrival in Stralsund on 18 May 1813 and his departure for England nearly a year later, he was to write letters from over twenty different addresses, most of these sent to Madame de Staël. It is hard to keep track of his movements. We can gain some of the big picture from the Prince Royal's own despatches[523], or from the memoirs of the French-born Swedish general Jean Baptiste de Suremain.[524]

---

520 *Was ich erlebte*, VII, 283-285.
521 *Briefe*, I, 299.
522 Pange, 451.
523 *Proclamations de S. A. R. le Prince-Royal de Suède et Bulletins publiés au Quartier-Général de l'Armée combinée du Nord de l'Allemagne* (Stockholm: Pierre Sohm, 1815).
524 [Jean Baptiste de Suremain], *La Suède sous la République et le Premier Empire. Mémoires du Lieutenant Général de Suremain (1794-1815)* [...] (Paris: Plon-Nourrit, 1902).

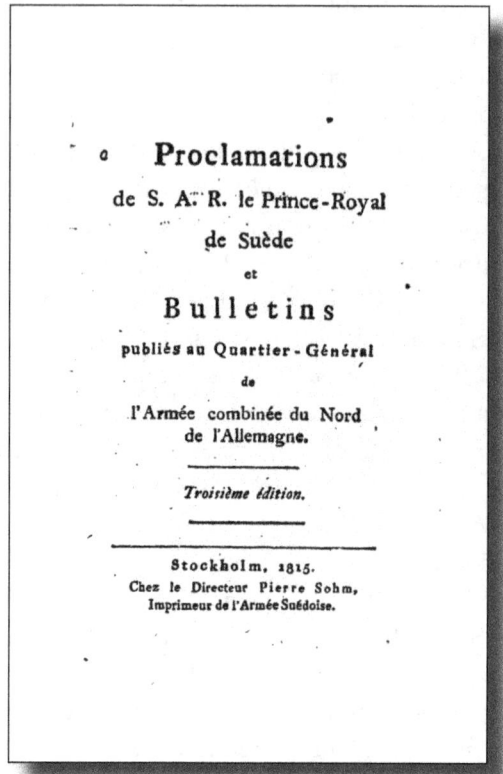

Fig. 20 *Proclamations de S. A. R. le Prince-Royal de Suède* (Stockholm, 1815). Title page. Image in the public domain.

Schlegel's letters to Madame de Staël are thus both an account of where he was on a particular day and what stage the political and military situation had reached. It was during these first weeks in Stralsund that Schlegel wrote his letters to Gentz and to Count Münster, articulating the frustrations felt in the Swedish headquarters about perceived Russian tergiversations, the ambitions of Baron Stein, and Austria's non-involvement in a new Germanic federation. Some of the hopes expressed in Schlegel's memoranda and pamphlets were beginning to appear more and more illusory in the face of the greater powers' *Realpolitik*.

These hopes had also been Madame de Staël's. Now, for the first time since 1804, she and Schlegel were to be separated one from another. His service under the Prince Royal, ultimately her doing, took him to the scene of military action (or as near as a private secretary came), while she had the task of convincing the still sceptical English that Bernadotte was an ally whom they could implicitly trust. She was learning how much she depended on Schlegel, sending out those *cris de coeur* about how she missed him, how he was a member of the family, and so forth. Of course he did belong to the family. He kept up his correspondence with Auguste. He knew about his infatuation with Madame Récamier and tried to give him advice, as man to man. It was to Auguste that he confided resignedly the reverses in his own life, his disappointments in love and friendship, his sense of isolation as he grew older (at the great age of 46), his 'petite célébrité littéraire'[525]—and somehow expected the younger man to understand.

Auguste made his way to Stockholm via Vienna and arrived on 10 May, 1813. He had to sit Latin examinations for the Royal Swedish chancellery. His mother could announce shortly after that he was now a 'gentleman of the chamber'.[526] In the summer of 1813, before their departure for England, Madame de Staël took the opportunity of seeing more of Sweden, travelling to Uppsala. It was an irony that she was able to see the *Codex argenteus*, the Gothic bible held there, and that Schlegel was not, he who at least knew the language.[527] On 8 June, she, Albertine, Auguste and Rocca embarked at Gothenburg for England. In her last letter before departure Albertine expressed the hope that they would be well received there. Madame de Staël added a note for Albert: 'I hope your next letter is better than your last one'. It was never to reach him. To Schlegel Staël added in English 'god bless you' [*sic*].[528] He had already left Karlskrona on 12 May to join Bernadotte at Stralsund, where he arrived eight days later.[529]

Madame de Staël was received triumphally in the highest echelons of English society. It was the unspoken background to Schlegel's reports on the military situation. Perhaps he could not quite compete with Lords Harrowby, Lansdowne, Liverpool or Holland, with Byron, with Sir James Mackintosh, with the Prince Regent, even with the exile Bourbons. Albertine was much admired. Auguste was a chargé d'affaires in the Swedish embassy in London. She was however to realise that England was not her 'patrie'.[530] Its notorious 'spleen' was infectious.[531] All this despite the 15,000 guineas

---

525 *Krisenjahre*, II, 258-261, ref. 261.
526 *Lettres inédites de Mme de Staël à Henri Meister*, ed. Paul Usteri and Eugène Ritter (Paris: Hachette, 1903), 258.
527 Schlegel claimed to have been there and, uncharacteristically, not to have found the time to see the Codex. Favre, lxxx.
528 Letter of (5) June, 1813. SLUB Dresden, Mscr. Dresd. e. 90, XIX (4), 1. Published separately by Norman King, 'Correspondances suédoises de Germaine de Staël (1812-1816)', *Cahiers staëliens*, 39 (1987-88), 11-137, ref. 115f.
529 Pange, 410, 413.
530 Gautier, 344.
531 Usteri/Ritter, 268.

that she received from John Murray for *De l'Allemagne*, an account of Germany that had lost some of its immediate relevance and that had to be updated in some sections. She assiduously lobbied on behalf of Bernadotte in London, proudly informing him that she had been intervening for him with the Prince Regent.[532] The later rumours that Bernadotte might be the ideal candidate to replace Napoleon (or the Bourbons) on the French throne, promptly denied by her once issued, emanated ultimately from her.

She devoured all the more Schlegel's despatches from Bernadotte's headquarters. Perhaps she was even piqued that he was in a male world where men made the decisions and where her otherwise formidable presence could effect nothing. The great events of the day could be heard in the distance as he wrote: the resumption of hostilities between Prussia and Napoleon, the armistice that followed, Austria's entry into the war on Russia's and Prussia's side (12 August), and the subsequent formation of three armies against Napoleon, Schwarzenberg's in Bohemia, Blücher's in Silesia, and Bernadotte's in North Germany. We hear of the victories at Grossbeeren, Katzbach and Dennewitz, the events that led up to the great confrontation at Leipzig in October.

A stream of notabilities and high-level negotiators passed through Bernadotte's headquarters, royal personages like the Duke of Cumberland (with whom Schlegel conversed in German),[533] or the Prince of Mecklenburg-Schwerin, diplomats and negotiators like Count Carlo Andrea Pozzo di Borgo, the wily Russian representative,[534] or Count Adam Albert Neipperg, Austria's assiduous soldier and go-between (later to marry Napoleon's imperial widow), Bernadotte's right-hand man Count Carl Gustav Löwenhielm or Sir Edward Thornton, the British minister plenipotentiary to Sweden. These would be some of the men who on 6 July met at Trachtenberg in Silesia with the Tsar and King Frederick William III of Prussia to work out a strategic plan, much of which was presented to them by Bernadotte himself. Despite his being, for the Austrians at least, an old adversary and a parvenu to boot, this was the high moment for Bernadotte in what were to be the Wars of Liberation from August to October of that year.[535]

---

532 Torvald Höjer, 'Madame de Staëls brev', 162-166.
533 Pange, 414.
534 Whose slipperiness the Staël circle would experience. See John McErlean and Norman King, 'Mme de Staël, A. W. Schlegel et Pozzo di Borgo', *Cahiers staëliens*, 16 (1973), 41-55.
535 Girod de l'Ain, 441-446.

3. The Years with Madame de Staël (1804-1817) 369

A source (not Schlegel) suggests that there were entertainments as well: the name of the famous actress Mademoiselle Georges is mentioned.[536] It was into the world of high living, gambling, women—and debts—that Albert de Staël, the Swedish cornet of hussars, was to find his way, with fatal results. Albert charmed everyone, but everybody also agreed with General Suremain that he was an 'étourdi', a scatterbrain.[537] The English admiral Hope had even prophesied his premature end.[538] He had crossed over to Germany before Schlegel and had obtained permission to join the forces of the Russian general Friedrich Karl von Tettenborn. Karl August Varnhagen von Ense had been on Tettenborn's staff and had witnessed the battle for Hamburg in March 1813, the subsequent re-taking of the city by French forces under Marshal Davout and its occupation by their Danish allies. The behaviour of both the French and Danes and the imposition of extortionate tribute monies had caused widespread indignation, and it was one reason for the denunciation of Danish policies in Schlegel's pamphlet.

Albert had shown himself to be courageous, but also foolhardy, insubordinate and insolent. He had been admonished in a fatherly way by Bernadotte himself and had been relegated to the nearby island of Rügen to regain his senses. He had become a compulsive gambler, and this was to prove his undoing. Schlegel wrote to Albert's mother from Demmin in Mecklenburg, to which the headquarters had moved, on 3 August, with some details. Albert had been in Doberan (now Bad Doberan) near Rostock. On 12 July, he had become involved in a quarrel over gambling debts with a certain Jorris, an adjutant to the Russian general Benckendorff. They agreed to fight it out with sabres, the encounter taking place on a bosky rise near the small town. Jorris's first blow severed Albert's jugular vein, killing him on the spot.[539]

'He had been splendidly prodigal with his life'[540] was how Schlegel expressed himself in this same long letter. It may also explain the tone of melancholy acceptance that pervades it, or even the wish in subsequent letters to see the business of war over and done with and to return to his

---

536 Suremain, 288.
537 *Ibid.*, 296. To this Varnhagen added 'liederlich' ('dissolute'), *Rahel-Bibliothek*, V, i, 66.
538 Pange, 435.
539 *Rahel-Bibliothek*, VI, i, 140. Cf. also Carl Schröder, 'Tagebuch des Erbprinzen Friedrich Ludwig von Mecklenburg-Schwerin aus den Jahren 1811-1813', *Jahrbücher des Vereins für Mecklenburgische Geschichte und Altertumskunde*, 65 (1900), 123-304, ref. 288, who supplies the names.
540 'il avait une belle prodigalité de sa vie'. Pange, 436.

first love of scholarship. A consolation had been the conferral on him by Bernadotte of the Order of Vasa. Despite its being the junior order of chivalry among the Swedish honours and usually bestowed on those in industry, commerce and education, Schlegel now insisted on being addressed as 'Chevalier'. Madame de Staël was willing to accede in this small display of vanity,[541] the first of several ribbons to wear on his coat.

Schlegel's letters do not tell us about the action proper; they come from one who followed in the armies' train, catching up with the generals as the headquarters moved rapidly from place to place. Before leaving Stralsund, he was able to meet up with General Jean Victor Marie Moreau, who had returned from American exile to throw in his lot with the anti-Napoleonic allies. Moreau and Bernadotte had not agreed on military matters, had parted company, Moreau joining the Tsar. 'Schleigel' (as Moreau calls him) had nevertheless managed to present the general with a copy of one of his pamphlets, which Moreau politely acknowledged. Three weeks later, he was killed at the Tsar's side outside Dresden.[542]

Oranienburg, Charlottenburg, Spandau, Treuenbrietzen, Jüterbog, Zerbst, Halle—these were the next halts in the military action. There were chance meetings along the way: with Fouqué in or near Berlin;[543] with his step-nephew Philipp Veit, who remarked disrespectfully on the 'Regierungsrat' wearing the Order of Vasa with its gold tassels;[544] in Zerbst, where his father Johann Adolf had been a professor and where August Wilhelm's older siblings had been born, also in uniform and with decorations, he met his aged godmother.[545] Unlike Steffens, who saw with his own eyes the great clash of armies at the 'Battle of the Nations' at Leipzig on 18-19 October,[546] Schlegel arrived there some time after and only saw the trail of destruction in the city he had known in the 1790s. To compensate, he saw the great parade of monarchs and generals and was received personally by the Prussian and Austrian chancellors, Hardenberg and Metternich.[547]

---

541 He is so addressed in her letter of 8 October, 1813. Usteri/Ritter, 265.
542 Moreau's note to AWS in SLUB Dresden, Mscr. Dresd. e. 90. XIX (15), 69. A memorial to Moreau is a short walk away from the present SLUB.
543 Pange, 447.
544 Raich, II, 226.
545 Pange 458. This was the 'Demoiselle Auguste Sophia Weissen' from Zerbst who features in the baptismal register. Hanover, Ev. Luth. Stadtkirchenkanzlei.
546 *Was ich erlebte*, VII, 296f.
547 Pange, 463; *Briefe*, I, 299.

Schlegel continued to have his uses for the 'Généralissime'.[548] He was an interpreter for the Prince Royal, who was no linguist (he taught Bernadotte the German for 'en avant, mes enfants!' [forward, lads!]).[549] His pen was still needed for propaganda purposes. There is textual evidence that Schlegel also had a hand in at least some of Bernadotte's proclamations.[550] It was more serious when on 5 October there appeared in the *Leipziger Zeitung* a defamatory article on the Prince Royal (Saxony had not yet changed sides) claiming congenital mental illness in the Bernadotte family. The implication was that this also applied to the Swedish pretender, the Jacobin, the renegade, the turncoat. Schlegel issued a counter-blast in the same newspaper, when Leipzig was no longer under French occupation, having it printed as a pamphlet in both French and German.[551] It did not take him long to demolish this calumny: parallels with Bayard and Gustavus Adolphus established the Prince Royal's credentials.[552]

An even better opportunity to demonstrate the righteousness of the Allied cause came when a cache of French official despatches was captured by General Tchernicheff's forces moving westwards towards Kassel. They were sent to Schlegel in Hanover, where they were duly published with his preface.[553] In a sense these documents spoke for themselves, uncovering as they did Napoleon's dealings with his own family, the losses incurred by his armies, the all-pervasiveness of his espionage system, and much besides.

Schlegel spent three weeks in Hanover with the oversight of these papers. He had an opportunity to visit his two older brothers Karl and Moritz and their families, in Göttingen and Hanover. Was there a conference between the brothers, at which the question of the family name was discussed? Did the other brothers hand over the original letters patent conferring the title of nobility, Schlegel von Gottleben, on their great-grandfather by Emperor

---

548 As he is called in *Proclamations* (1815), 7.
549 Pange, 452.
550 Brandt, 190f. The proclamation of August 15, 1813 seems to be the first. *Proclamations*, 8.
551 *Remarques sur un article de la Gazette de Leipsick du 5. Octobre 1813. Relatif au Prince Royal de Suède* (Altenburg: Brockhaus, 1813), translated into German as *Ueber Napoleon Buonaparte und den Kronprinzen von Schweden, eine Parallele in Beziehung auf einen Artikel der Leipziger Zeitung vom 5ten October 1813, von August Wilhelm Schlegel* ([n.p.], 1813, reissued Leipzig, 1814). *Briefe*, II, 126f.; Brandt, 184-187; Heberle, XVIII.
552 *Ueber Napoleon Buonaparte*, second ed., 28f.
553 *Dépêches et lettres interceptées par des partis détachés de l'armée combinée du nord de l'Allemagne* [...] (s.l., s.n. [Hanover] 1814). Also Paris 1814, London (bilingual edition) 1814. Preface published in: *Essais littéraires et historiques*, as 'Tableau de l'Empire français en 1813', 71-84. Brandt, 195f.; Pange, 471.

Ferdinand III?[554] Or had a decision already been made? Perhaps even being a 'chevalier' of the Vasa order gave August Wilhelm the impulse, for Madame de Staël already in October 1813 had written on a letter from London 'Monsieur A. Wilhelm de Schlegel'.[555] Whatever, Schlegel from December 1813 signed himself 'v. Schlegel'. Friedrich had already raised the matter, acutely aware as he was of the disadvantages of having a mere commoner's name in class-conscious Vienna. (The other brothers remained simply 'Schlegel'.) Of course his was not to be one of those new-fangled noble titles springing up in all directions in the Romantic age; it was the revival of a lapsed title, not the sign of recent imperial or royal favour, not like those 'von Müller', 'von Gentz' (or even those ultimate parvenus 'von Goethe' and 'von Schiller').

Bernadotte's army now moved northwards to deal with the Danes and secure the possession of Norway. There was no need to invade Denmark proper. On 13 December, Schlegel could write from the university town of Kiel, in Holstein. The army moved up in stages. It was a hard winter, so that, as one Holsteiner remembered, the war had left the land 'like a squeezed lemon'.[556] Schlegel's animus against the Danes had been aggravated by their behaviour towards his friend Wolf von Baudissin. The young diplomat had refused to accompany his superior on a mission to Dresden to cement the Franco-Danish alliance and had been sentenced to a year's imprisonment in the fortress of Friedrichsort near Kiel. It had not been too uncomfortable, but for Schlegel it was merely another instance of Danish inhumanity.[557] In the event, Baudissin was released after six months and enjoyed Schlegel's company before moving to Paris to take part in the peace negotiations there.[558] In Kiel, Schlegel reportedly read from his *Nibelungenlied* and from his Shakespeare translation:[559] Baudissin, with Dorothea Tieck, was later to take over where Schlegel had left off. There were even rumours of Schlegel having a romantic attachment, which however came to nothing.[560] (No doubt it would not have survived Madame de Staël's scrutiny.)

Schlegel meanwhile seized the political initiative. He had met up with Benjamin Constant in Göttingen and the two had dropped their

---

554 As he states in *SW*, VIII, 263.
555 Meister, 265.
556 Rudolph Schleiden, *Jugenderinnerungen eines Schleswig-Holsteiners* (Wiesbaden: Bergmann, 1886), 74.
557 *Krisenjahre*, II, 271.
558 Goldmann, 47f., 52f.
559 Schleiden, 74f.
560 *Ibid.*

old differences, to concentrate on the 'grand task' ['la grande oeuvre'].[561] Both were pushing Bernadotte's candidature for the French throne and were pressing for the pursuit of Napoleon over the French border and his overthrow. Madame de Staël's instincts rebelled against the idea of a punitive war against France, merely 'for the sake of one man',[562] and she was becoming resigned to the reality of the restoration of the Bourbons. Schlegel, she said, should give no credence to rumours of Bernadotte's candidature or his return as a king-maker in the style of 1660 or 1688: they emanated from the Bourbons and were intended to discredit him.[563]

Schlegel now turned his pen to give moral justification to Sweden's annexation of Norway, in the pamphlet *Réflexions sur l'état actuel de la Norvège* [Reflections on the present state of Norway] that John Murray was to publish in London in 1814. Broadsheets in London had commented adversely on Swedish ambitions and had even quoted *De l'Allemagne* against its authoress, not least her statement that 'the submission of one people to another is contrary to nature'.[564] Unflattering comparisons were made with the Tyrol or with Spain,[565] and 'the ingenious Mr. Schlegel'[566] did not emerge well. Schlegel's response was mainly sophistry: already his epigraph from *Hamlet* referring to 'young Fortinbras' was a veiled threat to the Danish royal house. Most conflicts, Schlegel states, end with some cession of territory, so why not Denmark too? Denmark was to be compensated with Swedish Pomerania, so what was the concern? (In the event, this did not happen.) Norway had suffered under Denmark because of the continental system and the Danish absolute monarchy: Sweden would guarantee ancient Norwegian rights. The speciousness of the argument knew no end. Denmark had backed the wrong horse, was going to lose Norway, and that was that.

As it was, the Danes agreed to Sweden's conditions in the treaty of Kiel, signed on 14 January, 1814. Bernadotte could now turn his army westwards to join in the push against Napoleon. This took Schlegel back again to Hanover. The soon to be restored kingdom of Hanover became for a short period a kind of propaganda factory, with both Schlegel and

---

561 Pange, 475.
562 Usteri/Ritter, 274.
563 *Ibid.*, 270-272.; Höjer, 'Madame de Staëls brev', 167.
564 A. Andersen Feldborg, 'An Appeal to the English Nation on Behalf of Norway', in: *The Pamphleteer*, IV, vii, Aug. 1814 (London: Valpy, 1814), 233-285, ref. 259.
565 [Anon.], *Cursory Remarks on the Meditated Attack on Norway; Comprising Strictures on Madame de Staël Holstein's 'Appeal to the Nations of Europe'* (London: Blacklock, [1813]), 49.
566 Feldborg, 272.

Benjamin Constant at the workplace. Constant had met the Prince Royal in November and had been delighted.[567] It gave him the spur to complete the work which became known as *L'Esprit de conquête* [The Spirit of Conquest] and to attach himself to the Prince's train. It was to Constant that Madame de Staël wrote: 'Send Schlegel over here: I can't live without him'.[568] Perhaps it was time for Schlegel to free himself of his duties to Bernadotte and re-enter Staëlian servitude. Varnhagen, who had met him in Göttingen and Kiel, had found him stiff, lifeless, a kind of 'prince of letters', and that had not been intended as flattery. He had also heard that the Prince Royal was finding Schlegel's writing increasingly prolix.[569]

Schlegel produced two more draft memoranda before events made them redundant. *Idées sur l'avenir de la France* [Ideas on the Future of France][570] is essentially an account of Napoleon's rule and its excesses and what might happen in the event of his death or removal. Did he really want peace, or was this merely another of his ruses? In any case, there would have to be a complete change in the personnel of government in France to guarantee the transition to a régime acceptable to the Allies. Perhaps this was a last glimmer of hope on Schlegel's part for Bernadotte's candidature for the French throne.

Analyse de la Proclamation de Louis XVIII aux Français. Au mois de Février 1814[571] does what it says, namely glosses the 'king-pretendant's' claim to the French throne and asks several pertinent questions. What right had the Bourbons to revert to a hereditary monarchy when it had been succeeded by a republic (that Bonaparte had then destroyed)? Was there not the danger of replacing one absolute system by another? What was Louis XVIII's 'authority? Was it the same as Louis XIV's? What of the instruments of state? Were they to be restored, and in what fashion? If Schlegel intended his analysis to gain time for Bernadotte's contention, events soon caught up with him, and the pamphlet, bereft of any further relevance, remained unpublished.

It could nevertheless be said that the extended Staël-Schlegel-Constant circle had been assiduous in its anti-Napoleonic publishing during the year 1814. *De l'Allemagne* had come out late in 1813; German translations were

---

567 *Journaux intimes*, 393f.
568 Pange, 488.
569 *Rahel-Bibliothek*, V, i, 245, 284.
570 SLUB Dresden, Mscr. Dresd. e. 90. VII (12); Brandt, 197f.
571 SLUB Dresden, Mscr. Dresd. e. 90. VII (11); Brandt, 199-203.

not slow in appearing.⁵⁷² Schlegel's own pamphlets, the *Dépêches et lettres interceptées* and *Réflexions sur l'état actuel de la Norvège* were being issued in London by John Murray⁵⁷³ and in pirate editions. There was Constant's *Esprit de conquête,* and there were Rocca's *Mémoires sur la guerre des Français en Espagne,* published in Paris in 1814 and then with Murray in 1815, a reminder that the first setbacks suffered by Napoleon had been on the Iberian Peninsula. Friedrich Schlegel had been an official mouthpiece for Habsburg policy. Not to be outdone, their older brother Moritz Schlegel, still superintendent and pastor in Göttingen, published later in 1814 his *Auswahl einiger Predigten* [Selection of Some Sermons].⁵⁷⁴ They were a reminder to the Schlegel family that not everyone had turned Rome-wards (or had flirted with the idea), that at least one son was producing sermons, not hour-long homilies in the manner of their father Johann Adolf, but like his oriented to the biblical text and its application. Moritz used the lectionary to comment on the 'Zeitgeist' and the momentous events of the times, the parallels between sacred history and these 'last days'. The tone is never strident; the Hanoverian preacher stayed within the acceptable limits of Lutheran teaching on church and state. It is conceivable that this family publication was one factor among several in August Wilhelm's later rediscovery of his Protestant roots.

The hard winter (the rivers Elbe and Weser froze over) caused Schlegel to miss out on the rapid westward advance of the Allied armies. A severe chest infection detained him in Hanover during February and March. Fortunately, his other brother Karl was able to find a good doctor. A consolation was meeting another royal prince, the Duke of Cambridge, but he was not to be present when Bernadotte issued his proclamation to the French people, his wish for peace, his desire not to have to fight on French soil. He was not there when the Prince Royal moved his headquarters to Cologne, Liège, Kaiserslautern and then finally to Brussels. Constant, with Auguste de Staël, had moved with Bernadotte and thus to Paris, to witness the capitulation on 30 March and the abdication on 6 April.

In March, we then hear of Schlegel in Soest, in Westphalia, and in Brussels in April. Events were not in his favour. His opposition to the

---

572 Pange, 491.
573 Heberle, XVIIIf.
574 Karl August Moritz Schlegel, *Auswahl einiger Predigten in Beziehung auf die bisherigen Zeitereignisse, und nach wichtigen Zeitbedürfnissen* [...] (Göttingen: Vandenhoek & Ruprecht, 1814).

Confederation of the Rhine, his disapproval of the settlements agreed between the Tsar, the king of Prussia, and the emperor of Austria (and their effective exclusion of Bernadotte), were of no avail. Madame de Staël had bowed to the inevitable and had accepted the Bourbon restoration with as good a grace as she could muster. It was now time for Schlegel to ask Bernadotte's permission to leave his service and join the Staël family in England.[575] The Prince Royal and his secretary were never to meet again in an official capacity.

England and France 1814

We know next to nothing about Schlegel's visit to England in April-May 1814. The brief mention in his self-justification against Voss in 1828[576] and one or two scattered references are all that we have.[577] In Paris later in 1814 he told Henry Crabb Robinson that 'he was there only for a fortnight'; he had not had time to meet Flaxman.[578] Flaxman! Not Byron, not Coleridge— his great admirer[579]—not Sir James Mackintosh (whose review of *De l'Allemagne* in the *Edinburgh Review* had put the work on the map), not the whole string of notabilities who had waited on Madame de Staël. Not of course the Sanskrit scholars: that was for the future.

We do know that he embarked at Calais, most likely on 30 April.[580] It was the day on which the newly proclaimed Louis XVIII made his triumphant progress through London on his way to Paris. Schlegel recalled that he wrote out the Dauphin's words from Shakespeare's *King John*:

> Have I not heard these islanders shout out,
> Vive le Roi! as I have bank'd their towns?[581]

He recollected having referred to these lines in society in the house of Lord Harrowby, once Pitt's foreign secretary and one of the grandees in Madame

---

575 Pange, 497.
576 *SW*, VII, 295, VIII, 255.
577 Such as Kohler, *Madame de Staël et la Suisse*, 622.
578 *Henry Crabb Robinson und seine deutschen Freunde. Brücke zwischen England und Deutschland im Zeitalter der Romantik.* Nach Briefen, Tagebüchern und anderen Aufzeichnungen unter Mithilfe von Kurt Schreinert bearb. v. Herta Marquardt, Palaestra, 237, 249, 2 vols (Göttingen: Vandenhoek & Ruprecht, 1964, 1967), II, 36.
579 Meister/Usteri, 265.
580 *SW*, VII, 295.
581 Quoted *ibid.*

de Staël's circle. Everyone admired Schlegel's serendipity (he knew, having translated it, that 'bank'd' meant 'sailed along').[582] Shakespeare supplied the right word for the situation and in quoting him Schlegel was announcing his own disillusionment with the recent turn of political events.

Circumstantial evidence in the form of a letter to John Murray of May 1814[583] suggests that he also met Lord Liverpool, the prime minister, and Sir James Mackintosh, who had been almost everything from lawyer to judge to MP, and who would later be the most prominent of Schlegel's British contacts. They and Lord Harrowby were to receive copies of the London bilingual edition of *Dépêches et lettres interceptées* that Murray was about to bring out (paying Schlegel 250 guineas).[584] He gave as his forwarding address the Swedish embassy in Chesterfield St. Baron Gotthard Maurits von Rehausen, the envoy and also Auguste de Staël's superior, had been responsible for putting the Swedish case to Castlereagh, the foreign minister. A rumour had gone the rounds that the Prince Regent had refused to receive Schlegel, his Hanoverian subject, on account of his association with Bernadotte.[585] Clearly not even Madame de Staël's lobbying on behalf of the Prince Royal had been successful.

Madame de Staël, Albertine, Rocca and Schlegel left London on 8 May and arrived in Paris on 12 May. Auguste had already left, to join in the great political events that were unfolding. She had once rashly spoken of travelling to Scotland with Schlegel or even settling in Germany.[586] Now, it was to be her triumphal return to the city in which she had not legally been since 1809. In addition she was the author of *De l'Allemagne*, the grandest public persona, the subject of the *mot*: 'There are three powers, England, Russia and Madame de Staël'.[587] Yet for many Staël biographers, 1814-17 is a kind of epilogue. True, there is no diminution of her fame and influence, but these last years usher in the end nevertheless. For Schlegel, receiving a few rays of her reflected glory, the same years were to witness the beginnings of a new orientation, the first hints that there might be a life beyond Madame de Staël.

---

582 *Ibid.*
583 Murray Archive, Ms. 41065. Edinburgh, National Library of Scotland. See also Murray to Auguste de Staël 21 January, 1814, agreeing to publish the *Dépêches*. SLUB Dresden, Mscr. Dresd. e. 90, XII (3).
584 As: *Copies of the Original Letters and Dispatches* [...] (London, 1814).
585 *Briefe*, II, 128.
586 Pange, 490.
587 Gautier, 358.

Depending on who one was, one would see Schlegel, now back in Paris, shining in the Staël circle (although never as brilliantly as she), and wearing the Russian Order of St Vladimir (Fourth Class, but no matter);[588] or merely as her pedantic appendage, her *petit maître*; or as a scholar, closeted again with his books after two years of enforced abstinence. These conflicting views make a proper assessment of the real man in these years difficult. They all contained some elements of truth: they only needed the right distribution.

He was disenchanted with politics. All of his abnegation of the scholarly life, his pamphleteering, his wandering existence, had ended in the restoration of the Bourbons. Some wryly cynical poems by him in French from the time of the first Restoration contained this sentiment: Bonaparte may have been bad, but not as bad as the bunch now in power.[589] The irrepressible gossip Crabb Robinson, hurrying over to Paris after the Restoration, noted of Schlegel that he 'did not speak with enthusiasm on politics'.[590] It was over dinner at Madame de Staël's, where the subjects were almost exclusively literary and seemed to reflect the need to catch up: Tieck, Schelling, Byron, Wordsworth, above all Goethe's new autobiography *Dichtung und Wahrheit* [Poetry and Truth] that was not well received by the extended Schlegel family.

He no longer talked politics with Madame de Staël—they would merely disagree[591]—but with Karl August Varnhagen von Ense, soon after the Restoration, he had done just that. All of Varnhagen's ambivalence towards Schlegel (he was 'pedantic', 'silly', if undeniably learned and adroit)[592] comes out in his letter from Paris to Rahel of 21 May. After an unflattering description of Madame de Staël's person, Varnhagen noted their diverging views on the Hanseatic cities: Schlegel would have incorporated them into his 'Empire'; Varnhagen represented their traditional rights.

To his old friend and fellow-antiquarian Guillaume Favre in Geneva Schlegel could drop his guard completely. Writing from Paris in October 1814, he stated that he was living in the Staël retreat at Clichy, away from the 'monde brillant' and concentrating on the main task.[593] Even so, living

---

588 Due in large measure to Pozzo di Borgo's good offices. McErlean/King, 'Mme de Staël, A. W.Schlegel et Pozzo di Borgo', 49. *Krisenjahre*, III, 541.
589 *Oeuvres*, I, 15.
590 Crabb Robinson, II, 35f., ref. 35.
591 *Krisenjahre*, II, 294.
592 *Rahel-Bibliothek*, V, i, 363.
593 Favre, lxxivf.

in the Staël *ménage*, he would not be able to avoid his social duties entirely. What was the object of this withdrawal from society?

Already while he was in Bernadotte's camp, he could write to Madame de Staël about 'vastes projets' that he had yet to undertake, Germanic, or 'Bramanic'.[594] His brother Friedrich had been urging him to return to his real métier of literature and scholarship, conveniently suggesting places— Vienna, Hanover—or persons—the Duke of Wellington—where or with whom he might work. Now, however, reinstalled in Paris, August Wilhelm spoke to Favre of three major concurrent projects, the two linked projects on the etymology of the French language and on Provençal; there was the old *Nibelungenlied* project, dormant since his essays in the *Deutsches Museum* in 1812; and, to cap it all, an 'enfantillage' [childish thing], he was learning Sanskrit.[595] Perhaps there was something youthfully injudicious about taking on so much at the same time, although for Schlegel this was nothing new.

The substance of these studies will occupy us presently. They and the related reviews were not undertaken in ideal conditions. One senses that he had to utilise the moment and the place to best effect: in Paris, to pursue the study of Sanskrit; in Coppet, to be near Favre and meet him or borrow from his vast library all the antiquarian arcana on the Goths for his studies on the *Nibelungenlied*; in Italy, to profit from scholarship there, mainly on classical archaeology or the Etruscans. How was this to be done? In 1814, Jacob Grimm had commented on Schlegel's professorial mien, the punctilious order of his desk—and the social commitments that kept him from it.[596] By 1817, he had however established a regimen of work. The young American traveller and scholar, George Ticknor, reported as follows:

> Schlegel's [manner of living] is such, indeed, as partly to account for his success as a man of letters, and as a member of the gay society of Paris. He wakes at four o'clock in the morning, and, instead of getting up, has his candle brought to him and reads five or six hours, then sleeps two or three more, and then gets up and works till dinner at six. From this time till ten o'clock he is a man of the world, in society and overflowing with amusing conversation; but at ten he goes again to his study and labours until midnight, when he begins the same course again.[597]

---

594 Pange, 426f., 437f.
595 Favre, lxxvi.
596 *Briefwechsel zwischen Jacob und Wilhelm Grimm aus der Jugendzeit*, ed. Herman Grimm and Gustav Hinrichs, 2nd edn, ed. Wilhelm Schoof (Weimar: Böhlau, 1963), 336.
597 Ticknor, I, 107.

The Return to Scholarship

It is doubtful whether this régime was able to withstand the incursions of Madame de Staël's lifestyle and the demands that it made. It was also clearly devised for a bachelor existence. In view of Schlegel's marriage plans in 1816 and their actual fulfilment in 1818 (however disastrous) one wonders if he ever gave a thought to the consequences for marital life of such a semi-monastic existence. As his brother Friedrich was to experience, being a public intellectual (and a public servant) meant subjecting one's personal life to privations and absences. His wife Dorothea, finding more and more solace in her Catholic piety and the welfare of her talented sons, accepted her lot. Not every wife looked up to her husband as she did.

Unlike August Wilhelm, who had followed the twisting paths of Madame de Staël and had only permitted himself one act of insubordination (staying in Germany with Bernadotte), Friedrich was harnessed to Habsburg service in Vienna, dependent on good words here and recommendations there. He had become Metternich's pamphleteer and mouthpiece, not always the best use for his multiform talents. When finally in 1815 he was appointed 'Legationssekretär' to the Imperial Diet in Frankfurt (at a salary of 3,000 florins, the most he ever earned), he had to accept separation and often demeaning superiors. Small wonder that his letters from 1813 onwards pleaded with August Wilhelm to come back to the German lands,[598] to foster the German cause, to ensure their continued activity together.[599]

It was not to be, and the brothers were only to meet once again, in 1818, in Frankfurt. Yet their public image perpetuated the symbiosis of earlier days. Brockhaus's biographical periodical *Zeitgenossen* [Contemporaries] ran in its 1816 number an article simply called 'August Wilhelm und Friedrich Schlegel'.[600] (It was by their brother Moritz, hence there was no 'von'.)[601] It traced their respective careers (with no direct mention of Caroline or Lucinde), down to the involvement of the one with Tsar Alexander and the other with Metternich. It may not have been the image that they sought to promote. If celebrities, they were at most minor ones. Certainly August Wilhelm wanted to move on from such involvement in political matters.

---

598 *Friedrich Schlegels Briefe an seinen Bruder August Wilhelm*, ed. Oskar F. Walzel (Berlin: Speyer & Peters, 1890), 544.
599 *KA*, XXIX, 82.
600 *Zeitgenossen. Biographieen und Charakteristiken* (Leipzig and Altenburg: Brockhaus, 1816), I, iv, 179-186.
601 *Briefe*, II, 152.

3. The Years with Madame de Staël (1804-1817)

One solution would be to find some kind of position as a scholar and public intellectual in Restoration France. Yet his only attachment there was to Madame de Staël. That was fine if he wished to enjoy the company of the Tsar, Talleyrand, Gentz, Wellington, Grand Duke Karl August and the many others assembled in Paris who sought her salon in Clichy. There was Alexander von Humboldt, now at the apogee of his considerable fame. Nobody held it against him that he was a Prussian: he was a citizen of the world and spoke and wrote in several languages. His famous works of scientific travel were appearing in Paris. Schlegel was different. He had never been forgiven the *Comparaison* of 1807. His Vienna Lectures, now available in French, seemed to augment and consolidate his animus against France. A younger generation had not yet seized on them as an alternative voice to official classicism. There was no question of his seeking office in France. At most he could keep his eyes and ears open for possibilities in Germany.

During those closely-guarded hours of study in Clichy or in Coppet, Schlegel sought to take advantage of what the great institutes in Paris had to offer. There would be more than enough on subjects of earlier study, like the Etruscans, Troubadours, or Provençal. Favre in Geneva was adding to Schlegel's collection of erudite references to the Goths. He met Jacob Grimm in Paris, he too part of the delegations that were filling the city after Napoleon's abdication. With him he could discuss matters Germanic.[602] Above all Paris offered him the chance to learn Sanskrit. It brought him into contact or renewed his acquaintance with the specialized scholarly world, so different from the whirl of the salons.

Antoine-Léonard de Chézy he already knew. Chézy had been learning Sanskrit from Alexander Hamilton with Friedrich at the time of *Ueber die Sprache und Weisheit der Indier*. Now in 1815 Chézy was to become the first professor of Sanskrit at the Collège de France. By that year Schlegel had acquired enough of the rudiments of the language to review Chézy's translations from the Sanskrit. Louis-Mathieu Langlès, who had catalogued the oriental collections of the Bibliothèque du Roi, was professor of Persian. He would send Schlegel texts when he was away from Paris. There was however now no Hamilton, as there had been for Friedrich.

The young Franz Bopp from Aschaffenburg and a Bavarian citizen, had however been in Paris since 1812.[603] The experts there had received

---

602 *Briefwechsel zwischen Jacob und Wilhelm Grimm aus der Jugendzeit*, 334, 336.
603 For Bopp see S. Lefmann, *Franz Bopp, sein Leben und seine Wissenschaft*, 3 vols (Berlin: Reimer, 1891-97) esp. I, 1-53.

him kindly, but he had taught himself Sanskrit with whatever texts were available, piecing the grammar together.[604] It was with him that Schlegel gained his first knowledge of the language. Yet Schlegel's attitude to Bopp was always ambivalent, even before the latter became Berlin's first professor of Sanskrit and comparative grammar. In 1815 in a letter to Langlès, who knew him, Schlegel wrote 'l'excellent Mr Bopp',[605] whereas to Favre in the same year he was merely 'a young German whom I have found here'.[606] Later he left him out of the record entirely.[607]

We can only guess at reasons. Bopp felt that Schlegel looked down on him:[608] he was from a humble background, had not been to a 'real' university, was dependent on others' support, lived in a garret in Saint Germain while 'von' Schlegel enjoyed the Staël salon. Schlegel may have felt that Bopp, for all of his extraordinary knowledge as a grammarian, was too narrow a specialist, whereas he, Schlegel, never lost his interest in all the manifestations of art and poetry and was the author of the Vienna Lectures and the translator of Shakespeare. There was certainly professional jealousy. Bopp as a young man had already in 1816 produced a study of the conjugation system of Sanskrit.[609] It made deferential references, as it must, to Friedrich Schlegel's *Ueber die Sprache und Weisheit der Indier*; but it was clear that he regarded Friedrich's ideas on inflections as unsound.[610] His edition also contained metrically translated extracts from the *Râmâyana* and the *Mahâbhârata*. The older Schlegel's knowledge of the language was not nearly so advanced. Bopp went on to be a distinguished comparative Indo-European grammarian and textual scholar, translated into English and French. He produced results. His studies, although multifarious, were related: he did not allow himself to be distracted. His output was not scattered and all over the place, as we have to admit Schlegel's was. Bopp produced a much-acclaimed grammar of Sanskrit: Schlegel too attempted one, but it remained in note form in his

---

604 'Entziffern und Enträtseln', Lefmann, I, 23.
605 *Briefe*, I, 307.
606 Favre, lxxvi.
607 *Opuscula*, 413f.
608 Lefmann, I, 36.
609 Franz Bopp, *Über das Conjugationssystem der Sanskritsprache in Vergleichung mit jenem der griechischen, lateinischen, persischen und germanischen Sprache*, ed. K. J. Windischmann (Frankfurt am Main: Andreä, 1816). Modern reprint ed. Roy Harris, Foundations of Indo-European Comparative Philology, 1800-1850, 1 (London, New York: Routledge, 1999).
610 Lefmann, I, 44f.

papers.⁶¹¹ Once Schlegel was in Bonn, there was an element of competition with Bopp, the Sankritist in the 'other place' (Berlin) to which Schlegel had not chosen to go, a rival for the funds and resources that the Prussian state was prepared to invest in pure scholarship. He would use his *Indische Bibliothek* as a critical forum against Bopp.⁶¹²

All of this lay in the future. Schlegel meanwhile could in 1815 claim to Friedrich Wilken the editor of the *Heidelberger Jahrbücher*, that his grammatical and etymological studies hitherto, of Greek and Latin and the Germanic dialects, gave him an access to Sanskrit which English scholars certainly did not have.⁶¹³This was true, although Bopp might have made the same claim with equal justification. Schlegel's approach was to be philological and rigorous. With the formidable resources of his own knowledge, he could, as he wrote to Favre, even work away from Paris.⁶¹⁴

Italy, Coppet, Paris: The Death of Madame de Staël

This was just as well, for Madame de Staël during these last years was variously on the move. The causes were several: her own state of health, Rocca's precarious condition, the need to find a husband for Albertine, and not unconnected, the restitution of the Necker loan. A candidate for Albertine's hand had been found in the person of Victor, duke of Broglie. He had in some respects impeccable Staëlien qualifications. He came from an old and distinguished military family. His father had been guillotined in the Terror; his mother had been part of Madame de Staël's circle; he had enjoyed a liberal education; he had been in the diplomatic service during the First Empire; he was anglophile. All he lacked was money, at least enough to marry the granddaughter of Jacques Necker. Hence the need for the Necker dotation.

Madame de Staël abstracted herself from the social bustle of Paris and spent the months of July to September 1814 in Coppet. She and Rocca saw their love-child for the first time in two years, the poor, retarded Alphonse, still fostered with the same pastor and his wife. If the list of visitors to Coppet is anything to go by, the time was hardly restful: Sir James Mackintosh, Sir Humphry and Lady Davy, Caroline von Humboldt, Count

---

611 SLUB Dresden, Mscr. Dresd. e. 90, LV (i).
612 *Indische Bibliothek*, III, i (1830), 1-113.
613 *Briefe*, I, 305.
614 Favre, lxxvii.

Neipperg, even Joseph Bonaparte.[615] The gap in Schlegel's correspondence with Favre indicates that he saw him in Coppet or Geneva during that time. Then it was back to Paris until 11 March 1815.

On 6 March 1815, Napoleon left Elba and embarked for France. Madame de Staël, Rocca, Albertine and Schlegel departed precipitately for Coppet. There was no certainty how the Emperor would behave towards this 'third power'. With liberals like Benjamin Constant flocking to serve the new regime, there were hopes for a better future. Lucien Bonaparte was living not far from Coppet, clearly placed to make discreet contact. Auguste was charged with making representations regarding his mother's interests. The Emperor seemed not unfavourable, but promised nothing. She tried to influence the 'peace party' in England, using as her intermediary the American minister Crawford. To no avail, as there ensued Waterloo, Napoleon's exile, the second Restoration of the Bourbons, and a second occupation of Paris.

The Staël party was in Coppet from 17 March, with interruptions, until 26/27 July 1815, when they left for Italy.[616] Rocca's health—he had tuberculosis—required a milder climate. The cavalcade was later augmented by Sismondi, as on the first Italian journey, also by Auguste and Victor de Broglie.[617] It was however no longer the Italy of those days; it was not possible simply to resume where *Corinne* had left off. The route this time did not take them to Rome or Naples, the places so much associated with 1805. Plague, not the floods that had hindered them on the first journey, now prevented their going further south than Florence.[618] Travelling from Lausanne, down to Lake Como and to Milan, one now entered Austrian territory. They encountered the surveillance that they had found so irksome when last in the Habsburg lands. Her old friend Monti, no longer a servant of the French, was now languishing in Austrian service.[619] The author of these restorations, Prince Metternich, even refused to allow her to purchase property in Lombardy.

Her beloved Italy seemed to be falling behind where France, England and especially Germany had embraced a cosmopolitan culture. Everyone was reading everybody else's literature through the device of translation. It

---

615 Jaskinski, 'Liste des principaux visiteurs', 482-485.
616 Details in Balayé, *Carnets de voyage*, 407-432.
617 *Souvenirs—1785-1870—du feu duc de Broglie*, 3 vols (Paris: Calmann Lévy, 1886), I, 337f.
618 *Krisenjahre*, III, 549.
619 Broglie, I, 337f.

3. The Years with Madame de Staël (1804-1817)

was the link between civilisations, the means of enrichment across national borders, the transfer of ideas. This was the burden of her pamphlet, *De l'esprit des traductions* [On the Spirit of Translations] that she brought out in Milan in 1816.[620] The French and English were doing it with varying degrees of success. The Germans however had excelled in it, and they should be the model for the Italians. Consider Voss's Homer, the most exact in any language, even more so works written for the theatre:

> If translations of poems enrich belles-lettres, those of works for the theatre could exercise an even greater influence; for the theatre is truly the executive power of literature. A. W. Schlegel has done a translation of Shakespeare which, joining exactness with inspiration, is completely national in Germany. English plays transmitted in this way are performed on the German stage, and Shakespeare and Schiller have become fellow-countrymen.[621]

These were proud words and a fine tribute to Schlegel whose Vienna Lectures were about to appear in Italian translation. If the Italians were piqued at Madame de Staël telling them how to run their literary affairs, it did not diminish the validity of her sentiments.

Schlegel, whose decorations entitled him to be called 'Eccelenza' in Italy,[622] did not neglect his wider contacts while there. He kept Friedrich Wilken of the *Heidelberger Jahrbücher* apprised of developments in Italian letters.[623] For Giuseppe Acerbi's periodical *Bibliotheca Italiana* he produced a piece on the horses of St Mark's in Venice.[624] From Genoa he wrote to the brothers Marc-Auguste and Charles Pictet in Geneva, agreeing to contribute to their *Bibliothèque britannique* (better known as *Bibliothèque universelle et revue de Genève*) and writing a critical essay on the figures of Niobe and her children. In Florence, he was made a member of the Società Fiorentina la Colombaria, the distinguished society for letters and history.[625]

Not for the first time, the Tieck family made its unruly presence felt in Italy. It was also one of those coincidences at which the Tiecks were

---

620 First published in Italian in *Biblioteca Italiana*, Jan. 1816, 9-18, as 'Sulla maniera e la utilità delle traduzione'.
621 *Oeuvres complètes de Madame de Staël*, 19 vols (Brussels: Wahlen, 1820-24), XVIII (Mélanges), 335.
622 *Krisenjahre*, II, 287.
623 *Briefe*, I, 308-310.
624 'Lettres aux éditeurs de la Bibliothèque italienne, à Milan, sur les chevaux de bronze sur la basilique de Saint-Marc, à Venise', *Oeuvres*, II, 30-62.
625 *Krisenjahre*, III, 556. The diploma, which Josef Körner found in the old Sächsische Landesbibliothek, is lost.

experts. In May 1816, a letter to Schlegel arrived from Sophie in farthest Estonia.[626] She had worked out an elaborate plan to suit her purposes. She and Knorring would sell their Estonian estate, move to Italy, set up her brother Friedrich in Rome as a sculptor, while Schlegel was to act as tutor to Felix Theodor, the object of that valedictory poem written over ten years ago. She had not forgotten her own epic poem, *Flore und Blanscheflur*, for which Schlegel was to find a publisher.

None of this came to anything, at least not yet. Certainly she did nothing to alleviate the sculptor brother's financial and material state. Madame de Staël, again not for the first time, was to do that in some measure. Friedrich had been at the marble quarries in Carrara since May of 1812, executing busts for Crown Prince Ludwig's Walhalla. He was as usual in financial straits, the result partly of his own misfortune and partly the improvidence of his siblings. He had tried to secure a post at the Academy in Berlin: success came only in 1819. He was therefore very gratified when the Staëls, on their way from Genoa to Pisa, called in at Carrara and took him with them to Pisa from December 1815 until February of 1816. In April-May he accompanied them to Florence.[627] It was agreed that he should do busts of Albertine and Rocca, and a full-size statue of Necker. For the latter he was to receive 600 sequins.[628]

Again, as usual with Friedrich Tieck, not all went well. Madame de Staël did not like the marble bust of Rocca and cancelled it, leaving him out of pocket.[629] (The furious sculptor smashed the nose off.) Only a plaster bust has survived. The Necker statue did however meet her wishes: the statesman, in modern dress but draped with a mantle in the antique mode, his hand raised as if in the gesture of speaking.[630] Whatever influences may have been at work in its conception—Etruscan motifs have been suggested[631]—its creator was not happy with the result. It is certainly true that he and Schlegel studied Etruscan works of art in Florence, as part of the preparation for Schlegel's review of Niebuhr.[632] The bust of Albertine is lost.[633]

---

626 *Krisenjahre*, II, 297-299.
627 Ibid., 293; Balayé, *Carnets de voyage*, 430f.; Maaz, 18.
628 Contract drawn up 14 May, 1816 in Florence. SLUB Dresden, Mscr. Dresd. e. 90, XIX (28), 18. The sequin [zecchino] was equivalent to the ducat, which was worth 3 Reichstalers.
629 Maaz, 154, 304; Mscr. Dresd. *ibid*.
630 Maaz, 159f., 307.
631 Ibid., 161.
632 Most likely the folder marked 'Origines italicae'. SLUB Dresden, Mscr. Dresd. e. 90, LX.
633 Maaz, 303.

The Necker restitution having been guaranteed after the Restoration of 1815, it was now possible for Albertine to marry Victor de Broglie and become a duchess. There were formalities to be observed, the drawing up of a marriage contract (witnessed by Sismondi and Schlegel), [634]a papal dispensation for an interconfessional union.[635] The marriage was solemnized in Pisa by the resident Anglican clergyman[636] and again at Leghorn by a Catholic priest.[637] In consideration of the two grand families thus united, their sons were to be brought up Catholic, their daughters Protestant. In the event, Albertine inclined towards an un-Staëlian orthodoxy,[638] quietism and mysticism even: it was she who tried to win over a now sceptical Schlegel in 1838, eliciting from him that response abjuring his Catholicising past.[639] For the moment, he contented himself with an epithalamium.

That poem, 'An Fräulein Albertina von Staël bei ihrer Vermählung. Pisa 20. Februar 1816' [To Mademoiselle Albertina von Staël on the Occasion of her Marriage'] was privately printed in Pisa and even translated into Italian.[640] It was written in *ottava rima*,[641] a verse for special occasions, for objects near to his heart and affections. The poem to Caroline all those years ago had been in this stanza; that celebrating the union of the church and the arts similarly. Now it was Albertine's turn. It was also a kind of symbolic leave-taking from the Staël children. Auguste had reached full manhood; poor Albert was in his grave in Mecklenburg; now Albertine, who had been a small girl when he first joined their household, was stepping out into full womanhood (and soon motherhood). It was not yet a question of real separation; still, only Madame de Staël remained seemingly unchanged from those early years. It was therefore appropriate that Schlegel's poem should invoke the mother almost as much as the daughter. Nor could Jacques Necker be absent from his verses, the tutelary spirit summoned up from the shores of Lake Geneva to the banks of the Arno, the intellectual

---

634 Victor de Pange, 'La fortune de Victor de Broglie et d'Albertine de Staël d'après leur contrat de mariage et le testament de Madame de Staël', *Cahiers staëliens*, 13 (1971), 3-30.
635 Victor de Pange, 'L'affaire de la dispense pour le mariage catholique de Victor de Broglie et d'Albertine de Staël', *Cahiers staëliens*, 24 (1978), 23-35.
636 Broglie, I, 340; Victor de Pange, *Madame de Staël et le duc de Wellington. Correspondance inédite 1815-1817* (Paris: Gallimard, 1962), 52.
637 Paola Luciani and Patrizia Urbani, 'Neuf lettres inédites de Mme de Staël au cavaliere Giovanni Battista Ruschi (1816)', *Cahiers staëliens*, 47 (1995-96), 49-75, ref. 66.
638 Broglie, II, 178.
639 *Oeuvres*, I, 189-201.
640 *Applausi poetici per le faustissime nozze fra S. E. il signore Vittorio duca di Broglio pari di Francia principe del Sacro Romano Impero e la signora Albertina de Staël* (Pisa: Sebastiano Nistri, 1816).
641 *SW*, I, 154f.

and moral (and also ultimately financial) force behind this marriage. As if on cue, Brockhaus's *Zeitgenossen* brought out a short biography of Necker in its 1816 number, attributed to Schlegel.[642]

Albertine retained some affection for Schlegel and after her mother's death kept up a correspondence with him for the rest of her relatively short life. Those letters are a salutary reminder that his existence was not limited to the ultimately provincial affairs of Bonn and took in Paris, the affairs of state in which her husband was involved and her family. Victor de Broglie shared Albertine's interests, but one senses that his involvement with Schlegel was out of duty rather than inclination. When for instance he decided to spend Holy Week of 1816 in Rome, he pointedly did not ask for 'courses' from Schlegel.[643] References to Schlegel in the Broglie memoirs are also so sparing as to be almost absent.

Schlegel's own emotional life was not so fortunate. Madame de Staël was finding Pisa dull and moved to Florence to be among the 'monde'.[644] She renewed her acquaintance with the Countess of Albany; she was presented to the grand duke and duchess of Tuscany; she met Priscilla, Lady Burghersh, the Duke of Wellington's niece, the wife of the British envoy. In these circles[645] Schlegel was made acquainted with the reconstruction of the Niobe group from the Aegina temple in the Uffizi, produced by the English neo-classical architect Charles Robert Cockerell. He studied it with Friedrich Tieck in order to ascertain its authenticity.[646]

Schlegel also met an acquaintance, Nina Schiffenhuber-Hartl, the ward of the director of the court theatre in Vienna.[647] He had met her there in 1808, and she was a close friend of his sister-in-law, Dorothea. It seems that Dorothea was scheming to bring Schlegel and this piously Catholic young woman together. Finding her now in Florence, Schlegel needed no encouragement. In his usual way, he wrote two or three poems for her;[648]

---

642 'Jakob Necker', *Zeitgenossen*, I, iii (1816), 91-112. It appears to be a shortened and edited version of Madame de Staël's *Du caractère de M. Necker, et de sa vie privée* (1804), *SW*, VIII, 176-202.
643 Pange, 515.
644 Broglie, I, 346.
645 Notably those of the grand duke and of Madame de Staël. Cf. David Watkin, *The Life and Works of C. R. Cockerell* (London: Zwemmer, 1974), 22f.
646 Who is the 'sculpteur fort expérimenté dans les marbres de Carrare' referred to in *Oeuvres*, II, 25. AWS seems to have met Cockerell later in London. He writes to John Murray there on 2 April 1832 of 'Mon ami Mr. Cockerell'. Murray Archive, Ms. 41065, Edinburgh, National Library of Scotland.
647 *KA*, XXIX, 590f.
648 'Der Geliebten' and 'Lied', *SW*, I, 29-32 (Böcking's dating needs correcting).

in her fashion, Madame de Staël put an abrupt stop to any matrimonial plans that he might have.[649] As it was, Nina married the Nazarene painter Friedrich Overbeck instead. His images of her are certainly better than Schlegel's poetic gallantries.

We leave aside the question: would such a marriage have worked? What remains are the Staël-Schlegel emotional entanglements, the moral pressures (some might say blackmail), the protestations of his indispensability, the teasings, the ultimate affront of Rocca's presence. There is surely some symbolic significance in the fact that when Staël and Rocca finally sealed their union at Coppet on 10 October, 1816, it was Fanny Randall who represented the household at the private ceremony, not Schlegel.

The group returned via Milan, Mont Cenis and Savoy, to Coppet.[650] It was to be the last of the Coppet summers, but in many ways the most interesting. It was this summer that led Stendhal to write of the 'estates general of European opinion' being assembled there.[651] Of course these included Bonstetten, Ludovico di Breme, the acerbically witty *abate* and proponent of Romanticism, Henry Brougham, Lord and Lady Lansdowne, Lord and Lady Jersey and various others.[652] No-one could however compete with Lord Byron, later joined by his entourage, his friend Hobhouse and his physician Polidori:

> The society at Copet [sic] is agreeable—The D. de Broglie is sensible & well informed—and Schlegel is very piquant—Rocca (whom she has certainly "made an honest man") is better tho' in a bad way—and Stael herself much in her usual manner—[...]
>
> Lord Byron lives on the other side of the lake, shunned by all—both English & Genevese—except Mad. Stael—who can't resist a little celebrity— of what kind soever & and with whatever vice or meanness allied—[...][653]

This was how Henry Brougham summed up the situation. Victor de Broglie, referred to in this extract, saw Byron rather prissily as a 'braggart of vice', without any particular distinguishing features (except perhaps the lame

---

649 'he wanted to have proposed to her, but Madame de Staël would not let him'. Augustus J. C. Hare, *The Life and Letters of Frances Baroness Bunsen*, 2 vols (London: Daldy, Isbister, 1879), I, 133; Kohler, *Madame de Staël et la Suisse*, 658.
650 Broglie, I, 354f.
651 Stendhal, *Rome, Naples et Florence*, 155.
652 Jasinski, 'Liste des principaux visiteurs', 485-487.
653 *Shelley and His Circle, 1773-1822*, ed. Kenneth Neill Cameron *et al.*, 10 vols (Cambridge, Mass: Harvard UP, 1961-2002), VII, 13f.

foot that he shared with Talleyrand).[654] Broglie's mother-in-law clearly saw Byron as less diabolic and invited him on various occasions to cross the lake from Villa Diodati in Cologny to Coppet.[655] Once Hobhouse and Polidori arrived, there were diary descriptions and *médisances* about the company. Schlegel was described as 'a presumptuous literato, contradicting *à outrance*' (Polidori), [656] and

> I was between Schlegel and the Duke of Broglie: the conversation was lively, and ran chiefly to Sheridan. Schlegel would have his *School for Scandal* had no invention, and talked, I thought, rather dogmatically. He is a little thin man with a largish sharp face, thin grey hair, intelligent-looking, talks English well. (Hobhouse)[657]

Hobhouse also passed on anecdotes of scenes he himself had not witnessed:

> Madame de Staël was one day saying that she was glad she published her "Allemagne" some time ago; if she had done so now it would have been too late. Nobody cares about Germany—literature was on the decline. "Quoi, Madame, vous osez dire ça du pays de Frederick Schlegel devant William Schlegel!" [What, Madam, you dare to say that of the country of FS in front of AWS] "Ah," said Madame de Staël, throwing herself back in her chair, "comme la vanité est bête!" [how stupid vanity is]
> Schlegel was one day talking English to Miss Randall. Brême said, "It seems to me that the English, for a man that does not understand it, is rather a hard language." Schlegel went up to Madame de Staël, and said, "I see, Madame, that there is a conspiracy in your house against me; everybody is resolved to offend me." Madame de Staël was writing; she threw down her pen: "Dites-moi donc, M. de Brême, qu'avez-vous fait pour offenser M. Schlegel?" [Tell me, M. de Breme, what have you done to offend M. Schlegel?] Brême explained, but in vain. He said that he did not know that Schlegel was hired defender of all nations. "Sir," said Schlegel, "any one could see you meant to laugh at my way of pronouncing English."[658]

It was unfortunate that 'Augustus William Schlegel', the author of the now translated *Course of Lectures on Dramatic Art and Literature*, came over in the Byron circle as merely fractious and hypersensitive. It is also true that Di Breme, a friend and correspondent of Sismondi, who saw Madame de

---

654 Broglie, I, 360-362.
655 Schedule of Byron's movements and guests at Coppet in *Bonstettiana*, XI, ii, 680-682.
656 *Ibid.*, 774.
657 Lord Broughton (John Cam Hobhouse), *Recollections of a Long Life. With Additional Extracts From His Private Diaries*, ed. Lady Dorchester, 6 vols (London: Murray, 1909-11), II, 15.
658 *Ibid.*, 42f.

Staël as an 'aging python' and Schlegel as her 'lemur spirit', went out of his way to make fun of 'il dottissimo e celebre Sig. Schlegel'.[659] For it was through Schlegel, if not a 'hired defender of all nations', that the spirit of national literatures was being transferred across borders and Di Breme was one of its recipients.[660] These aspersions were all the more regrettable in that the real importance of the visits in the summer of 1816 lay in the fact that Madame de Staël was prepared to receive a Byron shunned by the rest of Europe, was receptive to his poetry (he responded with a reference in Canto Three of *Childe Harold*), and attempted to effect a reconciliation between him and his wife.[661] Madame de Staël also gave Byron a copy of the French translation of Schlegel's Vienna Lectures.[662]

It was therefore a pity that Byron, by his own account, failed to find common ground with Schlegel. Byron resolutely refused to flatter him: for him, Schlegel was 'William the testy'.[663] They disagreed over the status of Alfieri,[664] whom Schlegel in his Vienna Lectures had effectively written off as a further manifestation of European neo-classicism. Later, someone suggested that Byron had plagiarized the elegy *Rom*:[665] one can be certain that Byron did not need this particular source of inspiration. There was no question of Byron ceding ground to Schlegel, whose tendency to carp and to ride the high horse ('Schlegel is in high force')[666] were well known in Coppet. Byron did not know German, but someone must have taught him the rude word 'Hundsfot' [sic] which he used of Schlegel.[667] As Ludwig Tieck was to find out in 1817 when he met Coleridge, Anglo-German literary encounters, especially between persons of established reputation and marked personality, seldom went off well. Of course contrasts can be made with Goethe's enthusiastic reception of Byron—after the younger man's death. But if they had met? What then?

---

659 Ludovico di Breme, *Lettere*, ed. Piero Camporesi, Nuova Universale Einaudi, 73 (Turin: Einaudi, 1966), 326, 503.
660 Wolfram Krömer, *Ludovico di Breme 1780-1820. Der erste Theoretiker der Romantik in Italien*, Kölner Romanistische Arbeiten, 19 (Geneva and Paris: Droz; Paris: Minard, 1961), 137-143.
661 Cf. Norman King, 'La correspondance de Mme de Staël et de Byron en 1816', in: Ceri Crossley and Dennis Wood (eds), *Constant in Britain*, Annales Benjamin Constant, 7 (Lausanne: Institut Benjamin Constant; Paris: Touzot, 1987), 93-100.
662 *Ibid.*, 97. Duly received. Byron, *Letters and Journals*, V, 88.
663 *Ibid.*, VIII, 166f., 172f.
664 *Ibid.*, 164f.
665 *Ibid.*, VIII, 164.
666 *Ibid.*, V, 86.
667 *Ibid.*, VIII, 167.

The last Coppet summer came to an end. After the departure of the last duchesses and princes, it was time for the Staël entourage to return to Paris. Her secret marriage with Rocca was followed by the drawing up of her will. In this she left her literary papers to Schlegel, a decision that was to prove unacceptable to the Staël heirs and the subject of some renegotiation. Her circle reconvened at 6, rue Royale, and George Ticknor left a vignette of a dinner party at that house, not omitting this description of Schlegel: 'a careworn, wearied courtier, with the manners of a Frenchman of the gayest circles, and the habits of a German scholar'.[668] It was that seeming contradiction between the man whom he found 'poring over a Sanskrit Grammar' yet in society uniting 'German enthusiasm and force to French lightness and vivacity'. Madame de Staël had suffered a stroke on February 21, 1817. In May, speaking to Ticknor, she claimed that it was not her old self that he saw, but merely her shadow.[669]

Despite her physical deterioration, her old interest in politics and affairs of state was not quite extinguished. As usual, she went straight to the centre of power. She renewed her acquaintance with the Duke of Wellington, now commander-in-chief of the Allied armies of occupation, with proconsular powers. The Duke had an eye for ladies, but not for clever ones: 'She was a most agreeable woman, if only you *kept her light*, & away from politics'.[670] He gave her more than one 'petit *warning*'[671] and claimed that she was 'confoundedly afraid of me',[672] yet in June she moved to 9, rue neuve des Mathurins, which was next door to him, and he is reported as having visited her daily.[673] Clearly there was enough common ground between him, who hated talking politics, and her, for whom talking politics was living.[674]

---

668 Ticknor, I, 106.
669 *Ibid.*, 110.
670 Quoted in Elizabeth Longford, *Wellington: Pillar of State* (Frogmore, St Albans: Panther, 1975), 65. The anecdote in the Wellington literature that Madame de Staël became a Catholic on her deathbed, is of course pure invention. *Ibid.* There is Byron's doggerel poem to Murray with these lines on the death of Madame de Staël: '[...] the fellow Schlegel/Was very likely to inveigle/A dying person in compunction/To try the extremity of Unction'. Byron, *Letters and Journals*, V, 260.
671 Victor de Pange, *Madame de Staël et le duc de Wellington*, 77.
672 *Correspondence of Lady Burghersh with the Duke of Wellington*, ed. Lady Rose Weigall (London: Murray, 1903), 16.
673 *Bonstettiana*, XI, ii, 854.
674 Victor de Pange, 140.

Her illness—illnesses—treated under demeaning and distressing circumstances, grew worse and the end came on July 14, 1817. She had already taken leave of those closest to her, including Schlegel. Fanny Randall was there at her side. Schlegel, faithful as ever, described the circumstances to Lady Burghersh, the Duke's niece. The letter expressed his personal grief, but also quoted 'There broke a noble heart' and 'The rest is silence'.[675] The manners of a Frenchman and the habits of a German scholar.

3.4 Scholarly Matters

In these years the Dresden engraver Gustav Adolph Zumpe produced the image of Schlegel that has become one of the standard representations of his mature years.[676]

Fig. 21 Portrait engraving of August Wilhelm Schlegel by Gustav Adolph Zumpe (c. 1817). Image in the public domain.

---

675 *The Correspondence of Priscilla, Countess of Westmorland Edited by her Daughter Lady Rose Weigall* (London: Murray, 1909), 27f.
676 Zumpe did engravings for 'Bildnisse der berühmtesten Männer aller Völker und Zeiten'. Thieme-Becker dates the Schlegel portrait at 1822. Ulrich Thieme and Felix Becker, *Allgemeines Lexikon der bildenden Künstler von der Antike bis zur Gegenwart* (Leipzig: Engelmann, 1907-50), XXXVI, 597f.

Where and under what circumstances Schlegel sat for it (if at all), we do not know. It shows him in sharp profile, looking straight ahead, the mouth firm, the figure straight; there is the usual high stock; the coat has elegantly tailored lapels. Quite the man about town, perhaps, but also the scholar-critic with his eye fixed on the task in hand. If so, it is a reminder that these last years with Madame de Staël—and one or two before them—were also times of critical activity and saw a last flurry of enthusiasm for things medieval. It showed that Schlegel, like Lessing in his father's generation, was able to extend a review far beyond a journal's requirements and raise issues—of accuracy, of integrity—that were relevant for the wider republic of letters. Like Lessing's, Schlegel's eye was also always lighting on things that distracted from the main task. How else could he claim to George Ticknor in 1817 that he was 'now wholly devoted to Sanskrit'[677] when in the same year he produced a description of engravings of Fra Angelico that were as unrelated as one could imagine?

The reviews extend over six years (1810-16),[678] the products of very different periods in time, ones of upheaval and scene-change, seemingly done in odd moments between editing his own Vienna Lectures or keeping *De l'Allemagne* out of Savary's clutches, evidence of Schlegel's ability to snatch some utility out of the disjointed and chaotic last years in Coppet and Berne, then in Paris; they owe much to his withdrawal in Coppet to the sanctum of his 'blue room', or to seclusion in Berne (where distractions

---

677 Ticknor, I, 106.
678 They are, in chronological order: 'Buch der Liebe. Herausgegeben durch Dr. Johann Gustav Büsching und Dr. Friedrich Heinrich von der Hagen. Erster Band. Berlin, bey J. Hitzig. 1809', *Heidelberger Jahrbücher der Literatur für Philologie, Historie, schöne Literatur*, 1810, 3. Jg. 1. Bd., 3. Heft, 97-118, *SW*, XII, 225-243; 'Ludovico Ariosto's Rasender Roland, übersetzt von J. D. Gries, 1804-1808. IV Theile', *ibid.*, 3. Jg., 5. Heft, 193-234, *SW*, XII, 243-288; 'Erstes Sendschreiben über den Titurel… von B. J. Docen. Berlin und Leipzig b. Salfeld. 1810', *Heidelberger Jahrbücher der Literatur*, 4. Jg., Nr. 68-70, 1073-1111, *SW*, XII, 288-321; 'Winckelmann's Werke, herausgegeben von C. L. Fernow. 1. Band. 1808. 3. 4. Band, herausgegeben von Heinrich Meyer und Joh. Schulze. 1809. 1811', *ibid.*, 1812, Nr. 5-7, 65-112, *SW*, XII, 321-383; 'Altdeutsche Wälder herausgegeben durch die Brüder Grimm. Erster Band. Cassel, bey Thurneisen 1813', *ibid.*, 8. Jg., 2. Hälfte, Nr. 46-48, 1815, 721-766, *SW*, XII, 383-426; 'Yadjnadatta-Badha ou La mort d'Yadjnadatta, épisode extrait et traduit du Ramayana, poème épique Sanskrit. Par A. L. Chézy. Paris 1814'. 'Discours prononcé au Collége Royal de France, à l'Ouverture du cours de langue et de littérature Sanskrite, par A. L. Chézy. Paris 1815', *ibid.*, Nr. 56, 1815, 881-893, *SW*, XII, 427-438; 'Sui quattro cavalli della basilica di S. Marco in Venezia. Lettera di Andrea Mustoxidi Corcirese. Padova 1816', *ibid.*, 9. Jg., 2. Hälfte, Nr. 42, 1816, 657-664, *SW*, XII, 438-444; 'Römische Geschichte von B. G. Niebuhr. Berlin, in der Realschulbuchhandlung. Erster Theil. 1811. Zweyter Theil 1812', *ibid.*, No. 53-57, 1816, 833-906, *SW*, XII, 444-512.

were few), less to the polished salon discourse around Madame de Staël's table; keeping up learned correspondence, adding to the folders of textual collations and collectanea that evidence his wide-encompassing reading, and relying on a formidable memory for detail. The three-year gap in publication dates between 1812 and 1815 reflects the interruption of scholarly activity in Stockholm and in Bernadotte's camp. Yet for all that they cohere as a corpus of learned writing.

They may seem intensely specialized, but they are by the same token interconnected, showing the humanist scholar ranging at will across the terrains that he had staked out as his own: the languages that humankind spoke (and still speaks), the historical structures that they inhabit, the characteristic ways of organizing and presenting knowledge, our attitudes to myth, our way of commemorating the dead, the works of art that ensure their continuing life, and how these came about. They are an attempt to explain continuities and ruptures, to see these in terms of historical rhythms and cycles.

This is of course to see systematically what in reality was produced in haphazard form, as editors (Wilken of the *Heidelberger Jahrbücher* or Pictet of the *Bibliothèque universelle*) approached him and thought how best to bring his knowledge to bear on the most recent issues of scholarship. They are— especially if we add in the contributions to Friedrich Schlegel's *Deutsches Museum*—also first fulfilments of older, long-term preoccupations. The *Nibelungenlied* had been exercising him ever since his exchange of letters with Ludwig Tieck in 1802 and his section in the Berlin Lectures. He had long since taken note of Sanskrit: there had been his early interest in Georg Forster's translation of Sir William Jones's version of the *Śakuntalâ*;[679] his stated intention in the *Athenaeum* to learn Sanskrit (and other oriental languages);[680] his hope, expressed in the Berlin Lectures, that India would open up new realms of poetry, religion and myth; the fascination with which he followed his brother Friedrich;[681] his statement in the still unpublished *Considérations* that India was the 'cradle of mankind'.[682] Now, in 1815, the year of his review of Chézy, he could write to Favre that he was 'sorting out the characters and finding his way in the grammar'.[683]

---

679 *SW*, VII, 40.
680 *Ibid.*, 215; 'Nachschrift des Uebersetzers an Ludwig Tieck', *Athenaeum*, II, ii, 281.
681 *SW*, VIII, 150.
682 *Oeuvres*, I, 305.
683 Favre, lxxvi.

They seem at odds with his other activity in the years 1812-14, and they appear to be unrelated to his preoccupations before the flight to Russia: helping with *De l'Allemagne* and seeing his own Vienna Lectures to press. It is hard enough keeping track of his movements physically and geographically, let alone with his disparate literary and philological projects. Some of these reviews, as said, simply resulted from Wilken, the editor of the *Heidelberger Jahrbücher*, knowing what he was looking for (and paying well) and finding in Schlegel the right reviewer. Some came closer to Schlegel's own medieval project and were an opportunity to formulate thoughts that had to date remained private or limited to scholarly interchange: the only published statements by Schlegel on the *Nibelungenlied* were to be found in his brother's periodical. August Wilhelm's breakneck journey to Vienna in 1811 was not just about saving a proof of *De l'Allemagne* for Madame de Staël but was also about handing over copy for Friedrich's *Deutsches Museum*.

It is tempting to see a grand Coppet narrative encompassing *De l'Allemagne*, Schlegel's Lectures and Sismondi's Lectures on Romance Literature—and it has its justification. But what we have in these reviews is essentially a Schlegel construction. It was allied in some regards to the grand sweep of Friedrich Schlegel's Vienna Lectures on literature, *Geschichte der alten und neuen Literatur* (1814), but it was characteristic of August Wilhelm in that he was drawing on the reservoirs of his knowledge and of necessity limiting himself to disjointed stones in an edifice that took in ancient languages and cultures, the medieval world, art and archaeology, historiography and translation.

When in 1817, after Madame de Staël's death and thoughts of an academic career had begun to take shape in his mind, he could point to this body of learning and criticism—and to much else besides—as a testimony to his learned qualifications. It would link up with that brief interlude in Jena twenty years earlier, where it had been the erudite Latinity of *De geographia Homerica* that had counted, not so much his translations of Dante or Shakespeare or what he had written in their support. They would remind readers—as if it were necessary—that nothing touched by the Schlegel brothers—the *Athenaeum, Europa*, their various courses of lectures—could be free of erudition; it was so much part of their natures. They could also wear that learning lightly, as when at different times they gave public lectures in Vienna. But reviews were another matter.

Learned Reviews

These reviews were a further reminder. In the early decades of the nineteenth century, before specialisms and demarcations took over the academy, it was still possible to aspire to universal knowledge. They are in some ways the demonstration of those Berlin lectures on 'Enzyclopädie', given in 1803 to a partly discriminating and partly uncomprehending audience. There, Schlegel had defined the encyclopedic principle as: method, thoroughness of approach, universality, drawing on the widest areas of the mind, theory but also empirical experience, a philosophical base that enabled past and present, abstract and concrete, to cohere as a whole. That is why Schlegel's 1812 review of Winckelmann is so important, for it had been Winckelmann who had first freed the study of classical art and archaeology from the merely polymathic, the unrelieved accumulation of facts for their own sake, and who had injected into it insights drawn from human history and climate, poetry, religion, philosophy, to explain in part what made the Greek sense of beauty and proportion unique and universally valid, and in a style that was a work of art in itself. Schlegel's reviews also have a sense of style, but they have by the same token their sections of severe factual strictures, pedantry even, that draw on the huge range of notes that he made—and never published.

Of course these reviews were not without their hints to the general (and also learned) readership of the *Heidelberger Jahrbücher* that here was no novice. He, too (in the review of Gries's translation of *Orlando Furioso*) had once translated a canto of Ariosto (and, in his opinion, better than Gries). He, too (in the reviews of Büsching, von der Hagen, Docen and the Grimms) was (or would be) the author of a significant essay on the Middle Ages that had just come out in his brother's periodical *Deutsches Museum*, where he had made no secret of the fact that he was preparing an edition of the *Nibelungenlied*. He (in the Grimm review) had been pursuing antiquarian and learned studies on medieval subjects, as his correspondence with the erudite Favre in Geneva testified; he had been working on the etymology of the German language, to which a mass of notes bore witness. He had been to Italy (the Mustoxidi and Niebuhr reviews), had met there the savants Carlo Feà and Pierre-François d'Harcarville, had seen everything of archaeological or palaeographical interest (earning from Sismondi that appellation 'naturalist', not meant as a compliment) and had seen the statuary and the art works that mattered (he had visited the collections in Paris looted by Napoleon). He was in 1815, after his return to Paris, now learning Sanskrit in earnest (the Chézy review), so that his remarks on it, while not yet from one equal to another, already possessed some gravity (also as the brother of Friedrich Schlegel the Sanskritist). Above all (the Niebuhr review), he had been to places that Niebuhr, the Roman historian, had not yet visited and which Schlegel believed he should have done before advancing some of his theories. He had read everything, and an examination of the sources cited in these reviews reveals a formidable arsenal of knowledge, from old Renaissance humanist antiquarianism right up to the beginnings of German academic scholarship. He had a good eye for archaeological inscriptions—and he had a terrifying memory for textual references and quotations.

Several of these reviews refer to projects never carried out (the *Nibelungenlied* edition and the etymological dictionary would be but two). Sometimes they show their place in the transition from the scholarly world of the eighteenth to the nineteenth century and reflect the state of knowledge in areas that were emerging out of the archaeological and antiquarian into specialized disciplines. His review of the Grimms is part of the narrative of Germanic philology that would make its way into the university curriculum. Of course reminders were still in season. He used the review of Gries to reacquaint readers with his own proficiency in poetic form. Despite Goethe's masterly handling of Romance stanzas, it was clear that not everyone grasped their underlying structures: there was the need for a prosodic approach. All the learning displayed here could not disguise the fact that medieval studies, in spite of pioneering efforts over the last half century, still suffered from indifference in some quarters and needed to be placed on a firmer footing.[684] Even so, he could have been more gracious to the Grimm brothers by acknowledging that they, even despite points of major disagreement, were with him adding pieces to the mosaic of awareness, popular as well as scholarly. The same might be said for Roman history. It was entering into a phase of 'higher criticism',

---

684 Cf. the Wolfenbüttel librarian Ernst Theodor Langer writing sarcastically in 1813 to Johann Joachim Eschenburg on the 'bis zur Abgötterey sich versteigernde Bewundrung und Empfehlung des *Nibelungen, Edda* etc'. Quoted by Matthias Buschmeier, 'Zwischen allen Stühlen. Eschenburgs "Popularphilologie"', in: Cord-Friedrich Berghahn and Till Kinzel (eds), *Johann Joachim Eschenburg und die Künste und Wissenschaften zwischen Aufklärung und Romantik. Netzwerke und Kulturen des Wissens*, GRM-Beiheft 50 (Heidelberg: Winter, 2013), 95-114, ref. 112.

where inscriptions and sources would be subjected to a scrutiny hitherto unimagined.

Yet each review had its own note and its own agenda. Some were restatements of old positions under new guise. The review of Gries's Ariosto, for example, reiterated Schlegel's inerrant belief in the efficacy of such translations, especially where Schleiermacher and Wilhelm von Humboldt were issuing doubts and caveats on the subject. It restated his insistence on 'the metrical form of the original' ['eigne metrische Form'],[685] but without too much strictness (Goethe was a good model). Nevertheless his own taste had changed since 1799. Whereas Schlegel had then filled up a whole section of the *Athenaeum* with the translation of a canto from Ariosto, he now found him less attractive. There was too much *esprit* and striving for effect. He lacked Dante's 'soul' ['Gemüth'].[686] He was closer to the popular romances of chivalry and the *Amadis de Gaules*.

One side of Schlegel was drawn to those old courtly *romans,* the *Amadis* and its like, the chapbooks, in short almost anything that predated 1500. Thus his reviews of Büsching/von der Hagen and of Docen stress the need to pass on to contemporary readers the wealth of older German language and literature. It would be worth doing this for its own sake: the 'Zeitumstände',[687] the times in which they were living (Schlegel was writing these reviews in 1810) rendered it all the more necessary. He was even prepared to make concessions to popular taste if need be. Here was a basic contradiction. There were echoes of the Vienna Lectures, but pointers too towards the patriotic message of his brother's periodical *Deutsches Museum* that came out in Vienna in 1812. This, too, had its qualifications. For all our eagerness to promulgate the riches of the past, he says, we should not forget philological scruples in the process. Language, the vehicle in which these texts are handed down, represents the very highest that our culture contains ['Palladium unsrer Bildung'].[688] We need a high standard of grammatical, linguistic and lexical accuracy.

One part of his review of Bernhard Joseph Docen's *Erstes Sendschreiben über den Titurel* [*First Letter on Titurel*] illustrates this crux nicely (the work was even dedicated to Schlegel). It acknowledges Docen's informative and pioneering work on the Munich manuscript of this thirteenth-century

---

685 *SW*, XII, 246.
686 *Ibid.*, 280.
687 *Ibid.*, 242.
688 *Ibid.*, 231.

Arthurian text.[689] That is one side. Yet the philologist in him asserts itself, and Schlegel establishes, with considerable acumen, who the author is. This older fragment of *Titurel* must be by Wolfram von Eschenbach; it is not to be confused with the later and greatly expanded *Der jüngere Titurel* of 1477. Thus, as it were in a few learned asides, Schlegel takes his place in the early history of Wolfram studies.[690]

Still, it would not be by philology alone that editions were to come into being: dating, learned perspicacity were fine, but so was also a 'poetic sense' ['dichterisches Gefühl'],[691] one might say some poetic imagination or inventiveness. This Schlegel illustrates by drawing a distinction between *Titurel* and the *Nibelungenlied*. *Titurel*, as part of the Grail cycle, was unhistorical, foreign, learned, chivalric. The *Nibelungenlied*, on the other hand, was primeval, native, of the people, tragic, heroic. It was like comparing Dante with Homer—and here Schlegel has recourse to some of the forced polarities of Romantic doctrine. It also formed part of Schlegel's preference in esteem for the Germanic heroic lay as against the Charlemagne and Grail cycles that were of Romance origin. Not only that: the reviewer was also setting out his stall as a potential future editor of the *Nibelungenlied*.

Schlegel was relatively kind to von der Hagen, Büsching and Docen, for they represented much of what he also was striving for. When in 1815 he came to review the Grimm brothers' *Altdeutsche Wälder* [*Old German Miscellany*], the tone was different. It is worth reflecting that Schlegel by then was becoming increasingly polemical and (some might say) pedantic, having in 1812 subjected Fernow and Meyer's edition of Winckelmann to a merciless scrutiny. Johann Diederich Gries, too, had been less than pleased at Schlegel's detailed 'suggestions' for his Ariosto rendering.[692] Of course from the very outset of his reviewing career Schlegel had hardly ever been able to suppress learned polemics (witness the Voss review), textual quibbles, parades of knowledge. One might except his piece on Bürger, which was also a review and arguably his best in the genre. Thus there is more than merely a difference in tone between these reviews and his articles

---

689 Edith Höltenschmidt, *Die Mittelalter-Rezeption der Brüder Schlegel* (Paderborn, etc.: Schöningh, 2000), 97-101.
690 For which he received no credit in his own lifetime. Cf. *Wolfram von Eschenbach*, ed. Karl Lachmann, 6th ed. (Berlin, Leipzig: de Gruyter, 1926) (1833 preface), xxviii.
691 *SW*, XII, 293.
692 *Briefe*, I, 275-282.

for the *Deutsches Museum*. The former punish defaults of scholarship. The latter set out the author's own position.

Winckelmann could no longer feel Schlegel's lash, but the Grimm brothers could. It should be remembered that Jacob and Wilhelm Grimm, if not quite at the beginning of their careers, were still finding their way as scholars and were not yet the authors of the standard grammatical and philological works that are associated with their names. The title 'Wälder', 'silvae', suggested the tentative, the fragmentary, the experimental. Put at its most disarmingly simple, the Grimms had postulated a people, no, a 'folk' — the Germanic root is important — that out of its collective unconscious had produced poetry. There was no evidence for this hypothesis, only feeling or intuition, the sense that it must be so. Nevertheless they had not only conjectured the existence of such poetry from the mists of time, but had come perilously close to claiming some historical truth for it. Schlegel by contrast believed in clear stages, first myth, then poetic utterance, then historical content. Instead, he saw here risky conjectures and shaky etymologies.[693] A vague mythical entity could not also express history; there must be, in his term, 'art' (a poet) as well as 'nature' (mythical origins). In addition, care was needed: much older poetry was unreliable and deliberately distorted the historical record. Turning to textual studies (citing his own edition of the *Nibelungenlied*, a chimaera that in 1815 he still believed in), he urged the need to establish a grammatical and a lexical base; there must be no rushing into guess-work. Here Schlegel throws the book, in fact several books, at the future lexicographers, pointing out that German does not yet have the kind of satisfactory etymological dictionary that other linguistic cultures had had for decades and indeed for centuries.[694] In the case of the *Nibelungenlied*, he restated what he had said in 1812, that the poem was a mixture of the undated heroic lay and also of a specific moment in historical time, the great barbarian invasions. It had moved northwards into Scandinavia, not the other way round, from a Christian base into a pagan theogony.

Not all of this was itself free of mythologizing, but the Grimms, predictably and understandably piqued at this attack on their integrity and

---

693 Cf. AWS's warning against 'étymologie spéculative' in his essay *De l'Étymologie en général*. *Oeuvres*, II, 108.

694 Schlegel cites the dictionaries by George Hickes (1689), Lambert den Kate (1723), Edward Lye (1772), Pierre Carpentier (1772) and Jean-Baptiste Roquefort (1808).

going into print to defend themselves,[695] were nevertheless forced to rethink some of their positions and turned as a result to grammar, comparative philology and lexicography, for which they still remain famous. Their beating at Schlegel's hands may not have seemed salutary at the time, but it proved to be so in the long run. Whether Barthold Georg Niebuhr, the historian of Rome, similarly chastened, had cause to see things this way, is less certain.

Niebuhr had in Schlegel's eyes erred on several counts. He had—a rather cheap piece of point-scoring on Schlegel's part—not been to Italy to see the monuments and inscriptions for himself, a reminder all the same that Schlegel's association with Madame de Staël had not been a mere frivolous grand tour. He had rushed in with hypotheses where older scholarship had counselled caution (witness already Louis de Beaufort's speaking title of 1738 *Sur l'incertitude des cinq premiers siècles de l'histoire romaine* [On the Uncertainty of the First Five Centuries of Roman History]), and crucially, he had advanced theories that did not fit in with Schlegel's own. Thus his 'lay theory' that postulated songs, sagas, in which the ancestors of the Romans sang about their early history, was a 'basic error'[696] (for Theodor Mommsen one of Niebuhr's 'brilliant aberrations'),[697] because no amount of historical legerdemain could summon up texts that essentially did not exist; and even the later founding myths of the Romans (Aeneas, Romulus etc.) were pure invention. It was, as it were, the Grimms' unsustainable folk theories as applied to Italy.

Schlegel was however as interested as Niebuhr in early human origins and always had been, but his notions of the theory of time were different. He diverged in his view of language. For him languages did not evolve out of climate but out of assimilation and imitation.[698] It was yet another reason for sound etymological principles. The Greek and Italic

---

695 *Achim von Arnim und die ihm nahe standen*, hg. v. Reinhold Steig and Herman Grimm, 3 vols (Stuttgart and Berlin: Cotta, 1894-1913), III: *Achim von Arnim und Jacob und Wilhelm Grimm*, ed. Reinhold Steig, 360. Predictably, the Grimms take Niebuhr's side against Schlegel. Ibid., 370; *Briefe der Brüder Grimm an Savigny*, ed. Ingeborg Schnack and Wilhelm Schoof (Berlin: Erich Schmidt, 1953), 252. Their defence is in vol. 3 of the *Altdeutsche Wälder* (1816). Wilhelm Grimm, *Kleinere Schriften*, ed. Gustav Hinrichs, 4 vols (Berlin: Dümmler, 1881-83; Gütersloh: Bertelsmann, 1887), II, 156-161.
696 *SW*, XII, 449.
697 'glänzende Verirrungen'. Susanne Stark, 'Behind Inverted Commas'. *Translation and Anglo-German Cultural Relations in the Nineteenth Century*, Topics in Translation, 15 (Clevedon etc.: Multilingual Matters, 1999), 131. For the influence of Niebuhr's lay theory in the Anglo-Saxon world, see also 120-141.
698 *SW*, XII, 458.

languages were related—on that both agreed—but Schlegel would not accept that they intercommunicated on the Italian peninsula. Rather, they had common Caucasian origins in some shadowy Central Asian 'Ursitze' [primeval places of abode]. Schlegel does little for his case by throwing in the mysterious Pelasgians, a people upon which already *De geographia Homerica* had expounded, except by way of saying that Niebuhr's account of early Mediterranean peoples needed revision.[699] Schlegel may have been on more secure ground than Niebuhr in his account of the Etruscans, their inscriptions, their artefacts, their cultural heritage; stating that we basically do not know where they came from was safer than speculation. Was he right about their architecture? Niebuhr claimed that their walled cities were the products of serf labour; for Schlegel, they were evidence of a high state of theoretical and technical knowledge imparted by a priestly caste. Like that of the Greeks, they were monumental, built for eternity; the beginnings of culture were manifested in complexity of design and sophistication of execution. He had said so in his unpublished *Considérations* of 1805: here he was saying it in public, and it would be always in the background of his later historical thinking. It linked in easily with his remarks on Sanskrit in 1815, where the 'perfection in construction' [Vollkommenheit ihres Baues][700] of this ancient language was evidence of its venerability and sophistication. Myth-making was clearly not limited to one party.

His review of Fernow's and Meyer's edition of Winckelmann's works that had come out in 1808-09 touches on similar themes. Pelasgians and Etruscans, about whom Winckelmann's (or his editors') knowledge was shaky, would occur again, but also Egyptians. Their temples, 'the wonder of the world',[701] the monumental repose of these earliest surviving edifices of humankind, their immutability and symmetry, the evidence of technical mastery that they evinced: these it was that seized the beholder (he would later add Indian and Aztec monuments to this list). Whereas Winckelmann

---

699 Giuseppe Micali, an authority for Schlegel, refers to the Pelasgians as 'oscura stirpe' and generally casts doubts on their origins. *L'Italia avanti il dominio dei Romani*, 4 vols (Florence: Piatti, 1810), I, 63, 65. A hundred years later, the Pelasgians were being referred to as 'a peg upon which to hang all sorts of speculation'. J. L. Myres, 'A History of the Pelasgian Theory', *Journal of Hellenic Studies* 27 (1907), 170-222, ref. 170. Roughly half a century later, all the sources were made known but still no consensus had been reached. Fritz Lochner-Hüttenbach, *Die Pelasger*, Arbeiten aus dem Institut für Sprachwissenschaft Graz, 6 (Vienna: Gerold, 1960).

700 *SW*, XII, 427.

701 *Ibid.*, 361. Cf. 'cette architecture majestueusement solide'; *Oeuvres*, II, 9; 'une certaine grandeur primitive'. *Ibid.*, 104.

had been dismissive of Egyptian art and had seen Egypt at most as receptive of Greece, Schlegel reversed the order and made the Greeks the debtors. True, the Egyptians did not reach such perfection in their depiction of the human figure, but in animal statuary they were hardly inferior, witness the lions on the Capitol that he, with Alexander von Humboldt's assistance, had traced back to their Egyptian provenance, even down to their geological content.

There were, however, more basic issues at stake. There was no denying Winckelmann's status as writer and art historian. Perhaps Friedrich Schlegel's superlatives like 'divine' or 'bible' [702] were no longer appropriate, and August Wilhelm in 1812 did not subscribe as wholeheartedly as he had done in his Berlin Lectures to the view that had Winckelmann, Hemsterhuis and Goethe as the only significant figures emerging out of an otherwise dismal eighteenth century. 'Classical' is however a word he is still prepared to use of Winckelmann in 1812, but with qualifications.[703] For all its sensuously enthusiastic passages, one would have to acknowledge defects in Winckelmann's style; his notion of symbol could no longer satisfy; he was not sound on Greek painting (or on Greek sources, for that matter); his definition of beauty inclined too much to what pleased the eye; he failed to see movements and developments in history and was unwilling to admit that the Greeks, too, were subject to the processes of decline. Some of this was expecting Winckelmann to be Herder or Friedrich Schlegel,[704] but it was also an acknowledgment that aesthetics and the history of art had moved on since Winckelmann's day.

Schlegel, as he admitted in his short review in 1816 on the horses at St Mark's in Venice, had seen all the statuary in Europe that mattered;[705] he had admired this equestrian group from its translation from Venice to the Tuileries and back; he knew all about Greek bronze casting (more at least than Winckelmann did); he was au fait with the latest discoveries

---

702 *KA*, XVIII, 199.
703 Next to Herder, Schlegel is the authority most quoted in Carl Justi's classic biography of Winckelmann.
704 The Fernow-Meyer edition of Winckelmann did not contain the essay 'Vom mündlichen Vortrag der neueren allgemeinen Geschichte' (1754?), which was indebted to Voltaire's view of history. See Katherine Harloe, *Winckelmann and the Invention of Antiquity. History and Aesthetics in the Age of* Altertumswissenschaft (Oxford: Oxford UP, 2013), 112f.
705 *SW*, XII, 444.

and excavations. His article on the Niobe group[706] sifted the archaeological evidence for declaring these figures to be the originals from the Aegina temple. Charles Robert Cockerell believed they were (Winckelmann, too). Only Schlegel, with Friedrich Tieck's expertise to help him, had examined the marble.[707] They might be copies done from Roman marble, or from imported Greek stone. The important thing was that the 'spirit of the original' had been copied. One must accept, as with paintings done after Raphael cartoons, that competent imitation also had its place.[708]

Winckelmann studies, therefore, must progress and take these and other new developments into account.[709] There was—although he did not say this in so many words—no point in subjecting Winckelmann to hagiography, as Goethe had done in 1805, overlooking his personal frailties (his conversion, for instance).[710] To highlight the inadequacies of this edition, when the editors were, respectively, the ducal librarian in Weimar (Carl Ludwig Fernow, now dead), and Goethe's right-hand man in art matters (the rigidly neo-classical Heinrich Meyer, still very much alive), was to register a point: that another generation of criticism had come of age and that its standards required more rigour than the one which it had succeeded.

Above all, with two exceptions, it was German intellectual and scholarly endeavours that Schlegel had discussed in his reviews. They were a German voice, a statement of German achievement. Where fufilment was lacking, he was hortatory, pointing to what must be done and could be done. That applied, too, to Antoine-Léonard de Chézy's translations from the Sanskrit of 1815. Schlegel was insistent that his approach to Sanskrit was different from others', knowing as he did Latin and Greek, and the whole range of the Germanic dialects. It was related to his general studies of etymology that he had already set out in a treatise called *De l'Étymologie en général* and which dates from roughly this period.[711] Thus he was coming to it from the

---

706 'Niobé et ses enfants. Sur la composition originale de ces statues', *Oeuvres*, II, 3-29. Emil Sulger-Gebing, *Die Brüder A. W. und F. Schlegel in ihrem Verhältnisse zur bildenden Kunst*, Forschungen zur neueren Litteraturgeschichte, 3 (Munich: Haushalter, 1897), 167-170.
707 SW, XII, 25.
708 Ibid., 27f.
709 For instance, Giuseppe Micali's *L'Italia avanti il dominio dei Romani* (1810).
710 Schlegel makes the point, often overlooked, that Goethe's hagiography is in the preface to an edition of Winckelmann's letters that show him to be anything but the young Achilles there apostrophized. SW, XII, 382.
711 *Oeuvres*, II, 103-141.

angle of grammar and etymology. But he was not yet in any position to review Chézy on this basis.

Rather, his remarks have a tri-cultural thrust: what the English have achieved in the area of Sanskrit studies, what the French have done with this inheritance, and what the Germans may yet be able to accomplish. Schlegel was of course speaking as the brother of Friedrich, of *Ueber die Sprache und Weisheit der Indier*, not yet as competent in the language, but learning fast and aware of its problems and the challenges involved. He was writing from Paris, where Chézy, as already mentioned, was now professor of oriental languages at the Collège de France and where Louis-Mathieu Langlès was professor of Persian. Paris was clearly the place to be, and when Schlegel set out his list of desideranda[712] it was with Parisian conditions and holdings in mind: the need for editions using devanagari type; the desirability of translating the key accessible Sanskrit texts into German (not just extracts, as Friedrich had done), the epic *Râmâyana*, *Hitopadeśa* the collection of fables; the urgency of training young men in the necessary skills and sending them to Paris, but also to London: Franz Bopp had been there since 1812 and others must follow. Clearly this was more a statement of intent than one of achievement. Nevertheless, his *Ueber den gegenwärtigen Zustand der Indischen Philologie* [On the Present State of Indian Philology], with which he inaugurated his career as a Sanskritist in Bonn in 1819,[713] would show how much he had assimilated in the mean time.

There was however a distinctly German note sounded, and one that would echo through all of Schlegel's later career as an orientalist: the especially ordained appropriateness of the Germans as disinterested academic scholars. If the Germans had not achieved the nation-state that had been forged by the French or the British, they at least had the *république des lettres*, the academy of scholars. The French and the British, for all their scholarly and learned achievements—and Schlegel was never too proud to avail himself of them—did not have real universities in the German sense; pure, untainted scholarship could only be found in the German academic community. Much (but not all) of this was admittedly true, and the history of Anglo-German academic relations in the nineteenth century was to bear

---

712 *SW*, XII, 435-438.
713 *Jahrbuch der Preußischen Rhein-Universität*, 1 (1819), 224-250; *Indische Bibliothek*, 1 (1820), 1-27; also in *Bibliothèque universelle des sciences, belles-lettres, et arts*, XII: Littérature (1819), 349-370.

it out. By this account, oriental studies elsewhere were compromised by association with colonial and commercial expansion. True, all scholars were indebted to Sir William Jones, to Wilkins, to the *Asiatick Researches*, to Colebrooke (Schlegel and he were later to become friends), to Chézy, but there hung, over British oriental endeavours at least, always that ominous phrase 'Honourable East India Company' and its links with the even more dreaded word 'commerce'. How could unperjured scholarship thrive where enrichment and territorial gain were the underlying motives? Of course there were ways of turning this argument on its head—through colonial conquests the texts had become available to Western scholars—but this Schlegel never chose to do. If, writing in 1815, Schlegel saw scant hope of a German nation-in-being issuing forth from the Napoleonic upheavals, at least the German university had emerged strengthened and ready for greater things. There was, of course, as he wrote in 1815, no question of his joining (or re-joining) the body academic: he could only express the hope that the Germans would succeed—and more—where the French, and even the British, had already excelled. It was evident that the years with Madame de Staël had not made him into an uncritical Francophile, nor had they succeeded in suppressing his latent Anglophobia.

Medieval Studies

All of this he had expressed through critical reviews of others' work. What of his own studies? As a medievalist, Schlegel stands somewhere between the 'heroic' first age of German medieval studies ('heroic' in both senses), with its volumes of essays, its engravings of 'Wolfram von Eschilbach' [*sic*], its pull-out illustrations of manuscripts, its learned antiquarianism— essentially the world of Docen, Büsching and von der Hagen—and the severe scholarship of the Grimm brothers and Karl Lachmann. These last-named had made their position symbolically clear in their disdain for the old German black-letter type[714] and their adoption of the unfrilled lower case for spelling. Schlegel has this median position between these two medievalist schools because on the one hand he favoured modernisation as being the only way of assuring a wider dissemination of the Old German heritage; but on the other he pounced on speculation and guesswork, had

---

714 Cf. Jacob Grimm's remark on Schlegel's intention of publishing his edition of the Nibelungenlied in black-letter type. *Briefwechsel aus der Jugendzeit*, 336.

an unrivalled linguistic and grammatical knowledge, collated manuscripts, identified versions (that *Titurel* fragment, for instance).

What did he have to show for it all? There was the undated essay in French *De l'Étymologie en général*,⁷¹⁵ which was little more than a general account of what his reviews had stated in detail. Otherwise, folders and folders of etymological notes, fascicule after convolute of collated material on the *Nibelungenlied*—plus an essay, unpublished⁷¹⁶—all of which finished up in his *Nachlass*,⁷¹⁷ and all of this done with the same intensity as his other literary and scholarly work. It was not to lie completely fallow, finding use, but on a very limited scale, in his Bonn lectures (also unpublished for nearly a century). One is put in mind of his friend Ludwig Tieck, who had been corresponding with him in 1802-03 on these subjects, who had also been to Rome, Munich and St Gall and who had written the variants of the *Nibelungenlied* manuscripts interlinearally into his copy of Christoph Heinrich Myller's edition, and who—to the frustration and despair of several publishers—had never produced the promised product. He had, of course, that influential *Minnelieder aus dem Schwäbischen Zeitalter* of 1803 and an edition of Ulrich von Lichtenstein (1812) to his credit, but there were also unfulfilled plans, notes, for an edition of the *Heldenbuch*, not to speak of marginalia on Elizabethan drama.⁷¹⁸

It may seem inappropriate to bracket the punctilious and fussily detailed Schlegel with the dilatory Ludwig Tieck (although he too could be pernickety over Shakespearean glosses). In the history of German medieval studies, however, Schlegel has to stand comparison with fragmentists, modernisers, populariser, translators like Tieck, Görres, Docen, Büsching, von der Hagen, even those Heidelberg amateurs Arnim and Brentano, rather than with the Grimm brothers or Lachmann. It is to their credit that the Grimms, the philologists and editors, despite all misgivings of a personal nature,⁷¹⁹ later came to acknowledge the debt that they owed to Schlegel;

---

715 *Oeuvres*, II, 103-114.
716 Now published in extract in Höltenschmidt, 804-831.
717 SLUB Dresden, the folders marked Mscr. Dresd. e. 90, LXXII, LXXIII a/b, LXXIV. These comprise his annotated copy of Myller; his variants of the Munich ms., his variants of *Die Klage* from the Munich ms., 'Historische Notizen' and the ms. of the article in *Deutsches Museum*.
718 Tieck's medieval studies set out succinctly by Uwe Meves, '"Altdeutsche" Literatur. Tiecks Hinwendung zur altdeutschen Dichtung', in: Claudia Stockinger and Stefan Scherer (eds), *Ludwig Tieck. Leben-Werk-Wirkung* (Berlin, Boston: de Gruyter, 2011), 207-218.
719 *Briefwechsel der Brüder Jacob und Wilhelm Grimm mit Karl Lachmann*, ed. Albert Leitzmann, 2 vols (Jena: Frommann, 1927), I, 509, 608.

Lachmann, the editor of the *Nibelungenlied* and of *Titurel*, never did. There is no reference to Schlegel in Lachmann's essay which is regarded as the foundation of *Nibelungenlied* studies, at most a mention of the 'theory of *one* poet', nor is Schlegel referred to in Lachmann's standard edition.[720]

Thus Schlegel's reputation has suffered for his not being an academic professional in the nineteenth century's perception of the term;[721] he is disparaged for the sheer breadth of his knowledge in so many fields, an amnesia that overlooks the Grimms' universality of approach or Lachmann's 'other career' as an editor of classical Latin texts (or as a translator of Shakespeare's sonnets), not just of Wolfram or of the *Nibelungenlied*. He is overlooked because his Berlin lectures remained largely unpublished for generations, as did his Bonn lectures on German literature—Karl Simrock the later Germanist, and Heinrich Heine, both of them in their separate ways considerable connoisseurs of the Middle Ages, sat at his feet in Bonn. But they were not intended to train experts: only the lectures on Sanskrit had that aim. All of this shows the dilemma of Romantic scholarship.

There is another factor. Writing to Lachmann in 1819,[722] Jacob Grimm held out little hope for Schlegel's continuing his studies on *Titurel* or the *Nibelungenlied*. The reason did not lie in Schlegel's declared espousal of things Indian. No: he was too taken up with French elegance and airs, he was all 'Geist und Scharfsinn' [esprit and acuteness]; he lacked 'eine gewisse einfache Gründlichkeit' [a certain basic thoroughness] without which nothing substantial comes about. There we have it: the Francophile, the 'Frenchified' Schlegel versus German seriousness, gravitas, meticulousness, 'bottom'. It is a key text for Schlegel's negative image during the nineteenth century.

The *Nibelungenlied*

In 1812, when he was already on his way to Russia and Sweden with Madame de Staël and her family, Schlegel published three articles in his

---

720 Karl Lachmann, *Über die ursprüngliche Gestalt des Gedichts von der Nibelungen Noth* (Berlin: Dümmler, 1816), ref. 87; *Der Nibelungen Noth mit der Klage. In der ältesten Gestalt mit den Abweichungen der gemeinen Lesart*, hg. von Karl Lachmann (Berlin: Reimer, 1826).
721 Cf. in the late nineteenth century Schlegel's perceived 'Alexandrismus' as opposed to the more acceptable 'folk' theories of the Grimm brothers. Anton E. Schönbach, *Die Brüder Grimm. Ein Gedenkblatt zum 4. Januar 1885* (Berlin: Dümmler, 1885), 20.
722 Grimm-Lachmann, I, 22.

brother Friedrich's short-lived periodical *Deutsches Museum* (1812-13).[723] The place of publication was Vienna, which had been a brief staging post on the flight northwards; the date of Friedrich's preface, 1 December 1811, would suggest that his brother had brought his contributions with him during his brief visit in the summer of that year.

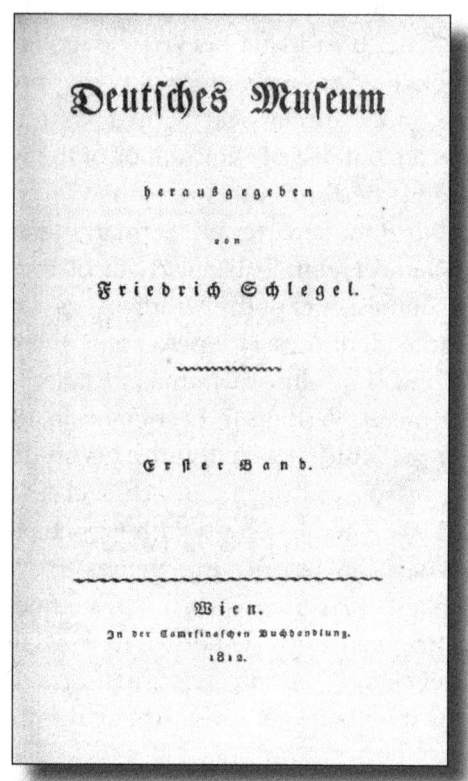

Fig. 22 Friedrich Schlegel, *Deutsches Museum* (Vienna, 1812). Title page. Image in the public domain.

The preface stressed the idea of the 'Nation': it had hitherto been conceived in too narrow a fashion; one must now open it up in all directions, moral, religious, historical. To that end, Friedrich cast his net very widely indeed,

---

723 *Deutsches Museum herausgegeben von Friedrich Schlegel*, 3 vols (Vienna: Camesina, 1812-13). AWS's contributions are, in order: 'Aus einer noch ungedruckten historischen Untersuchung über das *Lied der Nibelungen*', I, i, 9-36; 'Ueber das Nibelungen-Lied', I, vi, 505-536, II, i, 1-23; 'Gedichte auf Rudolf von Habsburg von Zeitgenossen', I, iv, 289-323; 'Ueber das Mittelalter. Eine Vorlesung, gehalten 1803', II, xi, 432-462. None in SW. There is in addition his announcement ('Ankündigung') dated June, 1812, of a forthcoming edition of the Nibelungenlied (II, x, 366).

to include himself and his brother, but also Caroline Pichler, Jean Paul, Adam Müller, Fouqué, Büsching, Görres, Zacharias Werner (now a priest in Vienna), Wilhelm von Humboldt (now the Prussian minister to Vienna), even Jacob Grimm. It intended to bring together all men and women of good will, like so many Romantic periodicals, and like them all, it had a brave start and a short duration.[724] It could be said to have caught some of the national upsurge consequent on Napoleon's reverses in Russia (the last number had a poem on the burning of Moscow),[725] but the literary fare that it offered was never going to attract a wide readership, let alone produce the *levée en masse* of 1813.[726] Only one contributor, the young poet Theodor Körner, was to achieve the distinction of being both a national hero and a poetic icon, but not in these pages.

Yet it is fair to say that an appeal to the Middle Ages had a different resonance in 1812-13 than, say, in 1803, when Ludwig Tieck's acclaimed *Minnelieder* appeared. There were two reasons. The Middle Ages had been caught up in Romantic myth-making, had become a wondrous, fabled, far-off time when faith and deed were one, when all was springtide and love, knights and ladies: Tieck's *Minnelieder* or Görres's *Volksbücher* (1807) had expressed themselves in such florid and extravagant terms. But Tieck, Görres, Büsching, Docen, von der Hagen, too, had also given serious thought to texts and authors, origins and dates, that were contingent on that first heroic age of Germanic studies. They had stressed the national heritage that, were it not for their efforts, they feared would be lost. As the nation (however defined) began to suffer successive humiliations at Napoleon's hands, its past constitution and temper were of renewed relevance. It is perhaps no coincidence that the first major published articles on the *Nibelungenlied* by this generation, by Jacob and Wilhelm Grimm, date from 1807, the year of Eylau and Friedland.[727] Both Schlegel brothers had sensed this as well; there had been plans (Friedrich's), also in 1807, for a joint periodical, *Das Mittelalter* [The Middle Ages].[728] As it was,

---

724 Friedrich attributes its suspension to the effects of war and difficulties of distribution, and hopes to resume in 1815. *Deutsches Museum*, IV, xii, 542. On this periodical see Johannes Bobeth, *Die Zeitschriften der Romantik* (Leipzig: Haessel, 1911), 261-286.
725 'Moskau's Brand' by Count Franz von Enzenberg, IV, xii, 449-453.
726 Bobeth, 284-286.
727 Wilhelm Grimm, 'Über die Originalität des Nibelungenlieds und des Heldenbuchs', *Kleinere Schriften*, I, 34f. Körner (1911), 79. A bibliographical account of the early literature on the Nibelungenlied to be found in Mary Thorp, *The Study of the Nibelungenlied. Being the History of the Study of the Epic and Legend from 1755 to 1937* (Oxford: Clarendon, 1940).
728 Krisenjahre, I, 390f.; Höltenschmidt, 82-87.

Friedrich's patriotic poetry was to be his major public expression. Again it is not entirely fortuitous that August Wilhelm's first reviews for the *Heidelberger Jahrbücher* were of popularizing medieval editions (Büsching/ von der Hagen, Docen) and that they generally met his approval.

For that outlet, he had had a learned, academic readership in mind. For his brother's *Deutsches Museum*, with its appeal to the 'Nation', with its speaking title that proclaimed Germanness and also the products of the Muses, the tone would have to be a little different. These articles, all three on the Middle Ages, are in their several ways symbolic of the varying sides to Schlegel's medievalism. Two of them, the ones on the *Nibelungenlied* and on the Middle Ages, were reformulations of notes from the Berlin Lectures of 1803, the first greatly expanded, the second simply made a little more readable.

The longest, on the *Nibelungenlied*, extending over three numbers, was scholarly, detailed, historical and textual; it was accompanied by a declaration announcing the imminent publication of a critical edition of this heroic lay. It aligned Schlegel with those other antiquarians and scholars who at roughly the same time were bringing out similar editions, Friedrich Heinrich von der Hagen, or Johann Gustav Büsching, but it also pointed forward to the definitive form that the *Nibelungenlied* would take at the hands of Karl Lachmann in 1826. It raised hopes that Schlegel might be the first to publish an edition with an established text based on manuscript variants. It was something that Johann Gustav Büsching was still looking forward to in 1815,[729] a forlorn wish, as it turned out.

The essay rehearsed the history of the poem's discovery; it echoed (with qualifications) Johannes von Müller, who had mentioned it in one breath with Homer; it listed the manuscripts that the scholar-editor must compare and collate.[730] It set out reasons why this poem must have precedence in the national consciousness: unlike the ultimately French Grail cycles it was German in origin ('vaterländischen Ursprungs'),[731] based ultimately (but not directly) on Germanic history. One could trace the stages of its conception,

---

729 *Das Lied der Nibelungen. Metrisch übersetzt von D. Johann Gustav Büsching* (Altenburg and Leipzig: Brockhaus, 1815), ix.
730 These are A (the second, so-called Hohenems ms., now in Munich), B (the St Gall ms. in the Stiftsbibliothek there), C (the so-called Hohenems-Lassberg, formerly in the Fürstenberg library in Donaueschingen and now in the Badische Landesbibliothek in Karlsruhe) and D (the so-called Prünn-Münchener, now in Munich). See *Der Nibelungen Liet und Diu Klage. Die Donaueschinger Handschrift 63 [Laßberg 174]*, ed. Werner Schröder, Deutsche Texte in Handschriften, 3 (Cologne, Vienna: Böhlau, 1969).
731 *Deutsches Museum*, I, i, 27.

from a postulated original (possibly sung) in an older Germanic form at the time of Theodoric and Attila, receiving Nordic admixtures up to the time of Charlemagne, when it would have been written down, and thence to its final written state, first between the tenth and twelfth centuries and then by one individual author, whom one could identify as Austrian, in the thirteenth (Schlegel suggests Klingsohr or Heinrich von Ofterdingen). (Lachmann, by contrast, believed in multi-authorship.) Telling as it did of nobility and chivalry, respect for the Christian religion, history and poetry, it was ideal for the nation's youth and its instruction in 'proper' values.

It would reverse notions, that had not yet quite died out, of the Middle Ages as monkish darkness. For it predated modern ideas of monarchy; it was pre-capitalist; it was pre-individual, pre-Enlightenment, pre-Reformation. It told of 'great men', not the Machiavellian politicians of more recent times; its warriors went forth in the service of their liege lords, not as modern standing armies. Add to this account of the *Nibelungenlied* Schlegel's articles in the *Deutsches Museum* on the poetic apostrophes to Rudolf of Habsburg and on the Middle Ages themselves, and one had, if not quite a 'national euphoria',[732] at least a set of counter-values to those current in the eighteenth century: papal and imperial dignity (Rudolf), the spirit of chivalry, which united Orient and Occident, North and South, equality under arms, wars of religion not of conquest, also a religion that cultivated manly virtues and higher ideals of love.

Clearly not all of this could apply to the *Nibelungenlied*; it was more apposite to other epic cycles, or to Minnesang, or to Provençal poetry that Schlegel already in his Berlin Lectures had linked with its German equivalent and which he had declared to be the *fons et origo* of the Romance lyric. Schlegel was to devote much more time to Provençal once he returned to Paris,[733] but in the mean time this view of the Middle Ages shared a number of general features with the Coppet circle. For them, too, the Middle Ages, the age of Troubadours, of chivalry—the exact terminology did not matter—was a time of values that the present age seemed to lack or that enlightenment notions of progress had occluded. Of course, there was much more stress on the fusion of 'Nord' and 'Midi', that was one of Madame de Staël's favourite notions, shared also by Constant and

---

732 The phrase used by Otfrid Ehrismann, *Das Nibelungenlied in Deutschland. Studien zur Rezeption des Nibelungenlieds von der Mitte des 18. Jahrhunderts bis zum Ersten Weltkrieg*, Münchner Germanistische Beiträge, 14 (Munich: Fink, 1975), 90.
733 His review of Raynouard (1818).

Sismondi.[734] Feudal society had had a vigour and resilience that the later unified state, exemplified by Louis XIV, did not possess; from there, one could easily trace the origins of modern tyranny. Madame de Staël's *Considérations sur les principaux événemens de la Révolution Française* (1819, but drafted much earlier) had explicitly praised the 'régime féodal'[735] in those terms and had applauded Germany, as *De l'Allemagne* already had, for its essentially feudal constitution.

Of course neither Madame de Staël nor Schlegel wanted a return to the Middle Ages in real terms: 'feudal' meant something more like 'federal'; it was the point that Schlegel made to Bernadotte in 1812, advocating the recreation of the old system of territorial checks and balances, if need be under a strong figure (a kind of Rudolf of Habsburg) with other neighbouring countries in loose alliance. For Madame de Staël, 'chevalerie' simply meant the opposite of tyranny,[736] the downfall of the notably unchivalrous Napoleon. If 'medieval' expressed the Germanic virtues necessary for the restoration of freedom (however defined), well and good. As it was, Schlegel's attitude to the Middle Ages had its inconsistencies, depending on the context: whether he was writing in a concrete political situation, as to Bernadotte in 1812; whether it was a general hankering after a pre-Reformation settlement, insouciant of historical details; or whether the Middle Ages were seen merely as the forcing-ground of the Golden Ages of England and Spain, united under strong monarchies, such as had informed the latter part of his Vienna Lectures on drama. Nevertheless it is fair to say that the once-cherished notions of an all-encompassing, all-enfolding embrace of faith and feudal rule and the arts, still just present in Schlegel's essay on the Middle Ages in 1812, were quietly dropped and did not form part of his thinking after 1815.

---

734 See esp. Norman King, 'Le Moyen Âge à Coppet', *Colloque 1974*, 375-399; and Henri Duranton, 'L'interprétation du mythe troubadour par le Groupe de Coppet', *ibid.*, 349-373.

735 Madame de Staël, *Considérations sur les principaux évémenents de la Révolution Française*, second edition, 3 vols (London: Baldwin, Cradock and Joy, 1819), I, 6, 13.

736 King (1974), 388.

4. Bonn and India (1818-1845)[1]

4.1 Bonn

'Chevalier de plusieurs ordres'[2]

The death of Madame de Staël marked for Schlegel the end of his middle years. He was now fifty, free and for the first time in thirteen years his own master. At first it was hard to take in. He accompanied the cortege—with himself, Auguste and the duke de Broglie as the chief mourners—that bore her body back to Coppet and saw it walled up in the family mausoleum, closed ever since. He was at liberty to remain in Coppet in his previous existence as a private scholar, but life would never be the same again. The Staël children, Auguste and Albertine, still saw him, with Fanny Randall, as part of the extended family and had no wish to exclude him after his long and sometimes selfless service to their mother. True, they challenged his title to the exclusive stewardship of her papers; in compensation, he was allowed the rights of *Considérations sur les principaux événements de la Révolution Française*, and he translated into German Madame Necker de Saussure's memoir of her famous cousin. With this, and the pension that Madame de Staël had agreed at the beginning of their association, he was

---

1 For a general biographical account of Schlegel's last years see Ruth Schirmer, *August Wilhelm Schlegel und seine Zeit. Ein Bonner Leben* (Bonn: Bouvier, 1986). Entertainingly written, it nevertheless needs to be taken with very considerable care. An important corrective to the standard view of the later AWS is offered by Jochen Strobel, 'Der Romantiker als homo academicus. August Wilhelm Schlegel in der Wissenschaft', *Jahrbuch des Freien Deutschen Hochstifts*, 2010, 298-338.
2 'Knight of various orders'.

© Roger Paulin, CC BY   http://dx.doi.org/10.11647/OBP.0069.04

comfortably off, and he had always put a little aside. The correspondence with the younger Staëls, the baron and the duchess, remained on the level of openness, not perhaps as children to a father, but certainly as nephews and nieces to an older uncle whom they were glad to see and whose foibles they tolerated. Albertine, among the three children the one with the greatest common sense and human understanding, also watched this avuncular figure with occasional and justified concern. They knew of his little vanities and made sure that they put 'Chevalier de plusieurs ordres' on the covers of their letters to him.

Madame de Staël's death was also a liberation from emotional and material servitude. He could move as he chose, not as she decreed. He could go to Paris or to London as his own man, in his own interests, not just when the spirit moved her. He could follow up those tentative movements towards a career that crop up in his correspondence with Favre, putting down roots after years of peregrination and nomadism. He was free to marry: she could no longer put a veto on his emotional life. That was the positive side. Perhaps this was not the appropriate time to take stock of what Madame de Staël had kept him from. For she had come at just the right moment to save him from the clutches of Sophie Tieck-Bernhardi and keep him at a distance from the emotional and matrimonial entanglements that ensued. It might not have been just jealousy, but also Staël-Necker native shrewdness, that intervened to prevent Schlegel's association with a married woman (Marianne Haller) or a much younger pious Catholic girl (Nina Hartl). (The Staël love life was of course a law unto itself). Even her daughter Albertine might have kept Schlegel back from what she was to call an 'étourderie', an act of folly, when eventually he did marry.

Madame de Staël had always injected a healthy scepticism into their relationship, despite all those occasional pleadings, blandishments and near moral blackmails. She had kept his feet on the ground, reined in his quarrelsomeness, kept his tendency to speculation within bounds, had subjected him and his views to the sometimes merciless and always critical causerie of her circle. She had not completely bridled his vanity, but she could temper it by seating him next to a duke or introducing him to a princess (or a Prince Royal). With her, he would not have needed those later grandiloquent gestures like his twelve-roomed house in Bonn (she had somewhat more), his carriage, his liveried servant, and she would have spared him much of the associated ridicule that was to come his way because of it.

She had shepherded him more than perhaps he realised; it was she who had set up the introductions that had made the Vienna Lectures such a success; it was her prompting that saw him enter Bernadotte's service. True, critical writing and dealings with publishers had been his concern alone, and here he had shown himself to be assiduous and if need be hardheaded. But if one compared the Berlin lectures, which were fragmented and largely unpublished and delivered against a background of some emotional turmoil, with those in Vienna, with their carefully chosen audience, the comparative leisure in Coppet to see them to the press, and their enormous subsequent international reception[3]—Coleridge, Stendhal, Hugo, Oehlenschläger, Kierkegaard, Mickiewicz, Pushkin are among their most famous recipients—one could see what a difference the Staël component made.

Auguste and Albertine

Thus it is only right that an account of Schlegel's last years should begin under this long shadow of Madame de Staël as it spread over her children and grandchildren and continued to take him in as part of their extended family. For if he was now of his own choice at last again domiciled in Germany, much of his heart and affections were nevertheless still in France. 'Stick the soul of a German into the mind [esprit] and body of a Frenchman, and you would have the perfect man',[4] was what he wrote to Auguste de Staël in 1821, a sentiment with which Alexander von Humboldt would not have disagreed. (Madame de Staël would have had an Englishman somewhere in the equation.) Of course this Staël-Broglie family was also staunchly anglophile. In 1822, Auguste de Staël and his brother-in-law Victor de Broglie spent some months in England, meeting the abolitionists Zachary Macaulay and Wilberforce, the economists Ricardo, Mill and Malthus, and the Holland House set.[5] These connections also enabled Schlegel to be received with equally open arms in England in 1823. For all that he made use of his Hanoverian connections when it suited him, being part of a grand French family and sharing in their culture tipped the

---

3 See Josef Körner, *Die Botschaft der deutschen Romantik an Europa*, Schriften zur deutschen Literatur für die Görresgesellschaft, 9 (Augsburg: Filser, 1929), esp. 69-74.

4 *Krisenjahre der Frühromantik. Briefe aus dem Schlegelkreis*, ed. Josef Körner, 3 vols (Brno, Vienna, Leipzig: Rohrer, 1936-37; Berne: Francke, 1958), II, 381f.

5 *Souvenirs—1785-1870—du feu duc de Broglie*, 3 vols (Paris: Calmann Lévy, 1886), II, 234-247.

balance in favour of France. (It is not by chance that the only really useful biographical accounts of Schlegel in these later years are by Frenchmen, first by Philippe de Golbéry,[6] the translator of Niebuhr, and after Schlegel's death, by Charles Galusky.)[7]

The letters written to him by Albertine, duchess de Broglie, from 1818 to 1838, along with those from Victor de Broglie and their son Albert, bulk large in the corpus of Schlegel's later correspondence.[8] To them can be added the letters from Ximénès Doudan,[9] the tutor to Alphonse de Rocca. One may regret that Schlegel's own letters are missing, but no matter.

These are letters from a grand family—Victor de Broglie was to hold various important ministerial posts under Louis-Philippe from 1830 to 1834—but with no pretensions to grandeur, written from Coppet, from the château of Broglie in Normandy, and from their town house in Paris, 76, rue de Bourbon. It was a family that kept open house for the *haute volée*, but one would hardly know it from these letters. It elicited great works of art— Gérard's painting 'Corinne at Cape Miseno' (1819), the lithograph of which Schlegel reviewed enthusiastically in 1822 in Sulpiz Boisserée's *Kunstblatt*[10] (and which his niece Auguste von Buttlar copied),[11] Lamartine's moving *Cantique sur la mort de Madame la duchesse de Broglie* of 1838, Ingres's splendid portrait of Louise d'Haussonville, Albertine's and Victor's daughter (1845), and his even more wonderful preliminary drawings—but these letters do not hint at them.

---

6   With whom Schlegel corresponded and to whom he passed on bibliographical details. *Briefe von und an August Wilhelm Schlegel*, ed. Josef Körner, 2 vols (Zurich, Leipzig, Vienna: Amalthea, 1930), II, 139, 230. Golbéry's letters to AWS in SLUB Dresden, Mscr. Dresd. e. 90, XIX (9), 31-39. Golbéry's account goes into the *Biographie universelle et portative* […], 5 vols (Supplément) (Paris, Strasbourg: Levraut, 1834), V, 731-735, then into *Biographie universelle, ancienne et moderne*, 85 vols (Paris: Michaud, 1811-62), LXXXI, 300-316. Chetana Nagavajara, *August Wilhelm Schlegel in Frankreich. Sein Anteil an der französischen Literaturkritik 1807-1835*, intr. Kurt Wais, Forschungsprobleme der vergleichenden Literaturgeschichte, 3 (Tübingen: Niemeyer, 1966), 335-338. The point is made that Jakob Minor had recourse to largely French sources when first writing up Schlegel's life at the end of the nineteenth century.

7   Ch[arles] Galusky, 'Notice sur la vie et les ouvrages de M. A. W. de Schlegel', *Revue des deux mondes*, 1 February 1846, 159-190, and issued separately.

8   With a few exceptions, these letters are unpublished. SLUB Dresden, Mscr. Dresd. e. 90, XIX (4), 1-86.

9   Published in X. Doudan, *Mélanges et lettres avec une introduction par M. le comte d'Haussonville et des notices part MM. de Sacy Cuvillier-Fleury*, 4 vols (Paris: Calmann Lévy, 1876), III, 1-25, 49-55, 126-128.

10   *August Wilhelm von Schlegel's sämmtliche Werke*, ed. Eduard Böcking, 12 vols [*SW*] (Leipzig: Weidmann, 1846-47), IX, 360-368.

11   Kupferstich-Kabinett, Staatliche Kunstsammlungen Dresden.

Albertine[12] writes of her family, the children that survived and those that did not, her state of mind and soul, her reading (always serious), her search for inner calm and assurance, and all this amid the social and political pressures that impinged. They tell of those left over from the old Coppet days, Auguste de Staël, whose death in 1827 saw the extinction of the male Staël line, or Alphonse de Rocca. They speak of good sense, reconciliation (of issues now unknown), of affection, even if not all of the Broglie family shared it. Victor's letters are always matter-of-fact: he kept up the correspondence after Albertine's death; Pauline wrote a dutiful letter in German, Louise one in French;[13] Albert de Broglie, by contrast, the schoolboy and the later law student, wrote long and spirited letters that showed that he did not seem to mind the conundrums, comic verse (Pythagoras's theorem explained in rhyming couplets)[14] or corrections to his Latinity that interlarded Schlegel's correspondence with him.

Near the end of the correspondence come the two long letters that Schlegel and Albertine wrote to each other in 1838 on the subject of his religious affiliations; it is their only published exchange.[15] It is to the pious, pietistic, Albertine and no-one else that he wrote that account of his religious development, his movements towards and away from Catholicism, his rejection of fanaticism and enthusiasm, his sense of a universal religion beyond confessions and affiliations. This to an Albertine who in 1829, one senses, had been more upset at the news of Friedrich Schlegel's death than his own brother was.

Of course this is but one side of Schlegel's later dealings with France. As it was, despite Albertine's constant pleadings, he only visited them twice, in 1820-21 and in 1832,[16] and they came once, in 1834, to Bonn. There is no doubt that Broglie influence saw Schlegel introduced at court and receiving the Légion d'honneur. Ximénès Doudan agreed to cast an eye over the French in Schlegel's articles for the *Journal des débats*.[17] But the main part

---

12 See Daniel Halévy, 'La duchesse de Broglie', *Cahiers staëliens*, 56 (2005), 117-167.
13 Victor's letters SLUB Dresden, Mscr. Dresd. e. 90, XIX (4), 113-136; Albert, *ibid.*, 102-136; Pauline, 138; Louise, 140.
14 *Oeuvres de M. Auguste-Guillaume de Schlegel écrites en français*, ed. Édouard Böcking, 3 vols (Leipzig: Weidmann, 1846), I, 95f.
15 *Ibid.*, 189-201.
16 As far as can be ascertained, AWS stayed with them in Paris. Proust's Madame de Villeparisis claimed to have met him at the Broglie country estate. Whom do we believe? Marcel Proust, *À la recherche du temps perdu*, ed. Pierre Clarac and André Ferré, Bibliothèque de la Pléiade, 3 vols (Paris: Gallimard, 1954), II, 275.
17 Doudan, III, 9.

of Schlegel's business in France was scholarly, and it was very largely in French that he was to display the breadth of those interests.

In the mean time, in the year immediately after Madame de Staël's death, Schlegel's links with the Staël-Broglie family were more mundane, matter-of-fact and mercenary. The will drawn up by Madame de Staël on 12 August, 1816, giving Schlegel the rights to her papers and especially to the manuscript later to be known as *Considérations sur les principaux événements de la Révolution Française*, was a source of some vexation to the Staël heirs; seizing on the 'laconisme' of the will and its 'actual intentions', they had another document framed, dated 31 January 1818, which defined Schlegel's rights but made it clear that they were their mother's literary executors.[18] Instead, he was to receive the sum of 34,500 francs, payable in instalments as the different volumes of Madame de Staël's posthumous works appeared.[19] The 10,000 francs that he received in February, 1818 would have come in useful as he began setting up house in Bonn in the summer of that year.

In keeping with the agreement, Schlegel's name did not appear on the title page of the *Considérations*: he was still too much associated with the anti-French sentiments of the *Comparaison* and the Vienna Lectures. The reader would only learn of his part in the enterprise through a short mention in the preface. He was not to be entrusted with a general account of Madame de Staël's life, either, this going to her cousin Madame Necker de Saussure, the translator of the Lectures. He in his turn was to translate this work into German.[20]

It seems that Schlegel, usually very tidy in his financial affairs, had followed Auguste in placing some of his assets (well over £1,000) with the London banking house of Tottie and Compton. A bank crisis, brought about by Allied demands for immediate repayment of French war indemnities,[21] caused Tottie and Compton to get into difficulties, then to declare bankruptcy and go into administration. Both Auguste and Schlegel were heavy losers. Schlegel showed the generosity of spirit that he always

---

18 I am quoting from the copy in AWS's papers, SLUB Dresden, Mscr. Dresd. e. 90, XII (1-2). There is another agreement published in Comtesse Jean de Pange, née Broglie, *Auguste-Guillaume Schlegel et Madame de Staël. D'après des documents inédits* (Paris: Albert, 1938), 523-525. Briefe, II, 138f.
19 Mscr. Dresd. *ibid.*
20 As *Ueber den Charakter und die Schriften der Frau von Staël von Frau Necker gebohrne von Saussure. Uebersetzt von A. W. von Schlegel* (Paris, London, Strasbourg: Treuttel & Würtz, 1820). AWS's preface *SW*, VIII, 202-206.
21 *Krisenjahre*, III, 574f.

evinced towards the Staël sons, telling Auguste to take it philosophically: one only needed some etymology or some Homeric problems to take one's mind off these matters!²²

The European Celebrity

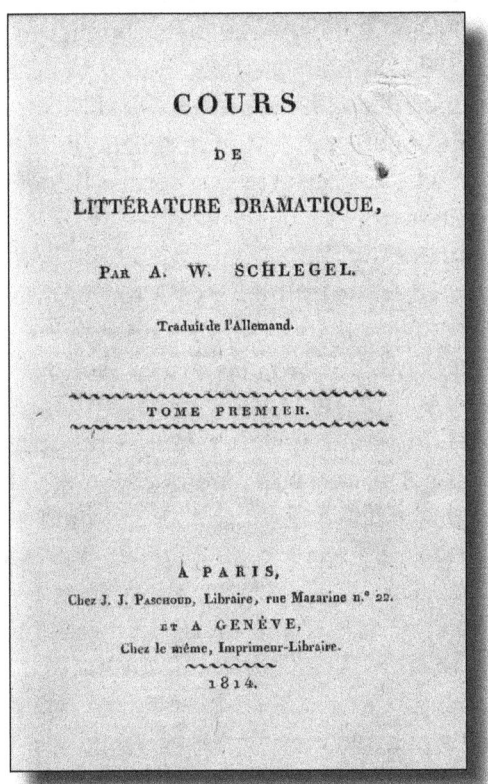

Fig. 23 August Wilhelm Schlegel, *Cours de littérature dramatique. Traduit de l'allemand* (Paris, Geneva, 1814). Title page of vol. 1. © and by kind permission of the Master and Fellows of Trinity College, Cambridge, CC BY-NC 4.0.

What of Schlegel's critical reputation? He was later to claim that his Vienna Lectures had spread his name and influence from 'Cadiz to Edinburgh, Stockholm and St Petersburg'.²³ By that he meant the cultivated readership, the educated elite. In terms of translations, his statement was certainly true. Whereas once, notably in his lectures on 'Encyclopedia' in Berlin (1803), he

---

22 *Ibid.*, II, 333; III, 579. SLUB Dresden, Mscr. Dresd. e. 90, XII (6a-e). Schlegel had already placed £500 with the bank in 1814. *Ibid.* (8b).
23 *SW*, VII, 285.

had shown a wide interest in national and historical cultures, his focus in the later years was directed at France and England, as the two places, the one with its institutes and libraries, the other with its overeas possessions, that could serve as the base for his all-consuming interest in India. Böhl von Faber, his Spanish translator and disciple, complained that Schlegel had buried himself in Sanskrit and had no further interest in things Hispanic (in fact, Schlegel disliked Böhl's 'reactionary' politics).[24] Adam Mickiewicz, on his visit to Schlegel in Bonn in 1829, found that his host evinced no interest in Polish matters and showed him Sanskrit manuscripts instead.[25] Despite a continuing interest in Indo-European philology and etymology, the spread of languages from an primeval source, he defied all the evidence and excluded the Celts from this linguistic family.

Others saw it differently. It had started with *De l'Allemagne*. When that work finally appeared late in 1813, it put Schlegel into the wider context that it encompassed, with its thirty-first chapter of Book Two announcing 'Des richesses littéraires de l'Allemagne et de ses critiques les plus renommés, A. W. et F. Schlegel' [On the literary treasures of Germany and its most renowned critics] and its short but important section on the Vienna Lectures. Thus Schlegel's name became associated with hers in the reviews of *De l'Allemagne* that followed.[26] In Britain it would be Hazlitt's and Sir James Mackintosh's. These were to be followed by reviews of the French translation of the Lectures, Francis Hare-Naylor's enthusiastic account in the *Quarterly Review* in 1815, and then by others of the English version which came out in the same year.[27] Madame de Staël's departure for France in 1814 had possibly prevented John Murray from taking on the English translation of the Vienna Lectures, but Robert Baldwin did so in 1815, with John Black as his translator.

Schlegel had every reason to be satisfied with this translation, especially when compared with Madame Necker de Saussure's of it into French. Where hers made no pretence to doing a literal version (and got quite a few

---

24 Camille Pitollet, *La Querelle caldéronienne de Johan Nikolas Böhl von Faber et José Joaquín de Mora reconstituée d'après les documents originaux*, doctoral thesis University of Toulouse (Paris: Alcan, 1909), 136.
25 Albert Zipper, 'Aus Odyniec' Reisebriefen', *Studien zur vergleichenden Literaturgeschichte* 4 (1904), 175-187, ref. 181.
26 See generally the excellent account in Thomas G. Sauer, *A. W. Schlegel's Shakespearean Criticism in England, 1811-1846*, Studien zur Literatur der Moderne, 9 (Bonn: Bouvier, 1981), and here specifically 54-64.
27 Sauer, 61-64.

things wrong),[28] Black's made every effort to keep to the original. One need only compare a crux passage in each translation, the section on ancient and modern poetry, to see the difference. Hers is adjusted (as perhaps it must be) to the needs of French lexis;[29] his tries to do justice to the nuances of Schlegel's text.[30] British critics were of course less interested in the quality of the translation than in its content; for here was a Shakespearean criticism that seemed quite different from Johnson or Richardson or Malone. Hazlitt's enthusiastic review in the *Edinburgh Review* set the tone,[31] and others, notably Thomas Campbell,[32] were to follow, not counting almost the whole British Romantic school who knew the work, Byron, Scott, Southey, Leigh Hunt, Wordsworth.[33] Nathan Drake, the first Shakespearean biographer of this generation, was indebted to 'the admirable Schlegel'.[34] Small wonder that Sir James Mackintosh could write, to Schlegel's considerable gratification, that he was 'our National Critic'.[35]

Samuel Taylor Coleridge, as is now well known, had come to Schlegel through the Vienna Lectures in the German original, when in 1812 and 1813 he lectured in London and Bristol on drama and Shakespeare.[36] Leaving aside questions of indebtedness (or plagiarism), the real point is that Coleridge's reading of Schlegel introduced into English Shakespearean criticism the images and philosophical terminology of German idealism and the historical sense of German Romanticism. Thus the organicist language that Coleridge employed in his critical writing was indebted to Herder, the common source for Schlegel but also for Schelling. When in

---

28 The preface states that it is adjusted to the needs of French readers. *Cours de littérature dramatique. Par A.W. Schlegel. Traduit de l'Allemand*, 2 vols (Paris and Geneva: Paschoud, 1814), I, v. AWS's indignation over misapprehensions in the translation registered in undated letter to Welcker. Bonn Universitätsbibliothek, S 686 (9).
29 Cf. *Cours de littérature dramatique*, II, 329.
30 Cf. Black's version of the same passage. *A Course of Lectures on Dramatic Art and Literature, by Augustus William Schlegel*, 2 vols (London: Baldwin, Cradock and Joy; Edinburgh: William Blackwood; Dublin: John Cumming, 1815), II, 99.
31 Sauer, 100-109.
32 *Ibid.*, 116f.
33 *Ibid.*, 112.
34 Nathan Drake, *Shakspeare and His Times*, 2 vols (London: Cadell and Davies, 1817), II, 614. See S. Schoenbaum, *Shakespeare's Lives* (Oxford: Clarendon, 1991), 193.
35 *Krisenjahre*, III, 584.
36 Sauer, 81-100. The issue of Coleridge's debt to Schlegel, which has engendered much controversy, is treated, most recently and with commendable succinctness, by Reginald Foakes, 'Samuel Taylor Coleridge', in: Roger Paulin (ed.), *Voltaire, Goethe, Schlegel, Coleridge, Great Shakespeareans*, III (London, New York: continuum, 2010), 128-172, esp. 143-148.

1823 he made his first longer visit to London in his newly-assumed status as a Sanskritist, Schlegel was already a European celebrity on account of the wide dissemination and reception of his Vienna Lectures. They were his major asset; they were what most people associated with his name.

It is fair to say that the English-language reaction to Schlegel was very largely reflected in Shakespeare criticism, coming as it did at a time of reaction against Johnsonian strictures or Richardsonian character study. It was natural for the British to seize on what was familiar—or, until they read Schlegel, was thought to be familiar. For others, he had many more aspects. Thomas Campbell had known Schlegel since the Staël days,[37] but in Bonn he saw a different side. Bonn itself as an institution gave him the first idea for a university along German lines, out of which London's University College would eventually emerge.[38] Schlegel—despite, or even because of his penchant to hold forth—was a man of letters with a difference,[39] one who on the basis of having to translate the works into German, knew Shakespeare better than most of the Bard's countrymen.[40] Cyrus Redding, Campbell's assistant editor on the *New Monthly Review* from 1821 to 1830, found that he had 'nothing of the pedant, and for a German scholar much of a man of the world'.[41] Perhaps this was the reason why Redding devoted more space to Schlegel than to Goethe in his important conspectus of the German literature that seemed significant in his lifetime, tracing Schlegel's development (even translating that 'Union of the Arts with the Church' poem that Schlegel had now in part retracted).[42]

Coleridge and Wordsworth visited Schlegel briefly during the summer of 1828 during their tour of the Moselle and Rhine. Needless to say, both came with a pre-knowledge of things German, in Wordsworth's case fairly extensive,[43] in Coleridge's hugely eclectic. Coleridge, whom one campanion described as resembling a 'dissenting minister' in appearance[44]

---

37 *Life and Letters of Thomas Campbell*, ed. William Beattie, 3 vols (London: Moxon, 1849), II, 257.
38 Ibid., 355.
39 Ibid., 363.
40 Cyrus Redding, *Fifty Years' Recollections, Literary and Personal, With Observations of Men and Things*, 3 vols (London: Skeet, 1858), II, 232-234.
41 Ibid., 235.
42 Cyrus Redding, *Yesterday and Today*, 3 vols (London: Cautley Newby, 1863), II, 5-71, ref. 48.
43 Theodor Zeiger, 'Beiträge zur Geschichte der deutsch-englischen Litteraturbeziehungen III: Wordsworths Stellung zur deutschen Litteratur', in: Max Koch (ed.), *Studien zur vergleichenden Literaturgeschichte*, 1 (Berlin: Duncker, 1901), 273-290.
44 Julian Charles Young, *A Memoir of Charles Mayne Young, Tragedian, with Extracts from his Son's Journal* (London, New York: Macmillan, 1871), 172f.

(Wordsworth like a 'mountain farmer'),[45] conversed volubly with a bewigged Schlegel; that is, once their language problems had been resolved. Coleridge's German was rusty, forcing Schlegel to say: 'Mein lieber Herr, would you speak English: I understand it; but your German I cannot follow'.[46] That worked: there was reciprocal praise of Schlegel's Shakespeare and of Coleridge's *Wallenstein*. If Coleridge had read Schlegel's less than enthusiastic remarks on Schiller, he did not let on. On Scott and Byron they disagreed (Wordsworth too);[47] for Schlegel, as indeed for most nineteenth-century German readers, they remained the paramount representatives of English letters.

In France, of course, things were different.[48] As said, for obvious reasons, Schlegel was caught up in the reception of *De l'Allemagne*, but his name was also involved in much more: the formation of opinion on Schiller, and above all the massive presence of Shakespeare. French readers were aware that the Vienna Lectures were not the first of Schlegel's challenges to their *drame classique*. Although neither of the two great acts of defiance against the dominance of classical French drama—Stendhal's *Racine et Shakespeare* (1823, 1825) and Victor Hugo's *Préface de Cromwell* (1827)—was directly influenced by Schlegel's formulations, the polarisations that underlay them had something of the abrupt and occasionally arbitrary distinctions that came with Romantic thought.[49] (Interestingly enough, the most thorough and thoughtful German review of the Vienna Lectures, by Karl Wilhelm Ferdinand Solger, who had been in the audience in Berlin, took issue with this, for him, 'artificial' forcing apart of cultures and traditions.)[50] Of course the 'accommodations' that Madame Necker de Saussure had made may have rendered these partitions less forcible in French (her translation was also used as the basis for the Italian version of the Lectures, not Schlegel's original).[51] The point stands nevertheless.

---

45 Thomas Colley Grattan, *Beaten Paths; and Those Who Trod Them*, 2 vols (London: Chapman Hall, 1862), I, 109.
46 Young, I, 180.
47 *Ibid.*, 174f.
48 This cannot be the place for a full discussion of Schlegel in France. This has been supplied by Chetana Nagavajara. My remarks are very much indebted to his study.
49 Such as Hugo's borrowing of Schlegel's distinction between the 'mechanical' and the 'organic'. Christian A. E. Jensen, *L'Évolution du romantisme. L'année 1826* (Geneva: Droz; Paris: Minard, 1959), 188f.
50 *Jahrbücher der Literatur*, VII (1819), 80-155; most accessible in: *Solger's nachgelassene Schriften und Briefwechsel*, ed. Ludwig Tieck and Friedrich von Raumer, 2 vols (Leipzig: Brockhaus, 1826), II, 493-628.
51 Navagajara, 230.

Schlegel's name remained associated first and foremost with the old members of the 'Groupe de Coppet'—Bonstetten, Constant, Sismondi, Barante—and its younger survivors—Auguste de Staël and Victor de Broglie—and their circles of political and literary influence.[52] Although his name did not appear on the title page, Schlegel had been as much involved as they had in the production of Staël's *Considérations sur les principaux événements de la Révolution Française*. Auguste's edition of *Dix Années d'exil*, in which Schlegel's role was given some prominence (perhaps not as much as he deserved) had come out in 1823, with nice timing, to coincide with the Napoleonic apologia, Émmanuel-Auguste-Dieudonné de Las Casas's *Mémorial de Sainte-Hélène*.[53] Schlegel, now fully engaged in the Prussian Rhineland, could not share their liberal political and social views except as a disinterested observer; writing resignedly to Auguste de Staël in 1819, he concluded that 'Germany was fine, so long as one did not get involved in politics'.[54]

Thus it is interesting to find Schlegel producing his own 'Ten Years of Exile', not in French, not even in German, but in Latin, in his oration as outgoing rector of Bonn university in 1825. He set out briefly his anti-Napoleonic credentials, covering with Latin *brevitas* what Madame de Staël had expanded in her extensive self-justification.[55] These remarks were delivered under the shadow of the Carlsbad Decrees, with colleagues in trouble, Ernst Moritz Arndt silenced and Friedrich Gottlieb Welcker not completely exonerated. They are also an exhortation to political prudence and avoidance of extremes. Only in 1828, under great provocation from Johann Heinrich Voss, did Schlegel 'go public' in German about his role in the struggle against the Usurper (unlike Voss in his 'Heidelberg

---

52 See esp. John Isbell, 'Présence de Coppet et romantisme libéral en France, 1822-1827', in: Françoise Tilkin (ed.), *Le Groupe de Coppet et le monde moderne: conceptions-images-débats*. Actes du VIe Colloque de Coppet organisé par la Société des Études Staëliennes (Paris) et l'Association Benjamin Constant (Lausanne) Liège, 10-12 juillet 1997, Bibliothèque de la Faculté de Philosophie et Lettres de l'Université de Liège, 277 (Geneva: Droz, 1998), 395-418.

53 Isbell (1998), 397.

54 *Krisenjahre*, II, 343.

55 *Opuscula quae Augustus Guilelmus Schlegelius Latine scripta reliquit. Collegit et edidit Eduardus Böcking* (Lipsiae: Weidmann, 1848), 385-396. See Karl August Neuhausen, 'August Wilhelm von Schlegel in Bonn als heute vergessener lateinischer Autor: Zu seinen autobiographischen Reden—vor allem zur Selbstdarstellung als <paene Ulysses quidam> im Exil auf der Flucht vor dem Tyrannen Napoleon', in: Uwe Baumann and Karl August Neuhausen (eds), *Autobiographie: Eine interdisziplinäre Gattung zwischen klassischer Tradition und (post-)moderner Variation* (Göttingen: V&R unipress, 2013), 225-257 (with translation of the Latin text).

cabbage-patch'), part of a general critique of fanatical anti-Romanticism. In his role as a university professor, however, he had to be careful about what he said. As we shall see, his most trenchant remarks of a political nature were to be about British India, not Europe.

Auguste consulted Schlegel over the choice of the German texts to be included in Pierre-François Ladvocat's huge twenty-five-volume undertaking, *Chefs-d'oeuvre des théâtres étrangers* [Masterpieces of Foreign Theatre] (1821-23).[56] He, his brother-in-law Broglie, Barante and Constant were to be among the contributors (and in the event were not). Schlegel, now claiming to have nothing but contempt for literature and to be interested only in 'antediluvian poetry', suggested Werner's *Der vierundzwanzigste Februar* [The Twenty-Fourth of February] that had been one of the highlights of the Coppet circle back in 1808. But why not Goethe's *Faust*? (He had already given some tips to an English translator.)[57] Above all, they must do Calderón. As it happened, *El principe constante*, the play that Schlegel had once translated, featured among these *chefs-d'oeuvre*.[58]

Whether Schlegel had cause to be pleased with an article by Broglie in the liberal *Revue française* in 1830, is open to question.[59] In a review of *Othello*, Broglie took the opportunity of examining some of the causes of post-Napoleonic French Shakespeare enthusiasm—idolatry. He rehearsed Schlegel's old strictures against Racine or Molière: clearly they still rankled. He subjected to an ironic deflation Schlegel's high esteem for all aspects of Shakespeare, applying the criteria of good taste and proper sense.

Yet even this article, from within the Staël circle, showed that one could not be indifferent to Schlegel, even if there was no question of his being declared, as in England, the 'national critic'. Of the French periodicals from the 1820s it was perhaps *Le Catholique* (1826-29) that came closest to the spirit of critical enquiry for which Schlegel stood. Edited by the convert Baron d'Eckstein, it was not above taking over whole tracts of Schlegel's

---

56 *Krisenjahre*, II, 390-392. On this undertaking see John Isbell, 'Les *Chefs-d'oeuvre des théâtres étrangers* de Ladvocat, 1821-1823', *Cahiers staëliens*, 50 (1999), 105-133.

57 Erich Schmidt, 'Ein verschollener Aufsatz A. W. Schlegels über Goethes "Triumph der Empfindsamkeit"', *Festschrift zur Begrüßung des fünften Allgemeinen Deutschen Neuphilologentages zu Berlin Pfingsten 1892* [...], ed. Julius Zupitza (Berlin: Weidmann, 1892), 77-92, ref. 83-85.

58 Isbell, 120.

59 'Sur Othello, traduit en vers français par M. Alfred de Vigny, et sur l'état de l'art dramatique en France en 1830 par M. le duc de B....', *Revue française* (Jan. 1830), republished in François Guizot, *Shakspeare et son temps. Étude littéraire* (Paris: Didier, 1852), 264-313, ref. to Schlegel 306f.

criticism;⁶⁰ its openness to other literatures—Slavonic, Germanic, Indian, Arabic—and its attempt to feel the pulse of European literary culture, aligned it in some ways with what Schlegel had once stood for. Yet it was the statement in this periodical, made in 1827, 'M. A. G. de Schlegel est à moitié catholique' ⁶¹ [M. A. G. Schlegel is half Catholic] that was to lead to Schlegel's riposte and his final break with his brother Friedrich.

The position in Spain was different again. To explain the item 'Cadiz' in Schlegel's later self-promoting account of his Vienna Lectures and their dissemination, we have to bring in the name of Johann Nikolas Böhl von Faber.⁶² A younger contemporary of Schlegel's, Böhl differed from his British or French counterparts in that, though German, he had a Spanish wife, and from 1813 lived in Cadiz and played an active part in making known there those parts of Schlegel's Lectures that bore on Spain and its dramatic culture. Moreover Böhl had in 1813 become a convert to Catholicism. His reception of Schlegel thus shows much of the zeal of the newly converted in an adopted country, one already noted for the pervasiveness of its religious culture.

Not only that: Böhl and his wife Frasquita had been early admirers of the Vienna Lectures as they came out, not least the sections on the Spanish drama that appeared in 1811. She even wrote (in Spanish) in 1813 to Schlegel in Stockholm, expressing her high esteem and appending three poems written in the metre of the *romance* by their friend (and later polemical adversary) José Joaquín de Mora.⁶³ Schlegel replied (in French) in mid-April, ⁶⁴ full of the hope that Spain, now freed of the French yoke, might learn from English and German literature and bring about the revival and rejuvenation of their national culture. When Böhl began to identify with the

---

60 As for instance the section 'De la littérature dramatique chez les modernes'. *Le Catholique, ouvrage périodique dans lequel on traite de l'universalité des connaissances humaines sous le point de vue de l'unité de doctrine; publié sous la direction de M. le baron d'Eckstein* (Paris: Sautelet, 1826-29), II (1826), 5-61. On Eckstein, see Louis Le Guillou, *Le 'baron' d'Eckstein et ses contemporains* [...] (Paris, Champion, 2003); Nagavajara, 274, 281; Jensen, 85-90; Isbell (1998), 398f., 408.
61 *Le Catholique*, VI (1827), 531-612, ref. 607.
62 On Böhl see Carol Tully, *Johann Nikolas Böhl von Faber (1770-1836). A German Romantic in Spain* (Cardiff: University of Wales Press, 2007); Pitollet, *La Querelle caldéronienne de Johan Nikolas Böhl von Faber*; on the link with Schlegel see Guadalupe Reyes Ponce, 'August Wilhelm Schlegel's *Wiener Vorlesungen* and Böhl von Faber's *Sobre el teatro español'*, *Bulletin of the John Rylands University Library of Manchester* 71 (1989), 105-124.
63 This letter is published by Josef Körner, 'Johann Nikolas Böhl von Faber und August Wilhelm Schlegel', *Die neueren Sprachen* 37 (1929), 53-58, ref. 53-55.
64 Pitollet, 75; Reyes Ponce, 108f.

restoration in Spain, Schlegel turned away from him completely:[65] it was part of his general reflection, not so much on 'reaction', as on the aftermath of upheaval, a general recidivism into superstition and fanaticism, that he was increasingly to associate with his brother Friedrich.[66]

Böhl's is a more extreme case of the transference of Schlegel's Lectures into a foreign medium. It can of course be argued that Schlegel's text ceased to be his own once the conventions of another language took over and the translator sought equivalents for a hitherto alien critical terminology. Böhl however went further than Madame Necker de Saussure or John Black: he translated only Lectures Twelve and Fourteen of Schlegel's cycle, the two that, respectively, compared English and Spanish drama, and characterized the Spanish dramatic tradition.

Böhl could not resist the opportunity of giving Schlegel's careful formulations a political edge that the original did not have. True, Schlegel was in 1808 lecturing to a Habsburg audience, aware of the historical links between Austria and Spain. His account of the Spanish Golden Age, although mythologically underpinned, was not intended to glorify it uncritically, but rather to explain how a high culture came about. The same could be said of his account of the age of Elizabeth. Even so, he did leave the impression that nothing of substance had happened in the cultural life and on the stage in both countries since these high moments in their history.

Böhl was less nuanced in his approach. 1814 — the date of his translation — was not 1808, and he could express hopes for a recrudescence of the Siglo de Oro in the terms of the more strident German advocates of the idea of nationhood, like Fichte or Görres. This involved the attenuation of Schlegel's fine distinctions and the blurring into one account of his strictures against neo-classical culture and his advocacy of a national drama in a national state. With this, Böhl also stepped into controversies relating to current Spanish politics (the restoration of the Bourbon monarchy) and literature (the dominance of classical taste in Spain).

The enthusiastic reception of the Vienna Lectures in the Slavic lands remained completely one-sided.[67] There is no evidence that Schlegel knew who Pushkin was, let alone being aware of the Russian's admiration. Adam Mickiewicz was to learn this in 1829 when he called in on Schlegel in Bonn on his way from Weimar. It had been one of the few high points in an

---

65 Tully, 176.
66 *SW*, VIII, 283.
67 Körner, *Botschaft*, 73f.

otherwise fruitless journey.[68] Schlegel's memories of his travels in Slavic parts were restricted to the grand receptions accorded to Madame de Staël, and he showed no interest in Poland or the Slavs in general. Politically, he supported the Tsar (a Staëlian legacy), and he seems to have been unconcerned at Russian (or Austrian) domination of other Slavic peoples. None of this had prevented his Vienna Lectures, mainly in Madame Necker de Saussure's version, from becoming a force in the formulation of Slavic national aspirations in literature.[69] It was his colleague in Bonn, Ernst Moritz Arndt, who was to utter anti-Polish remarks; but he had travelled through the Polish lands in 1812, and his negative judgment was based on the worst possible image, and on his desire to return from the perceived 'chaos' to the 'order' of his native Germany.[70]

Friedrich Schlegel in Frankfurt

The death of Madame de Staël and August Wilhelm's decision to return to Germany also brought about a change in the relations between the brothers Schlegel. Metternich finally overcame his scruples (but only just) and appointed Friedrich legation secretary to the Imperial Diet in Frankfurt am Main ('Legationsrath bei der k.k. Gesandtschaft am Deutschen Bundestag')[71] with a salary of 3,000 florins, finally satisfying his ambition of being a member of the Austrian imperial official class. From this time on, too, he was signing himself 'von Schlegel'. It was from here that he made those various appeals to August Wilhelm to return to Germany, to the Rhine, to Bavaria, to Vienna as secretary of some Academy of Sciences not yet in being. Part of this was the need for his brother's company and intellectual stimulus, for his letters betray a continuing interest in things Sanskrit (which produced notes, nothing more), and encouragement

---

68   Roman Koropeckyj, *Adam Mickiewicz. The Life of a Romantic* (Ithaca, London: Cornell UP, 2008), 129; Zipper, Odyniec, 180-182.
69   On Schlegel's knowledge of the Slavs see Josef Körner, 'Die Slawen im Urteil der deutschen Romantik', *Historische Vierteljahrschrift* 31 (1937-39), 565-576.
70   Dorota Masiakowska, 'Die Infamie der Diffamie—Zur Abwertung der Slawen bei Ernst Moritz Arndt und August Wilhelm Schlegel', in: Hubertus Fischer (ed.), *Die Kunst der Infamie. Vom Sängerkrieg zum Medienkrieg* (Frankfurt am Main, etc.: Peter Lang, 2003), 169-200.
71   *Kritische Friedrich-Schlegel-Ausgabe*, ed. Ernst Behler *et al.*, 35 vols [KA] (Paderborn, Munich, Vienna: Schöningh; Zurich: Thomas, 1958-, in progress), XXIX, 81. On the years in Frankfurt and subsequently see Harro Zimmermann, *Friedrich Schlegel oder die Sehnsucht nach Deutschland* (Paderborn etc.: Schöningh, 2009), 295-320.

to August Wilhelm to complete his editions of the *Nibelungenlied* or of Shakespeare. Of course there was no question of their meeting up until the older brother was freed of his commitments to the Staël family in 1818.

All was not as well as it seemed. Dorothea did not join Friedrich for the whole time, and then their quarters were unsatisfactory. In 1818 and 1819 she was an entire year in Italy keeping a solicitous eye on the artistic development of her sons Johannes and Philipp Veit (when not at Mass or otherwise piously engaged). Friedrich's health was indifferent, and his eating disorder if anything worse: George Ticknor, while stimulated by his conversation, found in Friedrich 'a short, thick little gentleman, with the ruddy vulgar health of a full-fed father of the Church'.[72] Friedrich had hoped for a post with the Austrian legation in Rome, and accepting Frankfurt as second-best, he found his work dull, his colleagues uncongenial and his superior 'imbecilic'.[73] They in their turn were not best pleased that he claimed a special relationship with Metternich. Even so, Friedrich's notions of the organic unity of all nations in the imperial German federation did not go down well in Metternich's circles, where maintaining Austrian hegemony was to the fore.

Above all, Friedrich felt that he was not being given recognition as a writer and an intellectual. Already in 1817 he was asking Schleiermacher if he would not like to contribute to a periodical, perhaps setting out a Protestant view of things.[74] Seeing that this was to become *Concordia*, a journal with pronounced Catholic leanings and solely Catholic contributors, it is not surprising that Schleiermacher showed no interest.[75] For the moment, Friedrich had recourse to the journal that enjoyed Metternich's favour, the Vienna *Jahrbücher der Literatur*, that had started in 1818. Friedrich stands out among the contributors, most of them more moderate than he, men who unlike him were part of the nineteenth-century advance of the humanist disciplines into academia: the Austrian historian and statesman Joseph von Hormayr, the distinguished orientalist Joseph von Hammer-Purgstall, Goethe's informant for the *West-östlicher Divan* (1819), Friedrich von Raumer, soon to be professor of history in Berlin and a friend of Tieck's, or Johann Gustav Büsching, the medievalist. It was for this journal that

---

72 George Ticknor, *Life, Letters, and Journals*, 2 vols (London: Sampson Low, Marston, 1876), I, 101. References to Schlegel's corpulence are legion.
73 *KA*, XXIX, 420.
74 *Ibid.*, 370f.
75 Cf. Johannes Bobeth, *Die Zeitschriften der Romantik* (Leipzig: Haessel, 1911), 288.

Karl Wilhelm Solger, also a professor in Berlin, wrote his important review of August Wilhelm's Vienna Lectures.

Friedrich Schlegel, as he watched his brother August Wilhelm move into these circles, felt increasingly excluded and embattled. He and Dorothea (especially she) had felt outrage that Goethe in the first parts of his autobiography *Dichtung und Wahrheit* [Poetry and Truth] (1811-14) had not acknowledged Friedrich's part in the rediscovery of medieval and religious art. After Goethe's journey to the Rhine and Main in 1814-15 with Friedrich's protégé Sulpiz Boisserée and the publication of his periodical *Ueber Kunst und Alterthum* [On Art and Antiquity] it might seem that he was becoming more reconciled to the religious Middle Ages. But then in 1817 had come that affront to Romantic sensitivities, Heinrich Meyer's *Neu-deutsche religios-patriotische Kunst* [New German Religious-Patriotic Art], fully sponsored by Goethe.[76] Friedrich, the step-father of the Veit brothers, at that moment in Rome and in the forefront of the group of German religious artists that called itself the Nazarenes, was prompted to issue a counterblast in the *Jahrbücher der Literatur*,[77] but essentially the damage had been done. It had been written when Friedrich was finally recalled from Frankfurt and had at last visited Italy in 1819 in the suite of Prince Metternich himself.

When the two brothers did meet up again in Frankfurt in May, 1818, after a six-year separation, August Wilhelm had already been in negotiation with the Prussian authorities and, having been offered Berlin, was also asked to consider Bonn. Friedrich expected imminently to be recalled to Austria (this did not happen until much later in the year), so time was of the essence. There was so much to catch up on; August Wilhelm had been sent the prospectus of *Concordia*,[78] so he knew where his brother stood on the religious and political issues which that periodical would raise. The younger brother found August Wilhelm in good heart and much less given to fractious behaviour; in fact Friedrich von Gentz maliciously contrasted the 'Schlegel of steel' (August Wilhelm) with the 'Schlegel of lead' (Friedrich).[79]

---

76 First in *Kunst und Alterthum. Von Goethe*, 6 vols (Stuttgart: Cotta, 1816-27), I, ii, [5]-62.
77 'Ueber die Deutsche Kunstausstellung in Rom, im Frühjahr 1819, und über den gegenwärtigen Stand der deutschen Kunst in Rom', *Jahrbücher der Literatur*, VII (1819), Anzeige-Blatt 1-16.
78 KA, XXIX, 367.
79 *Ibid.*, 864f.

4. Bonn and India (1818-1845)

Almost immediately, the brothers set off on a journey down the Rhine. The Congress of Princes had been announced, to take place in Aachen: there might be notabilities to meet in the vicinity. In Nassau (Bad Ems) it was Baron Stein: political events had overtaken all of them since St Petersburg and Paris, and Stein was no friend of the current political reaction. There too they met Grand Duke Karl August of Saxe-Weimar and August von Kotzebue, important figures from the past. From Mainz, they went to Coblenz, where the new and the old Prussia converged, with Joseph Görres, the Rhenish patriot, soon to be exiled for sedition, and General von Müffling, who had been military governor of Paris. In Bonn, which August Wilhelm now saw for the first time, they met his future colleague, Ernst Moritz Arndt, whose views on Schlegel had changed but little since they had seen each other in St Petersburg (less than two years later, he would be another victim of Prussian reaction). The down-river journey ended in Cologne, the town that had missed out to Bonn for the choice of the new Rhenish university.

Friedrich now took the waters in Wiesbaden, while August Wilhelm returned to Heidelberg, to write his first lectures, which would be delivered in Bonn, not in Berlin. Friedrich, knowing of his brother's negotiations with the Prussian authorities and his decision to go to Bonn, counselled him to discuss this matter with the state chancellor Hardenberg himself (an old Hanoverian). The Congress of Princes was now to be in Coblenz (16-22 September): it was imperative that August Wilhelm go there in person. This he did, accompanied by his teenage brother-in-law, Wilhelm Paulus. In Coblenz, he met Hardenberg and his secretary David Ferdinand Koreff and proceeded to Bonn to find the house in the Sandkaule in which he was to remain until his death. He also made arrangements with Fanny Randall for his library to be transferred from Coppet to Bonn.[80]

It was during these days and months, Friedrich's last in Frankfurt, as the saga of his marriage unfolded, that August Wilhelm had good reason to be grateful for his brother's wisdom and calming influence. Although himself facing outlays for house and travel, August Wilhelm made a loan to Friedrich of up to 300 florins to see him safely re-installed in Vienna:[81] it was this advance that was to cause such vexation ten years later when August Wilhelm requested its repayment.

---

80   *Krisenjahre*, II, 318.
81   FS actually asks for between 200 and 300 florins. *KA*, XXIX, 519; *ibid*., 885 says 200.

They were never to see each other again. For the moment, their letters (Friedrich's) suggested a good deal of common interest—in the Troubadours, in the *Indische Bibliothek*.⁸² Friedrich's review of Johann Gottlieb Rhode's *Ueber den Anfang unserer Geschichte und die letzte Revolution der Erde* [On The Beginnings of our History and the Last Revolution of the Earth]⁸³ in 1819 dealt with matters similar to August Wilhelm's set of Bonn lectures *Einleitung in die allgemeine Weltgeschichte* [Introduction to a General History of the World] (first delivered in 1821)—the evidence of mythology, the theory of the earth, the origins of language, the rise of religious belief—and they drew on a common set of sources. August Wilhelm even quoted Friedrich's review with approval.⁸⁴

It was a different matter when *Concordia* made its appearance.⁸⁵ This short-lived periodical—Friedrich's last—was written, as his preface stated, in response to the 'times, troubled and confused'.⁸⁶ By that he meant the events since 1818, the murder of Kotzebue, the Carlsbad Decrees, the persecution of the so-called 'demagogues', the revolutions in Spain, Portugal and Italy, the murder of the duke de Berry, the revolt in Greece, the repressions in Italy. It was no doubt these factors that led Metternich to tolerate this journal, for he might justifiably have believed that the settlements of the Congresses of Vienna were beginning to unravel. It was different in Prussia, as August Wilhelm was learning in unrevolutionary Bonn. Joseph Görres, in Coblenz in Rhenish Prussia, had in his *Europa und die Revolution* of 1821 addressed essentially the same issues as Friedrich had in 1819, but with less caution. It could not be published in Prussia,⁸⁷ and its author only just escaped arrest and spent the next eight years in exile in Strasbourg.

To that extent, both Schlegel brothers were reacting to the 'Zeitgeist'. August Wilhelm's counteraction had been to seek withdrawal from political events; Friedrich's was to confront them head on. His long article 'Signatur des Zeitalters' [Mark of the Times] that extended through the whole of *Concordia*, was quick to find reasons for, as he saw it, the moral decline of the nations, and was equally prompt to advance the means for their

---

82   Ibid., XXX, 298-300.
83   *Jahrbücher der Literatur*, VIII (1819), 413-468.
84   SLUB Dresden, Mscr. Dresd. e. 90, XXVIII, 42.
85   *Concordia. Eine Zeitschrift herausgegeben von Friedrich Schlegel*, 6 parts (Vienna: Wallishauser, 1820, 1823).
86   *Concordia*, Vorrede, 1.
87   *Krisenjahre*, II, 342.

regeneration, through the organic unity of church, state and the educational outreach of the state. This Metternich could hardly object to, although he may not have cared for some of the other contributors, a Catholic and conservative rump, most of them converts, dedicated to restoration and (some might say) reaction: Franz von Baader, Zacharias Werner, Adam Müller, Karl Ludwig von Haller.

Marriage

Then in 1818 Schlegel decided to marry Sophie Paulus. Every instinct ought to have told him that he was embarking on something unadvised, unwise, foolish. But perhaps that is merely wisdom after the event. He saw no reason why at the age of nearly 51 he should not marry and start a family. Having been close to others' children, seeing them grow up (or, in the case of Auguste Böhmer and Albert de Staël, cruelly cut off), he had a natural desire to have his own. He wanted what his colleagues-to-be in Bonn had, Arndt, Niebuhr, Windischmann: a household presided over by a capable wife, and full of children. And why not? He knew no physical reasons why this should not happen, and he was never short of romantic gallantries. True, there was an age-gap: Sophie was just short of her twenty-eighth birthday when they married, but the nineteenth century was very matter-of-fact about such unions. In 1823 at Carlsbad none other than Goethe (aged nearly 74) was paying assiduous court to a nineteen-year-old and even asking for her hand. Goethe is forgiven this act of silliness because her rejection produced some of his most moving late poetry.[88] Schlegel's portion was different. In the tradition of European comedy, where old men with young wives are a stock burlesque motif, he was instead to be the butt of ridicule.

It is also the case that those who gave him good advice when all had gone wrong, Albertine de Broglie and his own brother Friedrich, did not intervene until it was too late. Madame de Staël, as Albertine wrote, would certainly have kept him from this folly had she been alive.[89] The trouble was that she had also stunted Schlegel's emotional life and left him open to this kind of amorous infatuation. In fact nobody emerges especially well from this whole unfortunate affair, which cast a shadow over the rest of Schlegel's life.

---

88 The poems known as 'Trilogie der Leidenschaft'.
89 *Briefe*, II, 153.

It was natural that Schlegel, coming to Heidelberg after the Rhine trip with his brother, should pay his respects to the Paulus family. The theologian Friedrich Eberhard Gottlob Paulus and his wife Caroline had been friendly with the whole Romantic circle during his days as a professor in Jena; it had even been rumoured that Schlegel had flirted with Caroline (she wrote novels under the pseudonym of Eleutheria Holberg). Certainly the Paulus house in Jena had been the first to welcome Friedrich and Dorothea, and the friendship had lasted. Among the many children to be found in this Romantic circle was Sophie Karoline Eleutherie Paulus, a little younger than Auguste Böhmer, a little older than Philipp Veit (or Albertine de Staël). The Paulus parents had of course known Goethe and Schiller; in fact Goethe later visited them in Heidelberg, and the 'cup-bearer' ('Mundschenk') in his *West-östlicher Divan* is said to be based on Wilhelm, the young and short-lived Paulus son. Paulus had taken part in the great exodus from Jena, had gone like Schelling to Würzburg, and was now, a surviving representative of eighteenth-century rationalist exegetical criticism, a professor in Heidelberg. It was he who had been responsible for his fellow-Swabian Hegel coming to this university before his translation to Berlin.

The Paulus family knew everyone of note in Heidelberg: Friedrich Creuzer, Greek scholar and mythologist; Johann Heinrich Voss, Schlegel's old adversary (and to be Creuzer's),[90] and the brothers Sulpiz and Melchior Boisserée, Friedrich Schlegel's former protégés who had brought a good part of their important collection of Old German art to Heidelberg in 1810. They also knew Jean Paul, and it was perhaps unfortunate that the celebrated novelist (especially among his female readers) was in Heidelberg at exactly the same time as Schlegel.[91]

There was no love lost between the two (it did not help that Jean Paul was friendly with the Voss family). Jean Paul had never been part of a 'school'; he had preserved his own independence of mind. His review of *Corinne*

---

90 On this and on the whole affair see Karl Alexander von Reichlin-Meldegg, *Friedrich Eberhard Gottlob Paulus und seine Zeit, nach dessen literarischem Nachlasse, bisher ungedrucktem Briefwechsel und mündlichen Mittheilungen dargestellt*, 2 vols (Stuttgart: Verlags-Magazin, 1853), II, 245 (Voss), 196-213 (Schlegel and Sophie). The important cache of letters in Dresden (SLUB) and Heidelberg UB, published by Josef Körner in *Briefe* are a salutary corrective to Reichlin-Meldegg's sanitized account. There is further important material in Bonn UB, Nachlass Lambertz, to which reference will be made.

91 On Jean Paul's visits to Heidelberg and whole affair see Helmut Pfotenhauer, *Jean Paul. Das Leben als Schreiben* (Munich: Hanser, 2013), 369-375.

had been faint praise. Now there was his account of *De l'Allemagne*.⁹² It had essentially called into doubt the ability of a foreign author and critic to subject a literary culture not her own to scrutiny and judgment. It (rightly) questioned the capacity of another language to render the essential subtleties of German (including Jean Paul's). It found questionable the assertion that German poetry owed so much of its worth to its openness to other literatures. Was Jean Paul's own style not quintessentially German? In all this Schlegel had merely been Staël's 'concubine' ('Kebsmann'), ⁹³ a sentiment Jean Paul fortunately reserved for a letter.

But finding Schlegel staying at the same hotel was altogether too galling.⁹⁴ Jean Paul received an ovation from citizenry and students. Schlegel was also to have one, but it was feared it might be mistaken for a homage to another guest, the heir to the deposed king of Sweden. It was better to avoid a diplomatic incident. Worse still, Jean Paul found that the 'fop'⁹⁵ Schlegel was ingratiating himself into the Paulus household. For Jean Paul, although long married, was nevertheless not averse to a little flirtation—as here with both the Paulus mother and daughter—that bordered on the amorous and sometimes even crossed that threshold. Now Schlegel of all people was about to snatch Sophie from under his nose.

Schlegel meanwhile had caught sight of Sophie Paulus. Who could be better suited to be a professor's wife than someone with good looks, who also knew French, English and Latin and who played the piano beautifully? Writing to Koreff in Berlin, his former physician and now his academic adviser, he could say that she was a 'jewel'.⁹⁶ The parents seemed convinced of his suitability to be their son-in-law (they asked his colleague Welcker for a character reference).⁹⁷ And Schlegel used all the charm, gallantry and coquetry at his disposal. It was a pity that his brother Friedrich, also an occasional guest in the Paulus house, had not advised him earlier against adopting a hectoring and superior tone towards Sophie ('Hofmeisterton'). But for the moment all was well. The couple were engaged at the end of July and married in the Providenzkirche, the smaller of the two city-centre

---

92   'De l'Allemagne par Mme la Baronne de Staël-Holstein' (1814), Jean Paul, *Sämtliche Werke. Historisch-kritische Ausgabe hg. von der Deutschen Akademie der Wissenschaften zu Berlin*, 31 vols in 3 sections, 1. Abt. (Weimar: Böhlau, 1927-), XVI, 297-328.
93   *Ibid.*, 3. Abt. Briefe. 9 vols, VII, 228.
94   Walter Harich, *Jean Paul* (Leipzig: Haessel, 1928), 787.
95   'Geckerei und Glanzsucht', Jean Paul, *Sämtliche Werke*, Briefe, VII, 219.
96   *Briefe*, II, 329f.
97   SLUB Dresden, Mscr. Dresd. e. 90, XIX (23), 112.

Protestant churches in Heidelberg, on 30 August. In the register Schlegel was given the noble title of 'Freiherr', with his Swedish and Russian orders; Sophie was a mere 'spinster' ('Jungfer').[98] Melchior Boisserée stood in for the father, who was indisposed.

More than that we do not safely know. All as yet seemed fine. She called him in jest 'Herr Rembrandt', as perhaps befitted an academic husband, but signed a letter, hardly two weeks into their marriage, as 'Kind' ('child').[99] His in-laws, as was customary, addressed him as 'Herr Sohn', he them as 'Frau Mutter' and 'Herr Vater'. Yet things soon took a turn for the worse. It is only fair to hear Schlegel's own account. Writing on 10 January 1819 to the lawyer Jacob Lambertz in Bonn, Schlegel set out what he believed to be the course of events.[100]

He had, he stated, entered into the marriage in good faith, and it had been based on mutual affection. He had agreed with the Prussian authorities to go to Bonn, instead of Berlin as originally mooted, in order for his new wife to be nearer her parents in Heidelberg and to spare her the rigours of the Berlin climate. Thus the decision to go to the new Rhenish university had been taken very largely on her account, and her parents had never raised any objection to their proposed removal to Bonn. Ten days after their wedding he had needed to attend to university matters and see the chancellor Hardenberg in Coblenz, the second of Schlegel's two Rhine journeys in that year. The letters that they exchanged had been affectionate. Writing to Auguste de Staël he was full of marital bliss.[101] On his return, this time to Stuttgart where the Paulus family was staying, he noticed a difference, which he put down to his mother-in-law's interference. Sophie then contracted measles. On her recovery, 'she came every morning to his bed' (presumably not just to pass the time of day). When it became clear that Schlegel was indeed going to take her beloved Sophie from her and install her in Bonn, Frau Paulus went into paroxysms ('convulsivische Wuth'). They returned to Heidelberg; on 1 November he had to leave for Bonn, to set up house for the two of them. Sophie shed tears when he went.

By mid-November the tone had worsened. It was clear that Sophie was not going to join him in Bonn. Paulus stepped in and took over the

---

98 Reichlin-Meldegg, II, 200.
99 *Briefe*, I, 336f.
100 This letter is partly published by Paul Kaufmann, 'Auf den Spuren August Wilhelm von Schlegels', *Preußische Jahrbücher*, 234 (1933), 226-243, esp. 226-234. The whole letter is in Bonn UB, Nachlass Lambertz, S 2537, Mappe II, 1-4.
101 *Krisenjahre*, II, 320f.

correspondence. There were no more letters from Sophie, and nobody seems to have consulted her further on what was to be her fate. Paulus came straight to the point with Schlegel: no amount of ostentation and luxury (the house in Bonn) would compensate for what, he added darkly, he 'now knew'.[102] Schlegel, responding, then insisted not only on 'faith and love' but also his legal marital rights.[103] This elicited from Paulus a terrible letter[104] that accused Schlegel of all manner of lasciviousness with his innocent daughter, coupled with physical impotence. By this account Schlegel had entered into marriage under false pretences and without the necessary 'powers':

> You dared to speak of knowing your sacred legal rights, whereas what you really know is that you planned to sacrifice to enervated voluptuousness and vanity the deepest love, health and life's enjoyment of the purest, most noble and most artless of creatures and it has become inwardly a hell of shame, reproaching yourself for irrevocable wrongs done. [...]
>
> And now at last you wish to insist on rights, seek, like the rattlesnake charms its prey by its gaze alone, in hinting at claims to bring the deceived one into your presence and your clutches, whereas I have come to the conviction that you wished to make the purest, noblest and most simple-hearted of creatures an object of the most impotent debauchery and that you, depite all your clever talk of good health beyond your years, are, with all your stimulants, incapable of anything else. Fie and for shame at your abominations. Were you to flee to the Indus, what abhorrence, what judgment of depravity would not pursue you from all of Germany and half of Europe, where you are so proud of your celebrity [...][105]

One does not wish to quote more, and the letter took an ominous turn when Paulus indicated that he would sue for annulment and for appropriate compensation.

At this stage, Schlegel did the only wise thing left to him: he contacted his brother Friedrich, still in Frankfurt. Friedrich, hopeless in financial and other matters, nevertheless had more *savoir-vivre* than his older brother. The 'superior tone' he said,[106] had been unfortunate, but the important thing was to restore their relationship, and that could only be done in person, and not through letters. It would need time to heal any wrongs,

---

102 This letter in *Briefe*, I, 341f.
103 *Ibid.*, 342f.
104 *Ibid.*, 343-347.
105 *Ibid.*, 343f.
106 *KA*, XXX, 44-47; 'in einem kalten, hofmeisternden Tone', 45.

not mere expressions of affection. True, the mother's antics might be partly to blame, but he should not have recourse to law. Slightly later, he suggested that Windischmann, Schlegel's colleague in Bonn, should act as an intermediary; or that there might be a trial period, with Sophie living in Bonn for, say, six months and then deciding. Friedrich also wrote to both mother[107] and daughter. To the former, expressing himself delicately, he cited Sophie's 'lack of experience' ['Unerfahrenheit'].

By this time it was too late. Paulus was insisting on litigation and was bringing up heavy ordnance in the person of his Heidelberg colleague, the jurist, 'Professor und Geheimrath', Karl Salomo Zachariae, to manage his case. It was at this stage that Schlegel turned to Lambertz. To Paulus's allegations, Schlegel said that he would never have contemplated marriage without taking medical advice; moreover, the marriage settlement had been based on a spoken agreement, not a written contract. Paulus, now showing his true colours, was clearly not above using blackmail to get his hands on Schlegel's money: either he should agree to an indenture, or there would be a court case with embarrassing revelations.[108]

The nature of these possible revelations no-one knows. Perhaps it was Schlegel's *impuissance* or Sophie's 'Unerfahrenheit', or a mixture of both. Perhaps it was none of these things. Maybe Sophie's parents extracted from their innocent daughter only what they wished to hear. We shall never know. The parents had achieved what they clearly wanted all along: they did not lose their daughter. It was Paulus and his wife who broadcast the story of Schlegel's alleged impotence: Jean Paul knew; Sulpiz Boisserée spoke of 'swinish goings-on';[109] Heinrich Heine later made use of it to cruellest effect. It served to confirm all the unpleasant things that people claimed to know about Schlegel, his insufferable vanity, his pedantry, his superior tone. According to Jean Paul (not a disinterested witness), Sophie had no hatred in her heart for Schlegel, only contempt.[110]

Fortunately the lawyers were wiser than their clients. They sought ways and means to extricate Schlegel ('quid juris?', 'quo modo?').[111] (There was

---

107 *Ibid.*, 89-91; 'Unerfahrenheit', 90.
108 Lambertz also made the same points in a letter to Paulus. SLUB Dresden, Mscr. Dresd. e. 90, XIX (23), 113.
109 'schändliche Geschichte', 'Schlegelsche Sau-Geschichte'. Sulpiz Boisserée, *Tagebücher 1808-1854. Im Auftrag der Stadt Köln hg. von Hans-J. Weitz*, 4 vols plus index (Darmstadt: Roether, 1978-95), I, 523, 541.
110 Jean Paul, *Sämtliche Werke*, Briefe, VII, 278.
111 'What does the law say?', 'Which way shall we proceed?'. Bonn UB, Lambertz 2537, 7-10.

the further complication of Heidelberg being subject to Baden law and the Prussian Rhineland still recognizing the 'code civil'). Paulus wanted Schlegel to agree to a voluntary separation, with appropriate financial compensation. Lambertz informed Paulus that he might have to read out his letters in court. Did he really wish to subject his daughter to that? The result was that Schlegel was never legally separated from his wife and that the Paulus family never pressed a claim on his estate. Schlegel refused to have the matter settled, although advised by Lambertz to do so. When Schlegel died in 1845, Lambertz had to write formally to Sophie von Schlegel, as she still was, asking whether she wished to exercise her rights to Schlegel's estate. Her father believed she should.[112] To her credit, she waived them.

Schlegel nevertheless had the threat of Paulus's rapacity hanging over him for the rest of his life, not to speak of the scandal that might be involved. Paulus continued to collect further evidence of Schlegel's alleged turpitude: his papers hold the full documentation of the affair of the painter Peter Busch that was to cause Schlegel heartache in 1841.[113] They also contain letters of a different nature, concerning Madame de Staël's correspondence with Schlegel. In January 1819, when relations with the Paulus family were at their worst, Schlegel made arrangements for Sophie to send the packet of Staël letters to him.[114] This clearly did not happen: Sophie held on to them.[115] In 1831, when Albertine de Broglie asked him for the return of her mother's letters, he suggested that she write directly to Sophie, which she did in the politest of terms.[116] Circumstantial evidence (there were no further requests) suggests that they were returned, but the trail ends there. Their disappearance, which we must now assume, is one of the great losses of documentary material on Staël and Schlegel.

His brother Friedrich, predictably, was deeply upset, even suggesting as late as 1820 that August Wilhelm make another attempt at reconciliation,[117] and writing in 1823 of how painful the thought of their separation was.[118] Albertine de Broglie was more matter-of-fact.[119] She feared that he had

---

112 Cf. Paulus to both Lambertz and Böcking, December 1845, *Briefe*, II, 158.
113 Heidelberg UB, Heid. Hs. 860, 649.
114 *Briefe*, I, 357.
115 Cf. Sophie von Schlegel to Carl Winter 26 January, 1819. SLUB Dresden, Mscr. Dresd. e. 90, XIX (23), 117b.
116 The letter is published in *Briefe*, II, 225f.
117 *KA*, XXX, 250-252.
118 *Ibid.*, 413f.
119 *Briefe*, I, 355.

committed an 'étourderie' [act of folly], perhaps that he had really only imagined that he was in love and had come to realize this once he was married. Above all, he should avoid 'éclat'. There was much to ponder in her words. With a deep sense of inner distress but also of the resignation that he had learned to practise over the years, Schlegel wrote to his superior Altenstein[120] that he was despite all willing to remain in Bonn in the hope of adding to the lustre of this new university. In a letter to Koreff he stressed the need to forget the rumours and allegations and put the affair behind him.[121] Under the circumstances, it is a wonder that he achieved as much as he did in these Bonn years, for the failed marriage was not the last chagrin that he was to experience. An undated sonnet, 'Abschied' [Leave-Taking], though unrelated to these events, expressed not only the drying up of his poetic powers, but also a sense of inner death.[122] It may serve as a kind of epitaph to this unhappy episode.

Was anyone to blame? A much wiser Goethe had written *Der Mann von funfzig Jahren* [The Man of Fifty], a story of late passion which ended in renunciation.[123] Should Schlegel have been similarly prudent? Should the parents have thought again? Should others have warned him? These are imponderables. As it was, Sophie and Schlegel lived apart for over twenty-five years, she in the enveloping bosom of her parents, he searching hard for other fulfilments of his affections and essentially finding none.

The University of Bonn

> The road from the neighbourhood of the Seven Mountains to Bonn lies through an open country. The view of that flourishing Prussian town, and rising university, was very pleasing. The first buildings that meet the traveller's eye are the cupola-crowned Academy, which is appropriated by the medical faculty—and the Castle, now devoted to the uses of the University. The town-gate is handsome, the streets lively. If Bonn be inferior to Carlsruhe in beauty, it possesses commercial activity, one of the moral embellishments of a town. Groups of students, sauntering through the streets, or gazing from the windows, diminishes nought from the sprightliness of Bonn.

---

120 *Ibid.*, 356.
121 Friedrich v. Oppeln-Bronikowski, *David Ferdinand Koreff. Serapionsbruder, Magnetiseur, Geheimrat und Dichter. Der Lebensroman eines Vergessenen* (Berlin: Paetel, 1928), 331.
122 *SW*, I, 379.
123 It eventually became part of *Wilhelm Meisters Wanderjahre* (1829).

In the Castle is a gallery of casts, for the use of young artists. Several specimens are copied from pieces in the Louvre, and in the Elgin collection. The College Park, or Court Garden, forms a handsome promenade, communicating by a chestnut-alley with Poppelsdorf, which is situated at the foot of the Kreuzberg, and contains a castle and garden. From the *Alte Zoll*, a bastion at one end of the park, there is an admirable view of the Rhine, with the Seven Mountains rising dim in the distance, and the hills about Poppelsdorf. The *Münster-Kirche*, or Cathedral, is a Gothic building. The Jesuits' Church and College are now deserted, that order being suppressed in the Prussian dominions. The Town-house, which is modern, stands in the market-place.

The celebrated Augustus von Schlegel, the friend of Madame de Staël, is now a professor at this university. I had to apply to him for admission to an interesting collection of antiques, not yet arranged for public exhibition.[124]

We have to trace the course that led Schlegel to come to Bonn in 1818 and become the local celebrity described by an Irish visitor in 1832.

The Prussian Rhine province,[125] made up very largely of the former territories of the archbishop-elector of Cologne and the duchies of Jülich, Berg and Cleve, was proclaimed on 5 April, 1815. It was however not simply the result of a transfer from the ancien régime to a victorious Prussia. There had been the short revolutionary interlude from 1797 to 1814 when they were French. Cities and towns of the historic importance of Cologne, Coblenz, Düsseldorf, Aachen or Trier had been rudely shaken out of the restful late eighteenth century into the harsher realities of the nineteenth. Cologne, with the hulk of its unfinished Gothic cathedral, had become the symbol of German past greatness and the need for its revival. Friedrich Schlegel, the Boisserée brothers, Joseph Görres, had lent their voices to these aspirations.

Now, in 1815, the Rhine provinces, largely Catholic, found themselves ruled by an alien power, largely Protestant. Gestures of benevolence were the order of the day. Conscious that the Revolution and its aftermath had swept away the old Rhenish universities, King Frederick William III of Prussia had in the same proclamation promised the Rhineland a university of its own. There had of course been vague undertakings for Cologne or Düsseldorf under French administration (Friedrich Schlegel had entertained hopes in 1806), but the Prussian promise was not an empty

---

124 George Downes, *Letters from Continental Countries*, 2 vols (Dublin: Curry, 1832), II, 130f.
125 See generally Rudolf Vierhaus, 'Preußen und die Rheinlande 1815-1915', *Rheinische Vierteljahrsblätter* 30 (1965), 152-175.

one. These were the background circumstances to Schlegel's translation from Coppet and Paris to the banks of the Rhine.[126]

The principle was laudable, the details less straightforward. During the Napoleonic years—despite their being also the times of the Stein-Hardenberg reforms in Prussia—the universities had suffered badly. Some ancient academies, like Cologne or Mainz, had simply not survived the upheaval, while the medieval University of Heidelberg had emerged effectively as a new institution. After a sustained campaign for its creation, the Prussian education reforms had seen the foundation of Berlin university in 1810, with Breslau in 1811 to satisfy the needs of the province of Silesia. The Rhine provinces were a different proposition. There were several serious contenders; a perceived need too to provide a western university in the gap that extended from the Low Countries to the nearest academies, Heidelberg and Freiburg in the south.[127]

Not only that: the new territories contained a total of four former universities. Paderborn and Duisburg could be safely discounted, leaving Cologne and Bonn in the running. Cologne, founded in 1405, might seem to have the edge, especially as a centre of Roman and medieval antiquities. But the short-lived University of Bonn (1786-98), founded by the last prince-bishop and elector and reflecting the spirit of the late Enlightenment, could by no means be discounted.[128] (The young Ludwig van Beethoven had been briefly enrolled there.) Moreover, Bonn's former archiepiscopal palace, a grand and spacious building in the baroque style, was standing empty. That was more or less the situation when Goethe made his journey to the Rhine and Main in 1814-15 and remarked of Bonn that its setting for a university was advantageous.[129]

In the event, the matter was settled by the royal decree that created the University of Bonn on 8 April, 1818. The crucial decisions that would affect Schlegel had been taken by the Prussian state chancellor, Prince

---

126 The main sources for this section are Christian Renger, *Die Gründung und Einrichtung der Universität Bonn und die Berufungspolitik des Kultusmininsters Altenstein*, Academica Bonnensia, 7 (Bonn: Röhrscheid, 1982) and *idem*, 'August Wilhelm Schlegels frühe Bonner Jahre', diploma thesis University of Bonn, 1973, Bonn Universitätsarchiv Slg. Bib. 1554.
127 CF. Ludwig Petry, 'Die Gründung der drei Friedrich-Wilhelms-Universitäten Berlin, Breslau und Bonn', in: Otto Brunner *et al.* (eds), *Festschrift Hermann Aubin zum 80. Geburtstag*, 2 vols (Wiesbaden: Steiner, 1965), II, 687-709, ref. 704.
128 See Max Braubach, *Die erste Bonner Hochschule. Maxische Akademie und kurfürstliche Universität 1774/77 bis 1798*, Academica Bonnensia, 1 (Bonn: Bouvier, Röhrscheid, 1966).
129 *Ueber Kunst und Alterthum*, I, i, 36-38.

4. Bonn and India (1818-1845)

Hardenberg, and his minister of education (from 1817), Baron Karl vom Stein zum Altenstein. As Hardenberg's slightly improbable right-hand man was David Ferdinand Koreff, the 'Wunderdoktor' who had cured Schlegel in Vincelles back in 1806. Now, when not magnetizing titled ladies, he had found himself successively responsible for organizing the medical services in the new provinces, then Hardenberg's personal physician, a professor in Berlin, and finally, from 1815 to 1818, an official in the Prussian state service.

It was not automatic that Schlegel should embark—or re-embark—on an academic career. Philipp Joseph Rehfues, his later superior as 'Kurator' of the University of Bonn, reflected that Schlegel, after having been in Bernadotte's employ, could have made a career in Prussian, Russian or Austrian service; or he might have become an *homme de lettres* in France, a major contributor to the *Journal des débats*, perhaps a *pair de France*, even a minister, like Victor Cousin, also an academic.[130] Yet the signs pointed inexorably in the direction of academia.

It was Koreff (or so he maintained) who had first conceived the idea of attracting Schlegel to a university post in Prussia.[131] He claimed to have written to Schlegel immediately on hearing of Madame de Staël's death, using Alexander von Humboldt as an intermediary. Wilhelm von Humboldt also asserted that it was his idea. Whichever way, it was clear that the authorities in Berlin wanted Schlegel. Writing on 17 December, 1817 to his friend and colleague Guillaume Favre in Geneva, Schlegel could tell him that he had received a flattering offer of a chair at the University of Berlin. His espoused hope had been the life of private scholar, now in Coppet, now in Geneva, but here was an approach in which he was being asked to state his own terms.[132] At first, in Koreff's private communications[133] but also in Altenstein's official letters, there was only mention of Berlin. A chair would be created to suit his particular accomplishments, 'literature and aesthetics, German language and literature' ['Litteratur und schöne Wissenschaft, deutsche Sprache und Litteratur']. His Indian studies would

---

130 Alex. Kaufmann, 'Zur Erinnerung an August Wilhelm von Schlegel', *Monatsschrift für rheinisch-westfälische Geschichtsforschung und Alterthumskunde* 1 (1875), 239-254, ref. 245f.
131 See Oppeln-Bronikowsi, 90.
132 *Mélanges d'histoire littéraire par Guillaume Favre avec des lettres inédites d'Auguste-Guillaume Schlegel et d'Angelo Mai receuillis par sa famille et publiés par J. Adert*, 2 vols (Geneva: Ramboz & Schuchardt, 1886), I, CVII.
133 The correspondence between Koreff and AWS in Oppeln-Bronikowski, 225-236, 239, 251-253, 274-276, 325-339, 343-347, 423-426.

not be neglected either; on the contrary, he could take steps to have a Sanskrit typeface created and could travel to Paris or London if necessary. The ideas expressed in the Chézy review of 1815 were clearly going to find fulfilment.

His qualifications spoke for themselves. No-one mentioned that he did not have the 'Habilitation' normally required for professorial chairs.[134] Nobody specified the grounds for his eminence. His Berlin and Vienna Lectures would have suggested themselves, although they were not strictly academic in form or conception. The corpus of reviews between 1810 and 1816, now augmented by the authoritative *Observations sur la langue et la littérature provençales* (1818) bespoke a scholar of widest competence.

Koreff then sounded a slightly different note. Would Schlegel perhaps consider a year or two at the new University of Bonn? His chair would of course remain linked to Berlin, but his presence on the Rhine would give the new institution some early resplendence. Schlegel was not taken with the idea, citing the advantages, academic and cultural, of the capital city. After the Rhine journey in the early summer of 1818, however, where he saw the new university town for the first time, and, crucially, met the governor of the Rhine province, Count Friedrich zu Solms-Laubach, he seemed not averse to sharing his energies between Berlin and Bonn. The appointment memorandum signed on 20 July indicated this. It suited the thinking, briefly entertained at the time, that Berlin would be the central academic institution in Prussia, surrounded by a group of satellites.[135]

Schlegel's next move put paid to that idea. To Altenstein's consternation, he announced that he would after all prefer Bonn. The reason for this was Sophie Paulus and his forthcoming marriage, the need to soften the blow of her separation from her parents and the wish to protect her delicate frame from the rigours of the Berlin climate. Koreff and Hardenberg thereupon gave up all hope of securing Schlegel for Berlin, although his appointment to Bonn was not finally ratified until 1822. Bonn had as yet no library to speak of, but he was having his own books sent from Coppet. The small number of students that a new university could command would mean a reduced income from their fees. But Bonn, in attracting scholars like Schlegel, could stand comparison with Berlin and its luminaries, such as Schleiermacher or Hegel, Savigny or Raumer.

---

134 Renger (1983), 269.
135 Cf. Friedrich von Bezold, *Geschichte der Rheinischen Friedrich-Wilhelms-Universität von der Gründung bis zum Jahr 1870* (Bonn: Marcus & Weber, 1920), 63.

4. Bonn and India (1818-1845)

All this might suggest that Schlegel could expect special favours from the Prussian authorities and that these were also granted. This is only partly true, for all professors were subject to the practical needs of the state and the injunction for its universities to train men who were 'tüchtig', that is qualified, proficient and morally sound, for the requirements of the civil administration and church or the private sphere.[136] This clearly did not mean 'pure' scholarship for its own sake. True, the writings of professors were not subject to censorship; in Bonn, on the other hand, they were required each semester to give one public and free lecture of at least two hours per week.[137]

Applied to Schlegel's career in Bonn, it meant the broad transmission of general knowledge, a kind of *studium generale*, in classics, history, archaeology, literature, the fine arts, poetics, as we see in the almost universally wide range of lectures that he offered over twenty-five years.[138] These lectures were for the already educated, whose knowledge nevertheless stood in need of deepening. Concurrent with this lecture programme was the communication of a specialised knowledge of Sanskrit, pure linguistic science that was to produce a small and highly-trained elite, also 'tüchtig', but not of immediate relevance to the pragmatic needs of the state. It was the justification for Schlegel's claim that his Indian studies were disinterested scholarship, untainted by commerce or territorial gain, and this was largely true. That these unperjured studies were also dependent

---

136 Karl Th. Schäfer, *Verfassungsgeschichte der Universität Bonn 1818 bis 1960. 150 Jahre Rheinische Friedrich-Wilhelms-Universität zu Bonn 1818-1968* (Bonn: Bouvier, Röhrscheid, 1968), 82f., also 387-390.
137 *Ibid.*, 426, 453.
138 Schlegel lectured variously on Academic Study, Ancient History (up to Cyrus, up the the Fall of the Roman Empire; History of the Greeks and Romans), the History of German Language and Poetry (including the *Nibelungenlied* and Modern German Poetry), the History of European Literature (Italian, Spanish, French, English), the Theory and History of the Fine Arts, Greek and Latin Prosody, German Prosody and Recitation, German Grammar, Etruscan Antiquities, General History, Herodotus, Homer, Propertius, Ancient Geography, Introduction to the Study of History, Introduction to the Study of Philology; he lectured nearly every term from the summer of 1819 on Sanskrit and Indian Language and/or Literature (various titles), including *Râmâyana, Bhagavat-Gîtâ* and *Hitopadeśa*. Information on the Lectures, term by term, can be gained (for 1819-21) in *Jahrbuch der Preußischen Rhein-Universität* (Bonn: Weber, 1819-21), 27f., 32, 283f., 462f.; *Index praelectionum auspiciis augustissimi et serenissimi regis Friderici Guilelmi III. in academia Borussica Rhenana recens condita* [...] *publice privatimque habendarum* [title varies] (Bonn: various publishers, 1818/19-1839), from 1840-41 with sub-title '*auspiciis regis augustissimi Friderici Guilelmi IIII*'; Schlegel's 'Inskriptionslisten seiner Zuhörer' are a further source of information. SLUB Dresden, Mscr. Dresd. e. 90, V (21). Ag. 62000, 201.

on the scholarship of a Colebrooke, a Carey, a Wilson, tinged therefore by 'colonialism' in its widest sense, was an irony of which he was subliminally aware but which he had no cause to voice too loudly.

The Bonn Professor

Writing to Koreff on 19 January, 1820, in the first part of a long letter,[139] Schlegel dilated upon the advantages of Bonn as a town and a university. To his former physician he could state that he had put behind him the 'calumniations' that had accompanied his first arrival. By this he meant the disastrous marriage. Would that he had been able to shake off the memory of that 'étourderie' so quickly. For gossip-mongers and critics during his lifetime and writers of memoirs after his death found it a convenient stick with which to beat him while living and to strike him when dead. His reaction is typical of the stoical acceptance of things as they were that we find in the letters to the few genuine confidants left to him in later life.

Unlike his brother Friedrich, he could not fall back on the consolations of faith: the Protestantism that he claimed increasingly to profess in these Bonn years was really another way of saying 'non-Catholic'. An awareness of a deep religious instinct in humankind, profounder than any doctrine or cosmogony, that accompanied his philological and historical studies, could offer little stay against life's real tribulations.

In his best moments Schlegel was like those old humanist neo-stoics and Latinists for whom Seneca or Lucretius were not mere objects of study, and he was of course very much at home in their scholarly world. Thus Friedrich Tieck's neo-classically Roman bust, that now adorns the Great Hall of Bonn university, best symbolizes Schlegel in these years of muted triumph, not that disdainful and bemedalled portrait painting by Hohneck that has so much become his later image. For if indeed Schlegel at his worst was carping, captious, snide—and his vanity proverbial—at his best he was generous and altruistic: one does well to steer a middle course.

Bonn's climate and setting, Schlegel continued to Koreff,[140] its proximity to France, his good standing with his colleagues, the social ease of a small town, the distinguished visitors he had already received, the generosity of the monarch and his ministers, the influx of students to the new university (he was that winter lecturing to two hundred): all this showed that he had made the right choice in not going to Berlin.

---

139 Oppeln-Bronikowski, 330-334.
140 *Ibid.*, 332-334.

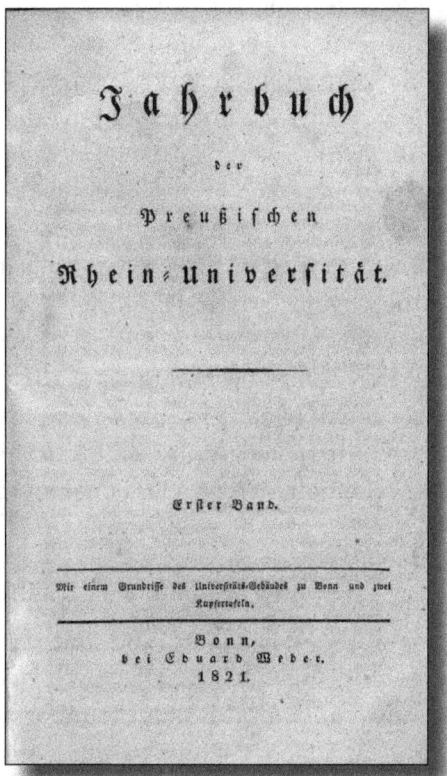

Fig. 24 *Jahrbuch der Preußischen Rhein-Universität* (Bonn, 1819). Frontispiece issued 1821. © and by kind permission of the Master and Fellows of Trinity College, Cambridge, CC BY-NC 4.0.

These same points were being made, but on a much larger scale, by the university's own publication, *Jahrbuch der Preußischen Rhein-Universität*, the first number of which Schlegel edited.[141] One could see there the results of the recruiting policy initiated by Count Solms-Laubach, now advanced to 'Kurator' of the university: also the colleagues with whom Schlegel was most closely associated, and the lectures that they offered.[142] Karl Joseph Windischmann,[143] Bopp's teacher at Aschaffenburg and a friend of Friedrich Schlegel, moved between medicine and philosophy. At first, Schlegel was sufficiently close to Windischmann to write a poem for the wedding of one

---

141 Renger (1973), 46.
142 *Jahrbuch*, 25-33, 279-291, 445-464.
143 On Windischmann see Adolf Dyroff, *Carl Jos. Windischmann (1775-1839) und sein Kreis*, Görres-Gesellschaft, Erste Vereinsschrift 1916 (Cologne: Bachem, 1916), on relations with AWS, 88; Renger (1982), 187-190.

of his daughters,[144] but the relationship cooled when August Wilhelm began his attacks on Friedrich. August Ferdinand Naeke taught classics (Schlegel held an oration in his memory),[145] Johann Friedrich Ferdinand Delbrück history and philosophy, which did not prevent overlaps between him and Schlegel. Ernst Moritz Arndt, whom Schlegel had met in St Petersburg, now a historian and commentator on the 'Zeitgeist', was a disrespectful, querulous and troublesome colleague whose outspokenness soon attracted the attention of the authorities. Of his Bonn colleagues, Schlegel was perhaps closest to the classics scholar Friedrich Gottlieb Welcker, who was also for a time in political trouble. Welcker had been tutor to Wilhelm von Humboldt's children before becoming an academic. Schlegel's notes to Welcker[146] and his general respect for his scholarship—he attended the younger man's lectures on paleography and inscriptions[147]—suggested common interests and outlook. (He was less taken with Welcker's studies on mythology.)

An anonymous contribution to the *Jahrbuch* was devoted to the charms and advantages of the town of Bonn itself.[148] True, it was small and easily traversed (its population was between nine and ten thousand), but so were Jena, Göttingen and Heidelberg. The town had suffered in wars and conflagrations, and although a Roman foundation, it did not match Cologne's historic pre-eminence. Then there was the setting on the Rhine, with the Siebengebirge range on its opposite bank, the vineyards, the forests, 'God's garden'. And if one wanted excursions, there were romantic hills and promontories within easy reach.

This small university town was—for the moment at least—where Schlegel was to settle after thirteen itinerant years. Everybody knew each other, nothing went unnoticed. Would Schlegel's foibles and petty extravagances have been registered in Paris or even Berlin? Would for instance anyone there have stopped to look, as they did in Bonn, when he

---

144 'An Windischmann, bei Vermählung seiner Tochter. 1821'. *SW*, I, 378.
145 *Opuscula*, 415-420.
146 Bonn Universitätsbibliothek, S 686.
147 Reinhard Kekulé, *Das Leben Friedrich Gottlieb Welcker's* (Leipzig: Teubner, 1880), 174, 192. See also Adolf Köhnken, 'Friedrich Gottlieb Welcker: Aspekte der Altertumswissenschaft in den ersten fünfzig Jahren der Universität Bonn', in: Heijo Klein (ed.), *Bonn— Universität in der Stadt. Beiträge zum Stadtjubiläum am DIES ACADEMICUS 1989 der Rheinischen Friedrich-Wilhelms-Universität Bonn*, Veröffentlichungen des Stadtarchivs Bonn, 48 (Bonn: Bouvier, 1990), 57-68.
148 *Jahrbuch*, 61-70; the same effectively by AWS in Latin, *Opuscula*, 418.

overbalanced while admiring a pretty face?[149] (In Berlin perhaps: Theodor Fontane deplored the Berliners' nosiness.) Would the relative opulence of his establishment in Sandkaule 529 have been otherwise noteworthy? But in Bonn this was the house in which he was to live in grand style,[150] grander than a professor needed to—with just a hint of competition, not with Wilhelm von Humboldt's seat of Tegel near Berlin, but certainly with Goethe's house on the Frauenplan in Weimar—and which he was to stuff with his treasures,[151] his Indian miniatures and bronzes (not to everyone's taste), presided over by the ever-loyal housekeeper Marie Löbel, with Heinrich von Wehrden, a coachman and factotum, in addition. This is where he was to receive a stream of visitors—the Broglies, Ludwig Tieck, Adam Mickiewicz, David d'Angers, Sir James Mackintosh, to mention some of the more prominent—but where he would also take in his niece Auguste von Buttlar and those honorary nephews, John Colebrooke and Patrick Johnston.

His life was to be ruled by the events of the new university and its institutions (some still to be created), its visitations, the absorbing minutiae and trivia of senate and faculty, by the rhythm of his lecturing. He would play his part in improving the town and its amenities. It was essentially here that his Sanskrit studies, which brought him new eminence, were to be carried out. Others, 'from Edinburgh to Cadiz' might translate and adapt his Vienna Lectures, while the torch of the Shakespeare translation was to be entrusted to the unsteady hands of Ludwig Tieck. Yet paradoxically it was those very Sanskrit studies, to be pursued to the standards of the German philological tradition, that provided him with a link to the 'monde', that greater outside world centred in Paris and London. They linked him ultimately, too, with the even wider 'monde' of India itself, not in real terms of course, but through those who had actually been there, members of the Royal Asiatic Society in London or the Asiatic Society in Calcutta; they were the surrogate for that passage to India which he never made, the one from which his older brother Carl, all those years ago, had never returned. These studies—not in the first instance the Staël-Broglie connection or the former circle of Madame de Staël in England—were the primary reason for those two visits each to Paris and London.

---

149 Wolfgang Menzel, *Denkwürdigkeiten. Herausgegeben von dem Sohne Konrad Menzel* (Bielefeld, Leipzig: Velhagen & Klasing, 1877), 137.
150 'vornehme Geselligkeit'. Kekulé, *Welcker*, 177f.
151 Description in Kaufmann, 'Auf den Spuren August Wilhelm von Schlegels', 235.

There were two further articles in the *Jahrbuch*, this time by Schlegel himself and an indication of the standing that he already enjoyed. Each could be seen as a statement of intent on behalf of Bonn and its university. There was his description of the collection left by canon Franz Pick, dated 'February, 1819'.[152] No-one seemed better qualified to pronounce on it than Schlegel: one ancient Roman head, he claimed, was better than anything he had seen in Rome, Florence or Paris. The ancient coins, but also the stained glass, the paintings and the manuscripts (including a Carolingian item) all spoke for their retention in Bonn. In the event the university only purchased the coin collection.[153]

The longer of the two articles by Schlegel had more significance for the future: *Ueber den gegenwärtigen Zustand der Indischen Philologie* [On the Present State of Indian Philology].[154] It had all the authority of a programmatic statement: it was to introduce his *Indische Bibliothek* in 1820, and it was translated into French.[155] 'Philologie' was the operative word here, for it was the generally accepted term for 'classics', Greek and Latin, as used in the lecture lists of universities. It underlined one of the key points that he was to make: the same standards as applied to the study of classical texts, as had motivated Heyne or Friedrich August Wolf, the same rigour in choosing versions, the same vigilance over manuscripts, the same acumen in determining meaning, must apply to the study of Sanskrit. It was Heyne or Friedrich August Wolf in a different context. It was a point that he had made in 1815; it was also the basis of Franz Bopp's studies (although Schlegel

---

152 *Jahrbuch*, 94-98.
153 The collection had been auctioned in 1817. Dietrich Höroldt (ed.), *Bonn. Von einer französischen Bezirksstadt zur Bundeshauptstadt 1794-1989*, in: *idem* and Manfred van Rey (eds), *Geschichte der Stadt Bonn in vier Bänden*, 4 (Bonn: Dümmler, 1989), 58. AWS and Welcker had recommended the purchase in December, 1818. Renger (1982), 243. The items were later destroyed. See Nikolaus Himmelmann, 'Die Archäologie im Werk F. G. Welckers', in: William M. Calder III *et al.* (eds), *Friedrich Gottlieb Welcker. Werk und Wirkung* […], *Hermaea* Einzelschriften, 49 (Stuttgart: Franz Steiner, 1986), 277-280, ref. 278. Other items were purchased for the Rheinisches Museum vaterländischer Altertümer. See Wilhelm Dorow, *Opferstätte und Grabhügel der Germanen und Römer am Rhein* (Wiesbaden: Schellenberg, 1826), 93. (ii-v contain AWS's and Welcker's expert opinion on Dorow's excavations.)
154 *Jahrbuch*, 224-250.
155 *Indische Bibliothek. Eine Zeitschrift von August Wilhelm von Schlegel*, 2 vols (Bonn: Weber, 1820, 1827, 1830), I, 1-27; *Bibliothèque universelle des sciences, belles-lettres, et arts* […] XII: Littérature (1819), 349-370. Despite what AWS says in his preface (and despite *Krisenjahre*, III, 585) there was no translation in the *Revue encyclopédique*. There is a condensed version in Latin in the oration for Friedrich Windischmann, *Opuscula*, 410-414.

did not press the point). Now, in 1819, he knew much more Sanskrit; he was acquainted with the manuscript situation, the textual and lexical position. He had assembled at considerable expense his own collection of texts and commentaries, making it at first unnecessary for the university library to duplicate it.[156] He knew what he wanted: professionally produced editions (there would be the *Bhagavad-Gîtâ*, *Râmâyana* and *Hitopadeśa*). He would have to have a press made with devanagari type. 'Philology' in its widest sense also took in comparative linguistics and ethnology, ancient history, and philosophy, what in effect Friedrich Schlegel had introduced into European oriental studies.[157]

While Schlegel, as said, could not afford to be dismissive of the British role in all this, he was not overawed either. He was duly appreciative of the work of Colebrooke, Wilkins and Carey, as indeed he must be, yet the British approach had of necessity to be defined by administration, law, and commerce. Even the great Sir William Jones, fine scholar as he was, a savant in his own right, had been a judge in British India. The French, too, spurred on by Bonaparte's Egyptian campaign, had begun to take a keener interest in inscriptions and monuments. But German universities could bring their particular, if not unique, skills to bear on this most ancient culture and language. Where else but in Germany, and in Bonn, would a general lecture on Indian antiquities and literature be on offer and who else could deliver it but Schlegel?[158]

The Carlsbad Decrees

All of these positive points were registered in the first half of Schlegel's letter to Koreff. The second part, alas, took them all back. It seemed that Schlegel imagined himself enjoying an academic idyll amid vineyards and boskiness, where he could put together the pieces of his existence, recently so rudely shattered. It was not to be. Even as he was negotiating with the Prussian authorities about coming to Bonn, the Congress of Aachen had received a memorandum from the Tsar's representative and counsel of state,

---

156 Wilhelm Erman, *Geschichte der Bonner Universitätsbibliothek (1818-1901)*, Sammlung bibliothekswissenschaftlicher Arbeiten, 37-38, II. Serie, 20-21 (Halle: Erhardt Karras, 1919), 108. Cf. also AWS's report to Rehfues of April 1829. SLUB Dresden, Mscr. Dresd. e. 90, XIX (38).
157 *Jahrbuch*, 226f.
158 AWS gave such a lecture, but under the rubric of History, in the summer semester of 1819. *Ibid.*, 284.

Alexander Stourdza, *Mémoire sur l'état actuel de l'Allemagne* [Memorandum on the Present State of Germany]. The Tsar, his head already turned by the ministrations of Frau von Krüdener and her Holy Alliance, was with Metternich's acquiescence extending his long arm into German university affairs. The universities, this pamphlet averred, were repositories of 'all the errors of the century', hotbeds of 'academic freedom'; it was time to suppress their privileges and police their conduct.[159] Already on 11 January, 1819, a 'Reskript' from the Prussian authorities ordered professors under their jurisdiction to refrain from political journalism.[160] Schlegel's days as a political pamphleteer were well and truly past, but this directive was primarily meant for Ernst Moritz Arndt in Bonn, the last volume of whose *Geist der Zeit* [Spirit of the Age] had displeased the king. All this had caused consternation in Bonn. Then, on 23 March, 1819, August von Kotzebue was murdered in Mannheim by the Jena student Karl Sand. Universities again: first there had been the—in every sense—fiery proclamations on the Wartburg in 1817, where Kotzebue's works had been publicly burned, and now this.

Rejoicing would have been tasteless, but there was no mourning for Kotzebue in former Romantic circles. Schlegel never retracted his anti-Kotzebue parody *Ehrenpforte* [Triumphal Arch] of 1800; he told his students in 1833 that Kotzebue's material was a 'slippery moral, whitewashed with magnanimity'.[161] For all that, it was, as he wrote to Auguste de Staël, a 'deplorable catastrophe', given that Kotzebue, already a dubious character (a Russian police spy as well as a dramatist), was now being seen as a martyr.[162] Sympathising with Sand or his family did not pay either: the Berlin theologian Wilhelm Martin Leberecht de Wette was summarily dismissed for doing just that. In Bonn, the Prussian authorities took steps to suppress any activity seen as inimical to the state. On 15 July, Friedrich Welcker, his brother, and Arndt received a visitation from the Prussian ministry of police, backed up by a battalion of infantry, had their rooms ransacked and their papers confiscated. Charges of sedition were preferred against all three: Arndt was suspended (the *Jahrbuch*, announcing the

---

159 [Alexander Stourdza], *Mémoire sur l'état actuel de l'Allemagne. Par M. de S..., conseiller d'état de S. M. I. de Toutes les Russies* (Paris: Libraire Grecque-Latine-Allemande, 1818), 39, 40, 44-46.
160 Renger (1973), 50f.
161 *A. W. Schlegel's Lectures on German Literature from Gottsched to Goethe Given at the University of Bonn and Taken Down by George Toynbee in 1833* [...], ed. H. G. Fiedler (Oxford: Blackwell, 1944), 31.
162 'un mauvais sujet, et le voilà martyre'. *Krisenjahre*, II, 335.

lectures for the summer of 1821, stated discreetly that he would 'notify the recommencement of his lectures in due course'),[163] and not reinstated until 1840. Welcker, an outspoken upholder of political rights, remained in office, but did not receive an explanation until 1822 and an acquittal until 1825.[164]

All this was followed by the so-called Carlsbad Decrees of 20 September, 1819, whose implementation in Prussia was to lead to reaction and repression in the universities. To their credit, the Bonn professors, Schlegel among them, protested against this flouting of due process.[165] Not only that: in a series of agitated letters, to Auguste, to Altenstein, to Johannes Schulze, a high official in the ministry of education, Schlegel expressed his disillusionment. An added factor was that Count Solms, who was generally well-liked, had been replaced by a new 'Kurator', who seemed less benign, Philipp Joseph (later 'von') Rehfues.[166] The Carlsbad Decrees also involved the temporary suspension of professors' exemption from censorship.[167] On 7 December, Schlegel actually tendered his resignation.[168] Albertine de Broglie offered him a safe haven in Coppet; to Auguste, too, he expressed the thought of returning to Switzerland, perhaps to Geneva.[169]

In the event, nothing came of these rumours of departure. The Prussian ministry—Altenstein, Schulze, Koreff, even the state chancellor Hardenberg himself—were not going to let this academic prize slip from their grasp over a few mere inconveniences. They used flattery and blandishments, Schulze indicating that Altenstein would accede to any reasonable request;[170] to Hardenberg himself Schlegel wrote that a 'nod from Your Serene Highness' was what was keeping him in Bonn.[171] Schlegel was not long in stating his terms. To Schulze he set out his plans for Indian studies and the need for a visit to Paris, his intention of conducting etymological researches and then of publishing Sanskrit texts.[172] In a long letter to Altenstein,[173] with the appendix, 'On the Means of Thoroughly Establishing the Study of the

---

163 *Jahrbuch*, 463. The *Index praelectionum* for the same year has 'Lectiones suas iusto tempore continuabit' (Bonnae: Weber, 1820-21), 7. His name is later simply dropped.
164 Kekulé, 160-163, 170; Köhnken, 59f.
165 *Krisenjahre*, II, 339.
166 On Rehfues see Karl Th. Schäfer, *Verfassungsgeschichte der Universität Bonn*, appendix by Gottfried Stein von Kaminiski, 'Bonner Kuratoren 1818 bis 1933', 532-537.
167 Schäfer, 23.
168 To Altenstein, *Briefe*, I, 362, to Schulze, 367-369.
169 *Krisenjahre*, II, 347f.
170 *Briefe*, I, 369-371.
171 Ibid., 371f.
172 Ibid., 372f.
173 Ibid., 373-377.

Indian Language in Germany', he was more specific, giving a historical conspectus (not omitting his brother Friedrich), then a set of desiderata: an Indian letterpress, editions of basic elementary texts. Knowing the man with whom he was dealing, Schlegel emphasized that Sanskrit had hitherto only been studied in Paris or London. Now it was to be Germany's turn, and to the 'renown of a royal Prussian regional university'.[174] That worked. A letter from Hardenberg himself, of 25 March 1820, effectively granted him everything he wanted, not least six months' leave in Paris and 2,000 talers to help set up the letterpress. The chancellor's envoi was pure Herder, and caught the tone of the late eighteenth century's fascination with India: he hoped for 'awarenesses of the highest importance for the history of human progress from the cradle of culture'.[175] Schlegel was to bring that enthusiasm into the nineteenth and give it an academic foundation that the previous century had lacked. Rehfues, as it turned out, proved to be much more sympathetic to Schlegel than originally feared; Schlegel's correspondence with him is largely official, but it also records private invitations and even the receipt of asparagus.[176]

It cannot be said that Schlegel's manoeuvrings were conducted in the spirit of pure academic freedom. He was not ignorant of the position of a professor in the educational organisation of the state or of the arrangement, the pact, between the state and its servants. He knew that academics, in the final analysis, could not say or do exactly as they pleased. Fichte in Jena all those years ago had exemplified this, and his case been compounded more recently by another Jena professor, Lorenz Oken, for whose dismissal the Carlsbad Decrees had been invoked. While Schlegel was right to be appalled at the authorities' treatment of Welcker and Arndt, he was naïve if he believed academics to be immune to such interventions. The case of the 'Göttingen Seven' in 1837 would show that so-called academic freedom was still dependent on the whim of a local ruler.[177] Two of his own three Latin orations as rector of the University of Bonn, in 1824 and 1825, were to stress obedience to the law, not rocking the boat (with words in season for student corporations, which the Prussian authorities had banned).[178] He

---

174 *Ibid.,* 377.
175 'die bedeutendsten Aufschlüsse für die Bildungs-Geschichte der Menschheit im Allgemeinen aus der Wiege der Cultur'. *Briefe,* I, 379.
176 Mainly in Bonn, Universitätsbibliothek, S 1392.
177 On all these matters see Roger Paulin, *Goethe, the Brothers Grimm and Academic Freedom,* Inaugural Lecture University of Cambridge (Cambridge: Cambridge UP, 1990), esp. 12-16.
178 'Ante omnia, cives, legibus est obtemperandum'. 'Oratio cum rectoris in universitate litteraria Bonnensi munus die XVIII. octobris anni MDCCCXXIIII. in se susciperet

had wanted a quiet life, hoping to retreat, as he had done in Coppet, when things became too turbulent. Now, he was a public persona.

It is clear from all this that the University of Bonn knew what an acquisition Schlegel was and was prepared to make accommodations on his behalf. He was one of the few professors with a noble title: it gave the university a certain cachet. His permanent appointment as a professor in 1822 was in one sense a mere formality, but it was also seen as a great honour.[179] Even by then he was beginning to fulfil his promise to Altenstein of putting Bonn on the map with his Sanskrit studies. He was not above reminding Rehfues the 'Kurator' subsequently of what he had achieved in respect of older literatures, Shakespeare, and Sanskrit (which he had had to learn the 'hard way', he said, not with help from Indians, like Wilkins); he cited his honours and decorations; he quoted letters from Henry Brougham and Sir James Mackintosh, where his agreeing to lecture in London would be regarded as an 'unspeakable obligation'.[180] The implication was that few if any other persons in Bonn were similarly obliged, Niebuhr perhaps, but Schlegel would not wish to press that particular analogy.

This needs stressing, in view of the prevailingly disrespectful and malicious tone of German memoirs of Schlegel in Bonn (Dorow, Menzel, Heine, David Friedrich Strauss), the personal dislike shown him by Niebuhr and Arndt, and the feeling expressed in official or semi-official histories of the university that Schlegel was 'past his best'.[181] It was, as we saw, not a view shared in France or in England, where he was the 'first critic of modern times'.[182]

---

habita'. *Opuscula*, 384. Similar calls for general vigilance in: 'Oratio natalibus Friderici Guilelmi III [...]' (1824); 'Iure itaque cavetur, ne diuturna quies in desidiam delabatur'. *Ibid.*, 365.

179 Cf. the memorandum of the Faculty of Philosophy of 16 July, 1822, to this effect. 'Personalakte der philosophischen Fakultät betreffend Prof. von Schlegel'. Bonn Universitätsarchiv PF-PA 478 (1).

180 These in letters to Rehfues, in chronological order of mention. Bonn Universitätsbibliothek, S 1392 (4), (8), (13), (unnumbered); *Briefe*, II, 226.

181 As, for instance, Bezold, 239-246; Erich Rothacker, 'Berühmte Bonner Professoren', *Kriegsvorträge der Rheinischen Friedrich-Wilhelms-Universität, Bonn am Rhein* (Bonn: Universitäts-Druckerei, 1943), 11-43, ref. 14; Walter Schirmer, 'August Wilhelm Schlegel als Bonner Professor 1818-1845', in: Konrad Repgen and Stephan Skalweit (eds), *Spiegel der Geschichte. Festgabe für Max Braubach zum 10. April 1964* (Münster: Aschendorff, 1964), 699-710; idem, 'August Wilhelm von Schlegel 1767-1845', in: *Bonner Gelehrte. Beiträge zur Geschichte der Wissenschaften in Bonn. Sprachwissenschaften, 150 Jahre Rheinische Friedrich-Wilhelms-Universität zu Bonn 1818-1968* (Bonn: Bouvier, Röhrscheid, 1970), 11-20. A more balanced view in Max Braubach, *Kleine Geschichte der Universität Bonn 1818-1968* (Bonn: Röhrscheid, 1968), 20.

182 Cf. Bisset Hawkins, *Germany; the Spirit of her History, Literature, Social Condition, and National Economy* [...] (London: Parker, 1838), ix, 117-121, ref. 118; [Anon.], *The University of Bonn: its Rise, Progress, & Present State* [....] (London: Parker, 1844), 78f.

The Professor's Day

Schlegel's day had always had a full twenty-four hours (he told Auguste de Staël in 1821 that he needed forty-eight).[183] For the last thirteen years before coming to Bonn, his life had of course been ordered by Madame de Staël. The exacting regimen dividing the day neatly into sections, noted in 1817 by George Ticknor, the strict separation of work and leisure, had been his method of accommodating both scholarly needs and social commitments. In Bonn, the Staëlian organizing genius was no longer there, and with his life as a professor and international scholar, the calls on his time and energy were correspondingly greater. Back in 1803, at a time of emotional turmoil, he had written of the ideal contemplative life of 'philosophical asceticism', achieved by keeping the mind and soul free of earthly cares, passions and amusements, cultivating moderation, cleanliness, order, and silence.[184] By 1820 or 1830, this had become more a kind of resigned stoicism. Yet his day, with its set course laid down, had echoes of a kind of Brahmanic ritual, not in any detail of course, and without any kind of religious foundation except the achievement of some kind of inner tranquillity; the desire, as he set it out in 1827, to act as teacher, counsellor, a kind of secular priest of scholarship and learning.[185] He admired Brahmanic 'impassivity' in controversy and 'their wise maxims',[186] if not always heeding this wisdom himself. His personal neatness and fastidiousness (his frequent baths)[187] could therefore not be put down solely to vanity, but were part of the persona of the scholar-ascetic.

Others, closer to earthly matters, enabled this scholarly existence to function smoothly. Maria Löbel was his housekeeper until her death in 1843. He relied on her implicitly, and there developed between them a kind of affection, separated of course by status and natural deference. At her death, he mourned her like a member of his family. She coped with the running of this huge house, the many visitors, the generous hospitality he extended. The letters they exchanged during his absences from Bonn form a kind of domestic counterbalance to the Broglie correspondence, behind

---

183 *Krisenjahre*, II, 380.
184 *Vorlesungen über Encyclopädie* [1803]. *Kritische Ausgabe der Vorlesungen* [*KAV*], III, ed. Frank Jolles and Edith Höltenschmidt (Paderborn etc: Schöningh, 2006), 371.
185 *Indische Bibliothek*, II, 466.
186 *Oeuvres*, III, 245.
187 *Briefe*, I, 605; *'Meine liebe Marie'—'Werthester Herr Professor'. Briefwechsel zwischen August Wilhelm von Schlegel und seiner Bonner Haushälterin Maria Löbel. Historisch-kritische Ausgabe*, ed. Ralf Georg Czapla and Franca Victoria Schankweiler (Bonn: Bernstein, 2012), 41. (This exemplary edition is generally informative of AWS's Bonn years.)

which are similarly unseen persons who minister and wait.[188] The much younger Heinrich von Wehrden looked after the stable and also doubled as a domestic servant.

Was it he who brought Schlegel his candles at five in the morning (or earlier),[189] so that his master could work in bed? No wonder that Schlegel complained of eyesight problems (not helped by consulting an incompetent oculist in Paris in 1820 or reading Sanskrit manuscripts in various states of legibility). The candles on the lectern when he lectured in the university were not, as Heine was maliciously to maintain, part of an elaborate ritual of self-promotion, but a simple aid to reading.

It was in these early hours, as well as late in the evening, that Schlegel found the time for reading, for writing lectures, for attending to the various calls on his time and attention, references for colleagues or young hopefuls (who inundated him with verse or translations), drafts on academic matters, and letters, letters, letters. As he became more and more a part of the local scene in Bonn, there would be city matters (he was elected to the town's 'Society for Extension and Improvement')[190] or fund-raising for a Beethoven monument.

Fig. 25 'Aula'. Illustration from *Die rheinische Friedrich-Wilhelms-Universität zu Bonn* (Bonn, 1839). Image in the public domain.

---

188 *Ibid.*
189 *Briefe*, I, 379.
190 Höroldt, 97.

Six years into his professorship and only two after being finally confirmed in office, he found himself 'Rector magnificus' of the university for the academic year 1824-25. The university's language for official occasions and pronouncements was Latin, and in Schlegel they had not only a conscientious rector but also one who was a Latinist. This of course he had always been — *De geographia Homerica* and even the lecture on *Antiquitates Etruscae* of 1822 bore witness — but the full unfolding of his Latin rhetorical style came only with his rectorial orations of 1824-25,[191] not least that one of 1825 in which he seized on the conceit of Ulysses to recount his wanderings on the face of the earth as a fugitive from Napoleon and — post-Carlsbad — exhorted his young hearers (but perhaps also older ones like Arndt or Welcker) to avoid political extremes. With all this Schlegel also found himself the university's public orator, delivering Latin tributes to the living and the dead (as to his former Göttingen teacher Johann Friedrich Blumenbach when the university honoured him on his seventy-fifth birthday),[192] for doctoral ceremonies, panegyrics (for his deceased colleague Naeke in 1839). When the king visited Bonn in 1825 and astounded the local populace by making his advent in a steamboat, it was Schlegel who delivered the *carmen*.[193] For who else combined metrical correctness in Latin with the inventiveness, the tropes and the mythology that the occasion elicited? To Coleridge may go the honour (just) of the first poem about a steamship, and Turner may have exploited in more spectacular fashion the effects of smoke, sky and water,[194] but Schlegel is surely the first (and doubtless the last) to have essayed it in Latin.

His opinion was solicited in matters to do with art or archaeology. He was sent to Cologne to assess the authenticity of a painting by a minor

---

191   *Opuscula*, 360-379, 380-385, 385-396. See Neuhausen, 'August Wihelm Schlegel in Bonn'.
192   *Opuscula*, 397-399.
193   'Faustam navigationem regis augustissimi et potentissimi Frederici Guilemi III. Quum universo populo acclamante navi vaporibus acta Bonnam praeterveheretur [...]'. Trans. as *Die Rheinfahrt Sr. Majestät des Königs von Preußen* [...], bilingual edition Berlin: Nauck, 1825. *Opuscula*, 434-435; *SW*, II, 41f. (as 'Die Huldigung des Rheins'). See Georg Czapla, 'Der Rhein als Bühne des technischen Fortschritts. August Wilhelm von Schlegels Elegie auf die Dampfschiffahrt des Preußenkönigs Friedrich Wilhelm III', in: Carmen Cardelle de Hartmann and Ulrich Eigler (eds), *Latein am Rhein* (Berlin, Boston: de Gruyter, 2015), 1-20.
194   The first poem may well be Coleridge's 'Youth and Age' (1823). *The Collected Works of Samuel Taylor Coleridge. Poetical Works*, I, ii, ed. J. C. C. Mays, Bollingen Series, LXXV (Princeton: Princeton UP, 2001), 1011-1013. Cf. Richard Holmes, *The Age of Wonder. How the Romantic Generation Discovered the Beauty and Terror of Science* (London: HarperPress, 2008), 382f.

seventeenth-century master.¹⁹⁵ The Great Hall of the university, in the former archiepiscopal palace, was bare and uninviting. It was to be enlivened with frescoes.¹⁹⁶ He knew from first hand all of the great Italian models; he believed the Germans, unlike the French, to be the true heirs of Renaissance fresco technique. And so it was the painters of the Düsseldorf school who decorated these walls with figures, allegorical and historical, of the four Faculties. He encouraged them to work according to the best authenticated images. Not everyone was enamoured: where Luther or Schleiermacher sat among the tiaras, mitres and tonsures of Theology; Manu and Solon expounded Law with Bacon and Grotius; Galen and Hippocrates dealt out Medicine with Haller and Linné; while Shakespeare, Goethe and Schiller represented Philosophy (nor has posterity much mourned the frescoes' loss).¹⁹⁷

Similarly, Schlegel was very much to the fore in the setting up of both the Rhenish Museum of Antiquities, into which much of the Pick collection had been absorbed, and the university's own academic museum. In the first-named institution a notice in Schlegel's hand invited visitors to apply to him in person for an entrance ticket.¹⁹⁸ A duty on his first visit to Paris had been to order casts of the most significant antique works of statuary, for inclusion in this institution, not least those of the Parthenon frieze.¹⁹⁹

Schlegel's lectures now represented a major incursion, sometimes up to three in one day.²⁰⁰ They were usually at six o'clock in the evening. Schlegel

---

195 Emil Sulger-Gebing, *Die Brüder A. W. und F. Schlegel in ihrem Verhältnisse zur bildenden Kunst*, Forschungen zur neueren Litteraturgeschichte, 3 (Munich: Haushalter, 1897), 173, 181-187.
196 On this subject see Sulger-Gebing, 187-189; Heinrich Schrörs, *Die Bonner Universitätsaula und ihre Wandgemälde* (Bonn: Hanstein, 1906); Schlegel's memorandum, 73-75. On fresco technique, Latin description, *Opuscula*, 368f.
197 The figures are explained by Schrörs, 50-62 and illustrated in Ilse Riemer, *Bildchronik der Bonner Universität. Ein Rückblick ins 19. Jahrhundert* (Bonn: Stollfuss, 1968), 28f. The frescoes were destroyed in the air raid on Bonn of 18 October, 1944.
198 'Anschlag für auswärtige Besucher am Schwarzen Brett des Königlichen Museums vaterländischer Alterthümer der Rheinlande und Westphalens', Bonn Universitätsbibliothek, Autogr. ['Handschrift von A. W. v. Schlegel'].
199 For a contemporary account of its setting up and of the works on display see F. G. Welcker, *Das akademische Kunstmuseum zu Bonn* (Bonn: Weber, 1827). See also *Jahrbuch*, 424. Correspondence relating to the University collection in Peter Hesselmann, 'Unveröffentlichte Briefe von August Wilhelm Schlegel', *Athenäum* (1995-96), 345-350, ref. 346f. See also Wilfred Geominy, 'Die Welckersche Archäologie', in: Calder III (1986), 230-250, ref. 242-244; Himmelmann, *ibid.*, 278.
200 *Briefwechsel zwischen Wilhelm von Humboldt und August Wilhelm Schlegel*, ed. Albert Leitzmann (Halle: Niemeyer, 1908), 46.

might go riding (as rector he encouraged his hearers to do so),[201] or go out in his carriage (with Wehrden as coachman) to take the air.[202] Bonn was generally noted for its gregariousness and sociability,[203] so perhaps he made calls: on the industrialist Friedrich aus'm Weerth, with his house full of art treasures,[204] on the city councillor Nikolaus Forstheim and his attractive wife, for instance;[205] later the Flotow family, with whom he exchanged verses; certainly he was renowned for his 'Mittagsgesellschaften' [lunch parties] and 'Abendgesellschaften' [dinner parties] (and his cuisine).[206] Perhaps he caught up with the foreign newspapers in the reading and dining club, 'Lese- und Erholungs-Gesellschaft' of which he and most other Bonn professors were members.[207] He could call in at the chess club which he founded and that met once a week.[208] There could be visitors: Niebuhr's boy, coming over on an errand, would be shown some of the treasures,[209] perhaps the peacock in the garden.[210]

But guests in the evening would arrive at the plain front of the Sandkaule, with its three storeys, a carriage entrance with archway, five windows on the ground floor and seven on each of the two upper levels.[211] The full panoply would unfold once one was inside, the Chinese and Indian rooms on the ground floor, with Chinese wall coverings, tablecloths and stone figures, Indian coloured engravings and bronzes, 'idols' (Schlegel's word),[212] a collection assembled mainly in Paris and London, a clock with elephants, Friedrich Tieck's marble bust of Schlegel himself. Furniture, china, glass and cellar were of the highest quality: they were, after all, intended for the professor's wife who never joined him.

---

201 *Opuscula*, 394.
202 'Fast täglich durchfliege ich die schöne Umgegend auf edlen und muthigen Rossen.' *Ludwig Tieck und die Brüder Schlegel. Briefe*. Auf der Grundlage der von Henry Lüdeke besorgten Edition neu herausgegeben und kommentiert von Edgar Lohner (Munich: Winkler, 1972), 184.
203 Höroldt, 177.
204 *Ibid.*, 59.
205 Kaufmann (1933), 235.
206 Werner Deetjen, 'August Wilhelm Schlegel in Bonn', *Spenden aus der Weimarer Bibliothek*, 15, *Zeitschrift für Bücherfreunde* NF 20 (1928), 16-20, ref. 17f., 20.
207 Schlegel since 1818. Adolf Dyroff, *Festschrift zur Feier des 150jährigen Bestehens der Lese- und Erholungs-Gesellschaft zu Bonn 1787-1937* (Bonn: Scheur, 1937), 111.
208 Georg Christian Burchardi, *Lebenserinnerungen eines Schleswig-Holsteiners*, ed. Wilhelm Klüver, Bücher Nordelbingens, Reihe I, ii (Flensburg: Verlag des Kunstgewerbemuseums, 1927), 104.
209 SLUB Dresden, Mscr. Dresd. e. 90, XIX (17), 26.
210 *Ibid*. (29), 45.
211 An illustration in Czapla/Schankweiler, between pp. 108 and 109 [plate 2].
212 'ich besitze selbst eine kleine Sammlung von Idolen'. *Indische Bibliothek*, II, 43.

The day would end with his withdrawal to the much less grand living quarters upstairs, to the solitude of scholarship.

Teacher and Taught

Schlegel's career as a lecturer may have reached its high point in Vienna. If it did not scale new heights in Bonn, it achieved a breadth and scope unattained elsewhere. True, he still enjoyed the rhetorical gesture to a larger audience and took an almost homiletical pleasure in the spoken word.[213] It was his father Johann Adolf's legacy, but secularized. His father, too, had taught his own sons (the gifted ones, that is) and catechised others', had pointed from the pulpit to universal truths. Schlegel, similarly, took seriously his role as an academic teacher and mentor. There was something of 'pädagogischer Eros', by which German denotes the desire to reach out and impart knowledge to the young.

Thus what one could call his educational experiments with others' children, with Auguste Böhmer, the Staëls, his interest in Pestalozzi, his watchful eye over the artistic career of his niece Auguste von Buttlar, the avuncular care for the Colebrooke and Johnston boys, even his ministrations to the Broglie son—not to speak of his later solicitude for those problem nephews Johann August Adolph and Hermann Wolper—were a outpouring of genuine affection for the young but were also motivated by the principles on which he was brought up and which he continued to maintain throughout his academic career. Childhood—he quoted the opening of the *Hitopadeśa* in his *Indische Bibliothek* in 1827—is the time of susceptibility to all impressions, like clay that can be formed to any shape, and when hardened, preserves these.[214] That was the theory. 'Languages and mathematics are the basis of all the rest', he told Auguste de Staël.[215] This principle he set out later in a systematic memorandum which has Latin as the foundation of all humanist, historical and philological endeavour,[216] his defence of Latin as an academic language and a means of international

---

213 'Neigung zu mündlichen Vorträgen'. Leitzmann, 102.
214 *Indische Bibliothek*, II, 17.
215 *Krisenjahre*, II, 409.
216 'Abriß vom Studium der classischen Philologie'. SLUB Dresden, Mscr. Dresd. e. 90, IV (4). See Josef Körner, 'Ein philologischer Studienplan August Wilhelm Schlegels', *Die Erziehung* 7 (1932), 373-379. See also AWS's draft 'Historischer Studienplan' of 1835, ibid., IV (3). Cf. 'Iure itaque doctae antiquitatis opes litterarae, quarum in atrio quasi ianitrix ars grammatica sedet, ad penetralia deducit ars critica, in erudienda pueritia atque adolescentia ingenuorum principum locum occupant'. *Opuscula*, 430.

communication.[217] It was the basis of his *De studio etymologico* that appeared in the *Indische Bibliothek* in 1820.[218] This involved the training of the memory as the means to acquire structures and patterns and the ability to analyse, the basic tools of the philologist and the historian which Schlegel in Bonn now essentially was.

He had not had the chance to experiment with children of his own; he had no gifted daughter like his Göttingen teacher Schlözer or even his friend Ludwig Tieck. He had failed with Albert de Staël (as all had) — except perhaps in those Rousseau-like 'promenades' through Switzerland in 1806. He was unable to see the English boys' education through to its final fruition.

The great cycles of Jena, Berlin and Vienna stood him in good stead for lecturing in Bonn, but only to some degree. In Jena, he had attempted too much and had extended himself too far; in Berlin, the grand schemes of art and literature had failed to cohere and were fragmented; in Vienna, the subdivision into Ancient and Modern was not without its forced character. Nevertheless it is possible to discern links with his Bonn lectures — inasmuch as we have them, for of the over thirty sets of lectures given in various guises and permutations, only seven of his scripts have survived.[219] Even then, with the sole and significant exception of his lectures on Sanskrit and Indian literature, which (Bopp in Berlin notwithstanding) represent an innovation for the whole of the German university system, it may well be that Schlegel was relying on earlier drafts: the lectures on Propertius which Karl Marx heard are possibly a revision of the Jena cycle on the Roman elegiacs; the lectures on classical or German metrics were so much second

---

217 Ibid., 427.
218 *Indische Bibliothek*, I, 277-294.
219 These are: 'Vorlesungen über das akademische Studium' (first 1819-20), published as: *Vorlesungen über das akademische Studium*, ed. Frank Jolles, Bonner Vorlesungen, 1 (Heidelberg: Stiehm, 1971); 'Geschichte der deutschen Sprache und Poesie' (first 1818-19), full text published as: A. W. Schlegel, *Geschichte der Deutschen Sprache und Poesie. Vorlesungen, gehalten an der Universität Bonn seit dem Wintersemester 1818/19*, ed. Josef Körner, Deutsche Literaturdenkmale des 18. und 19. Jahrhunderts, 147 (Berlin: Behr, 1913), with additions in Fiedler, *A. W. Schlegel's Lectures* (1944) (Bisset Hawkins's remarks on German literature are based on Toynbee's notes, Bisset Hawkins, viiif.); 'Entwurf zu Vorlesungen über die allgemeine Weltgeschichte' (first 1821-22), unpublished, SLUB Dresden, Mscr. Dresd. e. 90, XXIX; 'Einleitung in die allgemeine Weltgeschichte' (first 1821), unpublished, *ibid.* XXVIII; 'Antiquitates Etruscae' (1822), *Opuscula*, 115-286; 'Geschichte der Griechen und Römer' (first 1822-23), unpublished, SLUB Dresden, Mscr. Dresd. XXX (now only partially decipherable). The lectures on the fine arts given in Bonn, while covering similar ground, are textually different from those given in in Berlin in 1827. 'Vorlesungen über Theorie und allgemeine Geschichte der bildenden Künste' (first 1819), *ibid.*, XXXI.

nature as perhaps not even to require a text; those on ancient history are linked with his Göttingen origins, Heyne, Schlözer, Blumenbach, and are by the author of *De geographia Homerica*, now attained to maturity. He had enough material from Berlin and Vienna to lecture on Romance literatures, on German poetry likewise. The important general lectures on academic study reflected earlier views on the origins of language, on the acquisition of knowledge, on the structure and subdivisions of 'science'; they echoed, too, Hardenberg's and Humboldt's notions of the university and its stated purpose, stressing as well the old humanist 'nosce te ipsum' [know thyself]. The lectures on the fine arts had first been drafted in the early Berlin cycle, were partly published in *Prometheus* in 1808, and were to form the basis of the only public series that he gave in later life outside of the university, those in Berlin in 1827.

Much of what has survived therefore is very largely in note form or draft, aides-mémoire for public speaking. There are indications of adjustments or verbal qualifications that he made as he went along. With the exception of those 1827 lectures on the fine arts they were not destined to have an immediate afterlife except in the minds and memories of his student hearers. Their exclusion from the standard edition of his works means that we as readers are deprived of a substantial part of his later intellectual output. Thus it is all the more unfortunate that Heine's or Menzel's memoirs are almost entirely malicious, while Marx said nothing about his experience of Schlegel. All the more important are those letters and testimonies to their 'revered teacher' from the Sanskritists and philologists who had sat at his feet and whom he trained.

It is true that his lecturing style tended towards the 'occasion' or the ceremonial (if not exactly as Heine described it), and doubtless there were witty asides (but not necessarily the salacious remarks recorded by Dorow and Menzel).[220] Yet one cannot overlook his own stated requirement for the lecturer: that there should be a sympathetic bond between an attentive audience and the teacher.[221] The Englishman George Toynbee's notes from 1833 are therefore all the more important as coming from someone less encumbered with *parti pris*:

> A gentleman told me the other day to be sure and call on him as he would feel flattered by having an Englishman to attend his lectures, and he liked to hear himself talk English. Schlegel was first known by his critical writings

---

220 Menzel, 137; Wilhelm Dorow, *Erlebtes*, 4 vols (Leipzig: Hinrichsen, 1843-45), III, 270.
221 *Vorlesungen über das akademische Studium*, 61.

and his lectures on Dramatic Literature. Then appeared his great work, a translation of Shakespeare. He is now about 65 and occupies himself principally with oriental literature. His lecture today was interesting from the situation of the author. When a man gives us the history of literature he gives us in some measure the history of himself. Schlegel's appearance is not imposing, his stature is rather low, there is at first sight a look of obeseness and infirmity about him, which however is quickly destroyed as his eye brightens and sheds (as one may say) acute glances into the subject before him. His delivery is clear, distinct, melodious. In hearing this purely literary lecture the students present the same earnestness and attention. They all take copious notes. The utmost silence prevails. No one enters after the lecture has commenced. When it terminates, they sit still until the Lecturer has left the Hall[…][222]

It was a general principle in nineteenth-century German universities that professors could step over the strict bounds of their subjects and lecture in other related areas. Karl Windischmann in Bonn was an extreme example, being a professor in two faculties; but historians and philosophers lecturing on aesthetics or the history of literature were not uncommon, witness the cases elsewhere of Hegel, Gervinus or Hettner; Karl Lachmann in Berlin was a classical scholar who also edited German medieval texts. Schlegel's own pupil Lassen read on English literature as well as Sanskrit in the 1840s, indeed Prince Albert of Saxe-Coburg-Gotha was recommended to attend his lectures.[223] In Bonn at least, it seemed not uncommon for professors to listen to their own colleagues, as Schlegel did for Welcker and possibly later for Friedrich Ritschl;[224] Arndt, surprisingly, sat in on one or two of Schlegel's lectures.

Even so, Schlegel's lecturing range was extraordinary, not of course for anyone who had followed his intellectual career and noted his authority in so many fields of endeavour. Wilhelm von Humboldt, writing to him in 1822, summed it up: 'a man of your mind, with such many-sided command of scholarship and a marked penchant for philosophy and poetry, should not restrict himself to the philological study of one sole language'.[225] By all means teach Sanskrit, but not exclusively.

---

[222] Toynbee, 9f. On Toynbee see Gustav Hübener, 'Ein Engländer über Bonn vor hundert Jahren', *Bonner Mitteilungen* 13 (1934), 28-32.

[223] Franz Bosbach, 'Einleitung—Fürstliche Studienplanung und Studiengestaltung', in: FB (ed.), *Die Studien des Prinzen Albert an der Universität Bonn (1837-1838)*, Prinz-Albert-Forschungen, 5 (Berlin, New York: de Gruyter, 2010), 13-44, ref. 33.

[224] Otto Ribbeck, *Friedrich Wilhelm Ritschl. Ein Beitrag zur Geschichte der Philologie*, 2 vols (Leipzig: Teubner, 1879, 1881), II, 13-14, 476.

[225] Leitzmann, 110.

It was natural that he should wish to lecture on German literature, sometimes just on the 'Lied der Nibelungen' alone. 'Germanistik' as an academic subject was in its infancy and nobody could claim to know the material better than he, indeed he had helped to shape its recent development. As the translator of Shakespeare, Dante and Calderón and much else besides, he could cover all of modern European literature until Friedrich Christian Diez gained a full chair of Romance studies in 1830 and effectively founded the academic subject. Schlegel had produced in 1818 the first important critique of François Just Marie Raynouard's edition of the Troubadours, *Observations sur la langue et la littérature provençales* [Observations on Provençcal Language and Literature], but had not pursued the subject further. It had also been one of the first instances of an association between a French and a German scholar on a subject in Romance literature, soon to be augmented by his close relationship with Claude-Charles Fauriel.[226] Who better than a practising poet (if no longer writing in a serious vein) to expound metrics and prosody, classical or modern, especially when there were several budding poets in the audience, one destined to be great (Heine) and others to be minor (Geibel, Karl Simrock, Hoffmann von Fallersleben, Nikolaus Becker). 'Theory and History of the Fine Arts' would be second nature to someone who had seen all that was to be seen in Italy and France and who both revered and criticised Winckelmann. Once Eduard d'Alton, connoisseur and collector, received a full professorship of art in 1827, Schlegel left the field to him, only to return after D'Alton's death, when he was no more at the height of his powers. The same happened when August Ferdinand Naeke died in 1838 and Schlegel reasserted his right to lecture on classics. Ancient or Roman history he clearly was not going to leave to Welcker or Naeke or indeed to the historian Karl Dietrich Hüllmann, certainly not to Niebuhr, when in 1823 that scholar decided to settle privately in Bonn and finish the third volume of his Roman History, the first two of which Schlegel had savaged. His public lectures on Ancient History would enable him to draw on all the resources of language, history, geography, ethnography, and give a universal conspectus of human civilization. Similarly, no other

---

226 See Gertrud Richert, *Die Anfänge der romanischen Philologie und die deutsche Romantik*, Beiträge zur Geschichte der romanischen Sprachen und Literaturen, 10 (Halle: Niemeyer, 1914), 37-68, correspondence with Raynouard (48f.), Fauriel (54-56) and Diez (59-62).

professor could command the range of competence and experience that went into his public cycle on Academic Study.

Schlegel only occasionally lectured to a public audience on Indian literature and antiquities, but every semester he taught Sanskrit grammar, unspectacularly, unrelentingly, to the small group who had both the enthusiasm and the staying-power, hard going, making his students copy down from his dictation.[227] The 'Grammatica Sanscrita' in his papers and the comparative grammar of Greek, Latin, Etruscan, Germanic there,[228] are part of the philological apparatus that merged teaching and research into one process. For if Schlegel's other lectures in Bonn could be seen as drawing on resources long since acquired and no longer in the forefront of his academic interests, his Sanskrit studies demonstrated in exemplary fashion that Humboldtian ideal, so rarely attained, where the university teacher and the researcher were one and the same person.

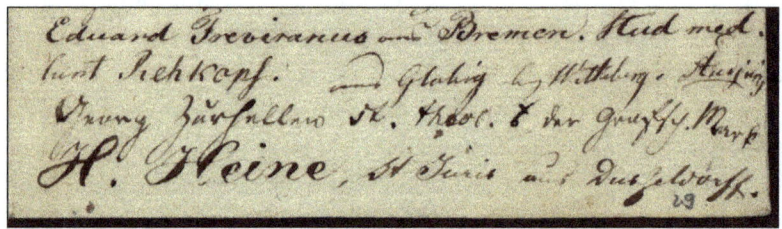

Fig. 26 'Inskriptions-Liste'. Attendance list for August Wilhelm Schlegel's lecture 'Deutsche Verskunst', summer semester 1820, showing Heinrich Heine's name at the bottom. © SLUB Dresden, all rights reserved.

Fig. 27 'Inskriptions-Liste'. Attendance list for August Wilhelm Schlegel's lecture 'Einige homerische Fragen', winter semester 1835-36. Karl Marx's name is marked '+6'. © SLUB Dresden, all rights reserved.

---

227 Leitzmann, 61f., 110. 'pourvu qu'ils aient du talent et de la persévérance'. *Oeuvres*, III, 239.
228 SLUB Dresden, Mscr. Dresd. e. 90, LIV, LV.

4. Bonn and India (1818-1845)

Who came to his lectures? And how many? We can reconstruct this, and much more besides from his 'Inscriptionslisten'.[229] The names listed there are of those who actually signed up for his public and private lectures and paid their fees.[230] They received a printed receipt, with details of the course and the venue, signed by the professor.[231] Not surprisingly, his numbers were small during the first years of the university's existence, and most of his students came from the Rhineland. That applied to Karl Simrock, the son of the Bonn music publisher (Haydn's and Beethoven's) and much later a professor; it held, too, for the son of the former 'Kurator' Count Solms, and for Windischmann's sons. Above all, it was the case with the young man who signed the register first as 'Harry Heine', then 'H: Heine St Juris' and finally, flamboyantly, 'H: Heine, St Juris aus Dußeldorff' [sic].[232] Jewish names are not uncommon on these lists, reflecting the processes of emancipation and assimilation, although neither 'Moses Hess aus Trier', the later socialist and Zionist,[233] nor notably 'Karl Heinrich Marx aus Trier'[234] was to find joy in their German homeland, nor was the said 'Harry Heine'.

Eduard Böcking is there, the later law professor in Bonn and (also as 'Édouard' or 'Eduardus') the editor of Schlegel's works. Names once resonant in German culture feature, but now in a younger generation: Stolberg, Görres, Boisserée, Eichendorff, Brockhaus, even 'von Goethe' (his grandson). August Heinrich Hoffmann von Fallersleben, Heinrich Düntzer, Moritz Haupt,[235] Karl Simrock and Nikolaus Delius were figures who learned their philological skills from Schlegel and who were to form part of the institutionalizing process of Germanic and English studies in German universities.

---

229 'Inscriptionslisten seiner Zuhörer'. SLUB Dresden, Mscr. Dresd. e. 90, V, 21. Ag. No. 62000, 201.
230 The fees charged by a professor for attendance at a private lecture seem to have averaged at about 100 talers per semester, and were often much more. Bosbach, 'Fürstliche Studienplanung', 37f.
231 Such a one for Schlegel's lecture on 'Alte Weltgeschichte' is reproduced in Reinhard Tgahrt et al. (ed.), *Weltliteratur. Die Lust am Übersetzen im Jahrhundert Goethes* (Munich: Kösel, 1982), 507, 522.
232 Heine was inscribed for 'Geschichte der deutschen Sprache und Poesie' (winter 1819-20), and 'Lied der Nibelungen' and 'Deutsche Verskunst' (summer 1820).
233 Hess heard 'Römische Geschichte' (winter 1828-29, summer 1831), 'Deutsche Sprache' (winter 1830-31) and 'Deutsche Verskunst' (summer 1833).
234 Marx heard 'Einige Homerische Fragen' (winter 1835-36) and 'Ausgewählte Elegien des Propertius' (summer 1836).
235 Letter of Haupt to AWS expressing indebtedness to his studies on the *Nibelungenlied*. SLUB Dresden, Mscr. Dresd. e. 90, XIX (10), 21.

By the time that Karl Marx was a student in Bonn, Schlegel was commanding audiences of between one and two hundred. From the early 1820s, non-German students occur in his lists, mainly from England (George Toynbee being but one). That anonymous London publication, *The University of Bonn: Its Rise, Progress, & Present State*, of 1844, while making capital out of the Prince Consort's recent sojourn in Bonn,[236] was telling prospective English students what they had known for almost twenty years: that this was the nearest German university to the British Isles, a fashionable one at that, and hosting 'the celebrated translator of Shakspeare'.[237] French students feature much less frequently, but one is Charles Galusky,[238] his later biographer, another is the son of Prosper de Barante, formerly of the Coppet circle.

Schlegel's lists also record another sociological process, the increasing number of German aristocrats and high nobility who were drawn to Bonn, especially from the middle of the 1830s onwards: 'the Heirs-apparent of Sovereign Princes are often found cordially and affectionately mingling with the sons of the lowly and the unknown', was how *The University of Bonn* saw it,[239] and indeed the years 1838 to 1841 alone see up to six heirs to grand ducal and ducal thrones there,[240] even 'Prinz Georg von Preußen' in one of Schegel's last lectures. In the summer semester of 1838, Prince Chlodwig zu Hohenlohe-Schillingsfürst, later to be chancellor of the German Empire, could have rubbed shoulders with three Swiss students and two Englishmen, all attending Schlegel's lectures on The History of German Literature.

It may have been thought that Bonn would offer these young gentlemen from the high nobility fewer distractions than a big city like Berlin; certainly the university's academic reputation, in which Schlegel played his part, would be another consideration. It was a deciding factor in the education of the two young Saxe-Coburg princes, Ernst and Albert.[241] Albert (while not inscribed among the student hearers) heard Schlegel's lectures on

---

236 *The University of Bonn*, 171.
237 Ibid., 78.
238 Undated letters to AWS. SLUB Dresden, Mscr. Dresd. e. 90, XIX (9), 2-3.
239 *The University of Bonn*, xiv.
240 Information in *Amtliches Verzeichniß des Personals und der Studirenden auf der Königlichen Rheinischen Friedrich-Wilhelms-Universität zu Bonn* (unpag.) for 1838-39, 1839-40, 1840, 1840-41, 1841.
241 See Franz Bosbach, 'Prinz Albert und das universitäre Studium in Bonn und Cambridge', in: Christa Jansohn (ed.), *In the Footsteps of Queen Victoria: Wege zum Viktorianischen Zeitalter*, Studien zur englischen Literatur, 15 (Münster, etc.: LIT, 2003), 201-224, ref. 208.

General Introduction to Historical Studies (winter 1837-38) and History of German Literature (summer 1838).²⁴² If he took notes from Schlegel, they have not survived.²⁴³There were also private lectures. *The University of Bonn* stated deferentially: 'He [Albert] delighted in the brilliant conversation of that patriarchal Professor, and the latter always contrived to render it so peculiarly interesting, that the Prince would never get tired of listening to him'.²⁴⁴ Maybe.

Yet no group of students attending his lectures owed him loyalty and testified its indebtedness more than the Sanskritists. The classes on Sanskrit were private, but most of them also attended other lectures by him, above all his star pupil Christian Lassen from Bergen in Norway, his assistant, his colleague and then his successor. This applied also to Hermann Brockhaus, later Max Müller's teacher; to Theodor Goldstücker from Königsberg, eventually to be a professor at University College London; to his colleague's son Friedrich Heinrich Hugo Windischmann; to Otto Böhtlingk from St Petersburg, the later compiler of the great Sanskrit-German lexicon (1853-75); to Martin Hammerich who was to translate *Śakuntalâ* into Danish (1845). Their letters express thanks and respect.²⁴⁵ They attest to Schlegel's aim, stated already in 1823 to Lassen, of founding a school, of making Bonn a centre of oriental scholarship.²⁴⁶

The Content of the Lectures²⁴⁷

What of the content of the lectures themselves? They are essentially broad surveys that combine Schlegel's notions of philology, together with the

---

242 Bosbach, 'Fürstliche Studienplanung', 33, 37f.
243 Not for the reason adduced by Renger (1983), that they were already published (222). They were not.
244 *The University of Bonn*, 171.
245 Brockhaus to AWS 1840 (SLUB Dresden, Mscr. Dresd. e. 90, XIX (3), 86); Goldstücker to AWS 1840 (*ibid.* (9), 41); Hammerich to AWS 1837 (*ibid.* (14), 7). Lassen's letters, much more extensive, in: *Briefwechsel A. W. von Schlegel Christian Lassen*, ed. W. Kirfel [Kirfel] (Bonn: Cohen, 1914).
246 Kirfel, 13. On AWS's school see Ernst Windisch, *Geschichte der Sanskrit-Philologie und indischen Altertumskunde*, 2 vols (Grundriss der indo-arischen Philologie und Altertumskunde [Encyclopedia of Indo-Aryan Research], I, iB) (Strasbourg: Trübner, 1917; Berlin, Leipzig: de Gruyter, 1920), II, 210-215.
247 On the links between the Berlin, Bonn and Berlin (1827) cycles see Frank Jolles, 'August Wilhelm Schlegel und Berlin: Sein Weg von den Berliner Vorlesungen von 1801-04 zu denen vom Jahre 1827', in: Otto Pöggeler and Annemarie Gethmann-Siefert (eds), *Kunsterfahrung und Kulturpolitik im Berlin Hegels, Hegel-Studien*, Beiheft 22 (Bonn: Bouvier, 1983), 153-[175].

widest acquisition of factual knowledge; with more than a touch of the old humanist tradition, but with Winckelmann's and Humboldt's ideal of 'Bildung', the development of every faculty of the human mind towards a full moral and aesthetic perception. Judging from the surviving scripts, edited or unedited, we can say that they fall into two categories: those that have long sections of formulated prose and then subside into notes and headings (the lectures on the History of German Language and Poetry and on the Fine Arts exemplify this); and those that are from the start really only aides-mémoire for the lecturer, headings separated by dashes, that would need his voice and his presence to supply the expanded remarks, the ad libitum asides, the quotations read out (the Lectures on General World History, the Greeks and Romans, on Academic Study). That would be the formal side. But whether the lectures contain large sections of informative material, dilate for instance on the notion of aesthetics and the subdivisions of the art forms, or trace German poetry from its beginnings down to the present day, there is always the underlying theme of origins.

This is not merely a question of needing to know primeval developments in order to understand later processes, or of wanting to have as complete and unbroken an account as possible of historical developments. As Schlegel states, warming to his subject in his second Lecture on General World History:

> Many people have had no history at all, at least not such as would deserve a place in universal history. Anyway, contributed nothing to the development of human capabilities. Isolated position of several very civilized peoples. India. China. Only rare contacts between Europe and inner Asia. [margin: Gog and Magog] Examples of the Cimmerians, Huns, Arabs, Tatars, Turks. No contacts at all between Europe and the centre of Africa, with America, etc.
>
> Comparison of the history of the whole human race with a river with several arms, whose source and mouth are unknown. [margin: Still a lot to correct and fill out. But main outlines are there. Statistics of all states, if that was possible]. Survey of oikumene [community of nations] according to our present geographical knowledge and general traits, the ethnographical task of universal history, to explain the present state of the human race by linking cause and effect and tracing down to the earliest beginnings. The more recent can be solved by its being closer, but perhaps never completely. [margin: The way Schiller saw it. Inaugural lecture. What is and to what end do we study universal history? My view of it. Wrong about the age, in which he was caught up. Nescia mens hominum fati sortisque futurae [The mind of men ignorant of fate or future destiny].[248]

---

248 SLUB Dresden, Mscr. Dresd. e. 90, XVIII, [p. 15f.].

Much of the essential Schlegel is here. The universal view (ideally, the need to know everything), expressed in terms of geography, ethnography, statistics, historical records; the interreaction of peoples (where this is known); our guessings at knowledge of earliest beginnings and our ignorance of the future (the side-swipe at Schiller and basically at all philosophers of history for imposing a scheme on events and not letting these speak for themselves); the notion of *oikumene*, standing for historical associations now only traceable through common roots of language or mythology, leading to questions, posed in all of these lectures, of the primeval base of the human race ('Ursitze'), its spreading out through incursions, migrations, colonies, 'families of languages' (the handy quotation from Virgil[249] demonstrating the uses of memorisation).

Schlegel in fact wants to go back further than that, to a point from which everything else may irradiate and illumine all aspects of human existence. In his Lectures on the History of Art, he confesses to being a Platonist,[250] believing in an Idea whose reflection we sense in nature and in art, where all physical manifestations and all philosophical notions are based on 'Urbilder' [primal images] and we have but intimations of a higher nature.[251] To Humboldt he speaks of 'divinatorische Erkenntniß' [divinatory cognition].[252] None of his contemporaries, Goethe, Schiller, Schelling, or his brother Friedrich, would have disputed this: it was at the time an essential tenet of any kind of aesthetic awareness and basic for the explication of any system of art. He is also restating his Hemsterhuisian beginnings that informed his Berlin lectures on the same subject.

Schlegel the historian knows on the one hand that art emanates from an Ideal that must be represented through the human senses and their limitations. He is also acutely aware that art reflects the highest strivings in all areas of human endeavour; that as such the work of art cannot be seen in isolation from religion, customs, mythology, poetry, politics, *mores*, and style of living. Thus the study of art and its origins is essentially a kind of archaeology,[253] a delving down into the past to find the traces of what once

---

249 *Aeneid*, X, 501.
250 Cf. Thomas Campbell: 'In fine, Mons. Schlegel is a visionary and a Platonist, who really believes that the external universe is only a shadow or reflexion of the inward principle of mind.' *Thomas Campbell*, II, 262.
251 'Theorie und allgemeine Geschichte der bildenden Künste', 33f.; AWS, *Vorlesungen über Ästhetik (1803-1827)*, ed. Ernst Behler assist. Georg Braungart, *Kritische Ausgabe der Vorlesungen* [*KAV*], II, i (Paderborn, etc.: Schöningh, 2007), 333.
252 Leitzmann, 72.
253 *Ibid.*

was, an 'Urwelt',²⁵⁴ the roots of language, the primordial 'Sitz' of the human race.²⁵⁵ It is not by chance that Schlegel in three separate lecture series and elsewhere uses the image of the comparative anatomist,²⁵⁶ reconstructing and restoring on the basis of archaeological and scientific evidence the 'antediluvian origins' of humankind, or through fragmentary inscriptions finding hints of languages now lost (Etruscan, Pelasgian) that might lead us back to the 'Ursprache'.

Hence the need for all those documents, all the study of human striving, the 'theory of the earth', the diversity of human types ('Raçen' in Schlegel's and his contemporaries' terminology: he follows Blumenbach's division of humanity into five 'racial types');²⁵⁷ not out of any mere antiquarian interest, although Schlegel is not one to despise old humanist scholarship as mere 'archaeology'. For, whether he is discussing the dramatic movements of the earth, the natural catastrophes and revolutions and their origins (which are reflected in mythology); whether it is a question of siting humankind in the physical roots of its culture (where languages and communities evolve); whether he is talking of the arts, of religion, of technology, of language, of poetry (the evidence of human accomplishment); in all this he is convinced that our species developed from common types and that all human records refer back to a 'centre' [Mittelpunkt]. There is no place here for the eighteenth century's belief in an animal-like, primitive state out of which mankind first had to evolve in order to attain to rational capabilities. On the contrary: the records that we have, of language, of religion, of technology, point to a high degree of cognition, of early wisdom, 'homo faber' [man the maker and doer].

None of this was essentially new. It can be related to the notion of 'prisca theologia', the belief in an ancient theological wisdom from which later civilization and language proceeds. It may have come to him through Herder or Hemsterhuis or Novalis.²⁵⁸ Schlegel had already said much of it

---

254 'Geschichte der Griechen und Römer', 16a.
255 *Geschichte der Deutschen Sprache und Poesie*, 24.
256 'Einleitung in die alte Weltgeschichte', 37; *Geschichte der Deutschen Sprache und Poesie*, 30f.; 'Griechen und Römer', 17. His *Indische Bibliothek* also quotes Alexander von Humboldt. I, i, 35. Cf. also the later fragment, 'Ueber historische und geographische Bestimmungen der Zoologie', SW, VIII, 334-336.
257 'Einleitung in die allgemeine Weltgeschichte', 68; 'Theorie und allgemeine Geschichte der bildenden Künste', *KAV*, II, i, 307.
258 Cf. H. B. Nisbet, 'Die naturphilosophische Bedeutung von Herders "Aeltester Urkunde des Menschengeschlechts"', in: Brigitte Poschmann (ed.), *Bückeburger Gespräche über Johann Gottfried Herder 1988. Älteste Urkunde des Menschengeschlechts*, Schaumburger Studien, 49 (Rinteln: Bösendahl, 1989), 210-226, and generally D. P. Walker, *The Ancient Theology. Studies in Christian Platonism from the Fifteenth to the Eighteenth Century* (London: Duckworth, 1972), esp. 20, 220f.

in his unpublished *Considérations sur la civilisation en général* of 1805, but in the context of a general critique of the Enlightenment. Some more of it had gone into his major essays on the *Nibelungenlied* and his review of Chézy in 1815. By then however he was learning Sanskrit, taking in the whole discourse, into which his own brother Friedrich had tapped, of a postulated Indic 'Ursprache', certainly an ancient mother language of a linguistic family 'from the Ganges to the Arctic',[259] and he had conducted philological studies of his own. True, his notions of the perfectibility and dignity of original language and its derivatives could not be explained in solely rational or scientific terms; language must be of divine origin[260] (Schlegel remained unrepentantly Romantic in that regard); comparative philology can however establish traces of those roots in the related languages of which we have records (the essay of around 1815, *De l'Étymologie en général*, had set out the principles).

Thus Germanic and by extension modern-day German, could be invested with the dignity reserved for Indian, Persian, Greek or Latin, through tracing its development from Gothic, which shared similar links with the primal language in the notional Central Asian 'Sitz' of this language family. (Schlegel does not yet use the term 'Indo-Germanic', current since Julius Klaproth's coining in 1823, but the same is meant nevertheless.) While, says Schlegel, we do not know with any certainty where the Germanic peoples came from, we can adduce linguistic evidence to supply what is lacking in historical documentation. If early Germanic is lost, at least Gothic will tell us of peoples in migration, spreading out in tribes and their dialects, from those fragments recorded by Tacitus, to Ulfilas's bible translation and notional epic poetry in Gothic. All of this gives historical authenticity and dignity to the *Nibelungenlied*, in a later form of Germanic, and invests it with the same venerability as the epic poetry of Persia and India. When Schlegel spends what may seem to be a disproportionate amount of time and energy on this Germanic epic, in order then to abandon it and consign it to his papers, he is satisfying part of the same philological and scholarly urge as when he does eventually edit and publish the *Râmâyana* instead.

Religion, a basic expression of man's experience of the world around him, is for Schlegel similarly not the expression of humankind's allegedly crude beginnings. Quite the other way round: there must have been a pure 'Naturreligion' at first, an intimation of the cognition of natural truth,[261] a

---

259 'De l'Origine des Hindous', *Oeuvres*, III, 62.
260 *Geschichte der Deutschen Sprache und Poesie*, 30.
261 'Griechen und Römer', 15.

belief even in the immortality of the soul.²⁶² Its overlaying and occluding by 'superstition', or the rise of polytheism, does not disprove its existence (or, rather, does not invalidate our inner sense of religious truth). We will of course wish to show the development of religion through sacred writings, while aware that they contain no ultimate explanations: the biblical Flood, for instance, is for Schlegel but one account among many of a terrestrial catastrophe in deep time. Instead, we will use the insights of Protestant hermeneutics and of philological criticism to illuminate religious and priestly record.²⁶³

Part of Schlegel's reversal of eighteenth-century notions of progress is his insistence on a high degree of technical accomplishment among so-called 'primitive man'. The massive architecture of early peoples (Indians, Egyptians, Greeks, Aztecs) shows a mastery of mathematics and of technology that goes hand in hand with their desire to build for eternity, not for the moment, to leave a permanent record for later generations of peoples ('wonders of colossal works of the ancient world').²⁶⁴

Schlegel's earlier essay of 1805 had cited as authorities Hemsterhuis, Bailly, Sir William Jones. In the Bonn lectures, other, more recent, names crop up: his own brother Friedrich, not only of course his *Ueber die Sprache und Weisheit der Indier*, but also his 1819 review of Rhode's *Ueber den Anfang unserer Geschichte* [On the Beginnings of our History]. Georges Cuvier is the authority for those remarks on comparative anatomy scattered throughout Schlegel's different lectures. James Cowles Prichard mediated many of the insights of Schlegel's Göttingen mentor Blumenbach in his *Researches into the Physical History of Mankind* (first 1813), and it was largely from him that Schlegel was to draw notions of a common human stock spreading out into diversity and intermixture. Schlegel in 1837 wrote a—not entirely uncritical—preface to the German translation of Prichard's *An Analysis of the Egyptian Mythology* (1819).²⁶⁵ Above all one notices the presence and influence of both brothers Humboldt. Like them, he was of his times in branching out into the widest areas of knowledge: the theory of the physical world (Alexander von Humboldt), the theory of language (Wilhelm von Humboldt), a 'world philology' (Schlegel).

---

262 'Einleitung in die allgemeine Weltgeschichte', 120.
263 'Entwurf zu Vorlesungen über die allgemeine Weltgeschichte', 62.
264 'Colossale Wunderwerke der alten Welt', 'Einleitung in die allgemeine Weltgeschichte', 145.
265 I. C. Prichard, *Darstellung der Aegyptischen Mythologie* […] (Bonn: Weber, 1837), v-xxxiv.

4. Bonn and India (1818-1845)

Much had happened to both since Alexander von Humboldt had identified the geological content of the lions in the Roman forum in 1805. Humboldt had been feted in the Paris of the Empire and the Restoration; now, from 1826-27 court chamberlain to King Frederick William III of Prussia, he was still as polyglot and culturally international as ever and as enterprising. There had been in 1818 plans to complete the circumnavigation that had been broken off in South America, now to take in India and Tibet (the East India Company, however, was not letting a pronounced liberal like Humboldt into its territories). In 1817, Schlegel had written a highly favourable and laudatory review of the quarto edition of Humboldt's *Vues des cordillères et monumens des peuples indigènes de l'Amérique* [Views of the Cordilleras and Monuments of the Indigenous Peoples of America] (1816), which for some reason he never published.[266]

Of course Schlegel, despite those foot journeys in Switzerland with the Staël boys, was never going to join Humboldt on Chimborazo; Humboldt was ever the 'hands-on' scientist,[267] Schlegel the sedentary scholar. Yet Schlegel's review made the point that Humboldt's account of the Americas, while primarily directed at the scientific reader, had much to offer the historian and the philosopher. It would of course be his many-sidedness, his striving for synthesis, his universal conception, his constant relating of individual manifestations to some greater whole, but more concretely, his descriptions of Aztec monuments and inscriptions, that attracted Schlegel's attention, his notions of language families, and much more besides.

Alexander von Humboldt was altogether more informal in his dealings with Schlegel than his rather austere brother Wilhelm. Alexander could write 'Cher et excellent Confrère' to Schlegel,[268] whereas Wilhelm always used the formal address 'Ew. Hochwohlgebornen' (and Schlegel 'Ew. Excellenz'). He passed on snippets of information to Schlegel and also asked him for favours (could, for instance, the 'oldest of his friends in Germany' inform him of references to poetic nature description in antiquity?).[269] He drew his attention to a drawing of Mayan gods that he thought Schlegel might wish to compare with their Indian counterparts;[270] not to give

---

266 *SW*, XII, 513-528; Roger Paulin, *August Wilhelm Schlegels Kosmos* (Dresden: Thelem, 2011), 9f.
267 'Weltumsegler der Wißenschaft', *SW*, VIII, 213.
268 SLUB Dresden, Mscr. Dresd. e. 90, XIX (11), 26.
269 *Ibid.*, 35.
270 *Ibid.*, LI (17). On this Roger Paulin, 'Die Ähnlichkeit der Götter. Ein Billet Alexander von Humboldts an August Wilhelm Schlegel in der SLUB Dresden', *BIS: Das Magazin der Bibliotheken in Sachsen* 3 (September 2010), 174f.

credence to some of the more fantastic exodus theories, but out of a general interest in comparative civilization theory, mythology and its expression in art. He may also have been slightly teasing Schlegel, knowing that the editor of the *Indische Bibliothek* was never going to concede any superiority over India, the cradle of all cultures, especially not from practitioners of human sacrifice.

Wilhelm von Humboldt, the former minister of state and Prussian envoy in Rome and London, the theoretician of classicism, the philologist, grammarian and translator, treated Schlegel with great respect, even receiving him in 1827 at his seat in Tegel when Schlegel visited Berlin. Yet they agreed to differ over a number of crucial points. It was Schlegel's example that had led him to teach himself Sanskrit and conduct a correspondence on issues of grammar, even to contribute to Schlegel's *Indische Bibliothek* (some of it hard going for non-specialists). They agreed on the task of the historian, to present facts (not a philosophy), but to do so creatively and with imagination. But they were to disagree publicly and radically on the role of translation, for Humboldt never more than a *pis-aller*, for Schlegel the gateway to alien cultures.

4.2 India

In a much-quoted letter to Goethe of 1 November, 1824, Schlegel wrote:

> From the very outset of my career as a writer I had made it my especial business to bring to light forgotten and unrecognized material. Thus I progressed from Dante to Shakespeare, to Petrarch, to Calderón, to the Old German epics; almost everywhere I did not achieve anything like half of what I intended; but I did succeed in providing a stimulus. In this way, I had to some extent exhausted European literature and turned to Asia to provide a new adventure. It was a good choice: for in the later years of life it is an amusing diversion to solve riddles; and here I need not worry about running out of material. Leaving aside the historical importance, the philosophical and poetical content, the very form of the language would draw me, which in comparison with its younger sisters provides such remarkable insights into the laws of language formation.[271]

This letter could easily—if misleadingly—be construed as a statement of bankruptcy on Schlegel's part, an admission to the ever-productive, ever

---

271 *August Wilhelm und Friedrich Schlegel im Briefwechsel mit Schiller und Goethe*, ed. Josef Körner and Ernst Wieneke [Wieneke] (Leipzig: Insel, 1926), 161f.

self-renewing Goethe of the depletion of his powers, the abandonment of poetry for philology. Of course it is no such thing. It may have seemed to Schlegel in the early 1820s, as he wrote to Auguste de Staël, that his interest lay solely in 'antediluvian poetry'.[272] Yet against that one can set his genuine interest in the continuation of the Shakespeare project (while no longer believing that he had the powers to carry it out), the reissue in 1828 in his *Kritische Schriften* of significant reviews from the 1790s, and his statement there of the European role of modern German literature and 'Wissenschaft'. He was also, as we saw, lecturing in Bonn on the widest spectrum of European, of world, literature. The second of his two long articles on European knowledge of India (1831)[273] provided the background to Luis de Camões's *Lusiadas*, promised, but not delivered, in his *Blumensträuße* of 1804; it also supplied his mature judgment on this late Renaissance epic, which he now preferred to Ariosto or Tasso. He was as well reminding his German readers of the significant Portuguese presence in India, long before an Englishman had set foot there. By coincidence or not, it echoed much of what his friend Ludwig Tieck was also saying.[274]

But could Schlegel really be claiming to Goethe that he had turned to the Orient as it were *faute de mieux*? There was enough evidence—that early poem for Bürger on the death of the Brahmin, the various statements on the East from his first maturity, the elegy to Carl Schlegel, his *Considérations* of 1805, his approbation and admiration of Friedrich Schlegel's Sanskrit studies—to suggest that at any moment he might simply drop Germanic or Romance if given the chance. But of course the Staël years were not conducive; there was no opportunity for the frenetic bursts of language acquisition that his brother Friedrich had performed in Paris.

There were for a start Schlegel's and Goethe's respective attitudes to India: Schlegel's unreserved belief that 'everything in ancient India is original; everything bears the stamp of the creative, inventive, speculative

---

272 *Krisenjahre*, II, 394.
273 'Indien in seinen Hauptbeziehungen. Einleitung. Über die Zunahme und den gegenwärtigen Stand unserer Kenntnisse von Indien', *Berliner Kalender auf das Gemein-Jahr 1829* (Berlin: Kön. Preuß. Kalender-Deputation [1828], 'Erste Abtheilung bis auf Vasco de Gama', 3-86; Zweite Abtheilung. 'Von Vasco de Gama bis auf die neueste Zeit', *Berliner Kalender auf das Gemein-Jahr 1831* (Berlin: Kön: Preuß: Kalender-Deputation [1830]), 3-160, on the *Lusiads* 68-75.
274 Cf. the minor Camões renaissance around 1830, esp. Tieck's novel *Tod des Dichters* (1833).

mind',[275] 'theology of the most profound';[276] Goethe's much more selective approach,[277] affirming great poetry where he saw it (the Jones/Forster version of the Śakuntalâ, for instance), but withdrawing, sometimes with marked distaste, from other aspects, the teeming cosmogony, or those 'Fratzen',[278] the grotesque faces that he saw staring out of Indian art. It did not prevent him from taking an intellectual interest—ordering Schlegel's *Râmâyana* edition for Weimar[279]—and generally keeping his finger on the pulse of travel and discovery in those regions.[280]

Whereas Schlegel's 'Orient' had India, and to a lesser extent also Egypt, as its two main points of reference, Goethe's took in Persia and the Arabic and Judaic world (both of them of course knew their Bible). Goethe's *Westöstlicher Divan* of 1819, bearing a dedication to the leading French orientalist, Silvestre de Sacy, presented an Orient that brought together his early poetic interest in Koranic motifs with a serious study of Persian and Arabic. Yet everything in the *Divan* touched on poetry: we read his *Noten und Abhandlungen* [Notes and Treatises] to the *Divan* because they contain the key to poetry. A vision of Persia came alive, a private world that drew on the Orient as it chose, playful, sometimes seriously playful, protean, taking notions and motifs that he found fruitful and attractive for poetic purposes; but always symbolic of a higher synthesis of man, nature, time and history, the individual and the universe. For Schlegel, India *had* poetry; it did not immediately *become* it: others must bring it alive. India had formed part of the Romantic urges that had *led* to poetry, where mythology and translation, the transference of great poetry from one cultural sphere to another, were an enriching and enlivening force. Novalis's vision of 'Indostan' in the *Athenaeum* in 1800 had been poetry representing religious myth and historical fulfilment. Schlegel, no less a Romantic mythologizer

---

275 *Briefe*, I, 528.
276 *Krisenjahre*, II, 428.
277 Well summarized in the article by Johannes Mehlig, 'Indien', in: *Goethe-Handbuch*, ed. Bernd Witte *et al.*, 4 vols in 5 (Stuttgart, Weimar: Metzler, 1996-99), IV, i, 521-524. Cf. also Anil Bhatti, 'Der Orient als Experimentierfeld. Goethes "Divan" und der Aneignungsprozess kolonialen Wissens', *Goethe Jahrbuch*, 126 (2009), 115-128, esp. 126f.
278 'Von Pfaffen und Fratzen uns befreit'. *Zahme Xenien*, II. Goethe, *Gedenkausgabe der Werke, Briefe und Gespräche*, ed. Ernst Beutler, 3rd edn, 27 vols (Zurich: Artemis, 1986 [1949]), I, 615.
279 Wieneke, 162f., 260.
280 Karl S. Guthke, *Goethes Weimar und 'Die große Öffnung in die weite Welt'*, Wolfenbütteler Forschungen, 93 (Wiesbaden: Harrassowitz, 2001), 20-22.

than Novalis when it suited him, was to pass this on as *ideas* through the readers of his editions, especially of the *Bhagavat-Gîtâ*, who included certainly Schopenhauer, possibly also Hegel and Nietzsche. They contained enough poetic potential for others to exploit creatively.

Goethe and Schlegel were in agreement that Orient and Occident were equal partners in giving and receiving. But Schlegel could not accept all the premises of the *Divan*. He was not basically interested in Persian poetry; above all, the Persian language was for him essentially a derivative of Sanskrit. Crucially, Persia, once the land and home of Zoroastrianism, had been subjected to Islamic conquest, and that was that. Muslim power or influence—Arab, Persian, Mughal—was for him inimical to culture, essentially uncreative, destructive, at most borrowing from 'superior' cultures.[281] Hence his conviction that the *Thousand and One Nights* must ultimately be of Indian origin, not Persian or Arab.[282] This did not make Schlegel an uncritical admirer of Hinduism—it, too, had its later accretions—and not of Buddhism. He could certainly identify with the status, spiritual depth, repose,[283] and intellectual achievement that he perceived in Brahmanic culture, its commitment to peace, its absence of a priestly hierarchy (or so Schlegel wished to believe). Entering into the world of the primeval language of Sanskrit, reading its great texts, also meant acquiring its lore: one needed to be familiar with its mythology, which deities were which and where their sway held, which aspects they bore, which legends had clustered round which. It extended to architecture: the figures of Indian gods and goddesses permitted comparison with other ancient cultures, Egyptian or Aztec. He was of his time in referring to them as 'idols',[284] but certainly they were to be preferred to a culture that banned the figural representation of the divine altogether.

Like Goethe's of the Orient, Schlegel's knowledge of India was at second hand. It was not the only paradox or contradiction that he shared with Goethe. There was his preoccupation with what can generally be called 'origins': the beginnings of human utterance, technical achievement,

---

281 Cf. 'Die Religion Mahomets, des unwissendensten aller Menschen, war freilich darauf eingerichtet, die Unwissenheit und den Stumpfsinn gegen jede Art der Geistesbildung unter ihren Anhängern zu verewigen'. *Berliner Kalender auf das Gemein-Jahr 1829*, 69.
282 'Les Mille et une nuits. Receuil de contes originairement indiens', *Oeuvres*, III, 3-23.
283 'Nous devons imiter l'impassibilité de ces brahmanes dont nous admirons les sages maximes', *ibid*, 245.
284 'ich besitze selbst eine kleine Sammlung von Idolen'. *Indische Bibliothek*, II, 431.

culture, poetry, mythology, religious observance, as it might have been and was now traceable through monuments in language or in stone; but also through a living memory of observance, rite and oral tradition. This is what made Schlegel different from Greek and Latin classical scholars and why he needed to move out and beyond them, while of course retaining the skills and insights that they had taught him. Unlike Classical Greece and Rome, India was still alive. Sanskrit was still present in India and was the undying expression of a civilization still in being. This culture, as he saw it, compared with so many others, had been able to maintain its essential integrity, its timeless calm and serenity, the uninterrupted line of its mythology. The origins, that in the case of Greek and Latin needed to be traced through painstaking philological and archaeological processes, were for Sanskrit still there. Once one had acquired the language, the whole of this civilization, superior to any that succeeded or overlaid it, became the possession of the 'Indianist'. Especially the German academic Indianist, so much better qualified than others to bring that civilization alive. This is what lies behind Schlegel's Sanskrit studies, his three editions of classical Sanskrit texts, and much of his *Indische Bibliothek*.

But the conviction that this culture was superior was not enough. For it, too, had been subjected to incursions, challenges, conquests, from within, but especially from without. That Indian culture had withstood these, was surmounting them now and was adapting to foreign military and administrative rule, was also part of the narrative of India. There was no escaping the fact that European contact and conquest—for good or ill, and much of it was for ill—had made this world and its culture accessible. It was the dilemma faced by Schlegel himself, the younger brother of a Hanoverian officer in the service of the East India Company, or by Henry Colebrooke or Sir James Mackintosh, the proconsuls of a colonizing power, yet all involved intellectually in the cultural heritage that they were administering. By extension, it even applied to Alexander von Humboldt too, Schlegel's authority in matters pertaining to the theory of the earth. One half of Schlegel found the East India Company distasteful—pragmatic, commercial, political—but the other, despite itself, had to be grateful when the Company's servants helped to open up India to the European gaze. Schlegel's analogy of British rule in India with ancient Rome[285] was right in terms of their respective imperial hegemonies; but was there not also

---

285 *Berliner Kalender* (1831), 122.

something of Horace's *Graecia capta*,[286] the conqueror taken captive, the vanquisher vanquished by the culture that it had encountered?

Above all, it elicited a 'Zivilisationskritik'.[287] This was not, say, of the Enlightenment, as in that early essay of 1805, but of European contact with India in general. It formed the substance of those major articles in the *Berliner Kalender*. Both of them hanker, Romantic-style, but also set out the historical record—such as it was—of 'civilisations' that claimed superiority, and in many ways still did; which however failed to measure up to the civilisation over which their rule extended. It explains his ambivalence to the East India Company as both boon and bugbear. His critique of Christian missionary zealotry and arrogance in India also fits very well his mood in the 1820s and 1830s, involving a much wider scrutiny of the phenomenon of religion itself, touched off by his brother Friedrich. Someone who had to examine the role of religion in his own life, as Schlegel did, was in a good position to consider its effects when, as with Christian missionary activity in India, it developed into fanaticism and assumed cultural supremacy. While lacking Humboldt's geopolitical and physiocratic thrust, and crucially, not being based on personal observation, it is fair to say that Schlegel's two essays in the *Berliner Kalender* have affinities with Humboldt's *Vues des cordillères* and his surveys of Cuba and Mexico, those writings that ensured his blacklisting by the East India Company when he hoped to continue them with a narrative of India. These same essays also set Schlegel apart from academic Sankritists like Bopp or Lassen. They represent a voice addressed to a different audience, non-specialist, only generally informed and interested. They epitomize the 'half-way' status that Schlegel occupies as an orientalist, the stringent editor but also the unashamed populariser.

Because of those lines of continuity from deep time, one could not be indifferent to the physical opening up of India. Like his contemporaries Cuvier, Malte-Brun, and especially Humboldt, Schlegel wanted to know everything about the 'cosmos'. Understanding Indian geography and topography (the source of the Ganges) opened up vistas of 'higher peaks

---

[286] 'Graecia capta ferum victorem cepit'. [Captured Greece captured the uncouth victor]. Horace, Epistles, 2, I, 156.
[287] Cf. Josef Körner, 'Indologie und Humanität', most accessible in: JK, *Philologische Schriften und Briefe*, ed. Ralf Klausnitzer, intr. Hans Eichner, Marbacher Wissenschaftsgeschichte, 1 (Göttingen: Wallstein, 2001), 137-162; Anil Bhatti, 'August Wilhelm Schlegels Indienrezeption und der Kolonialismus', in: Jürgen Lehmann et al. (eds), *Konflikt Grenze Dialog. Kulturkontrastive und interdisziplinäre Textzugänge. Festschrift für Horst Turk zum 60. Geburtstag* (Frankfurt am Main etc.: Peter Lang, 1997), 185-205.

than Chimborazo, that a second Saussure or Humboldt will hardly ever scale'.²⁸⁸ There was no need, as there once was, to travel there: the onus fell on European 'Indianisten' to give an accurate and sympathetic account.²⁸⁹ He met people who had been there; he collected artefacts; he was familiar with the relevant historical, geographical and topographical sources, which form the basis of those two articles in the *Berliner Kalender*.

Passage after passage in Schlegel's *Berliner Kalender* and *Indische Bibliothek* illustrated this, none better than his note on a recent publication by the Asiatic Society in Calcutta:²⁹⁰

> Nature description promises directly applicable results, and it follows that the present and future preoccupy the owners of the land more pressingly than the remote past. Of course the more exact knowledge gained of India in respect of its physical characteristics and its present state must be of no inconsiderable benefit to the investigation of its prehistory.²⁹¹

Thus, he says, Captain Webb and others, in giving us an exact topographical description of the fabled sources of the Yamuna and the Ganges, have linked the geographical precision of a Saussure or a Humboldt with the *Râmâyana*, with Indian creation myths and their still living presence. Schlegel, too, sought to give his readers a physical description, but as a European who had never been there and had no intention of ever doing so, he had recourse to its ultimate European counterpart in the Swiss Alps and the conventions of the sublime.²⁹² One must only magnify a little, he claimed, and the 'majesty' of the Himalaya will become present in the valleys, ravines and passes of the Jura and Rigi, the avalanches and cascades, the peaks and icefields—his own recollection of the river Aar in spate, a rainbow over its cataract. This is Schlegel at his most spirited, and we might wish for more. The engravers of the *Berliner Kalender* in 1829 had encountered the same problem. To illustrate an article on the topography of India,²⁹³ they produced a distinctly Swiss-like *veduta* of the sources of the Ganges, a temple and some turbaned figures supplying the oriental costume.

---

288 *Berliner Kalender* (1829), 5.
289 *Berliner Kalender* (1831), 138f., 155.
290 'Neueste Mittheilungen der Asiatischen Gesellschaft zu Calcutta', *Indische Bibliothek*, I, 371-390.
291 *Ibid.*, 371.
292 *Ibid.*, 388.
293 C. Ritter, 'Landeskunde von Indien', *Berliner Kalender auf das Gemein-Jahr 1829*, 87-210, plate facing p. 364.

4. Bonn and India (1818-1845)

Schlegel's Indian studies in the 1820s and 1830s did not take up some hermetically sealed compartment in his intellectual, academic—or even personal—life. They were integral to his whole existence; they represented the essential Schlegel. In that respect they cannot be divorced from the ups and downs of his private or academic life, although it is worth observing that more and more of his time and substance was being given up to these matters than to anything else. If, as he told Christian Lassen, he took on academic burdens like the rectorship, it was ultimately to further his position in the university and through this the status of India in the university's hierarchy.[294] Or if, as he confided to Wilhelm von Humboldt, he became a member of the city council or the 'Society for Civic Improvement' (from 1825), behind this lay similar, less selfless motives.[295] It is also true to say that the polemical and adversarial tone that marked his public persona in these years was audible in his oriental studies as well. There was less of the 'impassibilité des bramanes' than of those 'curious polemical dances'—his words later to August Böckh[296]—that he performed with Chézy, with Simon Alexandre Langlois (whom Chézy used as a front to criticise Schlegel's *Bhagavad-Gîtâ* edition),[297] with Heeren, with H. H. Wilson. It was part of other processes: the chagrin at seeing Ludwig Tieck continuing a Shakespeare that he could have done better had he had the time or inclination; the fracas with Voss; the love-hate relationship with his brother Friedrich; the affront of Goethe's correspondence with Schiller—all of them opening up old wounds and stirring up old resentments.

It was noticeable, too, that his Indian studies shared the shift into French which characterizes so much of his writing in the 1830s—after the *Indische Bibliothek* had ceased publication—and which was later to take up a considerable part of his posthumous *Oeuvres publiées en français*, confirming the nineteenth-century view of him as less-than-German or even a mere appendage of Madame de Staël.

Schlegel had had to acquire a knowledge of the ancient language to the highest professional standards. It all might have happened earlier, had Madame de Staël not taken him on her travels. Apart from the crucial factor of language—he and Franz Bopp would eye each other

---

294 Kirfel, 74f.
295 Leitzmann, 245f.
296 *Briefe*, I, 531.
297 In: *Journal Asiatique* 4 (1824), 105-116, 236-252; 5 (1824), 240-252; 6 (1825), 232-250.

as the premier Sanskritists in Germany and possibly in France (Bopp's knowledge being superior)—there was nothing in his method or approach to Sanskrit studies that was essentially new. What was needed was a new focus and status. His brother Friedrich had of course acted as a spur, but no more than that. August Wilhelm knew Sanskrit better and he edited texts that Friedrich had published in only partial or imperfect translations; nor would he follow Friedrich into philosophical speculation. He could draw on his own recent preoccupations. The two major works of 1817-18, on etymology in general, and on Provençal literature, converged with his Sanskrit researches as their methodology was reapplied to new subjects of study. His various publications on the *Nibelungenlied*, too, had had to do with origins, habitations, migrations from 'Ursitze', the spread of languages from a common source, ideas that were basic to his notions of India, and they, as well, stressed the centrality of the text. Where the text did not exist in a reliable form or was present in variants only, it must be re-established in a definitive edition. This is what links his *Nibelungenlied* studies with his three Sanskrit editions: *Bhagavad-Gîtâ*, *Râmâyana*, and *Hitopadeśa*.

The analogy went even further: those three were the essential texts conducive to a first understanding, respectively, of ancient Indian philosophy, epic poetry, and fable, and thus eminently suitable for both scholarly and pedagogic purposes. No less a person than the professor of Sanskrit at Oxford, Horace Hayman Wilson, would be told this. The *Nibelungenlied*, allowing for differences, was to serve a similar function in an even wider national consciousness: the effort in collating and editing was in proportion to the status of the poetry itself. Yet anyone comparing Schlegel's essays on the *Nibelungenlied* or even the (unpublished) edition with the Sanskrit texts will notice immediate differences. There was no concession to the non-expert. Readers had to know Sanskrit (of course): Schlegel told Wilhelm von Humboldt that ten readers in Europe and Asia would suffice.[298] Should they need a translation, it was in Latin, as were the notes to further understanding. It is interesting that Wilhelm von Humboldt, despite his scepticism otherwise on the subject of translation, urged Schlegel more than once to do a free version of the *Bhagavat-Gîtâ* for German readers,[299] or even a joint Indian project, Humboldt to do the

---
298 Leitzmann, 61.
299 *Ibid.*, 165.

philosophical writings, Schlegel the epic.³⁰⁰ Schlegel did not take up the idea. In this respect, he had come a long way from translating Shakespeare or Calderón, where questions of editions were of little relevance and the assimilation of the foreign poetic text to the needs of German was all in all.

The analogies with his other endeavours also end there. As he reminded his readers and interlocutors at every turn, the study of India encompassed the Sanskrit language and texts, but also philology and etymology, philosophy, theology, geography, astronomy, architecture. Above all language, without which the rest made little sense. Indian studies could not be like Ritter's, he told Koreff in 1821, for Carl Ritter had been one of those scholars who had collected every conceivable reference in Greek and Latin to—in his case—the Caucasus³⁰¹ but not in the ancient indigenous languages spoken there. He was to reiterate this in various contexts and combinations, temperately to the readers of the *Indische Bibliothek*, in the reissue of his statement of intent (and achievement), *Ueber den gegenwärtigen Zustand der Indischen Philologie*; intemperately in the same journal to the hapless Arnold Hermann Ludwig Heeren, the Göttingen historian who, in Schlegel's eyes, had presumed to embark on an account of the trade and politics of the ancient peoples without the requisite language tools;³⁰² emphatically in his published letter to Sir James Mackintosh of 1832,³⁰³ where issues of translation also obtruded; or in its appendix, addressed to the (in Schlegel's oversensitive eyes) disdainful Horace Hayman Wilson who had seen fit to question the linguistic credentials of continental Sanskrit scholarship.³⁰⁴

The discourse in this wide area of study was conducted in a variety of contexts, and—it has to be said—with a certain repetitiveness. But not everyone read Sanskrit, not everyone even read German. Thus the later

---

300 *Ibid.*, 214.
301 Oppeln-Bronikowski, 426; Carl Ritter, *Die Vorhalle Europäischer Völkergeschichten vor Herodotus, um den Kaukasus und an den Gestaden des Pontus. Eine Abhandlung zur Alterthumskunde* (Berlin: Reimer, 1820).
302 *Indische Bibliothek*, II, 373-473; Heeren's ignorance is also alluded to in *Râmâyana*, Praef., lv; Heeren had informed AWS of his election to honorary membership of the Göttingen Academy. *Briefe*, I, 338. Cf. his dignified reply: *Etwas über meine Studien des alten Indiens von A. H. L. Heeren. Antwort an Herrn Prof. A. W. v. Schlegel auf dessen an mich gerichtete drei ersten Briefe in seiner Indischen Bibliothek* (Göttingen: Vandenhoek & Ruprecht, 1827).
303 *Réflexions sur l'étude des langues asiatiques adressées à Sir James Mackintosh, suivies d'une lettre à M. Horace Hayman Wilson, ancien secrétaire de la Société Asiatique à Calcutta, élu professeur à Oxford* (Bonn: Weber, 1832); *Oeuvres*, III, 95-275.
304 'Lettre à M. Horace Hayman Wilson', *ibid.*, 212-246.

essay, *De l'Origine des Hindous* (1834, republished in 1838 and 1842)[305] rehearsed essentially what he had had to say on etymology in 1818 or what he was telling his Bonn students about geography, movement, settlement, 'Raçe'. What was new in 1834 were some words in season for 'celtomanes', who happened to be in France, and their 'chimères celtiques'.[306] For all his resounding phrases about a common language 'from the banks of the Ganges [...] to the confines of the Arctic ocean',[307] he was to exclude the Celts from his scheme of things, despite proof to the contrary from James Cowles Prichard or in spite of Adolphe Pictet,[308] at most ceding a little ground.

One could find essentially the same points being made in an altogether more popular context, those two long articles on European contacts with India for the *Berliner Kalender* of 1829 and 1831.[309] Here Schlegel recognized the need for a more general readership, especially after his art lectures in Berlin in 1827. Had they been republished, these essays would have shown later readers a Schlegel not only setting out his encyclopedic knowledge of this fascinating area of human exploration and cultural transfer, but doing so in a highly readable fashion. The subject involved whatever Europeans—Greeks, Portuguese, Dutch, French, British (not forgetting Arabs)—had brought back from India through trade or conquest and how in so doing they had made known an ancient civilization and its manifestations. The price was a high one, and Schlegel spares no-one, whether their motives were material gain or religious proselytism, who sought to impose Western 'superiority' on to a culture more ancient than their own. All things considered, Schlegel is relatively lenient on the British political administration and its role in opening up the country both

---

305 *Ibid.*, 24-94. Published three times in AWS's lifetime: *Transactions of the Royal Society of Literature in the United Kingdom* 2 (1834), 405-446; *Nouvelles Annales des voyages* 4 (1838), 137-214; *Essais littéraires et historiques*, 439-518.
306 *Oeuvres*, II, 281.
307 *Ibid.*, III, 62.
308 *Ibid.*, II, 80, 83. On Celts cf. his 'Aphorismen die Etymologie des Französischen betreffend', *SW*, VII, 269-271. James Cowles Prichard, *The Eastern Origin of the Celtic Nations* [...] (1831); Adolphe Pictet, 'Lettres à M. A. W. de Schlegel, sur l'affinité des langues celtiques avec le sanscrit', *Journal asiatique*, 3e série, 1 (1836), 263-290, 417-448; 2 (1836), 440-466. AWS's position retracted somewhat in the foreword to his translation of Prichard (1838), vf.
309 *Briefe*, I, 472f., II, 208f.; the insights of these essays summed up in Latin, *Opuscula*, 402-414. Karl S. Guthke, 'Benares am Rhein—Rom am Ganges. Die Begegnung von Orient und Okzident im Denken A. W. Schlegels', *Jahrbuch des Freien Deutschen Hochstifts*, 1978, 396-419.

physically, through topographical survey and description, and culturally. His own brother Carl Schlegel had after all had his brief part in this process. His remark that British rule in India was akin to Rome's power after the Punic Wars[310] was a tribute to the administrators whom by now he had met and respected: Mackintosh, Colebrooke, Malcolm, Johnston, Tod. It was also prescient: British imperial domination was to be no more lasting that Roman; it was a 'golden colossus with feet of clay'.[311]

Not everything was intended for public scrutiny. Learned correspondence provided an intellectual exchange, as with Baron Paul Ludwig Schilling von Canstatt, the itinerant Russo-German inventor and scholar of Tibetan and Chinese, who caused him to cast his eye both northwards and further eastwards;[312] or with Wilhelm von Humboldt, whose study of the Javanese Kâwi language gave evidence of a once wider spread of Sanskrit. Despite all the necessary deference, Schlegel was able to drop his guard with Humboldt and postulate, Romantic-style, a primeval language in deep time, a primordial event akin to the moment of creation itself, when language came into being in all of its original forms. Human amnesia, neglect, confusion, had led to the loss of originary form and expression; but Sanskrit was the language least affected by these abrading processes. Its wealth was discernible in Persian, Greek, Latin, Germanic (not Celtic, of course).[313] For Humboldt, this was too unhistorical, too much redolent of a superhuman (i.e. divine) intervention in language creation.[314] Altogether, the more cautious Humboldt showed a restraining hand, both in personal matters as well as linguistic: he urged Schlegel to be less unkind to Bopp, their fellow-labourer in the field, and not to overreact to Langlois,[315] (which he manifestly did).[316]

---

310 *Berliner Kalender* (1831), 122.
311 *Ibid.*, 125.
312 Correspondence with Schilling von Canstatt, *Briefe*, I, 630f.; *Choix de lettres d'Eugène Bournouf 1825-1852* (Paris: Champion, 1891), 508f.; SLUB Dresden, Mscr. Dresd. e. 90, XX (48-51).
313 Leitzmann, 73f., 187f.
314 *Ibid.*, 195.
315 *Ibid.*, 231-238.
316 AWS, 'Observations sur la critique du Bhagavad-Gîtâ, insérée dans le Journal Asiatique', *Journal Asiatique* 9 (1826), 3-27; cf. also [Wilhelm von Humboldt], 'Ueber die Bhagavad-Gita. Mit Bezug auf die Beurtheilung der Schlegelschen Ausgabe im Pariser Asiatischen Journal', *Indische Bibliothek* II (1826), Heft 2, 218-258, Heft 3, 328-372, which appeared concurrently.

The *Indische Bibliothek*

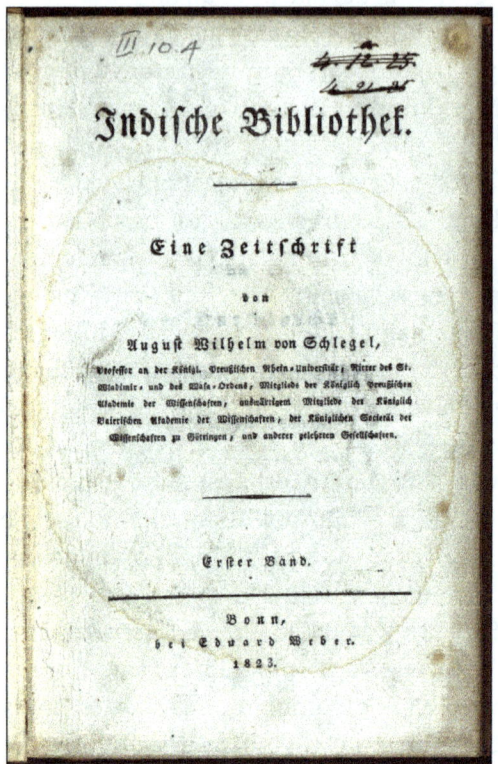

Fig. 28 *Indische Bibliothek. Eine Zeitschrift von August Wilhelm von Schlegel* (Bonn, 1820-1830). Title page issued in 1823. © and by kind permission of the Master and Fellows of Trinity College, Cambridge, CC BYNC 4.0.

All of these things find their confluence in the *Indische Bibliothek* (1820-23, 1826-27 and 1830),[317] issued by the Bonn publisher Weber in irregular

---

317 Contents (by AWS unless otherwise indicated): I (1820, reissued 1823 with new title page): Heft 1 (1820) [ii-xiii] dedication; ix-xvi Vorrede; 1-27 'Ueber den gegenwärtigen Zustand der Indischen Philologie'; 28-96 'Indische Dichtungen' (incl. 'Die Herabkunft der Göttin Ganga'); 97-128 'Ausgaben Indischer Bücher' (review of Bopp's 1819 ed. of *Nalus*); Heft 2 (1820): 129-231 'Zur Geschichte des Elephanten'; 232-256 'Indische Sphinx' (a miscellany of the learned and the curious); Heft 3 (1822): 257-273 'Die Einsiedelei des Kandu' (Chézy); 274-294 'De studio etymologico'; 295-364 'Wilsons Wörterbuch'; 365-370 'Nachrichten' (miscellany); Heft 4 (1823): 371-432 'Neueste Mittheilungen der Asiatischen Gesellschaft zu Calcutta'; 433-467 'Ueber die in der Sanskrit-Sprache […] gebildeten Verbalformen' (W. von Humboldt); II (reissued 1827 with a new title page): Heft 1 (1824); 1-70 'Allgemeine Uebersicht'; 72-134 'Ueber die in der Sanskrit-Sprache […] gebildeten Verbalformen' (W. von Humboldt); Heft 2 (1826): 135-148 'Ankündigung' (prospectus of *Râmâyana*); 149-217 'Briefwechsel' (synopsis of Sanskrit dramas; letter of German missionary in South India); 218-258 'Ueber die Bhagavat-Gita. Mit Bezug auf die Beurtheilung der Schlegelschen Ausgabe im Pariser Asiatischen

numbers. As is so often the case with Schlegel, it is difficult to pin down its significance to one single factor. First and foremost, however, it was the only journal that he edited on his own.

It was also—this needs saying at the outset—the first German journal devoted solely to India, as opposed to general oriental ('morgenländisch') matters, unlike the periodical that his own father-in-law Paulus had once edited in Jena with 'morgenländisch' in its subtitle,[318] or Julius Klaproth's *Asiatisches Magazin*, issued in Weimar in 1802-03. Despite its resounding opening—a dedication to Prince Hardenberg and a reissue of his manifesto *Ueber den gegenwärtigen Zustand der Indischen Philologie*—the *Indische Bibliothek* was, if not an outright failure, at least not the success that Schlegel might have hoped for. Then again conflicting priorities, as so often with him, became evident. It did sell 400 copies, but it really was little more than an occasional miscellany. It could not escape the influence of the *Asiatick Researches*, published in Calcutta, nor could it shake off entirely the extreme eclecticism of those periodicals. His dedication promised to cast the net over the immeasurable areas of India's past and present, to interrelate ancient and modern, all aspects, geography, natural history, sacred writings, religion, politics, art and architecture—not forgetting comparative linguistics. It was also a one-man band, or almost, with Schlegel as editor-in-chief and main contributor. By contrast, the *Journal Asiatique* in Paris, founded in 1822, had an editorial board that included Chézy, Fauriel, Klaproth, Abel-Rémusat and Silvestre de Sacy, and its content was by no means restricted to India. A German organisation, the Deutsche Morgenländische Gesellschaft, Germany's Asiatic society, was not founded until 1845. By then oriental studies would stand on a much more secure footing than they did in 1820, but even so there was no question of a journal devoted to India only.

The *Indische Bibliothek* has, in addition, along with the rest of Schlegel's Indian writings, suffered from the comparison with his brother's *Ueber die Sprache und Weisheit der Indier*, which has been edited and explicated and integrated into the main stream of oriental studies in a way that the *Indische Bibliothek* has not. The older perception is hard to shake off—Max

---

Journal' (Wilhelm von Humboldt); Heft 3 (1826): 259-283 'Indische Erzählungen'; 284-327 'Indische Sphinx'; 328-372 'Ueber die Bhagavad-Gita' (cont.); Heft 4 (1827): 373-473 'An Herrn Professor Heeren in Göttingen'; 474 'Zwei Epigramme'; III (1830): 1-113 'Ueber Professor Bopps grammatisches System der Sanskrit-Sprache' (Lassen); 114 'Denksprüche aus dem Sanskrit'.

318 *Neues Repertorium für Biblische und Morgenländische Litteratur*, 2 parts (Jena, 1790). See Andrea Polaschegg, *Der andere Orientalismus. Regeln deutsch-morgenländischer Imagination im 19. Jahrhundert*, Quellen und Forschungen zur Literatur- und Kulturgeschichte, 35 (269) (Berlin, New York: de Gruyter, 2005), 160, 181.

Müller in 1861 can stand for many others—that Friedrich, a 'man of genius', discovered a 'new world' with his 'poetic vision', while August Wilhelm, as set out in his letter to Goethe, merely expanded his literary interests.[319]

This may sound too negative. Schlegel did actually want to reach a wider educated audience, but then again he became increasingly disdainful of such a body, writing to Wilhelm von Humboldt that the *Indische Bibliothek* was not intended for entertainment.[320] That it certainly was not, especially once a knowledge of Sanskrit was assumed. German, French and Latin were taken for granted, indeed the *Indische Bibliothek* was living proof, if any was needed, that German was a language of international academic and scholarly discourse and that one required it for the full spectrum of oriental studies. It was the assumption behind the flattering mention that Schlegel received in 1831 in John Murray's *Quarterly Review*, before his last triumphant visit to England.[321] The essay on the elephant offered one of the few pieces for a general readership, but the same readers were also expected to cope with *De studio etymologico* in the original. There was clearly an element of 'take it or leave it'.

Were these not also the failings of the Romantic journals with which he had been associated, especially that youthful enterprise, the *Athenaeum*, boldly pronouncing the brothers Schlegel to be its sole creators and aiming deliberately to affront the 'average reader'? The *Indische Bibliothek* could not adopt such an uncompromising stance towards its readers: dedicated as it was to the state chancellor, Prince Hardenberg, the patron and benefactor of Schlegel's Indian projects, it required a more deferential tone. It did no harm to remind Hardenberg in dedication and preface that the generosity of the Prussian state was not going to be expended on half measures. Hardenberg, who had studied in Göttingen, would find here echoes of the historical school that had produced both Schlegel and himself and that had seen India as the 'cradle of civilisation'. And so it was in these pages that Schlegel set out his knowledge of India, his aims, his principles, his disagreements with other Sanskritists; it was as near as he ever got to enunciating in public his most cherished views on India, the history of Sanskrit studies and their challenges (as in that statement of intent originally written for an academic audience in Bonn), or an account of Sanskrit poetry (with some samples).

It made, as said, but few accommodations to the general reader. Its very title—not *Indisches Magazin* or *Indisches Journal*—suggested some solidity,

---

319 Max Müller, *Lectures on the Science of Language Delivered at the Royal Institution of Great Britain in April, May, & June, 1861*, 3rd edn (London: Longman, Green, 1862), 164, 167.
320 Leitzmann, 87.
321 'Sanscrit Poetry', *The Quarterly Review*, XLV (1831), 1-57, ref. 4.

accented less the miscellany that the journal essentially was, and more the solid repository, the 'library'. It had slightly eighteenth-century echoes, of Eschenburg perhaps, of endeavours far back in the 1780s, pioneering in their time, a connection with an older antiquarianism now of course overtaken by new academic scholarship. By 1823, however, when Schlegel reissued the first volume, he had largely abandoned any concessions. Hereafter a knowledge of Sanskrit became increasingly desirable. When one considers that the only major contributors to the *Indische Bibliothek* apart from Schlegel himself were Chézy, Wilhelm von Humboldt and Lassen, the last two in a strict Sanskritist mode, it was clear that it was becoming a journal for specialists or enthusiasts, or both.

Did it have a message for that other late Romantic periodical, his brother's *Concordia*, battling in rearguard actions against the *Zeitgeist* and really, as he wrote, a *Discordia*?[322] *Ex negativo* perhaps, by pointing eastwards away from Europe; directly, in its sharp attack on missionary zealotry (privately, he was to equate Jesuits and Methodists in their conversion tactics) and its disdain for a wisdom not of its own revelation.[323] As it was, the *Indische Bibliothek* itself was to devote more pages than was good for it to controversies. There was Humboldt's detailed rebuttal of Langlois's (Chézy's) critique of his *Bhagavad-Gîtâ* edition, delivered in the *Journal Asiatique*, that added to the discomfiture in Paris (Chézy's 'fureur').[324] Was there any need to devote a hundred pages to gratuitously and tediously punishing the unsuspecting Heeren for not knowing Sanskrit, and over a hundred to letting Christian Lassen loose on Bopp's Sanskrit grammar? This was not Brahmanic calm, as Schlegel understood it, but part of a general fractiousness in public discourse into which Schlegel allowed himself to be drawn in these Bonn years.

This however lay in the future. The first numbers of the *Indische Bibliothek*, reissued as one volume in 1823, were generally informative and civilized. Schlegel's review of Bopp's *Nalus* edition had a moderate, although authoritative, tone; his discussion of H. H. Wilson's Sanskrit dictionary gave him an opportunity to discourse on the essential purity of the ancient language, its freedom from modern admixtures and contaminations: as it came into being, so too did customs, religion and poetry. There was the extraordinary essay on the elephant.[325] This is the other Schlegel, who

---

322 *Friedrich Schlegels Briefe an seinen Bruder August Wilhelm*, ed. Oskar F. Walzel [Walzel] (Berlin: Speyer & Peters, 1890), 653.
323 *Indische Bibliothek*, I, 34f. Cf. Josef Körner, 'Indologie und Humanität', 137-160; Guthke (1978), 413-417.
324 Burnouf, *Choix de lettres*, 34.
325 *Indische Bibliothek*, I, 129-231.

in the Vienna Lectures, in the essays on the *Nibelungenlied*, later in the *Berliner Kalender*, could wear his learning lightly and use to advantage his considerable skills as a prose writer. Unfortunately, Böcking chose not to republish it—it might have changed later views on Schlegel—but it has found its way subsequently into Meyer's encyclopedia (it still winks complicitly out of Meyer's article 'Elefanten' in 1925).[326] A human and accessible Schlegel perhaps, proud of the four-inch high bronze elephants in his own house, a modest reminder of the attention once lavished by the patriarchal and heroic culture of India on this noble creature? We are not spared sources; it could not be otherwise: Bochart, Robertson, Cuvier, Gesner, Langlès, Sir John Malcolm, and the *Asiatick Researches*. We go from Ophir to Alexander, to Hannibal—and then to India. We have to learn the elephant's various names and their etymology; more importantly, we see elephants as the companions of gods and men (the god Ganesha is elephant-headed); their bulk, but also their delicacy of movement, symbolise the mythical link between the world of the senses and non-corporeal truth; they step through that multi-figured world into the realm of poetry.

We see the elephant's place in Sanskrit literature and in art: Schlegel describes the Elephanta cave near Bombay and calls for an understanding of Indian sculpture. Start with its animal depictions, he says, and you will find your way into these otherwise alien art forms. It was a veiled replique to Goethe's poem in his *Zahme Xenien*, turning in feigned horror from elephant-headed deities.[327]

Many of the ideas in the periodical were not new; at most their addressee had changed. One finds Schlegel in the *Indische Bibliothek* returning quite openly to what, for want of a better name, one could call Romantic preoccupations: mythology and translation. His conspectus of Indian poetry[328] is nothing less than a call for a return to origins, to the oldest texts (as he saw them), to deepest time, to the common source of mythology and poetry, to that moment when they were one and the same; where, with all peoples and all religions of all ages and climes, nature was mirrored in the human spirit, expressing basic human needs, intimations and strivings.[329]

---

326 *Meyers Lexikon*. 7. Auflage, 12 vols and 3 supplements (Leipzig: Bibliographisches Institut, 1924-33), III, 1435-1437.
327 'Und so will ich, ein- für allemal,
    Keine Bestien in dem Götter-Saal!
    Die leidigen Elefanten-Rüssel,
    Das umgeschlungene Schlangen-Genüssel'.
    Zahme Xenien, II. Goethe, *Gedenkausgabe*, I, 615.
328 *Indische Bibliothek*, I, 28-96.
329 *Ibid.*, 31.

He could also be more specific. The hypothesised spread out from an Indian 'Ursitz' took Schlegel back to the world of the *Nibelungenlied*. Did the twelfth-century *Annolied*, a preoccupation of his last years in Coppet, contain a reference to Germanic settlement in the Caucasus?³³⁰ Or: take the Kâwi language of Java, which showed the prehistoric transmission of Sanskrit, now of course overlayered by subsequent incursions.³³¹ On translation, he was at first surprisingly cautious, stressing its limits and inadequacies;³³² but he could not resist the opportunity of giving his readers two cantos from the *Râmâyana* in German hexameters. There was no question of his doing a literal translation into German of the Sanskrit classics: word-for-word translating he reserved for scholarly contexts, the Latin prose versions in his editions (*Bhagavad-Gîtâ, Râmâyana*) with their demonstrable complexity, without even taking into consideration the Indian metre. Hence his 'free version', based on *Râmâyana* I, xxxii-xxxv, 'Die Herabkunft der Göttin Ganga' [The Descent of the Goddess Ganga].³³³ He never repeated the experiment. It read too much like his own elegy *Rom* transferred to an alien cosmogony; it gave too much opportunity for the use of those accretive compounds that German shares with Sanskrit, but which require better poetic talents—Goethe's, Klopstock's, even Voss's—to carry them off. There are too many linguistic echoes of Christian mythology (Klopstock again). Clearly he could still write hexameters, but enough was enough. Perhaps Friedrich Schlegel had had the right idea back in 1808,³³⁴ with his less metrically severe versions, or Friedrich Windischmann in 1816.³³⁵

It was different when in 1827, in the pages of the *Indische Bibliothek*, Wilhelm von Humboldt presumed to call into question the very notion of translation itself. Humboldt, even as Schlegel was embarking on his Shakespeare, had always been sceptical on the subject. Hemsterhuis, Schlegel's philosophical mentor in those days, had not been encouraging, either. Schlegel writes:

> For all that I did not allow myself to be frightened off: I tried all manner of things: Dante, Shakespeare, Calderón, Ariosto, Petrarch, Camões etc., also some poets of classical antiquity. I could now say that after all these labours

---

330 *Ibid.*, 235-242.
331 *Ibid.*, 400-425.
332 *Ibid.*, 32f.
333 *Ibid.*, 50-96.
334 Cf. the section 'Indische Gedichte' in his *Ueber die Sprache und Weisheit der Indier* (Heidelberg: Mohr und Zimmer, 1808), 221-324.
335 The sections 'Wiswamitra's Büßungen. Eine Episode aus dem Ramajana', 'Der Kampf mit dem Riesen. Aus dem Mahâbhârat' and 'Einige Stellen aus den Veda's' by Windischmann, appended to Franz Bopp, *Über das Conjugationssystem der Sanskritsprache* (Frankfurt am Main: Andreä, 1816), 159-235, 237-269, 271-312.

I have come to the conviction that translation is, though freely chosen, nevertheless a laborious bondage, an art without sustenance, a thankless craft; thankless, not just because the best translation is never esteemed as equal to an original, but also because the translator, the more he gains insight, must feel even more the inevitable imperfection of his work. But I will rather emphasise the other side. The true translator, one could state boldly, who is able to render not just the content of a masterpiece, but also to preserve its noble form, its peculiar idiom, is a herald of genius who, over and beyond the narrow confines set by the separation of language, spreads abroad its fame and broadcasts its high gifts. He is a messenger from nation to nation, who mediates mutual respect and admiration, where otherwise all is indifference or even enmity.[336]

These are dignified and noble words that may stand as a monument to his Romantic achievement and his continuing sense that it was good. Their spirit could also be applied to the Sanskrit editions, although the letter—in Latin—was different. For by the time Schlegel was next to dilate on the subject of translation—in his published letter to Sir James Mackintosh of 1832—he had an axe to grind and ventured into controversial territory. He had not been pleased with the policy of the Oriental Translation Committee of the Royal Asiatic Society, indeed riled at the centrality of Persian and Arabic texts, not Sanskrit, in their prospectus. Once, over a generation ago, the actual edition of the text to be translated had not exercised him greatly (Bell's Shakespeare, instead of the more authoritative Johnson-Steevens, for instance), but solely the end result. With Sanskrit texts, it was different. One could not approach this task without the requisite 'philologie asiatique', and Schlegel proceeded to set out what in his view that involved. It was essentially a statement of what he had been doing since 1818. 'Fervour and enthusiasm',[337] which sufficed for the author of the article in the *Quarterly Review* in 1831, were not enough. The means of acquisition of Sanskrit by the British—'in the field', at the feet of pandits—was not always an absolutely reliable basis for translation as Schlegel envisaged it. The British would need to set up Sanskrit studies on a footing commensurate with their European counterparts.[338]

---

336 *Indische Bibliothek*, II, 254f. Reprinted in Hans Joachim Störig (ed.), *Das Problem des Übersetzens*, Wege der Forschung, 8 (Darmstadt: Wissenschaftliche Buchgesellschaft, 1969), 98.
337 *Quarterly Review* (1831), 5.
338 *Oeuvres*, III, 183.

Paris and London 1820-1823

The first fruits of Schlegel's Sanskrit studies were the two visits, to Paris in 1820-21, and to London in 1823, the fulfilment of the confidence and generosity vested in him by the Prussian government, and concretely, the 2,000 talers that Hardenberg had authorized.[339] His *Indische Bibliothek* had already started to appear in 1820. It could not however reproduce satisfactorily Sanskrit characters, which a learned Asiatic journal must be able to do, at least to Schlegel's specifications and satisfaction. Lithography would not suffice: the hapless Würzburg professor Othmar Frank, who had produced a lithographed chrestomathy of ancient Indian texts, received very short shrift indeed.[340] Franz Bopp had been able to use the London press set up by Charles Wilkins for his edition of *Nalus* in 1819, a fact that Schlegel was obliged to mention. But not without due words in season:[341] charity among the new Sanskritists in Germany did not come easily, it seems, Schlegel elsewhere complaining that Bopp gave himself airs,[342] Bopp claiming the same of Schlegel, Schlegel for good measure concluding his *Indische Bibliothek* in 1830 with a severe critique (by Lassen) of Bopp's Sanskrit grammar. And this was to be but one controversy among several.

More importantly, the editions of Sanskrit texts promised severally to Hardenberg, to Altenstein, to Solms, to Schulze, to Rehfues, needed a devanagari typeface. Paris was the only place in Europe that possessed the necessary technology. Thus Schlegel spent eight months in the royal capital, not only straining his eyes over manuscript variants of the *Bhagavad-Gîtâ* (to appear in 1823),[343] but also acquiring the practical skills of a type-founder and compositor—of Sanskrit.[344]

Schlegel rightly saw himself as a pioneer in this technique—he used the analogy with the Italian Renaissance printers who had set up the first Byzantine Greek texts[345]—not completely without predecessors, of course. Charles Wilkins's *Grammar of the Sanskrita Language*, for instance, had been

---

339 *Briefe*, I, 378f.
340 *Indische Bibliothek*, II, 45f.; also *Bhagavad-Gîtâ*, Praef., xiif.
341 *Indische Bibliothek*, I, i, 97-128.
342 *Briefe*, I, 387f.
343 *Krisenjahre*, II, 365f.; Czapla/Schankweiler, 32.
344 For most of what follows see W. Kirfel, 'Die Anfänge des Sanskrit-Druckes in Europa', *Zentralblatt für Bibliothekswesen* 32 (1915), 274-280.
345 *Indische Bibliothek*, I, 22.

published in London in 1808, using it;[346] Wilkins, similarly, had produced an edition of the *Hitopadeśa* in London in 1810, the first Indian textual edition in Europe. These were the two main factors spurring Schlegel on in this endeavour, both of equal rank in importance: pride that a German (Prussian) university now had a printing facility that the English had only privately, and that the French, for all their university chairs of oriental languages, did not have at all; and satisfaction at having designed the type, the one that he wanted and that was appropriate for reproducing the 'sacred' originals.

Being back in Paris[347] after an absence of little more than two years restored him to the Staël-Broglie family, renewed contact with Cuvier and Alexander von Humboldt (who praised the essay on the elephant).[348] He also needed to consult his booksellers and publishers Treuttel & Würtz over sales. (Was there time to visit Madame Récamier, whose address he had?) He certainly did have time to visit the studio of Baron François Pascal Gérard, in order to arrange for his niece Auguste von Buttlar to work there. It brought him back into the world of French oriental studies, to Silvestre de Sacy, to the young sinologist Jean-Pierre Abel-Rémusat—in 1823 Rémusat would congratulate him on his appointment as a corresponding member of the Société Asiatique[349]—and to his former mentor Chézy. There were copies of the *Indische Bibliothek* to give away. But the hypochondriac Chézy was moody and unhelpful, refusing him access to a manuscript of the *Bhagavad-Gîtâ*, a foretaste of that later carping critique of Schlegel's edition for which he used a front-man, Langlois. It was in fact the scholar Claude-Charles Fauriel, the celebrated translator of popular Greek songs, also an acquaintance from Staël days, who made himself most useful, being flattered with the address of 'pandita' and the assurance that Vishnu would reward his efforts.[350] Schlegel produced drawings, based on Paris manuscripts, of the letters he required, of the right size and clarity. He entrusted these to the engraver Vibert at the Didot printers, who cut them and had them cast by the Lion letter-foundry.[351] We have detailed instructions to the printer,

---

346 *Ibid.*, 97.
347 Paris address list SLUB Dresden, Mscr. Dresd. e. 90, XI, IVb.
348 *Briefe*, I, 380.
349 SLUB Dresden, Mscr. Dresd. e. 90, XIX (18) 89. Abel-Rémusat's letters to AWS *ibid.*, 87-99.
350 'M. Fauriel', in Charles-Augustin de Sainte-Beuve, *Portraits contemporains*, ed. Michel Brix (Paris: PUPS, 2008), 1227-1316, ref. 1302f. A letter of Fauriel to AWS ('mon toujours cher Pandita') in Gertrud Richert, *Die Anfänge der romanischen Philologie*, 94-96.
351 *Indische Bibliothek*, I, 368-370; technical description II, 36f.

in French and German, about type sizes, about ligatures and other technical matters.³⁵² The first trial of this type was only a few pages long, but it bore the resounding title *Specimen novae typographiae Indicae*,³⁵³ with 'curavit Aug. Guil. Schlegel' as a reminder of whose intellectual property it was. It was this press which Schlegel later had installed in the rear part of his house, when he and Lassen oversaw the devanagari sections of his editions and the *Indische Bibliothek*. Having footed the bill, the Prussian authorities also wanted the press to be available to Bopp in Berlin:³⁵⁴ Schlegel could only acquiesce, however unwillingly. It gave him greater satisfaction when the French asked permission to use it.³⁵⁵ The visit to London was equally important, but for different reasons. To the British customs authorities at Dover we owe the only surviving official description of Schlegel: 'five feet six inches; grey hair; fresh complexion; grey eyes'.³⁵⁶ He had crossed by steam packet, without being seasick.³⁵⁷

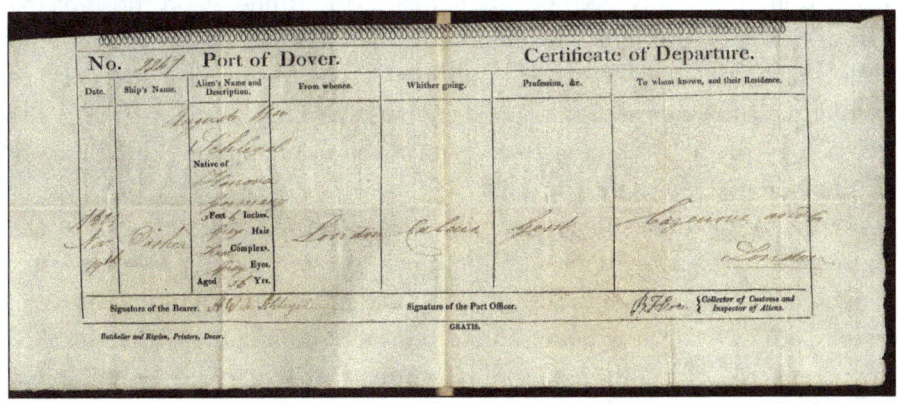

Fig. 29 Schlegel's Certificate of Departure from the Port of Dover, 19 November 1823, with description of his appearance. © SLUB Dresden, all rights reserved.

If the *Courier de Londres* of 4 November 1823 expressed his distinction primarily in terms of his famous Lectures, it did go on to say that he was

---

352 Bonn UB, S 1435.
353 There follow a further 12 lines of title page. (Lutetiae Parisiorum: Crapelet, 1821).
354 Rehfues to Schlegel 26 April 1822, in: Kirfel (1915), 278.
355 The *Journal Asiatique* prints a letter from Altenstein authorizing the Sanskrit press to be placed at the disposal of the society. *Journal Asiatique* 4 (1824), 117. The society was soliciting AWS's advice still in 1832. Burnouf, 459f.
356 SLUB Dresden, Mscr.Dresd. e. 90. XI, I, 4.
357 *Krisenjahre*, II, 421.

'at present one of the orientalists of the first rank in Europe'.³⁵⁸ It did not mention that he was accompanied by Christian Lassen, his pupil and amanuensis, for whom Schlegel had secured a travelling scholarship from the Prussian government and whose task was to compare manuscripts of the *Râmâyana* and the *Hitopadeśa* for the editions that Schlegel was planning. It was to involve both Schlegel and Lassen in more than they bargained for.

The presentation copies of the *Indische Bibliothek* listed on their title page all of his decorations and memberships of learned societies. If most of these were in respect of an earlier existence, surely nobody noticed. There had not been time to add the honorary membership of the Asiatic Society in Calcutta;³⁵⁹ the Prussian Red Eagle would not follow until 1824.³⁶⁰ As a corresponding member of the Royal Asiatic Society in London he was able to attend the annual general meeting at its foundation late in 1823. To the older Asiatic Society he could express himself: 'the printing of Sanskrit is being done under my eyes on the banks of the Rhine as on those of the Ganges', and warming to his theme, 'the comparative study of languages cuts across the limits of history and enables us to know where peoples belong, and their migrations. The venerable religion, the law-giving, the mythology of the Brahmins touches at a thousand points the history of civilization in the ancient world'.³⁶¹

Whereas his domestic needs in Paris were served in the Broglie house in the rue de l'Université, in London he had to find lodgings: 14 Leicester Square was certainly central, but quite a step from the British Museum (where a new wing was being added to accommodate the Elgin Marbles) and even farther from the East India Company Library in Leadenhall Street. Nevertheless he was feted and fussed over more than ever in his career. Doubtless the visit to England of Auguste de Staël and Victor de Broglie earlier in the year, although concerned with institutions (agronomy),³⁶² revived links with names from the Staël days. Sir James Mackintosh, who had been sending him Indian books since 1816,³⁶³ was away in the country, but his name was an entrée to the right circles.³⁶⁴ Mackintosh too had long

---

358 SLUB Dresden, Mscr. Dresd. e. 90, II, 17.
359 *Briefe*, I, 392f.
360 *Ibid.*, 405.
361 *Ibid.*, 393.
362 SLUB Dresden, Mscr. Dresd. e. 90, II, 57.
363 Cf. Norman King, 'Lettres de Madame de Staël à Sir James Mackintosh', *Cahiers staëliens*, 10 (1970), 27-54, ref. 44.
364 *Krisenjahre*, II, 421.

since recognized that Schlegel had philological accomplishments 'which our Anglo Indians cannot possess'.[365] Mackintosh was able to arrange for his proper reception in Oxford:[366] amid the Augean stable of the Bodleian's oriental manuscripts he spotted a fragment of the *Râmâyana*.[367] James Cowles Prichard came over from Bristol to meet him.[368]

Other Staëlian connections would prove useful: one was Sir Humphry Davy, now president of the Royal Society; Sir John Malcolm, general, ambassador and administrator, who took him to Cambridge; Sir Alexander Johnston, who had held highest administrative positions in Ceylon and whom Auguste de Staël had met, used his good offices.[369] Doors were opened, facilities granted, so that this now famous scholar could consult the holdings of the East India Company and the British Museum (where his fellow-countryman Georg Heinrich Noehden made himself useful). Davy and Johnston received Auguste von Buttlar and doubtless helped her to gain portrait commissions among the high aristocracy: there was a portrait of a Brougham child; the duchesses of Kent and Clarence asked to see her prices. There must have been a visit to John Flaxman, the object of Schlegel's enthusiasm twenty-five years earlier, for he advised Auguste not to overcharge.[370] Edward Moor, whose *Hindu Pantheon* (1810) Schlegel was to use in the notes to his *Râmâyana* edition, offered to help him in assembling a collection of Indian art.[371]

But the main object was to meet Henry Thomas Colebrooke.[372] Although near-contemporaries, Colebrooke and Schlegel could hardly have been more different, had not a common interest in Sanskrit brought them together. Of the second generation of high officials in the East India Company (although his father, chairman of the company, had fallen spectacularly from grace), Colebrooke was on his retirement from India in 1814 a judge and member of the Supreme Council in Calcutta, a trustee of the Fort William College as

---

365 SLUB Dresden, Mscr. Dresd. e. 90, XIX, 15 (21).
366 *Ibid.* (6).
367 *Râmâyana*, Praefatio, xlvii.
368 SLUB Dresden, Mscr. Dresd. e. 90, XLIX (21).
369 For much of which follows see the informative edition by Rosane Rocher and Ludo Rocher, *Founders of Western Indology. August Wilhelm von Schlegel and Henry Thomas Colebrooke in Correspondence 1820-1837*, Abhandlungen für die Kunde des Morgenlandes, 84 (Wiesbaden: Harrassowitz, 2013), here 85.
370 SLUB Dresden, Mscr. Dresd. e. 90, XIX (14), 14.
371 *Râmâyana*, I, i, 161; SLUB Dresden, Mscr. Dresd. e. 90, XIX (15), 68; Rocher and Rocher (2013), 88f.
372 Rocher and Rocher (2013), 80-87.

well as professor of Hindu law there, and the President of the Asiatic Society in Calcutta. He was the author of a Sanskrit grammar, based on indigenous systems (1805), had edited a Sanskrit dictionary (1808), written numerous papers on astronomy, inscriptions, prosody, geography (including the headwaters of the Ganges), and had translated source works on the law of inheritance. In 1815 he had returned to London with his young family, including John Colebrooke, the Anglo-Indian son whom he had fathered and who with Patrick Johnston was to live with Schlegel in 1824-26.

Colebrooke's interests were now more in the fields of astronomy and mathematics (subjects to which Schlegel himself was not indifferent). He was however a collector. His decision in 1819 to donate his amassed 2,000 volumes of Indian manuscripts to the East India Company Library made London overnight a centre of Sanskrit studies to throw into the shade Paris, which hitherto had the most extensive holdings. Both Othmar Frank and Franz Bopp had felt the need to come to London—before Schlegel—to consult manuscripts, and in Bopp's case to oversee the printing of his *Nalus* edition.[373]

Schlegel meanwhile had delivered a promissory note to the Prussian government in the form of a reissue of his essay on the current state of Indian philology (repeated from 1819) that had ushered in the first number of his *Indische Bibliothek*. That essay was much more informative and much less presumptuous than his last public statement, the review of Chézy in 1815. It had a more balanced and conciliatory attitude towards British India and efforts being fostered there to secure the preservation of the Sanskrit language, lexical, grammatical and textual, while not conceding the 'principles of classical philology' and their primacy.[374] In this context, the name of Colebrooke received an honorific mention.[375] Now, to fulfil his obligations, Schlegel needed to turn to the authority himself.

Schlegel's first approach to Colebrooke thus had every reason to be deferential,[376] writing in French as with all of his English-language correspondents.[377] But not obsequious either: he could write that other

---

373 *Ibid.*, 28; on Colebrooke see Rosane Rocher and Ludo Rocher, *The Making of Western Indology. Henry Thomas Colebrooke and the East India Company*, Royal Asiatic Society Books (London, New York: Routledge, 2011), 139-146.
374 *Indische Bibliothek*, I, 22.
375 *Ibid.*, I, 12f.
376 Rocher and Rocher (2013), 29-32.
377 A rare exception is his letter to the Directors of the East India Company, *Oeuvres*, III, 255-257.

Schlegels too had had their connections with India (Carl and Friedrich). Not knowing of Colebrooke's own interest in these matters,[378] he set out his stall as a comparative philologist, the great etymological project that never got beyond a few first beginnings. Names were dropped—Sir James Mackintosh and Thomas Campbell—and a copy of the *Indische Bibliothek* promised. It worked, and there ensued a correspondence in which Schlegel reported on the progress of his typographical and textual undertakings and made specific enquiries, while Colebrooke informed him on the London holdings and on the availability of manuscripts for purchase. It was Colebrooke, who on 1 August, 1822, informed Schlegel that he had been elected an honorary member of the Asiatic Society of Calcutta.[379]

Schlegel's letter to Johannes Schulze of 20 February, 1824,[380] is therefore of considerable interest in that it records Schlegel's impressions of England. This was an England without Madame de Staël, although that old connection had eased his way into some echelons of society. She had been interested in social and political institutions; he was concerned with these only as they affected education, or—this to Schulze—showed how much (or indeed how little) England was doing for 'Bildung'. Restricting himself to what he actually saw, Schlegel claimed that scholarship was restricted to Oxford and Cambridge (he did not know Scotland: Mackintosh had studied at Aberdeen and Edinburgh); University College in London, in whose founding Mackintosh was closely involved, was not yet in being (it would soon be teaching both German and Sanskrit). The two ancient universities were in the 1820s unreformed, at ease with themselves, unresponsive to outward stimuli. True, one knew Latin and Greek there, but there was no real theology, philosophy or history to enhance the linguistic knowledge. A germanophile wave was about to break over Cambridge, but not yet: the polymath William Whewell, whom Schlegel met and with whom he vied in omniscience,[381] was to be an early representative. Despite meeting the bookseller Bohte, Schlegel seemed unaware of the extent of translation activity from German into English. Yet he was generally right in stating that England's primacy lay in practical subjects like mathematics, physics

---

378 Rocher and Rocher (2011), 41.
379 *Ibid.*, 61.
380 *Briefe*, I, 405-411.
381 SLUB Dresden, Mscr. Dresd. e. 90, XIX (25), 63 (letter of Adam Sedgwick, 10 January, 1845).

or mechanics (Sir Humphry Davy, who had not been to university, would bear this out).

This was by way of impressing on Schulze the need for continuing support for the Sanskrit project, an object of pure scholarship, not of pragmatic application. Of course, England had Colebrooke, it had Wilkins, it had Haughton; between them these men covered astronomy, epic literature, and language. But (to read between the lines) the initiative lay with Germany: forty copies of his *Bhagavat-Gîtâ* had gone off to London for distribution, and the *Râmâyana* edition would not be far behind. Whereas no English university taught Sanskrit (as opposed to the East India Company's college at Haileybury), there were now four in Prussia alone that did (Bonn, Berlin, Greifswald and Königsberg). German scholarship had but to avail itself of the resources of Paris and London. As he was to say in another context, the ideal combination would be English money and German scholarly expertise.[382]

The letter to Schulze should not be read as belittling Schlegel's respect for the likes of Colebrooke, his 'vir summus' [the very best of men][383] (Schlegel would never know as much Sanskrit as he). Indeed when in 1824 Colebrooke made the unusual suggestion that his son John go to Bonn to have his schooling placed on a firmer footing, it was a request that Schlegel did not feel in a position to refuse. Nor, one feels, would he have wished to do so, even when Sir Alexander Johnston asked if his son Patrick might join John Colebrooke.

Educating the Young

This gesture was part of that extraordinary renewal of selfless devotion to the children of others, interrupted since the death of poor Albert de Staël. It was something that his contemporaries either did not notice or chose to overlook: the kindness extended to the young student Heinrich Heine is part of it. The first beneficiary was his niece Auguste von Buttlar, not as young as the boys, indeed already married. The only child of Ludwig Emanuel and Charlotte Ernst in Dresden, she was embarking on an artistic career, no easy task for a woman without patronage. (Her cousins by marriage, the Veit brothers, by contrast, had been to the Dresden academy and had their

---

382 Leitzmann, 154.
383 'De zodiaci antiquitate et origine', *Opuscula*, 349.

careers watched over assiduously by Friedrich and Dorothea Schlegel.) The Schlegel family was in agreement that it disliked her husband, a former officer in Russian service; her uncles Friedrich and August Wihelm had genuine affection for her. She had visited Friedrich in Frankfurt; now it was August Wilhelm in Bonn.

He spared no effort in promoting Auguste's career and supporting her financially. It was of course useful to have an uncle who was also an art connoisseur and a critic. Knowing Baron Gérard—and writing an enthusiastic article on his painting of Corinne at Cape Miseno, one of the more famous representations of Madame de Staël—he enabled Auguste to work in the painter's studio and to copy in the Louvre.[384] (There is a pencil drawing of the Corinne by her.)[385] In England, as seen, he recommended 'Madame de Buttlar' to his high social connections. None of her society portraits is traceable today, but we do have a fine pencil drawing of her uncle Friedrich Schlegel, the last image of him made before his death.

Fig. 30 Auguste von Buttlar, pencil drawing after the engraving by Jean Bein based on the painting by François Gérard, 'Corinne au cap Misène' (1819), 1824. © Kupferstich-Kabinett, Staatliche Kunstsammlungen Dresden, all rights reserved.

---

384 SLUB Dresden Mscr. Dresd. e. 90, XIX (3), 123.
385 Kupferstich-Kabinett, Staatliche Kunstsammlungen Dresden.

Alas, Auguste became embroiled in the religious politics of the Schlegel family. In 1826, she and her husband converted to Catholicism. She had waited until the deaths of her parents, both staunchly Protestant, also knowing that they would have disinherited her had she taken such a step in their lifetime. Her uncle, too, had proprietary claims, writing to her in pained anger:

> How gladly would I have been a father to you, dear niece, but you have placed yourself beyond my reach, have turned against me. If you can turn again, to join the sacred memory of your parents, of your venerable grandfather, and so many other forebears, I will receive you and your children with open arms.[386]

He accused his brother Friedrich of leading her astray, indeed all of these remarks were intended for his hearing in distant Vienna. One can discern nothing in these years that shows Schlegel returning to the substance of the family's Protestantism; he was of course still interested in the phenomenon of religion and its association with myth and culture, but not in doctrinal matters. One must conclude that his anti-Catholic stance was not without its element of ancestor-worship, with him as the guardian of the family flame. It was part of his growing detestation of converts and clericalism in general.[387] On the other hand, the increasingly apocalyptic tone of Friedrich's late lectures was an embarrassment to him and led to vigorous denials of the 'taint' of Catholicism.

If Schlegel could not pardon Friedrich, at least he forgave Auguste. Widowed and with a child, she became a frequent guest at the Sandkaule and in 1845 a major beneficiary of her uncle's will. She later deposited his collection of Indian miniature paintings in the Dresden gallery, the only art works from his house in Bonn that are readily identifiable today.

Already in 1823 his brother Moritz had written to him asking for advice in placing his son Johann Karl August Schlegel.[388] This nephew seemed to be the son that Schlegel might have wished for. He had studied classics at Göttingen and was set on a career as a 'Philologe' (a teacher of Greek and Latin),[389] thus the preserver of the male Schlegel line in every respect. His uncle could do nothing for him at this stage; later, when old and infirm, he had to accept responsibility for his nephew, who was by then mentally ill.

---

386 *Briefe*, I, 461.
387 Kaufmann, 'Zur Erinnerung', 246f.; Deetjen, 'August Wilhelm Schlegel in Bonn', 18.
388 SLUB Dresden, Mscr. Dresd. e. 90, XIX (23), 100.
389 Czapla/Schankweiler, 165f.

4. Bonn and India (1818-1845)

Would the care of others' children, outside of the family, produce less heartache? This too was not to be free of sorrow, but in the short term all went well. John Colebrooke and Patrick Johnston were in a sense living links with India and its high administration (John of mixed parentage). John's ancestry excluded him from East India Company service (there was talk of the Cape bar), but Patrick could aspire to it. Henry Colebrooke and Schlegel shared similarly stringent educational principles: mathematics and Latin as the base, with the full range of subjects offered by the German *Gymnasium*. The unreformed, pre-Arnoldian English public school—John had been at Charterhouse and Patrick at Eton—was in every respect deficient. German pedagogy would make up for English laxities.

It was all set up on a proper and businesslike basis, with accounts of expenses presented and approved. Needless to say it required of Schlegel time and energy, in the year that he was also rector of the university. Christian Lassen, whom Schlegel had left in London to work on the manuscripts in East India House, had to interrupt his researches to bring the boys over. They meant extra work for his housekeeper Marie. A tutor had to be found for them, Johann Nicolaus Bach, a pupil of Schlegel's,[390] who was to get them up to the required standard—in mathematics, the classics, history, geography, French (French was spoken at the dinner table, doubtless a daunting and formidable experience for the fifteen-year-olds). Their social attainments were not overlooked: there were fencing and dancing lessons; a touch of Pestalozzi saw them learning to ride and swim. There were echoes of Schlegel's and Albert's excursions when they went on a walking tour with their tutor up the Rhine as far as Mainz and the Rheingau. Paternal 'encouragement', admonition even, was not lacking. Schlegel was able to observe what the German school system could do for two English boys of the right aptitude, background—and means. They had arrived shy and retiring (no wonder) and had become outgoing, healthy, scholastically inclined even.

Yet this 'Pedagogical Province' on the Rhine ended as abruptly as it began. On 13 May, 1826, letters arrived from Colebrooke and Johnston recalling both boys with immediate effect. No reason was given for the termination, except that Patrick was to take the examinations for Haileybury, the East India Company college, John to study at a Scottish university. Schlegel remained on good terms with both fathers until 1828-29, when the

---

[390] A testimonial for him by AWS in SLUB Dresden, Mscr. Dresd. e. 90, XX (1), 4.

correspondence ceased; there were polite letters from each boy, doubtless paternally inspired. Poor John Colebrooke had only a year to live. Late in 1827 he was found dead in a Paris hotel. He had taken cyanide. Still young and inexperienced, he had contracted debts and in his own eyes had compromised and disgraced the family.

Schlegel had, as he said, 'paternal affection' for John and had wept on receiving the news.[391] He had lost Auguste Böhmer and Albert de Staël: Auguste von Buttlar was effectively lost through her 'defection'; Auguste de Staël had died in 1827. Now John Colebrooke was gone. He would not lose Christian Lassen.

The young Norwegian was quite a different proposition. For a start he was Schlegel's best pupil in Sanskrit, in a sense therefore his intellectual and academic son. Schlegel used the phrase 'fatherly concern',[392] but their correspondence suggests that, as a real father, he would have been fairly demanding, if not overbearing. There were exhortations to thriftiness, Schlegel reminding him that he too had once been a tutor and had known strict 'Oeconomie'.[393] Lassen spent from the autumn of 1823 until May, 1825 in London, the rest of 1825 until the spring of 1826 in Paris, on the scholarship that Schlegel had secured for him. Should further encouragement be necessary, Schlegel told Lassen that it was for his sake and for the furtherance and future of Sanskrit studies that he had pulled strings, taken on the rectorship, written that Latin ode on the king's steamship junket (of which he was proud nevertheless). He encouraged Lassen to diversify,[394] to take advantage of whatever foreign countries could offer (especially France), and to cultivate social graces ('Weltton').

That was all very well, given that Lassen was doing the donkey work for Schlegel's editions: the *Râmâyana* had appeared with only Schlegel's name on the title page (Lassen is thanked in the preface);[395] in the *Hitopadeśa* his role is acknowledged. Back in Bonn he would be helping with the devanagari press, and his presence was required at table with the young Englishmen. He could not move in the same circles as Schlegel in London and was living with the German bookseller Bohte. His views on England and the English were if anything even less flattering than Schlegel's. In Paris, he was caught up in the factions there, with Chézy being unhelpful

---

391 Rocher and Rocher (2013), 179, 181.
392 Kirfel, 22.
393 *Ibid.*, 29.
394 *Ibid.*, 87f.
395 *Râmâyana*, Praef., lxixf.

and obstructive, until Chézy's pupil Burnouf smoothed things over and received him as Schlegel's protégé and 'mon cher *fellow student*'.[396]

Schlegel also had very clear ideas about Lassen's career: doctorate, 'Habilitation', and chair. Missives went off at any sign of seeming unpunctuality. He had to do his master's bidding; it was he who wielded the critical hatchet on Bopp in the last number of the *Indische Bibliothek*. While Lassen duly completed his doctorate and fulfilled all the remaining plans of his fatherly mentor, including a chair in 1840, he also developed enough independence of mind and resilience: his first piece of important scholarship was completed with Burnouf in Paris.[397] His lectures in Bonn — he is listed as a 'professor extraordinarius' from the summer of 1831, a full professor from the winter of 1841-42[398] — suggested that he took much of the burden of teaching elementary Sanskrit off Schlegel's shoulders but also complemented and extended his master's range both in Indian literature and Persian. Apart from those courses on English literature that he gave on the side, Lassen's lectures suggested that oriental studies in Bonn now reflected a professional specialism, not Schlegel's universal approach to knowledge.

Nevertheless theirs is an important correspondence (Schlegel's letters mainly) that tells us of domestic arrangements, the visits to Berlin, Paris and London, Schlegel's larger and smaller vanities, and even the march of technological progress. For if the king's steamboat trip in 1825 had been a sensation, by 1827 a steamer took one to Mainz and back in seven hours.[399] In 1840, a railway was announced for Bonn.[400]

Paris and London Again

It was ultimately Indian matters that took Schlegel again to Paris and London in 1831-32. Leaving Lassen in charge of the proofs of the *Râmâyana*, he was absent in Paris from September 1831 until March 1832, comparing manuscripts of the third editorial project, the *Hitopadeśa*. When not doing this, or when not socially engaged, he was translating into French the lectures that he hoped to deliver in London.[401] He had escaped the cholera that was ravaging Germany (Hegel was its most prominent victim): his letters from

---

396 Burnouf, 2.
397 *Essai sur le pali* […] *par E. Burnouf et Chr. Lassen* (Paris: Dondey-Dupré, 1826).
398 Information in the *Index praelectionum*.
399 Kirfel, 204.
400 *Ibid.*, 229. The section from Bonn to Cologne was completed in 1844.
401 *Ibid.*, 218.

Lassen had been soaked in vinegar by the French border authorities.[402] It was doubtless agreeable to find Chézy in a good frame of mind, or to meet again the ever-friendly Burnouf. Above all, he renewed his links with the Broglie family: the children, Albert and Pauline, were growing up, and he showed an interest in their education. He took a particular shine to Albert, even going to the theatre with him to see the latest play by Victor Hugo.[403] He was sufficiently well-known to be invited by the Prussian ambassador, by Baron Rothschild, by Guizot, but one senses that Broglie influence may have been behind the invitation to the minister of the interior, Casimir-Périer.[404]

Schlegel had noted in the *Indische Bibliothek* in 1827 that the duke of Orleans was the patron of the French Société Asiatique.[405] In that capacity, the duke had also subscribed to the *Râmâyana*.[406] Since the July Revolution of 1830, the duke was now King Louis-Philippe. It was therefore extremely gratifying for Schlegel to receive an invitation to dine at the Tuileries Palace on 8 October, 1831 ('gentlemen to wear uniforms').[407] Full of pride he could report to Altenstein that he had received the Légion d'honneur, had been presented at court, and had walked arm in arm with the king in deep conversation.[408] His detractors might claim that Victor de Broglie, as a minister of state, had orchestrated all this, but Schlegel could count on the king's interest when he sent his Indian writings to him.[409]

The new chevalier was to be showered with invitations and honours during his stay in London, which followed in March and April. Evidently he chose to live in style:[410] lodging in the Brunswick Hotel, enjoying oysters and sherry, purchasing a razor from suppliers to his Majesty or a hat from the Duke of Cumberland's 'hatter, hosier & glover'.[411] *Le tout* of London received him: the Duke of Sussex at Kensington Palace (as President of the Royal Society and the only royal duke remotely interested in things of

---

402 Ibid., 209.
403 SLUB Dresden. Mscr. Dresd. e. 90, XIX, 4 (3), 1. Letter of 21 December 1832 (they had seen *Marion Delorme*).
404 Addresses and invitations SLUB Dresden, Mscr. Dresd. e. 90, XI, V. B.
405 *Indische Bibliothek*, II, 68.
406 List of subscribers in a letter to Treuttel & Würtz 1828. SLUB Dresden, Mscr. Dresd. e. 90, XIX (27) 29.
407 SLUB Dresden, Mscr. Dresd. e. 90, XI, V. B.
408 *Briefe*, I, 497f.
409 Kirfel, 214f.
410 'hat entsetzlich viel gekostet'. Lohner, 210.
411 SLUB Dresden, Mscr. Dresd. e. 90, II, 51.

the mind), Lord Munster (as President of the Royal Asiatic Society), Lord Lansdowne (an old friend of the Staëls); Prince Talleyrand, languishing in 'exile' as ambassador, had him to dinner, as did the Duke of Wellington (another old Staël connection).[412] The Athenaeum, The Royal Society of Literature, the Geographical Society, the Royal Institution all welcomed him. If Henry Colebrooke was too indisposed to see him, at least Sir James Mackintosh had him to breakfast; he met Charles Wilkins; Colonel Tod was absent, but he saw his collection of coins (the Bactrian Greek ones that so interested him);[413] Sir Alexander Johnston entertained him at the Asiatic Society Club.

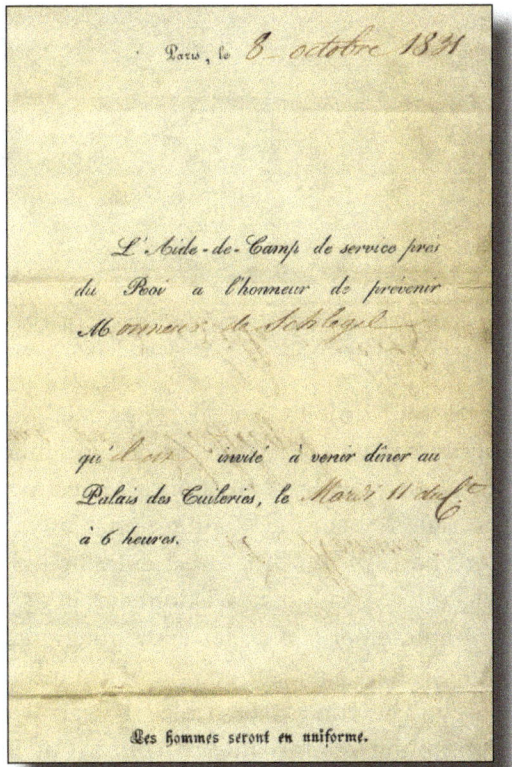

Fig. 31 Schlegel's invitation to the palace of the Tuileries, dated 8 October, 1831. © SLUB Dresden, all rights reserved.

---

412 *Ibid.*, XIX (29), 13.
413 *Oeuvres*, III, 311.

Fig. 32 Schlegel's receipt for the 'Silver Dress Star of the Royal Hanoverian Guelphic Order', 20 March, 1832. © SLUB Dresden, all rights reserved.

One invitation stands out: Sir John Herschel suggested that it might 'not be disagreeable' for him to come to his house near Slough to meet 'the Rajah Ram Ramoham Roy' [sic].[414] Schlegel mentions the meeting with Rammohan Roy but once—he refers to him as 'Râma-mohanaraya'—in a late letter to Rehfues.[415] There he calls him 'the most enlightened of all Brahmins', gratified at Western interest in Indian wisdom and poetry. The symbolism of that encounter would emerge only later: the religious, educational and social reformer, the 'Maker', the 'Father' of modern India, with the 'father' of German Indology. The context of Schlegel's recollection is however significant: his continuing interest in and concern at British policies in India, not least their insensitivities, the 'fanaticism' of missionaries towards local religious beliefs, of whatever kind. It was part of his indignation at Parliament's renewal of the East India Company's privileges, that 'golden colossus with feet of clay'.[416]

---

414 SLUB Dresden, Mscr. Dresd. e. 90, XIX (10), 42.
415 Körner, 'Indologie und Humanität', 160; Bhatti, 'Indienrezeption', 201.
416 Körner, 159.

Schlegel meanwhile was received by King William IV, presenting the king with his Sanskrit works and alluding deferentially to the monarch's protective sceptre extended over his Asiatic subjects. He reminded William too that he was the son of Johann Adolf Schlegel, who had received preferment from King George III, 'of glorious memory'.[417] He was invested with the silver star of the Royal Hanoverian Guelphic Order,[418] another ribbon to stick on his coat.

One would have expected his bliss to be complete. But he did not like England or the English ('the most banausic of people'),[419] despite the outward splendour of their institutions. Lord Munster had to tell him that there was more interest in the Reform Bill than in Asiatic antiquities, Sir James Mackintosh averring optimistically that 'The general Indifference of our Public to all Subjects but one will doubtless be conquered by your Genius & your Fame'.[420] Above all, nothing went according to his wishes or expectations. It was fine to be invited to the general meeting of the Royal Asiatic Society,[421] but less agreeable to find that library opening hours were not as generous as in Bonn (or Paris): he could not pull rank with professorial privilege. Having been treated with due courtesy by German publishers, he found himself let down by none other than John Murray in London.[422] It was all very well for Sir James Mackintosh to write disdainfully about a 'vile trader in Books';[423] these people knew what would really sell, and acted accordingly.

It was not Schlegel's first encounter with British publishers. His Vienna Lectures, as translated by John Black, were out of his hands and brought in no payment, but Murray had published his last political pamphlet in 1814. He and Auguste had had in 1817 to reject Murray's proposals for an 'ephemeral' and unauthorized biography of Madame de Staël.[424] In 1825 John Lockhart had written on Murray's behalf to invite Schlegel to contribute to the *Quarterly Review* (nothing came of this).[425] The idea of Schlegel giving lectures in London went back certainly to 1829, when Sir James Mackintosh and Henry Brougham invited him to deliver a series, in either French or

---

417 *Briefe*, I, 500f.
418 *Ibid.*, II, 227.
419 Kirfel, 217.
420 SLUB Dresden, Mscr. Dresd. e. 90, XIX (15), 95 (Lord Munster), *ibid.*, 12 (Mackintosh).
421 SLUB Dresden, Mscr. Dresd. e. 90, XIX (15), 19.
422 The account of what follows set out in Rocher and Rocher (2013), 165f.
423 SLUB Dresden, Mscr. Dresd. e. 90, XIX (15), 13.
424 Letter of 29 Sept 1817, Murray Archive Ms. 40165, Edinburgh, National Library of Scotland.
425 *Briefe*, I, 632.

English, at the institution they had co-founded: University College in London. It was this highly flattering invitation which Schlegel had quoted at Rehfues as an instance of his international esteem: 'any branch of literature most suited to your own taste', wrote Brougham; 'higher Criticism of German literature', were Mackintosh's words.[426] By 1831 the subject had been narrowed down to Indian literature, and the chosen language was to be French: the ever-punctilious Schlegel, although manifestly fluent and idiomatic in English,[427] may have been afraid of compromising himself. The lectures were to be framed in the form of a letter to Sir James Mackintosh, in which he set out his criteria and principles for the study of Sanskrit. Murray blew hot and cold, until the idea of public lectures and their publication was quietly dropped.[428] In fairness to Murray and Mackintosh, it is hard to imagine lectures by a German professor, delivered in French, drawing in crowds in the year of the Reform Bill, with so many of his potential audience politically engaged. His lectures would have to be dressed up differently if he were to compete with the former successes of Humphry Davy or Coleridge—or even his own minor triumph in Berlin.

In the event Schlegel published his text both in Bonn and Paris, but not in London. These *Réflexions sur l'étude des langages asiatiques*, with their pronounced views on translation from Sanskrit and the tools needed for its acquisition, while impeccable in their recommendations and seeking to exhort British Sanskritists to even greater things, were nevertheless not without their element of hectoring and stridency. Perhaps Schlegel's approach was the right one—it surely was—and academically the British were lagging behind. But did one say this in public and over the name of the now deceased Sir James Mackintosh, to whom Schlegel had been indebted since the days of Madame de Staël?

Nevertheless it is one of the important statements on Sanskrit that Böcking chose to republish. By contrast his essay *De l'Origine des Hindous*, which was brought out in 1833 by the Royal Society of Literature and subsequently republished, would not tell British experts much that they did not know already (or what he had already written himself), and they may have found his anti-Celtic animadversions tiresome, or just plain wrong.

But that letter to Sir James Mackintosh had an appendix. Another source of displeasure had been the filling of the Oxford chair of Sanskrit, the

---

426 To Rehfues (undated) UB Bonn S 1392.
427 Thomas Campbell less flattering. *Campbell*, I, 362.
428 Correspondence AWS to Murray, 9 Nov., 1831, 6 March and 2 April, 1832. AWS's manuscript received by Murray 1 March and returned 7 March, 1832. Murray Archive, Ms. 40165 and 42633, Edinburgh, National Library of Scotland.

newly created Boden professorship.⁴²⁹ It was flattering to be consulted over potential appointees: he saw the young Friedrich Rosen, a pupil of Bopp's recently appointed to University College, as a suitable candidate, but in unreformed Oxford (as opposed to the godless institution in London), one had to subscribe to the Thirty-Nine Articles. Schlegel would really have preferred Graves Chamney Haughton, but he withdrew in favour of H. H. Wilson. This was the same Wilson who, in order to pre-empt Rosen's possible candidature, had presumed to make disparaging remarks about continental orientalists and their acquisition of Sanskrit 'at second hand' (that is, not in India). This caused Schlegel to mount a very high horse indeed, in his general and specific—and public—attack on English academic Sanskrit as practised at the University of Oxford. 'We no longer consult pandits', Wilson would be told; the seat of 'historical and critical philology' was in Europe. The tone was unfortunate. Schlegel overreacted: there was no restraining hand to tell him to play it all down. It brought out prejudices and grievances, a clear failure (or unwillingness) on his part to understand the Oxford collegiate system, unjustified resentment at the East India Company and Haileybury: he had hoped, without any basis for these hopes, for generous subscriptions to his *Hitopadeśa* and they had not materialised.⁴³⁰ All this was compounded by the thought that his Sanskrit editions were not going to pay for themselves, with most of the expenses coming from his own pocket.⁴³¹ There may have been more than a touch of anti-clericalism in his remarks: Wilson's referees seemed to be clergymen. Whatever, there is an abrasiveness of tone paralleled by the satirical verse that he had been writing at the time, none of it good and none of it worthy of him or his intended victims.

The Sanskrit Editions

It was the Sanskrit editions that were, in his eyes, the crowning achievement. When he spoke of Sanskrit, these were the authorities to which he need point. The biographer cannot be concerned with the technical detail of these editions—the business of experts—but with their significance in the scheme of Schlegel's Indian endeavours. Certainly, in a notional Bibliotheca Schlegeliana, a collection of everything that he wrote, they would bulk

---

429 See Rocher and Rocher (2013), 167 and sources quoted there.
430 They subscribed to just ten copies. *Oeuvres*, III, 257.
431 'Eh, monsieur, si je n'avais pas honte de parler des sacrifices pécuniaires que j'ai faits pour faciliter l'étude du Sanscrit.' *Ibid.*, 242.

large: hefty quarto volumes, one of the *Bhagavad-Gîtâ*, three of *Râmâyana*, and two of *Hitopadeśa*.[432] They are a fulfilment of all the promises made to and by Schlegel after his arrival in Bonn, the earnest of the confidence placed in him by Hardenberg, by Altenstein, and so many others (the *Bhagavad-Gîtâ* is in fact dedicated to Altenstein, and its preface stresses 'Regia munificentia').[433]

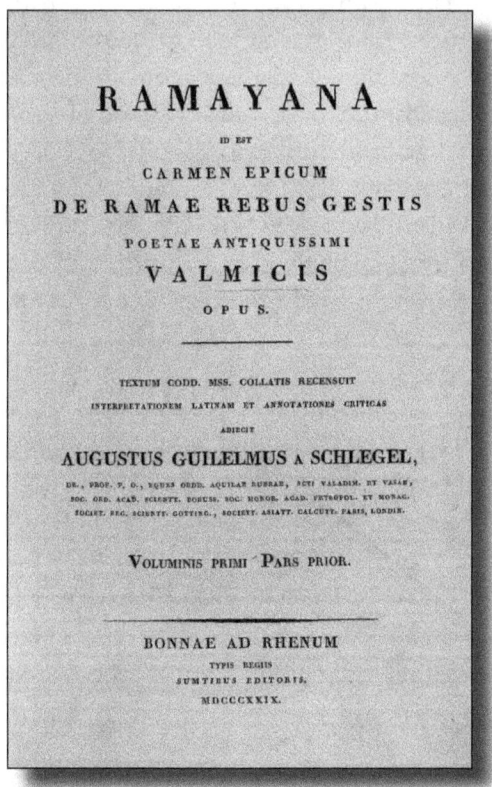

Fig. 33 *Râmâyana*. Schlegel's edition, part 1 of vol. 1 (Bonn, 1829). Title page. © and by kind permission of the Master and Fellows of Trinity College, Cambridge, CC BY-NC 4.0.

---

432 *Bhagavad-Gita, id est* ΘΕΣΠΕΣΙΟΝ ΜΕΛΟΣ, *sive almi Krishnae et Arjunae colloquium de rebus divinis, Bharateae episodium. Textum recensuit, adnotationes criticas et interpretationem Latinam adiecit Augustus Guilelmus a Schlegel* (Bonn: In Academia Borussica Rhenana typis regiis MDCCCXXIII [Bonn: Weber, 1823]); *Ramayana id est carmen epicum de Ramae rebus gestis poetae antiquissimi Valmicis opus. Textum codd. mss. collatis recensuit interpretationem Latinam et annotationes criticas adiecit Augustus Guilelmus a Schlegel,* 2 vols in 3 (Bonnae ad Rhenum: Typis Regiis. Sumtibus Editoris 1828, 1829); *HITOPADESAS id est institutio salutaris. Textum codd. mss. collatis recensuerunt interpretationem Latinam et annotationes criticas adiecerunt Augustus Guilelmus a Schlegel et Christianus Lassen,* 2 parts (Bonnae ad Rhenum: Weber, 1829, 1831) (AWS was responsible for Book 1, Lassen for Book 2).

433 *Bhagavat-Gîtâ*, Praef., vii.

What he says elsewhere in learned asides, in reviews, in letters, in footnotes, in statements of intent, in 'advertisements', is here given the focus of a text and a concrete application. These volumes, and the *Indische Bibliothek*, were what he presented to sovereigns and patrons, the evidence that here was no dilettante, here were no half-measures, but a serious scholar following the most stringent of editorial principles.[434] They had been set and printed in devanagari type on the press paid for by the Prussian government and as such were models of how it was done.[435]

They had exclusivity: the subscription to the *Râmâyana* was the very considerable sum of £4 or 28 talers per volume.[436] The print-runs were correspondingly low: 200 on better paper and 200 on plain for the *Râmâyana*,[437] 200 for *Hitopadeśa*. Hence Schlegel's anxieties as to the East India Company's subscription policies, generous in the case of the former text, seemingly niggardly in respect of the latter.[438] For Schlegel was paying for all this himself: 'my Brahmins have cost me at least 30,000 francs', he confessed ruefully to Victor de Broglie in 1844.[439] Like almost everything else of Schlegel's, the project was unable to fulfil its original ambitious design: the *Râmâyana* was conceived as a seven-volume edition, with a supplement (three appeared);[440] its third volume lacks the Latin translation, and the whole has none of the mythological and geographical index that it promised;[441] the 'Index radicum', the list of Sanskrit roots, to the *Hitopadeśa* never appeared.[442] Such recognition as these editions had—and this applied to the *Indische Bibliothek* as well—was mainly outside Germany (for this he blamed Bopp).

These were editions by a scholar for fellow-scholars. For those who knew Sanskrit, there was the text, established from all the manuscripts known to exist at the time and available for Schlegel to consult. For the Latinate—and who of his readers was not?—there were the learned notes,

---

434 *Briefe*, II, 222.
435 Cf. Schlegel's report to Altenstein in 1829, *Briefe*, II, 212-224.
436 *Râmâyana* [...] *Adverstisement* (London, November, 1823), 8; Briefe, II, 213; SLUB Dresden Mscr. Dresd. e. 90, X.
437 *Briefe*, II, 213.
438 The East India College subscribed generously to AWS's *Bhagavad-Gîtâ* (40 copies), because it was a useful new edition; it subscribed to his *Râmâyana* to the tune of 10 copies (a considerable outlay); but it had sufficient copies of an older edition of the *Hitopadeśa* (communication from Rosane and Ludo Rocher).
439 *Briefe*, I, 612f. The half-title of vol. 1 of *Râmâyana* has 'Rameidos Valmiceiae libri septem'.
440 *Indische Bibliothek*, II, 141, 147; *Râmâyana* [...] *Advertisement*, 1-8, ref. 7.
441 *Indische Bibliothek*, II, 138, 146.
442 SLUB Dresden, Mscr. Dresd. e. 90, LIII.

and for the non-Sanskritists (but not just for them) a translation. Sanskrit text, translation and notes together established an authority of textual reading and interpretation. Arthur Schopenhauer was such a Latinate general reader of the *Bhagavad-Gîtâ*,[443] and an early twentieth-century translator of the same text could claim that Schlegel's Latin version was still the best.[444] The commitment to Latinity in the 1820s and 1830s was part of an older scholarly discourse; Schlegel also was in no doubt that Latin, with its constructions, its abstracts and compounds, was the appropriate vehicle into which to render the ancient and venerable language.[445]

It did not call for 'user-friendliness', not a marked feature of nineteenth-century textual scholarship: the reader of Schlegel's *Bhagavad-Gîtâ* was faced with Sanskrit text, then notes, then the translation itself (Bopp's *Nalus*, by contrast, printed the Latin translation beneath the Sanskrit text, but 'Boppius', about whose Latin Schlegel and Lassen were dismissive, had done a literal version, altogether lacking Schlegel's sense of style).[446] The *Râmâyana* edition by contrast had footnotes to the Latin translation.

Schlegel had of course never intended it to be other than hard going, and his priorities make this clear. A scholarly edition proceeded from the primacy of and respect for the text (he salutes the author of the *Bhagavad-Gîtâ*, acknowledges its eternal truths, and hopes that none of his readings will detract from its message).[447] In this he differed markedly from his brother Friedrich ('frater dilectissime' 'dearest brother'—still in 1823),[448] who back in 1808 had not been able to resist speculation about the status of a perceived monotheism in the *Bhagavad-Gîtâ* and its relationship to the sacred writings of the Hebrews; or from Wilhelm von Humboldt, who had devoted a whole treatise to the philosophical content of the work,[449] and

---

443 Arthur Schopenhauer, *Werke in fünf Bänden*, ed. Ludger Lütkehans, 5 vols and 1 supplement, Haffmanns Taschenbuch, 121-126 (Zurich: Haffmans, 1988-91), III, 631; V, 348.
444 *Bhagavad- Gîtâ. Des Erhabenen Sang*, trans. Leopold von Schroeder, Religiöse Stimmen der Völker: Die Religion des Alten Indien, 2 (Jena: Diederichs, 1919), ii.
445 *Bhagavad-Gîtâ*, Praef., xxiii; *Hitopadeśa*, I, xvi.
446 *Nalus Maha-Bharati episodium. Textus Sanscritus cum interpretatione Latina et annotationibus criticis curante Francisco Bopp*, 2nd ed (Berlolini: Nicolai, 1827). On Schlegel's fraught relationship with Bopp see Ralf Georg Czapla, 'Annäherungen an das ferne Fremde. August Wilhelm Schlegels Kontroverse mit Friedrich Rückert und Franz Bopp über die Vermittlung von indischer Religion und Mythologie', *Jahrbuch der Rückert-Gesellschaft*, 17 (2006-07), 131-151.
447 *Bhagavad-Gîtâ*, Praef., xxvi, Adnott., 126.
448 *Ibid.*, Praef., xxvi.
449 'Ueber die unter dem Namen Bhagavad-Gita bekannte Episode des Maha-Bharata' (1825-26).

for whom the study of Sanskrit was more than a metrical, grammatical or philological exercise. It would of course be unfair to impute this to Schlegel or reduce his labours to this one aspect only (although his correspondence with Humboldt does circle mainly around language). Yet the 'Advertisement' of the *Râmâyana* edition that Treuttel & Würtz issued for its English subscribers in 1823 made his priorities clear:[450] first, 'genuineness and correctness of the text', the 'duty of an editor to clear up every thing that is obscure', then and only then remarks about the 'classical literature of the ancient Brahmins' and 'ancient religion' but also about '*Comparative Grammar*'. There follows a short description of the ancient Indian epic, not without a nod in the direction of Homer, then the technical details of the edition and its 'typographical execution'.[451]

Staying with the *Râmâyana*, as the most complex of the three textual editions, we note in its preface a similar set of priorities: an account of the ancient poet Vâlmîki, but also, the oral tradition, the stages of transmission, the analogy with Homer (F. A. Wolf is the authority cited). We hear of the interpolation of episodes from older sources, the writing down of the text (on palm leaves); we learn of the language itself and its fullness and richness ('ubertas').[452] A long section on his use of commentaries follows, then the account of his archival searches in Paris and London (and, briefly and shamefully, Oxford). Last of all he lists the names of those to whom he is indebted: Wilkins, Davy, Tod, Colebrooke, Noehden, Malcolm, Mackintosh, Johnston, Haughton, Abel-Rémusat, Wilhelm and Alexander von Humboldt, a roll-call of excellence and expertise. Before this resounding peroration of names, we find also '*Christianus Lassen*': only he and Schlegel knew how much the edition owed to this 'olim discipulus meus' [former pupil of mine].[453] Chézy's name is absent.

In a sense Schlegel wished his texts to speak for themselves, always his practice as a translator. But this was a philological exercise as well: the notes to the *Râmâyana* gloss points of scansion, but dilate also on matters botanical, zoological, geographical, astrological and mythological. As such the Sanskrit editions became also a focus and repository for a universal antiquarianism, an 'omni-philology', a tireless search to the utmost bounds of 'science' as understood at its fullest and most encyclopaedic.

---

450 *Râmâyana* [...] *Advertisement* (London, November 1823), 1-8. The same in French and German in *Indische Bibliothek*, II, 135-148.
451 *Advertisement*, refs 3, 4, 5, 6, 7.
452 *Râmâyana*, Praef., xx.
453 *Râmâyana*, Praef., lxix.

5. The Past Returns

All this might suggest years preoccupied with things Indian. The reality was different. His life could not be neatly compartmentalized in order to shut out other pressing realities. Such as Sophie von Knorring (as she now was), the baroness from Livonia. Schlegel may have forgotten his promise to write a preface for her medievalising epic *Flore und Blanscheflure*.[1] She had not. Effusive as ever, and appealing to their old friendship, she took advantage of a visit to Germany in 1821-22 to remind him of his undertaking. She even used her son Felix Theodor Bernhardi, now a student in Heidelberg—and a broad hint at what their relationship had once been—to jog his memory. If Schlegel did not reply soon enough, she wrote again, and yet again. He finally caved in, found a publisher (Reimer in Berlin) and wrote a preface.[2] Reimer, cutting his losses, left out her own foreword.[3]

Schlegel, taking time out from his *Indische Bibliothek* and his lecturing, did not disappoint her. He had, his preface states, never given up his belief that 'simple, energetic and godfearing ages' had been strongest in poetic invention. But we have their texts often only in the original languages, which few can now read, or in prose corruptions. Imitations are problematic: either they take liberties (like Ariosto) or they fail to render the subtleties of the original verse. Where did *Flore und Blanscheflur*—a story of love across the Muslim-Christian divide—come from? Certainly not from France (definitely not from the Charlemagne cycle), and most likely from the East (one almost expects him to say: India). Sophie Tieck had captured well both

---

[1]   Her letters in *Krisenjahre*, II, 382-408, Felix Theodor's 405f.; unpublished letters SLUB Dresden, Mscr. Dresd. e. 90, XIX (13), 25-26.

[2]   *Flore und Blanscheflur. Ein episches Gedicht in zwölf Gesängen von Sophie v. Knorring, geb. Tieck. Herausgegeben und mit einer Vorrede begleitet von A. W. von Schlegel* (Berlin: Reimer, 1822), iii-xxxiv. *SW*, VII, 272-280. On this work see Richert, *Die Anfänge*, 68f.

[3]   *Krisenjahre*, II, 406-408.

the letter and the spirit: it was what he had once tried himself with his poem *Tristan*. He did not say her brother Ludwig had once essayed this genre with far greater success. The market had changed since then: *Flore und Blanscheflur* remained a literary curiosity, not a reminder of Sophie Tieck's real literary talent.

With this, the Knorring correspondence ebbed away. He was spared a visitation in Bonn. Yet as late as 1838, Sophie's husband Knorring wondered if there was a chance of a French or English translation of *Flore und Blanscheflur*. It was an act of piety: Sophie had died in 1833.[4]

Friedrich Schlegel

This was as nothing compared with the rift between the brothers Schlegel. Strong expressions have been used: Schlegel's nineteenth-century editors Minor and Walzel spoke of fratricide.[5] Some sober facts are therefore in order. Apart from Schlegel's last three letters, of which he appears to have kept copies, only Friedrich's have survived, themselves sporadic. August Wilhelm seems to be making peremptory demands, but these may well be a final, exasperated repetition of things already stated. But even this we do not know with any certainty. Sometimes they were open with each other, sometimes not. There had been Friedrich's wise counsel to his brother in the matter of his marriage, but he had not told August Wilhelm about his own quasi-mystical, quasi-erotic relationship with Frau Christine von Stransky, one of the circumstances attending his journey to Munich in 1827 'for his health's sake'.[6] It does seem that the brothers could find a common basis of agreement and interest when in private conversation, as last in 1818. When Friedrich went into print, however, the tone changed, his position became more extreme. August Wilhelm claimed that he had not been prepared for the 'reactionary' tone of *Concordia* ('Discordia'); by the time the second volume appeared, in 1823, he had experienced the Carlsbad Decrees, Metternich's anti-liberal clamp-down on the German lands. Friedrich, by contrast, was unworried by the muzzling of the press;[7] he had allegedly written a poem to the queen of Spain, welcoming the restoration of the

---

4 Ibid., 507f.
5 Jakob Minor, 'August Wilhelm von Schlegel in den Jahren 1804-1845', *Zeitschrift für die Österreichischen Gymnasien* 38 (1887), 590-613, 733-753, ref. 745; Walzel, xx.
6 Walzel, 652.
7 Ibid., 658.

Bourbons there and the reaction that went with it.[8] August Wilhelm had wanted to make a public statement as early as 1822, dissociating himself from his brother. Henriette Mendelssohn, Dorothea's sister living in Paris, had dissuaded him, for the sake of family harmony.[9] He had on the other hand nothing but praise for his brother's pioneering work on Sanskrit: it was convenient to remind all and sundry that a Schlegel had been there first, not, say, Bopp. But Friedrich had not reissued *Ueber die Sprache und Weisheit der Indier* in the *Sämmtliche Werke*, the edition of his works that he had been bringing out since 1822. Those volumes contained much that was not to his brother's liking.

For all that, Schlegel hesitated to attack his brother openly and by name. In the preface that he wrote in 1825 to Johann Heinrich Bohte's catalogue of German literature for sale in London (*Abriß von den Europäischen Verhältnissen der Deutschen Litteratur*),[10] he had stressed the autonomy of scholarly investigation, the free flow of ideas, the freedom of the press. He cited Frederick the Great's edict of tolerance, so different from the English who had a habit of prosecuting publishers and booksellers. It would apply equally to Friedrich Schlegel's adopted country, Metternich's Austria. This was the Prussian professor setting himself against the servant of the Austrian state.

Again, he did not mention Friedrich by name in the long pamphlet that Reimer published in 1828, *Berichtigung einiger Missdeutungen* [Correction of Some Misapprehensions].[11] This was to be his most comprehensive public autobiographical account, the most unequivocal statement of his later views on religion. It was in response to that article in 'Baron' d'Eckstein's *Le Catholique*, claiming that August Wilhelm Schlegel was 'half-Catholic' (which half, it did not say); more extensively, it was a rebuttal of allegations of crypto-Catholicism directed posthumously at him by Johann Heinrich Voss, in the second part of his polemic, *Anti-Symbolik* (1827). It was an extraordinary performance of self-justification against the ever-rampageous Voss, whose mind was slightly unhinged by the wave of conversions that he saw Romanticism as having initiated. On the one hand Schlegel set out his impeccable anti-Napoleonic credentials against Voss's secure professorial existence in Heidelberg during those same years, when

---

8   Kaufmann, 'Zur Erinnerung', 247.
9   *KA*, XXX, 242.
10 *SW*, VIII, 207-219.
11 *Ibid.*, 220-284.

the nation might have needed him. On the other it was a part-recantation of the Catholicizing attitudes of his early manhood, part, because, for all the whiffs of incense and rustlings of vestments, his concern had always been with the highest things in art. He could justify that poem on the union of the church with the arts as a statement of art history, *Die Gemälde* from the *Athenaeum* similarly (reissued in the same year in his *Kritische Schriften*), similarly.

Now, he was all for tolerance, freedom of esteem, liberty of the press, the right of reply. Let there be conversations by all means, but they must not involve the stifling of intellectual debate, the surrender to a spiritual authority, the descent into Catholic apologetics, and—here surely meaning Friedrich—polemics on the 'Zeitgeist' that were in reality only the immutable positions of Rome. We must be on our guard against reaction, as in the restorations in France and Spain. All this was compatible with a continuing interest in Christian art, as evidenced by his article on Fra Angelico: Sulpiz Boisserée hoped that he might write something on Cologne cathedral for his *Kunstblatt*.[12]

It was to be seen against the background of Friedrich's lectures on the 'philosophy of life' in Vienna in 1827 and on the philosophy of history in Dresden in 1828, and finally, on the philosophy of language and word, also in Dresden. In the last letters that they exchanged, Friedrich returned to those good days on the Rhine in 1818, when there had been no differences; he regretted August Wilhelm's absence from the last family gathering in the autumn of 1824. Now, within a short space of time, their brother Moritz had died, then their sister Charlotte and her husband Ludwig Emanuel Ernst.[13] Then came the news of Auguste von Buttlar's conversion; she was living in Vienna, and August Wilhelm automatically blamed his brother Friedrich's malign influence.[14] By now, August Wilhelm had had enough. He asked Friedrich to contribute towards the support of Moritz's widow. Friedrich could not: he had been in debt since 1818, to Windischmann and above all to his brother August Wilhelm. Adopting a slightly self-pitying tone, he claimed that Moritz, 'whom he had esteemed as a brother and a father',[15] would not have wished any family discord. There it was, between the lines: Friedrich, the youngest sibling, the 'problem child', taken under

---

12 *Briefe*, I, 412.
13 Walzel, 653.
14 SLUB Dresden, Mscr. Dresd. e. 90, XIX (3), 136.
15 Walzel, 655.

his brother Moritz's wing, while August Wilhelm, clever and precocious, had been smiled upon by their father. But surely their common, collective presence was better than public disagreement.

These arguments could not move August Wilhelm. He announced that he would declare his 'public antagonism' to Friedrich as a writer,[16] believing that the late Moritz would have shared his views on *Concordia*, as 'anti-philosophical, anti-historical, and anti-social'.[17] Of course he never attacked his brother personally in public, only the ideas he believed him to represent. He then asked—yet again—for repayment of the old bad debt of 1818, the 300 florins that Friedrich had needed for his return from Frankfurt to Vienna. A death—he did not say whose—had placed him in financial embarrassment. Did Schlegel really need 300 florins all that urgently, and what for?[18] In a letter to Schulze of November, 1826, he mentions financial difficulties, even having to pawn an Indian statue: rumours about his wealth and life-style were not justified. The *Râmâyana* was keeping him poor, the Sanskrit editions were a constant drain on his finances.[19] His house, into which he had sunk most of his capital, was another burden. But surely he would not wish to bankrupt his brother. His life-style was not extravagant, only comfortable. Friedrich, too, enjoyed the good things of life, but without the means to afford them. It was a symbolic calling in of all those advances and loans that had disappeared into the bottomless pit of Friedrich and Dorothea's financial mismanagement. But the patience and goodwill that had once accompanied them were now exhausted.

Friedrich was in bad health, grossly corpulent and subject to a series of minor strokes.[20] He had been upset at the death of his fellow-convert Adam Müller, one of the contributors to *Concordia*. Yet nothing could stem the flow of his thoughts and his lecturing.[21] Now, he was staying in Dresden with his niece Auguste von Buttlar (she was sorting out her parents' estate) and had given his last lecture on 10 January, 1829. That morning he had received the sacrament. In the evening, while sitting with Auguste, he was taken ill with a massive stroke. A doctor could not be summoned, and the distraught Auguste had to watch her beloved uncle, struggling for breath,

---

16 *Ibid.,* 653.
17 *Ibid.,* 656.
18 *Ibid.,* 666.
19 *Briefe,* I, 443f., II, 223.
20 'Anfälle von apoplektischer Natur'. *Briefe,* I, 477.
21 *Ibid.,* I, 477.

his face distorted, until 'a serenity covered his features in death'.[22] He was buried in the Catholic cemetery in Dresden.

Schlegel made no claim on his brother's estate, remaining on polite terms with his sister-in-law Dorothea, consoled by her sons and her piety. He took in Moritz's son Johann August Adolph,[23] already displaying signs of mental disorder. He made his peace with Auguste. On the subject of Friedrich's literary *Nachlass* he remained equivocal. In a long letter to Windischmann, of 29 December, 1834,[24] he set out his considered views. His brother's writings on philosophy and theology were clearly still a stumbling-block. All of his work, he said, early and late, was marked by paradox and abrupt change. Whether or not one chose to republish his early works—those from the *Lyceum* or the *Athenaeum* (but not the 'foolish rhapsody' *Lucinde*)—the many turnings in his way of thinking must be manifest. 'Comet-like' was the word he used to characterize his brother, with its connotations of brilliance, eccentricity, and eye-catching changes of trajectory.

Ludwig Tieck

To compound the feelings aroused by his family, old friends came back into his ambit. Above all, there was Ludwig Tieck, a notoriously bad correspondent. Their once fairly frequent exchange of letters had come to a standstill. He and Schlegel had actually not met since Jena; they had missed each other in Rome in 1805, in Paris and Frankfurt in 1817. It was the other Tieck siblings, Sophie and Friedrich, who had written, with their catalogue of woes, some real, some imaginary. A constant theme had been the feline egoism of their brother Ludwig, his free use of others' money, his absences and disappearances. Now, since 1819, he was installed in a ménage à trois in Dresden, with his wife and Countess Henriette von Finckenstein, plus his daughters, the talented Dorothea and the less talented Agnes. Since 1825, he had been 'Dramaturg' at the royal theatre in Dresden, as well as re-inventing himself as a writer of short fiction. He, too, had been in Italy, England and France. On the subject of Friedrich Schlegel, to whom he had once been close, he inclined towards August Wilhelm's position.

---

22   *Ibid.*, 479f., II, 211.
23   *Ibid.*, 489.
24   *SW*, VIII, 285-293.

Thus when he came to stay for two weeks in Bonn in 1828,[25] they had more or less to reconstruct their friendship. Tieck had paved the way by dedicating a volume of his recently reissued works to Schlegel.[26] No doubt Tieck's charm and conversation helped, for there was an issue between them in the figure of William Shakespeare.[27] It was to strain their newly reforged friendship to the utmost (Tieck, as usual, wondering what all the fuss was about). It mattered to Schlegel, because a section of the German reading public still associated his name with his Shakespeare translation. To the public's chagrin and his publisher's vexation, he had left it unfinished. Reimer, who had taken the enterprise over from Unger's widow, tried to stir Schlegel into action by republishing the nine volumes in 1816-18 and again in 1821-23.[28] Schlegel was however never going to be in a position to deliver. Against his better judgment—and, as it emerged, his publisher's too—he allowed Reimer to enter into a contract with Ludwig Tieck to complete the task. He had never had a particularly high opinion of Tieck's skills as a Shakespeare translator—he had pointedly refused the offer of a version of *Love's Labour's Lost* from Tieck as far back as 1808[29]—and Tieck's renderings of pseudo-Shakespeareana and 'Old Plays', *Alt-Englisches Theater* (1811) and *Shakspeare's Vorschule* (1823, 1829) were hardly the 'real thing'.

Tieck had further surprises up his sleeve. He was not going to do the actual translating himself, entrusting this to Wolf von Baudissin and to his own daughter Dorothea. Schlegel could not object to Baudissin, whom he knew personally and whose own translation of *King Henry VIII* (1818) could be regarded as the completion of his own versions of the Histories.[30] Dorothea was as yet an unknown factor. In the event both proved to be highly competent. The problem was Tieck himself. He subjected their versions to his scrutiny, which was understandable. He also went much further: he appended a scholarly apparatus which enabled him to set out

---

25 Lohner, 183-185, 187-189.
26 Ludwig Tieck, *Schriften*, 20 vols (Berlin: Reimer, 1828-46). IV is dedicated to Schleiermacher but contains (3f.), as part of the opening of *Phantasus*, the warm tribute, 'An A.W. Schlegel'. V is dedicated to AWS and is similarly cordial in its remarks [iii-viii].
27 Most of this set out in 'Schreiben an Herrn Buchhändler Reimer in Berlin', *SW*, VII, 281-302.
28 Details in Christine Roger, *La Réception de Shakespeare en Allemagne de 1815 à 1850. Propagation et assimilation de la référence étrangère*, Theatrica, 24 (Berne etc.: Peter Lang, 2008), 367.
29 Lohner, 165f.
30 Bernd Goldmann, *Wolf Heinrich Graf Baudissin. Leben und Werk eines großen Übersetzers* (Hildesheim: Gerstenberg, 1981), 115f.

his own—often highly wayward—ideas on Shakespeare's datings, editions and readings. Schlegel, having seen Eschenburg's edition and its unhappy merging of translation and scholarly apparatus, had resolutely set his face against the 'contamination' of his own. He certainly never had the ambition of being an editor of Shakespeare, giving his readers the text, nothing else.

Tieck was also dilatory. The edition started coming out in 1825, but was not completed until 1833. By then the 'Cyclopian family' (Friedrich Schlegel's uncomplimentary name)[31] that was Johann Heinrich Voss and his sons Abraham and Heinrich, had finished the first ever complete German metrical Shakespeare. Voss had for good measure ensured that his preface contained some uncomplimentary words for Schlegel.[32] No-one willingly reads Voss today. In the nineteenth century however his was one among many Shakespeares that jostled on the market.[33] Carl Joseph Meyer's was another, and it was far cheaper than Reimer's. Worse still, Tieck put on the title page 'translated by August Wilhelm von Schlegel and Ludwig Tieck', never revealing the identity of either collaborator (who had done all the work in his name), and making 'corrections' to Schlegel's text. Not that this itself was beyond improvement: it would have been only fair to have allowed Schlegel the option of carrying out such a revision. One could even argue that Tieck's suppression of his own daughter's role was no worse than Schlegel's reticence on Caroline's: neither is laudable.

For the time being Schlegel was too preoccupied with other matters to be able to influence the issue. In 1838-39, however, he returned to the subject, pressing Reimer with demands for changes. It was almost as if he recognized, as his career was ebbing away, that this translation would remain his supreme achievement when everything else was forgotten, and that his Shakespeare essays were 'classics' of their kind. (One also notes a major reworking of the Vienna Lectures about this time.) He even harried Reimer to accept re-revisions, restorations of his original: he was only able to do *King John*, *King Richard II* and *1 King Henry IV*, before his energy ran out. A revised 'Schlegel-Tieck' came out in 1839-41,[34] neither the original text nor a proper revision, and a misnomer as such. For the 'Schlegel-Tieck',

---

31 Walzel, 573.
32 Roger Paulin, *The Critical Reception of Shakespeare in Germany 1682-1914. Native Literature and Foreign Genius*, Anglistische und Amerikanistische Texte und Studien, 11 (Hildesheim etc.: Olms, 2003), 334.
33 See Roger, *La Réception de Shakespeare*, esp. 367-373. Cf. AWS's poem on the many versions of the witches' chorus in *Macbeth*. SW, II, 223f.
34 Roger, 376.

as the standard German translation is known and as such is still in print, is not the one of 1797-1810 and it represents a back-handed compliment to Germany's greatest translator. If one wishes to cite Shakespeare according to Schlegel, it is to Unger's and Reimer's originals that one must return. There has never been a full reissue of Schlegel's text since 1823, which is surely a national disgrace.

Goethe

Schlegel forgave Ludwig Tieck: he liked him as a person and he had a weakness for his friend's Romantic verse. The dedication of a volume of Tieck's *Schriften* and the re-evocation there of the spirit of Jena mollified him, also the reminder that it was Schlegel who first discovered Tieck's talent.[35] Tieck was a friend, if an occasionally wayward one. What of Goethe, whom he (and his brother Friedrich) had always enshrined as the incarnation of the modern in German poetry, the consummate artist, a kind of 'Weltgeist', a name that stood comparison with Dante or Shakespeare or Calderón? Goethe, to whom Schlegel had been close in Jena and who had extended his patronage to the younger man, who had used Schlegel's Shakespeare for the Weimar stage (not Schlegel's 'pure' text, but no matter); who had received Madame de Staël—the list could be extended. Of course it had not been all deference: there was Schlegel's published letter from Rome in 1805 that can hardly have pleased Goethe, or the faint praise in the Vienna Lectures. Schlegel could appreciate Friedrich's and Dorothea's indignation that Goethe had failed to mention the Romantic contribution to the understanding of German medieval art and shared their displeasure at his sponsoring of Heinrich Meyer's attack on the Nazarene painters in Rome. If Goethe did not care for Indian art, he took a ready interest in Indian poetry and thought, noting the receipt of the *Bhagavad-Gîtâ* edtion and ensuring that the ducal library in Weimar subscribed to the *Râmâyana*.[36]

On August 28, 1826 admirers of Goethe in Bonn had foregathered to celebrate his seventy-seventh birthday in the romantic setting of Nonnenwörth island, on the Rhine. Schlegel had written the birthday ode (where 'Göthe' rhymed with 'Morgenröthe' [dawn]).[37] On his way to Berlin,

---

35   Tieck, *Schriften*, IV, [4].
36   Wieneke, 261.
37   Ibid., 260; SW, I, 156; Josef Körner, *Romantiker und Klassiker. Die Brüder Schlegel in ihren Beziehungen zu Schiller und Goethe* (Darmstadt: Wissenschaftliche Buchgesellschaft, 1971 [1924]), 211.

at the end of April, 1827, he had been received in Weimar by Goethe with full honours: Goethe listened with interest as Schlegel explained matters of Indian art and poetry.[38] Goethe had thanked Schlegel with a copy of his printed poem 'Am acht und zwanzigsten August 1826' [On the 28th of August 1826], with a lithographed signature, adding a personal greeting to a similar note on the same day in 1829.[39]

All this seemed fine, but for Goethe there was always the unseen presence of Schiller. For all his proclamation of an age of 'Weltliteratur' (which others, unacknowledged, had already ushered in, Wieland and Schlegel among them), Goethe's real literary canon in his later years, what really mattered, consisted of the Greek and Latin classics, Schiller, and himself.[40] Schiller's canonization was proceeding apace, but not fast enough for Goethe (his statue in Stuttgart, the first to a national poet, would follow in 1838). He remembered the Romantics'—the Schlegel brothers'— acts of disloyalty and disparagement to Schiller, their seeming duplicity, sidling up to him, Goethe, while writing Schiller out of the account in the *Athenaeum*, for instance. Schlegel's curt treatment of Schiller in the Vienna Lectures had not gone unnoticed. Already in 1815, in a particularly fierce remark to Sulpiz Boisserée, he had vowed to 'be revenged on the whole pack' of the Romantics.[41] Thus, primarily to remind the world of the wide significance of their 'Commercium', their symbiotic collaboration and intellectual exchange, but also to set the record straight, he decided as a first step to publish his correspondence with Schiller.[42]

It was part of a general settling of scores. Schlegel had issued his own *Kritische Schriften* in 1828,[43] containing almost entirely the production of

---

38 Wieneke, 261f.
39 SLUB Dresden, Mscr. Dresd. e. 90, XIX (9), 29-30.
40 Cf. Benedikt Jessing, 'Der Kanon des späten Goethe', in: Anett Lütteken et al. (eds), *Der Kanon im Zeitalter der Aufklärung. Beiträge zur historischen Kanonforschung* (Göttingen: Wallstein, 2009), 164-177, ref. 177.
41 Boisserée, *Tagebücher*, II, i, 228.
42 *Briefwechsel zwischen Schiller und Goethe in den Jahren 1794 bis 1805*, 6 parts (Stuttgart and Tübingen: Cotta, 1828-29). The correspondence from 1794 up to the end of 1796 was published in 1828 (parts 1-2), the rest, up to 1805, in 1829 (parts 3-6).
43 August Wilhelm von Schlegel, *Kritische Schriften*, 2 parts (Berlin: Reimer, 1828). I: iii-xviii Vorrede; 1-14 'Abriß von den Europäischen Verhältnissen der Deutschen Litteratur'; 15-73 'Ueber einige Werke von Goethe'; 74-163 'Homers Werke von Voß'; 164-178 'Die Gesundbrunnen'; 179-257 'Der Wettstreit der Sprachen'; 258-264 'Ueber kritische Zeitschriften'; 265-321 'Beurtheilung einiger Schauspiele und Romane'; 322-324 'Rollenhagens Froschmeuseler'; 325-330 'Jakob Balde'; 331-337 'Salomon Geßner'; 338-364 'Chamfort'; 365-386 'Ueber den dramatischen Dialog'; 387-416 'Ueber Shakspeare's Romeo und Julia'; 417-436 'Urtheile, Gedanken und Einfälle'. II: 1-81

the past, some of it ephemeral, but most of it good and solid, occasionally even brilliant, the best things he ever wrote, one might say of some of them, but associated with a Romantic movement that many, Heinrich Heine among them, wished to see consigned to history. Novalis was long dead; Friedrich Schlegel's multiform talents were being directed more and more to the Ultramontane and the chiliastic; Ludwig Tieck had abandoned the 'wondrous fairy-tale world' [wunderbare Märchenwelt] for the more prosaic and everyday; Schleiermacher had returned to theology; Schelling's star was being occluded by 'Sanct Hegelius' (Alexander von Humboldt in uncomplimentary vein to Schlegel).[44] Schlegel toyed with the idea of issuing his collected works, as his brother Friedrich was doing (minus the literary sins of his youth), or Tieck, or Jean Paul. It might have assembled much that was for so long to sink out of public consciousness or was republished only in 1846-47 when his reputation was already beginning to slump.

There was no question of Schlegel using his *Kritische Schriften* as a response to Goethe; at most, the general tone of self-justification might have annoyed the great man, nothing more. There was no reason for him to be displeased with what Schlegel had had to say in the 1790s, now reprinted, on his *Roman Elegies*, *Tasso*, or *Hermann und Dorothea*, if anything some slightly pedantic additional remarks might irk. But the various small pin-pricks against Schiller, especially his versification, made it clear where Schlegel stood. The tone was otherwise generally unrepentant:[45] Schlegel reprinted his essay on Bürger (a corrective to Schiller), various contributions to the *Athenaeum*, not least *Die Gemälde* and the Flaxman essay, his piece on *Ion*, his letter to Goethe from Rome, his more recent review of Fra Angelico, even his appreciation of Gérard's Staël-Corinne. And indeed why not?

Goethe also had no reason for repentance. His act of piety towards Schiller did not prevent him from striking quite a hard bargain with Cotta and with Schiller's widow, but no matter.[46] In the six parts that came out in 1828 and 1829, containing the letters from 1794 to the end of 1796, Schlegel, as he cut the volumes open, would have found little to upset him

---

'Bürger'; 82-121 'Matthisson, Voß und F. W. A. Schmidt'; 122-127 'Regulus'; 128-144 'Ueber den Deutschen Ion'; 145-252 'Die Gemälde'; 253-309 'Ueber Zeichnungen zu Gedichten und John Flaxman's Umrisse'; 310-336 'Ueber das Verhältniß der schönen Kunst zur Natur'; 337-370 'Schreiben an Goethe'; 371-411 'Johann von Fiesole'; 412-420 'Corinna auf dem Vorgebirge Miseno'.

44 SLUB Dresden, Mscr. Dresd. e. 90, XIX (11), 34.
45 *Kritische Schriften*, I, iiif.
46 Siegfried Unseld, *Goethe und seine Verleger* (Frankfurt am Main, Leipzig: Insel, 1991), 572-600.

personally. His brother Friedrich might be less pleased, but then again back in the 1790s he had been consorting with Schiller's *bête noire,* the hated Reichardt. The remaining parts of his correspondence with Schiller, that appeared in 1829—Friedrich was by now dead—contained Schiller's unflattering remarks on Friedrich Schlegel and his almost physical disgust at the *Athenaeum.* It was not so much Schiller's individual remarks as the awareness that these Romantics, for Goethe's and Schiller's concerns, were at worst an irrelevance and at best useful allies. It might appear that Goethe's tolerance towards them, his conciliatory words to Schiller, were little more than a front. The correspondence could give the impression that there was no outside world, no affairs of state, no domesticity (not for Goethe, at least), only the common pursuit. It would not emerge that both Goethe and Schiller for brief periods had exchanged notes with Schlegel with similar frequency.

How different, how much more intimate and natural the correspondence between Schiller and Wilhelm von Humboldt, that Humboldt published in 1830, and how much more conciliatory his 80-page preface ('Ueber Schiller und den Gang seiner Geistesentwicklung' [On Schiller and the Development of his Mind]). Above all, Humboldt had deliberately left out any remarks of Schiller's that might offend Schlegel.[47] There was much more of Schlegel's being a 'splendid acquisition' for *Die Horen*.[48]

Goethe however had some more shots in his locker and they were to be delivered posthumously. It was inevitable that the hagiography that started in earnest after his death would wish to publish more of his *obiter dicta*. In the correspondence between Goethe and Zelter that was brought out in 1833-34, Schlegel could read:

> The brothers Schlegel, for all their fine gifts, are and have been unhappy men all their lives; they wanted to present more than their nature had endowed them with, and achieve more than they were able. Thus they have wrought much havoc in art and literature. From the false doctrines in the fine arts that they preached and spread abroad, that conjoined egoism with weakness, German artists and connoisseurs have not yet recovered.[49]

---

47 As Humboldt makes clear to AWS. Leitzmann, 251f.
48 *Briefwechsel zwischen Schiller und Wilhelm v. Humboldt. Mit einer Vorerinnerung über Schiller und den Gang seiner Geistesentwicklung von W. von Humboldt* (Stuttgart and Tübingen: Cotta, 1830), 312, 347.
49 Letter to Zelter of 26 October, 1831. *Briefwechsel zwischen Goethe und Zelter in den Jahren 1796 bis 1832. Herausgegeben von Dr. Friedrich Wilhelm Riemer*, 6 vols (Berlin: Duncker und Humblot, 1833-34), VI, 318.

In an odd inversion of Schlegel's letter to him of 1 November, 1824, Goethe continued:

> Seen it its true light, their turning to India was no more than a pis-aller. They were clever enough to see that in the fields of German and Greek and Latin there was nothing brilliant for them to do; and so they threw themselves into the Far East, and here August Wilhelm's talent displays itself in an honourable fashion.[50]

That was an elegant put-down. It would have been much more galling to find oneself reading, in the conversations attributed to Goethe by Johann Peter Eckermann and published in 1836, this remark following Schlegel's visit to Weimar, on 24 April, 1827, but Eckermann suppressed it for the time being:

> He is in many respects not a man, but one can compensate that to some extent on account of his many-sided scholarly knowledge and his achievements.[51]

Would this perhaps confirm the otherwise implausible hypothesis, seriously advanced by a modern scholar, that Schlegel is the sexless 'Homunculus' in the second part of *Faust*, published in 1832?[52] Or was it part of Goethe's general dictum expressed to Eckermann on 2 April, 1827 (and published in 1836) that Romanticism equalled 'sickness'.[53] Where the early Goethe hagiographers, Carl Gustav Carus or Bettina von Arnim, were to stress his Olympian brow and his god-like physique, this correspondence and these conversations seemed to confirm a counter-image. It started with the Romantics' mentors, Reichardt a 'noxious insect' (Schiller), Georg Forster sexually and politically compromised, Bürger morally disqualified; then came the Romantics proper, the consumptive Novalis (Schiller, too, but that was different), a rheumaticky Tieck, a gross Friedrich Schlegel, an unmanned August Wilhelm Schlegel—one could go on. The so-called Young Germans, having the advantage of youth, perpetuated this image of a outdated generation, one also of converts and reactionaries (Friedrich Schlegel, Werner, Adam Müller, Gentz, now all safely dead). This general paying back with interest, this drawing up of fronts, formed the

---

50 *Ibid.*, 319.
51 Goethe, *Gedenkausgabe*, XXIV, 626.
52 Otto Höfler, *Homunculus— eine Satire auf A. W. Schlegel. Goethe und die Romantik* (Vienna, Cologne and Graz: Böhlau, 1972).
53 *Gespräche mit Goethe in den letzten Jahren seines Lebens. 1823-1832. Von Johann Peter Eckermann*, 2 parts (Leipzig: Brockhaus, 1836), II, 92.

background to Heinrich Heine's *Die Romantische Schule* of 1835 and the thrust it delivered. It had not come from nowhere: one feature of the 1820s and 1830s had been the reissue of the works of this older generation—some already deceased—with autobiographical self-justification or a retouched Life. It was a key motive in Schlegel's own *Kritische Schriften*, a reminder that the Bonn professor of belles-lettres and Indian literature was still a critic of formidable dimensions. He could put in their place the proponents of Johann Heinrich Voss (who included Goethe) or the detractors of Bürger (principally Schiller), Shakespearean sceptics (Goethe, in part), or would-be classicists (like Goethe and Schiller) who could not scan correctly.

It also brought out a less attractive side of Schlegel: the polemicist and satirist. It was related, as already seen, to his anti-Vossiade, his demolition of Langlois, his testy response to H. H. Wilson; it was to colour his later correspondence with Jean Antoine Letronne on the origins of the Zodiac (Indian versus Greek), until Letronne in 1838 finally spoke an irenic word: 'There cannot be any question, between us, of *war* or *tussle*; we are only in a discussion that can be turned to the benefit of science, because you are taking the trouble of being involved in it'.[54] It put an end to the buzzing of that particular bee in Schlegel's bonnet. But one notes that word 'war' all the same.

There was nothing of Brahmanic repose in the satirical verse (some of it in French) which Schlegel produced in the 1820s and 1830s, indeed right up to his death. It was more in the spirit of the *Athenaeum*, of the *Ehrenpforte* for Kotzebue. It saw him returning to almanacs and magazines, as he had done in the years up to his departure from Coppet, the Leipzig *Blätter für literarische Unterhaltung* or Amadeus Wendt's *Musenalmanach*. It was, as he told Wendt, a response to 'inimical and ridiculous things in recently-published correspondence',[55] but not only. There were other issues to settle. It was all very well informing his readers—and his victims—as he did in the poem *Epilog*:

> Nur ein poetisch Feuerwerk
> War, Publicum, mein Augenmerk.
> Doch ärgerst du dich an den Scherzen,
> Als kämen sie aus schwarzem Herzen,
> So geh' ich dir zu Leib' im Ernst,
> Damit du Spaß verstehen lernst.[56]

---

54 *Briefe*, I, 642.
55 *Ibid.*, 516.
56 *SW*, II, 256.

[It was only poetic fireworks,
Reading public, that I had in mind.
But if my jokes displease you,
And seem to you black-hearted,
I'll really go for you
So that you know what poking fun is.]

It did not prevent his satires on Schiller (fewer on Goethe) from being largely puerile (although even their correspondence can stand being cut down to size). One example:

Morgenbillet.
Damit mein Freund bequem in's Schauspiel rutsche,
So steht ihm heut zu Diensten meine Kutsche.
Antwort.
Ich zweifle, daß ich heut in's Schauspiel geh';
Mein liebes Fritzchen hat die Diarrhee.[57]

[Morning Note.
So that my friend can go with ease to the play,
My carriage is at his disposal today.
Answer.
I doubt that I will get to the play today.
My dearest little Fritz has the diarrhée.]

These reactions to the washing of Goethean linen in public,[58] the impugnments of Goethe's 'sacred' person, had their effect: Schlegel was himself more vulnerable to attacks from all quarters. Part of Heine's strategy was to play Goethe off against an 'unmanly' Schlegel. Karl August Varnhagen von Ense, once in the audience of the Berlin Lectures, recorded an altercation with Schlegel in 1844 over Goethe, saying that his disrespect towards Goethe would not harm the great man's name, but Schlegel's own.[59]

It would not have consoled Niebuhr, the butt of nearly a dozen of Schlegel's lampoons, especially after he had had a fire in his house and had lost his manuscripts. There is a poem (unpublished at the time) directed at a 'Sanct Obesus',[60] who could well be Friedrich Schlegel. Ernst Moritz Arndt received some verses in season, even his colleague Welcker as well. The

---

57 Ibid., 207.
58 'der Goethesche Aufwasch und Auskehricht', Lohner, 210.
59 *Rahel-Bibliothek. Rahel Varnhagen, Gesammelte Werke*, ed. Konrad Feilchenfeldt, Uwe Schweikert and Rahel E. Steiner, 10 vols (Munich: Matthes & Seitz, 1983), VI, 366f.
60 *SW*, II, 166f.

poets of the day—Grillparzer, Raupach, Müllner, the Voss family, Rückert, Mundt, Hoffmann von Fallersleben, Freiligrath—were not forgotten, and there were little jokes at Bopp's,[61] Schleiermacher's and Schelling's expense. It mattered little that many of these same names were among the contributors to Wendt's *Musenalmanach*, suggesting an inclusiveness, an ecumenicity of talent, old and new. Schlegel's fierce humour was also part of this age, its factionalisms, its fractiousness, the shrill tone of much of its public discourse. Schlegel could occasionally turn his wit against himself:[62] there is a poem on the wearing of wigs, which observers of his vanity could note with satisfaction. Readers of his epigrams lampooning titles and orders could point to the list of honours attached to his own name on the title pages of the *Indische Bibliothek* or the later *Essais littéraires et historiques*.

The 1827 Art Lectures in Berlin

Writing to Johannes Schulze in November, 1826, complaining of having too few students, Schlegel wondered if he might again be able to give lectures in the style of Vienna or Berlin.[63] There were hankerings here after the great moments of his public career, not as a professor, but as a man of letters, a connoisseur, a celebrity. They were to be revived again in 1828 when he had that flattering invitation to lecture in London which alas came to nothing. Schulze meanwhile replied that there was no objection to his lecturing in Berlin; as an honorary member of the Academy he was in fact entitled to do so. Ladies might be a problem, so the venue would have to be carefully chosen. In the event, he lectured in the then just new Singakademie (today's Gorki-Theater), near the university precinct. The models that Schulze cited were hardly encouraging: Karl von Holtei and Franz Horn were minor Berlin literati who nevertheless had had some success as public lecturers. Schlegel would not be competing in the same class as Davy or Coleridge in London or Cuvier or Alexander von Humboldt in Paris (although Humboldt followed him with popular lectures on science at the same venue during the winter of 1827-28). He had of course once done so, but that was in the past and could not be so easily revived. These lectures might provide a counterweight to those that his brother was giving at the same

---

61 See Czapla, 'Annäherungen an das ferne Fremde', 146. The contributions to Wendt's *Musenalmanache* are listed in: Karl Goedeke, *Grundriss der deutschen Dichtung aus den Quellen*, 2nd edn, 9 vols in 13 (Dresden: Ehlermann, 1884-1913), VIII, i, 129.
62 *SW*, II, 164f., 177-180.
63 *Briefe*, I, 443.

time in Vienna.⁶⁴ Family pride prevailed nevertheless: August Wilhelm, at the appropriate moment in Berlin, mentioned with approval the view that the Gothic style was an imitation of the Nordic forests,⁶⁵ a theory which many would associate with Friedrich Schlegel.

As it turned out, the lectures—Lectures on the Theory and History of the Fine Arts⁶⁶—went off to his satisfaction. It was a triumphal progress in a lower key. On the way to Berlin he called on the Grimm brothers in Kassel and renewed his acquaintance. There were bridges to be repaired, Schlegel recognizing what the Grimms had achieved since his stringent review of Jacob in 1814 (and having recommended him to Schulze in 1825 for a chair in Berlin); the brothers accepting that behind the vanity and the affectation there was a solid if not formidable base of philological and textual knowledge.⁶⁷ Continuing on his way, he was received in Weimar by the grand duke and by Goethe, whom the Berlin lectures were to mention honorifically. The people who mattered to him in Berlin came to his lectures or welcomed him personally: Wilhelm and Alexander von Humboldt;⁶⁸ his publisher Reimer; the Berlin sculptors and architects Rauch, Schinkel and Friedrich Tieck (the Lectures alluded to Schinkel's Altes Museum, soon to be built a short walk from where Schlegel was standing;⁶⁹ and to Friedrich Tieck's relief sculptures on the Royal Theatre, no great distance away).⁷⁰ He did not mention the luminaries of Berlin university, like Hegel, Schleiermacher, Lachmann, Bopp or Raumer. There were the inevitable disrespectful voices, like Bettina von Arnim's, that saw only the external foibles.⁷¹ Ludwig Tieck was to write an uncharacteristically stern letter to his friend Friedrich von Raumer, defending his old friend's small failures, his playing the 'Chevalier'; it was preferable, he said, to the usual professorial arrogance.⁷²

---

64   *Ibid.*, I, 459f.
65   Or Fiorillo, or Georg Forster. *KAV*, II, i, 347.
66   Text in *KAV*, II, i, 289-348.
67   Cf. his three long letters to J. Grimm October 1832-February 1834. *Briefe*, I, 501-515.
68   To Welcker, 28 June, 1827. UB Bonn S 686.
69   *KAV*, II, i, 312. Did AWS devise the inscription over the front of the Altes Museum? Wilhelm von Humboldt asked his advice, but we have no evidence that it was given. Leitzmann, 219, 290.
70   *KAV*, II, i, 311.
71   *Achim und Bettina in ihren Briefen. Briefwechsel Achim von Arnim und Bettina Brentano*, ed. Werner Vordtriede, intr. Rudolf Alexander Schröder, 2 vols (Frankfurt: Suhrkamp, 1961), II, 656, 660f., 671.
72   Friedrich von Raumer, *Lebenserinnerungen und Briefwechsel*, 2 vols (Leipzig: Brockhaus, 1861), II, 311-313.

It may come as a surprise that Schlegel wished to renew his credentials as an art historian, but despite everything to the contrary he had never ceased to see himself in this role. In 1817, at the end of his association with Madame de Staël, he had written a long essay on Fra Angelico's Crowning of the Virgin, to accompany a giant folio lithograph of the painting, by Wilhelm Ternite.[73] There was nothing Nazarene about this essay; it used the few sources then available; above all, it was based on close observation of the original (now in the Louvre). It was a technical description that sought to bring alive the dimensions, the colours, the groupings of the almost six-foot square work. It addressed the means at the disposal of a pre-Raphaelite painter, the limitations placed on him and the moments when he transcended them. It recognized that the painting was originally an object of religious veneration and spiritual contemplation.

The essay on Gérard's *Corinne*, written for Sulpiz Boisserée's *Kunstblatt* in 1822,[74] was of course different, tinged as it was with personal memory and association. Boisserée hoped that Schlegel would review his great work on Cologne cathedral—Schlegel would have no difficulty in switching from classical to Gothic—but it was not to be.[75] It was natural that he should be consulted about the frescoes for Bonn university's Aula[76] and that he should visit the Düsseldorf academy and its director Peter Cornelius and give his professional judgment on the cartoons being produced there, based on his knowledge 'from St. Petersburg to Naples'. Thus, in his rectorial speech in Bonn on the king's birthday, 3 August, 1824, he could point to the paintings in the unfinished Great Hall as a symbolic linking of all the disciplines under the aegis of the fine arts.[77] The king, he said, had continued the legacy of Frederick the Great, in the grand public buildings in Berlin.[78]

That had been in Latin. Now, amid those same edifices in the Prussian capital, he was delivering a comprehensive account in German of the history of art. There was of course a certain element of *déjà vu*, in that Schlegel had

---

73 *Le Couronnement de la Sainte Vierge et les Miracles de Saint Dominique; tableau de Jean de Fiesole, publié par Guillaume Ternite, avec une notice sur la vie du peintre et une explication du tableau* (Paris: Librairie grecque-latine-allemande, 1817), *Oeuvres*, II, 63-99; Sulger-Gebing, 170-172; letter of AWS to Ternite, *ibid.*, 181.
74 *SW*, IX, 360-368.
75 *Briefe*, I, 412.
76 *Ibid.*, 428-432; Sulger-Gebing, 187-189.
77 *Opuscula*, 368-377.
78 *Ibid.*, 376f.

given a similar series in Berlin nearly twenty-five years earlier. There were very few in his audience who would have heard both, and they could note that he was showing the same general deference to Goethe and Schiller as he had done then. In the intervening years, he had seen everything that most travellers could see. Not Greece, of course, but neither Winckelmann nor Goethe had been there, at most the Elgin Marbles (or casts of them),[79] Greek temples in Italy, the Greek statuary extant in Rome, Naples and Florence, everything looted by Napoleon. He now had much less time for the aesthetics of art and dismissed most of the eighteenth century in a few chosen sentences—except of course Winckelmann. Winckelmann had been a Platonist, and Schlegel remained one, unrepentantly. If the history of art showed a linear progression[80] and was not merely a series of technical descriptions, it was through the Platonic Idea of beauty that the historian or beholder was enabled to enter into its inner processes.

The relatively long sections on Egyptian and Indian art—he is said to have argued with Schinkel over the relative merits of Greek and Indian architecture[81]—inserted before the section on the Greeks, were new. Not everything now appealed—like Goethe he now had reservations about animal-headed gods—but it supported his general thesis, expressed in so many other contexts, of the monumentality, repose and gravity of ancient architecture. It was something shared by the most distinguished member of his audience, Alexander von Humboldt.

The Lectures, which Schlegel claimed to have delivered without recourse to notes (these exist nevertheless), came out in published form, then in an expanded French translation.[82] Perhaps for that reason Böcking did not see fit to include them in his edition of Schlegel's works.

---

79 If not the originals, certainly copies, such as the casts in the Louvre. Cf. William St. Clair, *Lord Elgin and the Marbles. The Controversial History of the Parthenon Sculptures* (Oxford, New York: Oxford UP, 1998 [1967]), 268, 271.
80 *KAV*, II, i, 320.
81 *Achim und Bettina*, II, 656, 660.
82 First in *Berliner Conversations-Blatt für Poesie, Literatur und Kritik*, No. 113, 118, 121/3, 127, 130, 134, 137, 141/2, 144, 148, 155, 157/9, 9 June-13 August, 1827; *Briefe*, II, 199. Then in: *Leçons sur l'histoire et la théorie des beaux arts, par A. G. Schlegel, professeur à l'université de Bonn; suivies des articles du Conversations-Lexicon, concernant l'architecture, la sculpture et la peinture; traduites par A. F. Couturier de Vienne* (Paris: Pichon et Didier, 1830). AWS's text published in *KAV*, II, i, 289-348 as: 'A. W. von Schlegels Vorlesungen über Theorie und Geschichte der bildenden Künste. Gehalten in Berlin, im Sommer 1827'.

Heinrich Heine[83]

This was how I imagined a German poet to be. How agreeably surprised I was then when in the year of 1819, when I, quite a young fellow, came up to the university of Bonn and had the honour there of seeing the Poet himself, the public genius, face to face. He was, with the exception of Napoleon, the first great man whom I had seen at that time, and I will never forget that sight and its sublimity. Still today I feel the thrill of sacred awe that went through my soul, as I stood before his lectern and heard him speak. In those days I wore a white frieze coat, a red cap, long fair hair and no gloves. But Herr A. W. Schlegel was wearing kid gloves and was dressed according to the latest Paris fashion; he was still perfumed by good society and eau de mille fleurs; he was daintiness and elegance itself, and when he spoke of the Lord Chancellor of England, he added 'My friend', and next to him stood a servant in the most baronial Schlegel house livery and trimmed the wax candles that were burning in a silver candelabrum, and stood next to a glass of sugared water before the great man at the lectern. Liveried servants! Wax candles! My friend the Lord Chancellor of England! Kid gloves! What things unheard of in the lecture of a German professor! This brilliance dazzled us young people in no small way, myself especially, and I wrote at that time three odes to Herr Schlegel, each beginning with the words: O thou who, etc. But it was only in poetry that I would have dared to address such a distinguished man. His outward appearance conferred on him a certain distinction. On his thin little pate gleamed a few silver hairs, and his body was so thin, so emaciated, so transparent, that he seemed to be all spirit, and almost looked like an emblem of spiritualism.[84]

These are the recollections of the year 1819 by the young Heinrich Heine, from *Die Romantische Schule* in 1835. Even as satire, this is may just be acceptable. But it gets worse. Heine turns his attention to Schlegel's marriage. He likens him to the god Osiris, who was castrated by Typhon: 'Herewith a scandalous myth came into being in Egypt, and in Heidelberg a mythical scandal'.[85] There then follows the account—real or imagined—of Heine's meeting with Schlegel in Paris in 1831, the insignia, the wig, the mincing coquetry, the rejuvenation ('second edition of his youth'), the rouge, with the peroration, 'Herr A.W. Schlegel, the German Osiris'.[86]

---

83 For the biographical and critical background to the Heine-Schlegel affair see Jeffrey L. Sammons, *Heinrich Heine. A Modern Biography* (Princeton, N.J.: Princeton UP, 1979), esp. 57f., 141-147, 192-197.
84 Heinrich Heine, *Historisch-kritische Gesamtausgabe der Werke*, ed. Manfred Windfuhr, 16 vols in 23 (Hamburg: Hoffmann und Campe, 1975-97), VIII, i, 174f.
85 *Ibid.*, 175.
86 *Ibid.*, 176f.

An attentive reader of Heine's writings from the early 1830s could observe that Schlegel's name kept cropping up in unflattering contexts. In the *Conditions in France* of 1832, he was the 'capon' in Madame de Staël's nest;[87] in *The Baths of Lucca*, famous for the demolition of August, Count Platen, his name appears juxtaposed with those of Karl Wilhelm Ramler and Platen himself,[88] associated in many minds with desiccated metrical formalism. To Platen's name was now of course added the charge of (homo) sexual deviancy. Others had said similarly unkind things about Schlegel's appearance and had expressed them in equally unflattering terms, but they had had the decency to keep them private or to suppress them during his lifetime: Varnhagen, Dorow, the Grimm brothers. Yet others, while noting the superficial mannerisms of vanity, as they must, remembered the essential point about Schlegel: once one overlooked his idiosyncrasies, there emerged a man of immense learning, acuity and perspicacity, whom one would not hesitate to mention in one breath with Lessing; a man, too, who was generous with his time and learning.[89]

Clearly Heine was having none of this. There were to be no mitigating circumstances—almost none—and the emphasis was to be on what he saw (or claimed to have seen), not on what he heard or read. Following Aristophanic principles—and here Schlegel would have agreed—the more outrageous and sexually compromising the better. As a Heine scholar of an older generation has remarked, it stretches satire to its very limits, but in making sexual imputations, it is also an attack on personal integrity.[90] Thus, in the context of Schlegel and Bonn, it is the longer passage quoted above that stays in most minds: Adolf Strodtmann, Heine's first editor and biographer, quoted it verbatim in 1867 (although he had the delicacy not to quote the other sections);[91] it has even found its way subsequently into standard works of reference.[92] Schlegel's reputation has never quite

---

87 Ibid., XII, i, 95. This admittedly does not quite render the sense of the original, 'Capaun im Korb' for 'Hahn im Korb' ('cock of the walk').
88 Ibid., VII, i, 139.
89 Cf. the accounts by Ludwig Rellstab and Emanuel Geibel, *Charakteristiken. Die Romantiker in Selbstzeugnissen und Äußerungen ihrer Zeitgenossen*, Deutsche Literatur in Entwicklungsreihen. Reihe Romantik, 1, ed. Paul Kluckhohn (Darmstadt: Wissenschaftliche Buchgesellschaft, 1964 [1950]) 75f., 76.
90 E. M. Butler, *Heinrich Heine. A Biography* (London: Hogarth Press, 1956), 121f.
91 Adolf Strodtmann, *H. Heine's Leben und Werke*, 2 vols (Berlin, Munich, Vienna: Tendler; New York: Steiger, 1867-69), II, 59f.
92 Cf. *Chambers's Encyclopaedia. A Dictionary of Universal Knowledge*, 10 vols (London, Edinburgh: Chambers; Philadelphia: Lippincott, 1925-27), IX, 148 (article 'Schlegel').

recovered from it. Cruel, nasty and appalling though it may be, it has nevertheless not greatly affected Heine's status. Nor need it, for there is so much more to Heine than this kind of demeaning—if outrageously witty— polemic. But Schlegel is less resilient: apart from the Vienna Lectures and the Shakespeare, it is Heine's attack that remains in the general consciousness. It is also fair to say that the other Romantics 'treated' in *Die Romantische Schule*—Friedrich Schlegel, Tieck, Brentano—have survived in a way that Schlegel has not, rehabilitated by institutions or organisations and—in the case of Friedrich Schlegel—monumentalized or canonized. Not so August Wilhelm Schlegel. India cannot compensate, indeed the image here is of a professorial Schlegel in decline, *déchéance*, decrepitude, impotence.

Schlegel, even assuming that he read *Die Romantische Schule*, reacted with dignified silence, under the circumstances the only prudent thing to do.[93] He had offered Heine no personal offence.[94] He may have disliked Jewish bankers,[95] but then Heine had disrespectful things to say about them too; what he did have to say on Judaism was in private, and it was about the bad state of Jewish-Christian relations.[96] Heine's attack had nothing to do with religion. It belonged instead to that line of German polemics where those who were already down (or perceived to be) were given another kick for good measure: Lessing (and later Goethe) with Gottsched, Schiller with Bürger. Of course Schlegel, by reissuing in his *Kritische Schriften* his lampoon of Voss from the year 1800, attacking his memory in *Berichtigung einiger Missdeutungen*, and by publishing bad verse on Schiller, might be said to be inviting satire on his own person, but then again he had never gone beyond the limits of this, admittedly flexible, genre.

One could say that Heine's account of Schlegel was merely a continuation of his notorious attack on Platen. Superficially, there are affinities: aristocracy of the mind (Heine) versus nobility of rank (Platen, and now Schlegel with his Légion d'honneur and what not), flexibility of form (Heine) versus perceived formalism (a charge both Platen and Schlegel could have rebutted). But Platen had nettled Heine with an anti-Jewish jibe, nothing of course compared with the rabid anti-Semitism of Achim von Arnim, whom Heine actually praises in *Die Romantische Schule*. Raising questions of consistency will not get us very far in this area.

---

93 *Briefe*, I, 508 speaks of other attacks before mentioning Heine as 'wildgewordener Jude'. To Golbéry, he claimed not to have read anything by Heine. *Ibid.*, II, 230.
94 I see no evidence that the poem 'An einen Dichter' (*SW*, II, 214) is directed at Heine.
95 'juiverie baronnisée', 'Parodies', *Oeuvres*, I, 83.
96 *Ibid.*, 228f.

Thus provoked, Heine went for Platen's sexuality. Schlegel had offered him no such direct provocation. The issue went even deeper. Writing to Varnhagen just a few years before, on 1 April, 1830, Heine had likened Goethe's and Schiller's literary campaigns of the 1790s to mere skirmishings in the realm of art:

> now it is a matter of the highest interest, of life itself: the *Revolution* makes its way into literature, and the war is more in earnest. Perhaps, with the exception of Voss, I am the sole representative of this revolution in literature.[97]

Heine, with his urbane and cosmopolitan stiletto-work, and Voss laying about him against 'crypto-Jesuits' and 'symbolists', are of course unlikely allies. But it suited Heine's purpose to invoke the blustering old Romantic-hater.

Defending himself in *Die Romantische Schule* against the charge of disloyalty and disrespect towards his old mentor in Bonn, Heine says this of Schlegel:

> But did Herr A.W. Schlegel spare Bürger when old, his literary father? No, he followed hallowed custom. For in literature as in the forests of the North American savages the fathers are slain by the sons before they become old and feeble.[98]

Or at Lake Nemi perhaps. For we are here in the realm of Frazer or Freud and the mythical and anthropological significance of patricide. Schlegel, in his essay of 1801, had of course not slain his literary father, Bürger: this is merely Heine's selective quoting, a prominent feature of *Die Romantische Schule*. He had, as we saw, regretted Bürger's tendency to embellish, not to leave well alone where simplicity would have been better. He had not written a hagiography, and for this we may be grateful: uncritical adulation served no good purpose, and these were sentiments which he had repeated in the reissue of his essay in 1828. By contrast, he had attacked Voss in self-defence and had dispraised Schiller because the older man's disparagements had now been made public.

Heine in his turn used this mythological analogy to slay his own spiritual father. For Strodtmann—also, incidentally, the editor of Bürger's

---

97 Heinrich Heine, *Säkularausgabe*, hg. von den Nationalen Forschungs- und Gedenkstätten der klassischen deutschen Literatur in Weimar und dem Centre National de la Recherche Scientifique in Paris, 27 vols (Berlin: Akademie-Verlag; Paris: Éditions du CNRS, 1970-), XX, 385.
98 Heine, *Gesamtausgabe*, VIII, i, 385.

letters—had made the point that Schlegel had given Heine the young student and budding poet 'many a useful hint' that had stood him in good stead for the rest of his poetic career.[99] It is also fair to say that a whole generation, one that included Platen as well, had learned the craft of verse from Schlegel: whichever form one chose, he had done it in well-turned fashion, classical metres, Italian sonnets, Spanish romances, and much else besides. Schlegel, says Strodtmann, had aroused his hearers' interest in the Middle Ages:[100] we know that Heine attended Schlegel's lectures on the *Nibelungenlied*. Schlegel was, according to Strodtmann, at the height of his powers, not yet the 'childish fop' of his later years.

He quotes the passage from *Die Romantische Schule* nevertheless, the biographer, as it were, carrying out Heine's wishes and performing the ritual slaughter. Heine had in fact written two (not very good) sonnets addressed to Schlegel,[101] neither beginning with 'O thou', but one containing the word 'Master'; they thank him, respectively, for opening up the prodigal wealth of world literature, and for encouraging the 'tender plant' of Heine's talent. He had in addition written a short article entitled *Die Romantik*,[102] which set its face against modish romanticizing, and pleaded instead for plastic form: the clear outlines of Goethe's *Iphigenie* or *Hermann und Dorothea*, or of Schlegel's elegy *Rom*.[103] *Rom*! Was this merely youthful flattery, or did the elegy for Madame de Staël still have some hold on young readers? Whatever, in 1835 these were things that needed to be lived down. Add to them Heine's so-called 'Petrarchist' phase, perhaps inspired by Schlegel's versions of the Italian master. Plus the fact that Schlegel was the successful poet turned academic: Heine had had hopes in this direction in 1829, but they had come to nothing. But all this hardly constituted the grounds for human sacrifice, even of the literary kind. It went still deeper.

There are two strands. In *Die Romantische Schule* Heine was setting the record straight, very largely with French readers in mind (the work had appeared partly in French). The 'record' was Madame de Staël's *De l'Allemagne*. It owed much to Schlegel, even identifying the Schlegel brothers as Germany's foremost critics, which in 1809 or 1813 was surely right, but it

---

99 Strodtmann, I, 59.
100 See the older study by Georg Mücke, *Heines Beziehungen zum deutschen Mittelalter*, Forschungen zur neueren Litteraturgeschichte, 34 (Berlin: Duncker, 1908) and the sources cited there.
101 Heine, *Gesamtausgabe*, I, i, 438f.
102 *Ibid.*, X, 194-196.
103 *Ibid.*, 195.

was nevertheless the product of her own inventive mind. (In *Conditions in France* Heine had also had uncomplimentary things to say about her father, Jacques Necker).[104] Her perception of Germany could not be Heine's: it was too backward-looking, too tolerant of superannuated institutions, too cosily close to a political system based on autocrats and aristocrats. It was anti-Napoleonic, one of the graver sins in Heine's scheme of things, and not without its own set of inner contradictions.

A cardinal sin of equal gravity was German Romanticism's perceived pact with Catholicism and the Middle Ages. It had turned its back on progress, enlightenment, political emancipation, in favour of monkish obscurantism, feudal systems, intellectual and political enslavement. The Schlegel brothers, the one with his conversion and his devotion to Metternich, the other with his aesthetic Catholicising, had, in Heine's view, been the leading force behind this reaction. By 1835, Friedrich Schlegel was of course dead. The full force of the assassination thrust intended for both brothers was therefore directed towards August Wilhelm alone. Hence the devastating weapons that Heine used against him, the blow aimed at the sexual parts (where, Heine claimed, there was nothing manly left to kick);[105] hence, too, the image of the foppish, bemedalled courtier-professor, consorting with aristocrats, receiving the Légion d'honneur from Louis-Philippe. The attack extended to Schlegel's real achievement, his Shakespeare. In his later *Shakespeares Mädchen und Frauen* [Shakespeare's Girls and Ladies] of 1838, Heine reduced Schlegel's translation to mere 'artifice'.[106] It involved the elevation of Goethe, natural and as of right, but also his sponsoring of some less likely anti-Romantics like Johann Heinrich Voss. At its most succinct and destructive the message was: Romantic Catholicism, especially the converted variety, got you the Carlsbad Decrees and the consequences. Thus it was that no other Romantics received such attention from Heine. Ludwig Tieck, their old friend and associate, was in Heine's eyes too good a poet, and nobody took rumours of his 'conversion' too seriously.

Had Heine wished to be fair — and he did not — he might have noted that he and Schlegel, despite the gap of generation and ideology, nevertheless had much in common. Neither ever wrote slack verse: Schlegel had proved to be too good a prosodic father. Both hated the English; both loved the French, but not without considerable qualifications; both were critics (there

---

104 *Ibid.,* XII, i, 146f.
105 *Ibid.,* VIII, i, 470.
106 *Ibid.,* X, 19.

were Schlegel's *Kritische Schriften* to prove it). Schlegel had in the 1820s recanted his Catholicizing and his critique of the Reformation; he was now a confessing Protestant (for whatever reason); he supported the freedom of the press. One could go on, but it would have been to no avail against Heine's patricidal intentions.

Does it all matter? Only to the extent that Schlegel's reputation has never quite recovered and that the spirit, not the letter, of Heine's attack has lived on in his reception (even the great editor Josef Körner is not free of it).[107] Similar disrespectful accounts kept coming out during Schlegel's lifetime.[108] The dart has remained embedded in the flesh. Heine must not be allowed the last word.[109]

5.1 The Last Years 1834-1845

Two portraits of Schlegel from the latter years of his life record the processes of ageing and decline. There is the painting by August Hohneck, from around 1830, in half-profile, showing a firm mouth, if slightly shrunken, a fine head of dark hair (not his own), the fashionable stock, the cloak slung over the shoulders, the left hand holding a sheet of writing symbolic of his calling. The painter also lavishes loving detail on those decorations: one sees on the original, and the engravings based on it, the White Horse of Hanover or the Red Eagle of Prussia, and so on, those 'Orden-pompons' about which he joked to Ludwig Tieck[110] but of which he was nevertheless inordinately proud. There is a 'look of cold command' that bespeaks the poet, the critic, the professor, the man of letters feted in Paris or London.

Then there is the old man at seventy, rendered around 1840 by Christian Hoffmeister, retreating from the public eye, in dressing-gown and skullcap, with woolly whiskers, the private scholar almost voluntarily subsiding into senescence (the so-called 'Pavianbild' [baboon portrait]). Perhaps it was better than trying to keep up a public image, for his attempts at fashion, like the brown court dress ('Galarock') that he sported in Berlin, were becoming a joke. His health was precarious and he was beset from all sides.

---

107 Körner tends to give Heine, rather than AWS, the benefit of the doubt. Cf. *Briefe*, II, 230.
108 Deetjen, 'August Wilhelm Schlegel in Bonn', 16f.
109 The point made by Hans Mayer in his afterword to the reissue of Bernhard von Brentano, *August Wilhelm Schlegel. Geschichte eines romantischen Geistes* (Frankfurt: Insel, 1986), 285f.
110 Lohner, 210.

Fig. 34 Lithograph by Henry & Cohen in Bonn, after the portrait engraving of August Wilhelm Schlegel by Adolf August Hohneck (c. 1830). © and by kind permission of the Master and Fellows of Trinity College, Cambridge, CC BY-NC 4.0.

Fig. 35 Portrait engraving of August Wilhelm Schlegel by Christian Hoffmeister (1841). Image in the public domain.

Perhaps we should add a third. The French sculptor Pierre-Jean David d'Angers came to Bonn in 1840 to model a profile medallion of Schlegel. As always with David, there is a tendency towards monumentality, fortunately not a colossal bust such as he did of Goethe and Tieck. Instead we have a Roman head with noble brow and hair receding, imperial-style, essentially the image on Schlegel's own gravestone.

The Romantic generation was not spared its share of infirmities, yet compared with Coleridge or Benjamin Constant in their last years, Schlegel was relatively active. He had outlived so many, not a victim to consumption like Novalis or Keats (or to the cholera, like Auguste and Caroline). But he was no longer well: 'subterranean goings-on', a souvenir of Coppet, a 'troglodyte', a tapeworm,[111] was affecting his digestion (it is just as well that Heine never knew).

He seemed to be generally distracted in all directions. No-one apparently appreciated all the thankless work that he had put in as director of the Royal Rhenish Museum (as late as 1839 he was writing a note on a recent archaeological discovery).[112] He had to be a member of the 'Greek committee', setting up a university in Athens; or the 'cathedral committee' in Cologne, delegated to seek Prince Albert's support;[113] it was he who wrote to Franz Liszt asking for a benefit concert for a blind musician (and receiving a fairly dusty answer);[114] when the queen of Prussia made an official visit to Bonn, he was the one who wrote the poem in homage.[115] Then he was president of the panel set up to produce a Beethoven statue.[116]

The statue—it was not unveiled until August, 1845, three months after Schlegel's death—proved to be particularly time-consuming, and the story of its commissioning also provided a microcosm of its age. There was no doubt that Beethoven deserved a monument, and a committee, with Schlegel as its president, was formed in Bonn in 1835 to that effect. He personally

---

111 *Briefe*, I, 381, 385, and graphic details there.
112 *Ibid.*, 522f.; 'Beschreibung eines bei Lechenich im Regierungsbezirke Köln ausgegrabenen, jetzt dem Alterthums-Museum der Universität Bonn zugehörigen Gefäßes von Erz mit halb erhobener Arbeit', *SW*, IX, 369-371.
113 Sulger-Gebing, 189-191.
114 SLUB Dresden, Mscr. Dresd. e. 90, XIX (14), 73-74.
115 *SW*, I, 165f.
116 See esp. Horst Hallensleben, 'Das Bonner Beethoven-Denkmal als frühes "bürgerliches Standbild"'; Susan Schaal, 'Das Beethovendenkmal von Ernst Julius Hähnel in Bonn', both in Ingrid Bodsch (ed.), *Monument für Beethoven. Zur Geschichte des Beethoven-Denkmals (1845) und der frühen Beethoven-Rezeption in Bonn*. Katalog zur Ausstellung des Stadtmuseums Bonn und des Beethoven-Hauses (Bonn: Stadtmuseum, 1995), 28-37, 39-133.

signed a pre-printed letter that had wide distribution.[117] Beethoven may have been born in Bonn, but under an elector-archbishop. Now, the town was Prussian, and in Prussia only monuments to rulers were tolerated, the sole exception being Luther's statue in Wittenberg of 1821. Would the authorities change their minds for Beethoven? Schlegel made enquiries of Karl Friedrich Schinkel in Berlin, to be told that King Frederick William III was not in favour. Schlegel now realized what he had let himself in for. He was supposed to be the expert: he wanted something in bronze, with a rotunda and bas-reliefs on the base. He asked Friedrich Tieck if he was interested, but his friend showed his characteristic dilatoriness.[118] Schlegel suggested the Münsterplatz as a suitable site—where in fact the statue now stands—but that was again vetoed 'from on high'. Faced with these seemingly insurmountable problems, Schlegel resigned in 1838. The accession of Frederick William IV in 1840 changed things, but Schlegel was not party to the choice of Ernst Julius Hähnel as sculptor (the statue was in bronze and had bas-reliefs, but no rotunda), nor could he be present at the official opening gala in the presence of the king and queen of Prussia, Queen Victoria and Prince Albert and so many other notables.

There were tussles with academic colleagues over fussy pedantic matters; he continued tenaciously to support Christian Lassen; in 1839, though over 70, he took on the deanship of his faculty. When the classicist August Ferdinand Naeke died in 1838, he stepped in until Friedrich Ritschl's arrival. The death of his friend and colleague and 'oracle',[119] the art historian Eduard d'Alton in 1840 saw him not only taking over the history of art but doing his utmost to prevent a replacement whom he considered inadequate.[120] He also produced a catalogue of D'Alton's considerable art collection, confirming his colleague's view that three very special items in it, ascribed respectively to Pontormo, Correggio and Rubens, were indeed genuine. On the basis of this authority, several paintings collected by D'Alton found their way via Prince Albert into the British royal collections (Albert had had private lessons from D'Alton).[121] As the university's public

---

117 Ibid., [catalogue], 213.
118 Bernhard Maaz, *Christian Friedrich Tieck 1776-1851. Leben und Werk unter besonderer Berücksichtigung seines Bildnisschaffens, mit einem Werkverzeichnis*, Bildhauer des 19. Jahrhunderts (Berlin: Gebr. Mann, 1995), 41.
119 *Verzeichniss einer von Eduard d'Alton [...] hinterlassenen Gemälde-Sammlung. Nebst einer Vorerinnerung und ausführlichen Beurtheilung dreier darin befindlichen Bilder. Herausgegeben von A.W. von Schlegel* (Bonn: Georgi, 1840), v.
120 *Briefe*, I, 548f.
121 See Margaret Rose, 'Eduard Joseph d'Alton and the Origin of Prince Albert's Collection', *The Burlington Magazine* 129 (1987), 532-538.

orator, he delivered the academic oration for Naeke.[122] Bonn's luminaries did not enjoy being the butt of his satirical verses, but Arndt made no pretence of his dislike of Schlegel, while Niebuhr had stated publicly that the precedence Schlegel accorded to India and Sanskrit over Greek was a fraud;[123] it was however unfair to lampoon Welcker,[124] a good colleague, merely because his views on mythology seemed suspect.

Then there were the needs of his immediate family. After the deaths of his brothers Moritz (1826) and Karl (1829), he seemed to be regarded as the all-providing brother-in-law and uncle. He managed to ward off Karl's adopted daughter, Wilhelmine Spall (later Büchting, then Hunter) when she and her husband saw in him a 'soft touch'. It was different with Moritz's children. There was his nephew Johann August Adolph Schlegel. He had secured a post in Hanoverian service at the Gymnasium in Verden, but his mental condition began to deteriorate. By late 1839 he was found to be suffering from 'paroxyms'. Schlegel made arrangements for his welfare and found an institution in Verden, also paying for the expenses incurred. Johann Karl died at Hildesheim in 1841.[125] His sister Amalie Wolper had lost her husband in 1832 and was supporting her mother and her son. It appears that Amalie and her son Hermann, briefly also her mother Charlotte Schlegel, stayed with Schlegel intermittently in the winter of 1834-35. Hermann had been a 'handful', but his great-uncle was kept abreast of his later progress, to a Gymnasium and then to Göttingen. The Schlegel genes seem to have prevailed.[126]

Schlegel felt obliged to support his extended family, but it was his essential generosity to others that caused him to assist the young painter and lithographer Peter Busch.[127] Busch, the son of a stocking weaver in Bonn, had displayed a precocious natural talent. As early as 1828, while Busch was apprenticed to a local painter, Schlegel had arranged through his solicitor Lambertz for first payments to be made to him. He proceeded

---

122 *Opuscula*, 413-420.
123 *Briefe*, I, 531.
124 *SW*, II, 237f.
125 Correspondence and invoices SLUB Dresden, Mscr. Dresd. e. 90, II, 32; Czapla/Schankweiler, 166f.
126 SLUB Dresden, Mscr. Dresd. e. 90, XIX (29), 44-78.
127 Most of this set out in Czapla/Schankweiler, 104, 246f., 274f.; see also Josef Körner, 'Ein unehelicher Sohn August Wilhelm Schlegels?', *Jahrbuch des Kölnischen Geschichtsvereins*, 15 (1933), 120-129; three caches of ms. material in, respectively, UB Bonn S 2537 Nachlass Lambertz, 1-20; SLUB Dresden, Mscr. Dresd. e. 90, XIIb, II, 1-10; UB Heidelberg, Heid. Hs. 860, 649 (Nachlass Paulus).

to the academy in Düsseldorf, to join the history painting section, after this to Stuttgart, and it was there that the tragedy of his last days unfolded. Schlegel's support for him had by then lapsed. Depressed, and in bad health, in doubts about his career, Busch turned to Schlegel for help. Receiving no response, he arranged an elaborate suicide in his lodgings, by inhaling the monoxide fumes from a charcoal brazier. Allegations then began to circulate, not least in the printed 'Words at the Graveside', that Busch was Schlegel's natural son and that his 'father' had coldly and disdainfully refused to recognize him. 'May his shade pursue you for ever', was one of the sentiments expressed.[128] Of course anyone capable of elementary calculation could work out that there was no question of Schlegel's paternity, and even his detractors had to admit this. His father-in-law Paulus in Heidelberg asked for the documentation, no doubt hoping for proof of moral turpitude and a chance to press charges. The excellent Lambertz managed to secure a public apology, which however did not appear until November of 1841,[129] meanwhile allowing the reading public a good six months to indulge their worst thoughts about Schlegel's alleged heartlessness.

The days of great projects were over: he seemed to be caught up in questions of detail, off-cuts of the grand schemes, occasional pieces. It goes without saying that they showed the enormous and eclectic range of his competence. While still engaged on the *Indische Bibliothek*, he had produced a short notice on Bactrian Greek coins for the *Nouveau Journal Asiatique* in 1828.[130] In that same journal, he respectfully challenged Silvestre de Sacy's theory of the Arab origin of *A Thousand and One Nights*, not surprisingly promoting Indian sources. After serving its purpose for an English readership, *De l'Origine des Hindous* was republished in Paris in 1838.[131] He was approached by the *Journal des débats* in 1834 to review Fauriel's work on French courtly romance. It was a link with his earlier studies on Wolfram and the *Nibelungenlied*, for both the Old French Charlemagne and Arthurian cycles had left their impact on German medieval literature, on Dante similarly. It also gave him an opportunity to disparage those 'chimères celtiques' to which French scholars seemed to be wedded. This time in

---

128 SLUB Dresden, Mscr. Dresd. e. 90, XIIb, II, 3.
129 Bonn UB S 2537, 18.
130 'Observations sur quelques médailles bactriennes et indo-scythiques nouvellement découvertes', *Oeuvres*, III, 311-337.
131 *Nouvelles annales des voyages etc. publ. par M. Eyriès et de Humboldt*, IV (Paris: Gide, 1838), 137-214.

the *Revue des deux mondes*,[132] he reviewed Gabriele Rossetti's extraordinary thesis that Dante, Petrarch and Boccaccio were part of a Cathar conspiracy aimed at overthrowing the papacy, unfolding his knowledge of all three poets, once liberally displayed in *Die Horen* or the first Berlin Lectures, and rebutted the patent absurdities of Rossetti's claims.

The invitation to provide a preface for the German translation of James Cowles Prichard's *The Analysis of the Egyptian Mythology* (first 1819)[133] brought Schlegel closer to home and provided the moment to set out his views on 'Indo-Germanic' (a term he now used),[134] and retract some, but not all, of his anti-Celtic prejudices (Prichard's etymological work had brought him round). Prichard's linking of the Indian and Egyptian religions could however not stand unchallenged. There were of course undeniable affinities: both had their origins, like all religious worship, in the veneration of a Supreme Being, and both had lapsed into cosmological mythology and polytheism; both had sacred writings and a priestly caste to watch over them and to be guardians of scientific knowledge (that Zodiac again). In the detail, however, they differed and it was the task of historical criticism and textual chronology to set this out.[135] Between the lines one reads the awareness that the Englishman had provided useful material, but that German methodology was needed to underpin it.

With one major exception, the essays and reviews from the 1830s were in French, which had established itself, along with Latin, as his language of antiquarian and philological expression and of civilized discourse as well. It was, as he said, his second mother tongue.[136] In his very last years, he may not have been quite sure of which language he was using, as his letters in French to August Böckh and Alexander von Humboldt testify. It was in French, too, that he cast the corpus of epigrams on the current state of (French) politics and his so-called 'Pensées détachées', those random thoughts on mainly religious issues. Was it the escape—intellectually and socially—from the confines of Bonn into a wider sphere where one's interlocutors were Silvestre de Sacy, Fauriel, Burnouf or Letronne, where, as he had said to Lassen, world society met? At least he was appreciated

---

132 'Le Dante, Pétrarque et Boccace, justifiés de l'imputation d'hérésie et d'une conspiration tendant au renversement du Saint-Siége', *Oeuvres*, II, 307-332.
133 I. C. Prichard, *Darstellung der Aegyptischen Mythologie* […], trans. L. Haymann, pref. A. W. von Schlegel (Bonn: Weber, 1837), v-xxxiv.
134 *Ibid.*, vii.
135 *Ibid.*, xxxiii.
136 *Briefe*, I, 575.

there: the Belgian orientalist Eugène Jacquet wrote to him in 1836 that the French were no longer used to the combination of 'littérature élégante' and 'littérature scientifique' that Schlegel so effectively represented.[137]

There was inevitably a less wide circulation for his material in Latin. In 1822, he had lectured in Bonn on *Antiquitates Etruscae*,[138] planned in fifteen sections, of which only the prolegomena and the first three survive.[139] It gave him the opportunity to retrace his steps from his early Göttingen dissertation on the geography of Homer; above all he could advance hypotheses on the basis of having explored the archaeological sites (on the second Italian journey), his communications with experts, and his projects on etymology. The Etruscans were not Pelasgians any more than they were Celts: their origins lay south of the Apennines, but where? The text breaks off. Not content with his animated correspondence in French with Letronne on the signs of the Zodiac, Schlegel set out his views in a learned paper in Latin in Bonn in 1839.[140] Of course there was no question for him but that these symbols were of Indian origin (possibly Chaldean or Egyptian, too), and not Greek.

All this—with so much more existing in note form in his papers—was part of an intended whole that never took shape, that lacked a sense of completion. But even the achievement on which hitherto he firmly stood—Shakespeare and the Vienna Lectures—was beginning to fray at the edges. His revision of the Shakespeare translation, intended to counteract Tieckian liberties, hardly got under way. At least Reimer agreed to reissue a new edition without Tieck's notes,[141] but it was not a full restoration of his original text. He returned to the Vienna Lectures and began a major revision of the section on the Greek theatre, adding a considerable amount of technical detail, much of it supplied by his new colleague Ritschl.[142] It interrupted the flow of his original narrative: the aristocratic audience of 1808 would have shifted uneasily in their seats had they been subjected to it. It was also by way of a critique of classical studies, now so taken up with, as he saw it, hair-splitting issues and not the main narrative and the aesthetic

---

137 SLUB Dresden, Mscr. Dresd. e. 90, XIX (12), 4.
138 *Opuscula quae Augustus Guilelmus Schlegelius Latine scripta reliquit*, ed. Eduardus Böcking (Lipsiae: Weidmann, 1848), 115-286.
139 'reliqua desunt', *ibid.* 286.
140 'Progr. acad. Bonn', 'De Zodiaci antiquitate et origine', *Opuscula*, 326-359.
141 *Briefe*, I, 593; Roger, *La Réception de Shakespeare*, 376.
142 *Briefe*, II, 247.

pleasure that it afforded.¹⁴³ Schlegel's revision was long and drawn out, his publisher Winter's patience not inexhaustible. Schlegel's plan to edit the works of Frederick the Great supervened, so that it was left to Schlegel's editor Böcking to rescue these revisions and include them in his edition of Schlegel's works of 1846-47.¹⁴⁴ One may regret this, for it meant that the famous Lectures of 1809-11 were never subsequently reprinted in exactly their original form.¹⁴⁵ Other publishers still had some hopes pinned on him. Reimer suggested a separate reissue of the Bürger essay, or a third edition of his poems (minus the satirical verse);¹⁴⁶ Cotta asked for anything he might wish, the *Nibelungenlied* perhaps.¹⁴⁷ It came to nothing.

Instead, he produced a volume of *Essais littéraires et historiques*.¹⁴⁸ He paid for it himself (the equivalent of 1,200 francs) and sold a mere 120 copies.¹⁴⁹ It was his general feeling that the German reading public had lost interest in his writings, whereas readers from Cadiz to St Petersburg (where French was spoken: Tsar Nicholas I received a copy)¹⁵⁰ had not. The nine and a half lines of orders and distinctions attached to his name on the title page would underline his status. In a way, the *Essais* are the French equivalent of his *Kritische Schriften* of 1828, the gathering together of pieces that had become scattered 'like the leaves of the Sybil', as the preface rather grandly states,¹⁵¹ the evidence that he had 'undertaken many things and finished little',¹⁵² an altogether too modest summary of his achievement.

But were these two volumes not also evidence that Schlegel was, in Josef Körner's insensitive words, but a 'Casanova des Geistes',¹⁵³ moving

---

143 *SW*, V, 253f.
144 See Körner, *Botschaft*, 75-80.
145 Amoretti's edition is based on the 1817 revision. A new edition in *KAV* is forthcoming.
146 *Briefe*, I, 517, 564f.
147 *Ibid*., 554f.
148 *Essais littéraires et historiques par A. W. de Schlegel* (Bonn: Weber, 1842) contains: v-xxiii Avant-propos; 1-70 'Du système continental'; 71-84 'Tableau de l'état politique et moral de l'Empire français en 1813'; 85-170 'Comparaison entre la Phèdre de Racine et celle d'Euripide'; 171-210 'Lettre [...] sur les chevaux de bronze'; 211-340 'Observations sur la langue et la littérature provençales'; 341-406 'De l'Origine des romans de chevalerie'; 407-437 'Le Dante, Pétrarque et Boccace, justifiés'; 439-518 'De l'Origine des Hindous'; 519-544 'Les Mille et une nuits'.
149 *Briefe*, I, 613.
150 *Ibid*., 590.
151 *Essais*, Avant-propos, v.
152 *Ibid*., xxiii.
153 Ref. Rainer Kolk, 'Liebhaber, Gelehrte, Experten. Das Sozialsystem der Germanistik bis zum Beginn des 20. Jahrhunderts', in: Jürgen Fohrmann and Wilhelm Vosskamp (eds), *Wissenschaftsgeschichte der Germanistik im 19. Jahrhundert* (Stuttgart, Weimar: Metzler, 1994), 48-114, ref. 53.

from conquest to conquest, without the application and staying-power of the true scholar? Rather, they were a testimony to a versatility and many-sidedness that was typical of an age not satisfied by academic 'Wissenschaft' and its specialisms, the same spirit that in the sphere of science animated Alexander von Humboldt to start writing his *Kosmos* in this very decade. The volumes assembled the recent pieces from the Paris journals of the 1830s, on courtly romance, on Dante, *A Thousand and One Nights*, or the Hindus; but also the long essay on Provençal of 1818, and the one on the horses of St Mark's in Venice of 1816. But as if almost to coincide with the return of Napoleon's remains to the Invalides, the volume opened with two of the pamphlets for Bernadotte, the one on the continental system, and the other on the intercepted despatches, a reminder that the professor had not always been sedentary,[154] but had once also been a man of action, a policy-maker, a small cog in the anti-Napoleonic machine. Then there was his *Comparaison entre la Phèdre de Racine et celle d'Euripide*. Nowhere had the reading public reacted with more vehemence, had been more divided among itself, than in France when this pamphlet appeared in 1807, a reaction rumbling on until that very day, that went to the heart of the nation's literary life. Here it was. None of his German contemporaries had written anything quite so influential or so controversial, nor had any of their works had been banned by Fouché or Savary on the Usurper's orders.

Already in 1837 Schlegel had described himself as an 'Antimodernist'.[155] Certainly his recantation in French of all the 'works of the devil' ('Formule d'abjuration') from the early 1840s[156] seemed like a renunciation of all progress, all civilization, all technical and cultural advances, but with tongue in cheek. It was part of a whole 'Résumé épigrammatique de l'histoire de nos jours' [Epigrammatic Survey of the History of Our Times], a survey of recent French politics from the early 1840s,[157] a wry review of constitutional crises, rumours of war, royal visits, changes of ministry, above all the repatriation of Napoleon's mortal remains and what it portended (his informant on much of this was Albert de Broglie).[158] There was, understandably, no such account of German politics: the age of Metternich hardly lent itself. His series does, however, end on this note:

---

154 *Essais*, Avant-propos, xxiii.
155 *Briefe*, I, 532.
156 *Oeuvres*, I, 83.
157 *Ibid.*, 13-73.
158 Albert's last extant letter, dated 12 May, 1842, is on the notepaper of the 'Ministère des Affaires Étrangères. Direction Politique'. SLUB Dresden, Mscr. Dresd. e. 90, XIX, [4], 23.

Le Michel Tudesque
[The German Michael]

Jusqu'à quand ronflera ce gros Michel tudesque
Et ne sentira point sa force gigantesque?
Chaque voisin le pince et rit de son sommeil.
Mais gare le réveil!¹⁵⁹

[How long will this big German Michael snore
Unaware of his gigantic strength?
All his neighbours pinch him, laugh at his slumbers.
But watch out when he wakes up.]

This is not Schlegel assuming powers of prophecy, no seer's eye foretelling a German awakening as it actually happened. At most it is a sense that the German nation, that once appeared in triumph in Paris in 1814-15, might some day again flex its muscles and surprise the French builders of 'les arcs de triomphe érigés par les battus' [triumphal arches put up by the vanquished].[160]

Perhaps more significant is his late return to religious issues, the reassessment of his own spiritual development. It was a journey into the past, a self-examination, a turning in on himself. In August, 1838 he had exchanged letters with Albertine de Broglie (almost the last). She pleaded the cause of the Christian faith, while he, as a 'solitaire contemplatif',[161] refused to be tied down to any revelation or cult that limited humankind's natural capacity to seek the ultimate, the divine; not wishing to be confined, as he said, to a house made by hands, when the starry vault declared the existence of some higher agency.[162] It meant retracing the steps of his own religious progression, from early scepticism, to a mystical aestheticism, a solace in the 'magical power of the rite'[163] (under the effects of Auguste Böhmer's death), to a revulsion against 'fanaticism and bigotry' (his brother Friedrich's),[164] to his present, and last, position. What was left? A hatred of the 'priestly yoke',[165] sacerdotal manipulations and constructions, their

---

159 *Oeuvres*, I, 73.
160 *Ibid.*, 83.
161 The exchange published as 'Fragments extraits du porte-feuille d'un solitaire contemplatif'. *Oeuvres*, I, 189-201.
162 *Ibid.*, 200f.
163 *Ibid.*, 191.
164 *Ibid.*, 192.
165 *Ibid.*, 193.

establishment of 'sacred texts' (there are a number of 'Pensées' devoted to the perceived inconsistencies of the New Testament), an abhorrence of any violence in the name of religion (which included the Christian Middle Ages), any restriction on the human imagination. One by one he had shed his mentors and preceptors:

> *Mes Adieux*
>
> Je vous quitte à jamais, tristes Nazaréens,
> Disciples de Saül, vains théologiens:
> Vos sacrés auteurs juifs sont pour moi des profanes.
> Pythagore, Platon, les sublimes Brahmanes
> Sont mes oracles saints, interprètes des dieux,
> Ma boussole sur mer et mon vol vers les cieux.[166]
>
> [I leave you forever, sad Nazarenes,
> Disciples of Saul, theologians in vain;
> Your sacred Jewish writings are for me profane;
> Pythagoras, Plato, the sublime Brahmins
> Are my sacred oracles, interpreters of the gods,
> My compass on the seas and my flight to the stars.]

A belief in the immortality of the soul, its transmigration, a rebirth in some other sphere.[167] Aesthetically, it was the Platonic position that had once drawn him to Hemsterhuis and which Winckelmann had translated into a sense of the divine in art. Now, it was extended back in time to take in India. It was a summation of where he had been and what he yet aspired to.

The Works of Frederick the Great

Schlegel's role in the Prussian Academy of Sciences' huge and monumental, thirty-volume edition of the works of Frederick the Great has been described as a 'tragicomedy'.[168] One could add 'farce', for it certainly had elements of both. It showed him at his most obstinate and pedantic, obstructive even. The work that he put into it, the mass of general remarks but also of detailed stylistic suggestions that he made to the Academy, repose unheeded and unedited among his papers. His sole published memorandum on the subject—*Vorläufiger Entwurf zu einer neuen Ausgabe*

---

166 *Ibid.*, 188.
167 Kaufmann, 'Zur Erinnerung', 253.
168 *Briefe*, II, 281.

der Werke Friedrichs des Großen [Preliminary Draft of a New Edition of the Works of Frederick the Great], dated 1844[169]—came out only after his death. Yet it is splendidly written, full of good sense, and shows a high degree of connoisseurship and a detailed knowledge of the eighteenth century. That the Academy approached him in the first place was an acknowledgment that no-one in their midst could claim to know French as well as he did or could write it with such elegance (Alexander von Humboldt perhaps, too busy carrying out the often capricious will of his sovereign).

It was all part of an enterprise of erecting a monument in print and bronze to the memory of Frederick the Great, and over it stood the unpredictable figure of King Frederick William IV of Prussia, the 'Romantic on the throne'. Monuments were in vogue: examples were Cotta's edition of Schiller's works and the Thorwaldsen statue in Stuttgart, or the musical apotheosis of Beethoven in Bonn. But these were the result largely of citizens' initiatives—Schlegel had chaired the Bonn committee from 1835 to 1838—not of royal fiats. By contrast, King Ludwig I of Bavaria's Walhalla of 1842, on the banks of the Danube, full of Friedrich Tieck's busts, was done in consultation with no-one but himself.

Although thoughts of a commemoration of Frederick were not new, it was Frederick William's cabinet order of 1840 that galvanized the efforts on behalf of his famous ancestor. 1840, the date of Frederick William's own succession, was the centenary of Frederick's accession to the throne and of the re-founding by him of the Prussian Academy of Sciences.[170] The Prussian Academy had been working on the idea of an edition of the works since at least 1837,[171] and it only needed the new king's advent to set the great work in motion. On 1 June, 1840 the foundation stone of Christian Rauch's equestrian statue of Frederick had been laid, that monument unveiled in 1851 and still standing (again) on Unter den Linden. The plinth of the statue was itself a piece of ideological myth-making, with extraordinary constellations of figures to bring out both the 'Herrscher' [ruler] and the 'Weiser auf dem Thron' [sage on the throne]. These were

---

169 *SW*, VIII, 294-333.
170 On the general background see Thomas Nipperdey, 'Nationalidee und Nationaldenkmal in Deutschland', *Historische Zeitschrift* 206 (1968), 529-585; on the monument Richard Nürnberger, 'Rauch's Friedrich-Denkmal historisch-politisch gesehen', *Jahrbuch preußischer Kulturbesitz*, 8 (1979), 115-124.
171 The history of the edition and of AWS's involvement is traced in *Briefe*, I, 541-621 and II, 247-281; on AWS's sojourn in Berlin see Czapla/Schankweiler, 102-108, 270-284. These form the basis of my remarks.

the very same words used by Alexander von Humboldt in a speech to the Academy in 1840;[172] his sentiments on Frederick as a patron of the sciences and arts were to be echoed by the Academy when it received the king's order later in the year. A standing committee of the Academy, including the classicist August Böckh, one of the secretaries (and the long-suffering recipient of Schlegel's increasingly testy missives), the historians Leopold von Ranke and Friedrich von Raumer, also Alexander von Humboldt and later Jacob Grimm, agreed that Schlegel, with his knowledge of French and his experience of literary and typographical matters, should be invited to take part in the undertaking on an advisory basis. With his elegant French style, he also seemed the appropriate person to write a general preface to the edition, possibly also to edit the king's letters and verse.[173]

Schlegel far exceeded his brief. He saw wider implications and bombarded the Academy with memoranda (in French), a whole 400 pages.[174] Clearly he had lost all sense of proportion. The issue at stake was the integrity of the text, and his short preliminary draft in German set out his views in eminently sensible fashion. But the Academy could not agree on what constituted a properly edited text, free of 'errors' but close to the originals.[175] It brought out the philologist—and controversialist—in Schlegel, hence those huge missives that the Academy most likely never read.

It was not helped by Schlegel coming in person to Berlin from May to July of 1841. He lived in some style in the Hôtel de Russie, not far from the royal palace.[176] He took part in Academy sessions, was feted and dined and met old friends and acquaintances. But he was plagued by ill-health and found Berlin's climate taxing.[177] It was a great honour to be invited to luncheon with the king at Sanssouci, but his donning a court dress that reflected the fashion of the Tuileries in 1815 was the subject of malicious comment.[178] The company seemed to consist very largely of that 'seniority', those 'superannuitants', about whom Varnhagen and others made

---

172 Nürnberger, 120.
173 Cf. *Briefe*, II, 247, 251, 253.
174 SLUB Dresden, Mscr. Dresd. e. 90, LXXV, 27-30, LXXVI, 1-2. (LXXV contains a whole mass of other more or less relevant material, some, but by no means all, published in *Briefe*).
175 *SW*, VIII, 306f.
176 Lohner, 222.
177 *Briefe*, II, 256.
178 Czapla/Schankweiler, 272f.

disrespectful comments,[179] part of the king's policy of reactivating culture — but through figures who were largely past it. He was made a member of the king's new Order of Merit.

Ludwig Tieck was not present on the occasion at Sanssouci, but now, at 69, he was the king's pensioner and about to direct the famous performance of *A Midsummer Night's Dream* at Potsdam in 1843, with Felix Mendelssohn Bartholdy's music. It was to Charlotte von Hagn, the actress who was to play Puck there, that Schlegel now paid court, full of gallantries, writing a poem in French (and leaving her a jewelled brooch in his will).[180] Although invited, Schlegel did not attend the gala dinner given in Tieck's honour, but they did meet, and it would be for the last time. There were less happy notes: it was in Berlin that the news of the Peter Busch affair reached him.

After his return to Bonn, the irreconcilable differences between him and the Academy came to a head. Despite conciliatory tones from Böckh and interventions from Alexander von Humboldt, he declared that he could not continue, even with the promised preface. The king now got involved. He, too, had some views about certain of Frederick's poems and wanted them excluded.[181] Beyond a few notes, the preface never materialized.[182] The edition as we have it does have a general preface, but not the one that Schlegel might have written, and there is no mention anywhere of him.[183] The Academy later received from Böcking copies of papers relating to the edition, but made no use of them and generally showed little gratitude for what Schlegel had done.[184]

Illness and Death

One has the impression of an old man going to pieces. To the outside observer, however, it looked different. An American visitor to Bonn in 1842 has left us this report:

> At Bonn, a few miles above Cologne, I went to see A. W. Schlegel. He is a striking-looking old gentleman of seventy-five, quite gray, but not bent by

---

179 Roger Paulin, *Ludwig Tieck: A Literary Biography* (Oxford: Clarendon Press, 1985), 402.
180 *Briefe*, I, 572f., II, 265; *SW*, I, 173; *Oeuvres*, I, 85.
181 *Briefe*, I, 618-620.
182 See Josef Körner, 'August Wilhelm Schlegel über Friedrich den Großen', *Die Neueren Sprachen* 40 (1932), 157-161.
183 *Oeuvres de Frédéric le Grand*, 30 vols plus 1 (Berlin: Decker, 1846-57).
184 *Briefe*, II, 281.

age, nor weakened in his mental powers. He still lectures in the University on subjects connected with the arts, and, as he told me, has just published a volume of his miscellaneous pieces, heretofore printed in different journals. The collection is in the French language. He farther said that he was soon to publish an enlarged and improved edition of his Lectures on Dramatic Art and Literature. He kept us for about an hour, making many enquiries respecting Americains [sic], whom he knew, as the Everetts and Mr. Ticknor, and mentioning with evident delight the republication of his writings in America. In the preface of his new book, he declares his consciousness that even beyond the Atlantic his name is still a living thing.[185]

This is the other side to the Academy affair, the proud awareness that he was not only read from Cadiz to St Petersburg, but in North America as well and even as far as Asia.[186] There was also the rueful admission to Schulze that the edition of Frederick the Great had kept him from the revision of the Vienna Lectures. Perhaps he had identified too much with the great king, the historian, the thinker, the poet, the wit, the man of society, all roles in which he fancied himself. How much better to be away from the heat and dust of Berlin, to be back in Bonn and receive guests like Rehfues in 'cool rooms, with the temperature never above 18 degrees, a sofa or divan among the roses in the garden, a fresh draught from the well-stocked cellar—my life in the country'.[187]

The one who had supplied those creature comforts and had ensured the smooth running of the household, who had kept a watchful eye on servants and tradesmen, who wrote faithfully when he was away, Maria Löbel, became seriously ill later in the summer of 1842. Despite signs of recovery, she died on 14 March, 1843, a pious Catholic to the last. Schlegel mourned her as he had mourned no member of his family, as he had Auguste Böhmer and Madame de Staël, all close but ultimately beyond his reach. Rehfues concluded: 'Her heart, her loyalty, had raised her to him, and had she been his wife, he could not have mourned her with deeper grief, or honoured her'.[188]

He was, as his American visitor observed, still lecturing; an advanced course in Sanskrit, courses on the history of art and on modern European

---

185 'Extrait d'un journal américain: Mills point Mercury, dans l'état de Kentucky', SLUB Dresden, Mscr. Dresd. e. 90, II (18).
186 *Briefe*, I, 556.
187 UB Bonn, S 1392 (46), 13 June, 1842.
188 Czapla/Schankweiler, 296.

history are announced in the university's lecture lists up to the summer of 1844.[189] He told Victor de Broglie that he was 'abounding in epigrams'.[190] It was a way of warding off thoughts of death. For he had seen all that he wished to see and he had outlived everyone.[191] His state of health had however been precarious since late 1842. He complained to Rehfues of 'melancholy and sleepiness', 'sea-sickness';[192] the 'taena lata' in his intestines caused associated digestive problems;[193] there was asthma,[194] all this despite following a quasi-Brahmanic regime of ablutions and baths.[195] Physical dissolution was not however accompanied by a clouding of his mind; he seemed instead intent on dying 'en philosophe', with no late recantations, perhaps more of the scepticism of Frederick the Great, on whom he had lavished such a disproportionate amount of time and energy. Even as his bodily state announced the approaching end, his colleague Friedrich Welcker found him in good spirits and displaying a sharp mind. He told Welcker an anecdote about Montaigne on his deathbed, set about by his family, and calling for a domino cloak to be put round him, 'ut moriamur in domino'.[196] Recondite and witty to the end.

Schlegel died on 12 March 1845, aged 77. The cause of death was given as 'debilitation caused by a gastric complaint'.[197] He was buried in the Alter Friedhof (Old Graveyard) in Bonn. His grave, designed by the sculptor Ernst von Bandel, best known for his huge monument of Arminius in the Teutoburg Forest, adapted David d'Angers's profile medallion, with that rather Roman image, stern, critical. Death merged friendships, enmities, and celebrities. A short walk from Schlegel's grave will take one to those of Rehfues, Niebuhr (conjoined Roman-style with his wife), of Schiller's widow and their son Ernst, of Beethoven's mother, of Robert and Clara Schumann.[198]

---

189 The course on Sanskrit until the winter of 1843-44; art history in the summer of 1842, the winter of 1842-43, and the summer of 1844; on history in the summers of 1843 and 1844. *Vorlesungen auf der Rheinischen Friedrich-Wilhelms-Universität Bonn* (Bonn: Georgi), Sommerhalbjahr 1842, 7; Winterhalbjahr 1842-43, 7; Sommerhalbjahr 1843, 6f.; Winterhalbjahr 1843-44, 6f.; Sommerhalbjahr 1844, 7. There is nothing for 1845.
190 *Briefe*, I, 614; Deetjen, 20.
191 *Ibid.*, 20.
192 UB Bonn S 1392 (51, 52); Deetjen, *ibid.*
193 *Briefe*, I, 573f.
194 *Ibid.*, 617.
195 *Ibid.*, 605.
196 A pun on 'so that I may die in the Lord'. Kekulé, *Welcker*, 405.
197 UB Bonn Lambertz S 2537, II (24).
198 Edith Ennen *et al.*, *Der Alte Friedhof in Bonn. Geschichtlich, biographisch, kunst- und geistesgeschichtlich* (Bonn: Stadt Bonn, 1981), 55f., plates 2, 3, 9, 12, 26, 27.

Epilogue

What of Schlegel's legacy? Already in 1829, when his solicitor Lambertz finally broke off relations with the Paulus family, Schlegel stated that he wished his will to benefit those who had contributed to his wellbeing, his scholarly collection to go to a public institution.[199] The will copied out and dated 23 March 1845 was more specific. Christian Lassen received part of his Indian material; to his nieces Amalie Wolper and Auguste von Buttlar went the bulk of his estate; the thankless Academy in Berlin gained his papers on Frederick the Great; his order of Pour le Mérite was returned to the king; Bonn university library was given his bust by Friedrich Tieck and the family psalter of 1525. Auguste in addition received back her own paintings and drawings, but more importantly she inherited his collection of Indian miniatures;[200] Friedrich Tieck acquired an antique head of Silenus and his own drawings. Countess d'Haussonville, née Broglie became the possessor of a golden medallion containing a lock of hair of her grandmother, Madame de Staël; Amalie Wolper came by a wisp of the hair of Johanna Erdmuthe Schlegel, her grandmother and Schlegel's beloved mother. The coachman and factotum Heinrich von Wehrden was left his carriage, his horses, and his wardrobe.[201] (The puce-coloured court dress finished up in a carnival stunt.)[202]

The bookseller J. M. Heberle in Bonn was entrusted with the sale by auction of Schlegel's library.[203] It has gone to the four winds. For sheer bulk, it ranks as one of the great Romantic collections, like Ludwig Tieck's and Clemens Brentano's, yet different from theirs for its emphasis on orientalia, history and geography, or classics; the parts on Romance and English literatures do not compare with Tieck's, but the sections on German literature are full of rare items including incunabula. His interest in reprographic techniques is reflected in his collection of lithographs and aquatints. In its coverage it has affinities with Eschenburg's library, auctioned twenty-five years earlier. The catalogue also represents as complete a bibliography of

---

199 UB Bonn Lambertz S 2537, II (21-22).
200 Now in Kupferstich-Kabinett, Staatliche Kunstsammlungen Dresden. It is not clear how these relate to the 95 paintings offered for sale in Heberle's catalogue (107).
201 Kaufmann, 239.
202 Ribbeck, *Ritschl*, II, 72.
203 *Katalog der von Aug. Wilh. von Schlegel, Professor an der Königl. Universität zu Bonn, Ritter etc., nachgelaßenen Büchersammlung, welche Montag den 1sten Dezember 1845 und an den folgenden Tagen Abends 5 Uhr präcise bei J. M. Heberle in Bonn öffentlich versteigert und dem Letztbietenden gegen gleich baare Zahlung verabfolgt wird.*

Schlegel's works as one will find anywhere. This is the working library of a polymath scholar, not that of a compulsive collector or a book fanatic: Ludwig Tieck possessed *Der jüngere Titurel* of 1477 because he must have it, Schlegel, because he needed it for learned study and discourse.

Lambertz was of course obliged to inform Schlegel's widow, Sophie von Schlegel, and Böcking sent her a copy of the will.[204] According to Baden law, his estate remained sealed until receipt of a statement of renunciation. This she produced on 19 May 1845.[205] For Lambertz, this was in keeping with her character.[206] Her father, Heinrich Eberhard Gottlob Paulus, in accordance with his less generous nature, wrote to Lambertz and Böcking in December 1845, enquiring whether there might not be a widow's pension from the University of Bonn, to which his daughter might have entitlement. There was not, and on this suitably mercenary note ended the saga of Schlegel's unhappy marriage.[207]

Eduard Böcking, also wearing his hat as 'Édouard' and 'Eduardus', was Schlegel's literary executor. It is to him that we owe the twelve volumes of *Sämmtliche Werke* in German, the three of *Oeuvres* in French and the single *Opuscula* in Latin, that came out with the Leipzig publisher Weidmann in 1846-48. This was not the edition that Reimer might have produced, or Cotta, had they been interested. Schlegel's meticulousness and the general tidiness of his papers meant that Böcking found most of the material in the *Nachlass* (nearly all of Schlegel's reviews and articles, for instance). He made small orthographical changes for consistency's sake, so minor as to be of no consequence. One may regret, as already said, his decision to publish Schlegel's revised version of the Vienna Lectures, which is not the text that secured his fame. The *Indische Bibliothek* and the *Berliner Kalender* were marked up for the printer, but never reissued as such, only extracts from the former, none of the latter. None of the pamphlets for Bernadotte is included, although they are all there in the *Nachlass*. The *Nibelungenlied* essays are missing, a regrettable omission. Doubtless copyright considerations meant the exclusion of the translations of Shakespeare and Calderón: clearly it was not an area into which Böcking wished to stray. We must be grateful for such hitherto unpublished material as he allotted space for, the *Considérations* of 1805, for instance, or the exchange of letters

---

204 UB Bonn, Lambertz S 2537, II (24).
205 *Ibid.* (27-28).
206 *Ibid.* (29).
207 *Briefe*, II, 158f.

with Albertine in 1838. Schlegel's Berlin and Bonn lectures remained largely unpublished, some of them until this day. It was to be Rudolf Haym's account of the Berlin Lectures in 1870 that first alerted attention to them, with Jakob Minor publishing the main Berlin series in the 1880s. The *Sämmtliche Werke* therefore present us with a Schlegel full of lacunae, a series of gaps around which we must construct a man and his works as an integrated whole. How extensive that whole is can be established from the acres of *Nachlass* that Böcking presented to the then Royal Library in Dresden in 1873 and which have very largely survived changes of name and regime, and the onslaught of war.

Short Biographies[1]

Arndt, Ernst Moritz (1769-1860): patriotic author and historian. Born on the island of Rügen, he studied at the University of Greifswald, where in 1806 he was appointed professor of history. He expressed strongly anti-Napoleonic views (esp. in his *Geist der Zeit*, 1806) and attached himself to Blücher, Gneisenau, and notably Friedrich Karl vom Stein (q.v.), whose amanuensis in St Petersburg he became. Appointed a professor at Bonn in 1818, he soon fell foul of the Carlsbad Decrees in 1819 and was suspended until 1840. In 1848, he was a member of the Frankfurt Parliament. He was noted for his Francophobia and anti-Semitism. He died at Bonn.

Arnim, Bettina von, née Elisabeth Brentano (1785-1859): writer; hagiographer of Goethe. Born Elisabeth Brentano in Frankfurt am Main, the sister of the poet Clemens Brentano, the granddaughter of Sophie von La Roche, the sister-in-law of Karl  Friedrich von Savigny and linked by close friendship with the Grimm brothers (q.v.). Her main publications were based on her association with Karoline von Günderrode (*Die Günderode*, 1840) and with Goethe (*Goethes Briefwechsel mit einem Kinde*, 1835). In 1811, she married Ludwig Achim von Arnim (q.v.). They lived at Wiepersdorf, in Brandenburg, and had seven children. After his death in 1831, she settled in Berlin, where she died.

Arnim, Ludwig Achim von (1781-1831): Romantic poet, dramatist and novelist. Born at Berlin, he studied at Halle and Göttingen, followed by a grand tour of Italy, France and the British Isles. A close friend of Clemens Brentano and of the Grimm brothers (q.v.), he was in 1805 in Heidelberg, where the first volume of *Des Knaben Wunderhorn* appeared (I-III,

---

1 For details about the images in this section please refer to the List of Illustrations.

© Roger Paulin, CC BY http://dx.doi.org/10.11647/OBP.0069.06

1806-08). He edited the periodical *Zeitung für Einsiedler* (1808), to which AWS contributed. After his marriage to Bettina Brentano (q.v.) in 1811, he lived at Wiepersdorf, where he died. He wrote the novels *Gräfin Dolores* (1810) and *Die Kronenwächter* (1817), the collection of plays *Die Schaubühne* (1813) and numerous short stories. Noted for his pronounced anti-Semitic views.

Baudissin, Wolf Heinrich von (1789-1878): Danish diplomat; translator of Shakespeare into German. Born at Copenhagen of an old Holstein noble family, he was educated by tutors, then at Berlin, where he attended AWS's lectures. He attended the Universities of Kiel, Göttingen and Heidelberg, then entered the Danish diplomatic service. In 1810 he was posted to Stockholm as legation secretary, where in 1813 he met Madame de Staël and AWS. For refusing to act in a diplomatic mission to further links between Denmark and Napoleon, he was imprisoned at Friedrichsort, near Kiel. After leaving the diplomatic service in 1814, he visited Italy (later, France and Greece) and in 1827 settled in Dresden. He was a close collaborator in the translation of Shakespeare edited by Ludwig Tieck (q.v.), for which he translated thirteen plays. He later translated Ben Jonson and Molière.

Bernadotte, Jean Baptiste (1763-1844): marshal of the Empire; Prince of Pontecorvo; Prince Royal, later king of Sweden. Born at Pau, in humble circumstances, he joined the royal army as a private soldier. During the Revolutionary Wars, he rose very quickly and by 1794 was a full general. He was briefly the Revolutionary government's first ambassador to Austria. Although never close to Napoleon, he was prominent at the battles of Ulm, Austerlitz, Jena and Auerstädt, and Wagram, becoming a Marshal of the Empire. Napoleon, although never  satisfied with his performance, made him Prince of Pontecorvo in 1806. He was governor of the Hanseatic towns during the French occupation. In 1810, he was approached by a Swedish intermediary as a possible successor to the childless king of Sweden, Charles XIII. As Charles John, he was proclaimed crown prince (Prince Royal) in the same year and assumed command of the Swedish forces. In 1812-13 he negotiated with the Tsar, then with Great Britain, finally breaking with France. AWS was his private secretary during this time. He pursued an anti-Danish policy with the intention of securing a personal union of Sweden and Norway (1814). He led the Swedish forces during the campaigns against Napoleon in 1813-14, in North Germany, Saxony, and the in the west. In 1818 he was crowned King Karl XIV Johan (Charles John) of Sweden and Norway. Died at Stockholm.

Bernhardi, August Ferdinand (1769-1820): critic and schoolmaster in Berlin; married to Sophie Tieck. Born in Berlin. After studying at university in Halle, he became a schoolmaster at the Friedrichswerder Gymnasium in Berlin (head in 1808), where he was the teacher, then friend of the young Ludwig Tieck (q.v.) and was part of the early Romantic circle. In 1799, he married Sophie Tieck (q.v.); there were two surviving children, Wilhelm and Felix Theodor (q.v.). He was associated with the Schlegel brothers in Berlin in 1801-03. The marriage failed; Sophie left him, taking her sons eventually to Rome and then Munich. Bernhardi obtained custody of Wilhelm after protracted divorce proceedings. He frequented the circle of Varnhagen von Ense in Berlin, was also noted for his writings on linguistics (*Sprachlehre*, 1801-03; *Anfangsgründe der Sprachwissenschaft*, 1805). Prominent in Prussian educational reform, he was in 1820 appointed head of the Friedrich-Wilhelms-Gymnasium. He died at Berlin.

Bernhardi, Felix Theodor (von) (1802-1887): diplomat; writer on military subjects. Born at Berlin, the son of August Ferdinand Bernhardi and Sophie Bernhardi, née Tieck (claims have been made for Karl Gregor von Knorring's and AWS's paternity), the nephew of Ludwig and Friedrich Tieck (q.v.). After the collapse of his parents' marriage, he moved with his mother and Knorring to Rome and Munich. He went in 1812 with Sophie Bernhardi and Knorring to the latter's estate in Estonia, returning to Germany in 1820-23 to study in Heidelberg. He then entered Russian service (1834-51), finally settling in Germany. He became a prominent writer on military affairs and was ennobled in 1873. He died at Schöpstal in Silesia.

Böhmer, Auguste (1785-1800): Caroline Schlegel's (q.v.) daughter by her first marriage with Johann Franz Wilhelm Böhmer; AWS's step-daughter; the granddaughter of Johann David Michaelis. Born at Claustal in the Harz. After the early death of her father, she moved with her mother to Göttingen, then to Marburg and finally, in 1792, to Mainz. She was with her mother in prison in the Königstein and in Kronberg in the Taunus and accompanied her to Lucka, where her half-brother Wilhelm Julius Crancé was born, then to Gotha and Brunswick. On her mother's marriage to AWS in 1796, she became his step-daughter and FS's step-niece. She was a precocious child in the Romantic circle in Jena. She accompanied Caroline and Schelling  (q.v.) to Bocklet in 1800 and died after a short illness there. Tieck's and AWS's *Musen-Almanach auf das Jahr 1802* is partly devoted to her memory, while Friedrich Tieck did a bust of her.

Boisserée, Melchior (1786-1851) **and Boisserée, Sulpiz** (1783-1854): Cologne patrician's sons; protégés of Friedrich Schlegel; important collectors of medieval art. Sulpiz was born at Cologne. In 1803 the brothers attended lectures in Paris given by

Friedrich Schlegel, continued in Cologne, and these founded their interest in the Christian art of the Middle Ages. Sulpiz began collecting in 1804; his collection, housed from 1810 in Heidelberg, attracted much attention, especially Goethe's. He edited the *Kunstblatt* (to which AWS contributed) and was prominent in the campaign to complete Cologne cathedral. The brothers sold their collection in 1827 to King Ludwig I of Bavaria (q.v.), where it is now part of the Alte Pinakothek. He died at Bonn. Melchior, also born in Cologne, continued the family business and provided the financial basis for their art acquisitions. He died at Bonn.

Bonstetten, Karl Viktor von (1745-1832): Bernese patrician; administrator; philosopher; member of Coppet circle. Born at Berne, he studied in Leyden, Cambridge and Paris. He was active in the reform of the administration in Berne and was closely associated with Johannes (von) Müller (q.v.). After Napoleon's seizure of Berne, he was in Copenhagen in the circle of Friederike Brun. He settled at Geneva in 1803 and became a member of Madame de Staël's circle in Coppet, where he also met AWS. His writings deal with national character (*Über Nationalbildung*, 1803), and climate and character (*L'Homme du Midi et l'homme du Nord*, 1824). He died at Geneva.

Broglie, Albert de, prince, then duke (1821-1901): diplomat, politician and historian. The son of Victor and Albertine de Broglie, and the grandson of Madame de Staël, he was born at Paris. After a brief diplomatic career, he devoted himself to travel and literature. Succeeding his father as duke in 1870, he entered politics and was successively minister of foreign affairs and minister of the interior, and briefly prime minister. He retired from politics in 1885.

Broglie, Albertine de, duchess, née de Staël-Holstein (1797-1838). The daughter of Madame de Staël and Baron Erik Magnus Staël von Holstein, she went on all the journeyings of her mother, to Italy, to Germany, to Russia and Sweden, and to England. On the second journey to Italy (1816), she was married to Victor, duke of Broglie (q.v.), with whom she had two sons and two daughters. Noted for her piety, she kept up a correspondence with AWS during the years of her marriage until her death at the château de Broglie in 1838.

Short Biographies 571

Broglie, Victor de, duke (1785-1870): French politician and statesman; husband of Albertine de Staël. He was born at Paris. His father was guillotined during the  Terror. After a brief exile, he returned to Paris and received a liberal education, entering the diplomatic service under Napoleon. At the Restoration, he became a liberal member of the House of Peers. In 1816, he married Albertine de Staël and alternated between Paris and the Broglie estate in Normandy. Under the July Monarchy, he was minister of education and minister of foreign affairs. He resigned from politics in 1836. Later, he was an implacable opponent of the Second Empire.

Bürger, Gottfried August (1747-1794): poet and translator, Schlegel's mentor in Göttingen. Born at Molmerswende, he studied law at the Universities of Halle and Göttingen and was a justice official, first near, then in Göttingen itself. After 1784, he gave lectures on philosophy and aesthetics at the university. He was closely linked with the Göttingen 'Hainbund' (Voss, Hölty, Stolberg), wrote ballads in a popular style, and translated Homer's *Iliad* and Shakespeare's *Macbeth*. He befriended AWS after his arrival in Göttingen and was his mentor in poetic matters. His marital arrangements (two marriages ended in death, the third was dissolved) and his financial disarray compromised his reputation, not least Schiller's  devastating review of the edition of his poems in 1791 (AWS's review 'Bürger' (1801) was written in his defence). He died at Göttingen.

Buttlar, Auguste von, née Ernst (1796-1857): painter. The daughter of Charlotte Ernst, née Schlegel, and Ludwig Emanuel Ernst, AWS's and FS's niece. Born at Pillnitz, she grew up in Dresden. In 1816, she married Baron von Buttlar, an officer in Russian service. After some training in Munich, she entered the studio of Baron Gérard in Paris, largely through the influence of her uncle, AWS. He also helped her with portrait commissions in England and France. She was estranged from him after her conversion to Catholicism in 1827, but they were later reconciled. After her husband's death, she painted portraits for a living, mainly in Austria. A major beneficiary of AWS's will, she inherited his Indian miniatures, which she later presented to the royal collections in Dresden. She died at Florence.

Chézy, Antoine-Léonard de (1773-1832): Orientalist. Born at Neuilly. He learned oriental languages, esp. Arabic and Persian, from Antoine-Isaac de Silvestre de Sacy and Louis-Mathieu Langlès, later adding Sanskrit. He married Wilhelmine von Klenke, who after her separation from him continued her writing career as Helmine von Chézy. The first occupant of a chair of Sanskrit in France (1814), he was also one of the founders of the Société asiatique in 1822, later also holding a chair of Persian. AWS visited him in Paris, but their relationship was more correct than cordial. He died at Paris. *Yadjinadatta-badha* (1814, reviewed by AWS), *Théorie du Sloka* (1827), *La Reconnaissance de Sacountala* (1830).

Colebrooke, Henry Thomas (1765-1837): Indologist. Born at London, he went as a young man to India, rising in the Bengal administration, eventually as judge in the court of appeal. In 1805, he was appointed professor of Hindu law and Sanskrit at the College of Fort William. He returned to England with his family in 1814. He presented his huge collection of Indian material to the Royal Asiatic Society, of which he was a co-founder. He corresponded with AWS from 1820 to 1828 and received him on his visit to London in 1823. His son John lived for nearly a year in AWS's house in Bonn, while preparing for university. He wrote  extensively on Hindu law, on astronomy and mathematics, on religion, and edited a Sanskrit dictionary. He died at London.

 **Constant, Henri-Benjamin Constant de Rebeque** (1767-1830): political theorist and activist; novelist; lover of Madame de Staël. Born at Lausanne to Protestant parents, he was educated in the Netherlands, then at Edinburgh university. He held a court post in Brunswick until forced to leave by the Revolutionary Wars. In Paris, he met Germaine de Staël and became her lover. After involvement in politics, he was obliged to leave France for Coppet. He accompanied Madame de Staël for part of her first journey to Germany and returned with her and AWS to Coppet. For the next few years, he moved in and out of the Coppet circle. His marriage in 1809 strained his relationship with Staël. He met up with AWS again in Hanover in 1814, returned to Paris and became deeply involved in politics during the Restoration, the Hundred Days, and the Bourbon monarchy. The author of *Des Réactions politiques* (1797), *Wallstein* (1809, which AWS reviewed), *Adolphe* (1816), *De la Religion* (1824-31).

Cotta, Johann Friedrich von (1764-1832): publisher. He was born at Stuttgart and studied law in Tübingen. In 1787 he took over his father's publishing business and extended it to include many of the major figures of the Classical and Romantic period, including Schiller and Goethe, Tieck and AWS. The firm moved to Stuttgart in 1810. Ennobled, he played a prominent role in politics in Württemberg after 1815.

Eschenburg, Johann Joachim (1743-1820): critic and literary historian. Born at

Hamburg, he studied at Leipzig (where he met Goethe) and Göttingen. In 1767 he was appointed tutor, subsequently professor, at the Collegium Carolinum in Brunswick. He was a poet and dramatist in his own right and translated widely, esp. English criticism and aesthetics, also producing standard handbooks of rhetoric and literary history, notably his *Beispielsammlung* (1788-95). He is best known for his complete prose translation of Shakespeare (1775-82) and for his compendium, *Ueber W. Shakspeare* (1787). In 1792, he used his influence to secure AWS his tutorship in Amsterdam. Died at Brunswick.

Fauriel, Claude Charles (1772-1844): French literary scholar and professor. Born at St Étienne and educated at Lyon, he served in the Revolutionary army and was involved in politics, making in 1801 the decision to become a private scholar. He was close to Madame de Staël, Constant, Manzoni and Guizot, and was the companion of Madame de Condorcet. He became especially noted for his translation of Greek popular songs (1824-25) and his studies on oriental languages and notably on Provençal. In 1830 he was appointed professor of foreign literature at the Sorbonne. He was associated with AWS during his visits to Paris.

Fichte, Johann Gottlieb (1762-1814): philosopher. Born at Rammenau, Saxony, the son of a ribbon weaver, through the good offices of a nobleman, he was able to study at Jena. There followed years as a tutor, including two in Zurich. He secured first prominence with his *Versuch einer Kritik aller Offenbarung* (1792), which met with Kant's approval. In 1794, he was appointed professor in Jena, where he was a popular lecturer and developed his system of transcendental idealism (*Wissenschaftslehre*, 1798-99). He was close to the Romantics, Novalis, AWS and FS, and
Schelling. The so-called 'atheism affair' led to his dismissal in 1799. He lived first in Berlin, and was briefly a professor in Erlangen. In 1808 he delivered the highly contentious and xenophobic *Reden an die deutsche Nation* in Berlin. In 1810, he was appointed professor at the newly founded University of Berlin, and was its rector in 1812. He died during a typhus epidemic in Berlin.

Fiorillo, Johann Domenik (Domenico) (1748-1821): art historian. Born at Hamburg, the son of an Italian composer, he studied art at Bologna and Rome, and was appointed history painter to the court in Brunswick. In 1781 he moved to Göttingen as drawing master. In this capacity he was the mentor to AWS, then to Tieck and Wackenroder. AWS assisted him with the first proofs of his monumental *Geschichte* *der zeichnendnen Künste* (1798-1808). He was appointed an assistant professor in 1799 and a full professor in 1813. Died at Göttingen.

Flaxman, John (1755-1826): neo-classical engraver and sculptor. Born at York, he studied at the Royal Academy. Working for Josiah Wedgwood, he first developed the neo-classical outline forms that secured him European fame with his later engravings for the works of Homer and Dante. He spent 1787-94 in Italy, and was thereafter a much sought-after sculptor in the classical style. AWS reviewed his Homer and Dante engravings in the *Athenaeum* in 1799, and he visited him in London in 1823. Died at London.

Forster, Georg (1754-1794): naturalist, explorer, journalist. Born at Nassenhuben, near Danzig, the son of Johann Reinhold Forster, who took Georg with him on journeys in Russia, England and then on James Cook's second circumnavigation of the world in 1772-75. His English account of Cook's voyage, *A Voyage Round the World* in 1777 (German, *Reise um die Welt*, 1778-80) established his reputation as a botanist and ethnographer. He taught natural history in Kassel, then at the academy in Vilna, before becoming university librarian in Mainz in 1788. Through his marriage to Therese Heyne,  he was linked with Caroline Böhmer, later Schlegel (q.v.), and both families lived in Mainz until 1793. His translation into German of Sir William Jones's version of *Śakuntalâ* (1791) was a major influence on later writers. In the spring of 1790, Forster and the young Alexander von Humboldt (q.v.) undertook a long journey on the lower Rhine. Forster's account, *Ansichten von Niederrhein* (1791-94), is important for its discussion of art and architecture. After the capture of Mainz by the French in 1792, he was involved in the Jacobin club, and was a delegate of the Mainz republic in Paris in 1793. After the capture of Mainz by the coalition forces, he was outlawed and forced to return to Paris, where he died in straitened circumstances.

Fouqué, Friedrich de la Motte, pseud. Pellegrin (1777-1843): dramatist and novelist. Born at Brandenburg, of Huguenot descent, the son of a Prussian officer and the grandson of one of Fredrick the Great's generals. After studying at Halle, he became an officer in the Prussian army. Upon his marriage, he settled on his estate at Nennhausen and devoted himself to literature. Publishing under a pseudonym, he attracted AWS's attention, who then issued his *Dramatische Spiele von Pellegrin* (1804). It was to Fouqué that AWS wrote the letter calling for more patriotic themes in German poetry. He published his Nibelungen trilogy, *Der*

Held des Nordens, in 1808-10, and continued, with diminishing quality, to produce prose and dramas on popular medieval-inspired themes. He is today best known for his tale *Undine* (1811). He served in the Wars of Liberation as a comrade-in-arms of Philipp Veit (q.v.).

Gentz, Friedrich (von) (1764-1832): statesman. Born at Breslau, after study in Königsberg, he entered the Prussian civil service. He first came to prominence with his translation of Edmund Burke's *Reflections* (1794), part of his general interest in the English constitution and financial system. He called for press freedom and was an energetic pamphleteer on contemporary issues. He received substantial payments from the British and Austrians, which supported his raffish life-style. He entered Austrian service in 1802, but was first employed in 1809. His anti-Napoleonic stance made him useful to Metternich (q.v.) whose right-hand man and draftsman he became and whose political system he supported in the later part of his career. He heard AWS's Berlin lectures, met him with Madame de Staël in 1808, and corresponded during AWS's time with Bernadotte. He died at Vienna.

Görres, Joseph (von) (1776-1848): Romantic nature philosopher and patriot. Born at Koblenz and educated in a Catholic Latin school, he was initially a supporter of the French Revolution and was a delegate of the Rhine Provinces in Paris. Changing orientation, he moved in 1806 to Heidelberg, where his lectures on natural philosophy attracted much attention and brought him into the circle around Clemens Brentano and Achim von Arnim (q.v.). He published his *Die teutschen Volksbücher* in 1807. Returning to Koblenz in 1808, he steeped himself in the Orient and produced his *Mythengeschichte der asiatischen Welt* in 1810. In 1813, at the outbreak of the Wars of Liberation, he published the strongly anti-Napoleonic periodical *Rheinischer Merkur*, which was eventually suppressed in 1816. His *Teutschland und die Revolution* (1819) fell foul of the Carlsbad Decrees; he was forced to flee, first to Strasbourg, then to Switzerland. His interests became more Ultramontane, and in 1827 he was appointed professor of history at the new University of Munich. *Die christliche Mystik* (1836-42) is his major later work. Died at Munich.

Goethe, Johann Wolfgang (von) (1749-1832): poet, dramatist, novelist. Born of patrician parentage at Frankfurt am Main. He studied law at Leipzig and Strasbourg, having in Strasbourg a close association with Johann Gottfried Herder. Major works from this period are the drama *Götz von Berlichingen* (1773) and poetry. In 1773 he was an assessor at the Imperial Chamber Court in Wetzlar, where an unhappy love affair formed the basis of his first novel *Die Leiden des jungen Werthers*

(1774), that caused a European-wide sensation. In 1775 he went on his first journey to Switzerland. In 1776, he was appointed companion, later minister of state, by duke Carl August of Saxe-Weimar, and remained resident in Weimar thereafter. In this time he showed his first interest in geology and botany. He travelled in Italy during the years 1786-8, followed by the publication of the more restrained *Iphigenie auf Tauris* (first 1779, revised 1786) and *Torquato Tasso* (1788), the works reviewed by the young AWS. His association with Schiller in the 1790s was expressed in *Die Horen* and the *Xenien*. After the publication of the novel *Wilhelm Meisters Lehrjahre* (1795-96), his *Römische Elegien* (1795) and his verse epic *Hermann und Dorothea* (1798), Goethe was the object of the young Romantics' devotion, and a close association developed, with Goethe the minister of state when Fichte, Schelling and the Schlegel brothers were at the university in Jena. Differences, however, emerged as Goethe remained true to his neo-classicism, whereas the Romantics favoured more the Catholic Middle Ages. Goethe nevertheless praised Arnim and Brentano's *Wunderhorn*, and was a friend of the Boisserée brothers (q.v.). While the first part of *Faust* (1808) was well received in Romantic circles, the novel *Die Wahlverwandtschaften* and his memoirs, *Dichtung und Wahrheit* (1811-14) were read as anti-Romantic in tendency. Despite a common interest in India, AWS's relations with Goethe in the 1820s became strained, culminating in the publication of Goethe's correspondence with Schiller (1828-29). His late works, the novel *Wilhelm Meisters Wanderjahre* (1829) and the second part of *Faust* (1832), were little appreciated. After Goethe's death, the publication of his conversations further accentuated the gulf between him and the Romantic generation.

Grimm, Jacob (1785-1863): grammarian; editor; lexicographer. Born at Hanau in Hesse, he attended Marburg university. There, he heard lectures by Karl Ludwig von Savigny and followed him to Paris to work on old German texts. In 1808, he was appointed librarian to King Jérôme of Westphalia, in Kassel. After the fall of Napoleon, he was part of the Hessian legation in Paris, then librarian in Kassel. He formed a close friendship with Clemens Brentano and Achim von Arnim (q.v.). With his brother Wilhelm (q.v.) he published on Germanic subjects, but the *Kinder- und Hausmärchen* (1812-15) first brought the brothers to a wider readership. AWS savaged their first scholarly collection, *Altdeutsche Wälder* (1813-15), but was reconciled by the later *Deutsche Grammatik* (1819) and their writings on the

history of the German language. AWS met the Grimm brothers in the 1820s, and a mutual respect developed, although for them AWS lacked the gravitas of the true scholar. They were appointed professors at Göttingen in 1830, but in 1837 fell foul, as members of the 'Göttingen Seven', of the Hanoverian king's reactionary politics. In 1840, both brothers were invited to Berlin, where they embarked on the Academy's project of a German dictionary (first vol. 1854). He died at Berlin.

Grimm, Wilhelm (1786-1859): grammarian; editor, lexicographer. Born at Hanau, the younger brother of Jacob (q.v.), from whom he was inseparable all his life and whose biography very closely parallels that of his brother. Wilhelm remained in Germany and became a librarian in Kassel, where he and Jacob worked until 1830. In 1825, Wilhelm married, but continued to live next to Jacob. Wilhelm's main independent work was *Die deutsche Heldensage* (1829). He died at Berlin.

Hardenberg, Friedrich von (known as Novalis) (1772-1801): poet. Born at the family estate of Oberwiederstedt in Thuringia, of a pious aristocratic family (Moravian Brethren), he attended school at Eisleben and studied law at the Universities of Leipzig, Wittenberg and Jena. At Jena he fell under the strong influence of Fichte (q.v.) and in 1794, he met Sophie von Kühn, the 'child bride' to whom he became engaged and who after her death in 1797 became an inspiration for his poetry. While at Jena, he also met the Romantic circle, esp. FS and Tieck, but also AWS, Caroline and Schelling (q.v.). In 1797, he attended the  mining academy at Freiberg, studying technical subjects, and in 1799 was appointed director of the salt mines at Weissenfels. The *Athenaeum* published his collection of aphorisms, *Blütenstaub* (1798) and his mystical *Hymnen an die Nacht* (1800). He died of tuberculosis at Weissenfels. FS and Tieck published his posthumous works (first 1802), the visionary novel *Heinrich von Ofterdingen*, and the treatise on nature philosophy, *Die Lehrlinge zu Sais*. The radical historical essay, *Die Christenheit oder Europa*, did not come out until 1826.

 **Hardenberg, Karl August von, prince** (1750-1822): minister of state. Born near Hanover, he studied at Leipzig and Göttingen. After travels in France, the Netherlands and England (where his wife had an affair with the Prince of Wales) he entered the service of the dukedom of Brunswick. In 1791, the Prussian state appointed him administrator of the territories of Ansbach and Bayreuth. In 1797 he was admitted to the cabinet; in 1804 he was foreign minister. He guided Prussian policy during the difficult years leading up to 1806 and after. In 1810, he was

appointed chancellor and presided over a series of military, civil and educational reforms. He was able to bring King Frederick William III over into the anti-Napoleon alliance in 1813, and he was Prussia's representative at the congresses in Vienna, Paris, and Aachen. Now a prince, he approved AWS's appointment in Bonn and was instrumental in securing him a grant for his Sanskrit studies. He died at Genoa.

Heine, Heinrich (1797-1856): poet. Born at Düsseldorf, until 1815 under French occupation, he was known as 'Harry' until his conversion to Christianity in 1825 (he signed the register of AWS's lectures in that style). Apprenticed to a banker in Hamburg, he showed no aptitude and embarked on the study of law, first at Bonn (where he attended AWS's lectures), then Göttingen, and finally Berlin (where he heard Hegel and met Varnhagen and Rahel, q.v.). There followed his journey to the Harz mountains, commemorated in his *Reisebilder* (I: 1826, II, 1827). He first made a name for himself with his *Buch der Lieder* (1827). Journeys to England and Italy followed. The third part of his *Reisebilder* (1829) contained his attack on Count Platen. He moved to Paris in 1831, working as a foreign correspondent. The main works of this period are *Der Salon, Französische Zustände, Zur Geschichte der Religion und Philosophie in Deutschland*, and *Die Romantische Schule* (1835) in which he made his unkind remarks on AWS and Madame de Staël, also in *Shakespeares Mädchen und Frauen* (1838). He became more and more involved in politics and was associated with the so-called Young Germans. His *Neue Gedichte* appeared in 1844, the satirical verse epics *Deutschland. Ein Wintermärchen* in 1844 and *Atta Troll* in 1847, and his final major collection of poetry, *Romanzero* in 1851. He died at Paris.

Hemsterhuis, Frans (François) (1721-1790): philosopher. Born at Franeker, Netherlands, he studied at Leyden. He was for most of his active life the secretary of state to the United Provinces. He was close to the Platonist and mystical circle in Münster around Princess Gallitzin and F.H. Jacobi. AWS was influenced by his Platonist aesthetic writings and by his notion of a golden age. *Lettre sur la sculpture* (1769), *Lettre sur l'homme et ses rapports* (1772), *Alexis* (1787). Died at The Hague.

Herder, Johann Gottfried (von) (1745-1803): theologian, philosopher, critic, poet. Born at Mohrungen, East Prussia, he studied at Königsberg and came under the influence of Kant and Johann Georg Hamann and esp. his idea of 'origins'. His first publication, *Kritische Wälder* (1767-68), was a voice advocating new directions in poetry and thought. Ordained a clergyman, he travelled in 1769 from Riga to Nantes, then to

Paris. From there, he went through north Germany as chaplain to a prince, and on to Strasbourg, where he met Goethe. There followed his significant essays on Shakespeare, Ossian, the origins of language and the philosophy of history. He took a post as court preacher in Bückeburg in 1771, moving in 1776 at Goethe's suggestion to Weimar, as 'General superintent'. Of especial importance were his notions of the organic development of history and of its cultural expression, and their natural forces, as set out in his *Ideen zur Philosophie der Geschichte der Menschheit* (1784-91), which was especially influential on the young Romantics. He died at Weimar.

Heyne, Christian Gottlob (1729-1812): classical scholar. Born at Chemnitz, the son of a weaver, he attended university at Leipzig, but lived in penury until appointed to the chair of classics at Göttingen in 1761. He had by now produced editions of Tibullus and Epictetus, and was to edit Virgil and Pindar. As university librarian and director of the classical seminar in Göttingen, he was an important mentor for the young AWS.

Humboldt, Alexander von (1769-1859): scientist and explorer. Born at Berlin and privately educated. He developed his precocious interests in natural history, esp. botany and mineralogy, at the Universities of Frankfurt an der Oder and Göttingen, then at the mining academy at Freiberg. A journey up the Rhine with Georg Forster quickened his interest in the interrelation of natural phenomena. He travelled extensively in Germany and Austria and was appointed a senior mining official by the Prussian state. Plans to join Napoleon's expedition to Egypt came to nothing, but in 1799, accompanied by Aimé Bonpland, he was able to persuade the authorities in Madrid to allow him to explore extensively in the Spanish possessions in the New World. Humboldt and Bonpland traversed the area of modern Venezuela and discovered the course of the Orinoco (*Voyage aux régions équinoctiales du Nouveau Continent*). The explorers proceeded through modern Colombia and  Peru, climbing Chimborazo (*Vues des Cordillères et monuments des peuples indigènes de l'Amérique*, 1810, reviewed 1817 by AWS). Unable to do the planned circumnavigation, they moved to Mexico and Cuba, on which Humboldt wrote important economic and political studies. After a short visit to the United States, he returned in 1804, He lived in Paris, 'the most famous man in Europe', writing up the results of his scientific and ethnological studies and laying the foundations of plant geography. Finally returning to Berlin in 1827, he was a courtier and chamberlain under Frederick William III and IV, making one last scientific journey, to Russia, in 1829. The synthesis of his scientific studies is his *Kosmos* (1845-62). He died at Berlin.

Humboldt, Wilhelm von (1767-1835): classical scholar, linguistician and Prussian minister of state. Born at Potsdam and privately educated. He attended university  at Frankfurt an der Oder and Göttingen (where he met AWS), followed by a grand tour which took him to Paris. He entered the Prussian civil service, but soon gave this up for the life of a private scholar. He moved in 1794 to Jena and was close to Schiller (q.v.). From 1797-1801 he was in Paris (meeting Madame de Staël) and Spain, engaged in linguistic studies (Basque). From 1803 to 1808 he was Prussian resident in Rome, where among other things he translated Pindar and Aeschylus. With his classical and liberal humanism, he was the natural choice to be Prussian minister of education, when during 1808-10 he carried out important school and university reforms. He was appointed Prussian minister to Vienna during the congresses, then ambassador in London. His proposals for a liberal constitution in Prussia were rejected, and he was dismissed in 1819. He spent the rest of his life on his estate at Tegel near Berlin, engaged on linguistic studies, including Sanskrit (correspondence with AWS) and the Kâwi langage of Java. He died at Tegel.

Iffland, August Wilhelm (1759-1814): actor and dramatist. Born at Hanover, he went to Gotha to learn acting from the great director Ekhof, moving to the National Theatre in Mannheim, where he was the first Franz Moor in Schiller's *Die Räuber*. He was briefly in Weimar before moving in 1796 to Berlin, where he became director of the state theatres there. He excelled in comic roles, but he was also Hamlet in AWS's translation, and Xuthus in *Ion*. He died at Berlin.

Jean Paul see **Richter**

Jones, Sir William (1746-1794): judge in the service of the East India Company;  orientalist, linguist. Born at London, he attended Oxford and studied law at the Middle Temple. In 1784 he was appointed a judge at Calcutta. He devoted himself to all aspects of India, laws, astronomy, language, poetry, and founded the Asiatic Society. He is best known for his study of the language family that linked Sanskrit with Persian, Greek, Latin, Germanic and Celtic, that would later be called 'Indo-European'. He died at Calcutta.

Klopstock, Friedrich Gottlieb (1724-1803): poet. Born at Quedlinburg, he attended the Pforta school in Naumburg (with Johann Adolf Schlegel, q.v.) and Jena and Leipzig universities. In Leipzig he gathered round him the group of young writers

 known as the 'Bremer Beiträger', many of them celebrated in his odes 'Auf meine Freunde' (Ebert, Gellert, Gärtner, Giseke, J.A. Schlegel) and 'Der Zürchersee'. He experimented with classical verse forms, adapting them for the needs of German metrics and creating a new poetic language. His great hexameter epic, *Der Messias*, in twenty cantos (1748-73), was his lasting poetic achievement. In 1750 he visited Bodmer in Zurich. In 1751, he received a pension from King Frederick V of Denmark and lived in Copenhagen until 1770. He returned to Hamburg, where, except for a year at the court of the margrave of Baden in Karlsruhe in 1775, he remained until his death. His views on language were expressed in his *Grammatische Gespräche* of 1794, the subject of AWS's *Die Sprachen*.

Körner, Josef (1888-1950): Schlegel scholar and editor. Born at Rohatetz in Moravia, he attended the Universities of Vienna and Prague, serving in World War One. He became a Gymnasium professor in Prague, his university career being blocked by anti-Semitic intrigues. He knew Kafka, Stefan Zweig and many other prominent writers. He produced numerous important publications on German Romanticism, esp. on AWS: *Romantiker und Klassiker* (1924), *Die Botschaft der deutschen Romantik an Europa* (1929), *Briefe von und an August Wilhelm Schlegel* (1930) and *Krisenjahre der Frühromantik* (1936-37, 1958). He was sent to Theresienstadt in 1944; on his release in 1945, he was threatened with deportation by the Czechs as a 'German'. He died at Prague.

Koreff, David Ferdinand (1783-1851): physician. Born at Breslau of Jewish parentage, he studied medicine at Halle (taught by Steffens q.v.) and Berlin, qualifying in 1803. He was strongly influenced by theories of animal magnetism and effected a number of cures through magnetic means. He moved to Paris and became a successful doctor there, with links to Saint-Martin and Chateaubriand, Madame de Staël, and AWS, whom  he treated. He returned to Germany and lived in Berlin and Vienna. Through Caroline von Humboldt he was introduced to the chancellor Hardenberg (q.v.), whose personal physician he became. He was entrusted with the organization of medical services in the new Rhine provinces, and was then called to the Prussian ministry of education under Altenstein, corresponding with AWS over his appointment to Bonn. In Berlin, he was part of the 'Serapion' brotherhood around E.T.A. Hoffmann. He fell into disfavour and returned to Paris in 1822 and became a well-known society doctor.

Kotzebue, August (von) (1761-1819): dramatist. Born at Weimar, he studied law at Jena and Duisburg. He moved to Russia and became secretary to the governor of St Petersburg, was ennobled in 1785, and became a high official in Estonia. Already a prolific writer of prose and plays, he retired to Reval (Tallin) in 1795. In 1800, on his way to St Petersburg, he was arrested as a supposed Jacobin and transported to Siberia. This incident prompted AWS's satire, *Ehrenpforte*. He was pardoned and became theatre director in St Petersburg, living thereafter as an independent writer in Berlin. After 1806, he sought safety in Estonia. In 1816, he was appointed to the ministry of  foreign affairs in St Petersburg and was sent in that capacity to Germany, being widely accused of acting as a spy. He was immensely successful as a dramatist and was performed all over Europe. His illiberal and anti-Romantic views led to his works being burned at the student rally on the Wartburg in 1817. In 1819, while at Mannheim, he was murdered by a student, Karl Sand. His son, Otto von Kotzebue (1787-1846), carried out the first Russian-sponsored circumnavigation of the world.

 **Lassen, Christian** (1800-1876): orientalist. Born at Bergen, Norway, he studied in Oslo, Heidelberg and Bonn. He became AWS's star pupil in Bonn and assisted him with his editions of the *Râmâyana* and *Hitopadeśa*. The years 1824-26 he spent in London and Paris and collaborated with Eugène Bournouf in the *Essai sur le Pali* (1826). He became an assistant professor in Bonn in 1830 and a full professor in 1840. His interests extended much father than AWS's, including Persia, as seen in his *Indische Alterthumskunde* (1849-61). Died at Bonn.

Lessing, Gotthold Ephraim (1729-1781): dramatist and critic. Born at Kamenz, Saxony, educated at Meissen, then at Leipzig university. He embarked on a career as a dramatist and critic, noted for his tragedy *Miss Sara Sampson* (1755), and his *Literaturbriefe*, which are important for the reception of Shakespeare in Germany. 1760-65 he was the secretary to General von Tauenzien in Breslau. There followed *Laokoon* (1766), his treatise on the functions of painting and poetry. In 1767 he moved to Hamburg as the critic at the National Theatre. Here he wrote his comedy,  *Minna von Barnhelm* (1767) and his set of reviews, *Hamburgische Dramaturgie* (1767-69), which were important in advocating a new approach not beholden to French models. In 1770, he moved to Wolfenbüttel as ducal librarian. He became involved in theological disputes, but also wrote the tragedy *Emilia Galotti* (1772), and the play on religious tolerance, *Nathan der Weise* (1779). He died at Brunswick.

Ludwig, crown prince, later king Ludwig I of Bavaria (1786-1868). Born at Strasbourg, the son of the Count Palatine Maximilian Joseph of Palatinate-

Zweibrücken (1799 Elector of Bavaria, 1806 king), he studied at Landshut and Göttingen. He commanded Bavarian forces during the Napoleonic wars, on the French side, until Bavaria changed allegiance in 1813. Succeeding his father as king in 1825, he changed the shape of his royal residence, Munich, lavishly supported the arts (Alte Pinakothek) and built the Walhalla near Regensburg (for which Friedrich Tieck did many of the busts, q.v.). His policies and his affairs led to his abdication in 1848. He died at Nice.

Mackintosh, Sir James (1765-1832): lawyer and politician. Born at Aldourie near Inverness, he studied at Aberdeen and Edinburgh, where he met Benjamin Constant. He became involved in political journalism and published the main rebuttal of Burke's *Reflections*, *Vindiciae Gallicae* (1791). He was called to the bar in 1795. His defence of a French refugee was translated by Madame de Staël, whose lifelong friend he became. He was appointed chief judge of Bombay (Mumbai) in

1804, staying in India until 1811. He became a member of parliament on the Whig side, supporting liberal causes, including the Reform Bill. From 1818 to 1824 he was professor of law and politics at the East India College at Haileybury. He was a founding member of the Royal Asiatic Society and was one of founders of University College, London. His *History of the Revolution in England in 1688* was published in 1834, after his death.

Metternich, Klemens, count, later prince (1773-1859): Austrian chancellor. Born at Koblenz, he studied (with Benjamin Constant) at Strasbourg, and at Mainz. He entered Austrian service and soon made his mark. He was appointed ambassador

to Saxony and then to Prussia, subsequently Austrian envoy to Paris. At the outbreak of war with France in 1809, he became minister of foreign affairs, and it was he who promoted the idea of a marriage between Napoleon and an Austrian archduchess (Marie-Louise). Raised to the rank of prince, he conducted the negotiations for a grand alliance against Napoleon, and he was the most prominent negotiator at the congresses that followed. In 1820 he was appointed chancellor of the Empire and Austrian state chancellor, ensuring the existing state of things by police action and despotic measures. The revolutions of 1848 led to his fall. He died at Vienna.

Müller, Adam Heinrich (von) (1779-1829): publicist and political theorist. Born at Berlin and studied at Göttingen. He was strongly influenced by Friedrich von Gentz (q.v.) in the direction of a political career. He attended AWS's lectures in Berlin. After a short period in Prussian service, and foreign travel, he moved to Vienna in 1805 and embraced the Catholic faith. From 1806-09 he was in Dresden as tutor to Prince Bernhard of Saxe-Weimar, where he gave lectures on dramatic art and on political science (*Die Elemente der Staatskunst*, 1809). With Heinrich von Kleist he edited the periodical *Phöbus* (1808). He entered Austrian service in 1813, first as an envoy, then as a framer of the Carlsbad Decrees. He  was a strong advocate of the links between the state and religion, an opponent of free trade and a proponent of the religious basis of economics. He died at Vienna.

 **Müller, Johannes (von)** (1752-1809): Swiss historian. Born at Schaffhausen, he studied at Göttingen. After teaching at Schaffhausen, encouraged by Karl Viktor von Bonstetten (q.v.), he began his historical studies. He gave lectures on universal history (admired by AWS). In 1786, he accepted a post as librarian to the elector of Mainz, having commenced work on his history of Switzerland, *Geschichte der Schweizer*, which appeared between 1780 and 1808. Forced to leave Mainz, he became chief imperial librarian in Vienna until 1804, when he accepted a post as academician and historiographer in Berlin. In 1806, he became secretary of state to the kingdom of Westphalia at Kassel. He died at Kassel.

Necker, Jacques (1732-1804): banker. Born at Geneva, he co-established the bank of Thellusson and Necker in Paris. He married Suzanne Curchod: their only daughter Germaine became Madame de Staël (q.v.). Suzanne's salon gathered in all the notabilities of Paris. In 1776, Necker was made director-general of finance, an office which he held against mounting difficulties until his dismissal in 1783. He retired to his estate  at Coppet, but was recalled in 1788. The outbreak of the Revolution made his position untenable, and he retired in 1790, having lent the French exchequer two million francs of his own. He died at Coppet.

Niebuhr, Barthold Georg (1776-1831): historian. Born at Copenhagen, the son of the explorer Carsten Niebuhr. He studied at Kiel, then in London and Edinburgh. He entered the Danish state administration in 1800, resigning in 1806 to make a career in the Prussian civil service. 1810-12 he gave lectures on Roman history at the new University of Berlin. His use of historical evidence opened up new fields in historiography. The first two volumes of his *Römische Geschichte* (1811-12) were savaged by AWS in 1816. He became Prussian ambassador to the papal court in Rome from 1816 to 1823. He retired to Bonn, where he gave lectures on classical archaeology. He died at Bonn.

Pange, Pauline, comtesse de, née de Broglie (1888-1972): doyenne of Staël studies. Daughter of the fifth duke of Broglie, sister of the Nobel laureates, Maurice and Louis de Broglie, the great-great-granddaughter of Madame de Staël. A grande dame, she was with her husband closely involved in post-war European rapprochements and was a leading Staël scholar (*Madame de Staël et la découverte de l'Allemagne*, 1929; *Auguste-Guillaume Schlegel et Madame de Staël*, 1938; edition *of De l'Allemagne*, 1958-60).

Paulus, Heinrich Eberhard Gottlob (1761-1851): theologian. Born at Leonberg, Württemberg, he attended university at Tübingen. A leading proponent of rational theology, advocating natural explanation for miracles, and an oriental scholar, he became in 1793 professor in Jena. With his wife Caroline he had close contact with Goethe, Schiller and the Romantics. Leaving Jena, he was 1803-08 professor in Würzburg, and from 1811 in Heidelberg (as a colleague of Hegel). After AWS married Sophie Paulus in 1818, Paulus was his father-in-law. Died at Heidelberg. (*Philologisch-kritischer und historischer Kommentar über das Neue Testament*, 1804-08; *Das Leben Jesu*, 1828).

Récamier, Juliette, née Jeanne-Françoise Julie Adélaïde Bernard (Madame Récamier) (1777-1849): Born at Lyon. A salonnière and famous beauty, her salon in Paris attracted all the notabilities of the time, and most especially Chateaubriand, Constant, Montmorency and Prince August of Prussia. Her anti-Napoleonic stance linked her with Madame de Staël, whose close friend she became (Auguste de Staël falling in love with her). Exiled from Paris, she settled in Naples, returning after the Restoration. She was the subject of paintings by Louis David and François Gérard. Died at Paris.

Rehfues, Philipp Joseph (von) (1779-1843): 'Kurator' of the University of Bonn. Born at Tübingen, he went as tutor to Italy and was involved in diplomatic negotiations there. In 1806 he became librarian to the king of Württemberg. Entering Prussian service, he was appointed governor of Trier and Koblenz after 1815, then administrator in Bonn, where he supported the founding of the university. In 1818 he became 'Kurator' of the new university, an office he held until 1842, being closely associated with AWS during this period. Died at Bonn.

Reichardt, Johann Friedrich (1752-1814): composer. Born at Königsberg, he studied  there and at Leipzig. He gained an early reputation as a keyboard virtuoso and in 1774 was appointed Kapellmeister in Berlin by Frederick the Great. He travelled widely in Italy, France, Austria and England. Through his second marriage, he became Tieck's brother-in-law, and he was an important influence on the young man. His sympathy for the French Revolution led to his dismissal. He retired to Giebichenstein, near Halle, which became a gathering-place for the Romantic generation. In 1796 he was appointed director of the salt mines there. In 1807, after Giebichenstein had been plundered by French troops, Reichardt accepted King Jérôme's offer to become theatre director in Kassel, but soon returned to Giebichenstein, where he died. He is important for his Singspiele and for his settings of songs, notably by Goethe.

Reimer, Georg Andreas (1776-1842): Berlin publisher. Born at Greifswald, he was apprenticed to a Berlin publisher and soon took over the business. In 1800, he gained control of the 'Realschule' impress and ran it as the 'Realschulbuchhandlung' until 1817, thereafter under his own name. He was the major publisher of the authors of the German Romantic generation, including Tieck, Jean Paul, Hoffmann, Arnim, Arndt, Fichte, the brothers Grimm and AWS. He was a noted liberal and supported progressive causes. His house in the Wilhelmstrasse was a centre of social and intellectual life in Berlin. Died at Berlin.

Richter, Jean Paul Friedrich (Jean Paul) (1763-1825): the most-read German novelist of his day. Born at Wunsiedel, Franconia. he attended the Gymnasium in Hof and university in Leipzig. His first years, later as a tutor, were spent in straitened circumstances. Choosing the pen name of Jean Paul in honour of Jean-Jacques Rousseau, he made his first breakthrough as a novelist with *Hesperus* in 1795. In 1798 he was in Weimar, where he was lionized (but not by Goethe or Schiller). He finally settled in Bayreuth, supported by a  pension from the Prince-Primate Dalberg and then from King Ludwig I of Bavaria. He died at Bayreuth. His other major novels are *Die unsichtbare Loge* (1793), *Siebenkäs* (1796-97), *Titan* (1800-03), *Flegeljahre* (1804), *Der Komet* (1820-22). His *Vorschule der*

Ästhetik (1804) and *Levana* (1807) are important forays, respectively, into aesthetics and education.

Robinson, Henry Crabb (1775-1867): barrister at law. Born at Bury St Edmunds. As  a Unitarian, he was unable to go to university, and was articled to an attorney in Colchester. From 1800 to 1805 he studied in Germany, notably at Jena, meeting everyone of note in Weimar, including Goethe and Schiller. During Madame de Staël's visit there, he explained to her the rudiments of German philosophy. He was called to the bar in 1813, but went abroad frequently to France and Germany. He was a founder of University College London. As a note-taker, diarist and gossip, he is a great source of information about Germany in the 'Goethezeit'. Died at London.

Schelling, Friedrich Wilhelm Joseph (von) (1775-1854): philosopher. Born at Leonberg in Württemberg, he attended the Tübinger Stift (where he was friendly with Hölderlin and Hegel) and the universites of Tübingen and Leipzig. In Dresden he met up with the Schlegel brothers, Caroline and Novalis (q.v.). Goethe, who found his notion of 'Weltseele' attractive, saw him appointed professor extraordinarius at Jena from 1798 to 1803. He became Caroline's lover, and in 1800 he was involved in the tragedy  of Auguste Böhmer's death (q.v.). In 1803, he married Caroline and moved as professor to Würzburg. In 1806, he accepted posts as secretary to the academy of sciences and the academy of arts, but also gave lectures in Stuttgart (1810) and Erlangen (1820-27). In 1841, as a member of the academy of sciences, he moved to Berlin and gave lectures (attended by Kierkegaard, Burckhardt, Bakunin and Engels) until 1845. He remained in Berlin until his death at Bad Ragatz, Switzerland. *Ideen zu einer Philosophie der Natur* (1797), *System des transzendentalen Idealismus* (1800), *Bruno* (1802), *Philosophie der Kunst* (1802-03).

Schiller, Friedrich (von) (1759-1805): poet, dramatist, philosopher. Born at Marbach, Württemberg, he attended the elite Hohe Karlsschule at Ludwigsburg, then at Stuttgart. He studied medicine and was appointed a army surgeon. A performance of his play, *Die Räuber*, at Mannheim in 1783 caused a sensation and scandal, and as a result he was forbidden to leave Württemberg. He escaped in disguise to Mannheim, moving to Bauerbach near Meiningen, where he completed his plays, *Fiesco* and *Kabale und Liebe* (both 1783). He was appointed dramatist at the Mannheim theatre, but the position was not renewed. He founded the journal, *Die Rheinische Thalia* in 1784, in which he published his most important stories, including *Der Geisterseher*. In 1785, he was able to move to Leipzig, then Dresden, where his friend Christian Gottfried Körner supported him. He finished *Don Karlos* in 1787. He moved to Weimar, then to Jena, in 1788 being appointed to a professorship of history at Jena, with a small pension, and thus able to marry Charlotte von Lengefeld. The *Briefe über die ästhetische Erziehung des Menschen* (1795) were the first major product of these years. He made the acquaintance of Fichte and Wilhelm von Humboldt and began his association and friendship with Goethe. He launched his periodical *Die Horen* (1795-98), securing AWS's collaboration. His *Musenalmanache* (1797-99) published the *Xenien* (with Goethe) and his major elegies and ballads, while *Wallenstein* (1798-99) was the pinnacle of his dramatic production. In 1799 he settled in Weimar to be nearer Goethe, producing in rapid succession his dramas *Maria Stuart* (1800), *Die Jungfrau von Orleans* (1801), *Die Braut von Messina* (1803) and *Wilhelm Tell* (1804). His break with AWS in 1797 made him a decided opponent of the Romantics. After many illnesses, and in broken health, he died at Weimar.

Schlegel, Carl August (1761-1789): AWS's older brother. As a lieutenant in Hanoverian service he went in 1782 with his regiment to India, seeing action against the French and against Tipu Sultan and being employed in a surveying expedition in the Carnatic. Died at Madras.

Schlegel, Caroline, née Michaelis (1763-1809): born at Göttingen, the daughter of Johann David Michaelis, the orientalist. In 1784 she married Johann Franz Wilhelm Böhmer (1755-1788) and moved with him to Clausthal in the Harz. There were

three children, Auguste (1785-1800), Therese (1787-89) and Wilhelm (1789). Böhmer died in 1788. She lived alternately in Göttingen and Marburg, and from this time date AWS's first serious attentions. In 1792, she moved to Mainz to be near her friend Therese Huber. A brief liaison with the French officer Crancé left her pregnant. She was arrested and incarcerated after the fall of the Mainz republic. AWS rescued her and brought her back to Brunswick. The child, Julius Crancé (or Kranz) died in 1795. After his return from Amsterdam, AWS married her in 1796 and they moved to Jena. She took a full part in his literary activities, and worked on the Shakespeare translation and the essay, *Die Gemälde*. An attraction developed for Schelling after his arrival in Jena. On the death of Auguste in 1800, she separated from AWS, divorcing him in 1803 and marrying Schelling. She moved with him to Würzburg and then to Munich. She died at Bad Maulbronn.

Schlegel, Caroline Sophie Eleutheria von, née Paulus (Sophie) (1791-1847): AWS's second wife. Born at Jena, the daughter of Heinrich Eberhard Gottlob Paulus (q.v.) and Caroline Paulus. She moved with her parents to Würzburg and then to

Heidelberg, marrying AWS in 1818 and separating from him in the same year. She died at Heidelberg.

Schlegel, Christoph (1613-1678): pastor; AWS's great-great-grandfather. Born at Kmehlen, Saxony, he studied in Leipzig. He was successively tutor, court preacher in Zerbst, then professor and pastor in Breslau. He received a doctorate of theology from Wittenberg in 1645. He moved next to Leutschau (Levoča) in the kingdom of Hungary, where Emperor Ferdinand III ennobled him as 'Schlegel von Gottleben'. In 1660 he was 'Superintendent' in Herzberg, 1662 in Grimma, where he died.

Schlegel, Dorothea (von), née Brendel Mendelssohn (1764-1839): novelist and translator. Born at Berlin, the daughter of Moses Mendelssohn. In 1783, she married the banker Simon Veit. Their two sons, Philipp and Johannes, became prominent painters of the Nazarene school. A nephew was Felix Mendelssohn Bartholdy. In 1797, she met FS in Henriette Herz's salon, and an intensive liaison developed, of which his novel *Lucinde* (1799) was the  expression. She moved with him to Jena during the period of the closest Romantic association, and in 1802 went with him to Paris. Her unfinished novel *Florentin* appeared in 1801, and in 1807 her translation of Madame de Staël's *Corinne*. In 1804, on her conversion to Protestantism, she and FS were married. In 1808, she and FS were received into the Catholic faith in Frankfurt. She moved with FS to Vienna, sharing the vicissitudes of his life there, moving mainly in pious Catholic circles. In 1818-20 she accompanied her artist sons to Rome. After FS's death, she moved to Frankfurt, where Johannes Veit was director of the Städelsches Kunstinstitut. She died at Frankfurt.

Schlegel, Johan Frederik Wilhelm (1765-1836) jurist, the son of Johann Heinrich Schlegel, and thus AWS's first cousin. Born at Copenhagen, he studied at Göttingen 1786-87, then travelled in Holland and England. In 1800, he became professor of law at Copenhagen university, later its rector, and the author of legal textbooks, notably on maritime law, and studies in legal history. Died at Søllerød.

Schlegel, Johann Adolf (1721-1793): AWS's father; the son of Johann Friedrich Schlegel. Born at Meissen, he attended the elite Pforta school in Naumburg, at the same time as Klopstock (q.v.), whose friend he became. He studied at Leipzig and was a member of the anti-Gottschedian 'Bremer Beiträger' (Gellert, Giseke, Cramer, Ebert, Gärtner etc.). In 1751 he became 'Diaconus' at the Pforta, where he married Johanna Christiane Erdmuthe Hübsch, with whom he had nine children. In 1754 he was

appointed pastor in Zerbst and professor at the Gymnasium; in 1759 he moved to the Marktkirche in Hanover, in 1775 to the Neustadt Hof- und Marktkirche, becoming 'Superintendent' of Hoya in 1782, and of Calenberg in 1787. He died at Hanover. His collected poems, esp. fables, appeared as *Vermischte Gedichte* in 1787-89, his sermons between 1754 and 1785. He revised the Hanoverian hymnary. He translated Batteux's *Les Beaux-Arts réduits à un même principe* (first 1751 and subsequently revised), (with Johann August Schlegel) Banier's *La Mythologie* (1754-66) and Leprince de Beaumont's *Éducation* (1766-80).

Schlegel, Johann August (1731-1776): pastor; AWS's uncle; the son of Johann Friedrich Schlegel (q.v.). Born at Meissen, he attended the St. Afra school there and studied at Leipzig, becoming a member of the 'Bremer Beiträger'. He assisted JAS with his translation of Banier. In 1759, he moved to Hanover and became pastor at Pattensen, later at Rehburg, where he briefly cared for the young FS.

Schlegel, Johann August Adolph (1790-1840): classical scholar; Moritz's son; AWS's nephew. He studied at Göttingen and was then a teacher of classics at the Johanneum in Hamburg, in Ilfeld and at Verden. He did a scholarly edition of Tacitus's *Agricola* (1816). He died in a mental institution in Verden.

Schlegel, Johann Elias (1664-1718): AWS's great-grandfather, born in Grimma, he was a lawyer ('Appellationsrat') in Wurzen.

Schlegel, Johann Elias (1719-1749): dramatist, translator and critic. Born at Meissen, the son of Johann Friedrich Schlegel, the brother of Johann Adolf, Johann August and Johann Heinrich. He attended the Pforta school at Naumburg and studied law and philosophy at Leipzig. He came under the influence of Gottsched and wrote dramas in the French style advocated by him, notably the tragedy *Hermann* and the comedy *Die stumme Schönheit* (both 1743). His *Vergleichung Shakespears und Andreas Gryphs* (1741) is the first independent voice in the reception of Shakespeare in Germany. He turned away from Gottsched, contributing to the 'Bremer Beiträge' and developing his own theory of imitation (*Von der Nachahmung*, 1742-45) and of individual national style (*Gedanken zur Aufnahme des dänischen Theaters*, 1747). In 1743 he became the secretary to the Saxon envoy in Copenhagen. He settled there and was appointed a professor at the Sorø academy in 1748. He died at Sorø.

Schlegel, Johann Friedrich (1689-1748): jurist; AWS's grandfather. Born at Wurzen. He became 'Domherr' in Meissen, with important legal responsibilities. Removed from office in 1741, he lived at Sörnewitz near Meissen, where he died.

Schlegel, Johann Heinrich (1726-1780): translator and historian in Copenhagen; AWS's uncle. Born at Meissen, the son of Johann Friedrich and the brother of Johann Adolf, Johann Elias and Johann August, the father of Johan Frederik Wilhelm (q.v.).

He attended the St. Afra school in Meissen, and was befriended by Lessing, then studying at Leipzig and becoming a member of the 'Bremer Beiträger'. He followed his brother Johann Elias to Copenhagen and was after 1750 a member of Klopstock's circle. Thereafter he was chancery secretary, then professor of history and royal librarian in Copenhagen. He translated from the English (James Thomson's *Agamemnon*, *Sophonisba* and *Coriolanus*).

Schlegel, Johann Karl Fürchtegott (Karl) (1758-1831): jurist; AWS's older brother. Born at Zerbst, he attended school in Hanover and university in Göttingen. From 1782 he was a lawyer with the church consistory in Hanover (later, 'Konsistorialrat'). In this capacity he pleaded for an improved status for Jews. *Kurhannoversches Kirchenrecht* (1801-06), *Kirchen- und Reformationsgeschichte Norddeutschlands* (1828-32).

Schlegel, Johanna Christiane Erdmuthe, née Hübsch (1735-1811): the mother of the nine Schlegel children. Born at Naumburg, the daughter of Johann Georg Gotthelf Hübsch, mathematics professor at the Pforta school. In 1751 she married Johann Adolf Schlegel. In the Klopstock circle she was known as 'Muthchen'. After the death of JAS she lived in straitened circumstances in Hanover, where she died.

Schlegel, Karl August Moritz (Moritz) (1756-1826): pastor and superintendent; AWS's older brother. Born at Zerbst, he attended school in Hanover and studied theology at Göttingen. In 1786 he was ordained pastor at Bothfeld; in 1792 he moved to Harburg, then in 1796 to Göttingen, where he became 'Superintendent'. In 1816 he was appointed 'Generalsuperintendent' in Harburg, where he died. His sermons were published as *Auswahl einiger Predigten* (1814).

Schlegel, Karl Wilhelm Friedrich (von) (Friedrich) (1772-1829): critic, philosopher; the youngest child of Johann Adolf and Johanna Christiane Erdmuthe Schlegel, and AWS's younger brother. Born at Hanover, as a child he spent some time with his uncle Johann August, then with his brother Moritz. He had little formal education, being in 1788 apprenticed to a banker in Leipzig. Unsuited to this profession, he spent the years 1788-89 preparing for university. He commenced law studies at

Göttingen in 1790, moving in 1791 to Leipzig. At the same time, he made the decision to live as an independent critic. In 1792 he first met Novalis and Schiller (q.v.). In 1793, he helped to look after Caroline and her children. In 1794 he moved to Dresden and produced *Von den Schulen der griechischen Poesie*. He reviewed for Reichardt's periodical *Deutschland* (1796) and moved to Jena. The break with Schiller followed. In 1797 he moved to Berlin and published *Die Griechen und Römer* and wrote for Reichardt's *Lyceum*. In Berlin he met Ludwig Tieck (q.v.), Henriette Herz, and Friedrich Schleiermacher (q.v.) and began his liaison with Dorothea Veit (*Lucinde* appeared in 1799). He and AWS began the *Athenaeum* in 1798, FS moving in 1799 to Jena with

Dorothea. He lectured on transcendental philosophy in Jena in 1800. He returned to Berlin in 1801 and published *Charakteristiken und Kritiken* with AWS. In 1802 he moved to Dresden, then to Leipzig. His play *Alarcos* was premiered in May of that year amid scandal. In July, he and Dorothea arrived in Paris. He gave lectures on literature and philosophy to the brothers Boisserée (q.v.) and Johann Baptist Bertram, edited the periodical *Europa* (until 1805) and took Sanskrit lessons with Alexander Hamilton. In 1804, he and Dorothea married. October to November 1804 saw him in Coppet with AWS and Madame de Staël. 1805 he and Dorothea moved to Cologne, where he gave lectures on universal history and literature and edited the *Poetisches Taschenbuch* (1806). The latter part of 1806 he spent at Acosta with AWS. In 1808 apppeared *Ueber die Sprache und Weisheit der Indier*. He and Dorothea converted to Catholicism in Frankfurt in the same year. They moved to Vienna, where he was appointed 'Hofsekretär' with the army administration. He edited the *Österreichische Zeitung* and moved with the army to Hungary after the battles of Wagram and Aspern. Back in Vienna, he gave lectures on history, which appeared in 1811 as *Über die neuere Geschichte*. In 1812-13 he edited the periodical *Deutsches Museum* and in 1814 his lectures on literature were published as *Geschichte der alten und neuen Literatur*. In 1815 he was appointed 'Legationssekretär' to the German Federal Diet at Frankfurt and remained there until 1818, AWS visiting him. He returned to Vienna, in 1819 visiting Italy with Emperor Francis and Metternich. His last periodical, *Concordia*, came out in 1820-23. This, bad debts, and his increasingly Ultramontane views led to a alienation from AWS, culminating in 1827. In 1828-29 he lectured in Vienna on 'Philosophie des Lebens' and on history, and in Dresden on language He died suddenly at Dresden.

Schlegel, Martin(us) (1581-1640): AWS's great-great-great grandfather. Born at Dippoldswalde, later pastor in Blochwitz and Zabeltitz, then court preacher in Dresden. He died as 'Superintendent' in Weissensee, in Thuringia.

Schlegel, Rebekka, née Wilke (1695-1736): AWS's grandmother, the mother of Johann Adolf, Johann August, Johann Elias and Johann Heinrich. Through her, the Cranach inheritance entered into the Schlegel family.

Schleiermacher, Friedrich Daniel Ernst (1768-1834): theologian. Born at Breslau, he attended schools at Breslau and Niesky. In 1785 he entered the Moravian academy at Barby, but left after differences for the University of Halle. There followed years as a tutor until he was appointed preacher at the Charité hospital in Berlin in 1796. In Berlin he was close to FS, Henriette Herz, the brothers Humboldt and Ludwig Tieck (q.v.). The first product of these years was his *Über die Religion*

(1799). In 1802 he became court preacher in Stolp in Pomerania. It was here that he commenced his version of Plato (1804-28) and developed his ideas on translation. In 1804 he became professor of theology in Halle. After the closure of the university he became a member of Wilhelm von Humboldt's staff in the ministry of education, and in 1810 he was appointed to a chair of theology in the new University of Berlin, where he was several times rector. He was instrumental in the Prussian Union between Lutherans and Reformed. He died at Berlin. *Der christliche Glaube* (1821-22, 1830-31).

Schütz, Christoph Gottfried (1747-1832): professor and editor. Born at Dederstedt. He attended university at Halle and in 1777 was a professor there. In 1779 he was appointed professor of poetry and rhetoric in Jena. In 1785 he became editor of the *Allgemeine Literatur-Zeitung*, for which AWS did numerous reviews. He returned to Halle as a professor in 1804. He counts as one of the first supporters of Kant. He died at Halle.

Sismondi, Jean-Charles-Léonard Simonde de (1773-1842): Swiss historian. Born at Geneva. The family took refuge in England during the Terror (1793-94), then moved to Italy. He devoted himself to economics (*Traité de la richesse commerciale*, 1803). He met Madame de Staël and was a close member of her circle (he and AWS were never on good terms). He travelled with her to Italy in 1804-05 and commenced his *Histoire des républiques italiennes* (1807-18). He was in Vienna in 1808 and attended AWS's lectures. He was appointed secretary to the chamber of commerce for the department of Léman, returning to Paris in 1813. Through marriage he was linked with Sir James Mackintosh (q.v.) and the Wedgwood family. He spent the latter part of his life in Geneva, dying at Chêne-Bougeries. *Littérature du midi de l'Europe* (1813), *Histoire de la chute de l'Empire romain* (1835).

Staël-Holstein, Albert de (1792-1813). Erik Magnus von Staël-Holstein's and Germaine de Staël's younger son, he was born at Coppet. He was left with his grandparents during his mother's exile in 1792 and subsequently shared her various places of residence. After his father's death in 1802, Mathieu de Montmorency was his legal guardian. He was left in his grandfather Necker's charge during the period 1803-04 when Madame de Staël was in France, then in Germany. In 1804 AWS was appointed tutor to the children. He accompanied his mother and siblings and AWS to Italy in 1804-05, then to France (Acosta). Back in Coppet in the summer of 1807, he did a journey on foot with AWS through the Swiss alps. He was with his mother in Vienna, where he was left in a military academy, under the care of FS and Maurice O'Donnell. Late in 1810, he was in Chaumont with the Staël ménage, then back in Coppet, and wth his mother in 1811 during her short sojourn in Aix-les-Bains. With

Eugène Uginet, he fled to Vienna in 1812, joining his mother, Auguste and Albertine and AWS there, then as a member of the cavalcade to Russia and Sweden. Albert was made a Swedish cornet of hussars and took part in action in Hamburg under General Tettenborn. He was killed in a duel at Doberan.

Staël-Holstein, Auguste de (1790-1827): Erik Magnus von Staël-Holstein's and Germaine de Staël's elder son. Born at Paris (Louis de Narbonne was reputedly the father). Left with his grandparents during his mother's first exile in England, he was subsequently with her in her various places of residence. He accompanied her to Germany in 1803-4, attending school briefly in Berlin. He went with her, his siblings and AWS to Italy in 1804-05, and was thereafter in France and Coppet. Prepared for entrance to the École polytechnique in Paris, his application was blocked by Napoleon. In December, 1807 he was received by Napoleon himself in Chambéry, where he put to the Emperor the case for the restitution of his grandfather Necker's loan to the French state (q.v.). Thereafter he was in Chaumont and Coppet. He fled with his mother and Albertine in 1812, but took a different route and arrived independently at Stockholm in 1813. He joined his mother and Albertine to London, where he was employed in the Swedish embassy. He went on his mother's second Italian journey, and was present at Albertine's wedding. After his mother's death, he was occupied with the publication of her works. He accompanied Victor de Broglie to England in 1822 and wrote pamphlets on agronomy. He was a noted opponent of the slave trade and a supporter of bible societies.

Staël-Holstein. Erik Magnus von (1749-1802): Swedish diplomat. Born at Loddby, Sweden. He was chamberlain to Queen Sophia Magdalena of Sweden and was appointed in 1783 first chargé d'affaires, then in 1785 ambassador to the court of France. In 1786, he married Germaine Necker (q.v.). There were five children, of whom three survived. He was in Stockholm in 1792 at the time of the assassination of King Gustav III. He met up again with his wife and family in Geneva  in 1793 and in 1795 was reinstated as ambassador. Dismissed in 1796, he continued to live in France and Switzerland and was separated from Madame de Staël in 1800. He died at Poligny.

Staël-Holstein, Anne Louise Germaine de, née Necker, baroness (Madame de Staël) (1766-1817). Born at Paris, the daughter of Jacques Necker and Suzanne Curchod, she grew up in the world of the Paris salons. In 1776 she went with her parents to England. In 1786 she married Erik Magnus von Staël-Holstein (q.v.), with whom (or with others, such as Louis de Narbonne, Mathieu de Montmorency, Benjamin Constant) she had five children, of whom Auguste, Albert and Albertine

 survived (q.v.). Caught up in the French Revolution, she was forced to retreat to Coppet, then to England in 1793. She returned to Switzerland and commenced her long affair with Benjamin Constant (q.v.). She returned to Paris with her husband after the Terror, but was forced back to Switzerland in 1796 after being suspected of Royalist involvement. In 1797 she returned to Paris and was there during Napoleon's coup d'état. Napoleon was wary of her after this, moving eventually to outright opposition. In 1802 her first novel, *Delphine*, was published. Banned from Paris in 1803, she went to Germany with Auguste and Albertine and (as far as Weimar) Constant, with sojourns at Gotha, Weimar and Berlin. At Berlin in 1804 she met AWS and appointed him tutor to her children. She was forced to return precipitately to Coppet on the death of her father. In 1804-05 she went on her first Italian journey, taking in Rome and Naples. Thereafter, in 1806, she was permitted to return to France, but not to Paris. After breaking this undertaking, she was obliged to return to Coppet in 1807. Her second novel *Corinne, ou l'Italie* appeared at the end of 1807. With her children and AWS, she left for Vienna at the end of 1807, staying there until the spring of 1808. There, she had close dealings with Maurice O'Donnell, Prince de Ligne and Gentz. She was back in Coppet until late 1809, where notable visitors were Zacharias Werner and Madame de Krüdener. She returned with her retinue to France (Chaumont sur Loire), to finish her great study of Germany, *De l'Allemagne*, which was competed in 1810. The book was seized and pulped, and she was ordered to leave for America. Instead, she was allowed back to Coppet, but under strict surveillance. She began her affair with John Rocca, and their son Alphonse was born in 1812. In May, 1812, leaving Alphonse with foster-parents, she and eventually all of her children, Rocca, AWS and Uginet fled Switzerland for Austria, Russia and Sweden. In St Petersburg, she was received by Tsar Alexander I. In Sweden, she used her influence on Bernadotte for an anti-Napoleonic course. She left for London in May 1813. It was there that *De l'Allemagne* appeared, published by John Murray. After Napoleon's defeat, she was able to return to Paris, although during the Hundred Days she was forced back to Coppet. In 1815-16 she made her second journey to Italy (Pisa, Florence), where Albertine was married to Victor de Broglie. Back in Coppet, she received Byron. She herself formally married John Rocca in Coppet later that year, returning to Paris at the end of 1816. Early in 1817, she fell ill, dying at Paris. She was interred in the Necker mausoleum in Coppet. Her *Dix Années d'exil* and *Réflexions sur les principaux événements de la Révolution française* appeared posthumously in 1818. *Lettres sur les ouvrages et le caractère de J.-J. Rousseau* (1788), *De la littérature considérée dans ses rapports avec les institutions sociales* (1800), *Réflexions sur le suicide* (1813), *De l'Esprit des traductions* (1816).

Steffens, Henrik (1773-1845): nature philosopher. Born at Stavanger, Norway (then Danish), he studied natural science at Copenhagen and Kiel, then went to Jena in  1798 to be with Schelling. He continued his mineralogical studies at Freiberg, returning to Denmark to lecture on philosophy. In 1804, he was made a professor at Halle, then at Breslau in 1811. He took part in the Wars of Liberation (as 'Sekonde-Lieutenant und Professor'). In 1832 he was appointed to a chair in Berlin. *Beiträge zur inneren Naturgeschichte der Erde* (1801), *Grundzüge der philosophischen Naturwissenschaft* (1806), *Anthropologie* (1824), *Was ich erlebte* (1840-44).

Stein, Friedrich Karl, Freiherr vom und zum (baron) (1757-1831): Prussian statesman and minister. Born at Nassau, he studied at Göttingen and entered Prussian state service in 1780, working mainly in the administration of mines and commerce. In 1804 he was summoned to take over trade and commerce in Prussia, but, hampered by traditional methods, he resigned in 1807. He was recalled by King Frederick William III to  preside over a series of sweeping reforms ('Stein-Hardenberg') in all aspects of civil and military organization. Napoleon insisted on his dismissal in 1808. He withdrew, first to Austria, then to St Petersburg (with Arndt as his secretary, and visited by Madame de Staël, q.v.), where he gave support to the cause of a coalition against Napoleon. Disappointed with the outcome of the congresses of Vienna, he retreated into private life. AWS met him at Nassau in 1818. He died at Cappenberg.

 **Stein zum Altenstein, Freiherr vom (baron)** (1770-1840): Prussian minister of education. Born at Schalkhausen near Ansbach, he studied law at Erlangen, Göttingen and Jena. He entered the Prussian civil service in 1793, where his talents were soon spotted by Hardenberg (q.v.). In 1808 he became Stein's successor as head of the finance administration. Dismissed in 1810, he was reinstated in 1813, as governor of Silesia. He was with Wilhelm von Humboldt in Paris in 1815. In 1817 he became the first Prussian minister of culture under Hardenberg, reforming the Prussian school system and introducing among other things compulsory schooling. He also played a significant role in the founding of Bonn university in 1818. He died at Berlin.

Tieck, Dorothea (1799-1841): Ludwig Tieck's elder daughter; translator. Born at Berlin. After her mother's conversion, she was brought up a Catholic. She lived with her parents in Berlin and Ziebingen, moving in 1819 with the Tieck family to Dresden. For her father, she translated part of *Shakspeare's Vorschule* (1823-29), Shakespeare's sonnets (1826; the whole set published in 1992), six plays, including

Macbeth, for the so-called 'Schlegel-Tieck' edition of Shakespeare, the life of Marcos Obregón (1827), Cervantes's *Persiles y Sigismunda* (1837); also Jared Sparks's *Life of Washington* (1839). She died at Dresden.

Tieck, Friedrich (1776-1851): sculptor; Ludwig Tieck's and Sophie Tieck's brother. Born at Berlin, he attended the Friedrichswerder Gymnasium. In 1789 he was

apprenticed to the sculptor Bettkober, from 1794 living with his brother Ludwig (q.v.) and taking part in the salon life in Berlin (Rahel Levin, Wilhelm von Humboldt, q.v.). After journeys to Dresden and Vienna, unable to travel to Italy, he left in 1797 for Paris, where he worked in Louis David's studio. He returned to Germany and secured the commission to do the reliefs on the Weimar palace, and carried out other work, such as Goethe's bust. He spent the years 1802-04 in Berlin, where he first met AWS. In 1805, after visits to Coppet and Berlin, he left for Rome and lived there until 1808. He spent six months in 1808-09 at Coppet, and secured commissions from Madame de Staël (Necker monument). In 1809 he was in Munich, where he received work from Crown Prince Ludwig (q.v.). During 1810-11 he was detained in Zurich and Berne by illness. The period 1812-19 was spent in Carrara, executing busts for the Walhalla, with a short interruption in 1815-16 when he joined Madame de Staël and AWS in Pisa and Florence. In 1819 he was appointed professor in Berlin and in 1830 director of the sculpture collection. He died at Berlin.

Tieck, Ludwig (1773-1853): poet, dramatist, translator. Born at Berlin, he attended the Friedrichswerder Gymnasium. In Berlin he had close contact with Karl Philipp Moritz and Johann Friedrich Reichardt (q.v.) and was linked by friendship with Wilhelm Heinrich Wackenroder. He studied at the Universities of Halle, Göttingen (where he heard lectures on art from Fiorillo, q.v.), and in the summer of 1792 at Erlangen,

where he and Wackenroder saw the art treasures of Franconia, esp. Nuremberg. On his return to Berlin in 1794, he embarked on a career as an independent writer, first under the tutelage of Friedrich Nicolai: the main works were *William Lovell* (1795-96), *Straußfedern* (1795-98), *Peter Lebrecht* (1795-96), *Volksmährchen* (1797). In 1797, he and Wackenroder published the *Herzensergießungen,* the first expression of Romantic art enthusiasm, followed in 1798 by Tieck's novel *Franz Sternbalds Wanderungen.* In Berlin he made the acquaintance of FS and AWS. He and his family joined the Romanrtic circle in Jena, marred by his illness with a rheumatic complaint that persisted throughout his life. 1799-1800 saw the publication of his *Romantische Dichtungen (Prinz Zerbino, Genoveva),* and 1803 the first fruit of his medieval studies, *Minnelieder aus dem Schwäbischen Zeitalter.* He withdrew to Berlin, then to Dresden, and finally to Ziebingen in Brandenburg, the estate of his friend Wilhelm von Burgsdorff. Here began the liaison with Henriette von Finckenstein that was to last for the rest of his life. In 1805, after the break-up of his sister Sophie's marriage, he travelled to Rome and moved in German literary and artistic circles there. He returned to Ziebingen, but left again in 1808 to be with his sister in Munich, where he fell seriously ill. He finally returned to Ziebingen in 1810, to continue his medieval studies and his work on Shakespeare and his contemporaries (*Alt-Englisches Theater*, 1811; *Shakspeare's Vorschule*, 1823-29; *Vier Schauspiele von Shakspeare*, 1836). The main work of this period is his collection of stories and plays, *Phantasus* (1812-16). In 1819, he and his family, with Countess Finckenstein, moved to Dresden. He was appointed dramaturge to the royal theatre in 1825 (*Dramaturgische Blätter*, 1826). 1825-33 he edited the Shakespeare translation commenced by AWS and had it completed by Wolf von Baudissin and his daughter Dorothea ('Schlegel-Tieck'). He was part of the cultivated circle around Prince John of Saxony (Carus, Baudissin). There is a wide variety of prose works from his Dresden years, notably *Der Aufruhr in den Cevennen* (1826), *Der junge Tischlermeister* (1836) and *Vittoria Accorombona* (1840) and numerous Novellen. After Dorothea's death, he accepted King Frederick William IV's invitation to live in Potsdam and Berlin. The performance of *A Midsummer Night's Dream*, with music by Felix Mendelssohn Bartholdy, took place under his direction in 1843. He died at Berlin.

Tieck, Sophie (see also Bernhardi) (1775-1833): writer; sister of Ludwig and Friedrich Tieck. Born at Berlin, she had no formal education, but contributed anonymously to literary collections by her brother and by August Ferdinand Bernhardi (esp. *Bambocciaden*, 1798-99). She married Bernhardi in 1799. The couple had two surviving children (Wilhelm, Felix Theodor, q.v.). On AWS's arrival in Berlin in 1800, he stayed with the Bernhardis and a love affair ensued (raising the question of AWS's alleged paternity of Felix Theodor). Her marriage broke down, and in 1803 she left for Dresden, eventually for Munich and Rome (1805), supported financially by AWS. She had meanwhile begun a relationship with Karl Gregor von Knorring, a Baltic nobleman. She returned via Munich and Vienna. She was divorced from Bernhardi in 1807 and married Knorring in 1810. Bernhardi took custody of Wilhelm and she of Felix Theodor. She had meanwhile published in the *Musen-Almanach* for 1802 and in Rostorf's *Dichtergarten* (1807). She moved with Knorring to Estonia, where, except for a visit to Heidelberg in 1820, she remained until her death. She died at Reval (Tallin). *Wunderbilder und Träume* (1802), *Dramatische Phantasien* (1804), *Egidio und Isabella* (1807), *Flore und Blanscheflur* (ed. AWS, 1822), *St. Evremond* (1836, posthumous).

Unger, Johann Friedrich (1753-1804): printer and publisher. Born at Berlin, he founded his own printing and publishing business in the city. A noted type-founder, he experimented with Roman, and then Fraktur ('Unger-Fraktur'). He was also a skilled wood engraver. He was publisher to the Berlin academy. Notable works published by Unger were Goethe's *Wilhelm Meister*, Tieck's and Wackenroder's *Herzensergießungen* and AWS's Shakespeare translation. He died at Berlin.

Varnhagen von Ense, Karl August (1785-1858): diplomat, essayist. Born at Düsseldorf, he studied medicine at Berlin, Halle and Tübingen. As a tutor he met various members of Berlin's literary scene (Fouqué, q.v., Chamisso) and founded the 'Nordsternbund' circle. He was an officer in Austrian and Russian service and was present at the battles of Wagram (1809) and Hamburg (1814). From 1815 to 1819, he was in the Prussian diplomatic service, but was forced to resign because of his 'democratic' leanings. In 1814 he married Rahel Levin (q.v.). He settled in Berlin and became an independent writer and biographer, editing Rahel's works. His letters and diaries are an invaluable source of information and gossip. He died at Berlin. *Biographische Denkmale* (1824-30), *Denkwürdigkeiten* (1837-1846), *Rahel. Ein Buch des Andenkens* (1833-34), *Tagebücher* (1861-70).

Varnhagen von Ense, Rahel (née Levin) (1771-1833): salonnière in Berlin. Born at Berlin. With Henriette Herz, she was the founder of the Berlin salon. She was close to the Mendelssohn sisters, Dorothea and Henriette. Her salon was frequented by men and women of all stations and professions, from Prince Louis Ferdinand of Prussia to the Tiecks, Schleiermacher, the brothers Humboldt, Gentz, later Heinrich Heine (q.v). She attended the first of AWS's  Berlin lectures. After 1806, she lived away from Berlin. In 1814, after converting to Christianity, she married Karl August Varnhagen von Ense (q.v.), who collected her letters, epigrams and memorabilia.

Veit, Philipp (1793-1877): painter. Born at Berlin, the son of Simon Veit and Brendel (Dorothea) Mendelssohn later FS's step-son. He followed his mother to Jena, then to Paris and Cologne; he received his artistic training at Dresden and Vienna. He served 1813-14 in the Wars of Liberation, and went to Rome in 1815. From 1830-43 he was director of the Städelsches Kunstinstitut in Frankfurt and from 1853-77 of the gallery in Mainz. Died at Mainz.

Voss, Johann Heinrich (1751-1826): poet, classical scholar, translator. Born at Sommerstorf in Mecklenburg, the grandson of a freed serf, he attended school at Neubrandenburg and was then a tutor. He came to Göttingen in 1772 and was, with Hölty, Boie and Stolberg, one of the founders of the 'Hainbund', also editing the Göttingen *Musenalmanach* from 1775 to 1800. He moved to Wandsbek, then to

Otterndorf on the Elbe as head of the Latin school there. From 1782 to 1802 he was rector of the Gymnasium in Eutin. He gained first prominence as the translator of

Homer (1781, 1793) and the author of his popular hexameter poem *Luise* (1795). He also translated Hesiod, Vergil, Ovid, Tibullus and Propertius.The version of Shakespeare that he undertook with his sons Abraham and Heinrich (1818-29) was the first complete German translation into verse. AWS's review of his Homer and his treatment in the *Athenaeum* made Voss an implacable enemy of the Schlegel brothers and of the Romantics in general. He became outspokenly anti-Catholic after Friedrich Stolberg's conversion in 1800. From 1802 to 1805 he was a private scholar in Jena. He went in 1805 as professor to Heidelberg. Died at Heidelberg.

Wackenroder, Wilhelm Heinrich (1773-1798): jurist. Born at Berlin, he attended the Friedrichswerder Gymnasium with Ludwig Tieck (q.v.), whose close friend he became. Like Tieck, he was influenced by Karl Philipp Moritz, whose lectures on aesthetics he attended, and by Johann Friedrich Reichardt (q.v.). He studied with Tieck at Erlangen, where they discovered Franconia and Nuremberg, then at Göttingen, where he received lectures on art from Johann Domenik Fiorillo (q.v.). He became an 'assessor' in the Prussian legal administration. In 1796 (published date 1797), he co-authored with Tieck the enthusiastic *Herzensergießungen*. After his death in 1797, Tieck published the *Phantasien über die Kunst*, very largely by Wackenroder. He died at Berlin.

Welcker, Friedrich Gottlieb (1784-1868): classicist. Born at Grünberg, he studied classics at Giessen. In 1806 he was in Italy as tutor to the family of Wilhelm von Humboldt (q.v.), becoming in 1809 professor of Greek and archaeology in Giessen. He served in the Wars of Liberation. In 1816 he became a professor in Göttingen, and in 1819 in Bonn. His liberal views brought him into conflict with the authorities at the time of the Carlsbad Decrees. AWS valued him as a colleague. *Die griechischen Tragödien* (1839-41); *Griechische Götterlehre* (1857-62).

Werner, Friedrich Ludwig Zacharias (1768-1823): dramatist. Born at Königsberg, he studied law and estate management at the university there and also attended Kant's lectures. He held various posts in the Prussian administration in the Polish provinces, meeting E. T. A. Hoffmann in Warsaw. Transferred to Berlin in 1805, he left Prussian service in 1807 and travelled through Germany, Switzerland, Austria and France. In 1808-09 he stayed twice at Coppet, where his fate tragedy *Der vierundzwanzigste Februar* was performed by him and AWS. Goethe was initially favourable to him and had his play *Wanda* staged in Weimar. In 1809 he went to Rome and in 1810 he converted to Catholicism. He was consecrated a priest in 1814 and was a noted preacher in Vienna. He died at Vienna. *Die Söhne des Tals* (1804-04), *Das Kreuz an der Ostsee* (1806), *Martin Luther* (1806), *Der vierundzwanzigste Februar* (1808), *Attila* (1809), *Wanda* (1810), *Kunigunde* (1815).

Wieland, Christoph Martin (1733-1813): poet, novelist. Born at Biberach an der Riss, he studied at Tübingen, but was from the beginning a prolific writer, first in a sentimental and religious vein. He spent some months in 1752 in Zurich as a house guest of Bodmer, remaining in Switzerland until 1760. He returned to Biberach in 1760, frequentlng the circle of Count Stadion and coming under the influence of French and English sensualism. The works from this period gained him a reputation for  frivolity, 'light-hearted philosophy': *Don Sylvio von Rosalva* (1764), *Comische Erzählungen* (1765), *Agathon* (1766-67), *Musarion* (1768), *Der neue Amadis* (1771). From 1769 to 1772 he was a professor of philosophy in Erfurt, when he was appointed tutor to the young duke Carl August of Saxe-Weimar. He became part of the Weimar circle around duchess Anna Amalia, including Herder and Goethe. His part-translation of Shakespeare in prose (1762-66) marked an important stage in German Shakespearean reception. From 1773 to 1789 he edited the influential periodical *Der Teutsche Merkur*. His late work *Oberon* (1780) gained him international fame. He was excoriated by the serious-minded young men of the Göttingen 'Hainbund' and by the Jena Romantics. Died at Weimar.

Winckelmann, Johann Joachim (1717-1768): art historian. Born at Stendal, he attended university at Halle. After tutorships and teaching, and amid great poverty, he became librarian to Count Bünau, at Nöthnitz near Dresden in 1748. It was here that he wrote his famous work, *Gedanken über die Nachachmung der griechischen Werke* (pub. 1755). After the visit of the papal nuncio, Winckelmann converted to Catholicism; he was given a grant by the Elector of Saxony and enabled to travel to Rome. He arrived in 1755 and became successively  librarian to three cardinals, notably Cardinal Albani. His work on the archaeology of Greek antiquity led to his masterpiece, *Geschichte der Kunst des Altertums* (1764). In 1768, he decided to make a visit to Germany. He reached Munich and Vienna, but decided to return. He was murdered in an inn at Trieste.

Windischmann, Karl Joseph Hieronymus (1775-1839): physician and philosopher. Born at Mainz, he studied medicine at Mainz and Würzburg. He was appointed professor at the Gymnasium at Aschaffenburg in 1803 (teacher of Franz Bopp). In 1818 he became professor of medicine and philosophy at Bonn and a colleague of AWS's. *Die Philosophie im Fortgang der Geschichte* (1827-34).

Zimmer, Johann Georg (1777-1853): publisher. Born at Homburg v.d.H., he learned the book trade in Göttingen and Hamburg. In 1805 he set up a publishing house with J. C. B. Mohr in Heidelberg (Mohr und Zimmer, later Mohr und Winter). They published the works of most of the Romantics, Arnim, Brentano, Tieck, Görres, including *Des Knaben Wunderhorn* and the *Zeitung für Einsiedler*. They also founded the *Heidelberger Jahrbücher* and published the works of Heidelberg scholars (Creuzer, Daub, etc.). Zimmer secured AWS's *Vorlesungen über dramatische Kunst und Litteratur*. After 1815, he became a full-time Protestant minister. He died at Frankfurt.

Select Bibliography

No attempt is made here to do a full bibliography of Schlegel's oeuvre. Unless otherwise indicated, only published works by him not included in *SW*, *Oeuvres* or *Opuscula* (see below), or those reissued in a substantially new form, are listed here singly (as 'Individual Works').

Primary Texts

Texts and Editions of August Wilhelm Schlegel

Collected Works:

August Wilhelm Schlegel, *Sämmtliche Werke* [*SW*], ed. Eduard Böcking, 12 vols (Leipzig: Weidmann, 1846-47).

Oeuvres de M. Auguste-Guillaume de Schlegel écrites en français, éd. Édouard Böcking, 3 vols (Leipzig: Weidmann, 1846).

Opuscula quae Augustus Guilemus Schlegelius Latine scripta reliquit, ed. Eduardus Böcking (Lipsiae: Weidmann, 1848).

Kritische Schriften, 2 vols (Berlin: Reimer, 1828).

Essais littéraires et historiques (Bonn: Weber, 1842).

Katalog der von Aug. Wilh. von Schlegel, Professor an der Königl. Universität zu Bonn, Ritter etc., nachgelaßenen Büchersammlung, welche Montag den 1sten Dezember 1845 und an den folgenden Tagen Abends 5 Uhr präcise bei J. M. Heberle in Bonn öffentlich versteigert und dem Letztbietenden gegen gleich baare Zahlung verabfolgt wird.

Individual Works:

Die Gemählde. Gespräch [1799], ed. Lothar Müller, Fundus-Bücher, 143 (Dresden: Verlag der Kunst, 1996).

'Brief eines Reisenden aus Lyon. Im May 1807', *Allgemeine Literatur-Zeitung*, Intelligenzblatt 50, 28 June, 1807, col. 433-437. In *Krisenjahre*, III, 81-86.

'Wallstein. Tragédie par Benj. Constant de Rebeque', *Morgenblatt für gebildete Stände* 41, 17 Feb. 1809, 161-63. Reprinted in *Annales Benjamin Constant*, 4 (1984), 90-95.

'Mémoire sur l'état de l'Allemagne et sur les moyens d'y former une insurrection nationale'. In: Norman King, 'A. W. Schlegel et la guerre de libération: le mémoire sur l'état de l'Allemagne', *Cahiers staëliens*, 16 (1973), 1-31.

Sur le système continental et sur ses rapports avec la Suède (Hambourg, [Stockholm], 1813).

Betrachtungen über die Politik der dänischen Regierung (s.l., s.n., [Stockholm], 1813).

Remarques sur un article de la Gazette de Leipsick du 5. Octobre 1813. Relatif au Prince Royal de Suède (Altenburg: Brockhaus, 1813), translated into German as *Ueber Napoleon Buonaparte und den Kronprinzen von Schweden, eine Parallele in Beziehung auf einen Artikel der Leipziger Zeitung vom 5ten October 1813, von August Wilhelm Schlegel* ([n.p.], 1813. reissued Leipzig, 1814).

Dépêches et lettres interceptées par des partis détachés de l'armée combinée du nord de l'Allemagne [...] (s.l., s.n. [Hanover], 1814).

'Idées sur l'avenir de la France'. In: Otto Brandt, *Schlegel und die Politik*, 197f.

'Analyse de la Proclamation de Louis XVIII aux Français. Au mois de Février 1814'. *Ibid.*, 199-203.

'Jakob Necker', In: *Zeitgenossen. Biographie und Charakteristiken*, vol. 1 (Leipzig and Altenburg: Brockhaus), I, iii (1816), 91-112.

'Ueber den gegenwärtigen Zustand der Indischen Philologie'. *In: Jahrbuch der Preußischen Rhein-Universität*, 1 (1819), 224-250; *Indische Bibliothek*, 1 (1820), 1-27; also in *Bibliothèque universelle des sciences, belles-lettres, et arts*, XII: Littérature (1819), 349-370.

Specimen novae typographiae Indicae curavit Aug. Guil. Schlegel (Lutetiae Parisiorum: Crapelet, 1821).

'Fragment d'une lettre originale de M. W. Schlegel, sur le Triomphe de la Sensibilité', in *Chefs d'oeuvre des théâtres étrangers*, [...] *traduits en français* [...], 25 vols (Paris: Ladvocat, 1822-23): I-VI: *Chefs d'oeuvre du théâtre allemand*, III, 373-378. Republished in Erich Schmidt, 'Ein verschollener Aufsatz A. W. Schlegels über Goethes "Triumph der Empfindsamkeit"', *Festschrift zur Begrüßung des fünften Allgemeinen Deutschen Neuphilologentages zu Berlin Pfingsten 1892* [...], ed. Julius Zupitza (Berlin: Weidmann, 1892), 77-92, text 86-90.

'Indien in seinen Hauptbeziehungen. Einleitung. Über die Zunahme und den gegenwärtigen Stand unserer Kenntnisse von Indien', *Berliner Kalender auf das Gemein-Jahr 1829* (Berlin: Kön. Preuß. Kalender-Deputation [1828], 'Erste Abtheilung bis auf Vasco de Gama', 3-86; Zweite Abtheilung. 'Von Vasco de Gama bis auf die neueste Zeit', *Berliner Kalender auf das Gemein-Jahr 1831* (Berlin: Kön: Preuß: Kalender-Deputation [1830]), 3-160.

Lectures:

Über dramatische Kunst und Litteratur. Vorlesungen von August Wilh. Schlegel, 2 vols (Heidelberg: Mohr und Zimmer, 1809, 1811).

Ueber dramatische Kunst und Litteratur. Vorlesungen von August Wilhelm von Schlegel (Heidelberg: Mohr und Winter, 1817).

A. W. von Schlegel's Vorlesungen über Theorie und Geschichte der bildenden Künste. *(Gehalten in Berlin, im Sommer 1827.)* In: Berliner Conversations-Blatt für Poesie, Literatur und Kritik (Berlin: Verlag der Schlesinger'schen Buch- und Musikhandlung, 9 June-13 August, 1827), Nr. 113, 118, 121-3, 127, 130, 134, 137, 141-2, 144, 148, 155, 157-9, pp. 449-51, 469-71, 483, 485-6, 489-90, 505-6, 517-19, 533-35, 545-47, 561-67, 573-75, 589-91, 619-20, 625-27, 629-30, 635-36.

Bisset Hawkins, *Germany; the Spirit of her History, Literature, Social Condition, and National Economy* […] (London: Parker, 1838).

August Wilhelm Schlegel, *Vorlesungen über schöne Litteratur und Kunst*, ed. Jakob Minor, Deutsche Litteraturdenkmale des 18. und 19. Jahrhunderts, 17-19 (Heilbronn: Henninger, 1884).

Aug. Wilhelm Schlegels Vorlesungen über Philosophische Kunstlehre […], ed. Aug. Wünsche (Leipzig: Dieterich, 1911).

August Wilhelm Schlegel, *Geschichte der Deutschen Sprache und Poesie. Vorlesungen, gehalten an der Universität Bonn seit dem Wintersemester 1818/19*, ed. Josef Körner, Deutsche Literaturdenkmale des 18. und 19. Jahrhunderts, 147 (Berlin: Behr, 1913).

A. W. Schlegel's Lectures on German Literature from Gottsched to Goethe Given at the University of Bonn and Taken Down by George Toynbee in 1833 […], ed. H. G. Fiedler (Oxford: Blackwell, 1944).

August Wilhelm Schlegel, *Vorlesungen über das akademische Studium*, ed. Frank Jolles, Bonner Vorlesungen, 1 (Heidelberg: Stiehm, 1971).

August Wilhelm Schlegel, *Kritische Ausgabe der Vorlesungen* (Paderborn, etc.: Schöningh, 1989- in progress [*KAV*]): I: *Vorlesungen über Ästhetik I* (1798-1803), ed. Ernst Behler (1989); II, i: *Vorlesungen über Ästhetik* (1803-1827), ed. Ernst Behler, then Georg Braungart (2007); III: *Vorlesungen über Encyklopädie* (1803), ed. Frank Jolles and Edith Höltenschmidt (2006).

Periodicals or collections edited by Schlegel or by others containing contributions by him:

Die Horen eine Monatsschrift herausgegeben von Schiller (Tübingen: Cotta, 1795-97).

[J. F. Reichardt], *Deutschland*, 4 parts (Berlin: Unger, 1796).

Athenaeum. Eine Zeitschrift von August Wilhelm Schlegel und Friedrich Schlegel, 3 vols (Berlin: Vieweg, 1798; Frölich, 1799-1800).

Charakteristiken und Kritiken. Von August Wilhelm Schlegel und Friedrich Schlegel, 2 vols (Königsberg: Nicolovius, 1801).

Musen-Almanach für das Jahr 1802. Herausgegeben von A. W. Schlegel und L. Tieck (Tübingen: Cotta, 1802).

Europa. Eine Zeitschrift. Herausgegeben von Friedrich Schlegel (Frankfurt: Wilmans, 1803, 1805).

Prometheus. Eine Zeitschrift. Herausgegeben von Leo v. Seckendorf und Jos. Lud. Stoll (Vienna: Geistinger, 1808).

Deutsches Museum herausgegeben von Friedrich Schlegel, 3 vols (Vienna: Camesina, 1812-13).

Indische Bibliothek. Eine Zeitschrift von August Wilhelm von Schlegel, 3 vols (Bonn: Weber, 1820-30).

Translations and Editions:

(Anon.), *Joachim Rendorps geheime Nachrichten zur Aufklärung der Vorfälle während des letzten Krieges zwischen England und Holland, aus dem Holländ. mit erläuternden Anmerkungen* (Leipzig: Heinsius, 1793).

Historische literarische und unterhaltende Schriften von Horatio Walpole, übersetzt von A. W. Schlegel (Leipzig: Hartknoch, 1800).

Shakespeare's dramatische Werke, übersetzt von August Wilhelm Schlegel, 9 vols (Berlin: Unger, 1797-1810).

Frank Jolles, *A. W. Schlegels Sommernachtstraum in der ersten Fassung vom Jahre 1789 nach den Handschriften herausgegeben*, Palaestra, 244 (Göttingen: Vandenhoek & Ruprecht, 1967).

[Wilhelm von Schütz], *Lacrimas, ein Schauspiel. Herausgegeben von August Wilhelm Schlegel* (Berlin: Realschulbuchhandlung, 1803).

Blumensträuße italiänischer, spanischer und portugiesischer Poesie. Nach dem Erstdruck [1803] neu hg. von Jochen Strobel (Dresden: Thelem, 2007).

Spanisches Theater. Herausgegeben von August Wilhelm Schlegel (Berlin: Reimer, 1803), part 2 (with a reprint of part 1) as: *Schauspiele von Don Pedro Calderon de la Barca. Übersetzt von August Wilhelm Schlegel* (Berlin: Hitzig, 1809).

Dramatische Spiele von Pellegrin [Friedrich de la Motte Fouqué]. *Herausgegeben von A. W. Schlegel* (Berlin: Unger, 1804).

Ueber den Charakter und die Schriften der Frau von Staël von Frau Necker gebohrne von Saussure. Uebersetzt von A. W. von Schlegel (Paris, London, Strasbourg: Treuttel & Würtz, 1820).

Flore und Blanscheflur. Ein episches Gedicht in zwölf Gesängen von Sophie v. Knorring, geb. Tieck. Herausgegeben und mit einer Vorrede begleitet von A. W. von Schlegel (Berlin: Reimer, 1822).

Bhagavad-Gita, id est ΘΕΣΠΕΣΙΟΝ ΜΕΛΟΣ, sive almi Krishnae et Arjunae colloquium de rebus divinis, Bharateae episodium. Textum recensuit, adnotationes criticas et interpretationem Latinam adiecit Augustus Guilelmus a Schlegel (Bonn: In Academia Borussica Rhenana typis regiis MDCCCXXIII [Bonn: Weber, 1823]).

Ramayana id est carmen epicum de Ramae rebus gestis poetae antiquissimi Valmicis opus. Textum codd. mss. collatis recensuit interpretationem Latinam et annotationes criticas adiecit Augustus Guilelmus a Schlegel, 2 vols in 3 (Bonnae ad Rhenum: Typis Regiis. Sumtibus Editoris 1828, 1829).

HITOPADESAS id est institutio salutaris. Textum codd. mss. collatis recensuerunt interpretationem Latinam et annotationes criticas adiecerunt Augustus Guilelmus a Schlegel et Christianus Lassen, 2 parts (Bonnae ad Rhenum: Weber, 1829, 1831).

I. C. Prichard, *Darstellung der Aegyptischen Mythologie [...] Uebersetzt von L. Haymann. Nebst einer Vorrede von A. W. von Schlegel* (Bonn: Weber, 1837).

Verzeichniss einer von Eduard d'Alton [...] hinterlassenen Gemälde-Sammlung. Nebst einer Vorerinnerung und ausführlichen Beurtheilung dreier darin befindlichen Bilder. Herausgegeben von A. W. von Schlegel (Bonn: Georgi, 1840).

Letters:

Mélanges d'histoire littéraire par Guillaume Favre avec des lettres inédites d'Auguste-Guillaume Schlegel et d'Angelo Mai receuilllis par sa famille et publiés par J. Adert, 2 vols (Geneva: Ramboz & Schuchardt, 1856).

Anton Klette, *Verzeichniss der von A. W. v. Schlegel nachgelassenen Briefsammlung* (Bonn: [n.p.], 1868).

Dreihundert Briefe aus zwei Jahrhunderten, ed. Karl von Holtei, 2 vols in 4 parts (Hanover: Rümpler, 1872).

Dorothea von Schlegel geb. Mendelssohn und deren Söhne Johannes und Philipp Veit. Briefwechsel im Auftrage der Familie Veit, hg. v. J. M. Raich, 2 vols (Mainz: Kirchheim, 1881).

Friedrich Schlegels Briefe an seinen Bruder August Wilhelm, ed. Oskar F. Walzel [Walzel] (Berlin: Speyer & Peters, 1890).

H. Blümner, 'Aus Briefen an J. J. Horner (1773-1831)', *Zürcher Taschenbuch auf das Jahr 1891* (Zurich: Höhr, 1891), 1-26.

Choix de lettres d'Eugène Burnouf, 1825-1852 [...] (Paris: Champion, 1891).

Ludwig Schmidt, 'Ein Brief August Wilhelm v. Schlegels an Metternich' [*recte* Sickingen], *Mitteilungen des Instituts für Österreichische Geschichtsforschung* 23 (1902), 490-495.

Ludwig Schmidt, 'Drei Briefe Aug. Wilh. Schlegels an Gentz', *Mitteilungen des Instituts für Österreichische Geschichtsforschung* 24 (1903), 412-423.

Briefwechsel zwischen Wilhelm von Humboldt und August Wilhelm Schlegel, ed. Albert Leitzmann [Leitzmann] (Halle: Niemeyer, 1908).

Caroline. Briefe aus der Frühromantik. Nach Georg Waitz vermehrt hg. von Erich Schmidt [*Caroline*], 2 vols (Leipzig: Insel, 1913).

Gertrud Richert, *Die Anfänge der romanischen Philologie und die deutsche Romantik*, Beiträge zur Geschichte der romanischen Sprachen und Literaturen, 10 (Halle: Niemeyer, 1914).

Briefwechsel A. W. von Schlegel Christian Lassen, ed. W. Kirfel (Bonn: Cohen, 1914).

August Wilhelm Schlegels Briefwechsel mit seinen Heidelberger Verlegern, ed. Erich Jenisch [Jenisch] (Heidelberg: Winter, 1922).

August Wilhelm und Friedrich Schlegel im Briefwechsel mit Schiller und Goethe, ed. Josef Körner and Ernst Wieneke [Wieneke] (Leipzig: Insel, 1926).

Briefe von und an August Wilhelm Schlegel, ed. Josef Körner [*Briefe*], 2 vols (Zurich, Leipzig, Vienna: Amalthea, 1930).

Krisenjahre der Frühromantik. Briefe aus dem Schlegelkreis, ed. Josef Körner [*Krisenjahre*], 3 vols (Brno, Vienna, Leipzig: Rohrer, 1936-37; Berne: Francke, 1958).

Comtesse Jean de Pange, née Broglie, *Auguste-Guillaume Schlegel et Madame de Staël. D'après des documents inédits* [Pange], doctoral thesis University of Paris (Paris: Albert, 1938).

Ludwig Tieck und die Brüder Schlegel. Briefe. Auf der Grundlage der von Henry Lüdeke besorgten Edition neu herausgegeben und kommentiert von Edgar Lohner [Lohner] (Munich: Winkler, 1972).

Friedrich Schiller-August Wilhelm Schlegel. Der Briefwechsel, ed. Norbert Oellers (Cologne: DuMont, 2005).

'Meine liebe Marie'—'Werthester Herr Professor'. Der Briefwechsel zwischen August Wilhelm von Schlegel und seiner Bonner Haushälterin Maria Löbel. Historisch-kritische Ausgabe, ed. Ralf Georg Czapla and Franca Victoria Schankweiler (Bonn: Bernstein, 2012).

Founders of Western Indology. August Wilhelm von Schlegel and Henry Thomas Colebrooke in Correspondence 1820-1837, ed. Rosane Rocher and Ludo Rocher, Abhandlungen für die Kunde des Morgenlandes, 84 (Wiesbaden: Harrassowitz, 2013).

'Geliebter Freund und Bruder'. Der Briefwechsel zwischen Christian Friedrich Tieck und August Wilhelm Schlegel in den Jahren 1804 bis 1811, ed. Cornelia Bögel, Tieck Studien 1 (Dresden: Thelem, 2015).

Other Primary Literature:

Ernst Moritz Arndt, *Ausgewählte Werke*, ed. Heinrich Meisner and Robert Geerds, 16 vols (Leipzig: Hesse, [1908]).

Sulpiz Boisserée, *Tagebücher 1808-1854*. Im Auftrag der Stadt Köln hg. von Hans-J. Weitz, 4 vols plus index (Darmstadt: Roether, 1978-95).

Bonstettiana. Historisch-kritische Ausgabe der Briefkorrespondenzen Karl Viktor von Bonstettens und seines Kreises, 1753-1832, ed. Doris and Peter Walser-Wilhelm [Bonstettiana], 14 vols in 27 (Berne: Peter Lang, 1996-2011).

Souvenirs—1785-1870—du feu duc de Broglie, 3 vols (Paris: Calmann Lévy, 1886).

Briefe von und an Gottfried August Bürger. Ein Beitrag zur Literaturgeschichte seiner Zeit. Aus dem Nachlasse Bürger's und anderen, meist handschriftlichen Quellen hg. von Adolf Strodtmann, 4 vols (Berlin: Paetel, 1874).

Byron's Letters and Journals, ed. Leslie A. Marchand, 12 vols plus 1 supplement (London: Murray, 1973-1994).

Life and Letters of Thomas Campbell, ed. William Beattie, 3 vols (London: Moxon, 1849).

Charakteristiken. Die Romantiker in Selbstzeugnissen und Äußerungen ihrer Zeitgenossen, ed. Paul Kluckhohn, Deutsche Literatur in Entwicklungsreihen, Reihe Romantik, 1 (Darmstadt: Wissenschaftliche Buchgesellschaft, 1964).

Benjamin Constant, *Journaux intimes*, ed. Alfred Roulin and Charles Roth [Journaux intimes] (Paris: Gallimard, 1952).

Briefe an Cotta. Das Zeitalter Goethes und Napoleons 1794-1815, ed. Maria Fehling (Stuttgart, Berlin: Cotta, 1925).

Ch[arles] Galusky, 'Notice sur la vie et les ouvrages de M. A. W. de Schlegel', *Revue des deux mondes*, 1 February 1846, 159-190.

Briefe von und an Friedrich Gentz, ed. Friedrich Carl Wittichen, 3 vols (Munich: Oldenbourg, 1909-14).

Johann Wolfgang Goethe, *Gedenkausgabe der Werke, Briefe und Gespräche*, ed. Ernst Beutler, 3rd edn, 27 vols (Zurich: Artemis, 1986 [1949]).

Goethes Briefwechsel mit Christian Gottlob Voigt, 4 vols, Schriften der Goethe-Gesellschaft, 53-56 (Weimar: Böhlau, 1949-62).

Philippe de Golbéry: 'Auguste-Guillaume de Schlegel'. In: *Biographie universelle et portative* […], 5 vols (Supplément) (Paris, Strasbourg: Levraut, 1834), V, 731-735, and *Biographie universelle, ancienne et moderne*, 85 vols (Paris: Michaud, 1811-62), LXXXI, 300-316.

Heinrich Heine, *Säkularausgabe*, hg. von den Nationalen Forschungs- und Gedenkstätten der klassischen deutschen Literatur in Weimar und dem Centre National de la Recherche Scientifique in Paris, 27 vols (Berlin: Akademie-Verlag; Paris: Éditions du CNRS, 1970-).

Heinrich Heine, *Historisch-kritische Gesamtausgabe der Werke*, ed. Manfred Windfuhr, 16 vols in 23 (Hamburg: Hoffmann und Campe, 1975-97).

Index praelectionum auspiciis augustissimi et serenissimi regis Friderici Guilelmi III. in academia Borussica Rhenana recens condita […] *publice privatimque habendarum* [title varies] (Bonn: various publishers, 1818/19-1839), from 1840-41 with sub-title *auspiciis regis augustissimi Friderici Guilelmi IIII.*

Jean Paul, *Sämtliche Werke. Historisch-kritische Ausgabe hg. von der Deutschen Akademie der Wissenschaften zu Berlin*, 31 vols in 3 sections (Weimar: Böhlau, 1927-).

Adam Müller, *Lebenszeugnisse*, ed. Jakob Baxa, 2 vols (Munich etc.: Schöningh, 1966).

Novalis, *Schriften. Die Werke Friedrich von Hardenbergs*, ed. Paul Kluckhohn and Richard Samuel, 6 vols in 7 [*HKA*] (Stuttgart: Kohlhammer, 1960-2006).

F. W. J. Schelling, *Briefe und Dokumente*, ed. Horst Fuhrmans, 3 vols (Bonn: Bouvier, 1962-75).

Briefwechsel zwischen Schiller und Wilhelm v. Humboldt. Mit einer Vorerinnerung über Schiller und den Gang seiner Geistesentwicklung von W. von Humboldt (Stuttgart and Tübingen: Cotta, 1830).

Der Briefwechsel zwischen Schiller und Goethe, ed. Hans Gerhard Gräf and Albert Leitzmann, 3 vols (Leipzig: Insel, 1955).

Kritische Friedrich-Schlegel-Ausgabe, ed. Ernst Behler et al., 30 vols [KA] (Paderborn, Munich, Vienna: Schöningh; Zurich: Thomas, 1958- in progress).

[Moritz Schlegel], 'August Wilhelm und Friedrich Schlegel', *Zeitgenossen. Biographieen und Charakteristiken*, vol. 1 (Leipzig and Altenburg: Brockhaus, 1816), iv, 179-186.

G. C. L. Sismondi, *Epistolario*, ed. Carlo Pellegrini, 4 vols. (Florence: La Nuova Italia, 1933-1954).

Lettres inédites de Mme. de Staël, ed. Paul Usteri and Eugène Ritter (Paris: Hachette, 1903).

Madame de Staël, *De l'Allemagne*, ed. Comtesse Jean de Pange and Simone Balayé, 5 vols (Paris: Hachette, 1958-60).

Madame de Staël, *Dix années d'exil*, ed. Simone Balayé (Paris: Bibliothèque 1018, 1966).

Madame de Staël, *Correspondance générale*, ed. Béatrice W. Jasinski and Othenin d'Haussonville, 7 vols [Correspondance générale] (Paris: Pauvert; Hachette; Klincksieck, 1962-; Geneva: Champion-Slatkine, 1962-2008).

Maria Ullrichová, *Lettres de Madame de Staël conservées en Bohème* (Prague: Czech Academy of Sciences, 1959).

Simone Balayé (ed.), *Les carnets de voyage de Madame de Staël. Contribution à la genèse de ses oeuvres* [Carnets de voyage] (Geneva: Droz, 1971).

Madame de Staël, *De la littérature considérée dans ses rapports avec les institutions sociales*, ed. Axel Blaeschke (Paris: Garnier, 1998).

Henrich Steffens, *Was ich erlebte. Aus der Erinnerung niedergeschrieben*, 12 vols (Breslau: Max, 1840-44).

Freiherr vom Stein, *Briefe und amtliche Schriften*, ed. Erich Botzenhart and Walther Hubatsch, 10 vols (Stuttgart: Kohlhammer, 1957-74).

George Ticknor, *Life, Letters and Journals*, 2 vols (London: Sampson Low, Marston, 1876).

Rahel-Bibliothek. Rahel Varnhagen. Gesammelte Werke, ed. Konrad Feilchenfeldt, Uwe Schweikert and Rahel E. Steiner, 10 vols [Rahel-Bibliothek] (Munich: Matthes & Seitz, 1983).

Caspar Voght und sein Hamburger Freundeskreis. Briefe aus einem tätigen Leben, ed. Kurt Detlev Möller and Anneliese Tecke, 3 vols, Veröffentlichung des Vereins für Hamburgische Geschichte, 15, i-iii (Hamburg: Christians, 1959-67).

Briefe des Dichters Friedrich Ludwig Zacharias Werner, ed. Oswald Floeck, 2 vols (Munich: Georg Müller, 1914).

Die Tagebücher des Dichters Zacharias Werner (Texte), ed. Oswald Floeck, Bibliothek des Literarischen Vereins in Stuttgart, 289 (Leipzig: Hiersemann, 1939).

Secondary Literature

Allgemeine Deutsche Biographie, ed. Historische Kommission der Königl. Akademie der Wissenschaften, 56 vols (Leipzig: Duncker & Humblot, 1875-1912).

Carl Alt, *Schiller und die Brüder Schlegel* (Weimar: Böhlau, 1904).

Simone Balayé, 'Madame de Staël et le gouvernement impérial en 1810, le dossier de la suppression de *De l'Allemagne*', *Cahiers staëliens*, 19 (1974), 3-77.

Simone Balayé, *Madame de Staël. Écrire, lutter, vivre*. Pref. Roland Mortier, afterword Frank Paul Bowman, Historie des idées et critique littéraire (Geneva: Droz, 1994).

Simone Balayé, 'Les rapports de l'écrivain et du pouvoir: Madame de Staël et Napoléon', in: Balayé (1994), 137-154.

Simone Balayé and Norman King et al., 'Madame de Staël et les polices françaises sous la Révolution et l'Empire', *Cahiers staëliens*, 44 (1992-93), 3-153.

Michael Bernays, *Zur Entstehungsgeschichte des Schlegelschen Shakespeare* (Leipzig: Hirzel, 1872).

Barbara Besslich, *Der deutsche Napoleon-Mythos. Literatur und Erinnerung 1800-1945* (Darmstadt: Wissenschaftliche Buchgesellschaft, 2007).

Waldtraut Beyer, 'Der Atheismusstreit um Fichte', in: Dahnke and Leistner, II, 154-245.

Friedrich von Bezold, *Geschichte der Rheinischen Friedrich-Wilhelms-Universität von der Gründung bis zum Jahr 1870* (Bonn: Marcus & Weber, 1920).

Anil Bhatti, 'August Wilhelm Schlegels Indienrezeption und der Kolonialismus', in: Jürgen Lehmann et al. (eds), *Konflikt Grenze Dialog. Kulturkontrastive und interdisziplinäre Textzugänge. Festschrift für Horst Turk zum 60. Geburtstag* (Frankfurt am Main etc.: Peter Lang, 1997), 185-205.

Ingrid Bodsch (ed.), *Monument für Beethoven. Zur Geschichte des Beethoven-Denkmals (1845) und der frühen Beethoven-Rezeption in Bonn*. Katalog zur Ausstellung des Stadtmuseums Bonn und des Beethoven-Hauses (Bonn: Stadtmuseum, 1995).

Cornelia Bögel, 'Fragment einer unbekannten autobiographischen Skizze aus dem Nachlass August Wilhelm Schlegels', *Athenäum* 22 (2012), 165-180.

Otto Brandt, *August Wilhelm Schlegel. Der Romantiker und die Politik* [Brandt] (Stuttgart, Berlin: Deutsche Verlags-Anstalt, 1919).

Max Braubach, *Kleine Geschichte der Universität Bonn 1818-1968* (Bonn: Röhrscheid, 1968).

Bernhard von Brentano, *August Wilhelm Schlegel. Geschichte eines romantischen Geistes* (Stuttgart: Cotta, 1943).

W. H. Bruford, *Germany in the Eighteenth Century: The Social Background of the Literary Revival* (Cambridge: Cambridge University Press, 1935).

W. H. Bruford, *Theatre, Drama and Audience in Goethe's Germany* (London: Routledge & Kegan Paul, 1950).

W. H. Bruford, *Culture and Society in Classical Weimar 1775-1806* (Cambridge: Cambridge University Press, 1962).

Hans-Dieter Dahnke and Bernd Leistner (eds), *Debatten und Kontroversen. Literarische Auseinandersetzungen in Deutschland am Ende des 18. Jahrhunderts*, 2 vols (Berlin, Weimar: Aufbau, 1989).

Robert Darnton, *The Great Cat Massacre and Other Episodes in French Cultural History* (Harmondsworth: Penguin, 2001 [1984]).

Werner Deetjen, 'August Wilhelm Schlegel in Bonn', *Spenden aus der Weimarer Bibliothek*, 15, Zeitschrift für Bücherfreunde NF 20 (1928), 16-20.

Carl Enders, *Friedrich Schlegel. Die Quellen seines Wesens und Werdens* (Leipzig: Haessel, 1913).

Ewa Eschler, *Sophie Tieck-Bernhardi-Knorring (1775-1833). Das Wanderleben und das vergessene Werk* (Berlin: Trafo, 2005).

K. F. von Frank, 'Schlegel von Gottleben', *Seftenegger Monatsblatt für Genealogie und Heraldik* 5 (1960-65), col. 314.

Paul Gautier, *Madame de Staël et Napoléon* (Paris: Plon, 1921).

Ludwig Geiger, *Dichter und Frauen. Abhandlungen und Mittheilungen. Neue Sammlung* (Berlin: Paetel, 1899).

Gabriel Girod de l'Ain, *Bernadotte, chef de guerre et chef d'état* (Paris: Perrin, 1968).

Alfred Götze, *Ein fremder Gast. Frau von Staël in Deutschland 1803/04. Nach Briefen und Dokumenten* (Jena: Frommann, 1928).

Bernd Goldmann, *Wolf Heinrich von Baudissin. Leben und Werk eines großen Übersetzers* (Hildesheim: Gerstenberg, 1981).

Bengt Hasselrot, *Nouveaux documents sur Benjamin Constant et Mme de Staël* (Copenhagen: Munksgaard, 1952).

Raymond Heitz and Roland Krebs (eds), *Schiller publiciste/Schiller als Publizist*, Convergences, 42 (Berne, etc.: Peter Lang, 2007).

J. Christopher Herold, *Mistress to an Age. A Life of Madame de Staël* (London: Hamish Hamilton, 1958).

Edith Höltenschmidt, *Die Mittelalter-Rezeption der Brüder Schlegel* (Paderborn, etc.: Schöningh, 2000).

Torvald Torvaldson Höjer, *Carl XIV Johan*, 3 vols (Stockholm: Norstedt, 1939-60).

John Isbell, *The Birth of European Romanticism. Truth and Propaganda in Staël's 'De l'Allemagne'*, Cambridge Studies in French, 49 (Cambridge: Cambridge University Press, 1994).

Béatrice W. Jasinski, 'Liste des principaux visiteurs qui ont séjourné à Coppet de 1799 à 1816', in: Simone Balayé and Jean-Daniel Candaux (eds), *Le Groupe de Coppet. Actes et documents du deuxième colloque de Coppet 1974* [...], Bibliothèque de la littérature comparée, 118 (Geneva and Paris: Slatkine, 1977), 461-492.

Walter Jesinghaus, 'August Wilhelm von Schlegels Meinungen über die Ursprache', doctoral thesis University of Leipzig (Düsseldorf: C. Jesinghaus, 1913).

Frank Jolles, 'August Wilhelm Schlegel und Berlin: Sein Weg von den Berliner Vorlesungen von 1801-04 zu denen vom Jahre 1827', in: Otto Pöggeler *et al.* (eds), *Kunsterfahrung und Kulturpolitik im Berlin Hegels*, Hegel-Studien, Beiheft 22 (Bonn: Bouvier, 1983), 153-73 plus [2].

Carl Justi, *Winckelmann und seine Zeitgenossen*, 3rd edn, 3 vols ([Justi] Leipzig: Vogel, 1923).

Gerhard R. Kaiser and Olaf Müller (eds), *Germaine de Staël und ihr erstes deutsches Publikum. Literaturpolitik und Kulturtransfer um 1800* (Heidelberg: Winter, 2008).

Alex. Kaufmann, 'Zur Erinnerung an August Wilhelm von Schlegel', *Monatsschrift für rheinisch-westfälische Geschichtsforschung und Alterthumskunde* 1 (1875), 239-54.

Paul Kaufmann, 'Auf den Spuren August Wilhelm von Schlegels', *Preußische Jahrbücher* 234 (1933), 226-43.

Reinhard Kekulé, *Das Leben Friedrich Gottlieb Welcker's* (Leipzig: Teubner, 1880).

Norman King, 'Un récit inédit du grand voyage de Madame de Staël (1812-1813)', *Cahiers staëliens*, 4 (1966), 4-23.

Norman King, 'Deux critiques de Wallstein', *Annales Benjamin Constant* 4 (1984), 61-89.

Josef Körner, 'August Wilhelm von Schlegel und die Frauen. Ein Gedenkblatt zum 150. Geburtstag des Romantikers', *Donauland* 1 (1918), 1219-1227.

Josef Körner, *Romantiker und Klassiker. Die Brüder Schlegel in ihren Beziehungen zu Schiller und Goethe* (Berlin: Askanischer Verlag, 1924).

Josef Körner, 'August Wilhelm Schlegel und der Katholizismus', *Historische Zeitschrift* 139 (1928-29), 62-83.

Josef Körner, *Die Botschaft der deutschen Romantik an Europa*, Schriften zur deutschen Literatur für die Görresgesellschaft, 9 (Augsburg: Filser, 1929).

Josef Körner, 'Ein philologischer Studienplan August Wilhelm Schlegels', *Die Erziehung* 7 (1932), 373-379.

Josef Körner, 'Die Slawen im Urteil der deutschen Romantik', *Historische Vierteljahrschrift* 31 (1937-39), 565-576.

Josef Körner, 'Indologie und Humanität', In: JK, *Philologische Schriften und Briefe*, ed. Ralf Klausnitzer, intr. Hans Eichner, Marbacher Wissenschaftsgeschichte, 1 (Göttingen: Wallstein, 2001), 137-162.

Peer Kösling, 'Die Wohnungen der Gebrüder Schlegel in Jena', *Athenäum* 8 (1998), 97-110.

Pierre Kohler, *Madame de Staël et la Suisse. Étude biographique et littéraire avec de nombreux documents inédits* (Lausanne and Paris: Payot, 1916).

Antje Middeldorf Kosegarten (ed.), *Johann Domenicus Fiorillo und die romantische Bewegung um 1800* (Göttingen: Wallstein, 1997).

S. Lefmann, *Franz Bopp, sein Leben und seine Wissenschaft*, 3 vols (Berlin: Reimer, 1891-97).

[Charles Lenormant], *Coppet et Weimar. Madame de Staël et la grande-duchesse Louise* (Paris: Lévy, 1862).

Perk Loesch, 'Der Nachlass August Wilhelm Schlegels in der Handschriftensammlung der Sächsischen Landesbibliothek-Staats- und Universitätsbibliothek Dresden', in: Ludger Syré (ed.), *Dichternachlässe. Literarische Sammlungen und Archive in den Regionalbibliotheken von Deutschland, Österreich und der Schweiz* (Frankfurt am Main: Klostermann, 2009), 183-193.

Bernhard Maaz, *Christian Friedrich Tieck 1776-1851. Leben und Werk unter besonderer Berücksichtigung seines Bildnisschaffens, mit einem Werkverzeichnis*, Bildhauer des 19. Jahrhunderts (Berlin: Gebr. Mann, 1995).

Jakob Minor, 'August Wilhelm von Schlegel in den Jahren 1804-1845', *Zeitschrift für die Österreichischen Gymnasien* 38 (1887), 590-613, 733-753.

York-Gothart Mix and Jochen Strobel (eds), *Der Europäer August Wilhelm Schlegel. Romantischer Kulturtransfer—romantische Wissenswelten*, Quellen und Forschungen 62 (296)[Mix-Strobel] (Berlin, New York: de Gruyter, 2010).

Chetana Nagavajara, *August Wilhelm Schlegel in Frankreich. Sein Anteil an der französischen Literaturkritik 1807-1835*, intr. Kurt Wais, Forschungsprobleme der vergleichenden Literaturgeschichte, 3 (Tübingen: Niemeyer, 1966).

Horst Neuper et al. (ed.), *Das Vorlesungsangebot an der Universität Jena von 1749 bis 1854* (Weimar: Verlag und Datenbank für Geisteswissenschaften, 2003).

Friedrich v. Oppeln-Bronikowski, *David Ferdinand Koreff. Serapionsbruder, Magnetiseur, Geheimrat und Dichter. Der Lebensroman eines Vergessenen* (Berlin: Paetel, 1928).

Comtesse Jean de Pange, *Mme de Staël et la découverte de l'Allemagne* (Paris: Malfère, 1929).

Roger Paulin, *Ludwig Tieck. A Literary Biography* (Oxford: Clarendon, 1985).

Roger Paulin, *The Critical Reception of Shakespeare in Germany 1682-1914. Native Literature and Foreign Genius*, Anglistische und amerikanistische Texte und Studien, 11 (Hildesheim, Zurich, New York: Olms, 2003).

Roger Paulin, *August Wilhelm Schlegels Kosmos* (Dresden: Thelem, 2011).

Christoph Perels (ed.), *'Ein Dichter hatte uns alle geweckt'. Goethe und die literarische Romantik*, exhibition catalogue (Frankfurt am Main: Freies Deutsches Hochstift Frankfurter Goethe-Museum, 1999).

Georg Reichard, *August Wilhelm Schlegels 'Ion'. Das Schauspiel und die Aufführungen unter der Leitung von Goethe und Iffland*, Mitteilungen zur Theatergeschichte der Goethezeit, 9 (Bonn: Bouvier, 1987).

Karl Alexander von Reichlin-Meldegg, *Friedrich Eberhard Gottlob Paulus und seine Zeit, nach dessen literarischem Nachlasse, bisher ungedrucktem Briefwechsel und mündlichen Mittheilungen dargestellt*, 2 vols (Stuttgart: Verlags-Magazin, 1853).

Doris Reimer, *Passion & Kalkül. Der Verleger Georg Andreas Reimer (1776-1842)* [Reimer] (Berlin: de Gruyter, 1999).

Christian Renger, 'August Wilhelm Schlegels frühe Bonner Jahre', typescript diploma thesis University of Bonn, 1973, Bonn Universitätsarchiv Slg. Bib. 1554.

Christian Renger, *Die Gründung und Einrichtung der Universität Bonn und die Berufungspolitik des Kultusmininsters Altenstein*, Academica Bonnensia, 7 (Bonn: Röhrscheid, 1982).

R[osane] Rocher, 'The Knowledge of Sanskrit in Europe Until 1800', in: Sylvain Auroux et al., *The History of the Language Sciences [...]*, 3 vols, Handbücher zur Sprach- und Kommunikationswissenschaft, 18, 1-3 (Berlin, New York: de Gruyter, 2000), II, 1156-1163.

Christine Roger, *La Réception de Shakespeare en Allemagne de 1815 à 1850. Propagation et assimilation de la référence étrangère*, Theatrica, 24 (Berne, etc.: Peter Lang, 2008).

Martine de Rougemont, 'Pour un répertoire des rôles et des représentations de Mme de Staël', *Cahiers staëliens*, 19 (1974), 79-92.

Martin J. S. Rudwick, *Bursting the Limits of Time. The Reconstruction of Geohistory in the Age of Revolution [...]* (Chicago and London: Chicago University Press, 2005).

Joyce S. Rutledge, *Johann Adolph Schlegel*, German Studies in America, 18 (Berne, Frankfurt am Main: Herbert Lang, 1974).

Thomas G. Sauer, *A. W. Schlegel's Shakespearean Criticism in England, 1811-1846*, Studien zur Literatur der Moderne, 9 (Bonn: Bouvier, 1981).

Karl Th. Schäfer, *Verfassungsgeschichte der Universität Bonn 1818 bis 1960. 150 Jahre Rheinische Friedrich-Wilhelms-Universität zu Bonn 1818-1968* (Bonn: Bouvier, Röhrscheid, 1968).

John William Scholl, 'August Wilhelm Schlegel and Goethe's Epic and Elegiac Verse', *Journal of English and Germanic Philology* 7, iii (1907-08), 61-98, iv, 54-86.

J. H. Scholte, 'August Wilhelm Schlegel in Amsterdam', *Jaarboek van het Genootschap Amstelodamum* 41 (Amsterdam: de Bussy, 1949), 102-146.

Rainer Schmitz (ed.), *Die ästhetische Prügeley. Streitschriften der antiromantischen Bewegung* (Göttingen: Wallstein, 1992).

Heinrich Schrörs, *Die Bonner Universitätsaula und ihre Wandgemälde* (Bonn: Hanstein, 1906).

Wilhelm Schwartz, *August Wilhelm Schlegels Verhältnis zur spanischen und portugiesischen Literatur*, Romanistische Arbeiten, 3 (Halle: Niemeyer, 1914).

Konrad Seeliger, 'Johann Elias Schlegel', *Mitteilungen des Vereins f. Geschichte der Stadt Meißen* 2, Heft 2 (1888), 145-188.

Wulf Segebrecht *et al.*, *Romantische Liebe und romantischer Tod. Über den Bamberger Aufenthalt von Caroline Schlegel, Auguste Böhmer, August Wilhelm Schlegel und Friedrich Wilhelm Schelling im Jahre 1800*, Fussnoten zur Literatur, 48 (Bamberg: Universität Bamberg, 2001).

Friedrich Sengle, *Das Genie und sein Fürst. Die Geschichte der Lebensgemeinschaft Goethes mit dem Herzog Carl August von Sachsen-Weimar-Eisenach. Ein Beitrag zum Spätfeudalismus und zu einem vernachlässigten Thema der Goetheforschung* (Stuttgart, Weimar: Metzler, 1993).

Margaret Stoljar, *Athenaeum: A Critical Commentary*, Australian and New Zealand Studies in German Language and Literature, 4 (Berne and Frankfurt am Main: Herbert Lang, 1973).

Friedrich Strack (ed.), *Evolution des Geistes: Jena um 1800. Natur und Kunst, Philosophie und Wissenschaft im Spannungsfeld der Geschichte*, Deutscher Idealismus, 17 (Stuttgart: Klett-Cotta, 1994).

Jochen Strobel, 'Der Romantiker als homo academicus. August Wilhelm Schlegel in der Wissenschaft', *Jahrbuch des Freien Deutschen Hochstifts*, 2010, 298-338.

Jochen Strobel, 'Eine digitale Edition der Korrespondenzen August Wihelm Schlegels', *Athenäum* 22 (2012), 145-151.

Emil Sulger-Gebing, *Die Brüder A. W. und F. Schlegel in ihrem Verhältnisse zur bildenden Kunst*, Forschungen zur neueren Litteraturgeschichte, 3 [Sulger-Gebing] (Munich: Haushalter, 1897).

Henry W. Sullivan, *Calderón in the German Lands and the Low Countries: His Reception and Influence, 1654-1980* (Cambridge, etc.: Cambridge University Press, 1983).

Paul Robinson Sweet, *Wilhelm von Humboldt: A Biography*, 2 vols (Columbus: Ohio State University Press, 1979-80).

Reinhard Tgahrt *et al.* (eds): *Weltliteratur. Die Lust am Übersetzen im Jahrhundert Goethes*, Marbacher Kataloge, 17 (Munich: Kösel, 1982).

Wilhelm Waetzoldt, 'August Wilhelm und Friedrich Schlegel', in: WW, *Deutsche Kunsthistoriker*, 2 vols (Berlin: Spiess, 1986 [1921, 1924]).

Oskar Walzel, 'Neue Quellen zur Geschichte der älteren romantischen Schule', *Zeitschrift für die Österreichischen Gymnasien* 42 (1891), 486-493.

Oskar Walzel, 'Neue Quellen zur Geschichte der älteren romantischen Schule', *Zeitschrift für die Österreichischen Gymnasien* 43 (1892), 289-296.

Ernst Windisch, *Geschichte der Sanskrit-Philologie und indischen Altertumskunde*, 2 vols (Grundriss der indo-arischen Philologie und Altertumskunde [Encyclopedia of Indo-Aryan Research], I, iB) (Strasbourg: Trübner, 1917; Berlin, Leipzig: de Gruyter, 1920).

Bernd Witte *et al.*, *Goethe-Handbuch*, 4 vols in 5 (Stuttgart, Weimar: Metzler, 1996-98).

Harro Zimmermann, *Friedrich Schlegel oder die Sehnsucht nach Deutschland* (Paderborn etc.: Schöningh, 2009).

List of Illustrations

Main Text

Frontispiece: The Schlegel Coat of Arms ('Schlegel von Gottleben'). SLUB Dresden. Mscr. Dresd. e. 90. 11. 10-1. © SLUB Dresden, all rights reserved.   x

1. August Wilhelm Schlegel, *De geographia Homerica* (Hanover, 1788). Title page. © and by kind permission of the Master and Fellows of Trinity College, Cambridge, CC BY-NC 4.0.   36
2. Portrait drawing of August Wilhelm Schlegel as a young man, by unknown artist, undated [early 1790s]. © and by kind permission of Hans-Joachim Dopfer, all rights reserved.   60
3. Portrait in oils of August Wilhelm Schlegel, by Johann Friedrich August Tischbein [1793]. http://www.zeno.org/nid/20004239346. Image in the public domain. (Attribution challenged by the present owners, Freies Deutsches Hochstift—Frankfurter Goethe-Museum, Frankfurt am Main).   61
4. *Die Horen eine Monatsschrift herausgegeben von Schiller* (Tübingen, 1795-98). Title page of vol. 1. Image in the public domain.   74
5. Manuscript page of Schlegel's and Caroline's translation of Shakespeare's *Romeo and Juliet* (1797), in Caroline's hand, open at Act 2, Scene 1 ('O Romeo, Romeo, wherefore art thou Romeo?'). SLUB Dresden. Mscr. Dresd. e. 90. XXII. 10. Bl. 24. © SLUB Dresden, all rights reserved.   97
6. Manuscript page of Schlegel's translation of Shakespeare's *The Tempest* (1798), open at Act 1, Scene 2 ('Full fathom five'). SLUB Dresden. Mscr. Dresd. e. 90. XXII. 13. Bl. 49. © SLUB Dresden, all rights reserved.   98
7. *Athenaeum. Eine Zeitschrift von August Wilhelm und Friedrich Schlegel* (Berlin, 1798-1800). Title page of vol. 2. Image in the public domain.   116
8. John Flaxman: illustration of Dante, *Inferno*, Canto 33 (Rome[?], 1802), showing Ugolino and his sons. © and by kind permission of the Master and Fellows of Trinity College, Cambridge, CC BY-NC 4.0.   164

9. August Wilhelm and Friedrich Schlegel, *Charakteristiken und Kritiken* (Königsberg, 1801), Title page of vol. 1. © and by kind permission of the Master and Fellows of Trinity College, Cambridge, CC BY-NC 4.0. — 172
10. A. W. Schlegel and L. Tieck, *Musenalmanach auf das Jahr 1802* (Tübingen, 1802). Title page. © and by kind permission of the Master and Fellows of Trinity College, Cambridge, CC BY-NC 4.0. — 181
11. 'Schlegel and Tieck Crowning Each Other With Laurels'. Extract from the caricature 'Die neuere Ästhetik' (1803). Image taken from *Die ästhetische Prügeley*, ed. Rainer Schmitz (Göttingen: Wallstein, 1992), [unpag.]. Courtesy of Wallstein Verlag, image in the public domain. — 191
12. *Europa. Eine Zeitschrift. Herausgegeben von Friedrich Schlegel* (Frankfurt am Main, 1803, 1805). Frontispiece and title page. © and by kind permission of the Master and Fellows of Trinity College, Cambridge, CC BY-NC 4.0. — 192
13. 'Artem penetrat'. Caricature drawing, undated [1805?], reproduced by J. G. van Gelder, 'Artem Penetrat', in: *Dancwerc. Opstellen aangeboden aan Prof. Dr. D. Th. Enklaar ter gelegenheid van zijn vijfenzestige verjaardag* (Groningen: Wolters, 1959), 308-317, ill. facing 312. Orphan work. — 266
14. August Wilhelm Schlegel, *Comparaison entre la Phèdre de Racine et celle d'Euripide* (Paris, 1807). Title page. © and by kind permission of the Master and Fellows of Trinity College, Cambridge, CC BY-NC 4.0. — 282
15. August Wilhelm Schlegel, *Über dramatische Kunst und Litteratur* (Heidelberg, 1809, 1811). Title page of vol. 1. Image in the public domain. — 303
16. 'Eintritts-Billett'. Admission ticket for Schlegel's lectures on Dramatic Art and Literature, Vienna 1808. SLUB Dresden. Mscr. Dresd. App. 2712. A8. 5. © SLUB Dresden, all rights reserved. — 306
17. August Wilhelm Schlegel, marble bust by Friedrich Tieck 1816-30. Image taken from the frontispiece of *Briefe von und an August Wilhelm Schlegel*, ed. Josef Körner (Zurich, Leipzig, Vienna: Amalthea, 1930), vol. 1. Image in the public domain. — 325
18. August Wilhelm Schlegel, *Poetische Werke* (Vienna, 1815). Frontispiece and title page. Image in the public domain. — 333
19. August Wilhelm Schlegel, *Betrachtungen über die Politik der dänischen Regierung* ([Stockholm], 1813). Title page. © and by kind permission of the Master and Fellows of Trinity College, Cambridge, CC BY-NC 4.0. — 363
20. *Proclamations de S. A. R. le Prince-Royal de Suède* (Stockholm, 1815). Title page. Image in the public domain. — 366
21. Portrait engraving of August Wilhelm Schlegel by Gustav Adolph Zumpe (c. 1817). Image in the public domain. — 393
22. Friedrich Schlegel, *Deutsches Museum* (Vienna, 1812). Title page. Image in the public domain. — 410
23. August Wilhelm Schlegel, *Cours de littérature dramatique. Traduit de l'allemand* (Paris, Geneva, 1814). Title page of vol. 1. © and by kind permission of the Master and Fellows of Trinity College, Cambridge, CC BY-NC 4.0. — 421

List of Illustrations 619

24. *Jahrbuch der Preußischen Rhein-Universität* (Bonn, 1819). Frontispiece issued 1821. © and by kind permission of the Master and Fellows of Trinity College, Cambridge, CC BY-NC 4.0. — 449
25. 'Aula'. Illustration from *Die rheinische Friedrich-Wilhelms-Universität zu Bonn* (Bonn, 1839). Image in the public domain. — 459
26. 'Inskriptions-Liste'. Attendance list for August Wilhelm Schlegel's lecture 'Deutsche Verskunst', summer semester 1820, showing Heinrich Heine's name at the bottom. SLUB Dresden. Mscr. Dresd. e. 90. V. 7. © SLUB Dresden, all rights reserved. — 468
27. 'Inskriptions-Liste'. Attendance list for August Wilhelm Schlegel's lecture 'Einige homerische Fragen', winter semester 1835-36. Karl Marx's name is marked '+6'. SLUB Dresden. Mscr. Dresd. e. 90. V. 4. © SLUB Dresden, all rights reserved. — 468
28. *Indische Bibliothek. Eine Zeitschrift von August Wilhelm von Schlegel* (Bonn, 1820-1830). Title page issued in 1823. © and by kind permission of the Master and Fellows of Trinity College, Cambridge, CC BY-NC 4.0. — 490
29. Schlegel's Certificate of Departure from the Port of Dover, 19 November 1823, with description of his appearance. SLUB Dresden. Mscr. Dresd. e. 90. XI. 1. 4. © SLUB Dresden, all rights reserved. — 499
30. Auguste von Buttlar, pencil drawing after the engraving by Jean Bein based on the painting by François Gérard, 'Corinne au cap Misène' (1819), 1824. Kupferstich-Kabinett, Kupferstich-Kabinett, Staatliche Kunstsammlungen Dresden, Inv. Nr. Ca 45/S.01 © Staatliche Kunstsammlungen Dresden, all rights reserved. — 505
31. Schlegel's invitation to the palace of the Tuileries, dated 8 October, 1831. SLUB Dresden. Mscr. Dresd. e. 90. XI. V. b. © SLUB Dresden, all rights reserved. — 511
32. Schlegel's receipt for the 'Silver Dress Star of the Royal Hanoverian Guelphic Order', 20 March, 1832. SLUB Dresden. Mscr. Dresd. e. 90. II. 51. © SLUB Dresden, all rights reserved. — 512
33. *Râmâyana*. Schlegel's edition, part 1 of vol. 1 (Bonn, 1829). Title page. © and by kind permission of the Master and Fellows of Trinity College, Cambridge, CC BY-NC 4.0. — 516
34. Lithograph by Henry & Cohen in Bonn, after the portrait engraving of August Wilhelm Schlegel by Adolf August Hohneck (c. 1830). Image from *Oeuvres de M. Auguste-Guillaume de Schlegel écrites en français*, ed. Éduouard Böcking, vol. 1 (Leipzig: Weidmann, 1846), frontispiece. © and by kind permission of the Master and Fellows of Trinity College, Cambridge, CC BY-NC 4.0. — 547
35. Portrait engraving of August Wilhelm Schlegel by Christian Hoffmeister (1841). Image taken from *Briefe von und an August Wilhelm Schlegel*, ed. Josef Körner (Zurich, Leipzig, Vienna, 1930), vol. 1, facing p. 521. Image in the public domain. — 547

Short Biographies

1. Ernst Moritz Arndt. Engraving by unknown artist (c. 1820). https:// commons.wikimedia.org/wiki/File:Ernst_Moritz_Arndt.gif — 567
2. Bettina von Arnim. Drawing by Ludwig Emil Grimm (c. 1810). https:// commons.wikimedia.org/wiki/File:Bettina-von-arnim-grimm.jpg — 567
3. Ludwig Achim von Arnim. Painting by Peter Eduard Ströhling (1805). http://commons.wikimedia.org/wiki/File:Ludwig_Achim_von_Arnim.jpg — 567
4. Wolf von Baudissin. Photograph from unknown source. http://commons.wikimedia.org/wiki/File:Wolf_Heinrich_Graf_von_Baudissin.jpg — 568
5. Jean Baptiste Bernadotte. Painting by François Gérard. http://commons.wikimedia.org/wiki/File:Charles_XIV_John_as_Crown_Prince_of_Sweden_-_François_Gérard.jpg — 568
6. Auguste Böhmer. Engraving based on a painting by Johann Friedrich August Tischbein (1798). http://commons.wikimedia.org/wiki/File:Böhmer_Auguste.jpg — 569
7. Sulpiz Boisserée. Drawing by Johann Joseph Schmeller (1827). http://commons.wikimedia.org/wiki/File:Sulpiz_Boisserée.jpg — 570
8. Albert de Broglie. Photograph by Bascard fils (late nineteenth century). http://commons.wikimedia.org/wiki/File:Broglie_Albert.JPG — 570
9. Victor de Broglie. Engraving by Lacoste (1843). http://commons.wikimedia.org/wiki/File:De_Broglie_1843.jpg — 571
10. Gottfried August Bürger. Engraving by unknown artist. http://commons.wikimedia.org/wiki/File:Gottfried_august_buerger.jpg — 571
11. Henry Thomas Colebrooke. Bust by Sir Francis Chantrey (1837). http://commons.wikimedia.org/wiki/File:HTColebrooke.jpg — 572
12. Benjamin Constant. Lithograph by Langlumé (undated). http://commons.wikimedia.org/wiki/File:BenjaminConstant.jpg — 572
13. Johann Friedrich von Cotta. Lithograph by unknown artist (c. 1830). http://commons.wikimedia.org/wiki/File:Johann_Friedrich_Freiherr_von_Cotta.png — 572
14. Johann Joachim Eschenburg. Painting by Johann Friedrich Weitsch (before 1803). http://commons.wikimedia.org/wiki/File:Johann_Joachim_Eschenburg.jpg — 573
15. Johann Gottlieb Fichte. Engraving after the drawing by Friedrich Bury (1801). http://commons.wikimedia.org/wiki/File:Johann_gottlieb_fichte.jpg — 573
16. John Flaxman. Self-portrait at the age of 24. http://commons.wikimedia.org/wiki/File:Selfportraitflaxman.jpg — 574
17. Georg Forster. Portrait painting by Johann Heinrich Wilhelm Tischbein (1785). http://commons.wikimedia.org/wiki/File:Georg_Forster-larger.jpg — 574
18. Friedrich de la Motte Fouqué. Engraving by L. Staub (undated, after 1815). http://commons.wikimedia.org/wiki/File:Staub_-_Friedrich_de_la_Motte_Fouqué.jpg — 574

List of Illustrations   621

19. Friedrich Gentz. Lithograph by Friedrich Lieder (1825). http://commons.   575
    wikimedia.org/wiki/File:Friedrich_Gentz.jpg
20. Joseph Görres. Portrait painting by Joseph Anton Nikolaus Settegast   575
    (1838). https://commons.wikimedia.org/wiki/File:Joseph_von_Görres.jpg
21. Johann Wolfgang Goethe. Drawing by Friedrich Bury (1800). https://   576
    commons.wikimedia.org/wiki/File:JohannWolfgangVonGoethe_
    FriedrichBury.jpg
22. Jacob and Wilhelm Grimm. Double portrait by Elisabeth Jerichau-   576
    Baumann (1855). https://commons.wikimedia.org/wiki/File:Grimm.jpg
23. Friedrich von Hardenberg (Novalis). Engraving by Eduard Eichens   577
    (1845) after a portrait by an unknown artist. http://commons.wikimedia.
    org/wiki/File:Novalis.jpg
24. Karl August von Hardenberg. Portrait painting by Friedrich Georg   577
    Weitsch (c. 1822). http://commons.wikimedia.org/wiki/File:Fürst_
    Hardenberg.jpg
25. Heinrich Heine. Etching by Eduard Mandel (1854) after a portrait   578
    drawing by Franz Kugler (1829). https://commons.wikimedia.org/wiki/
    File:Heinrich_Heine.jpg
26. Frans Hemsterhuis. Unidentified engraving. http://commons.   578
    wikimedia.org/wiki/File:Romein_erfl_Hemsterhuis.gif
27. Johann Gottfried Herder. Portrait painting by Anton Graff (1786). https:// 578
    commons.wikimedia.org/wiki/File:Johann_Gottfried_Herder_2.jpg
28. Christian Gottlob Heyne. Engraving based on a portrait painting by   579
    Johann Heinrich Wilhelm Tischbein (1789). https://commons.wikimedia.
    org/wiki/File:Christian_Gottlob_Heyne.jpg
29. Alexander von Humboldt. Portrait painting by Friedrich Georg   579
    Weitsch (1806). http://commons.wikimedia.org/wiki/Alexander_von_
    Humboldt#/media/File:Alexandre_humboldt.jpg
30. Wilhelm von Humboldt. Engraving by an unknown artist (undated).   580
    https://commons.wikimedia.org/wiki/File:W.v.Humboldt.jpg
31. August Wilhelm Iffland. Copy of a pastel portrait by Johann Heinrich   580
    Schröder (undated). https://commons.wikimedia.org/wiki/File:Iffland_
    after_Johann_Heinrich_Schröder.jpg
32. Sir William Jones. Engraving by William Evans (1804). https://commons.   580
    wikimedia.org/wiki/File:Sir_William_Jones_by_William_Evans_1804.jpg
33. Friedrich Gottlieb Klopstock. Portrait painting by Jens Juel (c.   580
    1779). http://commons.wikimedia.org/wiki/File:Friedrich_Gottlieb_
    Klopstock_1.jpg
34. David Ferdinand Koreff. Portrait drawing by Wilhelm Hensel   581
    (undated). https://commons.wikimedia.org/wiki/File:Wilhelm_
    Hensel_-_David_Ferdinand_Koreff.jpg
35. August von Kotzebue. Engraving by an unknown artist (1859). https://   582
    commons.wikimedia.org/wiki/File:August_von_Kotzebue.jpg

36. Christian Lassen. Drawing by Adolf Hohneck (1859). https://commons.wikimedia.org/wiki/File:Lassen2.jpg 582
37. Gotthold Ephraim Lessing. Portrait painting by Anton Graff (1771). https://commons.wikimedia.org/wiki/File:Gotthold_Ephraim_Lessing_Kunstsammlung_Uni_Leipzig.jpg 582
38. Ludwig I of Bavaria. Engraving by Albert Reindel after a portrait painting by Joseph Karl Stieler (1825). https://commons.wikimedia.org/wiki/File:Ludwig_I..jpg 583
39. Sir James Mackintosh. Engraving by T. W. Harland (undated) after the portrait by Sir Thomas Lawrence. https://commons.wikimedia.org/wiki/File:Charles_Wilkin06.jpg 583
40. Prince Klemens Metternich. Engraving by T.W. Harland (undated) after the portrait by Sir Thomas Lawrence. https://commons.wikimedia.org/wiki/File:ALISON(1850)_p12.092_METTERNICH.jpg 583
41. Adam Müller. Lithograph portrait of around 1815 by an unknown artist. https://commons.wikimedia.org/wiki/File:Adam_Heinrich_Müller.jpg 584
42. Johannes von Müller. Portrait painting by Anton Wilhelm Tischbein (1787-88). http://commons.wikimedia.org/wiki/File:MuellerJ.jpg 584
43. Jacques Necker. Portrait painting by Joseph-Siffrein Duplessis (1783). https://commons.wikimedia.org/wiki/File:Necker,_Jacques_-_Duplessis.jpg 584
44. Barthold Georg Niebuhr. Portrait drawing by Louise Seidler (undated). http://commons.wikimedia.org/wiki/File:Louise_Seidler_-_Niebuhr_-_Uhde_222.jpg 584
45. Juliette Récamier. Portrait painting by François Gérard. https://commons.wikimedia.org/wiki/File:François_Pascal_Simon_Gérard_003.jpg 585
46. Johann Friedrich Reichardt. Engraving by Karl Traugott Riedel (1814) after a portrait painting by Anton Graff (1794). https://commons.wikimedia.org/wiki/File:JohannFriedrichReichardtMusikerS130.jpg 586
47. Jean Paul (Richter). Portrait painting by Friedrich Meier (1810). https://commons.wikimedia.org/wiki/File:Jean_Paul_by_Friedrich_Meier_1810.jpg 586
48. Henry Crabb Robinson. Engraving by William Holl after a photographic portrait by Maull & Co. (1869). https://commons.wikimedia.org/wiki/File:Portrait_of_H_Crabb_Robinson_(crop).png 587
49. Friedrich Wilhelm Joseph Schelling. Pastel portrait by Friedrich Tieck (c. 1801). https://commons.wikimedia.org/wiki/File:FriedrichWilhelmSchelling.jpg 587
50. Friedrich Schiller. Portrait painting by Ludovike Simanowitz (1793-94). http://commons.wikimedia.org/wiki/File:Friedrich_Schiller_by_Ludovike_Simanowiz.jpg 587
51. Caroline Schlegel. Portrait painting by Friedrich August Tischbein (1798). https://commons.wikimedia.org/wiki/File:Tischbein_-_Caroline_Schelling.jpg 588

List of Illustrations 623

52. Dorothea Schlegel. Portrait painting by Anton Graff (c. 1790). https:// 589
    commons.wikimedia.org/wiki/File:Dorothea_Schlegel.jpg
53. Johann Adolf Schlegel. Portrait painting by G. W. Thielo (undated). 589
    https://commons.wikimedia.org/wiki/File:Johann_Adolf_Schlegel.jpg
54. Friedrich Schlegel. Engraving after the portrait drawing by Philipp 591
    Veit (1811). https://commons.wikimedia.org/wiki/File:Friederich_von_
    Schlegel.jpg
55. Friedrich Schleiermacher. Engraving by J. H. Lips (1800). https:// 592
    commons.wikimedia.org/wiki/File:Friedrich_Daniel_Ernst_
    Schleiermacher_2.jpg
56. Jean-Charles-Léonard Simonde de Sismondi. Engraving by de Pernel 593
    (undated). https://commons.wikimedia.org/wiki/File:Jean_Charles_de_
    Sismondi.jpg
57. Erik Magnus von Staël-Holstein. Portrait painting by Adolf Erik 594
    Wertmüller (c. 1782). https://commons.wikimedia.org/wiki/File:Erik_
    Magnus_Staël_von_Holstein.jpg
58. Germaine de Staël-Holstein. Portrait painting by François Gérard (c. 594
    1810). http://commons.wikimedia.org/wiki/File:Madame_de_Staël.jpg
59. Henrik Steffens. Lithograph by Friedrich Jentzen after a drawing 596
    by Franz Krüger (1828). https://commons.wikimedia.org/wiki/
    File:Henrich_Steffens2.jpg
60. Freiherr vom Stein. Drawing by Friedrich Olivier (1821). http:// 596
    commons.wikimedia.org/wiki/File:Woldemar_Friedrich_von_Olivier_-_
    Heinrich_Friedrich_Karl_Freiherr_Vom_Stein.jpg
61. Freiherr vom Stein zum Altenstein. Portrait by unknown artist 596
    (undated). http://commons.wikimedia.org/wiki/File:Altenstein.jpg
62. Friedrich Tieck. Lithograph by Johann Joseph Sprick after a drawing 597
    by Franz Krüger (early 1840s). https://commons.wikimedia.org/wiki/
    File:FriedrichTieck.jpg
63. Ludwig Tieck. Engraving after a portrait painting by Joseph Karl Stieler 597
    (1838). https://commons.wikimedia.org/wiki/File:Ludwig_Tieck.jpg
64. Karl August Varnhagen von Ense. Drawing by Samuel Friedrich Diez 599
    (1839). https://commons.wikimedia.org/wiki/File:Karl-Varnhagen-von-
    Ense-1839-Zeichnung-von-Samuel-Friedrich-Diez.jpg
65. Rahel Varnhagen. Engraving by an unknown artist (undated). https:// 599
    commons.wikimedia.org/wiki/File:Rahel_Varnhagen.jpg
66. Philipp Veit. Self-portrait (1816). https://commons.wikimedia.org/wiki/ 599
    File:Veitself.jpg
67. Johann Heinrich Voss. Portrait painting by Georg Friedrich Adolph 600
    Schöner (1797). http://commons.wikimedia.org/wiki/File:Johann_
    Heinrich_Voss_(Schöner).jpg
68. Friedrich Gottlieb Welcker. Engraving by Adolf Hohneck (1840). https:// 600
    commons.wikimedia.org/wiki/File:Friedrich_Gottlieb_Welcker_2.jpg

69. Zacharias Werner. Etching after a drawing by E. T. A. Hoffmann (undated). https://commons.wikimedia.org/wiki/File:E._T._A._Hoffmann_-_Zacharias_Werner.jpg   600

70. Christoph Martin Wieland. Portrait painting by Ferdinand Jagemann (1805). https://commons.wikimedia.org/wiki/File:Christoph_Martin_Wieland_by_Ferdinand_Jagemann_1805_Cut.jpg   601

71. Johann Joachim Winckelmann. Portrait painting by Anton Raphael Mengs (1761-62). http://commons.wikimedia.org/wiki/File:Johann_Joachim_Winckelmann_(Raphael_Mengs_after_1755).jpg   601

Index

Abel-Rémusat, Jean-Pierre (1783-1832): French sinologist and professor at the Collège de France 491, 498, 519
Acerbi, Giuseppe (1773-1846): travel writer and composer 385
Adams, John Quincy (1767-1848): American diplomat, politician, later president 345, 351, 352
Addison, Joseph (1672-1719): poet, essayist, editor 47
Adolphus, prince. *See* Cambridge
Aeschylus 158, 164, 187, 205, 208, 212, 244, 284, 286, 300, 303, 309, 312, 580
Akademie der schönen Redekünste 89
Albani, Alessandro (1672-1779): cardinal, connoisseur and patron of Winckelmann 601
Albany, Louise, princess Stolberg, called Countess of (1752-1824): married to Young Pretender, kept salon in Florence 252, 289, 388
Albert, prince of Saxe-Coburg-Gotha, later Prince Consort (1819-1861), attends AWS's lectures in Bonn 466, 548, 549
d'Alembert, Jean le Rond (1717-1763), mathematician, 'philosophe' 211, 218
Alexander I, tsar (1777-1825): Russian emperor 323, 348, 352, 380, 595
Alexander the Great 67, 494
Alfieri, Vittorio, count (1749-1803): poet and dramatist 236, 250, 252, 276, 287, 391

Algarotti, Francesco (1712-1764): philosopher, poet, essayist, connoisseur 125
Allgemeine Deutsche Bibliothek 118
Allgemeine Literatur-Zeitung 50, 64, 66, 68, 72, 73, 81, 85, 114, 115, 117, 118, 119, 120, 129, 140, 141, 142, 148, 151, 153, 167, 222, 244, 255, 267, 277, 279, 300, 593
Alpenrosen
  AWS contributions to 241, 280
d'Alton, Eduard (1772-1840): collector, professor of fine arts at Bonn, AWS edition of 467, 549
Anacreon 20, 208
Angelico, Fra (1387-1455): painter
  AWS essay on 254, 394, 524, 531, 538
Anna Amalia, duchess of Saxe-Weimar (1739-1807): mother of Carl August and patroness of the arts 68, 232, 601
Annolied 495
Ariosto, Ludovico (1474-1533): poet 123, 148, 156, 214, 236, 250, 334, 394, 397, 399, 400, 479, 495, 521
Aristophanes 156, 207, 208, 213, 303, 308, 309
Aristotle 168
Arminius 158, 336, 562
Arndt, Ernst Moritz (1769-1860): patriotic author and historian 339, 348, 350, 351, 352, 426, 430, 433, 435, 450, 454, 456, 457, 460, 466, 535, 550, 567, 586, 596

Arnim, Bettina von, née Brentano (1785-1859): writer, hagiographer of Goethe 231, 533, 537, 567
Arnim, Ludwig Achim von (1781-1831): Romantic poet, dramatist and novelist 206, 258, 317, 408, 542, 567, 575, 576, 586, 602
  works cited
    Des Knaben Wunderhorn 206, 567, 602
    Zeitung für Einsiedler 292, 317, 568, 602
Asiatick Researches 247, 344, 407, 491, 494
Ast, Friedrich (1776-1841): writer on aesthetics 128, 129, 166, 167
Athenaeum 65, 73, 75, 82, 83, 90, 92, 109, 110, 111, 115, 116, 117, 118, 119, 120, 121, 122, 125, 126, 129, 132, 133, 134, 135, 136, 137, 138, 139, 140, 141, 142, 146, 147, 148, 149, 151, 152, 154, 155, 156, 157, 159, 163, 164, 166, 169, 172, 176, 178, 179, 181, 183, 188, 189, 195, 204, 207, 208, 209, 236, 251, 258, 291, 308, 332, 334, 357, 395, 396, 399, 480, 492, 524, 526, 530, 531, 532, 534, 574, 577, 591, 511
Attila 336, 413
August, prince of Prussia (1779-1843): general, lover of Madame Récamier 208, 263, 274, 280, 585
aus'm Weerth, Peter Friedrich (1779-1852): manufacturer and art connoisseur in Bonn 462

Baader, Franz von (1765-1841): nature philosopher 435
Bachenschwanz, Leberecht (1729-1802): translator of Dante 89
Bach, Johann Nikolaus (1802-1841): tutor to John Colebrooke and Patrick Johnston 507
Bacon, Sir Francis (1561-1626): statesman, philosopher 218, 311, 461
Baggesen, Jens (1764-1826): poet in Danish and German 322
Bailly, Jean-Sylvain (1736-1793): astronomer, politician, source for AWS 264, 267, 268, 297, 476

Baldwin, Robert (n.d.): publisher of AWS's Vienna Lectures in English 422
Ballenstedt, Julius Bernhard (1744-1784): rector of the Lyceum in Hanover 29
Bandel, Ernst von (1800-1876): sculptor 562
Bandinellli, Baccio (1493-1560): sculptor 49
Banier, Antoine, abbé (1673-1741): historian of mythology and religion
  JAS's translation of 20, 590
Barante, Claude-Ignace Brugière, comte de (1745-1814): historian, prefect of Léman 1802-1810 330, 331
Barante, Prosper Brugière, comte de (1782-1866): statesman, historian, member of Coppet circle 238, 260, 264, 270, 274, 275, 289, 318, 327, 332, 426, 427, 470
Basedow, Johann Bernhard (1724-1790): educationalist 27, 29
Batoni, Pompeo (1708-1787): painter 49, 162
Batteux, Charles (1713-1780): normative aesthetician 283
  JAS's translation of 20, 28, 590
Batthyány: Hungarian magnate family 12, 306
Baudelaire, Charles (1821-1867): poet 85
Baudissin, Wolf von (1798-1878): Danish diplomat, translator of Shakespeare into German 203, 208, 210, 348, 355, 356, 372, 527, 568, 598
Bauer, Bernhard Philipp (1771-1840): Viennese publisher
  pirate edition of AWS 333, 334
Baumgarten, Alexander (1714-1762): philosopher and aesthetician 167, 168
Bayle, Pierre (1647-1706): philosopher, compiler of *Dictionnaire* 35
Beaufort, Louis de (1703-1795): historian of Rome 402
Beaumont, Marie Leprince de (1711-1789): children's writer
  JAS's translation of 28, 590

Becker, Nikolaus (1809-1842): minor poet, attends AWS's lectures in Bonn 467
Becker, Wilhelm Gottlieb (1753-1813): librarian in Dresden and publisher 69, 74, 79, 89, 122
Beethoven, Ludwig van (1770-1827): composer 289, 444, 459, 469, 548, 549, 558, 562
Behler, Ernst (1928-1997): Schlegel scholar and editor 3, 6, 7, 13, 66, 128, 129, 166, 233, 267, 273, 292, 430, 473
Bell, John (1745-1831): publisher 92, 496
Bellotto, Bernardo, called Canaletto (1721-1780): painter 125
Benckendorff, Alexander von (1783-1844): Russian general 369
Bennigsen, Levin August, count (1745-1826: Russian general 348
Bentinck, William, lord (1784-1813): British admiral and secret envoy to Sweden and Russia 352
Berliner Damen-Kalender 271
Berliner Kalender 479, 481, 482, 483, 484, 488, 489, 494, 564
BERNADOTTE, Jean Baptiste (1763-1844): marshal of the Empire, Prince of Pontecorvo, Prince Royal, later (1818-1844), as Charles XIV John [Karl Johan], king of Sweden 3, 228, 313, 316, 345, 346, 348, 352, 353, 354, 356, 357-375, 376, 377, 379, 380, 395, 414, 417, 445, 555, 564, 568, 575, 595
Bernhardi, August Ferdinand (1769-1820): critic and schoolmaster in Berlin 111, 142, 183, 197, 207, 569, 598
Bernhardi, Felix Theodor (von) (1802-1887): diplomat, writer on military subjects 521
    AWS 'paternity' 185, 521, 569
Bernhardi, Ludwig (1801-1802): infant son of August Ferdinand and Sophie Bernhardi 179
Bernhardi, Sophie. *See* Tieck
Bernhardi, Wilhelm (1800-1878): historical novelist 253, 569
Bernhard, prince of Saxe-Weimar-Eisenach (1792-1862): general in Dutch service 314, 584

Berry, Charles Ferdinand d'Artois, duc de (1778-1820): French royal prince assassinated in 1820 434
Bertram, Johann Baptist (1776-1841), attends Friedrich Schlegel's lectures in Paris and Cologne with the brothers Boisserée 194, 196, 223, 592
Bertuch, Friedrich Justin (1747-1822): entrepreneur and publisher in Jena 72, 130, 188
Bethmann, Simon Moritz (von) (1768-1826): banker in Frankfurt 231
Biblioteca Italiana 385
Bibliothèque universelle 385, 395, 406, 452
Black, John (1783-1855): translator of AWS's Vienna Lectures into English 10, 422, 423, 429, 513
Blackwell, Thomas (1701-1757): Homeric scholar 37
Blätter für literarische Unterhaltung 534
Blücher, Gebhard Leberecht von, count, then prince (1742-1819): Prussian field marshal 348, 368, 567
Blumenbach, Johann Friedrich (1752-1840): naturalist, physiologist, anthropologist, professor at Göttingen 33, 56, 460, 465, 474, 476
Boccaccio, Giovanni (1313-1375): writer 173, 196, 215, 217, 552
Bochart, Samuel (1599-1667): religious writer and lexicographer 494
Böckh, August (1785-1867): classicist, professor in Berlin and secretary to Prussian Academy of Sciences 485, 552, 559, 560
Böcking, Eduard (1802-1870): jurist, AWS's executor and the editor of his works 2, 6, 14, 144, 222, 242, 267, 304, 327, 351, 388, 418, 419, 426, 441, 469, 494, 514, 539, 553, 554, 560, 564, 565
Bodmer, Johann Jakob (1698-1783): Swiss poet, critic, and editor 331, 581, 601
Böhl von Faber, Frasquita (1775-1838): connoisseur of English and French literature and wife of the following 428

Böhl von Faber, Johann Nikolas (1770-1836): made AWS's Vienna Lectures known in Spain 422, 428, 429
Böhme, Jacob (1575-1624): theosophist, mystic philosopher 182, 191, 322
Böhmer, Auguste (1785-1800): Caroline Schlegel's daughter by her first marriage, AWS's step-daughter 26, 137, 143, 144, 145, 146, 169, 180, 182, 186, 233, 243, 259, 324, 332, 435, 436, 463, 508, 556, 561, 569, 587, 588
Böhmer, Caroline. *See* Schlegel
Böhmer, Johann Franz Wilhelm (1754-1788): physician, Caroline's first husband 51, 569, 588
Böhmer, Therese (1787-1789): infant daughter of Johann and Caroline Böhmer 52, 54, 145, 588
Bohte, Johann Heinrich (d. 1824): German bookseller in London 503, 508, 523
Böhtlingk, Otto (1815-1904): Sanskrit scholar, pupil of AWS's in Bonn 471
Boie, Heinrich Christian (1744-1806): editor of *Deutsches Museum* and of *Göttingen Musenalmanach* 23, 43, 599
Boisserée, Melchior (1786-1851) and Boisserée, Sulpiz (1783-1854): Cologne patrician's sons, protégés of Friedrich Schlegel, important collectors of medieval art 194, 223, 418, 432, 436, 438, 440, 443, 469, 524, 530, 538, 570, 576, 592
Bonaparte. *See* Napoleon
Bonaparte, Jérôme (1784-1860): king of Westphalia 576, 586
Bonaparte, Joseph (1768-1844): king of Naples and Sicily, then of Spain 228, 249, 384
Bonaparte, Lucien (1775-1840): prince of Musignano 195, 228, 384
Bonstetten, Karl Viktor von (1745-1832): Bernese patrician, administrator, philosopher, member of Coppet circle 244, 246, 247, 248, 249, 253, 260, 267, 318, 322, 323, 325, 338, 341, 389, 426, 570, 584

Bopp, Franz (1791-1867): Sankritist, professor in Berlin 381, 382, 383, 406, 449, 452, 464, 483, 485, 486, 489, 490, 493, 495, 497, 499, 502, 509, 515, 517, 518, 523, 536, 537, 602
Borck(e), Johann Friedrich von (1704-1747): officer and diplomat translation of *Julius Caesar* 14
Bossi, Luigi (1758-1835): archaeologist and antiquary 252, 254
Böttiger, Carl August (1760-1835): classical scholar in Weimar and Dresden and general busybody 78, 86, 94, 99, 165, 188, 190, 191, 203, 231, 232, 233, 236, 240, 300, 303
Bouterwek, Friedrich (1766-1828): literary historian in Göttingen 48, 49, 199, 308
Boydell, John (1719-1804): creator and publisher of the Shakespeare Gallery 164
di Breme, Ludovico (1780-1820): Italian man of letters, in Staël circle 389, 391
Brentano, Bernhard von (1901-1964): biographer of Schlegel 1, 3
Brentano, Clemens (1778-1841): poet and novelist associated with Romantic circle, co-compiler of *Des Knaben Wunderhorn* 142, 206, 258, 317, 335, 408, 542, 563, 567, 575, 576, 602
Brinkman, Karl Gustav von (1764-1847): Swedish diplomat, associated with the Schlegel brothers in Berlin and Paris 111, 113, 208, 227, 230, 234, 239
Brockhaus, Friedrich Arnold (1772-1823): publisher 380, 388, 469
Brockhaus, Hermann (1806-1877): Sankritist and pupil of AWS's 471
Brockmann, Johann Franz (1745-1812): actor 30, 301
Broglie, Albert de, prince, then duke (1821-1901): diplomat, politician and historian 418, 419, 510, 555, 570
BROGLIE, Albertine de, duchess, née de Staël-Holstein (1797-1838): the daughter of Madame de Staël and

Baron Erik Magnus Staël de Holstein 144, 145, 163, 230, 231, 234, 240, 243, 249, 253, 271, 272, 273, 294, 327, 343, 344, 347, 349, 355, 356, 367, 377, 383, 384, 386, 387, 388, 415, 416, 417, 418, 419, 435, 436, 441, 455, 556, 565, 570, 571, 594, 595

Broglie, Elséar Ferdinand de, count (1768-1837): soldier, 'maréchal des camps et armées du roi', tutored by AWS in Göttingen 36

Broglie, Louise de. *See* d'Haussonville

Broglie, Pauline de, princess (1817-1831): daughter of Victor and Albertine de Broglie 419

Broglie, Victor de, duke (1785-1870): French politician and statesman, husband of Albertine de Staël 347, 383, 384, 387, 388, 389, 390, 415, 417, 418, 419, 426, 427, 500, 517, 562, 570, 571, 594, 510

de Brosses, Charles (1709-1777): writer on exploration and anthropology, theory of language 84, 219

Brougham, Henry, later lord (1778-1868): British politician, member of Staël circle 389, 457, 501, 513, 514

Brumoy, Pierre, abbé (1688-1742): translator of *Le Théâtre des Grecs* 283

Brun, Friederike (1765-1835): writer, traveller 273

Brun, Ida (1791-1857): dancer, singer, attitude artist 273

Brunswick, Karl Wilhelm Ferdinand, duke of (1735-1806): Prussian field marshal 234

Brunswick, Ludwig Ernst, duke of (1718-1788): field marshal, regent of the Netherlands 60

Brunswick-Lüneburg, dukes of 21, 22

Bruzelius, Emanuel (1786-1832): Swedish publisher 304, 333
  pirate editions of AWS 304

Büchting, Wilhelmine, later Hunter (d. 1843): AWS's step-niece (Karl Schlegel's step-daughter) 550

Buffon, Georges Louis Leclerc, comte de (1707-1788): naturalist and philosophe 33, 195

BÜRGER, Gottfried August (1747-1794): poet and translator, Schlegel's mentor in Göttingen 3, 17, 23, 31, 37, 38, 39, 40, 41, 42, 43, 44, 46, 47, 48, 49, 51, 52, 53, 54, 59, 60, 64, 74, 79, 83, 84, 85, 86, 87, 89, 93, 105, 126, 127, 141, 147, 148, 157, 171, 172, 173, 174, 175, 176, 199, 400, 479, 531, 533, 534, 542, 543, 554, 571

Burghersh, Priscilla, lady, later Westmorland, countess of (1793-1879): niece of duke of Wellington, met Staël circle in Florence 388, 392, 393

Burgsdorff, Wilhelm von (1772-1822): friend and patron of Ludwig Tieck 194, 209, 597

Burke, Edmund (1729-1797): statesman and philosopher 62, 209, 314, 575, 583

Burnouf, Eugène (1801-1852): orientalist 493, 499, 509, 510, 552

Bury, Friedrich (1763-1823): neo-classical painter 180

Büsching, Johann Gustav (1783-1829): medievalist and antiquary 209, 394, 397, 399, 400, 407, 408, 411, 412, 431

Busch, Peter (1813-1841): painter 441, 550, 551, 560

BUTTLAR, Auguste von, née Ernst (1796-1857): painter, the daughter of Charlotte Ernst, née Schlegel, and Ludwig Emanuel Ernst, AWS's and FS's niece 11, 26, 125, 145, 164, 418, 451, 463, 498, 501, 504, 505, 508, 524, 525, 563, 571

Buttlar, Heinrich von (n.d.): officer in Russian service 505

Byron, Lord (1788-1824): met Mme de Staël and AWS at Coppet in 1816 246, 258, 342, 367, 376, 378, 389, 390, 391, 392, 423, 425, 595

Caesar, Julius 67

CALDERÓN de la Barca, Pedro (1600-1681): dramatist 123, 196, 198, 199,

200, 201, 202, 206, 213, 225, 236, 243, 261, 278, 287, 292, 300, 302, 303, 309, 310, 311, 319, 322, 326, 427, 467, 478, 487, 495, 529, 564
Callimachus 152
Cambridge, Adolphus duke of (1774-1850), meets AWS at Göttingen 32, 375
Camões, Luis de (1524-1580): Portuguese national poet 214, 341, 479, 495
Campbell, Thomas (1777-1844): poet 423, 424, 473, 503, 514
Canova, Antonio (1757-1822): neo-classical sculptor 255
Capelle, Guillaume Antoine Benoît (1775-1843): prefect of department of Léman 331, 341, 342
Carey, William (1761-1834): Sanskrit scholar, grammarian and lexicographer 448, 453
Carl August, duke, later grand duke, of Saxe-Weimar-Eisenach (1757-1828) 56, 70, 71, 99, 130, 131, 140, 147, 190, 576, 601
Carracci, Annibale (1560-1609): painter 49, 162
Carus, Carl Gustav (1789-1869): physician, psychologist, painter, hagiographer of Goethe 533, 598
Castel, Louis Bertrand, abbé (1688-1757): inventor of the *clavecin oculaire* 85
Castlereagh, Robert Stewart, marquis of Londonderry, known as Lord (1769-1822): British foreign secretary 377
Cathcart, William, viscount, then earl (1755-1843): British soldier and diplomat 352, 354
Catherine II, empress of Russia, 'the Great' (1729-1796) 18
Le Catholique 427, 428, 523
Caylus, Anne Claude Philippe de Tubières, comte de (1692-1765): archaeologist and art critic 124
Cellini, Benvenuto (1500-1571): goldsmith, sculptor
    Goethe's translation of 75, 80, 100

Cervantes Saavedra, Miguel de (1547-1616): Spanish national writer 141, 148, 173, 196, 198, 206, 207
Cesarotti, Melchiorre (1730-1808): man of letters, translator of Homer and Ossian into Italian 236, 252
Chambers's Encyclopaedia 541
Chamisso, Adelbert de, later von (1781-1838): poet and traveller 327, 330, 599
Charakteristiken und Kritiken 86, 133, 147, 169, 171, 172, 173, 236, 592
Charlemagne 336, 400, 413
Charles XII, king of Sweden (1682-1718) 354
Charles XIII, king of Sweden (1748-1818) 353, 568
Chateaubriand, François-René, vicomte de (1768-1848): writer, historian, diplomat 237, 246, 249, 255, 277, 323, 328, 581, 585
Chatterton, Thomas (1752-1770): forger, 'marvellous boy' 39
Chénier, Marie-Joseph de (1764-1811): poet and dramatist 328
Chézy, Antoine-Léonard de (1773-1832): Sanskrit scholar and professor in Paris 193, 275, 297, 381, 395, 398, 405, 406, 407, 446, 475, 485, 491, 493, 498, 502, 508, 510, 519, 571-572
Chézy, Helmine de (later 'von'), née von Klencke (1783-1856): writer, dramatist 327, 572
Chladni, Ernst Florens Friedrich (1756-1827): physicist, acoustician 85
Chodowieckii, Daniel Nikolaus (1726-1801): painter and engraver 164
Clairon, Mlle (1723-1803): celebrated French actress 269
Clarence, Adelaide of Saxe-Meiningen, duchess of, later queen Adelaide (1792-1849) 501
Claude, Claude Gelée called (1600-1682): landscape painter 160, 161
Clausewitz, Carl von: Prussian officer, later general and military theorist 246, 263, 281

Cockerell, Charles Robert (1788-1863): neo-classical architect 388, 405
Colebrooke, Henry Thomas (1765-1837): Indologist 26, 407, 448, 453, 482, 489, 501, 502, 503, 504, 507, 519, 511
Colebrooke, John (d. 1827): son of above 145, 451, 463, 502, 504, 507, 508
Coleridge, Samuel Taylor (1772-1834): poet and critic 26, 104, 134, 140, 203, 302, 309, 311, 376, 391, 417, 423, 460, 514, 536, 548
   meets AWS in 1829 424, 425
Collin, Heinrich Joseph von (1771-1811): Austrian dramatist 289, 299, 301, 308
Comenius, John Amos Komensky called (1592-1671): educational reformer 29
Condorcet, Jean Antoine Nicolas de Caritat, marquis de (1743-1794): mathematician, 'encyclopédiste', revolutionary 54, 64, 67, 267, 573
CONSTANT, Henri-Benjamin Constant de Rebeque (1767-1830): political theorist and activist, novelist, lover of Mme de Staël 227, 228, 230, 231, 232, 233, 234, 238, 239, 240, 241, 244, 245, 246, 247, 248, 260, 264, 267, 268, 269, 270, 274, 276, 279, 280, 281, 285, 288, 289, 290, 318, 319, 323, 325, 326, 356, 372, 374, 375, 384, 391, 414, 426, 427, 548, 572, 573, 583, 585, 594, 595
Cook, James (1728-1779): explorer and circumnavigator 56, 574
Corbigny, Louis Chicoilet de (1771-1811): prefect of Loir et Cher department 328, 329
Cornelius, Peter (1783-1867): Nazarene painter and engraver, director of the Düsseldorf Academy 166, 538
Correggio, Antonio Allegri da (1494-1534): painter 49, 125, 162, 196, 254, 549
Cotta, Georg Friedrich von (1796-1863): publisher in Tübingen and Stuttgart 554

Cotta, Johann Friedrich von (1764-1832): publisher in Tübingen and Stuttgart 8, 73, 75, 131, 146, 147, 180, 199, 261, 276, 277, 531, 558, 572
Courier de Londres 499
Courland, Dorothea von Medem, duchess of (1761-1821): grande dame at European courts 234, 245
Cousin, Victor (1792-1867): philosopher, educationalist, historian 445
Cramer, Johann Andreas (1723-1788): pastor, preacher, poet 16, 589
Cranach, Lukas (1472-1553): painter, ancestor of Schlegel's 12, 592
Crancé, Jean-Baptiste Dubois de (1773-1800): French officer, father of Caroline's child 57, 58, 588
Crancé (or Kranz), Wilhelm Julius (1793-1795): Caroline's child 59, 67-68, 145, 569, 588
Crawford, William Harris (1772-1834): American minister in Paris 384
Crébillon, Claude Prosper Jolyot de (1707-1777) ('Crébillon fils'): writer of piquant fiction 134
Creuzer, Friedrich (1771-1858): professor of classics in Heidelberg, co-editor of *Heidelberger Jahrbücher* 320, 436, 602
Cumberland, Ernest Augustus, duke of (1771-1851): king of Hanover 1837-1851 368, 510
Custine, Adam Philippe de (1740-1793): French revolutionary general 56, 57, 58
Cuvier, Georges, baron (1769-1832): comparative anatomist and paleontologist 195, 203, 241, 302, 476, 483, 494, 498, 536

Dacheröden, Caroline von. *See* Humboldt
Dalberg, Karl Theodor von (1744-1817): coadjutor archbishop of Mainz 58, 586

DANTE Alighieri (1265-1321): poet, 'Erzpoet' 40, 46, 50, 59, 64, 66, 69, 74, 81, 83, 88, 89, 90, 91, 92, 93, 105, 119, 127, 136, 148, 157, 164, 165, 173, 204, 206, 209, 213, 214, 215, 216, 230, 236, 250, 276, 344, 396, 399, 400, 467, 478, 495, 529, 551, 552, 554, 555, 574, 164

Daub, Karl (1765-1836): theology professor in Heidelberg, co-editor of *Heidelberger Jahrbücher* 320, 602

David d'Angers, Pierre-Jean (1788-1856): sculptor 451, 562
does medallion of AWS 548

David, Louis (1748-1825): neoclassical painter, teacher of Friedrich Tieck and Gottlieb Schick 165, 170, 185, 194, 255, 585, 597

Davout, Louis, prince of Eckmühl (1776-1823): marshal of the Empire 369

Davy, Sir Humphry (1778-1829): scientist and inventor, President of the Royal Society when AWS meets him 203, 246, 302, 383, 501, 504, 514, 519, 536

Delbrück, Johann Friedrich Ferdinand (1772-1848): professor of history and philosophy in Bonn 450

Delius, Nikolaus (1813-1888): Shakespearean scholar 469

De Quincey, Thomas (1785-1859): essayist and critic 118

Deutsches Museum 202, 205, 205-206, 331, 345, 357, 358, 379, 395, 396, 397, 399, 401, 408, 410, 411, 412, 413, 410

Deutschland 76, 77, 80, 93, 591

d'Haussonville, Louise, countess, née princess de Broglie (1818-1882): daughter of Victor and Albertine de Broglie, subject of painting by Ingres 418, 563

Diderot, Denis (1713-1784): philosopher, essayist, art critic 160, 272

Didot, Firmin (1764-1836): printer and engraver 498

Die Horen 8, 44, 45, 47, 60, 64, 65, 66, 68, 69, 72, 73, 74, 75, 77, 79, 80, 81, 82, 83, 84, 85, 89, 93, 94, 95, 96, 99, 101, 103, 105, 115, 118, 120, 127, 133, 147, 152, 153, 157, 204, 206, 227, 532, 552, 576, 588

Dieterich, Johann Christian (1722-1800): publisher in Göttingen 38, 40, 49, 129

Diez, Friedrich Christian (1794-1876): Romance scholar, professor at Bonn 467

Docen, Bernhard Joseph (1782-1828): librarian in Munich, antiquarian 331, 394, 397, 399, 400, 407, 408, 411, 412

Domenichino, Domenico Zampieri called (1581-1641): painter 254

Dornford, Josiah (1764-1797): lawyer and translator, tutored by AWS in Göttingen
36

Dorow, Wilhelm (1790-1846): archaeologist, author of memoir on AWS 452, 457, 465, 541

Doudan, Ximénès (1800-1872): French moralist and critic, tutor to Alphonse Rocca 418, 419

Drake, Nathan (1766-1836): Shakespearean biographer 423

Dryden, John (1631-1700): poet and translator 47

Dumouriez, Charles-François du Périer (1739-1823): Revolutionary general 59

Düntzer, Heinrich (1813-1901): German scholar, attends AWS's lectures in Bonn 469

Dürer, Albrecht (1471-1528): painter and engraver 121, 196, 215

Dussault, Jean-Joseph-François (1769-1824): journalist, critic, librarian 288

Ebert, Johann Arnold (1723-1795): translator, professor in Brunswick 16, 17, 68, 581, 589

Ebert, Louise (n.d.): wife of Johann Arnold Ebert 68

Eckermann, Johann Peter (1792-1854): records Goethe's conversations 533

d'Eckstein, Ferdinand, 'baron' (1790-1861): journalist and critic, editor of *Le Catholique* 427, 428, 523

Edinburgh Review 376, 423

Eichendorff, Joseph von (1788-1857): poet, playwright and novelist 162, 469

Eichhorn, Johann Gottfried (1752-1827): Protestant theologian at Göttingen, orientalist 32

Eichstädt, Heinrich Karl Albrecht (1772-1848): professor of classics at Jena, co-editor of *Allgemeine Literatur-Zeitung* 128, 167, 244

Elizabeth Alexeievna, tsarina, princess Louise of Baden (1779-1826) 352

d'Enghien, Louis Antoine, duke (1772-1804): French émigré accused of conspiracy against Napoleon and shot on his orders 234, 328, 353

Ernst, Charlotte, née Schlegel (d. 1826): AWS's sister 26, 121, 178, 189, 290, 297, 315, 504, 524, 571

Ernst, Henriette, née Schlegel (d. 1801): AWS's sister 26

Ernst, Ludwig Emanuel (d. 1826): court secretary in Dresden, AWS's brother-in-law 26, 504, 524, 571

Ernst, prince, later duke, of Saxe-Coburg-Gotha (1818-1893), attends AWS's lectures in Bonn 470

Erthal, Friedrich Karl Joseph von (1719-1802): Elector of Mainz 55

Ervoil d'Oyré, François-Ignace (1739-1799): French general 57

Eschenburg, Johann Joachim (1743-1820): critic and literary historian 13, 17, 46, 47, 52, 53, 68, 79, 88, 92, 93, 94, 95, 96, 99, 100, 103, 114, 156, 168, 310, 398, 493, 528, 563, 573

Esterházy, grand Hungarian princely family 264

Euripides 187, 191, 203, 207, 208, 213, 237, 272, 281, 282, 284, 286, 287, 288, 289, 303, 309
 works cited
  Bacchae 186, 286, 287
  Hippolytus 272, 284, 286, 287

Europa 166, 178, 183, 192, 193, 194, 195, 196, 197, 198, 202, 203, 206, 210, 212, 219, 223, 231, 236, 254, 278, 284, 285, 291, 298, 308, 340, 341, 396, 497, 592

Falk, Johann Daniel (1770-1826): writer, lampooner of the Romantics 190

Fauriel, Claude-Charles (1772-1844): French literary scholar and professor 467, 491, 498, 551, 552, 573

Favre, Guillaume (1770-1851): Genevan scholar and correspondent of AWS 242, 367, 378, 379, 381, 382, 383, 384, 395, 397, 416, 445

Feà, Carlo (1753-1836): archaeologist, translator of Winckelmann into Italian 251, 397

Fénelon, François de Salignac de la Mothe (1651-1715): archbishop of Cambrai, religious writer 284, 323, 343

Ferdinand III, Holy Roman Emperor and King of Hungary (1608-1657) 12, 372, 589

Fernow, Carl Ludwig (1763-1808): art critic and archaeologist, editor of Winckelmann's works 394, 400, 403, 404, 405

Fichte, Johann Gottlieb (1762-1814): philosopher 67, 71, 72, 73, 76, 79, 110, 111, 117, 118, 119, 127, 128, 129, 130, 131, 132, 135, 137, 138, 139, 141, 146, 155, 167, 168, 178, 184, 190, 199, 200, 203, 205, 209, 210, 224, 225, 227, 234, 237, 245, 280, 302, 303, 304, 305, 307, 330, 348, 429, 456, 573, 576, 577, 586, 588

Finck von Finckenstein, Henriette, countess (d. 1847): companion of Ludwig Tieck 222, 526, 598

Fiorillo, Johann Domenik (Domenico) (1748-1821): art historian 42, 48, 49, 50, 124, 126, 160, 254, 537, 573, 573-574, 597, 600

Fitzgerald, Penelope (1916-2000): novelist and biographer 110

Flaxman, John (1755-1826): neo-classical engraver and sculptor 111, 129, 148, 157, 164, 165, 166, 186, 214, 376, 501, 531, 164

Fleck, Johann Friedrich Ferdinand (1757-1801): actor 99

Fleming, Paul (1609-1640): poet 148, 216

Flotow (n.d.): family in Bonn 462
Fontane, Theodor (1819-1898): poet and novelist 235, 451
Forberg, Friedrich Karl (1770-1848): philosopher and educator 130, 131
Forster, Georg (1754-1794): explorer (on Cook's second voyage), writer, philosopher, revolutionary 45, 46, 51, 54, 55, 56, 57, 58, 64, 66, 67, 79, 82, 84, 112, 174, 178, 219, 395, 480, 533, 574, 579
Forster, Therese. *See* Huber
Forstheim, Nikolaus (n.d.): city councillor in Bonn 462
Fouché, Joseph, duke of Otranto (1759-1844): Napoleon's minister of police (until 1810) 228, 229, 264, 273, 275, 327, 353, 555
Fouqué, Friedrich de la Motte, pseud. Pellegrin (1777-1843): poet and novelist, AWS's protégé 156, 209, 210, 224, 225, 241, 259, 261, 262, 302, 333, 334, 342, 348, 357, 370, 411, 574, 599
Francis (1768-1835) Holy Roman Emperor (as Francis II) then emperor of Austria (as Francis I) 295, 300, 313, 323, 359, 360, 422, 592
Frank, Othmar (1770-1840): orientalist, professor in Würzburg 497, 502
Frazer, Sir James (1854-1941): anthropologist 543
Frederick II (the Great) (1712-1786): king of Prussia 4, 158, 208, 241, 523, 538, 554, 557, 558, 559, 560, 561, 562, 563, 586
Frederick William II (1744-1797): king of Prussia 58
Frederick William III (1770-1840): king of Prussia 120, 122, 210, 368, 443, 460, 477, 509, 538, 549, 578, 579, 596
Frederick William IV (1795-1861): king of Prussia 4, 549, 558, 560, 579, 598
Freiligrath, Ferdinand (1810-1876): poet and patriot 536
Fresny, Charles Rivière du (1657-1724): writer of comedies 30

Freud, Sigmund (1856-1939): father of psychoanalysis 543
Friedrich, Caspar David (1774-1840): Romantic painter 162
Frölich, Heinrich (d. 1805): publisher of *the Athenaeum* 92, 120, 133, 147, 251
Frommann, Friedrich (1765-1837): bookseller and publisher in Jena 135
Fulda, Friedrich Carl (1724-1788): linguist and grammarian 84
Füssli. *See* Orell, Gessner, Füssli

Galen 461
Gall, Franz Joseph (1758-1828): physician and phrenologist 203
Gallitzin, Adelheid Amalie, princess (1748-1806): centre of Platonist, later Catholic, circle in Münster 51, 578
Galusky, Louis-Charles (1817-?): journalist and translator, biographer of AWS 418, 470
Garve, Christian (1742-1798): philosopher of the Enlightenment 62
Gatterer, Johann Christoph (1727-1799): history professor at Göttingen 32, 33, 37
Geibel, Emanuel (1815-1884): poet 467, 541
Gellert, Christian Fürchtegott (1715-1769): poet, professor in Leipzig, friend of JAS 13, 14, 16, 24, 581, 589
Genelli, Hans Christian (1763-1823): neo-classical architect 189, 209
Gentz, Friedrich (von) (1764-1833): statesman 206, 208, 209, 210, 295, 314, 330, 338, 339, 348, 350, 357, 362, 366, 372, 381, 432, 533, 575, 584, 595, 599
George II, king of Great Britain and Hanover (1683-1760) 22
George III, king of Great Britain, Ireland and Hanover (1738-1820): signed JAS's letters of appointment 4, 18, 20, 21, 22, 35, 359, 513
George IV, Prince Regent, then king of Great Britain, Ireland and Hanover (1761-1830) 367, 368, 377

Georges, Mlle (1787-1867): celebrated French actress 368, 369
Georg, prince of Prussia (1826-1902), attends AWS's lectures in Bonn 470
Gérard, François, baron (1770-1837): French painter, tutored Auguste von Buttlar 274, 418, 498, 505, 531, 538, 571, 585
Gervinus, Georg Gottfried (1805-1871): literary historian and politician 466
Gesner, Johann Matthias (1691-1751): classical scholar, professor at Göttingen 33, 494
Gessner. *See* Orell, Gessner, Füssli
Gessner, Salomon (1730-1788): Swiss poet 174
Gibbon, Edward (1737-1794): historian 226
Giseke, Nikolaus Dietrich (1724-1765): poet, friend of JAS 16, 581, 589
Gneisenau, Neidhardt von (1760-1831): Prussian general 348, 567
GOETHE, Johann Wolfgang (von) (1749-1832): poet, dramatist, novelist 5, 9, 17, 20, 34, 37, 38, 39, 43, 44, 46, 51, 55, 56, 57, 62, 64, 65, 66, 67, 68, 69, 70, 71, 72, 73, 75, 76, 77, 78, 79, 80, 81, 82, 85, 86, 88, 89, 91, 92, 93, 94, 95, 99, 100, 103, 105, 109, 111, 116, 117, 118, 119, 120, 121, 122, 124, 126, 127, 130, 131, 132, 134, 135, 136, 137, 138, 139, 141, 147, 148, 150, 151, 152, 153, 154, 156, 159, 160, 161, 162, 165, 166, 167, 168, 169, 172, 173, 174, 175, 176, 178, 179, 180, 185, 186, 187, 188, 189, 190, 191, 196, 197, 198, 202, 212, 217, 221, 224, 225, 227, 228, 232, 233, 234, 236, 240, 245, 249, 250, 251, 252, 254, 255, 256, 257, 260, 263, 270, 271, 277, 278, 281, 282, 283, 287, 300, 303, 304, 310, 314, 321, 324, 332, 333, 339, 340, 372, 378, 391, 398, 399, 404, 405, 424, 427, 431, 432, 435, 436, 442, 444, 451, 461, 469, 473, 478, 479, 480, 481, 485, 492, 494, 495, 529, 530, 531, 532, 533, 534, 535, 537, 539, 542, 543, 544, 545, 548, 567, 570, 572, 573, 575, 576, 579, 585, 586, 587, 588, 597, 599, 601

AWS relations with 78, 79, 81, 95, 111, 116, 117, 118, 119, 120, 138, 151, 152, 153, 154, 167, 178, 179, 188, 189, 190, 196, 197, 200, 201, 212, 221, 224, 234, 236, 240, 250, 255, 256, 281, 283, 310, 332, 333, 378, 404, 478, 481, 485, 529-535, 537

major works cited
  Campagne in Frankreich 55, 56, 153
  Faust 78, 91, 137, 166, 190, 200, 304, 339, 427, 533, 576
  Hermann und Dorothea 55, 65, 73, 85, 88, 137, 141, 151, 152, 154, 173, 228, 531, 544, 576
  Iphigenie 186, 287, 544, 576
  Wilhelm Meister 62, 65, 66, 67, 69, 74, 78, 79, 93, 95, 99-101, 118, 119, 120, 134, 151, 156, 172, 185, 227
  Winckelmann und sein Jahrhundert 39, 169, 174, 255, 260
  Xenien 69, 70, 79, 80, 82, 86, 139, 576

Goethe, Wolfgang Maximilian von (1820-1883): jurist, Goethe's grandson 469
Golbéry, Philippe (1786-1854): French jurist and translator
  writes biographical account of AWS 418
Goldstücker, Theodor (1821-1872): Sanskrit scholar, pupil of AWS's in Bonn 471
Görres, Joseph (von) (1776-1848): Romantic nature philosopher, historian and patriot 334, 408, 411, 429, 433, 434, 443, 469, 575, 602
Göschen, Georg Joachim (1752-1828): publisher in Leipzig 58, 68, 94
Gotter, Friedrich Wilhelm (1746-1797): poet and dramatist in Gotha 58, 123
Gotter, Luise (1760-1826): close friend of Caroline Schlegel 57, 58, 69, 145
Gotter, Pauline. *See* Schelling
Gottfried von Strassburg 214, 216, 334

Göttinger Gelehrte Anzeigen 32, 38, 43, 45, 46, 53
Göttinger Musenalmanach
See *Musenalmanach*
Gottsched, Johann Christoph (1700-1766): literary pundit in Leipzig 14, 16, 30, 39, 542, 589, 590
Gottsched, Luise Adelgunde Victorie, née Kulmus (1713-1762): dramatist and translator 30
Grattenauer, Karl Wilhelm (1773-1838): jurist in Berlin 207
Gray, Thomas (1716-1771): poet 18
Gries, Johann Diederich (1775-1842): translator (Ariosto, Tasso, Calderón), associate of the Romantics in Jena 121, 123, 125, 156, 199, 200, 206, 394, 397, 398, 399, 400
Grillparzer, Franz (1791-1872): dramatist 326, 536
Grimm, Jacob (1785-1863): grammarian, editor, lexicographer 33, 159, 379, 381, 395, 397, 398, 400, 401, 402, 407, 408, 409, 411, 412, 537, 541, 559, 567, 576, 586
Grimm, Melchior, baron (1723-1807): French man of letters, 'Encyclopédiste' 227, 230
Grimm, Wilhelm (1786-1859): grammarian, editor, lexicographer 395, 397, 398, 400, 401, 402, 407, 408, 409, 411, 537, 541, 567, 577, 586
Guarini, Giovanni Battista (1538-1612): poet 214
Guattani, Giuseppe Antonio (1748-1830): archaeologist of Roman antiquities 253
Guizot, François Pierre Guillaume (1787-1874): politician and historian 246, 427, 510, 573
Günderrode, Karoline von (1780-1806): poet and dramatist 567
Günther, Johann Christian (1695-1723): poète maudit 174
Gustavus Adolphus, Gustav II Adolf (1594-1632): king of Sweden 354, 359, 365, 371
Guyon, Jeanne Marie Bouvier de la Mothe (1648-1717): mystical and quietist writer 343

Hackert, Philipp (1737-1807): neo-classical painter, friend of Goethe 160, 162, 255
Hafiz, Shems ud-Dīn Muhammed called (?-1389): Persian poet 200
Hagemann, Gottfried (1819-1890): Sankritist 194
Hagen, Friedrich Heinrich von der (1780-1856): mediaevalist, professor in Breslau and Berlin 209, 210, 334, 394, 397, 399, 400, 407, 408, 411, 412
Hagn, Charlotte von (1809-1891): actress in Berlin, admired by AWS 560
Hähnel, Ernst Julius (1811-1891): sculptor (Beethoven monument in Bonn) 548, 549
Haller, Albrecht von (1708-1777): physiologist, poet 461
Haller, Karl Ludwig von (1768-1854): Swiss jurist and proponent of restoration 435
Haller, Marianne (1782-1842): wife of city architect in Berne, linked with AWS 291, 331, 342, 416
Hamilton, Alexander (1762-1824): Scotsman in employ of East India Company, teaches Friedrich Schlegel Sanskrit in Paris 193, 194, 297, 381, 592
Hamilton, Emma, lady (1763-1815): performs 'attitudes' 355
Hammerich, Martin (1811-1881): Danish Sanskrit scholar, pupil of AWS's in Bonn 471
Hammer-Purgstall, Joseph von (1774-1856): orientalist 431
d'Harcarville, Pierre-François, known as baron (1719-1805): antiquarian 397
Hardenberg, Charlotte von (1769-1845): wife of Benjamin Constant 326
Hardenberg, Friedrich von (known as Novalis) (1772-1801): poet, in Jena circle 10, 39, 50, 66, 67, 71, 84, 103, 110, 111, 112, 118, 120, 121, 122, 123, 125, 129, 133, 134, 135, 136, 138, 143, 145, 161, 169, 178, 180, 181, 182, 190, 191, 210, 211, 222, 263, 280, 322, 474, 480, 481, 531, 533, 548, 573, 577, 587, 591

Hardenberg, Karl August von, prince (1750-1822): Prussian minister of state and chancellor 23, 99, 370, 433, 438, 444, 445, 446, 455, 456, 465, 491, 492, 497, 516, 577, 581, 596

Hardenberg, Karl von, pseud. Rostorf (1776-1813): brother of Novalis and editor of *Dichtergarten* 180, 222, 263, 333, 344, 598

Hardorff, Gerd Geroldt (1769-1864): Runge's art teacher in Hamburg 165

Hare-Naylor, Francis (1753-1815): historian, reviews AWS's Vienna Lectures 422

Harrowby, earl of (1762-1847): politician, friend of Mme de Staël 367, 376, 377

Hartmann von Aue 216

Haughton, Sir Graves Chamney (1788-1849): Sanskrit scholar 504, 515, 519

Haupt, Moritz (1808-1874): German philologist, attends AWS's lectures in Bonn 469

Haydn, Joseph (1732-1809): composer 469

Haydon, Benjamin (1786-1846): painter 166

Hazlitt, William (1778-1830): essayist 422, 423

Heberle, J.M. (n.d.): publisher in Bonn, issues catalogue of AWS's library 563

Heeren, Arnold Hermann Ludwig (1760-1842): professor of history at Göttingen 217, 485, 487, 491, 493

Hegel, George Wilhelm Friedrich (1770-1831): philosopher 262, 436, 446, 466, 481, 509, 531, 537, 578, 585, 587

Heidelberger Jahrbücher 127, 279, 292, 320, 331, 346, 383, 385, 394, 395, 396, 397, 412, 602

Heine, Heinrich (1796-1856): poet 3, 4, 5, 39, 139, 174, 207, 409, 440, 457, 459, 465, 467, 468, 469, 504, 531, 534, 535, 540, 541, 542, 543, 544, 545, 546, 548, 578, 599

Heine, Johann August (1769-1831): librarian 165

Heinse, Wilhelm (1749-1803): novelist, writer on art 50, 55, 134

Heinsius, Wilhelm (1768-1817): publisher in Leipzig 60

Heldenbuch 167, 216, 256, 331, 408

Hemsterhuis, Frans (François) (1721-1790): philosopher 51, 84, 91, 155, 157, 161, 197, 198, 237, 269, 404, 473, 474, 476, 495, 557, 578

Hendel-Schütz, Henriette (1772-1849): performer of attitudes and 'tableaux vivants' 355

Henry V, king of England (1387-1422) 313

Henry VIII, king of England (1491-1547) 313

Herder, Johann Gottfried: theologian, philosopher, critic, poet 15, 20, 29, 32, 38, 51, 56, 64, 78, 83, 84, 88, 95, 99, 101, 151, 153, 161, 168, 188, 210, 211, 214, 221, 232, 237, 247, 267, 268, 286, 299, 309, 310, 316, 317, 324, 338, 404, 423, 456, 474, 575, 578-579, 601

Hermesianax 152

Herodotus 37, 447, 487

Herschel, Sir John (1792-1871): astronomer 512

Herz, Henriette (1764-1847): salonnière in Berlin 113, 114, 115, 135, 140, 208, 599

Hess, Moses (1812-1875): socialist, Zionist, attends AWS's lectures in Bonn 469

Hettner, Hermann (1821-1882): literary historian 466

Heyne, Christian Gottlob (1729-1812): classical scholar, mentor to AWS in Göttingen 28, 32, 33, 34, 35, 36, 38, 43, 46, 48, 49, 51, 53, 54, 59, 79, 83, 99, 126, 157, 267, 333, 452, 465, 574, 579

Hippocrates 461

Hirt, Alois (1759-1837): professor in Berlin and writer on aesthetics 99

Hitopadeśa 406, 447, 453, 463, 486, 498, 500, 508, 509, 515, 516, 518, 582

Hitzig, Julius Eduard (1780-1849): publisher in Berlin 319

Hobhouse, John Cam, later Broughton, lord (1786-1869): politician, companion of Byron 389, 390

Hofer, Andreas (1767-1810): leader of the Tyrolean uprising 349

Hoffmann, Ernst Theodor Amadeus (1776-1822): writer, composer 303, 581, 586, 600
Hoffmann von Fallersleben, August Heinrich (1798-1874): poet, German scholar, attends AWS's lectures in Bonn 467, 469, 536
Hoffmeister, Christian (1818-1871): engraver 546
Hofmannswaldau, Christian Hoffmann von (1616-1679): poet 216
Hohenlohe-Schillingsfürst, Chlodwig zu, prince (1819-1901): German chancellor, attends AWS's lectures in Bonn 470
Hohneck, August (1812-1879): painter 546
    portrait of AWS 22, 448, 547
Holbein, Hans (?1497-1543): painter 161, 162
Holberg, Ludvig (1684-1754): Danish dramatist 136, 436
Hölderlin, Friedrich (1770-1843): poet 55, 74, 105, 128, 152, 587
Holland, lord (1773-1840): politician, friend of Mme de Staël 367
Holtei, Karl von (1798-1880): writer, actor, reciter 536
Hölty, Ludwig Heinrich (1748-1776): poet associated with Bürger 37, 38, 571, 599
Homer 34, 36, 37, 38, 64, 73, 83, 85, 86, 87, 88, 89, 91, 127, 151, 158, 164, 166, 168, 176, 205, 212, 213, 214, 216, 217, 238, 243, 247, 252, 312, 344, 385, 396, 400, 403, 412, 421, 447, 460, 465, 468, 469, 519, 530, 553, 571, 574, 600
Hope, Sir George Johnstone (1767-1818): British admiral 369
Horace 20, 44, 128, 167, 172, 212, 483
Hormayr, Joseph (1782-1848): Austrian historian 431
Horn, Franz (1781-1837): literary historian and lecturer 536
Huber, Ludwig Ferdinand (1764-1804): writer, associated with AWS and Caroline in Mainz 56, 57, 141, 240

Huber, Therese, née Heyne (1764-1829): writer, married to Georg Forster, then to Ludwig Ferdinand H., associated with AWS and Caroline in Mainz 57, 183, 240, 588
Hübsch, Erdmuthe. *See* Schlegel
Hübsch, Johann Georg Gotthelf (1690-1773): mathematics teacher at Pforta school, AWS's maternal grandfather 18, 591
Hufeland, Christoph Wilhelm (1762-1836): physician, professor of medicine in Jena and Berlin, founder of macrobiotics 28, 71, 76, 129, 132, 143, 221
Hufeland, Gottlieb (1760-1817): law professor in Jena, co-editor of the *Allgemeine Literatur-Zeitung* 72, 76, 119, 128, 188, 221
Hugo, Victor (1802-1885): poet, dramatist and novelist 417, 425, 510
Hüllmann, Karl Dietrich (1765-1846): history professor in Bonn 467
Hülsen, August Ludwig (1765-1810): philosopher 251
HUMBOLDT, Alexander von (1769-1859): scientist and explorer 28, 35, 37, 42, 55, 56, 78, 113, 194, 199, 203, 241, 251, 253, 264, 277, 290, 298, 302, 303, 330, 381, 404, 417, 445, 476, 477, 482, 483, 484, 498, 519, 531, 536, 537, 539, 552, 555, 558, 559, 560, 574, 579, 592, 599
Humboldt, Caroline von, née von Dacheröden (1766-1829): poet, wife of Wilhelm von Humboldt 41, 256, 383, 581
HUMBOLDT, Wilhelm von (1767-1835): classical scholar, linguistician and Prussian minister of state 28, 34, 41, 42, 44, 58, 71, 73, 76, 82, 101, 102, 113, 124, 185, 194, 199, 206, 209, 227, 228, 249, 253, 256, 258, 350, 399, 411, 445, 450, 451, 465, 466, 468, 472, 473, 476, 477, 478, 485, 486, 489, 490, 491, 492, 493, 495, 518, 519, 532, 537, 580, 588, 592, 593, 596, 597, 599, 600

Hume, David (1711-1776): philosopher, historian 268
Hunt, James Henry Leigh (1784-1859): essayist and critic 423
Hutton, James (1726-1797): geologist 35, 241

Iffland, August Wilhelm (1759-1814): actor and dramatist 19, 21, 23, 29, 30, 99, 122, 140, 184, 189, 301, 580
Indische Bibliothek 102, 159, 383, 434, 452, 463, 464, 478, 482, 484, 485, 487, 489, 490, 491, 492, 493, 494, 497, 498, 499, 500, 502, 503, 509, 517, 521, 536, 510
Ingres, Jean-Auguste-Dominique (1780-1867): painter 418
d'Ivernois, Sir Francis (1757-1842): economist and politician, opponent of the continental blockade 360

Jablonowski: grand Polish noble family 306
Jacobi, Friedrich Heinrich (1743-1819): philosopher, later president of Bavarian Academy of Sciences 228, 231, 293, 294, 338, 578
Jacquet, Eugène-Vincent-Stanislas (1811-1838): Belgian orientalist 553
Jagemann, Karoline (1777-1848): actress in Weimar 188
Jahn (n.d.): 'Hoftraiteur', restaurant owner in Vienna 305
Jahrbuch der Preußischen Rhein-Universität 406, 447, 449
Jahrbücher der Literatur 431, 432
Jahrbücher der Wissenschaft und Kunst für Deutschland (projected) 142
Jean Paul. *See* Richter
Jefferson, Thomas (1743-1826): US president
  receives a copy of *Corinne* 277
Jenisch, Daniel (1762-1804): writer, lampooner of Romantics 140
Jérôme. *See* Bonaparte
Jersey, earl of (1773-1859): British courtier and politician, in circle of Mme de Staël 389

Jerusalem, Friederike Magdalene (1750-1836): poet, sister of Karl Wilhelm Jerusalem 68
Jerusalem, Karl Wilhelm (1747-1772): the model for Goethe's Werther 68
John, king of England (1166-1216) 313
Johnson, Samuel (1709-1784): author of the *Lives of the English Poets* 39, 92, 100, 174, 310, 423, 424, 496
Johnston, Patrick (n.d.): son of below, lives in AWS's house in Bonn 1824-25 145, 451, 463, 502, 507
Johnston, Sir Alexander (1775-1849): chief justice of Ceylon, co-founder of the Royal Asiatic Society 489, 501, 504, 507, 511, 519
Jolles, Frank (1931-2014): Schlegel scholar and editor 6
Jones, Sir William (1746-1794): judge in service of East India Company, orientalist, linguist 45, 56, 219, 264, 267, 268, 297, 395, 407, 453, 476, 480, 574, 580
Jorris (n.d.): adjutant to general Benckendorff
  kills Albert de Staël in duel 369
Journal Asiatique 491, 493, 551
Journal de l'Empire 288
Journal des débats 419, 445, 551
Justi, Carl (1832-1912): art historian and biographer 14

Kant, Immanuel (1724-1804): philosopher 42, 43, 51, 56, 62, 67, 95, 130, 141, 168, 227, 228, 230, 231, 232, 233, 323, 329, 339, 573, 578, 593, 600
Karamzin, Nikolai (1786-1826): Russian poet and historian 351
Karl Friedrich, margrave, then grand duke of Baden (1728-1811) 317, 581
Keats, John (1795-1821): poet 169, 548
Kent, princess Victoria of Saxe-Coburg-Saalfeld, duchess of (1786-1861) 501
Kinsky: Austro-Bohemian princely family 306
Klaproth, Julius (1783-1835): orientalist, ethnographer 475, 491

Kleist, Heinrich von (1777-1811): dramatist 186, 303, 315, 341, 342, 362, 584

Klingemann, August (1777-1831): novelist and playwright
in AWS's audience in Jena 128

Klopstock, Friedrich Gottlieb (1724-1803): poet 14, 16, 17, 18, 38, 46, 83, 85, 90, 111, 118, 157, 158, 159, 167, 191, 192, 232, 324, 495, 580, 580-581, 589, 591
works cited
Auf meine Freunde 16, 581
Der Messias 89, 157, 158, 212, 581
Der Zürchersee 16, 581
Grammatische Gespräche 111, 157, 158, 159, 167, 581

Knebel, Karl Ludwig von (1744-1854): friend of Goethe's in Weimar, translator 153, 231, 232

Knorring, Karl Gregor von (1769-1837): Baltic nobleman, lover, then second husband, of Sophie Tieck-Bernhardi 185, 222, 256, 301, 302, 307, 315, 350, 386, 521, 522, 569, 598

Knorring, Sophie von. *See* Tieck

Koch, Johann Anton (1768-1839): Romantic landscape painter 255

Koreff, David Ferdinand (1783-1851): physician, attends AWS, in Prussian ministry 274, 275, 331, 337, 343, 433, 437, 442, 445, 446, 448, 453, 455, 487, 581

Körner, Christian Gottfried (1756-1831): civil servant in Dresden and friend of Schiller 76, 77, 122, 588

Körner, Josef (1888-1950): Schlegel scholar and editor 2, 3, 6, 7, 546, 554, 581

Körner, Theodor (1791-1813): patriotic poet 411

Körte, Friedrich Heinrich Wilhelm (1776-1846): literary historian and editor 209

Koselleck, Reinhart (1923-2006): German historian 65

Kotzebue, August von (1761-1819): dramatist, anti-Romantic 140, 141, 146, 188, 190, 191, 232, 234, 266, 301, 328, 332, 433, 434, 454, 534, 582

Kranz. *See* Crancé

Krause, Christoph Friedrich (1781-1832): philosopher 129

Krüdener, Barbara Juliane von, baroness (1764-1824): itinerant visionary, inspirer of the Holy Alliance 246, 323, 454, 595

Kühn, Sophie von (1782-1797): Novalis's child bride 138, 577

Kunstblatt 418, 524, 538, 570

Kutuzov, Mikhail (1745-1813): Russian field marshal 351, 352

Lachmann, Karl (1793-1851): philologist and editor 407, 408, 409, 412, 413, 466, 537

La Curne de Sainte-Palaye, Jean-Baptiste de (1697-1781): French medievalist and antiquary 214

Ladvocat, Pierre-François (1791-1854): editor and publisher 427

La Fayette, Gilbert du Motier, marquis de (1757-1834): general in American revolution 277

La Harpe, Jean-François de (1739-1803): critic and dramatist 227

Lamartine, Alphonse de (1790-1869): poet 418

Lambertz, Jacob (1779-1864): AWS's lawyer in Bonn 438, 440, 441, 550, 551, 563, 564

Langbein, August Friedrich (1757-1835): popular novelist 43

Langlès, Louis-Mathieu (1763-1824): keeper of oriental manuscripts in Bibliothèque nationale 275, 381, 382, 406, 494, 571

Langlois, Simon Alexandre (1785-1854): Sanskrit scholar 485, 489, 493, 498, 534

Lansdowne, marquess of (1780-1863): politician, friend of Mme de Staël 367, 389, 511

La Roche, Sophie von (1730-1807): novelist 54, 567
Las Casas, Emmanuel-Auguste-Dieudonné, comte de (1766-1842): author of *Mémorial de Sainte-Hélène* 426
Lassen, Christian (1800-1876): orientalist 466, 471, 483, 485, 493, 497, 499, 500, 507, 508, 509, 510, 518, 519, 549, 552, 563, 582
Lawrence, Sir Thomas (1769-1830): painter 64, 166
Leibniz, Gottfried Wilhelm (1646-1716): mathematician and philosopher 23
Leipziger Monatsschrift für Damen 89
Leipziger Zeitung 371
Le Moniteur 58
Lenz, Johann Reinhold Michael (1751-1792): dramatist 174
Leonardo da Vinci (1452-1519): painter, sculptor, architect 161
Le Publiciste 274
Lessing, Gotthold Ephraim (1729-1781): dramatist and critic 14, 15, 18, 20, 29, 32, 39, 64, 67, 68, 90, 92, 95, 112, 157, 174, 197, 199, 212, 232, 270, 283, 289, 394, 541, 542, 582-583, 591
Letronne, Jean Antoine (1787-1848): historian and archaeologist 534, 552, 553
Levin, Rahel. *See* Varnhagen von Ense
Liechtenstein: Austrian princely family 306
Ligne, Karl-Joseph Lamoral, prince de (1735-1814): Austrian field marshal and diplomat, friend of Mme de Staël 295, 318, 350, 595
Lips, Johann Heinrich (1758-1817): engraver 196
Liszt, Franz (1811-1886): composer, pianist 548
Liverpool, earl of (1770-1828): British prime minister 367, 377
Lobkowitz: Austro-Bohemian princely family 295, 306
Lockhart, John Gibson (1794-1854): man of letters, editor of the *Quarterly Review* 513

Löbel, Maria (1776-1843): AWS's housekeeper in Bonn 451, 458, 561
Löwenhielm, Carl von, count (1772-1861): Swedish soldier and diplomat 354, 368
Lohenstein, Daniel Casper von (1635-1683): poet, dramatist, diplomat 216
Louis XIV (1638-1715): king of France 285, 374, 414
Louis XV (1710-1774): king of France 4
Louis XVI (1754-1793): king of France 36, 226, 374
Louis XVIII (1755-1824): king of France 374, 376
Louise, duchess, then grand-duchess of Saxe-Weimar-Eisenach 232
L(o)uise, princess of Mecklenburg-Strelitz, queen of Prussia 1797-1810 (1776-1810) 122
Louis Ferdinand, prince of Prussia (1772-1806): composer, killed at battle of Saalfeld 113, 208, 234, 599
Louis-Philippe, duke of Orleans, then king of the French 1830-1848 (1773-1850) 4, 418, 545
  receives AWS 510
Lubomirski: Polish princely family 295, 306, 350
Lucian 44
Luden, Heinrich (1778-1847): historian in Jena 262
Ludwig, crown prince, later king of Bavaria (1786-1868), Walhalla 264, 320, 333, 558, 570, 583, 586
Ludwig Ernst, duke of Brunswick (1718-1788): captain-general of the Netherlands 60
Lüders, Ludwig (1776-1822): mathematician, opponent of continental blockade 360, 361
Luther, Martin (1483-1546): reformer 461, 549
Lützow, Ludwig Adolf Wilhelm, Freiherr von (1782-1844): Prussian volunteer corps commander 348

Macaulay, Zachary (1768-1838): slavery abolitionist 417
Mackintosh, Sir James (1765-1832): lawyer and politician, friend of Madame de Staël 367, 376, 377, 383, 422, 423, 457, 482, 487, 489, 496, 500, 501, 503, 513, 514, 519, 583, 511
Mahâbhârata 382
Malcolm, Sir John (1769-1833): general and governor in India 489, 494, 501, 519
Mallet, Paul-Henri (1730-1807): author of *Northern Antiquities* 247
Malone, Edmond (1741-1812): Shakespeare scholar and editor 92, 308, 423
Malte-Brun, Conrad (1755-1826): geographer 483
Malthus, Thomas (1766-1834): political economist 417
Manso, Johann Caspar Friedrich (1759-1826): historian and translator 79
Mantegna, Andrea (1431-1506): painter 254
Manu 297, 461
Maratta, Carlo (1625-1713): painter 125
Marie-Louise, archduchess of Austria, later Empress of the French (1791-1847): Napoleon's second wife, empress (1810-1814) 328, 349, 583
Marmontel, Jean François (1723-1799): poet and historiographer 227, 284
Marx, Karl (1818-1883), attends AWS's lectures in Bonn 4, 464, 465, 468, 469, 470
Maximilian I, Joseph (1756-1825): elector, then king of Bavaria (1806-1825) 294, 583
Mecklenburg-Schwerin, Friedrich Ludwig, prince of (1778-1819): general 264, 368, 369
Meinhard, Johann Nicolaus (1727-1767): translator from Italian 89
Meister, Henri (1744-1826): friend of Madame de Staël 227
Mendelssohn Bartholdy, Felix (1809-1847): composer, cousin of Veit brothers 137, 560, 589, 598

Mendelssohn, Henriette (1775-1831): educationalist, sister of Dorothea Schlegel 330, 523, 599
Mendelssohn, Moses (1729-1786): philosopher, father of Dorothea Schlegel, grandfather of Felix 110, 115, 589
Mengs, Anton Raphael (1728-1779): court painter 45, 162, 255
Menzel, Wolfgang (1798-1873): publicist and literary critic writes memoir of AWS 457, 465
Mereau, Sophie, née Schubart (1770-1806): writer 183
Merkel, Garlieb (1769-1850): writer, lampooner of the Romantics 140, 190
Metastasio, Pietro Trapassi pseud. (1698-1782): poet and librettist 250
Metternich, Klemens, count, later prince (1773-1859): Austrian chancellor 250, 275, 276, 306, 313, 314, 315, 335, 348, 350, 351, 353, 358, 359, 370, 380, 384, 430, 431, 432, 434, 435, 454, 522, 523, 545, 555, 575, 583-584, 592
Meyer, Carl Joseph (1796-1856): publisher, translator of Shakespeare, editor of *Conversations-Lexikon* 95, 528
Meyer, Friedrich Ludwig Wilhelm (1758-1840): poet, professor in Göttingen, confidant of Caroline Schlegel 41, 52, 54
Meyer, Heinrich (1759-1832): Goethe's art expert in Weimar 82, 148, 160, 188, 394, 400, 403, 405, 432, 529
Meyers Lexikon 494
Michaelis, Charlotte (1766-1793): Caroline's sister 54
Michaelis, Johann David (1717-1791): orientalist, professor in Göttingen, Caroline Schlegel's father 32, 34, 247, 316, 569, 588
Michaelis, Luise (1770-1846): Caroline's sister 57
Michaelis, Salomon Heinrich Karl (1768-1844): publisher 94
Michaud, Louis-Gabriel (1773-1858): publisher of *Biographie Universelle* 322, 341

Michelangelo Buonarroti (1475-1564): sculptor, painter, architect 49, 90, 165, 259
Mickiewicz, Adam (1798-1855): Polish national poet, visits AWS in 1829 417, 422, 429, 451
Mill, James (1773-1836): political economist 417
Milton, John (1608-1674): poet 90, 158, 191, 212, 311
Minor, Jakob (1855-1912): German scholar and editor of AWS's lectures 6, 522, 565
Mirabeau, Honoré Gabriel Riqueti, comte de (1749-1791): statesman of French Revolution 56
Mohr und Zimmer. *See* Zimmer
Molière, Jean-Baptiste Poquelin known as (1622-1673): playwright 295, 310, 312, 427, 568
Mommsen, Theodor (1817-1903): historian of Rome 402
Montgelas, Maximilan Joseph Garnerin, count (1759-1838): Bavarian minister and reformer 294
Monthly Review 190
Monti, Vincenzo (1754-1828): Italian neo-classical poet, friendship with Madame de Staël 236, 238, 252, 259, 264, 267, 276, 277, 278, 384
Montmorency, Jean Félicité Mathieu de, later duc de M-Laval (1767-1826): fought in American and French Revolutions, member of Coppet circle 238, 245, 274, 318, 320, 327, 331, 343, 585, 593, 594
Montor, Alexis-François Artaud de (1772-1849): secretary to French legation in Rome, connoisseur 253
Moor, Edward (1771-1848): soldier and Indologist 501
Mora, José Joaquín de (1783-1864): Spanish writer, educator and politician 428
Moreau, Jean-Victor Marie (1763-1813): French general, involved in conspiracy against Napoleon and exiled 234, 348, 353, 370

Morgenblatt für gebildeten Stände 277
Moritz, Karl Philipp (1756-1793): novelist, psychologist, aesthetician 29, 30, 203, 597, 600
Müffling, Friedrich Karl Ferdinand, Freiherr von (1775-1851): Prussian field marshal, governor of Paris 1815 433
Muhrbeck, Friedrich (1775-1827): philosopher, friend of Hölderlin's in Jena 128
Muilman, Henric (1743-1812): merchant at Amsterdam in whose house AWS was tutor 52, 59, 60, 64
Muilman, Willem Ferdinand Mogge (1778-1849): merchant at Amsterdam, tutored by AWS 1791-95 53, 145
Müller, Adam Heinrich (von) (1779-1829): publicist and political theorist 209, 210, 262, 278, 303, 304, 312, 314, 315, 372, 411, 435, 525, 533, 584
Müller, Friedrich Max (1823-1900): orientalist 471, 491, 492
Müller, Johannes (von) (1752-1809): Swiss historian 64, 214, 219, 233, 234, 244, 247, 262, 267, 317, 320, 338, 412, 570, 584
Müllner, Adolf (1774-1829): writer of 'fate tragedies' 326, 536
Münchhausen, Gerlach Adolf von (1688-1770): Hanoverian minister, 'Kurator' of Göttingen university 18, 31, 32
Mundt, Theodor (1808-1861): critic and novelist 536
Münster, Ernst Friedrich, count (1766-1839): Hanoverian minister in London 357, 361, 366
Munster, George FitzClarence, earl of (1794-1842): President of the Royal Asiatic Society 511, 513
Murat, Joachim (1767-1815): marshal of the Empire, king of Two Sicilies (1806-1815) 353
Murray, John (1778-1843): publisher (of *De l'Allemagne*) 346, 368, 373, 375, 377, 388, 392, 393, 422, 492, 513, 514, 595

Musen-Almanach für das Jahr 1802 169, 181, 569, 598
Musenalmanach (Göttingen) 37, 40, 41, 44, 46, 54, 199, 599
Musenalmanach (Schiller) 70, 79, 82, 105, 106, 180, 588
Musenalmanach (Wendt) 534, 536
Mustoxidi, Andrea (1785-1860): scholar of antiquity 394, 397
Myller, Christoph Heinrich (1740-1807): antiquarian and editor (notably of the *Nibelungenlied*) 408

Naeke, August Ferdinand (1788-1838): classics professor in Bonn 450, 460, 467, 549, 550
Nalus 490, 493, 497, 502, 518
NAPOLEON Bonaparte, emperor of the French (1769-1821): implacable opponent of Madame de Staël 3, 4, 5, 15, 21, 24, 118, 139, 170, 185, 194, 195, 205, 224, 226, 227, 228, 229, 230, 234, 237, 245, 246, 249, 252, 262, 263, 264, 274, 276, 285, 292, 293, 294, 295, 312, 313, 314, 317, 321, 326, 327, 328, 329, 330, 331, 335, 336, 339, 341, 345, 346, 349, 350, 352, 353, 354, 356, 357, 358, 359, 360, 361, 362, 364, 365, 368, 370, 371, 373, 374, 375, 378, 381, 384, 398, 407, 411, 414, 426, 427, 444, 453, 460, 523, 539, 540, 545, 555, 567, 568, 570, 571, 575, 576, 578, 579, 583, 585, 594, 595, 596
Necker de Saussure, Albertine (1768-1841): cousin of Madame de Staël, and her first biographer, translator of AWS's Vienna Lectures into French 240, 343, 415, 420, 422, 425, 429, 430
Necker, Jacques (1732-1804): banker 226, 229, 231, 239, 240, 242, 243, 256, 259, 267, 269, 273, 294, 324, 341, 342, 383, 386, 387, 416, 545, 584, 594, 595, 597
Necker, Suzanne, née Curchod (1737-1794): Madame de Staël's mother 226, 242
Neipperg, Adam Albert, count (1775-1829): Austrian general and diplomat, later married the empress Marie-Louise 354, 368, 384
Neues Deutsches Museum 23, 43

Nibelungenlied 7, 33, 166, 167, 205, 209, 210, 214, 216, 243, 244, 255, 292, 312, 320, 331, 332, 344, 372, 379, 395, 396, 397, 398, 400, 401, 407, 408, 409, 410, 411, 412, 413, 431, 447, 469, 475, 486, 494, 495, 544, 551, 554, 564
Nicholas I, tsar (1796-1855): emperor of Russia 554
Nicolai, Friedrich (1733-1811): Berlin publisher and novelist, Romantic-hater 51, 79, 94, 112, 118, 140, 184, 190, 203, 207, 234, 236, 597
Nicolle, Gabriel-Henri (1767-1829): Paris publisher, ruined by confiscation of *De l'Allemagne* 276, 328, 329, 330
Nicolovius, Friedrich (1768-1836): publisher 171, 173
Niebuhr, Barthold Georg (1776-1831): historian 312, 386, 394, 397, 398, 402, 403, 418, 435, 457, 462, 467, 535, 550, 562, 585
  AWS review of 386, 397, 398, 402, 403
  Römische Geschichte 585
Niebuhr, Carsten (1733-1815): traveller in Arabia 51, 585
Nietzsche, Friedrich (1844-1900): classical scholar and philosopher 14, 481
Nodier, Charles (1780-1844): French Romantic writer 328
Noehden, Georg Heinrich (1770-1826): translator in London 501, 519
Nouveau Journal Asiatique 551
Novalis. *See* Hardenberg, Friedrich von
Nuys, Elisabeth Wilhelmine van (1770-1835): society lady, friend of AWS 222, 290, 295, 301, 307, 333

O'Donnell, Maurice, count (1788-1843): Austrian nobleman, associated with Madame de Staël 238, 293, 294, 295, 305, 314, 315, 318, 335, 342, 593, 595
Oehlenschläger, Adam (1779-1850): Danish poet 321, 417
Oken, Lorenz (1779-1851): professor of natural philosophy at Jena
  dismissal 456

Opitz, Martin (1597-1639): poet 216
Orange, William V, prince of (1748-1806): last Stadtholder of the Dutch Republic 60, 234
Orell, Gessner, Füssli: publishers in Zurich 94, 96
Ossian 34, 229, 237, 238, 247, 252, 579
Österreichischer Beobachter 336
Österreichische Zeitung 335, 592
Otfrîd von Weissenburg 167
Overbeck, Friedrich (1789-1869): Nazarene painter 389
Ovid 152, 230, 273, 600

Pálffy: Hungarian magnate family 12, 306
Palma, Jacopo (1480-1528): painter 125
Pange, Pauline, comtesse de, née de Broglie (1888-1972): doyenne of Staël studies 585
Parmigianino, Girolamo Mazzola called (1504-1540): painter 49
Parny, Évariste Desiré de Forges, vicomte de (1753-1814): French writer 134
    AWS review of *La Guerre des dieux* 111, 156, 207, 213, 308
Paul I, emperor of Russia (1754-1801) 131
Paulus, Caroline (1767-1844): novelist, mother of Sophie, AWS's mother-in-law 588
Paulus, Heinrich Eberhard Gottlob (1761-1851): theologian, AWS father-in-law 72, 86, 128, 129, 132, 135, 137, 143, 178, 221, 436, 437, 438, 439, 440, 491, 551, 563, 564, 585, 588
Paulus, Sophie. *See* Schlegel
Paulus, Wilhelm (1802-1819): son of Heinrich Eberhard and Caroline Paulus, AWS's brother-in-law 433
Percy, Thomas (1729-1811): compiler of the *Reliques* 38, 41
Périer, Casimir Pierre (1777-1832): French prime minister and minister of the interior 510
Pervigilium Veneris 46
Pestalozzi, Johann Heinrich (1746-1827): Swiss educationalist 27, 321, 338, 463, 507

Petrarch, Francesco Petrarca called (1304-1374): poet 46, 64, 148, 204, 216, 217, 236, 265, 333, 478, 495, 552
Phanokles 152
Phöbus 315, 584
Pichegru, Jean-Charles (1761-1804): French general, involved in conspiracy against Napoleon 234, 353
Pichler, Caroline (1769-1843): Viennese writer and salonnière 289, 299, 301, 307, 411
Pick, Franz, canon (1750-1819): art collector in Bonn 452, 461
Pictet, Adolphe (1799-1875): Swiss linguist 247, 395, 488
Pictet, Charles (1755-1824) 385
Pictet, Marc-Auguste (1752-1825): Genevan scientist 242
Piroli, Tommaso (1752-1824): engraver of Flaxman's outline illustrations of Homer 164
Platen-Hallermünde, August von, count (1796-1853): poet, dramatist, subject of attack by Heine 39, 541, 542, 543, 544, 578
Plato 51, 168, 178, 557, 593
Pluche, Noël-Antoine, abbé (1686-1761): author of *Spectacle de la nature* 29
Polidori, John William (1795-1821): Byron's physician 389, 390
Polidoro Caldara (1499-1543): painter 49
Pontormo, Jacopo da (1494-1557): painter 549
Potocki: family of Polish magnates 295
Poussin, Gaspar Dughet called (1613-1675): landscape painter 160, 162
Pozzo di Borgo, Carlo Andrea, count (1764-1842): Russian diplomat 348, 368, 378
Prichard, James Cowles (1786-1848): physician, anthropologist 488, 501, 552
    AWS preface to 476, 552
Prometheus 202, 205, 280, 283, 291, 292, 299, 300, 302, 305, 307, 321, 332, 465
Propertius 152, 153, 212, 232, 447, 464, 469, 600
Propyläen 119, 120, 121, 124, 126, 147, 148, 152, 159, 160, 161, 165, 255

Pushkin, Alexander Sergievitch (1799-1837): Russian national poet 417, 429
Pütter, Johann Stephan (1725-1807): jurist in Göttingen 36

Quarterly Review 422, 492, 496, 513

Rabener, Gottlieb Wilhelm (1714-1771): satirist 16
Racine, Jean (1639-1699): dramatist 156, 207, 225, 237, 261, 270, 271, 272, 281, 284, 286, 287, 288, 289, 303, 310, 355, 425, 427, 554, 282
  work cited
    Phèdre 156, 207, 225, 261, 270, 271, 272, 281, 284, 285, 286, 287, 288, 289, 301, 352, 554, 282
Radziwill: Polish princely family 234
Râmâyana 10, 88, 297, 298, 382, 394, 406, 447, 453, 475, 480, 484, 486, 487, 490, 495, 500, 501, 504, 508, 509, 516, 517, 518, 519, 525, 529, 510
Ramdohr, Friedrich Wilhelm Basilius von (1757-1822): conservative art critic 79
Ramler, Karl Wilhelm (1725-1798): poet, metricist and editor 541
Rammohan Roy, Rajah (1772-1833): Indian religious reformer, 'the Maker of Modern India' 512
Randall, Fanny (1777-1833): Albertine de Staël's governess, member of Coppet household 294, 328, 342, 389, 390, 393, 415, 433
Ranke, Leopold (von) (1795-1886): historian 559
Raphael, Raffaello Santi known as (1483-1520): painter 49, 69, 90, 121, 125, 162, 163, 165, 196, 259, 405
Rauch, Christian Daniel (1777-1858): neo-classical sculptor 186, 537, 558
Raumer, Friedrich von (1781-1873): professor of history in Berlin 209, 210, 425, 431, 446, 537, 559
Raupach, Ernst (1784-1852): dramatist 536

Raynouard, François Just Marie (1761-1836): dramatist, Romance scholar 413, 467
Récamier, Juliette, Jeanne-Françoise Julie Adelaïde Bernard, Madame Récamier (1777-1849): salonnière 274, 275, 276, 279, 280, 281, 291, 325, 326, 327, 349, 353, 367, 498, 585
Redding, Cyrus (1785-1870): journalist and memoirist 424
Rehausen, Gotthard Maurits von, baron (1761-1822): Swedish envoy in London 377
Rehberg, Caroline (d. 1806): painter 19, 324
Rehfues, Philipp Joseph (von) (1779-1843): Kurator of the University of Bonn 445, 453, 455, 456, 457, 497, 499, 514, 561, 562, 512
Reichardt, Johann Friedrich (1752-1814): composer 76, 77, 79, 80, 82, 93, 112, 114, 123, 187, 188, 317, 532, 533, 586, 591, 597, 600
Reimer, Georg Andreas (1776-1842): Berlin publisher 9, 10, 92, 161, 193, 198, 199, 204, 208, 209, 223, 243, 261, 298, 319, 331, 332, 521, 523, 527, 528, 529, 530, 537, 553, 554, 564, 586
Reinhart, Johann Christian (1764-1847): painter and engraver 255
Rendorp, Joachim (1728-1792): brother-in-law of Henric Muilman, controversialist and opponent of popular rule 60
Reni, Guido (1575-1642): painter 42, 49, 125
Revue des deux mondes 552
Revue française 427
Rhode, Johann Gottlieb (1762-1827): writer and editor 434, 476
Ricardo, David (1772-1823): political economist 417
Richard I, Coeur de Lion, king of England (1157-1199) 341
Richard II, king of England (1367-1400) 313

Richard III, king of England (1452-1485) 313, 332
Richardson, William (1743-1814): Shakespeare critic 423, 424
Richter, Jean Paul Friedrich, pseud. Jean Paul (1763-1825): novelist 27, 122, 151, 278, 338, 411, 436, 437, 440, 531, 580, 586, 587
Ritschl, Friedrich Wilhelm (1806-1876): classicist, professor in Bonn 466, 549, 553
Ritter, Carl (1779-1859): geographer 487
Ritter, Johann Wilhelm (1776-1810): experimental scientist in Jena 136
Rivington, John (1720-1792): publisher 92
Robertson, William (1721-1793): historian 494
Robespierre, Maximilien de (1758-1794): Revolutionary politician 118
Robinson, Henry Crabb (1775-1867): barrister at law, diarist, gossip 232, 233, 587
   dealings with Madame de Staël and AWS 233-234, 376, 378
Rocca, Albert-Jean-Michel de (known as John) (1788-1818): French soldier, lover, then second husband, of Madame de Staël 238, 342, 344, 347, 349, 354, 367, 375, 377, 383, 384, 386, 389, 392, 595
Rocca, Louis-Alphonse de (1812-1842): son of John Rocca and Madame de Staël 343, 383, 418, 419, 595
Romano, Giulio (1499-1546): painter 49
Rosa, Salvator (1615-1673): landscape painter 161
Rosen, Friedrich (1805-1837): professor of Sanskrit in London 515
Rossetti, Gabriele (1783-1854): Italian poet and scholar, emigrated to London 552
Rostopchin, Fyodor, count (1763-1826): governor of Moscow 351
Rothschild, James Mayer, baron (1792-1868): banker in Paris 510

Rousseau, Jean-Jacques (1712-1778): model for Madame de Staël and counter-model for AWS 27, 28, 84, 209, 242, 243, 269, 464, 586, 595
Rowlandson, Thomas (1756-1827): caricaturist 190
Rubens, Peter Paul (1577-1640): painter 50, 162, 549
Rückert, Friedrich (1788-1866): poet, orientalist 518, 536
   AWS on 518, 536
Rudolf, count of Habsburg, German king (1218-1291) 336
   AWS account of 413
Rühlmann, Christian Friedrich (1753-1815): rector of the Lyceum in Hanover 30
Runge, Philipp Otto (1777-1840): Romantic painter 162, 165, 166
Ruysdael, Jacob van (1629-1682): landscape painter 161

Sabran, Elzéar de (1774-1846): writer, member of Coppet circle 260, 269, 270, 274, 279, 318, 319, 320, 325
Sachs, Hans (1494-1576): Mastersinger 215
Saint-Martin, Louis-Claude de, pseud. 'le philosophe inconnu' (1743-1803): religious writer, translator of Jakob Böhme into French 322, 343, 581
Śakuntalâ 42, 45, 56, 168, 219, 297, 395, 471, 480, 574
Sand, Karl (1795-1820): student, assassin of Kotzebue 454, 582
Sarto, Andrea del (1486-1531): painter 162
Saussure, Horace-Bénédicte de (1740-1799): Genevan scientist and alpinist 240, 241
Savage, Richard (1697-1743): 'poète maudit', subject of Dr Johnson's famous Life 39, 174
Savary, Anne Jean Marie René, later duke of Rovigo (1774-1833): French general and Napoleon's chief of

police 328, 329, 330, 346, 350, 352, 354, 394, 555
  orders the destruction of *De l'Allemagne* 329
Savigny, Friedrich von (1779-1861), law professor in Berlin 66, 128, 129, 167, 446, 567, 576
Schadow, Johann Gottfried (1764-1850): neo-classical sculptor 99, 144, 170, 186, 190, 204
Scharnhorst, Gerhard von (1755-1813): Prussian general 235, 348
Schelling, Friedrich Wilhelm Joseph (von) (1775-1854): philosopher, professor in Jena 78, 110, 111, 117, 121, 122, 123, 125, 126, 127, 128, 129, 132, 135, 137, 138, 142, 143, 144, 145, 146, 148, 161, 167, 169, 170, 171, 172, 178, 180, 181, 186, 188, 190, 209, 210, 213, 221, 222, 224, 233, 240, 260, 294, 302, 308, 320, 323, 324, 333, 338, 347, 378, 423, 436, 473, 531, 536, 569, 573, 576, 577, 587, 588, 596
Schelling, Pauline, née Gotter (1786-1851): Schelling's second wife 347
Schick, Gottlieb (1776-1812): neo-classical painter 194, 255
Schiffenhuber-Hartl, Nina (?-1853): mentioned in connection with AWS 388
Schiller, Charlotte, née von Lengefeld (1776-1826): Schiller's wife 77, 588
SCHILLER, Friedrich (von) (1759-1805): poet, dramatist, philosopher 5, 8, 9, 18, 38, 39, 41, 43, 44, 45, 46, 47, 52, 53, 55, 56, 60, 62, 63, 64, 65, 66, 67, 68, 69, 70, 71, 72, 73, 74, 75, 76, 77, 78, 79, 80, 81, 82, 83, 84, 85, 86, 87, 88, 89, 90, 91, 92, 93, 94, 95, 99, 100, 103, 105, 106, 112, 117, 118, 119, 122, 124, 127, 128, 129, 131, 134, 137, 139, 141, 147, 148, 151, 152, 153, 154, 159, 167, 168, 169, 171, 173, 174, 175, 180, 186, 188, 196, 197, 198, 207, 208, 225, 227, 232, 233, 236, 268, 271, 284, 289, 300, 301, 304, 310, 313, 315, 318, 319, 320, 321, 324, 339, 340, 372, 385, 425, 436, 461, 472, 473, 478, 485, 529, 530, 531, 532, 533, 534, 535, 539, 542, 543, 558, 562, 571, 572, 576, 580, 585, 586, 587-588, 591

  AWS's dealings with 8, 39, 44, 45, 53, 60, 64, 66, 67, 68, 70, 72, 73, 74, 75-84, 89, 92, 93, 95, 96, 99, 103, 105, 106, 122, 127, 128, 147, 167, 188, 200
  later attitudes to 117, 119, 137, 152, 154, 159, 171, 173, 174, 175, 196, 236, 284, 300, 310, 313, 318, 339, 425, 472, 473, 485, 530, 531, 532, 533, 534, 535, 539, 542, 543
  major works cited
    Die Horen 8, 44, 45, 47, 60, 64, 65, 66, 68, 69, 72, 73, 74, 75, 77, 79, 80, 81, 82, 83, 84, 85, 89, 93, 94, 95, 96, 99, 101, 103, 105, 115, 118, 120, 127, 133, 147, 152, 153, 157, 204, 206, 227, 532, 552, 576, 588
    Macbeth 137, 171, 300, 301
    Maria Stuart 232, 271, 319, 588
    Thalia 45, 60, 588
    Wallenstein 65, 137, 318, 319, 425, 588
    Xenien 70, 79, 80, 82, 86, 139, 576, 588
Schilling von Canstatt, Paul Ludwig, baron (1786-1837): Russo-German inventor, scholar of Tibetan and Chinese 489
Schinkel, Karl Friedrich (1781-1841): architect 537, 539, 549
Schink, Johann Friedrich (1755-1835): dramatist, critic, producer 174
SCHLEGEL, AUGUST WILHELM (VON) (1767-1845)
  family background 13-23
  siblings 23-26
  schooling in Hanover 27-31
  studies at Göttingen 30-52
  relations with Bürger 37-48
  relations with Fiorillo 48-50
  first meeting with Caroline, shares her tribulations 50-59
  in Amsterdam 59-64
  marries Caroline and moves to Jena 65-109
  collaboration on Schiller's *Die Horen* 72-112

Dante and Shakespeare translations 88-109
part of the Jena group 109-146
produces *Athenaeum* with FS 115-121, 154-166
professor in Jena 166-168
death of Auguste Böhmer and separation from Caroline 143-146
end of the Jena group 169-179
moves to Berlin 172-220
liaison with Sophie Bernhardi 182-185
Ion fiasco 186-189
Calderón translation 198-201
Berlin Lectures 202-220
meets Madame de Staël 235-241
Coppet group 241-249
in Italy 249-260
in Coppet again and Acosta 260-289
reviews of Staël's tragic roles 269-273
reviews of *Corinne* 273-289
Comparaison entre la Phèdre de Racine et celle d'Euripide 282-290
in Vienna and elsewhere with Madame de Staël 290-318
Vienna Lectures 299-314
return to Coppet 318-344
De l'Allemagne 325-330, 337-340
in Berne 330-334
dash to Vienna 334-337
flight with the Staël family to Austria 345-350
to Russia 350-355
to Sweden 355
secretary to Bernadotte and writer of political pamphlets 356-364
caught up in the campaigns of 1813-14 364-375
in England 376-377
return to France 378-393
with the Staël family in Italy, Coppet and Paris 384-392
death of Madame de Staël 392
scholarly writing, reviews, medieval studies 1810-1815 393-414

relations with the Staël family 415-421
reputation in Europe 421-431
with FS 430-435
marriage to Sophie Paulus 435-442
professor in Bonn 442-463
lectures given and their audience 463-478
Sanskrit studies 478-520
Indische Bibliothek 490-498
visits to Paris and London 497-515
Sanskrit editions 515-519
protégés and pupils 504-509. *See also* Auguste Böhmer, Elséar de Broglie, Auguste von Buttlar, John Colebooke, Josaiah Dornford, Patrick Johnston, Christian Lassen, Friedrich de la Motte Fouqué, Willem Muilman, Wilhelm von Schütz, George Thomas Smith, Albert de Staël, Albertine de Staël, Auguste de Staël
later relations with FS 522-526
later relations with Ludwig Tieck 526-529
later relations with Goethe 529-536
art lectures in Berlin 536-539
Heine affair 540-546
later works 546-557
Beethoven monument 548-549
Frederick the Great edition 557-561
illness and death 562-563
last will and testament 563-565
publishers. *See* Baldwin, Bauer, Becker, Bruzelius, Cotta, Frölich, Hitzig, Michaelis, Mohr & Zimmer, Murray, Nicolovius, Reimer, Schmid, Tourneisen, Treuttel & Würtz, Unger, Vieweg, Weber, Winter, Zimmer
WORKS (including those edited, translated and prefaced by AWS), 'r' = review, 'p' = poem
   Abendlied für die Entfernte (p) 333
   Abriß vom Studium der classischen Philologie 29, 463

Abriß von den europäischen Verhältnissen der deutschen Litteratur 523, 530
Abschied (p) 442
Adonis (p) 42
Altdeutsche Wälder herausgegeben durch die Brüder Grimm (r) 394, 402
À Madame de Staël après la représentation d'Agar (p) 272
À Madame Unzelmann à son logis (p) 271
Analyse de la Proclamation de Louis XVIII 374
An Bürgers Schatten (p) 42, 176, 177
An die Jungfrau von Orleans (p) 262
An einen Helden (p) 237
An einen Kunstrichter (p) 44
An Frau Händel-Schütz (p) 355
An Friederike Unzelmann als Nina (p) 271
An Friederike Unzelmann bei Uebersendung meiner Gedichte (p) 271
An Friedrich Schlegel (p) 192, 291, 300, 332
An Herrn Professor Heeren in Göttingen 491
An Ida Brun (p) 273
Ankündigung 410, 490
An Schelling (p) 148
Antiquitates Etruscae 460, 464, 553
An Windischmann (p) 450
Aphorismen die Etymologie des Französischen betreffend 488
Ariosto, Orlando Furioso 397
Auf die Taufe eines Negers (p) 327
Aus einer noch ungedruckten historischen Untersuchung über das Lied der Nibelungen 410
Aus Shakespeares Julius Cäsar 66
Berichtigung einiger Mißdeutungen 3, 136, 263, 317, 346, 523, 542

Beschreibung eines…Gefäßes 548
Betrachtungen über die Politik der dänischen Regierung 356, 363
Betrachtungen über Metrik 85
Bhagavat-Gîtâ 447, 481, 486, 504, 516
Blumensträuße italienischer, spanischer und portugiesischer Poesie 9, 204, 214, 479
Bopp: Nalus (r) 490, 493
Brief eines Reisenden aus Lyon 279
Briefe über Poesie, Silbenmaaß und Sprache 66, 84
Briefwechsel 490
Buch der Liebe. Herausgegeben von Dr. Johann Gustav Büsching und Dr. Friedrich Heinrich von der Hagen (r) 394
Bürger [Ueber Bürgers Werke] (r) 3, 84, 127, 147, 171, 173, 174, 175, 176, 400, 531, 533, 543, 554, 571
Comparaison entre la Phèdre de Racine et celle d'Euripide 156, 207, 225, 237, 261, 272, 276, 281, 283, 285, 286, 288, 289, 300, 308, 309, 329, 331, 381, 420, 554, 282
Considérations sur la civilisation en général 267, 268, 269, 297, 403, 475, 479, 564
Corinna auf dem Vorgebirge Miseno 531
Dante's Hölle 66
Das Sonett (p) 148
De geographia Homerica 36, 37, 86, 127, 396, 403, 460, 465
De l'Étymologie en général 401, 405, 408, 475
De l'Origine des Hindous 475, 488, 514, 551
Dépêches et lettres interceptées 371, 375, 377
Der Abschied (p) 331
Der Besuch und Abschied des Wanderers (p) 331

Der Bund der Kirche mit den Künsten (p) 125, 136, 148, 155, 357, 387, 424, 524
Der Dom zu Mailand (p) 254, 300
Der Geliebten (p) 388
Der gestiefelte Kater (r) 114
Der rasende Roland. Eilfter Gesang 111
De Zodiaci antiquitate et origine 553
Die gefangenen Sänger (p) 333
Die Gemälde 121, 124, 125, 126, 127, 129, 136, 142, 147, 148, 156, 157, 159, 160, 161, 164, 254, 344, 524, 531, 588
Die Herabkunft der Göttin Ganga (p) 490, 495
Die Horen (r) 73, 152, 153
Die Huldigung des Rheins (p) 4, 460, 508
Die Kunst der Griechen (p) 111, 119, 149, 151, 152, 156, 332
Die Rheinfahrt (p) 4, 460, 508
Die Schauspielerin Friederike Unzelmann (p) 271
Die Sprachen/Der Wettstreit der Sprachen 111, 117, 156, 157, 158, 159, 530, 581
Die verfehlte Stunde (p) 333
Dramatische Spiele von Pellegrin 574
Ehrenpforte und Triumphbogen für den Theater-Präsidenten von Kotzebue 141, 146, 190, 332, 454, 534, 582
Einleitung in die allgemeine Weltgeschichte 56, 434, 464, 474, 476
Ein schön kurzweilig Fastnachtspiel (p) 179
Elegien aus dem Griechischen 111, 152
Entwurf zu Vorlesungen über die allgemeine Weltgeschichte 464, 476
Epilog (p) 534-535

Erstes Sendschreiben über den Titurel ... von B. J. Docen (r) 394, 399
Essais littéraires et historiques 288, 536, 554
Etwas über William Shakespeare bey Gelegenheit Wilhelm Meisters 66, 99-102
Fragments extraits du porte-feuille d'un solitaire contemplatif 4, 556
Gedichte 147, 258, 332
Gedichte auf Rudolf von Habsburg von Zeitgenossen 410
Gedichte von Gottfried August Bürger (r) 43
Geschichte der Deutschen Sprache und Poesie 6, 464, 469, 474, 475
Geschichte der Griechen und Römer 464, 474
Goethe, Herrmann und Dorothea (r) 73, 137, 141, 151, 173, 531
Goethe, Schriften (r) 44
Herder, Terpsichore (r) 83
Historische literarische und unterhaltende Schriften von Horatio Walpole 126
Hitopadeśa 406, 447, 453, 463, 486, 498, 500, 508, 509, 515, 516, 517, 582
Homers Werke (r) 73, 85, 86, 87, 99, 141, 154, 173, 244, 400, 530, 600
Idées sur l'avenir de la France 374
Idyllen aus dem Griechischen 111
In der Fremde (p) 262
Ion 13, 154, 184, 186, 187, 189, 190, 204, 212, 213, 225, 270, 272, 283, 286, 531, 580
Jakob Necker 388
Joachim Rendorps geheime Nachrichten 60
Johannes in der Wüste (p) 163
Johann von Fiesole 254, 394, 524, 531, 538
Kosmopolit der Kunst und Poesie (p) 2

Kritische Schriften 9, 65, 86, 310, 479, 524, 530, 531, 534, 542, 546, 554
Lacrimas 200
Le Dante, Pétrarque et Boccace 552, 554
Lettre ... sur les chevaux de bronze 195, 385, 405, 554, 555
Lied (p) 188
Lied ('Laue Lüfte') (p) 300
Lob der Tränen (p) 333
Ludovico Ariosto's Rasender Roland, übersetzt von J. D. Gries (r) 394, 397, 399, 400
Mémoire sur l'état de l'Allemagne et sur les moyens d'y former une insurrection nationale 347, 358
Mes Adieux (p) 557
Mir schlug das Herz, es rasselte der Wagen (p) 256
Montbard (p) 300
Morgenbillet (p) 535
Nachschrift des Uebersetzers an Ludwig Tieck 141, 148, 173, 207, 386, 388, 395
Neoptolemus an Diocles 26, 149-151
Niobé et ses enfants 405
Observations sur la critique du Bhagavad-Gîtâ 489
Observations sur la langue et la littérature provençales 446, 467, 554
Observations sur quelques médailles bactriennes , 510
Opuscula 2, 14, 351, 426, 460, 553, 564
Oratio cum magistratum academicum ... deponeret habita 3
Oratio cum rectoris in universitate litteraria Bonnensi munus ... in se susceperit habita 456
Oratio natalibus Friderici Guilelmi III ... habita 457, 538
Pensées détachées 552
Poetische Werke 146, 151, 176, 177, 291, 332, 333, 334

Prichard, Darstellung der Aegyptischen Mythologie 476, 488, 552
Probe einer neuen Uebersetzung von Shakespeare's Werken 93
Proclamations de S. A. R. le Prince-Royal de Suède 365, 366, 371
Prometheus (p) 82, 105, 148, 155
Prometheus (r) 300
Pygmalion (p) 148, 155
Râmâyana 10, 88, 297, 298, 334, 382, 406, 447, 453, 475, 480, 484, 486, 487, 490, 495, 500, 501, 504, 508, 509, 516, 517, 518, 519, 525, 529, 510
Réflexions sur la situation politique du Danemarc 362
Réflexions sur l'état actuel de la Norvège 373, 375
Réflexions sur l'étude des langues asiatiques 487
Remarques sur un article de la Gazette de Leipsick 371
Résumé épigrammatique de l'histoire de nos jours 555
Ritter Blaubart (r) 114
Römische Geschichte von B. G. Niebuhr (r) 33, 312, 386, 394, 397, 402-405, 585
Sämmtliche Werke 2, 222, 418, 564, 565
Salomon Geßner (r) 174, 530
Scenen aus Romeo und Julie von Shakespeare 66, 93, 100
Schauspiele von Don Pedro Calderon de la Barca 198
Schreiben an Goethe über einige Arbeiten in Rom lebender Künstler 255, 256, 531
Schreiben an Herrn Buchhändler Reimer 92, 527
Selbstbeschreibung 3, 31, 33, 52, 54, 146, 346
Shakespeare's dramatische Werke 91, 95, 102, 175
Soltau's Don Quixote (r) 111, 148
Sonette, Von A. W. Schlegel (p) 111

Sonett I, II, III (p) 333
Spanisches Theater 198, 199
Specimen novae typographiae Indicae 499
Sprache der Liebe (p) 333
Staël, Corinne ou l'Italie (r) 251, 277, 278
Sui quattro cavalli della basilica di S. Marco in Venezia (r) 394
Sur le système continental et sur ses rapports avec la Suède 360-361
Szenen aus Shakespeare. Der Sturm 66
Tableau de l'état politique et moral de l'Empire français en 1813 554
Thränen und Küße (p) 331
Tristan (p) 175, 214, 334, 522
Über das Mittelalter 203, 205, 409
Über dramatische Kunst und Litteratur (Vienna Lectures) 2, 3, 5, 6, 23, 90, 101, 168, 197, 202, 209, 212, 225, 227, 238, 240, 285, 287, 288, 289, 290, 292, 299, 302-313, 304, 308, 317, 319, 320, 325, 329, 332, 339, 343, 345, 346, 357, 381, 382, 385, 391, 394, 396, 399, 414, 417, 420-425, 428, 429, 430, 432, 446, 451, 494, 513, 528, 529, 530, 542, 553, 303
Über Zeichnungen zu Gedichten und John Flaxmans Umrisse 111, 129, 148, 157, 164-166, 186, 501, 531, 510
Ueber das Nibelungen-Lied 410
Ueber das spanische Theater 198
Ueber das Verhältniß der schönen Kunst zur Natur 300, 531
Ueber den Charakter und die Schriften der Frau von Staël 420
Ueber den gegenwärtigen Zustand der Indischen Philologie 406, 452, 487, 490, 491
Ueber die Vermählungsfeyer Sr. K.K. Majestät Franz I. (p) 300

Ueber Litteratur, Kunst und Geist des Zeitalters 197, 202
Ueber Napoleon Buonaparte und den Kronprinzen von Schweden 371
Ueber Shakespeares Romeo und Julia 66, 74, 93, 103-105, 149, 161, 173, 311, 530
Umriße, entworfen auf einer Reise durch die Schweiz 241, 280
Verzeichniss einer von Eduard d'Alton ... hinterlassenen Gemälde-Sammlung 549
Volksmährchen (r) 73
Vollständiges Verzeichniß meiner zur Allg. Lit. Zeit. beygetragenen Rezensionen 111
Vorläufiger Entwurf zu einer neuen Ausgabe der Werke Friedrichs des Großen 557-558
Vorlesungen über das akademische Studium 6, 28, 464
Vorlesungen über Encyclopädie 202, 205, 216-219, 458
Vorlesungen über philosophische Kunstlehre 128, 166, 167
Vorlesungen über schöne Literatur und Kunst (Berlin Lectures) 132, 148, 173, 176, 179, 182, 190, 197, 198, 202-220, 225, 236, 251, 264, 271, 272, 273, 286, 301, 308, 318, 355, 395, 397, 404, 409, 411, 413, 417, 473, 535, 537, 552, 565, 575, 599
Vorlesungen über Theorie und allgemeine Geschichte der bildenden Künste 464
Vorlesungen über Theorie und Geschichte der bildenden Künste 202, 539
Werke (Bruzelius) 304
Wiedersehen (p) 333
Wieland, Lucian (r) 44
Wilsons Wörterbuch (r) 490
Winckelmann's Werke (r) 33, 251, 252, 254, 394, 398, 400, 403, 404, 467

Würde der Frauen (p) 82, 137
Zueignung des Trauerspiels Romeo und Julia (p) 106-109
Zuschrift (p) 332, 333
Schlegel, Carl August (1761-1789): AWS's older brother 24-26, 42, 149, 150, 332, 479, 489
SCHLEGEL, Caroline, née Michaelis (1763-1809): woman of letters, AWS's first wife 17, 26, 31, 32, 34, 41, 50, 51, 52, 54, 55, 56, 57, 58, 59, 61, 62, 64, 66, 67, 68, 69, 70, 76, 77, 78, 80, 81, 89, 93, 96, 97, 101, 102, 103, 104, 105, 109, 110, 111, 115, 117, 119, 121, 122, 123, 125, 126, 128, 129, 131, 132, 134, 135, 137, 138, 139, 141, 142, 143, 144, 145, 146, 148, 159, 161, 165, 169, 170, 171, 172, 177, 178, 183, 185, 188, 189, 191, 192, 207, 208, 221, 222, 224, 237, 240, 260, 294, 299, 301, 311, 316, 318, 324, 332, 380, 387, 528, 548, 569, 574, 577, 587, 588, 591. *See also* Böhmer and Schelling
Schlegel, Charlotte (1757-1853): Moritz Schlegel's wife 24, 550
Schlegel, Christoph (1613-1678): pastor, AWS's great-great-grandfather 11, 12, 589
SCHLEGEL, Dorothea (von), née Brendel (Veronica) Mendelssohn (1764-1839): novelist and translator, FS's wife 26, 110, 111, 115, 122, 123, 132, 133, 134, 135, 136, 137, 138, 140, 142, 145, 151, 154, 169, 170, 172, 177, 178, 183, 188, 190, 192, 193, 223, 276, 281, 291, 296, 297, 315, 330, 372, 380, 388, 431, 432, 436, 505, 523, 525, 526, 527, 529, 589, 591, 592. *See also* Veit
  works cited
    Corinne 223, 589
    Florentin 138, 589
Schlegel, Johan Frederik Wilhelm (1765-1836): jurist, AWS Danish cousin, writes on continental blockade 15, 360, 589
SCHLEGEL, Johann Adolf: pastor, poet, translator, AWS's father 13, 14, 16, 17, 18, 19, 20, 21, 22, 23, 24, 26, 27, 28, 29, 30, 31, 33, 34, 35, 40, 41, 51, 53, 62, 68, 89, 149, 150, 157, 158, 302, 323, 324, 343, 370, 375, 393, 463, 506, 513, 525, 580, 589, 590, 591, 592
Schlegel, Johann August (1731-1776): pastor 590
Schlegel, Johann August Adolph (1790-1840): classical scholar, Moritz's son, AWS's nephew 24, 526, 550, 590
Schlegel, Johann Elias (1664-1718): AWS's great-grandfather 12
Schlegel, Johann Elias (1719-1749): dramatist, translator and critic 13, 14, 16, 79-80, 91, 186, 284
Schlegel, Johann Friedrich (1689-1748): jurist, AWS's grandfather 11-13, 589, 590
SCHLEGEL, (Johann) Friedrich (von) (1772-1829): critic, philosopher, AWS younger brother and youngest Schlegel sibling 1, 6, 7, 9, 10, 12, 13, 16, 17, 18, 19, 21, 24, 26, 27, 28, 29, 30, 42, 49, 50, 51, 52, 54, 55, 58, 59, 60, 61, 62, 63, 64, 65, 66, 67, 68, 69, 70, 71, 72, 73, 76, 77, 78, 79, 80, 81, 82, 83, 84, 85, 87, 88, 92, 93, 94, 99, 100, 103, 104, 105, 110, 111, 112, 113, 114, 115, 116, 117, 118, 119, 120, 121, 123, 125, 126, 128, 129, 132, 133, 134, 135, 136, 137, 138, 140, 145, 146, 147, 148, 151, 152, 155, 156, 157, 159, 160, 161, 163, 166, 169, 170, 171, 172, 173, 174, 177, 178, 179, 183, 187, 188, 189, 190, 191, 192, 193, 194, 195, 196, 197, 198, 201, 202, 203, 206, 210, 216, 219, 222, 223, 224, 225, 231, 239, 243, 244, 247, 248, 250, 254, 256, 261, 262, 263, 264, 268, 275, 276, 278, 280, 284, 285, 291, 295, 296, 297, 298, 299, 300, 301, 302, 303, 315, 322, 323, 331, 332, 335, 336, 337, 340, 341, 346, 357, 372, 375, 379, 380, 381, 382, 383, 395, 396, 398, 404, 405, 406, 410, 411, 412, 419, 428, 429, 430, 431, 432, 433, 434, 435, 436, 437, 439, 440, 441, 442, 443, 448, 449, 453, 456, 473, 475, 476, 478, 479, 483, 485, 486, 492, 495, 503, 505, 506, 518, 522, 523, 524, 525, 526, 528, 529, 531, 532, 533, 535, 537, 542, 545, 556, 172, 410

childhood, youth and early manhood 15, 24, 27, 29, 42, 51, 59, 323, 524-525
early literary career 62-64, 65, 80-83
Berlin and Jena 76, 109
in Jena circle 113-147, 171-172
collaboration with AWS on *Athenaeum* 115-121
liaison with Dorothea, *Lucinde* 115, 132-135
Alarcos fiasco 190
in Paris and Cologne, Sanskrit studies 223, 244, 247, 264, 275, 291-292, 296-299, 443
conversion 296
political career in Vienna 295, 315, 335-337, 357, 375, 380-381
Deutsches Museum 357, 395, 410-411
delegate in Frankfurt 430-435
last years in Vienna 250
Concordia 432, 434
break with AWS 522-526
death 525-526
major works cited
    Alarcos 13, 178, 189, 190, 200, 592
    Athenaeum 65, 73, 75, 82, 83, 90, 92, 109, 110, 111, 115, 116, 117, 118, 119, 120, 121, 122, 125, 126, 129, 132, 133, 134, 135, 136, 137, 138, 139, 140, 141, 142, 146, 147, 148, 149, 151, 152, 154, 155, 156, 157, 159, 163, 164, 166, 169, 172, 176, 178, 179, 181, 183, 188, 195, 204, 206, 207, 208, 236, 251, 258, 291, 308, 332, 334, 357, 395, 396, 399, 480, 492, 524, 526, 530, 531, 532, 534, 574, 577, 591, 600
    Charakteristiken und Kritiken 86, 133, 147, 169, 171, 172, 173, 236, 172
    Concordia 431, 432, 434, 493, 522, 525, 592
    Deutsches Museum 202, 205, 331, 345, 357, 358, 379, 395, 396, 397, 399, 401, 408, 410, 411, 412, 413, 410
    Europa 166, 178, 183, 192, 193, 194, 195, 196, 197, 198, 202, 206, 210, 212, 219, 223, 231, 236, 254, 278, 284, 285, 291, 298, 308, 340, 341, 396, 434, 592
    Gespräch über die Poesie 136, 142, 148
    Lucinde 117, 126, 132, 133, 134, 138, 140, 141, 190, 191, 380, 526, 589, 591
    Ueber die Sprache und Weisheit der Indier 26, 247, 264, 292, 297, 300, 303, 304, 323, 332, 381, 382, 406, 476, 491, 495, 523, 592
relations with AWS 6, 21, 52, 54, 60-62, 66-67, 73, 84, 93, 103-104, 115-121, 152-153, 178, 192, 262, 275, 291, 323, 337, 346, 379, 380, 398, 429, 433, 435, 437, 439-441, 448, 456, 475-476, 479, 483, 485-486, 506, 519, 522-526, 535
Schlegel, Johann Heinrich (1726-1780): translator and historian in Copenhagen, AWS's uncle 13, 14, 15, 17, 91, 186, 589, 590-591
Schlegel, Johann Karl Fürchtegott (Karl) (1758-1831): jurist, AWS's older brother 21, 24, 34, 251, 371, 550, 591
SCHLEGEL, Johanna Christiane Erdmuthe, née Hübsch (1735-1811): AWS's mother 18, 23, 589, 591
Schlegel, Julie (d. 1838): Karl Schlegel's wife 24, 270, 326, 343
Schlegel, Karl August Moritz (Moritz) (1756-1826): pastor and superintendent, AWS older brother 21, 24, 27, 30, 68, 371, 375, 380, 506, 524, 525, 526, 550, 590, 591
Schlegel, Martin(us) (1581-1640): AWS's great-great-great grandfather 11, 592
Schlegel, Rebekka, née Wilke (1695-1736): AWS's grandmother 12, 592
Schlegel, Sophie Karoline Eleutherie von, née Paulus (1791-1847): AWS's second wife 72, 137, 435, 436, 437,

438, 439, 440, 441, 442, 446, 564, 585, 588-589
Schleiermacher, Friedrich Daniel Ernst (1768-1834): theologian 99, 110, 111, 113, 114, 116, 122, 133, 135, 136, 138, 140, 142, 178, 179, 181, 191, 199, 200, 209, 224, 245, 302, 316, 399, 431, 446, 461, 527, 531, 536, 537, 591, 592-593, 599
Schlichtegroll, Friedrich (1765-1822): biographer, compiler of the *Nekrolog* 16, 17, 19, 24, 31, 35
Schlözer, August Ludwig von (1735-1809): history professor at Göttingen 32, 58, 60, 464, 465
Schmid, Johann Wilhelm (n.d.): publisher in Hanover 37
Schmidt, Heinrich (1779-1857): actor and producer, attends AWS's lectures in Jena 129
Schmidt (von Werneuchen), Friedrich Wilhelm August (1766-1829): minor poet, parodied by Goethe and the Romantics 41
Schönborn: Austrian counts 306
Schopenhauer, Arthur (1788-1860): philosopher 481, 518
Schröder, Friedrich Ludwig (1744-1816): dramatist and actor 30, 301
Schubert, Franz (1797-1828), composer sets AWS's poems to music 333
Schubert, Gotthilf Heinrich (von) (1780-1860): nature philosopher 303, 304
Schulze, Johannes (1786-1869): official in Prussian ministry of education 455, 497, 503, 504, 525, 536, 537, 561
Schumann, Clara, née Wieck (1819-1896): musician and composer 562
Schumann, Johann Daniel (1714-1787): rector of the Lyceum in Hanover 29
Schumann, Robert (1810-1856): composer 327, 562
Schütz, Christian Gottfried (1747-1832): professor and editor 68, 72, 73, 83, 119, 127, 128, 140, 141, 167, 188, 593
Schütz, Wilhelm von (1776-1847): dramatist, protégé of AWS 154, 180, 186, 191, 200, 201, 207, 209, 224, 292

Schwarzenberg: Austrian princely family 306, 328, 368
Scott, Sir Walter (1771-1832): poet and novelist 423, 425
Seckendorf, Leo von (1775-1809): Austrian writer, editor of *Prometheus* 202, 205, 280, 283, 291, 299, 313
Sedgwick, Adam (1785-1873): geologist 241, 503
Seneca, L. Annaeus 312, 448
SHAKESPEARE, William (1564-1616) 3, 5, 8, 13, 14, 15, 17, 19, 22, 40, 42, 46, 47, 60, 64, 66, 68, 73, 74, 76, 80, 81, 83, 86, 87, 88, 89, 90, 91, 92, 93, 94, 95, 96, 97, 98, 99, 100, 101, 102, 103, 104, 109, 112, 113, 114, 115, 117, 119, 122, 126, 129, 137, 140, 149, 152, 156, 164, 168, 171, 173, 175, 176, 182, 184, 196, 198, 199, 200, 201, 202, 206, 207, 213, 225, 236, 244, 261, 271, 278, 286, 287, 288, 292, 300, 301, 308, 309, 310, 311, 312, 318, 319, 332, 334, 344, 372, 376, 377, 382, 385, 396, 409, 423, 424, 425, 427, 431, 451, 457, 461, 466, 467, 478, 479, 485, 487, 495, 496, 527, 528, 529, 534, 542, 545, 553, 564, 568, 571, 573, 578, 579, 582, 588, 590, 596, 597, 598, 599, 600, 601

plays cited
A Midsummer Night's Dream 47, 91, 93, 94, 99, 310, 311, 560, 598
As You Like It 91, 96, 129
Hamlet 30, 59, 60, 62, 64, 80, 91, 93, 96, 100, 102, 123, 287, 301, 311, 373, 580
Julius Caesar 14, 91, 93, 96, 265
1 & 2 King Henry IV 91, 528
King Henry VIII
  Baudissin's version of 527
King John 91, 96, 129, 313, 376, 528
King Lear 90, 171, 287, 311, 318
King Richard II 91, 129, 313, 528
King Richard III 91, 184, 244, 310, 318
Love's Labour's Lost
  Tieck's version of 527

Macbeth 38, 46, 90, 137, 171, 176, 287, 300, 301, 309, 311, 332, 528, 571, 597
Othello 90, 171, 301, 318, 427
Romeo and Juliet 60, 66, 74, 77, 91, 92, 93, 94, 96, 97, 99, 100, 103, 104, 105, 106, 107, 148, 149, 161, 172, 173, 278, 287, 311
The Merchant of Venice 91, 96, 129
Sheridan, Richard Brinsley (1751-1816): playwright 390
Sickingen, Franz, count (1760-1834): Austrian diplomat 20, 306, 351, 357, 359
Silvestre de Sacy, Antoine Isaac, baron (1758-1838): orientalist, professor of Arabic in Paris 480, 491, 498, 551, 552, 571
Simrock, Karl (1802-1876): German scholar, pupil of AWS's at Bonn 409, 467, 469
Sismondi, Jean-Charles-Léonard Simonde de (1773-1842): Swiss historian, in Coppet circle 245, 246, 248, 249, 252, 253, 254, 289, 295, 307, 318, 325, 332, 341, 384, 387, 390, 396, 397, 414, 426, 593
Smith, George Thomas (n.d.): young Englishman whom AWS tutors in Göttingen 35, 43
Solger, Karl Wilhelm Ferdinand (1780-1819): professor of philosophy 209, 210, 425, 432
Solms-Laubach, Friedrich zu, count (1769-1822): Kurator of Bonn university 446, 449, 455, 469, 497
Solon 461
Soltau, Dietrich Wihelm (1745-1827): translator of Cervantes 111, 148
Sömmering, Samuel Thomas (1755-1830): physician 55, 56, 57, 231
Sophocles 187, 205, 208, 210, 213, 284, 286, 287, 303, 309, 312
 Oedipus in Colonos 213, 287
Southey, Robert (1774-1843): poet 423
Souza, dom Pedro de Souza e Holstein (1781-1850): Portuguese nobleman and admirer of Madame de Staël 238, 252, 257, 273, 274
Spee, Friedrich von (1591-1635): poet 216
Spenser, Edmund (1552-1599): poet 311
Stadion, Johann Philipp von, count Stadion-Warthausen (1763-1824): Austrian diplomat and statesman 294, 301, 335, 601
STAËL-HOLSTEIN, Albert de (1792-1813): Erik Magnus von Staël-Holstein's and Germaine de Staël's younger son 131, 235, 240, 249, 253, 271, 272, 273, 274, 279, 280, 293, 295, 314, 315, 326, 344, 347, 349, 356, 367, 369, 387, 435, 464, 504, 507, 508, 593-594
Staël-Holstein, Albertine de (1797-1838). *See* Broglie
STAËL-HOLSTEIN, Anne Louise Germaine de, née Necker, baroness (Madame de Staël) (1766-1817): woman of letters
 early life and career 193, 225-229
 exile 230
 visits Germany 230-235
 meets Schlegel 234-240
 returns to Coppet with AWS 239-240
 Coppet group 244-249
 first Italian journey 249-260
 in Coppet and France 264-266, 273-276, 280-281
 tragic roles 269-272
 Corinne 276-279
 journey to Vienna 293-295, 314-318
 return to Coppet and France 318-325, 341-344
 De l'Allemagne 325-330, 337-340
 flight to Germany, Austria, Russia and Sweden 345-355
 political activity in Sweden 355-364
 in England 366-368, 376-377
 return to France 377, 381
 second Italian journey 383-388
 return to Coppet and Paris 389-391
 death 393

major works cited
- *Agar dans le désert* 270, 272
- *Considérations sur les principaux événements* 414, 415, 420, 426
- *Corinne* 223, 238, 239, 249, 250, 251, 252, 253, 254, 258, 260, 264, 273, 276, 277, 278, 315, 328, 338, 384, 418, 436, 505, 531, 538, 589, 595
- *De la littérature* 338
- *De l'Allemagne* 3, 5, 230, 231, 234, 235, 238, 250, 260, 288, 289, 290, 292, 293, 295, 305, 316, 317, 318, 319, 320, 321, 325, 326, 328, 329, 330, 334, 337, 338, 339, 340, 346, 350, 352, 368, 373, 374, 376, 377, 394, 396, 414, 422, 425, 437, 544, 585, 595
- *De l'Esprit des traductions* 385, 595
- *Delphine* 229, 231, 232, 595
- *Dix Années d'exil* 234, 249, 326, 328, 361, 426, 595
- *Réflexions sur le suicide* 341, 345, 361, 362, 595

relations with AWS 3, 4, 5, 7, 8, 9, 10, 15, 21, 22, 189, 202, 235-240, 244-249, 264-265, 270-273, 290, 292, 339, 359, 366, 378, 385, 389, 391, 392, 414, 415-416, 420, 426, 435, 437, 441, 485, 513, 541, 544, 561

short biography 594-595

STAËL-HOLSTEIN, Auguste de (1790-1827): Erik Magnus von Staël-Holstein and Germaine de Staël's elder son 145, 211, 235, 243, 249, 264, 269, 273, 274, 276, 294, 325, 327, 329, 344, 349, 356, 367, 375, 377, 384, 386, 387, 415, 417, 419, 420, 421, 426, 438, 454, 455, 458, 463, 479, 500, 501, 508, 513, 585, 594

Staël-Holstein, Erik Magnus von (1749-1802): Swedish diplomat, marries Germaine Necker 226, 570, 593, 594

Steffens, Henrik (1773-1845): nature philosopher, in Wars of Liberation 135, 136, 348, 349, 360, 362, 365, 366, 581, 596

Stein, Charlotte von (1742-1827): Goethe's friend and inspiration 109

Stein, Friedrich Karl, Freiherr vom und zum (baron) (1757-1831): Prussian statesman and minister 339, 348, 350, 351, 352, 358, 359, 361, 362, 366, 433, 444, 567, 596

Stein zum Altenstein, Freiherr vom (baron) (1770-1840): Prussian minister of education 130, 442, 445, 446, 455, 457, 497, 499, 516, 517, 581, 596, 615, 624, 510

Stendhal, Henri Beyle known as (1783-1842): novelist and essayist 245, 249, 288, 310, 389, 417, 425

Stolberg, Friedrich Leopold von, count (1750-1819): poet and translator 38, 50, 163, 244, 249, 469, 571, 599, 600

Stoll, Joseph Ludwig (1778-1815): co-editor with Seckendorff of the periodical *Prometheus* 202

Stourdza, Alexander (1791-1854): Russian official, author of memorandum on German universities 454

Stransky, Christina von, née von Schleich (1785-1862): FS's 'mystical love' 522

Strauss, David Friedrich (1808-1874): theologian, writes memoir on AWS 457

Strodtmann, Adolf (1829-1879): writer and translator, editor of Bürger, first biographer of Heine 541, 543, 544

Stuart, James (1741-1815): British general in India 25

Suard, Jean-Baptiste-Antoine (1732-1817): permanent secretary to French Academy 230, 274

Suchtelen, Jan Pieter van, count (1751-1836): Russian general and diplomat 352, 354, 357

Sulzer, Johann Georg (1720-1779): normative aesthetician 29

Suremain, Jean Baptiste de (1762-1835): French general in Swedish service 365, 369

Sussex, Augustus Frederick duke of (1773-1843): President of the Royal Society when AWS meets him 22, 510

Talleyrand-(Périgord), Charles-Maurice de, prince of Bénévent (1754-1838): statesman, ambassador in London when AWS meets him 381, 390, 511

Taschenbuch zum geselligen Vergnügen 89

Tasso, Torquato (1544-1595): poet 44, 123, 214, 334, 479, 531, 576

Tatter, Georg (1757-1805): tutor to British royal princes at Göttingen 52

Tchernicheff, Alexander (1779-1857): Russian general in Napoleonic wars 371

Ternite, Wilhelm (1786-1871): painter and engraver 538

Tettenborn, Friedrich Karl von (1778-1845): Russian general 348, 369, 594

Thalia 45, 60, 588

Theodoric 413

Thielo, Johann Gerhard Wilhelm (1735-1796): painter 19

Thomson, James (1700-1748): poet and dramatist 15, 91, 591

Thornton, Sir Edward (1766-1852): British diplomat 368

Thorwaldsen, Bertel (1770-1844): Danish neo-classical sculptor 255, 558

A Thousand and One Nights 481, 551
  AWS essay on 555

Thucydides 37

Thümmel, Moritz August von (1736-1817): novelist 43

Tibullus 152, 579, 600

Ticknor, George (1791-1871): American man of letters 234, 379, 392, 394, 431, 458, 561

Tieck, then Alberti, Agnes (1802-1880): Ludwig Tieck's younger daughter and his executor 526

Tieck, Amalia, née Alberti (1769-1837): Ludwig Tieck's wife and the mother of Dorothea and Agnes 137

Tieck, Dorothea (1799-1841): Ludwig Tieck's elder daughter, translator 97, 137, 372, 526, 527, 596-597, 598

TIECK, Friedrich (1776-1851): sculptor, Ludwig Tieck's and Sophie Tieck's brother 7, 17, 113, 139, 144, 165, 170, 179, 185, 186, 204, 214, 222, 243, 256, 259, 283, 301, 302, 320, 321, 323, 324, 331, 386, 388, 405, 448, 462, 526, 537, 549, 558, 563, 569, 583, 598, 325

TIECK, Ludwig (1773-1853): poet, dramatist, translator 10, 17, 28, 39, 41, 42, 49, 55, 62, 66, 69, 73, 77, 78, 90, 92, 93, 95, 96, 102, 104, 110, 111, 113, 114, 115, 116, 117, 118, 120, 121, 122, 124, 134, 135, 136, 137, 138, 141, 142, 143, 144, 145, 146, 147, 148, 156, 159, 160, 162, 164, 169, 173, 178, 179, 180, 181, 182, 183, 184, 185, 186, 189, 191, 192, 199, 200, 201, 203, 205, 206, 213, 222, 224, 239, 241, 250, 256, 262, 280, 301, 310, 322, 323, 324, 332, 333, 334, 335, 342, 348, 378, 385, 391, 395, 408, 411, 431, 451, 464, 479, 485, 526, 527, 528, 529, 531, 533, 537, 542, 545, 553, 560, 563, 564, 568, 569, 572, 577, 586, 591, 546, 592, 596, 597, 598, 599, 600, 602

  major works cited
    Alt-Englisches Theater 527, 598
    Der Sturm 73, 93, 102
    Franz Sternbalds Wanderungen 121, 162, 597
    Herzensergießungen eines kunstliebenden Klosterbruders 74, 95, 114, 121, 173, 597, 599, 600
    Minnelieder aus dem Schwäbischen Zeitalter 182, 206, 408, 411, 597
    Phantasus 332, 348, 527, 598
    Shakespeare's dramatische Werke 528, 598
    Shakspeare's Vorschule 527, 596, 598
    Volksmährchen 73, 114, 597
    William Lovell 114, 134, 597

TIECK, Sophie (1775-1833): writer, sister of Ludwig and Friedrich Tieck 10, 113, 138, 142, 179, 180, 182, 183, 184, 185, 209, 222, 223, 242, 243, 250, 251, 252, 256, 259, 260, 263, 275, 291, 292, 301, 307, 320, 324, 350, 386, 416, 521, 522, 526, 569, 597, 598
   works cited
      Egidio und Isabella 222, 263, 598
      Flore und Blanscheflur 252, 256, 320, 386, 521, 522, 598
Tiedge, Christoph August (1752-1841): didactic poet 231
Tilly, Johann Tserclaes, count of (1559-1632): Imperial general 365
Tipu Sultan (1750-1799): ruler of Mysore 25, 588
Tischbein, Johann Friedrich August (1750-1812): painter 61, 170, 324
Titian, Tiziano Vecellio called (1485/90-1576): painter 49
Der jüngere Titurel 400, 564
Tod, James (1782-1835): colonel in Indian Army, oriental scholar 489, 511, 519
Tottie and Compton: London bankers 420
T(o)urneisen: Paris publisher 281
Toynbee, George (1812-1841), attends AWS's lectures in Bonn 454, 464, 465, 466, 470
Treuttel & Würtz: publishers in Paris and London 10, 498, 519
Turgot, Anne Robert Jacques (1727-1781): statesman, economist and 'philosophe' 267
Turner, Joseph Mallord William (1775-1851): painter 460
Tychsen, Thomas Christian (1758-1834): orientalist and theologian at Göttingen 217

Uginet, Joseph Eugène (1771-1853): secretary and factotum to Madame de Staël 294, 344, 346, 349, 594, 595
Ulrich von Lichtenstein (ca. 1200-1275) 408
Unger, Friederike Helene (1751-1813): publisher 112, 184, 318, 332, 527

Unger, Johann Friedrich (1753-1804): printer and publisher 8, 95, 99, 112, 121, 171, 184, 243, 529, 598, 599
Unzelmann, Friederike (1760-1815): actress in Berlin, much admired by AWS 123, 184, 187, 189, 202, 221, 271

Varnhagen von Ense, Karl August (1785-1858): diplomat, essayist 209, 289, 348, 362, 369, 374, 378, 535, 599
Varnhagen von Ense, Rahel (née Levin) (1771-1833): salonnière in Berlin 113, 208, 234, 289, 362, 369, 374, 378, 535, 578, 597, 599
Vasari, Giorgio (1511-1574): painter and biographer 160
Veit, Johannes (Jonas) (1790-1854), painter 281, 431, 589
Veit, Philipp (1793-1877): painter, son of Simon Veit and Dorothea Mendelssohn, stepson of FS 137, 163, 281, 297, 336, 348, 370, 431, 436, 575, 599
Veit, Simon (1754-1819): banker, first husband of Dorothea Mendelssohn and father of Johannes and Philipp 115, 589, 599
Veronese, Paolo (1528-1588): painter 125, 162
Victoria, queen of Great Britain and Ireland (1819-1901) 4, 470, 549
Vieweg, Friedrich (1761-1835): publisher (of the first part of the *Athenaeum*) 116, 120, 133, 147
Villers, Charles de (1765-1816): French scholar of German literature and philosophy 228, 230, 231
Virgil 12, 35-36, 40, 49, 212, 267, 473, 579
Voght, Caspar von, baron (1752-1839): Hamburg merchant, traveller, philanthropist, in circle of Mme de Staël 205, 208, 318, 319, 322, 325, 337
Voigt, Christoph Gottlob (1743-1819): official and minister in Weimar 15, 71, 127, 131, 132, 221
Volney, Constantin-François de Chasseboeuf, comte de (1757-1820): historian, politician, orientalist 258

Voltaire, François-Marie Arouet known as (1764-1778): dramatist, philosopher, historian 16, 187, 191, 199, 242, 268, 270, 271, 272, 275, 281, 283, 284, 303, 305, 316, 404
Voss, Abraham (1785-1847): classical scholar and translator, the son of Johann Heinrich Voss 318, 528, 600
Voss, Gisela, countess, née von Berg (1780-1865): friend and correspondent of AWS 224, 263
Voss, Heinrich (1779-1822): classical scholar and translator, the son of Johann Heinrich Voss 318, 528, 600
Voss, Johann Heinrich (1751-1826): poet, classical scholar, translator 29, 37, 38, 44, 46, 73, 79, 85, 86, 87, 88, 95, 99, 111, 117, 141, 154, 157, 158, 173, 176, 224, 244, 261, 263, 300, 317, 318, 324, 347, 376, 385, 400, 426, 436, 485, 495, 523, 528, 534, 536, 542, 543, 545, 571, 599-600
Vulpius, Christiane (1765-1816): Goethe's mistress, then his wife 78

Wackenroder, Wilhelm Heinrich (1773-1798): jurist 49, 66, 69, 74, 90, 95, 114, 117, 124, 144, 159, 160, 162, 163, 169, 173, 203, 241, 280, 324, 573, 597, 599, 600
Wallenstein, Albrecht von, duke of Friedland (1584-1634): Imperial general 365
Wallis, George Augustus (1770-1847): landscape painter 254
Walpole, Horace, later earl of Orford (1717-1797): man of letters, politician, connoisseur 126
Waltharius 214
Warton, Thomas (1726-1790): poet, historian and antiquary 214
Webb, captain (n.d.): officer in Indian survey 484
Weber, Eduard (1791-1868): bookseller and publisher in Bonn 28, 102, 281, 360, 490
Weckherlin, Georg Rudolph (1584-1653): poet 216

Wehrden, Heinrich von (n.d.): AWS coachman and domestic servant in Bonn 451, 459, 462, 563
Weidmann: Leipzig publisher 564
Welcker, Friedrich Gottlieb (1784-1868): classicist, AWS colleague in Bonn 423, 426, 437, 450, 452, 454, 455, 456, 460, 466, 467, 535, 550, 562, 600
Wellington, Arthur Wellesley, duke of (1769-1852): commander of Allied troops in Paris when Madame de Staël knows him, former prime minister when AWS meets him 59, 379, 381, 387, 388, 392, 511
Wendt, Amadeus (1783-1836): professor of philosophy in Leipzig, writer, editor 534, 536
Werner, Friedrich Ludwig Zacharias (1768-1823): dramatist 156, 200, 269, 321, 322, 323, 325, 326, 328, 330, 335, 338, 340, 343, 411, 427, 435, 533, 595, 600-601
  works
    Attila 321, 330, 340, 413, 601
    Der vierundzwanzigste Februar 325, 427, 601
    Martin Luther 321, 601
de Wette, Wilhelm Martin Leberecht (1780-1849): theology professor in Berlin 454
Whewell, William (1794-1866): polymath, professor at Cambridge and Master of Trinity College 503
Wieland, Christoph Martin (1733-1813): poet, novelist 13, 18, 43, 44, 46, 47, 48, 78, 88, 92, 93, 94, 99, 100, 117, 134, 151, 168, 191, 216, 217, 232, 236, 301, 315, 334, 530, 601
Wilberforce, William (1749-1833): slavery abolitionist 327, 417
Wilken, Friedrich (1777-1840): professor of history in Heidelberg and Berlin 383, 385, 395, 396
Wilke, Rebekka. *See* Schlegel
Wilkins, Charles (1749-1836): grammarian of Sanskrit 407, 453, 457, 497, 498, 504, 511, 519

William IV, king of Great Britain, Ireland and Hanover (1765-1837): receives AWS 513
William V. *See* Orange
Wilmans, Friedrich (1764-1830): publisher 193, 195
Wilson, Horace Hayman (1786-1760): Sanskrit scholar, professor at Oxford 448, 485, 486, 487, 490, 493, 515, 534
Winckelmann, Johann Joachim (1717-1768): art historian 14, 28, 32, 33, 39, 45, 51, 64, 90, 124, 125, 160, 168, 169, 174, 197, 198, 217, 218, 219, 250, 251, 253, 254, 255, 260, 261, 269, 277, 283, 309, 344, 394, 397, 400, 401, 403, 404, 405, 467, 472, 539, 557, 601
Windischmann, Friedrich Heinrich Hugo (1811-1861): Sanskrit scholar, pupil of AWS's in Bonn 471
Windischmann, Karl Joseph Hieronymus (1775-1839): physician and philosopher, AWs colleague in Bonn 435, 440, 449, 452, 466, 469, 495, 524, 526, 602
Winter, Christian Friedrich (1773-1858): publisher 304, 554
Wolf, Friedrich August (1759-1824): classical scholar, professor in Halle and Berlin 85, 87, 88, 210, 247, 312, 452, 519
  Prolegomena ad Homerum 85, 312
Wolfram von Eschenbach 216, 400
  Titurel 216, 394, 400, 408, 409
Wollstonecraft, Mary (1759-1797): novelist, defender of women's rights 138
Wolper, Amalie (n.d.): Moritz's daughter, AWS's niece 550, 563
Wolper, Hermann (n.d.): AWS's great-nephew 463

Wolzogen, Caroline von, née von Lengefeld (1763-1847): novelist 183
Wood, Robert (1717-1771): Homeric scholar 37
Wordsworth, William (1770-1850): poet, meets AWS in 1829 105, 378, 423, 424, 425
Wrbna-Freudenthal, Rudolf, count (1761-1832): high court official in Vienna 306
Wyss, Johann Rudolf (1782-1830): Swiss writer, editor 280

Young, Edward (1683-1765): poet and dramatist 15, 18

Zachariae, Karl Salomo (1769-1843): law professor in Heidelberg 440
Zeitgenossen, AWS contribution to 380, 388
Zeitung für die elegante Welt, AWS contributions to 187, 189, 202
Zeitung für Einsiedler, AWS contribution to 292, 317, 568, 602
Zelter, Karl Friedrich (1758-1832): composer, corresponded with Goethe 234, 532
Zeuner, Fräulein von (n.d.): former lady-in-waiting at the court in Berlin 325
Zimmer, Johann Georg (1777-1853): publisher 8, 292, 298, 317, 320, 331, 333, 602
Zimmermann, Johann Georg (1728-1795): physician to Frederick the Great, author of *On Solitude* 35
Zinzendorf: German noble family 295
Zoëga, Johann Georg (1755-1809): Danish archaeologist 253
Zumpe, Gustav Adolph (1793-1854): engraver, portrait of AWS 393

This book need not end here...

At Open Book Publishers, we are changing the nature of the traditional academic book. The title you have just read will not be left on a library shelf, but will be accessed online by hundreds of readers each month across the globe. We make all our books free to read online so that students, researchers and members of the public who can't afford a printed edition can still have access to the same ideas as you.

Our digital publishing model also allows us to produce online supplementary material, including extra chapters, reviews, links and other digital resources. Find *The Life of August Wilhelm Schlegel* on our website to access its online extras. Please check this page regularly for ongoing updates, and join the conversation by leaving your own comments:

http://www.openbookpublishers.com/isbn/9781909254954

If you enjoyed this book, and feel that research like this should be available to all readers, regardless of their income, please think about donating to us. Our company is run entirely by academics, and our publishing decisions are based on intellectual merit and public value rather than on commercial viability. We do not operate for profit and all donations, as with all other revenue we generate, will be used to finance new Open Access publications.

For further information about what we do, how to donate to OBP, additional digital material related to our titles or to order our books, please visit our website: http://www.openbookpublishers.com

You may also be interested in...

Fiesco's Conspiracy at Genoa
Friedrich Schiller.
Translated by Flora Kimmich,
with an Introduction by John Guthrie

http://dx.doi.org/10.11647/OBP.0058
http://www.openbookpublishers.com/product/261

The End and the Beginning: The Book of My Life
Hermynia Zur Mühlen.
Translation, Introduction and Comments
by Lionel Gossman.

http://dx.doi.org/10.11647/OBP.0010
http://www.openbookpublishers.com/product/65

*Telling Tales: The Impact of Germany
on English Children's Books 1780-1918*
By David Blamires

http://dx.doi.org/10.11647/OBP.0004
http://www.openbookpublishers.com/product/23

*Brownshirt Princess
A Study of the 'Nazi Conscience'*
Lionel Gossman

http://dx.doi.org/10.11647/OBP.0003
http://www.openbookpublishers.com/product/18

www.ingramcontent.com/pod-product-compliance
Lightning Source LLC
Chambersburg PA
CBHW071711300426
44115CB00010B/1379